Advance Praise for
Inside Literature

"I think the use of classical rhetoric here is wonderful! As a tool for analyzing texts and coming up with arguments about texts, these classical elements—particularly ethos, pathos, and logos and the topoi —are quite helpful."

—Brad Sullivan
Western New England College

"The most compelling advantage of *Inside Literature* is its emphasis on classical rhetoric. This emphasis sets it apart from similar texts. . . . the thematic arrangements and choice of texts . . . the practical approach to writing papers, along with the tone that is inviting and helpful towards students, also makes this text stand out."

—Daniel Schierenbeck
Central Missouri State University

"Of critical importance here is that students are introduced to how texts harbor hidden agendas and complexities . . . students will hopefully learn to be writers themselves as they see the inner workings of the process."

—Timothy Kiogora
Eastern Kentucky University

"I like the fact that 'Crafting Arguments' is the first chapter, thus emphasizing critical reading and argument, setting the tone for the book as a whole. Addressing fundamental questions about a literary text in the opening chapter seems wise."

—Robert Lesman
Northern Virginia Community College

". . . apparatus that addresses how to interpret and read closely, and how to write on the readings. I really like the idea of arguing about literature and the logic involved."

—Rosemary Day
Albuquerque TVI Community College

"The sections on ethos, pathos, and logos and the topoi and introductory strategies were excellent."

—Edward Shannon
Ramapo College of New Jersey

"There are several advantages to *Inside Literature*. First is the uncluttered nature of the material, specifically the general strategies for writing about literature. The first three chapters do a good job of presenting an overview of reading, thinking about, and writing about the selections. The section on writing compelling introductions and the section on research are excellent."

—Michael Minassian
Broward County Community College

"... the breadth and depth of the readings are excellent. There's far more material here than one could use in any one semester, which means that any instructor has a very wide range of options. That's all one could hope for."

—Arnold Bradford
Northern Virginia Community College, Loudoun

"... placing the apparatus primarily in the first chapters and then leaving the anthology relatively apparatus-free (except for questions following the entries) is an excellent idea."

—Lois Feuer
California State University @ Dominguez Hills

"I see the value of this approach and it fits with my approach on 'critical thinking' skills that students can employ in a variety of situations."

—Shelly Dorsey
Pima Community College, Downtown Campus

"This book approaches the concepts behind writing from a workshop perspective. The reader feels involved in the process of discovering how to develop better writing skills."

—Alette Corley
Bethune-Cookman College

"What impressed me most was its practicality."

—Bridget Moss
Student Reviewer

"I like the thematic breakdown a great deal. . . . The categories are broad and general enough that these categories could also be applied to discussions of current issues and topics."

—Brenda Boudreau
McKendree College

"I am impressed by the greater emphasis on student's primary responses and on being aware of what they 'want' from the reading experience."

—Robert Lunday
Houston Community College/Southeast

"This is a well thought-out text... It has plentiful introductory and explanatory material, but not so much as to overwhelm the student."

—Keith Huneycutt
Florida Southern College

R. S. Gwynn has edited several other books, including *Poetry: A Pocket Anthology, Drama: A Pocket Anthology, Fiction: A Pocket Anthology, Literature: A Pocket Anthology, The Longman Anthology of Short Fiction* (with Dana Gioia), *Contemporary American Poetry: A Pocket Anthology* (with April Linder), and two volumes of *The Dictionary of Literary Biography.* He has also authored five collections of poetry, including *No Word of Farewell: Selected Poems: 1970–2000.*

Professor Gwynn teaches at Lamar University in Beaumont, Texas.

Steven J. Zani has recent publications in a number of journals and books, including *The Byron Journal, Lovecraft Studies,* and *James Bond and Philosophy*, and has co-authored a book on critical strategies to accompany *Literature: A Pocket Anthology.* His teaching accolades include an "Outstanding Commitment to Teaching" Award from Binghamton University and a listing in "Best Classes" in *Texas Monthly.*

Dr. Zani teaches at Lamar University in Beaumont, Texas.

R. S. Gwynn has edited several other books, including Poetry: A Pocket Anthology, Drama: A Pocket Anthology, Fiction: A Pocket Anthology, Literature: A Pocket Anthology, The Longman Anthology of Short Fiction (with Dana Gioia), Contemporary American Poetry: A Pocket Anthology (with April Lindner), and two volumes of The Dictionary of Literary Biography. He has also authored five collections of poetry, including No Word of Farewell: Selected Poems 1970–2000.

Professor Gwynn teaches at Lamar University in Beaumont, Texas.

Steven J. Zani has recent publications in a number of journals and books, including The Byron Journal, Literary Studies, and James Bond and Philosophy, and has co-authored a book on critical strategies to accompany Literature: A Pocket Anthology. His teaching accolades include an Outstanding Commitment to Teaching Award from Binghamton University and a ranking in "Best Classes" in Texas Monthly.

Dr. Zani teaches at Lamar University in Beaumont, Texas.

Inside
Literature

Reading · Responding · Arguing

Edited by

R. S. Gwynn
Lamar University

Steven J. Zani
Lamar University

PENGUIN ACADEMICS

PEARSON
Longman

New York   San Francisco   Boston
London   Toronto   Sydney   Tokyo   Singapore   Madrid
Mexico City   Munich   Paris   Cape Town   Hong Kong   Montreal

Managing Editor: Erika Berg
Development Editor: Anne Brunell Ehrenworth
Executive Marketing Manager: Ann Stypuloski
Production Manager: Denise Phillip
Project Coordination, Text Design, and Electronic Page Makeup: Pre-Press
   Company, Inc.
Senior Cover Design Manager/Designer: Nancy Danahy
Cover Image: © Getty Images, Inc.
Manufacturing Manager: Mary Fischer
Printer and Binder: Courier Corporation/Westford
Cover Printer: Phoenix Color Corporation

For more information about the Penguin Academics series, please contact us by
mail at Longman Publishers, attn. Marketing Department, 1185 Avenue of the
Americas, 25th Floor, New York, NY 10036, or by e-mail at www.ablongman.com

For permission to use copyrighted material, grateful acknowledgment is made
to the copyright holders on pp. 1354–1360, which are hereby made part of this
copyright page.

Library of Congress Cataloging-in-Publication Data

Gwynn, R. S.
    Inside literature / R. S. Gwynn and Steven Zani.
        p. cm. — (Penguin academics)
    Includes bibliographical references and index.
    ISBN 0-321-43874-4 (pbk. : alk. paper)
    1. College readers. 2. English language—Rhetoric—Problems, exercises, etc.
3. Report writing—Problems, exercises, etc. I. Zani, Steven. II. Title. III. Series.

PE1417.G89 2007
808'.0668—dc22   2006014071

Please visit us at http://www.ablongman.com/penguinacademics

ISBN 0-321-43874-4

1 2 3 4 5 6 7 8 9 10—CRW—09 08 07 06

Contents

(✱ Supported by *www.myliteraturelab.com*)

Who We Are: Personal and Communal Identities   129

FICTION

POETRY

Where We Come From: Cultures and Places   345

What We Believe: Language, Values, and Wisdom   523

Where We Stand: The Individual and the Institution 777

Where We Are Going: Time, Aging, and Death 1111

Alternate Contents by Genre

Preface

Inside Literature: Reading, Responding, Arguing encourages students to think for themselves—from engaging with literary works, to coming up with insightful things to say about literature, to crafting persuasive and well-supported argumentative essays. We've seen how elaborate apparatus can squelch original thought in introductory students. By telling students exactly what to do, good intentions often backfire, undermining students' initiative and confidence. *Inside Literature* takes a different approach, an approach which has worked well for our students and was well-received by reviewers. We have combined a rich body of thematically arranged literature with three foundational chapters that guide and encourage students through the process of developing compelling arguments about literature.

Our Approach

To develop a true appreciation for something—whether for the multitude of swirling colors in a van Gogh painting, the sleek art-deco design of the Chrysler Building in New York City, or the playful line breaks and punctuation of an e. e. cummings poem—we need to delve *inside* it, to explore the work for all its aspects: theme, style, genre, figurative language, meaning, and so forth. With this in mind, our approach to literary exploration and writing about literature is based on three basic principles: *reading, responding, and arguing.*

Reading

Chapter 1, *Crafting Arguments: Getting Started,* engages students in close reading. Students are used to having to "get something" out of a text. We turn this expectation around and ask, "What do you *want* to get out of it?" Students are prompted to reflect on their personal impressions of a work. Once they recognize that their initial reactions are valid, they are eased into a deeper examination of those impressions via various critical strategies of reading and writing. That's when they start to understand the process—and appreciate the benefits—of literary analysis.

Responding

Chapter 2, *Reading and Responding to Literature,* takes students' reactions to a work a step further. Here, students learn about the various literary genres, investigate the elements that each genre contains, and examine how those elements can affect their personal responses to a work. This chapter emphasizes analysis of these different elements individually and collectively, as well as shows how they function within a single work and genre. For example, students will find themselves considering how their initial impressions of a plot can change if that same plot is used in a play instead of a short story. They may wonder what difference it makes if the point-of-view of a poem is first-person narration rather than third-person narration. They may also question how a particular narrative might be more effectively presented as a graphic work than as a non-illustrated, fictional text. This line of inquiry and personal response enables students to develop more thoughtful and persuasive arguments about the texts.

Writing and Arguing

Students critically consider questions of genre and genre elements in greater depth in Chapter 3, *Writing and Arguing about Literature.* This chapter combines discussion of the particular stylistic challenges that students face when writing about the different genres (illustrated by numerous short excerpts from student essays, as well as a complete essay at the end of the chapter) with a comprehensive discussion of strategies of argumentation. Students discover how time-honored rhetorical methods can help them build compelling arguments. They learn how to generate ideas about a work, how to find internal and external support for their opinions, and how to present their interpretations of a work in writing. At the same time, we encourage students to go beyond mechanical correctness by demonstrating that no strategy of literary analysis should neglect common sense or the goal of generating clear, innovative, persuasive writing.

The Thematically Arranged Anthology

The anthology section of *Inside Literature* arranges stories, poems, plays, essays, and excerpts from graphic works in six thematic sections that take into consideration the changing faces of today's students. We believe our configuration is conversant with twenty-first century students while sensitive to the concerns and interests of older, returning students. The selections go beyond relating a tale or describing a pretty picture. They present a diversity of perspectives on individuality, culture, gender, mortality, love, and community—topics about which students can argue and write persuasively.

"Who We Are" showcases the challenging moments of establishing and coming to terms with race, class, gender, and, ultimately, personal identity; "Where We Come From" celebrates and challenges notions of culture and place; "What We Believe" examines individual and communal perspectives on religion, values, and ethics; "Where We Stand" presents the ever-altering role of the individual and the greater social community or institution; "How We Care" examines different types of romantic, familial, platonic, and sexual love (and hate); and "Where We Are Going" travels the course across time, through aging and death. The thematic introductions for each of these groupings not only explains how these topics speak to students but also returns students to the book's primary goal: to get *inside* literature—to read, respond, and argue.

Reading, Responding, Arguing

A number of features work at maintaining the thematic thread of *Inside Literature*.

- *Questions for Reading, Responding, Arguing* Questions designed to stimulate students' responses follow each of the selections. In general, they parallel the sequence of the first three foundational chapters. The initial set of questions tests students' comprehension of content; the second set of questions encourages interpretive thinking; and the third set helps students develop more sophisticated, critical insights into the work.
- *Sample Student Paper* A full sample student argument paper, at the end of Chapter 3, illustrates proper MLA documentation style, effective synthesis, argument, analysis, and use of sources.
- *Sectional Checklists* General inquiries intended to enhance students' recall of major concepts conclude each of the genre discussions in Chapter 2, as well as each of the primary discussions in Chapter 3. The thread of inquiry, so important in argumentative writing, is stressed throughout.

- *End-of-Chapter Checklists* The chapter's most salient points are summarized in question form. Students are reminded to ask themselves these questions during their critical reading and writing process. The theme of inquiry, argument, and "getting inside" literature is again brought to the forefront.
- *Appendix of Critical Strategies* This appendix supplements strategies introduced in Chapter 1; students and instructors can refer to it for further explanation of a strategy and to see each strategy in action.
- *Biographical Notes* Our notes are more than just biographical sketches; we provide pertinent details about the work as well. Such details are intended to support students' understanding and analysis of the work, as well as to help students build a persuasive argument about the text.

Acknowledgments

In closing, we would like to express our gratitude to the instructors who have reviewed the contents of *Inside Literature* from its initial proposal stage to its final form: Mary Amato, Rider University; Arnold J. Bradford, Northern Virginia Community College—Loudoun; Alette W. Corley, Bethune-Cookman College; Rosemary B. Day, Albuquerque TVI Community College; Robert Dial, University of Akron; Shelly Dorsey, Pima Community College—Downtown Campus; Noreen L. Duncan, Mercer County Community College; Lois Feuer, California State University Dominguez Hills; Robert Lesman, Northern Virginia Community College; Alan Lindsay, New Hampshire Technical Institute; Michael Minassian, Broward Community College; Edward Shannon, Ramapo College of New Jersey; and Brad Sullivan, Western New England College. Special thanks to our student reviewers, Luke Garlock, Bridget Moss, and Lauren Puccio.

Also, the editors wish to express their gratitude to Beverly Williams for her assistance in preparing this book.

R. S. Gwynn
Steven J. Zani
Lamar University

A Note From The Publisher

MyLiteratureLab MyLiteratureLab http://www.myliteraturelab.com is a state-of-the-art, Web-based interactive learning system designed to support Longman's introductory literature texts, including *Inside Literature*. The centerpiece of this password-protected site, the Longman Lecture Series, features 50 richly illustrated audio lectures about commonly taught literary texts, 37 of which appear in *Inside Literature* and are indicated by an ♣ both in the Contents and the text. Each multimedia lecture presents an engaging reading of an influential work and insights on the author and cultural context combined with evocative imagery and animation. The Longman Lectures are narrated by a host of Longman authors, including R.S. Gwynn and Steven Zani. Each six- to nine-minute lecture is organized into three parts—Reading, Interpreting, and Writing—each of which is followed by critical thinking questions to help students reflect on what they've just heard and viewed. To learn more about the benefits of MyLiteratureLab and how to order MyLiteratureLab with *Inside Literature* please see the inside front cover of this text.

What Every Student Should Know About Supplement Series These brief guides give students the kind of information they need on a wide range of important topics, including:

- *Avoiding Plagiarism*—students learn to take plagiarism seriously, understand its consequences, and to avoid its practice.
- *Researching Online*—students learn how to conduct research in the first place they will look: the Web.
- *Citing Sources with MLA Documentation*—students learn to write papers using proper Modern Language Association (MLA) style.

Any one of these WESSKA titles may be packaged with a Longman book for no extra charge.

Penguin Discount Novel Program One or more of a large selection of Penguin paperbacks can be value-packed at a significant discount with *Inside Literature*. Titles of special interest are listed on the last page of this book. For details or to arrange for a value-pack, please contact your Longman representative.

Inside
Literature

1
Crafting Arguments: Getting Started

Why Read and Argue About Literature?

We are all readers. However, what we want from the experience of reading varies widely. A few of us may want very little, confining our reading to signs, ads, memos, websites, or written instructions to help get us through the day. Others, at the other end of the spectrum, may stay up past midnight devouring the latest thriller, fully aware that an unwelcome alarm clock awaits us, unable to stop turning the pages. Most of us fall somewhere between these extremes. We read to be informed or entertained, or, occasionally, enlightened.

In a college course that focuses on reading, responding, and writing as a discipline, we may find ourselves challenged by some of the selections we are asked to read. Meaning in literature is rarely spelled out for us; thus, we often are asked to delve deep into a text—whether a story, poem, play, or essay—to question, discuss, and formulate an interpretive response to it; in other words, to craft an *argument*. After having done this, we may be asked to write an original literary analysis. While the immediate reasons for reading and arguing about literature aren't always clear, the reality is that analysis is crucial for living in the world. Reading and analysis, on some level, are processes that we perform every day, at all times and in all places. We make judgments about people, and about the world, every time we have a conversation or go to school or work. The tools and skills of literary analysis are basic components for learning, navigating through, and performing our daily tasks, and, ultimately, living a meaningful life. Arguing about literature, then, is practice in experiencing the world and what it has to offer.

What we think about the world is based on the conclusions that we draw from learning about, reading, and analyzing our relationships with others and the vast amount of information that bombards us daily. For example, in our relationships we learn how people feel about us, and we learn what we believe about people, places, and things, all based on how we "read" them. We often form judgments based on the contents of Internet blogs, television commercials, printed advertisements, and news stories. If we ask ourselves "what are the benefits of critical reading and argumentation," our answers should go beyond a desire to get one step closer to a coveted degree, career, life. That is, we should also ask what we *want* from reading a story, a poem, a play, or an essay. With that question in mind, let's look at a story that deals with the question of *wants*.

Reading Critically: Ways of Looking at a Literary Text

Grace Paley (b. 1922)

Wants

I saw my ex-husband in the street. I was sitting on the steps of the new library.

Hello, my life, I said. We had once been married for twenty-seven years, so I felt justified. He said, What? What life? No life of mine.

I said, O.K. I don't argue when there's real disagreement. I got up and went into the library to see how much I owed them.

The librarian said $32 even and you've owed it for eighteen years. I didn't deny anything. Because I don't understand how time passes. I have had those books. I have often thought of them. The library is only two blocks away.

My ex-husband followed me to the Books Returned desk. He interrupted the librarian, who had more to tell. In many ways, he said, as I look back, I attribute the dissolution of our marriage to the fact that you never invited the Bertrams to dinner.

That's possible, I said. But really, if you remember: first, my father was sick that Friday, then the children were born, then I had those Tuesday-night meetings, then the war began. Then we didn't seem to know them any more. But you're right. I should have had them to dinner.

I gave the librarian a check for $32. Immediately she trusted me, put my past behind her, wiped the record clean, which is just what most other municipal and/or state bureaucracies will not do.

I checked out the two Edith Wharton books I had just returned because I'd read them so long ago and they are more apropos now than ever. They were *The House of Mirth* and *The Children*, which is about how life in the United States in New York changed in twenty-seven years fifty years ago.

A nice thing I do remember is breakfast, my ex-husband said. I was surprised. All we ever had was coffee. Then I remembered there was a hole in the back of the kitchen closet which opened into the apartment next door. There, they always ate sugar-cured smoked bacon. It gave us a very grand feeling about breakfast, but we never got stuffed and sluggish.

That was when we were poor, I said.

When were we ever rich? he asked.

Oh, as time went on, as our responsibilities increased, we didn't go in need. You took adequate financial care, I reminded him. The children went to camp four weeks a year and in decent ponchos with sleeping bags and boots, just like everyone else. They looked very nice. Our place was warm in winter, and we had nice red pillows and things.

I wanted a sailboat, he said. But you didn't want anything.

Don't be bitter, I said. It's never too late.

No, he said with a great deal of bitterness. I may get a sailboat. As a matter of fact I have money down on an eighteen-foot two-rigger. I'm doing well this year and can look forward to better. But as for you, it's too late. You'll always want nothing.

He had had a habit throughout the twenty-seven years of making a narrow remark which, like a plumber's snake, could work its way through the ear down the throat, half-way to my heart. He would then disappear, leaving me choking with equipment. What I mean is, I sat down on the library steps and he went away.

I looked through *The House of Mirth*, but lost interest. I felt extremely accused. Now, it's true, I'm short of requests and absolute requirements. But I do want *something*.

I want, for instance, to be a different person. I want to be the woman who brings these two books back in two weeks. I want to be the effective citizen who changes the school system and addresses the Board of Estimate on the troubles of this dear urban center.

I *had* promised my children to end the war before they grew up.

I wanted to have been married forever to one person, my ex-husband or my present one. Either has enough character for a whole life, which as it turns out is really not such a long time. You couldn't exhaust either man's qualities or get under the rock of his reasons in one short life.

Just this morning I looked out the window to watch the street for a while and saw that the little sycamores the city had dreamily planted a couple of years before the kids were born had come that day to the prime of their lives.

Well! I decided to bring those two books back to the library. Which proves that when a person or an event comes along to jolt or appraise me I *can* take some appropriate action, although I am better known for my hospitable remarks.

—1980

"Wants" is a story that, on the surface, seems to raise few questions and leave little room for argument. It is so short and economically written that the reader is likely to dismiss it at first as "not a story at all, just some loosely connected jottings." To be sure, it has little in the way of conventional plot. It contains virtually no description of people or places, and it does not build to any earth-shaking conclusion: a woman goes to a library to return two long-overdue books, she runs into her ex-husband, they talk briefly, and he leaves her sitting on the library steps. But suppose you are in the position of having to write an argumentative paper about "Wants." Where would you begin?

Well, the title is always a good choice for a starting point, even if the title is only a single word. First, consider that *wants* is usually a verb, as in a sentence like "He wants a steak for supper." Here it is a noun, a synonym for "desires." What, exactly, are *wants*? Necessities? Luxuries? Material things or nonmaterial things? Looking carefully at the story, we can see that the word, or variant forms of it, appears eight times in the story. Those repetitions occur in a span of seven short paragraphs. Whenever a word, especially so prominent a word as *wants*, is repeated in a literary text, we can assume that the author is directing our attention toward it.

Now look again at those eight repetitions: seven of them relate to the narrator and only one ("I wanted a sailboat, he said.") relates to her ex-husband. In his case, *want* is for a sailboat—a nonessential, material thing. When the ex-husband applies the word twice to the narrator, it is in the negative sense: "But you didn't want anything" and "You'll always want nothing." Her echoing remark, at first, isn't very specific: "But I do want *something*." Then she goes on to list her own wants: "to be a different person," to be less tardy (eighteen years!) about returning library books, to be "the effective citizen" who makes a difference in the community, and finally to be the kind of woman who "wanted to have been married forever to one person." It should be clear from the list that her desires have to do with character, not with tangible things.

So, in crafting an initial argument, you could reflect on how these different *wants* underscore a conflict between the two characters. Is it possible that their long marriage ended for reasons that go beyond the husband's complaint? "I attribute the dissolution of our marriage to the fact that you never invited the Bertrams to dinner," he says. Is this a joke, or is he dead serious? And what do their lines reveal about them? He wanted a "proper" social life and a symbol of his worldly success; she wanted to be a better person in a better world.

Let's take a look at other details. Is anything else repeated in the story? Several things, for example, the uses of *life* three times in the opening paragraphs and the way that it is echoed later in the narrator's statements that both her ex-husband and her present one have "enough character for a whole life" and that "You couldn't exhaust either man's qualities or get under the rock of his reasons in one short life." Similar are the references to time (though the narrator claims, "I don't understand how time passes"): the coincidence of the twice-mentioned twenty-seven-year marriage and the Wharton novel in which "life in the United States in New York changed in twenty-seven years," the narrator's explanation that "as time went on . . . our responsibilities increased," and the observation that the sycamore trees, planted before the couple's children were born, are now in "the prime of their lives."

Paley also makes repeated references to the overdue books, which are immediately checked out again for the curious reason that "I'd read them so long ago and they are more apropos now than ever." And even the eighteen-year period that the books have been overdue is echoed in the ex-husband's down payment on "an eighteen-foot two-rigger."

Additionally, there's the matter of the two books themselves. The narrator makes several references to the couple's children. One of the books is titled *The Children*. Is the fact that the other one is titled *The*

House of Mirth somehow an ironic reflection of what must have become a home with little mirth in it? The narrator indicates more than
once that the marriage began to change with the coming of children,
and the ex-husband nostalgically recalls their coffee-only breakfasts
when they were poor and presumably childless. And finally there's the
wife's comment on the long-delayed, long-desired sailboat: "Don't be
bitter, I said. It's never too late." This is followed immediately by the
husband's response, which is "said with a great deal of bitterness":
"But as for you, it's too late." About this quality of his "character,"
she says, "He had had a habit throughout the twenty-seven years of
making a narrow remark which, like a plumber's snake, could work
its way through the ear down the throat, half-way to my heart." She is
left, "choking with equipment," feeling "extremely accused." At the
end of the story, she characterizes her own "remarks" as "hospitable."

As should be clear from this brief attempt at "close reading,"
Paley's story indeed has quite a bit going on beneath the surface, and
this underlying structure of repetition and variation helps us to formulate questions that may lead to strategies for argument. For example,
what do the repetitions imply about the fundamental difference between the two characters and what do they suggest as causes for the
failure of their marriage? What is the narrator's attitude toward her ex-
husband? Because we hear about the marriage primarily from her, can
we trust her account? What does she mean when she claims, "I don't
argue when there's real disagreement"? If she says at the end that it
takes "a person or an event . . . to jolt or appraise me" and force her to
do things ("I *can* take appropriate action"), then what does this self-
assessment tell us about her own assignment of blame for the end of
her first marriage?

There is no substitute for actually *reading* a literary text, that is,
paying close attention to the details, which are always details of
language. But what strategies can be used to help us *respond* to a text
in such a way that will then inspire the desire to *write*, or to formulate
an argument about it? In the next section we explore several widely
used critical strategies for reading and responding to a text. This deeper
investigation will give rise to even more questions about a literary
text—in this case, Paley's "Wants"—and, thus, inspire the urge to develop a larger argument about its textual meaning.

Writing an Argument: Putting Critical Strategies to Work

First of all, remember that when you respond to a text and produce an argument about it, you're not primarily concerned with stating the *facts* about what happens in it but with weighing the implications of the information that the author provides. In this sense, a literary argument arises from employing a certain critical strategy. A *critical strategy* is nothing but a decision to treat something as more important than something else, to treat particular words, ideas, or themes as more relevant than others. Even an interpretation based on your purely personal response is a critical strategy, although you may be completely unaware that it is. For example, if the woman and man in "wants" remind you of a long-divorced aunt and uncle whose goals in life led them in different directions, then you are applying your personal experience as a type of literary response.

The process of making an argument about a text is taking that response and articulating it to others. In our earlier look at the eight repetitions of the word *want*, for instance, when we discovered that one of those repetitions did not fit the pattern of the others, our focus fell on the details of the text itself—the structure and formal consistency of its language. Paying attention to details of linguistic structure and language is a critical strategy known as *formalism*. A formalist argument focuses on the language of a work and minimizes other considerations. Whenever we read a text, we are to some degree employing an element of formalism just by following the basic grammar and sentence structure of a work, or by noting, as in the case of "Wants," that Paley has chosen not to use traditional punctuation for her passages of dialogue. If just noticing where sentences end or how punctuation is used is employing a critical strategy, you might then ask, how else can a text be read? What other things can be considered?

An author's personal history can also be used to move beyond our first impressions in examining the meaning of a text. When we find ourselves using details of the author's life to form an argument for a text, we are engaging in a *biographical criticism* of the work. In its simplest form, biographical criticism assumes that the narrator is the same person as the author, and that the narrator's intentions and messages are also the same. Although this strategy is most valuable in analyzing lyric poetry, where the speaker of a poem is determined to be the author, it also has some use in examining a piece of fiction, even though we recognize that to say that something is "fictional" means that it differs from autobiography, which we assume to be a "true" account of events.

In the case of "wants," Paley's life corresponds in several ways with the characters and events of the story. If we read the author biography on page 1346, we will discover that Grace Paley was born in the 1920s, in New York City, and her background can be compared to that of the nameless narrator. The setting of the story is ambiguous, but we are told it is a "city," and it could be New York City with its apartments, winters, and institutions like the library. The narrator even mentions her interest in New York when discussing the Edith Wharton novels. Paley was married twice, like the narrator, similarly had children with her first husband, and was an outspoken political activist, details that also correspond to our narrator, who mentions her attendance at weekly meetings (political?) and her promise to her children to end the war (Given the story's 1974 publication date, one assumes the Vietnam War). Following this argument, we can say that Paley may be attempting to tell us—in the indirect way that fiction uses—about herself and what it is like to live in her world. By reading more about an author and more works by an author, we can determine the degree to which personal experience is reflected in a given text.

Even if a narrator's life corresponds exactly to the author's, however, it is still possible to analyze the meaning of a text without referencing the author's life. Better yet, we can see how an author may place him- or herself in the text in the form of a narrator, but simultaneously leave signs that the narrator's voice is not to be trusted as the author's own. The woman in "Wants," for instance, seems straightforward and sympathetic, but we only have a brief moment to gain insight into her character, and what we see is not completely promising. She is a woman whose motivations and desires are not clear, as her husband asserts when he says that, as far as he could see, she "never wanted anything." With a woman who takes eighteen years to return her library books only to check them out again immediately, we can have little faith that all of her actions are meant to be understandable or logical.

By introducing herself in thinly veiled form in the narrative, Paley is perhaps not trying to convince us that her narrator is correct, rather she is providing a self-critique. Unlike her narrator, Paley may recognize her own flaws and inconsistencies, and by playing them off of an equally ambiguous former husband, who may or may not bear the responsibility for their divorce, she can reveal a "jolt" of understanding to both the narrator and the reader. Just like Paley, we can see ourselves not only from our own perspective but from the perspective of how others, husbands, readers, may see us. Bearing in mind that the word *fiction* derives from a Latin word that means a shaping or fashioning, we can conclude that any text, no matter how closely it corresponds with the facts of an author's life, always involves a degree of "shaping."

When we read a literary text from the perspective of *historical criticism,* we pay attention to the history that surrounds a story or an author. For "Wants," which appeared in Paley's 1974 collection *Enormous Changes at the Last Minute,* one useful historical strategy is to think about the characters in relation to the culture and events in which the story places them. What is the history that surrounds this story? Much of Paley's upbringing took place in the 1930s, during America's Great Depression. That in itself allows us to consider certain "economic" issues in the story. Moreover, Paley's parents were socialists, a pair of Russian Jews who immigrated to America, and who spoke English, Russian, and Yiddish around the house. Her parents were not particularly religious, but the family members saw themselves as being committed to maintaining their Jewish heritage in terms of culture and ethics. The author, then, comes from a family that was committed to an awareness of its heritage and language, and interested in preserving a sense of Jewish American identity in a multicultural New York City community.

Thus, if we consider that history and the conditions of Paley's life, several interesting details become more meaningful in the story. For example, one of the differences between the narrator and her ex-husband is that he always had several *wants,* material goods such as a sailboat. The narrator, on the other hand, does not value such things. Like many children of the Depression, the narrator's interests are not for luxury items. When she considers the apparent level of wealth of their household, she mentions a few concrete items such as their "red pillows," but her most immediate judgment of their wealth is in how well the children were provided for, not what goods she and her husband had accumulated. In short, the values of the narrator reflect Depression-era considerations or the influence of socialist parents who would have been critical of extravagant material goods.

The argument one can make is not just that Paley believed these things, but that the story makes a specific point of elaborating those values. Issues of Jewish identity, too, can be found in the narrator's *wants.* What she wants, among other things, is to be "married forever to one person," which can be seen in the context of an ethical, if not overtly religious upbringing, a desire for stability and continuity in family and community. Even in the most general sense, Paley's urban life is reflected in every line of the story, in the basic background of a neighborhood life of apartments, libraries, and school bureaucracies.

Paley's history as a Jewish American and as a Depression-era child do not exhaust the possible arguments to make about the story. She also was a political activist for a number of causes, among them local Manhattan issues, involvement with antinuclear and antiwar groups, and the woman's movement. If we know that Paley herself was a political activist and a feminist, how do her beliefs manifest themselves in the story? How many references does the story make to the relationship of the individual to the state or to a commitment to changing the political status quo? Does it matter that the narrator is a woman? What can we say about the role of women in the story?

When we emphasize the gender (whether male or female) of the authors and characters connected to a work, we may develop a *feminist* argument about a text. Paley's story is about how women interact with men. It portrays a breakdown between the sexes and begins to ask questions about why that breakdown occurred.

One feminist strategy here is to take yet another look at the story's material goods. By portraying the difference between the *wants* of the characters, the story is not just saying that her ex-husband was more interested in tangible things, but that it may be a masculine trait to have those interests, whereas women are more interested in intangibles, such as questions of empowerment, identity, and self that men may be more likely to be insensitive to or ignore. Similarly, the woman is more forgiving and accepting of the relationship between them, willing to acknowledge the close bond between them. The narrator says that her husband was "my life," whereas his male reaction is one of emotional detachment, "no life of mine."

Another feminist argument to make about the story is that it is concerned with revealing the life of a woman. Many feminists argue that literature written by men has often either ignored or misrepresented women's lives and women's concerns. "Wants" looks at one woman's life from up close, in the minutiae of her paying a library fine and sitting on the steps. It is concerned with what she feels and thinks about the encounter of her day. In that sense, it is a woman's text, because it argues that it is worth listening to and writing about a woman's desires and opinions. Above all, a feminist strategy asks readers to remember that stories are not just about individuals, but about individuals who have a gender, and who may think differently or be treated differently because of it.

There are a great deal more strategies for arguing about literature than the ones we've briefly described here, each of which may have its own advantages or disadvantages. In later chapters we'll apply several of these strategies. For now, it is enough to know that a number of approaches can form the basis of writing analytically about literature. Each of them can offer a starting point for thinking about and writing about literature, at the very least by providing a set of questions to ask ourselves when beginning to formulate an argument. In "Wants," for example, we already have raised many questions. How do the structure and language of the story help to convey its meaning? What was the Paley's intention in telling the story, and how can we see messages particular to her in the text? How does her biography inform what the story means? How do historical events have a bearing on the meaning of the work? How does the gender of the narrator change our attitudes about her situation? These questions, and many more, are created by remembering that when we read a literary text, we're not just reading it, we're already formulating an argument, at the very least for ourselves, about what it means. Ultimately, the process of reading and responding critically will lead us to what we "want" to say about it.

2
Reading and
Responding to
Literature

Before we discuss the finer points of writing argumentative essays about literature, we must first look at the different literary *genres,* or types—fiction, poetry, drama, and the essay—and discuss the qualities that distinguish each genre from the other. Each genre of literature has its own history and terminology, some of which may be shared with other genres. In the introductory discussions of fiction, poetry, drama, and the essay that follow, certain important terms appear in **boldface** type. An index of critical terms can be found at the end of this book.

FICTION

Applying the Elements of Fiction

Plot

If you tell a friend about a short story that you have enjoyed, you will probably give a **synopsis** or brief summary of its incidents. Let's look at a *very* short story by an American master, John Cheever's "Reunion" (page 963). In the case of a very brief story like "Reunion," the synopsis would only be a few sentences long:

```
    In "Reunion" the narrator, a teenaged boy
traveling by train, meets his estranged father during
a stop for lunch in New York City. Over the course of
```

an hour and a half the father's alcoholism and potentially abusive personality are revealed. The story ends with the narrator boarding his train, indicating that this was the last time he saw his father, possibly by choice.

Plot may be defined as a story's sequence of incidents, arranged in dramatic order. We may be tempted to insert the word *chronological,* but doing so would exclude many stories that depart from this strict ordering of events.

Though its use is more characteristic in longer works like novels, many stories employ the **flashback** to narrate incidents in the past. (See, for example, William Faulkner's "A Rose for Emily" [page 356] and Margaret Atwood's "Happy Endings" [page 1231].) In opposite fashion, writers sometimes use **foreshadowing** to provide hints of future actions in the story; when foreshadowing is used effectively, the story's outcome seems less haphazard or contrived.

Of course, the manner in which stories handle time is largely illusory. The opening sentence of the second paragraph ("We went out of the station and up a side street to a restaurant.") of "Reunion," for example, compresses into a second or two an action that in reality would have taken at least several minutes. The ninety minutes of action in the story is compressed into about ten minutes of the reader's time. A plot like this is called a **unified plot.** Action that stretches over weeks or even longer periods and comprises a series of isolated scenes is called an **episodic plot.**

The **dramatic structure** of a story refers to the manner in which the plot is organized. The first part of this structure, the **exposition,** provides the reader with essential information—the *who, what, when, where*—of the story. The exposition of "Reunion," for example, is fairly straightforward: In the first paragraph we learn the *who* (Charlie and his father), the *what* (a lunchtime meeting between trains), the *when* (noon to 1:30 P.M.), and the *where* (in and near Grand Central Station in Manhattan). Cheever might have begun the story with a slightly more "dramatic" sentence ("At twelve o'clock sharp I saw him coming through the crowd.") but he would have to have provided the essential contextual information in short order to avoid unnecessarily confusing the reader. This type of beginning is called the **in medias res** ("in the middle of things"), which follows the conventions of old epic poems and opens with a "blind" bit of action in the story before supplying its context.

Exposition in a story usually describes a stable situation, even if it is not an entirely happy one. The appearance of "trouble" constitutes the second part of a plot—the **complication**—and it typically marks the rising action of the story. A stroke of fortune such as illness or accident is a typical example of an *external complication*—a problem that the characters cannot ignore. An *internal complication*, in contrast, might not be immediately apparent, for it may result from a character's deep-seated uncertainties, dissatisfactions, and fears. The external complication in "Reunion" is the father's series of confrontations with waiters; the internal complication is Charlie's growing sense of pity and revulsion. Typically the complication of a plot is heightened by **conflict** between two characters that have different personalities and goals. Charlie is overjoyed to see his father at the beginning of the story, but, despite his knowledge that he will grow up to "be something like him," he is more than eager to escape his company at the end, even if he is unconsciously trying to run away from his own "future and . . . doom."

Other elements of the short story include:

- **Rising action**—the body of the story comprising a number of action and dialogue scenes.
- **Moments of crisis**—points in the story where a resolution of the complication momentarily seems at hand but quickly disappear.
- **Climax**—the central moment of crisis in a plot, or the moment of greatest tension.
- **Falling action**—the point in which the built-up tension is finally released.
- **Epiphany**—a term that represents a moment of spiritual insight or revelation.
- **Dénouement**—a French term literally meaning "the untying of a knot," and referring to the emotional release of a story's ending. The dénouement returns the characters to another stable situation and may be termed either *closed* or *open*.
- **Closed dénouement**—ties up everything neatly and explains all unanswered questions that the reader might have.
- **Open dénouement**—leaves us with a few tantalizing questions; the last phrase of "Reunion," which consciously mirrors the story's opening sentence, does not explicitly state *why* Charlie never sees his father again. Was it strictly his own choice? Did the father die soon after their meeting? Were other factors involved? Such an ending invites us to speculate.

One final word about plots: It is no exaggeration to say that there is nothing (or at least not much) new under the sun where plots of short stories are concerned. Plots may be refurbished with new characters and settings, but still draw on what psychologist Carl Jung called **archetypes**— universal types of characters and situations that all human beings carry in their unconscious minds. Plots deriving from archetypes may be found in ancient mythologies, fairy tales, and even in contemporary fiction. Among a few of the most familiar are the *triangle plot,* a love story involving three people; *the quest plot,* which is unified around a group of characters on a journey; and the *transformation plot,* in which a weak or physically unattractive character changes radically in the course of the story. "Reunion" is an example of one of the most widely used of all archetypal plots, *the initiation story.* In a plot of this type the main character, usually a child or an adolescent, undergoes an experience (or a *rite of passage*) that prepares him or her for adulthood.

Determining Plot in Fiction

1. Identify the synopsis. What are the major events, spoken or unspoken, of the plot?
2. Does the plot proceed in a chronological fashion, or does it jump from time to time? Is there a reason for the ordering of time in the story?
3. Is the plot unified (that is, continuous in development), or episodic? How would the narrative change if the plot were organized differently?
4. How does the author give the exposition? When, if at all, does the reader learn important details about time, place, and so on?
5. What is the complication of the story, and when does it first become evident?
6. Is there a moment of epiphany, or revelation, for the characters? For the reader?
7. What is the dénouement, or resolution, of the story?
8. Is the dénouement closed or open? Could the story have a sequel?
9. What archetypes, if any, do you recognize in the narrative? Is there a pattern to the story that you've seen, or experienced before in your own life? In other stories?

Characterization

Every story hinges on the actions undertaken by its main character, or **protagonist,** a term drawn from ancient Greek tragedy (literally *first debater*) and a term less misleading than *hero* or *heroine.* Additionally, stories may contain an opposing character, or **antagonist,** with whom the protagonist is drawn into conflict. In many modern stories there is little, in any traditional sense, that is heroic about the protagonists; thus, **anti-hero** may be a more appropriate designation for one who occupies center stage but otherwise seems incapable of fitting the traditional heroic mold.

A character in a short story may be termed either a **flat character** or a **round character,** depending on the depth of detail the writer supplies. In "Reunion" the father is essentially a flat character, rendered with a few quick strokes and reduced to a single personality trait, his alcoholic rudeness. Flat minor characters are often **stock characters,** stereotypes necessary to advance the plot but otherwise are not deserving of more than the barest outlines of description, like the waiters in "Reunion." Round characters are given more than one trait, some of which may even seem contradictory, and are explored in depth as the author delves into the character's past and even into his or her unconscious mind. Characters of this type, usually the protagonists of stories, begin to approach the level of complexity that we associate with real human beings.

Development and motivation are also important in any consideration of a story's characters. Characters can be termed either **static** or **dynamic** depending on the degree to which they change in the course of the story. In "Reunion" the father is a static character. His personality was fixed long before the story opens, and Cheever holds out no likelihood that he will ever alter his course. But Charlie does attain some understanding in the course of the story, even if it is at the cost of his own disillusionment with what he wants his father to be. If development in a character is usually clear in a story, motivation—the reasons the reader is given for a character's actions—may not be so obvious. In many cases, an author simply tells us what is going on in a character's mind, but in others we are denied access to this level of understanding. Although we can speculate about Charlie's father's strange behavior, we are not given any direct insight into his own view of his actions. In some stories writers may try to plug directly into a character's thoughts by using **interior monologue,** a direct presentation of thought that is somewhat like a soliloquy in drama, or **stream of consciousness,** an attempt to duplicate raw information in the same disordered state that the mind receives it.

Description of characters also helps us to understand the author's intent. In real life we are told from an early age not to judge people by external appearance, but in fiction the opposite is more often the case: physical description is invariably a sign of what lurks beneath the surface. Given the brevity of most short stories, these physical details may be minimal but revealing in the author's choice of particulars. Cheever has Charlie describe his father at first as only "a big, good-looking man." Remarkably, the author then uses his protagonist's sense of smell to make the character vivid: Charlie breathes in "a rich compound of whiskey, after-shave lotion, shoe polish, woolens, and the rankness of a mature male." In that burst of **imagery** we may momentarily overlook the most important item in the list, the evidence that Charlie's father has been drinking in the morning.

Other elements may add to our understanding of characters. Many writers take particular care in naming their characters in such a way as to draw attention to aspects of their personalities. This device (called **characternym**) is sometimes obvious, as is the case with Hawthorne's Young Goodman Brown and his wife Faith. In one of her stories Flannery O'Connor calls an unscrupulous seducer Manley Pointer, a name that a moment's thought reveals as an outrageous pun. Similarly, actions in the story such as speech patterns and mannerisms may also disclose personality traits. A character's misuse of grammar or stilted vocabulary can *show* us a great deal more about background and self-image than a whole page of background information or analysis. Charlie's father's gestures and loud attempts at ordering in various foreign languages grow more embarrassing until his tongue-tied request for two "Bibson Geefeaters" (a Beefeater Gibson is a potent martini made from a well known brand of gin) comes as the punch line to a grotesque joke on himself.

Determining Characterization in Fiction

1. Who is the protagonist of the story, if any? The antagonist?
2. Is the protagonist heroic or antiheroic? How?
3. Are the characters flat or round? How well developed are they?
4. Are the characters static or dynamic? Do they change as the story progresses?

5. Does the story use stereotypical or stock characters? If so, how? Is there a personality type that you've seen, or experienced before in your own life? In other stories?
6. Does character development relate to the plot? Is development part of the rising action, the falling action, an epiphany, or other story element?
7. What is the motivation of the characters? Are their motivations evident to others in the story?
8. Is a stream-of-conscious narrative employed in the story? Do readers have access to the interior thoughts of the characters?
9. How are the characters described? In depth, or without much description?
10. How do physical descriptions of the characters reveal other details of their personalities?
11. Do the names of the characters have any significance?

Point of View

In fiction, the term **point of view** refers to the *authority* in the story. Every story has a **narrator**, a voice that provides the reader with information about and insight into characters and incidents. The narrative voice may be that of a character in the story, or it may come from outside the story. Almost all narrative points of view can be classified as either first person or third person.

First-person ("I") narration.   In first-person narration, the narrator is a **participant** (or the I) in the action. He or she may be either a major character (which is the case with Charlie in "Reunion") or a minor character, close to the event in time or distant from it. Though it is never directly stated, it seems likely that the adult Charlie is narrating an account of something that happened years before; thus, his repeated phrase about the last time he saw his father has a finality about it that goes far beyond a simple statement like "The last time I saw my father was a week ago in Grand Central Station."

In general, first-person stories may seem more immediate than third-person stories, but they are limited by the simple fact that the narrator must be present at all times and must also have some knowledge of what is going on. If, for example, an attempt had been made to tell "Reunion" from the point of view of one of the restaurant waiters, the narrator might have to resort to eavesdropping on Charlie and his father in order to report their circumstances. The ability of the narrator to tell the story accurately is also important. An **unreliable narrator,** either through naiveté, ignorance, deception, or impaired mental processes, relates events in such a distorted manner that the reader, who has come to recognize the narrator's unreliability, has literally to turn his reporting on its head to make sense. Imagine how we would read "Reunion" if it had been told from the boozy, self-deluding point of view of Charlie's father.

Third-person (she or he) narration. Third-person narration, by definition, employs a **nonparticipant** narrator, a voice of authority that never reveals its source and is capable of moving from place to place to describe action and report dialogue. In third-person stories the question of reliability is rarely an issue, but the matter of **omniscience**—the degree to which the "all-knowing" narrator can reveal the thoughts of characters—is. The degrees of omniscience vary, and those varying degrees include:

- **Total omniscience**—the narrator knows everything about the character's lives—their pasts, presents, and futures—and may reveal the thoughts of anyone in the story.
- **Editorial point of view**—the author has the godlike authority to comment directly on the action; this type of omniscience is also called **authorial intrusion.**
- **Limited omniscience**—the authors limit themselves to the thoughts and perceptions of a single character. Most contemporary authors avoid total omniscience in short fiction, perhaps sensing that a story's strength is dissipated if more than one perspective is used. Also called **selective omniscience** or the **method of central intelligence,** this point of view is perhaps the most flexible of all because it allows the writer to compromise between the immediacy of first-person narration and the mobility of third person.
- **Dramatic point of view**—(also called the **objective point of view**) a further departure from omniscience; here the narrator simply reports dialogue and action with minimal interpretation and no delving into characters' minds. The dramatic point of view, as the name implies, approximates the experience of reading a play; readers are provided only with set descriptions, stage directions, and dialogue, and thus must supply motivations that are based solely on this external evidence.

Technically, other points of view are possible, though they are rarely used. Stories have been told from a first-person plural ("we") and a second-person point of view ("you"), but such points of view are difficult to sustain and may quickly prove distracting to readers. Also, there is an unwritten rule that point of view should be consistent throughout a story, although occasionally a writer may use multiple perspectives to illustrate how the "truth" of any incident is always relative to the way in which it is witnessed.

Determining Point of View in Fiction

1. Is the story told in first, second, or third person? How would changing the point of view affect the way that the story is told?
2. In a first-person narration, is the narrator a minor or a major character in the plot?
3. In a third-person narration, is the narrator involved in the story at all?
4. Is the narrator reliable? If not, why?
5. Is the narrator omniscient in perspective? If the omniscience is limited, what are those limitations?
6. Are the thoughts of a character or characters available to the reader?
7. Are the narrator's motivations the same as the author's?
8. Does the story involve a dramatic point of view? Could it easily be a screenplay for a drama or movie?

Theme

Aesop's fables and the parables of the gospels make their purposes clear by explicitly stating a moral or interpretation at the end of the story. Literary fiction, however, is usually much more subtle in revealing its **theme,** the overall meaning the reader derives from the story. Thus, many readers complain, "If the author was trying to say that then why didn't she just come right out and *say* it!" To further complicate matters, the theoretical manner in which we analyze stories and the preconceptions we bring to bear on them may result in multiple interpretations of meaning. No single statement of theme is likely to be the "correct" one, though it is fair to say that some seem more likely than others.

What, then, is the theme of "Reunion"? A reader insistent on a moral might denounce Charlie's father, inveighing against alcoholism and its destructive effect on "family values." Another reader, slightly more charitable, might recognize alcoholism as a disease and feel some amount of sympathy for the father. Yet another, perhaps entirely too self-righteous, might fault Charlie for running away from his father, interpreting the older man's actions as a subconscious cry for help. If we investigate Cheever's own troubled biography and note his own serious problems with both parenthood and alcoholism, we may read the story as a psychological confession, with Cheever himself simultaneously playing the roles of father and son. Referring to plots and archetypes we can summarize a story's theme broadly: "'Reunion,' like most initiation stories, is about growth through loss of innocence. Children have to learn, often through painful experience, that they are not responsible for their parents' well-being, and sometimes they must distance themselves from their parents in order to survive." Such a statement does not encompass every possible nuance of the story's theme, but it does at least provide a starting point for arguing about the finer points of Cheever's meanings.

Still, many modern authors are not reticent about revealing their themes. A moralist like Flannery O'Connor perceives her characters' shortcomings and judges them according to her own Roman Catholic moral standards. Alice Walker has tackled social themes like female genital mutilation. Margaret Atwood's feminism is rarely hidden in her stories and poems. Many stories, especially those which imitate parables and fables, are in fact **allegorical tales,** in which the literal events point to a parallel sequence of symbolic ideas. In many stories the literal setting of the story, a doctor's waiting room, say, or a crowded city bus, is a **microcosm,** a "small world" that reflects the tensions of the larger world outside.

Determining Theme in Fiction

1. What is the theme of the story? Is there more than one theme?
2. Is the theme explicit and obvious, or implicit or hidden?
3. Is the story allegorically using symbols and situations to represent larger considerations?

Setting

Short story writers, hemmed in by limitations of space, must limit themselves to very selective descriptions of time and place. When a writer like Edgar Allan Poe goes into great detail in his Gothic descriptions, it is likely that **atmosphere,** the emotional aura surrounding a certain setting, is more important than the actual physical locale.

Setting is simply the time and place of a story, and in most cases the narrator provides the details of description given to the reader. A story may employ multiple locations in its different scenes, and its time frame may encompass a few hours or many years. "Reunion" is a story with relatively few details of setting. Because Cheever wrote his stories almost exclusively for the *New Yorker,* it is not necessary for him to describe the interior of Grand Central Station to an audience doubtless familiar with it; excessive details here would probably be irrelevant. The time setting is also relatively unimportant here. We know that the action is taking place during the lunch hour on a weekday, probably in the summer, but as far as a more specific time is concerned, we know little or nothing.

Some stories, however, depend on their **locale** or time setting much more heavily and thus demand fuller exposition of setting. **Historical fiction** usually pays great attention to the altered landscapes and customs of bygone eras. A writer who carelessly lets an electric alarm clock go off in a story set in the early 1800s has committed an anachronism that may be only slightly more obvious than another writer's use of contemporary slang in the same setting. **Local color fiction** depends heavily on the unique characteristics of a particular area, usually a rural one that is off the beaten path. Some southern writers, like William Faulkner or Flannery O'Connor, first established their reputations as practitioners of **regionalism,** setting most of their work in a particular area or country. A South American writer like Gabriel García Márquez continually draws us into the strange world of Colombian villages cut off from the contemporary world, places where past and present, history and folklore, natural and supernatural, seamlessly join in what has been labeled **magic realism.**

Stories contain both specific and general settings. The *specific setting* is the precise time(s) and place(s) where the action occurs. The *general setting* of a story, what is called its **enveloping action,** is its sense of the "times" and how its characters interact with events and social currents in the larger world. We have already mentioned how the specific setting of a story often is a microcosm that reflects the doings of society at large. It is impossible to read stories by Flannery O'Connor or Alice Walker and not be made aware of the social changes that have transformed the rural South in the last thirty years. Stories sometimes depend on readers' ability to bring their knowledge of history and culture to bear on the events taking place. In reading a story like Ralph Ellison's "A Party Down at the Square" (page 537) younger readers may be unaware of the widespread horrors of lynchings in an America that only older readers can painfully recall.

Determining Setting in Fiction

1. What is the setting of the narration? Is there more than one setting?
2. How much detail is used in describing the setting? Does the setting influence the atmosphere of the narrative?
3. Is the story historical fiction, employing a very specific past, present, or future? Would the meaning of the story change in a different historical setting?
4. Is the story regional fiction, employing a very specific location or community? Would the meaning of the story change in a different locale?
5. Is the setting realistic? Familiar? Does it employ magic or other fantastic elements?
6. What is the enveloping action of the story, if any? How relevant is it to the plot? To the story's theme?
7. How is the setting (enveloping action, specific locale, and so on) relevant to the characters' actions, or knowledge of their situation?

Style, Imagery, and Symbolism

Style in fiction refers equally to the characteristics of language in a particular story and to the same characteristics in a writer's complete works. A detailed analysis of the style in an individual story might include attention to such matters as vocabulary, sentence structure, punctuation (or the lack thereof), use of figurative language, and even the verb tenses that are used. In English we usually make a distinction between the differing qualities of words—standard versus slang usage, abstract versus concrete diction, and so on. We can clearly see the difference between one character who says, "I have profited to a great degree from the educational benefits of the realm of experience," and another who says, "I graduated from the school of hard knocks." However, in analyzing style we must be sensitive to the literary fashions of periods other than our own; it is senseless to fault Poe for "flowery diction" when we compare his use of language to that of his contemporaries. The prevailing fashion in fiction today, however, is for the unadorned starkness of writers like Bobbie Ann Mason and Raymond Carver, a type of literature that has been disparagingly called "KMart realism" by one critic.

The style of "Reunion" is for the most part straightforward, with few flourishes of vocabulary (if we don't count the foreign phrases) or sentence structure. About the only significant departure from this plain style is in the opening paragraph, where Charlie momentarily rises to a slightly elevated rhetorical plateau: "as soon as I saw him I felt that he was my father, my flesh and blood, my future and my doom." The **tone** of the story, or what we can indirectly determine about the author's own feelings about its events from his choice of words, is also carefully controlled. Cheever avoids the twin pitfalls of sentimentality on the one hand and cynicism on the other by deftly walking an emotional tightrope. After the opening paragraph, at no point does Charlie tell us how he feels, instead he lets his father's actions speak for themselves. At points in "Reunion" we may laugh, but it is an uncomfortable laugh at which we probably feel a little guilty. The range of possible tones available for use in any given story may run through the whole range of human emotions, from outright comedy or satirical contempt to *pathos* of the most wrenching sort.

Like tone of voice, **symbolism** in stories is often troublesome, as is indicated by the oft-heard phrase "hidden meanings." Understanding what a symbol *means* is often less important than merely realizing that it *exists*. The exact meaning of an incidental symbol is usually open to "interpretation," and multiple "readings" of its implications do not necessarily contradict one another. Symbolism may occur in any of the elements discussed above: A plot or character or setting may have some symbolic value. There is little heavy symbolism in "Reunion," but if we think about the title, with its suggestions of emotional warmth, and the setting, a busy train station, we can see that Cheever has chosen his title carefully, and it has both ironic and symbolic overtones.

If the details of a plot seem consistently symbolic, with each detail clearly pointing the way to some obvious larger meaning, then we are reading **allegory.** An allegorical reading of Hawthorne's "Young Goodman Brown" (page 525) might focus on how the protagonist's and his wife's names represent untested virtue and religious fidelity, respectively, and how the dark forest mirrors the confusion of Brown's soul. In a given story, an author may employ a *traditional symbol,* a thing that most members of a culture instantly recognize as possessing a shared symbolic meaning. Familiarity with an individual author's works may also help us to recognize a *private symbol,* a symbol that the author has made his or her own by repeated usage. To cite one example, Flannery O'Connor's use of bursts of bright light generally herald some kind of dawning spiritual revelation in the mind of one of her characters. Another writer may use certain colors, situations, and actions repeatedly;

it is hard to read much of Poe's fiction without becoming aware of the personal horror that small, confined spaces represent for the author. Finally, we may identify an *incidental symbol,* in a story. This symbol may be a thing or action that ordinarily would have not deeper meaning but acquires one in a particular story. Paying close attention to the way an author repeats certain details or otherwise points to their significance is the key.

Determining Style, Imagery, and Symbolism in Fiction

1. How can you characterize the author's style? Is it abstract? Concrete? Does the author use slang? Overly complicated words or sentences?
2. What is the tone of the story? Relaxed? Angry? Controlled? How is tone revealed through diction and sentence structure?
3. Does the tone reveal the attitudes of the author, or the narrator?
4. Are there any traditional symbols in the narrative? Are they employed in a straightforward manner, or does the story give them additional or ironic meaning?
5. Are there any private symbols in the narrative? Where else does the author employ these symbols and do those other instances have any influence on their meaning in this story?

Insight: GRAPHIC WORKS AS LITERARY TEXTS

Traditionally, graphic works have not been given much consideration in the study of literature. However, on some fundamental level, graphic art is no different from the plain written word. Given in a particular sequence, both letters and graphics can generate an amazing complexity of ideas and messages.

In recent years, a number of comics have begun to garner critical acclaim, some of which are represented in this anthology. The genre of the comic book might be associated with juvenile thinking and poor artwork, but the reality of the medium is that sequential art offers many of the same possibilities for artistry as other forms of art, and it in fact may offer readers and writers the possibility of creating and understanding things that could not be accomplished in other works and mediums of expression. Art Spiegelman's *Maus,* for example, juxtaposes images of cats, mice, and other animals onto otherwise human forms, and by interlacing these images with a Holocaust narrative he provides a metaphor that would have been difficult, if not impossible, to accomplish with such immediacy and effect in another medium. Sequential art can be analyzed and argued about in the same ways as traditional narrative, according to plot, characterization, theme, and any number of other elements, but it also opens an entirely new world of contrast, foregrounding, framing, and other techniques for generating and interpreting meaning in a work.

POETRY

Likely, the most famous and most often quoted poem written by an American is the following:

> O say, can you see, by the dawn's early light,
>> What so proudly we hailed at the twilight's last gleaming?
> Whose broad stripes and bright stars thro' the perilous fight,
>> O'er the ramparts we watched, were so gallantly streaming!
> And the rockets' red glare, the bombs bursting in air,
>> Gave proof through the night that our flag was still there:
> O say, does that star-spangled banner yet wave
>> O'er the land of the free and the home of the brave?

What this history demonstrates is that in order for us to understand any poem fully, we need some background information, like the exposition that opens a short story. However, in many cases this information, or **dramatic situation** of the poem, is often implied and not directly stated.

Yes, it's a song, but Francis Scott Key originally wrote it as a poem titled "The Defense of Fort McHenry." Some may know the poem's background. The events that the poem describes took place on September 13 and 14, 1814, during the War of 1812. A lawyer, Key came aboard a British warship anchored off Baltimore to argue for the release of a client and friend who had been taken hostage by the British. Key won his friend's release, but the British captain, fearing that he might reveal information he had learned on board, kept Key overnight, releasing him and his client in the morning. It was during that night that Key witnessed the bombardment and, with it, the failure of the British to take Baltimore. The other three stanzas of the poem celebrate the victory and offers a hopeful prayer that God will continue to smile on America "when our cause . . . is just."

Identifying Speaker, Listener, and Context

The details of speaker, listener, and context of a poem are called the **dramatic situation** of a poem and can be summed up in a question: *Who is speaking to whom under what circumstances?* If the poet fails to provide us with clues or if we are careless in picking up the information that is provided, then we may begin reading with no sense of reference and, thus, may go far astray. Even such words as *on, upon,* or *to* in titles can be crucial to our understanding of dramatic situation, telling us something about an event or object that provided the stimulus for the poem or about the identity of the "you" addressed in the poem. A poem like "The Star-Spangled Banner" (page 26) has the most specific type of dramatic situation a poem can have, for it is an example of **occasional verse**—a poem that is written about or for an important event (or occasion), sometimes private but usually of some public significance. Although poems of this type are not often printed on the front pages of newspapers as they once were, they are still being written. The thousands of poems written after September 11, 2001, bear witness to the staying power of occasional verse.

Let us consider the dramatic situation of the poem "My Husband Discovers Poetry" by Diane Lockward (page 1007). *Who* is speaking? A technical word often used to designate the speaker of a poem is **persona** (plural: **personae**), a word that meant "mask" in ancient Greek. Because Lockward uses first person and is a poet (and married as well), a first assumption would be that she is the speaker in her poem. Still, we have to ask the question of *how* we are meant to "take" what Lockward says—what kind of "mask" she is wearing here. Is this an account of something that literally happened between the poet and her husband, or is she sardonically imagining a rather extreme way of "getting back at" a man who has perhaps been inattentive one time too many? You might notice how the verb tenses in the poem shift from past to present midway through. This shift may indicate that Lockward's poem is closer to a fantasy than to an autobiographical vignette.

When you read any poem, look at it carefully for any evidence that the speaker is someone other than the poet. Poems like "Ulysses" by Alfred, Lord Tennyson (page 1237) or "Porphyria's Lover" by Robert Browning (page 987) have titles that identify personae who are, respectively, a character from ancient epic poetry and an unnamed man who is confessing the murder of his lover, Porphyria. In neither case is the persona to be identified with the poet himself. Even Sylvia Plath, a poet usually associated with an extremely candid form of autobiographical poetry known as **confessional poetry,** on a BBC broadcast identified the persona of her masterpiece "Daddy" (page 212) as an invented character. Sometimes poems have more than one persona, which is the case with Thomas Hardy's "The Ruined Maid" (page 823) and Robert Frost's "Home Burial" (page 992), two poems that consist almost entirely of dialogue. In other poems, for instance in many ballads, the voice may simply be a third-person narrator such as that found in a short story or novel. Thus, although it is perhaps true that many poems are in fact spoken by the poet out of his or her most private feelings, it is not a good idea to leap too quickly to the assumption that the persona of a poem is identical to the poet and shares his or her views. Conclusions about the degree to which a poem is autobiographical can be verified only by research and familiarity with a poet's life and other works.

To return to our question: Who is speaking to *whom*? Another useful term is **auditor,** the person or persons spoken to in a poem. Some poems identify no auditor; others clearly do specify an auditor or auditors, in most cases by name or by the second person pronoun "you" (or "thee/thou" in older poetry). The figure of speech **apostrophe** is used when a nonhuman, inanimate, or abstract thing is directly addressed. Relatively few poems are addressed directly to the reader, so when we read the opening of William Shakespeare's "Sonnet 18" ("Shall I compare thee to a summer's day?") (page 974) we should keep in mind that he is not addressing us but another individual, in this case a young male friend who is referred to in many of the sonnets. Lockward's poem does in fact have a "you" in it, but the identity of the auditor is unclear. Are we to think of her telling this story to another person, a friend perhaps, or is this the same kind of general "you" we use when we say, "You know what I mean"? Is the "you" the reader, here being addressed directly, or could it, in some strange way, be the husband who is elsewhere referred to in the third person (after all, if the poem shifts its tenses, it could as well shift its pronoun references).

Now the final part of the question: Who is speaking to whom *under what circumstances*? First, we might ask if there is a relationship, either implied or stated, between persona and auditor. Obviously many love poems take the form of verbal transactions between two parties, and, because relationships have their ups and downs, these shifts of mood are reflected in the poetry. One famous example is Michael Drayton's sonnet "Since There's No Help" (Sonnet 61 from his sequence *Idea*), which begins with the persona threatening to end the relationship with the auditor but that ends with an apparent reconciliation. Such "courtship ritual" poems as Andrew Marvell's "To His Coy Mistress" (page 978) are witty arguments in favor of the couple's engaging in sexual relations. An example from poetry about marital love is Matthew Arnold's "Dover Beach" (page 1241), which ends with the plea "Ah, love, let us be true / To one another" as the only hope for stability the persona can find in a world filled with uncertainty and fear. In Lockward's poem, this question involves the "you" less than the speaker's relationship to the husband. And what's even more interesting about the poem's situation is that it is actually a poem *about* a poem, one that may exist only in the author's fantasy of revenge. (By the way, if you're feeling sorry for the poor man in the poem, Lockward has said that this poem is her "real" husband's favorite!)

Other questions relating to circumstances of the dramatic situation might concern the poem's physical setting (if any), time (of day, year, historical era), and even such matters as weather. Thomas Hardy's "Neutral Tones" (page 989) provides a good example of a poem in which the setting, a gray winter day in a barren outdoor location, symbolically reinforces the persona's memory of the bitter end of a love affair. The shift in setting from the springtime idyll to the "cold hillside" in John Keats's "La Belle Dame sans Merci" (page 979) cannot be overlooked in discussing the persona's disillusionment. Of course, many poems are explicitly occasional and may even contain an **epigraph** (see Gwendolyn Brooks's "We Real Cool," page 210), a brief explanatory statement or quotation, or a **dedication** that explains the setting. Sometimes footnotes or even outside research may be necessary. Robert Browning's "My Last Duchess" (page 579) makes little sense to readers if they do not know that the poem is based on the life of a real 16th century Italian Duke whose wife died under suspicious circumstances. A great deal of subtlety and meaning in the poem will be lost on those who are unaware of history of the Duke and the particular occasion of the poem, as he addresses a broker to negotiate the details of his next marriage.

Determining Speaker, Listener, and Context in Poetry

1. How does reading the poem aloud, rather than simply reading it on the page, change its meaning? Are certain words in the poem confused or clarified (such as homynyms) when spoken out loud?
2. What is the dramatic situation of the poem? Who is speaking to whom under what circumstances?

3. Does the title of the poem reveal anything about its speaker, auditor, or subject?
4. Was the poem originally intended to be read to an audience, or was it written specifically for print publication?
5. Is the poem "occasional verse"—specific to some particular occasion or event—or is it more general in its context?
6. Who is the auditor of the poem, if any?
7. Is there a significant difference (in age, race, class, and so on) between the speaker and the auditor?
8. Does the poem involve any familiar patterns or situations (courtship rituals, reunions, heroic narratives, and so on) that you've seen in other poems or in your own life?
9. What is the setting of the poem? Does it take place in a particular season, time, or locale? Would the poem have the same meaning with a different setting?

Lyric, Narrative, and Dramatic Modes

Lyric Mode

The elements of dramatic situation vary from poem to poem or genre to genre. The most familiar genre for most readers is **lyric poetry,** which originally comprised brief poems that were meant to be sung or chanted to the accompaniment of a lyre. Today we still use the word *lyrics* in a specialized sense when referring to the words of a song, but lyric poetry has become such a large category that it includes virtually all poems that are primarily *about* a subject and contain little narrative content. The subject of a lyric poem may be the poet's emotions, an abstract idea, a satirical insight, or a description of a person or place. The persona in a lyric is usually closely identified with the poet him- or herself; because we tend to identify the essence of poetry with personal, subjective expression of feelings or ideas, lyric poetry is the largest genre, with various subgroups like the *ode,* a long, serious meditative lyric, or the *elegy,* a lyric composed on the occasion of someone's death; W. S. Merwin's "For the Anniversary of My Death" (page 1253) is what might be called a "future-tense" elegy.

Narrative Mode

The second genre is **narrative poetry,** that is, poetry whose main function is to tell a story. Like prose fiction, narrative poems have plots, characters, setting, and point of view, and may be discussed in similar terms as, say, a short story. One of the most familiar types of narrative poems is the *ballad,* which is a narrative with songlike qualities that often include rhyme and repeated refrains. Most American folk songs and many popular songs (especially country songs) are ballads. Other types of narrative poetry have been popular through the centuries. Many of Robert Frost's poems are medium-length, realistic narratives, virtually short stories written in verse; one of the most admired is "Home Burial" (page 992).

Dramatic Mode

The third type is usually called **dramatic poetry,** because it has much in common with the separate genre of drama. In general, the persona in a dramatic poem is an invented character not to be identified with the poet. The poem is presented as a speech or dialogue that might be acted out like a soliloquy or scene from a play. The *dramatic monologue* is a speech for a single character, usually delivered to a silent auditor. Notable examples are Tennyson's "Ulysses" and Browning's "Porphyria's Lover." At the close of "Ulysses," the aged hero urges his listening "mariners" to listen closely and to observe the ship in the harbor waiting to take them off on a final voyage. Dramatic poetry can also take the form of *dialogue poetry,* in which two personae speak alternately. One example is Christina Rossetti's allegorical dialogue, "Up-Hill" (page 581).

Although it is easy enough to find examples of "pure" lyric, narrative, and dramatic poems, sometimes the distinction between the three major types may become blurred, even in the same poem. Should Robert Frost's "Home Burial," which almost totally consists of dialogue between a husband and wife, be considered narrative or dramatic? Lockward's poem is a narrative, to be sure, for it does have a character and a plot, but is the poet's intent here just to tell an amusingly cruel story or to vent, in the lyric manner, some of her emotional "steam"?

Determining Lyric, Narrative, and Dramatic Modes of Poetry

1. Is the poem a lyric poem? What is its subject? Does it contain a narrative or is it a general discussion of a topic or theme?
2. Does the poem fit into any subgenres of the lyric? Is it an elegy? An ode?

3. Is the poem a narrative poem? Does it employ a narrator or narrators, and have plot or character development?
4. Does the poem invoke "dramatic" conventions, such as monologue or dialogue?
5. Does the poem use a single genre only, or does it invoke more than one genre or convention?

Applying the Elements of Poetry

Language

One of the most persistent myths about poetry is that its language is artificial, "flowery," and essentially different from the language that people speak in their daily lives. Although these beliefs may be true of some poetry, poems demonstrate varied poetic diction. **Diction** refers to the individual choice of words, ranging between conversational and standard levels, which a poet uses. Today's modern poets can be self-consciously formal (perhaps for ironic effect) or go to the opposite extreme to imitate the language of the streets. In the past *poetic diction* was used to indicate a level of refined speech or mistakenly deemed "superior"; today, however, the term is often used to refer negatively to a poet's language. We should keep in mind that the slang of one era may become the standard usage of another, as is the case with "OK," which has become a universal expression.

It is impossible to characterize poetic language narrowly, for poetry covers the widest possible range of linguistic possibilities. For example, here are several passages from different poets, all describing birds:

Hail to thee, blithe Spirit!
    Bird thou never wert—
That from Heaven, or near it,
    Pourest thy full heart
In profuse strains of unpremeditated art.

Higher still and higher
    From the earth thou springest
Like a cloud of fire;
    The blue deep thou wingest,
And singing still dost soar, and soaring ever singest.

Percy Bysshe Shelley, "To a Skylark"

I caught this morning morning's minion, king-
dom of daylight's dauphin, dapple-dawn-drawn Falcon, in his
riding
Of the rolling level underneath him steady air, and striding
High there, how he rung upon the rein of a wimpling wing
In his ecstasy!

Gerard Manley Hopkins, "The Windhover"

When the lilac-scent was in the air and Fifth-month grass was
growing,
Up this seashore in some briers,
Two feather'd guests from Alabama, two together,
And their nest, and four light-green eggs spotted with brown,
And every day the he-bird to and fro near at hand,
And every day the she-bird crouch'd on her nest, silent, with
bright eyes,
And every day I, a curious boy, never too close, never disturbing
them,
Cautiously peering, absorbing, translating.

Walt Whitman, "Out of the Cradle Endlessly Rocking"

The blue booby lives
on the bare rocks
of Galápagos
and fears nothing.
It is a simple life:
they live on fish,
and there are few predators.

James Tate, "The Blue Booby"

Of these quotes only Shelley's, from the early nineteenth century, possesses the characteristics of what many people mean when they use the term *poetic* to talk about language. Poetry, like any art form, follows fashions that change over the years; in Shelley's day, the artificially heightened grammatical forms of "thee" and "thou" and their related verb forms ("wert" and "wingest") were reserved for prayers and poetry. The language used in Hopkins's poem from the 1870s is artificial in an entirely different way; here the poet's **idiom** (in a phrase like "dapple-dawn-drawn falcon"), the personal use of words that marks his poetry, is highly idiosyncratic; indeed, it would be hard to mistake a poem by Hopkins, with its muscular monosyllables and rich texture of sound patterns, with one by any other poet. Compare this to a jazz singer like the late Ella Fitzgerald who invents words (this is called "scat") based solely on their sounds or a rapper who combines or invents new slang. These inventive uses of language are essentially no different from Hopkins's creativity with words. When we move to the contemporary period, we can find little difference between the language of many poems and conversational speech, as Tate's lines indicate.

Other linguistic devices that characterize poetic language include:

- **Archaisms**—words that are no longer in common use, for example, "barks of yore," from a poem by Edgar Allan Poe titled, "To Helen" (page 986). Looking up the literal sense of a word in a dictionary discloses its **denotation,** or literal meaning. Thus, we find that "barks" are small sailing ships and that "yore" refers to the distant past. Of course, Poe could have said "ships of the past" or a similar phrase, but his word choice was perhaps dictated by **connotation,** the implied meaning or feel that some words have acquired; it may be that even in Poe's day "barks of yore" had a remote quality that somehow evoked ancient Greece in a way that, say, "ancient ships" would not.
- **Syncope**—a contraction created by the dropping of a letter ("o'er" instead of "over"; "falt'ring" instead of "faltering") for the sake of maintaining the poem's meter.
- **Coinage** or **neologism**—a word made up by the poet, for example, "Nicean," from Poe's "To Helen" is a proper adjective that sounds geographical but does not appear in either the dictionary or gazetteer. Speculation on the source of "Nicean" has ranged from Nice, in the South of France, to Phoenician, but it is likely that Poe simply coined the word for its exotic sound.

Concrete and Abstract Diction   Several other matters relevant to poetic language are worth mentioning. A final tension exists in poems between their use of **concrete diction** and **abstract diction.** Concrete words denote that which can be perceived by the senses, and the vividness of a poem's language resides primarily in the way it uses **imagery,** sensory details denoting specific physical experiences. Because it is the most important of the five senses, *visual imagery* ("a dim light," "a dirty rag," "a golden daffodil") predominates in poems, but we should also be alert for striking examples of the other types of imagery:

auditory ("a pounding surf"), **tactile** ("a scratchy beard"), *olfactory* ("the scent of apple blossoms"), and *gustatory* ("the bitter tang of gin"). In his prologue to *The Canterbury Tales*, for example, Chaucer uses brilliantly chosen concrete details—a nun's coral jewelry, a monk's hood lined with fur, a festering sore on a cook's shin—to bring his pilgrims to life.

In the early twentieth century, a group of poets led by Americans Ezra Pound and H. D. (Hilda Doolittle) pioneered a poetic movement called **Imagism,** in which concrete details predominate in short descriptive poems. "Go in fear of abstractions," commanded Pound, and his friend William Carlos Williams modified the remark to become a poetic credo: "No ideas but in things."

Still, for most poets abstract words remain important because they carry the burden of a poem's overall meaning or theme. William Butler Yeats's "Leda and the Swan" (page 582) provides a good example of how concrete and abstract diction coexists in a poem. Reading this account of the myth in which Zeus, in the form of a swan, rapes and impregnates a human woman and thus sets in action the chain of events that leads to the Trojan War (Leda was the mother of Helen of Troy), we will probably be struck at first by the way that tactile imagery ("a sudden blow," fingers attempting to "push / The feathered glory" away, "A shudder in the loins") is used to describe an act of sexual violation. Even though some abstract words ("terrified," "vague," "glory," "strange") appear in the first eight lines of the poem, they are all linked closely to concrete words like "fingers," "feathered," and "heart." In the last two lines of the poem, Yeats uses three large abstractions—"knowledge," "power," and "indifferent"—to state his theme. More often than not, one can expect to encounter the largest number of abstract words near the conclusions of poems. Probably the most famous abstract statement in English poetry is John Keats's " 'Beauty is truth, truth beauty, that is all / Ye know on earth, and all ye need to know,'" which appears in the last two lines of a fifty-line poem that is filled with lush, sensory details of description.

Two other devices sometimes govern a poet's choice of words. **Onomatopoeia** refers to individual words like "splash" or "thud" whose meanings are closely related to their sounds. Auditory imagery in a poem can often be enhanced by the use of onomatopoeic words. In some cases, however, a whole line can be called onomatopoeic, even if it contains no single word that illustrates the device. Thomas Hardy uses this line to describe the pounding of distant surf: "Where hill-hid tides throb, throe on throe." Here the repetition of similar sounds helps to imitate the sound of the ocean. A second device is the **pun**, the use of one word to imply the additional meaning of a similar-sounding word. Thus, when Anne Bradstreet is comparing her first book to an illegitimate child, she addresses the book in this manner: "If for thy Father asked, say thou had'st none; / And for thy Mother, she alas is poor, / Which caused her thus to send thee out of door." The closeness of the interjection "alas" to the article and noun "a lass" is hardly coincidental. Poets in Bradstreet's day considered the pun a staple of their repertoire, even in serious poetry, but contemporary poets are more likely to use it primarily for comic effect

To return briefly to Lockward's poem, the level of diction here, like that of many contemporary poems, is simple, casual, and conversational, and doesn't raise any immediate questions. Still, take another look at the phrase "paying tribute" in the last line and think of both denotation and connotation. To "pay tribute" means, in one sense, to praise, but "pay" is a word that also has some negative connotations: "I'll make you pay for that remark!" And one of the denotations of "tribute" is "a sum . . . paid by one ruler or nation to another as acknowledgement of submission." Aha!

Determining the Language of Poetry

1. What kind of language does the poem use? Is it flowery? Common? Specific or general?
2. Is the poet idiomatic? Does the poet employ language in style, rhyme, or grammar that is very particular to that author alone?
3. How does the language of the poem relate to the era in which it was written? Would "archaic" language in a poem read today be considered archaic when it was written?
4. What is a brief paraphrase of the poem? How does the poem differ from such a "normal" prose version of its apparent meaning?
5. Does the etymology (or linguistic history) of any of the words in the poem add to its meaning?
6. Is the poem concrete or abstract? How does it use details?
7. What senses, if any, does the poem invoke (tactile, auditory, and so on)? Do these senses have any particular relation to the message or meaning of the poem?
8. Are there any puns in the poem or other passages that seem to be deliberately invoking more than one meaning at a time?

Syntax

Syntax in poetry, particularly in poems that use rhyme, is likely to differ from that of both speech and prose; if a poet decides to rhyme in a certain pattern, word order must be modified to fit the formal design, and this order may present difficulties to readers in understanding the grammar of a passage. Here is the opening of a familiar piece of American patriotic verse: "My country, 'tis of thee, / Sweet land of liberty, / Of thee I sing." What is the subject of this sentence? Would you be surprised to learn that the subject is "it" (contained in the contraction " 'tis"—"It is of thee, my country, sweet land of liberty, of thee [that] I sing")?

Poe's poem "To Helen" presents few difficulties of this order but does contain one example of **inversion,** words that fall out of their expected order: a related syntactical problem lies in **ellipsis,** words that are consciously omitted by the poet. If we do not allow for this, we are likely to be confused by such lines as "the weary, way-worn wanderer bore / To his own native shore." The wanderer bore *what*? A quick mental sentence diagram shows that "wanderer" is the direct object of "bore," not its subject. A good **paraphrase** (that is, text that we put into our own words) should simplify both diction and syntax: "Helen, to me your beauty is like those Nicean (?) ships of the ancient past that carried the weary, travel-worn wanderer gently over a perfumed sea to his own native land." In paraphrasing, only the potentially troublesome words and phrases should be substituted, leaving the original language as intact as possible. Paraphrasing is a useful first step toward unfolding a poem's literal sense, but it obviously takes few of a poet's specific nuances of language into account; words like "cool," "cold," "chilly," and "frigid" may denote the same thing, but each has its own connotation. "Poetry," Robert Frost famously remarked, "is what is lost in translation." He might have extended the complaint to include paraphrase as well.

Determining Syntax of Poetry

1. Is the syntax of the poem clear or difficult?
2. Are there inverted or missing terms?
3. Why did the poet decide to write in such a fashion?

Figures of Speech

We can always relate experience in a purely literal fashion: "His table manners were deplorable. Mother scolded him severely, and Dad said some angry words to him. He left the table embarrassed and with his feelings hurt." But a more vivid way of saying the same thing might be to use figurative language: "He made an absolute pig of himself. Mother jumped on his back about it, and Dad scorched his ears. You should have seen him slink off like a scolded puppy." All of the types of figurative language, what are called **figures of speech** or **tropes,** involve some kind of comparison, either explicit or implied. Thus, two of the figures in the above example specifically compare aspects of the character's behavior to animal behavior. The other two imply parental words that were delivered with strong physical force or extreme anger. In every case, the thing being described, what is called the **tenor** of the figure of speech, is linked with a concrete image or **vehicle.** Some of the most common figures of speech are:

Metaphor—a direct comparison between two unlike things. Lockward uses a metaphor when she speaks of

> the strange sounds
> that floated up the stairs that day,
> the sounds of an animal, its paw caught
> in one of those traps with teeth of steel . . .

Implied metaphor—a metaphor in which either the tenor or vehicle is implied, not stated.

> While smoke on its chin, that slithering gun
> Coiled back from its windowsill.

In this passage from X. J. Kennedy's poem about the assassination of President John F. Kennedy, Lee Harvey Oswald's rifle is indirectly compared to a snake ("coiled back" and "slithering") that has struck its victim.

Simile—a comparison using like, as, or than as a connective device.

> My love is like a red, red rose (*Robert Burns*)

Conceit—an extended or far-fetched metaphor, in most cases comparing things that apparently have almost nothing in common.

> Make me, O Lord, thy spinning wheel complete. . . .

Edward Taylor spins a conceit that compares the process of salvation to the manufacture of cloth, ending with the persona attired in "holy robes for glory."

Hyperbole—overstatement, a comparison using conscious exaggeration.

> And I will love thee still, my dear,
> Till a' the seas gang dry. (*Robert Burns*)

Understatement—the opposite of hyperbole.

> *The space between is but an hour,*
> *The frail duration of a flower.*

Philip Freneau is understating a wildflower's life span by saying it is "but an hour." Because, by implication, he is also talking about human life, the understatement is even more pronounced.

Allusion—metaphor making a direct comparison to a historical or literary event or character.

> He dreamed of Thebes and Camelot,
> And Priam's neighbors. (*Edwin Arlington Robinson*)

Metonymy—use of a related object to stand for the thing actually being talked about.

> He stood among a crowed a Drumahair;
> His heart hung all upon a silken dress.

The title character of William Butler Yeats's "The Man Who Dreamed of Faeryland" was interested in the woman *in* the dress, not the dress itself.

Synecdoche—use of a part for the whole, or vice versa.

> Before the indifferent beak could let her drop.

Here Yeats is retelling the myth of Leda, who was raped by Zeus in the form of a swan—represented by "beak" in the line.

Personification—giving human characteristics to nonhuman things or to abstractions.

> Of all her train, the hands of Spring
> First plant thee in the watery mould

William Cullen Bryant personifies spring by giving it hands with which to plant a yellow violet.

Apostrophe—variety of personification in which a nonhuman thing, abstraction, or person not physically present is directly addressed as if it could respond.

> Is it, O man, with such discordant noises,
>   With such accursed instruments as these,
> Thou drownest Nature's sweet and kindly voices,
>   And jarrest the celestial harmonies?

Henry Wadsworth Longfellow is addressing the human race in general, not a single man.

Paradox—an apparent contradiction or illogical statement.

> His hand hath made this noble work which Stands,
> His Glorious Handiwork not made by hands.

Edward Taylor is describing the Christian God's creation of the universe, which he *willed* into being.

Oxymoron—a short paradox, usually consisting of an adjective and noun with conflicting meanings.

> Progress is a comfortable disease. (*e. e. cummings*)

Synesthesia—a conscious mixing of two different types of sensory experience.

> Leaves cast in casual potpourris
> Whisper their scents from pits and cellar-holes.
> (*Richard Wilbur*)

Determining Figures of Speech in Poetry

1. Are figures of speech used frequently or infrequently in the poem? How do they invoke, or generate, meaning in the text?
2. Does the poem use any metaphors or implied metaphors? How do they influence the meaning of the poem?
3. Are there any similes in the poem? How do they influence meaning? Why did the author choose a simile rather than a metaphor to make the comparison?
4. Are there any conceits in the poem? Why did the author choose an elaborate metaphor rather then something less complex?

5. Are there any traditional poetic conceits in the poem? Does the poem use any other metaphoric structures that are familiar from other poems or texts?
6. Does the poem contain hyperbole, understatement, or both? How do these figurative devices affect the meaning of the poem?
7. Are there any allusions in the poem to other events, people, or works of literature?
8. Does the poem invoke synesthesia or any other paradoxes, oxymorons, or other contradictory messages? How, if at all, is the reader meant to resolve such problems?

Theme and Symbolism

In a sense, the theme of a poem is like the thesis sentence of an essay; it's not enough just to say that a poem is about love, we need to express, based on our reading of the poem's details of language, figures of speech, and tone, some sense of what it is saying about love. Because many poems indirectly express their themes through the use of symbols, we need to be aware of how some details in a poem may have meanings beyond their literal implications.

The **poetic allegory** is usually a narrative that exists on at least two levels simultaneously, a concrete literal level and an abstract meaning level; throughout an allegory there is a consistent sequence of parallels between the literal and the abstract. Few readers of Christina Rossetti's "Up-Hill" (page 581) would take this poem to be some kind of advertisement for a Victorian motel chain; it's fairly clear that she is speaking allegorically of a *spiritual* journey.

Many poems contain symbolic elements that are somewhat more elusive in meaning than the simple one-for-one allegorical equivalences. A **symbol**, then, is any concrete thing or any action in a poem that implies a meaning beyond its literal sense. Many of these things or actions are called *traditional symbols*, that is, symbols that hold roughly the same meanings for members of a given society. It would be unlikely for a poet to mention a cross without expecting readers think of its Christian symbolism.

Other types of symbols can be identified in poems that are otherwise not allegorical. A *private symbol* is one that has acquired certain meanings from a single poet's repeated use of it. William Butler Yeats's use of "gyres" in several of his poems is explained in some of his prose writings as a symbol for the turning of historical cycles, and his use of the word in his poems obviously goes beyond the literal level. Other poets may employ *incidental symbols,* things that are not usually considered symbolic but may be in a particular poem, or symbolic acts, a situation or response that seems of greater than literal import. Think about that trunk in the basement in Lockward's poem. What do we usually associate with such an object? And think about the title of the Lockward book from which this poem was taken—*Eve's Red Dress*!

Determining Theme and Symbolism in Poetry

1. Does the poem have a meaning beyond its literal, manifest details? If there is an allegorical level to the poem, is there only one?
2. Does the poem invoke any obvious or traditional symbols? Is there a difference between a symbol's meaning on the literal level versus the allegorical one?
3. Does the poem employ symbols that you have seen elsewhere in poems or texts?
4. Does the poet employ private symbols that have connections to other works written by the same author? How does it alter the meaning of the poem to consider these additional connections?

Tone of Voice

Even the simplest statement is subject to multiple interpretations if it is delivered in different tones of voice. Consider the shift in emphasis between saying "I *gave* you the money," "I gave *you* the money," and "I gave you the *money.*" Even a seemingly innocent compliment like "You look lovely this morning!" takes on a different meaning if it is delivered by a woman to her obviously hungover husband. Still, these variations in **tone,** the speaker's implied attitude toward the words he or she says, depend primarily on vocal inflection. Because a poet only rarely gets the opportunity to elucidate his or her tones in a public performance, it is possible that readers may have difficulties in grasping the tone of a poem printed on the page. Still, many poets establish tone in poems quite clearly from the outset. The opening of Marge Piercy's poem "What's That Smell in the Kitchen?" ("All over America women are burning dinners. / It's lambchops in Peoria . . .") (page 597) establishes a tone of comedic anger that is consistent throughout the poem. John

Donne's initial lines in "A Valediction: Forbidding Mourning" ("As virtuous men pass mildly away / And whisper to their souls to go . . .") (page 976) strike the reader with a solemn reverence. Thus, in many cases we can relate the tone of voice in poems to the emotions we employ in our own speech, and we would have to violate quite a few rules of common sense to argue that Piercy is being solemn or to argue that Donne is invoking rage or sarcasm.

Irony is used to imply an attitude that is in fact contrary to what his or her words appear to say. Of course, the simplest form of irony is *sarcasm,* the wounding tone of voice we use to imply exactly the opposite of what we say: "That's really a *great* excuse!" or "What a *wonderful* performance!" For obvious reasons, sarcasm is appropriate primarily to spoken language. It has become almost universal to follow a bit of gentle sarcasm in an e-mail message with a symbolic emoticon :) to indicate that the remark is not to be taken "straight." *Verbal irony* is the conscious manipulation of tone by which the poet's actual attitude is the opposite of what he or she says. Verbal irony is a conspicuous feature of **verse satire,** poetry that exists primarily to mock or ridicule, though often with serious intent. One famous example, in the form of a short satirical piece, or **epigram,** is Sarah N. Cleghorn's "The Golf Links," a poem written before the advent of child-labor laws:

> The golf links lie so near the mill
>   That almost every day
> The laboring children can look out
>   And see the men at play.

Here the weight of the verbal irony falls on two words, "laboring" and "play," and the way each is incongruously applied to the wrong group of people.

"The Golf Links," taken as a whole, also represents a second form of irony, **situational irony,** in which the setting of the poem (laboring children watching playing adults) contains a built-in incongruity. **Dramatic irony,** the third type of irony, occurs when the persona of a poem is less aware of the full import of his or her words than is the reader. William Blake's "The Chimney Sweeper" (from *Songs of Innocence*) (page 202) is spoken by a child who does not seem to fully realize how badly he is being exploited by his employer, who has apparently been using the promises of religion as a way of keeping his underage workers in line. Dramatic irony, as the term implies, is most often found in dramatic monologues, where the gap between the speaker's perception of the situation and the reader's may be wide indeed.

Determining Tone of Voice in Poetry

1. Can the tone be immediately established or understood in the poem?
2. Can ironic or sarcastic meanings be taken from the words of the poem?
3. Is the poem an epigram, a verse satire, or written in some other poetic genre that regularly employs tone to deliver its meaning?
4. Is there verbal, situational, or dramatic irony in the work? What words, lines, situations, or settings reveal one literal meaning while also suggesting another?

Repetition: Sound and Schemes

Because poetry uses language at its most intense level, we are aware of the weight of individual words and phrases to a degree that is usually lacking when we read prose. Poets have long known that the meanings that they attempt to convey often depend as much on the sound of the words as their meaning. We have already mentioned one sound device, onomatopoeia. Consider how much richer the experience of "the murmuring of innumerable bees" is than a synonymous phrase, "the low sound of a lot of bees." It has often been said that all art aspires to the condition of music in the way that it affects an audience on some unconscious, visceral level. By carefully exploiting the repetition of sound devices, a poet may attempt to produce some of the same effects that the musical composer does.

Of course, much of this sonic level of poetry is subjective; what strikes one listener as pleasant may overwhelm the ear of another. Still, it is useful to distinguish between a poet's use of **euphony,** a series of pleasant sounds, and **cacophony,** sounds that are deliberately unpleasant. Note the following passage from Alexander Pope's "An Essay on Criticism," a didactic poem that attempts to illustrate many of the devices poets use:

> Soft is the strain when Zephyr gently blows,
> And the smooth stream in smoother numbers flows . . .

The repetition of the initial consonant sounds is called **alliteration,** and here Pope concentrates on the s sound. The vowel sounds are generally long: str*ai*n, bl*ow*s, sm*oo*th, and fl*ow*s. Here the description of the gentle west wind is assisted by the generally pleasing sense of euphony.

But Pope, to illustrate the opposite quality, follows this couplet with a second:

> But when loud surges lash the sounding shore,
> The hoarse, rough verse should like the torrent roar.

Now the wind is anything but gentle, and the repetition of the *r* sounds in su*r*ges, sho*r*e, hoa*r*se, *r*ough, ve*r*se, to*r*rent, and *r*oar force the reader to speak from the back of the throat, making sounds that are anything but euphonious.

Repetition of sounds has no inherent meaning values (though some linguists might argue that certain sounds do stimulate particular emotions), but this repetition does call attention to itself and can be particularly effective when a poet wishes to emphasize a certain passage. We have already mentioned alliteration. Other sound patterns are **assonance,** the repetition of similar vowel sounds (st*ee*p, *e*v*e*n, rec*ei*ve, v*ea*l), and **consonance,** the repetition of similar consonant sounds (du*ck*, tor*que*, stri*ke*, tri*ck*le). It should go without saying that spelling has little to do with any sound pattern; an initial *f* will alliterate with an initial *ph.*

Rhyme is the most important sound device, and our pleasures in deftly executed rhymes go beyond mere sound to include the pleasure we take when an unexpected word is magically made to fit with another. There are several types of rhyme:

- *Masculine rhyme* occurs between single stressed syllables: *fleece, release, surcease, niece,* and so on.
- *Feminine rhyme,* also called *double rhyme,* matches two syllables, the first stressed and the second usually unstressed: *stinging, upbringing, flinging.*
- *Triple rhyme* goes further: *slithering, withering.*
- *Slant rhyme* (also called *near rhyme* and *off rhyme*) contains hints of sound repetition (sometimes related to assonance and consonance): *chill, dull, sale* are possibilities, though poets often grant themselves considerable leeway in counting as rhyming words pairs that often have only the slightest similarity.
- *End rhymes* occur at the ends of lines and fall in a pattern in a poem. This pattern makes it possible to assign letters to the sounds and speak of a **rhyme scheme.** Thus, a stanza of four lines ending with *heaven, hell, bell, eleven* would be said to have a rhyme scheme of *abba.*
- *Internal rhymes* are found in the interior of lines.

More complicated patterns of repetition involve more than mere sounds but whole phrases and grammatical units. Ancient rhetoricians, teaching the art of public speaking, identified several of these, and they are also found in poetry. **Parallel structure** is simply the repetition of grammatically similar phrases or clauses: Tennyson's "To strive, to seek, to find, and not to yield." **Anaphora** and **epistrophe** are repeated words or phrases at, respectively, the beginnings and ends of lines. Walt Whitman uses these schemes extensively, often in the same lines. This passage from "Song of Myself" illustrates both anaphora and epistrophe:

> If they are not yours as much as mine they are nothing, or next
>   to nothing,
> If they are not the riddle and the untying of the riddle they are
>   nothing,
> If they are not just as close as they are distant they are nothing.

Antithesis is the matching of parallel units that contain contrasting meanings, such as Whitman's "I am of old and young, of the foolish as much as the wise, / Regardless of others, ever regardful of others, / Maternal as well as paternal, a child as well as a man." Although the rhetorical schemes are perhaps more native to the orator, the poet can still make occasional effective use of them. Whitman's poetry was influenced by many sources but by none perhaps so powerfully as the heavily schematic language of the King James Bible.

Determining Repetition: Sound and Schemes in Poetry

1. How does the poem invoke sound, in general, in generating or influencing meaning?
2. Does the poem use euphony or cacophony? Why? What effect does it have?
3. Does the poem contain alliteration, assonance, or consonance? How does this contribute to the overall meaning?
4. What kind of rhyming does the poem use? Does the poem use a consistent kind of rhyme (only masculine rhymes, for example) or is there variation?
5. Are there parallel structures, such as repetitive rhymes or duplication in sentence structure, in the poem?

Meter and Rhythm

The subject of poetic meter and rhythm can be a difficult one, to say the least, and it is doubtless true that such phrases as *trochaic octameter* or *spondaic substitution* have an intimidating quality. Still, discussions of meter need not be limited to experts, and even beginning readers should be able to apply a few of the metrical principles that are commonly found in poetry written in English.

To start, let's distinguish between two terms that are often used synonymously: **poetry** and **verse.** On the one hand, poetry refers to a whole genre of literature and thus stands with fiction and drama as one of the three major types of writing; *verse* refers to a mode of writing in lines of a certain length; thus, many poets still retain the old practice of capitalizing the first word of each line to indicate its integrity as a unit of composition. Virtually any piece of writing can be versified (and sometimes rhymed as well). Perhaps the simplest way to think of **meter** in verse is to think of its synonym **measure** (think of the use of meter in words like odometer or kilometer). Thus, meter refers to the method by which a poet determines line length.

If a writer is unconcerned about the length of individual lines and is governed only by the width of the paper being used, then he or she is not writing verse but **prose.** All verse is metrical writing; prose is not. Surprisingly enough, there is a body of writing called **prose poetry,** writing that uses language in a poetic manner but avoids any type of meter.

When we talk about meter in poetry we ordinarily mean that the poet is employing some kind of consistent **prosody** or system of measurement. There are many possible prosodies, depending on what the poet decides to count as the unit of measurement in the line, but only three of these systems are common in English poetry.

Syllabic verse is perhaps the simplest. In verse of this type the length of the line is determined by counting the total number of syllables the line contains. Because English is a language of strong stresses, most English-language poets have favored other prosodic systems.

More natural to the English language is **accentual verse,** a prosodic system in which only accented or strongly stressed syllables are counted in a line, which can also contain a varying number of unaccented syllables. Much folk poetry, perhaps intended to be recited to the beat of a percussion instrument, retains this stress-based pattern, as do contemporary rap and hip-hop. We identify the various patterns of stress by **scanning** each line. (An example of scanned verse shortly follows.)

Accentual-syllabic verse is the most important prosodic system in English, dominating English-language poetry for the five centuries from Chaucer's time down to the early years of this century. Even though in the last fifty years free verse has become the prevailing style in which

poetry is written, accentual-syllabic verse still has many able practitioners. An accentual-syllabic prosody is somewhat more complicated than
the two systems we have mentioned, because it requires that the poet
count both the strongly stressed syllables and the total number of syllables in the line. Because stressed and unstressed syllables alternate
fairly regularly in this system, four **metrical feet,** representing the most
common patterns, designate the subdivisions of rhythm that make up
the line (think of a yardstick divided into three feet). These feet are
the **iamb** (or *iambic foot*), one unstressed and one stressed syllable; the
trochee (or *trochaic foot*), one stressed and one unstressed syllable;
the **anapest** (or *anapestic foot*), two unstressed syllables and one
stressed syllable; and the **dactyl** (or *dactylic foot*), one stressed and two
unstressed syllables. Simple repetition of words or phrases can give us
the sense of how these lines sound in a purely schematic sense. The
breve (∪) is used to denote unstressed syllables and **ictus** (′) is used to
denote stressed syllables.

Iambic:

release / release / release

to fall / into / despair

Marie / discov / ers candy

Trochaic:

melting / melting / melting / melting

Peter / disa / greed en / tirely

clever / writing / filled the / page

Anapestic

to the top / to the top

a retriev / er appeared

and a ter / ri ble thunder

Dactylic:

shivering / shivering / shivering / shivering / shivering

terribly / ill with the / symptoms of / viral pneu / monia

note how the / minister / whispered at / Emily's / grave

Because each of these lines contains a certain number of feet, a second term is used to denote how many times a foot is repeated in a line:

one foot	**monometer**
two feet	**dimeter**
three feet	**trimeter**
four feet	**tetrameter**
five feet	**pentameter**
six feet	**hexameter**
seven feet	**heptameter**
eight feet	**octameter**

Thus, in the examples above, the first set of lines is iambic trimeter; the second, trochaic tetrameter; the third, anapestic dimeter; and the fourth, dactylic pentameter. The iambic foot is most common in English, followed by the anapest and the trochee; the dactylic foot is relatively rare. Line lengths tend to be from three to five feet, with anything shorter or longer used only sparingly. Probably the most important of all English-language meters is iambic pentameter. Here are some lines from Tennyson's "Ulysses," marked to show his slight variations from the regular meter and his use of the **caesura (‖)**, a pause in a line.

This is / my son, ‖ / mine own / Telem / achus,

To whom / I leave / the scep / ter and / the isle,

Well-loved / of me, ‖ / discern / ing to / fulfill

This la / bor, ‖ by / slow pru / dence to / make mild

A rug / ged peo / ple, ‖ and / through soft / degrees

Subdue / them to / the use / ful and / the good.

Nothing has been so exhaustively debated in English-language poetry as the exact nature of **free verse**. The simplest definition may be the best: Free verse is verse with no consistent metrical pattern. In free verse, line length is a subjective decision made by the poet, and length may be determined by grammatical phrases, the poet's own sense of individual "breath units," or even by the visual arrangement of lines on the page. The extensive use of free verse is a fairly recent phenomenon in the history of poetry. Even though there are many examples of free verse from the past (the Psalms, Ecclesiastes, and the Song of Solomon from the King James Bible), the modern history of free verse begins in 1855 with the publication of Walt Whitman's *Leaves of Grass*. Lockward's poem is typical of many being written today in that it is written in free-verse lines that average nine or ten syllables. It's interesting that the "other" poem, the one her poem describes, is said to be in "lines of strict iambic pentameter," while "My Husband Discovers Poetry" has only a few lines (the first and last lines, for example) that scan as with this accent-syllabic scheme.

Determining Meter and Rhythm in Poetry

1. What kind of prosody does the poem employ? Does the number of syllables in the lines shape the poem? The number of accented or unaccented syllables?
2. Does the prosody of the poem correspond in any way to its meaning? How would meaning change in the poem if it were arranged so that different syllables or words were accented?
3. Does the poem employ very common metrical styles (iambic feet, for example), or is it less traditional?

Form

Closed form denotes the existence of some kind of regular pattern of meter, stanza, rhyme, or repetition. **Stanza forms** are consistent patterns in the individual units of the poem (stanza means "room" in Italian). We limit our discussion to only a few examples of forms; *The New Princeton Encyclopedia of Poetry and Poetics* is probably the most exhaustive reference book on this and virtually any other element of poetry.

Blank verse is not, strictly speaking, a stanza form because it consists of individual lines of iambic pentameter that do not rhyme. However, long poems in blank verse may be arranged into *verse paragraphs* or *stanzas* with a varying number of lines. Paired rhyming lines (*aabbcc . . .*) are called **couplets,** though they are only rarely printed as separate stanzas. *Short couplets* have a meter of iambic tetrameter, and *heroic couplets* have a meter of iambic pentameter. A four-line stanza is known as a **quatrain,** and poets have used many different combinations of rhyme scheme and meters. Alternating lines of tetrameter and trimeter in any foot, rhyming *abcb* or *abab,* make up a *ballad stanza;* if the feet are strictly iambic, the quatrain is called *common meter,* the form of many popular hymns like "Amazing Grace" and many of Emily Dickinson's poems. Other common stanza forms range from three to nine lines.

Fixed forms are combinations of meter, rhyme scheme, and repetition that make up complete poems. One familiar three-line fixed form is the **haiku,** a Japanese import consisting of lines of five, seven, and five syllables, respectively. The most important of the fixed forms is the **sonnet,** which consists of fourteen lines of rhymed iambic pentameter. The original form of the sonnet is called the **Italian sonnet** or the **Petrarchan sonnet** after the fourteenth-century poet who popularized it. An Italian sonnet is usually cast in two stanzas, an *octave* rhyming *abbaabba* and a *sestet* with a variable rhyme scheme; *cdcdcd, cdecde,* and *cddcee* are some of the possible patterns. A *volta* or "turn," usually a conjunction or conjunctive adverb like "but" or "then," may appear at the beginning of the sestet, signifying a slight change of direction in thought. Many Italian sonnets have a strong logical connection between octave and sestet—problem/solution, cause/effect, question/answer— and the volta helps to clarify the transition.

The **English sonnet,** also known as the **Shakespearean sonnet** after its prime exemplar, was developed in the sixteenth century after the sonnet was imported to England and employs a different rhyme scheme that considers the relative scarcity of rhymes in English (as compared to Italian). The English sonnet has a rhyme scheme of *ababcdcdefefgg* and is usually printed as a single stanza. The pattern of three English quatrains plus a heroic couplet often forces a slightly different organizational scheme on the poet, though many of Shakespeare's sonnets still employ a strong volta at the beginning of the ninth line. Other English sonnets may withhold the turn until the beginning of the closing couplet. Many other sonnets written over the years have other rhyme schemes, often hybrids of the Italian and English types. These are usually termed *nonce sonnets.* Several other fixed forms, all continental imports, have appeared frequently in English poetry. One of the most popular is the **villanelle,** a nineteen-line poem, usually written in iambic pentameter, employing two refrain lines, A_1 and A_2, in a pattern of five tercets and a final quatrain: $A_1bA_2\ abA_1\ abA_2\ abA_1\ abA_2\ abA_1A_2$. Other popular fixed forms include the 28-line *ballade* and the 39-line *sestina.*

Lockward's poem is written in what is usually called **open form,** meaning that it has no set meter, rhyme scheme, and regular stanza length. Most poems being written and published today are written in open form, though poets may occasionally use metrical lines and rhymes in them.

Determining Form in Poetry

1. If the poem is written in free verse, what elements of form does it still contain? What, if anything, still makes it a poem?

2. Does the poem have an open or a closed form? For example, does the poem employ a consistent rhyme scheme or have consistent, separate stanzas?

3. Where does the poem deviate, if at all, from traditional forms, or forms internal to the poem itself? How do these structures impact the meaning?

4. Does the poem employ traditional or nonce stanzaic forms? Both? What effect is created by using these forms?

5. If the poem uses stanzaic forms, does it employ rhyme or meter in combination with those forms?

6. Does the poem employ traditional stanzaic forms (such as common meter)? If so, does it depart from those traditional forms at any point? Why or why not?

7. Does the poem employ any rare stanzaic forms, such as the quintet?

8. How does the use of stanzaic forms in the poem relate it to other poems with either a similar form or on similar subject matter?

9. Is the poem written in a fixed, traditional form, such as a sonnet, haiku, or villanelle? What expectations, if any, does this place on the poem?

10. If the poem is written in a fixed form, does it deviate from that pattern at any time, and to what end? Does the way that the poem maintains (or deviates from) its form reveal anything about its meaning?

Insight: POPULAR SONGS AS POETRY

Consider for a moment that songs and poems are not exactly equivalent to one another.

Take the example of "emblematic" poetry, "concrete" poetry, or other work that forms particular visual shapes on the page. A poem by e. e. cummings, for example, might employ spacing and line breaks to give visual support to its meaning. If such a poem were read aloud to an audience, even using different readers for each voice, the visual craft of the piece would be lost, impossible to "hear."

However, most fans of popular music, and we consider ourselves in that group, are happy to point out that songs and poems are for the most part equivalent. That detail might seem obvious or irrelevant, but it's important to realize that there is a reason for making such an argument. By granting songs the status of "poetry," what we're saying is that songs can potentially be more than entertainment, and that we think of a quality song just as we do a quality poem, as a vital form of literary expression that is somehow capable of being more refined, elevated, or important than normal language. The fact that most people agree with this argument, perhaps without even knowing they do, can be seen in the immense popularity of songs in practically every known culture—if songs were mere entertainment, we wouldn't work so hard to produce and preserve them. Further proof of the correlation lies in the fact that many poems in the history of literature were originally from an oral tradition. Either they were created as songs originally, or at the very least they were originally intended to be heard, rather than read silently.

Still, we want to close with one caveat: Because songs are meant to be heard and not read, song lyrics lose their musical dimension when printed on a page. Suppose you had to study the history of sculpture primarily by looking at photographs. Wouldn't the whole third dimension that makes sculpture what it is be lost? We feel the same way about song lyrics when they are separated from the music that makes them so memorable.

DRAMA

In our earlier discussions of fiction and poetry, we made use of terminology originally derived from Aristotle's *Poetics*, the earliest work of literary criticism in western civilization. Aristotle attempts to define and classify the different literary genres that use rhythm, language, and harmony. Aristotle comments most fully on tragedy, and his definition of the genre demands close examination:

> A tragedy, then, is the imitation of an action that is serious and also, as having magnitude, complete in itself; in language with pleasurable accessories, each kind brought in separately in the parts of the work; in a dramatic, not in a narrative form; with incidents arousing pity and fear, wherewith to accomplish its catharsis of such emotions.

First we should note that the imitation here is of *action*. Later in the passage, when Aristotle differentiates between narrative and dramatic forms of literature, it is clear that he is referring to tragedy as a type of literature written primarily for public performance. Furthermore, tragedy must be serious and must have magnitude. By this Aristotle implies that issues of life and death must be involved and that these issues must be of public import. In many Greek tragedies the fate of the *polis,* or city, of which the chorus is the voice, is bound up with the actions taken by the main character in the play. Despite their rudimentary form of democracy, the people of Athens would have been perplexed by a tragedy with an ordinary citizen at its center; magnitude in tragedy demands that only the affairs of persons of high rank are of sufficient importance for tragedy. Aristotle further requires that this imitated action possess a sense of completeness. At no point does he say that a tragedy has to end with a death or even in a state of unhappiness; he does require, however, that the audience sense that after the last words are spoken no further story cries out to be told.

The next part of the passage may confuse the modern reader. By "language with pleasurable accessories" Aristotle means the poetic devices of rhythm and, in the choral parts of the tragedy, music and dance as well. Reading the choral passages in a Greek tragedy, we are likely to forget that these passages were intended to be chanted or sung ("chorus" and "choir" share the same root word in Greek) and danced ("choreography" comes from this root as well).

The rest of Aristotle's definition dwells on the emotional effects of tragedy on the audience. Pity and fear are to be evoked—pity because we must care for the characters and to some extent empathize with them, fear because we come to realize that the fate they endure involves actions that civilized men and women most abhor; in William Shakespeare's *Hamlet* (page 602) these actions involve murder, deception, and suicide. Finally, Aristotle's word **catharsis** has proven controversial over the centuries. The word literally means "a purging," but readers have debated whether Aristotle is referring to a release of harmful emotions or a transformation of them. In either case, the implication is that viewing a tragedy has a beneficial effect on an audience, perhaps because the viewers' deepest fears are brought to light in a make-believe setting. The protagonist of a tragedy remains, in many ways, a "scapegoat" on whose head we project our own unconscious terrors.

Aristotle identifies six elements of a tragedy, and these elements are still useful in analyzing not only tragedies but other types of plays as well, including comedies. In order of importance they are plot, characterization, theme, diction, melody, and spectacle.

Applying the Elements of Drama

Plot

Aristotle considers **plot** the chief element of a play, and it is easy to see this when we consider that in discussing a film with a friend we usually give a brief summary, or *synopsis,* of the plot, stopping just short of "giving it away" by telling how the story concludes. Aristotle defines plot as "the combination of incidents, or things done in the story," going on to give the famous formulation that a plot "is that which has beginning, middle, and end." Aristotle notes that the best plots are selective in their use of material and have an internal coherence and logic. Aristotle seems to favor plays with *unified plot,* that is, one that takes place in a single day; in a short play with a unified plot like Susan Glaspell's *Trifles* (page 230), the action is continuous and imitates the amount of time that the events would have taken in real life. By *episodic plot* we mean one that spreads its action out over a longer period of time. A play that has a unified plot, a single setting, and no subplots is said to observe the **three unities,** which critics in some past eras virtually insisted on as ironclad rules. Although most plots are chronological, playwrights in the last half-century have experimented, sometimes radically, with such straightforward progression through time. David Ives's *Sure Thing* (page 1081) plays havoc with chronology, allowing his protagonist to "replay" his previous scenes until he has learned the way to the "sure thing" of the title.

Two other important elements of plots that Aristotle considers most successful are **reversal** (*peripeteia* in Greek, also known as *peripety*) and **recognition** (*anagnorisis* in Greek, also known as *discovery*). By reversal he means a change "from one state of things within the play to its opposite." Most plays have more than a single reversal; each episode or act builds on the main character's hopes that his or her problems will be dissolved, only to dash those expectations as the play proceeds. Recognition, the second term, is perhaps more properly an element of characterization because it involves a character's "change from ignorance to knowledge." If the events of the plot have not served to illuminate the character about his or her failings then the audience is likely to feel that the story has lacked depth. The kind of self-knowledge that tragedies provide is invariably accompanied by suffering and won at great emotional cost, while in comedies reversals may bring relief to the characters and recognition may bring about the happy conclusion of the play.

As earlier noted in the discussion of fiction, a typical plot may be broken down into several components. First comes the **exposition**, which provides the audience with essential information—who, what, when, where—that it needs to know before the play can continue. A novelist or short story writer can present information directly with some sort of variation on the "Once upon a time" opening. But dramatists have particular problems with exposition because facts must be presented in the form of dialogue and action. Greek dramatists used the first two parts of a tragedy, a prologue and the first appearance of the chorus, to refresh the audience's familiarity with the myths being retold and to set up the initial situation of the play. Other types of drama use a single character to provide expository material. Some of Shakespeare's plays employ a single character named "Chorus" who speaks an introductory prologue and sets the scene for later portions of the plays as well. Occasionally, we even encounter the least elegant solution to the problem of dramatic exposition, employing minor characters whose sole function is to provide background information in the play's opening scene. Countless drawing-room comedies have raised the curtain on a pair of servants in the midst of a gossipy conversation that catches the audience up on the doings of the family members who make up the rest of the cast.

The second part of a plot is called the **complication**, the interjection of some circumstance or event that shakes up the stable situation that has existed before the play's opening and begins the **rising action** of the play, during which the audience's tension and expectations become tightly intertwined and involved with the characters and the events they experience. Complication in a play may be both external and internal. A plague, a threatened invasion, or a conclusion of a war are typical examples of external complications, outside events that affect the characters' lives. However, many plays rely primarily on an internal complication, a single character's weakness in his or her personality. Often the complication is heightened by **conflict** between two characters whom events have forced into collision with each other. In Terrence McNally's *Andre's Mother*, for example, the external complication is Andre's lovers trouble in communicating with Andre's mother, but the internal complication is her inability to deal with Andre's lifestyle and death. No matter how it is presented, the complication of the plot usually introduces a problem that the characters cannot avoid. The rising action, which constitutes the body of the play, usually contains a number of moments of **crisis**, when solutions crop up momentarily but quickly disappear. These critical moments in the scenes may take the form of the kinds of reversals discussed above, and the audience's emotional involvement in the plot generally hinges on the characters' rising and falling hopes.

The central moment of crisis in the play is the **climax,** or the moment of greatest tension, which initiates the **falling action** of the plot. Perhaps "moments" of greatest tension would be a more exact phrase, for skillful playwrights know how to wring as much tension as possible from the audience. In the best plots everything in earlier parts of the play has pointed to this scene—a duel, a suicide, a murder—and the play's highest pitch of emotion.

The final part of a plot is the **dénouement,** or **resolution.** As noted in our discussion of plots in fiction, the French word literally refers to the untying of a knot, the release of the tension that has built up during the play. The dénouement returns the play and its characters to a stable situation, though not the same one that existed at the beginning of the play, and gives some indication of what the future holds for them. A dénouement may be either closed or open. A *closed dénouement* ties up everything neatly and explains all unanswered questions the audience might have; an *open dénouement* leaves a few tantalizing loose ends.

Several other plot terms should also be noted. Aristotle mentions, not altogether favorably, plots with "double issues." The most common word for this is **subplot,** a less important story involving minor characters that may mirror the main plot of the play. Some plays may even have more than one subplot. Occasionally a playwright finds it necessary to drop hints about coming events in the plot, perhaps to keep the audience from complaining that certain incidents have happened "out of the blue." This is called **foreshadowing.** If a climactic incident that helps to resolve the plot has not been adequately prepared for, the playwright may be accused of having resorted to a *deus ex machina* ending, which takes its name from the *mechane* that once literally lowered a god or goddess into the midst of the dramatic proceedings.

Finally the difference between **suspense** and **dramatic irony** should be addressed. Both of these devices generate tension in the audience, though through opposite means—suspense when the audience does not know what is about to happen; dramatic irony, paradoxically, when it does. Much of our pleasure in reading a new play lies in speculating about what will happen next, but in Greek tragedy the original audience would be fully familiar with the basic outlines of the mythic story before the action even began. Dramatic irony, thus, occurs at moments when the audience is more knowledgeable about events than the onstage characters are. In *Hamlet* we know that Hamlet has "put an antic disposition on" and is pretending to be mad. In some plays, our fore-knowledge of certain events is so strong that we may want to cry out a warning to the characters.

You may have noticed that Ives's unified plot in *Sure Thing*, although it's certainly unconventional in the way it uses time, does in fact have a clear beginning, middle, and (happy!) ending. Also, every **peripety** or reversal is signaled by a bell and is quickly followed by Bill's recognition of his error and his next step in correcting it.

Determining Plot in Drama

1. Think of a synopsis of the play. What are the major events, spoken or unspoken, of the plot?
2. Is the plot unified (that is, continuous in development), or episodic? How would the narrative change if the plot were organized differently?
3. Are Aristotle's "unities" observed in the play? Does the play obey or disobey Aristotle's rules of traditional drama?
4. How is time portrayed in the play? Does the play show events in chronological order, or does the playwright use flashbacks or other experiments with the progression of events?
5. How does the author give their exposition? When, if at all, does the reader learn important details about time, place, and so on?
6. What is the complication of the story, and when does it first become evident?
7. Does complication lead to conflict in the plot?
8. What is the rising action of the drama?
9. What is the crisis of the drama? Is there more than one?
10. Is there a climax?
11. Is there a moment of reversal, or peripety?
12. How does the falling action of the drama take place? How does it relate to the rising action?
13. Is there a moment of epiphany, or revelation, for the characters? For the reader?
14. What is the dénouement, or resolution, of the story?
15. Is the dénouement closed or open? Could the drama have a sequel?
16. Are there any subplots to the narrative? How do they reflect, or add meaning to, the central plot of the drama?

17. Does the play invoke dramatic irony? Are there details known to the audience that are unknown to certain characters?

18. What traditional patterns or archetypes, if any, do you recognize in the drama? Is there a pattern to the story that you've seen, or experienced before in your own life? In other plays?

Characterization

The Greek word **agon** means "debate," and refers to the central issue or conflict of a play. From *agon* we derive two words commonly used to denote the chief characters in a play: **protagonist,** literally the "first speaker," and **antagonist,** one who speaks against him. Often the word *hero* is used as a synonym for protagonist, and it is difficult not to think of Antigone or Hamlet as tragic heroes. In many modern plays it may be more appropriate to speak of the protagonist as an **anti-hero** since he or she may possess few, if any, of the traditional attributes of a hero, a point that Arthur Miller discusses in his essay "Tragedy and the Common Man." Similarly, the word *villain* brings to mind a black-mustached, sneering character in a top hat and opera cloak from and old-fashioned **melodrama** (a play whose complications are solved happily at the last minute by the "triumph of good over evil") and usually has little application to the complex characters one encounters in a serious play.

Aristotle, in his discussion of characterization, stresses the complexity that marks the personages in the greatest plays. Nothing grows tiresome more quickly that a perfectly virtuous man or woman at the center of a play, and nothing is more offensive to the audience than seeing absolute innocence despoiled. Though Aristotle stresses that a successful protagonist must be better than ordinary men and women, he also insists that the protagonist be somewhat less than perfect:

> There remains, then, the intermediate kind of personage, a man not pre-eminently virtuous and just, whose misfortune, however, is brought upon him not by vice and depravity but by some error of judgment.

Aristotle's word for this error is **hamartia,** which is commonly translated as "tragic flaw" but might more properly be termed a "great error." In ordinary circumstances, the protagonist's strength of character may allow him or her to prosper, but under the pressure of events he or she may crack as one small chink in the armor widens and leaves the protagonist vulnerable. A typical flaw in tragedies is **hubris**, arrogance or excessive pride, which leads a character into errors that might have been avoided if he or she had listened to the advice of others. In *Antigone,* for example, Creon is told by Teiresias that he has made a wrong decision, and his prideful refusal to change his mind results in further tragedy. Although he does not use the term himself, Aristotle touches here on the concept of **poetic justice,** the audience's sense that virtue and vice have been fairly dealt with in the play and that punishment is to some degree deserved.

In reading, keep in mind several points about main characters. Physical description, while it may be minimal at best, is worth paying close attention to. For example, in *Antigone,* the character Teiresias is blind, but he "sees" the implications of situations better than many of the other characters. Sometimes a playwright will give a character a name that is an indicator of personality or has some other additional relevance. Antigone's name, in Greek, literally means "against" or opposed to "childbirth" or the womb, a significant name to give to a character who brings about her own death.

Character motivation is another point of characterization to ponder. Why do characters act in a certain manner? What do they hope to gain from their actions? In some cases, these motives are clear enough and may be discussed openly by the characters. In other plays, motivation is more elusive, as the playwright deliberately mystifies the audience by presenting characters who perhaps are not fully aware of the reasons for their compulsions. Modern dramatists, influenced by advances in psychology, have often refused to reduce characters' actions to simple equations of cause and effect.

Two conventions that the playwright may employ in revealing motivation are **soliloquy** and **aside.** A soliloquy is a speech a single character makes on stage alone. Hamlet's soliloquies, among them some of the most famous passages in all drama, show us the process of his mind as he toys with various plans of revenge but delays putting them into action. The aside is a brief remark (traditionally delivered to the side of a raised hand) that an actor makes directly to the audience and that the other characters on stage cannot hear. Occasionally an aside reveals a reason for a character's behavior in a scene. Neither of these devices is as widely used in today's theater as in earlier periods, but they remain part of the dramatist's collection of techniques.

Minor characters are also of great importance in a successful play, and there are several different traditional types:

- A **foil,** a minor character with whom a major character sharply contrasts, is used primarily as a sounding board for ideas, as in the way Hamlet banters with Polonius.
- A **confidant** like Nora Helmer's friend Dr. Rank in Ibsen's *A Doll's House* is a trusted friend or servant to whom a major character speaks frankly and openly; confidants fulfill in some respects one role that the chorus plays in Greek tragedy.
- **Stock characters** are stereotypes that are useful for advancing the plot and fleshing out the scenes, particularly in comedies. Hundreds of plays have employed a pair of innocent young lovers, sharp-tongued servants, and meddling mothers-in-law as part of their casts.
- **Comic relief** in a tragedy may be provided by minor characters like Shakespeare's fools or clowns.

Bill and Betty in *Sure Thing* are a classic pairing of protagonist versus antagonist, and the way that they exemplify something basic about their respective genders as they go through the ritual of courtship is the cause of much of the laughter that usually accompanies performances of this play (a few years ago it was the most-performed play in America, a special favorite of scholastic drama competitions).

Determining Characterization in Drama

1. Who is the protagonist of the story, if any? The antagonist?
2. Is the protagonist heroic? Admirable? Good? Or is he or she an antihero?
3. Does the protagonist have a flaw, such as excessive pride or some other negative quality? How is this flaw revealed in the narrative?
4. Do the characters receive what they deserve in the drama? Is there justice in the work? Why or why not, and what bearing does this have on the meaning of the play?
5. If the play is being watched rather than read, how do the performances alter the meaning? Do different actors portray the same characters differently, and how does this change the drama?
6. Are the characters static or dynamic? Do they change as the plot progresses?
7. Does character development relate to the plot? Is their development part of the rising action, the falling action, or an epiphany?

8. What is the motivation of the characters? Are their motivations evident to others in the story? To the audience?
9. Is a soliloquy, or an aside, employed to reveal information to the audience?
10. How does the appearance of characters (including gender, race, height, and so on), alter audience perception of them? Would the meaning of the play change if the actors were different people, or if they were dressed differently?
11. Are any characters clearly allegorical, or representative of something (such as an attribute or concept like Humility, Truth, or Evil)? How does the drama reveal them as such?
12. Do the names of the characters have any significance?

Theme

Aristotle has relatively little to say about the theme of a play, simply noting that "Thought of the personages is shown in everything to be effected by their language." Because he focuses to such a large degree on the emotional side of tragedy—its stimulation of pity and fear—he seems to give less importance to the role of drama as a serious forum for the discussion of ideas, referring his readers to another of his works, *The Art of Rhetoric*, where these matters have greater prominence. Nevertheless, **theme,** the central idea or ideas that a play discusses, is important in Greek tragedy and in the subsequent history of the theater.

Some dramas are explicitly **didactic** in their intent, existing with the specific aim of instructing the audience in ethical, religious, or political areas. A **morality play,** a popular type of drama in the late Middle Ages, is essentially a sermon on sin and redemption rendered in dramatic terms, with allegorical characters with names like "Everyman" or "Good Deeds." More subtle in its didacticism is the **problem play** of the late nineteenth century, popularized by Ibsen, which uses the theater as a forum for the serious debate of social issues like industrial pollution or women's rights. The **drama of ideas** of playwrights like George Bernard Shaw does not merely present social problems; it goes further, actually advancing programs of reform. In the United States during the Great Depression of the 1930s Broadway theaters featured a great deal of **social drama,** in which radical social and political programs were openly propagandized. In the ensuing decades the theater has remained a popular forum for debating issues of race, class, and gender, as plays like *A Raisin in the Sun* demonstrate. Even *Sure Thing,* in a lighthearted way, raises some important gender issues.

Determining Theme in Drama

1. What is the theme of the story? Is there more than one?
2. Does the play dramatize the origin of some tradition, social custom, or holiday? If so, what does it reveal about the meaning of its topic?
3. Is the play didactic, delivering a message such as in a morality play?
4. Is the play allegorical—using symbols and situations to represent larger considerations?
5. Is the work a problem play, or similarly a drama of ideas? Does it discuss or debate particular social problems or ideas? How far does the play go in advocating one idea over another?
6. Is there some clear characterization of the playwright's opinions on theme?

Diction

Aristotle was also the author of the first important manual of argumentation, *The Art of Rhetoric,* so it should come as no surprise that he devotes considerable attention in the *Poetics* to the precise words, either alone or in combinations, that playwrights use. Instead of "diction" we would probably speak today of a playwright's "style," or discuss his or her handling of various levels of idiom in the dialogue. Although much of what Aristotle has to say about parts of speech and the sounds of words in Greek is of little interest here, his emphasis on clarity and originality in word choice remains relevant. For Aristotle, the language of tragedy should be "poetic" in the best sense, somehow elevated above the level of ordinary speech but not so ornate that it loses the power to communicate feelings and ideas to an audience. Realism in speech is largely a matter of illusion, and close inspection of the actual lines of modern dramatists reveals a discrepancy between the carefully chosen words that characters speak in plays, often making up lengthy **monologues,** and the halting, often inarticulate ("Ya know what I mean?") manner in which we express ourselves in everyday life. The language of the theater has always been an artificial one. The idiom of plays, whether by Shakespeare or by August Wilson, *imitates* the language of life; it does not duplicate it.

Ancient Greek is a language with a relatively small vocabulary, and, even in translation, we encounter a great deal of repetition of key words. *Polis,* the Greek word for city, appears many times in Sophocles's plays, stressing the communal fate that the protagonist and the chorus, representing the citizens, share. Shakespeare's use of the full resources of the English language has been the standard against which all subsequent writers in the language have had to measure themselves. However, Shakespeare's language presents some special difficulties for the modern reader. His vocabulary is essentially the same as ours, but many words have changed in meaning or become obsolete over the last four hundred years. Shakespeare is also a master of different levels of diction. In the space of a few lines he can range from self-consciously flowery heights to the slangy level of the streets—he is a master of the off-color joke and the sarcastic put-down. We should remember that Shakespeare's poetic drama lavishly uses figurative language; his lines abound with similes, metaphors, personifications, and hyperboles, all characteristic devices of the language of poetry. Shakespeare's theater had little in the way of scenery and no "special effects," so a passage from *Hamlet* like "But, look, the morn, in russet mantle clad / Walks o'er the dew of yon high eastward hill" is not merely pretty or picturesque; it has the dramatic function of helping the audience visualize the welcome end of a long, fearful night.

It is true that playwrights since the middle of the nineteenth century have striven for more fidelity to reality, more verisimilitude, in the language their characters use, but even realistic dramatists often rise to rhetorical peaks that have little relationship to the way people actually speak. *Sure Thing,* we hope you'll agree, captures the way that men and women actually speak, even if the "sure thing" of the title means something different to each character.

Determining Diction in Drama

1. Is the style of speech in the play elevated? Common? What does the language that the characters use reveal about them?
2. Is the language artificial—characters employing monologues, for example, or using other stylistic devices that are unnatural in more realistic speech?

3. Is the language complex or simple? Does it employ many metaphors or figures of speech? Is sarcasm or irony frequently employed?
4. Do different characters employ different diction from one another? Why or why not?

Melody

Greek tragedy was accompanied by music. None of this music survives, and we cannot be certain how it was integrated into the drama. Certainly the choral parts of the play were sung and danced, and it is likely that even the dialogue involved highly rhythmical chanting, especially in passages employing **stichomythia,** rapid alternation of single lines between two actors, a device often encountered during moments of high dramatic tension and, incidentally, present throughout *Sure Thing.* In the original language the different poetic rhythms used in Greek tragedy are still evident, though these rhythms are for the most part lost in English translation. At any rate it is apparent that the skillful manipulation of a variety of **poetic meters,** combinations of line lengths and rhythms, for different types of scenes was an important part of the tragic poet's repertoire.

Both tragedies and comedies have been written in verse throughout the ages, often employing rhyme as well as rhythm. *Antigone* is written in a variety of poetic meters, with some of them appropriate for dialogue between actors and others for the choral odes. Shakespeare's *Hamlet* is composed, like all of his plays, largely in **blank verse,** that is, unrhymed lines of iambic pentameter (lines of ten syllables, alternating unstressed and stressed syllables). He also uses rhymed pairs of lines called **couplets,** particularly for emphasis at the close of scenes; songs (Ophelia's song); and even prose passages, especially when dealing with comic or "low" characters like *Hamlet*'s gravedigger. A study of Shakespeare's versification is beyond the scope of this discussion, but suffice it to say that a trained actor must be aware of the rhythmical patterns that Shakespeare used if he or she is to deliver the lines with anything approaching accuracy.

Of course, not only verse drama has rhythm. Tom Wingfield's last speech in Tennessee Williams's *The Glass Menagerie,* a play written in prose, can be broken into lines of fairly regular blank verse (Williams wrote a considerable amount of poetry):

Then all at once my sister touches my shoulder.
I turn around and look into her eyes . . .

Oh, Laura, Laura, I tried to leave you behind me,
but I am more faithful than I intended to be!
I reach for a cigarette, I cross the street,
I run into the movies or a bar,
I buy a drink, I speak to the nearest stranger—
anything that can blow your candles out!
for nowadays the world is lit by lightning!
Blow your candles out, Laura—and so good-bye. . . .

The ancient verse heritage of tragedy lingers on in the modern theater
and has proven resistant to even the prosaic rhythms of what Williams
calls a "world lit by lightning."

Determining Melody in Drama

1. Does the playwright use stichomythia, or any other complex
   variation of poetic meter? What effect does this use of
   melody have on the audience, or on the meaning of the play?
2. Does the play use particular forms of meter or rhythm, such
   as rhymed couplets or iambic pentatmeter? What effect does
   this style have on meaning?

Spectacle

Spectacle (sometimes called **mise en scène,** French for "putting on
stage") is the last of Aristotle's elements of tragedy and, in his view, the
least important. By spectacle we mean the purely visual dimension of a
play; in ancient Greece, this meant costumes, a few props, and effects
carried out by the use of the *mechane.* Costumes in Greek tragedy were
simple but impressive. The tragic mask, or **persona,** and a high-heeled
boot (**cothurnus**), were apparently designed to give characters a larger-
than-life appearance. Historians also speculate that the mask might
have additionally served as a crude megaphone to amplify the actors'
voices, a necessary feature when we consider that the open air theater
in Athens could seat over 10,000 spectators. Other elements of set dec-
oration were kept to a minimum, though playwrights occasionally employed a few well-chosen spectacular effects like the triumphant entrance
of the victorious king in Aeschylus's *Agamemnon,* which involves a
horse-drawn chariot and brilliant red carpet on which the protagonist
walks to his death. Elizabethan drama likewise relied little on spectacular
stage effects. Shakespeare's plays call for few props, and little attempt

was made at historical accuracy in costumes, a noble patron's cast-off clothing dressing Caesar one week, Othello the next.

Advances in technology since Shakespeare's day have obviously facilitated more elaborate effects in what we now call **staging** than patrons of earlier centuries could have envisioned. In the nineteenth century, first gas and then electric lighting not only made effects like sunrises possible but also, through the use of different combinations of color, added atmosphere to certain scenes. By Ibsen's day, realistic **box sets** were designed to resemble, in the smallest details, interiors of houses and apartments with an invisible "fourth wall" nearest the audience. Modern theater has experimented in all directions with set design, from the bare stage to barely suggested walls and furnishings, from revolving stages to scenes that "break the plane" by involving the audience in the drama. The most impressive uses of spectacle in today's Broadway productions may represent anything from the catacombs beneath the Paris Opera House in *Phantom of the Opera* to thirty-foot-high street barricades manned by soldiers firing muskets in *Les Misérables*. Modern technology can create virtually any sort of stage illusion; the only limitations in today's professional theater are imagination and budget. Still, many contemporary plays (*Sure Thing*) dispense with most props entirely, relying almost totally on the language of the play and the performers' skill with it.

Before we leave our preliminary discussion, one further element should be mentioned—**setting.** Particular locales—Thebes, Corinth, and Mycenæ—are the sites of different tragedies, and each city has its own history; in the case of Thebes, this history involves a family curse that touches the members of three generations. But for the most part specific locales in the greatest plays are less important than the universal currents that are touched. If we are interested in the particular features of middle-class marriage in Oslo in the late nineteenth century, we would perhaps do better going to sociology texts than to Ibsen's *A Doll's House* (page 1010).

Still, every play implies a larger sense of setting, a sense of history that is called the **enveloping action.** The conflicts and tensions of Lorraine Hansberry's *A Raisin in the Sun* cannot be understood without referencing the social dynamics of race relations in the America in which the drama is set. *Andre's Mother* will not have the same resonance without some understanding of the AIDS epidemic and how it impacted communities of gay males in the 1980s. Even though a play from the past may still speak eloquently today, it also provides a "time capsule" whose contents tell us how people lived and what they most valued during the period when the play was written and first performed.

Determining Spectacle in Drama

1. How do costumes affect audience perception of characters? Do the characters change their costumes? Why or why not?
2. Does the play invoke stage effects or use a great deal of props, or does it instead have a minimal, sparse set with few effects? How does the use of these effects and props create or alter the meaning of the drama?
3. Does the drama break the "fourth wall" and involve the audience in the work? What effect does this involvement have on audience perception of dramatic meaning?
4. Is the setting realistic? Familiar? Does it employ spectacular, shocking, or other "fantastic" elements?
5. How do the visual elements of the play reveal its enveloping action? Is the setting (time, locale, and so on) specific or general? Are those visual elements relevant to the plot? To the drama's theme?
6. How do the characters react to their setting (the enveloping action, props, and so on). Do their actions supplement their spoken words, or do they seem unconnected?

Insight: DRAMA INTO FILM

The differences between print and film versions of plays (as well as film versions of short stories) offer many challenging topics for argumentation. Of course, the two media differ radically. In some cases, the film versions, especially those from past decades when censors ruled, badly compromise the original plays; in others, however, it can be seen that absolute fidelity to the text of a play is not necessarily a wise decision when it is transferred to the screen. We should also bear in mind that the greatest burden of characterization in drama falls on the actor or actress who undertakes a role. No matter how well-written a part is, in the hands of an incompetent or inappropriate performer the character will not be credible. Vocal inflection, gesture, and even the strategic use of silence are the stock in trade of actors, for it is up to them to convince us that we are involved in the sufferings and joys of real human beings. No two actors will play the same part in the same manner. We are lucky to have several excellent film versions of Shakespeare's *Hamlet* available. Comparing Laurence Olivier with Mel Gibson or Kenneth Branagh provides wonderful instruction in the equal validity of radically different approaches to the same role.

The late O. B. Hardison, director of the Folger Shakespeare Library, once observed two important differences between plays and films. The first is that attending a play is a social function; the audience members and the performers are aware of one another's presence, and laughter in the wrong place can signal the beginning of a disaster. But film is typically a private experience; it was with good reason that one film critic titled a collection of her reviews *A Year in the Dark*. The other chief difference, Hardison notes, is that drama is a realistic medium, whereas film is surrealistic. Watching a play, we see real persons who have a physical reality, and we see them from a uniform perspective. But film has close-ups, jump cuts, and panoramas, and we view the action from a variety of perspectives. These differences, as fundamental as they seem, may largely go unnoticed. If you ever take a course in film (and we hope you will) you might be amazed by the sheer complexity of this art form, and we're not just talking about special effects!

THE ESSAY

Reading and analyzing essays, rather than poems or short stories, might seem to be the easiest task for students of literature, because we typically understand the purpose of an essay to be clearly written nonfiction. We assume that essays are texts where the message will be evident, or else the essay is not very well written. However, this assumption is challenged if we realize just how diverse nonfiction essays can be. In fact, the majority of the texts that people read everyday are nonfiction "essays" of one sort or another, which means that the subjects, styles, and organizational techniques of the form can have extraordinary variety. It's helpful to remember that "nonfiction" is really another word for any text, even of the simplest variety, that claims to be only what it is— not just a fantasy of how life could be, but a representation of life itself. In that sense, a stop sign along the side of the road is as much a nonfiction "essay" as Martin Luther King, Jr.'s "Letter from Birmingham Jail" (page 747). The former is not nearly as sophisticated, interesting, or strategically complex, but what it lacks in complexity it makes up for in brevity.

Journalism, for example, fits into this category of writing, and we encounter it in the morning newspaper, or in the online articles we read as we sip our orange juice. Similarly, when a newscaster reads from a teleprompter on the evening news, that too is an essay, albeit one given to its audience in an oral form. The advertisements on those newspaper pages, in online pop-up ads, and on commercials between news stories are all essays too, each making a nonfiction claim about the world—factual data about a product—and trying to convince you that its argument—purchase this product—is a correct one. Other forms of essays include the letters we receive in the mail.

The speeches we hear on television are another obvious form of the essay format. The president's "State of the Union Address" is an attempt to explain the current state of affairs in the nation and to convince us at the same time that things are going well under the hands of capable leadership. The memorandum an office worker gets is an essay too, as is the diary that you read after you sneak into your sister's room.

With this kind of diversity, finding a singular way to approach and understand an essay may at first seem like a daunting task. An immediate question you can ask of any nonfiction text is what it is arguing. Look for the "thesis" of the work. Although most good essays will be too sophisticated to have single sentences that summarize their arguments, nonetheless a good way to begin analysis of a work is to find some initial assertion it is trying to make. From that starting point, many different approaches can be useful, such as those we have already discussed with poetry, fiction, and other kinds of art. Many of the same techniques and methods employed for fiction work for nonfiction as well, including analyzing the various ways (style, tone, symbolism, and so on) with which an essay makes its point.

Applying the Elements of the Essay

Modes of Organization

As a model, the five-paragraph essay is a good conceptual way to frame an argument, and it is a good way to begin thinking about constructing arguments. The form uses one paragraph of introduction, giving a basic thesis, then three paragraphs of support and elaboration, and finally summarizes and concludes. However, the limitations of the five-paragraph essay lie in the fact that good arguments are inevitably more complex and variable than such a simple format allows. That said, take a look at Hendrik Hertzberg's essay, "Bah Humbug" on p. 766. Hertzberg's essay is a good example of how much more effective an author can be when he doesn't follow simple rules of introduction, support, and conclusion, but rather mixes different essay formats. Given that you may be asked to write many different kinds of essays in your classes, and in your life, it is a good idea to keep in mind both simple organizational formats, which can provide much needed structure for your arguments, and the benefits of mixing or combining argumentative techniques, voices, or styles.

Hertzberg's work can be understood more completely if we look at more of the typical **modes,** or types, of essay organization and see how his compares. The piece reads like a newspaper article in that it is informative, giving quotations and numbers of support, merging abstract ideas and concrete data. Unlike a newspaper article, however, it is sarcastic. In this sense, the work is a **classification essay.** Through exposition, it organizes the world in a particular way, and gives categories for our understanding. If we were to glance at the article very quickly, we might assume through a process such as comparison and contrast that it classifies people into two different categories, those who are for the "War on Christmas" and those who are against it. A closer reading, however, reveals the opposite, that Hertzberg uses sarcasm and tone to mock people who categorize the world in that way. Rather than comparing and contrasting the two groups, Hertzberg's point is to explain that the categories themselves are not valid.

In that sense, the work is **argumentative,** attempting to convince its readers of a particular point. This kind of essay is also often called **persuasive.** Of course, in some extended sense practically every essay is argumentative, because every text is trying to convince its reader of something. What makes a text specifically argumentative is a question of organization. Does the essay present a particular point of view, support it with evidence, and attempt to convince its readers of the truth of that view? One way Hertzberg's essay conforms to the category is that it uses **examples** or **illustrations** to make its point. Hertzberg discusses the anti-Semitism of Henry Ford, and quotes lines from the Fox News Channel and a book by John Gibson.

Other types of essays include the **narrative essay,** which attempts to make its point through narration, much as a work of fiction would, but recounting details of events that have actually happened. Narrative essays usually proceed from one sequence of events to another, and the only real difference between a narrative essay on the one hand and a short story on the other is that a narrative essay makes the claim of being factual and relating events that actually occurred to the author of the story.

Another format for essay writing that is often employed at the same time as narration is the **descriptive essay,** which uses detail, usually with specific sensory references, to describe a scene or event, and uses those descriptions to make an argument or communicate an impression. For obvious reasons the narrative essay can be, and very likely will be, descriptive at the same time, because description is one easy way to narrate a sequence of events. Such an essay could also easily be argumentative, too.

There are more types of essays, but it is less important that you learn the categories than it is you learn that essays employ rhetorical strategies or organizational tactics such as these to focus and arrange their points.

Determining Modes of Organization

1. What is the thesis of the work? Does it have a single, clear thesis, or is there more than one argument?
2. Is the essay in recognizable form such as a letter, diary, or satire? If so, does it follow your expectations for that form or deviate from them?
3. Does the essay employ classification of any sort? Does it divide the subjects or topics into separate groups? If so, does this division relate to a central argument?
4. Is the essay argumentative? If so, what is it trying to argue?
5. Does the essay employ a narrative? Why or why not? Would a narrative get across a point that some other essay format could not do as easily?
6. Does the essay use description, or give details and examples? If so, how do these things contribute to the point of the essay?

The Point of View

Another way to analyze essays is to look at the author's point of view employs. We've already examined the definitions of first-person and third-person narration in the previous fiction section, and they are used just as frequently in essay writing as they are in most of genres. A form of voice rarely used in fiction, however, that often gets used in the essay format is that of **second-person narration**, the use of "you" as a mode of address. In presenting an argument or idea, there is an express, frank acknowledgment that one person, the author, is addressing another, "you" the reader. Nonetheless, you will find that very few works, even in nonfiction, employ second-person narration with much frequency or consistency, instead leaving the reader only an assumed, but not mentioned, structural component of the essay.

Determining Point of View in an Essay

1. What point of view does the author use? First person? Second? More than one? Why does the author employ the voice that he or she does?
2. Is the author or the reader explicitly mentioned ("I" or "you") in the essay? Does the argument become more or less effective because of voice?

Personal Essay

The **personal essay** is one in which the writer presents his or her personality and qualities to the reader. It is an essay format that is very often written in the first person and is often required of college and job applicants (see Christopher Buckley's parody "College Essay" on page 336).

Determining Personal Essay

1. If the essay is a personal essay, how sympathetic is the author? Is the author entirely positive or negative about him- or herself? Why?
2. Why did the author choose to employ the intimacy of the personal essay form in this case? Does this form of writing help with the argument or point?

Journalistic Essay, the Review, and the Critical Essay

Another familiar essay form we have already mentioned is the **journalistic essay,** which presents a narrative or gives factual details to inform the reader and convey information. Yet a similar essay form is the **review,** which focuses on another work and giving a summation or opinion about it. Reviews can take many forms, from being simple "book reports" that do little more than summarize or simplify, to being highly opinionated evaluative arguments that make judgments on the craft or value of the work they address.

Another, more elaborate version of the review is an essay that you very likely will be called on to write during your college career, the **critical essay.** A critical essay is like a review, in that it takes up another text as its topic, but critical essays address much more thoroughly the meaning and structure of the texts they treat. A good critical essay is often one that attempts to present a detached, objective perspective of the material it covers but at the same time argues for some kind of interpretation of it.

Determining Journalistic Essay, the Review, and the Critical Essay

1. Is the essay journalistic? How does it convey its information?
2. Is the work a review or critical essay? Is it simple or does it make a highly elaborate argument? If so, what opinion does it give, or argument does it make, about the work it is addressing?

Insight: ADVERTISING AND THE USES OF PERSUASION

In our consumer society, advertising is a multibillion dollar industry, so pervasive that we are bombarded every day with hundreds of messages to buy or use products. Even the roofer's sign that sits in a neighbor's yard has a implicit message that says "Look at this new roof and give us a call!" Take, for one example, the topic of *testimony,* where so-called authorities are used to support an argument. One of the most common techniques of advertising is the use of the celebrity testimonial, even if the celebrity has little knowledge about the product being pitched. Tiger Woods, a famous and admired golfer, may know what he's talking about when it comes to selling golf equipment, but can we be necessarily convinced that he has the qualifications for recommending automobiles?

The audiences for ads and the claims they make are fun to speculate about. Watch, for example, a segment of network evening news. What do the many commercials for laxatives, denture adhesives, pain relievers, and "ED" medications tell you about the demographics of the audience? Can you identify this audience based on the products being sold? Likewise, think about the claims that ads make—for example, a commercial for one of the early grammar-check programs for word processing. The slogan was "Now, help is available for whomever needs it!" Unfortunately, "whomever" is grammatically incorrect in this claim!

We are all influenced by advertising, though perhaps in many cases less by the claims that ads make than by the entertainment they provide. On Superbowl Sunday every year, we wonder how many viewers, bored by a football game in which the score is lopsided, derive most of their second-half pleasure from watching and laughing at the parade of commercials for cars, chips, and beer.

✓ *Checklist:* READING AND RESPONDING TO LITERATURE

Have you . . .

❑ Read the author's biographical note? Can you get any insight into the work from the biographical details?

❑ Considered the title carefully? Asked how the title is appropriate or effective?

❑ In a short story, asked and answered questions about the individual elements—plot, characterization, dramatic structure, point of view, theme, and so forth?

❑ In a poem, examined dramatic situation or the speaker, listener, and context? Asked and answered questions about language, figures of speech, meter, syntax, irony, the various poetic modes, and so forth?

❑ In a play, tried to apply Aristotle's definition of tragedy to the work you've read? If the play is not a tragedy, how could it be classified? Have you asked and answered questions about Artistotle's six elements: plot, characterization, theme, diction, melody, and spectacle?

❑ In an essay, noticed the way that it's organized? What is the author's point of view? Have you asked and answered questions about its style, its method of argument, and so forth?

❑ Prepared yourself well enough to argue and write about the work?

3

Writing and Arguing About Literature

Reading, responding to, and writing about literature also involves the
art of argumentation. As a reader and responder, you are the audience,
asking yourself how a story has kept you in suspense, how a poem has
moved you, or how a character in a play relates to your own life. As a
writer, you must think of how you can generate, organize, and state
your own arguments to persuade your primary audience—that is, your instructor and your classmates—that your ideas are valid. **Argumentation,**
if not quite a science, is a complex art with many time-proven strategies, and by understanding the way that they work you can begin to
ask questions about literary texts and formulate your own written responses to them. With these thoughts in mind, let's look at ways—judg-
ing your first impressions, finding a topic and a thesis sentence, and selecting a strategy of argumentation—to proceed toward writing
successful critical essays about literary works.

Judging First Impressions

Writing about literature, however, unlike writing about your personal
life, involves more than just correcting errors in spelling, punctuation,
and grammar. When writing about literature, you need to go beyond
what you have discussed about a work in the classroom to formulate
your own critical responses. You then need to develop those responses
in order to turn them into well-supported arguments. Although you
may have confidently written thesis papers and completed research
projects in high school or other college courses, you need an

entirely different type of confidence to write, and therefore argue, about literature.

Initially, you might consider your first impressions of the work under discussion. If you are lucky, you will be able to write about an author with whom you're already familiar and whose other works you have enjoyed. If so, you have a favorable impression that is likely to carry over into the essay you write. But what happens when you're confronted with a new work by an author you've never heard of, and you find that work difficult, obscure, and unrelated to your own life? Your first impression is likely to be less than enthusiastic, but you must change your perspective long enough to write an essay that demonstrates you are compelled enough by the work to argue effectively about it.

Your first impression does not have to be a lasting one. It could change after you have read a bit about the author and his or her circumstances, for example. You may discover that you and the author share an area of interest. Try to put yourself in the author's situation of having to create a history for a character. Imagine, say, that you are a young man spending an hour with an alcoholic father, a woman angry at the husband who has dismissed her work, or just a young man and woman having a conversation in a café. It may be that doing this—trying on the author's shoes for a few moments—will cause you to raise "what if?" questions about yourself, your own assumptions about the world, and therefore the work itself. When you do these things, you may discover that your initial lack of interest or even dislike of a work, if not exactly transformed into enthusiastic admiration of it, has been modified to a level of respect and even empathy, that is, *understanding*, for the author and the author's characters. If you can reach this point, your response can help you find a topic to formulate an argument and to develop a thesis sentence for it.

Finding a Topic and Thesis

Generally, your instructor will give you a topic, and out of that topic you must find a workable thesis to guide your arguments about a single work or several works. Writing assignments differ greatly, and instructions may range from general to very specific. On the one hand, you might be asked to discuss the symbolic importance of three minor characters in one of the plays from this anthology. Or, you might be asked to compare and contrast the plot, characterization, and setting of Joyce Carol Oates's short story "Where Are You Going, Where Have You Been?" (page 1216) against Joyce Chopra's 1985 film version, *Smooth Talk*. In some cases, especially in essay-type examinations, your instructor may give the whole class the same topic; in others, you may be allowed considerable freedom in selecting one. Length requirements will vary depending on the type of assignment. They may range from a single paragraph of personal reaction to a standard five-hundred-word essay to a full-scale research paper of three or four times that length. The assignment will probably ask you to support your assertions with quotes from the story, poem, or play; or it may require that you add further supporting evidence from secondary critical sources.

Consider a typical assignment for an essay on poetry: *Argue the relationships among any three poems that share a similar theme.* Although this topic allows you some latitude in selecting the poems you wish to write about, paradoxically it is just this type of assignment that may cause you the most distress. Why? Because you have more than one hundred poems to choose from in this anthology. Before despairing, though, consider the different ways you could limit the topic. Instead of "three poems" you might narrow the field by selecting three specific types of poems, for example, three ballads, three war poems, or three poems by contemporary African-American poets. You may even decide to choose three sonnets. Then you could tackle the second half of the assignment—to find three sonnets with a similar theme.

Let's take a look at the sonnets available in *Inside Literature*. After reading a dozen or so of them, three of Shakespeare's sonnets seem to connect thematically. For example, you might observe that sonnets 18, 20 (page 975), and 73 (page 1235) deal with intimate relationships and are all addressed to another person. Before going further with any research, you decide to look for an overview of the sonnets on electronic resources from your library. You've had good luck using the multivolume *Dictionary of Literary Biography* before, and a quick search of the articles on Shakespeare reveals a general discussion of his sonnets.

After reading the three sonnets again, you decide that Shakespeare, in addressing these sonnets to a young man, first dwells on his physical beauty, then mocks himself for thinking of him only in physical terms, and finally values their spiritual bond much more than the physical one. You can now begin thinking about formulating a thesis statement. Always keep in mind that the process of choosing, limiting, and developing a topic and thesis sentence should follow the same steps that you practiced in earlier composition courses, namely engaging in prewriting techniques before you begin any formal drafting of your essay. Techniques such as brainstorming, freewriting, and idea mapping are intended to help you explore various aspects of a particular topic, which then enable you to develop a coherent and arguable thesis statement, such as, "In three of his sonnets, Shakespeare moves from mere admiration of the physical beauty of the young man whom he addresses to a deeper appreciation of their spiritual and emotional bonds of friendship."

Keep in mind that a certain amount of informal preparation is always useful. In addition to practicing prewriting exercises, you can also take notes on a text and refine those initial ideas further by discussing them with your peers and instructor. Many composition and introduction to literature courses now include group discussion and peer review of rough drafts as part of the writing process. Even if your class does not use formal group discussion as part of its prewriting activities, nothing prevents you from talking over your ideas with your classmates or scheduling a conference with your instructor. The conference, especially, is a good idea, because it allows you to get a clearer sense of what is expected from you. In many cases, after a conference with your instructor, you may discover that you could have limited your topic even further or that you could have selected other more pertinent examples to support your thesis. Let's take a closer look at these prewriting activities.

Determining First Impressions, Finding Topics, and Developing Theses

1. Review the instructions of the writing assignment. What are the specific requirements? Should your paper be a specific length? What details should be discussed in the content of the paper? Do you need to consult outside critical sources?
2. Have you thought of several possible strategies for approaching the work(s)?
3. Does your thesis statement show the range of your subject and the argument you will be making about it?

Brainstorming, Peer Reviewing, and Conferencing

The amount of prewriting activity you undertake will probably be determined by your instructor. Some instructors spend several classes "walking you through" a writing assignment, but others may simply announce a topic and deadline for a completed paper. If your class uses special techniques such as submitting a rough draft, reviewing your and other students' drafts in peer groups, or requiring a one-on-one conference with your instructor, then we suggest that you simply follow your instructor's guidelines and schedule for the writing process. If, however, your class does not include these activities, some methods follow that may help you to clarify your arguments and assemble them in written form.

First, take notes on your reading. How you do this will vary, including looking up the definitions of any words you do not know or any references that aren't explained in the footnotes in your textbook. But arriving for an instructor conference with a story that has notes written in the margins and important passages highlighted indicates that you've done more than just "skim" the text you're writing about.

Second, after you've asked and answered some of the questions suggested in the discussion of the *topoi* (page 92), the "common topics" that will help you to find specific arguments about a work, (located at the ends of each section of the explanations of the appropriate genre), formulate your thesis and decide on the order of your arguments. Formal outlining, which was once a mainstay of any writing course, may not be something you're familiar with, but some degree of "blocking out" your ideas is always a good idea.

Third, talk it over. Friends, classmates, and your instructor can always provide good "sounding boards" for your ideas. If your roommate says, "Hey, I don't get this at all," it might be worth your while to take a second look at the passage he or she is focusing on. And if your instructor says, "Well, it's an interesting argument, but, see, it's really not going to hold up if you look at this scene," you shouldn't be afraid to ask how you can modify your ideas to take care of the discrepancy. Although it's true that most instruction goes on in the classroom, some of the most valuable feedback you may ever receive can come when you're sitting across the desk from a professor who is eager to explore the text with you.

Finally, be flexible. Remember that no argument is so watertight that it can't be improved and that no sentence or paragraph is going to be absolutely perfect. With these points in mind, assemble your notes and your copies of any research materials roughly in the order you want to present them and write your first draft. Remember, while writing any rough draft, that "rough" means exactly what it sounds like. If you see a gap in your argument, make yourself a note to look for more supporting materials. The main thing to accomplish in any draft is to set forth the "bare bones" of your arguments—the beginning, middle, and end. You can "flesh out" your paper as you proceed through the next stages of the writing process.

Drafting and Revising the Essay: The Importance of Style

At some point, you may have gotten your paper back with comments on its contents and marks on spelling, grammar, usage, and other aspects of the mechanics of writing. "Spelling?" you ask. "I ran my spell-check program!" As useful as they are, such word-processing "miracles" don't account for everything, especially proper nouns and homophones like "it's" and "its." Nothing is more catastrophic to your *ethos* as a writer than an author's name misspelled or the title of a poem given incorrectly. Grammar and spell-checking software can be useful, but such tools are not failure-proof. You are doubtless familiar with some of the more serious writing errors—sentence fragments, subject-verb agreement errors, misplaced modifiers, missing apostrophes—so now is the time to get out the handbook and correct them.

Developing an appropriate style is the major stumbling block that many students find in writing an effective piece of literary argument. Aware perhaps that your vocabulary and sentence structures are less sophisticated than those found in the primary and secondary materials being discussed, you may be tempted to overcompensate by adopting the language of professional critics. This practice can result in garbled sentences and jargon-filled writing. It is much better to write simple, direct sentences, avoiding slang and too many contractions and using only words with which you are familiar. Writing in a style with which you are comfortable allows you to make clear transitions between your own writing and the sources that you are citing for supporting evidence. In introducing a quote from a critic, use a phrase like "As so-and-so notes in his essay on . . . " to guide the reader from your own style into one that may be very different. As we've noted before, be wary of including a statement from a critical work that you do not understand yourself, and do not hesitate to go on for a sentence or two after a supporting quote to explain it in your own words. Remember that literary criticism has its own technical vocabulary and that many of these literary terms are discussed elsewhere in this book. The appropriate terminology should be used instead of homemade substitutes. Thus, to talk about the "high-point of the story-line" instead of "the climax of the plot" or the "style of the rhythm and rhyme" instead of "the formal strategies of the poem" is to invite an unfavorable response.

Always remember to take another look at your previous attempts at written work. We wish you success with your writing assignments. For a model student paper, one that we find successful in every respect, see page 122 of this chapter.

Determining Prewriting Activities

1. Read the text closely: are there words with which you are unfamiliar? Does the text make reference to outside sources or situations? Have you identified all the areas of the text that will help you formulate a thesis for your argument?
2. What is the structure of your paper? Formal or informal?
3. Share your work with your peers and instructor. What corrections or suggestions did they make on your first draft? Did you note these on your second draft, and correct any errors in spelling, punctuation, and grammar? Are your thoughts and ideas well organized and well supported?

Selecting a Strategy of Argumentation: The Three Appeals

Although revising your work for style and correct structure is certainly a major step to ensuring that you've written a successful critical essay, it is also essential that you make sure your argument is sound, effective, and well-supported throughout. Effective argumentation first hinges on what are known as the three *appeals,* which are the strategies by which we engage an audience and stimulate their interest and trust in our arguments. The three appeals are *ethos,* the appeal to character, *logos,* the appeal to reason, and *pathos,* the appeal to the emotions.

Ethos

Ethos comes from the same Greek word that gives us "ethics"; in its original sense it means "character" and concerns how a writer *appears* to an audience. In some ways, it is like the phrase "public image" when we apply it to political figures or sports stars. When you read an author's biographical note and learn that he or she has won many awards and honors, you look at that author's work as a reflection of the author's literary reputation, the *ethos* of a successful literary career. Even small amounts of biographical information can provide insights into an author's *ethos.* If you learn, for example, that a certain poet has been passionately involved for years in various ecological movements, this knowledge may give you insight into his attitude toward nature in one of his poems. If, you learn that another author is regarded as an effective satirist, you can perhaps use that fact to determine the tone of voice and level of irony in one of her essays.

Usually, you won't have to worry about validating an author's literary credentials—especially an author like William Shakespeare. With over four centuries of admiration to back him up, Shakespeare does not have to be referred to as, say, "an important Elizabethan playwright." Furthermore, *ethos* applies not just to authors and playwrights but to their characters and their characters' actions as well. If you feel that a character has acted dishonorably or immorally, you then bring to the table your own definitions of honor and morality, and you may be challenged to examine the reasons for your standards of values. Thus, these judgments are not merely based on credibility and authority, but on ethics as well.

As a writer developing an argument about a particular work or works, you are also faced with the question of *ethos*: How have you presented yourself in your essay? Obviously, paying close attention to grammar, spelling, and punctuation as well as following the appropriate guidelines for manuscript form and documentation are important external marks of your *ethos*. Even the critics you use for support in an essay reflect an *ethos,* for an opinion taken from a critical journal has more value in crafting effective arguments than an anonymous remark found on an Internet page. Finally, the *ethos* of your attitude toward a literary work is an important factor. Your instructor realizes that you are not a professional literary critic but does expect that you take your task seriously by not letting your personal response outweigh everything else in your essay. For example, to reject an author's work outright because of what you may have discovered about his sexual orientation or her political beliefs is not likely to win points for fairness.

Logos

The second of the appeals is **logos**, the appeal to reason. *Logos* is ancient Greek for *word,* but here it means the way in which words are connected to one another to create logically sound thoughts and statements. When a writer uses statistics or historical facts to support an argument, he or she is using *logos*. When we rely on *logos* as our primary persuasive strategy, we expect that a text will consistently exhibit logical qualities in the way that its characters act or the manner in which its themes are developed; this expectation is often thwarted, however, when we enter the realm of the imagination. Thus, in order to argue effectively using this appeal to reason, we must, as Samuel Taylor Coleridge would advise, employ a "willing suspension of disbelief" or, in other words, "go with the flow" of the author's imagination. Literary works often hinge on seemingly supernatural events, irrational actions, or the fantastic. It is common, to cite one notable example, for a character to confess to a crime while seemingly in the act of defending him- or herself to interrogators. Likewise, many works of recent centuries, influenced by the theories of literary modernism, deliberately use fragmentation, shifts in tone and scene, logical dislocations, and even tricks with time to manipulate our everyday sense of the rational or reasonable.

Although it's clear that many works don't conform to the logical rules of the world as you would "normally" experience it, it may well be that the work has an internal logic of its own. Consider, for example, Shakespeare's mixture of the literal with the figurative at the beginning of Sonnet 73:

> That time of year thou mayst in me behold,
> When yellow leaves, or none, or few do hang
> Upon those boughs which shake against the cold,
> Bare ruined choirs where late the sweet birds sang.

It is important to realize here that an imaginative leap has been made. You don't need to think of a man with leaves hanging from his arms to appreciate Shakespeare's metaphor; he is comparing his aging, in a general way, to the details of what we can observe when a year winds down. When, in the next eight lines of the poem he compares himself first to the end of a day, and then to a dying fire, the internal logic of his sonnet's pattern is revealed: his metaphors grow steadily smaller and more intimate—year, day, fire—as the poem develops the argument and concludes that its auditor should "love that well which thou must leave ere long."

As you may have guessed, most of the burden of *logos* falls on you as the reader, and then on you as the writer; you are being asked to make claims about a literary work and to bear the burden of proof that makes those claims valid. Thus, your use of *logos* will come under close scrutiny when your essay is read and evaluated. At the simplest level, ask yourself if you have clearly stated your thesis and the rationale for your organization of ideas. For example, in discussing three poems from a poet's collected works, how have you arranged the order of the poems? If you wish to demonstrate that the poems reveal a heightened understanding of a certain theme as the poet ages, then it would make sense to discuss the poems in chronological order. Intuitive logic, so-called common sense, should not be abandoned as an essential tool of literary analysis.

Logos has traditionally been divided into two areas: deductive logic and inductive logic. Although a formal study of their methods cannot be attempted here, it is good to keep in mind a few basic concepts of each. In deductive logic, the three-step *syllogism* is employed to advance an argument. A syllogism consists of a major premise, a minor premise, and a conclusion, or, If A, then B. Therefore C. Thus, the classic example is:

A. All men are mortal. (Major premise)
B. Socrates is a man. (Minor premise)
C. Thus, Socrates is mortal. (Conclusion)

Even if the conclusion is worded differently ("Thus, Socrates must eventually die.") the syllogism is still valid because one quality of mortality (the major premise) is death. However, validity and truth are often at odds when syllogisms are concerned.

Take, for example, this syllogistic argument:

A. English poets of the early nineteenth century embraced Romanticism. (Major premise)
B. George Crabbe lived from 1754 to 1832. (Minor premise)
C. Thus, George Crabbe is a Romantic poet. (Conclusion)

Although the syllogism is technically valid, the truth of the argument here depends on the major premise: Did *all* English poets of this era wholeheartedly embrace Romanticism, or did *most*? Further examination of criticism of Crabbe's poetry reveals that in some ways it resembles that of his Romantic near-contemporaries Wordsworth and Coleridge but that in others it is more closely akin to the neoclassical style of poetry of the late eighteenth century. It may be well to keep in mind that literary analysis rarely deals in such absolute statements as the one above. Here's an even more absurd example of deductive reasoning gone astray (and notice that here the syllogism appears in a shortened form called an *enthymeme*):

If Robert Frost's poems have New England settings,
then his "Once by the Pacific" must be a poem about New England.

Valid, yes; true, no, as any glance at a map will demonstrate. An argument that combines validity with truth might run:

> Although Robert Frost's poems typically have New England settings, "Once by the Pacific" possibly reflects his childhood in San Francisco, where he was born in 1874. Frost did not move to New England until 1885, following his father's death.

The argument here is not concerned with establishing the geographical location of the Pacific Ocean; rather, it's trying to demonstrate why Frost left San Francisco only after his father's death. If you were to read the poem you would see how the ominous imagery depicts tumultuous events that took place during Frost's childhood. Further research reveals that his father, an alcoholic, died when Frost was eleven, forcing his mother to take her two children, Robert and his sister, to Massachusetts, where she had family.

The other form of *logos*, inductive reasoning, is likely to be even more useful in the kind of critical arguments you will be writing. Inductive reasoning depends on the marshaling of evidence that leads to a likely conclusion; in other words, it proceeds from specific examples to a general statement. Even though this general statement is probably going to be stated early in the paper as a thesis sentence, it is still up to you to provide examples that convince your audience that you have not leapt to a conclusion or have selected your supporting evidence haphazardly. Let's look at an example of inductive *logos*.

Suppose you want to argue that Ernest Hemingway's short story "Big Two-Hearted River" (page 365) is about a war veteran's attempts to come to terms with his battle experiences and readjust to society. On first reading, "Big Two-Hearted River" doesn't seem to offer much in the way of support for this argument, for on the surface is a simple narrative about Nick Adams, Hemingway's protagonist, camping out by himself and fishing for trout. The story doesn't mention the war, and Nick allows himself to think about the past only once. After doing a bit of reading in secondary sources, you begin to assort bits of evidence for your argument: First, you learn that Nick Adams appears in several Hemingway stories and that he is usually considered an autobiographical character. Next, you discover that other Nick Adams stories deal directly with Nick's war experience, including his recovery from wounds in a military hospital, and that these experiences closely parallel Hemingway's own. Then, you find a letter from Hemingway explaining that "Big Two-Hearted River" was originally a much longer story that incorporated scenes from battle but that the author decided to cut them all out, with the notion that Nick's desire to "cleanse" himself of his bad memories was the motivation behind his fishing trip and his conscious wish not to let thoughts of anything other than the basics—making camp, eating, and fishing—intrude on his solitude. With this evidence in mind, you can return to the story and locate passages that symbolically reflect the past that Nick is leaving behind (the ruined town and burned-out landscape described in the opening paragraphs) and the future to which Nick must return (the complex swamp that he leaves for a later day's fishing). All of these details—from critical and biographical sources, from the author's own words about his story, and from the story itself—support your argument and persuade your audience that you have made a valid conclusion.

Of course, like deductive reasoning, inductive reasoning can be faulty as well. If you have been too selective in choosing your supporting examples, you may overlook contrary interpretations of a text. To cite a further example, suppose you tried to argue that Sylvia Plath's famous poem "Daddy" (page 212) revealed that she was the victim of some sort of abuse at the hands of her father. Here, investigation of Plath's biographies, her letters, and criticism of her poetry would indicate little support for your argument. You can either forge ahead, relying on the selective details you pick from the poem, or you can modify your thesis, in the light of reading and research, to incorporate Plath's complex feelings about the father whom she could not forgive for dying when she was eight years old. Again, common sense should tell you that if there is little or no support for an argument in the thousands of pages of commentary on a writer's work, then the argument is unlikely to be a good "fit" for the inductive method.

Pathos

The third appeal, **pathos,** is perhaps the trickiest of the three to employ effectively in literary arguments, simply because arguments based on personal emotional responses to a text are so subjective, so personal, that they rarely find a place in critical writing.

Like the other two appeals, *pathos* is a Greek word, from which we get such English words as "sympathize." Surely one of the main purposes of literature is to affect us emotionally—to be made happy by the final embrace in a comedy, to be moved to "pity and tears," as Aristotle put it, by the events of a tragedy, or to be excited to anger and outrage by a political poem or essay. You would also not be in error if you were to cite an emotionally intense passage from a text in order to support an argument that the language and emotion of a powerful poem or story can affect a reader's *pathos* strongly. However, you should take care not to state outright, "*I* was moved to tears by this beautiful poem." Nor would it be out of order to call attention to the author's *pathos* when discussing a single work. For example, if you were writing about one of the poems that John Keats, who died at the age of twenty-six, wrote during the last "marvelous year" of his life, it would be entirely appropriate to speak of how the poet's own sense of mortality lies behind some of his greatest poems.

We are all moved by writers who manage to triumph over circumstances, even if, in the cases of poets like Antwone Fisher, the subject of a popular film, or Mattie Stepanek, the child poet who died at thirteen of a neuromuscular disease, the poems may be overly sentimental. Remember that the downside of *pathos* is sentimentality, when the heartstrings are plucked a little too loudly or obviously. The best way to demonstrate that a literary work has affected you emotionally is to treat it with dignity and seriousness, not by "wearing your heart on your sleeve." Your emotional involvement with the text will be apparent to your audience from the energy, the passion that you demonstrate in analyzing and arguing about it. As you will see later, your personal use of *pathos,* used sparingly, may provide an effective way of concluding an argument.

Determining Strategies of Argumentation: The Three Appeals

1. What details reveal the author's literary reputation, and how are they important to his or her *ethos*?
2. Who is making the ethical decisions in the text? The characters? The author? Which ones are stated or implied? How can you make the distinction?
3. Have you adopted a tone of voice that displays your own competence and confidence as a writer?
4. Are the actions or events and structure of the text logical? Illogical?
5. How have you organized your paper? Is the structure logical and sound? Have you supplied sufficient evidence to support your conclusions?
6. Did you consider how the work emotionally affects the reader or reveals the author's own feelings?

Titling and Introducing an Argument

We all remember being introduced for the first time to people; how often, however, have we found ourselves struggling to recall their names five minutes later because they didn't quite make lasting impressions upon us? Why do we remember some but forget others? Perhaps it was because one person had a very unusual name or because another had an original way of saying, "How do you do?" A title and introduction to an essay are similar; not only should they inform the audience about where the argument is eventually heading, they should also put the audience in a receptive mood to read what the writer has to say.

Let's consider two possible paper titles that neither inform the audience nor interest them: "Ernest Hemingway's 'Big Two-Hearted River'" and "Emily Dickinson's Reputation." The first tells us only that the argument is going to focus on a single story; it tells us nothing about the contents of the essay and is about as inspiring as some kind of generic brand of canned food with a black and white label announcing that "Creamed Corn" is inside. The second is too vague. What kind of reputation are we talking about? Dickinson's reputation as a local eccentric in her hometown of Amherst or her *literary* reputation? One way to improve a title is to use a short quote from the work itself as part of the title, followed by an explanatory subtitle: "'His Mind Was Starting to Work': The Untold Story of Hemingway's 'Big Two-Hearted River.'" The use of "untold" in the title generates a small amount of suspense in the audience. How can a story be both "told" and "untold" at the same time? "'Selects Her Own Society': The Curious History of Emily Dickinson's Literary Reputation" not only uses an appropriate quote from one of Dickinson's best known poems, it also shows that you are dealing with the poet's literary reputation only and that that reputation was unusual. If your paper contains a significant number of important argumentative points, then a title that reflects this may be a good choice: "Discover, Debate, Delay: Three Reasons for Hamlet's Indecision." A good title should be more than merely functional; it should act in the same way that a title in the table of contents of a popular magazine immediately makes you turn to the article's first page.

Even more important are introductory paragraphs, beginning with their first sentences. Too many student essays start out by saying something like "In this essay, I will argue that the author, Ernest Hemingway, in his story, 'Big Two-Hearted River,' is symbolically showing how a war veteran prepares himself to return to society" or "Emily Dickinson was an important nineteenth-century American poet." In the first case, the audience, your instructor, *knows* that you are writing an argumentative essay, and, if you have given the essay an effective title, you are simply repeating yourself. In other words, why begin by telling her what she already knows? In the second, no one would argue that Emily Dickinson was not an important poet; she is universally considered the most important woman poet America has ever produced. If your instructor has spent a whole class period on a few of Dickinson's short poems, it should be clear that he is aware of the poet's importance.

In either case, think of more interesting alternatives. It might be more effective to begin the first essay with "On first glance, 'Big Two-Hearted River' appears to be a story with no depth whatsoever; indeed, many readers may totally miss the point and wonder why it is in a literature anthology instead of a magazine like *Field & Stream*." The second essay might begin more provocatively by asking, "How important a poet was Emily Dickinson in her own century?" In both cases you have at least "hooked" the reader by, in the first case, indicating that you are not going to deal with the obvious surface of a work of literature but that you are going to look for a "depth" that is not immediately apparent. In the second, you are raising a historical question, and it immediately is clear that you are going to answer your own question by arguing that Dickinson, so widely admired now, was little known during her own lifetime for several compelling reasons.

Richard Whately, an early nineteenth-century writer on argumentation, outlined five possible ways that an audience's interest could be stirred by well-chosen opening sentences:

- **Use a question (as in the second Dickinson example above) that is provocative and immediately raises other questions.** Are contemporary tastes in poetry different from those of the nineteenth century? Was reaching a large audience important to Dickinson? Did the editors who brought out her posthumous poems alter them in a way that made her appear much less original than she now appears? In many cases, this second set of questions may give you a clue about how to proceed with the rest of the essay.

- **Attempt to correct a popular or standard view of a writer or a work.** The Hemingway example in the paragraph above refutes the idea that Hemingway is a "simple" writer and says that, although the standard view has become so universally accepted that it seems unassailable, there may be another way of arguing about it. Let's take a poem by Robert Frost, "The Road Not Taken" (page 206), as a further example.

This famous poem is usually read as an allegory encouraging us to choose difficult tasks, because those tasks will be more rewarding than simple ones, a reading encouraged by the end of the poem "I took the one less traveled by, / And that has made all the difference." But that popular conception of the poem can be challenged by several other lines of the poem, including one that asserts the roads are "about the same." It is always possible to examine a text and discover a reading or an insight that has been previously overlooked.

- **State a paradox or curious fact about the work or works you are discussing.** Here are a few sentences from the beginning of one of critic Kenneth Tynan's essays on the English theatre: "The most characteristic English play on the subject of physical love is Shakespeare's *Antony and Cleopatra*. It is characteristic because it has no love scenes. The English, as their drama represents them, are a nation endlessly communicative about love without ever enjoying it." How can a "play on the subject of physical love . . . have no love scenes"? For another example, suppose you are writing about a Walt Whitman poem that has had a strange history: You might begin by saying, "'O Captain! My Captain!'" is the one poem that literally made Whitman a famous poet, the kind of poem that, during Whitman's life and for many years after, was widely reprinted, posted on classroom bulletin boards, and recited by schoolchildren. Yet it has virtually vanished from contemporary textbooks and anthologies of American literature, and, indeed, Whitman himself once stated that he was 'half sorry' that he had written it!" This is the kind of paradox, a mystery if you will, that invites the audience to explore further with you.

- **Prepare the audience for a method of arguing that might be unconventional or unfamiliar.** Suppose you are writing about the unusual technique of another story included here, J. G. Ballard's "Time of Passage" (page 1205), a story that begins with the main character's death and ends with his birth. You might begin by saying, "In order to understand the technique of J. G. Ballard's 'Time of Passage,' it is first necessary to give a brief plot summary, beginning with the story's last sentence and proceeding backward to its first." Or, having been assigned to write about the gender implications of Shakespeare's Sonnet 20, you might begin, "We know so few details about Shakespeare's personal life that any attempt to read his sonnets as autobiographical is very dangerous; however, Sonnet 20 indicates that he must have had significant questions about his own sexual orientation."

- **Open with a narrative.** We have all heard banquet speakers who begin by saying, "Before I get to my speech, I'd like to tell a little story. . . ." Such a story may be either amusing or sentimental, but it does have the effect of getting the attention of the audience, perhaps even "loosening them up." In writing about Nathaniel Hawthorne's "Young Goodman Brown" (page 525), you might begin at an intense point of the narrative: "It is a dark night in a forest. A young man, frightened and confused, is running. Suddenly and mysteriously, a familiar pink ribbon drifts down from the sky." Or you might use a narrative from the author's life as part of your introduction: "Sometime late in the night of February 10, 1963, Sylvia Plath, who had separated from her husband Ted Hughes and who was raising their two small children in a London flat, decided to take her own life." If your paper is going on to discuss one of Plath's final poems, then this dramatic opening not only stirs the reader's interest but builds *pathos* as well.

Titling and Introducing an Argument

1. Did you select a title that both reveals the content of your argument and interests your audience?
2. In what ways have you considered opening the paper? Do you think you selected the method that seems most effective for your argument? Is your thesis clearly stated?

Discovering Arguments

One of the most common questions about writing assignments usually sounds like this: "I've read the work I'm supposed to write about and I think I understand it but, aside from just summarizing it, how am I going to come up with five hundred words to say about it?" This cry for help is not a new one, and the ancient teachers of argumentation devised a system known as the **topoi,** or common topics, that would enable writers to discover ideas that they could use in developing their writing. We have already discussed, in talking about the three appeals, how some ideas can be generated by thinking of *ethos, logos,* and *pathos* in literary works. Now, let's go further and look at the five areas of *topoi.*

Definition

The first of the topics is **definition.** In Chapter 2, we discussed the four literary genres and broke down each into several components. So, in writing about a work from one of the genres, you have already begun to define it by your knowledge that a poem differs from a short story, a play, or an essay. In other words, anything is defined first by putting it into a class of things and, second, by showing how it differs from other things in the same class. For example, if you had to define "elephant," you might first put it in a class ("a large land mammal") and then give details that show how it is different from, say, a bear or a giraffe. These differences might include unique features (trunk), habitat (Africa and southeast Asia), size (up to twelve tons!), and other characteristics. Further, you might subdivide elephants into two subgroups, African and Asian, and note the differences between them. Thus, in writing about one of Shakespeare's sonnets, you might first define what a sonnet is (a fourteen-line poem, usually lyrical, written in iambic pentameter with a rhyme scheme) and then go on to discuss how the "Shakespearean" (or English) sonnet differs from the other types of sonnets (Petrarchan and Spenserian). Surely the most famous set of definitions in literary history are to be found in Aristotle's *Poetics,* where he defines *tragedy* and then breaks it down into its component parts.

Comparison

After you ask, "What is it?" the next logical step is to ask, "What is it like?" or "How is it different from . . . ?" **Comparison,** then, is the second of the topics. If you are writing about a short story, ask yourself if it is like other stories you have read or if it is like other stories by the same author. One of the most familiar types of writing assignments is the comparison-contrast essay in which you are asked to find both similarities and differences between two literary texts, sometimes in different genres. Is comparing a poem to a story feasible, or is it an "apples versus oranges" situation? Even though poems and stories differ in most regards, they can still share common ground; for example, their themes may be similar, or they both may employ narrative techniques like plot and characterization. In such a writing assignment you would not dwell on the differences between a poem and a short story but would instead focus on their similarities in one or more specific areas. One further aspect of *comparison* is the question of degree. If, in reading Tolstoy's "The Death of Ivan Ilyich" (page 1113), you argue that the more the protagonist's physical health declines the more his spiritual self-awareness grows, then you are employing a classic logical strategy called *a fortiori* (Latin for "from or to the stronger"); in essence, you are saying that if a small degree of pain causes Ivan to awaken spiritually, then a greater degree of pain will lead him to even more important self-revelations. John Donne, in "Holy Sonnet 10" (page 576), paradoxically argues that Death should "be not proud" and uses *a fortiori* when he says, "From rest and sleep, which but thy [Death's] pictures be, / [Comes] Much pleasure; then from thee [Death] much more must flow." In other words, if we derive pleasure from rest and sleep, which merely resemble death, then it follows that we will derive more pleasure from the real thing.

Relationship

The third topic is **relationship.** In reading any literary text, you should ask how one part affects another part. In a plot, for example, the obvious level of relationship is time. In most plots, one event follows another in a chronological sequence; if an author deviates from chronology, then you should ask why. But more important than time relationships are causes and effects. How, for instance, does a single event set off a chain of events that are all connected in cause-effect relationships? Aristotle famously defined plot not merely as a sequence of events but as a sequence that has a beginning, a middle, and an end, none of which could exist outside of its cause-effect relationship to the other two parts. Causes and effects are also important topics to employ when discussing character motivation in fiction and drama. Surely one of the most debated works of literature in this regard is Shakespeare's *Hamlet,* for critics have been asking for centuries why Hamlet delays so long in avenging his father's death. Plays always seem to raise a large number of questions about cause and effect, perhaps because, unlike short stories, they rarely have a narrator to provide insight into characters' minds. What we learn about the causes of a character's dilemma is based primarily on what he says and does; if a playwright does not use soliloquies to reveal inner thoughts, the reader has to judge only from externals and supply plausible motivations based on what is *not* said, the so-called **subtext** of the play.

Circumstance

Because most arguments about literary works hinge on probabilities instead of certainties, the fourth topic, **circumstance,** raises many useful questions. If, for example, you learn that an author once made a general statement about his or her works, then it is likely that the same statement would apply to a specific work by the same author. If we know that a political journalist belongs to a certain party, then it is probable that many of his or her columns will reflect the views of that party. Similarly, what an author has done in the past is likely to be done again in later years. Writers may change their views or techniques, naturally, but more often than not they display some type of consistency throughout their careers.

In "Letter from Birmingham Jail" (page 747), Dr. Martin Luther King, Jr. employs another aspect of circumstance, the relationship between past and present facts (the history of racial oppression and his incarceration for protesting against it) and future probabilities (the eventual success of these nonviolent protests): "I hope that the church as a whole will meet the challenge of this decisive hour. But even if the church does not come to the aid of justice, I have no despair about the future. I have no fear about the outcome of our struggle in Birmingham, even if our motives are at present misunderstood. We will reach the goal of freedom in Birmingham and all over the nation, because the goal of America is freedom. . . . We will win our freedom because the sacred heritage of our nation and the eternal will of God are embodied in our echoing demands."

Testimony

The four *topoi* we've looked at so far are primarily *internal*; that is, they may be explored simply by asking questions about a given text. The fifth topic, **testimony,** is what you may call an *external* topic, for here you go beyond the text to the Internet and the library to find support for your arguments from critics, historians, and biographers, the "authorities" or experts who have the specific knowledge that you need to validate the claims that you have made. Later, we will look in detail at research methods, many of which you are doubtless already familiar with, and discuss the often troublesome question of whom we should trust when we explore the different things that have been said about a work of literature.

Discovering Arguments

1. Have you considered matters of definition that are essential to your argument?
2. How can the work be compared to or contrasted with other works?
3. What details reveal how cause and effect operate in plot, characterization, or development of theme?

4. Do some research on your author; what kind of general statements by or about your author can you include that may be relevant to the specific work you are dealing with?

5. Does your argument include support from authorities who are established and reliable? Do you agree with these authorities? Why or why not?

Concluding an Argument

You have probably been taught that the final paragraph of a paper should summarize and restate the facts and arguments set forth in the introduction and body paragraphs. In itself, this is not bad advice, but simply rewriting an opening paragraph that began "In this paper, I will show . . ." to say "Thus, in this paper, I have shown . . ." is only going to pair up an uninspiring introduction with an equally uninspired conclusion. If your paper is a short one, there is no need to give a detailed summary, for the points you have made should be fresh in the mind of your audience. Instead, consider three other options, any or all of which can be used to complement your final restatement of your points:

• **First, leave a good impression of your own abilities by adding to your *ethos*.** Suppose, at the conclusion of an essay in which you have argued that Hamlet is constitutionally incapable of swift action because of his overintellectual nature, you say, "only a few critics have mentioned that he is an overage schoolboy, a perpetual graduate student who is called to perform a duty that he has not been trained to do." What are you doing here? You are not only indicating that you have made a thorough search of the criticism of the play but that you have also taken a fairly original slant on the familiar topic of Hamlet's hesitations.

• **Second, amplify the statements you have made before, especially by a judicious use of emotional language or *pathos*.** In the final paragraph of the sample research paper at the end of this chapter, note how the writer has used a number of words that carry strong emotional connotations to reinforce the points that she has already made. If you have refrained from using first person earlier in the essay, now may be the time to make a brief personal observation.

• **Finally, admit your limitations and look forward to further investigations.** In a brief paper, no one can totally exhaust the implications of an argument; if you do not plan to write on the same topic again, you could say something like, "Although close reading of a poem can, in fact, reveal its details and their relationship to each other, using small amounts of biographical and historical information can enhance the reading of any poem and reveal further depths of understanding." Combined with summary, these techniques may give your final words on the subject an added degree of energy and involvement. At the least it may show your audience that, if you have not totally exhausted your subject, you are far from being exhausted by it.

Concluding an Argument

1. How does your argument conclude? Have you done more than merely summarize the contents of your paper?
2. What kind of impressions have you left on your audience?

Explicating, Analyzing, and Reviewing

In general, writing assignments on literature fall into three broad categories: explications, analyses, and reviews. **Explication,** which literally means "an unfolding" and is also known as "close reading," is a painstaking analysis of the details of a piece of writing. Because of its extremely limited focus—only on the specific words that the author uses—explication is a consistent favorite for writing assignments on individual poems. In such assignments the writer attempts to discuss every possible nuance of meaning that a poet has employed. The most useful aid to explication is the dictionary; a full-scale assignment of this type may even involve using the multivolume *Oxford English Dictionary* to demonstrate how a word in a poem may have once possessed a meaning different from what it presently has or to support your contention that a phrase may have several possible meanings. Explication assignments are also possible in writing about fiction and drama. You might be expected to focus closely on a single short passage from a story, for example, explicating the passages describing Arnold Friend in Joyce Carol Oates's "Where Are You Going, Where Have You Been?" (page 1216). Or you might be limited to one scene from a play, being asked to discuss how Othello's speeches in Act I, Scene 3 reveal both his strengths of character and the weaknesses that will prove his undoing. There are many useful critical sources to support assignments of this type, and some of them are mentioned later in the section on research methods.

Analysis uses the same general techniques of explication, that is, the use of specific details from the text to support your statements. But where explication attempts to exhaust the widest possible range of meanings, analysis is more selective in its focus, requiring that you examine how a single element—a theme, a technique, a structural device—functions in a single work or in a related group of works. Instead of being assigned to explicate Walt Whitman's "Song of Myself" (a formidable task given its 1,346-line length, and only a few short excerpts appear on pp. 1239–1240), you might be asked to analyze only the poet's use of various schemes of repetition or to examine his imagery or to focus exclusively on the structure of his free verse. Analysis assignments often take the form of comparison-contrast essays, for example, *Compare and contrast the sacrifices and motivations for them of the female protagonists of "Mother Savage" and "Where Are You Going, Where Have You Been?"* or essays that combine definition with example-illustration, *Define the ballad and discuss ballads written by three poets of this century, showing their links to the tradition of this type of poem.* In the case of these examples, general reference books like William Harmon and C. Hugh Holman's *A Handbook to Literature* or the exhaustive *The New Princeton Encyclopedia of Poetry and Poetics* will help you to establish your definitions and an overall context for your examples.

The third category, **reviewing**, is less common in introductory literature courses. A review is a firsthand reaction to a performance or a publication and combines literary analysis with the techniques of journalism. A review of a play or film would evaluate the theatrical elements—acting, direction, sets, and so forth—of the performance as well as the play itself. Reviews are largely descriptive reporting, but they should also provide evaluation and recommendation. Many of the stories and plays in this book have been filmed, and you could be asked to discuss how one of them has been adapted for a different medium. Even a local production of a play that you are reading in class is a possibility, and you might find yourself jotting down notes on how the quiet young woman who sits beside you in a chemistry lab has transformed herself into the vibrant role of Ibsen's Nora from *A Doll's House* (page 1010). It is even possible that you might find yourself reviewing a public reading given by a poet or fiction writer whose works you first encountered in this book, and you may find yourself commenting on the distance between the image that the writer projects in the poems or stories and his or her actual "stage presence" as a performer. On the purely literary side, book reviews of new collections of stories and poems regularly appear in periodicals like the *Hudson Review* or the literary sections of major newspapers (the *New York Times Book Review*, published as a separate section of the Sunday *Times*, is the most comprehensive of these), and it is simple enough to find many excellent models should you be assigned to write a paper of this type.

One last word of warning: Note that nowhere above are primarily biographical essays about authors listed as possible writing assignments. Research assignments may ask you to discuss how the particular circumstances of a writer's life may have influenced his or her works, but for the most part biographical information should reside in the background, not the foreground, of literary analysis. An explication of a single poem that begins "Richard Wilbur was born in 1921 in New York City . . . " gives the erroneous impression that you are writing about the poet's life instead of about his work. Try to find a more direct (and original) way of opening your paper by using one of the methods suggested above.

Developing Arguments from Fiction

As mentioned before, an explication assignment on a single short story demands close attention to detail because it focuses on the subtleties of a writer's language. Close reading means exactly what it sounds like: You should carefully weigh every word in the passage you are explicating. Typically, an explication assignment might ask you to look carefully at a key section of a short story, explaining how it contains some element on which the whole story hinges and without which it could not succeed. Suppose, for example, that you are asked to explicate the opening paragraph of John Cheever's "Reunion" (page 963) and must explain what the paragraph conveys beyond obvious expository information. After poring over the paragraph several times, you might decide that it contains ample foreshadowing of the disastrous events that are about to occur. In particular you might cite such telltale phrases as "His secretary wrote to say" or "my mother divorced him" as Cheever's way of dropping hints about the father's unstable personality. Then, you might go on to mention Charlie's forebodings of his own "doom," all leading up to the aroma of prelunch cocktails that Charlie notices when he and his father embrace. Any explication demands that you quote extensively from the text, explaining why certain choices of words and details are important and speculating about why the writer made these choices. You can see how close reading focuses on details by taking another look at the discussion of Grace Paley's "Wants" in Chapter 1 (page 2).

Student Michelle Ortiz decided to examine the significance of the colors and textures used in Alice Walker's "Everyday Use" (page 966). Her argument here is that the author is not just using these details randomly but as signs that indicate something about the differences of the three main characters.

> Walker establishes the color contrasts carefully. The opening paragraph describes the clean-swept "hard clay" of the front yard, which the mother says "is like an extended living room." She describes how she wears "flannel nightgowns to bed and overalls during the day." Maggie, the stay-at-home daughter, wears a "pink skirt and red blouse," colors that perhaps relate to the house fire years ago that scarred her. The items in the house that Dee wants to take away are drably colored, an old wooden bench and a wooden churn top. The handmade quilts, which become the chief bone of contention between the mother and Maggie and the acquisitive Dee are made from scraps of old clothing. The colors that Walker mentions are "one teeny faded blue piece" from an ancestor's Civil War uniform and some "lavender ones" from one of her great-grandmother's dresses. Contrasting with bright colors ("yellows and oranges") of the flamboyant Dee's outfit ("so loud it <u>hurts</u> my eyes," the mother says), the colors associated with the family home are muted and soft, suggesting things that have faded from years of "everyday use."

A typical analysis assignment in short fiction might ask you to explain what a "rites of passage" story is and demonstrate that "Reunion" has most of the characteristics of the type. You might want first to define the initiation story, using your lecture notes, general literary reference books, and your familiarity with other stories from popular sources like fairy tales or motion pictures. After demonstrating that this type of story is indeed well established and having described its chief characteristics, you might then focus on such matters in "Reunion" as Charlie's age, his naive expectations, his disillusioning experience, and his eventual "passage" out of his father's life at the end of the story.

A slightly more complicated analysis assignment might involve comparison and contrast. Generally, comparison seeks out common ground between two subjects while contrast finds differences; most papers of this type do both, first pointing out the similarities before going on to demonstrate how each story represents a variation on the theme.

Comparison-contrast essays may examine a single story, analyzing two characters' approaches to a similar situation, or even a single character's "before and after" view of another character or event. Or these essays may compare and contrast two or more works that have common threads. If you are examining a single author in depth, you might be required to locate other stories that deal with similar themes. Because Cheever writes extensively about alcoholism, family tensions, and divorce, you might choose several of his stories that reflect the same basic themes as "Reunion." Even more demanding might be a topic asking you to find stories (or even poems or plays) by other authors to compare or contrast. Among the stories in this book are several examples of initiation stories and others that deal with tensions between parents and children. Assignments in comparative analysis require careful selection and planning, and it is essential to find significant examples of both similarities and differences to support your thesis.

Developing Arguments from Poetry

Because explication of a poem involves careful close reading on a line-by-line basis, an assignment of this type usually deals with a relatively short poem or a passage from a longer one. Some poems yield most of their meaning on a single reading; others, however, may contain complexities and nuances that deserve a careful inspection of how the poet uses all of the resources at his or her command. A typical explication examines both form and content. Because assignments in analysis usually involve many of the same techniques as explication, we will look at explication more closely. Poetry explications usually require much more familiarity with the technical details of poems than do those explications about fiction and drama, so here are some sample answers to the questions about poetry that we raised in Chapter 2. Student Merritt Potter's informal responses apply to a poem from this book, Edwin Arlington Robinson's sonnet "Firelight" (page 991). They were later incorporated, revised, and rearranged in paragraph form with appropriate parenthetical citations, in her explication of the poem, which argued that Robinson used both the sonnet form and a number of ironic details to reveal that outward appearances don't always tell the whole story, especially when a couple's relationship is concerned.

```
I first decided that "Firelight" is an Italian sonnet
because it has fourteen lines and is divided into two
stanzas, an octave and sestet, like some of the other
sonnets we've read. And there's a shift, or what is
```

known in sonnets as a "turn" or <u>volta</u>, at the beginning of line nine, though here there isn't any single word that signals the shift.

There's not much that's visually unusual here. Punctuation is standard, and Robinson follows the traditional practice of capitalizing the first word of each line.

The lines are all ten syllables long, so iambic pentameter is a good guess for the poem's meter. Several lines are very regular when you read them out loud, like "Her thoughts a moment since of one who shines" and others have troches and spondees. The way the lines run on or flow into each other makes the rhymes less obvious and keeps the whole poem casual and conversational. I like the way the pause in the last line calls attention to "Apart," which ironically contrasts with the poem's opening phrase: "Ten years together."

This has a standard rhyme scheme for a Petrarchan sonnet, abbaabba cdecde. Robinson uses exact masculine rhymes, with the only possible exception is "intervals," where the meter forces a secondary stress on the third syllable.

I read the poem out loud several times and heard alliteration "<u>f</u>irelight" and "<u>f</u>our" and "wan" and "one." I wouldn't have noticed this second pair if I hadn't read out loud. I also heard some assonance like "W<u>i</u>ser for s<u>i</u>lence" and some consonance like "the w<u>an</u> face of <u>one</u> somewhere al<u>one</u>".

Sonnets are usually lyric poems, but "Firelight" is a short narrative. It's not really concerned with expressing the author's feelings, and it contains two characters in a specific setting who perform actions. That's not a plot exactly, but it's more narrative than anything else, mainly because of its third-person point of view.

As I said before, the persona here is a third-person omniscient narrator such as you'd find in a short story; the narrator has the ability to read the woman's thoughts and says that both of them are "Wiser for silence." The characters in the poem are a man and woman who have been married for ten years. The poem is set in their home, apparently in a comfortable room with a fireplace where they are spending a quiet evening together. Neither one of them speaks during the poem; they just look at "each other's eyes at intervals / Of gratefulness." Much of the poem's ironic meaning is in their silence: "what neither says aloud."

The syntax of "Firelight" is simple and so is the sentence structure. The first four lines make up a single sentence, and so do the second four lines. The final six lines also make up a long single sentence. The vocabulary of "Firelight" is not difficult, though "obliteration" stopped me. I looked it up and found that it meant "an erasure." There's also an easy allusion to Genesis in "snake" and "sword." The grammar in the sestet is a little more complicated in the way it uses "were" in three lines.

I found some figurative language and other things that might be symbolic. "Cloud" is a metaphor for something like a bad turn of events. "Four walls" is a synecdoche for the home. The allusion to the "snake" and "sword" made me think of the unhappy ending of the Garden of Eden story. "Wiser for silence" is what you'd call a paradox because you expect that keeping quiet about something would increase knowledge. I liked the metaphor in "The graven tale of lines / on the wan face" because it compares the lines on a person's face to a written story. I found out that "graven" means <u>engraved</u>. It also sounds like "grave," a word that has a lot of negative connotations. I don't think the poem is heavily symbolic, but maybe the title, "Firelight," doesn't just stand for cozy comfort but also has to

do with shedding light on the real situation.
Robinson is going beneath the surface to show us that
what the couple is thinking is ironically different
from what they appear to be. The more I thought about
it, I felt the simple title was very clever. It even
has a hint of danger to it. Maybe if there was enough
"light" in this relationship, the two people wouldn't
be as content as they appear to be.

Your instructor may ask you to employ specific strategies in your explication and may require a certain type of organization for the paper. In writing the body of the explication you will probably proceed through the poem from beginning to end, summarizing and paraphrasing some lines and quoting others fully when you feel an explanation is required. It should be stressed that there are many ways, in theory, to approach a poem and that no two explications of the same poem will agree in every detail.

A writing assignment in analysis might examine the way a single element—dramatic situation, meter, form, imagery, one or more figures of speech, theme—functions in poetry. An analysis would probably require that you write about two or more poems, using the organizational patterns of comparison-contrast or definition/example-illustration. Such an assignment might examine two or more related poems by the same poet, or it might inspect the way that several poets have used a poetic device or theme. Comparison-contrast essays might explore both similarities and differences found in two poems. Definition-illustration papers usually begin with a general discussion of the topic, say, a popular theme like the carpe diem motif, and then go on to illustrate how it may be found in several different poems. Assignments in analysis often lead to longer papers that may require the use of secondary sources. These two paragraphs are from Jennifer Haughton's paper arguing that A. D. Hope's "Imperial Adam" uses of various kinds of quatrains in his poetry alter the conventional uses of the stanza form. She includes parenthetical citations both to the poem and to works by two critics, Paul Fussell and Robert Darling, who have made comments she found relevant to her argument.

Another poem in which Hope uses quatrains
contrary to convention is "Imperial Adam," which is
written in elegiac stanzas (<u>Selected</u> 44).
Traditionally, the elegiac stanza was often (though

not always) employed to lament someone's death; however, it became so associated with this function over time that modern poets may now use it for irony (Fussell 135). Hope said he intended the poem "Imperial Adam" to be a satire of the profane image of Eve (thus the use of the elegiac stanza), yet at least one critic believes that he did his job too well and ended up perpetuating Eve's wicked image (Darling 44). The extent to which "Imperial Adam" succeeds as a satire depends on whether its content or its form becomes dominant in the poem.

The first two stanzas maintain a fairly regular iambic meter and show a "puzzled" Adam discovering the loss of his rib. By the fourth quatrain, Eve has been introduced, and a double spondaic substitution ("dark hairs winked crisp") in the last line spotlights a part of Eve's anatomy that will spark the fall. Instead of eating a forbidden apple, the taboo of this poem centers on sex: "She promised on the turf of Paradise / Delicious pulp of the forbidden fruit" (18-19). In the absence of a literal serpent in the poem tempting Adam and Eve, the origin of evil becomes the question.

Developing Arguments from Drama

A review of a play is an evaluation of an actual performance and focuses less on the text of the play itself (especially if it is well known) than on the actors' performances, the overall direction of the production, and the elements of staging. Because reviews are, first, news stories, basic information about the time and place of production should be given at the beginning of the review. A short summary of the play's plot might follow, and subsequent paragraphs evaluate the performers and the production. Remember that a review is chiefly a *recommendation*, either positive or negative, to readers. Films of most of the plays in this book are available on videotape or DVD, and you might also be asked to review one of these versions, paying attention to the ways in which directors have "opened up" the action by using the complex technical resources of motion pictures. Excellent examples of drama and film reviews can be found in almost any major newspaper or in the pages of popular magazines like *Time* or the *New Yorker*.

Explication assignments, like the examples from fiction and poetry given earlier, probably require that you pay close attention to a selected passage, giving a detailed account of all the fine shadings of language in a scene or perhaps a single speech. Because Shakespeare's poetry is often full of figurative language that may not be fully understood until it has been subjected to explication, close reading of one of the monologues or soliloquies for this type of writing assignment. Or you might be asked to explicate selected passages for a common thread of imagery, for example, identifying the various kinds of birds to which the condescending Helmer metaphorically compares his wife Nora throughout *A Doll's House.* For a short writing assignment in a Shakespeare class, Brandon Frank chose to explicate one speech from *Othello,* the title character's defense of himself to the Venetian senate against charges brought by his new bride Desdemona's father, Brabantio, that Othello has used witchcraft to seduce his daughter. Here is the opening part of Othello's speech in act one, scene three, followed by Brandon's explication:

> Most potent, grave, and reverend signiors,
> My very noble and approved good masters,
> That I have ta'en away this old man's daughter,
> It is most true; true, I have married her:
> The very head and front of my offending
> Hath this extent, no more. Rude am I in my speech,
> And little bless'd with the soft phrase of peace:
> For since these arms of mine had seven years' pith,
> Till now some nine moons wasted, they have used
> Their dearest action in the tented field,
> And little of this great world can I speak,
> More than pertains to feats of broil and battle,
> And therefore little shall I grace my cause
> In speaking for myself. Yet, by your gracious patience,
> I will a round unvarnish'd tale deliver
> Of my whole course of love; what drugs, what charms,
> What conjuration and what mighty magic,
> For such proceeding I am charged withal,
> I won his daughter.

```
    Othello is a subtle and intelligent man. He
realizes that the charges against him are serious,
and he also knows that the Duke and other members of
```

the senate are inclined to trust Brabantio, one of
their own to whom the Duke has just said, "Welcome
gentle signior, / We lacked your counsel and your
help tonight" (1.3.50-51). Othello counters, first,
by deferring to the "most potent, grave, and reverend
signiors" whom he calls his "very noble and approved
good masters" (1.3.76-77). Next, he freely admits to
one part of Brabantio's charge, that he and Desdemona
have married:

> That I have ta'en away this old man's
> daughter,
> It is most true--true, I have married her.
> The very head and front of my offending
> Hath this extent, no more. (1.3.78-81)

Having at least partially defused Brabantio's charges
by showing respect to the senate which will decide
his fate and by stating that has in fact wed
Desdemona, he makes a humble reference to how,
because he has spent most of his life "in the tented
field" (1.3.85) and then proceeds to the heart of his
defense, in which he will "a round unvarnished tale
deliver / Of my whole course of love" (1.3.90-91). He
will inform the senate that it was the power of love,
not "what drugs, what charms, / What conjuration and
mighty magic" (1.3.91-92), that brought him and
Desdemona together.

Analysis assignments typically hinge on only one of the elements of
the play like plot or characterization, or on a concept set forth by a
critic. For example, you might be asked to explain Aristotle's statements
about reversal and recognition and then apply his terminology to a
modern play like *The Piano Lesson* (page 412). Here you would attempt to locate relevant passages from the play to support Aristotle's
contentions about the importance of these reversals in the best plots. Or
you might be asked to provide a summary of his comments about the
tragic hero and then apply this definition to a character like Hamlet.
Again, comparison and contrast schemes are useful. You might be asked
to contrast two or more characters in a single play (Nora versus Mrs.
Linde as examples of two kinds of feminine strength) or to compare
characters in two different plays (Antigone and Hamlet as undeserving
victims of fate). In an extended essay comparing Christian references in

Tennessee Williams's two great family dramas, *The Glass Menagerie* and *Cat on a Hot Tin Roof,* Beverly Williams (no relation!) examines attitudes toward God and religion that are revealed by the characters. Here is her paragraph on family patriarch, Big Daddy, in the latter play:

> Unlike Amanda Wingfield, whose exclusively materialistic values largely reflect her struggle for her family to survive, for Big Daddy Pollitt, God does not exist in any religious order, and he tells Brick, "Church!--it bores the bejesus out of me but I go!" (1155). Instead, his God has two manifestations, money and his youngest son Brick. To Big Daddy, money means power and freedom from want, but there are some wants that money cannot buy, no matter how much a man acquires. Though he states his worth at "Close on ten million in cash an' blue-chip stocks" (1143), Big Daddy knows that "a man can't buy back his life with it when his life has been spent" (1143), and it cannot buy "life everlasting." No one can escape mortality. In The Broken World of Tennessee Williams, Esther Merle Jackson states it best, "Big Daddy has believed in the power of money. He speaks of its failure as a god" (142).

Developing Arguments from Essays

Because most essays are by their very nature argumentative, we don't need to dwell on their use at great length, and it is unlikely that you will be asked to write an explication of an essay. Essays, for the most part, differ from stories, poems, and plays in that they display their arguments directly rather than making them indirectly by implication or through the use of symbolism. It is more likely that you will be using the arguments in essays as a "springboard" to discuss texts from other genres. Suppose, for example, that you are asked to read Robert Flynn's antimilitaristic essay "John Wayne Must Die" (page 762) and compare his ideas to those in a poem or short story. Obviously, you would try to select a text that displays some of the same sentiments. In this case, a logical choice would be Wilfred Owen's "Dulce Et Decorum Est" (page 583), that attacks, from the point of view of a soldier who has seen the grim realities of war, the easy patriotism and pro-war slogans of those who have not. Another good choice might be Tim

O'Brien's "The Things They Carried" (page 795), a story set among the "grunts" who fought in the Vietnam War.

The other ways that essays may be employed for the purposes of argument are mentioned above in the section on the topic of *testimony* and later in the discussion of research methods. It should be obvious that the most important use of essays lies in how they can provide support from critics, the "authorities," in reinforcing and building your own arguments. The two main concerns here are *relevance* and *reliability*. The quotes you choose for support must be relevant to your own argument; if you do not understand what a piece of literary criticism is saying, it would probably be counterproductive to quote it in your essay. And, as we'll discuss below, literary scholars and critics are notorious for disagreeing with one another in their interpretations. Your dilemma may boil down to a question of "whom to trust" unless you want to cite contrary opinions as a way of showing the complexity of the subject that you're arguing about. A great deal depends, again, on the *ethos* of the critical source. A critic who is considered reliable enough to be quoted by other critics has an *ethos* that is much stronger than that of a maverick whom other critics have dismissed as eccentric or simply wrong. It cannot be stressed too much that you should carefully evaluate any critical source before deciding to use it. Most instructors would not consider any of the easily available print or online "notes" on literary texts (which consist primarily of plot summaries) to be reliable critical sources.

Developing Arguments

1. Review your argument. Does it require extensive explication of selected passages or a wider-ranging analytical approach?
2. How will the questions you ask about the work differ from genre to genre? What will those questions be? What is the appropriate technical vocabulary for each genre?
3. Have you evaluated your supporting materials for relevance and reliability?

Conducting Research

Research is a time consuming and sometimes frustrating process, but a few general principles may help you to streamline it. Bear in mind that about 90 percent of the time you spend on assembling research materials will take place in one section of the library, the reference room, and that a large amount of information about where to find certain materials and the critical materials themselves are now available on electronic databases. If you rush off to consult a book on the fifth-floor shelves every time you locate a mention of something that is potentially useful to you, you may gain more expertise in operating an elevator than in conducting effective research. Thus, use the reference room to assemble the "shopping list" of items you will have to find in other parts of the library. Also, remember that the CD-ROM reader and online indexes and sources have greatly enhanced the mechanics of research. It may be frustrating to learn that an article you spotted in a musty index and found, after a long search, in a bound volume of a journal could have been downloaded and printed out in seconds from a CD-ROM or online database.

Most contemporary students have literally grown up writing with computers and are familiar with the Internet. Still, a few words about the use of the Internet for online research may be helpful. In recent years, the Internet has facilitated the chores of research, and many online databases, reference works, and periodicals may be quickly located using search engines like Yahoo! (http://www.yahoo.com) and Google (http://www.google.com). The Internet also holds a wealth of information in the form of individual websites devoted to authors, many of which are run by universities or private organizations. You should be aware, however, that websites vary widely in quality. Some are legitimate sources displaying sound scholarship; others are little more that "fan pages" that may contain erroneous or misleading information. Online information, like any other kind of research material, should be carefully evaluated before using it.

Careful documentation of your sources is essential; if you use any material other than what is termed "common knowledge" you must cite it in your paper. Common knowledge includes biographical information, an author's publications, prizes and awards received, and other information that can be found in more than one reference book. Anything else—direct quotes or material you have put in your own words by paraphrasing—requires both a parenthetical citation in the body of your paper and an entry on your works cited pages.

The first step in successful research is very simple: Read the assigned text before looking for secondary sources. After you have read the story, poem, or play that you have been assigned, you may have already begun to formulate a workable thesis sentence. If you have done this before beginning your research, you eliminate any number of missteps and repetitions. Next, perform a subject search for books that will be useful to you. If, for example, you are writing on one of Keats's odes, a subject search may reveal one or more books devoted solely to this single type of poem.

Computerized library catalogs are set up in different configurations, but many of them allow multiple "keyword" searches; a command like FIND KEATS AND ODE might automatically cross-reference all books in the library that mention both subjects. If you are unfamiliar with your terminology and do not know, for example, how an ode differs from other kinds of poems, you should consult a reference book containing a discussion of literary terms. After you have located books and reference sources that will be of use, check the journals that publish literary criticism. The standard index for these is the *MLA International Bibliography*, which is available in bound volumes, CD-ROM, and online versions, and many items listed after a search may exist in full-text electronic versions. A reference librarian may also direct you to other indexes such as the *Literary Criticism Index* and the *Essay and General Literature Index*. It is a good idea to check indexes like these early in your research. No single college library carries all of the journals listed in the *MLA International Bibliography*, and you may discover that getting a reprint through interlibrary services can take a week or more.

Once you have located and assembled your sources, you can decide which of them will be most valuable to you. Again, if you have already formulated your thesis and perhaps completed a tentative outline as well, you can move more swiftly. Two blessed additions to almost every library are the photocopying machine and the network printer, which remove the tedious chore of taking notes by hand on 3 × 5 cards. Note cards may still be useful if you want to try different arrangements of your material, but most students have happily discarded them as relics of the distant past.

It is impossible to guess what research materials will be available in any given library, but most college libraries contain many different kinds of indexes and reference books for literary research. If you are writing about a living writer, we particularly recommend three popular reference sets published by Gale Research: *Dictionary of Literary Biography* (*DLB*), *Contemporary Authors* (*CA*), and *Contemporary Literary Criticism* (*CLC*). These two last reference works are also available in editions that cover the nineteenth and twentieth centuries. These references will provide you both with useful overviews of author careers and generous samples of criticism. *DLB* and *CA* articles also contain extensive bibliographies of other relevant sources; *CLC* contains reprints of book reviews and relevant passages from critical works. Similar to these reference works are those in the *Critical Survey* series from Magill Publishers, multivolume sets that focus on short and long fiction, poetry, drama, and film. Another reliable source of information on individual writers can be found in several series of critical books published by Twayne Publishers, which can be located in a subject search.

For locating explications, several indexes are available, including *Poetry Explication: A Checklist of Interpretations since 1925 of British and American Poems Past and Present* and *The Explicator Cyclopedia,* which reprints explications originally appearing in the periodical of the same name. *Poetry Criticism* and *Short Story Criticism* are multivolume reference works that reprint excerpts from critical essays and books. One of several popular indexes of book reviews, the annual *Book Review Digest* reprints brief passages from the most representative reviews. Two reference sources providing, respectively, examples of professional drama and film reviews are *The New York Times Theater Reviews, 1920–1970* (and subsequent volumes) and *The New York Times Film Reviews.* Popular magazines containing book, drama, and film reviews (and occasionally poetry reviews as well) include *Time, Newsweek,* and the *New Yorker,* and these reviews are indexed in the *Readers' Guide to Periodical Literature,* more recent volumes of which are available online. Also, yearbooks like *Theatre World* or the *Dictionary of Literary Biography Yearbook* provide a wealth of information about the literary activities of a given year.

Quoting, Citing, and Avoiding Plagiarism

You should always try to support the general statements you make about a story, poem, or play by quoting directly from the text or, if required, by using secondary sources for additional critical opinion. The *MLA Handbook for Writers of Research Papers,* 6th ed., which you will find in the reference section of almost any library, contains standard formats for bibliographies and manuscripts; indeed, most of the writing handbooks used in college composition courses follow MLA style guidelines. Purdue University maintains a useful online source on MLA style at http://owl.english.purdue.edu/handouts/research/r_mla.html. However, if you have doubts or if you have not been directed to use a certain format, ask your instructor which one he or she prefers.

The type of parenthetical citation used in MLA-style format to indicate the source of quotations is simple to learn and dispenses with such tedious and repetitive chores as footnotes and endnotes. In using parenthetical citations remember that your goal is to direct your reader from the quoted passage in the paper to the corresponding entry on your works cited pages and from there, if necessary, to the book or periodical from which the quote was taken. A good parenthetical citation gives only the *minimal* information needed to accomplish this task. Here are a few typical examples from student papers on fiction, poetry, and drama. The first discusses Cheever's "Reunion":

> Cheever moves very quickly to indicate that the "Reunion" may well be memorable but will not be happy. As soon as father and son enter the first restaurant and are seated, Charlie's father begins to act strangely: "We sat down, and my father hailed the waiter in a loud voice. 'Kellner!' he shouted. 'Garçon! Cameriere! You!' His boisterousness in the empty restaurant seemed out of place" (518).

You should note a couple of conventions of writing about fiction and literature in general. One is that the present tense is used in speaking of the events of the story; in general, use the present tense throughout your critical writing except when you are giving biographical or historical information.

Second, note the use of single and double quotation marks. Double quotes from the story are changed to single quotes here because they appear within the writer's own quotation marks. The parenthetical citation lists only a page number, for earlier in this paper the writer has mentioned Cheever by name and the context makes it clear that the quotation comes from the story. Only one work by Cheever appears among the works cited entries. If several works by Cheever had been listed there, the parenthetical citation would clarify which one was being referred to by adding a shortened form of the book's title: (Stories 518). The reader finds the following entry among the sources:

> Cheever, John. The Stories of John Cheever. New York: Knopf, 1978.

Similarly, quotes and paraphrases from secondary critical sources or from other pieces of nonfiction should follow the same rules of common sense:

> Cheever's daughter Susan, in her candid memoir of her father, observes that the author's alcoholism followed an increasingly destructive pattern:
>
> > Long before I was even aware that he was alcoholic, there were bottles hidden all

> over the house, and even outside in the
> privet hedge and the garden shed. Drink was
> his crucible, his personal hell. As early
> as the 1950s . . . he spent a lot of energy
> trying not to drink before 4 p.m., and then
> before noon, and then before 10 a.m., and
> then before breakfast. (43)
> But she goes on to observe that Cheever's drinking
> had not yet affected his skills as a writer.

This quotation is longer than four lines, so it is indented ten spaces. Indented quotes of this type do not require quotation marks. Also note how ellipses are used to omit extraneous information. Because the author of the quotation is identified, only the page number is included in the parenthetical citation. The reader knows where to look among the sources:

> Cheever, Susan. Home Before Dark. Boston: Houghton,
>   1984.

Notice that a paraphrase of the same passage requires the citation as well:

> Cheever's daughter Susan, in her candid memoir of her
> father, observes that the author's alcoholism
> followed an increasingly destructive pattern. She
> notes that as a child she found bottles hidden in the
> house, in outbuildings, and even in the hedge. She
> recalls that he spent a great deal of energy simply
> not trying to drink before a certain hour, at first
> before 4 p.m. but eventually before breakfast (43).

To simplify parenthetical citations, it is recommended that quotes from secondary sources be introduced, whenever possible, in a manner that identifies the author so that only the page number of the quote is needed inside of the parentheses.

Slightly different conventions govern quotations from poetry. Here are a few examples from papers on Edwin Arlington Robinson's poetry:

> Robinson's insights into character are never sharper
> than in "Miniver Cheevy," a portrait of a town drunk
> who loves "the days of old / When swords were bright

and steeds were prancing" and dreams incongruously "of Thebes and Camelot, / And Priam's neighbors" (347).

Pay attention to how only parts of lines are quoted here to support the sentence and how the parts fit smoothly into the writer's sentence structure. In general, ellipses (. . .) are not necessary at the beginning or end of these quotes because it is clear that they are quoted only in part; they should, however, be used if something is omitted from the middle of a quote ("the days of old / When . . . steeds were prancing"). The virgule or slash (/) is used to indicate line breaks; a double slash (//) indicates stanza breaks. Quotes of up to three lines should be treated in this manner. If a quote is longer than three lines it should be indented ten spaces (with no quotation marks) and printed as it appears in the original poem:

> Robinson opens one of his most effective and pitiless character sketches with an unsparing portrait of failure and bitterness:
>
> > Miniver Cheevy, child of scorn,
> >   Grew lean while he assailed the seasons;
> > He wept that he was ever born,
> >   And he had reasons. (347)

As in the example from the Cheever story, the parenthetical citation here lists only a page number because only one work by Robinson appears in the bibliography. If you are dealing with a classic poem that can be found in many editions (an ode by Keats or a Shakespeare sonnet, for example) the *MLA Handbook* recommends using line numbers instead of page numbers inside the parentheses. This practice should also be followed if you have included a copy of the poem that you are explicating with the paper.

Quoting from a play follows similar procedures. These papers discuss *Othello*:

> In a disarming display of modesty before the Venetian senators, Othello states that his military background has not prepared him to act as an eloquent spokesman in his own defense, readily admitting that "little shall I grace my cause / In speaking for myself" (1.3.90-91).

Classic poetic dramas like *Othello* may be cited by act, scene, and line numbers instead of by page numbers. The reader knows that Shakespeare is the author, so the citation here will simply direct him or her to the edition of Shakespeare listed in the works cited pages at the end of the paper. Also note that verse dramas should be quoted in the same manner as poems; quotations of more than three lines should be indented ten spaces. In this paper, a scene involving dialogue is quoted:

> In the climactic scene of <u>Othello</u>, Shakespeare's
> practice of fragmenting his blank verse lines into
> two or more parts emphasizes the violence that is
> about to occur:
>
> OTHELLO: He hath confessed.
> DESDEMONA: What, my lord?
> OTHELLO: That he hath used thee.
> DESDEMONA: How? Unlawfully?
> OTHELLO: Ay.
> DESDEMONA: He will not say so. (5.2.73-75)

If you are quoting from a prose drama, you would cite a page number from the edition of the play which you used:

> In <u>A Doll's House</u> Ibsen wants to demonstrate
> immediately that Nora and Helmer share almost
> childlike attitudes toward each other. "Is that my
> little lark twittering out there?" is Helmer's
> initial line in the play (43).

Remember that common sense is the best test to apply to any parenthetical citation. Have you given the reader enough information in the citation to locate the source from which the quote was taken?

Finally, here is a brief warning about plagiarism. Few students knowingly plagiarize, and those who do are usually not successful at it. An instructor who has read four or five weak papers from a student is likely to be suspicious if the same student suddenly begins to sound like an officer of the Modern Language Association, writing, with no citations, about "paradigms" or "*différance*" in the "*texte.*" A definition of "common knowledge," the kind of information that does not require a citation, is given above. Otherwise, any *opinion* about a writer and his or her work must be followed by a citation indicating its source. If the opinion is directly quoted, paraphrased, or even summarized in passing you should still include a citation. Doing less than this is to commit an act of plagiarism, for which the penalties are usually severe. Internet materials, which are so easily cut and pasted into a manuscript, provide an easy temptation but are immediately noticeable, and there has been much media scrutiny in recent years about the widespread "epidemic" of Internet plagiarism. Nothing is easier to spot in a paper than an uncited "lift" from a source; in most cases the vocabulary and sentence structure will be radically different from the rest of the paper, and a simple text search with Google will probably reveal its source. Particularly bothersome are the numerous websites offering "free" research papers; a quick perusal of some of these papers indicates that even at a free price they are significantly overpriced. Additionally, many educational institutions have subscribed to "plagiarism-detection" software services that maintain huge, searchable files of research papers that have seen more than one user.

Sample Works Cited Entries

Here are formats for some of the most commonly used types of materials used in literary research. More detailed examples may be found in the *MLA Handbook for Writers of Research Papers*.

BOOK BY A SINGLE AUTHOR

Reynolds, Clay. Ars Poetica. Lubbock: Texas Tech UP, 2003.

Sanderson, Jim. Semi-Private Rooms. Youngstown: Pig Iron, 1994.

Wilbur, Richard. Collected Poems 1943-2004. New York: Harcourt, 2004.

BOOK WITH AUTHOR AND EDITOR

Robinson, Edwin Arlington. Edwin Arlington Robinson's Letters to Edith Brower. Ed. Richard Cary. Cambridge: Harvard UP, 1968.

CASEBOOK OR EDITED COLLECTION OF CRITICAL ESSAYS

Dean, Leonard Fellows, ed. A Casebook on Othello. New York: Crowell, 1961.

Snyder, Susan, ed. Othello: Critical Essays. New York: Garland, 1988.

Individual Selection from a Casebook or Edited Collection

Urbanski, Marie Mitchell Oleson. "Existential Allegory: Joyce Carol Oates's 'Where Are You Going, Where Have You Been?'" "Where Are You Going, Where Have You Been?": Joyce Carol Oates. Ed. Elaine Showalter. New Brunswick: Rutgers UP, 1994. 75-79.

Woodring, Carl R. "Once More The Windhover." Gerard Manley Hopkins: The Windhover. Ed. John Pick. Columbus: Merrill, 1969. 52-56.

Story, Poem, or Play Reprinted in Anthology or Textbook

Cheever, John. "The Swimmer." The Longman Anthology of Short Fiction: Stories and Authors in Context. Ed. Dana Gioia and R. S. Gwynn. New York: Longman, 2001. 390-99.

Hansberry, Lorraine. A Raisin in the Sun. Black Theater: A Twentieth-Century Collection of the Work of Its Best Playwrights. Ed. Lindsay Patterson. New York: Dodd, 1971. 221-76.

Robinson, Edwin Arlington. "Richard Cory." Literature: An Introduction to Poetry, Fiction, and Drama. 9th ed. Ed. X. J. Kennedy and Dana Gioia. New York: Longman, 2005. 793.

Article in Reference Book

Johnson, Richard A. "Auden, W. H." Academic American Encyclopedia (Electronic Edition). 2002 ed. CD-ROM.Danbury: Grolier, 2002.

"Othello." The Oxford Companion to English Literature. Ed. Margaret Drabble. 5th ed. New York: Oxford UP, 1985.

Seymour-Smith, Martin. "Cheever, John." Who's Who in Twentieth Century Literature. New York: McGraw, 1976.

Article, Book Review, Story, or Poem in Scholarly Journal

Berry, Edward. "Othello's Alienation." Studies in English Literature, 1500-1900 30 (1990): 315-33.

Horgan, Paul. "To Meet Mr. Eliot: Three Glimpses."
    American Scholar 60 (1991): 407-13.
McDonald, Walter. "Sandstorms." Negative Capability
    3.4 (1983): 93.
Read, Arthur M., II. "Robinson's 'The Man Against the
    Sky.'" Explicator 26 (1968): 49.

ARTICLE, BOOK REVIEW, STORY, OR POEM IN MAGAZINE

Becker, Alida. Rev. of Morning, Noon, and Night, by
    Sidney Sheldon. New York Times Book Review 15
    Oct. 1995: 20.
Iyer, Pico. "Magic Carpet Ride." Rev. of The English
    Patient, by Michael Ondattje. Time 2 Nov. 1992:
    71. Time Man of the Year. CD-ROM. Compact. 1993.
Jones, Rodney. "TV." Atlantic Monthly Jan. 1993: 52.
Spires, Elizabeth. "One Life, One Art: Elizabeth Bishop
    in Her Letters." Rev. of One Art: Letters, by
    Elizabeth Bishop. New Criterion May 1994: 18-23.

INTERVIEW

Cheever, John. Interview. "John Cheever: The Art of
    Fiction LXII." By Annette Grant. Paris Review 17
    (1976): 39-66.

REVIEW OF PLAY PRODUCTION

Brantley, Ben. "Big Daddy's Ego Defies Death and His
    Family." New York Times. 3 Nov. 2003: E1.

FILM, VIDEO, OR AUDIO RECORDING

Harjo, Joy, and Poetic Justice. The Woman Who Fell
    from the Sky.Audiocassette. Norton, 1994.
Pygmalion. Dir. Anthony Asquith and Leslie Howard.
    Perf. Leslie Howard and Wendy Hiller. Paschal,
    1938.

ONLINE: ARTICLE OR REVIEW

Wasserstein, Wendy. "A Place They'd Never Been: The
    Theater." Theater Development Fund. 7 June 2000.
    1 Mar. 2005 <http://www.tdf.org/communications/
    wendy.htm>.

ONLINE: AUTHOR OR CRITICAL WEB SITE

```
"August Wilson." Literature Online. Rev. 12 May 2001.
    28 Feb. 2006 <http://longman.awl.com/kennedy/
    wilson/biography.html>.
"A Page for Edwin." 5 Feb. 1998. 12 Apr. 2006
    <http://www.du.edu/~dokonski/robin.html>.
```

ONLINE: PLAY PRODUCTION WEB SITE

```
"Death of a Salesman." 15 Nov. 2000. 12 Jan. 2006
    <http:www.deathofasalesman.com>.
```

ONLINE: REFERENCE WORK

```
"Sophocles." Britannica Online. 15 Feb. 2006
    <http://www.britannica.com/bcom/eb/article/0/
    0,5716,118260+1+109862,00.html?query=sophocles>.
```

Conducting Research

1. What types of materials have you searched to use as supporting materials for your argument? Are they electronic, print or both? What details should you keep in mind when preparing a works cited list?
2. Have you made notes on the publication data necessary for documenting sources and copied articles you may use?
3. Did you observe MLA guidelines for manuscript formatting and for works cited entries?
4. Have you ensured that you have adequately documented material taken from secondary sources, whether quoted directly or paraphrased?

"Reality, Responsibility, and Reinvention": Sample Student Essay

The following argumentative paper on Sandra Cisneros's "Woman Hollering Creek" (page 183) was written by Amanda Smith, who twice won awards for best undergraduate critical paper while a student at Lamar University. The critical strategy that Smith employs combines close reading with historical and sociological (mainly feminist and multicultural) approaches. Her title itself generates interest by its alliterative first three words, which also give a clue to the three-part development of her argument. Notice how, at the outset, the author gives a clear indication that she has given considerable thought to narrowing her topic, taking her cue from Cisneros's own analysis (quoted from a book by Deborah Madsen) of one of her major themes.

Smith's opening paragraph establishes her *ethos* as a critic by making it immediately apparent to the audience that she had done considerable research in secondary sources, applying the testimony of the author herself as support, and throughout the essay she uses support from the story and from critics to support her arguments. The first part of the introductory paragraph is mainly concerned with the topic of definition, for Smith wishes to deal with the perspective of a writer who labels herself a Chicana. At the end of the paragraph, Smith indicates the structure of the body of the paper, using the topic of relationship, by showing how she will move from the protagonist's own situation to the responsibility of the secondary characters to help her and, finally, to a discussion of how a figure from Mexican-American myth has become an archetype which the story follows.

Note how the second paragraph of the essay primarily uses the topics of comparison, circumstance, and relationship to discuss the situation of the protagonist. Comparison is used in contrasting Cleófilas's situation in Mexico with, first, her fantasies about and, later, her real experiences in Texas. Circumstance is used primarily to indicate the degrees to which her situation has altered; if a little patriarchy is bad (her previous life with her brothers and her fathers), then more patriarchy must be worse (her present life with her abusive husband). Relationship is employed when Smith links the development of her argument with a compact summary of the story's plot.

In the next paragraph, Smith further uses definition to clarify the Chicana figure and uses comparison to show how Cleófilas is incapable of being helped by her two similarly trapped neighbors but how she is assisted by the contrasting figures of the two Chicana women whom she meets at the clinic; also in this paragraph Smith reintroduces the figure of *La Llorona*, providing a link to her next paragraph and topic.

The fourth paragraph of the essay primarily uses the topic of relationship, for Smith wishes to demonstrate that the figure from myth has exercised a powerful cause-effect relationship on the Chicana who has come to understand her role and responsibility in society. Finally, the essay concludes with a strong recapitulation of the major themes of both the story and of the critical argument. With her *ethos* clearly established at the beginning of the paper, Smith has demonstrated her *logos* through her structured, well-supported argument. Fittingly, she has withheld her appeal to the emotions, her *pathos,* until the end of the essay when she speaks of the "dreams" and "disappointments" of women like Cleófilas and uses strong terms like "sacrificing." It has not been necessary for her to give a first-person response to the story, for her involvement with the story on both personal and critical levels is implicit throughout. If the author was perhaps first drawn to "Woman Hollering Creek" because of her own sense of multiethnic identity, she has chosen to leave that information unstated.

```
Amanda Smith
Professor Gwynn
ENG 3360
11 July 2006

     Reality, Responsibility, and Reinvention in Sandra
           Cisneros's "Woman Hollering Creek"

     The Chicana, a Mexican-American female, is a
marginalized being; on the one hand, she is neither
completely Mexican and, on the other, not fully
American. Sandra Cisneros is a Chicana author. In
Understanding Contemporary Chicana Literature by
Deborah Madsen, Sandra Cisneros is quoted as saying,
"'We're always straddling two countries, and we're
always living in that kind of schizophrenia that I
call being a Mexican woman living in American
society, but not belonging to either culture'" (108).
Cisneros seeks to "negotiate a cross-cultural
identity" through her work. The difficulty comes from
the necessity to "challenge the deeply rooted
patriarchal values of both Mexican and American
cultures" (108). In the short story "Woman Hollering
Creek," she challenges these patriarchal cultures in
three very specific ways. First she does this by
examining the reality of Cleófilas's situation as a
Mexican bride brought "to a town en el otro lado--on
the other side" of the Rio Grande (43).
     Cleófilas has many fantasies of what life will
be like on the northern side of the border, but these
are dispelled shortly after her marriage. Through
```

Smith 2

this story Cisneros also shows the reader that it is the liberated Chicana's responsibility to help her "sisters" out of the entrapment of these imprisoning patriarchies. Finally, and perhaps most importantly, one of the ways she has chosen to undermine these traditions is to reevaluate and redefine one of the three Mexican mythologies that most deeply impact female Mexican culture, that of La Llorona.

The protagonist, Cleófilas, is a young Mexican woman who has lived with her "six good-for-nothing brothers, and one old" man, her father, and has been waiting her entire life for "passion." "The kind books and songs and telenovelas describe when one finds, finally, the great love of one's life and does whatever one can, must do, at whatever the cost" (43-44). Before her marriage and uprooting, she also has grand imaginings of what life in Seguin, Texas will be like:

> A nice sterling ring to it. The tinkle of money. She would get to wear outfits like the women on the *tele*, like Lucía Méndez. And would have a lovely house, and wouldn't Chela be jealous. [. . .] and then they'll drive off in his new pickup- did you see it?- to their new home in Seguin. Well, not exactly new, but they're going to repaint the house. You know newlyweds. New paint and new furniture. Why not? He can afford it. (45)

She marries Juan Pedro and is transported away from her family and friends--all she has known in her life--and taken to Seguin. This is not the heaven on earth she has constructed in her mind. Marital bliss is short-lived, and she soon finds herself a battered wife completely at the mercy of her unfaithful husband. The reality of the situation is that she must

> remind herself why she loves him when she changes the baby's Pampers, or when she mops the bathroom floor, or tries to make the curtains for the doorways without doors, or whiten the linen. Or wonder a

little when he kicks the refrigerator door and says he hates this shitty house and is going out where he won't be bothered with the baby's howling and her suspicious questions. (49)

She has based all of her ideas of love on these telenovelas giving her the notion that "to suffer for love is good. The pain all sweet somehow. In the end" (45). This deeply held belief and the geography of a new land trap her in an abusive relationship: "Because the towns here are built so that you have to depend on husbands" (50-51). Jeff Thompson writes about this in "'What Is Called Heaven': Identity in Sandra Cisneros's Woman Hollering Creek." He states that "she is beaten by her husband and trapped in a suburban house between two women who are equally trapped" (420). These women are Cleófilas's only companions, Dolores and Soledad, aside from the creek which she believes calls to her in the voice of La Llorona. In the end, she decides, for the safety of her unborn child, that she must escape back to her father's home in Mexico. She does this with the aid of Felice, a Chicana woman who drives her from Seguin to the bus station in San Antonio. As the story is ending, the reader finds Cleófilas in Mexico explaining her escape and the strange woman who "when we crossed the arroyo she just started yelling like a crazy" (56). At this time Cleófilas notices that she has gained some of Felice's strength, her laughter, that comes "gurgling out of her own throat, a long ribbon of laughter, like water" (56).

In an article titled "On Not Being La Malinche: Border Negotiations of Gender in Sandra Cisneros's 'Never Marry a Mexican' and 'Woman Hollering Creek,'" Jean Wyatt explains that this "Chicana figure provides Cleófilas with a [. . .] positive role model" (257). In the context of this story, it is to the advantage of the Chicana woman that she is

Smith 4

marginalized. "The Chicana, who stands astride Anglo and Mexican cultures, is not captive to the myths of either culture" (257-58). Instead of having only one way of interpreting the world, Felice, one of the story's Chicana figures, can choose to hear La Llorona's wailing or to yell out like Tarzan. She chooses the latter, and as they cross over the creek she lets "out a yell as loud as any mariachi" (55). Wyatt claims "Felice's grito may also be read as a call to arms, to the cause of female solidarity, which now rescues Cleófilas from domestic abuse" (258). She also is not confined to one language. She speaks "in a Spanish pocked with English" (55). Felice asks Cleófilas if she has noticed "how nothing around here is named after a woman? Really. Unless she's the Virgin. I guess you're only famous if you're a virgin" (55). Wyatt also explains that while this is true and quite annoying to Felice, the creek is a "woman" but has both Spanish and English names, allowing "Felice to define 'woman' for herself" (258). Because of Felice, Cleófilas is able to see a type of woman she never knew existed--the type of woman who is not married, who has her own truck that she makes her own payments on, and who is not afraid to express herself by screaming at the top of her lungs and laughing out loud. Cleófilas has just gained the knowledge that women can express themselves and that there is more than one way to live and more than one way to interpret the world around her.

Similarly there are multiple ways to examine Mexican and pre-colonial Mexican myths. According to an essay by Alexandra Fitts, the three that impact the Mexican female psyche most dramatically are the images of La Malinche, the Virgin of Guadalupe, and La Llorona. In "Woman Hollering Creek," Cisneros specifically focuses on the myth of La Llorona. Fitts states "Part of this negotiation is the incorporation of key feminine archetypes from the Mexican tradition

and the reconsideration of these figures in a way that
will reflect the realities of the modern Chicana
experience (11). Cisneros reexamines the figure of La
Llorona, who according to Octavio Paz describes in
Fitts' essay, is

> the wailing woman in white [seeking] her
> children who died in childbirth. Originally
> an Aztec goddess who sacrificed babies and
> disappeared shrieking into lakes or rivers,
> La Llorona usually appears near a well,
> stream or washing place. The Hispanicized
> form has La Llorona murdering her own
> children born out of wedlock when her lover
> married a woman of his own station. (18)

Jacqueline Doyle examines this topic in her article
"Haunting the Borderlands: La Llorona in Sandra
Cisneros's 'Woman Hollering Creek.'" In this
analysis, she quotes Norma Alarcón's argument "that
these highly charged 'symbolic figures' have been
used as 'reference point[s] not only for controlling,
interpreting, or visualizing women' in Mexican-
American culture, 'but also to wage a domestic battle
of stifling proportions'" (55). As Cleófilas's
situation worsens she believes she hears La Llorona
calling out to her:

> La Llorona calling to her. She is sure of
> it. Cleófilas sets the baby's Donald Duck
> blanket on the grass. Listens. The day sky
> turning to night. The baby pulling up
> fistfuls of grass and laughing. La Llorona.
> Wonders if something as quiet as this
> drives a woman to the darkness under the
> trees. (51)

She is beginning to understand the kind of
desperation that potentially leads a woman to perform
such an act, but she resists following La Llorona's
example. Fitts suggests that this occurs because
Cleófilas has some "resources that La Llorona must
not have possessed, and it is through Cleófilas's

Smith 6
resolution of her desperate situation that Cisneros
rewrites the story of La Llorona" (19). The two
resources that Cleófilas has are her father back in
Mexico, who tells Cleófilas on her wedding day "I am
your father, I will never abandon you," and the
comadres she discovers at the doctor's office, Felice
and Graciela (43). Thus, Cisneros has succeeded in
her attempt "to chart the interstices and in-betweens
of the borderlands, to remap symbolic maternal
landscapes, and to open a protean space where La
Llorona's ghostly wail is replaced by 'a voice all
[her] own,' a high, silver voice' that calls
Cleófilas to a new spiritual birth" (55). Her goal of
reinventing a classic Mexican myth has been achieved.

"Woman Hollering Creek" is more than a
relatively short piece of prose fiction with simple
language; it is a political and emotional statement
about the plight of Mexican women in American
society: specifically, "Another one of those brides
from across the border" (54). Cisneros shows her
readers the dreams of these women and their
disappointments at the reality of the "American
Dream." She shows her audience that Chicana women
possess a responsibility, a kind of stewardship,
which must be shown towards women less liberated and
fortunate. But most importantly, she reinvents La
Llorona through the character of Cleófilas, who
instead of sacrificing her children and herself finds
a way of escape and personal liberation.

[New Page]

Works Cited

Cisneros, Sandra. Woman Hollering Creek. New York:
    Vintage, 1991.
Doyle, Jacqueline. "Haunting the Borderlands: La
    Llorona in Sandra Cisneros's 'Woman Hollering
    Creek.'" Frontiers: A Journal of Women Studies
    16.1 (1996): 53–70.

Fitts, Alexandra. "Sandra Cisneros's Modern Malinche:
     A Reconsideration of Feminine Archetypes in
     'Woman Hollering Creek.'" International Fiction
     Review 29.1-2 (2002): 11-22.

Madsen, Deborah L. Understanding Contemporary Chicana
     Literature. Columbia: U of South Carolina P,
     2000.

Thompson, Jeff. "'What Is Called Heaven': Identity in
     Sandra Cisneros's Woman Hollering Creek."
     Studies in Short Fiction 31 (1994): 415-24.

Wyatt, Jean. "On Not Being La Malinche: Border
     Negotiations of Gender in Sandra Cisneros's
     'Never Marry a Mexican' and 'Woman Hollering
     Creek.'" Tulsa Women's Literature 14 (1995):
     243-71.

✓ *Checklist:* WRITING AND ARGUING ABOUT LITERATURE

Have you . . .

❑ Examined the topic closely and thought about narrowing it so that you can manage it in the assigned length?

❑ Formulated a clear thesis for your overall argument?

❑ Thought about the uses of *ethos, pathos,* and *logos* in your writing?

❑ Decided how best to introduce your overall argument?

❑ Used the *topoi* to discover further arguments?

❑ Considered how to conclude your essay?

❑ Employed terminology and conventions appropriate to the genre you are writing about?

❑ Discussed your ideas or drafts with peers or your instructor?

❑ Conducted research thoroughly and evaluated your secondary sources?

❑ Followed MLA guidelines for quoting, citing, manuscript form, and works cited?

❑ Reread and revised your drafts into a final version?

Who We Are

Personal and Communal Identities

"Every man is a piece of the continent, a part of the main."
—John Donne, *Meditation 17*

As individuals, we have our own private thoughts, feelings, and reactions. Yet we grow up in a community of family and friends that gives us ideas about ourselves, who we are, and what place we have in relation to others. How do we face this apparent contradiction—that we are both ourselves and yet part of something else at the same time? These and many other questions can be asked in the texts in this chapter. As familiar as some of these issues may already be to you, you will see that authors have found many different or unusual ways to respond to the situations, classifications, and lives in which they've found themselves.

Anyone who has watched an episode of television or gone to the movies knows that race, class, and gender are dominant ways that we categorize one another in American culture. While sometimes we openly recognize these categories, they often act as unspoken influences on decisions about who our friends are, whom we want to date, what kind of neighborhoods we'll live in, and what opportunities we have in life. In the last several decades in particular, Americans have expressed great sensitivity to issues of race, which you will see reflected in some of the texts in our selections. Class has not been so explicitly addressed in our country. Nonetheless it has a major influence on personal identity. Class is the rationale behind the jobs we pursue, the products we purchase, and the expectations we have for life. Gender and the whole question of sexual identity have also received enormous attention in recent decades. However, even before writers explicitly addressed sexual inequalities in society as a topic, gender and its complications have been a major element in literary production since its earliest history. The purpose of the following selections is to introduce to you the many ways that we label, identify, and organize ourselves—having incalculable, pervasive influence both for good and bad on who we are as people.

> "We, whites, are not white at all, we are mauve at birth, then tea-rose, and later all kinds of repulsive colors."
>
> —Vladimir Nabokov, *Pale Fire*

From *The Qur'an* (c. 630)

The Story of Joseph

SURA 12. JOSEPH

[MECCA]

In the Name of God, the Compassionate, the Merciful

Alif lām rā. These are the verses of the Glorious Book. We have revealed the Koran in the Arabic tongue so that you may grow in understanding.

In revealing this Koran We will recount to you the best of narratives, though before it you were heedless.

Joseph said to his father: "Father, I dreamt of eleven stars and the sun and the moon; I saw them prostrate themselves before me."

"My son," he replied, "say nothing of this dream to your brothers, lest they plot evil against you: Satan is the sworn enemy of man. You shall be chosen by your Lord. He will teach you to interpret visions, and will perfect His favour to you and to the house of Jacob, as He perfected it to your forefathers Abraham and Isaac before you. Your Lord is wise and all-knowing."

Surely in Joseph and his brothers there are signs for doubting men.

They said to each other: "Joseph and his brother are dearer to our father than ourselves, though we are many. Truly, our father is much mistaken. Let us slay Joseph, or cast him away in some far-off land, so that we may have no rivals in our father's love, and after that be honourable men."

One of them said: "Do not slay Joseph; but if you must, rather cast him into a dark pit. Some caravan will take him up."

They said to their father: "Why do you not trust us with Joseph? Surely we wish him well. Send him with us tomorrow, that he may play and enjoy himself. We will take good care of him."

He replied: "It would much grieve me to let him go with you; for I fear lest the wolf should eat him when you are off your guard."

They said: "If the wolf could eat him despite our numbers, then we should surely be lost!"

And when they took Joseph with them, they decided to cast him into a dark pit. We revealed to him, saying: "You shall tell them of all this when they will not know you."

At nightfall they returned weeping to their father. They said: "We went off to compete together and left Joseph with our packs. The wolf devoured him. But you will not believe us, though we speak the truth." And they showed him their brother's shirt, stained with false blood.

"No!" he cried. "Your souls have tempted you to evil. Sweet patience! God alone can help me bear the loss you speak of."

And a caravan passed by, who sent their water-bearer to the pit. And when he had let down his pail, he cried: "Rejoice! A boy!"

They concealed him as part of their merchandise. But God knew what they did. They sold him for a trifling price, for a few pieces of silver. They cared nothing for him.

The Egyptian who bought him said to his wife: "Be kind to him. He may prove useful to us, or we may adopt him as our son."

Thus We established Joseph in the land, and taught him to interpret dreams. God has power over all things, though most men may not know it. And when he reached maturity We bestowed on him wisdom and knowledge. Thus We reward the righteous.

His master's wife sought to seduce him. She bolted the doors and said: "Come!"

"God forbid!" he replied. "My lord has treated me with kindness. Wrong-doers never prosper."

She made for him, and he himself would have succumbed to her had he not been shown a sign from his Lord. Thus did We shield him from wantonness, for he was one of Our faithful servants.

They both rushed to the door. She tore his shirt from behind. And at the door they met her husband.

She cried: "Shall not the man who wished to violate your wife be thrown into prison or sternly punished?"

Joseph said: "It was she who attempted to seduce me."

"If his shirt is torn from the front," said one of her people, "she is speaking the truth and he is lying. If it is torn from behind, then he is speaking the truth and she is lying."

And when her husband saw Joseph's shirt rent from behind, he said to her: "This is but one of your tricks. Your cunning is great indeed! Joseph, say no more about this. Woman, ask pardon for your sin. You have done wrong."

In the city women were saying: "The Prince's wife has sought to seduce her servant. She has conceived a passion for him. It is clear that she has gone astray."

When she heard of their intrigues, she invited them to a banquet at her house. To each she gave a knife, and ordered Joseph to present himself before them. When they saw him, they were amazed at him and cut their hands, exclaiming: "God preserve us! This is no mortal, but a gracious angel."

"This is the man," she said, "on whose account you blamed me. I sought to seduce him, but he was unyielding. If he declines to do my bidding, he shall be thrown into prison and shall be held in scorn."

"Lord," said Joseph, "sooner would I go to prison than give in to their advances. Shield me from their cunning, or I shall yield to them and lapse into folly."

His Lord heard his prayer and warded off their wiles from him. He hears all and knows all.

Yet for all the evidence they had seen, they thought it right to jail him for a time.

Two young men entered the prison with him. One of them said: "I dreamt that I was pressing grapes." And the other said: "I dreamt that I was carrying a loaf upon my head, and that the birds came and ate of it. Tell us the meaning of these dreams, for we can see you are a virtuous man."

Joseph replied: "I can interpret them long before they are fulfilled. Whatever food you are provided with, I can divine for you its meaning, even before it reaches you. This knowledge my Lord has given me, for I have left the faith of those that disbelieve in God and deny the life to come. I follow the faith of my forefathers, Abraham, Isaac, and Jacob. We will serve no idols besides God. Such is the grace which God has bestowed on us and on all mankind. Yet most men do not give thanks.

"Fellow-prisoners! Are sundry gods better than God, the One, the One who conquers all? Those you serve besides Him are nothing but names which you and your fathers have devised and for which God has revealed no sanction. Judgement rests only with God. He has commanded you to worship none but Him. That is the true faith: yet most men do not know it.

"Fellow-prisoners, one of you will serve his lord with wine. The other will be crucified, and the birds will peck at his head. This is the answer to your question."

And Joseph said to the prisoner who he knew would be freed: "Remember me in the presence of your lord."

But Satan made him forget to mention Joseph to his lord, so that he stayed in prison for several years.

The king said: "I saw seven fatted cows which seven lean ones devoured; also seven green ears of corn and seven others dry. Tell me the meaning of this vision, my nobles, if you can interpret visions."

They replied: "It is but a medley of dream; nor are we skilled in the interpretation of dreams."

Thereupon the man who had been freed remembered Joseph after all that time. He said: "I shall tell you what it means. Give me leave to go."

He said to Joseph: "Tell us, man of truth, of the seven fatted cows which seven lean ones devoured; also of the seven green ears of corn and the other seven which were dry: so that I may go back to my masters and inform them."

He replied: "You shall sow for seven consecutive years. Leave in the ear the corn you reap, except a little which you may eat. Then there shall follow seven hungry years which will consume all but little of what you have stored. Then there will come a year of abundant rain, in which the people will press the grape."

The king said: "Bring this man before me."

But when the envoy came to him, Joseph said: "Go back to your master and ask him about the women who cut their hands. My master knows their cunning."

The king questioned the women, saying: "What made you attempt to seduce Joseph?"

"God forbid!" they replied. "We know no evil of him."

"Now the truth must come to light," said the Prince's wife. "It was I who sought to seduce him. He has told the truth."

"From this," said Joseph, "my lord will know that I did not betray him in his absence, and that God does not guide the work of the treacherous. Not that I am free from sin: man's soul is prone to evil, except his to whom God has shown mercy. My Lord is forgiving and merciful."

The king said: "Bring him before me. I will choose him for my own."

And when he had spoken with him, the king said: "You shall henceforth dwell with us, honoured and trusted."

Joseph said: "Give me charge of the granaries of the realm. I shall husband them wisely."

Thus did We establish Joseph in the land, and he dwelt there as he pleased. We bestow Our mercy on whom We will, and never deny the righteous their reward. Better is the reward of the life to come for those who believe in God and keep from evil.

Joseph's brothers arrived and presented themselves before him. He recognized them, but they knew him not. And when he had given them their provisions, he said: "Bring me your other brother from your father. Do you not see that I give just measure and am the best of hosts?

If you do not bring him, you shall have no corn, nor shall you come near me again."

They replied: "We will endeavour to fetch him from his father. This we will surely do."

Joseph said to his servants: "Put their money into their packs, so that they may find it when they return to their people. Perchance they will come back."

When they returned to their father, they said: "Father, corn is henceforth denied us. Send our brother with us and we shall have our measure. We will take good care of him."

He replied: "Am I to trust you with him as I once trusted you with his brother? But God is the best of guardians: and of all those that show mercy He is the most merciful."

When they opened their packs, they discovered that their money had been returned to them. "Father," they said, "what more can we desire? Here is our money paid back to us. We will buy provisions for our people and take good care of our brother. We shall receive an extra camel-load; a camel-load should be easy enough."

He replied: "I will not let him go with you until you promise in God's name to bring him back to me, unless the worst befall you."

And when they had given him their pledge, he said: "God is the witness of your oath. My sons, enter the town by different gates. If you do wrong, I cannot ward off from you the wrath of God: judgement is His alone. In Him I have put my trust. In Him alone let the faithful put their trust."

And when they entered as their father had bade them, his counsel availed them nothing against the decree of God. It was but a wish in Jacob's soul which he had thus fulfilled. He was possessed of knowledge which We had given him, though most men have no knowledge.

When they went in to Joseph, he embraced his brother, and said: "I am your brother. Do not grieve at what they did."

And when he had given them their provisions, he hid a drinking-cup in his brother's pack.

Then a crier called out after them: "Travellers, you are thieves!"

They turned back and asked: "What have you lost?"

"We miss the king's drinking-cup," he replied. "He that brings it shall have a camel-load of corn. I pledge my word for it."

"In God's name," they cried, "you know we did not come to do evil in this land. We are no thieves."

The Egyptians said: "What penalty shall be his who stole it, if you prove to be lying?"

They replied: "He in whose pack the cup is found shall be your bondsman. Thus we punish the wrongdoers."

Joseph searched their bags before his brother's, and then took out the cup from his brother's bag.

Thus We directed Joseph. By the king's law he had no right to seize his brother: but God willed otherwise. We exalt in knowledge whom We will: but above those that have knowledge there is One more knowing.

They said: "If he has stolen—know then that a brother of his has committed theft before him."

But Joseph kept his secret and revealed nothing to them. He said: "Your deed was worse. God best knows the things you speak of."

They said: "Noble prince, this boy has an aged father. Take one of us, instead of him. We can see you are a generous man."

He replied: "God forbid that we should take any but the man with whom our property was found: for then we should be unjust."

When they despaired of him, they went aside to confer in private. The eldest said: "Have you forgotten that your father took from you a pledge in God's name, and that long ago you did your worst with Joseph. I will not stir from this land until my father gives me leave or God makes known to me His judgement: He is the best of judges. Return to your father and say to him: 'Father, your son has committed a theft. We testify only to what we know. How could we guard against the unforeseen? Inquire at the city where we lodged, and from the caravan with which we travelled. We speak the truth.' "

"No!" cried their father. "Your souls have tempted you to evil. But I will have sweet patience. God may bring them all to me. He alone is all-knowing and wise." And he turned away from them, crying: "Alas for Joseph!" His eyes went white with grief and he was oppressed with silent sorrow.

His sons exclaimed: "In God's name, will you not cease to think of Joseph until you ruin your health and die?"

He replied: "I complain to God of my sorrow and sadness. He has made known to me things that you know not. Go, my sons, and seek news of Joseph and his brother. Do not despair of God's spirit; none but unbelievers despair of God's spirit."

And when they went in to him, they said: "Noble prince, we and our people are scourged with famine. We have brought but little money. Give us some corn, and be charitable to us: God rewards the charitable."

"Do you know," he replied, "what you did to Joseph and his brother? You are surely unaware."

They cried: "Can you indeed be Joseph?"

"I am Joseph," he answered, "and this is my brother. God has been gracious to us. Those that keep from evil and endure with fortitude, God will not deny them their reward."

"By the Lord," they said, "God has exalted you above us all. We have indeed been guilty."

He replied: "None shall reproach you this day. May God forgive you: Of all those who show mercy, He is the most merciful. Take this shirt of mine and throw it over my father's face: he will recover his sight. Then return to me with all your people."

When the caravan departed their father said: "I feel the breath of Joseph, though you will not believe me."

"In God's name," said those who heard him, "it is but your old illusion."

And when the bearer of good news arrived, he threw Joseph's shirt over the old man's face, and he regained his sight. He said: "Did I not tell you that God has made known to me what you know not?"

His sons said: "Father, implore forgiveness for our sins. We have indeed done wrong."

He replied: "I shall implore my Lord to forgive you. He is forgiving and merciful."

And when they went in to Joseph, he embraced his parents and said: "Welcome to Egypt, safe, if God wills!"

He helped his parents to a couch, and they all fell on their knees and prostrated themselves before him.

"This," said Joseph to his father, "is the meaning of my old vision: my Lord has fulfilled it. He has been gracious to me. He has released me from prison and brought you out of the desert after Satan had stirred up strife between me and my brothers. My lord is gracious to whom He will. He alone is all-knowing and wise.

"Lord, You have given me authority and taught me to interpret dreams. Creator of the heavens and the earth, my Guardian in this world and in the hereafter. Allow me to die in submission, and admit me among the righteous."

That which We have now revealed to you is a tale of the unknown. You were not present when Joseph's brothers conceived their plans and schemed against him. Yet strive as you may, most men will not believe.

You shall demand of them no recompense for this. It is an admonition to all mankind.

Many are the marvels of the heavens and the earth; yet they pass them by and pay no heed to them. The greater part of them believe in God only if they can worship other gods besides Him.

Are they confident that God's scourge will not fall upon them, or that the Hour of Doom will not overtake them unawares, without warning?

Say: "This is my path. With sure knowledge I call on you to have faith in God, I and all my followers. Glory be to God! I am no idolater."

Nor were the apostles whom We sent before you other than mortals inspired by Our will and chosen from among their people.

Have they not travelled in the land and seen what was the end of those who disbelieved before them? Better is the world to come for those that keep from evil. Can you not understand?

And when at length Our apostles despaired and thought they were denied, Our help came down to them, delivering whom We pleased. The evil-doers could not be saved from Our scourge. Their annals point to a moral to men of understanding.

This is no invented tale, but a confirmation of previous scriptures, an explanation of all things, a guide and a blessing to true believers.

—c. 7th century

Questions: Reading, Responding, Arguing

1. Satan does not appear as a character in Genesis. What is his function here?
2. Compare this version of the story with the one in Genesis 37:39–45. Which incidents are similar and which are different?
3. Joseph explains God's purpose in Genesis 45:4–7. Is there a comparable passage in this version? How does Joseph's speech in both Genesis and the Qur'an reflect the Hebrews' belief in their unique status? Cite passages from both texts in your argument.

Kate Chopin (1851–1904)

Désirée's Baby*

As the day was pleasant, Madame Valmondé drove over to L'Abri to see Désirée and the baby.

It made her laugh to think of Désirée with a baby. Why, it seemed but yesterday that Désirée was little more than a baby herself; when Monsieur in riding through the gateway of Valmondé had found her lying asleep in the shadow of the big stone pillar.

The little one awoke in his arms and began to cry for "Dada." That was as much as she could do or say. Some people thought she might have strayed there of her own accord, for she was of the toddling age. The prevailing belief was that she had been purposely left by a party of Texans, whose canvas-covered wagon, late in the day, had crossed the ferry that Coton Maïs kept, just below the plantation. In time Madame Valmondé abandoned every speculation but the one that Désirée had been sent to her by a beneficent Providence to be the child of her affection, seeing that she was without child of the flesh. For the girl grew to be beautiful and gentle, affectionate and sincere,—the idol of Valmondé.

It was no wonder, when she stood one day against the stone pillar in whose shadow she had lain asleep, eighteen years before, that Armand Aubigny riding by and seeing her there, had fallen in love with her. That was the way all the Aubignys fell in love, as if struck by a pistol shot. The wonder was that he had not loved her before; for he had known her since his father brought him home from Paris, a boy of eight, after his mother died there. The passion that awoke in him that day, when he saw her at the gate, swept along like an avalanche, or like a prairie fire, or like anything that drives headlong over all obstacles.

Monsieur Valmondé grew practical and wanted things well considered: that is, the girl's obscure origin. Armand looked into her eyes and did not care. He was reminded that she was nameless. What did it matter about a name when he could give her one of the oldest and proudest in Louisiana? He ordered the *corbeille*[1] from Paris, and contained himself with what patience he could until it arrived; then they were married.

Madame Valmondé had not seen Désirée and the baby for four weeks. When she reached L'Abri she shuddered at the first sight of it, as

[1] *corbeille*: trousseau.

she always did. It was a sad looking place, which for many years had not known the gentle presence of a mistress, old Monsieur Aubigny having married and buried his wife in France, and she having loved her own land too well ever to leave it. The roof came down steep and black like a cowl, reaching out beyond the wide galleries that encircled the yellow stuccoed house. Big, solemn oaks grew close to it, and their thick-leaved, far-reaching branches shadowed it like a pall. Young Aubigny's rule was a strict one, too, and under it his negroes had forgotten how to be gay, as they had been during the old master's easygoing and indulgent lifetime.

The young mother was recovering slowly, and lay full length, in her soft white muslins and laces, upon a couch. The baby was beside her, upon her arm, where he had fallen asleep, at her breast. The yellow nurse woman sat beside a window fanning herself.

Madame Valmondé bent her portly figure over Désirée and kissed her, holding her an instant tenderly in her arms. Then she turned to the child.

"This is not the baby!" she exclaimed, in startled tones. French was the language spoken at Valmondé in those days.

"I knew you would be astonished," laughed Désirée, "at the way he has grown. The little *cochon de lait*![2] Look at his legs, mamma, and his hands and fingernails,—real finger-nails. Zandrine had to cut them this morning. Isn't it true, Zandrine?"

The woman bowed her turbaned head majestically, "Mais si, Madame."

"And the way he cries," went on Désirée, "is deafening. Armand heard him the other day as far away as La Blanche's cabin."

Madame Valmondé had never removed her eyes from the child. She lifted it and walked with it over to the window that was lightest. She scanned the baby narrowly, then looked as searchingly at Zandrine, whose face was turned to gaze across the fields.

"Yes, the child has grown, has changed," said Madame Valmondé, slowly, as she replaced it beside its mother. "What does Armand say?"

Désirée's face became suffused with a glow that was happiness itself.

"Oh, Armand is the proudest father in the parish, I believe, chiefly because it is a boy, to bear his name; though he says not,—that he would have loved a girl as well. But I know it isn't true. I know he says that to please me. And mamma," she added, drawing Madame Valmondé's head down to her, and speaking in a whisper, "he hasn't punished one of them—not one of them—since baby is born. Even

---

[2]*cochon de lait*: suckling pig.

Négrillon, who pretended to have burnt his leg that he might rest from work—he only laughed, and said Négrillon was a great scamp Oh, mamma, I'm so happy; it frightens me."

What Désirée said was true. Marriage, and later the birth of his son, had softened Armand Aubigny's imperious and exacting nature greatly. This was what made the gentle Désirée so happy, for she loved him desperately. When he frowned she trembled, but loved him. When he smiled, she asked no greater blessing of God. But Armand's dark, handsome face had not often been disfigured by frowns since the day he fell in love with her.

When the baby was about three months old, Désirée awoke one day to the conviction that there was something in the air menacing her peace. It was at first too subtle to grasp. It had only been a disquieting suggestion; an air of mystery among the blacks; unexpected visits from far-off neighbors who could hardly account for their coming. Then a strange, an awful change in her husband's manner, which she dared not ask him to explain. When he spoke to her, it was with averted eyes, from which the old love-light seemed to have gone out. He absented himself from home; and when there, avoided her presence and that of her child, without excuse. And the very spirit of Satan seemed suddenly to take hold of him in his dealings with the slaves. Désirée was miserable enough to die.

She sat in her room, one hot afternoon, in her *peignoir*, listlessly drawing through her fingers the strands of her long, silky brown hair that hung about her shoulders. The baby, half naked, lay asleep upon her own great mahogany bed, that was like a sumptuous throne, with its satin-lined half-canopy. One of La Blanche's little quadroon boys—half naked too—stood fanning the child slowly with a fan of peacock feathers. Désirée's eyes had been fixed absently and sadly upon the baby, while she was striving to penetrate the threatening mist that she felt closing about her. She looked from her child to the boy who stood beside him, and back again; over and over. "Ah!" It was a cry that she could not help; which she was not conscious of having uttered. The blood turned like ice in her veins, and a clammy moisture gathered upon her face.

She tried to speak to the little quadroon boy; but no sound would come, at first. When he heard his name uttered, he looked up, and his mistress was pointing to the door. He laid aside the great, soft fan, and obediently stole away, over the polished floor, on his bare tiptoes.

She stayed motionless, with gaze riveted upon her child, and her face the picture of fright. Presently her husband entered the room, and without noticing her, went to a table and began to search among some papers which covered it.

"Armand," she called to him, in a voice which must have stabbed him, if he was human. But he did not notice. "Armand," she said again. Then she rose and tottered towards him. "Armand," she panted once more, clutching his arm, "look at our child. What does it mean? Tell me."

He coldly but gently loosened her fingers from about his arm and thrust the hand away from him. "Tell me what it means!" she cried despairingly.

"It means," he answered lightly, "that the child is not white; it means that you are not white."

A quick conception of all that this accusation meant for her nerved her with unwonted courage to deny it. "It is a lie; it is not true, I am white! Look at my hair, it is brown; and my eyes are gray, Armand, you know they are gray. And my skin is fair," seizing his wrist. "Look at my hand; whiter than yours, Armand," she laughed hysterically.

"As white as La Blanche's," he returned cruelly; and went away leaving her alone with their child.

When she could hold a pen in her hand, she sent a despairing letter to Madame Valmondé.

"My mother, they tell me I am not white. Armand has told me I am not white. For God's sake tell them it is not true. You must know it is not true. I shall die. I must die. I cannot be so unhappy, and live."

The answer that came was brief:

"My own Désirée: Come home to Valmondé; back to your mother who loves you. Come with your child."

When the letter reached Désirée she went with it to her husband's study, and laid it open upon the desk before which he sat. She was like a stone image: silent, white, motionless after she placed it there.

In silence he ran his cold eyes over the written words.

He said nothing. "Shall I go, Armand?" she asked in tones sharp with agonized suspense.

"Yes, go."

"Do you want me to go?"

"Yes, I want you to go."

He thought Almighty God had dealt cruelly and unjustly with him; and felt, somehow, that he was paying Him back in kind when he stabbed thus into his wife's soul. Moreover he no longer loved her, because of the unconscious injury she had brought upon his home and his name.

She turned away like one stunned by a blow, and walked slowly towards the door, hoping he would call her back.

"Good-by, Armand," she moaned.

He did not answer her. That was his last blow at fate.

Désirée went in search of her child. Zandrine was pacing the sombre gallery with it. She took the little one from the nurse's arms with no word of explanation, and descending the steps, walked away, under the live-oak branches.

It was an October afternoon; the sun was just sinking. Out in the still fields the negroes were picking cotton.

Désirée had not changed the thin white garment nor the slippers which she wore. Her hair was uncovered and the sun's rays brought a golden gleam from its brown meshes. She did not take the broad, beaten road which led to the far-off plantation of Valmondé. She walked across a deserted field, where the stubble bruised her tender feet, so delicately shod, and tore her thin gown to shreds.

She disappeared among the reeds and willows that grew thick along the banks of the deep, sluggish bayou; and she did not come back again.

Some weeks later there was a curious scene enacted at L'Abri. In the centre of the smoothly swept back yard was a great bonfire. Armand Aubigny sat in the wide hallway that commanded a view of the spectacle; and it was he who dealt out to a half dozen negroes the material which kept this fire ablaze.

A graceful cradle of willow, with all its dainty furbishings, was laid upon the pyre, which had already been fed with the richness of a priceless layette. Then there were silk gowns, and velvet and satin ones added to these; laces, too, and embroideries; bonnets and gloves; for the *corbeille* had been of rare quality.

The last thing to go was a tiny bundle of letters; innocent little scribblings that Désirée had sent to him during the days of their espousal. There was the remnant of one back in the drawer from which he took them. But it was not Désirée's; it was part of an old letter from his mother to his father. He read it. She was thanking God for the blessing of her husband's love:—

"But above all," she wrote, "night and day, I thank the good God for having so arranged our lives that our dear Armand will never know that his mother, who adores him, belongs to the race that is cursed with the brand of slavery."

—1893

Questions: Reading, Responding, Arguing

1. Why is the account of Désirée's "obscure origin" important as part of the story's plot?

2. How does Chopin depict the deaths of Désirée and her child? How would you describe her method of depiction—direct? Indirect? Why do you think she chose this method?

3. After you have read the story's surprise ending, go back and look for instances of foreshadowing. Does Chopin adequately foreshadow the story's final development? Compare her uses of foreshadowing with Ray Bradbury's in "The Veldt" on page 543.

Charlotte Perkins Gilman (1860–1935)

The Yellow Wallpaper

It is very seldom that mere ordinary people like John and myself secure ancestral halls for the summer.

A colonial mansion, a hereditary estate, I would say a haunted house and reach the height of romantic felicity—but that would be asking too much of fate!

Still I will proudly declare that there is something queer about it.

Else, why should it be let so cheaply? And why have stood so long untenanted?

John laughs at me, of course, but one expects that.

John is practical in the extreme. He has no patience with faith, an intense horror of superstition, and he scoffs openly at any talk of things not to be felt and seen and put down in figures.

John is a physician, and *perhaps*—(I would not say it to a living soul, of course, but this is dead paper and a great relief to my mind)—*perhaps* that is one reason I do not get well faster.

You see, he does not believe I am sick! And what can one do?

If a physician of high standing, and one's own husband, assures friends and relatives that there is really nothing the matter with one but temporary nervous depression—a slight hysterical tendency—what is one to do?

My brother is also a physician, and also of high standing, and he says the same thing.

So I take phosphates or phosphites—whichever it is—and tonics, and air and exercise, and journeys, and am absolutely forbidden to "work" until I am well again.

Personally, I disagree with their ideas.

Personally, I believe that congenial work, with excitement and change, would do me good.

But what is one to do?

I did write for a while in spite of them; but it *does* exhaust me a good deal—having to be so sly about it, or else meet with heavy opposition.

I sometimes fancy that in my condition, if I had less opposition and more society and stimulus—but John says the very worst thing I can do is to think about my condition, and I confess it always makes me feel bad.

So I will let it alone and talk about the house.

The most beautiful place! It is quite alone, standing well back from the road, quite three miles from the village. It makes me think of English places that you read about, for there are hedges and walls and gates that lock, and lots of separate little houses for the gardeners and people.

There is a *delicious* garden! I never saw such a garden—large and shady, full of box-bordered paths, and lined with long grape-covered arbors with seats under them.

There were greenhouses, but they are all broken now.

There was some legal trouble, I believe, something about the heirs and coheirs; anyhow, the place has been empty for years.

That spoils my ghostliness, I am afraid, but I don't care—there is something strange about the house—I can feel it.

I even said so to John one moonlight evening, but he said what I felt was a *draught*, and shut the window.

I get unreasonably angry with John sometimes. I'm sure I never used to be so sensitive. I think it is due to this nervous condition.

But John says if I feel so I shall neglect proper self-control; so I take pains to control myself—before him, at least, and that makes me very tired.

I don't like our room a bit. I wanted one downstairs that opened onto the piazza and had roses all over the window, and such pretty old-fashioned chintz hangings! But John would not hear of it.

He said there was only one window and not room for two beds, and no near room for him if he took another.

He is very careful and loving, and hardly lets me stir without special direction.

I have a schedule prescription for each hour in the day; he takes all care from me, and so I feel basely ungrateful not to value it more.

He said he came here solely on my account, that I was to have perfect rest and all the air I could get. "Your exercise depends on your strength, my dear," said he, "and your food somewhat on your appetite; but air you can absorb all the time." So we took the nursery at the top of the house.

It is a big, airy room, the whole floor nearly, with windows that look all ways, and air and sunshine galore. It was a nursery first, and then playroom and gymnasium, I should judge, for the windows are barred for little children, and there are rings and things in the walls.

The paint and paper look as if a boys' school had used it. It is stripped off—the paper—in great patches all around the head of my bed, about as far as I can reach, and in a great place on the other side of the room low down. I never saw a worse paper in my life. One of those sprawling, flamboyant patterns committing every artistic sin.

It is dull enough to confuse the eye in following, pronounced enough constantly to irritate and provoke study, and when you follow the lame uncertain curves for a little distance they suddenly commit suicide—plunge off at outrageous angles, destroy themselves in unheard-of contradictions.

The color is repellent, almost revolting: a smouldering unclean yellow, strangely faded by the slow-turning sunlight. It is a dull yet lurid orange in some places, a sickly sulphur tint in others.

No wonder the children hated it! I should hate it myself if I had to live in this room long.

There comes John, and I must put this away—he hates to have me write a word.

● ● ●

We have been here two weeks, and I haven't felt like writing before, since that first day.

I am sitting by the window now, up in this atrocious nursery, and there is nothing to hinder my writing as much as I please, save lack of strength.

John is away all day, and even some nights when his cases are serious.

I am glad my case is not serious!

But these nervous troubles are dreadfully depressing.

John does not know how much I really suffer. He knows there is no *reason* to suffer, and that satisfies him.

Of course it is only nervousness. It does weight on me so not to do my duty in any way!

I meant to be such a help to John, such a real rest and comfort, and here I am a comparative burden already!

Nobody would believe what an effort it is to do what little I am able—to dress and entertain, and order things.

It is fortunate Mary is so good with the baby. Such a dear baby!

And yet I *cannot* be with him, it makes me so nervous.

I suppose John never was nervous in his life. He laughs at me so about this wallpaper!

At first he meant to repaper the room, but afterward he said that I was letting it get the better of me, and that nothing was worse for a nervous patient than to give way to such fancies.

He said that after the wallpaper was changed it would be the heavy bedstead, and then the barred windows, and then that gate at the head of the stairs, and so on.

"You know the place is doing you good," he said, "and really, dear, I don't care to renovate the house just for a three months' rental."

"Then do let us go downstairs," I said. "There are such pretty rooms there."

Then he took me in his arms and called me a blessed little goose, and said he would go down to the cellar, if I wished, and have it whitewashed into the bargain.

But he is right enough about the beds and windows and things.

It is as airy and comfortable a room as anyone need wish, and, of course, I would not be so silly as to make him uncomfortable just for a whim.

I'm really getting quite fond of the big room, all but that horrid paper.

Out of one window I can see the garden—those mysterious deep-shaded arbors, the riotous old-fashioned flowers, and bushes and gnarly trees.

Out of another I get a lovely view of the bay and a little private wharf belonging to the estate. There is a beautiful shaded lane that runs down there from the house. I always fancy I see people walking in these numerous paths and arbors, but John has cautioned me not to give way to fancy in the least. He says that with my imaginative power and habit of storymaking, a nervous weakness like mine is sure to lead to all manner of excited fancies, and that I ought to use my will and good sense to check the tendency. So I try.

I think sometimes that if I were only well enough to write a little it would relieve the press of ideas and rest me.

But I find I get pretty tired when I try.

It is so discouraging not to have any advice and companionship about my work. When I get really well, John says we will ask Cousin Henry and Julia down for a long visit; but he says he would as soon put fireworks in my pillow-case as to let me have those stimulating people about now.

I wish I could get well faster.

But I must not think about that. This paper looks to me as if it *knew* what a vicious influence it had!

There is a recurrent spot where the pattern lolls like a broken neck and two bulbous eyes stare at you upside down.

I get positively angry with the impertinence of it and the everlastingness. Up and down and sideways they crawl, and those absurd unblinking eyes are everywhere. There is one place where two breadths didn't match, and the eyes go all up and down the line, one a little higher than the other.

I never saw so much expression in an inanimate thing before, and we all know how much expression they have! I used to lie awake as a child and get more entertainment and terror out of blank walls and plain furniture than most children could find in a toy-store.

I remember what a kindly wink the knobs of our big old bureau used to have, and there was one chair that always seemed like a strong friend.

I used to feel that if any of the other things looked too fierce I could always hop into that chair and be safe.

The furniture in this room is no worse than inharmonious, however, for we had to bring it all from downstairs. I suppose when this was used as a playroom they had to take the nursery things out, and no wonder! I never saw such ravages as the children have made here.

The wallpaper, as I said before, is torn off in spots, and it sticketh closer than a brother—they must have had perseverance as well as hatred.

Then the floor is scratched and gouged and splintered, the plaster itself is dug out here and there, and this great heavy bed, which is all we found in the room, looks as if it had been through the wars.

But I don't mind it a bit—only the paper.

There comes John's sister. Such a dear girl as she is, and so careful of me! I must not let her find me writing.

She is a perfect and enthusiastic housekeeper, and hopes for no better profession. I verily believe she thinks it is the writing which made me sick!

But I can write when she is out, and see her a long way off from these windows.

There is one that commands the road, a lovely shaded winding road, and one that just looks off over the country. A lovely country, too, full of great elms and velvet meadows.

This wallpaper has a kind of subpattern in a different shade, a particularly irritating one, for you can only see it in certain lights, and not clearly then.

But in the places where it isn't faded and where the sun is just so—I can see a strange, provoking, formless sort of figure that seems to skulk about behind that silly and conspicuous front design.

There's sister on the stairs!

Well, the Fourth of July is over! The people are all gone, and I am tired out. John thought it might do me good to see a little company, so we just had Mother and Nellie and the children down for a week.

Of course I didn't do a thing. Jennie sees to everything now.

But it tired me all the same.

John says if I don't pick up faster he shall send me to Weir Mitchell[1] in the fall.

But I don't want to go there at all. I had a friend who was in his hands once, and she says he is just like John and my brother, only more so!

Besides, it is such an undertaking to go so far.

I don't feel as if it was worthwhile to turn my hand over for anything, and I'm getting dreadfully fretful and querulous.

I cry at nothing, and cry most of the time.

Of course I don't when John is here, or anybody else, but when I am alone.

And I am alone a good deal just now. John is kept in town very often by serious cases, and Jennie is good and lets me alone when I want her to.

So I walk a little in the garden or down that lovely lane, sit on the porch under the roses, and lie down up here a good deal.

I'm getting really fond of the room in spite of the wallpaper. Perhaps *because* of the wallpaper.

It dwells in my mind so!

I lie here on this great immovable bed—it is nailed down, I believe—and follow that pattern about by the hour. It is as good as gymnastics, I assure you. I start, we'll say, at the bottom, down in the corner over there where it has not been touched, and I determine for the thousandth time that I *will* follow that pointless pattern to some sort of a conclusion.

I know a little of the principle of design, and I know this thing was not arranged on any laws of radiation,[2] or alternation, or repetition, or symmetry, or anything else that I ever heard of.

It is repeated, of course, by the breadths, but not otherwise.

---

[1]*Weir Mitchell* (1829–1914): famed nerve specialist who actually treated the author, Charlotte Perkins Gilman, for nervous prostration with his well-known "rest cure." (The cure was not successful.) Also the author of *Diseases of the Nervous System, Especially of Women* (1881).

[2]*laws of radiation*: a principle of design in which all elements are arranged in some circular pattern around a center.

Looked at in one way, each breadth stands alone; the bloated curves and flourishes—a kind of "debased Romanesque" with *delirium tremens*—go waddling up and down in isolated columns of fatuity.

But, on the other hand, they connect diagonally, and the sprawling outlines run off in great slanting waves of optic horror, like a lot of wallowing seaweeds in full chase.

The whole thing goes horizontally, too, at least it seems so, and I exhaust myself trying to distinguish the order of its going in that direction.

They have used a horizontal breadth for a frieze, and that adds wonderfully to the confusion.

There is one end of the room where it is almost intact, and there, when the crosslights fade and the low sun shines directly upon it, I can almost fancy radiation after all—the interminable grotesque seems to form around a common center and rush off in headlong plunges of equal distraction.

It makes me tired to follow it. I will take a nap, I guess.

I don't know why I should write this.

I don't want to.

I don't feel able.

And I know John would think it absurd. But I *must* say what I feel and think in some way—it is such a relief!

But the effort is getting to be greater than the relief.

Half the time now I am awfully lazy, and lie down ever so much. John says I mustn't lose my strength, and has me take cod liver oil and lots of tonics and things, to say nothing of ale and wines and rare meat.

Dear John! He loves me very dearly, and hates to have me sick. I tried to have a real earnest reasonable talk with him the other day, and tell him how I wish he would let me go and make a visit to Cousin Henry and Julia.

But he said I wasn't able to go, nor able to stand it after I got there; and I did not make out a very good case for myself, for I was crying before I had finished.

It is getting to be a great effort for me to think straight. Just this nervous weakness, I suppose.

And dear John gathered me up in his arms, and just carried me upstairs and laid me on the bed, and sat by me and read to me till it tired my head.

He said I was his darling and his comfort and all he had, and that I must take care of myself for his sake, and keep well.

He says no one but myself can help me out of it, that I must use my will and self-control and not let any silly fancies run away with me.

There's one comfort—the baby is well and happy, and does not have to occupy this nursery with the horrid wallpaper.

If we had not used it, that blessed child would have! What a fortunate escape! Why, I wouldn't have a child of mine, an impressionable little thing, live in such a room for worlds.

I never thought of it before, but it is lucky that John kept me here after all; I can stand it so much easier than a baby, you see.

Of course I never mention it to them any more—I am too wise—but I keep watch for it all the same.

There are things in the wallpaper that nobody knows about but me, or ever will.

Behind that outside pattern the dim shapes get clearer every day.

It is always the same shape, only very numerous.

And it is like a woman stooping down and creeping about behind that pattern. I don't like it a bit. I wonder—I begin to think—I wish John would take me away from here!

It is so hard to talk with John about my case, because he is so wise, and because he loves me so.

But I tried it last night.

It was moonlight. The moon shines in all around just as the sun does.

I hate to see it sometimes, it creeps so slowly, and always comes in by one window or another.

John was asleep and I hated to waken him, so I kept still and watched the moonlight on that undulating wallpaper till I felt creepy.

The faint figure behind seemed to shake the pattern, just as if she wanted to get out.

I got up softly and went to feel and see if the paper *did* move, and when I came back John was awake.

"What is it, little girl?" he said. "Don't go walking about like that—you'll get cold."

I thought it was a good time to talk, so I told him that I really was not gaining here, and that I wished he would take me away.

"Why, darling!" said he. "Our lease will be up in three weeks, and I can't see how to leave before.

"The repairs are not done at home, and I cannot possibly leave town just now. Of course, if you were in any danger, I could and would, but you really are better, dear, whether you can see it or not. I am a doctor, dear, and I know. You are gaining flesh and color, your appetite is better, I feel really much easier about you."

"I don't weigh a bit more," said I, "nor as much; and my appetite may be better in the evening when you are here but it is worse in the morning when you are away!"

"Bless her little heart!" said he with a big hug. "She shall be as sick as she pleases! But now let's improve the shining hours by going to sleep, and talk about it in the morning!"

"And you won't go away?" I asked gloomily.

"Why, how can I, dear? It is only three weeks more and then we will take a nice little trip for a few days while Jennie is getting the house ready. Really, dear, you are better!"

"Better in body perhaps—" I began, and stopped short, for he sat up straight and looked at me with such a stern, reproachful look that I could not say another word.

"My darling," said he, "I beg you, for my sake and for our child's sake, as well as for your own, that you will never for one instant let that idea enter your mind! There is nothing so dangerous, so fascinating, to a temperament like yours. It is a false and foolish fancy. Can you trust me as a physician when I tell you so?"

So of course I said no more on that score, and we went to sleep before long. He thought I was asleep first, but I wasn't, and lay there for hours trying to decide whether that front pattern and the back pattern really did move together or separately.

On a pattern like this, by daylight, there is a lack of sequence, a defiance of law, that is a constant irritant to a normal mind.

The color is hideous enough, and unreliable enough, and infuriating enough, but the pattern is torturing.

You think you have mastered it, but just as you get well under way in following, it turns a back-somersault and there you are. It slaps you in the face, knocks you down, and tramples upon you. It is like a bad dream.

The outside pattern is a florid arabesque,[3] reminding one of a fungus. If you can imagine a toadstool in joints, an interminable string of toadstools, budding and sprouting in endless convolutions—why, that is something like it.

That is, sometimes!

There is one marked peculiarity about this paper, a thing nobody seems to notice but myself, and that is that it changes as the light changes.

---

[3]*arabesque:* a type of ornamental style (Arabic in origin) that uses flowers, foliage, fruit, or other figures to create an intricate pattern of interlocking shapes and lines.

When the sun shoots in through the east window—I always watch for that first long, straight ray—it changes so quickly that I never can quite believe it.

That is why I watch it always.

By moonlight—the moon shines in all night when there is a moon—I wouldn't know it was the same paper.

At night in any kind of light, in twilight, candlelight, lamplight, and worst of all by moonlight, it becomes bars! The outside pattern, I mean, and the woman behind it is as plain as can be.

I didn't realize for a long time what the thing was that showed behind, that dim subpattern, but now I am quite sure it is a woman.

By daylight she is subdued, quiet. I fancy it is the pattern that keeps her so still. It is so puzzling. It keeps me quiet by the hour.

I lie down ever so much now. John says it is good for me, and to sleep all I can.

Indeed he started the habit by making me lie down for an hour after each meal.

It is a very bad habit, I am convinced, for you see, I don't sleep.

And that cultivates deceit, for I don't tell them I'm awake—oh, no!

The fact is I am getting a little afraid of John.

He seems very queer sometimes, and even Jennie has an inexplicable look.

It strikes me occasionally, just as a scientific hypothesis, that perhaps it is the paper!

I have watched John when he did not know I was looking, and come into the room suddenly on the most innocent excuses, and I've caught him several times *looking at the paper!* And Jennie too. I caught Jennie with her hand on it once.

She didn't know I was in the room, and when I asked her in a quiet, a very quiet voice, with the most restrained manner possible, what she was doing with the paper, she turned around as if she had been caught stealing, and looked quite angry—asked me why I should frighten her so!

Then she said that the paper stained everything it touched, that she had found yellow smooches[4] on all my clothes and John's and she wished we would be more careful!

Did not that sound innocent? But I know she was studying that pattern, and I am determined that nobody shall find it out but myself!

[4]*smooches:* smudges or smears.

Life is very much more exciting now than it used to be. You see, I have something more to expect, to look forward to, to watch. I really do eat better, and am more quiet than I was.

John is so pleased to see me improve! He laughed a little the other day, and said I seemed to be flourishing in spite of my wallpaper.

I turned it off with a laugh. I had no intention of telling him it was *because* of the wallpaper—he would make fun of me. He might even want to take me away.

I don't want to leave now until I have found it out. There is a week more, and I think that will be enough.

I'm feeling so much better!

I don't sleep much at night, for it is so interesting to watch developments; but I sleep a good deal during the daytime.

In the daytime it is tiresome and perplexing.

There are always new shoots on the fungus, and new shades of yellow all over it. I cannot keep count of them, though I have tried conscientiously.

It is the strangest yellow, that wallpaper! It makes me think of all the yellow things I ever saw—not beautiful ones like buttercups, but old, foul, bad yellow things.

But there is something else about that paper—the smell! I noticed it the moment we came into the room, but with so much air and sun it was not bad. Now we have had a week of fog and rain, and whether the windows are open or not, the smell is here.

It creeps all over the house.

I find it hovering in the dining-room, skulking in the parlor, hiding in the hall, lying in wait for me on the stairs.

It gets into my hair.

Even when I go to ride, if I turn my head suddenly and surprise it— there is that smell!

Such a peculiar odor, too! I have spent hours in trying to analyze it, to find what it smelled like.

It is not bad—at first—and very gentle, but quite the subtlest, most enduring odor I ever met.

In this damp weather it is awful. I wake up in the night and find it hanging over me.

It used to disturb me at first. I thought seriously of burning the house—to reach the smell.

But now I am used to it. The only thing I can think of that it is like is the *color* of the paper! A yellow smell.

There is a very funny mark on this wall, low down, near the mopboard. A streak that runs round the room. It goes behind every piece of furniture, except the bed, a long, straight, even *smooch*, as if it had been rubbed over and over.

I wonder how it was done and who did it, and what they did it for. Round and round and round—round and round and round—it makes me dizzy!

I really have discovered something at last.

Through watching so much at night, when it changes so, I have finally found out.

The front pattern *does* move—and no wonder! The woman behind shakes it!

Sometimes I think there are a great many women behind, and sometimes only one, and she crawls around fast, and her crawling shakes it all over.

Then in the very bright spots she keeps still, and in the very shady spots she just takes hold of the bars and shakes them hard.

And she is all the time trying to climb through. But nobody could climb through that pattern—it strangles so; I think that is why it has so many heads.

They get through and then the pattern strangles them off and turns them upside down, and makes their eyes white!

If those heads were covered or taken off it would not be half so bad.

I think that woman gets out in the daytime!

And I'll tell you why—privately—I've seen her!

I can see her out of every one of my windows!

It is the same woman, I know, for she is always creeping, and most women do not creep by daylight.

I see her in that long shaded lane, creeping up and down. I see her in those dark grape arbors, creeping all round the garden.

I see her on that long road under the trees, creeping along, and when a carriage comes she hides under the blackberry vines.

I don't blame her a bit. It must be very humiliating to be caught creeping by daylight!

I always lock the door when I creep by daylight. I can't do it at night, for I know John would suspect something at once.

And John is so queer now that I don't want to irritate him. I wish he would take another room! Besides, I don't want anybody to get that woman out at night but myself.

I often wonder if I could see her out of all the windows at once.

But, turn as fast as I can, I can only see out of one at one time.

And though I always see her, she *may* be able to creep faster than I can turn! I have watched her sometimes away off in the open country, creeping as fast as a cloud shadow in a wind.

If only that top pattern could be gotten off from the under one! I mean to try it, little by little.

I have found out another funny thing, but I shan't tell it this time! It does not do to trust people too much.

There are only two more days to get this paper off, and I believe John is beginning to notice. I don't like the look in his eyes.

And I heard him ask Jennie a lot of professional questions about me. She had a very good report to give.

She said I slept a good deal in the daytime.

John knows I don't sleep very well at night, for all I'm so quiet!

He asked me all sorts of questions too, and pretended to be very loving and kind.

As if I couldn't see through him!

Still, I don't wonder he acts so, sleeping under this paper for three months.

It only interests me, but I feel sure John and Jennie are affected by it.

Hurrah! This is the last day, but it is enough. John is to stay in town over night, and won't be out until this evening.

Jennie wanted to sleep with me—the sly thing; but I told her I should undoubtedly rest better for a night all alone.

That was clever, for really I wasn't alone a bit! As soon as it was moonlight and that poor thing began to crawl and shake the pattern, I got up and ran to help her.

I pulled and she shook, I shook and she pulled, and before morning we had peeled off yards of that paper.

A strip about as high as my head and half around the room.

And then when the sun came and that awful pattern began to laugh at me, I declared I would finish it today!

We go away tomorrow, and they are moving all my furniture down again to leave things as they were before.

Jennie looked at the wall in amazement, but I told her merrily that I did it out of pure spite at the vicious thing.

She laughed and said she wouldn't mind doing it herself, but I must not get tired.

How she betrayed herself that time!

But I am here, and no person touches this paper but Me—not *alive!*

She tried to get me out of the room—it was too patent! But I said it was so quiet and empty and clean now that I believed I would lie down again and sleep all I could, and not to wake me even for dinner—I would call when I woke.

So now she is gone, and the servants are gone, and the things are gone, and there is nothing left but that great bedstead nailed down, with the canvas mattress we found on it.

We shall sleep downstairs tonight, and take the boat home tomorrow.

I quite enjoy the room, now it is bare again.

How those children did tear about here!

This bedstead is fairly gnawed!

But I must get to work.

I have locked the door and thrown the key down into the front path.

I don't want to go out, and I don't want to have anybody come in, till John comes.

I want to astonish him.

I've got a rope up here that even Jennie did not find. If that woman does get out, and tries to get away, I can tie her!

But I forgot I could not reach far without anything to stand on!

This bed will *not* move!

I tried to lift and push it until I was lame, and then I got so angry I bit off a little piece at one corner—but it hurt my teeth.

Then I peeled off all the paper I could reach standing on the floor. It sticks horribly and the pattern just enjoys it! All those strangled heads and bulbous eyes and waddling fungus growths just shriek with derision!

I am getting angry enough to do something desperate. To jump out of the window would be admirable exercise, but the bars are too strong even to try.

Besides I wouldn't do it. Of course not. I know well enough that a step like that is improper and might be misconstrued.

I don't like to *look* out of the windows even—there are so many of those creeping women, and they creep so fast.

I wonder if they all come out of that wallpaper as I did!

But I am securely fastened now by my well-hidden rope—you don't get *me* out in the road there!

I suppose I shall have to get back behind the pattern when it comes night, and that is hard!

It is so pleasant to be out in this great room and creep around as I please!

I don't want to go outside. I won't, even if Jennie asks me to:

For outside you have to creep on the ground, and everything is green instead of yellow.

But here I can creep smoothly on the floor, and my shoulder just fits in that long smooch around the wall, so I cannot lose my way.

Why, there's John at the door!

It is no use, young man, you can't open it!

How he does call and pound!

Now he's crying to Jennie for an axe.

It would be a shame to break down that beautiful door!

"John, dear!" said I in the gentlest voice. "The key is down by the front steps, under a plantain leaf!"

That silenced him for a few moments.

Then he said, very quietly indeed, "Open the door, my darling!"

"I can't," said I. "The key is down by the front door under a plantain leaf!" And then I said it again, several times, very gently and slowly, and said it so often that he had to go and see, and he got it of course, and came in. He stopped short by the door.

"What is the matter?" he cried. "For God's sake, what are you doing!"

I kept on creeping just the same, but I looked at him over my shoulder.

"I've got out at last," said I, "in spite of you and Jane.[5] And I've pulled off most of the paper, so you can't put me back!"

Now why should that man have fainted? But he did, and right across my path by the wall, so that I had to creep over him every time!

—1892

Questions: Reading, Responding, Arguing

1. How does the unnamed narrator describe the room she occupies? Is the wallpaper symbolic? How do you know? How does Gilman's description of it help the reader to interpret the symbol?

2. How would you characterize the narrator's perceptions of truth and reality? Can readers count on her to give a reliable account of what is happening around her? Why or why not?

[5] *Jane:* presumably the given name of the narrator's sister-in-law, Jennie. Some have argued that this is the protagonist's name.

In what ways could her account of the events be considered accurate?

3. Note the number of times the word "creep" or a variant of it appears in the story. What is the significance of this repetition?

4. What is unusual about the prose style in the story, especially of the way it is paragraphed? Why is this style appropriate?

5. How does the narrator's perception of the woman in the wallpaper change as the story progresses?

6. Compare the actual story with Gilman's account of how she wrote it. (See "Why I Wrote *The Yellow Wallpaper*" on page 329.) To what degree does she indicate she should be identified with her protagonist? Provide examples from both texts to support your argument.

Bobbie Ann Mason (b. 1940)

Shiloh*

Leroy Moffitt's wife, Norma Jean, is working on her pectorals. She lifts three-pound dumbbells to warm up, then progresses to a twenty-pound barbell. Standing with her legs apart, she reminds Leroy of Wonder Woman.

"I'd give anything if I could just get these muscles to where they're real hard," says Norma Jean. "Feel this arm. It's not as hard as the other one."

"That's 'cause you're right-handed," says Leroy, dodging as she swings the barbell in an arc.

"Do you think so?"

"Sure."

Leroy is a truckdriver. He injured his leg in a highway accident four months ago, and his physical therapy, which involves weights and a pulley, prompted Norma Jean to try building herself up. Now she is attending a body-building class. Leroy has been collecting temporary disability since his tractor-trailer jackknifed in Missouri, badly twisting his left leg in its socket. He has a steel pin in his hip. He will probably not be able to drive his rig again. It sits in the backyard, like a gigantic bird that has flown home to roost. Leroy has been home in Kentucky for three months, and his leg is almost healed, but the accident frightened him and he does not want to drive any more long hauls. He is not sure what to do next. In the meantime, he makes things from craft kits. He started by building a miniature log cabin from notched Popsicle sticks. He varnished it and placed it on the TV set, where it remains. It reminds him of a rustic Nativity scene. Then he tried string art (sailing ships on black velvet), a macramé owl kit, a snap-together B-17 Flying Fortress, and a lamp made out of a model truck, with a light fixture screwed in the top of the cab. At first the kits were diversions, something to kill time, but now he is thinking about building a full-scale log house from a kit. It would be considerably cheaper than building a regular house, and besides, Leroy has grown to appreciate how things are put together. He has begun to realize that in all the years he was on the road he never took time to examine anything. He was always flying past scenery.

"They won't let you build a log cabin in any of the new subdivisions," Norma Jean tells him.

"They will if I tell them it's for you," he says, teasing her. Ever since they were married, he has promised Norma Jean he would build her a new home one day. They have always rented, and the house they live in is small and nondescript. It does not even feel like a home, Leroy realizes now.

Norma Jean works at the Rexall drugstore, and she has acquired an amazing amount of information about cosmetics. When she explains to Leroy the three stages of complexion care, involving creams, toners, and moisturizers, he thinks happily of other petroleum products—axle grease, diesel fuel. This is a connection between him and Norma Jean. Since he has been home, he has felt unusually tender about his wife and guilty over his long absences. But he can't tell what she feels about him. Norma Jean has never complained about his traveling; she has never made hurt remarks, like calling his truck a "widow-maker." He is reasonably certain she has been faithful to him, but he wishes she would celebrate his permanent home-coming more happily. Norma Jean is often startled to find Leroy at home, and he thinks she seems a little disappointed about it. Perhaps he reminds her too much of the early days of their marriage, before he went on the road. They had a child who died as an infant, years ago. They never speak about their memories of Randy, which have almost faded, but now that Leroy is home all the time, they sometimes feel awkward around each other, and Leroy wonders if one of them should mention the child. He has the feeling that they are waking up out of a dream together—that they must create a new marriage, start afresh. They are lucky they are still married. Leroy has read that for most people losing a child destroys the marriage—or else he heard this on *Donahue*. He can't always remember where he learns things anymore.

At Christmas, Leroy bought an electric organ for Norma Jean. She used to play the piano when she was in high school. "It don't leave you," she told him once. "It's like riding a bicycle."

The new instrument had so many keys and buttons that she was bewildered by it at first. She touched the keys tentatively, pushed some buttons, then pecked out "Chopsticks." It came out in an amplified fox-trot rhythm, with marimba sounds.

"It's an orchestra!" she cried.

The organ had a pecan-look finish and eighteen preset chords, with optional flute, violin, trumpet, clarinet, and banjo accompaniments. Norma Jean mastered the organ almost immediately. At first she played Christmas songs. Then she bought *The Sixties Songbook* and learned every tune in it, adding variations to each with the rows of brightly colored buttons.

"I didn't like these old songs back then," she said. "But I have this crazy feeling I missed something."

"You didn't miss a thing," said Leroy.

Leroy likes to lie on the couch and smoke a joint and listen to Norma Jean play "Can't Take My Eyes Off You" and "I'll Be Back." He is back again. After fifteen years on the road, he is finally settling down with the woman he loves. She is still pretty. Her skin is flawless. Her frosted curls resemble pencil trimmings.

Now that Leroy has come home to stay, he notices how much the town has changed. Subdivisions are spreading across western Kentucky like an oil slick. The sign at the edge of town says "Pop: 11,500"—only seven hundred more than it said twenty years before. Leroy can't figure out who is living in all the new houses. The farmers who used to gather around the courthouse square on Saturday afternoons to play checkers and spit tobacco juice have gone. It has been years since Leroy has thought about the farmers, and they have disappeared without his noticing.

Leroy meets a kid named Stevie Hamilton in the parking lot at the new shopping center. While they pretend to be strangers meeting over a stalled car, Stevie tosses an ounce of marijuana under the front seat of Leroy's car. Stevie is wearing orange jogging shoes and a T-shirt that says CHATTAHOOCHEE SUPER-RAT. His father is a prominent doctor who lives in one of the expensive subdivisions in a new white-columned brick house that looks like a funeral parlor. In the phone book under his name there is a separate number, with the listing "Teenagers."

"Where do you get this stuff?" asks Leroy. "From your pappy?"

"That's for me to know and you to find out," Stevie says. He is slit-eyed and skinny.

"What else you got?"

"What you interested in?"

"Nothing special. Just wondered."

Leroy used to take speed on the road. Now he has to go slowly. He needs to be mellow. He leans back against the car and says, "I'm aiming to build me a log house, soon as I get time. My wife, though, I don't think she likes the idea."

"Well, let me know when you want me again," Stevie says. He has a cigarette in his cupped palm, as though sheltering it from the wind. He takes a long drag, then stomps it on the asphalt and slouches away.

Stevie's father was two years ahead of Leroy in high school. Leroy is thirty-four. He married Norma Jean when they were both eighteen, and their child Randy was born a few months later, but he died at the age of four months and three days. He would be about Stevie's age now. Norma Jean and Leroy were at the drive-in, watching a double feature *(Dr. Strangelove* and *Lover Come Back),* and the baby was sleeping in the back seat. When the first movie ended, the baby was dead. It was the sudden infant death syndrome. Leroy remembers handing Randy to a nurse at the emergency room, as though he were offering her a large doll as a present. A dead baby feels like a sack of flour. "It just happens sometimes," said the doctor, in what Leroy always recalls as a nonchalant tone. Leroy can hardly remember the child anymore, but he still sees vividly a scene from *Dr. Strangelove* in which the President of the United States was talking in a folksy voice on the hot line to the Soviet premier about the bomber accidentally headed toward Russia. He was in the War Room, and the world map was lit up. Leroy remembers Norma Jean standing catatonically beside him in the hospital and himself thinking: Who is this strange girl? He had forgotten who she was. Now scientists are saying that crib death is caused by a virus. Nobody knows anything, Leroy thinks. The answers are always changing.

When Leroy gets home from the shopping center, Norma Jean's mother, Mabel Beasley, is there. Until this year, Leroy has not realized how much time she spends with Norma Jean. When she visits, she inspects the closets and then the plants, informing Norma Jean when a plant is droopy or yellow. Mabel calls the plants "flowers," although there are never any blooms. She also notices if Norma Jean's laundry is piling up. Mabel is a short, overweight woman whose tight, brown-dyed curls look more like a wig than the actual wig she sometimes wears. Today she has brought Norma Jean an off-white dust ruffle she made for the bed; Mabel works in a custom-upholstery shop.

"This is the tenth one I made this year," Mabel says. "I got started and couldn't stop."

"It's real pretty," says Norma Jean.

"Now we can hide things under the bed," says Leroy, who gets along with his mother-in-law primarily by joking with her. Mabel has never really forgiven him for disgracing her by getting Norma Jean pregnant. When the baby died, she said that fate was mocking her.

"What's that thing?" Mabel says to Leroy in a loud voice, pointing to a tangle of yarn on a piece of canvas.

Leroy holds it up for Mabel to see. "It's my needlepoint," he explains. "This is a *Star Trek* pillow cover."

"That's what a woman would do," says Mabel. "Great day in the morning!"

"All the big football players on TV do it," he says.

"Why, Leroy, you're always trying to fool me. I don't believe you for one minute. You don't know what to do with yourself—that's the whole trouble. Sewing!"

"I'm aiming to build us a log house," says Leroy. "Soon as my plans come."

"Like *heck* you are," says Norma Jean. She takes Leroy's needlepoint and shoves it into a drawer. "You have to find a job first. Nobody can afford to build now anyway."

Mabel straightens her girdle and says, "I still think before you get tied down y'all ought to take a little run to Shiloh."

"One of these days, Mama," Norma Jean says impatiently.

Mabel is talking about Shiloh, Tennessee. For the past few years, she has been urging Leroy and Norma Jean to visit the Civil War battleground there. Mabel went there on her honeymoon—the only real trip she ever took. Her husband died of a perforated ulcer when Norma Jean was ten, but Mabel, who was accepted into the United Daughters of the Confederacy in 1975, is still preoccupied with going back to Shiloh.

"I've been to kingdom come and back in that truck out yonder," Leroy says to Mabel, "but we never yet set foot in that battleground. Ain't that something? How did I miss it?"

"It's not even that far," Mabel says.

After Mabel leaves, Norma Jean reads to Leroy from a list she has made. "Things you could do," she announces. "You could get a job as a guard at Union Carbide, where they'd let you set on a stool. You could get on at the lumberyard. You could do a little carpenter work, if you want to build so bad. You could—"

"I can't do something where I'd have to stand up all day."

"You ought to try standing up all day behind a cosmetics counter. It's amazing that I have strong feet, coming from two parents that never had strong feet at all." At the moment Norma Jean is holding on to the kitchen counter, raising her knees one at a time as she talks. She is wearing two-pound ankle weights.

"Don't worry," says Leroy. "I'll do something."

"You could truck calves to slaughter for somebody. You wouldn't have to drive any big old truck for that."

"I'm going to build you this house," says Leroy. "I want to make you a real home."

"I don't want to live in any log cabin."

"It's not a cabin. It's a house."

"I don't care. It looks like a cabin."

"You and me together could lift those logs. It's just like lifting weights."

Norma Jean doesn't answer. Under her breath, she is counting. Now she is marching through the kitchen. She is doing goose steps.

Before his accident, when Leroy came home he used to stay in the house with Norma Jean, watching TV in bed and playing cards. She would cook fried chicken, picnic ham, chocolate pie—all his favorites. Now he is home alone much of the time. In the mornings, Norma Jean disappears, leaving a cooling place in the bed. She eats a cereal called Body Buddies, and she leaves the bowl on the table, with the soggy tan balls floating in a milk puddle. He sees things about Norma Jean that he never realized before. When she chops onions, she stares off into a corner, as if she can't bear to look. She puts on her house slippers almost precisely at nine o'clock every evening and nudges her jogging shoes under the couch. She saves bread heels for the birds. Leroy watches the birds at the feeder. He notices the peculiar way goldfinches fly past the window. They close their wings, then fall, then spread their wings to catch and lift themselves. He wonders if they close their eyes when they fall. Norma Jean closes her eyes when they are in bed. She wants the lights turned out. Even then, he is sure she closes her eyes.

He goes for long drives around town. He tends to drive a car rather carelessly. Power steering and an automatic shift make a car feel so small and inconsequential that his body is hardly involved in the driving process. His injured leg stretches out comfortably. Once or twice he has almost hit something, but even the prospect of an accident seems minor in a car. He cruises the new subdivisions, feeling like a criminal rehearsing for a robbery. Norma Jean is probably right about a log house being inappropriate here in the new subdivision. All the houses look grand and complicated. They depress him.

One day when Leroy comes home from a drive he finds Norma Jean in tears. She is in the kitchen making a potato and mushroom-soup casserole, with grated-cheese topping. She is crying because her mother caught her smoking.

"I didn't hear her coming. I was standing here puffing away pretty as you please," Norma Jean says, wiping her eyes.

"I knew it would happen sooner or later," says Leroy, putting his arm around her.

"She don't know the meaning of the word 'knock,'" says Norma Jean. "It's a wonder she hadn't caught me years ago."

"Think of it this way," Leroy says. "What if she caught me with a joint?"

"You better not let her!" Norma Jean shrieks. "I'm warning you, Leroy Moffitt!"

"I'm just kidding. Here, play me a tune. That'll help you relax."

Norma Jean puts the casserole in the oven and sets the timer. Then she plays a ragtime tune, with horns and banjo, as Leroy lights up a joint and lies on the couch, laughing to himself about Mabel's catching him at it. He thinks of Stevie Hamilton—a doctor's son pushing grass. Everything is funny. The whole town seems crazy and small. He is reminded of Virgil Mathis, a boastful policeman Leroy used to shoot pool with. Virgil recently led a drug bust in a back room at a bowling alley, where he seized ten thousand dollars' worth of marijuana. The newspaper had a picture of him holding up the bags of grass and grinning widely. Right now, Leroy can imagine Virgil breaking down the door and arresting him with a lungful of smoke. Virgil would probably have been alerted to the scene because of all the racket Norma Jean is making. Now she sounds like a hard-rock band. Norma Jean is terrific. When she switches to a Latin-rhythm version of "Sunshine Superman," Leroy hums along. Norma Jean's foot goes up and down, up and down.

"Well, what do you think?" Leroy says, when Norma Jean pauses to search through her music.

"What do I think about what?"

His mind has gone blank. Then he says, "I'll sell my rig and build us a house." That wasn't what he wanted to say. He wanted to know what she thought—what she *really* thought—about them.

"Don't start in on that again," says Norma Jean. She begins playing "Who'll Be the Next in Line?"

Leroy used to tell hitchhikers his whole life story—about his travels, his hometown, the baby. He would end with a question: "Well, what do you think?" It was just a rhetorical question. In time, he had the feeling that he'd been telling the same story over and over to the same hitchhikers. He quit talking to hitchhikers when he realized how his voice sounded—whining and self-pitying, like some teenage-tragedy song. Now Leroy has the sudden impulse to tell Norma Jean about himself, as if he had just met her. They have known each other so long they have forgotten a lot about each other. They could become reacquainted. But when the oven timer goes off and she runs to the kitchen, he forgets why he wants to do this.

The next day, Mabel drops by. It is Saturday and Norma Jean is cleaning. Leroy is studying the plans of his log house, which have finally come in the mail. He has them spread out on the table—big sheets of stiff blue paper, with diagrams and numbers printed in white. While Norma Jean runs the vacuum, Mabel drinks coffee. She sets her coffee cup on a blueprint.

"I'm just waiting for time to pass," she says to Leroy, drumming her fingers on the table.

As soon as Norma Jean switches off the vacuum, Mabel says in a loud voice, "Did you hear about the datsun dog that killed the baby?"

Norma Jean says, "The word is 'dachshund.'"

"They put the dog on trial. It chewed the baby's legs off. The mother was in the next room all the time." She raises her voice. "They thought it was neglect."

Norma Jean is holding her ears. Leroy manages to open the refrigerator and get some Diet Pepsi to offer Mabel. Mabel still has some coffee and she waves away the Pepsi.

"Datsuns are like that," Mabel says. "They're jealous dogs. They'll tear a place to pieces if you don't keep an eye on them."

"You better watch out what you're saying, Mabel," says Leroy.

"Well, facts is facts."

Leroy looks out the window at his rig. It is like a huge piece of furniture gathering dust in the backyard. Pretty soon it will be an antique. He hears the vacuum cleaner. Norma Jean seems to be cleaning the living room rug again.

Later, she says to Leroy, "She just said that about the baby because she caught me smoking. She's trying to pay me back."

"What are you talking about?" Leroy says, nervously shuffling blueprints.

"You know good and well," Norma Jean says. She is sitting in a kitchen chair with her feet up and her arms wrapped around her knees. She looks small and helpless. She says, "The very idea, her bringing up a subject like that! Saying it was neglect."

"She didn't mean that," Leroy says.

"She might not have *thought* she meant it. She always says things like that. You don't know how she goes on."

"But she didn't really mean it. She was just talking."

Leroy opens a king-sized bottle of beer and pours it into two glasses, dividing it carefully. He hands a glass to Norma Jean and she takes it from him mechanically. For a long time, they sit by the kitchen window watching the birds at the feeder.

• • •

Something is happening. Norma Jean is going to night school. She has graduated from her six-week body-building course and now she is taking an adult-education course in composition at Paducah Community College. She spends her evenings outlining paragraphs.

"First, you have a topic sentence," she explains to Leroy. "Then you divide it up. Your secondary topic has to be connected to your primary topic."

To Leroy, this sounds intimidating. "I never was any good in English," he says.

"It makes a lot of sense."

"What are you doing this for, anyhow?"

She shrugs. "It's something to do." She stands up and lifts her dumbbells a few times.

"Driving a rig, nobody cared about my English."

"I'm not criticizing your English."

Norma Jean used to say, "If I lose ten minutes' sleep, I just drag all day." Now she stays up late, writing compositions. She got a B on her first paper—a how-to theme on soup-based casseroles. Recently Norma Jean has been cooking unusual foods—tacos, lasagna, Bombay chicken. She doesn't play the organ anymore, though her second paper was called "Why Music Is Important to Me." She sits at the kitchen table, concentrating on her outlines, while Leroy plays with his log house plans, practicing with a set of Lincoln Logs. The thought of getting a truckload of notched, numbered logs scares him, and he wants to be prepared. As he and Norma Jean work together at the kitchen table, Leroy has the hopeful thought that they are sharing something, but he knows he is a fool to think this. Norma Jean is miles away. He knows he is going to lose her. Like Mabel, he is just waiting for time to pass.

One day, Mabel is there before Norma Jean gets home from work, and Leroy finds himself confiding in her. Mabel, he realizes, must know Norma Jean better than he does.

"I don't know what's got into that girl," Mabel says. "She used to go to bed with the chickens. Now you say she's up all hours. Plus her a-smoking. I like to died."

"I want to make her this beautiful home," Leroy says, indicating the Lincoln Logs. "I don't think she even wants it. Maybe she was happier with me gone."

"She don't know what to make of you, coming home like this."

"Is that it?"

Mabel takes the roof off his Lincoln Log cabin. "You couldn't get me in a log cabin," she says. "I was raised in one. It's no picnic, let me tell you."

"They're different now," says Leroy.

"I tell you what," Mabel says, smiling oddly at Leroy.

"What?"

"Take her on down to Shiloh. Y'all need to get out together, stir a little. Her brain's all balled up over them books."

Leroy can see traces of Norma Jean's features in her mother's face. Mabel's worn face has the texture of crinkled cotton, but suddenly she looks pretty. It occurs to Leroy that Mabel has been hinting all along that she wants them to take her with them to Shiloh.

"Let's all go to Shiloh," he says. "You and me and her. Come Sunday."

Mabel throws up her hand in protest. "Oh, no, not me. Young folks want to be by theirselves."

When Norma Jean comes in with groceries, Leroy says excitedly, "Your mama here's been dying to go to Shiloh for thirty-five years. It's about time we went, don't you think?"

"I'm not going to butt in on anybody's second honeymoon," Mabel says.

"Who's going on a honeymoon, for Christ's sake?" Norma Jean says loudly.

"I never raised no daughter of mine to talk that-a-way," Mabel says.

"You ain't seen nothing yet," says Norma Jean. She starts putting away boxes and cans, slamming cabinet doors.

"There's a log cabin at Shiloh," Mabel says. "It was there during the battle. There's bullet holes in it."

"When are you going to *shut up* about Shiloh, Mama?" asks Norma Jean.

"I always thought Shiloh was the prettiest place, so full of history," Mabel goes on. "I just hoped y'all could see it once before I die, so you could tell me about it." Later, she whispers to Leroy, "You do what I said. A little change is what she needs."

"Your name means 'the king,'" Norma Jean says to Leroy that evening. He is trying to get her to go to Shiloh, and she is reading a book about another century.

"Well, I reckon I ought to be right proud."

"I guess so."

"Am I still king around here?"

Norma Jean flexes her biceps and feels them for hardness. "I'm not fooling around with anybody, if that's what you mean," she says.

"Would you tell me if you were?"

"I don't know."

"What does *your* name mean?"

"It was Marilyn Monroe's real name."

"No kidding!"

"Norma comes from the Normans. They were invaders," she says. She closes her book and looks hard at Leroy. "I'll go to Shiloh with you if you'll stop staring at me."

On Sunday, Norma Jean packs a picnic and they go to Shiloh. To Leroy's relief Mabel says she does not want to come with them. Norma Jean drives, and Leroy, sitting beside her, feels like some boring hitchhiker she has picked up. He tries some conversation, but she answers him in monosyllables. At Shiloh, she drives aimlessly through the park, past bluffs and trails and steep ravines. Shiloh is an immense place, and Leroy cannot see it as a battleground. It is not what he expected. He thought it would look like a golf course. Monuments are everywhere, showing through the thick clusters of trees. Norma Jean passes the log cabin Mabel mentioned. It is surrounded by tourists looking for bullet holes.

"That's not the kind of log house I've got in mind," says Leroy apologetically.

"I know *that*."

"This is a pretty place. Your mama was right."

"It's O.K.," says Norma Jean. "Well, we've seen it. I hope she's satisfied."

They burst out laughing together.

At the park museum, a movie on Shiloh is shown every half hour, but they decide that they don't want to see it. They buy a souvenir Confederate flag for Mabel, and then they find a picnic spot near the cemetery. Norma Jean has brought a picnic cooler, with pimiento sandwiches, soft drinks, and Yodels. Leroy eats a sandwich and then smokes a joint, hiding it behind the picnic cooler. Norma Jean has quit smoking altogether. She is picking cake crumbs from the cellophane wrapper, like a fussy bird.

Leroy says, "So the boys in gray ended up in Corinth. The Union soldiers zapped 'em finally. April 7, 1862."

They both know that he doesn't know any history. He is just talking about some of the historical plaques they have read. He feels awkward, like a boy on a date with an older girl. They are still just making conversation.

"Corinth is where Mama eloped to," says Norma Jean.

They sit in silence and stare at the cemetery for the Union dead and, beyond, at a tall cluster of trees. Campers are parked nearby, bumper to bumper, and small children in bright clothing are cavorting and squealing. Norma Jean wads up the cake wrapper and squeezes it tightly in her hand. Without looking at Leroy, she says, "I want to leave you."

Leroy takes a bottle of Coke out of the cooler and flips off the cap. He holds the bottle poised near his mouth but cannot remember to take a drink. Finally he says, "No, you don't."

"Yes, I do."

"I won't let you."

"You can't stop me."

"Don't do me that way."

Leroy knows Norma Jean will have her own way. "Didn't I promise to be home from now on?" he says.

"In some ways, a woman prefers a man who wanders," says Norma Jean. "That sounds crazy, I know."

"You're not crazy." Leroy remembers to drink from his Coke. Then he says, "Yes, you *are* crazy. You and me could start all over again. Right back at the beginning."

"We *have* started all over again," says Norma Jean. "And this is how it turned out."

"What did I do wrong?"

"Nothing."

"Is this one of those women's lib things?" Leroy asks.

"Don't be funny."

The cemetery, a green slope dotted with white markers, looks like a subdivision site. Leroy is trying to comprehend that his marriage is breaking up, but for some reason he is wondering about white slabs in a graveyard.

"Everything was fine till Mama caught me smoking," says Norma Jean, standing up. "That set something off."

"What are you talking about?"

"She won't leave me alone—*you* won't leave me alone." Norma Jean seems to be crying, but she is looking away from him. "I feel eighteen again. I can't face that all over again." She starts walking away. "No, it *wasn't* fine. I don't know what I'm saying. Forget it."

Leroy takes a lungful of smoke and closes his eyes as Norma Jean's words sink in. He tries to focus on the fact that thirty-five hundred soldiers died on the grounds around him. He can only think of that war as a board game with plastic soldiers. Leroy almost smiles, as he compares the Confederates' daring attack on the Union camps and Virgil Mathis's raid on the bowling alley. General Grant, drunk and furious, shoved the Southerners back to Corinth, where Mabel and Jet Beasley were married years later, when Mabel was still thin and good-looking. The next day, Mabel and Jet visited the battleground, and then Norma Jean was born, and then she married Leroy and they had a baby, which they lost, and now Leroy and Norma Jean are here at the same battleground. Leroy knows he is leaving out a lot. He is leaving out the insides of history. History was always just names and dates to him. It occurs to him that building a house of logs is similarly empty—too simple. And the real inner workings of a marriage, like most of history, have escaped him. Now he sees that building a log house is the dumbest idea he could have had. It was clumsy of him to think Norma Jean would want a log house. It was a crazy idea. He'll have to think of something else, quickly. He will wad the blueprints into tight balls and fling them into the lake. Then he'll get moving again. He opens his eyes. Norma Jean has moved away and is walking through the cemetery, following a serpentine brick path.

Leroy gets up to follow his wife, but his good leg is asleep and his bad leg still hurts him. Norma Jean is far away, walking rapidly toward the bluff by the river, and he tries to hobble toward her. Some children run past him, screaming noisily. Norma Jean has reached the bluff, and she is looking out over the Tennessee River. Now she turns toward Leroy and waves her arms. Is she beckoning to him? She seems to be doing an exercise for her chest muscles. The sky is unusually pale—the color of the dust ruffle Mabel made for their bed.

—*1982*

Questions: Reading, Responding, Arguing

1. Mason titled her story after Shiloh, Tennessee. Why did she choose this title and why is Shiloh significant to the story and the characters?
2. Discuss the role of houses in this story. Why is Leroy so determined to build a log house? Why is it important that the story is told primarily from his point of view?
3. Larry asks, "Is this one of those women's lib things?" Discuss the character of Norma Jean, and how her actions are connected, if at all, with feminism or the women's movement.
4. Connect Mason's treatment of Norma Jean with another author's treatment of a married woman. How are they similar? How are they different? How do each of these treatments carry out the theme of personal and communal identities? Citing specific examples from the texts, argue whether or not each of these treatments carries out the theme of personal and communal identities.

Amy Tan (b. 1952)

Two Kinds

My mother believed you could be anything you wanted to be in America. You could open a restaurant. You could work for the government and get good retirement. You could buy a house with almost no money down. You could become rich. You could become instantly famous.

"Of course, you can be prodigy, too," my mother told me when I was nine. "You can be best anything. What does Auntie Lindo know? Her daughter, she is only best tricky."

America was where all my mother's hopes lay. She had come here in 1949 after losing everything in China: her mother and father, her family home, her first husband, and two daughters, twin baby girls. But she never looked back with regret. There were so many ways for things to get better.

We didn't immediately pick the right kind of prodigy. At first my mother thought I could be a Chinese Shirley Temple. We'd watch Shirley's old movies on TV as though they were training films. My mother would poke my arm and say, *"Ni kan."*—You watch. And I would see Shirley tapping her feet, or singing a sailor song, or pursing her lips into a very round O while saying "Oh, my goodness."

"Ni kan," said my mother as Shirley's eyes flooded with tears. "You already know how. Don't need talent for crying!"

Soon after my mother got this idea about Shirley Temple, she took me to a beauty training school in the Mission district and put me in the hands of a student who could barely hold the scissors without shaking. Instead of getting big fat curls, I emerged with an uneven mass of crinkly black fuzz. My mother dragged me off to the bathroom and tried to wet down my hair.

"You look like Negro Chinese," she lamented, as if I had done this on purpose.

The instructor of the beauty training school had to lop off these soggy clumps to make my hair even again. "Peter Pan is very popular these days," the instructor assured my mother. I now had hair the length of a boy's, with straight-across bangs that hung at a slant two inches above my eyebrows. I liked the haircut and it made me actually look forward to my future fame.

In fact, in the beginning, I was just as excited as my mother, maybe even more so. I pictured this prodigy part of me as many different images, trying each one on for size. I was a dainty ballerina girl standing by the curtains, waiting to hear the music that would send me floating on my tiptoes. I was like the Christ child lifted out of the straw manger, crying with holy indignity. I was Cinderella stepping from her pumpkin carriage with sparkly cartoon music filling the air.

In all of my imaginings, I was filled with a sense that I would soon become *perfect*. My mother and father would adore me. I would be beyond reproach. I would never feel the need to sulk for anything.

But sometimes the prodigy in me became impatient. "If you don't hurry up and get me out of here, I'm disappearing for good," it warned. "And then you'll always be nothing."

Every night after dinner, my mother and I would sit at the Formica kitchen table. She would present new tests, taking her examples from stories of amazing children she had read in *Ripley's Believe It or Not,* or *Good Housekeeping, Reader's Digest,* and a dozen other magazines she kept in a pile in our bathroom. My mother got these magazines from people whose houses she cleaned. And since she cleaned many houses each week, we had a great assortment. She would look through them all, searching for stories about remarkable children.

The first night she brought out a story about a three-year-old boy who knew the capitals of all the states and even most of the European countries. A teacher was quoted as saying the little boy could also pronounce the names of the foreign cities correctly.

"What's the capital of Finland?" my mother asked me, looking at the magazine story.

All I knew was the capital of California, because Sacramento was the name of the street we lived on in Chinatown. "Nairobi!" I guessed, saying the most foreign word I could think of. She checked to see if that was possibly one way to pronounce "Helsinki" before showing me the answer.

The tests got harder—multiplying numbers in my head, finding the queen of hearts in a deck of cards, trying to stand on my head without using my hands, predicting the daily temperatures in Los Angeles, New York, and London.

One night I had to look at a page from the Bible for three minutes and then report everything I could remember. "Now Jehoshaphat had riches and honor in abundance and . . . that's all I remember, Ma," I said.

And after seeing my mother's disappointed face once again, something inside of me began to die. I hated the tests, the raised hopes and failed expectations. Before going to bed that night, I looked in the mirror above the bathroom sink and when I saw only my face staring back—and that it would always be this ordinary face—I began to cry. Such a sad, ugly girl! I made high-pitched noises like a crazed animal, trying to scratch out the face in the mirror.

And then I saw what seemed to be the prodigy side of me—because I had never seen that face before. I looked at my reflection, blinking so I could see more clearly. The girl staring back at me was angry, powerful. This girl and I were the same. I had new thoughts, willful thoughts, or rather thoughts filled with lots of won'ts. I won't let her change me, I promised myself. I won't be what I'm not.

So now on nights when my mother presented her tests, I performed listlessly, my head propped on one arm. I pretended to be bored. And I was. I got so bored I started counting the bellows of the foghorns out on the bay while my mother drilled me in other areas. The sound was comforting and reminded me of the cow jumping over the moon. And the next day, I played a game with myself, seeing if my mother would give up on me before eight bellows. After a while I usually counted only one, maybe two bellows at most. At last she was beginning to give up hope.

Two or three months had gone by without any mention of my being a prodigy again. And then one day my mother was watching *The*

Ed Sullivan Show on TV. The TV was old and the sound kept short-ing out. Every time my mother got halfway up from the sofa to adjust the set, the sound would go back on and Ed would be talking. As soon as she sat down, Ed would go silent again. She got up, the TV broke into loud piano music. She sat down. Silence. Up and down, back and forth, quiet and loud. It was like a stiff embraceless dance between her and the TV set. Finally she stood by the set with her hand on the sound dial.

She seemed entranced by the music, a little frenzied piano piece with this mesmerizing quality, sort of quick passages and then teasing lilting ones before it returned to the quick playful parts.

"*Ni kan,*" my mother said, calling me over with hurried hand ges-tures, "Look here."

I could see why my mother was fascinated by the music. It was be-ing pounded out by a little Chinese girl, about nine years old, with a Peter Pan haircut. The girl had the sauciness of a Shirley Temple. She was proudly modest like a proper Chinese child. And she also did this fancy sweep of a curtsy, so that the fluffy skirt of her white dress cas-caded slowly to the floor like the petals of a large carnation.

In spite of these warning signs, I wasn't worried. Our family had no piano and we couldn't afford to buy one, let alone reams of sheet music and piano lessons. So I could be generous in my comments when my mother bad-mouthed the little girl on TV.

"Play note right, but doesn't sound good! No singing sound," my mother complained.

"What are you picking on her for?" I said carelessly. "She's pretty good. Maybe she's not the best, but she's trying hard." I knew almost immediately I would be sorry I said that.

"Just like you," she said. "Not the best. Because you not trying." She gave a little huff as she let go of the sound dial and sat down on the sofa.

The little Chinese girl sat down also to play an encore of "Anitra's Dance,"[1] by Grieg. I remember the song, because later on I had to learn how to play it.

Three days after watching *The Ed Sullivan Show*, my mother told me what my schedule would be for piano lessons and piano practice. She had talked to Mr. Chong, who lived on the first floor of our apart-ment building. Mr. Chong was a retired piano teacher and my mother

[1] "*Anitra's Tanz*": a section from the incidental musc that Edvard Grieg (1843–1907) wrote for *Peer Gynt*, a play by Henrik Ibsen.

had traded housecleaning services for weekly lessons and a piano for me to practice on every day, two hours a day, from four until six.

When my mother told me this, I felt as though I had been sent to hell. I whined and then kicked my foot a little when I couldn't stand it anymore.

"Why don't you like me the way I am? I'm *not* a genius! I can't play the piano. And even if I could, I wouldn't go on TV if you paid me a million dollars!" I cried.

My mother slapped me. "Who ask you be genius?" she shouted. "Only ask you be your best. For you sake. You think I want you be genius? Hnnh! What for! Who ask you!"

"So ungrateful," I heard her mutter in Chinese. "If she had as much talent as she has temper, she would be famous now."

Mr. Chong, whom I secretly nicknamed Old Chong, was very strange, always tapping his fingers to the silent music of an invisible orchestra. He looked ancient in my eyes. He had lost most of the hair on top of his head and he wore thick glasses and had eyes that always looked tired and sleepy. But he must have been younger than I thought, since he lived with his mother and was not yet married.

I met Old Lady Chong once and that was enough. She had this peculiar smell like a baby that had done something in its pants. And her fingers felt like a dead person's, like an old peach I once found in the back of the refrigerator; the skin just slid off the meat when I picked it up.

I soon found out why Old Chong had retired from teaching piano. He was deaf. "Like Beethoven!" he shouted to me. "We're both listening only in our head!" And he would start to conduct his frantic silent sonatas.

Our lessons went like this. He would open the book and point to different things, explaining their purpose: "Key! Treble! Bass! No sharps or flats! So this is C major! Listen now and play after me!"

And then he would play the C scale a few times, a simple chord, and then, as if inspired by an old, unreachable itch, he gradually added more notes and running trills and a pounding bass until the music was really something quite grand.

I would play after him, the simple scale, the simple chord, and then I just played some nonsense that sounded like a cat running up and down on top of garbage cans. Old Chong smiled and applauded and then said, "Very good! But now you must learn to keep time!"

So that's how I discovered that Old Chong's eyes were too slow to keep up with the wrong notes I was playing. He went through the motions in half-time. To help me keep rhythm, he stood behind me, pushing down on my right shoulder for every beat. He balanced pennies on top of my wrists so I would keep them still as I slowly played scales and arpeggios. He had me curve my hand around an apple and keep that shape when playing chords. He marched stiffly to show me how to make each finger dance up and down, staccato like an obedient little soldier.

He taught me all these things, and that was how I also learned I could be lazy and get away with mistakes, lots of mistakes. If I hit the wrong notes because I hadn't practiced enough, I never corrected myself. I just kept playing in rhythm. And Old Chong kept conducting his own private reverie.

So maybe I never really gave myself a fair chance. I did pick up the basics pretty quickly, and I might have become a good pianist at that young age. But I was so determined not to try, not to be anybody different that I learned to play only the most ear-splitting preludes, the most discordant hymns.

Over the next year I practiced like this, dutifully in my own way. And then one day I heard my mother and her friend Lindo Jong both talking in a loud bragging tone of voice so others could hear. It was after church, and I was leaning against the brick wall wearing a dress with stiff white petticoats. Auntie Lindo's daughter, Waverly, who was about my age, was standing farther down the wall about five feet away. We had grown up together and shared all the closeness of two sisters squabbling over crayons and dolls. In other words, for the most part, we hated each other. I thought she was snotty. Waverly Jong had gained a certain amount of fame as "Chinatown's Littlest Chinese Chess Champion."

"She bring home too many trophy," lamented Auntie Lindo that Sunday. "All day she play chess. All day I have no time do nothing but dust off her winnings." She threw a scolding look at Waverly, who pretended not to see her.

"You lucky you don't have this problem," said Auntie Lindo with a sigh to my mother.

And my mother squared her shoulders and bragged: "Our problem worser than yours. If we ask Jing-mei wash dish, she hear nothing but music. It's like you can't stop this natural talent."

And right then, I was determined to put a stop to her foolish pride.

A few weeks later, Old Chong and my mother conspired to have me play in a talent show which would be held in the church hall. By then, my parents had saved up enough to buy me a secondhand piano, a black Wurlitzer spinet with a scarred bench. It was the showpiece of our living room.

For the talent show, I was to play a piece called "Pleading Child" from Schumann's *Scenes from Childhood*.[2] It was a simple, moody piece that sounded more difficult than it was. I was supposed to memorize the whole thing, playing the repeat parts twice to make the piece sound longer. But I dawdled over it, playing a few bars and then cheating, looking up to see what notes followed. I never really listened to what I was playing. I daydreamed about being somewhere else, about being someone else.

The part I liked to practice best was the fancy curtsy: right foot out, touch the rose on the carpet with a pointed foot, sweep to the side, left leg bends, look up and smile.

My parents invited all the couples from the Joy Luck Club to witness my debut. Auntie Lindo and Uncle Tin were there. Waverly and her two older brothers had also come. The first two rows were filled with children both younger and older than I was. The littlest ones got to go first. They recited simple nursery rhymes, squawked out tunes on miniature violins, twirled Hula Hoops, pranced in pink ballet tutus, and when they bowed or curtsied, the audience would sigh in unison, "Awww," and then clap enthusiastically.

When my turn came, I was very confident. I remember my childish excitement. It was as if I knew, without a doubt, that the prodigy side of me really did exist. I had no fear whatsoever, no nervousness. I remember thinking to myself, This is it! This is it! I looked out over the audience, at my mother's blank face, my father's yawn, Auntie Lindo's stiff-lipped smile, Waverly's sulky expression. I had on a white dress layered with sheets of lace, and a pink bow in my Peter Pan haircut. As I sat down I envisioned people jumping to their feet and Ed Sullivan rushing up to introduce me to everyone on TV.

And I started to play. It was so beautiful. I was so caught up in how lovely I looked that at first I didn't worry how I would sound. So it was a surprise to me when I hit the first wrong note and I realized something didn't sound quite right. And then I hit another and another followed that. A chill started at the top of my head and began to trickle down. Yet I couldn't stop playing, as though my hands were bewitched. I kept thinking my fingers would adjust themselves back, like a train switching to the right track. I played this strange jumble through two repeats, the sour notes staying with me all the way to the end.

[2]*Scenes from Childhood*: a piano work by Robert Shumann (1810–1856) with twelve titled sections and an epilogue.

When I stood up, I discovered my legs were shaking. Maybe I had just been nervous and the audience, like Old Chong, had seen me go through the right motions and had not heard anything wrong at all. I swept my right foot out, went down on my knee, looked up and smiled. The room was quiet, except for Old Chong, who was beaming and shouting, "Bravo! Bravo! Well done!" But then I saw my mother's face, her stricken face. The audience clapped weakly, and as I walked back to my chair, with my whole face quivering as I tried not to cry, I heard a little boy whisper loudly to his mother, "That was awful," and the mother whispered back, "Well, she certainly tried."

And now I realized how many people were in the audience, the whole world it seemed. I was aware of eyes burning into my back. I felt the shame of my mother and father as they sat stiffly throughout the rest of the show.

We could have escaped during intermission. Pride and some strange sense of honor must have anchored my parents to their chairs. And so we watched it all: the eighteen-year-old boy with a fake moustache who did a magic show and juggled flaming hoops while riding a unicycle. The breasted girl with white makeup who sang from *Madame Butterfly* and got honorable mention. And the eleven-year-old boy who won first prize playing a tricky violin song that sounded like a busy bee.

After the show, the Hsus, the Jongs, and the St. Clairs from the Joy Luck Club, came up to my mother and father.

"Lots of talented kids," Auntie Lindo said vaguely, smiling broadly.

"That was somethin' else," said my father, and I wondered if he was referring to me in a humorous way, or whether he even remembered what I had done.

Waverly looked at me and shrugged her shoulders. "You aren't a genius like me," she said matter-of-factly. And if I hadn't felt so bad, I would have pulled her braids and punched her stomach.

But my mother's expression was what devastated me: a quiet, blank look that said she had lost everything. I felt the same way, and it seemed as if everybody were now coming up, like gawkers at the scene of an accident, to see what parts were actually missing. When we got on the bus to go home, my father was humming the busy-bee tune and my mother was silent. I kept thinking she wanted to wait until we got home before shouting at me. But when my father unlocked the door to our apartment, my mother walked in and then went to the back, into the bedroom. No accusations. No blame. And in a way, I felt disappointed. I had been waiting for her to start shouting, so I could shout back and cry and blame her for all my misery.

I assumed my talent-show fiasco meant I never had to play the piano again. But two days later, after school, my mother came out of the kitchen and saw me watching TV.

"Four clock," she reminded me as if it were any other day. I was stunned, as though she were asking me to go through the talent-show torture again. I wedged myself more tightly in front of the TV.

"Turn off TV," she called from the kitchen five minutes later.

I didn't budge. And then I decided. I didn't have to do what my mother said anymore. I wasn't her slave. This wasn't China. I had listened to her before and look what happened. She was the stupid one.

She came out from the kitchen and stood in the arched entryway of the living room. "Four clock," she said once again, louder.

"I'm not going to play anymore," I said nonchalantly. "Why should I? I'm not a genius."

She walked over and stood in front of the TV. I saw her chest was heaving up and down in an angry way.

"No!" I said, and I now felt stronger, as if my true self had finally emerged. So this was what had been inside me all along.

"No! I won't!" I screamed.

She yanked me by the arm, pulled me off the floor, snapped off the TV. She was frighteningly strong, half pulling, half carrying me toward the piano as I kicked the throw rugs under my feet. She lifted me up and onto the hard bench. I was sobbing by now, looking at her bitterly. Her chest was heaving even more and her mouth was open, smiling crazily as if she were pleased I was crying.

"You want me to be someone that I'm not!" I sobbed. "I'll never be the kind of daughter you want me to be!"

"Only two kinds of daughters," she shouted in Chinese. "Those who are obedient and those who follow their own mind! Only one kind of daughter can live in this house. Obedient daughter!"

"Then I wish I wasn't your daughter. I wish you weren't my mother," I shouted. As I said these things I got scared. It felt like worms and toads and slimy things crawling out of my chest, but it also felt good, as if this awful side of me had surfaced, at last.

"Too late change this," said my mother shrilly.

And I could sense her anger rising to its breaking point. I wanted to see it spill over. And that's when I remembered the babies she had lost in China, the ones we never talked about. "Then I wish I'd never been born!" I shouted. "I wish I were dead! Like them."

It was as if I had said the magic words. Alakazam!—and her face went blank, her mouth closed, her arms went slack, and she backed out of the room, stunned, as if she were blowing away like a small brown leaf, thin, brittle, lifeless.

It was not the only disappointment my mother felt in me. In the years that followed, I failed her so many times, each time asserting my own will, my right to fall short of expectations. I didn't get straight As. I didn't become class president. I didn't get into Stanford. I dropped out of college.

For unlike my mother, I did not believe I could be anything I wanted to be. I could only be me.

And for all those years, we never talked about the disaster at the recital or my terrible accusations afterward at the piano bench. All of that remained unchecked, like a betrayal that was now unspeakable. So I never found a way to ask her why she had hoped for something so large that failure was inevitable.

And even worse, I never asked her what frightened me the most: Why had she given up hope?

For after our struggle at the piano, she never mentioned my playing again. The lessons stopped. The lid to the piano was closed, shutting out the dust, my misery, and her dreams.

So she surprised me. A few years ago, she offered to give me the piano, for my thirtieth birthday. I had not played in all those years. I saw the offer as a sign of forgiveness, a tremendous burden removed.

"Are you sure?" I asked shyly. "I mean, won't you and Dad miss it?"

"No, this your piano," she said firmly. "Always your piano. You only one can play."

"Well, I probably can't play anymore," I said. "It's been years."

"You pick up fast," said my mother, as if she knew this was certain. "You have natural talent. You could been genius if you want to."

"No I couldn't."

"You just not trying," said my mother. And she was neither angry nor sad. She said it as if to announce a fact that could never be disproved. "Take it," she said.

But I didn't at first. It was enough that she had offered it to me. And after that, every time I saw it in my parents' living room, standing in front of the bay windows, it made me feel proud, as if it were a shiny trophy I had won back.

Last week I sent a tuner over to my parents' apartment and had the piano reconditioned, for purely sentimental reasons. My mother had died a few months before and I had been getting things in order for my father, a little bit at a time. I put the jewelry in special silk pouches. The sweaters she had knitted in yellow, pink, bright orange—all the colors I hated—I put those in moth-proof boxes. I found some old Chinese silk dresses, the kind with little slits up the sides. I rubbed the old silk against my skin, then wrapped them in tissue and decided to take them home with me.

After I had the piano tuned, I opened the lid and touched the keys. It sounded even richer than I remembered. Really, it was a very good piano. Inside the bench were the same exercise notes with handwritten scales, the same secondhand music books with their covers held together with yellow tape.

I opened up the Schumann book to the dark little piece I had played at the recital. It was on the left-hand side of the page, "Pleading Child." It looked more difficult than I remembered. I played a few bars, surprised at how easily the notes came back to me.

And for the first time, or so it seemed, I noticed the piece on the right-hand side. It was called "Perfectly Contented." I tried to play this one as well. It had a lighter melody but the same flowing rhythm and turned out to be quite easy. "Pleading Child" was shorter but slower; "Perfectly Contented" was longer, but faster. And after I played them both a few times, I realized they were two halves of the same song.

—1989

Questions: Reading, Responding, Arguing

1. What are the "Two Kinds" referred to in the title of the story? Is there more than one set of "kinds"?
2. How does the relationship change between daughter and mother over the course of the story?
3. Is there a reason that the narrative reveals the mother speaking to her daughter in Chinese as well as English? What does this use of language tell us about the relationship between them?
4. Cite examples from the text to make an argument about the relevance of the two musical pieces played on the piano.
5. Why does Tan mention Shirley Temple in the narrative? Why does the mother encourage her daughter to watch an American movie star? Cite examples of the mother's methods of encouragement to make an argument about the major themes of the story.

Sandra Cisneros (b. 1954)

Woman Hollering Creek

The day Don Serafín gave Juan Pedro Martínez Sánchez permission to take Cleófilas Enriqueta DeLeón Hernández as his bride, across her father's threshold, over several miles of dirt road and several miles of paved, over one border and beyond to a town *en el otro lado*—on the other side—already did he divine the morning his daughter would raise her hand over her eyes, look south, and dream of returning to the chores that never ended, six good-for-nothing brothers, and one old man's complaints.

He had said, after all, in the hubbub of parting: I am your father, I will never abandon you. He *had* said that, hadn't he, when he hugged and then let her go. But at the moment Cleófilas was busy looking for Chela, her maid of honor, to fulfill their bouquet conspiracy. She would not remember her father's parting words until later. *I am your father, I will never abandon you.*

Only now as a mother did she remember. Now, when she and Juan Pedrito sat by the creek's edge. How when a man and a woman love each other, sometimes that love sours. But a parent's love for a child, a child's for its parents, is another thing entirely.

This is what Cleófilas thought evenings when Juan Pedro did not come home, and she lay on her side of the bed listening to the hollow roar of the interstate, a distant dog barking, the pecan trees rustling like ladies in stiff petticoats—*shh-shh-shh, shh-shh-shh*—soothing her to sleep.

• • •

In the town where she grew up, there isn't very much to do except accompany the aunts and godmothers to the house of one or the other to play cards. Or walk to the cinema to see this week's film again, speckled and with one hair quivering annoyingly on the screen. Or to the center of town to order a milk shake that will appear in a day and a half as a pimple on her backside. Or to the girlfriend's house to watch the latest *telenovela* episode and try to copy the way the women comb their hair, wear their makeup.

But what Cleófilas has been waiting for, has been whispering and sighing and giggling for, has been anticipating since she was old enough to lean against the window displays of gauze and butterflies and lace, is passion. Not the kind on the cover of the *¡Alarma!* magazines, mind you, where the lover is photographed with the bloody fork she used to salvage her good name. But passion in its purest crystalline essence. The kind the books and songs and *telenovelas* describe when one finds, finally, the great love of one's life, and does whatever one can, must do, at whatever the cost.

Tú o Nadie. "You or No One." The title of the current favorite *telenovela.* The beautiful Lucía Méndez having to put up with all kinds of hardships of the heart, separation and betrayal, and loving, always loving no matter what, because *that* is the most important thing, and did you see Lucía Méndez on the Bayer aspirin commercials—wasn't she lovely? Does she dye her hair do you think? Cleófilas is going to go to the *farmacia* and buy a hair rinse; her girlfriend Chela will apply it— it's not that difficult at all.

Because you didn't watch last night's episode when Lucía confessed she loved him more than anyone in her life. In her life! And she sings the song "You or No One" in the beginning and end of the show. *Tú o Nadie.* Somehow one ought to live one's life like that, don't you think? You or no one. Because to suffer for love is good. The pain all sweet somehow. In the end.

• • •

Seguín. She had liked the sound of it. Far away and lovely. Not like *Monclova. Coahuila.* Ugly.

Seguín, Tejas. A nice sterling ring to it. The tinkle of money. She would get to wear outfits like the women on the *tele*, like Lucía Méndez. And have a lovely house, and wouldn't Chela be jealous.

And yes, they will drive all the way to Laredo to get her wedding dress. That's what they say. Because Juan Pedro wants to get married right away, without a long engagement since he can't take off too much time from work. He has a very important position in Seguin with, with . . . a beer company, I think. Or was it tires? Yes, he has to be back. So they will get married in the spring when he can take off work, and then they will drive off in his new pickup—did you see it?—to their new home in Seguin. Well, not exactly new, but they're going to repaint the house. You know newlyweds. New paint and new furniture. Why not? He can afford it. And later on add maybe a room or two for the children. May they be blessed with many.

Well, you'll see. Cleófilas has always been so good with her sewing machine. A little *rrrr, rrrr, rrrr* of the machine and *¡zas!* Miracles. She's always been so clever, that girl. Poor thing. And without even a mama to advise her on things like her wedding night. Well, may God help her. What with a father with a head like a burro, and those six clumsy brothers. Well, what do you think! Yes, I'm going to the wedding. Of course! The dress I want to wear just needs to be altered a teensy bit to bring it up to date. See, I saw a new style last night that I thought would suit me. Did you watch last night's episode of *The Rich Also Cry?* Well, did you notice the dress the mother was wearing?

• • •

La Gritona. Such a funny name for such a lovely *arroyo*. But that's what they called the creek that ran behind the house. Though no one could say whether the woman had hollered from anger or pain. The natives only knew the *arroyo* one crossed on the way to San Antonio, and then once again on the way back, was called Woman Hollering, a name no one from these parts questioned, little less understood. *Pues, allá de los indios,*[1] *quién sabe*—who knows, the townspeople shrugged, because it was of no concern to their lives how this trickle of water received its curious name.

"What do you want to know for?" Trini the laundromat attendant asked in the same gruff Spanish she always used whenever she gave Cleófilas change or yelled at her for something. First for putting too much soap in the machines. Later, for sitting on a washer. And still later, after Juan Pedrito was born, for not understanding that in this country you cannot let your baby walk around with no diaper and his pee-pee hanging out, it wasn't nice, *¿ entiendes? Pues.*[2]

How could Cleófilas explain to a woman like this why the name Woman Hollering fascinated her. Well, there was no sense talking to Trini.

On the other hand there were the neighbor ladies, one on either side of the house they rented near the *arroyo*. The woman Soledad on the left, the woman Dolores on the right.

The neighbor lady Soledad liked to call herself a widow, though how she came to be one was a mystery. Her husband had either died, or run away with an ice-house floozie, or simply gone out for cigarettes one afternoon and never came back. It was hard to say which since Soledad, as a rule, didn't mention him.

In the other house lived *la señora* Dolores, kind and very sweet, but her house smelled too much of incense and candles from the altars that burned continuously in memory of two sons who had died in the last

[1] *Pues allá de los indies*: Well, that came from the Indians.
[2] *¿entiendes? Pues.*: You understand?

war and one husband who had died shortly after from grief. The neighbor lady Dolores divided her time between the memory of these men and her garden, famous for its sunflowers—so tall they had to be supported with broom handles and old boards; red red cockscombs, fringed and bleeding a thick menstrual color; and, especially, roses whose sad scent reminded Cleófilas of the dead. Each Sunday *la señora* Dolores clipped the most beautiful of these flowers and arranged them on three modest headstones at the Seguin cemetery.

The neighbor ladies, Soledad, Dolores, they might've known once the name of the *arroyo* before it turned English but they did not know now. They were too busy remembering the men who had left through either choice or circumstance and would never come back.

Pain or rage, Cleófilas wondered when she drove over the bridge the first time as a newlywed and Juan Pedro had pointed it out. *La Gritona*, he had said, and she had laughed. Such a funny name for a creek so pretty and full of happily ever after.

• • •

The first time she had been so surprised she didn't cry out or try to defend herself. She had always said she would strike back if a man, any man, were to strike her.

But when the moment came, and he slapped her once, and then again, and again; until the lip split and bled an orchid of blood, she didn't fight back, she didn't break into tears, she didn't run away as she imagined she might when she saw such things in the *telenovelas*.

In her own home her parents had never raised a hand to each other or to their children. Although she admitted she may have been brought up a little leniently as an only daughter—*la consentida*, the princess—there were some things she would never tolerate. Ever.

Instead, when it happened the first time, when they were barely man and wife, she had been so stunned, it left her speechless, motionless, numb. She had done nothing but reach up to the heat on her mouth and stare at the blood on her hand as if even then she didn't understand.

She could think of nothing to say, said nothing. Just stroked the dark curls of the man who wept and would weep like a child, his tears of repentance and shame, this time and each.

• • •

The men at the ice house. From what she can tell, from the times during her first year when still a newlywed she is invited and accompanies her husband, sits mute beside their conversation, waits and sips a beer until it grows warm, twists a paper napkin into a knot, then another into a fan, one into a rose, nods her head, smiles, yawns, politely grins, laughs at the appropriate moments, leans against her husband's sleeve, tugs at his elbow, and finally becomes good at predicting where the talk will lead, from this Cleófilas concludes each is nightly trying to find the truth lying at the bottom of the bottle like a gold doubloon on the sea floor.

They want to tell each other what they want to tell themselves. But what is bumping like a helium balloon at the ceiling of the brain never finds its way out. It bubbles and rises, it gurgles in the throat, it rolls across the surface of the tongue, and erupts from the lips—a belch.

If they are lucky, there are tears at the end of the long night. At any given moment, the fists try to speak. They are dogs chasing their own tails before lying down to sleep, trying to find a way, a route, an out, and—finally—get some peace.

• • •

In the morning sometimes before he opens his eyes. Or after they have finished loving. Or at times when he is simply across from her at the table putting pieces of food into his mouth and chewing. Cleófilas thinks. This is the man I have waited my whole life for.

Not that he isn't a good man. She has to remind herself why she loves him when she changes the baby's Pampers, or when she mops the bathroom floor, or tries to make the curtains for the doorways without doors, or whiten the linen. Or wonder a little when he kicks the refrigerator and says he hates this shitty house and is going out where he won't be bothered with the baby's howling and her suspicious questions, and her requests to fix this and this and this because if she had any brains in her head she'd realize he's been up before the rooster earning his living to pay for the food in her belly and the roof over her head and would have to wake up again early the next day so why can't you just leave me in peace, woman.

He is not very tall, no, and he doesn't look like the men on the *telenovelas*. His face still scarred from acne. And he has a bit of a belly from all the beer he drinks. Well, he's always been husky.

This man who farts and belches and snores as well as laughs and kisses and holds her. Somehow this husband whose whiskers she finds each morning in the sink, whose shoes she must air each evening on the porch, this husband who cuts his fingernails in public, laughs loudly, curses like a man, and demands each course of dinner be served on a separate plate like at his mother's, as soon as he gets home, on time or late, and who doesn't

care at all for music or *telenovelas* or romance or roses or the moon floating pearly over the *arroyo*, or through the bedroom window for that matter, shut the blinds and go back to sleep, this man, this father, this rival,
this keeper, this lord, this master, this husband till kingdom come.

· · ·

A doubt. Slender as a hair. A washed cup set back on the shelf wrong-
side-up. Her lipstick, and body talc, and hairbrush all arranged in the
bathroom a different way.

No. Her imagination. The house the same as always. Nothing.

Coming home from the hospital with her new son, her husband.
Something comforting in discovering her house slippers beneath the
bed, the faded housecoat where she left it on the bathroom hook. Her
pillow. Their bed.

Sweet sweet homecoming. Sweet as the scent of face powder in the
air, jasmine, sticky liquor.

Smudged fingerprint on the door. Crushed cigarette in a glass.
Wrinkle in the brain crumpling to a crease.

· · ·

Sometimes she thinks of her father's house. But how could she go back
there? What a disgrace. What would the neighbors say? Coming home
like that with one baby on her hip and one in the oven. Where's your
husband?

The town of gossips. The town of dust and despair. Which she has
traded for this town of gossips. This town of dust, despair. Houses farther
apart perhaps, though no more privacy because of it. No leafy *zócalo*[3] in
the center of the town, though the murmur of talk is clear enough all the
same. No huddled whispering on the church steps each Sunday. Because
here the whispering begins at sunset at the ice house instead.

This town with its silly pride for a bronze pecan the size of a baby
carriage in front of the city hall. TV repair shop, drugstore, hardware,
dry cleaner's, chiropractor's, liquor store, bail bonds, empty storefront,
and nothing, nothing, nothing of interest. Nothing one could walk to,
at any rate. Because the towns here are built so that you have to depend on husbands. Or you stay home. Or you drive. If you're rich
enough to own, allowed to drive, your own car.

There is no place to go. Unless one counts the neighbor ladies.
Soledad on one side, Dolores on the other. Or the creek.

---

[3] *zócalo*: central square

Don't go out there after dark, *mi'jita*. Stay near the house. *No es bueno para la salud.*[4] *Mala suerte.* Bad luck. *Mal aire.*[5] You'll get sick and the baby too. You'll catch a fright wandering about in the dark, and then you'll see how right we were.

The stream sometimes only a muddy puddle in the summer, though now in the springtime, because of the rains, a good-size alive thing, a thing with a voice all its own, all day and all night calling in its high, silver voice. Is it La Llorona, the weeping woman? La Llorona, who drowned her own children. Perhaps La Llorona is the one they named the creek after, she thinks, remembering all the stories she learned as a child.

La Llorona calling to her. She is sure of it. Cleófilas sets the baby's Donald Duck blanket on the grass. Listens. The day sky turning to night. The baby pulling up fistfuls of grass and laughing. La Llorona. Wonders if something as quiet as this drives a woman to the darkness under the trees.

• • •

What she needs is . . . and made a gesture as if to yank a woman's buttocks to his groin. Maximiliano, the foul-smelling fool from across the road, said this and set the men laughing, but Cleófilas just muttered. *Grosero,*[6] and went on washing dishes.

She knew he said it not because it was true, but more because it was he who needed to sleep with a woman, instead of drinking each night at the ice house and stumbling home alone.

Maximiliano who was said to have killed his wife in an ice-house brawl when she came at him with a mop. I had to shoot, he had said— she was armed.

Their laughter outside the kitchen window. Her husband's, his friends'. Manolo, Beto, Efraín, el Perico. Maximiliano.

Was Cleófilas just exaggerating as her husband always said? It seemed the newspapers were full of such stories. This woman found on the side of the interstate. This one pushed from a moving car. This one's cadaver, this one unconscious, this one beaten blue. Her ex-husband, her husband, her lover, her father, her brother, her uncle, her friend, her co-worker. Always. The same grisly news in the pages of the dailies. She dunked a glass under the soapy water for a moment—shivered.

• • •

---

[4] *No es bueno para la salud*: It's bad for the health
[5] *Mal aire*: bad air
[6] *Grosero*: gross

He had thrown a book. Hers. From across the room. A hot welt across the cheek. She could forgive that. But what stung more was the fact it was *her* book, a love story by Corín Tellado, what she loved most now that she lived in the U.S., without a television set, without the *telenovelas*.

Except now and again when her husband was away and she could manage it, the few episodes glimpsed at the neighbor lady Soledad's house because Dolores didn't care for that sort of thing, though Soledad was often kind enough to retell what had happened on what episode of *María de Nadie*, the poor Argentine country girl who had the ill fortune of falling in love with the beautiful son of the Arrocha family, the very family she worked for, whose roof she slept under and whose floors she vacuumed, while in that same house, with the dust brooms and floor cleaners as witnesses, the square-jawed Juan Carlos Arrocha had uttered words of love, I love you, María, listen to me, *mi querida*,[7] but it was she who had to say No, no, we are not of the same class, and remind him it was not his place nor hers to fall in love, while all the while her heart was breaking, can you imagine.

Cleófilas thought her life would have to be like that, like a *telenovela*, only now the episodes got sadder and sadder. And there were no commercials in between for comic relief. And no happy ending in sight. She thought this when she sat with the baby out by the creek behind the house. Cleófilas de . . . ? But somehow she would have to change her name to Topazio, or Yesenia, Cristal, Adriana, Stefania, Andrea, something more poetic than Cleófilas. Everything happened to women with names like jewels. But what happened to a Cleófilas? Nothing. But a crack in the face.

• • •

Because the doctor has said so. She has to go. To make sure the new baby is all right, so there won't be any problems when he's born, and the appointment card says next Tuesday. Could he please take her. And that's all.

No, she won't mention it. She promises. If the doctor asks she can say she fell down the front steps or slipped when she was out in the backyard, slipped out back, she could tell him that. She has to go back next Tuesday, Juan Pedro, please, for the new baby. For their child.

She could write to her father and ask maybe for money, just a loan, for the new baby's medical expenses. Well then if he'd rather she didn't.

[7] *mi querida*: my darling

All right, she won't. Please don't anymore. Please don't. She knows it's difficult saving money with all the bills they have, but how else are they going to get out of debt with the truck payments? And after the rent and the food and the electricity and the gas and the water and the who-knows-what, well, there's hardly anything left. But please, at least for the doctor visit. She won't ask for anything else. She has to. Why is she so anxious? Because.

Because she is going to make sure the baby is not turned around backward this time to split her down the center. Yes. Next Tuesday at five-thirty. I'll have Juan Pedrito dressed and ready. But those are the only shoes he has. I'll polish them, and we'll be ready. As soon as you come from work. We won't make you ashamed.

• • •

Felice? It's me, Graciela.

No, I can't talk louder. I'm at work.

Look, I need kind of a favor. There's a patient, a lady here who's got a problem.

Well, wait a minute. Are you listening to me or what?

I can't talk real loud 'cause her husband's in the next room.

Well, would you just listen?

I was going to do this sonogram on her—she's pregnant, right?—and she just starts crying on me. *Híjole*,[8] Felice! This poor lady's got black-and-blue marks all over. I'm not kidding.

From her husband. Who else? Another one of those brides from across the border. And her family's all in Mexico.

Shit. You think they're going to help her? Give me a break. This lady doesn't even speak English. She hasn't been allowed to call home or write or nothing. That's why I'm calling you.

She needs a ride.

Not to Mexico, you goof. Just to the Greyhound. In San Anto.

No, just a ride. She's got her own money. All you'd have to do is drop her off in San Antonio on your way home. Come on, Felice. Please? If we don't help her, who will? I'd drive her myself, but she needs to be on that bus before her husband gets home from work. What do you say?

I don't know. Wait.

Right away, tomorrow even.

Well, if tomorrow's no good for you . . .

[8] *Híjole*: a mild interjection

It's a date, Felice. Thursday. At the Cash N Carry off I-10. Noon. She'll be ready.

Oh, and her name's Cleófilas.

I don't know. One of those Mexican saints, I guess. A martyr or something.

Cleófilas. C-L-E-O-F-I-L-A-S. Cle. O. Fi. Las. Write it down.

Thanks, Felice. When her kid's born she'll have to name her after us, right?

Yeah, you got it. A regular soap opera sometimes. *Qué vida, comadre. Bueno*[9] bye.

• • •

All morning that flutter of half-fear, half-doubt. At any moment Juan Pedro might appear in the doorway. On the street. At the Cash N Carry. Like in the dreams she dreamed.

There was that to think about, yes, until the woman in the pickup drove up. Then there wasn't time to think about anything but the pickup pointed toward San Antonio. Put your bags in the back and get in.

But when they drove across the *arroyo*, the driver opened her mouth and let out a yell as loud as any mariachi. Which startled not only Cleófilas, but Juan Pedrito as well.

Pues, look how cute. I scared you two, right? Sorry. Should've warned you. Every time I cross that bridge I do that. Because of the name, you know. Woman Hollering. *Pues*, I holler. She said this in a Spanish pocked with English and laughed. Did you ever notice, Felice continued, how nothing around here is named after a woman? Really. Unless she's the Virgin. I guess you're only famous if you're a virgin. She was laughing again.

That's why I like the name of that *arroyo*. Makes you want to holler like Tarzan, right?

Everything about this woman, this Felice, amazed Cleófilas. The fact that she drove a pickup. A pickup, mind you, but when Cleófilas asked if it was her husband's, she said she didn't have a husband. The pickup was hers. She herself had chosen it. She herself was paying for it.

I used to have a Pontiac Sunbird. But those cars are for *viejas*.[10] Pussy cars. Now this here is a *real* car.

---

[9] *Qué vida, comadre. Bueno*: What a life, friend. Good
[10] *viejas*: old people

What kind of talk was that coming from a woman? Cleófilas thought. But then again, Felice was like no woman she'd ever met. Can you imagine, when we crossed the *arroyo* she just started yelling like a crazy, she would say later to her father and brothers. Just like that. Who would've thought?

Who would've? Pain or rage, perhaps, but not a hoot like the one Felice had just let go. Makes you want to holler like Tarzan, Felice had said.

Then Felice began laughing again, but it wasn't Felice laughing. It was gurgling out of her own throat, a long ribbon of laughter, like water.

—1992

Questions: Reading, Responding, Arguing

1. What are the names of Cleófilas's two neighbors? What do their names signify? What are the names of the two women who assist her? What do their names signify?
2. How have the *telenovelas* (soap operas) influenced Cleófilas's current disappointments? How else are they significant to her life in Mexico?
3. Why does Cleófilas remain with her abusive husband so long?
4. Read Amanda Smith's essay on page 122. Do you agree with her interpretation of the *La Llorona* figure? Why or why not? Present your argument using specific references from the text.

Louise Erdrich (b. 1954)

The Red Convertible

Lyman Lamartine

I was the first one to drive a convertible on my reservation. And of course it was red, a red Olds. I owned that car along with my brother Henry Junior. We owned it together until his boots filled with water on a windy night and he bought out my share. Now Henry owns the whole car, and his younger brother Lyman (that's myself), Lyman walks everywhere he goes.

How did I earn enough money to buy my share in the first place? My one talent was I could always make money. I had a touch for it, unusual in a Chippewa. From the first I was different that way, and everyone recognized it. I was the only kid they let in the American Legion Hall to shine shoes, for example, and one Christmas I sold spiritual bouquets for the mission door to door. The nuns let me keep a percentage. Once I started, it seemed the more money I made the easier the money came. Everyone encouraged it. When I was fifteen I got a job washing dishes at the Joliet Cafe, and that was where my first big break happened.

It wasn't long before I was promoted to bussing tables, and then the short-order cook quit and I was hired to take her place. No sooner than you know it I was managing the Joliet. The rest is history. I went on managing. I soon became part owner, and of course there was no stopping me then. It wasn't long before the whole thing was mine.

After I'd owned the Joliet for one year, it blew over in the worst tornado ever seen around here. The whole operation was smashed to bits. A total loss. The fryalator was up in a tree, the grill torn in half like it was paper. I was only sixteen. I had it all in my mother's name, and I lost it quick, but before I lost it I had every one of my relatives, and their relatives, to dinner, and I also bought that red Olds I mentioned, along with Henry.

The first time we saw it! I'll tell you when we first saw it. We had gotten a ride up to Winnipeg, and both of us had money. Don't ask me why, because we never mentioned a car or anything, we just had all our money. Mine was cash, a big bankroll from the Joliet's insurance. Henry had two checks—a week's extra pay for being laid off, and his regular check from the Jewel Bearing Plant.

We were walking down Portage anyway, seeing the sights, when we saw it. There it was, parked, large as life. Really as *if* it was alive. I thought of the word *repose,* because the car wasn't simply stopped, parked, or whatever. That car reposed, calm and gleaming, a FOR SALE sign in its left front window. Then, before we had thought it over at all, the car belonged to us and our pockets were empty. We had just enough money for gas back home.

We went places in that car, me and Henry. We took off driving all one whole summer. We started off toward the Little Knife River and Mandaree in Fort Berthold and then we found ourselves down in Wakpala somehow, and then suddenly we were over in Montana on the Rocky Boys, and yet the summer was not even half over. Some people hang on to details when they travel, but we didn't let them bother us and just lived our everyday lives here to there.

I do remember this one place with willows. I remember I laid under those trees and it was comfortable. So comfortable. The branches bent down all around me like a tent or a stable. And quiet, it was quiet, even though there was a powwow close enough so I could see it going on. The air was not too still, not too windy either. When the dust rises up and hangs in the air around the dancers like that, I feel good. Henry was asleep with his arms thrown wide. Later on, he woke up and we started driving again. We were somewhere in Montana, or maybe on the Blood Reserve—it could have been anywhere. Anyway it was where we met the girl.

All her hair was in buns around her ears, that's the first thing I noticed about her. She was posed alongside the road with her arm out, so we stopped. That girl was short, so short her lumber shirt looked comical on her, like a nightgown. She had jeans on and fancy moccasins and she carried a little suitcase.

"Hop on in," says Henry. So she climbs in between us.

"We'll take you home," I says. "Where do you live?"

"Chicken," she says.

"Where the hell's that?" I ask her.

"Alaska."

"Okay," says Henry, and we drive.

We got up there and never wanted to leave. The sun doesn't truly set there in summer, and the night is more a soft dusk. You might doze off, sometimes, but before you know it you're up again, like an animal in nature. You never feel like you have to sleep hard or put away the world. And things would grow up there. One day just dirt or moss, the next day flowers and long grass. The girl's name was Susy. Her family really took to us. They fed us and put us up. We had our own tent to live in by their house, and the kids would be in and out of there all day and night. They couldn't get over me and Henry being brothers, we looked so different. We told them we knew we had the same mother, anyway.

One night Susy came in to visit us. We sat around in the tent talking of this thing and that. The season was changing. It was getting darker by that time, and the cold was even getting just a little mean. I told her it was time for us to go. She stood up on a chair.

"You never seen my hair," Susy said.

That was true. She was standing on a chair, but still, when she unclipped her buns the hair reached all the way to the ground. Our eyes opened. You couldn't tell how much hair she had when it was rolled up so neatly. Then my brother Henry did something funny. He went up to the chair and said, "Jump on my shoulders." So she did that, and her hair reached down past his waist, and he started twirling, this way and that, so her hair was flung out from side to side.

"I always wondered what it was like to have long pretty hair," Henry says. Well we laughed. It was a funny sight, the way he did it. The next morning we got up and took leave of those people.

On to greener pastures, as they say. It was down through Spokane and across Idaho then Montana and very soon we were racing the weather right along under the Canadian border through Columbus, Des Lacs, and then we were in Bottineau County and soon home. We'd made most of the trip, that summer, without putting up the car hood at all. We got home just in time, it turned out, for the army to remember Henry had signed up to join it.

I don't wonder that the army was so glad to get my brother that they turned him into a Marine. He was built like a brick outhouse anyway. We liked to tease him that they really wanted him for his Indian nose. He had a nose big and sharp as a hatchet, like the nose on Red Tomahawk, the Indian who killed Sitting Bull, whose profile is on signs all along the North Dakota highways. Henry went off to training camp, came home once during Christmas, then the next thing you know we got an overseas letter from him. It was 1970, and he said he was stationed up in the northern hill country. Whereabouts I did not know. He wasn't such a hot letter writer, and only got off two before the enemy caught him. I could never keep it straight, which direction those good Vietnam soldiers were from.

I wrote him back several times, even though I didn't know if those letters would get through. I kept him informed all about the car. Most of the time I had it up on blocks in the yard or half taken apart, because that long trip did a hard job on it under the hood.

I always had good luck with numbers, and never worried about the draft myself. I never even had to think about what my number was. But Henry was never lucky in the same way as me. It was at least three years before Henry came home. By then I guess the whole war was solved in the government's mind, but for him it would keep on going. In those years I'd put his car into almost perfect shape. I always thought of it as his car while he was gone, even though when he left he said, "Now it's yours," and threw me his key.

"Thanks for the extra key," I'd said. "I'll put it up in your drawer just in case I need it." He laughed.

When he came home, though, Henry was very different, and I'll say this: the change was no good. You could hardly expect him to change for the better, I know. But he was quiet, so quiet, and never comfortable sitting still anywhere but always up and moving around. I thought back to times we'd sat still for whole afternoons, never moving a muscle, just shifting our weight along the ground, talking to whoever sat with us, watching things. He'd always had a joke, then, too, and now you couldn't get him to laugh, or when he did it was more the sound of a man choking, a sound that stopped up the throats of other people around him. They got to leaving him alone most of the time, and I didn't blame them. It was a fact: Henry was jumpy and mean.

I'd bought a color TV set for my mom and the rest of us while Henry was away. Money still came very easy. I was sorry I'd ever bought it though, because of Henry. I was also sorry I'd bought color, because with black-and-white the pictures seem older and farther away. But what are you going to do? He sat in front of it, watching it, and that was the only time he was completely still. But it was the kind of stillness that you see in a rabbit when it freezes and before it will bolt. He was not easy. He sat in his chair gripping the armrests with all his might, as if the chair itself was moving at a high speed and if he let go at all he would rocket forward and maybe crash right through the set.

Once I was in the room watching TV with Henry and I heard his teeth click at something. I looked over, and he'd bitten through his lip. Blood was going down his chin. I tell you right then I wanted to smash that tube to pieces. I went over to it but Henry must have known what I was up to. He rushed from his chair and shoved me out of the way, against the wall. I told myself he didn't know what he was doing.

My mom came in, turned the set off real quiet, and told us she had made something for supper. So we went and sat down. There was still blood going down Henry's chin, but he didn't notice it and no one said anything, even though every time he took a bite of his bread his blood fell onto it until he was eating his own blood mixed in with the food.

While Henry was not around we talked about what was going to happen to him. There were no Indian doctors on the reservation, and my mom was afraid of trusting Old Man Pillager because he courted her long ago and was jealous of her husbands. He might take revenge through her son. We were afraid that if we brought Henry to a regular hospital they would keep him.

"They don't fix them in those places," Mom said; "they just give them drugs."

"We wouldn't get him there in the first place," I agreed, "so let's just forget about it."

Then I thought about the car.

Henry had not even looked at the car since he'd gotten home, though like I said it was in tip-top condition and ready to drive. I thought the car might bring the old Henry back somehow. So I bided my time and waited for my chance to interest him in the vehicle.

One night Henry was off somewhere. I took myself a hammer. I went out to that car and I did a number on its underside. Whacked it up. Bent the tail pipe double. Ripped the muffler loose. By the time I was done with the car it looked worse than any typical Indian car that has been driven all its life on reservation roads, which they always say are like government promises—full of holes. It just about hurt me, I'll tell you that! I threw dirt in the carburetor and I ripped all the electric tape off the seats. I made it look just as beat up as I could. Then I sat back and waited for Henry to find it.

Still, it took him over a month. That was all right, because it was just getting warm enough, not melting, but warm enough to work outside.

"Lyman," he says, walking in one day, "that red car looks like shit."

"Well it's old," I says. "You got to expect that."

"No way!" says Henry. "That car's a classic! But you went and ran the piss right out of it, Lyman, and you know it don't deserve that. I kept that car in A-one shape. You don't remember. You're too young. But when I left, that car was running like a watch. Now I don't even know if I can get it to start again, let alone get it anywhere near its old condition."

"Well you try," I said, like I was getting mad, "but I say it's a piece of junk."

Then I walked out before he could realize I knew he'd strung together more than six words at once.

After that I thought he'd freeze himself to death working on that car. He was out there all day, and at night he rigged up a little lamp, ran a cord out the window, and had himself some light to see by while he worked. He was better than he had been before, but that's still not saying much. It was easier for him to do the things the rest of us did. He ate more slowly and didn't jump up and down during the meal to get this or that or look out the window. I put my hand in the back of the

TV set, I admit, and fiddled around with it good, so that it was almost impossible now to get a clear picture. He didn't look at it very often anyway. He was always out with that car or going off to get parts for it. By the time it was really melting outside, he had it fixed.

I had been feeling down in the dumps about Henry around this time. We had always been together before. Henry and Lyman. But he was such a loner now that I didn't know how to take it. So I jumped at the chance one day when Henry seemed friendly. It's not that he smiled or anything. He just said, "Let's take that old shitbox for a spin." Just the way he said it made me think he could be coming around.

We went out to the car. It was spring. The sun was shining very bright. My only sister, Bonita, who was just eleven years old, came out and made us stand together for a picture. Henry leaned his elbow on the red car's windshield, and he took his other arm and put it over my shoulder, very carefully, as though it was heavy for him to lift and he didn't want to bring the weight down all at once.

"Smile," Bonita said, and he did.

That picture. I never look at it anymore. A few months ago, I don't know why, I got his picture out and tacked it on the wall. I felt good about Henry at the time, close to him. I felt good having his picture on the wall, until one night when I was looking at television. I was a little drunk and stoned. I looked up at the wall and Henry was staring at me. I don't know what it was, but his smile had changed, or maybe it was gone. All I know is I couldn't stay in the same room with that picture. I was shaking. I got up, closed the door, and went into the kitchen. A little later my friend Ray came over and we both went back into that room. We put the picture in a brown bag, folded the bag over and over tightly, then put it way back in a closet.

I still see that picture now, as if it tugs at me, whenever I pass that closet door. The picture is very clear in my mind. It was so sunny that day Henry had to squint against the glare. Or maybe the camera Bonita held flashed like a mirror, blinding him, before she snapped the picture. My face is right out in the sun, big and round. But he might have drawn back, because the shadows on his face are deep as holes. There are two shadows curved like little hooks around the ends of his smile, as if to frame it and try to keep it there—that one, first smile that looked like it might have hurt his face. He has his field jacket on and the worn-in clothes he'd come back in and kept wearing ever since. After Bonita took the picture, she went into the house and we got into the car. There was a full cooler in the trunk. We started off, east, toward Pembina and the Red River because Henry said he wanted to see the high water.

The trip over there was beautiful. When everything starts changing, drying up, clearing off, you feel like your whole life is starting. Henry felt it, too. The top was down and the car hummed like a top. He'd really put it back in shape, even the tape on the seats was very carefully put down and glued back in layers. It's not that he smiled again or even joked, but his face looked to me as if it was clear, more peaceful. It looked as though he wasn't thinking of anything in particular except the bare fields and windbreaks and houses we were passing.

The river was high and full of winter trash when we got there. The sun was still out, but it was colder by the river. There were still little clumps of dirty snow here and there on the banks. The water hadn't gone over the banks yet, but it would, you could tell. It was just at its limit, hard swollen, glossy like an old gray scar. We made ourselves a fire, and we sat down and watched the current go. As I watched it I felt something squeezing inside me and tightening and trying to let go all at the same time. I knew I was not just feeling it myself; I knew I was feeling what Henry was going through at that moment. Except that I couldn't stand it, the closing and opening. I jumped to my feet. I took Henry by the shoulders and I started shaking him. "Wake up," I says, "wake up, wake up, wake up!" I didn't know what had come over me. I sat down beside him again.

His face was totally white and hard. Then it broke, like stones break all of a sudden when water boils up inside them.

"I know it," he says. "I know it. I can't help it. It's no use."

We start talking. He said he knew what I'd done with the car. It was obvious it had been whacked out of shape and not just neglected. He said he wanted to give the car to me for good now, it was no use. He said he'd fixed it just to give it back and I should take it.

"No way," I says, "I don't want it."

"That's okay," he says, "you take it."

"I don't want it, though," I says back to him, and then to emphasize, just to emphasize, you understand, I touch his shoulder. He slaps my hand off.

"Take that car," he says.

"No," I say, "make me," I say, and then he grabs my jacket and rips the arm loose. That jacket is a class act, suede with tags and zippers. I push Henry backwards, off the log. He jumps up and bowls me over.

We go down in a clinch and come up swinging hard, for all we're worth, with our fists. He socks my jaw so hard I feel like it swings loose. Then I'm at his ribcage and land a good one under his chin so his head snaps back. He's dazzled. He looks at me and I look at him and then his eyes are full of tears and blood and at first I think he's crying. But no, he's laughing. "Ha! Ha!" he says. "Ha! Ha! Take good care of it."

"Okay," I says, "okay, no problem. Ha! Ha!"

I can't help it, and I start laughing, too. My face feels fat and strange, and after a while I get a beer from the cooler in the trunk, and when I hand it to Henry he takes his shirt and wipes my germs off. "Hoof-and-mouth disease," he says. For some reason this cracks me up, and so we're really laughing for a while, and then we drink all the rest of the beers one by one and throw them in the river and see how far, how fast, the current takes them before they fill up and sink.

"You want to go on back?" I ask after a while. "Maybe we could snag a couple nice Kashpaw girls."

He says nothing. But I can tell his mood is turning again.

"They're all crazy, the girls up here, every damn one of them."

"You're crazy too," I say, to jolly him up. "Crazy Lamartine boys!"

He looks as though he will take this wrong at first. His face twists, then clears, and he jumps up on his feet. "That's right!" he says. "Crazier 'n hell. Crazy Indians!"

I think it's the old Henry again. He throws off his jacket and starts swinging his legs out from the knees like a fancy dancer. He's down doing something between a grouse dance and a bunny hop, no kind of dance I ever saw before, but neither has anyone else on all this green growing earth. He's wild. He wants to pitch whoopee! He's up and at me and all over. All this time I'm laughing so hard, so hard my belly is getting tied up in a knot.

"Got to cool me off!" he shouts all of a sudden. Then he runs over to the river and jumps in.

There's boards and other things in the current. It's so high. No sound comes from the river after the splash he makes, so I run right over. I look around. It's getting dark. I see he's halfway across the water already, and I know he didn't swim there but the current took him. It's far. I hear his voice, though, very clearly across it.

"My boots are filling," he says.

He says this in a normal voice, like he just noticed and he doesn't know what to think of it. Then he's gone. A branch comes by. Another branch. And I go in.

By the time I get out of the river, off the snag I pulled myself onto, the sun is down. I walk back to the car, turn on the high beams, and drive it up the bank. I put it in first gear and then I take my foot off the clutch. I get out, close the door, and watch it plow softly into the water. The headlights reach in as they go down, searching, still lighted even after the water swirls over the back end. I wait. The wires short out. It is all finally dark. And then there is only the water, the sound of it going and running and going and running and running.

—1984

Questions: Reading, Responding, Arguing

1. Discuss Erdrich's use of first-person narration. What impact does this type of narration have on the story?
2. Discuss Erdrich's use of the red convertible as a central metaphor. What does it represent? How does this metaphor change throughout the story?
3. How does Erdrich convey Henry's character and the changes he undergoes?
4. Select another work from this anthology, such as Tim O'Brien's "The Things They Carried" on page 797, that addresses the impact of war on individuals. Compare it to Erdrich's. How are they similar or different in terms of their discussion of war and the impact of war? Using specific examples from both texts, present your argument on the similarities or differences in terms of both texts' discussion of war and the impact of war.

William Blake (1757–1827)

The Chimney Sweeper

When my mother died I was very young,
And my father sold me while yet my tongue
Could scarcely cry "'weep! 'weep! 'weep! 'weep!"
So your chimneys I sweep & in soot I sleep.

There's little Tom Dacre, who cried when his head   5
That curl'd like a lamb's back, was shav'd, so I said,
"Hush, Tom! never mind it, for when your head's bare,
You know that the soot cannot spoil your white hair."

And so he was quiet, & that very night,
As Tom was a-sleeping, he had such a sight!   10
That thousands of sweepers, Dick, Joe, Ned, & Jack,
Were all of them lock'd up in coffins of black;

And by came an Angel who had a bright key,
And he open'd the coffins & set them all free;
Then down a green plain, leaping, laughing, they run,   15
And wash in a river and shine in the Sun.

Then naked & white, all their bags left behind,
They rise upon clouds, and sport in the wind.
And the Angel told Tom, if he'd be a good boy,
He'd have God for his father, & never want joy.   20

And so Tom awoke; and we rose in the dark,
And got with our bags & our brushes to work.
Tho' the morning was cold, Tom was happy & warm;
So if all do their duty, they need not fear harm.

—1789

Questions: Reading, Responding, Arguing

1. What function does the Angel play in this poem? Is the Angel an ironic figure? How do you know?
2. Discuss the poem as a social commentary or a social critique of child labor.
3. Examine Blake's use of light and dark imagery. How does his imagery help to convey his themes and ideas? What are his themes and ideas and how do they connect to personal and communal identity?

Emily Dickinson (1830–1886)

The Brain is wider than the Sky

The Brain—is wider than the Sky—
For—put them side by side—
The one the other will contain
With ease—and You—beside—   5

The Brain is deeper than the sea—
For—hold them—Blue to Blue—
The one the other will absorb—
As Sponges—Buckets—do—

The Brain is just the weight of God—   10
For—Heft them—Pound for Pound—
And they will differ—if they do—
As Syllable from Sound—

—1896

Questions: Reading, Responding, Arguing

1. Identify the hyperboles and paradoxes in this poem. How do
   they work together?
2. Why is the simile in the second stanza appropriate?
3. What does Dickinson mean in the final stanza's simile, "they
   will differ—if they do— / As Syllable from Sound—"? What
   does this say about personal and communal identity?
   Discuss what this stanza says about personal and communal
   identity, and use additional stanzas to support your answer.

Paul Laurence Dunbar (1872–1906)

We Wear the Mask

We wear the mask that grins and lies,
It hides our cheeks and shades our eyes,—
This debt we pay to human guile;
With torn and bleeding hearts we smile,
And mouth with myriad subtleties.   5

Why should the world be over-wise,
In counting all our tears and sighs?
Nay, let them only see us, while
    We wear the mask.

We smile, but, O great Christ, our cries   10
To thee from tortured souls arise.
We sing, but oh the clay is vile
Beneath our feet, and long the mile;
But let the world dream otherwise,
    We wear the mask!   15

—*1896*

Questions: Reading, Responding, Arguing

1. What does Dunbar mean by the mask? What does it symbolize?
2. What does the use of the word *we* contribute to the poem? Who is the "we"?
3. Explain the significance of the line "We sing, but oh the clay is vile." What does this line add to the poem? How would this poem be different without this line? Argue whether or not this poem would be different without this line.

Robert Frost (1874–1963)

The Road Not Taken

Two roads diverged in a yellow wood,
And sorry I could not travel both
And be one traveler, long I stood
And looked down one as far as I could
To where it bent in the undergrowth;   5

Then took the other, as just as fair,
And having perhaps the better claim,
Because it was grassy and wanted wear;
Though as for that, the passing there
Had worn them really about the same,   10

And both that morning equally lay
In leaves no step had trodden black.
Oh, I kept the first for another day!
Yet knowing how way leads on to way,
I doubted if I should ever come back.   15

I shall be telling this with a sigh
Somewhere ages and ages hence:
Two roads diverged in a wood, and I,
I took the one less traveled by,
And that has made all the difference.   20

—*1916*

Questions: Reading, Responding, Arguing

1. Look carefully at the description of the two roads. How much difference is there between them?
2. Is there any indication in the poem that the roads symbolize anything more than the persona's need to make a choice?
3. What is ambiguous about "with a sigh" in the poem's final stanza? Discuss what this phrase reveals about the persona's feelings toward the choices he makes. Use examples from the poem to support your answer.

Langston Hughes (1902–1967)

The Negro Speaks of Rivers

I've known rivers:
I've known rivers ancient as the world and older than the
  flow of human blood in human veins.

My soul has grown deep like the rivers.

I bathed in the Euphrates when dawns were young.
I built my hut near the Congo and it lulled me to sleep.   5
I looked upon the Nile and raised the pyramids above it.
I heard the singing of the Mississippi when Abe Lincoln
  went down to New Orleans, and I've seen its muddy
  bosom turn all golden in the sunset.

I've known rivers:
Ancient, dusky rivers.

My soul has grown deep like the rivers.   10

—*1921*

Questions: Reading, Responding, Arguing

1. Who is the persona in this poem, Hughes or a "representative" speaker?
2. What aspects of Black history are identified by the rivers mentioned in the poem?
3. How would you interpret the simile in the poem's final line? Support you interpretation with concrete examples from the selection.

Countee Cullen (1903–1946)

Yet Do I Marvel

I doubt not God is good, well-meaning, kind,
And did He stoop to quibble could tell why
The little buried mole continues blind,
Why flesh that mirrors Him must some day die,
Make plain the reason tortured Tantalus   5
Is baited by the fickle fruit, declare
If merely brute caprice dooms Sisyphus
To struggle up a never-ending stair.
Inscrutable His ways are, and immune
To catechism by a mind too strewn   10
With petty cares to slightly understand
What awful brain compels His awful hand.
Yet do I marvel at this curious thing:
To make a poet black and bid him sing!

—*1963*

Questions: Reading, Responding, Arguing

1. In what form is this poem written? Why do you think Cullen chose to connect to this tradition?
2. Identify the poem's themes, and explain how Cullen's allusions to mythology contribute to them.
3. Why does the speaker marvel at God's making a poet black and making him sing? What does this reveal about Cullen's treatment of race? Using specific examples from the poem, discuss what this reveals about Cullen's treatment of race.

Dudley Randall (1914–2000)

Ballad of Birmingham

(On the Bombing of a Church in
Birmingham, Alabama, 1963)°

"Mother dear, may I go downtown
Instead of out to play,
And march the streets of Birmingham
In a Freedom March today?"

"No, baby, no, you may not go,   5
For the dogs are fierce and wild,
And clubs and hoses, guns and jail
Aren't good for a little child."

"But, mother, I won't be alone.
Other children will go with me,   10
And march the streets of Birmingham
To make our country free."

"No, baby, no, you may not go,
For I fear those guns will fire.
But you may go to church instead   15
And sing in the children's choir."

She has combed and brushed her night-dark hair,
And bathed rose petal sweet,
And drawn white gloves on her small brown hands,
And white shoes on her feet.   20

The mother smiled to know her child
Was in the sacred place,
But that smile was the last smile
To come upon her face.

For when she heard the explosion,   25
Her eyes grew wet and wild.
She raced through the streets of Birmingham
Calling for her child.

Birmingham, Alabama, 1963 during the height of the civil rights movement

She clawed through bits of glass and brick,
Then lifted out a shoe.   30
"O, here's the shoe my baby wore,
But, baby, where are you?"

—*1969*

Questions: Reading, Responding, Arguing

1. What is the irony of the mother's statement in stanzas two, four, and six?
2. Using secondary sources, connect this poem with its social, political, and historical context. How is it related to the civil rights movement? What happened in Birmingham?
3. Explain the significance of stanza five's description of the daughter. Would the poem have a different meaning or make a different argument without this stanza?

Gwendolyn Brooks (1917–2000)

We Real Cool

The Pool Players.
Seven at the Golden Shovel.

We real cool. We
Left school. We

Lurk late. We
Strike straight. We

Sing sin. We   5
Thin gin. We

Jazz June. We
Die soon.

—*1960*

Questions: Reading, Responding, Arguing

1. Consider the poetic techniques Brooks applies to the poem: How does she use sound? Repetition? Rhythm? Line breaks? How do these techniques contribute to the poem's overall effectiveness?
2. What argument are the speakers making about school? Is it the same argument that her speakers are making?

Philip Larkin (1922–1985)

This Be The Verse

They fuck you up, your mum and dad.
    They may not mean to, but they do.
They fill you with the faults they had
    And add some extra, just for you.

But they were fucked up in their turn   5
    By fools in old-style hats and coats,
Who half the time were soppy-stern
    And half at one another's throats.

Man hands on misery to man.
    It deepens like a coastal shelf.   10
Get out as early as you can,
    And don't have any kids yourself.

—1971

Questions: Reading, Responding, Arguing

1. Describe Larkin's use of rhythm and diction.
2. Connect this poem with another that addresses themes of parents and children. Is Larkin's attitude merely cynical or is there similarity in it?
3. What argument is Larkin making with the line "Man hands on misery to man"? Is this the argument of the entire poem?

Adrienne Rich (b. 1929)

Aunt Jennifer's Tigers

Aunt Jennifer's tigers prance across a screen,
Bright topaz denizens of a world of green.
They do not fear the men beneath the tree;
They pace in sleek chivalric certainty.

Aunt Jennifer's fingers fluttering through her wool   5
Find even the ivory needle hard to pull.
The massive weight of Uncle's wedding band
Sits heavily upon Aunt Jennifer's hand.

When Aunt is dead, her terrified hands will lie
Still ringed with ordeals she was mastered by.   10
The tigers in the panel that she made
Will go on prancing, proud and unafraid.

—*1950*

Questions: Reading, Responding, Arguing

1. What is Rich describing in the poem? What are the tigers?
2. What does Rich achieve by juxtaposing the tigers with Aunt Jennifer?
3. What is Rich revealing about Aunt Jennifer and her life? How does she convey her message? Cite examples from the text to justify your argument.

Sylvia Plath (1932–1963)

Daddy

You do not do, you do not do
Any more, black shoe
In which I have lived like a foot
For thirty years, poor and white,
Barely daring to breathe or Achoo.   5

Daddy, I have had to kill you.
You died before I had time—
Marble-heavy, a bag full of God,
Ghastly statue with one gray toe
Big as a Frisco seal   10

And a head in the freakish Atlantic
Where it pours bean green over blue
In the waters off beautiful Nauset.
I used to pray to recover you.
Ach, du.°   15

In the German tongue, in the Polish town
Scraped flat by the roller
Of wars, wars, wars.
But the name of the town is common.
My Polack friend   20

Says there are a dozen or two.
So I never could tell where you
Put your foot, your root,
I never could talk to you.
The tongue stuck in my jaw.   25

It stuck in a barb wire snare.
Ich, ich, ich, ich,°
I could hardly speak.
I thought every German was you.
And the language obscene   30

An engine, an engine
Chuffing me off like a Jew.
A Jew to Dachau, Auschwitz, Belsen.°
I began to talk like a Jew.
I think I may well be a Jew.   35

The snows of the Tyrol, the clear beer of Vienna
Are not very pure or true.
With my gypsy ancestress and my weird luck
And my Taroc pack and my Taroc pack
I may be a bit of a Jew.   40

---

15 **Ach, du** "Oh, you"   27 **Ich, ich, ich, ich** "I, I, I, I"   33 **Dachau, Auschwitz, Belsen** German concentration camps

I have always been scared of *you*,
With your Luftwaffe,° your gobbledygoo.
And your neat mustache
And your Aryan eye, bright blue.
Panzer-man, panzer-man, O You—   45

Not God but a swastika
So black no sky could squeak through.
Every woman adores a Fascist,
The boot in the face, the brute
Brute heart of a brute like you.   50

You stand at the blackboard, daddy,
In the picture I have of you,
A cleft in your chin instead of your foot
But no less a devil for that, no not
Any less the black man who   55

Bit my pretty red heart in two.
I was ten when they buried you.
At twenty I tried to die
And get back, back, back to you.
I thought even the bones would do.   60

But they pulled me out of the sack,
And they stuck me together with glue.
And then I knew what to do.
I made a model of you,
A man in black with a Meinkampf° look   65

And a love of the rack and the screw.
And I said I do, I do.
So daddy, I'm finally through.
The black telephone's off at the root,
The voices just can't worm through.   70

If I've killed one man, I've killed two—
The vampire who said he was you
And drank my blood for a year,
Seven years, if you want to know.
Daddy, you can lie back now.   75

There's a stake in your fat black heart
And the villagers never liked you.

42 Luftwaffe German Air Force   **65 Meinkampf** title of Hitler's autobiography ("My Struggle")

They are dancing and stamping on you.
They always *knew* it was you.
Daddy, daddy, you bastard, I'm through.   80

—*1966*

Questions: Reading, Responding, Arguing

1. How does Plath characterize or convey the character of the father?
2. Describe the parent/child relationship depicted in this poem. Compare it to the father/child relationship depicted in Robert Hayden's poem, "Those Winter Sundays" on page 1005. In what ways are they similar? Different?
3. Explain Plath's references to Germans and Jews. How does she use these groups to convey theme? Cite examples from the text to justify your argument.

Mark Strand (b. 1934)

The Tunnel

A man has been standing
in front of my house
for days. I peek at him
from the living room
window and at night,   5
unable to sleep,
I shine my flashlight
down on the lawn.
He is always there.

After a while   10
I open the front door
just a crack and order
him out of my yard.
He narrows his eyes
and moans. I slam   15
the door and dash back
to the kitchen, then up
to the bedroom, then down.

I weep like a schoolgirl
and make obscene gestures
through the window. I
write large suicide notes
and place them so he
can read them easily.
I destroy the living
room furniture to prove
I own nothing of value.

When he seems unmoved
I decide to dig a tunnel
to a neighboring yard.
I seal the basement off
from the upstairs with
a brick wall. I dig hard
and in no time the tunnel
is done. Leaving my pick
and shovel below,

I come out in front of a house
and stand there too tired to
move or even speak, hoping
someone will help me.
I feel I'm being watched
and sometimes I hear
a man's voice,
but nothing is done
and I have been waiting for days.

—1968

Questions: Reading, Responding, Arguing

1. What does the man represent? What effect does he have on the narrator? Why?
2. Why does the speaker build a tunnel? Why is the poem titled after this tunnel?
3. Why does Strand end the poem with the narrator "waiting" as he does? What meaning does his "waiting" convey, and how is it related to the waiting of the other man? Use multiple stanzas from the text to support your argument.

Lucille Clifton (b. 1936)

lee°

my mother's people
belonged to the lees
my father would say
then spout a litany
of names   old lighthorse harry   5
old robert e

my father
who lied on his deathbed
who knew the truth
but didn't always choose it   10
who saw himself an honorable man

was proud of lee
that man of honor
praised by grant and lincoln
worshipped by his men   15
revered by the state of virginia
which he loved almost as much
as my father did

it may have been a lie
it may have been   20
one of my father's tales
if so there was an honor in it
if he was indeed to be
the child of slaves
he would decide himself   25
that proud old man

i can see him now
chaining his mother to lee

—*1996*

lee Robert E. Lee (1807–1870), Confederate general in American Civil War

Questions: Reading, Responding, Arguing

1. Who is Lee? Why does Clifton choose to title her poem after this character?
2. Contrast Clifton's attitude toward the past with that of her father.
3. What are the implications of the poem's final image? How does it alter the meaning of the poem as a whole? Cite examples from the text to justify your argument.

Florence Cassen Mayers (b. 1940)

All-American Sestina

One nation, indivisible
two-car garage
three strikes you're out
four-minute mile
five-cent cigar   5
six-string guitar

six-pack Bud
one-day sale
five-year warranty
two-way street   10
fourscore and seven years ago
three cheers

three-star restaurant
sixty-
four-dollar question   15
one-night stand
two-pound lobster
five-star general

five-course meal
three sheets to the wind   20
two bits
six-shooter
one-armed bandit
four-poster

four-wheel drive   25
five-and-dime
hole in one
three-alarm fire
sweet sixteen
two-wheeler
                                                                   30
two-tone Chevy
four rms, hi flr, w/vu
six-footer
high five
three-ring circus
one-room schoolhouse   35

two thumbs up, five-karat diamond
Fourth of July, three-piece suit
six feet under, one-horse town

—*1996*

Questions: Reading, Responding, Arguing

1. What is a *sestina*? How does this poem alter the *rules* of a traditional sestina?
2. Why is this poem called an "All-American Sestina"? What is Mayers saying about America? What is "all-American" about this sestina?
3. Examine the images or allusions Mayers makes in this poem. How does she connect the images? What argument does she make by doing so?

Gladys Cardiff (b. 1942)

Combing

Bending, I bow my head
And lay my hand upon
Her hair, combing, and think
How women do this for
Each other. My daughter's hair   5

Curls against the comb,
Wet and fragrant—orange
Parings. Her face, downcast,
Is quiet for one so young.

I take her place. Beneath   10
My mother's hands I feel
The braids drawn up tight
As a piano wire and singing,
Vinegar-rinsed. Sitting
Before the oven I hear   15
The orange coils tick
The early hour before school.

She combed her grandmother
Mathilda's hair using
A comb made out of bone.   20
Mathilda rocked her oak wood
Chair, her face downcast,
Intent on tearing rags
In strips to braid a cotton
Rug from bits of orange   25
and brown. A simple act,

Preparing hair. Something
Women do for each other,
Plaiting the generations.

                                                        —1976

Questions: Reading, Responding, Arguing

1. This poem is about combing hair but it's also about other
   things—name them. What does the combing signify or represent?
2. What does Cardiff mean when she writes about "plaiting the
   generations"?
3. Compare this poem with another that deals with generations. Which do you find more truthful? Cite examples from
   both texts to justify your argument.

Sharon Olds (b. 1942)

The One Girl at the Boys Party

When I take my girl to the swimming party
I set her down among the boys. They tower and
bristle, she stands there smooth and sleek,
her math scores unfolding in the air around her.
They will strip to their suits, her body hard and   5
indivisible as a prime number,
they'll plunge into the deep end, she'll subtract
her height from ten feet, divide it into
hundreds of gallons of water, the numbers
bouncing in her mind like molecules of chlorine   10
in the bright blue pool. When they climb out,
her ponytail will hang its pencil lead
down her back, her narrow silk suit
with hamburgers and french fries printed on it
will glisten in the brilliant air, and they will   15
see her sweet face, solemn and
sealed, a factor of one, and she will
see their eyes, two each,
their legs, two each, and the curves of their sexes,
one each, and in her head she'll be doing her   20
wild multiplying, as the drops
sparkle and fall to the power of a thousand from her body.

—*1983*

Questions: Reading, Responding, Arguing

1. According to Olds, what kind of relationship exists between the girls and the boys?
2. How does Olds describe her daughter?
3. Examine Olds's use of mathematical and numerical language. What does it add to the poem?
4. What is the impact of the choice of narrator and her point of view? How does it enhance the poem's themes? Cite examples from the text to justify your argument.

Jim Hall (b. 1947)

Maybe Dats Your Pwoblem Too

All my pwoblems,
who knows, maybe evwybody's pwoblems
is due to da fact, due to da awful twuth
dat I am SPIDERMAN.

I know, I know. All da dumb jokes: 5
No flies on you, ha ha,
and da ones about what do I do wit all
doze extwa legs in bed. Well, dat's funny yeah.
But you twy being
SPIDERMAN for a month or two. Go ahead.   10

You get doze cwazy calls fwom da
Gubbener askin you to twap some booglar who's
only twying to wip off color T.V. sets.
Now, what do I cawre about T.V. sets?
But I pull on da suit, da stinkin suit,   15
wit da sucker cups on da fingers,
and get my wopes and wittle bundle of
equipment and den I go flying like cwazy
acwoss da town fwom woof top to woof top.

Till der he is. Some poor dumb color T.V. slob   20
and I fall on him and we westle a widdle
until I get him all woped. So big deal.

You tink when you SPIDERMAN
der's sometin big going to happen to you.
Well, I tell you what. It don't happen dat way.   25
Nuttin happens. Gubbener calls, I go.
Bwing him to powice, Gubbener calls again,
like dat over and over.

I tink I twy sometin diffunt. I tink I twy
sometin excitin like wacing cawrs. Sometin to make   30
my heart beat at a difwent wate.

But den you just can't quit being sometin like
SPIDERMAN.
You SPIDERMAN for life. Fowever. I can't even
buin my suit. It won't buin. It's fwame wesistent.   35
So maybe dat's youwr pwoblem too, who knows.
Maybe dat's da whole pwoblem wif evwytin.
Nobody can buin der suits, dey all fwame wesistent.
Who knows?

—1980

Questions: Reading, Responding, Arguing

1. Explain Hall's approach to language. What does this approach contribute to the poem?
2. How does Hall's depiction of "Spiderman" differ or relate to
   popular culture's view of the character?
3. How does Hall create and use humor? Examine his mis-
   spellings/mispronunciations and justify them.
4. What does this poem say about personal identity? What arguments can you make about personal identity and the significance of the "suit"?

Timothy Murphy (b. 1950)

Case Notes

for Dr. Richard Kolotkin

MARCH 7, 2002

Raped at an early age
by older altar boy.
"Damned by the Church to Hell,
never to sire a son,
perhaps man's greatest joy,"   5
said father in a rage.
Patient was twenty-one.
Handled it pretty well.

MARCH 14, 2002

Curiously, have learned
patient was Eagle Scout.
Outraged that Scouts have spurned   10
each camper who is "out."
Questioned if taunts endured
are buried? "No, immured."

MARCH 21, 2002

Immersed in verse and drink   15
when he was just sixteen,
turned to drugs at Yale.
Patient began to sink,
to fear he was a "queen,"
a "queer" condemned to fail   20
or detox in a jail.

APRIL 1, 2002

Into a straight town
he brought a sober lover.
"Worked smarter, drank harder
to stock an empty larder,"   25
wrote poetry, the cover
for grief he cannot drown.

APRIL 9, 2002

Uneasy with late father,
feared for by his mother,
lover, and younger brother.   30
Various neuroses,
but no severe psychosis.
Precarious prognosis.

—2004

Questions: Reading, Responding, Arguing

1. What does the title of this poem refer to? How does the
   poem's language reflect the contents of the poem?
2. Who is the persona of the poem? What is his/her tone of voice?

3. Note the use of rhymes in the poem, especially in the final stanza. Are they effective in establishing the poem's tone of voice?
4. Do you think the persona's diagnosis of his patient is accurate? Citing examples from the text for support, what is your own argument for a diagnosis of the patient?

Joy Harjo (b. 1951)

She Had Some Horses

She had some horses.
She had horses who were bodies of sand.
She had horses who were maps drawn of blood.
She had horses who were skins of ocean water.
She had horses who were the blue air of sky.   5
She had horses who were fur and teeth.
She had horses who were clay and would break.
She had horses who were splintered red cliff.

She had some horses.

She had horses with eyes of trains.   10
She had horses with full brown thighs.
She had horses who laughed too much.
She had horses who threw rocks at glass houses.
She had horses who licked razor blades.

She had some horses.   15

She had horses who danced in their mother's arms.
She had horses who thought they were the sun and
their bodies shone and burned like stars.
She had horses who waltzed nightly on the moon.
She had horses who were much too shy, and kept quiet   20
in stalls of their own making.

She had some horses.

She had horses who liked Creek Stomp Dance songs.
She had horses who cried in their beer.
She had horses who spit at male queens who made   25

them afraid of themselves.
She had horses who said they weren't afraid.
She had horses who lied.
She had horses who told the truth, who were stripped   30
bare of their tongues.

She had some horses.

She had horses who called themselves "horse."
She had horses who called themselves "spirit,"
and kept their voices secret and to themselves.
She had horses who had no names.   35
She had horses who had books of names.

She had some horses.

She had horses who whispered in the dark, who were afraid to speak.
She had horses who screamed out of fear of the silence,
who carried knives to protect themselves from ghosts.   40
She had horses who waited for destruction.
She had horses who waited for resurrection.

She had some horses.

She had horses who got down on their knees for any savior.
She had horses who thought their high price had saved them.   45
She had horses who tried to save her,
who climbed in her bed at night and prayed as they raped her.

She had some horses.

She had some horses she loved.
She had some horses she hated.   50

They were the same horses.

—*1983*

Questions: Reading, Responding, Arguing

1. Discuss the ways that Harjo uses repetition in this poem.
2. Identify different horses and discuss the use of some of them in the poem. What do they reveal about personal and communal identities? At what point in the poem is it obvious that the poet is using horses as symbols? What do they symbolize?

3. Virtually every line contains a metaphor. Identify them and discuss their implications. What do they reveal about personal and communal identities? Use examples of metaphors from the text to justify your argument.

Julia Alvarez (b. 1953)

Bilingual Sestina

Some things I have to say aren't getting said
in this snowy, blond, blue-eyed, gum-chewing English:
dawn's early light sifting through *persianas*° closed
the night before by dark-skinned girls whose words
evoke *cama,*° *aposento,*° *sueños*° in *nombres*°   5
from that first world I can't translate from Spanish.

Gladys, Rosario, Altagracia—the sounds of Spanish
wash over me like warm island waters as I say
your soothing names: a child again learning the *nombres*
of things you point to in the world before English
turned *sol,*° *sierra,*° *cielo,*° *luna*° to vocabulary words—   10
sun, earth, sky, moon. Language closed

like the touch-sensitive *morivivi*° whose leaves closed
when we kids poked them, astonished. Even Spanish
failed us back then when we saw how frail a word is   15
when faced with the thing it names. How saying
its name won't always summon up in Spanish or English
the full blown genie from the bottled *nombre.*

Gladys, I summon you back by saying your *nombre.*
Open up again the house of slatted windows closed   20
since childhood, where *palabras*° left behind for English
stand dusty and awkward in neglected Spanish.
Rosario, muse of *el patio,*° sing in me and through me say
that world again, begin first with those first words

---

3 **persianas** venetian blinds   5 **cama** bed   **aposento** apartment   **sueños** dreams   **nombres** names
11 **sol** sun   **sierra** mountain   **cielo** sky   **luna** moon   13 **morivivi** a type of Caribbean bush
21 **palabras** words   23 **el patio** outdoor terrace

you put in my mouth as you pointed to the world—   25
not Adam, not God, but a country girl numbering
the stars, the blades of grass, warming the sun by saying,
¡Qué calor!° as you opened up the morning closed
inside the night until you sang in Spanish,
Estas son las mañanitas,° and listening in bed, no English   30

yet in my head to confuse me with translations, no English
doubling the world with synonyms, no dizzying array of words
—the world was simple and intact in Spanish—
luna, sol, casa,° *luz, flor,*° as if the *nombres*
were the outer skin of things, as if words were so close   35
one left a mist of breath on things by saying

their names, an intimacy I now yearn for in English—
words so close to what I mean that I almost hear my Spanish
heart beating, beating inside what I say *en inglés*°.

                                                        —1995

Questions: Reading, Responding, Arguing

1. What is a sestina? How is this poem representative of sestinas?

2. Discuss why this poem is called a bilingual sestina. What is Alvarez saying about language and language's ability to convey thoughts and emotions?

3. What does Alvarez say about the connections between the word and the world? Cite examples from the text to explain her position, and develop an argument for or against it.

---

28 Qué calor What heat!   30 Estas son las mañanitas These are birthday songs   34 casa house
flor flower   39 en ingles in English

Cathy Song (b. 1955)

Stamp Collecting

The poorest countries
have the prettiest stamps
as if impracticality were a major export
shipped with the bananas, t-shirts, and coconuts.
Take Tonga, where the tourists,   5
expecting a dramatic waterfall replete with birdcalls
are taken to see the island's peculiar mystery:
hanging bats with collapsible wings
like black umbrellas swing upside down from fruit trees.
The Tongan stamp is a fruit.   10
The banana stamp is scalloped like a butter-varnished seashell.
The pineapple resembles a volcano, a spout of green on top,
and the papaya, a tarnished goat skull.

They look impressive,
these stamps of countries without a thing to sell   15
except for what is scraped, uprooted and hulled
from their mule-scratched hills.
They believe in postcards,
in portraits of progress: the new dam;
a team of young native doctors   20
wearing stethoscopes like exotic ornaments;
the recently constructed "Facultad de Medicina,"°
a building as lack-lustre as an American motel.

The stamps of others are predictable.
Lucky is the country that possesses indigenous beauty.   25
Say a tiger or a queen.
The Japanese can display to the world
their blossoms: a spray of pink on green.
Like pollen, they drift, airborne.
But pity the country that is bleak and stark.   30

Beauty and whimsey are discouraged as indiscreet.
Unbreakable as their climate, a monument of ice,

22 Facultad de Medicina Medical Faculty (building)

they issue serious statements, commemorating
factories, tramways and aeroplanes;
athletes marbled into statues.   35
They turn their noses upon the world, these countries,
and offer this: an unrelenting procession
of a grim, historic profile.

                                                        —1988

Questions: Reading, Responding, Arguing

1. What does Song say about the stamps from Tonga?
2. What does Song say about images and realities?
3. What do the stamps signify? Cite examples from the text to
   make an argument about the meaning of the symbols/images
   on the stamps.

Susan Glaspell (1882–1948)

Trifles*

CHARACTERS

George Henderson, County Attorney
Mrs. Peters
Henry Peters, Sheriff
Lewis Hale, a neighbor
Mrs. Hale

SCENE: *The kitchen in the now abandoned farmhouse of John
Wright, a gloomy kitchen, and left without having been put in order—
unwashed pans under the sink, a loaf of bread outside the breadbox, a
dish towel on the table—other signs of incompleted work. At the rear
the outer door opens, and the Sheriff comes in, followed by the County
Attorney and Hale. The Sheriff and Hale are men in middle life, the
County Attorney is a young man; all are much bundled up and go at
once to the stove. They are followed by the two women—the Sheriff's
Wife first; she is a slight wiry woman, a thin nervous face. Mrs. Hale is*

*larger and would ordinarily be called more comfortable looking, but
she is disturbed now and looks fearfully about as she enters. The
women have come in slowly and stand close together near the door.*

COUNTY ATTORNEY: [*rubbing his hands*]: This feels good. Come up
to the fire, ladies.

MRS. PETERS [*after taking a step forward*]: I'm not—cold.

SHERIFF [*unbuttoning his overcoat and stepping away from the stove
as if to the beginning of official business*]: Now, Mr. Hale, before
we move things about, you explain to Mr. Henderson just what
you saw when you came here yesterday morning.

COUNTY ATTORNEY: By the way, has anything been moved? Are
things just as you left them yesterday?

SHERIFF [*looking about*]: It's just the same. When it dropped below
zero last night, I thought I'd better send Frank out this morning to
make a fire for us—no use getting pneumonia with a big case on;
but I told him not to touch anything except the stove—and you
know Frank.

COUNTY ATTORNEY: Somebody should have been left here yesterday.

SHERIFF: Oh—yesterday. When I had to send Frank to Morris Center
for that man who went crazy—I want you to know I had my hands
full yesterday. I knew you could get back from Omaha by today,
and as long as I went over everything here myself—

COUNTY ATTORNEY: Well, Mr. Hale, tell just what happened when
you came here yesterday morning.

HALE: Harry and I had started to town with a load of potatoes. We
came along the road from my place; and as I got here, I said, "I'm
going to see if I can't get John Wright to go in with me on a party
telephone." I spoke to Wright about it once before, and he put me
off, saying folks talked too much anyway, and all he asked was
peace and quiet—I guess you know about how much he talked
himself; but I thought maybe if I went to the house and talked
about it before his wife, though I said to Harry that I didn't know
as what his wife wanted made much difference to John—

COUNTY ATTORNEY: Let's talk about that later, Mr. Hale. I do want
to talk about that, but tell now just what happened when you got
to the house.

HALE: I didn't hear or see anything; I knocked at the door, and still it
was all quiet inside. I knew they must be up, it was past eight
o'clock. So I knocked again, and I thought I heard somebody say,
"Come in." I wasn't sure, I'm not sure yet, but I opened the door—

this door [*indicating the door by which the two women are still standing*], and there in that rocker—[*pointing to it*] sat Mrs. Wright. [*They all look at the rocker.*]

COUNTY ATTORNEY: What—was she doing?

HALE: She was rockin' back and forth. She had her apron in her hand and was kind of—pleating it.

COUNTY ATTORNEY: And how did she—look?

HALE: Well, she looked queer.

COUNTY ATTORNEY: How do you mean—queer?

HALE: Well, as if she didn't know what she was going to do next. And kind of done up.

COUNTY ATTORNEY: How did she seem to feel about your coming?

HALE: Why, I don't think she minded—one way or other. She didn't pay much attention. I said, "How do, Mrs. Wright, it's cold, ain't it?" And she said, "Is it?"—and went on kind of pleating at her apron. Well, I was surprised; she didn't ask me to come up to the stove, or to set down, but just sat there, not even looking at me, so I said, "I want to see John." And then she—laughed. I guess you would call it a laugh. I thought of Harry and the team outside, so I said a little sharp: "Can't I see John?" "No," she says, kind o' dull like. "Ain't he home?" says I. "Yes," says she, "he's home." "Then why can't I see him?" I asked her, out of patience. "'Cause he's dead," says she. "*Dead?*" says I. She just nodded her head, not getting a bit excited, but rockin' back and forth. "Why—where is he?" says I, not knowing what to say. She just pointed upstairs—like that [*himself pointing to the room above*]. I got up, with the idea of going up there. I walked from there to here—then I says, "Why, what did he die of?" "He died of a rope around his neck," says she, and just went on pleatin' at her apron. Well, I went out and called Harry. I thought I might—need help. We went upstairs, and there he was lyin'—

COUNTY ATTORNEY: I think I'd rather have you go into that upstairs, where you can point it all out. Just go on now with the rest of the story.

HALE: Well, my first thought was to get that rope off. I looked . . . [*Stops, his face twitches.*] . . . but Harry, he went up to him, and he said, "No, he's dead all right, and we'd better not touch anything." So we went back downstairs. She was still sitting that same way. "Has anybody been notified?" I asked. "No," says she, unconcerned. "Who did this, Mrs. Wright?" said Harry. He said it businesslike—and she stopped pleatin' of her apron. "I don't know," she says. "You don't *know?*" says Harry. "No," says she, "Weren't you sleepin' in the bed with him?" says Harry. "Yes," says she, "but I was on the inside." "Somebody slipped a rope round his neck and strangled him, and you didn't wake up?" says Harry. "I didn't wake up," she said after him. We must 'a looked as if we didn't see how that could be, for after a minute she said, "I sleep sound." Harry was going to ask her more questions, but I said maybe we ought to let her tell her story first to the coroner, or the sheriff, so Harry went fast as he could to Rivers' place, where there's a telephone.

COUNTY ATTORNEY: And what did Mrs. Wright do when she knew that you had gone for the coroner?

HALE: She moved from that chair to this over here . . . [*Pointing to a small chair in the corner.*] . . . and just sat there with her hands held together and looking down. I got a feeling that I ought to make some conversation, so I said I had come in to see if John wanted to put in a telephone, and at that she started to laugh, and then she stopped and looked at me—scared. [*The County Attorney, who has had his notebook out, makes a note.*] I dunno, maybe it wasn't scared. I wouldn't like to say it was. Soon Harry got back, and then Dr. Lloyd came, and you, Mr. Peters, and so I guess that's all I know that you don't.

COUNTY ATTORNEY [*looking around*]: I guess we'll go upstairs first—and then out to the barn and around there. [*To the Sheriff.*] You're convinced that there was nothing important here—nothing that would point to any motive?

SHERIFF: Nothing here but kitchen things.

[*The County Attorney, after again looking around the kitchen, opens the door of a cupboard closet. He gets up on a chair and looks on a shelf. Pulls his hand away, sticky.*]

COUNTY ATTORNEY: Here's a nice mess.

[*The women draw nearer.*]

MRS. PETERS [*to the other woman*]: Oh, her fruit; it did freeze. [*To the Lawyer.*] She worried about that when it turned so cold. She said the fir'd go out and her jars would break.

SHERIFF: Well, can you beat the women! Held for murder and worryin' about her preserves.

COUNTY ATTORNEY: I guess before we're through she may have something more serious than preserves to worry about.

HALE: Well, women are used to worrying over trifles.

[*The two women move a little closer together.*]

COUNTY ATTORNEY [*with the gallantry of a young politician*]: And yet, for all their worries, what would we do without the ladies? [*The women do not unbend. He goes to the sink, takes a dipperful of water from the pail and, pouring it into a basin, washes his hands. Starts to wipe them on the roller towel, turns it for a cleaner place.*] Dirty towels! [*Kicks his foot against the pans under the sink.*] Not much of a housekeeper, would you say, ladies?

MRS. HALE [*stiffly*]: There's a great deal of work to be done on a farm.

COUNTY ATTORNEY: To be sure. And yet . . . [*With a little bow to her.*] . . . I know there are some Dickson county farmhouses which do not have such roller towels. [*He gives it a pull to expose its full length again.*]

MRS. HALE: Those towels get dirty awful quick. Men's hands aren't always as clean as they might be.

COUNTY ATTORNEY: Ah, loyal to your sex, I see. But you and Mrs. Wright were neighbors. I suppose you were friends, too.

MRS. HALE [*shaking her head*]: I've not seen much of her of late years. I've not been in this house—it's more than a year.

COUNTY ATTORNEY: And why was that? You didn't like her?

MRS. HALE: I liked her all well enough. Farmers' wives have their hands full, Mr. Henderson. And then—

COUNTY ATTORNEY: Yes—?

MRS. HALE [*looking about*]: It never seemed a very cheerful place.

COUNTY ATTORNEY: No—it's not cheerful. I shouldn't say she had the homemaking instinct.

MRS. HALE: Well, I don't know as Wright had, either.

COUNTY ATTORNEY: You mean that they didn't get on very well?

MRS. HALE: No, I don't mean anything. But I don't think a place'd be any cheerfuler for John Wright's being in it.

COUNTY ATTORNEY: I'd like to talk more of that a little later. I want to get the lay of things upstairs now. [*He goes to the left, where three steps lead to a stair door.*]

SHERIFF: I suppose anything Mrs. Peters does'll be all right. She was to take in some clothes for her, you know, and a few little things. We left in such a hurry yesterday.

COUNTY ATTORNEY: Yes, but I would like to see what you take, Mrs. Peters, and keep an eye out for anything that might be of use to us.

MRS. PETERS: Yes, Mr. Henderson.

[*The women listen to the men's steps on the stairs, then look about the kitchen.*]

MRS. HALE: I'd hate to have men coming into my kitchen, snooping around and criticizing. [*She arranges the pans under sink which the Lawyer had shoved out of place.*]

MRS. PETERS: Of course it's no more than their duty.

MRS. HALE: Duty's all right, but I guess that deputy sheriff that came out to make the fire might have got a little of this on. [*Gives the roller towel a pull.*] Wish I'd thought of that sooner. Seems mean to talk about her for not having things slicked up when she had to come away in such a hurry.

MRS. PETERS [*who has gone to a small table in the left rear corner of the room, and lifted one end of a towel that covers a pan*]:   She had bread set. [*Stands still.*]

MRS. HALE [*eyes fixed on a loaf of bread beside the breadbox, which is on a low shelf at the other side of the room. Moves slowly toward it*]:   She was going to put this in there. [*Picks up loaf, then abruptly drops it. In a manner of returning to familiar things.*] It's a shame about her fruit. I wonder if it's all gone. [*Gets up on the chair and looks.*] I think there's some here that's all right, Mrs. Peters. Yes—here; [*Holding it toward the window.*] this is cherries, too. [*Looking again.*] I declare I believe that's the only one. [*Gets down, bottle in her hand. Goes to the sink and wipes it off on the outside.*] She'll feel awful bad after all her hard work in the hot weather. I remember the afternoon I put up my cherries last summer. [*She puts the bottle on the big kitchen table, center of the room, front table. With a sigh, is about to sit down in the rocking chair. Before she is seated realizes what chair it is; with a slow look at it, steps back. The chair, which she has touched, rocks back and forth.*]

MRS. PETERS: Well, I must get those things from the front room closet. [*She goes to the door at the right, but after looking into the other room steps back.*] You coming with me, Mrs. Hale? You could help me carry them. [*They go into the other room; reappear, Mrs. Peters carrying a dress and skirt, Mrs. Hale following with a pair of shoes.*]

MRS. PETERS: My, it's cold in there. [*She puts the cloth on the big table, and hurries to the stove.*]

MRS. HALE [*examining the skirt*]:   Wright was close. I think maybe that's why she kept so much to herself. She didn't even belong to the Ladies' Aid. I suppose she felt she couldn't do her part, and then you don't enjoy things when you feel shabby. She used to wear pretty clothes and be lively, when she was Minnie Foster, one of the town girls singing in the choir. But that—oh, that was thirty years ago. This all you was to take in?

MRS. PETERS: She said she wanted an apron. Funny thing to want, for there isn't much to get you dirty in jail, goodness knows. But I suppose just to make her feel more natural. She said they was in the top drawer in this cupboard. Yes, here. And then her little shawl that always hung behind the door. [*Opens stair door and looks.*] Yes, here it is. [*Quickly shuts door leading upstairs.*]

MRS. HALE [*abruptly moving toward her*]:   Mrs. Peters?

MRS. PETERS: Yes, Mrs. Hale?

MRS. HALE: Do you think she did it?

MRS. PETERS [*in a frightened voice*]:   Oh, I don't know.

MRS. HALE: Well, I don't think she did. Asking for an apron and her little shawl. Worrying about her fruit.

MRS. PETERS [*starts to speak, glances up, where footsteps are heard in the room above. In a low voice*]:   Mr. Peters says it looks bad for her. Mr. Henderson is awful sarcastic in speech, and he'll make fun of her sayin' she didn't wake up.

MRS. HALE: Well, I guess John Wright didn't wake when they was slipping that rope under his neck.

MRS. PETERS: No, it's strange. It must have been done awful crafty and still. They say it was such a—funny way to kill a man, rigging it all up like that.

MRS. HALE: That's just what Mr. Hale said. There was a gun in the house. He says that's what he can't understand.

MRS. PETERS: Mr. Henderson said coming out that what was needed for the case was a motive; something to show anger, or—sudden feeling.

MRS. HALE [*who is standing by the table*]:   Well, I don't see any signs of anger around here. [*She puts her hand on the dish towel which lies on the table, stands looking down at the table, one half of which is clean, the other half messy.*] It's wiped here. [*Makes a move as if to finish work, then turns and looks at loaf of bread outside the breadbox. Drops towel. In that voice of coming back to familiar things.*] Wonder how they are finding things upstairs? I hope she had it a little more red-up there. You know, it seems kind of *sneaking*. Locking her up in town and then coming out here and trying to get her own house to turn against her!

MRS. PETERS: But, Mrs. Hale, the law is the law.

MRS. HALE: I s'pose 'tis. [*Unbuttoning her coat.*] Better loosen up your things, Mrs. Peters. You won't feel them when you go out.

[*Mrs. Peters takes off her fur tippet, goes to hang it on hook at the back of room, stands looking at the under part of the small corner table.*]

MRS. PETERS: She was piecing a quilt. [*She brings the large sewing basket, and they look at the bright pieces.*]

MRS. HALE: It's log cabin pattern. Pretty, isn't it? I wonder if she was goin' to quilt or just knot it?

[*Footsteps have been heard coming down the stairs. The Sheriff enters, followed by Hale and the County Attorney.*]

SHERIFF: They wonder if she was going to quilt it or just knot it. [*The men laugh, the women look abashed.*]

COUNTY ATTORNEY [*rubbing his hands over the stove*]: Frank's fire didn't do much up there, did it? Well, let's go out to the barn and get that cleared up.

[*The men go outside.*]

MRS. HALE [*resentfully*]: I don't know as there's anything so strange, our takin' up our time with little things while we're waiting for them to get the evidence. [*She sits down at the big table, smoothing out a block with decision.*] I don't see as it's anything to laugh about.

MRS. PETERS [*apologetically*]: Of course they've got awful important things on their minds. [*Pulls up a chair and joins Mrs. Hale at the table.*]

MRS. HALE [*examining another block*]: Mrs. Peters, look at this one. Here, this is the one she was working on, and look at the sewing! All the rest of it has been so nice and even. And look at this! It's all over the place! Why, it looks as if she didn't know what she was about! [*After she has said this, they look at each other, then started to glance back at the door. After an instant Mrs. Hale has pulled at a knot and ripped the sewing.*]

MRS. PETERS: Oh, what are you doing, Mrs. Hale?

MRS. HALE [*mildly*]: Just pulling out a stitch or two that's not sewed very good. [*Threading a needle.*] Bad sewing always made me fidgety.

MRS. PETERS [*nervously*]: I don't think we ought to touch things.

MRS. HALE: I'll just finish up this end. [*Suddenly stopping and leaning forward.*] Mrs. Peters?

MRS. PETERS: Yes, Mrs. Hale?

MRS. HALE: What do you suppose she was so nervous about?

MRS. PETERS: Oh—I don't know. I don't know as she was nervous. I sometimes sew awful queer when I'm just tired. [*Mrs. Hale starts to say something, looks at Mrs. Peters, then goes on sewing.*] Well, I must get these things wrapped up. They may be through sooner than we think. [*Putting apron and other things together.*] I wonder where I can find a piece of paper, and string.

MRS. HALE: In that cupboard, maybe.

MRS. PETERS [*looking in cupboard*]:   Why, here's a birdcage. [*Holds it up.*] Did she have a bird, Mrs. Hale?

MRS. HALE: Why, I don't know whether she did or not—I've not been here for so long. There was a man around last year selling canaries cheap, but I don't know as she took one; maybe she did. She used to sing real pretty herself.

MRS. PETERS [*glancing around*]:   Seems funny to think of a bird here. But she must have had one, or why should she have a cage? I wonder what happened to it?

MRS. HALE: I s'pose maybe the cat got it.

MRS. PETERS: No, she didn't have a cat. She's got that feeling some people have about cats—being afraid of them. My cat got in her room, and she was real upset and asked me to take it out.

MRS. HALE: My sister Bessie was like that. Queer, ain't it?

MRS. PETERS [*examining the cage*]:   Why, look at this door. It's broke. One hinge is pulled apart.

MRS. HALE [*looking, too*]:   Looks as if someone must have been rough with it.

MRS. PETERS: Why, yes. [*She brings the cage forward and puts it on the table.*]

MRS. HALE: I wish if they're going to find any evidence they'd be about it. I don't like this place.

MRS. PETERS: But I'm awful glad you came with me, Mrs. Hale. It would be lonesome for me sitting here alone.

MRS. HALE: It would, wouldn't it? [*Dropping her sewing.*] But I tell you what I do wish, Mrs. Peters. I wish I had come over sometimes when *she* was here. I—[*Looking around the room.*]—wish I had.

MRS. PETERS: But of course you were awful busy, Mrs. Hale—your house and your children.

MRS. HALE: I could've come. I stayed away because it weren't cheerful—and that's why I ought to have come. I—I've never liked this place. Maybe because it's down in a hollow, and you don't see the road. I dunno what it is, but it's a lonesome place and always was. I wish I had come over to see Minnie Foster sometimes. I can see now—[*Shakes her head.*]

MRS. PETERS: Well, you mustn't reproach yourself, Mrs. Hale. Somehow we just don't see how it is with other folks until—something comes up.

MRS. HALE: Not having children makes less work—but it makes a quiet house, and Wright out to work all day, and no company when he did come in. Did you know John Wright, Mrs. Peters?

MRS. PETERS: Not to know him; I've seen him in town. They say he was a good man.

MRS. HALE: Yes—good; he didn't drink, and kept his word as well as most, I guess, and paid his debts. But he was a hard man, Mrs. Peters. Just to pass the time of day with him. [*Shivers.*] Like a raw wind that gets to the bone. [*Pauses, her eye falling on the cage.*] I should think she would 'a wanted a bird. But what do you suppose went with it?

MRS. PETERS: I don't know, unless it got sick and died. [*She reaches over and swings the broken door, swings it again; both women watch it.*]

MRS. HALE: You weren't raised round here, were you? [*Mrs. Peters shakes her head.*] You didn't know—her?

MRS. PETERS: Not till they brought her yesterday.

MRS. HALE: She—come to think of it, she was kind of like a bird herself—real sweet and pretty, but kind of timid and—fluttery. How—she—did—change. [*Silence; then as if struck by a happy thought and relieved to get back to everyday things.*] Tell you what, Mrs. Peters, why don't you take the quilt in with you? It might take up her mind.

MRS. PETERS: Why, I think that's a real nice idea, Mrs. Hale. There couldn't possibly be any objection to it, could there? Now, just what would I take? I wonder if her patches are in here—and her things. [*They look in the sewing basket.*]

MRS. HALE: Here's some red. I expect this has got sewing things in it [*Brings out a fancy box.*] What a pretty box. Looks like something somebody would give you. Maybe her scissors are in here. [*Opens box. Suddenly puts her hand to her nose.*] Why—[*Mrs. Peters bends nearer, then turns her face away.*] There's something wrapped up in this piece of silk.

MRS. PETERS: Why, this isn't her scissors.

MRS. HALE [*lifting the silk*]: Oh, Mrs. Peters—it's—[*Mrs. Peters bends closer.*]

MRS. PETERS: It's the bird.

MRS. HALE [*jumping up*]: But, Mrs. Peters—look at it. Its neck! Look at its neck! It's all—other side *to.*

MRS. PETERS: Somebody—wrung—its neck.

[*Their eyes meet. A look of growing comprehension of horror. Steps are heard outside. Mrs. Hale slips box under quilt pieces, and sinks into her chair. Enter Sheriff and County Attorney. Mrs. Peters rises.*]

COUNTY ATTORNEY [*as one turning from serious things to little pleasantries*]: Well, ladies, have you decided whether she was going to quilt it or knot it?

MRS. PETERS: We think she was going to—knot it.

COUNTY ATTORNEY: Well, that's interesting, I'm sure. [*Seeing the birdcage.*] Has the bird flown?

MRS. HALE [*putting more quilt pieces over the box*]: We think the—cat got it.

COUNTY ATTORNEY [*preoccupied*]: Is there a cat?

[*Mrs. Hale glances in a quick covert way at Mrs. Peters.*]

MRS. PETERS: Well, not now. They're superstitious, you know. They leave.

COUNTY ATTORNEY [*to Sheriff Peters, continuing an interrupted conversation*]: No sign at all of anyone having come from the outside. Their own rope. Now let's go up again and go over it piece by piece. [*They start upstairs.*] It would have to have been someone who knew just the—

[*Mrs. Peters sits down. The two women sit there not looking at one another, but as if peering into something and at the same time holding back. When they talk now, it is the manner of feeling their way over strange ground, as if afraid of what they are saying, but as if they cannot help saying it.*]

MRS. HALE: She liked the bird. She was going to bury it in that pretty box.

MRS. PETERS [*in a whisper*]: When I was a girl—my kitten—there was a boy took a hatchet, and before my eyes—and before I could get there—[*Covers her face an instant.*] If they hadn't held me back, I would have—[*Catches herself, looks upstairs where steps are heard, falters weakly.*]—hurt him.

MRS. HALE [*with a slow look around her*]: I wonder how it would seem never to have had any children around. [*Pause.*] No, Wright wouldn't like the bird—a thing that sang. She used to sing. He killed that, too.

MRS. PETERS [*moving uneasily*]: We don't know who killed the bird.

MRS. HALE: I knew John Wright.

MRS. PETERS: It was an awful thing was done in this house that night, Mrs. Hale. Killing a man while he slept, slipping a rope around his neck that choked the life out of him.

MRS. HALE: His neck. Choked the life out of him.

[*Her hand goes out and rests on the birdcage.*]

MRS. PETERS [*with a rising voice*]:   We don't know who killed him. We don't *know.*

MRS. HALE [*her own feeling not interrupted*]:   If there'd been years and years of nothing, then a bird to sing to you, it would be awful—still, after the bird was still.

MRS. PETERS [*something within her speaking*]:   I know what stillness is. When we homesteaded in Dakota, and my first baby died—after he was two years old, and me with no other then—

MRS. HALE [*moving*]:   How soon do you suppose they'll be through, looking for evidence?

MRS. PETERS: I know what stillness is. [*Pulling herself back.*] The law has got to punish crime, Mrs. Hale.

MRS. HALE [*not as if answering that*]:   I wish you'd seen Minnie Foster when she wore a white dress with blue ribbons and stood up there in the choir and sang. [*A look around the room.*] Oh, I *wish* I'd come over here once in a while! That was a crime! That was a crime! Who's going to punish that?

MRS. PETERS [*looking upstairs*]:   We mustn't—take on.

MRS. HALE: I might have known she needed help! I know how things can be—for women. I tell you, it's queer, Mrs. Peters. We live close together and we live far apart. We all go through the same things— it's all just a different kind of the same thing. [*Brushes her eyes, noticing the bottle of fruit, reaches out for it.*] If I was you, I wouldn't tell her her fruit was gone. Tell her it *ain't.* Tell her it's all right. Take this in to prove it to her. She—she may never know whether it was broke or not.

MRS. PETERS [*takes the bottle, looks about for something to wrap it in; takes petticoat from the clothes brought from the other room, very nervously begins winding this around the bottle. In a false voice*]:   My, it's a good thing the men couldn't hear us. Wouldn't they just laugh! Getting all stirred up over a little thing like a— dead canary. As if that could have anything to do with—with— wouldn't they *laugh!*

[*The men are heard coming downstairs.*]

MRS. HALE [*under her breath*]: Maybe they would—maybe they wouldn't.

COUNTY ATTORNEY: No, Peters, it's all perfectly clear except a reason for doing it. But you know juries when it comes to women. If there was some definite thing. Something to show—something to make a story about—a thing that would connect up with this strange way of doing it.

[*The women's eyes meet for an instant. Enter Hale from outer door.*]

HALE: Well, I've got the team around. Pretty cold out there.

COUNTY ATTORNEY: I'm going to stay here awhile by myself. [*To the Sheriff.*] You can send Frank out for me, can't you? I want to go over everything. I'm not satisfied that we can't do better.

SHERIFF: Do you want to see what Mrs. Peters is going to take in?

[*The Lawyer goes to the table, picks up the apron, laughs.*]

COUNTY ATTORNEY: Oh I guess they're not very dangerous things the ladies have picked up. [*Moves a few things about, disturbing the quilt pieces which cover the box. Steps back.*] No, Mrs. Peters doesn't need supervising. For that matter, a sheriff's wife is married to the law. Ever think of it that way, Mrs. Peters?

MRS. PETERS: Not—just that way.

SHERIFF [*chuckling*]: Married to the law. [*Moves toward the other room.*] I just want you to come in here a minute, George. We ought to take a look at these windows.

COUNTY ATTORNEY [*scoffingly*]: Oh, windows!

SHERIFF: We'll be right out, Mr. Hale.

[*Hale goes outside. The Sheriff follows the County Attorney into the other room. Then Mrs. Hale rises, hands tight together, looking intensely at Mrs. Peters, whose eyes take a slow turn, finally meeting, Mrs. Hale's. A moment Mrs. Hale holds her, then her own eyes point the way to where the box is concealed. Suddenly Mrs. Peters throws back quilt pieces and tries to put the box in the bag she is wearing. It is too big. She opens box, starts to take the bird out, cannot touch it, goes to pieces, stands there helpless. Sound of a knob turning in the other room. Mrs. Hale snatches the box and puts it in the pocket of her big coat. Enter County Attorney and Sheriff.*]

COUNTY ATTORNEY [*facetiously*]:   Well, Henry, at least we found out that she was not going to quilt it. She was going to—what is it you call it, ladies?

MRS. HALE [*her hand against her pocket*]:   We call it—knot it, Mr. Henderson.

CURTAIN

—1917

Questions: Reading, Responding, Arguing

1. Both the men and the women are doing investigations of the crime situation. Compare the two investigations. How are they similar? How are they different? Whose methodology works best?
2. Explain how Glaspell conveys the men's attitudes toward the women.
3. The character Hale says "women are used to worrying over trifles." What's meant by the title *Trifles*? Is there irony in Glaspell's use of the word *trifles*?
4. Glaspell chooses to tell the story of the death using dialogue, the past tense, and secondhand sources. What does she achieve by using this kind of approach?
5. Write a brief character comparison/contrast analysis of Mrs. Hale or Mrs. Peters. How is their character conveyed?
6. What is the symbolic significance of the bird?
7. Mrs. Wright isn't a present character yet we learn a lot about her. How do the various characters present information about Mrs. Wright? How do the different points of view see her? How does Glaspell use point of view for thematic purposes?
8. What is the significance of the quilt? What role does it play? Cite examples of its recurrence in the dialogue and make an argument about what it means.
9. Discuss the play as a commentary on women and men. What arguments can you make about how the play addresses the differences between men and women? The divisions between their lives? The relationships between them? How does Glaspell portray the relationship between the two women? How and why does the relationship develop? What do the women share?

Lorraine Hansberry (1930–1965)

A Raisin in the Sun*

CHARACTERS IN ORDER OF APPEARANCE

Ruth Younger *Walter's wife, about thirty*
Travis Younger *her son and Walter's*
Walter Lee Younger *(brother) Ruth's husband, mid-thirties*
Beneatha Younger *Walter's sister, about twenty*
Lena Younger *(Mama) mother of Walter and Beneatha*
Joseph Asagai *Nigerian, Beneatha's suito*
George Murchison *Beneatha's date, wealthy*
Karl Lindner *white, chairman of the Clybourne Park New Neighbors*
    Orientation Committee
Bobo *one of Walter's business partners*
Moving Men

The action of the play is set in Chicago's South Side, sometime between World War II and the present.

ACT I

SCENE I. FRIDAY MORNING

SCENE II. THE FOLLOWING MORNING

ACT II

SCENE I. LATER, THE SAME DAY

SCENE II. FRIDAY NIGHT, A FEW WEEKS LATER

SCENE III. MOVING DAY, ONE WEEK LATER

ACT III

An hour later

ACT I

SCENE I

The Younger living room would be a comfortable and well-ordered room if it were not for a number of indestructible contradictions to this state of being. Its furnishings are typical and undistinguished and their primary feature now is that they have clearly had to accommodate the living of too many people for too many years—and they are tired. Still, we can see that at some time, a time probably no longer remembered by the family (except perhaps for Mama*) the furnishings of this room were actually selected with care and love and even hope—and brought to this apartment and arranged with taste and pride.*

That was a long time ago. Now the once loved pattern of the couch upholstery has to fight to show itself from under acres of crocheted doilies and couch covers which have themselves finally come to be more important than the upholstery. And here a table or a chair has been moved to disguise the worn places in the carpet; but the carpet has fought back by showing its weariness, with depressing uniformity, elsewhere on its surface.

Weariness has, in fact, won in this room. Everything has been polished, washed, sat on, used, scrubbed too often. All pretenses but living itself have long since vanished from the very atmosphere of this room.

Moreover, a section of this room, for it is not really a room unto itself, though the landlord's lease would make it seem so, slopes backward to provide a small kitchen area, where the family prepares the meals that are eaten in the living room proper, which must also serve as dining room. The single window that has been provided for these "two" rooms is located in this kitchen area. The sole natural light the family may enjoy in the course of a day is only that which fights its way through this little window.

At left, a door leads to a bedroom which is shared by Mama *and her daughter,* Beneatha. *At right, opposite, is a second room (which in the beginning of the life of this apartment was probably a breakfast room) which serves as a bedroom for* Walter *and his wife,* Ruth.

Time: *Sometime between World War II and the present.*

Place: *Chicago's South Side.*

At rise: It is morning dark in the living room. Travis *is asleep on the make-down bed at center. An alarm clock sounds from within the bedroom at right, and presently* Ruth *enters from that room and closes the door behind her. She crosses sleepily toward the window. As she passes her sleeping son she reaches down and shakes him a little. At the window she raises the shade and a dusky South Side morning light comes in feebly. She fills a pot with water and puts it on to boil. She calls to the boy, between yawns, in a slightly muffled voice.*

Ruth *is about thirty. We can see that she was a pretty girl, even exceptionally so, but now it is apparent that life has been little that she expected, and disappointment has already begun to hang in her face. In a few years, before thirty-five even, she will be known among her people as a "settled woman."*

She crosses to her son and gives him a good, final, rousing shake.

RUTH: Come on now, boy, it's seven thirty! [*Her son sits up at last, in a stupor of sleepiness.*] I say hurry up, Travis! You ain't the only person in the world got to use a bathroom! [*The child, a sturdy, handsome little boy of ten or eleven, drags himself out of the bed and almost blindly takes his towels and "today's clothes" from drawers and a closet and goes out to the bathroom, which is in an outside hall and which is shared by another family or families on the same floor.* Ruth *crosses to the bedroom door at right and opens it and calls in to her husband.*] Walter Lee! . . . It's after seven thirty! Lemme see you do some waking up in there now! [*She waits.*] You better get up from there, man! It's after seven thirty I tell you. [*She waits again.*] All right, you just go ahead and lay there and next thing you know Travis be finished and Mr. Johnson'll be in there and you'll be fussing and cussing round here like a mad man! And be late too! [*She waits, at the end of patience.*] Walter Lee—it's time for you to get up! [*She waits another second and then starts to go into the bedroom, but is apparently satisfied that her husband has begun to get up. She stops, pulls the door to, and returns to the kitchen area. She wipes her face with a moist cloth and runs her fingers through her sleep-disheveled hair in a vain effort and ties an apron around her housecoat. The bedroom door at right opens and her husband stands in the doorway in his pajamas, which are rumpled and mismated. He is a lean, intense young man in his middle thirties, inclined to quick nervous* *movements and erratic speech habits—and always in his voice there is a quality of indictment.*]

WALTER: Is he out yet?

RUTH: What you mean *out?* He ain't hardly got in there good yet.

WALTER [*wandering in, still more oriented to sleep than to a new day*]: Well, what was you doing all that yelling for if I can't even get in there yet? [*stopping and thinking*] Check coming today?

RUTH: They *said* Saturday and this is just Friday and I hopes to God you ain't going to get up here first thing this morning and start talking to me 'bout no money—'cause I 'bout don't want to hear it.

WALTER: Something the matter with you this morning?

RUTH: No—I'm just sleepy as the devil. What kind of eggs you want?

WALTER: Not scrambled. [*Ruth starts to scramble eggs.*] Paper come? [*Ruth points impatiently to the rolled up* Tribune *on the table, and he gets it and spreads it out and vaguely reads the front page.*] Set off another bomb yesterday.

RUTH [*maximum indifference*]: Did they?

WALTER [*looking up*]: What's the matter with you?

RUTH: Ain't nothing the matter with me. And don't keep asking me that this morning.

WALTER: Ain't nobody bothering you. [*reading the news of the day absently again*] Say Colonel McCormick is sick.

RUTH [*affecting tea-party interest*]: Is he now? Poor thing.

WALTER [*Sighing and looking at his watch*]: Oh, me. [*He waits.*] Now what is that boy doing in that bathroom all this time? He just going to have to start getting up earlier. I can't be being late to work on account of him fooling around in there.

RUTH [*turning on him*]: Oh, no he ain't going to be getting up earlier no such thing! It ain't his fault that he can't get to bed no earlier nights 'cause he got a bunch of crazy good-for-nothing clowns sitting up running their mouths in what is supposed to be his bedroom after ten o'clock at night . . .

WALTER: That's what you mad about, ain't it? The things I want to talk about with my friends just couldn't be important in your mind, could they? [*He rises and finds a cigarette in her handbag on the table and crosses to the little window and looks out, smoking and deeply enjoying this first one.*]

RUTH [*almost matter of factly, a complaint too automatic to deserve emphasis*]: Why you always got to smoke before you eat in the morning?

WALTER [*at the window*]: Just look at 'em down there. . . . Running and racing to work. . . . [*He turns and faces his wife and watches her a moment at the stove, and then, suddenly.*] You look young this morning, baby.

RUTH [*indifferently*]: Yeah?

WALTER: Just for a second—stirring them eggs. It's gone now—just for a second it was—you looked real young again. [*then, drily*] It's gone now—you look like yourself again.

RUTH: Man, if you don't shut up and leave me alone.

WALTER [*looking out to the street again*]: First thing a man ought to learn in life is not to make love to no colored woman first thing in the morning. You all some evil people at eight o'clock in the morning. [Travis *appears in the hall doorway, almost fully dressed and quite wide awake now, his towels and pajamas across his shoulders. He opens the door and signals for his father to make the bathroom in a hurry.*]

TRAVIS [*watching the bathroom*]: Daddy, come on! [Walter *gets his bathroom utensils and flies out to the bathroom.*]

RUTH: Sit down and have your breakfast, Travis.

TRAVIS: Mama, this is Friday. [*gleefully*] Check coming tomorrow, huh?

RUTH: You get your mind off money and eat your breakfast.

TRAVIS [*eating*]: This is the morning we supposed to bring the fifty cents to school.

RUTH: Well, I ain't got no fifty cents this morning.

TRAVIS: Teacher say we have to.

RUTH: I don't care what teacher say. I ain't got it. Eat your breakfast, Travis.

TRAVIS: I *am* eating.

RUTH: Hush up now and just eat! [*The boy gives her an exasperated look for her lack of understanding, and eats grudgingly.*]

TRAVIS: You think Grandmama would have it?

RUTH: No! And I want you to stop asking your grandmother for money, you hear me?

TRAVIS [*outraged*]: Gaaaleee! I don't ask her, she just gimme it sometimes!

RUTH: Travis Willard Younger—I got too much on me this morning to be—

TRAVIS: Maybe Daddy—

RUTH: Travis! [*The boy hushes abruptly. They are both quiet and tense for several seconds.*]

TRAVIS [*presently*]:   Could I maybe go carry some groceries in front of the supermarket for a little while after school then?

RUTH: Just hush, I said. [*Travis jabs his spoon into his cereal bowl viciously, and rests his head in anger upon his fists.*] If you through eating, you can get over there and make up your bed. [*The boy obeys stiffly and crosses the room, almost mechanically, to the bed and more or less carefully folds the covering. He carries the bedding into his mother's room and returns with his books and cap.*]

TRAVIS *sulking and standing apart from her unnaturally*]:   I'm gone.

RUTH [*looking up from the stove to inspect him automatically*]: Come here. [*He crosses to her and she studies his head.*] If you don't take this comb and fix this here head, you better! [*Travis puts down his books with a great sigh of oppression, and crosses to the mirror. His mother mutters under her breath about his "stubbornness."*] 'Bout to march out of here with that head looking just like chickens slept in it! I just don't know where you get your stubborn ways . . . And get your jacket, too. Looks chilly out this morning.

TRAVIS [*with conspicuously brushed hair and jacket*]:   I'm gone.

RUTH: Get carfare and milk money—[*waving one finger*]—and not a single penny for no caps, you hear me?

TRAVIS [*with sullen politeness*]:   Yes'm. [*He turns in outrage to leave. His mother watches after him as in his frustration he approaches the door almost comically. When she speaks to him, her voice has become a very gentle tease.*]

RUTH [*mocking, as she thinks he would say it*]:   Oh, Mama makes me so mad sometimes, I don't know what to do! [*She waits and continues to his back as he stands stock-still in front of the door.*] I wouldn't kiss that woman good-bye for nothing in this world this morning! [*The boy finally turns around and rolls his eyes at her, knowing the mood has changed and he is vindicated; he does not, however, move toward her yet.*] Not for nothing in this world! [*She finally laughs aloud at him and holds out her arms to him and we see that it is a way between them, very old and practiced. He crosses to her and allows her to embrace him warmly but keeps his face fixed with masculine rigidity. She holds him back from her presently and looks at him and runs her fingers over the features of his face. With utter gentleness—*] Now—whose little old angry man are you?

TRAVIS [*The masculinity and gruffness start to fade at last.*]:   Aw gaalee—Mama . . .

RUTH [*mimicking*]: Aw—gaaaaalleeeee, Mama! [*She pushes him, with rough playfulness and finality, toward the door.*] Get on out of here or you going to be late.

TRAVIS [*in the face of love, new aggressiveness*]: Mama, could I *please* go carry groceries?

RUTH: Honey, it's starting to get so cold evenings.

WALTER [*coming in from the bedroom and drawing a make-believe gun from a make-believe holster and shooting at his son*]: What is it he wants to do?

RUTH: Go carry groceries after school at the supermarket.

WALTER: Well, let him go . . .

TRAVIS [*quickly, to the ally*]: I *have* to—she won't gimme the fifty cents . . .

WALTER [*to his wife only*]: Why not?

RUTH [*simply, and with flavor*]: 'Cause we don't have it.

WALTER [*to Ruth only*]: What you tell the boy things like that for? [*reaching down into his pants with a rather important gesture*] Here, son—[*He hands the boy the coin, but his eyes are directed to his wife's. Travis takes the money happily.*]

TRAVIS: Thanks, Daddy. [*He starts out. Ruth watches both of them with murder in her eyes. Walter stands and stares back at her with defiance, and suddenly reaches into his pocket again on an afterthought.*]

WALTER [*without even looking at his son, still staring hard at his wife*]: In fact, here's another fifty cents . . . Buy yourself some fruit today—or take a taxicab to school or something!

TRAVIS: Whoopee—[*He leaps up and clasps his father around the middle with his legs, and they face each other in mutual appreciation; slowly Walter Lee peeks around the boy to catch the violent rays from his wife's eyes and draws his head back as if shot.*]

WALTER: You better get down now—and get to school, man.

TRAVIS [*at the door*]: O.K. Good-bye. [*He exits.*]

WALTER [*after him, pointing with pride*]: That's *my* boy. [*She looks at him in disgust and turns back to her work.*] You know what I was thinking 'bout in the bathroom this morning?

RUTH: No.

WALTER: How come you always try to be so pleasant!

RUTH: What is there to be pleasant 'bout!

WALTER: You want to know what I was thinking 'bout in the bathroom or not!

RUTH: I know what you thinking 'bout.

WALTER [*ignoring her*]:   'Bout what me and Willy Harris was talking about last night.

RUTH [*immediately—a refrain*]:   Willy Harris is a good-for-nothing loudmouth.

WALTER: Anybody who talks to me has got to be a good-for-nothing loudmouth, ain't he? And what you know about who is just a good-for-nothing loudmouth? Charlie Atkins was just a "good-for-nothing loudmouth" too, wasn't he! When he wanted me to go in the dry-cleaning business with him. And now—he's grossing a hundred thousand a year. A hundred thousand dollars a year! You still call *him* a loudmouth!

RUTH [*bitterly*]:   Oh, Walter Lee . . . [*She folds her head on her arms over the table.*]

WALTER [*rising and coming to her and standing over her*]:   You tired, ain't you? Tired of everything. Me, the boy, the way we live—this beat-up hole—everything. Ain't you? [*She doesn't look up, doesn't answer.*] So tired—moaning and groaning all the time, but you wouldn't do nothing to help, would you? You couldn't be on my side that long for nothing, could you?

RUTH: Walter, please leave me alone.

WALTER: A man needs for a woman to back him up . . .

RUTH: Walter—

WALTER: Mama would listen to you. You know she listen to you more than she do me and Bennie. She think more of you. All you have to do is just sit down with her when you drinking your coffee one morning and talking 'bout things like you do and—[*He sits down beside her and demonstrates graphically what he thinks her methods and tone should be.*]—you just sip your coffee, see, and say easy like that you been thinking 'bout that deal Walter Lee is so interested in, 'bout the store and all, and sip some more coffee, like what you saying ain't really that important to you—And the next thing you know, she be listening good and asking you questions and when I come home—I can tell her the details. This ain't no fly-by-night proposition, baby. I mean we figured it out, me and Willy and Bobo.

RUTH [*with a frown*]:   Bobo?

WALTER: Yeah. You see, this little liquor store we got in mind cost seventy-five thousand and we figured the initial investment on the place be 'bout thirty thousand, see. That be ten thousand each. Course, there's a couple of hundred you got to pay so's you don't spend your life just waiting for them clowns to let your license get approved—

RUTH: You mean graft?

WALTER [*frowning impatiently*]: Don't call it that. See there, that just goes to show you what women understand about the world. Baby, don't *nothing* happen for you in this world 'less you pay *somebody* off!

RUTH: Walter, leave me alone! [*She raises her head and stares at him vigorously—then says, more quietly.*] Eat your eggs, they gonna be cold.

WALTER [*straightening up from her and looking off*]: That's it. There you are. Man say to his woman: I got me a dream. His woman say: Eat your eggs. [*sadly, but gaining in power*] Man say: I got to take hold of this here world, baby! And a woman will say: Eat your eggs and go to work. [*passionately now*] Man say: I got to change my life, I'm choking to death, baby! And his woman say—[*in utter anguish as he brings his fists down on his thighs*]—Your eggs is getting cold!

RUTH [*softly*]: Walter, that ain't none of our money.

WALTER [*not listening at all or even looking at her*]: This morning, I was lookin' in the mirror and thinking about it . . . I'm thirty-five years old; I been married eleven years and I got a boy who sleeps in the living room—[*very, very quietly*]—and all I got to give him is stories about how rich white people live . . .

RUTH: Eat your eggs, Walter.

WALTER: *Damn my eggs . . . damn all the eggs that ever was!*

RUTH: Then go to work.

WALTER [*looking up at her*]: See—I'm trying to talk to you 'bout myself—[*shaking his head with the repetition*]—and all you can say is eat them eggs and go to work.

RUTH [*wearily*]: Honey, you never say nothing new. I listen to you every day, every night and every morning, and you never say nothing new. [*shrugging*] So you would rather *be* Mr. Arnold than be his chauffeur. So—I would *rather* be living in Buckingham Palace.

WALTER: That is just what is wrong with the colored woman in this world . . . Don't understand about building their men up and making 'em feel like they somebody. Like they can do something.

RUTH [*drily, but to hurt*]: There *are* colored men who do things.

WALTER: No thanks to the colored woman.

RUTH: Well, being a colored woman, I guess I can't help myself none. [*She rises and gets the ironing board and sets it up and attacks a huge pile of rough-dried clothes, sprinkling them in preparation for the ironing and then rolling them into tight fat balls.*]

WALTER [*mumbling*]:   We one group of men tied to a race of women with small minds. [*his sister Beneatha enters. She is about twenty, as slim and intense as her brother. She is not as pretty as her sister-in-law, but her lean, almost intellectual face has a handsomeness of its own. She wears a bright-red flannel nightie, and her thick hair stands wildly about her head. Her speech is a mixture of many things; it is different from the rest of the family's insofar as education has permeated her sense of English—and perhaps the Midwest rather than the South has finally—at last—won out in her inflection; but not altogether, because over all of it is a soft slurring and transformed use of vowels which is the decided influence of the South Side. She passes through the room without looking at either Ruth or Walter and goes to the outside door and looks, a little blindly, out to the bathroom. She sees that it has been lost to the Johnsons. She closes the door with a sleepy vengeance and crosses to the table and sits down a little defeated.*]

BENEATHA: I am going to start timing those people.

WALTER: You should get up earlier.

BENEATHA [*Her face in her hands. She is still fighting the urge to go back to bed*]:   Really—would you suggest dawn? Where's the paper?

WALTER [*pushing the paper across the table to her as he studies her almost clinically, as though he has never seen her before*]:   You a horrible-looking chick at this hour.

BENEATHA [*drily*]:   Good morning, everybody.

WALTER [*senselessly*]:   How is school coming?

BENEATHA [*in the same spirit*]:   Lovely, Lovely. And you know, biology is the greatest. [*looking up at him*] I dissected something that looked just like you yesterday.

WALTER: I just wondered if you've made up your mind and everything.

BENEATHA [*gaining in sharpness and impatience*]:   And what did I answer yesterday morning—and the day before that?

RUTH [*from the ironing board, like someone disinterested and old*]:   Don't be so nasty, Bennie.

BENEATHA [*still to her brother*]:   And the day before that and the day before that!

WALTER [*defensively*]:   I'm interested in you. Something wrong with that? Ain't many girls who decide—

WALTER AND BENEATHA [*in unison*]: —"to be a doctor." [*silence*]

WALTER: Have we figured out yet just exactly how much medical school is going to cost?

RUTH: Walter Lee, why don't you leave that girl alone and get out of here to work?

BENEATHA [*exits to the bathroom and bangs on the door*]: Come on out of there, please! [*She comes back into the room.*]

WALTER [*looking at his sister intently*]: You know the check is coming tomorrow.

BENEATHA [*turning on him with a sharpness all her own*]: That money belongs to Mama, Walter, and it's for her to decide how she wants to use it. I don't care if she wants to buy a house or a rocket ship or just nail it up somewhere and look at it. It's hers. Not ours—hers.

WALTER [*bitterly*]: Now ain't that fine! You just got your mother's interest at heart, ain't you, girl? You such a nice girl—but if Mama got that money she can always take a few thousand and help you through school too—can't she?

BENEATHA: I have never asked anyone around here to do anything for me!

WALTER: No! And the line between asking and just accepting when the time comes is big and wide—ain't it!

BENEATHA [*with fury*]: What do you want from me, Brother—that I quit school or just drop dead, which!

WALTER: I don't want nothing but for you to stop acting holy 'round here. Me and Ruth done made some sacrifices for you—why can't you do something for the family?

RUTH: Walter, don't be dragging me in it.

WALTER: You are in it—Don't you get up and go work in somebody's kitchen for the last three years to help put clothes on her back?

RUTH: Oh, Walter—that's not fair . . .

WALTER: It ain't that nobody expects you to get on your knees and say thank you, Brother; thank you, Ruth; thank you, Mama—and thank you, Travis, for wearing the same pair of shoes for two semesters—

BENEATHA [*dropping to her knees*]: Well—I do—all right?—thank everybody . . . and forgive me for ever wanting to be anything at all . . . forgive me, forgive me!

RUTH: Please stop it! Your mama'll hear you.

WALTER: Who the hell told you you had to be a doctor? If you so crazy 'bout messing 'round with sick people—then go be a nurse like other women—or just get married and be quiet . . .

BENEATHA: Well—you finally got it said . . . It took you three years but you finally got it said. Walter, give up; leave me alone—it's Mama's money.

WALTER: *He was my father, too!*

BENEATHA: So what? He was mine, too—and Travis' grandfather—but the insurance money belongs to Mama. Picking on me is not going to make her give it to you to invest in any liquor stores—[*under breath, dropping into a chair*]—and I for one say, God bless Mama for that!

WALTER [*To Ruth*]: See—did you hear? Did you hear!

RUTH: Honey, please go to work.

WALTER: Nobody in this house is ever going to understand me.

BENEATHA: Because you're a nut.

WALTER: Who's a nut?

BENEATHA: You—you are a nut. Thee is mad, boy.

WALTER [*looking at his wife and his sister from the door, very sadly*]: The world's most backward race of people, and that's a fact.

BENEATHA [*turning slowly in her chair*]: And then there are all those prophets who would lead us out of the wilderness—[Walter *slams out of the house.*]—into the swamps!

RUTH: Bennie, why you always gotta be pickin' on your brother? Can't you be a little sweeter sometimes? [*Door opens. Walter walks in.*]

WALTER [*to Ruth*]: I need some money for carfare.

RUTH [*looks at him, then warms; teasing, but tenderly*]: Fifty cents? [*She goes to her bag and gets money.*] Here, take a taxi. [*Walter exits.* Mama *enters. She is a woman in her early sixties, full-bodied and strong. She is one of those women of a certain grace and beauty who wear it so unobtrusively that it takes a while to notice. Her dark-brown face is surrounded by the total whiteness of her hair, and, being a woman who has adjusted to many things in life and overcome many more, her face is full of strength. She has, we can see, wit and faith of a kind that keep her eyes lit and full of interest and expectancy. She is, in a word, a beautiful woman. Her bearing is perhaps most like the noble bearing of the women of the Hereros of Southwest Africa—rather as if she imagines that as she walks she still bears a basket or a vessel upon her head. Her speech, on the other hand, is as careless as her carriage is precise—she is inclined to slur everything—but her voice is perhaps not so much quiet as simply soft.*]

MAMA: Who that 'round here slamming doors at this hour? [*She crosses through the room, goes to the window, opens it, and brings in a feeble little plant growing doggedly in a small pot on the window sill. She feels the dirt and puts in back out.*]

RUTH: That was Walter Lee. He and Bennie was at it again.

MAMA: My children and they tempers. Lord, if this little old plant don't get more sun that it's been getting it ain't never going to see spring again. [*She turns from the window.*] What's the matter with you this morning, Ruth? You looks right peaked. You aiming to iron all them things? Leave some for me. I'll get to 'em this afternoon. Bennie honey, it's too drafty for you to be sitting 'round half dressed. Where's your robe?

BENEATHA: In the cleaners.

MAMA: Well, go get mine and put it on.

BENEATHA: I'm not cold, Mama, honest.

MAMA: I know—but you so thin . . .

BENEATHA [*irritably*]: Mama, I'm not cold.

MAMA [*seeing the make-down bed as* Travis *has left it*]: Lord have mercy, look at that poor bed. Bless his heart—he tries, don't he? [*She moves to the bed* Travis *has sloppily made up.*]

RUTH: No—he don't half try at all 'cause he knows you going to come along behind him and fix everything. That's just how come he don't know how to do nothing right now—you done spoiled that boy so.

MAMA: Well—he's a little boy. Ain't supposed to know 'bout housekeeping. My baby, that's what he is. What you fix for his breakfast this morning?

RUTH [*angrily*]: I feed my son, Lena!

MAMA: I ain't meddling—[*under breath, busy-bodyish*]: I just noticed all last week he had cold cereal, and when it starts getting this chilly in the fall a child ought to have some hot grits or something when he goes out in the cold—

RUTH [*furious*]: I gave him hot oats—is that all right!

MAMA: I ain't meddling. [*pause*] Put a lot of nice butter on it? [*Ruth shoots her an angry look and does not reply.*] He likes lots of butter.

RUTH [*exasperated*]: Lena—

MAMA [*To* Beneatha: Mama *is inclined to wander conversationally sometimes*]: What was you and your brother fussing 'bout this morning?

BENEATHA: It's not important, Mama. [*She gets up and goes to look out at the bathroom, which is apparently free, and she picks up her towels and rushes out.*]

MAMA: What was they fighting about?

RUTH: Now you know as well as I do.

MAMA [*shaking her head*]: Brother still worrying hisself sick about that money?

RUTH: You know he is.

MAMA: You had breakfast?

RUTH: Some coffee.

MAMA: Girl, you better start eating and looking after yourself better. You almost thin as Travis.

RUTH: Lena—

MAMA: Uh-hunh?

RUTH: What are you going to do with it?

MAMA: Now don't you start, child. It's too early in the morning to be talking about money. It ain't Christian.

RUTH: It's just that he got his heart set on that store—

MAMA: You mean that liquor store that Willy Harris want him to invest in?

RUTH: Yes—

MAMA: We ain't no business people, Ruth. We just plain working folks.

RUTH: Ain't nobody business people till they go into business. Walter Lee say colored people ain't never going to start getting ahead till they start gambling on some different kinds of things in the world—investments and things.

MAMA: What done got into you, girl? Walter Lee done finally sold you on investing.

RUTH: No. Mama, something is happening between Walter and me. I don't know what it is—but he needs something—something I can't give him any more. He needs this chance, Lena.

MAMA [*frowning deeply*]: But liquor, honey—

RUTH: Well—like Walter say—I spec people going to always be drinking themselves some liquor.

MAMA: Well—whether they drinks it or not ain't none of my business. But whether I go into business selling it to 'em is, and I don't want that on my ledger this late in life. [*stopping suddenly and studying her daughter-in-law*] Ruth Younger, what's the matter with you today? You look like you could fall over right there.

RUTH: I'm tired.

MAMA: Then you better stay home from work today.

RUTH: I can't stay home. She'd be calling up the agency and scream-ing at them, "My girl didn't come in today—send me somebody! My girl didn't come in!" Oh, she just have a fit . . .

MAMA: Well, let her have it. I'll just call her up and say you got the flu—

RUTH [*laughing*]: Why the flu?

MAMA: 'Cause it sounds respectable to 'em. Something white people get, too. They know 'bout the flu. Otherwise they think you been cut up or something when you tell 'em you sick.

RUTH: I got to go in. We need the money.

MAMA: Somebody would of thought my children done all but starved to death the way they talk about money here late. Child, we got a great big old check coming tomorrow.

RUTH [*sincerely, but also self-righteously*]: Now that's your money. It ain't got nothing to do with me. We all feel like that—Walter and Bennie and me—even Travis.

MAMA [*thoughtfully, and suddenly very far away*]: Ten thousand dollars—

RUTH: Sure is wonderful.

MAMA: Ten thousand dollars.

RUTH: You know what you should do, Miss Lena? You should take yourself a trip somewhere. To Europe or South America or some-place—

MAMA [*throwing up her hands at the thought*]: Oh, child!

RUTH: I'm serious. Just pack up and leave! Go on away and enjoy yourself some. Forget about the family and have yourself a ball for once in your life—

MAMA [*drily*]: You sound like I'm just about ready to die. Who'd go with me? What I look like wandering 'round Europe by myself?

RUTH: Shoot—these here rich white women do it all the time. They don't think nothing of packing up they suitcases and piling on one of them big steamships and—swoosh!—they gone, child.

MAMA: Something always told me I wasn't no rich white woman.

RUTH: Well—what are you going to do with it then?

MAMA: I ain't rightly decided. [*Thinking. She speaks now with em-phasis.*] Some of it got to be put away for Beneatha and her schoolin'—and ain't nothing going to touch that part of it. Nothing. [*She waits several seconds, trying to make up her mind about something, and looks at Ruth little tentatively before going on.*] Been thinking that we maybe could meet the notes on a little old two-story somewhere, with a yard where Travis could play in the summertime, if we use part of the insurance for a down payment and everybody kind of pitch in. I could maybe take on a little day work again, few days a week—

RUTH [*studying her mother-in-law furtively and concentrating on her ironing, anxious to encourage without seeming to*]: Well, Lord knows, we've put enough rent into this here rat trap to pay for four houses by now . . .

MAMA [*looking up at the words "rat trap" and then looking around and leaning back and sighing—in a suddenly reflective mood—*]: "Rat trap"—yes, that's all it is. [*smiling*] I remember just as well the day me and Big Walter moved in here. Hadn't been married but two weeks and wasn't planning on living here no more than a year. [*She shakes her head at the dissolved dream.*] We was going to set away, little by little, don't you know, and buy a little place out in Morgan Park. We had even picked out the house. [*chuckling a little*] Looks right dumpy today. But Lord, child, you should know all the dreams I had 'bout buying that house and fixing it up and making me a little garden in the back—[*She waits and stops smiling.*] And didn't none of it happen. [*dropping her hands in a futile gesture*]

RUTH [*keeps her head down, ironing*]: Yes, life can be a barrel of disappointments, sometimes.

MAMA: Honey, Big Walter would come in here some nights back then and slump down on that couch there and just look at the rug, and look at me and look at the rug and then back at me—and I'd know he was down then . . . really down. [*After a second very long and thoughtful pause; she is seeing back to times that only she can see.*] And then, Lord, when I lost that baby—little Claude—I almost thought I was going to lose Big Walter too. Oh, that man grieved hisself! He was one man to love his children.

RUTH: Ain't nothin' can tear at you like losin' your baby.

MAMA: I guess that's how come that man finally worked hisself to death like he done. Likely he was fighting his own war with this here world that took his baby from him.

RUTH: He sure was a fine man, all right. I always liked Mr. Younger.

MAMA: Crazy 'bout his children! God knows there was plenty wrong with Walter Younger—hard-headed, mean, kind of wild with women—plenty wrong with him. But he sure loved his children. Always wanted them to have something—be something. That's where Brother gets all these notions, I reckon. Big Walter used to say, he'd get right wet in the eyes sometimes, lean his head back with the water standing in his eyes and say, "Seem like God didn't see fit to give the black man nothing but dreams—but He did give us children to make them dreams seem worth while." [*She smiles.*] He could talk like that, don't you know.

RUTH: Yes, he sure could. He was a good man, Mr. Younger.

MAMA: Yes, a fine man—just couldn't never catch up with his dreams, that's all. [Beneatha *comes in, brushing her hair and looking up to the ceiling, where the sound of a vacuum cleaner has started up.*]

BENEATHA: What could be so dirty on that woman's rugs that she has to vacuum them every single day?

RUTH: I wish certain young women 'round here who I could name would take inspiration about certain rugs in a certain apartment I could also mention.

BENEATHA [*shrugging*]: How much cleaning can a house need, for Christ's sakes?

MAMA [*not liking the Lord's name used thus*]: Bennie!

RUTH: Just listen to her—just listen!

BENEATHA: Oh, God!

MAMA: If you use the Lord's name just one more time—

BENEATHA [*a bit of a whine*]: Oh, Mama—

RUTH: Fresh—just fresh as salt, this girl!

BENEATHA [*drily*]: Well—if the salt loses its savor—

MAMA: Now that will do. I just ain't going to have you 'round here reciting the scriptures in vain—you hear me?

BENEATHA: How did I manage to get on everybody's wrong side by just walking into a room?

RUTH: If you weren't so fresh—

BENEATHA: Ruth, I'm twenty years old.

MAMA: What time you be home from school today?

BENEATHA: Kind of late. [*with enthusiasm*] Madeline is going to start my guitar lessons today. [Mama *and* Ruth *look up with the same expression.*]

MAMA: Your *what* kind of lessons?

BENEATHA: Guitar.

RUTH: Oh, Father!

MAMA: How come you done taken it in your mind to learn to play the guitar?

BENEATHA: I just want to, that's all.

MAMA [*smiling*]: Lord, child, don't you know what to do with your-self? How long it going to be before you get tired of this now—like you got tired of that little play-acting group you joined last year? [*looking at* Ruth] And what was it the year before that?

RUTH: The horseback-riding club for which she bought that fifty-five-dollar riding habit that's been hanging in the closet ever since!

MAMA [*to* Beneatha]: Why you got to flit so from one thing to an-other, baby?

BENEATHA [*sharply*]: I just want to learn to play the guitar. Is there anything wrong with that?

MAMA: Ain't nobody trying to stop you. I just wonders sometimes why you has to flit so from one thing to another all the time. You ain't never done nothing with all that camera equipment you brought home—

BENEATHA: I don't flit! I—I experiment with different forms of ex-pression—

RUTH: Like riding a horse?

BENEATHA: —People have to express themselves one way or another.

MAMA: What is it you want to express?

BENEATHA [*angrily*]: Me! [Mama *and* Ruth *look at each other and burst into raucous laughter*] Don't worry—I don't expect you to understand.

MAMA [*to change the subject*]: Who you going out with tomorrow night?

BENEATHA [*with displeasure*]: George Murchison again.

MAMA [*pleased*]: Oh—you getting a little sweet on him?

RUTH: You ask me, this child ain't sweet on nobody but herself—[*under breath*] Express herself? [*They laugh.*]

BENEATHA: Oh—I like George all right, Mama. I mean I like him enough to go out with him and stuff, but—

RUTH [*for devilment*]: What does and stuff mean?

BENEATHA: Mind your own business.

MAMA: Stop picking at her now, Ruth. [*a thoughtful pause, and then a suspicious sudden look at her daughter as she turns in her chair for emphasis*] What does it mean?

BENEATHA [*wearily*]: Oh, I just mean I couldn't ever really be seri-ous about George. He's—he's so shallow.

RUTH: Shallow—what do you mean he's shallow? He's *Rich!*

MAMA: Hush, Ruth.

BENEATHA: I know he's rich. He knows he's rich, too.

RUTH: Well—what other qualities a man got to have to satisfy you, little girl?

BENEATHA: You wouldn't even begin to understand. Anybody who married Walter could not possibly understand.

MAMA [*outraged*]: What kind of way is that to talk about your brother?

BENEATHA: Brother is a flip—let's face it.

MAMA [*to Ruth, helplessly*]: What's a flip?

RUTH [*glad to add kindling*]: She's saying he's crazy.

BENEATHA: Not crazy. Brother isn't really crazy yet—he—he's an elaborate neurotic.

MAMA: Hush your mouth!

BENEATHA: As for George. Well. George looks good—he's got a beautiful car and he takes me to nice places and, as my sister-in-law says, he is probably the richest boy I will ever get to know and I even like him sometimes—but if the Youngers are sitting around waiting to see if their little Bennie is going to tie up the family with the Murchisons, they are wasting their time.

RUTH: You mean you wouldn't marry George Murchison if he asked you someday? That pretty, rich thing? Honey, I knew you was odd—

BENEATHA: No I would not marry him if all I felt for him was what I feel now. Besides, George's family wouldn't really like it.

MAMA: Why not?

BENEATHA: Oh, Mama—The Murchisons are honest-to-God-real-*live*-rich colored people, and the only people in the world who are more snobbish than rich white people are rich colored people. I thought everybody knew that. I've met Mrs. Murchison. She's a scene!

MAMA: You must not dislike people 'cause they well off, honey.

BENEATHA: Why not? It makes just as much sense as disliking people 'cause they are poor, and lots of people do that.

RUTH [*a wisdom-of-the-ages manner. To* Mama]: Well, she'll get over some of this—

BENEATHA: Get over it? What are you talking about, Ruth? Listen, I'm going to be a doctor. I'm not worried about who I'm going to marry yet—if I ever get married.

MAMA AND RUTH: *If!*

MAMA: Now, Bennie—

BENEATHA: Oh, I probably will . . . but first I'm going to be a doctor, and George, for one, still thinks that's pretty funny. I couldn't be bothered with that. I am going to be a doctor and everybody around here better understand that!

MAMA [*kindly*]: 'Course you going to be a doctor, honey, God willing.

BENEATHA [*drily*]: God hasn't got a thing to do with it.

MAMA: Beneatha—that just wasn't necessary.

BENEATHA: Well—neither is God. I get sick of hearing about God.

MAMA: Beneatha!

BENEATHA: I mean it! I'm just tired of hearing about God all the time. What has He got to do with anything? Does he pay tuition?

MAMA: You 'bout to get your fresh little jaw slapped!

RUTH: That's just what she needs, all right!

BENEATHA: Why? Why can't I say what I want to around here, like everybody else?

MAMA: It don't sound nice for a young girl to say things like that— you wasn't brought up that way. Me and your father went to trouble to get you and Brother to church every Sunday.

BENEATHA: Mama, you don't understand. It's all a matter of ideas, and God is just one idea I don't accept. It's not important. I am not going out and be immoral or commit crimes because I don't believe in God. I don't even think about it. It's just that I get tired of Him getting credit for all the things the human race achieves through its own stubborn effort. There simply is no blasted God—there is only man and it is he who makes miracles! [Mama *absorbs this speech, studies her daughter and rises slowly and crosses to* Beneatha *and slaps her powerfully across the face. After, there is only silence and the daughter drops her eyes from her mother's face, and* Mama *is very tall before her.*]

MAMA: Now—you say after me, in my mother's house there is still God. [*There is a long pause and* Beneatha *stares at the floor wordlessly.* Mama *repeats the phrase with precision and cool emotion.*] In my mother's house there is still God.

BENEATHA: In my mother's house there is still God. [*a long pause*]

MAMA [*Walking away from Beneatha, too disturbed for triumphant posture. Stopping and turning back to her daughter.*]: There are some ideas we ain't going to have in this house. Not long as I am at the head of this family.

BENEATHA: Yes, ma'am. [Mama *walks out of the room.*]

RUTH [*almost gently, with profound understanding*]: You think you a woman, Bennie—but you still a little girl. What you did was childish—so you got treated like a child.

BENEATHA: I see. [*quietly*] I also see that everybody thinks it's all right for Mama to be a tyrant. But all the tyranny in the world will never put a God in the heavens! [*She picks up her books and goes out.*]

RUTH [*goes to* Mama's *door*]:   She said she was sorry.

MAMA [*coming out, going to her plant*]:   They frightens me, Ruth. My children.

RUTH: You got good children, Lena. They just a little off some-times—but they're good.

MAMA: No—There's something come down between me and them that don't let us understand each other and I don't know what it is. One done almost lost his mind thinking 'bout money all the time and the other done commence to talk about things I can't seem to understand in no form or fashion. What is it that's changing, Ruth?

RUTH [*soothingly, older than her years*]:   Now . . . you taking it all too seriously. You just got strong-willed children and it takes a strong woman like you to keep 'em in hand.

MAMA [*looking at her plant and sprinkling a little water on it*]:   They spirited all right, my children. Got to admit they got spirit—Bennie and Walter. Like this little old plant that ain't never had enough sunshine or nothing—and look at it . . . [*She has her back to* Ruth, *who has had to stop ironing and lean against something and put the back of her hand to her forehead.*]

RUTH [*trying to keep* Mama *from noticing*]:   You . . . sure . . . loves that little old thing, don't you? . . .

MAMA: Well, I always wanted me a garden like I used to see some-times at the back of the houses down home. This plant is close as I ever got to having one. [*She looks out of the window as she re-places the plant.*] Lord, ain't nothing as dreary as the view from this window on a dreary day, is there? Why ain't you singing this morning, Ruth? Sing that "No Ways Tired." That song always lifts me up so—[*She turns at last to see that* Ruth *has slipped quietly into a chair, in a state of semiconsciousness.*] Ruth! Ruth honey—what's the matter with you . . . Ruth!

CURTAIN

SCENE II

It is the following morning; a Saturday morning, and house cleaning is in progress at the Youngers. Furniture has been shoved hither and yon and Mama is giving the kitchen-area walls a washing down. Beneatha, in dungarees, with a handkerchief tied around her face, is spraying in-secticide into the cracks in the walls. As they work, the radio is on and a South Side disk jockey program is inappropriately filling the house with a rather exotic saxophone blues. Travis, *the sole idle one, is leaning on his arms, looking out of the window.*

TRAVIS: Grandmama, that stuff Bennie is using smells awful. Can I go downstairs, please?

MAMA: Did you get all them chores done already? I ain't seen you doing much.

TRAVIS: Yes'm—finished early. Where did Mama go this morning?

MAMA [*looking at* Beneatha]: She had to go on a little errand.

TRAVIS: Where?

MAMA: To tend to her business.

TRAVIS: Can I go outside then?

MAMA: Oh, I guess so. You better stay right in front of the house, though . . . and keep a good lookout for the postman.

TRAVIS: Yes'm. [*He starts out and decides to give his* Aunt Beneatha *a good swat on the legs as he passes her.*] Leave them poor little old cockroaches alone, they ain't bothering you none. [*He runs as she swings the spray gun at him both viciously and playfully.* Walter *enters from the bedroom and goes to the phone.*]

MAMA: Look out there, girl, before you be spilling some of that stuff on that child!

TRAVIS [*teasing*]: That's right—look out now! [*He exits.*]

BENEATHA [*drily*]: I can't imagine that it would hurt him—it has never hurt the roaches.

MAMA: Well, little boys' hides ain't as tough as South Side roaches.

WALTER [*into phone*]: Hello—Let me talk to Willy Harris.

MAMA: You better get over there behind the bureau. I seen one marching out of there like Napoleon yesterday.

WALTER: Hello, Willy? It ain't come yet. It'll be here in a few minutes. Did the lawyer give you the papers?

BENEATHA: There's really only one way to get rid of them, Mama—

MAMA: How?

BENEATHA: Set fire to this building.

WALTER: Good. Good. I'll be right over.

BENEATHA: Where did Ruth go, Walter?

WALTER: I don't know. [*He exits abruptly.*]

BENEATHA: Mama, where did Ruth go?

MAMA [*looking at her with meaning*]: To the doctor, I think.

BENEATHA: The doctor? What's the matter? [*They exchange glances.*] You don't think—

MAMA [*with her sense of drama*]: Now I ain't saying what I think. But I ain't never been wrong 'bout a woman neither. [*The phone rings.*]

BENEATHA [*at the phone*]: Hay-lo ... [*pause, and a moment of recognition*] Well—when did you get back! ... And how was it? ... Of course I've missed you—in my way ... This morning? No ... house cleaning and all that and Mama hates it if I let people come over when the house is like this ... You *have?* Well, that's different ... What is it—Oh, what the hell, come on over ... Right, see you then.

[*She hangs up.*]

MAMA [*who has listened vigorously, as is her habit*]: Who is that you inviting over here with this house looking like this? You ain't got the pride you was born with!

BENEATHA: Asagai doesn't care how houses look, Mama—he's an intellectual.

MAMA: *Who?*

BENEATHA: Asagai—Joseph Asagai. He's an African boy I met on campus. He's been studying in Canada all summer.

MAMA: What's his name?

BENEATHA: Asagai, Joseph. Ah-sah-guy ... He's from Nigeria.

MAMA: Oh, that's the little country that was founded by slaves way back ...

BENEATHA: No, Mama—that's Liberia.

MAMA: I don't think I never met no African before.

BENEATHA: Well, do me a favor and don't ask him a whole lot of ignorant questions about Africans. I mean, do they wear clothes and all that—

MAMA: Well, now, I guess if you think we so ignorant 'round here maybe you shouldn't bring your friends here—

BENEATHA: It's just that people ask such crazy things. All anyone seems to know about when it comes to Africa is Tarzan—

MAMA [*indignantly*]: Why should I know anything about Africa?

BENEATHA: Why do you give money at church for the missionary work?

MAMA: Well, that's to help save people.

BENEATHA: You mean save them from *heathenism*—

MAMA [*innocently*]: Yes.

BENEATHA: I'm afraid they need more salvation from the British and the French. [Ruth *comes in forlornly and pulls off her coat with dejection. They both turn to look at her.*]

RUTH [*Dispiritedly*]: Well, I guess from all the happy faces—everybody knows.

BENEATHA: You pregnant?

MAMA: Lord have mercy, I sure hope it's a little old girl. Travis ought to have a sister. [Beneatha *and* Ruth *give her a hopeless look for this grandmotherly enthusiasm*]

BENEATHA: How far along are you?

RUTH: Two months.

BENEATHA: Did you mean to? I mean did you plan it or was it an accident?

MAMA: What do you know about planning or not planning?

BENEATHA: Oh, Mama.

RUTH [*wearily*]: She's twenty years old, Lena.

BENEATHA: Did you plan it, Ruth?

RUTH: Mind your own business.

BENEATHA: It is my business—where is he going to live, on the roof? [*There is silence following the remark as the three women react to the sense of it.*] Gee—I didn't mean that, Ruth, honest. Gee, I don't feel like that at all. I—I think it is wonderful.

RUTH [*dully*]: Wonderful.

BENEATHA: Yes—really.

MAMA [*looking at* Ruth, *worried*]: Doctor say everything going to be all right?

RUTH [*far away*]: Yes—she says everything is going to be fine . . .

MAMA [*Immediately suspicious*]: "She"—What doctor you went to? [Ruth *folds, over, near hysteria*]

MAMA [*worriedly hovering over* Ruth]: Ruth, honey—what's the matter with you—you sick? [Ruth *has her fists clenched on her thighs and is fighting hard to suppress a scream that seems to be rising in her.*]

BENEATHA: What's the matter with her, Mama?

MAMA [*working her fingers in* Ruth's *shoulder to relax her*]: She be all right. Women gets right depressed sometimes when they get her way. [*speaking softly, expertly, rapidly*] Now you just relax. That's right . . . just lean back, don't think 'bout nothing at all . . . nothing at all—

RUTH: I'm all right . . . [*The glassy-eyed look melts and then she collapses into a fit of heavy sobbing. The bell rings.*]

BENEATHA: Oh, my God—that must be Asagai.

MAMA [*to* Ruth]: Come on now, honey. You need to lie down and rest awhile . . . then have some nice hot food. [*They exit,* Ruth's *weight on her mother-in-law.* Beneatha, *herself profoundly disturbed, opens the door to admit a rather dramatic-looking young man with a large package.*]

ASAGAI: Hello, Alaiyo—

BENEATHA [*holding the door open and regarding him with pleasure*]: Hello . . . [*long pause*] Well—come in. And please excuse everything. My mother was very upset about my letting anyone come here with the place like this.

ASAGAI [*coming into the room*]: You look disturbed too . . . Is something wrong?

BENEATHA [*still at the door, absently*]: Yes . . . we've all got acute ghetto-itus. [*She smiles and comes toward him, finding a cigarette and sitting.*] So—sit down! How was Canada?

ASAGAI [*a sophisticate*]: Canadian.

BENEATHA [*looking at him*]: I'm very glad you are back.

ASAGAI [*looking back at her in turn*]: Are you really?

BENEATHA: Yes—very.

ASAGAI: Why—you were quite glad when I went away. What happened?

BENEATHA: You went away.

ASAGAI: Ahhhhhhhh.

BENEATHA: Before—you wanted to be so serious before there was time.

ASAGAI: How much time must there be before one knows what one feels?

BENEATHA [*Stalling this particular conversation. Her hands pressed together, in a deliberately childish gesture*]: What did you bring me?

ASAGAI [*handing her the package*]: Open it and see.

BENEATHA [*eagerly opening the package and drawing out some records and the colorful robes of a Nigerian woman*]: Oh, Asagai! . . . You got them for me! . . . How beautiful . . . and the records too! [*She lifts out the robes and runs to the mirror with them and holds the drapery up in front of herself.*]

ASAGAI [*coming to her at the mirror*]: I shall have to teach you how to drape it properly. [*He flings the material about her for the moment and stands back to look at her.*] Ah—*Oh-pay-gay-day, oh-gbah-mu-shay.* [*a Yoruba exclamation for admiration*] You wear it well . . . very well . . . mutilated hair and all.

BENEATHA [*turning suddenly*]: My hair—what's wrong with my hair?

ASAGAI [*shrugging*]: Were you born with it like that?

BENEATHA [*reaching up to touch it*]: No . . . of course not. [*She looks back to the mirror, disturbed.*]

ASAGAI [*smiling*]: How then?

BENEATHA: You know perfectly well how . . . as crinkly as yours . . . that's how.

ASAGAI: And it is ugly to you that way?

BENEATHA [*quickly*]: Oh, no—not ugly . . . [*more slowly, apologetically*] But it's so hard to manage when it's, well—raw.

ASAGAI: And so to accommodate that—you mutilate it every week?

BENEATHA: It's not mutilation!

ASAGAI [*laughing aloud at her seriousness*]: Oh . . . please! I am only teasing you because you are so very serious about these things. [*He stands back from her and folds his arms across his chest as he watches her pulling at her hair and frowning in the mirror.*] Do you remember the first time you met me at school? . . . [*He laughs.*] You came up to me and said—and I thought you were the most serious little thing I had ever seen—you said: [*He imitates her.*] "Mr. Asagai—I want very much to talk with you. About Africa. You see, Mr. Asagai, I am looking for my *identity!*" [*He laughs.*]

BENEATHA [*turning to him, not laughing*]: Yes—[*Her face is quizzical, profoundly disturbed.*]

ASAGAI [*still teasing and reaching out and taking her face in his hands and turning her profile to him*]: Well . . . it is true that this is not so much a profile of a Hollywood queen as perhaps a queen of the Nile—[*a mock dismissal of the importance of the question*] But what does it matter? Assimilationism is so popular in your country.

BENEATHA [*wheeling, passionately, sharply*]: I am not an assimilationist!

ASAGAI [*The protest hangs in the room for a moment and Asagai studies her, his laughter fading.*]: Such a serious one. [*There is a pause.*] So—you like the robes? You must take excellent care of them—they are from my sister's personal wardrobe.

BENEATHA [*with incredulity*]: You—you sent all the way home—for me?

ASAGAI [*with charm*]: For you—I would do much more. . . Well, that is what I came for. I must go.

BENEATHA: Will you call me Monday?

ASAGAI: Yes . . . We have a great deal to talk about. I mean about identity and time and all that.

BENEATHA: Time?

ASAGAI: Yes. About how much time one needs to know what one feels.

BENEATHA: You never understood that there is more than one kind of feeling which can exist between a man and a woman—or, at least, there should be.

ASAGAI [shaking his head negatively but gently]: No. Between a man and a woman there need be only one kind of feeling. I have that for you . . . Now even . . . right this moment . . .

BENEATHA: I know—and by itself—it won't do. I can find that anywhere.

ASAGAI: For a woman it should be enough.

BENEATHA: I know—because that's what it says in all the novels that men write. But it isn't. Go ahead and laugh—but I'm not interested in being someone's little episode in America or—[with feminine vengeance]—one of them! [Asagai has burst into laughter again.] That's funny as hell, huh!

ASAGAI: It's just that every American girl I have known has said that to me. White—black—in this you are all the same. And the same speech, too!

BENEATHA [angrily]: Yuk, yuk, yuk!

ASAGAI: It's how you can be sure that the world's most liberated women are not liberated at all. You all talk about it too much! [Mama enters and is immediately all social charm because of the presence of a guest.]

BENEATHA: Oh—Mama—this is Mr. Asagai.

MAMA: How do you do?

ASAGAI [total politeness to an elder]: How do you do, Mrs. Younger. Please forgive me for coming at such an outrageous hour on a Saturday.

MAMA: Well, you are quite welcome. I just hope you understand that our house don't always look like this. [chatterish] You must come again. I would love to hear all about—[not sure of the name]—your country. I think it's so sad the way our American Negroes don't know nothing about Africa 'cept Tarzan and all that. And all that money they pour into these churches when they ought to be helping you people over there drive out them French and Englishmen done taken away your land. [The mother flashes a slightly superior look at her daughter upon completion of the recitation.]

ASAGAI [taken aback by this sudden and acutely unrelated expression of sympathy]: Yes . . . yes . . .

MAMA [*smiling at him suddenly and relaxing and looking him over*]: How many miles is it from here to where you come from?

ASAGAI: Many thousands.

MAMA [*looking at him as she would* Walter]: I bet you don't half look after yourself, being away from your mama either. I spec you better come 'round here from time to time and get yourself some decent home-cooked meals . . .

ASAGAI [*moved*]: Thank you. Thank you very much. [*They are all quiet, then—*] Well . . . I must go. I will call you Monday, Alaiyo.

MAMA: What's that he call you?

ASAGAI: Oh—"Alaiyo." I hope you don't mind. It is what you would call a nickname, I think. It is a Yoruba word. I am a Yoruba.

MAMA [*looking at* Beneatha]: I—I thought he was from—

ASAGAI [*understanding*]: Nigeria is my country. Yoruba is my tribal origin—

BENEATHA: You didn't tell us what Alaiyo means . . . for all I know, you might be calling me Little Idiot or something . . .

ASAGAI: Well . . . let me see . . . I do not know how just to explain it . . . The sense of a thing can be so different when it changes languages.

BENEATHA: You're evading.

ASAGAI: No—really it is difficult . . . [*thinking*] It means . . . it means One for Whom Bread—Food—Is Not Enough. [*He looks at her.*] Is that all right?

BENEATHA [*understanding, softly*]: Thank you.

MAMA [*looking from one to the other and not understanding any of it*]: Well . . . that's nice. . . . You must come see us again—Mr.—

ASAGAI: Ah-sah-guy. . . .

MAMA: Yes . . . Do come again.

ASAGAI: Good-bye. [*He exits.*]

MAMA [*after him*]: Lord, that's a pretty thing just went out here! [*insinuatingly, to her daughter*] Yes, I guess I see why we done commence to get so interested in Africa 'round here. Missionaries my aunt Jenny! [*She exits.*]

BENEATHA: Oh, Mama! . . . [*She picks up the Nigerian dress and holds it up to her in front of the mirror again. She sets the headdress on haphazardly and then notices her hair again and clutches at it and then replaces the headdress and frowns at herself. Then she starts to wriggle in front of the mirror as she thinks a Nigerian woman might. Travis enters and regards her.*]

TRAVIS: You cracking up?

BENEATHA: Shut up. [*She pulls the headdress off and looks at herself in the mirror and clutches at her hair again and squinches her eyes as if trying to imagine something. Then, suddenly, she gets her raincoat and kerchief and hurriedly prepares for going out.*]

MAMA [*coming back into the room*]: She's resting now. Travis, baby, run next door and ask Miss Johnson to please let me have a little kitchen cleanser. This here can is empty as Jacob's kettle.

TRAVIS: I just came in.

MAMA: Do as you told. [*He exits and she looks at her daughter.*] Where you going?

BENEATHA [*halting at the door*]: To become a queen of the Nile! [*She exits in a breathless blaze of glory.* Ruth *appears in the bedroom doorway.*]

MAMA: Who told you to get up?

RUTH: Ain't nothing wrong with me to be lying in no bed for. Where did Bennie go?

MAMA [*drumming her fingers*]: Far as I could make out—to Egypt. [*Ruth just looks at her.*] What time is it getting to?

RUTH: Ten twenty. And the mailman going to ring that bell this morning just like he done every morning for the last umpteen years. [*Travis comes in with the cleanser can.*]

TRAVIS: She say to tell you that she don't have much.

MAMA [*angrily*]: Lord, some people I could name sure is tight-fisted! [*directing her grandson*] Mark two cans of cleanser down on the list there. If she that hard up for kitchen cleanser, I sure don't want to forget to get her none!

RUTH: Lena—maybe the woman is just short on cleanser—

MAMA [*not listening*]: —Much baking powder as she done borrowed from me all these years, she could of done gone into the baking business! [*The bell sounds suddenly and sharply and all three are stunned—serious and silent—mid speech. In spite of all the other conversation and distractions of the morning, this is what they have been waiting for, even* Travis, *who looks helplessly from his mother to his grandmother.* Ruth *is the first to come to life again.*]

RUTH [*to Travis*]: Get down them steps, boy! [*Travis snaps to life and flies out to get the mail.*]

MAMA [*her eyes wide, her hand to her breast*]: You mean it done really come?

RUTH [*excited*]: Oh, Miss Lena!

MAMA [*collecting herself*]: Well . . . I don't know what we all so excited about 'round here for. We known it was coming for months.

RUTH: That's a whole lot different from having it come and being able to hold it in your hands . . . a piece of paper worth ten thousand dollars . . . [Travis *bursts back into the room. He holds the envelope high above his head, like a little dancer, his face is radiant and he is breathless. He moves to his grandmother with sudden slow ceremony and puts the envelope into her hands. She accepts it, and then merely holds it and looks at it.*] Come on! Open it . . . Lord have mercy, I wish Walter Lee was here!

TRAVIS: Open it, Grandmama!

MAMA [*staring at it*]: Now you all be quiet. It's just a check.

RUTH: Open it . . .

MAMA [*still staring at it*]: Now don't act silly . . . We ain't never been no people to act silly 'bout no money—

RUTH [*swiftly*]: We ain't never had none before—*open it!* [Mama *finally makes a good strong tear and pulls out the thin blue slice of paper and inspects it closely. The boy and his mother study it raptly over* Mama's *shoulders.*]

MAMA: Travis! [*She is counting off with doubt.*] Is that the right number of zeros?

TRAVIS: Yes'm . . . ten thousand dollars. Gaalee, Grandmama, you rich.

MAMA [*She holds the check away from her, still looking at it. Slowly her face sobers into a mask of unhappiness.*]: Ten thousand dollars. [*She hands it to* Ruth.] Put it away somewhere, Ruth. [*She does not look at* Ruth; *her eyes seem to be seeing something somewhere very far off.*] Ten thousand dollars they give you. Ten thousand dollars.

TRAVIS [*to his mother, sincerely*]: What's the matter with Grandmama—don't she want to be rich?

RUTH [*distractedly*]: You go on out and play now, baby. [Travis *exits.* Mama *starts wiping dishes absently, humming intently to herself.* Ruth *turns to her, with kind exasperation.*] You've gone and got yourself upset.

MAMA [*not looking at her*]: I spec if it wasn't for you all . . . I would just put that money away or give it to the church or something.

RUTH: Now what kind of talk is that. Mr. Younger would just be plain mad if he could hear you talking foolish like that.

MAMA [*stopping and staring off*]: Yes . . . he sure would. [*sighing*] We got enough to do with that money, all right. [*She halts then, and turns and looks at her daughter-in-law hard;* Ruth *avoids her eyes and* Mama *wipes her hands with finality and starts to speak firmly to* Ruth.] Where did you go today, girl?

RUTH: To the doctor.

MAMA [*impatiently*]: Now, Ruth . . . you know better than that. Old Doctor Jones is strange enough in his way but there ain't nothing 'bout him make somebody slip and call him "she"—like you done this morning.

RUTH: Well, that's what happened—my tongue slipped.

MAMA: You went to see that woman, didn't you?

RUTH [*defensively, giving herself away*]: What woman you talking about?

MAMA [*angrily*]: That woman who—[Walter *enters in great excitement.*]

WALTER: Did it come?

MAMA [*quietly*]: Can't you give people a Christian greeting before you start asking about money?

WALTER [*to* Ruth]: Did it come? [Ruth *unfolds the check and lays it quietly before him, watching him intently with thoughts of her own.* Walter *sits down and grasps it close and counts off the zeros.*] Ten thousand dollars—[*He turns suddenly, frantically to his mother and draws some papers out of his breast pocket.*] Mama—look. Old Willy Harris put everything on paper—

MAMA: Son—I think you ought to talk to your wife . . . I'll go on out and leave you alone if you want—

WALTER: I can talk to her later—Mama, look—

MAMA: Son—

WALTER: WILL SOMEBODY PLEASE LISTEN TO ME TODAY!

MAMA [*quietly*]: I don't 'low no yellin' in this house, Walter Lee, and you know it—[Walter *stares at them in frustration and starts to speak several times.*] And there ain't going to be no investing in no liquor stores. I don't aim to have to speak on that again. [*a long pause*]

WALTER: Oh—so you don't aim to have to speak on that again? So you have decided . . . [*crumpling his papers*] Well, *you* tell that to my boy tonight when you put him to sleep on the living-room couch . . . [*turning to* Mama *and speaking directly to her*]:Yeah—and tell it to my wife, Mama, tomorrow when she has to go out of here to look after somebody else's kids. And tell it to *me*, Mama, every time we need a new pair of curtains and I have to watch *you* go out and work in somebody's kitchen. Yeah, you tell me then! [Walter *starts out*]

RUTH: Where you going?

WALTER: I'm going out!

RUTH: Where?

WALTER: Just out of this house somewhere—

RUTH [*getting her coat*]: I'll come too.

WALTER: I don't want you to come!

RUTH: I got something to talk to you about, Walter.

WALTER: That's too bad.

MAMA [*still quietly*]: Walter Lee—[*She waits and he finally turns and looks at her.*] Sit down.

WALTER: I'm a grown man, Mama.

MAMA: Ain't nobody said you wasn't grown. But you still in my house and my presence. And as long as you are—you'll talk to your wife civil. Now sit down.

RUTH [*suddenly*]: Oh, let him go on out and drink himself to death! He makes me sick to my stomach! [*She flings her coat against him.*]

WALTER [*violently*]: And you turn mine, too, baby! [Ruth *goes into their bedroom and slams the door behind her.*] That was my greatest mistake—

MAMA [*still quietly*]: Walter, what is the matter with you?

WALTER: Matter with me? Ain't nothing the matter with *me!*

MAMA: Yes there is. Something eating you up like a crazy man. Something more than me not giving you this money. The past few years I been watching it happen to you. You get all nervous acting and kind of wild in the eyes—[Walter *jumps up impatiently at her words.*] I said sit there now, I'm talking to you!

WALTER: Mama—I don't need no nagging at me today.

MAMA: Seem like you getting to a place where you always tied up in some kind of knot about something. But if anybody ask you 'bout it you just yell at 'em and bust out the house and go out and drink somewheres. Walter Lee, people can't live with that. Ruth's a good, patient girl in her way—but you getting to be too much. Boy, don't make the mistake of driving that girl away from you.

WALTER: Why—what she do for me?

MAMA: She loves you.

WALTER: Mama—I'm going out. I want to go off somewhere and be by myself for a while.

MAMA: I'm sorry 'bout your liquor store, son. It just wasn't the thing for us to do. That's what I want to tell you about—

WALTER: I got to go out, Mama—[*He rises.*]

MAMA: It's dangerous, son.

WALTER: What's dangerous?

MAMA: When a man goes outside his home to look for peace.

WALTER [*beseechingly*]: Then why can't there never be no peace in this house then?

MAMA: You done found it in some other house?

WALTER: No—there ain't no woman! Why do women always think there's a woman somewhere when a man gets restless. [*coming to her*] Mama—Mama—I want so many things. . .

MAMA: Yes, son—

WALTER: I want so many things that they are driving me kind of crazy . . . Mama—look at me.

MAMA: I'm looking at you. You a good-looking boy. You got a job, a nice wife, a fine boy and—

WALTER: A job. [*looks at her*] Mama, a job? I open and close car doors all day long. I drive a man around in his limousine and I say, "Yes, sir; no, sir; very good, sir; shall I take the Drive, sir?" Mama, that ain't no kind of job . . . that ain't nothing at all. [*very quietly*] Mama, I don't know if I can make you understand.

MAMA: Understand what, baby?

WALTER [*quietly*]: Sometimes it's like I can see the future stretched out in front of me—just plain as day. The future, Mama. Hanging over there at the edge of my days. Just waiting for me—a big, looming blank space—full of *nothing*. Just waiting for *me*. [*pause*] Mama—sometimes when I'm downtown and I pass them cool, quiet-looking restaurants where them white boys are sitting back and talking 'bout things . . . sitting there turning deals worth millions of dollars . . . sometimes I see guys don't look much older than me—

MAMA: Son—how come you talk so much 'bout money?

WALTER [*with immense passion*]: Because it is life, Mama!

MAMA [*quietly*]: Oh—[*very quietly*] So now it's life. Money is life. Once upon a time freedom used to be life—now it's money. I guess the world really do change. . .

WALTER: No—it was always money, Mama. We just didn't know about it.

MAMA: No . . . something has changed. [*She looks at him.*] You something new, boy. In my time we was worried about not being lynched and getting to the North if we could and how to stay alive and still have a pinch of dignity too . . . Now here come you and Beneatha—talking 'bout things we ain't never even thought about hardly, me and your daddy. You ain't satisfied or proud of nothing we done. I mean that you had a home; that we kept you out of trouble till you was grown; that you don't have to ride to work on the back of nobody's streetcar—You my children—but how different we done become.

WALTER: You just don't understand, Mama, you just don't understand.

MAMA: Son—do you know your wife is expecting another baby? [Walter *stands, stunned, and absorbs what his mother has said.*] That's what she wanted to talk to you about. [Walter *sinks down into a chair.*] This ain't for me to be telling—but you ought to know. [*She waits*] I think Ruth is thinking 'bout getting rid of that child.

WALTER [*slowly understanding*]: No—no—Ruth wouldn't do that.

MAMA: When the world gets ugly enough—a woman will do anything for her family. *The part that's already living.*

WALTER: You don't know Ruth, Mama, if you think she would do that. [Ruth *opens the bedroom door and stands there a little limp.*]

RUTH [*beaten*]: Yes I would too, Walter, [*pause*] I gave her a five-dollar down payment. [*There is total silence as the man stares at his wife and the mother stares at her son.*]

MAMA [*presently*]: Well—[*tightly*] Well—son, I'm waiting to hear you say something . . . I'm waiting to hear how you be your father's son. Be the man he was . . . [*pause*] Your wife say she going to destroy your child. And I'm waiting to hear you talk like him and say we a people who give children life, not who destroys them—[*She rises.*] I'm waiting to see you stand up and look like your daddy and say we done give up one baby to poverty and that we ain't going to give up nary another one . . . I'm waiting.

WALTER: Ruth—

MAMA: If you a son of mine, tell her! [Walter *turns, looks at her and can say nothing. She continues, bitterly.*] You . . . you are a disgrace to your father's memory. Somebody get me my hat.

CURTAIN

ACT II

SCENE I

Time: Later the same day.

At rise: Ruth *is ironing again. She has the radio going. Presently Beneatha's *bedroom door opens *and* Ruth's *mouth falls and she puts down the iron in fascination.*

RUTH: What have we got on tonight!

BENEATHA [*emerging grandly from the doorway so that we can see her thoroughly robed in the costume* Asagai *brought.*]:You are looking at what a well-dressed Nigerian woman wears—[*She parades for* Ruth, *her hair completely hidden by the headdress; she is coquettishly fanning herself with an ornate oriental fan, mistakenly more like Butterfly than any Nigerian that ever was.*] Isn't it beautiful? [*She promenades to the radio and, with an arrogant flourish, turns off the good loud blues that is playing.*] Enough of this assimilationist junk! [Ruth *follows her with her eyes as she goes to the phonograph and puts on a record and turns and waits ceremoniously for the music to come up. Then with a shout—*] OCOMOGOSIAY! [Ruth *jumps. The music comes up, a lovely Nigerian melody.* Beneatha *listens, enraptured, her eyes far away—"back to the past." She begins to dance.* Ruth *is dumbfounded.*]

RUTH: What kind of dance is that?

BENEATHA: A folk dance.

RUTH [*Pearl Bailey*]: What kind of folks do that, honey?

BENEATHA: It's from Nigeria. It's a dance of welcome.

RUTH: Who you welcoming?

BENEATHA: The men back to the village.

RUTH: Where they been?

BENEATHA: How should I know—out hunting or something. Anyway, they are coming back now . . .

RUTH: Well, that's good.

BENEATHA [*with the record*]:   *Alundi, alundi*
  Alundi alunya
  Jop pu a jeepua
  Ang gu soooooooooo
  Ai yai yae . . .

Ayehaye—alundi . . . [Walter *comes in during this performance; he has obviously been drinking. He leans against the door heavily and watches his sister, at first with distaste. Then his eyes look off—"back to the past"—as he lifts both his fists to the roof, screaming.*]

WALTER: YEAH . . . AND ETHIOPIA STRETCH FORTH HER HANDS AGAIN! . . .

RUTH [*drily, looking at him*]: Yes—and Africa sure is claiming her own tonight. [*She gives them both up and starts ironing again.*]

WALTER [*all in a drunken, dramatic shout*]: Shut up! . . . I'm digging them drums . . . them drums move me! . . . [*He makes his weaving way to his wife's face and leans in close to her.*] In my heart of hearts—[*He thumps his chest.*]—I am much warrior!

RUTH [*without even looking up*]: In your heart of hearts you are much drunkard.

WALTER [*coming away from her and starting to wander around the room, shouting*]: Me and Jomo . . . [*Intently, in his sister's face. She has stopped dancing to watch him in this unknown mood.*] That's my man, Kenyatta. [*Shouting and thumping his chest.*] FLAMING SPEAR! HOT DAMN! [*He is suddenly in possession of an imaginary spear and actively spearing enemies all over the room.*] OCOMOGOSIAY . . . THE LION IS WAKING . . . OWIMOWEH! [*He pulls his shirt open and leaps up on a table and gestures with his spear. The bell rings. Ruth goes to answer.*]

BENEATHA [*to encourage Walter, thoroughly caught up with this side of him*]: OCOMOGOSIAY, FLAMING SPEAR!

WALTER [*On the table, very far gone, his eyes pure glass sheets. He sees what we cannot, that he is a leader of his people, a great chief, a descendant of Chaka, and that the hour to march has come.*]: Listen, my black brothers—

BENEATHA: OCOMOGOSIAY!

WALTER: —Do you hear the waters rushing against the shores of the coastlands—

BENEATHA: OCOMOGOSIAY!

WALTER: —Do you hear the screeching of the cocks in yonder hills beyond where the chiefs meet in council for the coming of the mighty war—

BENEATHA: OCOMOGOSIAY!

WALTER: —Do you hear the beating of the wings of the birds flying low over the mountains and the low places of our land—[*Ruth opens the door, George Murchison enters.*]

BENEATHA: OCOMOGOSIAY!

WALTER: —Do you hear the singing of the women, singing the war songs of our fathers to the babies in the great houses . . . singing the sweet war songs? OH, DO YOU HEAR, MY BLACK BROTHERS?

BENEATHA [*completely gone*]: We hear you, Flaming Spear—

WALTER: Telling us to prepare for the greatness of the time— [*to George*] Black Brother! [*He extends his hand for the fraternal clasp.*]

GEORGE: Black Brother, hell!

RUTH [*having had enough, and embarrassed for the family*]: Beneatha, you got company—what's the matter with you? Walter Lee Younger, get down off that table and stop acting like a fool . . . [Walter *comes down off the table suddenly and makes a quick exit to the bathroom.*]

RUTH: He's had a little to drink . . . I don't know what her excuse is.

GEORGE [*to* Beneatha]: Look honey, we're going *to* the theatre—we're not going to be *in* it . . . so go change, huh?

RUTH: You expect this boy to go out with you looking like that?

BENEATHA [*looking at* George]: That's up to George. If he's ashamed of his heritage—

GEORGE: Oh, don't be so proud of yourself, Bennie—just because you look eccentric.

BENEATHA: How can something that's natural be eccentric?

GEORGE: That's what being eccentric means—being natural. Get dressed.

BENEATHA: I don't like that, George.

RUTH: Why must you and your brother make an argument out of everything people say?

BENEATHA: Because I hate assimilationist Negroes!

RUTH: Will somebody please tell me what assimila-who-ever means!

GEORGE: Oh, it's just a college girl's way of calling people Uncle Toms—but that isn't what it means at all.

RUTH: Well, what does it mean?

BENEATHA [*cutting George off and staring at him as she replies to* Ruth]: It means someone who is willing to give up his own culture and submerge himself completely in the dominant, and in this case, *oppressive* culture!

GEORGE: Oh, dear, dear, dear! Here we go! A lecture on the African past! On our Great West African Heritage! In one second we will hear all about the great Ashanti empires; the great Songhay civilizations; and the great sculpture of Benin—and then some poetry in the Bantu—and the whole monologue will end with the word *heritage!* [*nastily*] Let's face it, baby, your heritage is nothing but a bunch of raggedy-assed spirituals and some grass huts!

BENEATHA: *Grass huts!* [Ruth *crosses to her and forcibly pushes her toward the bedroom.*] See there . . . you are standing there in your splendid ignorance talking about people who were the first to smelt iron on the face of the earth! [Ruth *is pushing her through the door.*] The Ashanti were performing surgical operations when the

English—[Ruth *pulls the door to, with* Beneatha *on the other side, and smiles graciously at* George. Beneatha *opens the door and shouts the end of the sentence defiantly at* George.]—were still tattooing themselves with blue dragons . . . [*She goes back inside.*]

RUTH: Have a seat, George. [*They both sit.* Ruth *folds her hands rather primly on her lap, determined to demonstrate the civilization of the family.*] Warm, ain't it? I mean for September. [*pause*] Just like they always say about Chicago weather: If it's too hot or cold for you, just wait a minute and it'll change. [*She smiles happily at this cliché, of clichés.*] Everybody say it's got to do with them bombs and things they keep setting off. [*pause*] Would you like a nice cold beer?

GEORGE: No, thank you. I don't care for beer. [*He looks at his watch.*] I hope she hurries up.

RUTH: What time is the show?

GEORGE: It's an eight-thirty curtain. That's just Chicago, though. In New York standard curtain time is eight forty. [*He is rather proud of this knowledge.*]

RUTH [*properly appreciating it*]: You get to New York a lot?

GEORGE [*offhand*]: Few times a year.

RUTH: Oh—that's nice. I've never been to New York. [Walter *enters. We feel he has relieved himself, but the edge of unreality is still with him.*]

WALTER: New York ain't got nothing Chicago ain't. Just a bunch of hustling people all squeezed up together—being "Eastern." [*He turns his face into a screw of displeasure.*]

GEORGE: Oh—you've been?

WALTER: Plenty of times.

RUTH [*shocked at the lie*]: Walter Lee Younger!

WALTER [*staring her down*]: Plenty! [*pause*] What we got to drink in this house? Why don't you offer this man some refreshment. [*to* George] They don't know how to entertain people in this house, man.

GEORGE: Thank you—I don't really care for anything.

WALTER [*feeling his head; sobriety coming*]: Where's Mama?

RUTH: She ain't come back yet.

WALTER [*looking* Murchison *over from head to toe, scrutinizing his carefully casual tweed sports jacket over cashmere V-neck sweater over soft eyelet shirt and tie, and soft slacks, finished off with white buckskin shoes*]: Why all you college boys wear them fairyish-looking white shoes?

RUTH: Walter Lee! [George Murchison *ignores the remark.*]

WALTER [*to* Ruth]: Well, they look crazy as hell—white shoes, cold as it is.

RUTH [*crushed*]: You have to excuse him—

WALTER: No he don't! Excuse me for what? What you always excusing me for! I'll excuse myself when I needs to be excused! [*a pause*] They look as funny as them black knee socks Beneatha wears out of here all the time.

RUTH: It's the college *style*, Walter.

WALTER: Style, hell. She looks like she got burnt legs or something!

RUTH: Oh, Walter—

WALTER [*an irritable mimic*]: Oh, Walter! Oh, Walter! [*to* Murchison] How's your old man making out? I understand you all going to buy that big hotel on the Drive?[1] [*He finds a beer in the refrigerator, wanders over to* Murchison, *sipping and wiping his lips with the back of his hand, and straddling a chair backwards to talk to the other man.*] Shrewd move. Your old man is all right, man. [*tapping his head and half winking for emphasis*] I mean he knows how to operate. I mean he thinks big, you know what I mean, I mean for a home,[2] you know? But I think he's kind of running out of ideas now. I'd like to talk to him. Listen, man, I got some plans that could turn this city upside down. I mean I think like he does. *Big.* Invest big, gamble big, hell, lose *big* if you have to, you know what I mean. It's hard to find a man on this whole Southside who understands my kind of thinking—you dig? [*He scrutinizes* Murchison *again, drinks his beer, squints his eyes and leans in close, confidential, man to man.*] Me and you ought to sit down and talk sometimes, man. Man, I got me some ideas . . .

MURCHISON [*with boredom*]: Yeah—sometimes we'll have to do that, Walter.

WALTER [*understanding the indifference, and offended*]: Yeah—well, when you get the time, man. I know you a busy little boy.

RUTH: Walter, please—

WALTER [*bitterly, hurt*]: I know ain't nothing in this world as busy as you colored college boys with your fraternity pins and white shoes . . .

RUTH [*covering her face with humiliation*]: Oh, Walter Lee—

---

[1]*Drive:* Chicago's Outer Drive running along Lake Michigan
[2]*home:* home-boy; one of us

WALTER: I see you all all the time—with the books tucked under your arms—going to your [*British A—a mimic*] "clahsses." And for what! What the hell you learning over there? Filling up your heads—[*counting off on his fingers*]—with the sociology and the psychology—but they teaching you how to be a man? How to take over and run the world? They teaching you how to run a rubber plantation or a steel mill? Naw—just to talk proper and read books and wear white shoes . . .

GEORGE [*looking at him with distaste, a little above it all*]: You're all wacked up with bitterness, man.

WALTER [*intently, almost quietly, between the teeth, glaring at the boy*]: And you—ain't you bitter, man? Ain't you just about had it yet? Don't you see no stars gleaming that you can't reach out and grab? You happy?—You contented son-of-a-bitch—you happy? You got it made? Bitter? Man, I'm a volcano. Bitter? Here I am a giant—surrounded by ants! Ants who can't even understand what it is the giant is talking about.

RUTH [*passionately and suddenly*]: Oh, Walter—ain't you with nobody!

WALTER [*violently*]: No! 'Cause ain't nobody with me! Not even my own mother!

RUTH: Walter, that's a terrible thing to say! [Beneatha *enters, dressed for the evening in a cocktail dress and earrings.*]

GEORGE: Well—hey, you look great.

BENEATHA: Let's go, George. See you all later.

RUTH: Have a nice time.

GEORGE: Thanks. Good night. [*to* Walter, *sarcastically*] Good night, Prometheus. [Beneatha *and* George *exit.*]

WALTER [*to* Ruth]: Who is Prometheus?

RUTH: I don't know. Don't worry about it.

WALTER [*in fury, pointing after* George]: See there—they get to a point where they can't insult you man to man—they got to go talk about something ain't nobody never heard of!

RUTH: How do you know it was an insult? [*to humor him*] Maybe Prometheus is a nice fellow.

WALTER: Prometheus! I bet there ain't even no such thing! I bet that simpleminded clown—

RUTH: Walter—[*She stops what she is doing and looks at him.*]

WALTER [*yelling*]: Don't start!

RUTH: Start what?

WALTER: Your nagging! Where was I? Who was I with? How much money did I spend?

RUTH [*plaintively*]: Walter Lee—why don't we just try to talk about it . . .

WALTER [*not listening*]: I been out talking with people who understand me. People who care about the things I got on my mind.

RUTH [*wearily*]: I guess that means people like Willy Harris.

WALTER: Yes, people like Willy Harris.

RUTH [*with a sudden flash of impatience*]: Why don't you all just hurry up and go into the banking business and stop talking about it!

WALTER: Why? You want to know why? 'Cause we all tied up in a race of people that don't know how to do nothing but moan, pray and have babies! [*The line is too bitter even for him and he looks at her and sits down.*]

RUTH: Oh, Walter . . . [*softly*] Honey, why can't you stop fighting me?

WALTER [*without thinking*]: Who's fighting you? Who even cares about you? [*This line begins the retardation of his mood.*]

RUTH: Well—[*She waits a long time, and then with resignation starts to put away her things.*] I guess I might as well go on to bed . . . [*more or less to herself*] I don't know where we lost it . . . but we have. . . [*Then, to him.*] I—I'm sorry about this new baby, Walter. I guess maybe I better go on and do what I started . . . I guess I just didn't realize how bad things was with us. . . I guess I just didn't really realize—[*She starts out to the bedroom and stops.*] You want some hot milk?

WALTER: Hot milk?

RUTH: Yes—hot milk.

WALTER: Why hot milk?

RUTH: 'Cause after all that liquor you come home with you ought to have something hot in your stomach.

WALTER: I don't want no milk.

RUTH: You want some coffee then?

WALTER: No, I don't want no coffee. I don't want nothing hot to drink. [*almost plaintively*] Why you always trying to give me something to eat?

RUTH [*standing and looking at him helplessly*]: What else can I give you, Walter Lee Younger? [*She stands and looks at him and presently turns to go out again. He lifts his head and watches her going away from him in a new mood which began to emerge when he asked her, "Who cares about you?"*]

WALTER: It's been rough, ain't it, baby? [*She hears and stops but does not turn around and he continues to her back.*] I guess between two people there ain't never as much understood as folks generally thinks there is. I mean like between me and you—[*She turns to face him.*] How we gets to the place where we scared to talk softness to each other. [*He waits, thinking hard himself.*] Why you think it got to be like that? [*He is thoughtful, almost as a child would be.*] Ruth, what is it gets into people ought to be close?

RUTH: I don't know, honey. I think about it a lot.

WALTER: On account of you and me, you mean? The way things are with us. The way something done come down between us.

RUTH: There ain't so much between us, Walter . . . Not when you come to me and try to talk to me. Try to be with me . . . a little even.

WAITER [*total honesty*]:   Sometimes . . . sometimes . . . I don't even know how to try.

RUTH: Walter—

WALTER: Yes?

RUTH [*coming to him, gently and with misgiving, but coming to him*]:   Honey . . . life don't have to be like this. I mean sometimes people can do things so that things are better . . . You remember how we used to talk when Travis was born . . . about the way we were going to live . . . the kind of house . . . [*She is stroking his head.*] Well, it's all starting to slip away from us . . . [Mama *enters, and* Walter *jumps up and shouts at her.*]

WALTER: Mama, where have you been?

MAMA: My—them steps is longer than they used to be. Whew! [*She sits down and ignores him.*] How you feeling this evening, Ruth! [Ruth *shrugs, disturbed some at having been prematurely interrupted and watching her husband knowingly.*]

WALTER: Mama, where have you been all day?

MAMA [*still ignoring him and leaning on the table and changing to more comfortable shoes*]:   Where's Travis?

RUTH: I let him go out earlier and he ain't come back yet. Boy, is he going to get it!

WALTER: Mama!

MAMA [*as if she has heard him for the first time*]:   Yes, son?

WALTER: Where did you go this afternoon?

MAMA: I went downtown to tend to some business that I had to tend to.

WALTER: What kind of business?

MAMA: You know better than to question me like a child, Brother.

WALTER [*rising and bending over the table*]: Where were you, Mama? [*bringing his fists down and shouting*] Mama, you didn't go do something with that insurance money, something crazy? [*The front door opens slowly, interrupting him, and Travis peeks his head in, less than hopefully.*]

TRAVIS [*to his mother*]: Mama, I—

RUTH: "Mama I" nothing! You're going to get it, boy! Get on in that bedroom and get yourself ready!

TRAVIS: But I—

MAMA: Why don't you all never let the child explain hisself.

RUTH: Keep out of it now, Lena. [*Mama clamps her lips together, and Ruth advances toward her son menacingly.*]

RUTH: A thousand times I have told you not to go off like that—

MAMA [*holding out her arms to her grandson*]: Well—at least let me tell him something. I want him to be the first one to hear . . . Come here, Travis. [*the boy obeys, gladly*] Travis—[*She takes him by the shoulder and looks into his face.*]—you know that money we got in the mail this morning?

TRAVIS: Yes'm—

MAMA: Well—what you think your grandmama gone and done with that money?

TRAVIS: I don't know, Grandmama.

MAMA [*putting her finger on his nose for emphasis*]: She went out and she bought you a house! [*The explosion comes from Walter at the end of the revelation and he jumps up and turns away from all of them in a fury. Mama continues, to Travis.*] You glad about the house? It's going to be yours when you get to be a man.

TRAVIS: Yeah—I always wanted to live in a house.

MAMA: All right, gimme some sugar then—[*Travis puts his arms around her neck as she watches her son over the boy's shoulder. Then, to Travis, after the embrace.*] Now when you say your prayers tonight, you thank God and your grandfather—'cause it was him who give you the house—in his way.

RUTH [*taking the boy from Mama and pushing him toward the bedroom*]: Now you get out of here and get ready for your beating.

TRAVIS: Aw, Mama—

RUTH: Get on in there—[*closing the door behind him and turning radiantly to her mother-in-law*] So you went and did it!

MAMA [*quietly, looking at her son with pain*]: Yes, I did.

RUTH [*raising both arms classically*]: Praise God! [*Looks at Walter a moment, who says nothing. She crosses rapidly to her husband.*]

Please, honey—let me be glad . . . you be glad too. [*She has laid her hands on his shoulders, but he shakes himself free of her roughly, without turning to face her.*] Oh, Walter . . . a home . . . *a home.* [*She comes back to* Mama.] Well—where is it? How big is it? How much it going to cost?

MAMA: Well—

RUTH: When we moving?

MAMA [*smiling at her*]:   First of the month.

RUTH [*throwing back her head with jubilance*]:   *Praise God!*

MAMA [*tentatively, still looking at her son's back turned against her and* Ruth]:   It's—it's a nice house too . . . [*She cannot help speaking directly to him. An imploring quality in her voice, her manner, makes her almost like a girl now.*] Three bedrooms—nice big one for you and Ruth . . . Me and Beneatha still have to share our room, but Travis have one of his own—and [*with difficulty*] I figure if the—new baby—is a boy, we could get one of them double-decker outfits . . . And there's a yard with a little patch of dirt where I could maybe get to grow me a few flowers . . . And a nice big basement. . . .

RUTH: Walter honey, be glad—

MAMA [*still to his back, fingering things on the table*]:   'Course I don't want to make it sound fancier than it is. . . . It's just a plain little old house—but it's made good and solid—and it will be *ours.* Walter Lee—it makes a difference in a man when he can walk on floors that belong to *him.* . . .

RUTH: Where is it?

MAMA [*frightened at this telling*]:   Well—well—it's out there in Clybourne Park—[Ruth's *radiance fades abruptly, and* Walter *finally turns slowly to face his mother with incredulity and hostility.*]

RUTH: Where?

MAMA [*matter-of-factly*]:   Four o six Clybourne Street, Clybourne Park.

RUTH: Clybourne Park? Mama, there ain't no colored people living in Clybourne Park.

MAMA [*almost idiotically*]:   Well, I guess there's going to be some now.

WALTER [*bitterly*]:   So that's the peace and comfort you went out and bought for us today!

MAMA [*raising her eyes to meet his finally*]:   Son—I just tried to find the nicest place for the least amount of money for my family.

RUTH [*trying to recover from the shock*]: Well—well—'course I ain't one never been 'fraid of no crackers, mind you—but—well, wasn't there no other houses nowhere?

MAMA: Them houses they put up for colored in them areas way out all seem to cost twice as much as other houses. I did the best I could.

RUTH [*Struck senseless with the news, in its various degrees of goodness and trouble, she sits a moment, her fists propping her chin in thought, and then she starts to rise, bringing her fists down with vigor, the radiance spreading from cheek to cheek again.*]: Well—well!—All I can say is—if this is my time in life—my time—to say good-bye—[*And she builds with momentum as she starts to circle the room with an exuberant, almost tearfully happy release.*]—to these Goddamned cracking walls!—[*She pounds the walls*]—and these marching roaches!—[*She wipes at an imaginary army of marching roaches.*]—and this cramped little closet which ain't now or never was no kitchen! . . . then I say it loud and good, *Hallelujah! and good-bye misery . . . I don't never want to see your ugly face again!* [*She laughs joyously, having practically destroyed the apartment, and flings her arms up and lets them come down happily, slowly, reflectively, over her abdomen, aware for the first time perhaps that the life therein pulses with happiness and not despair.*] Lena?

MAMA [*moved, watching her happiness*]: Yes, honey?

RUTH [*looking off*]: Is there—is there a whole lot of sunlight?

MAMA [*understanding*]: Yes, child, there's a whole lot of sunlight. [*long pause*]

RUTH [*collecting herself and going to the door of the room* Travis *is in*]: Well—I guess I better see 'bout Travis. [*to Mama*] Lord, I sure don't feel like whipping nobody today! [*she exists*]

MAMA [*The mother and son are left alone now and the mother waits a long time, considering deeply, before she speaks.*]: Son—you—you understand what I done, don't you? [*Walter is silent and sullen.*] I—I just seen my family falling apart today . . . just falling to pieces in front of my eyes . . . We couldn't of gone on like we was today. We was going backwards 'stead of forwards—talking 'bout killing babies and wishing each other was dead . . . When it gets like that in life—you just got to do something different, push on out and do something bigger . . . [*She waits.*] I wish you say something, son . . . I wish you'd say how deep inside you you think I done the right thing—

WALTER [*crossing slowly to his bedroom door and finally turning there and speaking measuredly*]: What you need me to say you done right for? You the head of this family. You run our lives like you want to. It was your money and you did what you wanted with it. So what you need for me to say it was all right for? [*bitterly, to hurt her as deeply as he knows is possible*] So you butchered up a dream of mine—you—who always talking 'bout your children's dreams . . .

MAMA: Walter Lee—[*He just closes the door behind him. Mama sits alone, thinking heavily.*]

CURTAIN

Scene II

Time: Friday night. A few weeks later.

At rise: Packing crates mark the intention of the family to move. Beneatha and George come in, presumably from an evening out again.

GEORGE: O.K. . . . O.K., whatever you say . . . [*They both sit on the couch. He tries to kiss her. She moves away.*] Look, we've had a nice evening; let's not spoil it, huh? . . . [*He again turns her head and tries to nuzzle in and she turns away from him, not with distaste but with momentary lack of interest; in a mood to pursue what they were talking about.*]

BENEATHA: I'm trying to talk to you.

GEORGE: We always talk.

BENEATHA: Yes—and I love to talk.

GEORGE [*exasperated; rising*]: I know it and I don't mind it sometimes . . . I want you to cut it out, see—The moody stuff, I mean. I don't like it. You're a nice-looking girl . . . all over. That's all you need, honey, forget the atmosphere. Guys aren't going to go for the atmosphere—they're going to go for what they see. Be glad for that. Drop the Garbo routine. It doesn't go with you. As for myself, I want a nice—[*groping*]—simple [*thoughtfully*]—sophisticated girl . . . not a poet—O.K.? [*She rebuffs him again and he starts to leave.*]

BENEATHA: Why are you angry?

GEORGE: Because this is stupid! I don't go out with you to discuss the nature of "quiet desperation" or to hear all about your thoughts—because the world will go on thinking what it thinks regardless—

BENEATHA: Then why read books? Why go to school?

GEORGE [*with artificial patience, counting on his fingers*]: It's simple. You read books—to learn facts—to get grades—to pass the course— to get a degree. That's all—it has nothing to do with thoughts. [*a long pause*]

BENEATHA: I see. [*a longer pause as she looks at him*] Good night, George. [George *looks at her a little oddly, and starts to exit. He meets* Mama *coming in.*]

GEORGE: Oh—hello, Mrs. Younger.

MAMA: Hello, George, how you feeling?

GEORGE: Fine—fine, how are you?

MAMA: Oh, a little tired. You know them steps can get you after a day's work. You all have a nice time tonight?

GEORGE: Yes—a fine time. Well, good night.

MAMA: Good night. [*He exits.* Mama *closes the door behind her.*] Hello, honey. What you sitting like that for?

BENEATHA: I'm just sitting.

MAMA: Didn't you have a nice time?

BENEATHA: No.

MAMA: No? What's the matter?

BENEATHA: Mama, George is a fool—honest. [*She rises.*]

MAMA [*Hustling around unloading the packages she has entered with. She stops.*]: Is he, baby?

BENEATHA: Yes. [Beneatha *makes up* Travis' *bed as she talks.*]

MAMA: You sure?

BENEATHA: Yes.

MAMA: Well—I guess you better not waste your time with no fools. [Beneatha *looks up at her mother, watching her put groceries in the refrigerator. Finally she gathers up her things and starts into the bedroom. At the door she stops and looks back at her mother.*]

BENEATHA: Mama—

MAMA: Yes, baby—

BENEATHA: Thank you.

MAMA: For what?

BENEATHA: For understanding me this time. [*She exits quickly and the mother stands, smiling a little, looking at the place where* Beneatha *had stood.* Ruth *enters.*]

RUTH: Now don't you fool with any of this stuff, Lena—

MAMA: Oh, I just thought I'd sort a few things out. [*The phone rings.* Ruth *answers.*]

RUTH [*at the phone*]: Hello—Just a minute. [*goes to door*] Walter, it's Mrs. Arnold. [*Waits. Goes back to the phone. Tense.*] Hello.

Yes, this is his wife speaking . . . He's lying down now. Yes . . . well, he'll be in tomorrow. He's been very sick. Yes—I know we should have called, but we were so sure he'd be able to come in today. Yes—yes, I'm very sorry. Yes . . . Thank you very much. [*She hangs up.* Walter *is standing in the doorway of the bedroom behind her.*] That was Mrs. Arnold.

WALTER [*indifferently*]: Was it?

RUTH: She said if you don't come in tomorrow that they are getting a new man . . .

WALTER: Ain't that sad—ain't that crying sad.

RUTH: She said Mr. Arnold has had to take a cab for three days . . . Walter, you ain't been to work for three days! [*This is a revelation to her.*] Where you been, Walter Lee Younger? [Walter *looks at her and starts to laugh.*] You're going to lose your job.

WALTER: That's right . . .

RUTH: Oh, Walter, and with your mother working like a dog every day—

WALTER: That's sad too—Everything is sad.

MAMA: What you been doing for these three days, son?

WALTER: Mama—you don't know all the things a man what got leisure can find to do in this city . . . What's this—Friday night? Well—Wednesday I borrowed Willy Harris' car and I went for a drive . . . just me and myself and I drove and drove . . . Way out . . . way past South Chicago, and I parked the car and I sat and looked at the steel mills all day long. I just sat in the car and looked at them big black chimneys for hours. Then I drove back and I went to the Green Hat. [*pause*] And Thursday—Thursday I borrowed the car again and I got in it and I pointed it the other way and I drove the other way—for hours—way, way up to Wisconsin, and I looked at the farms. I just drove and looked at the farms. Then I drove back and I went to the Green Hat. [*pause*] And today—today I didn't get the car. Today I just walked. All over the Southside. And I looked at the Negroes and they looked at me and finally I just sat down on the curb at Thirty-ninth and South Parkway and I just sat there and watched the Negroes go by. And then I went to the Green Hat. You all sad? You all depressed? And you know where I am going right now—[Ruth *goes out quietly.*].

MAMA: Oh, Big Walter, is this the harvest of our days?

WALTER: You know what I like about the Green Hat? [*He turns the radio on and a steamy, deep blues pours into the room.*] I like this little cat they got there who blows a sax . . . He blows. He talks to me. He ain't but 'bout five feet tall and he's got a conked head and his eyes is always closed and he's all music—

MAMA [*rising and getting some papers out of her handbag*]:   Walter —

WALTER: And there's this other guy who plays the piano . . . and they got a sound. I mean they can work on some music . . . They got the best little combo in the world in the Green Hat . . . You can just sit there and drink and listen to them three men play and you realize that don't nothing matter worth a damn, but just being there—

MAMA: I've helped do it to you, haven't I, son? Walter, I been wrong.

WALTER: Naw—you ain't never been wrong about nothing, Mama.

MAMA: Listen to me, now. I say I been wrong, son. That I been doing to you what the rest of the world been doing to you. [*She stops and he looks up slowly at her and she meets his eyes pleadingly.*] Walter—what you ain't understood is that I ain't got nothing, don't own nothing, ain't never really wanted nothing that wasn't for you. There ain't nothing as precious to me . . . There ain't nothing worth holding on to, money, dreams, nothing else—if it means—if it means it's going to destroy my boy. [*She puts her papers in front of him and he watches her without speaking or moving.*] I paid the man thirty-five hundred dollars down on the house. That leaves sixty-five hundred dollars. Monday morning I want you to take this money and take three thousand dollars and put it in a savings account for Beneatha's medical schooling. The rest you put in a checking account—with your name on it. And from now on any penny that come out of it or that go in it is for you to look after. For you to decide. [*She drops her hands a little helplessly.*] It ain't much, but it's all I got in the world and I'm putting it in your hands. I'm telling you to be the head of this family from now on like you supposed to be.

WALTER [*stares at the money*]: You trust me like that, Mama?

MAMA: I ain't never stop trusting you. Like I ain't never stop loving you. [*She goes out, and* Walter *sits looking at the money on the table as the music continues in its idiom, pulsing in the room. Finally, in a decisive gesture, he gets up, and, in mingled joy and desperation, picks up the money. At the same moment,* Travis *enters for bed.*]

TRAVIS: What's the matter, Daddy? You drunk?

WALTER [*sweetly, more sweetly than we have ever known him*]:   No, Daddy ain't drunk. Daddy ain't going to never be drunk again. . . .

TRAVIS: Well, good night, Daddy. [*The father has come from behind the couch and leans over, embracing his son.*]

WALTER: Son, I feel like talking to you tonight.

TRAVIS: About what?

WALTER: Oh, about a lot of things. About you and what kind of man you going to be when you grow up. . . . Son—son, what do you want to be when you grow up?

TRAVIS: A bus driver.

WALTER [*laughing a little*]: A what? Man, that ain't nothing to want to be!

TRAVIS: Why not?

WALTER: 'Cause, man—it ain't big enough—you know what I mean.

TRAVIS: I don't know then. I can't make up my mind. Sometimes Mama asks me that too. And sometimes when I tell her I just want to be like you—she says she don't want me to be like that and sometimes she says she does . . .

WALTER [*gathering him up in his arms*]: You know what, Travis? In seven years you going to be seventeen years old. And things is going to be very different with us in seven years, Travis. . . . One day when you are seventeen I'll come home—home from my office downtown somewhere—

TRAVIS: You don't work in no office, Daddy.

WALTER: No—but after tonight. After what your daddy gonna do tonight, there's going to be offices—a whole lot of offices. . . .

TRAVIS: What you gonna do tonight, Daddy?

WALTER: You wouldn't understand yet, son, but your daddy's gonna make a transaction . . . a business transaction that's going to change our lives . . . That's how come one day when you 'bout seventeen years old I'll come home and I'll be pretty tired, you know what I mean, after a day of conferences and secretaries getting things wrong the way they do . . . 'cause an executive's life is hell, man—[*The more he talks the farther away he gets.*] And I'll pull the car up on the driveway . . . just a plain black Chrysler, I think, with white walls—no—black tires. More elegant. Rich people don't have to be flashy . . . though I'll have to get something a little sportier for Ruth—maybe a Cadillac convertible to do her shopping in. . . . And I'll come up the steps to the house and the gardener will be clipping away at the hedges and he'll say, "Good evening, Mr. Younger." And I'll say, "Hello, Jefferson, how are you this evening?" And I'll go inside and Ruth will come downstairs and meet me at the door and we'll kiss each other and she'll take my arm and we'll go up to your room to see you sitting on the floor with the catalogues of all the great schools in America around you. . . . All the great schools in the world! And—and I'll say, all right son—it's your seventeenth birthday, what is it you've decided? . . . Just tell me where you want to go to school and you'll go. Just tell me, what it is you want to be—and you'll be it. . . . Whatever you want to be—Yessir! [*He holds his arms open for* Travis.] You just name it, son . . . [Travis *leaps into them*] and I hand you the world! [Walter's *voice has risen in pitch and hysterical promise and on the last line he lifts* Travis *high*.]

Blackout

Scene III

Time: Saturday, moving day, one week later.

Before the curtain rises, Ruth's *voice, a strident, dramatic church alto, cuts through the silence.*

It is, in the darkness, a triumphant surge, a penetrating statement of expectation; "Oh, Lord, I don't feel no ways tired! Children, oh, glory hallelujah!"

As the curtain rises we see that Ruth *is alone in the living room, finishing up the family's packing. It is moving day. She is nailing crates and tying cartons.* Beneatha *enters, carrying a guitar case, and watches her exuberant sister-in-law.*

RUTH: Hey!

BENEATHA [*putting away the case*]: Hi.

RUTH [*pointing at a package*]: Honey—look in that package there and see what I found on sale this morning at the South Center. [Ruth *gets up and moves to the package and draws out some curtains.*] Lookahere—hand-turned hems!

BENEATHA: How do you know the window size out there?

RUTH [*who hadn't thought of that*]: Oh—Well, they bound to fit something in the whole house. Anyhow, they was too good a bargain to pass up. [Ruth *slaps her head, suddenly remembering something.*] Oh, Bennie—I meant to put a special note on that carton over there. That's your mama's good china and she wants 'em to be very careful with it.

BENEATHA: I'll do it. [Beneatha *finds a piece of paper and starts to draw large letters on it.*]

RUTH: You know what I'm going to do soon as I get in that new house?

BENEATHA: What?

RUTH: Honey—I'm going to run me a tub of water up to here ... [*with her fingers practically up to her nostrils*] And I'm going to get in it— and I am going to sit ... and sit ... and sit in that hot water and the first person who knocks to tell *me* to hurry up and come out—

BENEATHA: Gets shot at sunrise.

RUTH [*laughing happily*]: You said it, sister! [*noticing how large Beneatha is absentmindedly making the note*] Honey, they ain't going to read that from no airplane.

BENEATHA [*laughing herself*]: I guess I always think things have more emphasis if they are big, somehow.

RUTH [*looking up at her and smiling*]: You and your brother seem to have that as a philosophy of life. Lord, that man—done changed so 'round here. You know—you know what we did last night? Me and Walter Lee?

BENEATHA: What?

RUTH [*smiling to herself*]: We went to the movies. [*looking at Beneatha to see if she understands*] We went to the movies. You know the last time me and Walter went to the movies together?

BENEATHA: No.

RUTH: Me neither. That's how long it been. [*smiling again*] But we went last night. The picture wasn't much good, but that didn't seem to matter. We went—and we held hands.

BENEATHA: Oh, Lord!

RUTH: We held hands—and you know what?

BENEATHA: What?

RUTH: When we come out of the show it was late and dark and all the stores and things was closed up ... and it was kind of chilly and there wasn't many people on the streets ... and we was still holding hands, me and Walter.

BENEATHA: You're killing me. [*Walter enters with a large package. His happiness is deep in him; he cannot keep still with his newfound exuberance. He is singing and wiggling and snapping his fingers. He puts his package in a corner and puts a phonograph record, which he has brought in with him, on the record player. As the music comes up he dances over to* Ruth *and tries to get her to dance with him. She gives in at last to his raunchiness and in a fit of giggling allows herself to be drawn into his mood and together they deliberately burlesque an old social dance of their youth.*]

BENEATHA [*Regarding them a long time as they dance, then drawing in her breath for a deeply exaggerated comment which she does*

not particularly mean.]: Talk about—oldddddddddd—fashioned-
dddddd—Negroes!

WALTER [*stopping momentarily*]: What kind of Negroes? [*He says this in fun. He is not angry with her today, nor with anyone. He starts to dance with his wife again.*]

BENEATHA: Old-fashioned.

WALTER [*as he dances with* Ruth]: You know, when these *New Negroes* have their convention—[*pointing at his sister*]—that is going to be the chairman of the Committee on Unending Agitation. [*He goes on dancing, then stops.*] Race, race, race! . . . Girl, I do believe you are the first person in the history of the entire human race to successfully brainwash yourself. [Beneatha *breaks up and he goes on dancing. He stops again, enjoying his tease.*] Damn, even the N double A C P takes a holiday sometimes! [Beneatha *and* Ruth *laugh. He dances with* Ruth *some more and starts to laugh and stops and pantomimes someone over an operating table.*] I can just see that chick someday looking down at some poor cat on an operating table before she starts to slice him, saying . . . [*pulling his sleeves back maliciously*] "By the way, what are your views on civil rights down there?. . ." [*He laughs at her again and starts to dance happily. The bell sounds.*]

BENEATHA: Sticks and stones may break my bones but . . . words will never hurt me! [Beneatha *goes to the door and opens it as* Walter *and* Ruth *go on with the clowning.* Beneatha *is somewhat surprised to see a quiet-looking middle-aged white man in a business suit holding his hat and a briefcase in his hand and consulting a small piece of paper.*]

MAN: Uh—how do you do, miss. I am looking for a Mrs.—[*He looks at the slip of paper.*] Mrs. Lena Younger?

BENEATHA [*smoothing her hair with slight embarrassment*]: Oh—yes, that's my mother. Excuse me. [*She closes the door and turns to quiet the other two.*] Ruth! Brother! Somebody's here. [*Then she opens the door. The man casts a curious quick glance at all of them.*] Uh—come in please.

MAN [*coming in*]: Thank you.

BENEATHA: My mother isn't here just now. Is it business?

MAN: Yes . . . well, of a sort.

WALTER [*freely, the Man of the House*]: Have a seat. I'm Mrs. Younger's son. I look after most of her business matters. [Ruth *and* Beneatha *exchange amused glances.*]

MAN [*regarding* Walter, *and sitting*]: Well—My name is Karl Lindner . . .

WALTER [*stretching out his hand*]: Walter Younger. This is my wife—[Ruth *nods politely.*]—and my sister.

LINDNER: How do you do.

WALTER [*amiably, as he sits himself easily on a chair, leaning with interest forward on his knees and looking expectantly into the newcomer's face*]: What can we do for you, Mr. Lindner!

LINDNER [*some minor shuffling of the hat and briefcase on his knees*]: Well—I am a representative of the Clybourne Park Improvement Association—

WALTER [*pointing*]: Why don't you sit your things on the floor?

LINDNER: Oh—yes. Thank you. [*He slides the briefcase and hat under the chair.*] And as I was saying—I am from the Clybourne Park Improvement Association and we have had it brought to our attention at the last meeting that you people—or at least your mother—has bought a piece of residential property at—[*He digs for the slip of paper again.*]—four o six at Clybourne Street. . .

WALTER: That's right. Care for something to drink? Ruth, get Mr. Lindner a beer.

LINDNER [*upset for some reason*]: Oh—no, really, I mean thank you very much, but no thank you.

RUTH [*innocently*]: Some coffee?

LINDNER: Thank you, nothing at all. [Beneatha *is watching the man carefully.*]

LINDNER: Well, I don't know how much you folks know about our organization. [*He is a gentle man; thoughtful and somewhat labored in his manner.*] It is one of these community organizations set up to look after—oh, you know, things like block upkeep and special projects and we also have what we call our New Neighbors Orientation Committee . . .

BENEATHA [*drily*]: Yes—and what do they do?

LINDNER [*turning a little to her and then returning the main force to* Walter]: Well—it's what you might call a sort of welcoming committee, I guess. I mean they, we, I'm the chairman of the committee—go around and see the new people who move into the neighborhood and sort of give them the lowdown on the way we do things out in Clybourne Park.

BENEATHA [*with appreciation of the two meanings, which escape* Ruth *and* Walter]: Uh-huh.

LINDNER: And we also have the category of what the association calls—[*He looks elsewhere.*]—uh—special community problems . . .

BENEATHA: Yes—and what are some of those?

WALTER: Girl, let the man talk.

LINDNER [*with understated relief*]: Thank you. I would sort of like to explain this thing in my own way. I mean I want to explain to you in a certain way.

WALTER: Go ahead.

LINDNER: Yes. Well. I'm going to try to get right to the point. I'm sure we'll all appreciate that in the long run.

BENEATHA: Yes.

WALTER: Be still now!

LINDNER: Well—

RUTH [*still innocently*]: Would you like another chair—you don't look comfortable.

LINDNER [*more frustrated than annoyed*]: No, thank you very much. Please. Well—to get right to the point I—[*a great breath, and he is off at last*] I am sure you people must be aware of some of the incidents which have happened in various parts of the city when colored people have moved into certain areas—[Beneatha: *exhales heavily and starts tossing a piece of fruit up and down in the air.*] Well—because we have what I think is going to be a unique type of organization in American community life—not only do we deplore that kind of thing—but we are trying to do something about it. [Beneatha *stops tossing and turns with a new and quizzical interest to the man.*] We feel—[*gaining confidence in his mission because of the interest in the faces of the people he is talking to*]—we feel that most of the trouble in this world, when you come right down to it—[*He hits his knee for emphasis.*]—most of the trouble exists because people just don't sit down and talk to each other.

RUTH [*nodding as she might in church, pleased with the remark*]: You can say that again, mister.

LINDNER [*more encouraged by such affirmation*]: That we don't try hard enough in this world to understand the other fellow's problem. The other guy's point of view.

RUTH: Now that's right. [Beneatha *and* Walter *merely watch and listen with genuine interest.*]

LINDNER: Yes—that's the way we feel out in Clybourne Park. And that's why I was elected to come here this afternoon and talk to you people. Friendly like, you know, the way people should talk to each other and see if we couldn't find some way to work this thing out. As I say, the whole business is a matter of caring about the other fellow. Anybody can see that you are a nice family of folks, hard working and honest I'm sure. [Beneatha *frowns slightly, quizzically, her head tilted regarding him.*] Today everybody knows what it means to be on the outside of *something*. And of course, there is always somebody who is out to take the advantage of people who don't always understand.

WALTER: What do you mean?

LINDNER: Well—you see our community is made of people who've worked hard as the dickens for years to build up that little community. They're not rich and fancy people; just hardworking, honest people who don't really have much but those little homes and a dream of the kind of community they want to raise their children in. Now, I don't say we are perfect and there is a lot wrong in some of the things they want. But you've got to admit that a man, right or wrong, has the right to want to have the neighborhood he lives in a certain kind of way. And at the moment the overwhelming majority of our people out there feel that people get along better, take more of a common interest in the life of the community, when they share a common background. I want you to believe me when I tell you that race prejudice simply doesn't enter into it. It is a matter of the people of Clybourne Park believing, rightly or wrongly, as I say, that for the happiness of all concerned that our Negro families are happier when they live in their *own* communities.

BENEATHA [*with a grand and bitter gesture*]: This, friends, is the Welcoming Committee!

WALTER [*dumbfounded, looking at* Lindner]: Is this what you came marching all the way over here to tell us?

LINDNER: Well, now we've been having a fine conversation. I hope you'll hear me all the way through.

WALTER [*tightly*]: Go ahead, man.

LINDNER: You see—in the face of all things I have said, we are prepared to make your family a very generous offer . . .

BENEATHA: Thirty pieces and not a coin less!

WALTER: Yeah?

LINDNER [*putting on his glasses and drawing a form out of the briefcase*]: Our association is prepared, through the collective effort of our people, to buy the house from you at a financial gain to your family.

RUTH: Lord have mercy, ain't this the living gall!

WALTER: All right, you through?

LINDNER: Well, I want to give you the exact terms of the financial arrangement—

WALTER: We don't want to hear no exact terms of no arrangements. I want to know if you got any more to tell us 'bout getting together?

LINDNER [*taking off his glasses*]: Well—I don't suppose that you feel . . .

WALTER: Never mind how I feel—you got any more to say 'bout how people ought to sit down and talk to each other? . . . Get out of my house, man. [*He turns his back and walks to the door.*]

LINDNER [*looking around at the hostile faces and reaching and assembling his hat and briefcase*]: Well—I don't understand why you people are reacting this way. What do you think you are going to gain by moving into a neighborhood where you just aren't wanted and where some elements—well—people can get awful worked up when they feel that their whole way of life and everything they've ever worked for is threatened.

WALTER: Get out.

LINDNER [*at the door, holding a small card*]: Well—I'm sorry it went like this.

WALTER: Get out.

LINDNER [*almost sadly regarding* Walter]: You just can't force people to change their hearts, son. [*He turns and put his card on a table and exits.* Walter *pushes the door to with stinging hatred, and stands looking at it.* Ruth *just sits and* Beneatha *just stands. They say nothing.* Mama *and* Travis *enter.*]

MAMA: Well—this all the packing got done since I left out of here this morning. I testify before God that my children got all the energy of the dead. What time the moving men due?

BENEATHA: Four o'clock. You had a caller, Mama. [*She is smiling, teasingly.*]

MAMA: Sure enough—who?

BENEATHA [*her arms folded saucily*]: The Welcoming Committee. [Walter *and* Ruth *giggle.*]

MAMA [*innocently*]: Who?

BENEATHA: The Welcoming Committee. They said they're sure going to be glad to see you when you get there.

WALTER [*devilishly*]: Yeah, they said they can't hardly wait to see your face. [*laughter*]

MAMA [*sensing their facetiousness*]: What's the matter with you all?

WALTER: Ain't nothing the matter with us. We just telling you 'bout the gentleman who came to see you this afternoon. From the Clybourne Park Improvement Association.

MAMA: What he want?

RUTH [*in the same mood as* Beneatha *and* Walter]: To welcome you, honey.

WALTER: He said they can't hardly wait. He said the one thing they don't have, that they just dying to have out there is a fine family of colored people! [*to Ruth and* Beneatha] Ain't that right!

RUTH AND BENEATHA [*mockingly*]: Yeah! He left his card in case—[*They indicate the card, and* Mama *picks it up and throws it on the floor—understanding and looking off as she draws her chair up to the table on which she has put her plant and some sticks and some cord.*]

MAMA: Father, give us strength. [*knowingly—and without fun*] Did he threaten us?

BENEATHA: Oh—Mama—they don't do it like that any more. He talked Brotherhood. He said everybody ought to learn how to sit down and hate each other with good Christian fellowship. [*She and* Walter *shake hands to ridicule the remark.*]

MAMA [*sadly*]: Lord, protect us . . .

RUTH: You should hear the money those folks raised to buy the house from us. All we paid and then some.

BENEATHA: What they think we going to do—eat 'em?

RUTH: No, honey, marry 'em.

MAMA [*shaking her head*]: Lord, Lord, Lord . . .

RUTH: Well—that's the way the crackers crumble. Joke.

BENEATHA [*laughingly noticing what her mother is doing*]: Mama, what are you doing?

MAMA: Fixing my plant so it won't get hurt none on the way . . .

BENEATHA: Mama, you going to take that to the new house?

MAMA: Un-huh—

BENEATHA: That raggedy-looking old thing?

MAMA [*stopping and looking at her*]: It expresses *me*.

RUTH [*with delight, to* Beneatha]: So there, Miss Thing! [Walter *comes to* Mama *suddenly and bends down behind her and squeezes her in his arms with all his strength. She is overwhelmed by the suddenness of it and, though delighted, her manner is like that of* Ruth *with* Travis.]

MAMA: Look out now, boy! You make me mess up my thing here!

WALTER [*His face lit, he slips down on his knees beside her, his arms still about her.*]: Mama . . . you know what it means to climb up in the chariot?

MAMA [*gruffly, very happy*]: Get on away from me now . . .

RUTH [*near the gift-wrapped package, trying to catch* Walter's *eye*]: Psst—

WALTER: What the old song say, Mama . . .

RUTH: Walter—Now? [*She is pointing at the package.*]

WALTER [*speaking the lines, sweetly, playfully, in his mother's face*]: *I got wings . . . you got wings . . .*
All God's children got wings . . .

MAMA: Boy—get out of my face and do some work . . .

WALTER: *When I get to heaven gonna put on my wings, Gonna fly all over God's heaven . . .*

BENEATHA [*teasingly, from across the room*]: Everybody talking 'bout heaven ain't going there!

WALTER [*to Ruth, who is carrying the box across to them*]: I don't know, you think we ought to give her that . . . Seems to me she ain't been very appreciative around here.

MAMA [*eying the box, which is obviously a gift*]: What is that?

WALTER [*taking it from Ruth and putting it on the table in front of Mama*]: Well—what you all think? Should we give it to her?

RUTH: Oh—she was pretty good today.

MAMA: I'll good you—[*She turns her eyes to the box again.*]

BENEATHA: Open it, Mama. [*She stands up, looks at it, turns and looks at all of them, and then presses her hands together and does not open the package.*]

WALTER [*sweetly*]: Open it, Mama. It's for you. [Mama *looks in his eyes. It is the first present in her life without its being Christmas. Slowly she opens her package and lifts out, one by one, a brand-new sparkling set of gardening tools.* Walter *continues, prodding.*] Ruth made up the note—read it . . .

MAMA [*picking up the card and adjusting her glasses*]: "To our own Mrs. Miniver—Love from Brother, Ruth and Beneatha." Ain't that lovely . . .

TRAVIS [*tugging at his father's sleeve*]: Daddy, can I give her mine now?

WALTER: All right, son. [Travis *flies to get his gift.*] Travis didn't want to go in with the rest of us, Mama. He got his own. [*somewhat amused*] We don't know what it is . . .

TRAVIS [*racing back in the room with a large hatbox and putting it in front of his grandmother*]: Here!

MAMA: Lord have mercy, baby. You done gone and bought your grandmother a hat?

TRAVIS [*very proud*]:   Open it! [*She does and lifts out an elaborate, but very elaborate, wide gardening hat, and all the adults break up at the sight of it.*]

RUTH: Travis, honey, what is that?

TRAVIS [*who thinks it is beautiful and appropriate*]:   It's a gardening hat! Like the ladies always have on in the magazines when they work in their gardens.

BENEATHA [*giggling fiercely*]:   Travis—we were trying to make Mama Mrs. Miniver—not Scarlett O'Hara!

MAMA [*indignantly*]:   What's the matter with you all! This here is a beautiful hat! [*absurdly*] I always wanted me one just like it! [*She pops it on her head to prove it to her grandson, and the hat is ludicrous and considerably oversized.*]

RUTH: Hot dog! Go, Mama!

WALTER [*doubled over with laughter*]:   I'm sorry, Mama—but you look like you ready to go out and chop you some cotton sure enough! [*They all laugh except* Mama, *out of deference to* Travis's *feelings.*]

MAMA [*gathering the boy up to her*]:   Bless your heart—this is the prettiest hat I ever owned—[Walter, Ruth *and* Beneatha *chime in— noisily, festively and insincerely congratulating* Travis *on his gift.*] What are we all standing around here for? We ain't finished packin' yet. Bennie, you ain't packed one book. [*The bell rings.*]

BENEATHA: That couldn't be the movers . . . it's not hardly two o'clock yet—[Beneatha *goes into her room.* Mama *starts for door.*]

WALTER [*turning, stiffening*]:   Wait—wait—I'll get it. [*He stands and looks at the door.*]

MAMA: You expecting company, son?

WALTER [*just looking at the door*]:   Yeah—yeah . . . [Mama *looks at* Ruth, *and they exchange innocent and unfrightened glances.*]

MAMA [*not understanding*]:   Well, let them in, son.

BENEATHA [*from her room*]:   We need some more string.

MAMA: Travis—you run to the hardware and get me some string cord. [Mama *goes out and* Walter *turns and looks at* Ruth. Travis *goes to a dish for money.*]

RUTH: Why don't you answer the door, man?

WALTER [*suddenly bounding across the floor to her*]:   'Cause sometimes it hard to let the future begin! [*stooping down in her face*]

I got wings! You got wings!
All God's children got wings!

[*He crosses to the door and throws it open. Standing there is a very slight little man in a not too prosperous business suit and with haunted frightened eyes and a hat pulled down tightly, brim up, around his forehead.* Travis *passes between the men and exits.* Walter *leans deep in the man's face, still in his jubilance.*]

When I get to heaven gonna put on my wings,
Gonna fly all over God's heaven . . .
[*The little man just stares at him*]
Heaven—
[*Suddenly he stops and looks past the little man into the empty hallway.*] Where's Willy, man?

BOBO: He ain't with me.

WALTER [*not disturbed*]:   Oh—come on in. You know my wife.

BOBO [*dumbly, taking off his hat*]:   Yes—h'you, Miss Ruth.

RUTH [*quietly, a mood apart from her husband already, seeing* Bobo]:
Hello, Bobo.

WALTER: You right on time today . . . Right on time. That's the way!
[*He, slaps* Bobo *on his back.*] Sit down . . . lemme hear. [Ruth
*stands stiffly and quietly in back of them, as though somehow she
senses death, her eyes fixed on her husband.*]

BOBO [*his frightened eyes on the floor, his hat in his hands*]:   Could I
please get a drink of water, before I tell you about it, Walter Lee?
[Walter *does not take his eyes off the man.* Ruth *goes blindly to the
tap and gets a glass of water and brings it to* Bobo.]

WALTER: There ain't nothing wrong, is there?

BOBO: Lemme tell you—

WALTER: Man—didn't nothing go wrong?

BOBO: Lemme tell you—Walter Lee. [*Looking at* Ruth *and talking to
her more than to* Walter.] You know how it was. I got to tell you
how it was. I mean first I got to tell you how it was all the way . . .
I mean about the money I put in, Walter Lee . . .

WALTER [*with taut agitation now*]:   What about the money you put in?

BOBO: Well—it wasn't much as we told you—me and Willy—[*He
stops.*] I'm sorry, Walter. I got a bad feeling about it. I got a real
bad feeling about it . . .

WALTER: Man, what you telling me about all this for? . . . Tell me
what happened in Springfield . . .

BOBO: Springfield.

RUTH [*like a dead woman*]:   What was supposed to happen in
Springfield?

BOBO [*to her*]: This deal that me and Walter went into with Willy—
Me and Willy was going to go down to Springfield and spread
some money 'round so's we wouldn't have to wait so long for the
liquor license . . . That's what we were going to do. Everybody said
that was the way you had to do, you understand, Miss Ruth?

WALTER: Man—what happened down there?

BOBO [*a pitiful man, near tears*]: I'm trying to tell you, Walter.

WALTER [*screaming at him suddenly*]: THEN TELL ME, GOD-
DAMMIT . . . WHAT'S THE MATTER WITH YOU?

BOBO: Man . . . I didn't go to no Springfield, yesterday.

WALTER [*halted, life hanging in the moment*]: Why not?

BOBO [*the long way, the hard way to tell*]: 'Cause I didn't have no
reasons to . . .

WALTER: Man, what are you talking about!

BOBO: I'm talking about the fact that when I got to the train station
yesterday morning—eight o'clock like we planned . . . Man—*Willy
didn't never show up.*

WALTER: Why . . . where was he . . . where is he?

BOBO: That's what I'm trying to tell you . . . I don't know . . . I
waited six hours . . . I called his house . . . and I waited . . . six
hours . . . I waited in that train station six hours . . . [*breaking into
tears*] That was all the extra money I had in the world . . . [*looking
up at* Walter *with the tears running down his face*] Man, *Willy is
gone.*

WALTER: Gone, what you mean Willy is gone? Gone where? You
mean he went by himself. You mean he went off to Springfield by
himself—to take care of getting the license—[*turns and looks anxiously at* Ruth] You mean maybe he didn't want too many people
in on the business down there? [*looks to* Ruth *again, as before*]
You know Willy got his own ways. [*looks back to* Bobo] Maybe
you was late yesterday and he just went on down there without
you. Maybe—maybe—he's been callin' you at home tryin' to tell
you what happened or something. Maybe—maybe—he just got
sick. He's somewhere—he's got to be somewhere. We just got to
find him—me and you got to find him. [*grabs* Bobo *senselessly by
the collar and starts to shake him*] We got to!

BOBO [*in sudden angry, frightened agony*]: What's the matter with
you, Walter! *When a cat take off with your money he don't leave
you no maps!*

WALTER [*turning madly, as though he is looking for* Willy *in the very
room*]: Willy! . . . Willy . . . don't do it . . . Please don't do it . . .

Man, not with that money . . . Man, please, not with that money . . . Oh, God . . . Don't let it be true . . . [*He is wandering around, crying out for* Willy *and looking for him or perhaps for help from God.*] Man . . . I trusted you . . . Man, I put my life in your hands . . . [*He starts to crumple down on the floor as* Ruth *just covers her face in horror*, Mama *opens the door and comes into the room, with* Beneatha *behind her.*] Man . . . [*He starts to pound the floor with his fists, sobbing wildly.*] *That money is made out of my father's flesh* . . .

BOBO [*standing over him helplessly*]: I'm sorry, Walter . . . [*Only* Walter's *sobs reply.* Bobo *puts on his hat.*] I had my life staked on this deal, too . . . [*He exits.*]

MAMA [*to* Walter]: Son—[*She goes to him, bends down to him, talks to his bent head.*] Son . . . Is it gone? Son, I gave, you sixty-five hundred dollars. Is it gone? All of it? Beneatha's money too?

WALTER [*lifting his head slowly*]: Mama . . . I never . . . went to the bank at all.

MAMA [*not wanting to believe him*]: You mean . . . your sister's school money . . . you used that too . . . Walter? . . .

WALTER: Yessss! . . . All of it . . . It's all gone . . .

[*There is total silence.* Ruth *stands with her face covered with her hands;* Beneatha *leans forlornly against a wall, fingering a piece of red ribbon from the mother's gift.* Mama *stops and looks at her son without recognition and then, quite without thinking about it, starts to beat him senselessly in the face.* Beneatha *goes to them and stops it.*]

BENEATHA: Mama! [Mama *stops and looks at both of her children and rises slowly and wanders vaguely, aimlessly away from them.*]

MAMA: I seen . . . him . . . night after night . . . come in . . . and look at that rug . . . and then look at me . . . the red showing in his eyes . . . the veins moving in his head . . . I seen him grow thin and old before he was forty . . . working and working and working like somebody's old horse . . . killing himself . . . and you—you give it all away in a day . . .

BENEATHA: Mama—

MAMA: Oh, God . . . [*She looks up to Him.*] Look down here—and show me the strength.

BENEATHA: Mama—

MAMA [*folding over*]: Strength . . .

BENEATHA [*plaintively*]: MAMA . . .

MAMA: Strength!

CURTAIN

ACT III

An hour later.

At curtain, there is a sullen light of gloom in the living room, gray light not unlike that which began the first scene of Act I. At left we can see Walter *within his room, alone with himself. He is stretched out on the bed, his shirt out and open, his arms under his head. He does not smoke, he does not cry out, he merely lies there, looking up at the ceiling, much as if he were alone in the world.*

In the living room Beneatha *sits at the table, still surrounded by the now almost ominous packing crates. She sits looking off. We feel that this is a mood struck perhaps an hour before, and it lingers now, full of the empty sound of profound disappointment. We see on a line from her brother's bedroom the sameness of their attitudes. Presently the bell rings and* Beneatha *rises without ambition or interest in answering. It is* Asagai, *smiling broadly, striding into the room with energy and happy expectation and conversation.*

ASAGAI: I came over . . . I had some free time. I thought I might help with the packing. Ah, I like the look of packing crates! A household in preparation for a journey! It depresses some people . . . but for me . . . it is another feeling. Something full of the flow of life, do you understand? Movement, progress . . . It makes me think of Africa.

BENEATHA: Africa!

ASAGAI: What kind of a mood is this? Have I told you how deeply you move me?

BENEATHA: He gave away the money, Asagai . . .

ASAGAI: Who gave away what money?

BENEATHA: The insurance money. My brother gave it away.

ASAGAI: Gave it away?

BENEATHA: He made an investment! With a man even Travis wouldn't have trusted.

ASAGAI: And it's gone?

BENEATHA: Gone!

ASAGAI: I'm very sorry . . . And you, now?

BENEATHA: Me? . . . Me? . . . Me, I'm nothing . . . Me. When I was very small . . . we used to take our sleds out in the wintertime and the only hills we had were the ice-covered stone steps of some houses down the street. And we used to fill them in with snow and make them smooth and slide down them all day . . . and it was very dangerous you know . . . far too steep . . . and sure enough one day a kid named Rufus came down too fast and hit the sidewalk . . . and we saw his face just split open right there in front of us . . . And I remember standing there looking at his bloody open face thinking that was the end of Rufus. But the ambulance came and they took him to the hospital and they fixed the broken bones and they sewed it all up . . . and the next time I saw Rufus he just had a little line down the middle of his face . . . I never got over that . . . [Walter *sits up, listening on the bed. Throughout this scene it is important that we feel his reaction at all times, that he visibly respond to the words of his sister and* Asagai.]

ASAGAI: What?

BENEATHA: That that was what one person could do for another, fix him up—sew up the problem, make him all right again. That was the most marvelous thing in the world . . . I wanted to do that. I always thought it was the one concrete thing in the world that a human being could do. Fix up the sick, you know—and make them whole again. This was truly being God . . .

ASAGAI: You wanted to be God?

BENEATHA: No—I wanted to cure. It used to be so important to me. I wanted to cure. It used to matter. I used to care. I mean about people and how their bodies hurt . . .

ASAGAI: And you've stopped caring?

BENEATHA: Yes—I think so.

ASAGAI: Why? [Walter *rises, goes to the door of his room and is about to open it, then stops and stands listening, leaning on the door jamb.*]

BENEATHA: Because it doesn't seem deep enough, close enough to what ails mankind—I mean this thing of sewing up bodies or administering drugs. Don't you understand? It was a child's reaction to the world. I thought that doctors had the secret to all the hurts . . . That's the way a child sees things—or an idealist.

ASAGAI: Children see things very well sometimes—and idealists even better.

BENEATHA: I know that's what you think. Because you are still where I left off—you still care. This is what you see for the world, for Africa. You with the dreams of the future will patch up all Africa—you are going to cure the Great Sore of colonialism with Independence—

ASAGAI: Yes!

BENEATHA: Yes—and you think that one word is the penicillin of the human spirit: "Independence!" But then what?

ASAGAI: That will be the problem for another time. First we must get there.

BENEATHA: And where does it end?

ASAGAI: End? Who even spoke of an end? To life? To living?

BENEATHA: An end to misery!

ASAGAI [*smiling*]: You sound like a French intellectual.

BENEATHA: No! I sound like a human being who just had her future taken right out of her hands! While I was sleeping in my bed in there, things were happening in this world that directly concerned me—and nobody asked me, consulted me—they just went out and did things—and changed my life. Don't you see there isn't any real progress, Asagai, there is only one large circle that we march in, around and around, each of us with our own little picture—in front of us—our own little mirage that we think is the future.

ASAGAI: That is the mistake.

BENEATHA: What?

ASAGAI: What you just said—about the circle. It isn't a circle—it is simply a long line—as in geometry, you know, one that reaches into infinity. And because we cannot see the end—we also cannot see how it changes. And it is very odd but those who see the changes are called "idealists"—and those who cannot, or refuse to think, they are the "realists." It is very strange, and amusing too, I think.

BENEATHA: You—you are almost religious.

ASAGAI: Yes . . . I think I have the religion of doing what is necessary in the world—and of worshipping man—because he is so marvelous, you see.

BENEATHA: Man is foul! And the human race deserves its misery!

ASAGAI: You see: *you* have become the religious one in the old sense. Already, and after such a small defeat, you are worshipping despair.

BENEATHA: From now on, I worship the truth—and the truth is that people are puny, small and selfish . . .

ASAGAI: Truth? Why is it that you despairing ones always think that only you have the truth? I never thought to see *you* like that. You! Your brother made a stupid, childish mistake—and you are grateful to him. So that now you can give up the ailing human race on account of it. You talk about what good is struggle; what good is anything? Where are we all going? And why are we bothering?

BENEATHA: *And you cannot answer it!* All your talk and dreams about Africa and Independence. Independence and then what?

What about all the crooks and petty thieves and just plain idiots who will come into power to steal and plunder the same as before—only now they will be black and do it in the name of the new Independence—You cannot answer that.

ASAGAI [*shouting over her*]:   *I live the answer!* [*pause*] In my village at home it is the exceptional man who can even read a newspaper . . . or who ever *sees* a book at all. I will go home and much of what I will have to say will seem strange to the people of my village. . . . But I will teach and work and things will happen, slowly and swiftly. At times it will seem that nothing changes at all . . . and then again . . . the sudden dramatic events which make history leap into the future. And then quiet again. Retrogression even. Guns, murder, revolution. And I even will have moments when I wonder if the quiet was not better than all that death and hatred. But I will look about my village at the illiteracy and disease and ignorance and I will not wonder long. And perhaps . . . perhaps I will be a great man . . . I mean perhaps I will hold on to the substance of truth and find my way always with the right course . . . and perhaps for it I will be butchered in my bed some night by the servants of empire . . .

BENEATHA: *The martyr!*

ASAGAI: . . . or perhaps I shall live to be a very old man, respected and esteemed in my new nation . . . And perhaps I shall hold office and this is what I'm trying to tell you, Alaiyo; perhaps the things I believe now for my country will be wrong and outmoded, and I will not understand and do terrible things to have things my way or merely to keep my power. Don't you see that there will be young men and women, not British soldiers then, but my own black countrymen . . . to step out of the shadows some evening and slit my then useless throat? Don't you see they have always been there . . . that they always will be. And that such a thing as my own death will be an advance? They who might kill me even . . . actually replenish me!

BENEATHA: Oh, Asagai, I know all that.

ASAGAI: Good! Then stop moaning and groaning and tell me what you plan to do.

BENEATHA: Do?

ASAGAI: I have a bit of a suggestion.

BENEATHA: What?

ASAGAI [*rather quietly for him*]:   That when it is all over—that you come home with me—

BENEATHA [*slapping herself on the forehead with exasperation born of misunderstanding*]: Oh—Asagai—at this moment you decide to be romantic!

ASAGAI [*quickly understanding the misunderstanding*]: My dear, young creature of the New World—I do not mean across the city—I mean across the ocean; home—to Africa.

BENEATHA [*slowly understanding and turning to him with murmured amazement*]: To—to Nigeria?

ASAGAI: Yes! . . . [*smiling and lifting his arms playfully*]. Three hundred years later the African Prince rose up out of the seas and swept the maiden back across the middle passage over which her ancestors had come—

BENEATHA [*unable to play*]: Nigeria?

ASAGAI: Nigeria. Home. [*coming to her with genuine romantic flippancy*] I will show you our mountains and our stars; and give you cool drinks from gourds and teach you the old songs and the ways of our people—and, in time, we will pretend that—[*very softly*]—you have only been away for a day—[*She turns her back to him, thinking. He swings her around and takes her full in his arms in a long embrace which proceeds to passion*]

BENEATHA [*pulling away*]: You're getting me all mixed up—

ASAGAI: Why?

BENEATHA: Too many things—too many things have happened today. I must sit down and think. I don't know what I feel about anything right this minute. [*She promptly sits down and props her chin on her fist.*]

ASAGAI [*charmed*]: All right, I shall leave you. No—don't get up. [*touching her, gently, sweetly*] Just sit awhile and think . . . Never be afraid to sit awhile and think. [*He goes to door and looks at her.*] How often I have looked at you and said, "Ah—so this is what the New World hath finally wrought . . ." [*He exits. Beneatha sits on alone. Presently Walter enters from his room and starts to rummage through things, feverishly looking for something. She looks up and turns in her seat.*]

BENEATHA [*hissingly*]: Yes—just look at what the New World hath wrought! . . . Just look! [*She gestures with bitter disgust.*] There he is! *Monsieur le petit bougeois noir*—himself! There he is—Symbol of a Rising Class! Entrepreneur! Titan of the system! [*Walter ignores her completely and continues frantically and destructively looking for something and hurling things to the floor and tearing things out of their place in his search. Beneatha ignores the eccen-*

tricity of his actions and goes on with the monologue of insult.] Did you dream of yachts on Lake Michigan, Brother? Did you see yourself on that Great Day sitting down at the Conference Table, surrounded by all the mighty bald-headed men in America? All halted, waiting, breathless, waiting for your pronouncements on industry? Waiting for you—Chairman of the Board? [Walter *finds what he is looking for—a small piece of white paper—and pushes it in his pocket and puts on his coat and rushes out without ever having looked at her. She shouts after him.*] I look at you and I see the final triumph of stupidity in the world! [*The door slams and she returns to just sitting again.* Ruth *comes quickly out of* Mama's *room.*]

RUTH: Who was that?

BENEATHA: Your husband.

RUTH: Where did he go?

BENEATHA: Who knows—maybe he has an appointment at U.S. Steel.

RUTH [*anxiously, with frightened eyes*]: You didn't say nothing bad to him, did you?

BENEATHA: Bad? Say anything bad to him? No—I told him he was a sweet boy and full of dreams and everything is strictly peachy keen, as the ofay[3] kids say!

[Mama *enters from her bedroom. She is lost, vague, trying to catch hold, to make some sense of her former command of the world, but it still eludes her. A sense of waste overwhelms her gait; a measure of apology rides on her shoulders. She goes to her plant, which has remained on the table, looks at it, picks it up and takes it to the window sill and sets it outside, and she stands and looks at it a long moment. Then she closes the window, straightens her body with effort and turns around to her children.*]

MAMA: Well—ain't it a mess in here, though? [*a false cheerfulness, a beginning of something*] I guess we all better stop moping around and get some work done. All this unpacking and everything we got to do. [Ruth *raises her head slowly in response to the sense of the line; and* Beneatha *in similar manner turns very slowly to look at her mother.*] One of you all better call the moving people and tell 'em not to come.

RUTH: Tell 'em not to come?

---

[3]*ofay:* white (pig Latin meaning "foe")

MAMA: Of course, baby. Ain't no need in 'em coming all the way here and having to go back. They charges for that too. [*She sits down, fingers to her brow, thinking.*] Lord, ever since I was a little girl, I always remembers people saying, "Lena—Lena Eggleston, you aims too high all the time. You needs to slow down and see life a little more like it is. Just slow down some." That's what they always used to say down home—"Lord, that Lena Eggleston is a high-minded thing. She'll get her due one day!"

RUTH: No, Lena . . .

MAMA: Me and Big Walter just didn't never learn right.

RUTH: Lena, no! We gotta go. Bennie—tell her . . . [*She rises and crosses to Beneatha with her arms outstretched. Beneatha doesn't respond.*] Tell her we can still move . . . the notes ain't but a hundred and twenty-five a month. We got four grown people in this house—we can work . . .

MAMA [*to herself*]: Just aimed too high all the time—

RUTH [*turning and going to Mama fast—the words pouring out with urgency and desperation*]: Lena—I'll work . . . I'll work twenty hours a day in all the kitchens in Chicago . . . I'll strap my baby on my back if I have to and scrub all the floors in America and wash all the sheets in America if I have to—but we got to move . . . We got to get out of here . . . [*Mama reaches out absently and pats Ruth's hand.*]

MAMA: No—I sees things differently now. Been thinking 'bout some of the things we could do to fix this place up some. I seen a second-hand bureau over on Maxwell Street just the other day that could fit right there. [*She points to where the new furniture might go. Ruth wanders away from her.*] Would need some new handles on it and then a little varnish and then it look like something brand-new. And—we can put up them new curtains in the kitchen . . . Why this place be looking fine. Cheer us all up so that we forget trouble ever came . . . [*to Ruth*] And you could get some nice screens to put up in your room round the baby's bassinet . . . [*She looks at both of them, pleadingly.*] Sometimes you just got to know when to give up some things . . . and hold on to what you got. [*Walter enters from the outside, looking spent and leaning against the door, his coat hanging from him.*]

MAMA: Where you been, son?

WALTER [*breathing hard*]: Made a call.

MAMA: To who, son?

WALTER: To the Man.

MAMA: What man, baby?

WALTER: The Man, Mama. Don't you know who The Man is?

RUTH: Walter Lee?

WALTER: *The Man.* Like the guys in the street say—*the Man.* Captain Boss—Mistuh Charley . . . Old Captain Please Mr. Bossman . . .

BENEATHA [*suddenly*]: Linder!

WALTER: That's right! That's good. I told him to come right over.

BENEATHA [*fiercely, understanding*]: For what? What do you want to see him for?

WALTER [*looking at his sister*]: We are going to do business with him.

MAMA: What you talking 'bout, son?

WALTER: Talking 'bout life, Mama. You all always telling me to see life like it is. Well—I laid in there on my back today . . . and I figured it out. Life just like it is. Who gets and who don't get. [*He sits down with his coat on and laughs.*] Mama, you know it's all divided up. Life is. Sure enough. Between the takers and the "tooken." [*He laughs.*] I've figured it out finally. [*He looks around at them.*] Yeah. Some of us always getting "tooken." [*He laughs.*] People like Willy Harris, they don't never get "tooken." And you know why the rest of us do? 'Cause we all mixed up. Mixed up bad. We get to looking 'round for the right and the wrong; and we worry about it and cry about it and stay up nights trying to figure out 'bout the wrong and the right of things all the time . . . And all the time, man, them takers is out there operating, just taking and taking. Willy Harris? Shoot—Willy Harris don't even count. He don't even count in the big scheme of things. But I'll say one thing for old Willy Harris . . . he's taught me something. He's taught me to keep my eye on what counts in this world. Yeah—[*shouting out a little*] Thanks, Willy!

RUTH: What did you call that man for, Walter Lee!

WALTER: Called him to tell him to come on over to the show. Gonna put on a show for the man. Just what he wants to see. You see, Mama, the man came here today and he told us that them people out there where you want us to move—well they so upset they willing to pay us not to move out there. [*He laughs again.*] And— and oh, Mama—you would of been proud of the way me and Ruth and Bennie acted. We told him to get out . . . Lord have mercy! We told the man to get out. Oh, we was some proud folks this afternoon, yeah. [*He lights a cigarette.*] We were still full of that old-time stuff . . .

RUTH [*coming toward him slowly*]: You talking 'bout taking them people's money to keep us from moving in that house?

WALTER: I ain't just talking 'bout it, baby—I'm telling you that's what's going to happen.

BENEATHA: Oh, God! Where is the bottom! Where is the real honest-to-God bottom so he can't go any farther!

WALTER: See—that's the old stuff. You and that boy that was here today. You all want everybody to carry a flag and a spear and sing some marching songs, huh? You wanna spend your life looking into things and trying to find the right and the wrong part, huh? Yeah. You know what's going to happen to that boy someday—he'll find himself sitting in a dungeon, locked in forever—and the takers will have the key! Forget it, baby! There ain't no causes—there ain't nothing but taking in this world, and he who takes most is smartest—and it don't make a damn bit of difference *how*.

MAMA: You making something inside me cry, son. Some awful pain inside me.

WALTER: Don't cry, Mama. Understand. That white man is going to walk in that door able to write checks for more money than we ever had. It's important to him and I'm going to help him . . . I'm going to put on the show, Mama.

MAMA: Son—I come from five generations of people who was slaves and sharecroppers—but ain't nobody in my family never let nobody pay 'em no money that was a way of telling us we wasn't fit to walk the earth. We ain't never been that poor. [*raising her eyes and looking at him*] We ain't never been that dead inside.

BENEATHA: Well—we are dead now. All the talk about dreams and sunlight that goes on in this house. All dead.

WALTER: What's the matter with you all! I didn't make this world! It was give to me this way! Hell, yes, I want me some yachts someday! Yes, I want to hang some real pearls 'round my wife's neck. Ain't she supposed to wear no pearls? Somebody tell me—tell me, who decides which women is suppose to wear pearls in this world. I tell you I am a *man*—and I think my wife should wear some pearls in this world! [*This last line hangs a good while and* Walter *begins to move about the room. The word "Man" has penetrated his consciousness; he mumbles it to himself repeatedly between strange agitated pauses as he moves about.*]

MAMA: Baby, how you going to feel on the inside?

WALTER: Fine! . . . Going to feel fine . . . a man. . . .

MAMA: You won't have nothing left then, Walter Lee.

WALTER [*coming to her*]: I'm going to feel fine, Mama. I'm going to look that son-of-a-bitch in the eyes and say—[*He falters.*]—and say, "All right, Mr. Lindner—[*He falters even more.*]—that's your neighborhood out there. You got the right to keep it like you want. You got the right to have it like you want. Just write the check and—the house is yours." And, and I am going to say—[*His voice almost breaks.*] And you—you people just put the money in my hand and you won't have to live next to this bunch of stinking niggers!. . . [*He straightens up and moves away from his mother, walking around the room.*] Maybe—maybe I'll just get down on my black knees . . . [*He does so;* Ruth *and* Bennie *and* Mama *watch him in frozen horror.*] Captain, Mistuh, Bossman. [*He starts crying.*] A-hee-hee-hee! [*wringing his hands in profoundly anguished imitation*] Yasssssuh! Great White Father, just gi' ussen de money, fo' God's sake, and we's ain't gwine come out deh and dirty up yo' white folks neighborhood . . . [*He breaks down completely, then gets up and goes into the bedroom.*]

BENEATHA: That is not a man. That is nothing but a toothless rate.

MAMA: Yes—death done come in this here house. [*She is nodding, slowly, reflectively.*] Done come walking in my house. On the lips of my children. You what supposed to be my beginning again. You—what supposed to be my harvest. [*to Beneatha*] You—you mourning your brother?

BENEATHA: He's no brother of mine.

MAMA: What you say?

BENEATHA: I said that that individual in that room is no brother of mine.

MAMA: That's what I thought you said. You feeling like you better than he is today? [Beneatha *does not answer.*] Yes? What you tell him a minute ago? That he wasn't a man? Yes? You give him up for me? You done wrote his epitaph too—like the rest of the world? Well, who give you the privilege?

BENEATHA: Be on my side for once! You saw what he just did, Mama! You saw him—down on his knees. Wasn't it you who taught me—to despise any man who would do that? Do what he's going to do.

MAMA: Yes—I taught you that. Me and your daddy. But I thought I taught you something else too . . . I thought I taught you to love him.

BENEATHA: Love him? There is nothing left to love.

MAMA: There is always something left to love. And if you ain't learned that, you ain't learned nothing. [*looking at her*] Have you cried for that boy today? I don't mean for yourself and for the family 'cause we lost the money. I mean for him; what he been through and what it done to him. Child, when do you think is the time to love somebody the most; when they done good and made things easy for everybody? Well then, you ain't through learning—because that ain't the time at all. It's when he's at his lowest and can't believe in hisself 'cause the world done whipped him so. When you starts measuring somebody, measure him right, child, measure him right. Make sure you done taken into account what hills and valleys he come through before he got to wherever he is. [Travis *bursts into the room at the end of the speech, leaving the door open.*]

TRAVIS: Grandmama—the moving men are downstairs! The truck just pulled up.

MAMA [*turning and looking at him*]: Are they, baby? They downstairs? [*She sighs and sits.* Lindner *appears in the doorway. He peers in and knocks lightly, to gain attention, and comes in. All turn to look at him.*]

LINDNER [*hat and briefcase in hand*]: Uh—hello . . . [Ruth *crosses mechanically to the bedroom door and opens it and lets it swing open freely and slowly as the lights come up on* Walter *within, still in his coat, sitting at the far corner of the room. He looks up and out through the room to* Lindner.]

RUTH: He's here. [*A long minute passes and* Walter *slowly gets up.*]

LINDNER [*coming to the table with efficiency, putting his briefcase on the table and starting to unfold papers and unscrew fountain pens*]: Well, I certainly was glad to hear from you people. [Walter *has begun the trek out of the room, slowly and awkwardly, rather like a small boy, passing the back of his sleeve across his mouth from time to time.*] Life can really be so much simpler than people let it be most of the time. Well—with whom do I negotiate? You, Mrs. Younger, or your son here? [Mama *sits with her hands folded on her lap and her eyes closed as* Walter *advances.* Travis *goes close to* Lindner *and looks at the papers curiously.*] Just some official papers, sonny.

RUTH: Travis, you go downstairs.

MAMA [*opening her eyes and looking into* Walter's]: No. Travis, you stay right here. And you make him understand what you doing. Walter Lee. You teach him good. Like Willy Harris taught you. You show where our five generations done come to. Go ahead, son—

WALTER [*Looks down into his boy's eyes.* Travis *grins at him merrily and* Walter *draws him beside him with his arm lightly around his shoulders.*]: Well, Mr. Lindner. [Beneatha *turns away.*] We called you—[*There is a profound, simple groping quality in his speech.*]—because, well, me and my family [*He looks around and shifts from one foot to the other.*] Well—we are very plain people. . . .

LINDNER: Yes—

WALTER: I mean—I have worked as a chauffeur most of my life—and my wife here, she does domestic work in people's kitchens. So does my mother. I mean—we are plain people. . . .

LINDNER: Yes, Mr. Younger—

WALTER [*really like a small boy, looking down at his shoes and then up at the man*]: And—uh—well, my father, well, he was a laborer most of his life.

LINDNER [*absolutely confused*]: Uh, yes—

WALTER [*looking down at his toes once again*]: My father almost beat a man to death once because this man called him a bad name or something, you know what I mean?

LINDNER: No, I'm afraid I don't.

WALTER [*finally straightening up*]: Well, what I mean is that we come from people who had a lot of pride. I mean—we are very proud people. And that's my sister over there and she's going to be a doctor—and we are very proud—

LINDNER: Well—I am sure that is very nice, but—

WALTER [*Starting to cry and facing the man eye to eye*]: What I am telling you is that we called you over here to tell you that we are very proud and that this is—this is my son, who makes the sixth generation of our family in this country, and that we have all thought about your offer and we have decided to move into our house because my father—my father—he earned it. [*Mama has her eyes closed and is rocking back and forth as though she were in church, with her head nodding the amen yes.*] We don't want to make no trouble for nobody or fight no causes—but we will try to be good neighbors. That's all we got to say. [*He looks the man absolutely in the eyes.*] We don't want your money. [*He turns and walks away from the man.*]

LINDNER [*looking around at all of them*]: I take it then that you have decided to occupy.

BENEATHA: That's what the man said.

LINDNER [*to Mama in her reverie*]: Then I would like to appeal to you, Mrs. Younger. You are older and wiser and understand things better I am sure. . . .

MAMA [*rising*]: I am afraid you don't understand. My son said we was going to move and there ain't nothing left for me to say.

[*Shaking her head with double meaning.*] You know how these young folks is nowadays, mister. Can't do a thing with 'em. Goodbye.

LINDNER [*folding up his materials*]: Well—if you are that final about it . . . There is nothing left for me to say. [*He finishes. He is almost ignored by the family, who are concentrating on* Walter Lee. *At the door* Lindner *halts and looks around.*] I sure hope you people know what you're doing. [*He shakes his head and exits.*]

RUTH [*looking around and coming to life*]: Well, for God's sake—if the moving men are here—LET'S GET THE HELL OUT OF HERE!

MAMA [*into action*]: Ain't in the truth! Look at all this here mess. Ruth, put Travis' good jacket on him . . . Walter Lee, fix your tie and tuck your shirt in, you look just like somebody's hoodlum. Lord have mercy, where is my plant? [*She flies to get it amid the general bustling of the family, who are deliberately trying to ignore the nobility of the past moment.*] You all start on down . . . Travis child, don't go empty-handed . . . Ruth, where did I put that box with my skillets in it? I want to be in charge of it myself . . . I'm going to make us the biggest dinner we ever ate tonight . . . Beneatha, what's the matter with them stockings? Pull them things up, girl . . . [*The family starts to file out as two moving men appear and begin to carry out the heavier pieces of furniture, bumping into the family as they move about.*]

BENEATHA: Mama, Asagai—asked me to marry him today and go to Africa—

MAMA [*in the middle of her getting-ready activity*]: He did? You ain't old enough to marry nobody—[*Seeing the moving men lifting one of her chairs precariously.*] Darling, that ain't no bale of cotton, please handle it so we can sit in it again. I had that chair twenty-five years . . . [*The movers sigh with exasperation and go on with their work.*]

BENEATHA [*girlishly and unreasonably trying to pursue the conversation*]: To go to Africa, Mama—be a doctor in Africa . . .

MAMA [*distracted*]: Yes, baby—

WALTER: Africa! What he want to go to Africa for?

BENEATHA: To practice there . . .

WALTER: Girl, if you don't get all them silly ideas out your head! You better marry yourself a man with some loo t. . .

BENEATHA [*angrily, precisely as in the first scene of the play*]: What have you got to do with who I marry!

WALTER: Plenty. Now I think George Murchison—[*He and* Beneatha *go out yelling at each other vigorously;* Beneatha *is heard saying that she would not marry* George Murchison *if he were Adam and she were Eve, etc. The anger is loud and real till their voices diminish.* Ruth *stands at the door and turns to* Mama *and smiles knowingly.*]

MAMA [*fixing her hat at last*]: Yeah—they something all right, my children . . .

RUTH: Yeah—they're something. Let's go, Lena.

MAMA [*stalling, starting to look around at the house*]: Yes—I'm coming. Ruth—

RUTH: Yes?

MAMA [*quietly, woman to woman*]: He finally come into his manhood today, didn't he? Kind of like a rainbow after the rain. . .

RUTH [*biting her lip lest her own pride explode in front of* Mama]: Yes, Lena. [Walter's *voice calls for them raucously.*]

MAMA [*waving* Ruth *out vaguely*]: All right, honey—go on down. I be down directly. [Ruth *hesitates, then exits.* Mama *stands, at last alone in the living room, her plant on the table before her as the lights start to come down. She looks around at all the walls and ceilings and suddenly, despite herself, while the children call below, a great heaving thing rises in her and she puts her fist to her mouth, takes a final desperate look, pulls her coat about her, pats her hat and goes out. The lights dim down. The door opens and she comes back in, grabs her plant, and goes out for the last time.*]

CURTAIN

—1959

Questions: Reading, Responding, Arguing

1. What is the significance of the Langston Hughes poem and the play's title? What does Hughes mean by "a dream deferred?"
2. Are all the members of the Younger family similar? Which member differs?
3. What is Walter and Ruth's marital relationship like? What pressures do they face?
4. Does the play make an implicit statement about gender roles as well as racial ones? Are they comparable to those in Ibsen's *A Doll's House?*
5. How does the play deal with stereotypical portrayals of African Americans?
6. What changes occur to Walter's attitudes as the play progresses?

7. What role does money play in the plot? How do various characters view it?
8. What is the symbolism in Mama's plant?
9. What does the new house symbolize to the members of the Younger family?
10. How is the theme of assimilation dealt with in the play?
11. Some of the minor characters serve as foils to the major ones. Discuss their roles in the play.
12. The theme of race is obviously important in the play. How do the characters view their racial situations?
13. This play is almost fifty years old. How does it reflect its historical setting? Are its issues still relevant?
14. Many elements of the play are clearly symbolic, such as the plant that Mama tends, just as she tends the family. Find and cite examples of symbols in the text to generate your own argument about what it means.

Jonathan Swift (1667–1745)

A Modest Proposal

FOR PREVENTING THE CHILDREN OF POOR PEOPLE IN IRELAND FROM BEING A BURDEN TO THEIR PARENTS OR COUNTRY, AND FOR MAKING THEM BENEFICIAL TO THE PUBLIC

It is a melancholy object to those who walk through this great town or travel in the country, when they see the streets, the roads, and cabin doors, crowded with beggars of the female-sex, followed by three, four, or six children, all in rags and importuning every passenger for an alms. These mothers, instead of being able to work for their honest livelihood, are forced to employ all their time in strolling to beg sustenance for their helpless infants, who, as they grow up, either turn thieves for want of work, or leave their dear native country to fight for the Pretender in Spain, or sell themselves to the Barbadoes.

I think it is agreed by all parties that this prodigious number of children in the arms, or on the backs, or at the heels of their mothers, and frequently of their fathers, is in the present deplorable state of the kingdom a very great additional grievance; and therefore whoever could find out a fair, cheap, and easy method of making these children sound, useful members of the commonwealth would deserve so well of the public as to have his statue set up for a preserver of the nation.

But my intention is very far from being confined to provide only for the children of professed beggars; it is of a much greater extent, and shall take in the whole number of infants at a certain age who are born of parents in effect as little able to support them as those who demand our charity in the streets.

As to my own part, having turned my thoughts for many years upon this important subject, and maturely weighed the several schemes of other projectors, I have always found them grossly mistaken in their computation. It is true, a child just dropped from its dam may be supported by her milk for a solar year, with little other nourishment; at most not above the value of two shillings, which the mother may certainly get, or the value in scraps, by her lawful occupation of begging; and it is exactly at one year old that I propose to provide for them in such a manner as instead of being a charge upon their parents or the parish, or wanting food and raiment for the rest of their lives, they shall on the contrary contribute to the feeding, and partly to the clothing, of many thousands.

There is likewise another great advantage in my scheme, that it will prevent those voluntary abortions, and that horrid practice of women murdering their bastard children, alas, too frequent among us, sacrificing the poor innocent babes, I doubt, more to avoid the expense than the shame, which would move tears and pity in the most savage and inhuman breast.

The number of souls in this kingdom being usually reckoned one million and a half, of these I calculate there may be about two hundred thousand couple whose wives are breeders; from which number I subtract thirty thousand couples who are able to maintain their own children, although I apprehend there cannot be so many under the present distresses of the kingdom; but this being granted, there will remain an hundred and seventy thousand breeders. I again subtract fifty thousand for those women who miscarry, or whose children die by accident or disease within the year. There only remain an hundred and twenty thousand children of poor parents annually born. The question therefore is, how this number shall be reared and provided for, which, as I have already said, under the present situation of affairs, is utterly impossible by all the methods hitherto proposed. For we can neither employ them in handicraft or agriculture; we neither build houses (I mean in the country) nor cultivate land. They can very seldom pick up a livelihood by stealing till they arrive at six years old, except where they are of towardly parts; although I confess they learn the rudiments much earlier, during which time they can however be looked upon only as probationers, as I have been informed by a principal gentleman in the county of Cavan, who protested to me that he never knew above one or two instances under the age of six, even in a part of the kingdom so renowned for the quickest proficiency in that art.

I am assured by our merchants that a boy or a girl before twelve years old is no salable commodity; and even when they come to this age they will not yield above three pounds, or three pounds and half a crown at most on the Exchange; which cannot turn to account either to the parents or the kingdom, the charge of nutriment and rags having been at least four times that value.

I shall now therefore humbly propose my own thoughts, which I hope will not be liable to the least objection.

I have been assured by a very knowing American of my acquaintance in London, that a young healthy child well nursed is at a year old a most delicious, nourishing, and wholesome food, whether stewed, roasted, baked, or boiled; and I make no doubt that it will equally serve in a fricassee or a ragout.

I do therefore humbly offer it to public consideration that of the hundred and twenty thousand children, already computed, twenty thousand may be reserved for breed, whereof only one fourth part to be males, which is more than we allow to sheep, black cattle, or swine; and my reason is that these children are seldom the fruits of marriage, a circumstance not much regarded by our savages, therefore one male will be sufficient to serve four females. That the remaining hundred thousand may at a year old be offered in sale to the persons of quality and fortune through the kingdom, always advising the mother to let them suck plentifully in the last month, so as to render them plump and fat for a good table. A child will make two dishes at an entertainment for friends; and when the family dines alone, the fore or hind quarter will make a reasonable dish, and seasoned with a little pepper or salt will be very good boiled on the fourth day, especially in winter.

I have reckoned upon a medium that a child just born will weigh twelve pounds, and in a solar year if tolerably nursed increaseth to twenty-eight pounds.

I grant this food will be somewhat dear, and therefore very proper for landlords, who, as they have already devoured most of the parents, seem to have the best title to the children.

Infant's flesh will be in season throughout the year, but more plentiful in March, and a little before and after. For we are told by a grave author, an eminent French physician, that fish being a prolific diet, there are more children born in Roman Catholic countries about nine months after Lent than at any other season; therefore, reckoning a year after Lent, the markets will be more glutted than usual, because the number of popish infants is at least three to one in this kingdom; and therefore it will have one other collateral advantage, by lessening the number of Papists among us.

I have already computed the charge of nursing a beggar's child (in which list I reckon all cottagers, laborers, and four fifths of the farmers) to be about two shillings per annum, rags included; and I believe no gentleman would repine to give ten shillings for the carcass of a good fat child, which, as I have said, will make four dishes of excellent nutritive meat, when he hath only some particular friend or his own family to dine with him. Thus the squire will learn to be a good landlord, and grow popular among the tenants; the mother will have eight shillings net profit, and be fit for work till she produces another child.

Those who are more thrifty (as I must confess the times require) may flay the carcass; the skin of which artificially dressed will make admirable gloves for ladies, and summer boots for fine gentlemen.

As to our city of Dublin, shambles may be appointed for this purpose in the most convenient parts of it, and butchers we may be assured will not be wanting; although I rather recommend buying the children alive, and dressing them hot from the knife as we do roasting pigs.

A very worthy person, a true lover of his country, and whose virtues I highly esteem, was lately pleased in discoursing on this matter to offer a refinement upon my scheme. He said that many gentlemen of this kingdom, having of late destroyed their deer, he conceived that the want of venison might be well supplied by the bodies of young lads and maidens, not exceeding fourteen years of age nor under twelve, so great a number of both sexes in every county being now ready to starve for want of work and service; and these to be disposed of by their parents, if alive, or otherwise by their nearest relations. But with due deference to so excellent a friend and so deserving a patriot, I cannot be altogether in his sentiments; for as to the males, my American acquaintance assured me from frequent experience that their flesh was generally tough and lean, like that of our schoolboys, by continual exercise, and their taste disagreeable; and to fatten them would not answer the charge. Then as to the females, it would, I think with humble submission, be a loss to the public, because they soon would become breeders themselves: and besides, it is not improbable that some scrupulous people might be apt to censure such a practice (although indeed very unjustly) as a little bordering upon cruelty; which, I confess, hath always been with me the strongest objection against any project, how well soever intended.

But in order to justify my friend, he confessed that this expedient was put into his head by the famous Psalmanazar, a native of the island Formosa, who came from thence to London above twenty years ago, and in conversation told my friend that in his country when any young person happened to be put to death, the executioner sold the carcass to persons of quality as a prime dainty; and that in his time the body of a plump girl of fifteen, who was crucified for an attempt to poison the emperor, was sold to his Imperial Majesty's prime minister of state, and other great mandarins of the court, in joints from the gibbet, at four hundred crowns. Neither indeed can I deny that if the same use were made of several plump young girls in this town, who without one single groat to their fortunes cannot stir abroad without a chair, and appear at the playhouse and assemblies in foreign fineries which they never will pay for, the kingdom would not be the worse.

Some persons of a desponding spirit are in great concern about that vast number of poor people who are aged, diseased, or maimed, and I have been desired to employ my thoughts what course may be taken to ease the nation of so grievous an encumbrance. But I am not in the least pain upon that matter, because it is very well known that they are every day dying and rotting by cold and famine, and filth and vermin, as fast as can be reasonably expected. And as to the younger laborers, they are now in almost as hopeful a condition. They cannot get work, and consequently pine away for want of nourishment to a degree that if at any time they are accidentally hired to common labor, they have not strength to perform it; and thus the country and themselves are happily delivered from the evils to come.

I have too long digressed, and therefore shall return to my subject. I think the advantages by the proposal which I have made are obvious and many, as well as of the highest importance.

For first, as I have already observed, it would greatly lessen the number of Papists, with whom we are yearly overrun, being the principal breeders of the nation as well as our most dangerous enemies; and who stay at home on purpose to deliver the kingdom to the Pretender, hoping to take their advantage by the absence of so many good Protestants, who have chosen rather to leave their country than to stay at home and pay tithes against their conscience to an Episcopal curate.

Secondly, the poorer tenants will have something valuable of their own, which by law may be made liable to distress, and help to pay their landlord's rent, their corn and cattle being already seized and money a thing unknown.

Thirdly, whereas the maintenance of an hundred thousand children, from two years old and upwards, cannot be computed at less than ten shillings a piece per annum, the nation's stock will be thereby increased fifty thousand pounds per annum, besides the profit of a new dish introduced to the tables of all gentlemen of fortune in the kingdom who have any refinement in taste. And the money will circulate among ourselves, the goods being entirely of our own growth and manufacture.

Fourthly, the constant breeders, besides the gain of eight shillings sterling per annum by the sale of their children, will be rid of the charge of maintaining them after the first year.

Fifthly, this food would likewise bring great custom to taverns, where the vintners will certainly be so prudent as to procure the best receipts for dressing it to perfection, and consequently have their houses frequented by all the fine gentlemen, who justly value themselves upon their knowledge in good eating; and a skillful cook, who understands how to oblige his guests, will contrive to make it as expensive as they please.

Sixthly, this would be a great inducement to marriage, which all wise nations have either encouraged by rewards or enforced by laws and penalties. It would increase the care and tenderness of mothers toward their children, when they were sure of a settlement for life to the poor babes, provided in some sort by the public, to their annual profit instead of expense. We should see an honest emulation among the married women, which of them could bring the fattest child to the market. Men would become as fond of their wives during the time of their pregnancy as they are now of their mares in foal, their cows in calf, or sows when they are ready to farrow; nor offer to beat or kick them (as is too frequent a practice) for fear of a miscarriage.

Many other advantages might be enumerated. For instance, the addition of some thousand carcasses in our exportation of barreled beef, the propagation of swine's flesh, and improvement in the art of making good bacon, so much wanted among us by the great destruction of pigs, too frequent at our tables, which are no way comparable in taste or magnificence to a well-grown, fat, yearling child, which roasted whole will make a considerable figure at a lord mayor's feast or any other public entertainment. But this and many others I omit, being studious of brevity.

Supposing that one thousand families in this city would be constant customers for infants' flesh, besides others who might have it at merry meetings, particularly weddings and christenings, I compute that Dublin would take off annually about twenty thousand carcasses, and the rest of the kingdom (where probably they will be sold somewhat cheaper) the remaining eighty thousand.

I can think of no one objection that will possibly be raised against this proposal, unless it should be urged that the number of people will be thereby much lessened in the kingdom. This I freely own, and it was indeed one principal design in offering it to the world. I desire the reader will observe, that I calculate my remedy for this one individual kingdom of Ireland and for no other that ever was, is, or I think ever can be upon earth. Therefore let no man talk to me of other expedients: of taxing our absentees at five shillings a pound: of using neither clothes nor household furniture except what is of our own growth and manufacture: of utterly rejecting the materials and instruments that promote foreign luxury: of curing the expensiveness of pride, vanity, idleness, and gaming in our women: of introducing a vein of parsimony, prudence, and temperance: of learning to love our country, in the want of which we differ even from Laplanders and the inhabitants of Topinamboo: of quitting our animosities and factions, nor acting any longer like the Jews, who were murdering one another at the very moment their city was taken: of being a little cautious not to sell our country and conscience for nothing: of teaching landlords to have at least one degree of mercy toward their tenants: lastly, of putting a spirit of honesty, industry, and skill into our shopkeepers; who, if a resolution could now be taken to buy only our native goods, would immediately unite to cheat and exact upon us in the price, the measure, and the goodness, nor could ever yet be brought to make one fair proposal of just dealing, though often and earnestly invited to it.

Therefore I repeat, let no man talk to me of these and the like expedients, till he hath at least some glimpse of hope that there will ever be some hearty and sincere attempt to put them in practice.

But as to myself, having been wearied out for many years with offering vain, idle, visionary thoughts, and at length utterly despairing of success, I fortunately fell upon this proposal, which, as it is wholly new, so it hath something solid and real, of no expense and little trouble, full in our own power, and whereby we can incur no danger in disobliging England. For this kind of commodity will not bear exportation, the flesh being of too tender a consistence to admit a long continuance in salt, although perhaps I could name a country which would be glad to eat up our whole nation without it.

After all, I am not so violently bent upon my own opinion as to reject any offer proposed by wise men, which shall be found equally innocent, cheap, easy, and effectual. But before something of that kind shall be advanced in contradiction to my scheme, and offering a better, I desire the author or authors will be pleased maturely to consider two points. First, as things now stand, how they will be able to find food and raiment for an hundred thousand useless mouths and backs. And secondly, there being a round million of creatures in human figure throughout this kingdom, whose sole subsistence put into a common stock would leave them in debt two millions of pounds sterling, adding those who are beggars by profession to the bulk of farmers, cottagers, and laborers, with their wives and children who are beggars in effect; I desire those politicians who dislike my overture, and may perhaps be so bold to attempt an answer, that they will first ask the parents of these mortals whether they would not at this day think it a great happiness to have been sold for food at a year old in the manner I prescribe, and thereby have avoided such a perpetual scene of misfortunes as they have since gone through by the oppression of landlords, the impossibility of paying rent without money or trade, the want of common sustenance, with neither house nor clothes to cover them from the inclemencies of the weather, and the most inevitable prospect of entailing the like or greater miseries upon their breed forever.

I profess, in the sincerity of my heart, that I have not the least personal interest in endeavoring to promote this necessary work, having no other motive than the public good of my country, by advancing our trade, providing for infants, relieving the poor, and giving some pleasure to the rich. I have no children by which I can propose to get a single penny; the youngest being nine years old, and my wife past childbearing.

—*1729*

Questions: Reading, Responding, Arguing

1. Early in his essay, Swift declares his own humility, and argues that he has nothing to gain from his own proposal. What is his intention in stating these details?
2. What is Swift's one objection to his own plan, and why does he raise it?
3. Cite examples from the text where Swift is being satirical, and explain the target of his satire.
4. Moments in the text can be read as Swift revealing his sympathies for the Irish. Cite examples from the text to explain Swift's argument for support of the Irish people.

Charlotte Perkins Gilman (1860–1935)

Why I Wrote
The Yellow Wallpaper

Many and many a reader has asked that. When the story first came out, in the *New England Magazine* about 1891, a Boston physician made protest in *The Transcript.* Such a story ought not to be written, he said; it was enough to drive anyone mad to read it.

Another physician, in Kansas I think, wrote to say that it was the best description of incipient insanity he had ever seen, and—begging my pardon—had I been there?

Now the story of the story is this:

For many years I suffered from a severe and continuous nervous breakdown tending to melancholia—and beyond. During about the third year of this trouble I went, in devout faith and some faint stir of hope, to a noted specialist in nervous diseases, the best known in the country. This wise man put me to bed and applied the rest cure, to which a still-good physique responded so promptly that he concluded there was nothing much the matter with me, and sent me home with solemn advice to "live as domestic a life as far as possible," to "have but two hours' intellectual life a day," and "never to touch pen, brush, or pencil again" as long as I lived. This was in 1887.

I went home and obeyed those directions for some three months, and came so near the borderline of utter mental ruin that I could see over.

Then, using the remnants of intelligence that remained, and helped by a wise friend, I cast the noted specialist's advice to the winds and went to work again—work, the normal life of every human being; work, in which is joy and growth and service, without which one is a pauper and a parasite—ultimately recovering some measure of power.

Being naturally moved to rejoicing by this narrow escape, I wrote *The Yellow Wallpaper,* with its embellishments and additions, to carry out the ideal (I never had hallucinations or objections to my mural decorations) and sent a copy to the physician who so nearly drove me mad. He never acknowledged it.

The little book is valued by alienists and as a good specimen of one kind of literature. It has, to my knowledge, saved one woman from a similar fate—so terrifying her family that they let her out into normal activity and she recovered.

But the best result is this. Many years later I was told that the great specialist had admitted to friends of his that he had altered his treatment of neurasthenia since reading *The Yellow Wallpaper*.

It was not intended to drive people crazy, but to save people from being driven crazy, and it worked.

—*1913*

Questions: Reading, Responding, Arguing

1. What is significantly different in Gilman's own account of her illness and that of the story's protagonist?
2. What does Gilman mean by the story's "embellishments and additions?" To what additions does she specifically refer?
3. What is Gilman's attitude toward work? How is her attitude different from what might have been considered "normal" for a woman in the late 19th century? Justify your argument using research about 19th century attitudes toward women, comparing them to Gilman's attitude.

Jorge Luis Borges (1899–1986)

Borges and I

It's Borges, the other one, that things happen to. I walk through Buenos Aires and I pause—mechanically now, perhaps—to gaze at the arch of an entryway and its inner door; news of Borges reaches me by mail, or I see his name on a list of academics or in some biographical dictionary. My taste runs to hourglasses, maps, eighteenth-century typefaces, etymologies, the taste of coffee, and the prose of Robert Louis Stevenson; Borges shares those preferences, but in a vain sort of way that turns them into the accoutrements of an actor. It would be an exaggeration to say that our relationship is hostile—I live, I allow myself to live, so that Borges can spin out his literature, and that literature is my justification. I willingly admit that he has written a number of sound pages, but those pages will not save *me*, perhaps because the good in them no longer belongs to any individual, not even to that other man, but rather to language itself, or to tradition. Beyond that, I am doomed—utterly and inevitably—to oblivion, and fleeting moments will be all of me that survives in that other man. Little by little, I have been turning everything over to him, though I know the perverse way he has of distorting and magnifying everything. Spinoza believed that all things wish to go on being what they are—stone wishes eternally to be stone, and tiger, to be tiger. I shall endure in Borges, not in myself (if, indeed, I am anybody at all), but I recognize myself less in his books than in many others', or in the tedious strumming of a guitar. Years ago I tried to free myself from him, and I moved on from the mythologies of the slums and outskirts of the city to games with time and infinity, but those games belong to Borges now, and I shall have to think up other things. So my life is a point-counterpoint, a kind of fugue, and a falling away—and everything winds up being lost to me, and everything falls into oblivion, or into the hands of the other man.

I am not sure which of us it is that's writing this page.

—*1964*

Questions: Reading, Responding, Arguing

1. There are at least two different versions of Borges in the essay. Explain the differences between them.
2. Borges writes that "stone wishes eternally to be stone, and tiger, to be tiger." Explain how this relates to the themes of the essay.
3. Borges gives both specific details and abstract generalizations about his life. Cite examples of these dual personalities of Borges to make an argument about the meaning of the text.

Langston Hughes (1902–1967)

The Negro Artist and the Racial Mountain

One of the most promising of the young Negro poets said to me once, "I want to be a poet—not a Negro poet," meaning, I believe, "I want to write like a white poet"; meaning subconsciously, "I would like to be a white poet"; meaning behind that, "I would like to be white." And

I was sorry the young man said that, for no great poet has ever been afraid of being himself. And I doubted then that, with his desire to run away spiritually from his race, this boy would ever be a great poet. But this is the mountain standing in the way of any true Negro art in America—this urge within the race toward whiteness, the desire to pour racial individuality into the mold of American standardization, and to be as little Negro and as much American as possible.

But let us look at the immediate background of this young poet. His family is of what I suppose one would call the Negro middle class: people who are by no means rich yet never uncomfortable nor hungry— smug, contented, respectable folk, members of the Baptist church. The father goes to work every morning. He is a chief steward at a large white club. The mother sometimes does fancy sewing or supervises parties for the rich families of the town. The children go to a mixed school. In the home they read white papers and magazines. And the mother often says "Don't be like niggers" when the children are bad. A frequent phrase from the father is, "Look how well a white man does things." And so the word white comes to be unconsciously a symbol of all virtues. It holds for the children beauty, morality, and money. The whisper of "I want to be white" runs silently through their minds. This young poet's home is, I believe, a fairly typical home of the colored middle class. One sees immediately how difficult it would be for an artist born in such a home to interest himself in interpreting the beauty of his own people. He is never taught to see that beauty. He is taught rather not to see it, or if he does, to be ashamed of it when it is not according to Caucasian patterns.

For racial culture the home of a self-styled "high-class" Negro has nothing better to offer. Instead there will perhaps be more aping of things white than in a less cultured or less wealthy home. The father is perhaps a doctor, lawyer, landowner, or politician. The mother may be a social worker, or a teacher, or she may do nothing and have a maid. Father is often dark but he has usually married the lightest woman he could find. The family attend a fashionable church where few really colored faces are to be found. And they themselves draw a color line. In the North they go to white theaters and white movies. And in the South they have at least two cars and a house "like white folks." Nordic manners, Nordic faces, Nordic hair, Nordic art (if any), and an Episcopal heaven. A very high mountain indeed for the would-be racial artist to climb in order to discover himself and his people.

But then there are the low-down folks, the so-called common element, and they are the majority—may the Lord be praised! The people who have their hip of gin on Saturday nights and are not too important to themselves or the community, or too well fed, or too learned to watch the lazy world go round. They live on Seventh Street in Washington or State Street in Chicago and they do not particularly care whether they are like white folks or anybody else. Their joy runs, bang! into ecstasy. Their religion soars to a shout. Work maybe a little today, rest a little tomorrow. Play awhile. Sing awhile. O, let's dance! These common people are not afraid of spirituals, as for a long time their more intellectual brethren were, and jazz is their child. They furnish a wealth of colorful, distinctive material for any artist because they still hold their own individuality in the face of American standardizations. And perhaps these common people will give to the world its truly great Negro artist, the one who is not afraid to be himself. Whereas the better-class Negro would tell the artist what to do, the people at least let him alone when he does appear. And they are not ashamed of him—if they know he exists at all. And they accept what beauty is their own without question.

Certainly there is, for the American Negro artist who can escape the restrictions the more advanced among his own group would put upon him, a great field of unused material ready for his art. Without going outside his race, and even among the better classes with their "white" culture and conscious American manners, but still Negro enough to be different, there is sufficient matter to furnish a black artist with a lifetime of creative work. And when he chooses to touch on the relations between Negroes and whites in this country, with their innumerable overtones and undertones surely, and especially for literature and the drama, there is an inexhaustible supply of themes at hand. To these the Negro artist can give his racial individuality, his heritage of rhythm and warmth, and his incongruous humor that so often, as in the Blues, becomes ironic laughter mixed with tears. But let us look again at the mountain.

A prominent Negro clubwoman in Philadelphia paid eleven dollars to hear Raquel Meller sing Andalusian popular songs. But she told me a few weeks before she would not think of going to-hear "that woman," Clara Smith, a great black artist, sing Negro folksongs. And many an upper-class Negro church, even now, would not dream of employing a spiritual in its services. The drab melodies in white folks' hymnbooks are much to be preferred. "We want to worship the Lord correctly and quietly. We don't believe in 'shouting.' Let's be dull like the Nordics," they say, in effect.

The road for the serious black artist, then, who would produce a racial art is most certainly rocky and the mountain is high. Until recently he received almost no encouragement for his work from either white or colored people. The fine novels of Chesnutt go out of print with neither race noticing their passing. The quaint charm and humor of Dunbar's dialect verse brought to him, in his day, largely the same kind of encouragement one would give a sideshow freak (A colored man writing poetry! How odd!) or a clown (How amusing!).

The present vogue in things Negro, although it may do as much harm as good for the budding artist, has at least done this: it has brought him forcibly to the attention of his own people among whom for so long, unless the other race had noticed him beforehand, he was a prophet with little honor. I understand that Charles Gilpin acted for years in Negro theaters without any special acclaim from his own, but when Broadway gave him eight curtain calls, Negroes, too, began to beat a tin pan in his honor. I know a young colored writer, a manual worker by day, who had been writing well for the colored magazines for some years, but it was not until he recently broke into the white publications and his first book was accepted by a prominent New York publisher that the "best" Negroes in his city took the trouble to discover that he lived there. Then almost immediately they decided to give a grand dinner for him. But the society ladies were careful to whisper to his mother that perhaps she'd better not come. They were not sure she would have an evening gown.

The Negro artist works against an undertow of sharp criticism and misunderstanding from his own group and unintentional bribes from the whites. "Oh, be respectable, write about nice people, show how good we are," say the Negroes. "Be stereotyped, don't go too far, don't shatter our illusions about you, don't amuse us too seriously. We will pay you," say the whites. Both would have told Jean Toomer not to write *Cane*. The colored people did not praise it. The white people did not buy it. Most of the colored people who did read *Cane* hate it. They are afraid of it. Although the critics gave it good reviews the public remained indifferent. Yet (excepting the work of Du Bois) *Cane* contains the finest prose written by a Negro in America. And like the singing of Robeson, it is truly racial.

But in spite of the Nordicized Negro intelligentsia and the desires of some white editors we have an honest American Negro literature already with us. Now I await the rise of the Negro theater. Our folk music, having achieved world-wide fame, offers itself to the genius of the great individual American composer who is to come. And within the next decade I expect to see the work of a growing school of colored artists who paint and model the beauty of dark faces and create with new technique the expressions of their own soul-world. And the Negro dancers who will dance like flame and the singers who will continue to carry our songs to all who listen—they will be with us in even greater numbers tomorrow.

Most of my own poems are racial in theme and treatment, derived from the life I know. In many of them I try to grasp and hold some of the meanings and rhythms of jazz. I am as sincere as I know how to be in these poems and yet after every reading I answer questions like these from my own people: Do you think Negroes should always write about Negroes? I wish you wouldn't read some of your poems to white folks. How do you find anything interesting in a place like a cabaret? Why do you write about black people? You aren't black. What makes you do so many jazz poems?

But jazz to me is one of the inherent expressions of Negro life in America; the eternal tom-tom beating in the Negro soul—the tom-tom of revolt against weariness in a white world, a world of subway trains, and work, work, work; the tom-tom of joy and laughter, and pain swallowed in a smile. Yet the Philadelphia clubwoman is ashamed to say that her race created it and she does not like me to write about it. The old sub-conscious "white is best" runs through her mind. Years of study under white teachers, a lifetime of white books, pictures, and papers, and white manners, morals, and Puritan standards made her dislike the spirituals. And now she turns up her nose at jazz and all its manifestations—likewise almost everything else distinctly racial. She doesn't care for the Winold Reiss portraits of Negroes because they are "too Negro." She does not want a true picture of herself from anybody. She wants the artist to flatter her, to make the white world believe that all negroes are as smug and as near white in soul as she wants to be. But, to my mind, it is the duty of the younger Negro artist, if he accepts any duties at all from outsiders, to change through the force of his art that old whispering "I want to be white," hidden in the aspirations of his people, to "Why should I want to be white? I am a Negro—and beautiful!"

So I am ashamed for the black poet who says, "I want to be a poet, not a Negro poet," as though his own racial world were not as interesting as any other world. I am ashamed, too, for the colored artist who runs from the painting of Negro faces to the painting of sunsets after the manner of the academicians because he fears the strange unwhiteness of his own features. An artist must be free to choose what he does, certainly, but he must also never be afraid to do what he must choose.

Let the blare of Negro jazz bands and the bellowing voice of Bessie Smith singing the Blues penetrate the closed ears of the colored near-intellectuals until they listen and perhaps understand. Let Paul Robeson singing "Water Boy," and Rudolph Fisher writing about the streets of

Harlem, and Jean Toomer holding the heart of Georgia in his hands, and Aaron Douglas's drawing strange black fantasies cause the smug Negro middle class to turn from their white, respectable, ordinary books and papers to catch a glimmer of their own beauty. We younger Negro artists who create now intend to express our individual dark-skinned selves without fear or shame. If white people are pleased we are glad. If they are not, it doesn't matter. We know we are beautiful. And ugly too. The tom-tom cries and the tom-tom laughs. If colored people are pleased we are glad. If they are not, their displeasure doesn't matter either. We build our temples for tomorrow, strong as we know how, and we stand on top of the mountain, free within ourselves.

—1926

Questions: Reading, Responding, Arguing

1. Explain the metaphor of the "racial mountain."
2. Why does Hughes suspect that the promising young man who wants to be "a poet—not a Negro poet," will never become great?
3. How does Hughes explain why he writes about black topics and themes so frequently?
4. Explain Hughes's attitude toward jazz music. Citing examples, make an argument that explains how jazz music relates to the major themes of the essay.

Christopher Buckley (b. 1952)

College Essay

> . . . your entrance essay must not only demonstrate your grasp of grammar and ability to write lucid, structured prose, but also paint a vivid picture of your personality and character, one that compels a busy admissions officer to accept you.
>
> —*Online college-application editing service.*

It was a seventeenth-century Englishperson John Donne who wrote, "No man is an island." An excellent statement, but it is also true that "No woman is also an island."

The truth of this was brought home dramatically on September 11, 2001. Despite the fact that I was only twelve at the time, the images of that day will not soon ever be forgotten. Not by me, certainly. Though technically not a New Yorker (since I inhabit north-western Wisconsin), I felt, as Donne would put it, "Part of the main," as I watched those buildings come down. Coincidentally, this was also the day my young sibling came down with a skin ailment that the doctors have not yet been able to determine what it is. It's not like his skin condition was a direct result of the terrorist attack, but it probably didn't help.

I have a personal connection to the events of that day, for some years ago my uncle by marriage's brother worked in one of the towers. He wasn't working there on 9/11, but the fact that he had been in the building only years before brought the tragedy home to Muskelunge Township.

It is for this reason that I have resolved to devote my life to bringing about harmony among the nations of the world, especially in those nations who appear to dislike us enough to fly planes into our skyscrapers. With better understanding comes, I believe, the desire not to fly planes into each other's skyscrapers.

Also, I would like to work toward finding a cure for mysterious skin ailments. Candidly, I do not know at this point if I would be a premed, which indeed would be a good way to begin finding the cure. But I also feel that I could contribute vitally to society even if I were a liberal-arts major, for instance majoring in writing for television.

Many people in the world community, indeed probably most, watch television. Therefore I feel that by writing for TV I could reach them through that powerful medium, and bring to them a higher awareness of such problems as Global Warming, Avian Flu, earthquakes in places like Pakistan, and the tsumani. Also the situation in the White House with respect to Mr. Scooter Liddy. To be precise, I believe that television could play a key role in warning people living on shorelines that they are about to be hit by one humongous wave. While it is true that in northwest Wisconsin we don't have this particular problem, it is also true that I think about it on behalf of people who do. No man is an island. To be sure.

Another element in my desire to devote my life to service to humanity was my parents' divorce. Because I believe that this is valuable preparation for college and, beyond, life. At college, for instance, one is liable to find yourself living in a situation in which people don't get along, especially in bathrooms. Bathrooms are in that sense a microcosm of the macrocosm. Bathrooms also can be a truly dramatic crucible, as the playright Arthur Miller has demonstrated in his dramaturgical magnum opus by that title.

I am not one to say, "Omigod, like poor me," despite the fact that my dad would on numerable occasions drink an entire bottle of raspberry cordial and try to run Mamma over with the combine harvester. That is "Stinkin' Thinkin'." As the Danish composer Frederick Nietzche declared, "That which does not kill me makes me longer." This was certainly true of Mamma, especially after being run over.

Finally, what do I bring to the college experience? As President Kennedy observed in his second inaugural, "Ask not what your country can do to you. Ask, what can you do to your country."

I would bring two things, primarily. First, a positive attitude, despite all this crap I have had to deal with. Secondly, full tuition payment.

While Dad pretty much wiped out the money in the process of running over Mamma—she was in the house at the time—my grandparents say they can pay for my education, and even throw in a little "walking-around money" for the hardworking folks in the admissions department. Grandma says she will give up her heart and arthritis medications, and Grandpa says he will go back to work at the uranium mine in Utah despite the facts that he is eighty-two and legally blind.

In this way, the college won't have to give me scholarship money that could go to some even more disadvantaged applicant, assuming there is one.

—2005

Questions: Reading, Responding, Arguing

1. Who is the assumed reader of Buckley's essay? Is there more than one?
2. What is the satiric target of the essay?
3. What are the various stereotypes of writing that Buckley is exploring or exaggerating?
4. Buckley makes several references to literature, to real events, or to his family. Cite examples to argue that Buckley manipulates those references to pursue his own agenda.

Harvey Pekar (b. 1939) *and R. Crumb* (b. 1943)
The Harvey Pekar Name Story

Questions: Reading, Responding, Arguing

1. Explain all of the meanings and identities associated with the author's name in the story.
2. How do the illustrations convey Pekar's reactions and emotions from panel to panel?
3. Does Pekar eventually become satisfied with his name? With his identity? Cite examples to justify your argument.
4. The stark background and bland depiction of the narrator in Crumb's illustrations seem to stand in contrast to the anxiety Pekar reveals in his monologue. Why did the authors choose to make the text as they did? Compare and contrast the illustrations to the written text to make an argument about what the story means.

Where We Come From

Cultures and Places

"Where do you come from, Phaedrus my friend, and where are you going?"

—Plato, *Phaedrus*

Environment has a profound influence on who we are and what we believe. Yet, paradoxically, the limitations of our environment can also make it difficult for us to see where, or how profoundly, that influence has occurred. One of the advantages of literature is that it allows us to gain perspective on our own lives by experiencing other places and cultures we might otherwise not be able to experience directly. Reading allows us to travel elsewhere, in particular to those places that are impossible for us to go to—the past, the future, fantasy settings—or to places where the potential of coming face to face with grave personal risk is too great.

We can also travel to places that are not just physical locations or temporal moments in history—there are all of the symbolic places of our lives, such as "home." "Home" means different things to different people. For some, home is a place for peace and relaxation at the end of a busy day, but for others, home is a house filled with bustle and activity. What do *you* call home? Similarly, what do you think of when you think of nature? For some, trees, lakes, fields, or farmlands most accurately portray their idea of a natural setting, but someone who grew up in the middle of a city would find those locations "unnatural" or even threatening.

Finally, we can think about this question of "place" in terms of culture—the shared traditions, ideas, beliefs, and rules held by any significant collection of people. The inhabitants of countries other than the United States have radically different notions of comfort, of food, of love, and of truth. What does your country mean to you? What "spaces" are you a part of that might be smaller, or larger, than national boundaries? These are the kinds of questions that are asked, and answered, when we read literature. The purpose of the following selections is to spur you into thinking about the "setting" of your life and how that setting has contributed to your knowledge of the world.

> "What difference is there, do you think, between those in
> Plato's cave who can only marvel at the shadows and images
> of various objects, provided they are content and don't know
> what they miss, and the philosopher who has emerged from
> the cave and sees the real things?"
>
> —Erasmus, *The Praise of Folly*

Sarah Orne Jewett (1849–1909)

A White Heron

I

The woods were already filled with shadows one June evening, just before eight o'clock, though a bright sunset still glimmered faintly among the trunks of the trees. A little girl was driving home her cow, a plodding, dilatory, provoking creature in her behavior, but a valued companion for all that. They were going away from whatever light there was, and striking deep into the woods, but their feet were familiar with the path, and it was no matter whether their eyes could see it or not.

There was hardly a night the summer through when the old cow could be found waiting at the pasture bars; on the contrary, it was her greatest pleasure to hide herself away among the huckleberry bushes, and though she wore a loud bell she had made the discovery that if one stood perfectly still it would not ring. So Sylvia had to hunt for her until she found her, and call Co'! Co'! with never an answering Moo, until her childish patience was quite spent. If the creature had not given good milk and plenty of it, the case would have seemed very different to her owners. Besides, Sylvia had all the time there was, and very little use to make of it. Sometimes in pleasant weather it was a consolation to look upon the cow's pranks as an intelligent attempt to play hide and seek, and as the child had no playmates she lent herself to this amusement with a good deal of zest. Though this chase had been so long that the wary animal herself had given an unusual signal of her whereabouts. Sylvia had only laughed when she came upon Mistress Moolly at the swamp-side, and urged her affectionately homeward with a twig of birch leaves. The old cow was not inclined to wander farther, she even turned in the right direction for once as they left the pasture, and stepped along the road at a good pace. She was quite ready to be milked now, and seldom stopped to browse. Sylvia wondered what her grandmother would say because they were so late. It was a great while since she had left home at half-past five o'clock, but everybody knew the difficulty of making this errand a short one. Mrs. Tilley had chased the horned torment too many summer evenings herself to blame any one else for lingering, and was only thankful as she waited that she had Sylvia, nowadays, to give such valuable assistance. The good woman suspected that Sylvia loitered occasionally on her own account; there never was such a child for straying about out-of-doors since the world was made! Everybody said that it was a good change for a little maid who had tried to grow for eight years in a crowded manufacturing town, but as for Sylvia herself, it seemed as if she never had been alive at all before she came to live at the farm. She thought often with wistful compassion of a wretched geranium that belonged to a town neighbor.

" 'Afraid of folks,' " old Mrs. Tilley said to herself, with a smile, after she had made the unlikely choice of Sylvia from her daughter's houseful of children, and was returning to the farm. " 'Afraid of folks,' they said! I guess she won't be troubled no great with 'em up to the old place!" When they reached the door of the lonely house and stopped to unlock it, and the cat came to purr loudly, and rub against them, a deserted pussy, indeed, but fat with young robins, Sylvia whispered that this was a beautiful place to live in, and she never should wish to go home.

The companions followed the shady woodroad, the cow taking slow steps and the child very fast ones. The cow stopped long at the brook to drink, as if the pasture were not half a swamp, and Sylvia stood still and waited, letting her bare feet cool themselves in the shoal water, while the great twilight moths struck softly against her. She waded on through the brook as the cow moved away, and listened to the thrushes with a heart that beat fast with pleasure. There was a stirring in the great boughs overhead. They were full of little birds and beasts that seemed to be wide awake, and going about their world, or else saying goodnight to each other in sleepy twitters. Sylvia herself felt sleepy as she walked along. However, it was not much farther to the house, and the air was soft and sweet. She was not often in the woods so late as this, and it made her feel as if she were a part of the gray shadows and the moving leaves. She was just thinking how long it seemed since she first came to the farm a year ago, and wondering if everything went on in the noisy town just the same as when she was there; the thought of the great red-faced boy who used to chase and frighten her made her hurry along the path to escape from the shadow of the trees.

Suddenly this little woods-girl is horror-stricken to hear a clear whistle not very far away. Not a bird's-whistle, which would have a sort of friendliness, but a boy's whistle, determined, and somewhat aggressive. Sylvia left the cow to whatever sad fate might await her, and stepped discreetly aside into the brushes, but she was just too late. The enemy had discovered her, and called out in a very cheerful and persuasive tone, "Halloa, little girl, how far is it to the road?" and trembling Sylvia answered almost inaudibly. "A good ways."

She did not dare to look boldly at the tall young man, who carried a gun over his shoulder, but she came out of her bush and again followed the cow, while he walked alongside.

"I have been hunting for some birds," the stranger said kindly, "and I have lost my way, and need a friend very much. Don't be afraid," he added gallantly. "Speak up and tell me what your name is, and whether you think I can spend the night at your house, and go out gunning early in the morning."

Sylvia was more alarmed than before. Would not her grandmother consider her much to blame? But who could have foreseen such an accident as this? It did not seem to be her fault, and she hung her head as if the stem of it were broken, but managed to answer "Sylvy," with much effort when her companion again asked her name.

Mrs. Tilley was standing in the doorway when the trio came into view. The cow gave a loud moo by way of explanation.

"Yes, you'd better speak up for yourself, you old trial! Where'd she tucked herself away this time, Sylvy?" But Sylvia kept an awed silence; she knew by instinct that her grandmother did not comprehend the gravity of the situation. She must be mistaking the stranger for one of the farmer-lads of the region.

The young man stood his gun beside the door, and dropped a lumpy game-bag beside it; then he bade Mrs. Tilley good-evening, and repeated his wayfarer's story, and asked if he could have a night's lodging.

"Put me anywhere you like," he said. "I must be off early in the morning, before day; but I am very hungry, indeed. You can give me some milk at any rate, that's plain."

"Dear sakes, yes," responded the hostess, whose long slumbering hospitality seemed to be easily awakened. "You might fare better if you went out to the main road a mile or so, but you're welcome to what we've got. I'll milk right off, and you make yourself at home. You can sleep on husks or feathers," she proffered graciously. "I raised them all myself. There's good pasturing for geese just below here towards the ma'sh. Now step round and set a plate for the gentleman, Sylvy!" And Sylvia promptly stepped. She was glad to have something to do, and she was hungry herself.

It was a surprise to find so clean and comfortable a little dwelling in this New England wilderness. The young man had known the horrors of its most primitive housekeeping, and the dreary squalor of that level of society which does not rebel at the companionship of hens. This was the best thrift of an old-fashioned farmstead, though on such a small scale that it seemed like a hermitage. He listened eagerly to the old woman's quaint talk, he watched Sylvia's pale face and shining gray eyes with ever growing enthusiasm, and insisted that this was the best supper he had eaten for a month, and afterward the new-made friends sat down in the door-way together while the moon came up.

Soon it would be berry-time, and Sylvia was a great help at picking. The cow was a good milker, though a plaguy thing to keep track of, the hostess gossiped frankly, adding presently that she had buried four children, so Sylvia's mother, and a son (who might be dead) in California were all the children she had left. "Dan, my boy, was a great hand to go gunning," she explained sadly. "I never wanted for pa'tridges or gray squer'ls while he was to home. He's been a great wand'rer, I expect, and he's no hand to write letters. There, I don't blame him, I'd ha' seen the world myself if it had been so I could."

"Sylvy takes after him," the grandmother continued affectionately, after a minute's pause. "There ain't a foot o' ground she don't know her way over, and the wild creaturs counts her one o' themselves. Squer'ls she'll tame to come an' feed right out o' her hands, and all sorts o' birds. Last winter she got the jaybirds to bangeing[1] here, and I believe she'd 'a' scanted herself of her own meals to have plenty to throw out amongst 'em, if I hadn't kep' watch. Anything but crows, I tell her, I'm willin' to help support—though Dan he had a tamed one o' them that did seem to have reason same as folks. It was round here a good spell after he went away. Dan an' his father they didn't hitch,—but he never held up his head ag'in after Dan had dared him an' gone off."

The guest did not notice this hint of family sorrows in his eager interest in something else.

"So Sylvy knows all about birds, does she?" he exclaimed, as he looked round at the little girl who sat, very demure but increasingly sleepy, in the moonlight. "I am making a collection of birds myself. I have been at it ever since I was a boy." (Mrs. Tilley smiled.) "There are two or three very rare ones I have been hunting for these five years. I mean to get them on my own grounds if they can be found."

"Do you cage 'em up?" asked Mrs. Tilley doubtfully, in response to this enthusiastic announcement.

"Oh no, they're stuffed and preserved, dozens and dozens of them," said the ornithologist, "and I have shot or snared every one myself. I caught a glimpse of a white heron a few miles from here on Saturday, and I have followed it in this direction. They have never been found in this district at all. The little white heron, it is," and he turned

---

[1] *bangeing:* loitering

again to look at Sylvia with the hope of discovering that the rare bird was one of her acquaintances.

But Sylvia was watching a hop-toad in the narrow footpath.

"You would know the heron if you saw it," the stranger continued eagerly. "A queer tall white bird with soft feathers and long thin legs. And it would have a nest perhaps in the top of a high tree, made of sticks, something like a hawk's nest."

Sylvia's heart gave a wild beat; she knew that strange white bird, and had once stolen softly near where it stood in some bright green swamp grass, away over at the other side of the woods. There was an open place where the sunshine always seemed strangely yellow and hot, where tall, nodding rushes grew, and her grandmother had warned her that she might sink in the soft black mud underneath and never be heard of more. Not far beyond were the salt marshes just this side the sea itself, which Sylvia wondered and dreamed much about, but never had seen, whose great voice could sometimes be heard above the noise of the woods on stormy nights.

"I can't think of anything I should like so much as to find that heron's nest," the handsome stranger was saying. "I would give ten dollars to anybody who could show it to me," he added desperately, "and I mean to spend my whole vacation hunting for it if need be. Perhaps it was only migrating, or had been chased out of its own region by some bird of prey."

Mrs. Tilley gave amazed attention to all this, but Sylvia still watched the toad, not divining, as she might have done at some calmer time, that the creature wished to get to its hole under the door-step, and was much hindered by the unusual spectators at that hour of the evening. No amount of thought, that night, could decide how many wished-for treasures the ten dollars, so lightly spoken of, would buy.

The next day the young sportsman hovered about the woods, and Sylvia kept him company, having lost her first fear of the friendly lad, who proved to be most kind and sympathetic. He told her many things about the birds and what they knew and where they lived and what they did with themselves. And he gave her a jack-knife, which she thought as great a treasure as if she were a desert-islander. All day long he did not once make her troubled or afraid except when he brought down some unsuspecting singing creature from its bough. Sylvia would have liked him vastly better without his gun; she could not understand why he killed the very birds he seemed to like so much. But as the day waned, Sylvia still watched the young man with loving admiration. She had never seen anybody so charming and delightful; the woman's heart, asleep in the child, was vaguely thrilled by a dream of love. Some premonition of that great power stirred and swayed these young creatures who traversed the solemn woodlands with soft-footed silent care. They stopped to listen to a bird's song; they pressed forward again eagerly, parting the branches—speaking to each other rarely and in whispers; the young man going first and Sylvia following fascinated, a few steps behind, with her gray eyes dark with excitement.

She grieved because the longed-for white heron was elusive, but she did not lead the guest, she only followed, and there was no such thing as speaking first. The sound of her own unquestioned voice would have terrified her—it was hard enough to answer yes or no when there was need of that. At last evening began to fall, and they drove the cow home together, and Sylvia smiled with pleasure when they came to the place where she heard the whistle and was afraid only the night before.

II

Half a mile from home, at the farther edge of the woods, where the land was highest, a great pine-tree stood, the last of its generation. Whether it was left for a boundary mark, or for what reason, no one could say; the woodchoppers who had felled its mates were dead and gone long ago, and a whole forest of sturdy trees, pines and oaks and maples, had grown again. But the stately head of this old pine towered above them all and made a landmark for sea and shore miles and miles away. Sylvia knew it well. She had always believed that whoever climbed to the top of it could see the ocean; and the little girl had often laid her hand on the great rough trunk and looked up wistfully at those dark boughs that the wind always stirred, no matter how hot and still the air might be below. Now she thought of the tree with a new excitement, for why, if one climbed it at break of day could not one see all the world, and easily discover from whence the white heron flew, and mark the place, and find the hidden nest?

What a spirit of adventure, what wild ambition! What fancied triumph and delight and glory for the later morning when she could make known the secret! It was almost too real and too great for the childish heart to bear.

All night the door of the little house stood open and the whippoorwills came and sang upon the very step. The young sportsman and his old hostess were sound asleep, but Sylvia's great design kept her broad awake and watching. She forgot to think of sleep. The short summer night seemed as long as the winter darkness, and at last when the whippoorwills ceased, and she was afraid the morning would after all come too soon, she stole out of the house and followed the pasture path through the woods, hastening toward the open ground beyond, listening with a sense of comfort and companionship to the drowsy twitter of a half-awakened bird, whose perch she had jarred in passing. Alas, if the great wave of human interest which flooded for the first time this dull little life should sweep away the satisfactions of an existence heart to heart with nature and the dumb life of the forest!

There was the huge tree asleep yet in the paling moonlight, and small and silly Sylvia began with utmost bravery to mount to the top of it, with tingling, eager blood coursing the channels of her whole frame, with her bare feet and fingers, that pinched and held like bird's claws to the monstrous ladder reaching up, up, almost to the sky itself. First she must mount the white oak tree that grew alongside, where she was almost lost among the dark branches and the green leaves heavy and wet with dew; a bird fluttered off its nest, and a red squirrel ran to and fro and scolded pettishly at the harmless housebreaker. Sylvia felt her way easily. She had often climbed there, and knew that higher still one of the oak's upper branches chafed against the pine trunk, just where its lower boughs were set close together. There, when she made the dangerous pass from one tree to the other, the great enterprise would really begin.

She crept out along the swaying oak limb at last, and took the daring step across into the old pine-tree. The way was harder than she thought; she must reach far and hold fast, the sharp dry twigs caught and held her and scratched her like angry talons, the pitch made her thin little fingers clumsy and stiff as she went round and round the tree's great stem, higher and higher upward. The sparrows and robins in the woods below were beginning to wake and twitter to the dawn, yet it seemed much lighter there aloft in the pine-tree, and the child knew she must hurry if her project were to be of any use.

The tree seemed to lengthen itself out as she went up, and to reach farther and farther upward. It was like a great main-mast to the voyaging earth; it must truly have been amazed that morning through all its ponderous frame as it felt this determined spark of human spirit wending its way from higher branch to branch. Who knows how steadily the least twigs held themselves to advantage this light, weak creature on her way! The old pine must have loved his new dependent. More than all the hawks, and bats, and moths, and even the sweet voiced thrushes, was the brave, beating heart of the solitary gray-eyed child. And the tree stood still and frowned away the winds that June morning while the dawn grew bright in the east.

Sylvia's face was like a pale star, it one had seen it from the ground, when the last thorny bough was past, and she stood trembling and tired but wholly triumphant, high in the treetop. Yes, there was the sea with the dawning sun making a golden dazzle over it, and toward that glorious east flew two hawks with slow-moving pinions. How low they looked in the air from that height when one had only seen them before far up, and dark against the blue sky. Their gray feathers were as soft as moths: they seemed only a little way from the tree, and Sylvia felt as if she too could go flying away among the clouds. Westward, the woodlands and farms reached miles and miles into the distance; here and there were church steeples, and white villages, truly it was a vast and awesome world!

The birds sang louder and louder. At last the sun came up bewilderingly bright. Sylvia could see the white sails of ships out at sea, and the clouds that were purple and rose-colored and yellow at first began to fade away. Where was the white heron's nest in the sea of green branches, and was this wonderful sight and pageant of the world the only reward for having climbed to such a giddy height? Now look down again, Sylvia, where the green marsh is set among the shining birches and dark hemlocks; there where you saw the white heron once you will see him again; look, look! a white spot of him like a single floating feather comes up from the dead hemlock and grows larger, and rises, and comes close at last, and goes by the landmark pine with steady sweep of wing and outstretched slender neck and crested head. And wait! wait! do not move a foot or a finger, little girl, do not send an arrow of light and consciousness from your two eager eyes, for the heron has perched on a pine bough not far beyond yours, and cries back to his mate on the nest and plumes his feathers for the new day!

The child gives a long sigh a minute later when a company of shouting cat-birds comes also to the tree, and vexed by their fluttering and lawlessness the solemn heron goes away. She knows his secret now, the wild, light, slender bird that floats and wavers, and goes back like an arrow presently to his home in the green world beneath. Then Sylvia, well satisfied, makes her perilous way down again, not daring to look far below the branch she stands on, ready to cry sometimes because her fingers ache and her lamed feet slip. Wondering over and over again what the stranger would say to her, and what he would think when she told him how to find his way straight to the heron's nest.

"Sylvy, Sylvy!" called the busy old grandmother again and again, but nobody answered, and the small husk bed was empty and Sylvia had disappeared.

The guest waked from a dream, and remembering his day's pleasure hurried to dress himself that might it sooner begin. He was sure from the way the shy little girl looked once or twice yesterday that she had at least seen the white heron, and now she must really be made to tell. Here she comes now, paler than ever, and her worn old frock is torn and tattered, and smeared with pine pitch. The grandmother and the sportsman stand in the door together and question her, and the splendid moment has come to speak of the dead hemlock-tree by the green marsh.

But Sylvia does not speak after all, though the old grandmother fretfully rebukes her, and the young man's kind, appealing eyes are looking straight in her own. He can make them rich with money; he has promised it, and they are poor now. He is so well worth making happy, and he waits to hear the story she can tell.

No, she must keep silence! What is it that suddenly forbids her and makes her dumb? Has she been nine years growing and now, when the great world for the first time puts out a hand to her, must she thrust it aside for a bird's sake? The murmur of the pine's green branches is in her ears, she remembers how the white heron came flying through the golden air and how they watched the sea and the morning together, and Sylvia cannot speak; she cannot tell the heron's secret and give its life away.

Dear loyalty, that suffered a sharp pang as the guest went away disappointed later in the day, that could have served and followed him and loved him as a dog loves! Many a night Sylvia heard the echo of his whistle haunting the pasture path as she came home with the loitering cow. She forgot even her sorrow at the sharp report of his gun and the sight of thrushes and sparrows dropping silent to the ground, their songs hushed and their pretty feathers stained and wet with blood. Were the birds better friends than their hunter might have been,—who can tell? Whatever treasures were lost to her, woodlands and summertime, remember! Bring your gifts and graces and tell your secrets to this lonely country child!

—*1886*

Questions: Reading, Responding, Arguing

1. What is the significance of Sylvia's name?
2. Even though she is a child, Sylvia is attracted to the young man. Locate passages that show both her attraction to him and her doubts about him.
3. Examine the shift in Jewett's style near the end of the story. Why does she alter her style?

4. Why is "A White Heron" a good example of an initiation story? Explain what an invitation story is and cite examples from the text to argue that this story fits those qualifications.
5. Citing examples from the text, argue that the climax of the story symbolically represents Sylvia's increased maturity.

William Faulkner (1897–1962)

A Rose for Emily

I

When Miss Emily Grierson died, our whole town went to her funeral: the men through a sort of respectful affection for a fallen monument, the women mostly out of curiosity to see the inside of her house, which no one save an old manservant—a combined gardener and cook—had seen in at least ten years.

It was a big, squarish frame house that had once been white, decorated with cupolas and spires and scrolled balconies in the heavily lightsome style of the seventies, set on what had once been our most select street. But garages and cotton gins had encroached and obliterated even the august names of that neighborhood; only Miss Emily's house was left, lifting its stubborn and coquettish decay above the cotton wagons and the gasoline pumps—an eyesore among eyesores. And now Miss Emily had gone to join the representatives of those august names where they lay in the cedar-bemused cemetery among the ranked and anonymous graves of Union and Confederate soldiers who fell at the battle of Jefferson.

Alive, Miss Emily had been a tradition, a duty, and a care; a sort of hereditary obligation upon the town, dating from that day in 1894 when Colonel Sartoris, the mayor—he who fathered the edict that no Negro woman should appear on the streets without an apron—remitted her taxes, the dispensation dating from the death of her father on into perpetuity. Not that Miss Emily would have accepted charity. Colonel Sartoris invented an involved tale to the effect that Miss Emily's father had loaned money to the town, which the town, as a matter of business, preferred this way of repaying. Only a man of Colonel Sartoris' generation and thought could have invented it, and only a woman could have believed it.

When the next generation, with its more modern ideas, became mayors and aldermen, this arrangement created some little dissatisfaction. On the first of the year they mailed her a tax notice. February came, and there was no reply. They wrote her a formal letter, asking her to call at the sheriff's office at her convenience. A week later the mayor wrote her himself, offering to call or to send his car for her, and received in reply a note on paper of an archaic shape, in a thin, flowing calligraphy in faded ink, to the effect that she no longer went out at all. The tax notice was also enclosed, without comment.

They called a special meeting of the Board of Aldermen. A deputation waited upon her, knocked at the door through which no visitor had passed since she ceased giving china-painting lessons eight or ten years earlier. They were admitted by the old Negro into a dim hall from which a staircase mounted into still more shadow. It smelled of dust and disuse—a close, dank smell. The Negro led them into the parlor. It was furnished in heavy, leather-covered furniture. When the Negro opened the blinds of one window, they could see that the leather was cracked; and when they sat down, a faint dust rose sluggishly about their thighs, spinning with slow motes in the single sunray. On a tarnished gilt easel before the fireplace stood a crayon portrait of Miss Emily's father.

They rose when she entered—a small, fat woman in black, with a thin gold chain descending to her waist and vanishing into her belt, leaning on an ebony cane with a tarnished gold head. Her skeleton was small and spare; perhaps that was why what would have been merely plumpness in another was obesity in her. She looked bloated, like a body long submerged in motionless water, and of that pallid hue. Her eyes, lost in the fatty ridges of her face, looked like two small pieces of coal pressed into a lump of dough as they moved from one face to another while the visitors stated their errand.

She did not ask them to sit. She just stood in the door and listened quietly until the spokesman came to a stumbling halt. Then they could hear the invisible watch ticking at the end of the gold chain.

Her voice was dry and cold. "I have no taxes in Jefferson. Colonel Sartoris explained it to me. Perhaps one of you can gain access to the city records and satisfy yourselves."

"But we have. We are the city authorities, Miss Emily. Didn't you get a notice from the sheriff, signed by him?"

"I received a paper, yes," Miss Emily said. "Perhaps he considers himself the sheriff. . . . I have no taxes in Jefferson."

"But there is nothing on the books to show that, you see. We must go by the—"

"See Colonel Sartoris. I have no taxes in Jefferson."

"But, Miss Emily—"

"See Colonel Sartoris." (Colonel Sartoris had been dead almost ten years.) "I have no taxes in Jefferson. Tobe!" The Negro appeared. "Show these gentlemen out."

II

So she vanquished them, horse and foot, just as she had vanquished their fathers thirty years before about the smell. That was two years after her father's death and a short time after her sweetheart—the one we believed would marry her—had deserted her. After her father's death she went out very little; after her sweetheart went away people hardly saw her at all. A few of the ladies had the temerity to call, but were not received, and the only sign of life about the place was the Negro man—a young man then—going in and out with a market basket.

"Just as if a man—any man—could keep a kitchen properly," the ladies said; so they were not surprised when the smell developed. It was another link between the gross, teeming world and the high and mighty Griersons.

A neighbor, a woman, complained to the mayor, Judge Stevens, eighty years old.

"But what will you have me do about it, madam?" he said.

"Why, send her word to stop it," the woman said. "Isn't there a law?"

"I'm sure that won't be necessary," Judge Stevens said. "It's probably just a snake or a rat that nigger of hers killed in the yard. I'll speak to him about it."

The next day he received two more complaints, one from a man who came in diffident deprecation. "We really must do something about it, Judge. I'd be the last one in the world to bother Miss Emily, but we've got to do something." That night the Board of Aldermen met—three gray-beards and one younger man, a member of the rising generation.

"It's simple enough," he said. "Send her word to have her place cleaned up. Give her a certain time to do it in, and if she don't. . . ."

"Dammit, sir," Judge Stevens said, "will you accuse a lady to her face of smelling bad?"

So the next night, after midnight, four men crossed Miss Emily's lawn and slunk about the house like burglars, sniffing along the base of the brickwork and at the cellar openings while one of them performed a regular sowing motion with his hand out of a sack slung from his shoulder. They broke open the cellar door and sprinkled lime there, and in all the outbuildings. As they recrossed the lawn, a window that had been dark was lighted and Miss Emily sat in it, the light behind her, and her upright torso motionless as that of an idol. They crept quietly across the lawn and into the shadow of the locusts that lined the street. After a week or two the smell went away.

That was when people had begun to feel really sorry for her. People in our town, remembering how old lady Wyatt, her great-aunt, had gone completely crazy at last, believed that the Griersons held themselves a little too high for what they really were. None of the young men were quite good enough for Miss Emily and such. We had long thought of them as a tableau; Miss Emily a slender figure in white in the background, her father a spraddled silhouette in the foreground, his back to her and clutching a horsewhip, the two of them framed by the backflung front door. So when she got to be thirty and was still single, we were not pleased exactly, but vindicated; even with insanity in the family she wouldn't have turned down all of her chances if they had really materialized.

When her father died, it got about that the house was all that was left to her; and in a way, people were glad. At last they could pity Miss Emily. Being left alone, and a pauper, she had become humanized. Now she too would know the old thrill and the old despair of a penny more or less.

The day after his death all the ladies prepared to call at the house and offer condolence and aid, as is our custom. Miss Emily met them at the door, dressed as usual and with no trace of grief on her face. She told them that her father was not dead. She did that for three days, with the ministers calling on her, and the doctors, trying to persuade her to let them dispose of the body. Just as they were about to resort to law and force, she broke down, and they buried her father quickly.

We did not say she was crazy then. We believed she had to do that. We remembered all the young men her father had driven away, and we knew that with nothing left, she would have to cling to that which had robbed her, as people will.

III

She was sick for a long time. When we saw her again, her hair was cut short, making her look like a girl, with a vague resemblance to those angels in colored church windows—sort of tragic and serene.

The town had just let the contracts for paving the sidewalks, and in the summer after her father's death they began the work. The construction company came with niggers and mules and machinery, and a foreman named Homer Barron, a Yankee—a big, dark, ready man, with a big voice and eyes lighter than his face. The little boys would follow in groups to hear him cuss the niggers, and the niggers singing in time to the rise and fall of picks. Pretty soon he knew everybody in town. Whenever you heard a lot of laughing anywhere about the square, Homer Barron would be in the center of the group. Presently we began to see him and Miss Emily on Sunday afternoons driving in the yellow-wheeled buggy and the matched team of bays from the livery stable.

At first we were glad that Miss Emily would have an interest, because the ladies all said, "Of course a Grierson would not think seriously of a Northerner, a day laborer." But there were still others, older people, who said that even grief could not cause a real lady to forget *noblesse oblige*—without calling it *noblesse oblige*. They just said, "Poor Emily. Her kinsfolk should come to her." She had some kin in Alabama; but years ago her father had fallen out with them over the estate of old lady Wyatt, the crazy woman, and there was no communication between the two families. They had not even been represented at the funeral.

And as soon as the old people said, "Poor Emily," the whispering began. "Do you suppose it's really so?" they said to one another. "Of course it is. What else could . . ." This behind their hands; rustling of craned silk and satin behind jalousies closed upon the sun of Sunday afternoon as the thin, swift clop-clop-clop of the matched team passed: "Poor Emily."

She carried her head high enough—even when we believed that she was fallen. It was as if she demanded more than ever the recognition of her dignity as the last Grierson; as if it had wanted that touch of earthiness to reaffirm her imperviousness. Like when she bought the rat poison, the arsenic. That was over a year after they had begun to say "Poor Emily," and while the two female cousins were visiting her.

"I want some poison," she said to the druggist. She was over thirty then, still a slight woman, though thinner than usual, with cold, haughty black eyes in a face the flesh of which was strained across the temples and about the eyesockets as you imagine a lighthousekeeper's face ought to look. "I want some poison," she said.

"Yes, Miss Emily. What kind? For rats and such? I'd recom—"

"I want the best you have. I don't care what kind."

The druggist named several. "They'll kill anything up to an elephant. But what you want—"

"Arsenic," Miss Emily said. "Is that a good one?"

"Is . . . arsenic? Yes, ma'am. But what you want—"

"I want arsenic."

The druggist looked down at her. She looked back at him, erect, her face like a strained flag. "Why, of course," the druggist said. "If that's what you want. But the law requires you to tell what you are going to use it for."

Miss Emily just stared at him, her head tilted back in order to look him eye for eye, until he looked away and went and got the arsenic and wrapped it up. The Negro delivery boy brought her the package; the druggist didn't come back. When she opened the package at home there was written on the box, under the skull and bones—"For rats."

IV

So the next day we all said, "She will kill herself"; and we said it would be the best thing. When she had first begun to be seen with Homer Barron, we had said, "She will marry him." Then we said, "She will persuade him yet," because Homer himself had remarked— he liked men, and it was known that he drank with the younger men in the Elks' Club—that he was not a marrying man. Later we said, "Poor Emily" behind the jalousies as they passed on Sunday after-noon in the glittering buggy, Miss Emily with her head high and Homer Barron with his hat cocked and a cigar in his teeth, reins and whip in a yellow glove.

Then some of the ladies began to say that it was a disgrace to the town and a bad example to the young people. The men did not want to interfere, but at last the ladies forced the Baptist minister—Miss Emily's people were Episcopal—to call upon her. He would never divulge what happened during that interview, but he refused to go back again. The next Sunday they again drove about the streets, and the following day the minister's wife wrote to Miss Emily's relations in Alabama.

So she had blood-kin under her roof again and we sat back to watch developments. At first nothing happened. Then we were sure that they were to be married. We learned that Miss Emily had been to the jew-eler's and ordered a man's toilet set in silver, with the letters H. B. on each piece. Two days later we learned that she had bought a complete outfit of men's clothing, including a nightshirt, and we said, "They are married." We were really glad. We were glad because the two female cousins were even more Grierson than Miss Emily had ever been.

So we were not surprised when Homer Barron—the streets had been finished some time since—was gone. We were a little disappointed that there was not a public blowing-off, but we believed that he had gone on to prepare for Miss Emily's coming, or to give her a chance to get rid of the cousins. (By that time it was a cabal, and we were all Miss Emily's allies to help circumvent the cousins.) Sure enough, after another week they departed. And, as we had expected all along, within three days Homer Barron was back in town. A neighbor saw the Negro man admit him at the kitchen door at dusk one evening.

And that was the last we saw of Homer Barron. And of Miss Emily for some time. The Negro man went in and out with the market basket, but the front door remained closed. Now and then we would see her at a window for a moment, as the men did that night when they sprinkled the lime, but for almost six months she did not appear on the streets. Then we knew that this was to be expected too; as if that quality of her father which had thwarted her woman's life so many times had been too virulent and too furious to die.

When we next saw Miss Emily, she had grown fat and her hair was turning gray. During the next few years it grew grayer and grayer until it attained an even pepper-and-salt iron-gray, when it ceased turning. Up to the day of her death at seventy-four it was still that vigorous iron-gray, like the hair of an active man.

From that time on her front door remained closed, save for a period of six or seven years, when she was about forty, during which she gave lessons in china painting. She fitted up a studio in one of the downstairs rooms, where the daughters and granddaughters of Colonel Sartoris' contemporaries were sent to her with the same regularity and in the same spirit that they were sent to church on Sundays with a twenty-five cent piece for the collection plate. Meanwhile her taxes had been remitted.

Then the newer generation became the backbone and the spirit of the town, and the painting pupils grew up and fell away and did not send their children to her with boxes of color and tedious brushes and pictures cut from the ladies' magazines. The front door closed upon the last one and remained closed for good. When the town got free postal delivery, Miss Emily alone refused to let them fasten the metal numbers above her door and attach a mailbox to it. She would not listen to them.

Daily, monthly, yearly we watched the Negro grow grayer and more stooped, going in and out with the market basket. Each December we sent her a tax notice, which would be returned by the post office a week later, unclaimed. Now and then we would see her in one of the downstairs windows—she had evidently shut up the top floor of the house—like the carven torso of an idol in a niche, looking or not looking at us, we could never tell which. Thus she passed from generation to generation—dear, inescapable, impervious, tranquil, and perverse.

And so she died. Fell ill in the house filled with dust and shadows, with only a doddering Negro man to wait on her. We did not even know she was sick; we had long since given up trying to get any information from the Negro. He talked to no one, probably not even to her, for his voice had grown harsh and rusty, as if from disuse.

She died in one of the downstairs rooms, in a heavy walnut bed with a curtain, her gray head propped on a pillow yellow and moldy with age and lack of sunlight.

V

The Negro met the first of the ladies at the front door and let them in, with their hushed, sibilant voices and their quick, curious glances, and then he disappeared. He walked right through the house and out the back and was not seen again.

The two female cousins came at once. They held the funeral on the second day, with the town coming to look at Miss Emily beneath a mass of bought flowers, with the crayon face of her father musing profoundly above the bier and the ladies sibilant and macabre; and the very old men—some in their brushed Confederate uniforms—on the porch and the lawn, talking of Miss Emily as if she had been a contemporary of theirs, believing that they had danced with her and courted her perhaps, confusing time with its mathematical progression, as the old do, to whom all the past is not a diminishing road but, instead, a huge meadow which no winter ever quite touches, divided from them now by the narrow bottleneck of the most recent decade of years.

Already we knew that there was one room in that region above stairs which no one had seen in forty years, and which would have to be forced. They waited until Miss Emily was decently in the ground before they opened it.

The violence of breaking down the door seemed to fill this room with pervading dust. A thin, acrid pall as of the tomb seemed to lie everywhere upon this room decked and furnished as for a bridal: upon the valance curtains of faded rose color, upon the rose-shaded lights, upon the dressing table, upon the delicate array of crystal and the man's toilet things backed with tarnished silver, silver so tarnished that the monogram was obscured. Among them lay collar and tie, as if they had just been removed, which, lifted, left upon the surface a pale crescent in the dust. Upon a chair hung the suit, carefully folded; beneath it the two mute shoes and the discarded socks.

The man himself lay in the bed.

For a long while we just stood there, looking down at the profound and fleshless grin. The body had apparently once lain in the attitude of an embrace, but now the long sleep that outlasts love, that conquers even the grimace of love, had cuckolded him. What was left of him, rotted beneath what was left of the nightshirt, had become inextricable from the bed in which he lay; and upon him and upon the pillow beside him lay that even coating of the patient and biding dust.

Then we noticed that in the second pillow was the indentation of a head. One of us lifted something from it, and leaning forward, that faint and invisible dust dry and acrid in the nostrils, we saw a long strand of iron-gray hair.

—1930

Questions: Reading, Responding, Arguing

1. The narrator uses the perspective of "we." How does this affect the narrative? How does it relate to the story's non-chronological plot?

2. Explain Emily's relationship to the town and the people. What does the narrator mean by "Alive, Miss Emily had been a tradition, a duty, and a care"?

3. Compare this story with one by another writer who writes about the South. Do both contain an implicit criticism of Southern life? Cite examples from both texts to argue that the authors have different, or similar, attitudes about Southern life.

Ernest Hemingway (1899–1961)

Big Two-Hearted River

PART I

The train went on up the track out of sight, around one of the hills of burnt timber. Nick sat down on the bundle of canvas and bedding the baggage man had pitched out of the door of the baggage car. There was no town, nothing but the rails and the burned-over country. The thirteen saloons that had lined the one street of Seney had not left a trace. The foundations of the Mansion House hotel stuck up above the ground. the stone was chipped and split by the fire. It was all that was left of the town of Seney. Even the surface had been burned off the ground.

Nick looked at the burned-over stretch of hillside, where he had expected to find the scattered houses of the town and then walked down the railroad track to the bridge over the river. The river was there. It swirled against the log spiles of the bridge. Nick looked down into the clear, brown water, colored from the pebbly bottom, and watched the trout keeping themselves steady in the current with wavering fins. As he watched them they changed their positions by quick angles, only to hold steady in the fast water again. Nick watched them a long time.

He watched them holding themselves with their noses into the current, many trout in deep, fast moving water, slightly distorted as he watched far down through the glassy convex surface of the pool, its surface pushing and swelling smooth against the resistance of the log-driven piles of the bridge. At the bottom of the pool were the big trout. Nick did not see them at first. Then he saw them at the bottom of the pool, big trout looking to hold themselves on the gravel bottom in a varying mist of gravel and sand, raised in spurts by the current.

Nick looked down into the pool from the bridge. It was a hot day. A kingfisher flew up the stream. It was a long time since Nick had looked into a stream and seen trout. They were very satisfactory. As the shadow of the kingfisher moved up the stream, a big trout shot upstream in a long angle, only his shadow marking the angle, then lost his shadow as he came through the surface of the water, caught the sun, and then, as he went back into the stream under the surface, his shadow seemed to float down the stream with the current, unresisting, to his post under the bridge where he tightened facing up into the current.

Nick's heart tightened as the trout moved. He felt all the old feeling.

He turned and looked down the stream. It stretched away, pebbly-bottomed with shallows and big boulders and a deep pool as it curved away around the foot of a bluff.

Nick walked back up the ties to where his pack lay in the cinders beside the railway track. He was happy. He adjusted the pack harness around the bundle, pulling straps tight, slung the pack on his back, got his arms through the shoulder straps and took some of the pull off his shoulders by leaning his forehead against the wide band of the tump-line. Still, it was too heavy. It was much too heavy. He had his leather rod-case in his hand and leaning forward to keep the weight of the pack high on his shoulders he walked along the road that paralleled the railway track, leaving the burned town behind in the heat, and then turned off around a hill with a high, fire-scarred hill on either side onto a road that went back into the country. He walked along the road feeling the ache from the pull of the heavy pack. The road climbed steadily. It was hard work walking up-hill. His muscles ached and the day was hot, but Nick felt happy. He felt he had left everything behind, the need for thinking, the need to write, other needs. It was all back of him.

From the time he had gotten down off the train and the baggage man had thrown his pack out of the open car door things had been different. Seney was burned, the country was burned over and changed, but it did not matter. It could not all be burned. He knew that. He hiked along the road, sweating in the sun, climbing to cross the range of hills that separated the railway from the pine plains.

The road ran on, dipping occasionally, but always climbing. Nick went on up. Finally the road after going parallel to the burnt hillside reached the top. Nick leaned back against a stump and slipped out of the pack harness. Ahead of him, as far as he could see, was the pine plain. The burned country stopped off at the left with the range of hills. On ahead islands of dark pine trees rose out of the plain. Far off to the left was the line of the river. Nick followed it with his eye and caught glints of the water in the sun.

There was nothing but the pine plain ahead of him, until the far blue hills that marked the Lake Superior height of land. He could hardly see them, faint and far away in the heat-light over the plain. If he looked too steadily they were gone. But if he only half-looked they were there, the far-off hills of the height of land.

Nick sat down against the charred stump and smoked a cigarette. His pack balanced on the top of the stump, harness holding ready, a hollow molded in it from his back. Nick sat smoking, looking out over the country. He did not need to get his map out. He knew where he was from the position of the river.

As he smoked, his legs stretched out in front of him, he noticed a grasshopper walk along the ground and up onto his woolen sock. The grasshopper was black. As he had walked along the road, climbing, he had started many grasshoppers from the dust. They were all black. They were not the big grasshoppers with yellow and black or red and black wings whirring out from their black wing sheathing as they fly up. These were just ordinary hoppers, but all a sooty black in color. Nick had wondered about them as he walked, without really thinking about them. Now, as he watched the black hopper that was nibbling at the wool of his sock with its fourway lip, he realized that they had all turned black from living in the burned-over land. He realized that the fire must have come the year before, but the grasshoppers were all black now. He wondered how long they would stay that way.

Carefully he reached his hand down and took hold of the hopper by the wings. He turned him up, all his legs walking in the air, and looked at his jointed belly. Yes, it was black too, iridescent where the back and head were dusty.

"Go on, hopper," Nick said, speaking out loud for the first time. "Fly away somewhere."

He tossed the grasshopper up into the air and watched him sail away to a charcoal stump across the road.

Nick stood up. He leaned his back against the weight of his pack where it rested upright on the stump and got his arms through the shoulder straps. He stood with the pack on his back on the brow of the hill looking out across the country, toward the distant river and then struck down the hillside away from the road. Underfoot the ground was good walking. Two hundred yards down the hillside the fire line stopped. Then it was sweet fern, growing ankle high, to walk through, and clumps of jack pines; a long undulating country with frequent rises and descents, sandy underfoot and the country alive again.

Nick kept his direction by the sun. He knew where he wanted to strike the river and he kept on through the pine plain, mounting small rises to see other rises ahead of him and sometimes from the top of a rise a great solid island of pines off to his right or his left. He broke off some sprigs of the heathery sweet fern, and put them under his pack straps. The chafing crushed it and he smelled it as he walked.

He was tired and very hot, walking across the uneven, shadeless pine plain. At any time he knew he could strike the river by turning off to his left. It could not be more than a mile away. But he kept on toward the north to hit the river as far upstream as he could go in one day's walking.

For some time as he walked Nick had been in sight of one of the big islands of pine standing out above the rolling high ground he was crossing. He dipped down and then as he came slowly up to the crest of the bridge he turned and made toward the pine trees.

There was no underbrush in the island of pine trees. The trunks of the trees went straight up or slanted toward each other. The trunks were straight and brown without branches. The branches were high above. Some interlocked to make a solid shadow on the brown forest floor. Around the grove of trees was a bare space. It was brown and soft underfoot as Nick walked on it. This was the over-lapping of the pine needle floor, extending out beyond the width of the high branches. The trees had grown tall and the branches moved high, leaving in the sun this bare space they had once covered with shadow. Sharp at the edge of this extension of the forest floor commenced the sweet fern.

Nick slipped of his pack and lay down in the shade. He lay on his back and looked up into the pine trees. His neck and back and the small of his back rested as he stretched. The earth felt good against his back. He looked up at the sky, through the branches, and then shut his eyes. He opened them and looked up again. There was a wind high up in the branches. He shut his eyes again and went to sleep.

Nick woke stiff and cramped. The sun was nearly down. His pack was heavy and the straps painful as he lifted it on. He leaned over with the pack on and picked up the leather rod-case and started out from the pine trees across the sweet fern swale, toward the river. He knew it could not be more than a mile.

He came down a hillside covered with stumps into a meadow. At the edge of the meadow flowed the river. Nick was glad to get to the river. He walked upstream through the meadow. His trousers were soaked with the dew as he walked. After the hot day, the dew had come quickly and heavily. The river made no sound. It was too fast and smooth. At the edge of the meadow, before he mounted to a piece of high ground to make camp, Nick looked down the river at the trout rising. They were rising to insects come from the swamp on the other side of the stream when the sun went down. The trout jumped out of water to take them. While Nick walked through the little stretch of meadow alongside the stream, trout had jumped high out of water. Now as he looked down the river, the insects must be settling on the surface, for the trout were feeding steadily all down the stream. As far down the long stretch as he could see, the trout were rising, making circles all down the surface of the water, as though it were starting to rain.

The ground rose, wooded and sandy, to overlook the meadow, the stretch of river and the swamp. Nick dropped his pack and rod-case and looked for a level piece of ground. He was very hungry and he wanted to make his camp before he cooked. Between two jack pines, the ground was quite level. He took the ax out of the pack and chopped out two projecting roots. That leveled a piece of ground large enough to sleep on. He smoothed out the sandy soil with his hand and pulled all the sweet fern bushes by their roots. His hands smelled good from the sweet fern. He smoothed the uprooted earth. He did not want anything making lumps under the blankets. When he had the ground smooth, he spread his three blankets. One he folded double, next to the ground. The other two he spread on top.

With the ax he slit off a bright slab of pine from one of the stumps and split it into pegs for the tent. He wanted them long and solid to hold in the ground. With the tent unpacked and spread on the ground, the pack, leaning against a jackpine, looked much smaller. Nick tied the rope that served the tent for a ridge-pole to the trunk of one of the pine trees and pulled the tent up off the ground with the other end of the rope and tied it to the other pine. The tent hung on the rope like a canvas blanket on a clothesline. Nick poked a pole he had cut up under the back peak of the canvas and then made it a tent by pegging out the sides. he pegged the sides out taut and drove the pegs deep, hitting them down into the ground with the flat of the ax until the rope loops were buried and the canvas was drum tight.

Across the open mouth of the tent Nick fixed cheesecloth to keep out mosquitoes. He crawled inside under the mosquito bar with various things from the pack to put at the head of the bed under the slant of the canvas. Inside the tent the light came through the brown canvas. It smelled pleasantly of canvas. Already there was something mysterious and homelike. Nick was happy as he crawled inside the tent. He had not been unhappy all day. This was different though. Now things were done. there had been this to do. Now it was done. It had been a hard trip. He was very tired. That was done. He had made his camp. He was settled. Nothing could touch him. It was a good place to camp. He was there, in the good place. He was in his home where he had made it. Now he was hungry.

He came out, crawling under the cheesecloth. It was quite dark outside. It was lighter in the tent.

Nick went over to the pack and found, with his fingers, a long nail in a paper sack of nails, in the bottom of the pack. He drove it into the pine tree, holding it close and hitting it gently with the flat of the ax. He hung the pack up on the nail. All his supplies were in the pack. They were off the ground and sheltered now.

Nick was hungry. He did not believe he had ever been hungrier. He opened and emptied a can of pork and beans and a can of spaghetti into the frying pan.

"I've got a right to eat this kind of stuff, if I'm willing to carry it," Nick said. His voice sounded strange in the darkening woods. He did not speak again.

He started a fire with some chunks of pine he got with the ax from a stump. Over the fire he stuck a wire grill, pushing the four legs down into the ground with his boot. Nick put the frying plan on the grill over the flames. He was hungrier. The beans and spaghetti warmed. Nick stirred them and mixed them together. They began to bubble, making little bubbles that rose with difficulty to the surface. There was a good smell. Nick got out a bottle of tomato catchup and cut four slices of bread. The little bubbles were coming faster now. Nick sat down beside the fire and lifted the frying pan off. He poured about half the contents out into the tin plate. It spread slowly on the plate. Nick knew it was too hot. He poured on some tomato catchup. He knew the beans and spaghetti were still too hot. He looked at the fire, then at the tent, he was not going to spoil it all by burning his tongue. For years he had never enjoyed fried bananas because he had never been able to wait for them to cool. His tongue was very sensitive. He was very hungry. Across the river in the swamp, in the almost dark, he saw a mist rising. He looked at the tent once more. All right. He took a full spoonful from the plate.

"Chrise," Nick said, "Geezus Chrise," he said happily.

He ate the whole plateful before he remembered the bread. Nick finished the second plateful with the bread, mopping the plate shiny. He had not eaten since a cup of coffee and a ham sandwich in the station restaurant at St. Ignace. It had been a very fine experience. He had been that hungry before, but had not been able to satisfy it. He could have made camp hours before if he had wanted to. There were plenty of good places to camp on the river. But this was good.

Nick tucked two big chips of pine under the grill. The fire flared up. He had forgotten to get water for the coffee. Out of the pack he got a folding canvas bucket and walked down the hill, across the edge of the meadow, to the stream. The other bank was in a white mist. The grass was wet and cold as he knelt on the bank and dipped the canvas bucket into the stream. It bellied and pulled hard in the current. The water was ice cold. Nick rinsed the bucket and carried it full up to the camp. Up away from the stream it was not so cold.

Nick drove another big nail and hung up the bucket full of water. He dipped the coffee pot half full, put some more chips under the grill onto the fire and put the pot on. He could not remember which way he made coffee. He could remember an argument about it with Hopkins, but not which side he had taken. He decided to bring it to a boil. He remembered now that was Hopkins's way. He had once argued about everything with Hopkins. While he waited for the coffee to boil, he opened a small can of apricots. He liked to open cans. He emptied the can of apricots out into a tin cup. While he watched the coffee on the fire, he drank the juice syrup of the apricots, carefully at first to keep from spilling, then meditatively, sucking the apricots down. They were better than fresh apricots.

The coffee boiled as he watched. The lid came up and coffee and grounds ran down the side of the pot. Nick took it off the grill. It was a triumph for Hopkins. He put sugar in the empty apricot cup and poured some of the coffee out to cool. It was too hot to pour and he used his hat to hold the handle of the coffee pot. He would not let it steep in the pot at all. Not the first cup. It should be straight Hopkins all the way. Hop deserved that. He was a very serious coffee drinker. He was the most serious man Nick had ever known. Not heavy, serious. That was a long time ago. Hopkins spoke without moving his lips. He had played polo. He made millions of dollars in Texas. He had borrowed carfare to go to Chicago, when the wire came that his first big well had come in. He could have wired for money. That would have been too slow. they called Hop's girl the Blonde Venus. Hop did not mind because she was not his real girl. Hopkins said very confidently that none of them would make fun of his real girl. He was right. Hopkins went away when the telegram came. That was on the Black River. It took eight days for the telegram to reach him. Hopkins gave away his .22 caliber Colt automatic pistol to Nick. He gave his camera to Bill. It was to remember him always by. They were all going fishing again next summer. The Hop Head was rich. He would get a yacht and they would all cruise along the north shore of Lake Superior. He was excited but serious. They said good-bye and all felt bad. It broke up the trip. They never saw Hopkins again. That was a long time ago on the Black River.

Nick drank the coffee, the coffee according to Hopkins. The coffee was bitter. Nick laughed. It made a good ending to the story. His mind was starting to work. He knew he could choke it because he was tired enough. He spilled the coffee out of the pot and shook the grounds loose into the fire. He lit a cigarette and went inside the tent. He took off his shoes and trousers, sitting on the blankets, rolled the shoes up inside the trousers for a pillow and got in between the blankets.

Out through the front of the tent he watched the glow of the fire, when the night wind blew on it. It was a quiet night. The swamp was perfectly quiet. Nick stretched under the blanket comfortably. A mosquito hummed close to his ear. Nick sat up and lit a match. The mosquito was on the canvas, over his head. Nick moved the match quickly up to it. The mosquito made a satisfactory hiss in the flame. The match went out. Nick lay down again under the blanket. He turned on his side and shut his eyes. He was sleepy. He felt sleep coming. He curled up under the blanket and went to sleep.

PART II

In the morning the sun was up and the tent was starting to get hot. Nick crawled out under the mosquito netting stretched across the mouth of the tent, to look at the morning. The grass was wet on his hands as he came out. He held his trousers and his shoes in his hands. The sun was just up over the hill. There was the meadow, the river and the swamp. There were birch trees in the green of the swamp on the other side of the river.

The river was clear and smoothly fast in the early morning. Down about two hundred yards were three logs all the way across the stream. They made the water smooth and deep above them. As Nick watched, a mink crossed the river on the logs and went into the swamp. Nick was excited. He was excited by the early morning and the river. He was really too hurried to eat breakfast, but he knew he must. He built a little fire and put on the coffee pot. While the water was heating in the pot he took an empty bottle and went down over the edge of the high ground to the meadow. the meadow was wet with dew and Nick wanted to catch grasshoppers for bait before the sun dried the grass. He found plenty of good grasshoppers. They were at the base of the grass stems. Sometimes they clung to a grass stem. They were cold and wet with the dew, and could not jump until the sun warmed them. Nick picked them up, taking only the medium sized brown ones, and put them into the bottle. He turned over a log and just under the shelter of the edge were several hundred hoppers. It was a grasshopper lodging house. Nick put about fifty of the medium browns into the bottle. While he was picking up the hoppers the others warmed in the sun and commenced to hop away. They flew when they hopped. At first they made one flight and stayed stiff when they landed, as though they were dead.

Nick knew that by the time he was through with breakfast they would be as lively as ever. Without dew in the grass it would take him all day to catch a bottle full of good grasshoppers and he would have to crush many of them, slamming at them with his hat. He washed his hands at the stream. He was excited to be near it. then he walked up to the tent. The hoppers were already jumping stiffly in the grass. In the bottle, warmed by the sun, they were jumping in a mass. Nick put in a pine stick as a cork. It plugged the mouth of the bottle enough, so the hoppers could not get out and left plenty of air passage.

He had rolled the log back and knew he could get grasshoppers there every morning.

Nick laid the bottle full of jumping grasshoppers against a pine trunk. Rapidly he mixed some buckwheat flour with water and stirred it smooth, one cup of flour, one cup of water. He put a handful of coffee in the pot and dipped a lump of grease out of a can and slid it sputtering across the hot skillet. On the smoking skillet he poured smoothly the buckwheat batter. It spread like lava, the grease spitting sharply. Around the edges the buckwheat cake began to firm, then brown, then crisp. The surface was bubbling slowly to porousness. Nick pushed under the browned undersurface with a fresh pine chip. He shook the skillet sideways and the cake was loose on the surface. I won't try and flop it, he thought. He slid the chip of clean wood all the way under the cake, and flopped it over onto its face. It sputtered in the pan.

When it was cooked Nick regreased the skillet. He used all the batter. It made another big flapjack and one smaller one.

Nick ate a big flapjack and a smaller one, covered with apple butter. He put apple butter on the third cake, folded it over twice, wrapped it in oiled paper and put it in his shirt pocket. He put the apple butter jar back in the pack and cut bread for two sandwiches.

In the pack he found a big onion. He sliced it in two and peeled the silky outer skin. Then he cut one half into slices and made onion sandwiches. He wrapped them in oiled paper and buttoned them in the other pocket of his khaki shirt. He turned the skillet upside down on the grill, drank the coffee, sweetened and yellow brown with the condensed milk in it, and tidied up the camp. It was a nice little camp.

Nick took his fly rod out of the leather rod-case, jointed it, and shoved the rod-case back into the tent. He put on the reel and threaded the line through the guides. He had to hold it from hand to hand, as he threaded it, or it would slip back through its own weight. It was a heavy, double tapered fly line. Nick had paid eight dollars for it a long time ago. It was made heavy to lift back in the air and come forward flat and heavy and straight to make it possible to cast a fly which has no weight. Nick opened the aluminum leader box. The leaders were coiled between the damp flannel pads. Nick had wet the pads at the water cooler on the train up to St. Ignace. In the damp pads the gut leaders had softened and Nick unrolled one and tied it by a loop at the end to the heavy fly line. He fastened a hook on the end of the leader. It was a small hook; very thin and springy.

Nick took it from his hook book, sitting with the rod across his lap. He tested the knot and the spring of the rod by pulling the line taut. It was a good feeling. He was careful not to let the hook bite into his finger.

He started down to the stream, holding his rod, the bottle of grasshoppers hung from his neck by a thong tied in half hitches around the neck of the bottle. His landing net hung by a hook from his belt. Over his shoulder was a long flour sack tied at each corner into an ear. The cord went over his shoulder. The sack flapped against his legs.

Nick felt awkward and professionally happy with all his equipment hanging from him. The grasshopper bottle swung against his chest. In his shirt the breast pockets bulged against him with the lunch and his fly book.

He stepped into the stream. It was a shock. His trousers clung tight to his legs. His shoes felt the gravel. The water was a rising cold shock.

Rushing, the current sucked against his legs. Where he stepped in, the water was over his knees. He waded with the current. The gravel slid under his shoes. He looked down at the swirl of water below each leg and tipped up the bottle to get a grasshopper.

The first grasshopper gave a jump in the neck of the bottle and went out into the water. He was sucked under in the whirl by Nick's right leg and came to the surface a little way down stream. He floated rapidly, kicking. In a quick circle, breaking the smooth surface of the water, he disappeared. A trout had taken him.

Another hopper poked his head out of the bottle. His antennae wavered. He was getting his front legs out of the bottle to jump. Nick took him by the head and held him while he threaded the slim hook under his chin, down through his thorax and into the last segments of his abdomen. The grasshopper took hold of the hook with his front feet, spitting tobacco juice on it. Nick dropped him into the water.

Holding the rod in his right hand he let out line against the pull of the grasshopper in the current. He stripped off line from the reel with his left hand and let it run free. He could see the hopper in the little waves of the current. It went out of sight.

There was a tug on the line. Nick pulled against the taut line. It was his first strike. Holding the now living rod across the current, he brought in the line with his left hand. The rod bent in jerks, the trout pumping against the current. Nick knew it was a small one. He lifted the rod straight up in the air. It bowed with the pull.

He saw the trout in the water jerking with his head and body against the shifting tangent of the line in the stream.

Nick took the line in his left hand and pulled the trout, thumping tiredly against the current, to the surface. His back was mottled the clear, water-over-gravel color, his side flashing in the sun. The rod under his right arm, Nick stooped, dipping his right hand into the current. He held the trout, never still, with his moist right hand, while he unhooked the barb from his mouth, then dropped him back into the stream.

He hung unsteadily in the current, then settled to the bottom beside a stone. Nick reached down his hand to touch him, his arm to the elbow under the water. The trout was steady in the moving stream, resting on the gravel, beside a stone. As Nick's fingers touched him, touched his smooth, cool, underwater feeling he was gone, gone in a shadow across the bottom of the stream.

He's all right, Nick thought. He was only tired.

He had wet his hand before he touched the trout, so he would not disturb the delicate mucus that covered him. If a trout was touched with a dry hand, a white fungus attacked the unprotected spot. Years before when he had fished crowded streams, with fly fishermen ahead of him and behind him, Nick had again and again come on dead trout, furry with white fungus, drifted against a rock, or floating belly up in some pool. Nick did not like to fish with other men on the river. Unless they were of your party, they spoiled it.

He wallowed down the stream, above his knees in the current, through the fifty yards of shallow water above the pile of logs that crossed the stream. He did not rebait his hook and held it in his hand as he waded. He was certain he could catch small trout in the shallows, but he did not want them. There would be no big trout in the shallows this time of day.

Now the water deepened up his thighs sharply and coldly. Ahead was the smooth dammed-back flood of water above the logs. The water was smooth and dark; on the left, the lower edge of the meadow; on the right the swamp.

Nick leaned back against the current and took a hopper from the bottle. He threaded the hopper on the hook and spat on him for good luck. Then he pulled several yards of line from the reel and tossed the hopper out ahead onto the fast, dark water. It floated down towards the logs, then the weight of the line pulled the bait under the surface. Nick held the rod in his right hand, letting the line run out through his fingers.

There was a long tug. Nick struck and the rod came alive and dangerous, bent double, the line tightening, coming out of water, tightening, all in a heavy, dangerous, steady pull. Nick felt the moment when the leader would break if the strain increased and let the line go.

The reel ratcheted into a mechanical shriek as the line went out in a rush. Too fast. Nick could not check it, the line rushing out, the reel note rising as the line ran out.

With the core of the reel showing, his heart feeling stopped with the excitement, leaning back against the current that mounted icily his thighs, Nick thumbed the reel hard with his left hand. It was awkward getting his thumb inside the fly reel frame.

As he put on pressure the line tightened into sudden hardness and beyond the logs a huge trout went high out of water. As he jumped, Nick lowered the tip of the rod. But he felt, as he dropped the tip to ease the strain, the moment when the strain was too great; the hardness too tight. Of course, the leader had broken. There was no mistaking the feeling when all spring left the line and it became dry and hard. Then it went slack.

His mouth dry, his heart down, Nick reeled in. He had never seen so big a trout. There was a heaviness, a power not to be held, and then the bulk of him, as he jumped. He looked as broad as a salmon.

Nick's hand was shaky. He reeled in slowly. The thrill had been too much. He felt, vaguely, a little sick, as though it would be better to sit down.

The leader had broken where the hook was tied to it. Nick took it in his hand. He thought of the trout somewhere on the bottom, holding himself steady over the gravel, far down below the light, under the logs, with the hook in his jaw. Nick knew the trout's teeth would cut through the snell of the hook. The hook would imbed itself in his jaw. He'd bet the trout was angry. Anything that size would be angry. That was a trout. He had been solidly hooked. Solid as a rock. He felt like a rock, too, before he started off. By God, he was a big one. By God, he was the biggest one I ever heard of.

Nick climbed out onto the meadow and stood, water running down his trousers and out of his shoes, his shoes squlchy. He went over and sat on the logs. He did not want to rush his sensations any.

He wriggled his toes in the water, in his shoes, and got out a cigarette from his breast pocket. He lit it and tossed the match into the fast water below the logs. A tiny trout rose at the match, as it swung around in the fast current. Nick laughed. He would finish the cigarette.

He sat on the logs, smoking, drying in the sun, the sun warm on his back, the river shallow ahead entering the woods, curving into the woods, shallows, light glittering, big water-smooth rocks, cedars along the bank and white birches, the logs warm in the sun, smooth to sit on, without bark, gray to the touch; slowly the feeling of disappointment left him. It went away slowly, the feeling of disappointment that came sharply after the thrill that made his shoulders ache. It was all right now. His rod lying out on the logs, Nick tied a new hook on the leader, pulling the gut tight until it grimped into itself in a hard knot.

He baited up, then picked up the rod and walked to the far end of the logs to get into the water, where it was not too deep. Under and beyond the logs was a deep pool. Nick walked around the shallow shelf near the swamp shore until he came out on the shallow bed of the stream.

On the left, where the meadow ended and the woods began, a great elm tree was uprooted. Gone over in a storm, it lay back into the woods, its roots clotted with dirt, grass growing in them, rising a solid bank beside the stream. The river cut to the edge of the uprooted tree. From where Nick stood he could see deep channels, like ruts, cut in the shallow bed of the stream by the flow of the current. Pebbly where he stood and pebbly and full of boulders beyond; where it curved near the tree roots, the bed of the stream was marly and between the ruts of deep water green weed fronds swung in the current.

Nick swung the rod back over his shoulder and forward, and the line, curving forward, laid the grasshopper down on one of the deep channels in the weeds. A trout struck and Nick hooked him.

Holding the rod far out toward the uprooted tree and sloshing backward in the current, Nick worked the trout, plunging, the rod bending alive, out of the danger of the weeds into the open river. Holding the rod, pumping alive against the current, Nick brought the trout in. He rushed, but always came, the spring of the rod yielding to the rushes, sometimes jerking under water, but always bringing him in. Nick eased downstream with the rushes. The rod above his head he led the trout over the net, then lifted.

The trout hung heavy in the net, mottled trout back and silver sides in the meshes. Nick unhooked him; heavy sides, good to hold, big undershot jaw, and slipped him, heaving and big sliding, into the long sack that hung from his shoulders in the water.

Nick spread the mouth of the sack against the current and it filled, heavy with water. He held it up, the bottom in the stream, and the water poured out through the sides. Inside at the bottom was the big trout, alive in the water.

Nick moved downstream. The sack out ahead of him, sunk, heavy in the water, pulling from his shoulders.

It was getting hot, the sun hot on the back of his neck.

Nick had one good trout. He did not care about getting many trout. Now the stream was shallow and wide. There were trees along both banks. The trees of the left bank made short shadows on the current in the forenoon sun. Nick knew there were trout in each shadow. In the afternoon, after the sun had crossed toward the hills, the trout would be in the cool shadows on the other side of the stream.

The very biggest ones would lie up close to the bank. You could always pick them up there on the Black. When the sun was down they all moved out into the current. Just when the sun made the water blinding in the glare before it went down, you were liable to strike a big trout anywhere in the current. It was almost impossible to fish then, the surface of the water was blinding as a mirror in the sun. Of course, you could fish upstream, but in a stream like the Black, or this, you had to wallow against the current and in a deep place, the water piled up on you. It was no fun to fish upstream with this much current.

Nick moved along through the shallow stretch watching the banks for deep holes. A beech tree grew close beside the river, so that the branches hung down into the water. The stream went back in under the leaves. There were always trout in a place like that.

Nick did not care about fishing that hole. He was sure he would get hooked in the branches.

It looked deep though. He dropped the grasshopper so the current took it under water, back in under the overhanging branch. The line pulled hard and Nick struck. The trout threshed heavily, half out of water in the leaves and branches. The line was caught. Nick pulled hard and the trout was off. He reeled in and holding the hook in his hand, walked down the stream.

Ahead, close to the left bank, was a big log. Nick saw it was hollow; pointing up river the current entered it smoothly, only a little ripple spread each side of the log. The water was deepening. The top of the hollow log was gray and dry. It was partly in the shadow.

Nick took the cork out of the grasshopper bottle and a hopper clung to it. He picked him off, hooked him and tossed him out. He held the rod far out so that the hopper on the water moved into the current flowing into the hollow log. Nick lowered the rod and the hopper floated in. There was a heavy strike. Nick swung the rod against the pull. It felt as though he were hooked into the log itself, except for the live feeling.

He tried to force the fish out into the current. It came, heavily.

The line went slack and Nick thought the trout was gone. Then he saw him, very near, in the current, shaking his head, trying to get the hook out. His mouth was clamped shut. He was fighting the hook in the clear flowing current.

Looping in the line with his left hand, Nick swung the rod to make the line taut and tried to lead the trout toward the net, but he was gone, out of sight, the line pumping. Nick fought him against the current, letting him thump in the water against the spring of the rod. He shifted the rod to his left hand, worked the trout upstream, holding his weight, fighting on the rod, and then let him down into the net. He lifted him clear of the water, a heavy half circle in the net, the net dripping, unhooked him and slid him into the sack.

He spread the mouth of the sack and looked down in at the two big trout alive in the water.

Through the deepening water, Nick waded over to the hollow log. He took the sack off, over his head, the trout flopping as it came out of the water, and hung it so the trout were deep in the water. Then he pulled himself up on the log and sat, the water from his trousers and boots running down into the stream. He laid his rod down, moved along to the shady end of the log and took the sandwiches out of his pocket. He dipped the sandwiches in the cold water. The current carried away the crumbs. He ate the sandwiches and dipped his hat full of water to drink, the water running out through his hat just ahead of his drinking.

It was cool in the shade, sitting on the log. He took a cigarette out and struck a match to light it. The match sunk into the gray wood, making a tiny furrow. Nick leaned over the side of the log, found a hard place and lit the match. He sat smoking and watching the river.

Ahead the river narrowed and went into a swamp. The river became smooth and deep and the swamp looked solid with cedar trees, their trunks close together, their branches solid. It would not be possible to walk through a swamp like that. The branches grew so low. You would have to keep almost level with the ground to move at all. You could not crash through the branches. That must be why the animals that lived in swamps were built the way they were, Nick thought.

He wished he had brought something to read. He felt like reading. He did not feel like going on into the swamp. He looked down the river. A big cedar slanted all the way across the stream. Beyond that the river went into the swamp.

Nick did not want to go in there now. He felt a reaction against deep wading with the water deepening up under his armpits, to hook big trout in places impossible to land them. In the swamp the banks were bare, the big cedars came together overhead, the sun did not come through, except in patches; in the fast deep water, in the half light, the fishing would be tragic. In the swamp fishing was a tragic adventure. Nick did not want it. He did not want to go down the stream any further today.

He took out his knife, opened it and stuck it in the log. Then he pulled up the sack, reached into it and brought out one of the trout. Holding him near the tail, hard to hold, alive, in his hand, he whacked him against the log. The trout quivered, rigid. Nick laid him on the log in the shade and broke the neck of the other fish the same way. He laid them side by side on the log. They were fine trout.

Nick cleaned them, slitting them from the vent to the tip of the jaw. All the insides and the gills and tongue came out in one piece. They were both males; long gray-white strips of milt, smooth and clean. All the insides clean and compact, coming out all together. Nick tossed the offal ashore for the minks to find.

He washed the trout in the stream. When he held them back up in the water they looked like live fish. Their color was not gone yet. He washed his hands and dried them on the log. Then he laid the trout on the sack spread out on the log, rolled them up in it, tied the bundle and put it in the landing net. His knife was still standing, blade stuck in the log. He cleaned it on the wood and put it in his pocket.

Nick stood up on the log, holding his rod, the landing net hanging heavy, then stepped into the water and splashed ashore. He climbed the bank and cut up into the woods, toward the high ground. He was going back to camp. He looked back. The river just showed through the trees. There were plenty of days coming when he could fish the swamp.

—*1925*

Questions: Reading, Responding, Arguing

1. The story begins with a description of a burned town and ends with a description of a swamp. What do these signify to Nick?
2. How does Hemingway indicate that Nick's fishing trip is more than what it appears on the surface? What does he mean when he refers to Nick's "mind . . . starting to work." Why does Nick wish to "choke it"?
3. What is the importance of the memory of Hopkins in the story?
4. Would you agree that Nick's actions in the story have a certain ritualistic quality to them? Why do you think this is so?
5. How does this story compare with Thoreau's account on page 491 of why he went into the woods? Cite examples from both texts to argue for the differences and similarities in their motives.

Chinua Achebe (b. 1930)

Dead Men's Path

Michael Obi's hopes were fulfilled much earlier than he had expected. He was appointed headmaster of Ndume Central School in January 1949. It had always been an unprogressive school, so the Mission authorities decided to send a young and energetic man to run it. Obi accepted this responsibility with enthusiasm. He had many wonderful ideas and this was an opportunity to put them into practice. He had had sound secondary school education which designated him a "pivotal teacher" in the official records and set him apart from the other headmasters in the mission field. He was outspoken in his condemnation of the narrow views of these older and often less-educated ones.

"We shall make a good job of it, shan't we?" he asked his young wife when they first heard the joyful news of his promotion.

"We shall do our best," she replied. "We shall have such beautiful gardens and everything will be just *modern* and delightful. . . ." In their two years of married life she had become completely infected by his passion for "modern methods" and his denigration of "these old and superannuated people in the teaching field who would be better employed as traders in the Onitsha market." She began to see herself already as the admired wife of the young headmaster, the queen of the school.

The wives of the other teachers would envy her position. She would set the fashion in everything. . . . Then, suddenly, it occurred to her that there might not be other wives. Wavering between hope and fear, she asked her husband, looking anxiously at him.

"All our colleagues are young and unmarried," he said with enthusiasm which for once she did not share. "Which is a good thing," he continued.

"Why?"

"Why? They will give all their time and energy to the school."

Nancy was downcast. For a few minutes she became skeptical about the new school; but it was only for a few minutes. Her little personal misfortune could not blind her to her husband's happy prospects. She looked at him as he sat folded up in a chair. He was stoop-shouldered and looked frail. But he sometimes surprised people with sudden bursts of physical energy. In his present posture, however, all his bodily strength seemed to have retired behind his deep-set eyes, giving them an extraordinary power of penetration. He was only twenty-six, but looked thirty or more. On the whole, he was not unhandsome.

"A penny for your thoughts, Mike," said Nancy after a while, imitating the woman's magazine she read.

"I was thinking what a grand opportunity we've got at last to show these people how a school should be run."

Ndume School was backward in every sense of the word. Mr. Obi put his whole life into the work, and his wife hers too. He had two aims. A high standard of teaching was insisted upon, and the school compound was to be turned into a place of beauty. Nancy's dream-gardens came to life with the coming of the rains, and blossomed. Beautiful hibiscus and allamanda hedges in brilliant red and yellow marked out the carefully tended school compound from the rank neighborhood bushes.

One evening as Obi was admiring his work he was scandalized to see an old woman from the village hobble right across the compound, through a marigold flower-bed and the hedges. On going up there he found faint signs of an almost disused path from the village across the school compound to the bush on the other side.

"It amazes me," said Obi to one of his teachers who had been three years in the school, "that you people allowed the villagers to make use of this footpath. It is simply incredible." He shook his head.

"The path," said the teacher apologetically, "appears to be very important to them. Although it is hardly used, it connects the village shrine with their place of burial."

"And what has that got to do with the school?" asked the headmaster.

"Well, I don't know," replied the other with a shrug of the shoulders. "But I remember there was a big row some time ago when we attempted to close it."

"That was some time ago. But it will not be used now," said Obi as he walked away. "What will the Government Education Officer think of this when he comes to inspect the school next week? The villagers might, for all I know, decide to use the schoolroom for a pagan ritual during the inspection."

Heavy sticks were planted closely across the path at the two places where it entered and left the school premises. These were further strengthened with barbed wire.

Three days later the village priest of *Ani* called on the headmaster. He was an old man and walked with a slight stoop. He carried a stout walking-stick which he usually tapped on the floor, by way of emphasis, each time he made a new point in his argument.

"I have heard," he said after the usual exchange of cordialities, "that our ancestral footpath has recently been closed. . . ."

"Yes," replied Mr. Obi. "We cannot allow people to make a highway of our school compound."

"Look here, my son," said the priest bringing down his walking-stick, "this path was here before you were born and before your father was born. The whole life of this village depends on it. Our dead relatives depart by it and our ancestors visit us by it. But most important, it is the path of children coming in to be born. . . ."

Mr. Obi listened with a satisfied smile on his face.

"The whole purpose of our school," he said finally, "is to eradicate just such beliefs as that. Dead men do not require footpaths. The whole idea is just fantastic. Our duty is to teach your children to laugh at such ideas."

"What you say may be true," replied the priest, "but we follow the practices of our fathers. If you reopen the path we shall have nothing to quarrel about. What I always say is: let the hawk perch and let the eagle perch." He rose to go.

"I am sorry," said the young headmaster. "But the school compound cannot be a thoroughfare. It is against our regulations. I would suggest your constructing another path, skirting our premises. We can even get our boys to help in building it. I don't suppose the ancestors will find the little detour too burdensome."

"I have no more words to say," said the old priest, already outside.

Two days later a young woman in the village died in childbed. A diviner was immediately consulted and he prescribed heavy sacrifices to propitiate ancestors insulted by the fence.

Obi woke up next morning among the ruins of his work. The beautiful hedges were torn up not just near the path but right round the school, the flowers trampled to death and one of the school buildings pulled down. . . That day, the white Supervisor came to inspect the school and wrote a nasty report on the state of the premises but more seriously about the "tribal-war situation developing between the school and the village, arising in part from the misguided zeal of the new headmaster."

—*1953*

Questions: Reading, Responding, Arguing

1. What does the supervisor mean when he talks about the "misguided zeal" of the new headmaster?
2. Examine Achebe's deceptively simple style of writing. How does the simplicity of the style ironically reflect the headmaster's attitude toward the people of the village?
3. Discuss Achebe's use of the path as a metaphor. Cite examples from the text to argue that Achebe uses the path to convey the major themes of the story.

Toni Cade Bambara (1939–1995)

The Lesson*

Back in the days when everyone was old and stupid or young and foolish and me and Sugar were the only ones just right, this lady moved on our block with nappy hair and proper speech and no makeup. And quite naturally we laughed at her, laughed the way we did at the junk man who went about his business like he was some big-time president and his sorry-ass horse his secretary. And we kinda hated her too, hated the way we did the winos who cluttered up our parks and pissed on our handball walls and stank up our hallways and stairs so you couldn't halfway play hide-and-seek without a goddamn gas mask. Miss Moore was her name. The only woman on the block with no first name. And she was black as hell, cept for her feet, which were fish-white and spooky. And she was always planning these boring-ass things for us to do, us being my cousin, mostly, who lived on the block cause we all moved North the same time and to the same apartment then spread out gradual to breathe. And our parents would yank our heads into some kinda shape and crisp up our clothes so we'd be presentable for travel with Miss Moore, who always looked like she was going to church, though she never did. Which is just one of the things the grownups talked about when they talked behind her back like a dog. But when she came calling with some sachet she'd sewed up or some gingerbread she'd made or some book, why then they'd all be too embarrassed to turn her down and we'd get handed over all spruced up. She'd been to college and said it was only right that she should take responsibility for the young ones' education, and she not even related by marriage or blood. So they'd go for it. Specially Aunt Gretchen. She was the main gofer in the family. You got some ole dumb shit foolishness you want somebody to go for, you send for Aunt Gretchen. She been screwed into the go-along for so long, it's a blood-deep natural thing with her. Which is how she got saddled with me and Sugar and Junior in the first place while our mothers were in a la-de-da apartment up the block having a good ole time.

So this one day Miss Moore rounds us all up at the mailbox and it's puredee hot and she's knockin herself out about arithmetic. And school suppose to let up in summer I heard, but she don't never let up. And the starch in my pinafore scratching the shit outta me and I'm really hating this nappy-head bitch and her goddamn college degree. I'd much rather go to the pool or to the show where it's cool. So me and Sugar leaning on the mailbox being surly, which is a Miss Moore word. And Flyboy checking out what everybody brought for lunch. And Fat Butt already wasting his peanut-butter-and-jelly sandwich like the pig he is. And Junebug punchin on Q.T.'s arm for potato chips. And Rosie Giraffe shifting from one hip to the other waiting for somebody to step on her foot or ask her if she from Georgia so she can kick ass, preferably Mercedes'. And Miss Moore asking us do we know what money is, like we a bunch of retards. I mean real money, she say, like it's only poker chips or monopoly papers we lay on the grocer. So right away I'm tired of this and say so. And would much rather snatch Sugar and go to the Sunset and terrorize the West Indian kids and take their hair ribbons and their money too. And Miss Moore files that remark away for next week's lesson on brotherhood, I can tell. And finally I say we oughta get to the subway cause it's cooler and besides we might meet some cute boys. Sugar done swiped her mama's lipstick, so we ready.

So we heading down the street and she's boring us silly about what things cost and what our parents make and how much goes for rent and how money ain't divided up right in this country. And then she gets to the part about we all poor and live in the slums, which I don't feature. And I'm ready to speak on that, but she steps out in the street and hails two cabs just like that. Then she hustles half the crew in with her and hands me a five-dollar bill and tells me to calculate 10 percent tip for the driver. And we're off. Me and Sugar and Junebug and Flyboy hangin out the window and hollering to everybody, putting lipstick on each other cause Flyboy a faggot anyway, and making farts with our sweaty armpits. But I'm mostly trying to figure how to spend this money. But they all fascinated with the meter tick-ing and Junebug starts laying bets to how much it'll read when Flyboy can't hold his breath no more. Then Sugar lays bets as to how much it'll be when we get there. So I'm stuck. Don't nobody want to go for my plan, which is to jump out at the next light and run off to the first bar-b-que we can find. Then the driver tells us to get the hell out cause we there already. And the meter reads eighty-five cents. And I'm stalling to figure out the tip and Sugar say give him a dime. And I de-cide he don't need it as bad as I do, so later for him. But then he tries to take off with Junebug foot still in the door so we talk about his mama something ferocious. Then we check out that we on Fifth Avenue and everybody dressed up in stockings. One lady in a fur coat, hot as it is. White folks crazy.

"This is the place," Miss Moore say, presenting it to us in the voice she uses at the museum. "Let's look in the windows before we go in."

"Can we steal?" Sugar asks very serious like she's getting the ground rules squared away before she plays. "I beg your pardon," say Miss Moore, and we fall out. So she leads us around the windows of the toy store and me and Sugar screamin, "This is mine, that's mine, I gotta have that, that was made for me, I was born for that," till Big Butt drowns us out.

"Hey, I'm goin to buy that there."

"That there? You don't even know what it is, stupid."

"I do so," he say punchin on Rosie Giraffe. "It's a microscope."

"Whatcha gonna do with a microscope, fool?"

"Look at things."

"Like what, Ronald?" ask Miss Moore. And Big Butt ain't got the first notion. So here go Miss Moore gabbing about the thousands of bacteria in a drop of water and the somethinorother in a speck of blood and the million and one living things in the air around us is invisible to the naked eye. And what she say that for? Junebug go to town on that "naked" and we rolling. Then Miss Moore ask what it cost. So we all jam into the window smudgin it up and the price tag say $300. So then she ask how long'd take for Big Butt and Junebug to save up their allowances. "Too long," I say. "Yeh," adds Sugar, "outgrown it by that time." And Miss Moore say no, you never outgrow learning instruments. "Why, even medical students and interns and," blah, blah, blah. And we ready to choke Big Butt for bringing it up in the first damn place.

"This here costs four hundred eighty dollars," say Rosie Giraffe. So we pile up all over her to see what she pointin out. My eyes tell me it's a chunk of glass cracked with something heavy, and different-color inks dripped into the splits, then the whole thing put into a oven or something. But for $480 it don't make sense.

"That's a paperweight made of semi-precious stones fused together under tremendous pressure," she explains slowly, and her hands doing the mining and all the factory work.

"So what's a paperweight?" asks Rosie Giraffe.

"To weigh paper with, dumbbell," say Flyboy, the wise man from the East.

"Not exactly," say Miss Moore, which is what she say when you warm or way off too. "It's to weigh paper down so it won't scatter and make your desk untidy." So right away me and Sugar curtsy to each other and then to Mercedes who is more the tidy type.

"We don't keep paper on top of the desk in my class," say Junebug, figuring Miss Moore crazy or lyin one.

"At home, then," she say. "Don't you have a calendar and a pencil case and a blotter and a letter-opener on your desk at home where you do your homework?" And she know damn well what our homes look like cause she nosys around in them every chance she gets.

"I don't even have a desk," say Junebug. "Do we?"

"No. And I don't get no homework neither," says Big Butt.

"And I don't even have a home," say Flyboy like he do at school to keep the white folks off his back and sorry for him. Send this poor kid to camp posters, is his specialty.

"I do," says Mercedes. "I have a box of stationery on my desk and a picture of my cat. My godmother bought the stationery and the desk. There's a big rose on each sheet and the envelopes smell like roses."

"Who wants to know about your smelly-ass stationery," say Rosie Giraffe fore I can get my two cents in.

"It's important to have a work area all your own so that ..."

"Will you look at this sailboat, please," say Flyboy, cuttin her off and pointin to the thing like it was his. So once again we tumble all over each other to gaze at this magnificent thing in the toy store which is just big enough to maybe sail two kittens across the pond if you strap them to the posts tight. We all start reciting the price tag like we in assembly. "Handcrafted sailboat of fiberglass at one thousand one hundred ninety-five dollars."

"Unbelievable," I hear myself say and am really stunned. I read it again for myself just in case the group recitation put me in a trance. Same thing. For some reason this pisses me off. We look at Miss Moore and she lookin at us, waiting for I dunno what.

"Who'd pay all that when you can buy a sailboat set for a quarter at Pop's, a tube of glue for a dime, and a ball of string for eight cents? It must have a motor and a whole lot else besides," I say. "My sailboat cost me about fifty cents."

"But will it take water?" say Mercedes with her smart ass.

"Took mine to Alley Pond Park once," say Flyboy. "String broke. Lost it. Pity."

"Sailed mine in Central Park and it keeled over and sank. Had to ask my father for another dollar."

"And you got the strap," laugh Big Butt. "The jerk didn't even have a string on it. My old man wailed on his behind."

Little Q.T. was staring hard at the sailboat and you could see he wanted it bad. But he too little and somebody'd just take it from him. So what the hell. "This boat for kids, Miss Moore?"

"Parents silly to buy something like that just to get all broke up," say Rosie Giraffe.

"That much money it should last forever," I figure.

"My father'd buy it for me if I wanted it."

"Your father, my ass," say Rosie Giraffe getting a chance to finally push Mercedes.

"Must be rich people shop here," say Q.T.

"You are a very bright boy," say Flyboy. "What was your first clue?" And he rap him on the head with the back of his knuckles, since Q.T. the only one he could get away with. Though Q.T. liable to come up behind you years later and get his licks in when you half expect it.

"What I want to know is," I says to Miss Moore though I never talk to her, I wouldn't give the bitch that satisfaction, "is how much a real boat costs? I figure a thousand'd get you a yacht any day."

"Why don't you check that out," she says, "and report back to the group?" Which really pains my ass. If you gonna mess up a perfectly good swim day least you could do is have some answers. "Let's go in," she say like she got something up her sleeve. Only she don't lead the way. So me and Sugar turn the corner to where the entrance is, but when we get there I kinda hang back. Not that I'm scared, what's there to be afraid of, just a toy store. But I feel funny, shame. But what I got to be shamed about? Got as much right to go in as anybody. But somehow I can't seem to get hold of the door, so I step away for Sugar to lead. But she hangs back too. And I look at her and she looks at me and this is ridiculous. I mean, damn, I have never ever been shy about doing nothing or going nowhere. But then Mercedes steps up and then Rosie Giraffe and Big Butt crowd in behind and shove, and next thing we all stuffed into the doorway with only Mercedes squeezing past us, smoothing out her jumper and walking right down the aisle. Then the rest of us tumble in like a glued-together jigsaw done all wrong. And people lookin at us. And it's like the time me and Sugar crashed into the Catholic church on a dare. But once we got in there and everything so hushed and holy and the candles and the bowin and the handkerchiefs on all the drooping heads, I just couldn't go through with the plan. Which was for me to run up to the altar and do a tap dance while Sugar played the nose flute and messed around in the holy water. And Sugar kept givin me the elbow. Then later teased me so bad I tied her up in the shower and turned it on and locked her in. And she'd be there till this day if Aunt Gretchen hadn't finally figured I was lyin about the boarder takin a shower.

Same thing in the store. We all walkin on tiptoe and hardly touchin the games and puzzles and things. And I watched Miss Moore who is steady watchin us like she waitin for a sign. Like Mama Drewery watches the sky and sniffs the air and takes note of just how much slant is in the bird formation. Then me and Sugar bump smack into each other, so busy gazing at the toys, 'specially the sailboat. But we don't laugh and go into our fat-lady bumpstomach routine. We just stare at that price tag. Then Sugar run a finger over the whole boat. And I'm jealous and want to hit her. Maybe not her, but I sure want to punch somebody in the mouth.

"Whatcha bring us here for, Miss Moore?"

"You sound angry, Sylvia. Are you mad about something?" Givin me one of them grins like she tellin a grown-up joke that never turns out to be funny. And she's lookin very closely at me like maybe she plannin to do my portrait from memory. I'm mad, but I won't give her that satisfaction. So I slouch around the store bein very bored and say, "Let's go."

Me and Sugar at the back of the train watchin the tracks whizzin by large then small then gettin gobbled up in the dark. I'm thinkin about this tricky toy I saw in the store. A clown that somersaults on a bar then does chin-ups just cause you yank lightly at his leg. Cost $35. I could see me askin my mother for a $35 birthday clown. "You wanna who that costs what?" she'd say, cocking her head to the side to get a better view of the hole in my head. Thirty-five dollars could buy new bunk beds for Junior and Gretchen's boy. Thirty-five dollars and the whole household could go visit Granddaddy Nelson in the country. Thirty-five dollars would pay for the rent and the piano bill too. Who are these people that spend that much for performing clowns and $1000 for toy sailboats? What kinda work they do and how they live and how come we ain't in on it? Where we are is who we are, Miss Moore always pointin out. But it don't necessarily have to be that way, she always adds then waits for somebody to say that poor people have to wake up and demand their share of the pie and don't none of us know what kind of pie she talkin about in the first damn place. But she ain't so smart cause I still got her four dollars from the taxi and she sure ain't gettin it. Messin up my day with this shit. Sugar nudges me in my pocket and winks.

Miss Moore lines us up in front of the mailbox where we started from, seem like years ago, and I got a headache for thinkin so hard. And we lean all over each other so we can hold up under the draggy-ass lecture she always finishes us off with at the end before we thank her for borin us to tears. But she just looks at us like she readin tea leaves. Finally she say, "Well, what do you think of F. A. O. Schwarz?"

Rosie Giraffe mumbles, "White folks crazy."

"I'd like to go there again when I get my birthday money," says Mercedes, and we shove her out the pack so she has to lean on the mailbox by herself.

"I'd like a shower. Tiring day," say Flyboy.

Then Sugar surprises me by sayin, "You know, Miss Moore, I don't think all of us here put together eat in a year what that sailboat costs." And Miss Moore lights up like somebody goosed her. "And?"

she say, urging Sugar on. Only I'm standin on her foot so she don't continue.

"Imagine for a minute what kind of society it is in which some people can spend on a toy what it would cost to feed a family of six or seven. What do you think?"

"I think," say Sugar pushing me off her feet like she never done before, cause I whip her ass in a minute, "that this is not much of a democracy if you ask me. Equal chance to pursue happiness means an equal crack at the dough, don't it?" Miss Moore is besides herself and I am disgusted with Sugar's treachery. So I stand on her foot one more time to see if she'll shove me. She shuts up, and Miss Moore looks at me, sorrowfully I'm thinkin. And somethin weird is goin on, I can feel it in my chest.

"Anybody else learn anything today?" lookin dead at me. I walk away and Sugar has to run to catch up and don't even seem to notice when I shrug her arm off my shoulder.

"Well, we got four dollars anyway," she says.

"Uh hunh."

"We could go to Hascombs and get half a chocolate layer and then go to the Sunset and still have plenty money for potato chips and ice cream sodas."

"Uh hunh."

"Race you to Hascombs," she say.

We start down the block and she gets ahead which is O.K. by me cause I'm going to the West End and then over to the Drive to think this day through. She can run if she want to and even run faster. But ain't nobody gonna beat me at nuthin.

—1972

Questions: Reading, Responding, Arguing

1. How do the children view Miss Moore? How, apparently, does she view them?
3. What is Miss Moore's reason for taking the children to the toy store?
3. Explain the importance of point of view and voice in this story.
4. What is "the lesson"? Does Sylvia understand what it is? Cite examples from the story to argue how Sylvia's understanding reflects the story's theme of initiation.

Emma Lazarus (1849–1887)

The New Colossus

Not like the brazen giant of Greek fame,
With conquering limbs astride from land to land;
Here at our sea-washed, sunset gates shall stand
A mighty woman with a torch, whose flame
Is the imprisoned lightning, and her name   5
Mother of Exiles. From her beacon-hand
Glows world-wide welcome; her mild eyes command
The air-bridged harbor that twin cities frame.
"Keep, ancient lands, your storied pomp!" cries she
With silent lips. "Give me your tired, your poor,   10
Your huddled masses yearning to breathe free,
The wretched refuse of your teeming shore.
Send these, the homeless, tempest-tost to me,
I lift my lamp beside the golden door!"

—*1883*

Questions: Reading, Responding, Arguing

1. This is a sonnet. How does the way it develops reflect the
   sonnet's traditional structure?
2. To what is Lazarus alluding in the poem's first two lines?
   Why is her initial word, "Not," so important? What contrast is she making between the symbol that represents the
   "old" world with the "new" one?
3. What shift does the poem make in line 9? Who is speaking
   now? Explain why the identity of the speaker is important
   and make an argument about the meaning of the poem
   based on that identification.

William Butler Yeats (1865–1939)

The Lake Isle of Innisfree*

I will arise and go now, and go to Innisfree,
And a small cabin build there, of clay and wattles° made:
Nine bean-rows will I have there, a hive for the honey-bee,
And live alone in the bee-loud glade.

And I shall have some peace there, for peace comes dropping slow,   5
Dropping from the veils of the morning to where the cricket sings;
There midnight's all a glimmer, and noon a purple glow,
And evening full of the linnet's wings.

I will arise and go now, for always night and day
I hear lake water lapping with low sounds by the shore;   10
While I stand on the roadway, or on the pavements gray,
I hear it in the deep heart's core.

—*1892*

Questions: Reading, Responding, Arguing

1. How does Yeats characterize Innisfree? What kind of mood does his language convey?
2. How, where, and why does he use repetition of words and sounds? What effect does this create?
3. Why does the speaker talk about the "deep heart's core"? Use that phrase and other phrases or lines from the poem to make an argument about its meaning.

Robert Frost (1874–1963)

Mending Wall*

Something there is that doesn't love a wall,
That sends the frozen-ground-swell under it,
And spills the upper boulders in the sun;
And makes gaps even two can pass abreast.
The work of hunters is another thing: 5

2 **wattles** woven poles and reeds

I have come after them and made repair
Where they have left not one stone on a stone,
But they would have the rabbit out of hiding,
To please the yelping dogs. The gaps I mean,
No one has seen them made or heard them made,   10
But at spring mending-time we find them there.
I let my neighbor know beyond the hill;
And on a day we meet to walk the line
And set the wall between us once again.
We keep the wall between us as we go.   15
To each the boulders that have fallen to each.
And some are loaves and some so nearly balls
We have to use a spell to make them balance:
"Stay where you are until our backs are turned!"
We wear our fingers rough with handling them.   20
Oh, just another kind of outdoor game,
One on a side. It comes to little more:
There where it is we do not need the wall:
He is all pine and I am apple orchard.
My apple trees will never get across   25
And eat the cones under his pines, I tell him.
He only says, "Good fences make good neighbors."
Spring is the mischief in me, and I wonder
If I could put a notion in his head:
"*Why* do they make good neighbors? Isn't it   30
Where there are cows? But here there are no cows.
Before I built a wall I'd ask to know
What I was walling in or walling out,
And to whom I was like to give offense.
Something there is that doesn't love a wall,   35
That wants it down." I could say "Elves" to him,
But it's not elves exactly, and I'd rather
He said it for himself. I see him there
Bringing a stone grasped firmly by the top
In each hand, like an old-stone savage armed.   40
He moves in darkness as it seems to me,
Not of woods only and the shade of trees.
He will not go behind his father's saying,
And he likes having thought of it so well
He says again, "Good fences make good neighbors."   45

—*1914*

Questions: Reading, Responding, Arguing

1. What is the importance of "Something" as the opening word of the poem?
2. Contrast the speaker's ideas about walls with those of his neighbor.
3. The poem ends with one of the most quoted lines in all American poetry. What is ironic about the way that it is generally used? Does Frost seem to support what it says?

Once by the Pacific

The shattered water made a misty din.
Great waves looked over others coming in,
And thought of doing something to the shore
That water never did to land before.
The clouds were low and hairy in the skies,   5
Like locks blown forward in the gleam of eyes.
You could not tell, and yet it looked as if
The shore was lucky in being backed by cliff,
The cliff in being backed by continent;
It looked as if a night of dark intent   10
Was coming, and not only a night, an age.
Someone had better be prepared for rage.
There would be more than ocean-water broken
Before God's last *Put out the Light* was spoken.

—*1928*

Questions: Reading, Responding, Arguing

1. How does Frost's imagery in the poem establish its ominous quality?
2. What does he mean by "a night of dark intent"? Is he speaking of a single night?
3. What is ironic about the italicized words in the poem's final line? Cite examples from the text to support your argument about Frost's support of the line.

William Carlos Williams (1883–1963)

Spring and All

By the road to the contagious hospital°
under the surge of the blue
mottled clouds driven from the
northeast—a cold wind. Beyond, the
waste of broad, muddy fields   5
brown with dried weeds, standing and fallen

patches of standing water
the scattering of tall trees
All along the road the reddish
purplish, forked, upstanding, twiggy   10
stuff of bushes and small trees
with dead, brown leaves under them
leafless vines—

Lifeless in appearance, sluggish
dazed spring approaches—   15

They enter the new world naked,
cold, uncertain of all
save that they enter. All about them
the cold, familiar wind—

Now the grass, tomorrow   20
the stiff curl of wildcarrot leaf
One by one objects are defined—
It quickens: clarity, outline of leaf

But now the stark dignity of
entrance—Still, the profound change   25
has come upon them: rooted, they
grip down and begin to awaken

—*1923*

Questions: Reading, Responding, Arguing

1. Who is the "they" mentioned in the poem?
2. Describe how Williams uses language and sound to create an
   effect of starkness or harshness.

1 **contagious hospital** a hospital for quarantined patients

3. What is Williams's attitude toward nature? How do his diction and imagery convey his "unromantic" approach to nature? Cite examples from the text to argue that diction and imagery convey his "unromantic" approach to nature.

Ezra Pound (1885–1972)

The River-Merchant's Wife: A Letter°

While my hair was still cut straight across my forehead
I played about the front gate, pulling flowers.
You came by on bamboo stilts, playing horse,
You walked about my seat, playing with blue plums.
And we went on living in the village of Chokan: 5
Two small people, without dislike or suspicion.
At fourteen I married My Lord you.
I never laughed, being bashful.
Lowering my head, I looked at the wall.
Called to, a thousand times, I never looked back.   10

At fifteen I stopped scowling,
I desired my dust to be mingled with yours
Forever and forever and forever.
Why should I climb the lookout?

At sixteen you departed,   15
You went into far Ku-to-yen, by the river of swirling eddies,
And you have been gone five months.
The monkeys make sorrowful noise overhead.

You dragged your feet when you went out.
By the gate now, the moss is grown, the different mosses,   20
Too deep to clear them away!
The leaves fall early this autumn, in wind.
The paired butterflies are already yellow with August
Over the grass in the West garden;

The River-Merchant's Wife: A Letter imitation of a poem by Li-Po (AD 701–762)

They hurt me. I grow older.   25
If you are coming down through the narrows of the river Kiang,
Please let me know beforehand,
And I will come out to meet you
    As far as Cho-Fu-Sa.

                                                        —1915

Questions: Reading, Responding, Arguing

1. How does Pound use images to convey a narrative of the relationship between the wife and her husband?
2. What is the nature of the present emotional relationship between the "you" and the "I"?
3. The title is "The River-Merchant's Wife: A Letter": How
   does Pound use the letter form in his poem? Cite examples
   from the poem to argue that Pound uses the letter form to
   express his major themes for the poem.

Robinson Jeffers (1887–1962)

The Purse-Seine°

Our sardine fishermen work at night in the dark of the moon;
    daylight or moonlight
They could not tell where to spread the net, unable to see the
    phosphorescence of the shoals of fish.
They work northward from Monterey, coasting Santa Cruz; off New
    Year's Point or off Pigeon Point
The look-out man will see some lakes of milk-color light on the sea's
    night-purple; he points, and the helmsman
Turns the dark prow, the motorboat circles the gleaming shoal and
    drifts out her seine-net. They close the circle   5
and purse the bottom of the net, then with great labor haul it in.

Purse-Seine large circular fishing net; the bottom is closed (or pursed) before it is hauled in

                                           I cannot tell you
How beautiful the scene is, and a little terrible, then, when the
    crowded fish
Know they are caught, and wildly beat from one wall to the other of
    their closing destiny the phosphorescent
Water to a pool of flame, each beautiful slender body sheeted with
    flame, like a live rocket   10
A comet's tail wake of clear yellow flame; while outside the
    narrowing
Floats and cordage of the net great sea-lions come up to watch,
    sighing in the dark; the vast walls of night
Stand erect to the stars.

                         Lately I was looking from a night mountain-top
On a wide city, the colored splendor, galaxies of light: how could I
    help but recall the seine-net
Gathering the luminous fish? I cannot tell you how beautiful the   15
    city appeared, and a little terrible.
I thought, We have geared the machines and locked all together
    into interdependence; we have built the great cities; now
There is no escape. We have gathered vast populations incapable
    of free survival, insulated
From the strong earth, each person in himself helpless, on all
    dependent. The circle is closed, and the net
Is being hauled in. They hardly feel the cords drawing, yet they
    shine already. The inevitable mass-disasters   20
Will not come in our time nor in our children's, but we and our
    children
Must watch the net draw narrower, government take all powers—
    or revolution, and the new government
Take more than all, add to kept bodies kept souls—or anarchy, the
    mass-disasters.

                             These things are Progress;
Do you marvel our verse is troubled or frowning, while it keeps
    its reason? Or it lets go, lets the mood flow   25
In the manner of the recent young men into mere hysteria,
    splintered gleams, crackled laughter. But they are quite wrong.
There is no reason for amazement: surely one always knew that
    cultures decay, and life's end is death.

                                            —1937

Questions: Reading, Responding, Arguing

1. Describe Jeffers's use of syntax and line breaks. What effect does this create?
2. Explain how Jeffers uses the fish. What does it symbolize?
3. What does Jeffers mean by "These things are Progress"? What is his tone of voice here? Citing examples from the text, construct an argument that stanza three represents the overall theme of the poem.

Langston Hughes (1902–1967)

The Weary Blues*

Droning a drowsy syncopated tune,
Rocking back and forth to a mellow croon,
   I heard a Negro play.
Down on Lenox Avenue the other night
By the pale dull pallor of an old gas light   5
   He did a lazy sway. . . .
   He did a lazy sway. . . .
To the tune o' those Weary Blues.
With his ebony hands on each ivory key
He made that poor piano moan with melody.   10
   O Blues!
Swaying to and fro on his rickety stool
He played that sad raggy tune like a musical fool.
   Sweet Blues!
Coming from a black man's soul.   15
   O Blues!
In a deep song voice with a melancholy tone
I heard that Negro sing, that old piano moan—
   "Ain't got nobody in all this world,
   Ain't got nobody but ma self.   20
   I's gwine to quit ma frownin'
   And put ma troubles on the shelf."

Thump, thump, thump, went his foot on the floor.
He played a few chords then he sang some more—
   "I got the Weary Blues   25

And I can't be satisfied.
Got the Weary Blues
And can't be satisfied—
I ain't happy no mo'
And I wish that I had died."   30
And far into the night he crooned that tune.
The stars went out and so did the moon.
The singer stopped playing and went to bed
While the Weary Blues echoed through his head.
He slept like a rock or a man that's dead.   35

—*1926*

Questions: Reading, Responding, Arguing

1. What portion of the poem, strictly speaking, is "The Weary
   Blues"?
2. What is the structure of a typical blues lyric? How does
   Hughes employ it here?
3. The poem uses three distinct types of rhythm and several
   rhyme schemes. Identify them. Citing examples, argue how
   rhythm and rhyme help contribute to the characterization of
   the piano player.

Seamus Heaney (b. 1939)

Digging*

Between my finger and my thumb
The squat pen rests; snug as a gun.

Under my window, a clean rasping sound
When the spade sinks into gravelly ground:
My father, digging. I look down   5

Till his straining rump among the flowerbeds
Bends low, comes up twenty years away
Stooping in rhythm through potato drills°
Where he was digging.

8 drills furrows

The coarse boot nestled on the lug, the shaft   10
Against the inside knee was levered firmly.
He rooted out tall tops, buried the bright edge deep
To scatter new potatoes that we picked
Loving their cool hardness in our hands.

By God, the old man could handle a spade.   15
Just like his old man.

My grandfather cut more turf in a day
Than any other man on Toner's bog.
Once I carried him milk in a bottle
Corked sloppily with paper. He straightened up   20
To drink it, then fell to right away
Nicking and slicing neatly, heaving sods
Over his shoulder, going down and down
For the good turf. Digging.

The cold smell of potato mould, the squelch and slap   25
Of soggy peat, the curt cuts of an edge
Through living roots awaken in my head.
But I've no spade to follow men like them.

Between my finger and my thumb
The squat pen rests.   30
I'll dig with it.

—*1980*

Questions: Reading, Responding, Arguing

1. Who digs in the poem and for what?
2. What is the speaker saying about language and writing?
3. Discuss the poem in terms of fathers, sons, time, and generations. Construct an argument about how one or more of these terms contributes to the major themes of the poem.

Ted Kooser (b. 1939)

Abandoned Farmhouse

He was a big man, says the size of his shoes
on a pile of broken dishes by the house;
a tall man too, says the length of the bed
in an upstairs room; and a good, God-fearing man,
says the Bible with a broken back   5
on the floor below the window, dusty with sun;
but not a man for farming, say the fields
cluttered with boulders and the leaky barn.

A woman lived with him, says the bedroom wall
papered with lilacs and the kitchen shelves   10
covered with oilcloth, and they had a child,
says the sandbox made from a tractor tire.
Money was scarce, say the jars of plum preserves
and canned tomatoes sealed in the cellar hole.
And the winters cold, say the rags in the window frames.   15
It was lonely here, says the narrow country road.

Something went wrong, says the empty house
in the weed-choked yard. Stones in the fields
in the cellar say she left in a nervous haste.
And the child? Its toys are strewn in the yard   20
like branches after a storm—a rubber cow,
a rusty tractor with a broken plow,
a doll in overalls. Something went wrong, they say.

                                                        —1980

Questions: Reading, Responding, Arguing

1. What specific details does Kooser provide to help readers
   identify the former inhabitants of the house?
2. How do the details of the man in particular help explain
   what likely happened in the house?
3. Is it clear that all the inhabitants left at the same time, or did
   they leave at different times? Citing text from the poem, explain its major theme and make an argument that the time
   the inhabitants left is important to the theme of the poem as
   a whole.

Shirley Geok-lin Lim (b. 1944)

Pantoun° for Chinese Women

"At present, the phenomena of butchering, drowning and leaving to die female infants have been very serious."

(The People's Daily, Peking, March 3rd, 1983)

They say a child with two mouths is no good.
In the slippery wet, a hollow space,
Smooth, gumming, echoing wide for food.
No wonder my man is not here at his place.

In the slippery wet, a hollow space,   5
A slit narrowly sheathed within its hood.
No wonder my man is not here at his place:
He is digging for the dragon jar of soot.

That slit narrowly sheathed within its hood!
His mother, squatting, coughs by the fire's blaze   10
While he digs for the dragon jar of soot.
We had saved ashes for a hundred days.

His mother, squatting, coughs by the fire's blaze.
The child kicks against me mewing like a flute.
We had saved ashes for a hundred days.   15
Knowing, if the time came, that we would.

The child kicks against me crying like a flute
Through its two weak mouths. His mother prays
Knowing when the time comes that we would,
For broken clay is never set in glaze.   20

Through her two weak mouths his mother prays.
She will not pluck the rooster nor serve its blood,
For broken clay is never set in glaze:
Women are made of river sand and wood.

Pantoun Malayan term for the pantourn, a verse form in which the second and fourth lines of each stanza recur as the first lines of the stanza that follows

She will not pluck the rooster nor serve its blood. 25
My husband frowns, pretending in his haste
Women are made of river sand and wood.
Milk soaks the bedding. I cannot bear the waste.

My husband frowns, pretending in his haste.
Oh clean the girl, dress her in ashy soot! 30
Milk soaks our bedding, I cannot bear the waste.
They say a child with two mouths is no good.

—*1989*

Questions: Reading, Responding, Arguing

1. Who is the speaker in this poem?
2. What is the significance of "two mouths"?
3. Look up *pantoun* (or *pantoum*). Why is this form appropriate here? Using your research and lines from the text, argue how the form of the poem contributes to its meaning.

Robert Morgan (b. 1944)

Mountain Bride

They say Revis found a flatrock
on the ridge just
perfect for a natural hearth,
and built his cabin with a stick

and clay chimney right over it. 5
On their wedding night he lit
the fireplace to dry away the mountain
chill of late spring, and flung on

applewood to dye
the room with molten color while 10
he and Martha that was a Parrish
warmed the sheets between the tick

stuffed with leaves and its feather
cover. Under that wide hearth
a nest of rattlers, 15
they'll knot a hundred together,

had wintered and were coming awake.
The warming rock
flushed them out early.
It was she   20

who wakened to their singing near
the embers and roused him to go look.
Before he reached the fire
more than a dozen struck

and he died yelling her to stay   25
on the big four-poster.
Her uncle coming up the hollow
with a gift bearham two days later

found her shivering there
marooned above a pool   30
of hungry snakes,
and the body beginning to swell.

—1979

Questions: Reading, Responding, Arguing

1. What kind of expectations does the title set up? Does the poem fulfill these expectations?
2. Examine Morgan's use of details. What kind of details does he include? What do these details contribute to the poem?
3. How does the final stanza change the theme of the poem? Use the final stanza to construct an argument about the poem's meaning.

Leon Stokesbury (b. 1945)

Day Begins at Governor's Square Mall

Here, newness is all. Or almost all. And like
a platterful of pope's noses° at a White House dinner,
I exist apart. But these trees now—
how do you suppose they grow this high in here?

2 **pope's nose** rural expression for the tail-end of a chicken

They look a little like the trees I sat beneath in 1959   5
waiting with my cheesecloth net for butterflies.
It was August and it was hot. Late summer,
yes, but already the leaves in trees were
flecked with ochers and the umbers of the dead.
I sweated there for hours, so driven,   10
so immersed in the forest's shimmering life,
that I could will my anxious self not move
for half a day—just on the imagined chance
of making some slight part of it my own.
Then they came. One perfect pair of just-hatched   15
black-and-white striped butterflies. The white
lemon-tipped with light, in shade
then out, meandering. Zebra swallowtails,
floating, drunk in the sun, so rare to find
their narrow, fragile, two-inch tails intact.   20
At that moment I could only drop my net and stare.
The last of august. 1959. but these trees, now,
climb up through air and concrete never hot or cold.
And I suspect the last lepidoptera that found
themselves in here were sprayed then swept away.   25
Everyone is waiting though, as before a storm—
anticipating something. Do these leaves never fall?

Now, and with a mild surprise, faint
music falls. But no shop breaks open yet.
The people, like myself, range aimlessly;   30
the air seems thick and still. Then, lights blink on;
the escalators jerk and hum. And in the center, at
the exact center of the mall, a jet of water spurts
twenty feet straight up, then drops and spatters
in a shallow pool where signs announce that none   35
may ever go. O bright communion! O new cathedral!
where the appetitious, the impure, the old, the young,
the bored, the lost, the dumb, with wide dilated eyes°
advance with offerings to be absolved and be made clean.
Now, the lime-lit chainlink fronts from over one hundred   40
pleasant and convenient stalls and stores are rolled away.

---

38 dilated eyes "I remember I wrote this poem shortly after rereading Wordworth's 'Tintern Abbey'
and then seeing Goerge A. Romero's 1978 horror film *Dawn of the Dead* for the first time"
[Author's note]

Now, odors of frying won tons come wafting up from
Lucy Ho's Bamboo Garden. And this music, always
everywhere, yet also somehow strangely played as if
not to be heard, pours its soft harangue down now.   45
The people wander forward now. And the world begins.

—*1986*

Questions: Reading, Responding, Arguing

1. What is ironic about the poem's title? How does day begin in
   this environment?
2. Near the end of the poem Stokesbury uses "communion"
   and "cathedral" in reference to the mall. What connotations
   do these terms have?
3. The poem makes many comparisons between the natural
   world of the poet's childhood and the mall. Compare and
   contrast the natural world of the poet and the mall to make
   an argument about the poem's themes.

Amy Uyematsu (b. 1947)

Lessons from Central America

Always start with the male children.

Give them candy, Coca Cola, and guns.

Tell them secrets.
Teach them to doubt everything,
especially fathers and priests.   5
Show them what happens to men
who won't listen to reason
and necessity.

Take them to the grave of warm skulls.
Make them watch all the ways   10
for torturing a sister.

Do not trust them
too long with their mothers,
but do give them bread
and shoes for their feet.   15

—1998

Questions: Reading, Responding, Arguing

1. How do the "lessons" of the poem relate to recent historical events in Central America?
2. Why does the poet say, "Always start with the male children"?
3. The poem is written in the imperative (command) voice. Who is being told to follow these lessons?
4. How does the poem contrast material things with spiritual values? Does it imply how spiritual values can be under-minded? Use the comparison/contrast between material and spiritual things in the poem to construct an argument about the poem's themes.

Judith Ortiz Cofer (b. 1952)

The Latin Deli: An Ars Poetica[1]

Presiding over a formica counter,
plastic Mother and Child magnetized
to the top of an ancient register,
the heady mix of smells from the open bins
of dried codfish, the green plantains   5
hanging in stalks like votive offerings,
she is the Patroness of Exiles,
a woman of no-age who was never pretty,
who spends her days selling canned memories
while listening to the Puerto Ricans complain   10

[1]Ars Poetica: the art of poetry

that it would be cheaper to fly to San Juan
than to buy a pound of Bustelo coffee here,
and to Cubans perfecting their speech
of a "glorious return" to Havana—where no one
has been allowed to die and nothing to change until then,   15
to Mexicans who pass through, talking lyrically
of *dólares* to be made in El Norte—
                                      all wanting the comfort
of spoken Spanish, to gaze upon the family portrait
of her plain wide face, her ample bosom   20
resting on her plump arms, her look of maternal interest
as they speak to her and each other
of their dreams and their disillusions—
how she smiles understanding,
when they walk down the narrow aisles of her store   25
reading the labels of packages aloud, as if
they were the names of lost lovers: *Suspiros*,
Merengues, the stale candy of everyone's childhood.
                                      She spends her days
slicing *jamón y queso* and wrapping it in wax paper   30
tied with string: plain ham and cheese
that would cost less at the A&P, but it would not satisfy
the hunger of the fragile old man lost in the folds
of his winter coat, who brings her lists of items
that he reads to her like poetry, or the others,   35
whose needs she must divine, conjuring up products
from places that now exist only in their hearts—
closed ports she must trade with.

                                                              —*1995*

Questions: Reading, Responding, Arguing

1. What are the implications of the phrase "canned memories"?
2. The poem says that the items in the deli would cost less in a supermarket. Why, then, does the deli have such a steady stream of customers?
3. Why does Cofer call this poem an "ars poetica" (art of poetry)? What kind of aesthetic statement is she making? Cite examples from the poem to explain Cofer's argument about art and poetry.

Suji Kwock Kim (b. 1968)

Occupation

The soldiers
are hard at work
building a house.
They hammer
bodies into the earth   5
like nails,
they paint the walls
with blood.
Inside the doors
stay shut, locked   10
as eyes of stone.
Inside the stairs
feel slippery,
all flights go down.
There is no floor: 15
only a roof,
where ash is falling—
dark snow,
human snow,
thickly, mutely   20
falling.
Come, they say.
This house will
last forever.
You must occupy it.   25
And you, and you—
And you, and you—
Come, they say.
There is room
for everyone.   30

—*2003*

Questions: Reading, Responding, Arguing

1. Who are the soldiers in the poem? Are they defenders or invaders?
2. How does the poem develop its conceit or central metaphor? What is its significance?
3. How does the theme of this poem connect to recent military occupations of foreign countries? Use research to construct an argument about how this poem can provide insights into recent military occupations in the world.

August Wilson (1945–2005)

The Piano Lesson

Gin my cotton
Sell my seed
Buy my baby
Everything she need
—Skip James

CHARACTERS

Doaker
Boy Willie
Lymon
Berniece
Maretha
Avery
Wining Boy
Grace

The Setting: *The action of the play takes place in the kitchen and parlor of the house where Doaker Charles lives with his niece, Berniece, and her eleven-year-old daughter, Maretha. The house is sparsely furnished, and although there is evidence of a woman's touch, there is a lack of warmth and vigor. Berniece and Maretha occupy the upstairs* *rooms. Doaker's room is prominent and opens onto the kitchen. Dominating the parlor is an old upright piano. On the legs of the piano, carved in the manner of African sculpture, are mask-like figures resembling totems. The carvings are rendered with a grace and power of invention that lifts them out of the realm of craftsmanship and into the realm of art. At left is a staircase leading to the upstairs.*

ACT I   SCENE I

[*The lights come up on the Charles household. It is five o'clock in the morning. The dawn is beginning to announce itself, but there is something in the air that belongs to the night. A stillness that is a portent, a gathering, a coming together of something akin to a storm. There is a loud knock at the door.*]

BOY WILLIE [*offstage, calling*]:   Hey, Doaker . . . Doaker!

[*He knocks again and calls.*]

Hey, Doaker! Hey, Berniece! Berniece!

[*Doaker enters from his room. He is a tall, thin man of forty-seven, with severe features, who has for all intents and purposes retired from the world though he works full-time as a railroad cook.*]

DOAKER: Who is it?

BOY WILLIE: Open the door, nigger! It's me . . . Boy Willie!

DOAKER: Who?

BOY WILLIE: Boy Willie! Open the door!

[*Doaker opens the door and Boy Willie and Lymon enter. Boy Willie is thirty years old. He has an infectious grin and a boyishness that is apt for his name. He is brash and impulsive, talkative and somewhat crude in speech and manner. Lymon is twenty-nine. Boy Willie's partner, he talks little, and then with a straightforwardness that is often disarming.*]

DOAKER: What you doing up here?

BOY WILLIE: I told you, Lymon. Lymon talking about you might be sleep. This is Lymon. You remember Lymon Jackson from down home? This my Uncle Doaker.

DOAKER: What you doing up here? I couldn't figure out who that was. I thought you was still down in Mississippi.

BOY WILLIE: Me and Lymon selling watermelons. We got a truck out there. Got a whole truckload of watermelons. We brought them up here to sell. Where's Berniece?

[*Calls.*]

Hey, Berniece!
DOAKER: Berniece up there sleep.
BOY WILLIE: Well, let her get up.

[*Calls.*]

Hey, Berniece!
DOAKER: She got to go to work in the morning.
BOY WILLIE: Well she can get up and say hi. It's been three years since I seen her.

[*Calls.*]

Hey, Berniece! It's me . . . Boy Willie.
DOAKER: Berniece don't like all that hollering now. She got to work in the morning.
BOY WILLIE: She can go on back to bed. Me and Lymon been riding two days in that truck . . . the least she can do is get up and say hi.
DOAKER [*looking out the window*]: Where you all get that truck from?
BOY WILLIE: It's Lymon's. I told him let's get a load of watermelons and bring them up here.
LYMON: Boy Willie say he going back, but I'm gonna stay. See what it's like up here.
BOY WILLIE: You gonna carry me down there first.
LYMON: I told you I ain't going back down there and take a chance on that truck breaking down again. You can take the train. Hey, tell him Doaker, he can take the train back. After we sell them watermelons he have enough money he can buy him a whole railroad car.
DOAKER: You got all them watermelons stacked up there no wonder the truck broke down. I'm surprised you made it this far with a load like that. Where you break down at?
BOY WILLIE: We broke down three times! It took us two and a half days to get here. It's a good thing we picked them watermelons fresh.
LYMON: We broke down twice in West Virginia. The first time was just as soon as we got out of Sunflower. About forty miles out she

broke down. We got it going and got all the way to West Virginia before she broke down again.

BOY WILLIE: We had to walk about five miles for some water.

LYMON: It got a hole in the radiator but it runs pretty good. You have to pump the brakes sometime before they catch. Boy Willie have his door open and be ready to jump when that happens.

BOY WILLIE: Lymon think that's funny. I told the nigger I give him ten dollars to get the brakes fixed. But he thinks that funny.

LYMON: They don't need fixing. All you got to do is pump them till they catch.

[*Berniece enters on the stairs. Thirty-five years old, with an eleven-year-old daughter, she is still in mourning for her husband after three years.*]

BERNIECE: What you doing all that hollering for?

BOY WILLIE: Hey, Berniece. Doaker said you was sleep. I said at least you could get up and say hi.

BERNIECE: It's five o'clock in the morning and you come in here with all this noise. You can't come like normal folks. You got to bring all that noise with you.

BOY WILLIE: Hell, I ain't done nothing but come in and say hi. I ain't got in the house good.

BERNIECE: That's what I'm talking about. You start all that hollering and carry on as soon as you hit the door.

BOY WILLIE: Aw hell, woman, I was glad to see Doaker. You ain't had to come down if you didn't want to. I come eighteen hundred miles to see my sister I figure she might want to get up and say hi. Other than that you can go back upstairs. What you got, Doaker? Where your bottle? Me and Lymon want a drink.

[*To Berniece.*]

This is Lymon. You remember Lymon Jackson from down home.

LYMON: How you doing, Berniece. You look just like I thought you looked.

BERNIECE: Why you all got to come in hollering and carrying on? Waking the neighbors with all that noise.

BOY WILLIE: They can come over and join the party. We fixing to have a party. Doaker, where your bottle? Me and Lymon celebrating. The Ghosts of the Yellow Dog got Sutter.

BERNIECE: Say what?

BOY WILLIE: Ask Lymon, they found him the next morning. Say he drowned in his well.

DOAKER: When this happen, Boy Willie?

BOY WILLIE: About three weeks ago. Me and Lymon was over in Stoner County when we heard about it. We laughed. We thought it was funny. A great big old three-hundred-and-forty-pound man gonna fall down his well.

LYMON: It remind me of Humpty Dumpty.

BOY WILLIE: Everybody say the Ghosts of the Yellow Dog pushed him.

BERNIECE: I don't want to hear that nonsense. Somebody down there pushing them people in their wells.

DOAKER: What was you and Lymon doing over in Stoner County?

BOY WILLIE: We was down there working. Lymon got some people down there.

LYMON: My cousin got some land down there. We was helping him.

BOY WILLIE: Got near about a hundred acres. He got it set up real nice. Me and Lymon was down there chopping down trees. We was using Lymon's truck to haul the wood. Me and Lymon used to haul wood all around them parts.

[*To Berniece.*]

Me and Lymon got a truckload of watermelons out there.

[*Berniece crosses to the window to the parlor.*]

Doaker, where your bottle? I know you got a bottle stuck up in your room. Come on, me and Lymon want a drink.

[*Doaker exits into his room.*]

BERNIECE: Where you all get that truck from?

BOY WILLIE: I told you it's Lymon's.

BERNIECE: Where you get the truck from, Lymon?

LYMON: I bought it.

BERNIECE: Where he get that truck from, Boy Willie?

BOY WILLIE: He told you he bought it. Bought it for a hundred and twenty dollars. I can't say where he got that hundred and twenty dollars from . . . but he bought that old piece of truck from Henry Porter. [*To Lymon.*] Where you get that hundred and twenty dollars from, nigger?

LYMON: I got it like you get yours. I know how to take care of money.

[*Doaker brings a bottle and sets it on the table.*]

BOY WILLIE: Aw hell, Doaker got some of that good whiskey. Don't give Lymon none of that. He ain't used to good whiskey. He liable to get sick.

LYMON: I done had good whiskey before.

BOY WILLIE: Lymon bought that truck so he have him a place to sleep. He down there wasn't doing no work or nothing. Sheriff looking for him. He bought that truck to keep away from the sheriff. Got Stovall looking for him too. He down there sleeping in that truck ducking and dodging both of them. I told him come on let's go up and see my sister.

BERNIECE: What the sheriff looking for you for, Lymon?

BOY WILLIE: The man don't want you to know all his business. He's my company. He ain't asking you no questions.

LYMON: It wasn't nothing. It was just a misunderstanding.

BERNIECE: He in my house. You say the sheriff looking for him, I wanna know what he looking for him for. Otherwise you all can go back out there and be where nobody don't have to ask you nothing.

LYMON: It was just a misunderstanding. Sometimes me and the sheriff we don't think alike. So we just got crossed on each other.

BERNIECE: Might be looking for him about that truck. He might have stole that truck.

BOY WILLIE: We ain't stole no truck, woman. I told you Lymon bought it.

DOAKER: Boy Willie and Lymon got more sense than to ride all the way up here in a stolen truck with a load of watermelons. Now they might have stole them watermelons, but I don't believe they stole that truck.

BOY WILLIE: You don't even know the man good and you calling him a thief. And we ain't stole them watermelons either. Them old man Pitterford's watermelons. He give me and Lymon all we could load for ten dollars.

DOAKER: No wonder you got them stacked up out there. You must have five hundred watermelons stacked up out there.

BERNIECE: Boy Willie, when you and Lymon planning on going back?

BOY WILLIE: Lymon say he staying. As soon as we sell them watermelons I'm going on back.

BERNIECE [*starts to exit up the stairs*]: That's what you need to do. And you need to do it quick. Come in here disrupting the house. I don't want all that loud carrying on around here. I'm surprised you ain't woke Maretha up.

BOY WILLIE: I was fixing to get her now.

[*Calls.*]

Hey, Maretha!

DOAKER: Berniece don't like all that hollering now.

BERNIECE: Don't you wake that child up!

BOY WILLIE: You going up there . . . wake her up and tell her her uncle's here. I ain't seen her in three years. Wake her up and send her down here. She can go back to bed.

BERNIECE: I ain't waking that child up . . . and don't you be making all that noise. You and Lymon need to sell them watermelons and go on back.

[*Berniece exits up the stairs.*]

BOY WILLIE: I see Berniece still try to be stuck up.

DOAKER: Berniece alright. She don't want you making all that noise. Maretha up there sleep. Let her sleep until she get up. She can see you then.

BOY WILLIE: I ain't thinking about Berniece. You hear from Wining Boy? You know Cleotha died?

DOAKER: Yeah, I heard that. He come by here about a year ago. Had a whole sack of money. He stayed here about two weeks. Ain't offered nothing. Berniece asked him for three dollars to buy some food and he got mad and left.

LYMON: Who's Wining Boy?

BOY WILLIE: That's my uncle. That's Doaker's brother. You heard me talk about Wining Boy. He play piano. He done made some records and everything. He still doing that, Doaker?

DOAKER: He made one or two records a long time ago. That's the only ones I ever known him to make. If you let him tell it he a big recording star.

BOY WILLIE: He stopped down home about two years ago. That's what I hear. I don't know. Me and Lymon was up on Parchman Farm doing them three years.

DOAKER: He don't never stay in one place. Now, he been here about eight months ago. Back in the winter. Now, you subject not to see him for another two years. It's liable to be that long before he stop by.

BOY WILLIE: If he had a whole sack of money you liable never to see him. You ain't gonna see him until he get broke. Just as soon as that sack of money is gone you look up and he be on your doorstep.

LYMON [*noticing the piano*]: Is that the piano?

BOY WILLIE: Yeah . . . look here, Lymon. See how it's carved up real nice and polished and everything? You never find you another piano like that.

LYMON: Yeah, that look real nice.

BOY WILLIE: I told you. See how it's polished? My mama used to polish it every day. See all them pictures carved on it? That's what I was talking about. You can get a nice price for that piano.

LYMON: That's all Boy Willie talked about the whole trip up here. I got tired of hearing him talk about the piano.

BOY WILLIE: All you want to talk about is women. You ought to hear this nigger, Doaker. Talking about all the women he gonna get when he get up here. He ain't had none down there but he gonna get a hundred when he get up here.

DOAKER: How your people doing down there, Lymon?

LYMON: They alright. They still there. I come up here to see what it's like up here. Boy Willie trying to get me to go back and farm with him.

BOY WILLIE: Sutter's brother selling the land. He say he gonna sell it to me. That's why I come up here. I got one part of it. Sell them watermelons and get me another part. Get Berniece to sell that piano and I'll have the third part.

DOAKER: Berniece ain't gonna sell that piano.

BOY WILLIE: I'm gonna talk to her. When she see I got a chance to get Sutter's land she'll come around.

DOAKER: You can put that thought out your mind. Berniece ain't gonna sell that piano.

BOY WILLIE: I'm gonna talk to her. She been playing on it?

DOAKER: You know she won't touch that piano. I ain't never known her to touch it since Mama Ola died. That's over seven years now. She say it got blood on it. She got Maretha playing on it though. Say Maretha can go on and do everything she can't do. Got her in an extra school down at the Irene Kaufman Settlement House. She want Maretha to grow up and be a schoolteacher. Say she good enough she can teach on the piano.

BOY WILLIE: Maretha don't need to be playing on no piano. She can play on the guitar.

DOAKER: How much land Sutter got left?

BOY WILLIE: Got a hundred acres. Good land. He done sold it piece by piece, he kept the good part for himself. Now he got to give that up. His brother come down from Chicago for the funeral . . . he up there in Chicago got some kind of business with soda fountain equipment. He anxious to sell the land, Doaker. He don't want to be bothered with it. He called me to him and said cause of how long our families done known each other and how we been good friends and all, say he wanted to sell the land to me. Say he'd rather see me with it than Jim Stovall. Told me he'd let me have it for two thousand dollars cash money. He don't know I found out the most Stovall would give him for it was fifteen hundred dollars. He trying to get that extra five hundred out of me telling me he do-ing me a favor. I thanked him just as nice. Told him what a good man Sutter was and how he had my sympathy and all. Told him to give me two weeks. He said he'd wait on me. That's why I come up here. Sell them watermelons. Get Berniece to sell that piano. Put them two parts with the part I done saved. Walk in there. Tip my hat. Lay my money down on the table. Get my deed and walk on out. This time I get to keep all the cotton. Hire me some men to work it for me. Gin my cotton. Get my seed. And I'll see you again next year. Might even plant some tobacco or some oats.

DOAKER: You gonna have a hard time trying to get Berniece to sell that piano. You know Avery Brown from down there don't you? He up here now. He followed Berniece up here trying to get her to marry him after Crawley got killed. He been up here about two years. He call himself a preacher now.

BOY WILLIE: I know Avery. I know him from when he used to work on the Willshaw place. Lymon know him too.

DOAKER: He after Berniece to marry him. She keep telling him no but he won't give up. He keep pressing her on it.

BOY WILLIE: Avery think all white men is bigshots. He don't know there some white men ain't got as much as he got.

DOAKER: He supposed to come past here this morning. Berniece go-ing down to the bank with him to see if he can get a loan to start his church. That's why I know Berniece ain't gonna sell that piano. He tried to get her to sell it to help him start his church. Sent the man around and everything.

BOY WILLIE: What man?

DOAKER: Some white fellow was going around to all the colored peo-ple's houses looking to buy up musical instruments. He'd buy any-thing. Drums. Guitars. Harmonicas. Pianos. Avery sent him past here. He looked at the piano and got excited. Offered her a nice price. She turned him down and got on Avery for sending him past. The man kept on her about two weeks. He seen where she wasn't gonna sell it, he gave her his number and told her if she ever wanted to sell it to call him first. Say he'd go one better than what anybody else would give her for it.

BOY WILLIE: How much he offer her for it?

DOAKER: Now you know me. She didn't say and I didn't ask. I just know it was a nice price.

LYMON: All you got to do is find out who he is and tell him somebody else wanna buy it from you. Tell him you can't make up your mind who to sell it to, and if he like Doaker say, he'll give you anything you want for it.

BOY WILLIE: That's what I'm gonna do. I'm gonna find out who he is from Avery.

DOAKER: It ain't gonna do you no good. Berniece ain't gonna sell that piano.

BOY WILLIE: She ain't got to sell it. I'm gonna sell it. I own just as much of it as she does.

BERNIECE [offstage, hollers]:   Doaker! Go on get away. Doaker!

DOAKER [calling]:   Berniece?

[Doaker and Boy Willie rush to the stairs, Boy Willie runs up the stairs, passing Berniece as she enters, running.]

DOAKER: Berniece, what's the matter? You alright? What's the matter?

[Berniece tries to catch her breath. She is unable to speak.]

DOAKER: That's alright. Take your time. You alright. What's the matter?

[He calls.]

Hey, Boy Willie?

BOY WILLIE [offstage]:   Ain't nobody up here.

BERNIECE: Sutter . . . Sutter's standing at the top of the steps.

DOAKER [calls]:   Boy Willie!

[Lymon crosses to the stairs and looks up. Boy Willie enters from the stairs.]

BOY WILLIE: Hey Doaker, what's wrong with her? Berniece, what's wrong? Who was you talking to?

DOAKER: She say she seen Sutter's ghost standing at the top of the stairs.

BOY WILLIE: Seen what? Sutter? She ain't seen no Sutter.

BERNIECE: He was standing right up there.

BOY WILLIE [*entering on the stairs*]: That's all in Berniece's head. Ain't nobody up there. Go on up there, Doaker.

DOAKER: I'll take your word for it. Berniece talking about what she seen. She say Sutter's ghost standing at the top of the steps. She ain't just make all that up.

BOY WILLIE: She up there dreaming. She ain't seen no ghost.

LYMON: You want a glass of water, Berniece? Get her a glass of water, Boy Willie.

BOY WILLIE: She don't need no water. She ain't seen nothing. Go on up there and look. Ain't nobody up there but Maretha.

DOAKER: Let Berniece tell it.

BOY WILLIE: I ain't stopping her from telling it.

DOAKER: What happened, Berniece?

BERNIECE: I come out my room to come back down here and Sutter was standing there in the hall.

BOY WILLIE: What he look like?

BERNIECE: He look like Sutter. He look like he always look.

BOY WILLIE: Sutter couldn't find his way from Big Sandy to Little Sandy. How he gonna find his way all the way up here to Pittsburgh? Sutter ain't never even heard of Pittsburgh.

DOAKER: Go on, Berniece.

BERNIECE: Just standing there with the blue suit on.

BOY WILLIE: The man ain't never left Marlin County when he was living . . . and he's gonna come all the way up here now that he's dead?

DOAKER: Let her finish. I want to hear what she got to say.

BOY WILLIE: I'll tell you this. If Berniece had seen him like she think she seen him she'd still be running.

DOAKER: Go on, Berniece. Don't pay Boy Willie no mind.

BERNIECE: He was standing there . . . had his hand on top of his head. Look like he might have thought if he took his hand down his head might have fallen off.

LYMON: Did he have on a hat?

BERNIECE: Just had on that blue suit . . . I told him to go away and he just stood there looking at me . . . calling Boy Willie's name.

BOY WILLIE: What he calling my name for?

BERNIECE: I believe you pushed him in the well.

BOY WILLIE: Now what kind of sense that make? You telling me I'm gonna go out there and hide in the weeds with all them dogs and things he got around there . . . I'm gonna hide and wait till I catch him looking down his well just right . . . then I'm gonna run over and push him in. A great big old three-hundred-and-forty-pound man.

BERNIECE: Well, what he calling your name for?

BOY WILLIE: He bending over looking down his well, woman . . . how he know who pushed him? It could have been anybody. Where was you when Sutter fell in his well? Where was Doaker? Me and Lymon was over in Stoner County. Tell her, Lymon. The Ghosts of the Yellow Dog got Sutter. That's what happened to him.

BERNIECE: You can talk all that Ghosts of the Yellow Dog stuff if you want. I know better.

LYMON: The Ghosts of the Yellow Dog pushed him. That's what the people say. They found him in his well and all the people say it must be the Ghosts of the Yellow Dog. Just like all them other men.

BOY WILLIE: Come talking about he looking for me. What he come all the way up here for? If he looking for me all he got to do is wait. He could have saved himself a trip if he looking for me. That ain't nothing but in Berniece's head. Ain't no telling what she liable to come up with next.

BERNIECE: Boy Willie, I want you and Lymon to go ahead and leave my house. Just go on somewhere. You don't do nothing but bring trouble with you everywhere you go. If it wasn't for you Crawley would still be alive.

BOY WILLIE: Crawley what? I ain't had nothing to do with Crawley getting killed. Crawley three time seven. He had his own mind.

BERNIECE: Just go on and leave. Let Sutter go somewhere else looking for you.

BOY WILLIE: I'm leaving. Soon as we sell them watermelons. Other than that I ain't going nowhere. Hell, I just got here. Talking about Sutter looking for me. Sutter was looking for that piano. That's what he was looking for. He had to die to find out where that piano was at . . . If I was you I'd get rid of it. That's the way to get rid of Sutter's ghost. Get rid of that piano.

BERNIECE: I want you and Lymon to go on and take all this confusion out of my house!

BOY WILLIE: Hey, tell her, Doaker. What kind of sense that make? I told you, Lymon, as soon as Berniece see me she was gonna start something. Didn't I tell you that? Now she done made up that story about Sutter just so she could tell me to leave her house. Well, hell, I ain't going nowhere till I sell them watermelons.

BERNIECE: Well why don't you go out there and sell them! Sell them and go on back!

BOY WILLIE: We waiting till the people get up.

LYMON: Boy Willie say if you get out there too early and wake the people up they get mad at you and won't buy nothing from you.

DOAKER: You won't be waiting long. You done let the sun catch up with you. This the time everybody be getting up around here.

BERNIECE: Come on, Doaker, walk up here with me. Let me get Maretha up and get her started. I got to get ready myself. Boy Willie, just go on out there and sell them watermelons and you and Lymon leave my house.

[*Berniece and Doaker exit up the stairs.*]

BOY WILLIE [*calling after them*]: If you see Sutter up there . . . tell him I'm down here waiting on him.

LYMON: What if she see him again?

BOY WILLIE: That's all in her head. There ain't no ghost up there.

[*Calls.*]

Hey, Doaker . . . I told you ain't nothing up there.

LYMON: I'm glad he didn't say he was looking for me.

BOY WILLIE: I wish I would see Sutter's ghost. Give me a chance to put a whupping on him.

LYMON: You ought to stay up here with me. You be down there working his land . . . he might come looking for you all the time.

BOY WILLIE: I ain't thinking about Sutter. And I ain't thinking about staying up here. You stay up here. I'm going back and get Sutter's land. You think you ain't got to work up here. You think this the land of milk and honey. But I ain't scared of work. I'm going back and farm every acre of that land.

[*Doaker enters from the stairs.*]

I told you there ain't nothing up there, Doaker. Berniece dreaming all that.

DOAKER: I believe Berniece seen something. Berniece levelheaded. She ain't just made all that up. She say Sutter had on a suit. I don't believe she ever seen Sutter in a suit. I believe that's what he was buried in, and that's what Berniece saw.

BOY WILLIE: Well, let her keep on seeing him then. As long as he don't mess with me.

[*Doaker starts to cook his breakfast.*]

I heard about you, Doaker. They say you got all the women looking out for you down home. They be looking to see you coming. Say you got a different one every two weeks. Say they be fighting one another for you to stay with them.

[*To Lymon.*]

Look at him, Lymon. He know it's true.

DOAKER: I ain't thinking about no women. They never get me tied up with them. After Coreen I ain't got no use for them. I stay up on Jack Slattery's place when I be down there. All them women want is somebody with a steady payday.

BOY WILLIE: That ain't what I hear. I hear every two weeks the women all put on their dresses and line up at the railroad station.

DOAKER: I don't get down there but once a month. I used to go down there every two weeks but they keep switching me around. They keep switching all the fellows around.

BOY WILLIE: Doaker can't turn that railroad loose. He was working the railroad when I was walking around crying for sugartit. My mama used to brag on him.

DOAKER: I'm cooking now, but I used to line track. I pieced together the Yellow Dog stitch by stitch. Rail by rail. Line track all up around there. I lined track all up around Sunflower and Clarksdale. Wining Boy worked with me. He helped put in some of that track. He'd work it for six months and quit. Go back to playing piano and gambling.

BOY WILLIE: How long you been with the railroad now?

DOAKER: Twenty-seven years. Now, I'll tell you something about the railroad. What I done learned after twenty-seven years. See, you got North. You got West. You look over here you got South. Over there you got East. Now, you can start from anywhere. Don't care where you at. You got to go one of them four ways. And whichever way you decide to go they got a railroad that will take you there. Now, that's something simple. You think anybody would be able to understand that. But you'd be surprised how many people trying to go North get on a train going West. They think the train's supposed to go where they going rather than where it's going.

Now, why people going? Their sister's sick. They leaving before they kill somebody . . . and they sitting across from somebody who's leaving to keep from getting killed. They leaving cause they can't get satisfied. They going to meet someone. I wish I had a dollar for every time that someone wasn't at the station to meet them. I done seen that a lot. In between the time they sent the telegram and the time the person get there . . . they done forgot all about them.

They got so many trains out there they have a hard time keeping them from running into each other. Got trains going every whichaway. Got people on all of them. Somebody going where somebody just left. If everybody stay in one place I believe this would be a better world. Now what I done learned after twenty-seven years of railroading is this . . . if the train stays on the track . . . it's going to get where it's going. It might not be where you going. If it ain't, then all you got to do is sit and wait cause the train's coming back to get you. The train don't never stop. It'll come back every time. Now I'll tell you another thing . . .

BOY WILLIE: What you cooking over there, Doaker? Me and Lymon's hungry.

DOAKER: Go on down there to Wylie and Kirkpatrick to Eddie's restaurant. Coffee cost a nickel and you can get two eggs, sausage, and grits for fifteen cents. He even give you a biscuit with it.

BOY WILLIE: That look good what you got. Give me a little piece of that grilled bread.

DOAKER: Here . . . go on take the whole piece.

BOY WILLIE: Here you go, Lymon . . . you want a piece?

[*He gives Lymon a piece of toast. Maretha enters from the stairs.*]

BOY WILLIE: Hey, sugar. Come here and give me a hug. Come on give Uncle Boy Willie a hug. Don't be shy. Look at her, Doaker. She done got bigger. Ain't she got big?

DOAKER: Yeah, she getting up there.

BOY WILLIE: How you doing, sugar?

MARETHA: Fine.

BOY WILLIE: You was just a little old thing last time I seen you. You remember me, don't you? This your Uncle Boy Willie from down South. That there's Lymon. He my friend. We come up here to sell watermelons. You like watermelons?

[*Maretha nods.*]

We got a whole truckload out front. You can have as many as you want. What you been doing?

MARETHA: Nothing.

BOY WILLIE: Don't be shy now. Look at you getting all big. How old is you?

MARETHA: Eleven. I'm gonna be twelve soon.

BOY WILLIE: You like it up here? You like the North?

MARETHA: It's alright.

BOY WILLIE: That there's Lymon. Did you say hi to Lymon?

MARETHA: Hi.

LYMON: How you doing? You look just like your mama. I remember you when you was wearing diapers.

BOY WILLIE: You gonna come down South and see me? Uncle Boy Willie gonna get him a farm. Gonna get a great big old farm. Come down there and I'll teach you how to ride a mule. Teach you how to kill a chicken, too.

MARETHA: I seen my mama do that.

BOY WILLIE: Ain't nothing to it. You just grab him by his neck and twist it. Get you a real good grip and then you just wring his neck and throw him in the pot. Cook him up. Then you got some good eating. What you like to eat? What kind of food you like?

MARETHA: I like everything . . . except I don't like no black-eyed peas.

BOY WILLIE: Uncle Doaker tell me your mama got you playing that piano. Come on play something for me.

[*Boy Willie crosses over to the piano followed by Maretha.*]

Show me what you can do. Come on now. Here . . . Uncle Boy Willie give you a dime . . . show me what you can do. Don't be bashful now. That dime say you can't be bashful.

[*Maretha plays. It is something any beginner first learns.*]

Here, let me show you something.

[*Boy Willie sits and plays a simple boogie-woogie.*]

See that? See what I'm doing? That's what you call the boogie-woogie. See now . . . you can get up and dance to that. That's how good it sound. It sound like you wanna dance. You can dance to that. It'll hold you up. Whatever kind of dance you wanna do you can dance to that right there. See that? See how it go? Ain't nothing to it. Go on you do it.

MARETHA: I got to read it on the paper.

BOY WILLIE: You don't need no paper. Go on. Do just like that there.

BERNIECE: Maretha! You get up here and get ready to go so you be on time. Ain't no need you trying to take advantage of company.

MARETHA: I got to go.

BOY WILLIE: Uncle Boy Willie gonna get you a guitar. Let Uncle Doaker teach you how to play that. You don't need to read no paper to play the guitar. Your mama told you about that piano? You know how them pictures got on there?

MARETHA: She say it just always been like that since she got it.

BOY WILLIE: You hear that, Doaker? And you sitting up here in the house with Berniece.

DOAKER: I ain't got nothing to do with that. I don't get in the way of Berniece's raising her.

BOY WILLIE: You tell your mama to tell you about that piano. You ask her how them pictures got on there. If she don't tell you I'll tell you.

BERNIECE: Maretha!

MARETHA: I got to get ready to go.

BOY WILLIE: She getting big, Doaker. You remember her, Lymon?

LYMON: She used to be real little.

[*There is a knock on the door. Doaker goes to answer it. Avery enters. Thirty-eight years old, honest and ambitious, he has taken to the city like a fish to water, finding in it opportunities for growth and advancement that did not exist for him in the rural South. He is dressed in a suit and tie with a gold cross around his neck. He carries a small Bible.*]

DOAKER: Hey, Avery, come on in. Berniece upstairs.

BOY WILLIE: Look at him . . . look at him . . . he don't know what to say. He wasn't expecting to see me.

AVERY: Hey, Boy Willie. What you doing up here?

BOY WILLIE: Look at him, Lymon.

AVERY: Is that Lymon? Lymon Jackson?

BOY WILLIE: Yeah, you know Lymon.

DOAKER: Berniece be ready in a minute, Avery.

BOY WILLIE: Doaker say you a preacher now. What . . . we supposed to call you Reverend? You used to be plain old Avery. When you get to be a preacher, nigger?

LYMON: Avery say he gonna be a preacher so he don't have to work.

BOY WILLIE: I remember when you was down there on the Willshaw place planting cotton. You wasn't thinking about no Reverend then.

AVERY: That must be your truck out there. I saw that truck with them watermelons, I was trying to figure out what it was doing in front of the house.

BOY WILLIE: Yeah, me and Lymon selling watermelons. That's Lymon's truck.

DOAKER: Berniece say you all going down to the bank.

AVERY: Yeah, they give me a half day off work. I got an appointment to talk to the bank about getting a loan to start my church.

BOY WILLIE: Lymon say preachers don't have to work. Where you working at, nigger?

DOAKER: Avery got him one of them good jobs. He working at one of them skyscrapers downtown.

AVERY: I'm working down there at the Gulf Building running an elevator. Got a pension and everything. They even give you a turkey on Thanksgiving.

LYMON: How you know the rope ain't gonna break? Ain't you scared the rope's gonna break?

AVERY: That's steel. They got steel cables hold it up. It take a whole lot of breaking to break that steel. Naw, I ain't worried about nothing like that. It ain't nothing but a little old elevator. Now, I wouldn't get in none of them airplanes. You couldn't pay me to do nothing like that.

LYMON: That be fun. I'd rather do that than ride in one of them elevators.

BOY WILLIE: How many of them watermelons you wanna buy?

AVERY: I thought you was gonna give me one seeing as how you got a whole truck full.

BOY WILLIE: You can get one, get two. I'll give you two for a dollar.

AVERY: I can't eat but one. How much are they?

BOY WILLIE: Aw, nigger, you know I'll give you a watermelon. Go on, take as many as you want. Just leave some for me and Lymon to sell.

AVERY: I don't want but one.

BOY WILLIE: How you get to be a preacher, Avery? I might want to be a preacher one day. Have everybody call me Reverend Boy Willie.

AVERY: It come to me in a dream. God called me and told me he wanted me to be a shepherd for his flock. That's what I'm gonna call my church . . . The Good Shepherd Church of God in Christ.

DOAKER: Tell him what you told me. Tell him about the three hobos.

AVERY: Boy Willie don't want to hear all that.

LYMON: I do. Lots a people say your dreams can come true.

AVERY: Naw. You don't want to hear all that.

DOAKER: Go on. I told him you was a preacher. He didn't want to believe me. Tell him about the three hobos.

AVERY: Well, it come to me in a dream. See . . . I was sitting out in this railroad yard watching the trains go by. The train stopped and these three hobos got off. They told me they had come from Nazareth and was on their way to Jerusalem. They had three candles. They gave me one and told me to light it . . . but to be careful that it didn't go out. Next thing I knew I was standing in front of this house. Something told me to go knock on the door. This old woman opened the door and said they had been waiting on me. Then she led me into this room. It was a big room and it was full of all kinds of different people. They looked like anybody else except they all had sheep heads and was making noise like sheep make. I heard somebody call my name. I looked around and there was these same three hobos. They told me to take off my clothes and they give me a blue robe with gold thread. They washed my feet and combed my hair. Then they showed me these three doors and told me to pick one.

I went through one of them doors and that flame leapt off that candle and it seemed like my whole head caught fire. I looked around and there was four or five other men standing there with these same blue robes on. Then we heard a voice tell us to look out across this valley. We looked out and saw the valley was full of wolves. The voice told us that these sheep people that I had seen in the other room had to go over to the other side of this valley and somebody had to take them. Then I heard another voice say, "Who shall I send?" Next thing I knew I said, "Here I am. Send me." That's when I met Jesus. He say, "If you go, I'll go with you." Something told me to say, "Come on. Let's go." That's when I woke up. My head still felt like it was on fire . . . but I had a peace about myself that was hard to explain. I knew right then that I had been filled with the Holy Ghost and called to be a servant of the Lord. It took me a while before I could accept that. But then a lot of little ways God showed me that it was true. So I became a preacher.

LYMON: I see why you gonna call it the Good Shepherd Church. You dreaming about them sheep people. I can see that easy.

BOY WILLIE: Doaker say you sent some white man past the house to look at that piano. Say he was going around to all the colored people's houses looking to buy up musical instruments.

AVERY: Yeah, but Berniece didn't want to sell that piano. After she told me about it . . . I could see why she didn't want to sell it.

BOY WILLIE: What's this man's name?

AVERY: Oh, that's a while back now. I done forgot his name. He give Berniece a card with his name and telephone number on it, but I believe she throwed it away.

[*Berniece and Maretha enter from the stairs.*]

BERNIECE: Maretha, run back upstairs and get my pocketbook. And wipe that hair grease off your forehead. Go ahead, hurry up.

[*Maretha exits up the stairs.*]

How you doing, Avery? You done got all dressed up. You look nice. Boy Willie, I thought you and Lymon was going to sell them watermelons.

BOY WILLIE: Lymon done got sleepy. We liable to get some sleep first.

LYMON: I ain't sleepy.

DOAKER: As many watermelons as you got stacked up on that truck out there, you ought to have been gone.

BOY WILLIE: We gonna go in a minute. We going.

BERNIECE: Doaker. I'm gonna stop down there on Logan Street. You want anything?

DOAKER: You can pick up some ham hocks if you going down there. See if you can get the smoked ones. If they ain't got that get the fresh ones. Don't get the ones that got all that fat under the skin. Look for the long ones. They nice and lean.

[*He gives her a dollar.*]

Don't get the short ones lessen they smoked. If you got to get the fresh ones make sure that they the long ones. If they ain't got them smoked then go ahead and get the short ones.

[*Pause.*]

You may as well get some turnip greens while you down there. I got some buttermilk . . . if you pick up some cornmeal I'll make me some cornbread and cook up them turnip greens.

[*Maretha enters from the stairs.*]

MARETHA: We gonna take the streetcar?

BERNIECE: Me and Avery gonna drop you off at the settlement house. You mind them people down there. Don't be going down there showing your color. Boy Willie, I done told you what to do. I'll see you later, Doaker.

AVERY: I'll be seeing you again, Boy Willie.

BOY WILLIE: Hey, Berniece . . . what's the name of that man Avery sent past say he want to buy the piano?

BERNIECE: I knew it. I knew it when I first seen you. I knew you was up to something.

BOY WILLIE: Sutter's brother say he selling the land to me. He waiting on me now. Told me he'd give me two weeks. I got one part. Sell them watermelons get me another part. Then we can sell that piano and I'll have the third part.

BERNIECE: I ain't selling that piano, Boy Willie. If that's why you come up here you can just forget about it.

[*To Doaker.*]

Doaker, I'll see you later. Boy Willie ain't nothing but a whole lot of mouth. I ain't paying him no mind. If he come up here thinking he gonna sell that piano then he done come up here for nothing.

[*Berniece, Avery, and Maretha exit the front door.*]

BOY WILLIE: Hey, Lymon! You ready to go sell these watermelons.

[*Boy Willie and Lymon start to exit. At the door Boy Willie turns to Doaker.*]

Hey, Doaker . . . if Berniece don't want to sell that piano . . . I'm gonna cut it in half and go on and sell my half.

[*Boy Willie and Lymon exit.*]

[*The lights go down on the scene.*]

Scene II

[*The lights come up on the kitchen. It is three days later. Wining Boy sits at the kitchen table. There is a half-empty pint bottle on the table. Doaker busies himself washing pots. Wining Boy is fifty-six years old. Doaker's older brother, he tries to present the image of a successful musician and gambler, but his music, his clothes, and even his manner of presentation are old. He is a man who looking back over his life continues to live it with an odd mixture of zest and sorrow.*]

WINING BOY: So the Ghosts of the Yellow Dog got Sutter. That just go to show you I believe I always lived right. They say every dog gonna have his day and time it go around it sure come back to you. I done seen that a thousand times. I know the truth of that. But I'll tell you out-right . . . if I see Sutter's ghost I'll be on the first thing I find that got wheels on it.

[*Doaker enters from his room.*]

DOAKER: Wining Boy!

WINING BOY: And I'll tell you another thing . . . Berniece ain't gonna sell that piano.

DOAKER: That's what she told him. He say he gonna cut it in half and go on and sell his half. They been around here three days trying to sell them watermelons. They trying to get out to where the white folks live but the truck keep breaking down. They go a block or two and it break down again. They trying to get out to Squirrel Hill and can't get around the corner. He say soon as he can get that truck empty to where he can set the piano up in there he gonna take it out of here and go sell it.

WINING BOY: What about them boys Sutter got? How come they ain't farming that land?

DOAKER: One of them going to school. He left down there and come North to school. The other one ain't got as much sense as that frying pan over yonder. That is the dumbest white man I ever seen. He'd stand in the river and watch it rise till it drown him.

WINING BOY: Other than seeing Sutter's ghost how's Berniece doing?

DOAKER: She doing alright. She still got Crawley on her mind. He been dead three years but she still holding on to him. She need to go out here and let one of these fellows grab a whole handful of whatever she got. She act like it done got precious.

WINING BOY: They always told me any fish will bite if you got good bait.

DOAKER: She stuck up on it. She think it's better than she is. I believe she messing around with Avery. They got something going. He a preacher now. If you let him tell it the Holy Ghost sat on his head and heaven opened up with thunder and lightning and God was calling his name. Told him to go out and preach and tend to his flock. That's what he gonna call his church. The Good Shepherd Church.

WINING BOY: They had that joker down in Spear walking around talking about he Jesus Christ. He gonna live the life of Christ. Went through the Last Supper and everything. Rented him a mule on Palm Sunday and rode through the town. Did everything . . . talking about he Christ. He did everything until they got up to that crucifixion part. Got up to that part and told everybody to go home and quit pretending. He got up to the crucifixion part and changed his mind. Had a whole bunch of folks come down there to see him get nailed to the cross. I don't know who's the worse fool. Him or them. Had all them folks come down there . . . even carried the cross up this little hill. People standing around waiting to see him get nailed to the cross and he stop everything and preach a little sermon and told everybody to go home. Had enough nerve to tell them to come to church on Easter Sunday to celebrate his resurrection.

DOAKER: I'm surprised Avery ain't thought about that. He trying every little thing to get him a congregation together. They meeting over at his house till he get him a church.

WINING BOY: Ain't nothing wrong with being a preacher. You got the preacher on one hand and the gambler on the other. Sometimes there ain't too much difference in them.

DOAKER: How long you been in Kansas City?

WINING BOY: Since I left here. I got tied up with some old gal down there.

[*Pause.*]

You know Cleotha died.

DOAKER: Yeah, I heard that last time I was down there. I was sorry to hear that.

WINING BOY: One of her friends wrote and told me. I got the letter right here.

[*He takes the letter out of his pocket.*]

I was down in Kansas City and she wrote and told me Cleotha had died. Name of Willa Bryant. She says she know cousin Rupert.

[*He opens the letter and reads.*]

Dear Writing Boy: I am writing this letter to let you know Miss Cleotha Holman passed on Saturday the first of May she departed this world in the loving arms of her sister Miss Alberta Samuels. I know you would want to know this and am writing as a friend of

Cleotha. There have been many hardships since last you seen her but she survived them all and to the end was a good woman whom I hope have God's grace and is in His Paradise. Your cousin Rupert Bates is my friend also and he give me your address and I pray this reaches you about Cleotha. Miss Willa Bryant. A friend.

[*He folds the letter and returns it to his pocket.*]

They was nailing her coffin shut by the time I heard about it. I never knew she was sick. I believe it was that yellow jaundice. That's what killed her mama.

DOAKER: Cleotha wasn't but forty-some.

WINING BOY: She was forty-six. I got ten years on her. I met her when she was sixteen. You remember I used to run around there. Couldn't nothing keep me still. Much as I loved Cleotha I loved to ramble. Couldn't nothing keep me still. We got married and we used to fight about it all the time. Then one day she asked me to leave. Told me she loved me before I left. Told me, Wining Boy, you got a home as long as I got mine. And I believe in my heart I always felt that and that kept me safe.

DOAKER: Cleotha always did have a nice way about her.

WINING BOY: Man that woman was something. I used to thank the Lord. Many a night I sat up and looked out over my life. Said, well, I had Cleotha. When it didn't look like there was nothing else for me, I said, thank God, at least I had that. If ever I go anywhere in this life I done known a good woman. And that used to hold me till the next morning.

[*Pause.*]

What you got? Give me a little nip. I know you got something stuck up in your room.

DOAKER: I ain't seen you walk in here and put nothing on the table. You done sat there and drank up your whiskey. Now you talking about what you got.

WINING BOY: I got plenty money. Give me a little nip.

[*Doaker carries a glass into his room and returns with it half-filled. He sets it on the table in front of Wining Boy.*]

WINING BOY: You hear from Coreen?

DOAKER: She up in New York. I let her go from my mind.

WINING BOY: She was something back then. She wasn't too pretty but she had a way of looking at you made you know there was a whole lot of woman there. You got married and snatched her out from under us and we all got mad at you.

DOAKER: She up in New York City. That's what I hear.

[*The door opens and Boy Willie and Lymon enter.*]

BOY WILLIE: Aw hell . . . look here! We was just talking about you. Doaker say you left out of here with a whole sack of money. I told him we wasn't going see you till you got broke.

WINING BOY: What you mean broke? I got a whole pocketful of money.

DOAKER: Did you all get that truck fixed?

BOY WILLIE: We got it running and got halfway out there on Centre and it broke down again. Lymon went out there and messed it up some more. Fellow told us we got to wait till tomorrow to get it fixed. Say he have it running like new. Lymon going back down there and sleep in the truck so the people don't take the watermelons.

LYMON: Lymon nothing. You go down there and sleep in it.

BOY WILLIE: You was sleeping in it down home, nigger! I don't know nothing about sleeping in no truck.

LYMON: I ain't sleeping in no truck.

BOY WILLIE: They can take all the watermelons. I don't care. Wining Boy, where you coming from? Where you been?

WINING BOY: I been down in Kansas City.

BOY WILLIE: You remember Lymon? Lymon Jackson.

WINING BOY: Yeah, I used to know his daddy.

BOY WILLIE: Doaker say you don't never leave no address with nobody. Say he got to depend on your whim. See when it strike you to pay a visit.

WINING BOY: I got four or five addresses.

BOY WILLIE: Doaker say Berniece asked you for three dollars and you got mad and left.

WINING BOY: Berniece try and rule over you too much for me. That's why I left. It wasn't about no three dollars.

BOY WILLIE: Where you getting all these sacks of money from? I need to be with you. Doaker say you had a whole sack of money . . . turn some of it loose.

WINING BOY: I was just fixing to ask you for five dollars.

BOY WILLIE: I ain't got no money. I'm trying to get some. Doaker tell you about Sutter? The Ghosts of the Yellow Dog got him about three weeks ago. Berniece done seen his ghost and everything. He right upstairs.

[*Calls.*]

Hey Sutter! Wining Boy's here. Come on, get a drink!

WINING BOY: How many that make the Ghosts of the Yellow Dog done got?

BOY WILLIE: Must be about nine or ten, eleven or twelve. I don't know.

DOAKER: You got Ed Saunders. Howard Peterson. Charlie Webb.

WINING BOY: Robert Smith. That fellow that shot Becky's boy . . . say he was stealing peaches . . .

DOAKER: You talking about Bob Mallory.

BOY WILLIE: Berniece say she don't believe all that about the Ghosts of the Yellow Dog.

WINING BOY: She ain't got to believe. You go ask them white folks in Sunflower County if they believe. You go ask Sutter if he believe. I don't care if Berniece believe or not. I done been to where the Southern cross the Yellow Dog and called out their names. They talk back to you, too.

LYMON: What they sound like? The wind or something?

BOY WILLIE: You done been there for real, Wining Boy?

WINING BOY: Nineteen thirty. July of nineteen thirty I stood right there on that spot. It didn't look like nothing was going right in my life. I said everything can't go wrong all the time . . . let me go down there and call on the Ghosts of the Yellow Dog, see if they can help me. I went down there and right there where them two railroads cross each other . . . I stood right there on that spot and called out their names. They talk back to you, too.

LYMON: People say you can ask them questions. They talk to you like that?

WINING BOY: A lot of things you got to find out on your own. I can't say how they talked to nobody else. But to me it just filled me up in a strange sort of way to be standing there on that spot. I didn't want to leave. It felt like the longer I stood there the bigger I got. I seen the train coming and it seem like I was bigger than the train. I started not to move. But something told me to go ahead and get on out the way. The train passed and I started to go back up there and stand some more. But something told me not to do it. I walked away from there feeling like a king. Went on and had a stroke of luck that run on for three years. So I don't care if Berniece believe or not. Berniece ain't got to believe. I know cause I been there. Now Doaker'll tell you about the Ghosts of the Yellow Dog.

DOAKER: I don't try and talk that stuff with Berniece. Avery got her all tied up in that church. She just think it's a whole lot of nonsense.

BOY WILLIE: Berniece don't believe in nothing. She just think she believe. She believe in anything if it's convenient for her to believe. But when that convenience run out then she ain't got nothing to stand on.

WINING BOY: Let's not get on Berniece now. Doaker tell me you talking about selling that piano.

BOY WILLIE: Yeah . . . hey, Doaker, I got the name of that man Avery was talking about. The man what's fixing the truck gave me his name. Everybody know him. Say he buy up anything you can make music with. I got his name and his telephone number. Hey, Wining Boy, Sutter's brother say he selling the land to me. I got one part. Sell them watermelons get me the second part. Then . . . soon as I get them watermelons out that truck I'm gonna take and sell that piano and get the third part.

DOAKER: That land ain't worth nothing no more. The smart white man's up here in these cities. He cut the land loose and step back and watch you and the dumb white man argue over it.

WINING BOY: How you know Sutter's brother ain't sold it already? You talking about selling the piano and the man's liable to sold the land two or three times.

BOY WILLIE: He say he waiting on me. He say he give me two weeks. That's two weeks from Friday. Say if I ain't back by then he might gonna sell it to somebody else. He say he wanna see me with it.

WINING BOY: You know as well as I know the man gonna sell the land to the first one walk up and hand him the money.

BOY WILLIE: That's just who I'm gonna be. Look, you ain't gotta know he waiting on me. I know. Okay. I know what the man told me. Stovall already done tried to buy the land from him and he told him no. The man say he waiting on me . . . he waiting on me. Hey, Doaker . . . give me a drink. I see Wining Boy got his glass.

[*Doaker exits into his room.*]

Wining Boy, what you doing in Kansas City? What they got down there?

LYMON: I hear they got some nice-looking women in Kansas City. I sure like to go down there and find out.

WINING BOY: Man, the women down there is something else.

[*Doaker enters with a bottle of whiskey. He sets it on the table with some glasses.*]

DOAKER: You wanna sit up here and drink up my whiskey, leave a dollar on the table when you get up.

BOY WILLIE: You ain't doing nothing but showing your hospitality. I know we ain't got to pay for your hospitality.

WINING BOY: Doaker say they had you and Lymon down on the Parchman Farm. Had you on my old stomping grounds.

BOY WILLIE: Me and Lymon was down there hauling wood for Jim Miller and keeping us a little bit to sell. Some white fellows tried to run us off of it. That's when Crawley got killed. They put me and Lymon in the penitentiary.

LYMON: They ambushed us right there where that road dip down and around that bend in the creek. Crawley tried to fight them. Me and Boy Willie got away but the sheriff got us. Say we was stealing wood. They shot me in my stomach.

BOY WILLIE: They looking for Lymon down there now. They rounded him up and put him in jail for not working.

LYMON: Fined me a hundred dollars. Mr. Stovall come and paid my hundred dollars and the judge say I got to work for him to pay him back his hundred dollars. I told them I'd rather take my thirty days but they wouldn't let me do that.

BOY WILLIE: As soon as Stovall turned his back, Lymon was gone. He down there living in that truck dodging the sheriff and Stovall. He got both of them looking for him. So I brought him up here.

LYMON: I told Boy Willie I'm gonna stay up here. I ain't going back with him.

BOY WILLIE: Ain't nobody twisting your arm to make you go back. You can do what you want to do.

WINING BOY: I'll go back with you. I'm on my way down there. You gonna take the train? I'm gonna take the train.

LYMON: They treat you better up here.

BOY WILLIE: I ain't worried about nobody mistreating me. They treat you like you let them treat you. They mistreat me I mistreat them right back. Ain't no difference in me and the white man.

WINING BOY: Ain't no difference as far as how somebody supposed to treat you. I agree with that. But I'll tell you the difference between the colored man and the white man. Alright. Now you take and eat some berries. They taste real good to you. So you say I'm gonna go out and get me a whole pot of these berries and cook them up to make a pie or whatever. But you ain't looked to see them berries is sitting in the white fellow's yard. Ain't got no fence around them. You figure anybody want something they'd fence it in. Alright. Now the white man come along and say that's my land. Therefore everything that grow on it belong to me. He tell the sheriff, "I want you to put this nigger in jail as a warning to all the other niggers. Otherwise first thing you know these niggers have everything that belong to us."

BOY WILLIE: I'd come back at night and haul off his whole patch while he was sleep.

WINING BOY: Alright. Now Mr. So and So, he sell the land to you. And he come to you and say, "John, you own the land. It's all yours now. But them is my berries. And come time to pick them I'm gonna send my boys over. You got the land . . . but them berries, I'm gonna keep them. They mine." And he go and fix it with the law that them is his berries. Now that's the difference between the colored man and the white man. The colored man can't fix nothing with the law.

BOY WILLIE: I don't go by what the law say. The law's liable to say anything. I go by if it's right or not. It don't matter to me what the law say. I take and look at it for myself.

LYMON: That's why you gonna end up back down there on the Parchman Farm.

BOY WILLIE: I ain't thinking about no Parchman Farm. You liable to go back before me.

LYMON: They work you too hard down there. All that weeding and hoeing and chopping down trees. I didn't like all that.

WINING BOY: You ain't got to like your job on Parchman. Hey, tell him, Doaker, the only one got to like his job is the waterboy.

DOAKER: If he don't like his job he need to set that bucket down.

BOY WILLIE: That's what they told Lymon. They had Lymon on water and everybody got mad at him cause he was lazy.

LYMON: That water was heavy.

BOY WILLIE: They had Lymon down there singing:

[Sings.]

O Lord Berta Berta O Lord gal oh-ah
O Lord Berta Berta O Lord gal well

[Lymon and Wining Boy join in.]

Go 'head marry don't you wait on me oh-ah
Go 'head marry don't you wait on me well
Might not want you when I go free oh-ah
Might not want you when I go free well

BOY WILLIE: Come on, Doaker. Doaker know this one.

[*As Doaker joins in the men stamp and clap to keep time. They sing in harmony with great fervor and style.*]

O Lord Berta Berta O Lord gal oh-ah
O Lord Berta Berta O Lord gal well

Raise them up higher, let them drop on down oh-ah
Raise them up higher, let them drop on down well
Don't know the difference when the sun go down oh-ah
Don't know the difference when the sun go down well

Berta in Meridan and she living at ease oh-ah
Berta in Meridan and she living at ease well
I'm on old Parchman, got to work or leave oh-ah
I'm on old Parchman, got to work or leave well

O Alberta, Berta, O Lord gal oh-ah
O Alberta, Berta, O Lord gal well

When you marry, don't marry no farming man oh-ah
When you marry, don't marry no farming man well
Everyday Monday, hoe handle in your hand oh-ah
Everyday Monday, hoe handle in your hand well

When you marry, marry a railroad man, oh-ah
When you marry, marry a railroad man, well
Everyday Sunday, dollar in your hand oh-ah
Everyday Sunday, dollar in your hand well

O Alberta, Berta, O Lord gal oh-ah
O Alberta, Berta, O Lord gal well

BOY WILLIE: Doaker like that part. He like that railroad part.
LYMON: Doaker sound like Tangleye. He can't sing a lick.
BOY WILLIE: Hey, Doaker, they still talk about you down on Parchman. They ask me, "You Doaker Boy's nephew?" I say, "Yeah, me and him is family." They treated me alright soon as I told them that. Say, "Yeah, he my uncle."

DOAKER: I don't never want to see none of them niggers no more.

BOY WILLIE: I don't want to see them either. Hey, Wining Boy, come on play some piano. You a piano player, play some piano. Lymon wanna hear you.

WINING BOY: I give that piano up. That was the best thing that ever happened to me, getting rid of that piano. That piano got so big and I'm carrying it around on my back. I don't wish that on nobody. See, you think it's all fun being a recording star. Got to carrying that piano around and man did I get slow. Got just like molasses. The world just slipping by me and I'm walking around with that piano. Alright. Now, there ain't but so many places you can go. Only so many road wide enough for you and that piano. And that piano get heavier and heavier. Go to a place and they find out you play piano, the first thing they want to do is give you a drink, find you a piano, and sit you right down. And that's where you gonna be for the next eight hours. They ain't gonna let you get up! Now, the first three or four years of that is fun. You can't get enough whiskey and you can't get enough women and you don't never get tired of playing that piano. But that only last so long. You look up one day and you hate the whiskey, and you hate the women, and you hate the piano. But that's all you got. You can't do nothing else. All you know how to do is play that piano. Now, who am I? Am I me? Or am I the piano player? Sometime it seem like the only thing to do is shoot the piano player cause he the cause of all the trouble I'm having.

DOAKER: What you gonna do when your troubles get like mine?

LYMON: If I knew how to play it, I'd play it. That's a nice piano.

BOY WILLIE: Whoever playing better play quick. Sutter's brother say he waiting on me. I sell them watermelons. Get Berniece to sell that piano. Put them two parts with the part I done saved . . .

WINING BOY: Berniece ain't gonna sell that piano. I don't see why you don't know that.

BOY WILLIE: What she gonna do with it? She ain't doing nothing but letting it sit up there and rot. That piano ain't doing nobody no good.

LYMON: That's a nice piano. If I had it I'd sell it. Unless I knew how to play like Wining Boy. You can get a nice price for that piano.

DOAKER: Now I'm gonna tell you something, Lymon don't know this . . . but I'm gonna tell you why me and Wining Boy say Berniece ain't gonna sell that piano.

BOY WILLIE: She ain't got to sell it! I'm gonna sell it! Berniece ain't got no more rights to that piano than I do.

DOAKER: I'm talking to the man . . . let me talk to the man. See, now . . . to understand why we say that . . . to understand about that piano . . . you got to go back to slavery time. See, our family was owned by a fellow named Robert Sutter. That was Sutter's grandfather. Alright. The piano was owned by a fellow named Joel Nolander. He was one of the Nolander brothers from down in Georgia. It was coming up on Sutter's wedding anniversary and he was looking to buy his wife . . . Miss Ophelia was her name . . . he was looking to buy her an anniversary present. Only thing with him . . . he ain't had no money. But he had some niggers. So he asked Mr. Nolander to see if maybe he could trade off some of his niggers for that piano. Told him he would give him one and a half niggers for it. That's the way he told him. Say he could have one full grown and one half grown. Mr. Nolander agreed only he say he had to pick them. He didn't want Sutter to give him just any old nigger. He say he wanted to have the pick of the litter. So Sutter lined up his niggers and Mr. Nolander looked them over and out of the whole bunch he picked my grandmother . . . her name was Berniece . . . same like Berniece . . . and he picked my daddy when he wasn't nothing but a little boy nine years old. They made the trade-off and Miss Ophelia was so happy with that piano that it got to be just about all she would do was play on that piano.

WINING BOY: Just get up in the morning, get all dressed up and sit down and play on that piano.

DOAKER: Alright. Time go along. Time go along. Miss Ophelia got to missing my grandmother . . . the way she would cook and clean the house and talk to her and what not. And she missed having my daddy around the house to fetch things for her. So she asked to see if maybe she could trade back that piano and get her niggers back. Mr. Nolander said no. Said a deal was a deal. Him and Sutter had a big falling out about it and Miss Ophelia took sick to the bed. Wouldn't get out of the bed in the morning. She just lay there. The doctor said she was wasting away.

WINING BOY: That's when Sutter called our granddaddy up to the house.

DOAKER: Now, our granddaddy's name was Boy Willie. That's who Boy Willie's named after . . . only they called him Willie Boy. Now, he was a worker of wood. He could make you anything you wanted out of wood. He'd make you a desk. A table. A lamp. Anything you wanted. Them white fellows around there used to come up to Mr. Sutter and get him to make all kinds of things for them. Then they'd pay Mr. Sutter a nice price. See, everything my granddaddy made Mr. Sutter owned cause he owned him. That's why when Mr. Nolander offered to buy him to keep the family together Mr. Sutter wouldn't sell him. Told Mr. Nolander he didn't have enough money to buy him. Now . . . am I telling it right, Wining Boy?

WINING BOY: You telling it.

DOAKER: Sutter called him up to the house and told him to carve my grandmother and my daddy's picture on the piano for Miss Ophelia. And he took and carved this . . .

[*Doaker crosses over to the piano.*]

See that right there? That's my grandmother, Berniece. She looked just like that. And he put a picture of my daddy when he wasn't nothing but a little boy the way he remembered him. He made them up out of his memory. Only thing . . . he didn't stop there. He carved all this. He got a picture of his mama . . . Mama Esther . . . and his daddy, Boy Charles.

WINING BOY: That was the first Boy Charles.

DOAKER: Then he put on the side here all kinds of things. See that? That's when him and Mama Berniece got married. They called it jumping the broom. That's how you got married in them days. Then he got here when my daddy was born . . . and here he got Mama Esther's funeral . . . and down here he got Mr. Nolander taking Mama Berniece and my daddy away down to his place in Georgia. He got all kinds of things what happened with our family. When Mr. Sutter seen the piano with all them carvings on it he got mad. He didn't ask for all that. But see . . . there wasn't nothing he could do about it. When Miss Ophelia seen it . . . she got excited. Now she had her piano and her niggers too. She took back to playing it and played on it right up till the day she died. Alright . . . now see, our brother Boy Charles . . . that's Berniece and Boy Willie's daddy . . . he was the oldest of us three boys. He's dead now. But he would have been fifty-seven if he had lived. He died in 1911 when he was thirty-one years old. Boy Charles used to talk about that piano all the time. He never could get it off his mind. Two or three months go by and he be talking about it again. He be talking about taking it out of Sutter's house. Say it was the story of our whole family and as long as Sutter had it . . . he had us. Say we was still in slavery. Me and Wining Boy tried to talk him out of it but it wouldn't do any good. Soon as he quiet down about it he'd start up again. We seen where he wasn't gonna get it off his mind . . . so, on the Fourth of

July, 1911 . . . when Sutter was at the picnic what the county give every year . . . me and Wining Boy went on down there with him and took that piano out of Sutter's house. We put it on a wagon and me and Wining Boy carried it over into the next county with Mama Ola's people. Boy Charles decided to stay around there and wait until Sutter got home to make it look like business as usual.

Now, I don't know what happened when Sutter came home and found that piano gone. But somebody went up to Boy Charles's house and set it on fire. But he wasn't in there. He must have seen them coming cause he went down and caught the 3:57 Yellow Dog. He didn't know they was gonna come down and stop the train. Stopped the train and found Boy Charles in the boxcar with four of them hobos. Must have got mad when they couldn't find the piano cause they set the boxcar afire and killed everybody. Now, nobody know who done that. Some people say it was Sutter cause it was his piano. Some people say it was Sheriff Carter. Some people say it was Robert Smith and Ed Saunders. But don't nobody know for sure. It was about two months after that that Ed Saunders fell down his well. Just upped and fell down his well for no reason. People say it was the ghost of them men who burned up in the boxcar that pushed him in his well. They started calling them the Ghosts of the Yellow Dog. Now, that's how all that got started and that why we say Berniece ain't gonna sell that piano. Cause her daddy died over it.

BOY WILLIE: All that's in the past. If my daddy had seen where he could have traded that piano in for some land of his own, it wouldn't be sitting up here now. He spent his whole life farming on somebody else's land. I ain't gonna do that. See, he couldn't do no better. When he come along he ain't had nothing he could build on. His daddy ain't had nothing to give him. The only thing my daddy had to give me was that piano. And he died over giving me that. I ain't gonna let it sit up there and rot without trying to do something with it. If Berniece can't see that, then I'm gonna go ahead and sell my half. And you and Wining Boy know I'm right.

DOAKER: Ain't nobody said nothing about who's right and who's wrong. I was just telling the man about the piano. I was telling him why we say Berniece ain't gonna sell it.

LYMON: Yeah, I can see why you say that now. I told Boy Willie he ought to stay up here with me.

BOY WILLIE: You stay! I'm going back! That's what I'm gonna do with my life! Why I got to come up here and learn to do something I don't know how to do when I already know how to farm? You stay up here and make your own way if that's what you want to do. I'm going back and live my life the way I want to live it.

[*Wining Boy gets up and crosses to the piano.*]

WINING BOY: Let's see what we got here. I ain't played on this thing for a while.

DOAKER: You can stop telling that. You was playing on it the last time you was through here. We couldn't get you off of it. Go on and play something.

[*Wining Boy sits down at the piano and plays and sings. The song is one which has put many dimes and quarters in his pocket, long ago, in dimly remembered towns and way stations. He plays badly, without hesitation, and sings in a forceful voice.*]

WINING BOY: [*Singing.*]
I am a rambling gambling man
I gambled in many towns
I rambled this wide world over
I rambled this world around
I had my ups and downs in life
And bitter times I saw
But I never knew what misery was
Till I lit on old Arkansas.

I started out one morning
to meet that early train
He said, "You better work for me
I have some land to drain.
I'll give you fifty cents a day,
Your washing, board and all
And you shall be a different man
In the state of Arkansas."

I worked six months for the rascal
Joe Herrin was his name
He fed me old corn dodgers
They was hard as any rock
My tooth is all got loosened
And my knees begin to knock
That was the kind of hash I got
In the state of Arkansas.

Traveling man
I've traveled all around this world
Traveling man
I've traveled from land to land
Traveling man
I've traveled all around this world
Well it ain't no use
writing no news
I'm a traveling man.

[*The door opens and Berniece enters with Maretha.*]

BERNIECE: Is that . . . Lord, I know that ain't Wining Boy sitting there.

WINING BOY: Hey, Berniece.

BERNIECE: You all had this planned. You and Boy Willie had this planned.

WINING BOY: I didn't know he was gonna be here. I'm on my way down home. I stopped by to see you and Doaker first.

DOAKER: I told the nigger he left out of here with that sack of money, we thought we might never see him again. Boy Willie say he wasn't gonna see him till he got broke. I looked up and seen him sitting on the doorstep asking for two dollars. Look at him laughing. He know it's the truth.

BERNIECE: Boy Willie, I didn't see that truck out there. I thought you was out selling watermelons.

BOY WILLIE: We done sold them all. Sold the truck too.

BERNIECE: I don't want to go through none of your stuff. I done told you to go back where you belong.

BOY WILLIE: I was just teasing you, woman. You can't take no teasing?

BERNIECE: Wining Boy, when you get here?

WINING BOY: A little while ago. I took the train from Kansas City.

BERNIECE: Let me go upstairs and change and then I'll cook you something to eat.

BOY WILLIE: You ain't cooked me nothing when I come.

BERNIECE: Boy Willie, go on and leave me alone. Come on, Maretha, get up here and change your clothes before you get them dirty.

[*Berniece exits up the stairs, followed by Maretha.*]

WINING BOY: Maretha sure getting big, ain't she, Doaker. And just as pretty as she want to be. I didn't know Crawley had it in him.

[*Boy Willie crosses to the piano.*]

BOY WILLIE: Hey, Lymon . . . get up on the other side of this piano and let me see something.

WINING BOY: Boy Willie, what is you doing?

BOY WILLIE: I'm seeing how heavy this piano is. Get up over there, Lymon.

WINING BOY: Go on and leave that piano alone. You ain't taking that piano out of here and selling it.

BOY WILLIE: Just as soon as I get them watermelons out that truck.

WINING BOY: Well, I got something to say about that.

BOY WILLIE: This my daddy's piano.

WINING BOY: He ain't took it by himself. Me and Doaker helped him.

BOY WILLIE: He died by himself. Where was you and Doaker at then? Don't come telling me nothing about this piano. This is me and Berniece's piano. Am I right, Doaker?

DOAKER: Yeah, you right.

BOY WILLIE: Let's see if we can lift it up, Lymon. Get a good grip on it and pick it up on your end. Ready? Lift!

[*As they start to move the piano, the sound of Sutter's Ghost is heard. Doaker is the only one to hear it. With difficulty they move the piano a little bit so it is out of place.*]

BOY WILLIE: What you think?

LYMON: It's heavy . . . but you can move it. Only it ain't gonna be easy.

BOY WILLIE: It wasn't that heavy to me. Okay, let's put it back.

[*The sound of Sutter's Ghost is heard again. They all hear it as Berniece enters on the stairs.*]

BERNIECE: Boy Willie . . . you gonna play around with me one too many times. And then God's gonna bless you and West is gonna dress you. Now set that piano back over there. I done told you a hundred times I ain't selling that piano.

BOY WILLIE: I'm trying to get me some land, woman. I need that piano to get me some money so I can buy Sutter's land.

BERNIECE: Money can't buy what that piano cost. You can't sell your soul for money. It won't go with the buyer. It'll shrivel and shrink to know that you ain't taken on to it. But it won't go with the buyer.

BOY WILLIE: I ain't talking about all that, woman. I ain't talking about selling my soul. I'm talking about trading that piece of wood for some land. Get something under your feet. Land the only thing God ain't making no more of. You can always get you another piano. I'm talking about some land. What you get something out the ground from. That's what I'm talking about. You can't do nothing with that piano but sit up there and look at it.

BERNIECE: That's just what I'm gonna do. Wining Boy, you want me to fry you some pork chops?

BOY WILLIE: Now, I'm gonna tell you the way I see it. The only thing that make that piano worth something is them carvings Papa Willie Boy put on there. That's what make it worth something. That was my great-grandaddy. Papa Boy Charles brought that piano into the house. Now, I'm supposed to build on what they left me. You can't do nothing with that piano sitting up here in the house. That's just like if I let them watermelons sit out there and rot. I'd be a fool. Alright now, if you say to me, Boy Willie, I'm using that piano. I give out lessons on it and that help me make my rent or whatever. Then that be something else. I'd have to go on and say, well, Berniece using that piano. She building on it. Let her go on and use it. I got to find another way to get Sutter's land. But Doaker say you ain't touched that piano the whole time it's been up here. So why you wanna stand in my way? See, you just looking at the sentimental value. See, that's good. That's alright. I take my hat off whenever somebody say my daddy's name. But I ain't gonna be no fool about no sentimental value. You can sit up here and look at the piano for the next hundred years and it's just gonna be a piano. You can't make more than that. Now I want to get Sutter's land with that piano. I get Sutter's land and I can go down and cash in the crop and get my seed. As long as I got the land and the seed then I'm alright. I can always get me a little something else. Cause that land give back to you. I can make me another crop and cash that in. I still got the land and the seed. But that piano don't put out nothing else. You ain't got nothing working for you. Now, the kind of man my daddy was he would have understood that. I'm sorry you can't see it that way. But that's why I'm gonna take that piano out of here and sell it.

BERNIECE: You ain't taking that piano out of my house.

[*She crosses to the piano.*]

Look at this piano. Look at it. Mama Ola polished this piano with her tears for seventeen years. For seventeen years she rubbed on it till her hands bled. Then she rubbed the blood in . . . mixed it up with the rest of the blood on it. Every day that God breathed life into her body she rubbed and cleaned and polished and prayed over it. "Play something for me, Berniece. Play something for me, Berniece." Every day. "I cleaned it up for you, play something for me, Berniece." You always talking about your daddy but you ain't never stopped to look at what his foolishness cost your mama. Seventeen years' worth of cold nights and an empty bed. For what? For a piano? For a piece of wood? To get even with somebody? I look at you and you're all the same. You, Papa Boy Charles, Wining Boy, Doaker, Crawley . . . you're all alike. All this thieving and killing and thieving and killing. And what it ever lead to? More killing and more thieving. I ain't never seen it come to nothing. People getting burned up. People getting shot. People falling down their wells. It don't never stop.

DOAKER: Come on now, Berniece, ain't no need in getting upset.

BOY WILLIE: I done a little bit of stealing here and there, but I ain't never killed nobody. I can't be speaking for nobody else. You all got to speak for yourself, but I ain't never killed nobody.

BERNIECE: You killed Crawley just as sure as if you pulled the trigger.

BOY WILLIE: See, that's ignorant. That's downright foolish for you to say something like that. You ain't doing nothing but showing your ignorance. If the nigger was here I'd whup his ass for getting me and Lymon shot at.

BERNIECE: Crawley ain't knew about the wood.

BOY WILLIE: We told the man about the wood. Ask Lymon. He knew all about the wood. He seen we was sneaking it. Why else we gonna be out there at night? Don't come telling me Crawley ain't knew about the wood. Them fellows come up on us and Crawley tried to bully them. Me and Lymon seen the sheriff with them and give in. Wasn't no sense in getting killed over fifty dollars' worth of wood.

BERNIECE: Crawley ain't knew you stole that wood.

BOY WILLIE: We ain't stole no wood. Me and Lymon was hauling wood for Jim Miller and keeping us a little bit on the side. We dumped our little bit down there by the creek till we had enough to make a load. Some fellows seen us and we figured we better get it before they did. We come up there and got Crawley to help us load it. Figured we'd cut him in. Crawley trying to keep the wolf from his door . . . we was trying to help him.

LYMON: Me and Boy Willie told him about the wood. We told him some fellows might be trying to beat us to it. He say let me go back and get my thirty-eight. That's what caused all the trouble.

BOY WILLIE: If Crawley ain't had the gun he'd be alive today.

LYMON: We had it about half loaded when they come up on us. We seen the sheriff with them and we tried to get away. We ducked around near the bend in the creek . . . but they was down there too. Boy Willie say let's give in. But Crawley pulled out his gun and started shooting. That's when they started shooting back.

BERNIECE: All I know is Crawley would be alive if you hadn't come up there and got him.

BOY WILLIE: I ain't had nothing to do with Crawley getting killed. That was his own fault.

BERNIECE: Crawley's dead and in the ground and you still walking around here eating. That's all I know. He went off to load some wood with you and ain't never come back.

BOY WILLIE: I told you, woman . . . I ain't had nothing to do with . . .

BERNIECE: He ain't here, is he? He ain't here!

[*Berniece hits Boy Willie.*]

I said he ain't here. Is he?

[*Berniece continues to hit Boy Willie, who doesn't move to defend himself, other than back up and turning his head so that most of the blows fall on his chest and arms.*]

DOAKER [*grabbing Berniece*]: Come on, Berniece . . . let it go, it ain't his fault.

BERNIECE: He ain't here, is he? Is he?

BOY WILLIE: I told you I ain't responsible for Crawley.

BERNIECE: He ain't here.

BOY WILLIE: Come on now, Berniece . . . don't do this now. Doaker get her. I ain't had nothing to do with Crawley . . .

BERNIECE: You come up there and got him!

BOY WILLIE: I done told you now. Doaker, get her. I ain't playing.

DOAKER: Come on. Berniece.

[*Maretha is heard screaming upstairs. It is a scream of stark terror.*]

MARETHA: Mama! . . . Mama!

[*The lights go down to black. End of Act One.*]

ACT II   SCENE I

[*The lights come up on the kitchen. It is the following morning. Doaker is ironing the pants to his uniform. He has a pot cooking on the stove at the same time. He is singing a song. The song provides him with the rhythm for his work and he moves about the kitchen with the ease born of many years as a railroad cook.*]

DOAKER:
> Gonna leave Jackson Mississippi
> and go to Memphis
> and double back to Jackson
> Come on down to Hattiesburg
> Change cars on the Y. D.
> coming through the territory to
> Meridian
> and Meridian to Greenville
> and Greenville to Memphis
> I'm on my way and I know where

> Change cars on the Katy
> Leaving Jackson
> and going through Clarksdale
> Hello Winona!
> Courtland!
> Bateville!
> Como!
> Senitobia!
> Lewisberg!
> Sunflower!
> Glendora!
> Sharkey!
> And double back to Jackson
> Hello Greenwood
> I'm on my way Memphis
> Clarksdale
> Moorhead
> Indianola
> Can a highball pass through?
> Highball on through sir
> Grand Carson!

Thirty First Street Depot
Fourth Street Depot
Memphis!

[*Wining Boy enters carrying a suit of clothes.*]

DOAKER: I thought you took that suit to the pawnshop?

WINING BOY: I went down there and the man tell me the suit is too old. Look at this suit. This is one hundred percent silk! How a silk suit gonna get too old? I know what it was he just didn't want to give me five dollars for it. Best he wanna give me is three dollars. I figure a silk suit is worth five dollars all over the world. I wasn't gonna part with it for no three dollars so I brought it back.

DOAKER: They got another pawnshop up on Wylie.

WINING BOY: I carried it up there. He say he don't take no clothes. Only thing he take is guns and radios. Maybe a guitar or two. Where's Berniece?

DOAKER: Berniece still at work. Boy Willie went down there to meet Lymon this morning. I guess they got that truck fixed, they been out there all day and ain't come back yet. Maretha scared to sleep up there now. Berniece don't know, but I seen Sutter before she did.

WINING BOY: Say what?

DOAKER: About three weeks ago. I had just come back from down there. Sutter couldn't have been dead more than three days. He was sitting over there at the piano. I come out to go to work . . . and he was sitting right there. Had his hand on top of his head just like Berniece said. I believe he broke his neck when he fell in the well. I kept quiet about it. I didn't see no reason to upset Berniece.

WINING BOY: Did he say anything? Did he say he was looking for Boy Willie?

DOAKER: He was just sitting there. He ain't said nothing. I went on out the door and left him sitting there. I figure as long as he was on the other side of the room everything be alright. I don't know what I would have done if he had started walking toward me.

WINING BOY: Berniece say he was calling Boy Willie's name.

DOAKER: I ain't heard him say nothing. He was just sitting there when I seen him. But I don't believe Boy Willie pushed him in the well. Sutter here cause of that piano. I heard him playing on it one time. I thought it was Berniece but then she don't play that kind of music. I come out here and ain't seen nobody, but them piano keys was moving a mile a minute. Berniece need to go on and get rid of it. It ain't done nothing but cause trouble.

WINING BOY: I agree with Berniece. Boy Charles ain't took it to give it back. He took it cause he figure he had more right to it than Sutter did. If Sutter can't understand that . . . then that's just the way that go. Sutter dead and in the ground . . . don't care where his ghost is. He can hover around and play on the piano all he want. I want to see him carry it out the house. That's what I want to see. What time Berniece get home? I don't see how I let her get away from me this morning.

DOAKER: You up there sleep. Berniece leave out of here early in the morning. She out there in Squirrel Hill cleaning house for some bigshot down there at the steel mill. They don't like you to come late. You come late they won't give you your carfare. What kind of business you got with Berniece?

WINING BOY: My business. I ain't asked you what kind of business you got.

DOAKER: Berniece ain't got no money. If that's why you was trying to catch her. She having a hard enough time trying to get by as it is. If she go ahead and marry Avery . . . he working every day . . . she go ahead and marry him they could do alright for themselves. But as it stands she ain't got no money.

WINING BOY: Well, let me have five dollars.

DOAKER: I just give you a dollar before you left out of here. You ain't gonna take my five dollars out there and gamble and drink it up.

WINING BOY: Aw, nigger, give me five dollars. I'll give it back to you.

DOAKER: You wasn't looking to give me five dollars when you had that sack of money. You wasn't looking to throw nothing my way. Now you wanna come in here and borrow five dollars. If you going back with Boy Willie you need to be trying to figure out how you gonna get train fare.

WINING BOY: That's why I need the five dollars. If I had five dollars I could get me some money.

[*Doaker goes into his pocket.*]

Make it seven.

DOAKER: You take this five dollars . . . and you bring my money back here too.

[*Boy Willie and Lymon enter. They are happy and excited. They have money in all of their pockets and are anxious to count it.*]

DOAKER: How'd you do out there?

BOY WILLIE: They was lining up for them.

LYMON: Me and Boy Willie couldn't sell them fast enough. Time we got one sold we'd sell another.

BOY WILLIE: I seen what was happening and told Lymon to up the price on them.

LYMON: Boy Willie say charge them a quarter more. They didn't care. A couple of people give me a dollar and told me to keep the change.

BOY WILLIE: One fellow bought five. I say now what he gonna do with five watermelons? He can't eat them all. I sold him the five and asked him did he want to buy five more.

LYMON: I ain't never seen nobody snatch a dollar fast as Boy Willie.

BOY WILLIE: One lady asked me say, "Is they sweet?" I told her say, "Lady, where we grow these watermelons we put sugar in the ground." You know, she believed me. Talking about she had never heard of that before. Lymon was laughing his head off. I told her, "Oh, yeah, we put the sugar right in the ground with the seed." She say, "Well, give me another one." Them white folks is something else . . . ain't they, Lymon?

LYMON: Soon as you holler watermelons they come right out their door. Then they go and get their neighbors. Look like they having a contest to see who can buy the most.

WINING BOY: I got something for Lymon.

[*Wining Boy goes to get his suit. Boy Willie and Lymon continue to count their money.*]

BOY WILLIE: I know you got more than that. You ain't sold all them watermelons for that little bit of money.

LYMON: I'm still looking. That ain't all you got either. Where's all them quarters?

BOY WILLIE: You let me worry about the quarters. Just put the money on the table.

WINING BOY [*entering with his suit*]: Look here, Lymon . . . see this? Look at his eyes getting big. He ain't never seen a suit like this. This is one hundred percent silk. Go ahead . . . put it on. See if it fit you.

[*Lymon tries the suit coat on.*]

Look at that. Feel it. That's one hundred percent genuine silk. I got that in Chicago. You can't get clothes like that nowhere but New York and Chicago. You can't get clothes like that in Pittsburgh. These folks in Pittsburgh ain't never seen clothes like that.

LYMON: This is nice, feel real nice and smooth.

WINING BOY: That's a fifty-five-dollar suit. That's the kind of suit the bigshots wear. You need a pistol and a pocketful of money to wear that suit. I'll let you have it for three dollars. The women will fall out their windows they see you in a suit like that. Give me three dollars and go on and wear it down the street and get you a woman.

BOY WILLIE: That looks nice, Lymon. Put the pants on. Let me see it with the pants.

[*Lymon begins to try on the pants.*]

WINING BOY: Look at that . . . see how it fits you? Give me three dollars and go on and take it. Look at that, Doaker . . . don't he look nice?

DOAKER: Yeah . . . that's a nice suit.

WINING BOY: Got a shirt to go with it. Cost you an extra dollar. Four dollars you got the whole deal.

LYMON: How this look, Boy Willie?

BOY WILLIE: That look nice . . . if you like that kind of thing. I don't like them dress-up kind of clothes. If you like it, look real nice.

WINING BOY: That's the kind of suit you need for up here in the North.

LYMON: Four dollars for everything? The suit and the shirt?

WINING BOY: That's cheap. I should be charging you twenty dollars. I give you a break cause you a homeboy. That's the only way I let you have it for four dollars.

LYMON [*going into his pocket*]: Okay . . . here go the four dollars.

WINING BOY: You got some shoes? What size you wear?

LYMON: Size nine.

WINING BOY: That's what size I got! Size nine. I let you have them for three dollars.

LYMON: Where they at? Let me see them.

WINING BOY: They real nice shoes, too. Got a nice tip to them. Got pointy toe just like you want.

[*Wining Boy goes to get his shoes.*]

LYMON: Come on, Boy Willie, let's go out tonight. I wanna see what it looks like up here. Maybe we go to a picture show. Hey, Doaker, they got picture shows up here?

DOAKER: The Rhumba Theater. Right down there on Fullerton Street. Can't miss it. Got the speakers outside on the sidewalk. You can hear it a block away. Boy Willie know where it's at.

[*Doaker exits into his room.*]

LYMON: Let's go to the picture show, Boy Willie. Let's go find some women.

BOY WILLIE: Hey, Lymon, how many of them watermelons would you say we got left? We got just under a half a load . . . right?

LYMON: About that much. Maybe a little more.

BOY WILLIE: You think that piano will fit up in there?

LYMON: If we stack them watermelons you can sit it up in the front there.

BOY WILLIE: I'm gonna call that man tomorrow.

WINING BOY [*returns with his shoes*]: Here you go . . . size nine. Put them on. Cost you three dollars. That's a Florsheim shoe. That's the kind Staggerlee wore.

LYMON [*trying on the shoes*]: You sure these size nine?

WINING BOY: You can look at my feet and see we wear the same size. Man, you put on that suit and them shoes and you got something there. You ready for whatever's out there. But is they ready for you? With them shoes on you be the King of the Walk. Have everybody stop to look at your shoes. Wishing they had a pair. I'll give you a break. Go on and take them for two dollars.

[*Lymon pays Wining Boy two dollars.*]

LYMON: Come on, Boy Willie . . . let's go find some women. I'm gonna go upstairs and get ready. I'll be ready to go in a minute. Ain't you gonna get dressed?

BOY WILLIE: I'm gonna wear what I got on. I ain't dressing up for these city niggers.

[*Lymon exits up the stairs.*]

That's all Lymon think about is women.

WINING BOY: His daddy was the same way. I used to run around with him. I know his mama too. Two strokes back and I would have been his daddy! His daddy's dead now . . . but I got the nigger out of jail one time. They was fixing to name him Daniel and walk him through the Lion's Den. He got in a tussle with one of them white fellows and the sheriff lit on him like white on rice. That's how the whole thing come about between me and Lymon's mama. She knew me and his daddy used to run together and he got in jail and she went down there and took the sheriff a hundred dollars. Don't get me to lying about where she got it from. I don't know. The sheriff looked at that hundred dollars and turned his nose up. Told her, say, "That ain't gonna do him no good. You got to put another hundred on top of that." She come up there and got me where I was playing at this saloon . . . said she had all but fifty dollars and asked me if I could help. Now the way I figured it . . . without that fifty dollars the sheriff was gonna turn him over to Parchman. The sheriff turn him over to Parchman it be three years before anybody see him again. Now I'm gonna say it right . . . I will give anybody fifty dollars to keep them out of jail for three years. I give her the fifty dollars and she told me to come over to the house. I ain't asked her. I figure if she was nice enough to invite me I ought to go. I ain't had to say a word. She invited me over just as nice. Say, "Why don't you come over to the house?" She ain't had to say nothing else. Them words rolled off her tongue just as nice. I went on down there and sat about three hours. Started to leave and changed my mind. She grabbed hold to me and say, "Baby, it's all night long." That was one of the shortest nights I have ever spent on this earth! I could have used another eight hours. Lymon's daddy didn't even say nothing to me when he got out. He just looked at me funny. He had a good notion something had happened between me an' her. L. D. Jackson. That was one bad-luck nigger. Got killed at some dance. Fellow walked in and shot him thinking he was somebody else.

[*Doaker enters from his room.*]

Hey, Doaker, you remember L. D. Jackson?
DOAKER: That's Lymon's daddy. That was one bad-luck nigger.
BOY WILLIE: Look like you ready to railroad some.
DOAKER: Yeah, I got to make that run.

[*Lymon enters from the stairs. He is dressed in his new suit and shoes, to which he has added a cheap straw hat.*]

LYMON: How I look?
WINING BOY: You look like a million dollars. Don't he look good, Doaker? Come on, let's play some cards. You wanna play some cards?
BOY WILLIE: We ain't gonna play no cards with you. Me and Lymon gonna find some women. Hey, Lymon, don't play no cards with Wining Boy. He'll take all your money.
WINING BOY [*to Lymon*]:   You got a magic suit there. You can get you a woman easy with that suit . . . but you got to know the magic words. You know the magic words to get you a woman?

LYMON: I just talk to them to see if I like them and they like me.

WINING BOY: You just walk right up to them and say, "If you got the harbor I got the ship." If that don't work ask them if you can put them in your pocket. The first thing they gonna say is, "It's too small." That's when you look them dead in the eye and say, "Baby, ain't nothing small about me." If that don't work then you move on to another one. Am I telling him right, Doaker?

DOAKER: That man don't need you to tell him nothing about no women. These women these days ain't gonna fall for that kind of stuff. You got to buy them a present. That's what they looking for these days.

BOY WILLIE: Come on, I'm ready. You ready, Lymon? Come on, let's go find some women.

WINING BOY: Here, let me walk out with you. I wanna see the women fall out their window when they see Lymon.

[*They all exit and the lights go down on the scene.*]

SCENE II

[*The lights come up on the kitchen. It is late evening of the same day. Berniece has set a tub for her bath in the kitchen. She is heating up water on the stove. There is a knock at the door.*]

BERNIECE: Who is it?

AVERY: It's me, Avery.

[*Berniece opens the door and lets him in.*]

BERNIECE: Avery, come on in. I was just fixing to take my bath.

AVERY: Where Boy Willie? I see that truck out there almost empty. They done sold almost all them watermelons.

BERNIECE: They was gone when I come home. I don't know where they went off to. Boy Willie around here about to drive me crazy.

AVERY: They sell them watermelons . . . he'll be gone soon.

BERNIECE: What Mr. Cohen say about letting you have the place?

AVERY: He say he'll let me have it for thirty dollars a month. I talked him out of thirty-five and he say he'll let me have it for thirty.

BERNIECE: That's a nice spot next to Benny Diamond's store.

AVERY: Berniece . . . I be at home and I get to thinking you up here an' I'm down there. I get to thinking how that look to have a preacher that ain't married. It makes for a better congregation if the preacher was settled down and married.

BERNIECE: Avery . . . not now. I was fixing to take my bath.

AVERY: You know how I feel about you, Berniece. Now . . . I done got the place from Mr. Cohen. I get the money from the bank and I can fix it up real nice. They give me a ten cents a hour raise down there on the job . . . now Berniece, I ain't got much in the way of comforts. I got a hole in my pockets near about as far as money is concerned. I ain't never found no way through life to a woman I care about like I care about you. I need that. I need somebody on my bond side. I need a woman that fits in my hand.

BERNIECE: Avery, I ain't ready to get married now.

AVERY: You too young a woman to close up, Berniece.

BERNIECE: I ain't said nothing about closing up. I got a lot of woman left in me.

AVERY: Where's it at? When's the last time you looked at it?

BERNIECE [*stunned by his remark*]: That's a nasty thing to say. And you call yourself a preacher.

AVERY: Anytime I get anywhere near you . . . you push me away.

BERNIECE: I got enough on my hands with Maretha. I got enough people to love and take care of.

AVERY: Who you got to love you? Can't nobody get close enough to you. Doaker can't half say nothing to you. You jump all over Boy Willie. Who you got to love you, Berniece?

BERNIECE: You trying to tell me a woman can't be nothing without a man. But you alright, huh? You can just walk out of here without me—without a woman—and still be a man. That's alright. Ain't nobody gonna ask you, "Avery, who you got to love you?" That's alright for you. But everybody gonna be worried about Berniece. "How Berniece gonna take care of herself? How she gonna raise that child without a man? Wonder what she do with herself. How she gonna live like that?" Everybody got all kinds of questions for Berniece. Everybody telling me I can't be a woman unless I got a man. Well, you tell me, Avery—you know—how much woman am I?

AVERY: It wasn't me, Berniece. You can't blame me for nobody else. I'll own up to my own shortcomings. But you can't blame me for Crawley or nobody else.

BERNIECE: I ain't blaming nobody for nothing. I'm just stating the facts.

AVERY: How long you gonna carry Crawley with you, Berniece? It's been over three years. At some point you got to let go and go on. Life's got all kinds of twists and turns. That don't mean you stop living. That don't mean you cut yourself off from life. You can't go through life carrying Crawley's ghost with you. Crawley's been dead three years. Three years, Berniece.

BERNIECE: I know how long Crawley's been dead. You ain't got to tell me that. I just ain't ready to get married right now.

AVERY: What is you ready for, Berniece? You just gonna drift along from day to day. Life is more than making it from one day to another. You gonna look up one day and it's all gonna be past you. Life's gonna be gone out of your hands—there won't be enough to make nothing with. I'm standing here now, Berniece—but I don't know how much longer I'm gonna be standing here waiting on you.

BERNIECE: Avery, I told you . . . when you get your church we'll sit down and talk about this. I got too many other things to deal with right now. Boy Willie and the piano . . . and Sutter's ghost. I thought I might have been seeing things, but Maretha done seen Sutter's ghost, too.

AVERY: When this happen, Berniece?

BERNIECE: Right after I came home yesterday. Me and Boy Willie was arguing about the piano and Sutter's ghost was standing at the top of the stairs. Maretha scared to sleep up there now. Maybe if you bless the house he'll go away.

AVERY: I don't know, Berniece. I don't know if I should fool around with something like that.

BERNIECE: I can't have Maretha scared to go to sleep up there. Seem like if you bless the house he would go away.

AVERY: You might have to be a special kind of preacher to do something like that.

BERNIECE: I keep telling myself when Boy Willie leave he'll go on and leave with him. I believe Boy Willie pushed him in the well.

AVERY: That's been going on down there a long time. The Ghosts of the Yellow Dog been pushing people in their wells long before Boy Willie got grown.

BERNIECE: Somebody down there pushing them people in their wells. They ain't just upped and fell. Ain't no wind pushed nobody in their well.

AVERY: Oh, I don't know. God works in mysterious ways.

BERNIECE: He ain't pushed nobody in their wells.

AVERY: He caused it to happen. God is the Great Causer. He can do anything. He parted the Red Sea. He say I will smite my enemies. Reverend Thompson used to preach on the Ghosts of the Yellow Dog as the hand of God.

BERNIECE: I don't care who preached what. Somebody down there pushing them people in their wells. Somebody like Boy Willie. I can see him doing something like that. You ain't gonna tell me that Sutter just upped and fell in his well. I believe Boy Willie pushed him so he could get his land.

AVERY: What Doaker say about Boy Willie selling the piano?

BERNIECE: Doaker don't want no part of that piano. He ain't never wanted no part of it. He blames himself for not staying behind with Papa Boy Charles. He washed his hands of that piano a long time ago. He didn't want me to bring it up here—but I wasn't gonna leave it down there.

AVERY: Well, it seems to me somebody ought to be able to talk to Boy Willie.

BERNIECE: You can't talk to Boy Willie. He been that way all his life. Mama Ola had her hands full trying to talk to him. He don't listen to nobody. He just like my daddy. He get his mind fixed on something and can't nobody turn him from it.

AVERY: You ought to start a choir at the church. Maybe if he seen you was doing something with it—if you told him you was gonna put it in my church—maybe he'd see it different. You ought to put it down in the church and start a choir. The Bible say "Make a joyful noise unto the Lord." Maybe if Boy Willie see you was doing something with it he'd see it different.

BERNIECE: I done told you I don't play on that piano. Ain't no need in you to keep talking this choir stuff. When my mama died I shut the top on that piano and I ain't never opened it since. I was only playing it for her. When my daddy died seem like all her life went into that piano. She used to have me playing on it . . . had Miss Eula come in and teach me . . . say when I played it she could hear my daddy talking to her. I used to think them pictures came alive and walked through the house. Sometime late at night I could hear my mama talking to them. I said that wasn't gonna happen to me. I don't play that piano cause I don't want to wake them spirits. They never be walking around in this house.

AVERY: You got to put all that behind you, Berniece.

BERNIECE: I got Maretha playing on it. She don't know nothing about it. Let her go on and be a schoolteacher or something. She don't have to carry all of that with her. She got a chance I didn't have. I ain't gonna burden her with that piano.

AVERY: You got to put all of that behind you, Berniece. That's the same thing like Crawley. Everybody got stones in their passway.

You got to step over them or walk around them. You picking them up and carrying them with you. All you got to do is set them down by the side of the road. You ain't got to carry them with you. You can walk over there right now and play that piano. You can walk over there right now and God will walk over there with you. Right now you can set that sack of stones down by the side of the road and walk away from it. You don't have to carry it with you. You can do it right now.

[*Avery crosses over to the piano and raises the lid.*]

Come on, Berniece . . . set it down and walk away from it. Come on, play "Old Ship of Zion." Walk over here and claim it as an instrument of the Lord. You can walk over here right now and make it into a celebration.

[*Berniece moves toward the piano.*]

BERNIECE: Avery . . . I done told you I don't want to play that piano. Now or no other time.

AVERY: The Bible say, "The Lord is my refuge . . . and my strength!" With the strength of God you can put the past behind you, Berniece. With the strength of God you can do anything! God got a bright tomorrow. God don't ask what you done . . . God ask what you gonna do. The strength of God can move mountains! God's got a bright tomorrow for you . . . all you got to do is walk over here and claim it.

BERNIECE: Avery, just go on and let me finish my bath. I'll see you tomorrow.

AVERY: Okay, Berniece. I'm gonna go home. I'm gonna go home and read up on my Bible. And tomorrow . . . if the good Lord give me strength tomorrow . . . I'm gonna come by and bless the house . . . and show you the power of the Lord.

[*Avery crosses to the door.*]

It's gonna be alright, Berniece. God say he will soothe the troubled waters. I'll come by tomorrow and bless the house.

[*The lights go down to black.*]

SCENE III

[*Several hours later. The house is dark. Berniece has retired for the night. Boy Willie enters the darkened house with Grace.*]

BOY WILLIE: Come on in. This my sister's house. My sister live here. Come on, I ain't gonna bite you.

GRACE: Put some light on. I can't see.

BOY WILLIE: You don't need to see nothing, baby. This here is all you need to see. All you need to do is see me. If you can't see me you can feel me in the dark. How's that, sugar?

[*He attempts to kiss her.*]

GRACE: Go on now . . . wait!

BOY WILLIE: Just give me one little old kiss.

GRACE [*pushing him away*]: Come on, now. Where I'm gonna sleep at?

BOY WILLIE: We got to sleep out here on the couch. Come on, my sister don't mind. Lymon come back he just got to sleep on the floor. He run off with Dolly somewhere he better stay there. Come on, sugar.

GRACE: Wait now . . . you ain't told me nothing about no couch. I thought you had a bed. Both of us can't sleep on that little old couch.

BOY WILLIE: It don't make no difference. We can sleep on the floor. let Lymon sleep on the couch.

GRACE: You ain't told me nothing about no couch.

BOY WILLIE: What difference it make? You just wanna be with me.

GRACE: I don't want to be with you on no couch. Ain't you got no bed?

BOY WILLIE: You don't need no bed, woman. My granddaddy used to take women on the backs of horses. What you need a bed for? You just want to be with me.

GRACE: You sure is country. I didn't know you was this country.

BOY WILLIE: There's a lot of things you don't know about me. Come on, let me show you what this country boy can do.

GRACE: Let's go to my place. I got a room with a bed if Leroy don't come back there.

BOY WILLIE: Who's Leroy? You ain't said nothing about no Leroy.

GRACE: He used to be my man. He ain't coming back. He gone off with some other gal.

BOY WILLIE: You let him have your key?

GRACE: He ain't coming back.

BOY WILLIE: Did you let him have your key?

GRACE: He got a key but he ain't coming back. He took off with some other gal.

BOY WILLIE: I don't wanna go nowhere he might come. Let's stay here. Come on, sugar.

[*He pulls her over to the couch.*]

Let me heist your hood and check your oil. See if your battery needs charged.

[*He pulls her to him. They kiss and tug at each other's clothing. In their anxiety they knock over a lamp.*]

BERNIECE: Who's that . . . Wining Boy?

BOY WILLIE: It's me . . . Boy Willie. Go on back to sleep. Everything's alright.

[*To Grace.*]

That's my sister. Everything's alright, Berniece. Go on back to sleep.

BERNIECE: What you doing down there? What you done knocked over?

BOY WILLIE: It wasn't nothing. Everything's alright. Go on back to sleep.

[*To Grace.*]

That's my sister. We alright. She gone back to sleep.

[*They begin to kiss. Berniece enters from the stairs dressed in a nightgown. She cuts on the light.*]

BERNIECE: Boy Willie, what you doing down here?

BOY WILLIE: It was just that there lamp. It ain't broke. It's okay. Everything's alright. Go on back to bed.

BERNIECE: Boy Willie, I don't allow that in my house. You gonna have to take your company someplace else.

BOY WILLIE: It's alright. We ain't doing nothing. We just sitting here talking. This here is Grace. That's my sister Berniece.

BERNIECE: You know I don't allow that kind of stuff in my house.

BOY WILLIE: Allow what? We just sitting here talking.

BERNIECE: Well, your company gonna have to leave. Come back and talk in the morning.

BOY WILLIE: Go on back upstairs now.

BERNIECE: I got an eleven-year-old girl upstairs. I can't allow that around here.

BOY WILLIE: Ain't nobody said nothing about that. I told you we just talking.

GRACE: Come on . . . let's go to my place. Ain't nobody got to tell me to leave but once.

BOY WILLIE: You ain't got to be like that, Berniece.

BERNIECE: I'm sorry, Miss. But he know I don't allow that in here.

GRACE: You ain't got to tell me but once. I don't stay nowhere I ain't wanted.

BOY WILLIE: I don't know why you want to embarrass me in front of my company.

GRACE: Come on, take me home.

BERNIECE: Go on, Boy Willie. Just go on with your company.

[*Boy Willie and Grace exit. Berniece puts the light on in the kitchen and puts on the teakettle. Presently there is a knock at the door. Berniece goes to answer it. Berniece opens the door. Lymon enters.*]

LYMON: How you doing, Berniece? I thought you'd be asleep. Boy Willie been back here?

BERNIECE: He just left out of here a minute ago.

LYMON: I went out to see a picture show and never got there. We always end up doing something else. I was with this woman she just wanted to drink up all my money. So I left her there and came back looking for Boy Willie.

BERNIECE: You just missed him. He just left out of here.

LYMON: They got some nice-looking women in this city. I'm gonna like it up here real good. I like seeing them with their dresses on. Got them high heels. I like that. Make them look like they real precious. Boy Willie met a real nice one today. I wish I had met her before he did.

BERNIECE: He come by here with some woman a little while ago. I told him to go on and take all that out of my house.

LYMON: What she look like, the woman he was with? Was she a brown-skinned woman about this high? Nice and healthy? Got nice hips on her?

BERNIECE: She had on a red dress.

LYMON: That's her! That's Grace. She real nice. Laugh a lot. Lot of fun to be with. She don't be trying to put on. Some of these woman act like they the Queen of Sheba. I don't like them kind. Grace ain't like that. She real nice with herself.

BERNIECE: I don't know what she was like. He come in here all drunk knocking over the lamp, and making all kind of noise. I told them to take that somewhere else. I can't really say what she was like.

LYMON: She real nice. I seen her before he did. I was trying not to act like I seen her. I wanted to look at her a while before I said something. She seen me when I come into the saloon. I tried to act like I didn't see her. Time I looked around Boy Willie was talking to her. She was talking to him kept looking at me. That's when her friend Dolly came. I asked her if she wanted to go to the picture show. She told me to buy her a drink while she thought about it. Next thing I knew she done had three drinks talking about she too tired to go. I bought her another drink, then I left. Boy Willie was gone and I thought he might have come back here. Doaker gone, huh? He say he had to make a trip.

BERNIECE: Yeah, he gone on his trip. This is when I can usually get me some peace and quiet, Maretha asleep.

LYMON: She look just like you. Got them big eyes. I remember her when she was in diapers.

BERNIECE: Time just keep on. It go on with or without you. She going on twelve.

LYMON: She sure is pretty. I like kids.

BERNIECE: Boy Willie say you staying . . . what you gonna do up here in this big city? You thought about that?

LYMON: They never get me back down there. The sheriff looking for me. All because they gonna try and make me work for somebody when I don't want to. They gonna try and make me work for Stovall when he don't pay nothing. It ain't like that up here. Up here you more or less do what you want to. I figure I find me a job and try to get set up and then see what the year brings. I tried to do that two or three times down there . . . but it never would work out. I was always in the wrong place.

BERNIECE: This ain't a bad city once you get to know your way around.

LYMON: Up here is different. I'm gonna get me a job unloading boxcars or something. One fellow told me say he know a place. I'm gonna go over there with him next week. Me and Boy Willie finish selling them watermelons I'll have enough money to hold me for a while. But I'm gonna go over there and see what kind of jobs they have.

BERNIECE: You shouldn't have too much trouble finding a job. It's all in how you present yourself. See now, Boy Willie couldn't get no job up here. Somebody hire him they got a pack of trouble on their hands. Soon as they find that out they fire him. He don't want to do nothing unless he do it his way.

LYMON: I know. I told him let's go to the picture show first and see if there was any women down there. They might get tired of sitting at home and walk down to the picture show. He say he wanna look around first. We never did get down there. We tried a couple of places and then we went to this saloon where he met Grace. I tried to meet her before he did but he beat me to her. We left Wining Boy sitting down there running his mouth. He told me if I wear this suit I'd find me a woman. He was almost right.

BERNIECE: You don't need to be out there in them saloons. Ain't no telling what you liable to run into out there. This one liable to cut you as quick as that one shoot you. You don't need to be out there. You start out that fast life you can't keep it up. It makes you old quick. I don't know what them women out there be thinking about.

LYMON: Mostly they be lonely and looking for somebody to spend the night with them. Sometimes it matters who it is and sometimes it don't. I used to be the same way. Now it got to matter. That's why I'm here now. Dolly liable not to even recognize me if she sees me again. I don't like women like that. I like my women to be with me in a nice and easy way. That way we can both enjoy ourselves. The way I see it we the only two people like us in the world. We got to see how we fit together. A woman that don't want to take the time to do that I don't bother with. Used to. Used to bother with all of them. Then I woke up one time with this woman and I didn't know who she was. She was the prettiest woman I had ever seen in my life. I spent the whole night with her and didn't even know it. I had never taken the time to look at her. I guess she kinda knew I ain't never really looked at her. She must have known that cause she ain't wanted to see me no more. If she had wanted to see me I believe we might have got married. How come you ain't married? It seem like to me you would be married. I remember Avery from down home. I used to call him plain old Avery. Now he Reverend Avery. That's kinda funny about him becoming a preacher. I like when he told about how that come to him in a dream about them sheep people and them hobos. Nothing ever come to me in a dream like that. I just dream about women. Can't never seem to find the right one.

BERNIECE: She out there somewhere. You just got to get yourself ready to meet her. That's what I'm trying to do. Avery's alright. I ain't really got nobody in mind.

LYMON: I get me a job and a little place and get set up to where I can make a woman comfortable I might get married. Avery's nice. You ought to go ahead and get married. You be a preacher's wife you won't have to work. I hate living by myself. I didn't want to be no strain on my mama so I left home when I was about sixteen. Everything I tried seem like it just didn't work out. Now I'm trying this.

BERNIECE: You keep trying it'll work out for you.

LYMON: You ever go down there to the picture show?

BERNIECE: I don't go in for all that.

LYMON: Ain't nothing wrong with it. It ain't like gambling and sinning. I went to one down in Jackson once. It was fun.

BERNIECE: I just stay home most of the time. Take care of Maretha.

LYMON: It's getting kind of late. I don't know where Boy Willie went off to. He's liable not to come back. I'm gonna take off these shoes. My feet hurt. Was you in bed? I don't mean to be keeping you up.

BERNIECE: You ain't keeping me up. I couldn't sleep after that Boy Willie woke me up.

LYMON: You got on that nightgown. I likes women when they wear them fancy nightclothes and all. It makes their skin look real pretty.

BERNIECE: I got this at the five-and-ten-cents store. It ain't so fancy.

LYMON: I don't too often get to see a woman dressed like that.

[*There is a long pause. Lymon takes off his suit coat.*]

Well, I'm gonna sleep here on the couch. I'm supposed to sleep on the floor but I don't reckon Boy Willie's coming back tonight. Wining Boy sold me this suit. Told me it was a magic suit. I'm gonna put it on again tomorrow. Maybe it bring me a woman like he say.

[*He goes into his coat pocket and takes out a small bottle of perfume.*]

I almost forgot I had this. Some man sold me this for a dollar. Say it come from Paris. This is the same kind of perfume the Queen of France wear. That's what he told me. I don't know if it's true or not. I smelled it. It smelled good to me. Here . . . smell it see if you like it. I was gonna give it to Dolly. But I didn't like her too much.

BERNIECE: [*takes the bottle*]: It smells nice.

LYMON: I was gonna give it to Dolly if she had went to the picture with me. Go on, you take it.

BERNIECE: I can't take it. Here . . . go on you keep it. You'll find somebody to give it to.

LYMON: I wanna give it to you. Make you smell nice.

[*He takes the bottle and puts perfume behind Berniece's ear.*]

They tell me you supposed to put it right here behind your ear. Say if you put it there you smell nice all day.

[*Berniece stiffens at his touch. Lymon bends down to smell her.*]

There . . . you smell real good now.

[*He kisses her neck.*]

You smell real good for Lymon.

[*He kisses her again. Berniece returns the kiss, then breaks the embrace and crosses to the stairs. She turns and they look silently at each other. Lymon hands her the bottle of perfume. Berniece exits up the stairs. Lymon picks up his suit coat and strokes it lovingly with the full knowledge that it is indeed a magic suit. The lights go down on the scene.*]

SCENE IV

[*It is late the next morning. The lights come up on the parlor. Lymon is asleep on the sofa. Boy Willie enters the front door.*]

BOY WILLIE: Hey, Lymon! Lymon, come on get up.

LYMON: Leave me alone.

BOY WILLIE: Come on, get up, nigger! Wake up, Lymon.

LYMON: What you want?

BOY WILLIE: Come on, let's go. I done called the man about the piano.

LYMON: What piano?

BOY WILLIE [*dumps Lymon on the floor*]:   Come on, get up!

LYMON: Why you leave, I looked around and you was gone.

BOY WILLIE: I come back here with Grace, then I went looking for you. I figured you'd be with Dolly.

LYMON: She just want to drink and spend up your money. I come on back here looking for you to see if you wanted to go to the picture show.

BOY WILLIE: I been up at Grace's house. Some nigger named Leroy come by but I had a chair up against the door. He got mad when he couldn't get in. He went off somewhere and I got out of there before he could come back. Berniece got mad when we came here.

LYMON: She say you was knocking over the lamp busting up the place.

BOY WILLIE: That was Grace doing all that.

LYMON: Wining Boy seen Sutter's ghost last night.

BOY WILLIE: Wining Boy's liable to see anything. I'm surprised he found the right house. Come on, I done called the man about the piano.

LYMON: What he say?

BOY WILLIE: He say to bring it on out. I told him I was calling for my sister, Miss Berniece Charles. I told him some man wanted to buy it for eleven hundred dollars and asked him if he would go any better. He said yeah, he would give me eleven hundred and fifty dollars for it if it was the same piano. I described it to him again and he told me to bring it out.

LYMON: Why didn't you tell him to come and pick it up?

BOY WILLIE: I didn't want to have no problem with Berniece. This way we just take it on out there and it be out the way. He want to charge twenty-five dollars to pick it up.

LYMON: You should have told him the man was gonna give you twelve hundred for it.

BOY WILLIE: I figure I was taking a chance with that eleven hundred. If I had told him twelve hundred he might have run off. Now I wish I had told him twelve-fifty. It's hard to figure out white folks sometimes.

LYMON: You might have been able to tell him anything. White folks got a lot of money.

BOY WILLIE: Come on, let's get it loaded before Berniece come back. Get that end over there. All you got to do is pick it up on that side. Don't worry about this side. You wanna stretch you' back for a minute?

LYMON: I'm ready.

BOY WILLIE: Get a real good grip on it now.

[*The sound of Sutter's Ghost is heard. They do not hear it.*]

LYMON: I got this end. You get that end.

BOY WILLIE: Wait till I say ready now. Alright. You got it good? You got a grip on it?

LYMON: Yeah, I got it. You lift up on that end.

BOY WILLIE: Ready? Lift!

[*The piano will not budge.*]

LYMON: Man, this piano is heavy! It's gonna take more than me and you to move this piano.

BOY WILLIE: We can do it. Come on—we did it before.

LYMON: Nigger—you crazy! That piano weighs five hundred pounds!

BOY WILLIE: I got three hundred pounds of it! I know you can carry two hundred pounds! You be lifting them cotton sacks! Come on lift this piano!

[*They try to move the piano again without success.*]

LYMON: It's stuck. Something holding it.

BOY WILLIE: How the piano gonna be stuck? We just moved it. Slide you' end out.

LYMON: Naw—we gonna need two or three more people. How this big old piano get in the house?

BOY WILLIE: I don't know how it got in the house. I know how it's going out though! You get on this end. I'll carry three hundred and fifty pounds of it. All you got to do is slide your end out. Ready?

[*They switch sides and try again without success. Doaker enters from his room as they try to push and shove it.*]

LYMON: Hey, Doaker . . . how this piano get in the house?

DOAKER: Boy Willie, what you doing?

BOY WILLIE: I'm carrying this piano out the house. What it look like I'm doing? Come on, Lymon, let's try again.

DOAKER: Go on let the piano sit there till Berniece come home.

BOY WILLIE: You ain't got nothing to do with this, Doaker. This my business.

DOAKER: This is my house, nigger! I ain't gonna let you or nobody else carry nothing out of it. You ain't gonna carry nothing out of here without my permission!

BOY WILLIE: This is my piano. I don't need your permission to carry my belongings out of your house. This is mine. This ain't got nothing to do with you.

DOAKER: I say leave it over there till Berniece come home. She got part of it too. Leave it set there till you see what she say.

BOY WILLIE: I don't care what Berniece say. Come on, Lymon. I got this side.

DOAKER: Go on and cut it half in two if you want to. Just leave Berniece's half sitting over there. I can't tell you what to do with your piano. But I can't let you take her half out of here.

BOY WILLIE: Go on, Doaker. You ain't got nothing to do with this. I don't want you starting nothing now. Just go on and leave me alone. Come on, Lymon. I got this end.

[*Doaker goes into his room. Boy Willie and Lymon prepare to move the piano.*]

LYMON: How we gonna get it in the truck?

BOY WILLIE: Don't worry about how we gonna get it on the truck. You got to get it out the house first.

LYMON: It's gonna take more than me and you to move this piano.

BOY WILLIE: Just lift up on that end, nigger!

[*Doaker comes to the doorway of his room and stands.*]

DOAKER [*quietly with authority*]: Leave that piano set over there till Berniece come back. I don't care what you do with it then. But you gonna leave it sit over there right now.

BOY WILLIE: Alright . . . I'm gonna tell you this, Doaker. I'm going out of here . . . I'm gonna get me some rope . . . find me a plank and some wheels . . . and I'm coming back. Then I'm gonna carry that piano out of here . . . sell it and give Berniece half the money. See . . . now that's what I'm gonna do. And you . . . or nobody else is gonna stop me. Come on, Lymon . . . let's go get some rope and stuff. I'll be back, Doaker.

[*Boy Willie and Lymon exit. The lights go down on the scene.*]

SCENE V

[*The lights come up. Boy Willie sits on the sofa, screwing casters on a wooden plank. Maretha is sitting on the piano stool. Doaker sits at the table playing solitaire.*]

BOY WILLIE [*to Maretha*]: Then after that them white folks down around there started falling down their wells. You ever seen a well? A well got a wall around it. It's hard to fall down a well. You got to be leaning way over. Couldn't nobody figure out too much what was making these fellows fall down their well . . . so everybody says the Ghosts of the Yellow Dog must have pushed them. That's what everybody called them four men what got burned up in the boxcar.

MARETHA: Why they call them that?

BOY WILLIE: Cause the Yazoo Delta railroad got yellow boxcars. Sometime the way the whistle blow sound like an old dog howling so the people call it the Yellow Dog.

MARETHA: Anybody ever see the Ghosts?

BOY WILLIE: I told you they like the wind. Can you see the wind?

MARETHA: No.

BOY WILLIE: They like the wind you can't see them. But sometimes you be in trouble they might be around to help you. They say if you go where the Southern cross the Yellow Dog . . . you go to where them two railroads cross each other . . . and call out their names . . . they say they talk back to you. I don't know, I ain't never done that. But Uncle Wining Boy he say he been down there and talked to them. You have to ask him about that part.

[*Berniece has entered from the front door.*]

BERNIECE: Maretha, you go on and get ready for me to do your hair.

[*Maretha crosses to the steps.*]

Boy Willie, I done told you to leave my house.

[*To Maretha.*]

Go on, Maretha.

[*Maretha is hesitant about going up the stairs.*]

BOY WILLIE: Don't be scared. Here, I'll go up there with you. If we see Sutter's ghost I'll put a whupping on him. Come on, Uncle Boy Willie going with you.

[*Boy Willie and Maretha exit up the stairs.*]

BERNIECE: Doaker—what is going on here?

DOAKER: I come home and him and Lymon was moving the piano. I told them to leave it over there till you got home. He went out and got that board and them wheels. He say he gonna take that piano out of here and ain't nobody gonna stop him.

BERNIECE: I ain't playing with Boy Willie. I got Crawley's gun upstairs. He don't know but I'm through with it. Where Lymon go?

DOAKER: Boy Willie sent him for some rope just before you come in.

BERNIECE: I ain't studying Boy Willie or Lymon—or the rope. Boy Willie ain't taking that piano out this house. That's all there is to it.

[*Boy Willie and Maretha enter on the stairs. Maretha carries a hot comb and a can of hair grease. Boy Willie crosses over and continues to screw the wheels on the board.*]

MARETHA: Mama, all the hair grease is gone. There ain't but this little bit left.

BERNIECE [*gives her a dollar*]:   Here . . . run across the street and get another can. You come straight back, too. Don't you be playing around out there. And watch the cars. Be careful when you cross the street.

[*Maretha exits out the front door.*]

Boy Willie, I done told you to leave my house.

BOY WILLIE: I ain't in you' house. I'm in Doaker's house. If he ask me to leave then I'll go on and leave. But consider me done left your part.

BERNIECE: Doaker, tell him to leave. Tell him to go on.

DOAKER: Boy Willie ain't done nothing for me to put him out of the house. I told you if you can't get along just go on and don't have nothing to do with each other.

BOY WILLIE: I ain't thinking about Berniece.

[*He gets up and draws a line across the floor with his foot.*]

There! Now I'm out of your part of the house. Consider me done left your part. Soon as Lymon come back with that rope. I'm gonna take that piano out of here and sell it.

BERNIECE: You ain't gonna touch that piano.

BOY WILLIE: Carry it out of here just as big and bold. Do like my daddy would have done come time to get Sutter's land.

BERNIECE: I got something to make you leave it over there.

BOY WILLIE: It's got to come better than this thirty-two-twenty.

DOAKER: Why don't you stop all that! Boy Willie, go on and leave her alone. You know how Berniece get. Why you wanna sit there and pick with her?

BOY WILLIE: I ain't picking with her. I told her the truth. She the one talking about what she got. I just told her what she better have.

BERNIECE: That's alright, Doaker. Leave him alone.

BOY WILLIE: She trying to scare me. Hell, I ain't scared of dying. I look around and see people dying every day. You got to die to make room for somebody else. I had a dog that died. Wasn't nothing but a puppy. I picked it up and put it in a bag and carried it up there to Reverend C. L. Thompson's church. I carried it up there and prayed and asked Jesus to make it live like he did the man in the Bible. I prayed real hard. Knelt down and everything. Say ask in Jesus' name. Well, I must have called Jesus' name two hundred times. I called his name till my mouth got sore. I got up and looked in the bag and the dog still dead. It ain't moved a muscle! I say,

"Well, ain't nothing precious." And then I went out and killed me a cat. That's when I discovered the power of death. See, a nigger that ain't afraid to die is the worse kind of nigger for the white man. He can't hold that power over you. That's what I learned when I killed that cat. I got the power of death too. I can command him. I can call him up. The white man don't like to see that. He don't like for you to stand up and look him square in the eye and say, "I got it too." Then he got to deal with you square up.

BERNIECE: That's why I don't talk to him, Doaker. You try and talk to him and that's the only kind of stuff that comes out his mouth.

DOAKER: You say Avery went home to get his Bible?

BOY WILLIE: What Avery gonna do? Avery can't do nothing with me. I wish Avery would say something to me about this piano.

DOAKER: Berniece ain't said about that. Avery went home to get his Bible. He coming by to bless the house see if he can get rid of Sutter's ghost.

BOY WILLIE: Ain't nothing but a house full of ghosts down there at the church. What Avery look like chasing away somebody's ghost?

[*Maretha enters the front door.*]

BERNIECE: Light that stove and set that comb over there to get hot. Get something to put around your shoulders.

BOY WILLIE: The Bible say an eye for an eye, a tooth for a tooth, and a life for a life. Tit for tat. But you and Avery don't want to believe that.

You gonna pass up that part and pretend it ain't in there. Everything else you gonna agree with. But if you gonna agree with part of it you got to agree with all of it. You can't do nothing halfway. You gonna go at the Bible halfway. You gonna act like that part ain't in there. But you pull out the Bible and open it and see what it say. Ask Avery. He a preacher. He'll tell you it's in there. He the Good Shepherd. Unless he gonna shepherd you to heaven with half the Bible.

BERNIECE: Maretha, bring me that comb. Make sure it's hot.

[*Maretha brings the comb. Berniece begins to do her hair.*]

BOY WILLIE: I will say this for Avery. He done figured out a path to go through life. I don't agree with it. But he done fixed it so he can go right through it real smooth. Hell, he liable to end up with a million dollars that he done got from selling bread and wine.

MARETHA: OWWWWWW!

BERNIECE: Be still, Maretha. If you was a boy I wouldn't be going through this.

BOY WILLIE: Don't you tell that girl that. Why you wanna tell her that?

BERNIECE: You ain't got nothing to do with this child.

BOY WILLIE: Telling her you wished she was a boy. How's that gonna make her feel?

BERNIECE: Boy Willie, go on and leave me alone.

DOAKER: Why don't you leave her alone? What you got to pick with her for? Why don't you go on out and see what's out there in the streets? Have something to tell the fellows down home.

BOY WILLIE: I'm waiting on Lymon to get back with that truck. Why don't you go on out and see what's out there in the streets? You ain't got to work tomorrow. Talking about me . . . why don't you go out there? It's Friday night.

DOAKER: I got to stay around here and keep you all from killing one another.

BOY WILLIE: You ain't got to worry about me. I'm gonna be here just as long as it takes Lymon to get back here with that truck. You ought to be talking to Berniece. Sitting up there telling Maretha she wished she was a boy. What kind of thing is that to tell a child? If you want to tell her something tell her about that piano. You ain't even told her about that piano. Like that's something to be ashamed of. Like she supposed to go off and hide somewhere about that piano. You ought to mark down on the calendar the day that Papa Boy Charles brought that piano into the house. You ought to mark that day down and draw a circle around it . . . and every year when it come up throw a party. Have a celebration. If you did that she wouldn't have no problem in life. She could walk around here with her head held high. I'm talking about a big party! Invite everybody! Mark that day down with a special meaning. That way she know where she at in the world. You got her going out here thinking she wrong in the world. Like there ain't no part of it belong to her.

BERNIECE: Let me take care of my child. When you get one of your own then you can teach it what you want to teach it.

[*Doaker exits into his room.*]

BOY WILLIE: What I want to bring a child into this world for? Why I wanna bring somebody else into all this for? I'll tell you this . . . If

I was Rockefeller I'd have forty or fifty. I'd make one every day. Cause they gonna start out in life with all the advantages. I ain't got no advantages to offer nobody. Many is the time I looked at my daddy and seen him staring off at his hands. I got a little older I know what he was thinking. He sitting there saying, "I got these big old hands but what I'm gonna do with them? Best I can do is make a fifty-acre crop for Mr. Stovall. Got these big old hands capable of doing anything. I can take and build something with these hands. But where's the tools? All I got is these hands. Unless I go out here and kill me somebody and take what they got . . . it's a long row to hoe for me to get something of my own. So what I'm gonna do with these big old hands? What would you do?"

See now . . . if he had his own land he wouldn't have felt that way. If he had something under his feet that belonged to him he could stand up taller. That's what I'm talking about. Hell, the land is there for everybody. All you got to do is figure out how to get you a piece. Ain't no mystery to life. You just got to go out and meet it square on. If you got a piece of land you'll find everything else fall right into place. You can stand right up next to the white man and talk about the price of cotton . . . the weather, and anything else you want to talk about. If you teach that girl that she living at the bottom of life, she's gonna grow up and hate you.

BERNIECE: I'm gonna teach her the truth. That's just where she living. Only she ain't got to stay there.

[*To Maretha.*]

Turn you' head over to the other side.

BOY WILLIE: This might be your bottom but it ain't mine. I'm living at the top of life. I ain't gonna just take my life and throw it away at the bottom. I'm in the world like everybody else. The way I see it everybody else got to come up a little taste to be where I am.

BERNIECE: You right at the bottom with the rest of us.

BOY WILLIE: I'll tell you this . . . and ain't a living soul can put a come back on it. If you believe that's where you at then you gonna act that way. If you act that way then that's where you gonna be. It's as simple as that. Ain't no mystery to life. I don't know how you come to believe that stuff. Crawley didn't think like that. He wasn't living at the bottom of life. Papa Boy Charles and Mama Ola wasn't living at the bottom of life. You ain't never heard them say nothing like that. They would have taken a strap to you if they heard you say something like that.

[*Doaker enters from his room.*]

Hey, Doaker . . . Berniece say the colored folks is living at the bottom of life. I tried to tell her if she think that . . . that's where she gonna be. You think you living at the bottom of life? Is that how you see yourself?

DOAKER: I'm just living the best way I know how. I ain't thinking about no top or no bottom.

BOY WILLIE: That's what I tried to tell Berniece. I don't know where she got that from. That sound like something Avery would say. Avery think cause the white man give him a turkey for Thanksgiving that makes him better than everybody else. That's gonna raise him out of the bottom of life. I don't need nobody to give me a turkey. I can get my own turkey. All you have to do is get out my way. I'll get me two or three turkeys.

BERNIECE: You can't even get a chicken let alone two or three turkeys. Talking about get out your way. Ain't nobody in your way.

[*To Maretha.*]

Straighten your head, Maretha! Don't be bending down like that. Hold your head up!

[*To Boy Willie.*]

All you got going for you is talk. You' whole life that's all you ever had going for you.

BOY WILLIE: See now . . . I'll tell you something about me. I done strung along and strung along. Going this way and that. Whatever way would lead me to a moment of peace. That's all I want. To be as easy with everything. But I wasn't born to that. I was born to a time of fire.

The world ain't wanted no part of me. I could see that since I was about seven. The world say it's better off without me. See, Berniece accept that. She trying to come up to where she can prove something to the world. Hell, the world a better place cause of me. I don't see it like Berniece. I got a heart that beats here and it beats just as loud as the next fellow's. Don't care if he black or white. Sometime it beats louder. When it beats louder, then everybody can hear it. Some people get scared of that. Like Berniece. Some people get scared to hear a nigger's heart beating. They think you ought to lay low with that heart. Make it beat quiet and go along with everything the way it is. But my mama ain't birthed me for nothing. So what I got to do? I got to mark my passing on the road. Just like you write on a tree, "Boy Willie was here."

That's all I'm trying to do with that piano. Trying to put my mark on the road. Like my daddy done. My heart say for me to sell that piano and get me some land so I can make a life for myself to live in my own way. Other than that I ain't thinking about nothing Berniece got to say.

[*There is a knock at the door. Boy Willie crosses to it and yanks it open thinking it is Lymon. Avery enters. He carries a Bible.*]

BOY WILLIE: Where you been, nigger? Aw . . . I thought you was Lymon. Hey, Berniece, look who's here.

BERNIECE: Come on in, Avery. Don't you pay Boy Willie no mind.

BOY WILLIE: Hey . . . Hey, Avery . . . tell me this . . . can you get to heaven with half the Bible?

BERNIECE: Boy Willie . . . I done told you to leave me alone.

BOY WILLIE: I just ask the man a question. He can answer. He don't need you to speak for him. Avery . . . if you only believe on half the Bible and don't want to accept the other half . . . you think God let you in heaven? Or do you got to have the whole Bible? Tell Berniece . . . if you only believe in part of it . . . when you see God he gonna ask you why you ain't believed in the other part . . . then he gonna send you straight to Hell.

AVERY: You got to be born again. Jesus say unless a man be born again he cannot come unto the Father and who so ever heareth my words and believeth them not shall be cast into a fiery pit.

BOY WILLIE: That's what I was trying to tell Berniece. You got to believe in it all. You can't go at nothing halfway. She think she going to heaven with half the Bible.

[*To Berniece.*]

You hear that . . . Jesus say you got to believe in it all.

BERNIECE: You keep messing with me.

BOY WILLIE: I ain't thinking about you.

DOAKER: Come on in, Avery, and have a seat. Don't pay neither one of them no mind. They been arguing all day.

BERNIECE: Come on in, Avery.

AVERY: How's everybody in here?

BERNIECE: Here, set this comb back over there on that stove.

[*To Avery.*]

Don't pay Boy Willie no mind. He been around here bothering me since I come home from work.

BOY WILLIE: Boy Willie ain't bothering you. Boy Willie ain't bothering nobody. I'm just waiting on Lymon to get back. I ain't thinking about you. You heard the man say I was right and you still don't want to believe it. You just wanna go and make up anythin'. Well there's Avery . . . there's the preacher . . . go on and ask him.

AVERY: Berniece believe in the Bible. She been baptized.

BOY WILLIE: What about that part that say an eye for an eye a tooth for a tooth and a life for a life? Ain't that in there?

DOAKER: What they say down there at the bank, Avery?

AVERY: Oh, they talked to me real nice. I told Berniece . . . they say maybe they let me borrow the money. They done talked to my boss down at work and everything.

DOAKER: That's what I told Berniece. You working every day you ought to be able to borrow some money.

AVERY: I'm getting more people in my congregation every day. Berniece says she gonna be the Deaconess. I get me my church I can get married and settled down. That's what I told Berniece.

DOAKER: That be nice. You all ought to go ahead and get married. Berniece don't need to be by herself. I tell her that all the time.

BERNIECE: I ain't said nothing about getting married. I said I was thinking about it.

DOAKER: Avery get him his church you all can make it nice.

[*To Avery.*]

Berniece said you was coming by to bless the house.

AVERY: Yeah, I done read up on my Bible. She asked me to come by and see if I can get rid of Sutter's ghost.

BOY WILLIE: Ain't no ghost in this house. That's all in Berniece's head. Go on up there and see if you see him. I'll give you a hundred dollars if you see him. That's all in her imagination.

DOAKER: Well, let her find that out then. If Avery blessing the house is gonna make her feel better . . . what you got to do with it?

AVERY: Berniece say Maretha seen him too. I don't know, but I found a part in the Bible to bless the house. If he is here then that ought to make him go.

BOY WILLIE: You worse than Berniece believing all that stuff. Talking about . . . if he here. Go on up there and find out. I been up there I ain't seen him. If you reading from that Bible gonna make him leave out of Berniece imagination, well, you might be right. But if you talking about . . .

DOAKER: Boy Willie, why don't you just be quiet? Getting all up in the man's business. This ain't got nothing to do with you. Let him go ahead and do what he gonna do.

BOY WILLIE: I ain't stopping him. Avery ain't got no power to do nothing.

AVERY: Oh, I ain't got no power. God got the power! God got power over everything in His creation. God can do anything. God say, "As I commandeth so it shall be." God said, "Let there be light," and there was light. He made the world in six days and rested on the seventh. God's got a wonderful power. He got power over life and death. Jesus raised Lazareth from the dead. They was getting ready to bury him and Jesus told him say, "Rise up and walk." He got up and walked and the people made great rejoicing at the power of God. I ain't worried about him chasing away a little old ghost!

[*There is a knock at the door. Boy Willie goes to answer it. Lymon enters carrying a coil of rope.*]

BOY WILLIE: Where you been? I been waiting on you and you run off somewhere.

LYMON: I ran into Grace. I stopped and bought her drink. She say she gonna go to the picture show with me.

BOY WILLIE: I ain't thinking about no Grace nothing.

LYMON: Hi, Berniece.

BOY WILLIE: Give me that rope and get up on this side of the piano.

DOAKER: Boy Willie, don't start nothing now. Leave the piano alone.

BOY WILLIE: Get that board there, Lymon. Stay out of this, Doaker.

[*Berniece exits up the stairs.*]

DOAKER: You just can't take the piano. How you gonna take the piano? Berniece ain't said nothing about selling that piano.

BOY WILLIE: She ain't got to say nothing. Come on, Lymon. We got to lift one end at a time up on the board. You got to watch so that the board don't slide up under there.

LYMON: What we gonna do with the rope?

BOY WILLIE: Let me worry about the rope. You just get up on this side over here with me.

[*Berniece enters from the stairs. She has her hand in her pocket where she has Crawley's gun.*]

AVERY: Boy Willie . . . Berniece . . . why don't you all sit down and talk this out now?

BERNIECE: Ain't nothing to talk out.

BOY WILLIE: I'm through talking to Berniece. You can talk to Berniece till you get blue in the face, and it don't make no difference. Get up on that side, Lymon. Throw that rope around there and tie it to the leg.

LYMON: Wait a minute . . . wait a minute, Boy Willie. Berniece got to say. Hey, Berniece . . . did you tell Boy Willie he could take this piano?

BERNIECE: Boy Willie ain't taking nothing out of my house but himself. Now you let him go ahead and try.

BOY WILLIE: Come on, Lymon, get up on this side with me.

[*Lymon stands undecided.*]

Come on, nigger! What you standing there for?

LYMON: Maybe Berniece is right, Boy Willie. Maybe you shouldn't sell it.

AVERY: You all ought to sit down and talk it out. See if you can come to an agreement.

DOAKER: That's what I been trying to tell them. Seem like one of them ought to respect the other one's wishes.

BERNIECE: I wish Boy Willie would go on and leave my house. That's what I wish. Now, he can respect that. Cause he's leaving here one way or another.

BOY WILLIE: What you mean one way or another? What's that supposed to mean? I ain't scared of no gun.

DOAKER: Come on, Berniece, leave him alone with that.

BOY WILLIE: I don't care what Berniece say. I'm selling my half. I can't help it if her half got to go along with it. It ain't like I'm trying to cheat her out of her half. Come on, Lymon.

LYMON: Berniece . . . I got to do this . . . Boy Willie say he gonna give you half of the money . . . say he want to get Sutter's land.

BERNIECE: Go on, Lymon. Just go on . . . I done told Boy Willie what to do.

BOY WILLIE: Here, Lymon . . . put that rope up over there.

LYMON: Boy Willie, you sure you want to do this? The way I figure it . . . I might be wrong . . . but I figure she gonna shoot you first.

BOY WILLIE: She just gonna have to shoot me.

BERNIECE: Maretha, get on out the way. Get her out the way, Doaker.

DOAKER: Go on, do what your mama told you.

BERNIECE: Put her in your room.

[*Maretha exits to Doaker's room. Boy Willie and Lymon try to lift the piano. The door opens and Wining Boy enters. He has been drinking.*]

WINING BOY: Man, these niggers around here! I stopped down there at Seefus. . . . These folks standing around talking about Patchneck Red's coming. They jumping back and getting off the sidewalk talking about Patchneck Red this and Patchneck Red that. Come to find out . . . you know who they was talking about? Old John D. from up around Tyler! Used to run around with Otis Smith. He got everybody scared of him. Calling him Patchneck Red. They don't know I whupped the nigger's head in one time.

BOY WILLIE: Just make sure that board don't slide, Lymon.

LYMON: I got this side. You watch that side.

WINING BOY: Hey, Boy Willie, what you got? I know you got a pint stuck up in your coat.

BOY WILLIE: Wining Boy, get out the way!

WINING BOY: Hey, Doaker. What you got? Gimme a drink. I want a drink.

DOAKER: It look like you had enough of whatever it was. Come talking about "What you got?" You ought to be trying to find somewhere to lay down.

WINING BOY: I ain't worried about no place to lay down. I can always find me a place to lay down in Berniece's house. Ain't that right, Berniece?

BERNIECE: Wining Boy, sit down somewhere. You been out there drinking all day. Come in here smelling like an old polecat. Sit on down there, you don't need nothing to drink.

DOAKER: You know Berniece don't like all that drinking.

WINING BOY: I ain't disrespecting Berniece. Berniece, am I disrespecting you? I'm just trying to be nice. I been with strangers all day and they treated me like family. I come in here to family and you treat me like a stranger. I don't need your whiskey. I can buy my own. I wanted your company, not your whiskey.

DOAKER: Nigger, why don't you go upstairs and lay down? You don't need nothing to drink.

WINING BOY: I ain't thinking about no laying down. Me and Boy Willie fixing to party. Ain't that right, Boy Willie? Tell him. I'm fixing to play me some piano. Watch this.

[*Wining Boy sits down at the piano.*]

BOY WILLIE: Come on, Wining Boy! Me and Lymon fixing to move the piano.

WINING BOY: Wait a minute . . . wait a minute. This a song I wrote for Cleotha. I wrote this song in memory of Cleotha.

[*He begins to play and sing.*]

Hey little woman what's the matter with you now
Had a storm last night and blowed the line all down

Tell me how long
Is I got to wait
Can I get it now
Or must I hesitate

It takes a hesitating stocking in her hesitating shoe
It takes a hesitating woman wanna sing the blues

Tell me how long
Is I got to wait
Can I kiss you now
Or must I hesitate.

BOY WILLIE: Come on, Wining Boy, get up! Get up, Wining Boy! Me and Lymon's fixing to move the piano.

WINING BOY: Naw . . . Naw . . . you ain't gonna move this piano!

BOY WILLIE: Get out the way, Wining Boy.

[*Wining Boy, his back to the piano, spreads his arms out over the piano.*]

WINING BOY: You ain't taking this piano out the house. You got to take me with it!

BOY WILLIE: Get on out the way, Wining Boy! Doaker get him!

[*There is a knock on the door.*]

BERNIECE: I got him, Doaker. Come on, Wining Boy. I done told Boy Willie he ain't taking the piano.

[*Berniece tries to take Wining Boy away from the piano.*]

WINING BOY: He got to take me with it!

[*Doaker goes to answer the door. Grace enters.*]

GRACE: Is Lymon here?
DOAKER: Lymon.
WINING BOY: He ain't taking that piano.
BERNIECE: I ain't gonna let him take it.
GRACE: I thought you was coming back. I ain't gonna sit in that truck all day.
LYMON: I told you I was coming back.
GRACE: [*Sees Boy Willie.*] Oh, hi, Boy Willie. Lymon told me you was gone back down South.
LYMON: I said he was going back. I didn't say he had left already.
GRACE: That's what you told me.
BERNIECE: Lymon, you got to take your company someplace else.
LYMON: Berniece, this is Grace. That there is Berniece. That's Boy Willie's sister.
GRACE: Nice to meet you.

[*To Lymon.*]

I ain't gonna sit out in that truck all day. You told me you was gonna take me to the movie.
LYMON: I told you I had something to do first. You supposed to wait on me.
BERNIECE: Lymon, just go on and leave. Take Grace or whoever with you. Just go on get out my house.
BOY WILLIE: You gonna help me move this piano first, nigger!
LYMON: [*To Grace.*] I got to help Boy Willie move the piano first.

[*Everybody but Grace suddenly senses Sutter's presence.*]

GRACE: I ain't waiting on you. Told me you was coming right back. Now you got to move a piano. You just like all the other men.

[*Grace now senses something.*]

Something ain't right here. I knew I shouldn't have come back up in this house.

[*Grace exits.*]

LYMON: Hey, Grace! I'll be right back, Boy Willie.

BOY WILLIE: Where you going, nigger?

LYMON: I'll be back. I got to take Grace home.

BOY WILLIE: Come on, let's move the piano first!

LYMON: I got to take Grace home. I told you I'll be back.

[*Lymon exits. Boy Willie exits and calls after him.*]

BOY WILLIE: Come on, Lymon! Hey . . . Lymon! Lymon . . . come on!

[*Again, the presence of Sutter is felt.*]

WINING BOY: Hey, Doaker, did you feel that? Hey, Berniece . . . did you get cold? Hey, Doaker . . .

DOAKER: What you calling me for?

WINING BOY: I believe that's Sutter.

DOAKER: Well, let him stay up there. As long as he don't mess with me.

BERNIECE: Avery, go on and bless the house.

DOAKER: You need to bless that piano. That's what you need to bless. It ain't done nothing but cause trouble. If you gonna bless anything go on and bless that.

WINING BOY: Hey, Doaker, if he gonna bless something let him bless everything. The kitchen . . . the upstairs. Go on and bless it all.

BOY WILLIE: Ain't no ghost in this house. He need to bless Berniece's head. That's what he need to bless.

AVERY: Seem like that piano's causing all the trouble. I can bless that. Berniece, put me some water in that bottle.

[*Avery takes a small bottle from his pocket and hands it to Berniece, who goes into the kitchen to get water. Avery takes a candle from his pocket and lights it. He gives it to Berniece as she gives him the water.*]

Hold this candle. Whatever you do make sure it don't go out.

O Holy Father we gather here this evening in the Holy Name to cast out the spirit of one James Sutter. May this vial of water be empowered with thy spirit. May each drop of it be a weapon and a shield against the presence of all evil and may it be a cleansing and blessing of this humble abode.

Just as Our Father taught us how to pray so He say, "I will prepare a table for you in the midst of mine enemies," and in His hands we place ourselves to come unto his presence. Where there is Good so shall it cause Evil to scatter to the Four Winds.

[*He throws water at the piano at each commandment.*]

AVERY: Get thee behind me, Satan! Get thee behind the face of Righteousness as we Glorify His Holy Name! Get thee behind the Hammer of Truth that breaketh down the Wall of Falsehood! Father. Father. Praise. Praise. We ask in Jesus' name and call forth the power of the Holy Spirit as it is written . . .

[*He opens the Bible and reads from it.*]

I will sprinkle clean water upon thee and ye shall be clean.

BOY WILLIE: All this old preaching stuff. Hell, just tell him to leave.

[*Avery continues reading throughout Boy Willie's outburst.*]

AVERY: I will sprinkle clean water upon you and you shall be clean: from all your uncleanliness, and from all your idols, will I cleanse you. A new heart also will I give you, and a new spirit will I put within you: and I will take out of your flesh the heart of stone, and I will give you a heart of flesh. And I will put my spirit within you, and cause you to walk in my statutes, and ye shall keep my judgments, and do them.

[*Boy Willie grabs a pot of water from the stove and begins to fling it around the room.*]

BOY WILLIE: Hey Sutter! Sutter! Get your ass out this house! Sutter! Come on and get some of this water! You done drowned in the well, come on and get some more of this water!

[*Boy Willie is working himself into a frenzy as he runs around the room throwing water and calling Sutter's name. Avery continues reading.*]

BOY WILLIE: Come on, Sutter!

[*He starts up the stairs.*]

Come on, get some water! Come on, Sutter!

[*The sound of Sutter's Ghost is heard. As Boy Willie approaches the steps he is suddenly thrown back by the unseen force, which is choking him. As he struggles he frees himself, then dashes up the stairs.*]

BOY WILLIE: Come on, Sutter!

AVERY [*continuing*]:   A new heart also will I give you and a new spirit will I put within you: and I will take out of your flesh the heart of stone, and I will give you a heart of flesh. And I will put my spirit within you, and cause you to walk in my statutes, and ye shall keep my judgments, and do them.

[*There are loud sounds heard from upstairs as Boy Willie begins to wrestle with Sutter's Ghost. It is a life-and-death struggle fraught with perils and faultless terror. Boy Willie is thrown down the stairs. Avery is stunned into silence. Boy Willie picks himself up and dashes back upstairs.*]

AVERY: Berniece, I can't do it.

[*There are more sounds heard from upstairs. Doaker and Wining Boy stare at one another in stunned disbelief. It is in this moment, from somewhere old, that Berniece realizes what she must do. She crosses to the piano. She begins to play. The song is found piece by piece. It is an old urge to song that is both a commandment and a plea. With each repetition it gains in strength. It is intended as an exorcism and a dressing for battle. A rustle of wind blowing across two continents.*]

BERNIECE [*singing*]:
I want you to help me
I want you to help me
I want you to help me
I want you to help me
I want you to help me
I want you to help me
Mama Berniece
I want you to help me
Mama Esther
I want you to help me
Papa Boy Charles
I want you to help me
Mama Ola
I want you to help me

I want you to help me
I want you to help me
I want you to help me
I want you to help me

I want you to help me
I want you to help me
I want you to help me
I want you to help me

[*The sound of a train approaching is heard. The noise upstairs subsides.*]

BOY WILLIE: Come on, Sutter! Come back, Sutter!

[*Berniece begins to chant:*]

BERNIECE:
Thank you.
Thank you.
Thank you.

[*A calm comes over the house. Maretha enters from Doaker's room. Boy Willie enters on the stairs. He pauses a moment to watch Berniece at the piano.*]

BERNIECE:
Thank you.
Thank you.

BOY WILLIE: Wining Boy, you ready to go back down home? Hey, Doaker, what time the train leave?

DOAKER: You still got time to make it.

[*Maretha crosses and embraces Boy Willie.*]

BOY WILLIE: Hey Berniece . . . if you and Maretha don't keep playing on that piano . . . ain't no telling . . . me and Sutter both liable to be back.

[*He exits.*]

BERNIECE: Thank you.

[*The lights go down to black.*]

—1987

Questions: Reading, Responding, Arguing

1. How does the notion of legacy relate to the themes of the play? Who has a legacy, how are legacies revealed, and what message is the audience given about what a legacy means?

2. How does music relate to the themes of the play? Given the examples of many types of music in the play, pick one example and connect it to a larger overall message.

3. Ghosts are a recurrent theme in the work. How do ghosts reveal themselves and what do they have to do with the play's overall meaning?

4. Think about gender in the play. Do men and women act differently, or are they faced with different situations? What does the play say about gender roles?

5. What, if anything, does the piano symbolize? Is it seen by different characters in different ways? How does it contribute to the overall meaning of the play?

6. How does Wilson employ comedy in the play? Does the comedy undercut or help support and contribute to the more serious themes of the work?

7. Choose one or two characters you find most important in the play. What is their purpose in the narrative? Why are they important?

8. Think about the minor characters in the play (Lymon? Berniece?). Why are they less important than others? What is their purpose in the drama? Do they offer insights into the play's meaning that other characters do not?

9. What is the "lesson" of the play? Is there only one?

10. How does race play a part in the drama? Does history, particularly African-American history, influence or inform the overall message of the work? Explain the meaning of the play, using details from the text as well as historical research, to support your answer.

Henry David Thoreau (1817–1862)

Why I Went to the Woods

I went to the woods because I wished to live deliberately, to front only the essential facts of life, and see if I could not learn what it had to teach, and not, when I came to die, discover that I had not lived. I did not wish to live what was not life, living is so dear; nor did I wish to practice resignation, unless it was quite necessary. I wanted to live deep and suck out all the marrow of life, to live so sturdily and Spartan-like as to put to rout all that was not life, to cut a broad swath and shave close, to drive life into a corner, and reduce it to its lowest terms, and, if it proved to be mean, why then to get the whole and genuine meanness of it, and publish its meanness to the world; or if it were sublime, to know it by experience, and be able to give a true account of it in my next excursion. For most men, it appears to me, are in a strange uncertainty about it, whether it is of the devil or of God, and have somewhat hastily concluded that it is the chief end of man here to "glorify God and enjoy him forever."

Still we live meanly, like ants; though the fable tells us that we were long ago changed into men; like pygmies we fight with cranes; it is error upon error, and clout upon clout, and our best virtue has for its occasion a superfluous and evitable wretchedness. Our life is frittered away by detail. An honest man has hardly need to count more than his ten fingers, or in extreme cases he may add his ten toes, and lump the rest. Simplicity, simplicity, simplicity! I say, let your affairs be as two or three, and not a hundred or a thousand; instead of a million count half a dozen, and keep your accounts on your thumb-nail. In the midst of this chopping sea of civilized life, such are the clouds and storms and quicksands and thousand-and-one items to be allowed for, that a man has to live, if he would not founder and go to the bottom and not make his port at all, by dead reckoning, and he must be a great calculator indeed who succeeds. Simplify, simplify. Instead of three meals a day, if it be necessary eat but one; instead of a hundred dishes, five; and reduce other things in proportion. Our life is like a German Confederacy, made of up petty states, with its boundary forever fluctuating, so that even a German cannot tell you how it is bounded at any moment. The nation itself, with all its so-called internal improvements, which, by the way are all external and superficial, is just such an unwieldy and overgrown establishment, cluttered with furniture and tripped up by its own traps, ruined by luxury and heedless expense, by want of calculation and a worthy aim, as the million households in the lands; and the only cure for it, as for them, is in a rigid economy, a stern and more than Spartan simplicity of life and elevation of purpose. It lives too fast. Men think that it is essential that the Nation have commerce, and export ice, and talk through a telegraph, and ride thirty miles an hour, without a doubt, whether they do or not; but whether we should live like baboons or like men, is a little uncertain. If we do not get our sleepers, and forge rails, and devote days and nights to the work, but go to tinkering upon our lives to improve them, who will build railroads? And if railroads are not built, how shall we get to heaven in season? But if we stay at home and mind our business, who will want railroads? We do not ride on the railroad; it rides upon us. Did you ever think what those sleepers are that underlie the railroad? Each one is a man, an Irishman, or a Yankee man. The rails are laid on them, and they are covered with sand, and the cars run smoothly over them. They are sound sleepers, I assure you. And every few years a new lot is laid down and run over; so that, if some have the pleasure of riding on a rail, others have the misfortune to be ridden upon. And when they run over a man that is walking in his sleep, a supernumerary sleeper in the wrong position, and wake him up, they suddenly stop the cars, and make a hue and cry about it, as if this were an exception. I am glad to know that it takes a gang of men for every five miles to keep the sleepers down and level in their beds as it is, for this is a sign that they may sometimes get up again.

Why should we live with such hurry and waste of life? We are determined to be starved before we are hungry. Men say that a stitch in time saves nine, and so they take a thousand stitches to-day to save nine tomorrow. As for work, we haven't any of any consequence. We have the Saint Vitus' dance, and cannot possibly keep our heads still. If I should only give a few pulls at the parish bell-rope, as for a fire, that is, without setting the bell, there is hardly a man on his farm in the outskirts of Concord, notwithstanding that press of engagements which was his excuse so many times this morning, nor a boy, nor a woman, I might almost say, but would foresake all and follow that sound, not mainly to save property from the flames, but, if we will confess the truth, much more to see it burn, since burn it must, and we, be it known, did not set it on fire—or to see it put out, and have a hand in it, if that is done as handsomely; yes, even if it were the parish church itself. Hardly a man takes a half-hour's nap after dinner, but when he wakes he holds up his head and asks, "What's the news?" as if the rest of mankind had stood his sentinels. Some give directions to be waked every half-hour, doubtless for no other purpose; and then, to pay for it, they tell what they have dreamed. After a night's sleep the news is as indispensable as the breakfast. "Pray tell me anything new that has happened to a man anywhere on this globe"—and he reads it over his coffee and rolls, that a man has had his eyes gouged out this morning on the Wachito River; never dreaming the while that he lives in the dark unfathomed mammoth cave of this world, and has but the rudiment of an eye himself.

For my part, I could easily do without the post-office. I think that there are very few important communications made through it. To speak critically, I never received more than one or two letters in my life—I wrote this some years ago—that were worth the postage. The penny-post is, commonly, an institution through which you seriously offer a man that penny for his thoughts which is so often safely offered in jest. And I am sure that I never read any memorable news in a newspaper. If we read of one man robbed, or murdered, or killed by accident, or one house burned, or one vessel wrecked, or one steamboat blown up, or one cow run over on the Western Railroad, or one mad dog killed, or one lot of grasshoppers in the winter—we never need read of another. One is enough. If you are acquainted with the principle, what do you care for a myriad instances and applications? To a philosopher all news, as it is called, is gossip, and they who edit and read it are old women over their tea. Yet not a few are greedy after this gossip. There was such a rush, as I hear, the other day at one of the offices to learn the foreign news by the last arrival, that several large squares of plate glass belonging to the establishment were broken by the pressure—news which I seriously think a ready wit might write a twelvemonth, or twelve years, before-hand with sufficient accuracy. As for Spain, for instance, if you know how to throw in Don Carlos and the Infanta, and Don Pedro and Seville and Granada, from time to time in the right proportions—they may have changed the names a little since I saw the papers—and serve up a bull-fight when other entertainments fail, it will be true to the letter, and give us as good an idea of the exact state or ruin of things in Spain as the most succinct and lucid reports under this head in the newspapers; and as for England, almost the last significant scrap of news from that quarter was the revolution of 1649; and if you have learned the history of her crops for an average year, you never need attend to that thing again, unless your speculations are of a merely pecuniary character. If one may judge who rarely looks into the newspapers, nothing new does ever happen in foreign parts, a French revolution not excepted.

What news! how much more important to know what that is which was never old! "Kieou-he-yu (great dignitary of the state of Wei) sent a man to Khoung-tseu to know his news. Khoung-tseu caused the messenger to be seated near him, and questioned him in these terms: What is your master doing? The messenger answered with respect: My master desires to diminish the number of his faults, but he cannot come to the end of them. The messenger being gone, the philosopher remarked: What a worthy messenger! What a worthy messenger!" The preacher, instead of vexing the ears of drowsy farmers on their day of rest at the end of the week—for Sunday is the fit conclusion of an ill-spent week, and not the fresh and brave beginning of a new one—with this one other draggle-tail of a sermon, should shout with thundering voice, "Pause! Avast! Why so seeming fast, but deadly slow?"

Shams and delusions are esteemed for soundless truths, while reality is fabulous. If men would steadily observe realities only, and not allow themselves to be deluded, life, to compare it with such things as we know, would be like a fairy tale and the Arabian Nights' Entertainments. If we respected only what is inevitable and has a right to be, music and poetry would resound along the streets. When we are unhurried and wise, we perceive that only great and worthy things have any permanent and absolute existence, that petty fears and petty pleasures are but the shadow of the reality. This is always exhilarating and sublime. By closing the eyes and slumbering, and consenting to be deceived by shows, men establish and confirm their daily life of routine and habit everywhere, which still is built on purely illusory foundations. Children, who play life, discern its true law and relations more clearly than men, who fail to live it worthily, but who think that they are wiser by experience, that is, by failure. I have read in a Hindoo book, that "there was a king's son, who, being expelled in infancy from his native city, was brought up by a forester, and, growing up to maturity in that state, imagined himself to belong to the barbarous race with which he lived. One of his father's ministers having discovered him, revealed to him what he was, and the misconception of his character was removed, and he knew himself to be a prince. So soul," continues the Hindoo philosopher, "from the circumstances in which it is placed, mistakes its own character, until the truth is revealed to it by some holy teacher and then it knows itself to be Brahme." I perceive that we inhabitants of New England live this mean life that we do because our vision does not penetrate the surface of things. We think that that is which appears to be. If a man should walk through this town and see only the reality, where, think you, would the "Milldam" go to? If he should give us an account of the realities he beheld there, we should not recognize the place in his description. Look at the meetinghouse, or a courthouse, or a jail, or a shop, or a dwelling-house, and say what that thing really is before a true gaze, and they would all go to pieces in your account of them. Men esteem truth remote, in the outskirts of the system, behind the farthest star, before Adam and after the last man. In eternity there is indeed something true and sublime. But all these times and places and occasions are now and here. God himself culminates in the present moment, and will never be more divine in the lapse of all the ages. And we are enabled to apprehend at all what is sublime and noble only by the perpetual instilling and drenching of the reality that surrounds us. The universe constantly and obediently answers to our conceptions; whether we travel fast or slow, the track is laid for us. Let us spend our lives in conceiving then. The poet or the artist never yet had so fair and noble a design but some of his posterity at least could accomplish it.

Let us spend one day as deliberately as Nature, and not be thrown off the track by every nutshell and mosquito's wing that falls on the rails. Let us rise early and fast, or breakfast, gently and without perturbation; let company come and let company go, let the bells ring and the children cry—determined to make a day of it. Why should we knock under and go with the stream? Let us not be upset and overwhelmed in that terrible rapid and whirlpool called a dinner, situated in the meridian shallows. Weather this danger and you are safe, for the rest of the way is downhill. With unrelaxed nerves, with morning vigor, sail by it, looking another way, tied to the mast like Ulysses. If the engine whistles, let it whistle till it is hoarse for its pains. If the bell rings, why should we run? We will consider what kind of music they are like. Let us settle ourselves and work and wedge our feet downward through the mud and slush of opinion, and prejudice, and tradition, and delusion, and appearance, that alluvion which covers the globe, through Paris and London, through New York and Boston and Concord, through Church and State, through poetry and philosophy and religion, till we come to a hard bottom and rocks in place, which we can call reality, and say, This is, and no mistake; and then begin, having a point d'appui, below freshet and frost and fire, a place where you might found a wall or a state, or set a lamppost safely, or perhaps a gauge, not a Nilometer, but a Realometer, that future ages might know how deep a freshet of shams and appearances had gathered from time to time. If you stand right fronting and face to face to a fact, you will see the sun glimmer on both its surfaces, as if it were a cimeter, and feel its sweet edge dividing you through the heart and marrow, and so you will happily conclude your mortal career. Be it life or death, we crave only reality. If we are really dying, let us hear the rattle in our throats and feel cold in the extremities; if we are alive, let us go about our business.

Time is but the stream I go afishing in. I drink at it; but while I drink I see the sandy bottom and detect how shallow it is. Its thin current slides away but eternity remains. I would drink deeper; fish in the sky, whose bottom is pebbly with stars. I cannot count one. I know not the first letter of the alphabet. I have always been regretting that I was not as wise as the day I was born. The intellect is a cleaver; it discerns and rifts its way into the secret of things. I do not wish to be any more busy with my hands than is necessary. My head is hands and feet. I feel all my best faculties concentrated in it. My instinct tells me that my head is an organ for burrowing, as some creatures use their snout and fore paws, and with it I would mine and burrow my way through these hills. I think that the richest vein is somewhere hereabouts; so by the divining-rod and thin rising vapors, I judge; and here I will begin to mine.

—*1854*

Questions: Reading, Responding, Arguing

1. What is the main argument of Thoreau's essay?
2. Thoreau asserts that "Time is but a stream that I go afishing in." Explain his metaphor.
3. How do Thoreau's observations about life in his time relate to life today?
4. Explain Thoreau's attitude towards the "post-office." Citing details from the text, construct an argument that Thoreau uses mail service in his story as a way to reveal one of his major themes.

Pauline Kael (1919–2001)

Review of *The Godfather*

Alchemy

If ever there was a great example of how the best popular movies come out of a merger of commerce and art, *The Godfather* is it. The movie starts from a trash novel that is generally considered gripping and compulsively readable, though (maybe because movies more than satisfy my appetite for trash) I found it unreadable. You're told who and what the characters are in a few pungent, punchy sentences, and that's all they are. You're briefed on their backgrounds and sex lives in a flashy anecdote or two, and the author moves on, from nugget to nugget. Mario Puzo has a reputation as a good writer, so his potboiler was treated as if it were special, and not in the Irving Wallace-Harold Robbins class, to which, by its itch and hype and juicy *roman-â-clef*[1]

---

[1] *roman-â-clef:* a novel about real individuals

treatment, it plainly belongs. What would this school of fiction do without Porfirio Rubirosa, Judy Garland, James Aubrey, Howard Hughes, and Frank Sinatra? The novel *The Godfather,* financed by Paramount during its writing, features a Sinatra stereotype, and sex and slaughter, and little gobbets of trouble and heartbreak. It's gripping, maybe, in the same sense that Spiro Agnew's speeches were a few years back. Francis Ford Coppola, who directed the film, and wrote the script with Puzo, has stayed very close to the book's greased-lightning sensationalism and yet has made a movie with the spaciousness and strength that popular novels such as Dickens' used to have. With the slop and sex reduced and the whoremongering guess-who material minimized ("Nino," who sings with a highball in his hand, has been weeded out), the movie bears little relationship to other adaptations of books of this kind, such as *The Carpetbaggers* and *The Adventurers.* Puzo provided what Coppola needed: a storyteller's outpouring of incidents and details to choose from, the folklore behind the headlines, heat and immediacy, the richly familiar. And Puzo's shameless turn-on probably left Coppola looser than if he had been dealing with a better book; he could not have been cramped by worries about how best to convey its style. Puzo, who admits he was out to make money, wrote "below my gifts," as he puts it, and one must agree. Coppola uses his gifts to reverse the process—to give the public the best a moviemaker can do with this very raw material. Coppola, a young director who has never had a big hit, may have done the movie for money, as *he* claims—in order to make the pictures he really wants to make, he says—but this picture was made at peak capacity. He has salvaged Puzo's energy and lent the narrative dignity. Given the circumstances and the rush to complete the film and bring it to market, Coppola has not only done his best but pushed himself farther than he may realize. The movie is on the heroic scale of earlier pictures on broad themes, such as *On the Waterfront, From Here to Eternity,* and *The Nun's Story.* It offers a wide, startlingly vivid view of a Mafia dynasty. The abundance is from the book; the quality of feeling is Coppola's.

The beginning is set late in the summer of 1945; the film's roots, however, are in the gangster films of the early thirties. The plot is still about rival gangs murdering each other, but now we see the system of patronage and terror, in which killing is a way of dealing with the competition. We see how the racketeering tribes encroach on each other and why this form of illegal business inevitably erupts in violence. We see the ethnic subculture, based on a split between the men's conception of their responsibilities—all that they keep dark—and the sunny false Eden in which they try to shelter the women and children. The thirties films indicated some of this, but *The Godfather* gets into it at the primary level; the willingness to be basic and the attempt to understand the basic, to look at it without the usual preconceptions, are what give this picture its epic strength.

The visual scheme is based on the most obvious life-and-death contrasts; the men meet and conduct their business in deep-toned, shuttered rooms, lighted by lamps even in the daytime, and the story moves back and forth between this hidden, nocturnal world and the sunshine that they share with the women and children. The tension is in the meetings in the underworld darkness; one gets the sense that this secret life has its own poetry of fear, more real to the men (and perhaps to the excluded women also) than the sunlight world outside. The dark-and-light contrast is so operatic and so openly symbolic that it perfectly expresses the basic nature of the material. The contrast is integral to the Catholic background of the characters: innocence versus knowledge—knowledge in this sense being the same as guilt. It works as a visual style, because the Goyaesque shadings of dark brown into black in the interiors suggest (no matter how irrationally) an earlier period of history, while the sunny, soft-edge garden scenes have their own calendar pretty pastness. Nino Rota's score uses old popular songs to cue the varying moods, and at one climatic point swells in a crescendo that is both Italian opera and pure-forties movie music. There are rash, foolish acts in the movie but no acts of individual bravery. The killing, connived at in the darkness, is the secret horror, and it surfaces in one bloody outburst after another. It surfaces so often that after a while it doesn't surprise us, and the recognition that the killing is an integral part of business policy takes us a long way from the fantasy outlaws of old movies. These gangsters don't satisfy our adventurous fantasies of disobeying the law; they're not defiant, they're furtive and submissive. They are required to be more obedient than we are; they live by taking orders. There is no one on the screen we can identify with—unless we take a fancy to the pearly teeth of one shark in a pool of sharks.

Even when the plot strands go slack about two-thirds of the way through, and the passage of a few years leaves us in doubt whether certain actions have been concluded or postponed, the picture doesn't become softheaded. The direction is tenaciously intelligent. Coppola holds on and pulls it all together. The trash novel is there underneath, but he attempts to draw the patterns out of the particulars. It's amazing how encompassing the view seems to be—what a sense you get of a broad historical perspective, considering that the span is only from

1945 to the mid-fifties, at which time the Corleone family, already forced by competitive pressures into dealing in narcotics, is moving its base of operations to Las Vegas.

The enormous cast is headed by Marlon Brando as Don Vito Corleone, the "godfather" of a powerful Sicilian-American clan, with James Caan as his hothead son, Sonny, and Al Pacino as the thoughtful, educated son, Michael. Is Brando marvellous? Yes, he is, but then he often is; he was marvellous a few years ago in *Reflections in a Golden Eye*, and he's shockingly effective as a working-class sadist in a current film, *The Night-comers*, though the film itself isn't worth seeing. The role of Don Vito—a patriarch in his early sixties—allows him to release more of the gentleness that was so seductive and unsettling in his braggart roles. Don Vito could be played as a magnificent old warrior, a noble killer, a handsome bull-patriarch, but Brando manages to debanalize him. It's typical of Brando's daring that he doesn't capitalize on his broken-prow profile and the massive, sculptural head that has become the head of Rodin's Balzac—he doesn't play for statuesque nobility. The light, cracked voice comes out of a twisted mouth and clenched teeth; he has the battered face of a devious, combative old man, and a pugnacious thrust to his jaw. The rasp in his voice is particularly effective after Don Vito has been wounded; one almost feels that the bullets cracked it, and wishes it hadn't been cracked before. Brando interiorizes Don Vito's power, makes him less physically threatening and *deeper*, hidden within himself.

Brando's acting has mellowed in recent years; it is less immediately exciting than it used to be, because there's not the sudden, violent discharge of emotion. His effects are subtler, less showy, and he gives himself over to the material. He appears to have worked his way beyond the self-parody that was turning him into a comic, and that sometimes left the other performers dangling and laid bare the script. He has not acquired the polish of most famous actors; just the opposite—less mannered as he grows older, he seems to draw directly from life, and from himself. His Don is a primitive sacred monster, and the more powerful because he suggests not the strapping sacred monsters of movies (like Anthony Quinn) but actual ones—those old men who carry never-ending grudges and ancient hatreds inside a frail frame, those monsters who remember minute details of old business deals when they can no longer tie their shoelaces. No one has aged better on camera than Brando; he gradually takes Don Vito to the close of his life, when he moves into the sunshine world, a sleepy monster, near to innocence again. The character is all echoes and shadings, and no noise; his strength is in that armor of quiet. Brando has lent Don Vito some of his own mysterious, courtly reserve: the character is not explained; we simply assent to him and believe that, yes, he could become a king of the underworld. Brando doesn't dominate the movie, yet he gives the story the legendary presence needed to raise it above gang warfare to archetypal tribal warfare.

Brando isn't the whole show; James Caan is very fine, and so are Robert Duvall and many others in lesser roles. Don Vito's sons suggest different aspects of Brando—Caan's Sonny looks like the muscular young Brando but without the redeeming intuitiveness, while as the heir, Michael, Al Pacino comes to resemble him in manner and voice. Pacino creates a quiet, ominous space around himself; his performance—which is marvellous, too, big yet without ostentation—complements Brando's. Like Brando in this film, Pacino is simple; you don't catch him acting, yet he manages to change from a small, fresh-faced, darkly handsome college boy into an underworld lord, becoming more intense, smaller, and more isolated at every step. Coppola doesn't stress the father-and-son links; they are simply there for us to notice when we will. Michael becomes like his father mostly from the inside, but we also get to see how his father's face was formed (Michael's mouth gets crooked and his cheeks jowly, like his father's, after his jaw has been smashed). Pacino has an unusual gift for conveying the divided spirit of a man whose calculations often go against his inclinations. When Michael, warned that at a certain point he must come out shooting, delays, we are left to sense his mixed feelings. As his calculations will always win out, we can see that he will never be at peace. The director levels with almost everybody in the movie. The women's complicity in their husbands' activities is kept ambiguous, but it's naggingly there—you can't quite ignore it. And Coppola doesn't make the subsidiary characters lovable; we look at Clemenza (Richard Castellano) as objectively when he is cooking spaghetti as we do when he is garrotting a former associate. Many of the actors (and the incidents) carry the resonances of earlier gangster pictures, so that we almost unconsciously place them in the prehistory of this movie. Castellano, with his resemblance to Al Capone and Edward G. Robinson (plus a vagrant streak of Oscar Levant), belongs in this atmosphere; so does Richard Conte (as Barzini), who appeared in many of the predecessors of this movie, including *House of Strangers*, though perhaps Al Lettieri (as Sollozzo) acts too much like a B-picture hood. And perhaps the director goes off key when Sonny is blasted and blood-spattered at a toll booth; the effect is too garish.

The people dress in character and live in character—with just the gewgaws that seem right for them. The period details are there—a satin pillow, a modernistic apartment-house lobby, a child's pasted-together greeting to Grandpa—but Coppola doesn't turn the viewer into a guided tourist, told what to see. Nor does he go in for a lot of closeups, which are the simplest tool for fixing a director's attitude. Diane Keaton (who plays Michael's girl friend) is seen casually; her attractiveness isn't labored. The only character who is held in frame for us to see exactly as the character looking at her sees her is Apollonia (played by Simonetta Stefanelli), whom Michael falls in love with in Sicily. She is fixed by the camera as a ripe erotic image, because that is what she means to him, and Coppola, not having wasted his resources, can do it in a few frames. In general, he tries not to fix the images. In *Sunday Bloody Sunday*, John Schlesinger showed a messy knocked-over ashtray being picked up in closeup, so that there was nothing to perceive in the shot but the significance of the messiness. Coppola, I think, would have kept the camera on the room in which the woman bent over to retrieve the ashtray, and the messiness would have been just one element among many to be observed—perhaps the curve of her body could have told us much more than the actual picking-up motion. *The Godfather* keeps so much in front of us all the time that we're never bored (though the picture runs just two minutes short of three hours)— we keep taking things in. This is a heritage from Jean Renoir—this uncoercive, "open" approach to the movie frame. Like Renoir, Coppola lets the spectator roam around in the images, lets a movie breathe, and this is extremely difficult in a period film, in which every detail must be carefully planted. But the details never look planted: you're a few minutes into the movie before you're fully conscious that it's set in the past.

When one considers the different rates at which people read, it's miraculous that films can ever solve the problem of a pace at which audiences can "read" a film together. A hack director solves the problem of pacing by making only a few points and making those so emphatically that the audience can hardly help getting them (this is why many of the movies from the studio-system days are unspeakably insulting); the tendency of a clever, careless director is to go too fast, assuming that he's made everything clear when he hasn't, and leaving the audience behind. When a film has as much novelistic detail as this one, the problem might seem to be almost insuperable. Yet, full as it is, *The Godfather* goes by evenly, so we don't feel rushed, or restless, either; there's classic grandeur to the narrative flow. But Coppola's attitudes are specifically modern—more so than in many films with a more jagged surface. Renoir's openness is an expression of an almost pagan love of people and landscape; his style is an embrace. Coppola's openness is a reflection of an exploratory sense of complexity; he doesn't feel the need to comment on what he shows us, and he doesn't want to reduce the meanings in a shot by pushing us this way or that. The assumption behind this film is that complexity will engage the audience.

These gangsters *like* their life style, while we—seeing it from the outside—are appalled. If the movie gangster once did represent, as Robert Warshow suggested in the late forties, "what we want to be and what we are afraid we may become," if he expressed "that part of the American psyche which rejects the qualities and the demands of modern life, which rejects 'Americanism' itself," that was the attitude of another era. In *The Godfather* we see organized crime as an obscene symbolic extension of free enterprise and government policy, an extension of the worst in America—its feudal ruthlessness. Organized crime is not a rejection of Americanism, it's what we fear Americanism to be. It's our nightmare of the American system. When "Americanism" was a form of cheerful, bland official optimism, the gangster used to be destroyed at the end of the movie and our feelings resolved. Now the mood of the whole country has darkened, guiltily; nothing is resolved at the end of *The Godfather*, because the family business goes on. Terry Malloy didn't clean up the docks at the end of *On the Waterfront*; that was a lie. *The Godfather* is popular melodrama, but it expresses a new tragic realism.

—1972

Questions: Reading, Responding, Arguing

1. How does Kael view the novel on which the movie was based?
2. Kael generally devotes much of her reviews to discussing the genre to which the individual films belong. What does she mean when she says that the movie is a popular melodrama with its roots in the gangster films of the thirties, but "it expresses a new tragic realism"?
3. How does Kael relate the film to American corporate life and to the experience of immigrant groups?
4. Watch the movie *The Godfather* and construct an argument that either agrees or disagrees with Kael's major points.

John Edgar Wideman (b. 1941)

The Killing of Black Boys

I am a man. A first-time grandfather recently. Yet a nightmare from my childhood still haunts my sleep. A monster chases me. Some creature whose shape and face are too terrible for the nightmare to reveal. I can't escape. Run headlong down an unfamiliar street, duck into an alley, dart along shortcuts, dash in and out of all the hiding places in my old neighborhood. The monster still lumbers behind me and also sits, patient and hideous, waiting to seize me when I turn the next corner.

Trapped by the dream, I try to scream my way out. There is no way out, but I scream anyway. One scream or many. Screaming for mercy. Screaming for the worst to happen, anything, just so the nightmare ends. Muscles of my throat constrict. I can't breathe. One last choked yell as the face of death looms closer.

I die. Awaken again to whimpers and panting, the rapid, lonely thump of my heart, noises that survive one world's extinction, another world's birth, and I lie in my warm bed shivering, listening to myself, wondering how my wife slept through the tumult.

Sometimes she doesn't. A scream can startle her awake. Her fear, the first thing I see when I open my eyes.

Though the nightmare is as old as anything I can remember about myself, I've come to believe the face in the dream I can't bear to look upon is Emmett Till's. Emmett Till's face crushed, chewed, mutilated, gray and swollen, water dripping from holes punched in his skull. Warm gray water on that August day in 1955 when they dragged his corpse from the Tallahatchie River.

Both of us 14 the summer they murdered Emmett Till. My nightmare, an old acquaintance by then. The fact that the nightmare predates by many years the afternoon in Pittsburgh I came across Emmett Till's photograph in *Jet* magazine confounds me and seems to matter not at all, part of the mystery I must abide to heal myself.

I certainly hadn't been searching for Emmett Till's face when it found me. I peeked quickly, focused my eyes just enough to ascertain something awful on the page, a mottled, grayish something resembling an aerial shot of a landscape cratered by bombs or ravaged by natural disaster—something I registered with a sort of simultaneous glance at and glance away.

Refusing to look, lacking the power to look, to this day, shames me. That afternoon in Pittsburgh I think I sensed vaguely why a wrecked boy's face was displayed in the pages of a magazine. Guessed it would be dangerous not to look. Emmett Till had died instead of me and I needed to know how, why. Not returning his eyeless stare blinded me. In a faint, skittish fashion, I intuited all of this. Understood obscurely how the murdered boy's picture raised issues of responsibility, accountability. But Emmett Till was also just too dead, too horribly, unalterably dead to look at. I sensed that too.

Like Emmett Till, in 1955 I had just graduated from junior high. I'm trying to remember if, like Emmett Till, I carried pictures of White girls in my wallet. Can't recall whether I owned a wallet in 1955. Certainly it wouldn't have been a necessity because the little bit of cash I managed to get hold of passed rapidly through my hands. *Money burns a hole in your pocket, boy,* my mom said. Wanting to feel grown-up, wanting to radiate at least a show of what seemed to represent manliness, I probably stuffed some sort of hand-me-down billfold in my hip pocket. The same urge may have prompted me to carry around a White girl's picture. No doubt about it, possessing a White girl's photo was a merit badge for a Black boy. A sign of power. Your footprint in "their" world. Proof you could handle its opportunities and dangers. Any actual romance with a White girl would have to be underground, clandestine, so a photo served as prime evidence of things unseen. A ticket to status in my clan of brown boys in White Shadyside, a trophy copped in another country I could flaunt in Black Homewood. So I may have owned a wallet with pictures of White girlfriends or classmates in it, and if I'd traveled to Promised Land, South Carolina, with my grandfather Harry Wideman one of those summers he offered to take me down home to his briar patch, who knows? I was a bit of a smart aleck like Emmett Till. I liked to brag. Take on dares like him.

Okay, Emmett Till. You so bad. You talkin 'bout all those White gals you got up in Chicago. Bet you won't say boo to that White lady in the store.

Those of us who survived it understood in our bones that Emmett Till's murder was an attempt to slay an entire generation. Push us backward to the bad old days when the lives of Black people seemed to belong to Whites. When White power and racist ideology seemed unchallengeable forces of nature.

Emmett Till's dead body reminded us that the bad old days are never farther away than the thickness of skin, dark skin that some pale-skinned people claim the prerogative to strip away, burn or cut or shoot full of holes. It is not an accident that the hacked, dead face of Emmett Till looks inhuman. The point of killing and mutilating him, inflicting the agony of his last moments, was to prove he was not human.

And it almost worked. Comes close to working every time. Disfigured by drugs, crime, disease, homelessness, pathological poverty, drenched in hot-blooded or cold-blooded statistics, the brutalized Black body displayed in the media loses all vestiges of humanity. We are set back on our collective heels by the evidence, the warning, the prophecy that beneath Black skin something *other*, something less than human lurks. A so-called lost generation of young Black men dying in the streets today points backward, the way Emmett Till's battered corpse points backward, history and prophecy at once: This is the way things have always been, will always be, the way they're supposed to be.

The circle of racism, its perverse logic, is unbroken. Emmett Till violates the rules. Young Black men are born breaking the rules and thus forfeit all rights White people are bound to respect. Ugly consequences are inevitable. Why not jail Blacks, lynch them? Why not construct walls to separate them from decent citizens?

An apartheid mentality reigns in this country, not because most Americans consciously embrace racist attitudes or wish ill on their neighbors of African descent. Emmett Till dies again and again because his murder and the conditions that ensure and perpetuate it are more acceptable to the majority than placing themselves, their dominant position, at risk. Any serious attempt to achieve true economic, social and political equality must begin not with opening doors to selected minorities, but with the majority's willingness to relinquish a significant measure of power and privilege. There have always been open doors, of sorts—emancipation, emigration, education, economic success in sport or business. What's been missing is an unambiguous private and public decision by a majority of the majority to dismantle the wall, to give up the doors and keys, the identity and protection that comes with the wall.

Like the body of Emmett Till, the Black victims of drug and territory wars raging today are not taken as signs of a fatally flawed society failing its children. Once more the bodies of dead Black men, imprisoned Black men, jobless Black men, addicted Black men are being used to justify increasingly brutal policing of the racial divide.

In 1955, one year after the Supreme Court's *Brown v Board of Education* school-desegregation decision, as the last great campaign to secure civil rights for Black people commenced in the southern United States, the murder of Emmett Till clarified exactly what was at stake: life or death. And as long as race continues to legitimize one group's life-and-death power over another, the stolen face of Emmett Till will haunt the unresolved middle ground between so-called Whites and so-called Blacks, his face unburied, unmourned, unloved in the netherworld where incompatible versions of reality clash.

It was hard to bury Emmett Till, hard to bury Carole Robertson, Addie Mae Collins, Denice McNair and Cynthia Wesley, the four girls killed by a bomb in a Birmingham, Alabama, church. So hard an entire nation began to register the convulsions of Black mourning. The deaths of our children in the civil-rights campaigns changed us. Grief was collective; began to unify us, clarify our thinking, roll back the rock of our fear. Emmett Till's mangled face could belong to anybody's Black son who transgressed racial laws; anyone's little girl could be crushed in the rubble of a bombed church. We read the terrorist message inscribed upon Emmett Till's flesh and were shaken, but refused to comply with the terms it set forth.

Because we knew the killing of children was an effort to murder our future, we mourned our young martyrs but also fought with ferocity and dignity in the courts, churches and streets to protect them. Young people, after all, were the shock troops of the movement for social justice, on the front lines, the hottest, most dangerous spots in Alabama and Mississippi. And though they had the most to gain and the most to lose, they also carried on their shoulders the hopes of older generations and generations unborn.

Now in our rituals of mourning for our lost children, there seems to be no sense of a communal, general loss, no comprehension of larger forces or of the relationship of our immediate trials—drugs, gang violence, empty schools, empty minds, empty homes, empty values—to the ongoing struggle to liberate ourselves from the oppressive legacies of slavery and apartheid. Funerals for our young are daily, lonely occurrences. In some urban ghetto or another somewhere in America, at least once a day a small Black congregation will gather together to try and repair the hole in a brother or mother's soul with the balm of gospel singing, prayer, the laying on of dark hands on darkened spirits.

How many a week, how many repetitions of the same sad ceremony must there be? The hush afterward when the true dimensions of loss and futility begin to set in. A sense of isolation and powerlessness dogs the survivors who are burdened not only by the sudden death of a loved one but also with the knowledge it's going to happen again, today or tomorrow, and it's supposed to happen in a world where Black lives are expendable, can disappear, *click*, just like that, without a trace, so it seems almost as if the son or sister were hardly here at all and maybe Black people really ain't worth shit just like you've been hearing your whole sorry life.

Curtis Jones, a cousin who accompanied Emmett Till on the trip from Chicago to Leflore County, Mississippi, in August 1955, relates how close Emmett Till came to missing their train, reminding us how close Emmett Till's story came to not happening, or being another story altogether, and that in turn should remind us how any story, sad or happy, is always precariously close to being other than it is. Doesn't take much to turn a familiar scene into chaos. Difficult as it is to remember what does occur, we must also try to keep alive what doesn't—the missed trains, squandered opportunities, warnings not heeded. We carry forward these fictions because *what might have been* is part of what gives shape to our stories. We depend on memory's capacity to hold many lives, not just the one we appear to be leading at the moment. Memory is space for storing lives we didn't lead; it's room where they remain alive, room for mourning them, forgiving them. Memory is like all stories we tell, a tissue of remembering and forgetting, of *what if* and *once upon a time*, burying our dead so the dead may rise.

Curtis Jones goes on to tell us about everybody piling into Mose Wright's automobile and trundling down the dusty road to church. How he and his cousin Emmett Till took the car into Money that afternoon while Mose Wright preached.

A bunch of boys loafing outside Bryant's general store on Money's main drag. Sho' nuff country town. Wooden storefronts with wooden porches. Wooden sidewalks. Overhanging wooden signs. With its smatter of Black boys out front, its frieze of tire-size Coca Cola signs running around the eaves of its porch, Bryant's was probably the only game in town, Emmett Till guessed.

Climbing out of Mose Wright's old Ford, he sports the broad smile I recall from another photo, the one of him leaning, elbow atop a TV set, clean as a string bean in his white dress shirt and stylized checkerboard-stripe tie, his chest thrust out mannishly, baby fat in his cheeks, a softish, still-forming boy whose energy, intelligence and expectations of life are evident in the pose he's striking for the camera, just enough in-your-face swagger so you can't help smiling back at the wary eagerness-to-please of his smile.

To Emmett Till, the Black boys are a cluster of down-home country cousins. He sees a stage beckoning on which he can perform. Steps up on the sidewalk with his cousin Curtis, to whom he is *Bo* or *Bobo*, greets his audience. Like a magician, Emmett Till pulls a White girl from his wallet. Silences everybody. Mesmerizes them with tales of what they're missing living down here in the woods. If he'd been selling magic beans, all the boys would have dug into their overalls and extracted their last hot penny to buy some. They watch his fingers slip into his shirt pocket. Hold their breath waiting for the next trick.

Emmett Till's on a roll, can't help rubbing it in a little. What he's saying about himself sounds real good, so good he wants to hear more. All he wants really is for these brown faces to love him. As much as he's loved by the Black faces and White faces in the junior-high graduation pictures from Chicago he's showing around.

He winks at the half-dozen or so boys gathered round him. Nods. Smiles. Points to the prettiest girl, the Whitest, fairest, longest-haired one of all you can easily see, even though the faces in the class picture are tiny and gray. Emmett Till says she is the prettiest, anyway, so why not? Why not believe he's courted and won her and ain't youall lucky he came down here bringing youall the good news?

Though Emmett Till remains the center of attention, the other kids giggle, scratch their naps, stroke their chins, turn their heads this way and that around the circle, commence little conversations of eye-cutting and teeth-sucking and slack-jawed awe. Somebody pops a finger against somebody's shaved skull, somebody's hip bumps somebody else, a tall boy whistles a blues line and someone's been humming softly the whole time. Emmett Till's the preacher and it's Sunday morning and the sermon is righteous. Everybody's ready for a hymn or a responsive reading, even a collection plate circulating so they can participate, stretch a little, hear their own voices.

You sure is something, boy. You say you bad, Emmett Till. Got all them White gals up North, you say. Bet you won't say boo to the White lady in the store.

Curtis Jones is playing checkers with old Uncle Edmund on a barrel set in the shade around the corner from the main drag. One of the boys who sauntered into the store with Emmett Till to buy candy comes running. *He did it. Emmett Till did it. That cousin of yours crazy, boy. Said,* Bye-bye, Baby, *to Miss Bryant!* The old man gets up so fast he knocks over the crate he's been sitting on. *Lord have mercy. I know the boy didn't do nothing like that. Huh uh. No. No he didn't. Youall better get out here. That lady come out that store blow youalls' brains off.*

Several months later, after an all-White jury in the town of Sumner, Mississippi, had deliberated an hour—*would have been less, if we hadn't took time for lunch*—and found Roy Bryant and J. W. Milam not guilty of murdering Emmett Till, the two men were paid $4,000 by a journalist, William Bradford Huie, to tell the story of abducting, beating and shooting Emmett Till.

To get rid of his body they used barbed wire to lash a 100-pound cotton-gin fan to Emmett Till's neck and threw him in the Tallahatchie River. The journalist in a videotaped interview said: "It seems to a rational mind today, it seems impossible that they could have killed him."

The reporter muses for a moment, then remembers: "But J. W. Milam looked up at me and he says, 'Well, when he told me about this White girl he had, my friend, well, that's what this war's about down here now, that's what we got to fight to protect, and I just looked at him and say, '*Boy, you ain't never gone to see the sun come up again.*'"

To the very end, Emmett Till didn't believe the crackers would kill him. He was 14, from Chicago, he'd hurt no one; these strange, funny-talking White men were a nightmare he'd awaken from sooner or later. Milam found the boy's lack of fear shocking. Called it "belligerence." Here was this nigger should be shitting his drawers. Instead, he was making J. W. Milam uncomfortable. Brave or foolhardy or ignorant or blessed to be already in another place, a place these sick, sick men could never touch, whatever enabled Emmett Till to stand his ground, to be himself until the first deadly blow landed, be himself even after it landed, I hope Emmett Till understood that Milam or Bryant, whoever struck first with the intent to kill, was the one who flinched, not he.

When such thoughts come to me, I pile them like sandbags along the levees that protect my sleep. I should know better than to waste my time.

I ask my wife, Judy, who is flesh-and-blood embodiment of the nightmare J. W. Milam discovered in Emmett Till's wallet, what she thinks of when she hears *Emmett Till*.

"A Black kid whistling at a White woman somewhere down South and being killed for it is what I think," she says.

"He didn't whistle," I reply. I've heard the whistling story all my life and another that has him not moving aside for a White woman walking down the sidewalk. Both are part of the myth, but neither's probably true. The story Till's cousin Curtis Jones tells is different. And for what it's worth, his cousin was there. Something Emmett Till said to a White woman inside a store is what caused the shit to hit the fan.

She wants to know where I heard the cousin's version, and I launch into a riff on my sources—*Voices of Freedom,* an oral history of the Civil Rights Movement, Henry Hampton's video documentary *Eyes on the Prize,* a book *Representations of Black Masculinity in Contemporary American Art* organized around a museum exhibit of Black-male images. Then I realize I'm doing all the talking, when what I'd intended to elicit was Judy's spontaneous witness. What her memory carried forward, what it lost.

She's busy with something of her own—a law-school exam—and we just happened to cross paths a moment in the kitchen and she's gone before I get what I wanted. Gone before I know what I wanted. Except standing there next to the refrigerator, in the silence released by its hum, I feel utterly defeated. All the stuff spread out on my desk upstairs isn't getting me any closer to Emmett Till or a cure. Neither will man-in-the-street, woman-in-the-kitchen interviews. Only one other voice is required for the story I'm constructing to overcome a bad dream, and they shut him up a long time ago, didn't they?

Here's what happened. Four nights after the candy-buying and Byebye, Baby scene in Money, at 2:00 a.m. on August 28, 1955, Roy Bryant with a pistol in one hand and a flashlight in the other appears at Mose Wright's door. "This is Mr. Bryant," he calls into the darkness. Then demands to know if Mose Wright has two niggers from Chicago inside. He says he wants the nigger done all that talk.

When Emmett Till is delivered, Bryant marches him to a pickup truck and asks someone inside, "This is the right nigger?" And somebody says, "Yes he is."

Next time Mose Wright sees Emmett Till is three days later when the sheriff summons him to identify a corpse. The body's naked and too badly damaged to tell who it is until Mose Wright notices the initialed ring on his nephew's finger.

Where were you when JFK was shot? Where were you when a man landed on the moon? When Martin Luther King, Jr., was shot? When the Rodney King verdict was announced? Where were you when Emmett Till floated up to the surface of the Tallahatchie River for Byebye, Babying a White woman?

How many places can I be in at once? A Black boy asleep in my bed. A White man in the darkness outside a tar-paper cabin announcing the terror of my name, gripping a flashlight that yesterday was a flaming torch brandished in the fists of a white-sheeted ghost, a heavy-duty flashlight stuffed with thick D batteries that will soon become a club for bashing Emmett Till's skull. An old Black man in the shanty crammed with bodies, instantly alert when I hear *You got those niggers from Chicago in there with you?* An old man figuring the deadly odds, how many lives bought if one handed over. Calculating the rage of his ancient enemy, weighing the risk of saying words the other in his charge must hear, Emmett Till must hear, no matter what terrible things happen next.

Got my two grandsons and a nephew in here.

Black boy inside the cabin, a boy my age whose name I don't know yet, who will never know mine, rubbing his eyes, not sure he's awake or dreaming a scary dream, one of the tales buried deep, deep. He's been hearing since before he was born, about the old days in the Deep South when they cut off niggers' nuts and lynched niggers and roasted niggers over fires like marshmallows.

Black man in my bed, lying beside a pale, beautiful, long-haired woman rubbing my shoulder, a woman whose presence sometimes is as strange and unaccountable to me as mine must be to her, as snow would be falling softly through the bedroom ceiling, accumulating in drifts on the down comforter. Miracles and cheap trick of being many places, many people at once. Conjuring with words what I need, what I'm missing, what's lost. The nightmare dissolving as I decide she's real, as I pretend this loving moment together might last and last.

The name *Emmett* is spoiled for me. In any of its spellings. How could Black parents name a son Emmett? As big a kick as I get watching Emmitt Smith rush the football for the Dallas Cowboys, there is also the moment after a bone-shattering collision, and he's sprawled lifeless on the turf or the moment after he's stumbled or fumbled and slumps to the bench and lifts his helmet and I see a Black mother's son, a small, dark, round face, a boy's big, wide, scared eyes. All those yards gained, all that wealth, but like O.J., he'll never run far enough or fast enough. Inches behind them, the worst thing the people who hate him can imagine hounds him like a shadow.

Sometimes I think the only way to end this would be with Andy Warhol-like strips of images, the same face, Emmett Till's face, replicated 12, 24, 48, 96 times on a wall-size canvas. Like giant postage stamps end to end, top to bottom, each version of the face exactly like the other but different names printed below each one. Martin Till. Malcolm Till. Medgar Till. Nat Till. Gabriel Till. Huey Till. Bigger Till.

Nelson Till. Mumia Till. Colin Till. Jesse Till. Your daddy, your mama, your sister, brother aunt cousin uncle niece nephew Till . . .

Instead of the nightmare one night, this is what I dream: I'm marching with many, many men, a multitude of Black men of all colors, marching past the bier on which the body of Emmett Till rests. The casket, as his mother demanded, is open. *I want the world to see what they did to my baby.* One by one, from an endless line, the men detach themselves, pause, peer down into the satin-lined box. Pinned inside its upright lid, a snapshot of Emmett Till, young, smiling, whole, a jaunty Stetson cocked high across his brow. In the casket he is dressed in a dark suit, jacket wings spread to expose a snowy shroud pulled up to his chin. Then the awful face, patched together with string and wire, awaits each mourner.

My turn is coming soon. I'm grateful. Will not shy away this time. Will look hard. The line of my brothers and fathers and sons stretches ahead of me, behind me. I am drawn by them, pushed by them, steadied as we move each other along. We are a horizon girding the earth, holding the sky down. So many of us at one time in one place, it scares me. More than a million of us marching through this city of monumental buildings and dark alleys. Not very long ago we were singing, but now we march silently, more shuffle than brisk step as we approach the bier, wait our turn. Singing's over but it holds silently in the air, tangible as weather, as the bright sun disintegrating marble buildings, emptying alleys of shadows, warming us on a perfect October day we had no right to expect but would have been profoundly disappointed had it fallen out otherwise.

What I say when I lean over and speak one last time to Emmett Till is: *I love you. I'm sorry. I won't allow it to happen ever again.* And my voice is small and quiet when I say the words, not nearly as humble as it should be, fearful almost to pledge any good after so much bad. My small voice and short turn and then the next man and the next, close together, leading, following one another so the murmur of our voices beside the bier never stops. And immensity, a continuous muted shout and chant and benediction, a river gliding past the stillness of Emmett Till. Past this city, this hour, this place. River sound of blood I'm almost close enough to hear coursing in the veins of the next man.

In the dream we do not say, *Forgive us.* We are taking, not asking for something today. There is no time left to ask for things, even things as precious as forgiveness, only time to take one step, then the next and the next, alone in this great body of men, each one standing on his own feet, moving, our shadows linked, a coolness, a shield stretching nearly unbroken across the last bed where Emmett Till sleeps.

Where we bow and hope and pray he frees us. Ourselves seen sinking, then rising as in a mirror, then stepping away.

And then. And then this vision fades, too. I am there and not there. Not in Washington, D.C., marching with a million other Black men. My son Dan, my new granddaughter Qasima's father, marched. He was a witness, and the arc of his witness included me, as mine includes his, so yes, I was there in a sense, but not there to view the face of Emmett Till because Emmett Till was not there either, not in an open casket displayed to the glory of the heavens, the glories of this Republic, not there except as a shadow, a stain, a wound in the million faces of the marchers, the faces of their fathers, sons and brothers.

We have yet to look upon Emmett Till's face. No apocalyptic encounter, no ritual unveiling, no epiphany has freed us. The nightmare is not cured.

I cannot wish away Emmett Till's face. The horrific death mask of his erased features marks a place I ignore at my peril. The sight of a grievous wound. A wound unhealed because untended. Beneath our nation's pieties, our lies and self-delusions, our denials and distortions of history, our professed certainties about race, lies chaos. The whirlwind that swept Emmett Till away and brings him back.

—*1997*

Questions: Reading, Responding, Arguing

1. Why does Wideman compare himself to Emmett Till many times in the essay? What is the significance of his remarks about his marriage?
2. Explain Wideman's assertion that the murder of Till was an attempt to kill something else even larger and more important than the person.
3. How does Wideman connect the past death with present events?
4. Wideman's language is often very specific, and even shocking, in the essay. How do his stark descriptions change or affect the themes of the essay? Cite examples from the text to argue how the meaning of the essay would change without Wideman's particular use of language.

Maryjane Satrapi (b. 1969)

From *Persepolis*

THE VEIL

THIS IS ME WHEN I WAS 10 YEARS OLD. THIS WAS IN 1980.

AND THIS IS A CLASS PHOTO. I'M SITTING ON THE FAR LEFT SO YOU DON'T SEE ME. FROM LEFT TO RIGHT: GOLNAZ, MAHSHID, NARINE, MINNA.

IN 1979 A REVOLUTION TOOK PLACE. IT WAS LATER CALLED "THE ISLAMIC REVOLUTION".

THEN CAME 1980: THE YEAR IT BECAME OBLIGATORY TO WEAR THE VEIL AT SCHOOL.

WEAR THIS!

WE DIDN'T REALLY LIKE TO WEAR THE VEIL, ESPECIALLY SINCE WE DIDN'T UNDERSTAND WHY WE HAD TO.

IT'S TOO HOT OUT!

EXECUTION IN THE NAME OF FREEDOM.

GIVE ME MY VEIL BACK!

YOU'LL HAVE TO LICK MY FEET!

OOH! I'M THE MONSTER OF DARKNESS.

GIDDYAP!

AND ALSO BECAUSE THE YEAR BEFORE, IN 1979, WE WERE IN A FRENCH NON-RELIGIOUS SCHOOL.

WHERE BOYS AND GIRLS WERE TOGETHER.

AND THEN SUDDENLY IN 1980...

ALL BILINGUAL SCHOOLS MUST BE CLOSED DOWN.

THEY ARE SYMBOLS OF CAPITALISM.

BRAVO!

WHAT WISDOM!

OF DECADENCE.

THIS IS CALLED A "CULTURAL REVOLUTION."

WE FOUND OURSELVES VEILED AND SEPARATED FROM OUR FRIENDS.

AND THAT WAS THAT...

EVERYWHERE IN THE STREETS THERE WERE DEMONSTRATIONS FOR AND AGAINST THE VEIL.

AT ONE OF THE DEMONSTRATIONS, A GERMAN JOURNALIST TOOK A PHOTO OF MY MOTHER.

I WAS REALLY PROUD OF HER. HER PHOTO WAS PUBLISHED IN ALL THE EUROPEAN NEWSPAPERS.

AND EVEN IN ONE MAGAZINE IN IRAN. MY MOTHER WAS REALLY SCARED.

HAVE YOU SEEN THIS?

DON'T WORRY, DARLING.

SHE DYED HER HAIR,

AND WORE DARK GLASSES FOR A LONG TIME.

518 • *Maryjane Satrapi*

I REALLY DIDN'T KNOW WHAT TO THINK ABOUT THE VEIL. DEEP DOWN I WAS VERY RELIGIOUS BUT AS A FAMILY WE WERE VERY MODERN AND AVANT-GARDE.

I WAS BORN WITH RELIGION.

AT THE AGE OF SIX I WAS ALREADY SURE I WAS THE LAST PROPHET. THIS WAS A FEW YEARS BEFORE THE REVOLUTION.

O' Celestial light!

BEFORE ME THERE HAD BEEN A FEW OTHERS.

A WOMAN?

I AM THE LAST PROPHET.

I WANTED TO BE A PROPHET...

BECAUSE OUR MAID DID NOT EAT WITH US.

BECAUSE MY FATHER HAD A CADILLAC.

AND, ABOVE ALL, BECAUSE MY GRANDMOTHER'S KNEES ALWAYS ACHED.

COME HERE MARJI! HELP ME TO STAND UP.

DON'T WORRY. SOON YOU WON'T HAVE ANY MORE PAIN. YOU'LL SEE.

LIKE ALL MY PREDECESSORS I HAD MY HOLY BOOK.

THE FIRST THREE RULES CAME FROM ZARATHUSTRA. HE WAS THE FIRST PROPHET IN MY COUNTRY BEFORE THE ARAB INVASION.

YOU MUST BASE EVERYTHING ON THESE THREE RULES: BEHAVE WELL, SPEAK WELL, ACT WELL.

I ALSO WANTED US TO CELEBRATE THE TRADITIONAL ZARATHUSTRIAN HOLIDAYS. LIKE THE FIRE CEREMONY,

BEFORE THE PERSIAN NEW YEAR, NOROUZ, ON MARCH 21ST, THE FIRST DAY OF SPRING.

ONLY MY GRANDMOTHER KNEW ABOUT MY BOOK.

RULE NUMBER SIX: EVERYBODY SHOULD HAVE A CAR.

RULE NUMBER SEVEN: ALL MAIDS SHOULD EAT AT THE TABLE WITH THE OTHERS.

RULE NUMBER EIGHT: NO OLD PERSON SHOULD HAVE TO SUFFER.

IN THAT CASE, I'LL BE YOUR FIRST DISCIPLE.

REALLY?

BUT TELL ME HOW YOU'LL ARRANGE FOR OLD PEOPLE NOT TO SUFFER?

IT WILL SIMPLY BE FORBIDDEN.

EVERY NIGHT I HAD A BIG DISCUSSION WITH GOD.

GOD, GIVE ME SOME MORE TIME. I AM NOT QUITE READY YET.

YES YOU ARE, CELESTIAL LIGHT, YOU ARE MY CHOICE, MY LAST AND MY BEST CHOICE.

EXCEPT FOR MY GRANDMOTHER I WAS OBVIOUSLY THE ONLY ONE WHO BELIEVED IN MYSELF.

WHAT DO YOU WANT TO BE WHEN YOU GROW UP?

I'LL BE A PROPHET.

HAHA! HAHA! HAHA!

SHE'S CRAZY.

MY PARENTS WERE CALLED IN BY THE TEACHER.

YOUR CHILD IS DISTURBED, SHE WANTS TO BECOME A PROPHET.

WHAT ABOUT IT?

DOESN'T THIS WORRY YOU?

NO! NOT AT ALL!

NONETHELESS, MY PARENTS WERE PUZZLED.

SO TELL ME, MY CHILD, WHAT DO YOU WANT TO BE WHEN YOU GROW UP?

A PROPHET.

I WANT TO BE A DOCTOR.

THAT'S FINE MY LOVE. THAT'S FINE.

I FELT GUILTY TOWARDS GOD.

YOU WANT TO BE A DOCTOR? I THOUGHT THAT...

NO, NO, I WILL BE A PROPHET BUT THEY MUSTN'T KNOW.

I WANTED TO BE JUSTICE, LOVE AND THE WRATH OF GOD ALL IN ONE.

Questions: Reading, Responding, Arguing

1. Satrapi describes her family in one panel as both "modern and avant-garde." What does this mean? How does the accompanying illustration supplement that description?
2. Since it remains unspoken in the text, how can a reader determine the mother's attitude about coloring her own hair?
3. Explain Satrapi's understanding of what it meant to be a prophet.
4. How do the children react to wearing the veil? Are there different kinds of veils in the story? Construct an argument about the meaning of veils in the story, and how Satrapi uses them to develop her themes.

What We Believe
Language, Values, and Wisdom

"Suffice it that we lost our tempers very readily in pursuit of God and Truth, and said exquisitely foolish things on either side."

—H.G. Wells, *In the Days of the Comet*

Many of us use common sense to tell us what in life should be important. For example, we spend a great deal of time and effort devoted to nothing else but preserving life itself, through eating, breathing, and staying on the right side of the road. Yet we need only look at firefighters who rush into a burning building to save the occupants, or soldiers who risk their lives going into battle, to know that the human belief in self-preservation is potentially limited, or negotiable. Secret Service agents who deliberately step in front of a bullet do so because they feel one person's life, the President's, is more valuable than their own. A policewoman risking her life in the line of duty likely does so because of a belief that her life is less important than upholding an abstract concept, the Law. Many of us would sacrifice our lives for *something*, whether it be our country, our lovers, our children, or ideals such as Love or Freedom.

If even the supposedly universal value of sustaining life can be contested and debated, what beliefs do we hold with certainty? What do we find valuable, and how do we articulate and preserve our values? The selections in "What We Believe" all have something to do with beliefs, how those beliefs guide actions, and the ways that people transmit or reveal their values.

You may want to begin your investigation of these readings by questioning the source of the values in each, and connecting that source to your own perspective on values. Do values stem from religious faith, from family upbringing, from one's country? After thinking of the origins of belief, we can then form arguments about the way beliefs guide what we do in the here and now, and contemplate the most effective way to act on those beliefs. Finally, we can think about the future. Once people develop a set of values, what do they do to preserve them? What ideas and values have lasted over the centuries? Why are some more effective than others?

Arguably, it is the great tragedy of life that human values are not always shared. There are many different belief systems, and friction or outright disagreement between those systems forms the majority of the conflict we experience in this world, both on the personal scale and on much more global, political, and cultural scales. It is often precisely the attempt to *make* people agree with us, to *force* shared perceptions and shared values, that causes our conflicts. This tangle, our attempts to do what we feel is right and the difficulties that result from those attempts, lies at the core of what it means to be human.

> Faith is a fine invention
> When gentlemen can see,
> But microscopes are prudent
> In an emergency.
>
> —Emily Dickinson

Nathaniel Hawthorne (1804–1864)

Young Goodman Brown*

Young Goodman Brown came forth, at sunset, into the street at Salem village;[1] but put his head back, after crossing the threshold, to exchange a parting kiss with his young wife. And Faith, as the wife was aptly named, thrust her pretty head into the street, letting the wind play with the pink ribbons of her cap while she called to Goodman Brown.

"Dearest heart," whispered she, softly and rather sadly, when her lips were close to his ear, "Prithee put off your journey until sunrise and sleep in your own bed to-night. A lone woman is troubled with such dreams and such thoughts that she's afeared of herself sometimes. Pray tarry with me this night, dear husband, of all nights in the year."

"My love and my Faith," replied young Goodman Brown, "of all nights in the year, this one night must I tarry away from thee. My journey, as thou callest it, forth and back again, must needs be done 'twixt now and sunrise. What, my sweet, pretty wife, dost thou doubt me already, and we but three months married?"

"Then God bless you!" said Faith, with the pink ribbons; "and may you find all well when you come back."

"Amen!" cried Goodman Brown. "Say thy prayers, dear Faith, and go to bed at dusk, and no harm will come to thee."

So they parted; and the young man pursued his way until, being about to the corner by the meeting-house, he looked back and saw the head of Faith peeping after him with a melancholy air, in spite of her pink ribbons.

"Poor little Faith!" thought he, for his heart smote him. "What a wretch am I to leave her on such an errand! She talks of dreams, too. Methought as she spoke there was trouble in her face, as if a dream had warned her what work is to be done to-night. But no, no; 'twould kill her to think it. Well, she's a blessed angel on earth and after this one night, I'll cling to her skirts and follow her to heaven."

With this excellent resolve for the future, Goodman Brown felt himself justified in making more haste on his present evil purpose. He had taken a dreary road, darkened by all the gloomiest trees of the forest, which barely stood aside to let the narrow path creep through, and

[1]The story takes place several years before the "witch trials" of 1692. Goody Cloyse and Martha Carrier were among the persons sentenced by the courts.

closed immediately behind. It was all as lonely as could be; and there is this peculiarity in such a solitude, that the traveller knows not who may be concealed by the innumerable trunks and the thick boughs overhead; so that with lonely footsteps he may yet be passing through an unseen multitude.

"There may be a devilish Indian behind every tree," said Goodman Brown to himself and he glanced fearfully behind him as he added, "What if the devil himself should be at my very elbow!"

His head being turned back, he passed a crook of the road, and, looking forward again, beheld the figure of a man, in grave and decent attire, seated at the foot of an old tree. He arose at Goodman Brown's approach and walked onward side by side with him.

"You are late, Goodman Brown," said he. "The clock of the Old South was striking as I came through Boston, and that is full fifteen minutes agone."

"Faith kept me back a while," replied the young man, with a tremor in his voice, caused by the sudden appearance of his companion, though not wholly unexpected.

It was now deep dusk in the forest, and deepest in that part of it where these two were journeying. As nearly as could be discerned, the second traveller was about fifty years old, apparently in the same rank of life as Goodman Brown, and bearing a considerable resemblance to him, though perhaps more in expression than features. Still they might have been taken for father and son. And yet, though the elder person was as simply clad as the younger, and as simple in manner too, he had an indescribable air of one who knew the world, and who would not have felt abashed at the governor's dinner table, or in King William's court, were it possible that his affairs should call him thither. But the only thing about him that could be fixed upon as remarkable was his staff, which bore the likeness of a great black snake, so curiously wrought that it might almost be seen to twist and wriggle itself like a living serpent. This, of course, must have been an ocular deception, assisted by uncertain light.

"Come, Goodman Brown," cried his fellow-traveller, "this is a dull pace for the beginning of a journey. Take my staff, if you are so soon weary."

"Friend," said the other, exchanging his slow pace for a full stop, "having kept covenant by meeting thee here, it is my purpose now to return whence I came. I have scruples touching the matter thou wot'st of."

"Sayest thou so?" replied he of the serpent, smiling apart. "Let us walk on, nevertheless, reasoning as we go; and if I convince thee not thou shalt turn back. We are but a little way in the forest yet."

"Too far! Too far!" exclaimed the Goodman, unconsciously resuming his walk. "My father never went into the woods on such an errand, nor his father before him. We have been a race of honest men and good Christians since the days of the martyrs; and shall I be the first of the name of Brown that ever took this path and kept—"

"Such company, thou wouldst say," observed the elder person, interpreting his pause. "Well said, Goodman Brown! I have been as well acquainted with your family as with ever a one among the Puritans; and that's no trifle to say. I helped your grandfather, the constable, when he lashed the Quaker woman so smartly through the streets of Salem; and it was I that brought your father a pitch-pine knot, kindled at my own hearth, to set fire to an Indian village, in King Philip's war. They were my good friends, both; and many a pleasant walk have we had along this path, and returned merrily after midnight. I would fain be friends with you for their sake."

"If it be as thou sayest," replied Goodman Brown, "I marvel they never spoke of these matters, or, verily, I marvel not, seeing that the least rumor of the sort would have driven them from New England. We are a people of prayer, and good works to boot, and abide no such wickedness."

"Wickedness or not," said the traveller with the twisted staff, "I have a very general acquaintance here in New England. The deacons of many a church have drunk the communion wine with me; the selectmen of divers towns make me their chairman; and a majority of the Great and General Court are firm supporters of my interest. The governor and I, too—But these are state secrets."

"Can this be so!" cried Goodman Brown, with a stare of amazement at his undisturbed companion. "Howbeit, I have nothing to do with the governor and council; they have their own ways, and are no rule for a simple husbandman like me. But, were I to go on with thee, how should I meet the eye of that good old man, our minister, at Salem village? Oh, his voice would make me tremble both Sabbath day and lecture day!"

Thus far the elder traveller had listened with due gravity; but now burst into a fit of irrepressible mirth, shaking himself so violently that his snake-like staff actually seemed to wriggle in sympathy.

"Ha! ha! ha!" shouted he again and again; then composing himself, "Well, go on, Goodman Brown, go on; but, prithee, don't kill me with laughing."

"Well, then, to end the matter at once," said Goodman Brown, considerably nettled, "there is my wife, Faith. It would break her dear little heart; and I'd rather break my own."

"Nay, if that be the case," answered the other, "e'en go thy ways, Goodman Brown. I would not for twenty old women like the one hobbling before us that Faith should come to any harm."

As he spoke he pointed his staff at a female figure on the path, in whom Goodman Brown recognized a very pious and exemplary dame, who had taught him his catechism in youth, and was still his moral and spiritual adviser, jointly with the minister and Deacon Gookin.

"A marvel, truly, that Goody Cloyse should be so far in the wilderness at night fall," said he. "But with your leave, friend, I shall take a cut through the woods until we have left this Christian woman behind. Being a stranger to you, she might ask whom I was consorting with and whither I was going."

"Be it so," said his fellow-traveller. "Betake you the woods, and let me keep the path."

Accordingly the young man turned aside, but took care to watch his companion, who advanced softly along the road until he had come within a staff's length of the old dame. She, meanwhile, was making the best of her way, with singular speed for so aged a woman, and mumbling some indistinct words—a prayer, doubtless—as she went. The traveller put forth his staff and touched her withered neck with what seemed the serpent's tail.

"The devil!" screamed the pious old lady.

"Then Goody Cloyse knows her old friend?" observed the traveller, confronting her and leaning on his writhing stick.

"Ah, forsooth, and is it your worship indeed?" cried the good dame. "Yea, truly is it, and in the very image of my old gossip, Goodman Brown, the grandfather of the silly fellow that now is. But—would your worship believe it?—my broomstick hath strangely disappeared, stolen, as I suspect, by that unhanged witch, Goody Cory and that, too, when I was all anointed with the juice of smallage and cinquefoil and wolf's bane—"[2]

"Mingled with fine wheat and the fat of a new-born babe," said the shape of old Goodman Brown.

"Ah, your worship knows the recipe," cried the old lady, cackling aloud. "So, as I was saying, being all ready for the meeting, and no horse to ride on, I made up my mind to foot it; for they tell me there is a nice young man to be taken into communion to-night. But now your good worship will lend me your arm, and we shall be there in a twinkling."

---

[2]*smallage and cinquefoil and wolf's bane:* wild plants and herbs.

"That can hardly be," answered her friend. "I may not spare you my arm, Goody Cloyse; but here is my staff, if you will."

So saying, he threw it down at her feet, where, perhaps, it assumed life, being one of the rods which its owner had formerly lent to the Egyptian magi. Of this fact, however, Goodman Brown could not take cognizance. He had cast up his eyes in astonishment, and, looking down again, beheld neither Goody Cloyse nor the serpentine staff but his fellow-traveller alone, who waited for him as calmly as if nothing had happened.

"That old woman taught me my catechism," said the young man; and there was a world of meaning in this simple comment.

They continued to walk onward, while the elder traveller exhorted his companion to make good speed and persevere in the path, discoursing so aptly that his arguments seemed rather to spring up in the bosom of his auditor than to be suggested by himself. As they went, he plucked a branch of maple to serve for a walking-stick, and began to strip it of the twigs and little boughs, which were wet with evening dew. The moment his fingers touched them they became strangely withered and dried up as with a week's sunshine. Thus the pair proceeded, at a good free pace, until suddenly, in a gloomy hollow of the road, Goodman Brown sat himself down on the stump of a tree and refused to go any farther.

"Friend," said he, stubbornly, "my mind is made up. Not another step will I budge on this errand. What if a wretched old woman do choose to go to the devil when I thought she was going to heaven: is that any reason why I should quit my dear Faith and go after her?"

"You will think better of this by and by," said his acquaintance, composedly. "Sit here and rest yourself a while; and when you feel like moving again, there is my staff to help you along."

Without more words, he threw his companion the maple stick, and was as speedily out of sight as if he had vanished into the deepening gloom. The young man sat a few moments by the roadside, applauding himself greatly, and thinking with how clear a conscience he should meet the minister in his morning walk, nor shrink from the eye of good old Deacon Gookin. And what calm sleep would be his that very night, which was to have been spent so wickedly, but so purely and sweetly now, in the arms of Faith! Amidst these pleasant and praiseworthy meditations, Goodman Brown heard the tramp of horses along the road, and deemed it advisable to conceal himself within the verge of the forest, conscious of the guilty purpose that had brought him thither, though now so happily turned from it.

On came the hoof-tramps and the voices of the riders, two grave old voices, conversing soberly as they drew near. These mingled sounds appeared to pass along the road, within a few yards of the young man's hiding-place; but, owing doubtless to the depth of the gloom at that particular spot, neither the travellers nor their steeds were visible. Though their figures brushed the small boughs by the wayside, it could not be seen that they intercepted, even for a moment, the faint gleam from the strip of bright sky athwart which they must have passed. Goodman Brown alternately crouched and stood on tiptoe, pulling aside the branches and thrusting forth his head as far as he durst without discerning so much as a shadow. It vexed him the more, because he could have sworn, were such a thing possible, that he recognized the voices of the minister and Deacon Gookin, jogging along quietly, as they were wont to do, when bound to some ordination or ecclesiastical council. While yet within hearing, one of the riders stopped to pluck a switch.

"Of the two, reverend sir," said the voice like the deacon's, "I had rather miss an ordination dinner than to-night's meeting. They tell me that some of our community are to be here from Falmouth and beyond, and others from Connecticut and Rhode Island, besides several of the Indian powwows, who, after their fashion, know almost as much deviltry as the best of us. Moreover, there is a goodly young woman to be taken into communion."

"Mighty well, Deacon Gookin!" replied the solemn old tones of the minister. "Spur up, or we shall be late. Nothing can be done, you know, until I get on the ground."

The hoofs clattered again; and the voices, talking so strangely in the empty air, passed on through the forest, where no church had ever been gathered or solitary Christian prayed. Whither, then, could these holy men be journeying so deep into the heathen wilderness? Young Goodman Brown caught hold of a tree for support, being ready to sink down on the ground, faint and overburdened with the heavy sickness of his heart. He looked up to the sky, doubting whether there really was a heaven above him. Yet, there was the blue arch, and the stars brightening in it.

"With heaven above, and Faith below, I will yet stand firm against the devil," cried Goodman Brown.

While he still gazed upward into the deep arch of the firmament and had lifted his hands to pray, a cloud, though no wind was stirring, hurried across the zenith and hid the brightening stars. The blue sky was still visible, except directly overhead, where this black mass of cloud was sweeping swiftly northward. Aloft in the air, as if from the depths of the cloud, came a confused and doubtful sound of voices.

Once the listener fancied that he could distinguish the accents of towns-people of his own, men and women, both pious and ungodly, many of whom he had met at the communion table, and had seen others rioting at the tavern. The next moment, so indistinct were the sounds, he doubted whether he had heard aught but the murmur of the old forest, whispering without a wind. Then came a stronger swell of those familiar tones, heard daily in the sunshine at Salem village, but never until now from a cloud of night. There was one voice, of a young woman, uttering lamentations, yet with an uncertain sorrow, and entreating for some favor, which, perhaps it would grieve her to obtain; and all the unseen multitude, both saints and sinners seemed to encourage her onward.

"Faith!" shouted Goodman Brown, in a voice of agony and desperation; and the echoes of the forest mocked him, crying, "Faith! Faith!" as if bewildered wretches were seeking her all through the wilderness.

The cry of grief, rage, and terror was yet piercing the night, when the unhappy husband held his breath for a response. There was a scream, drowned immediately in a louder murmur of voices, fading into far-off laughter, as the dark cloud swept away, leaving the clear and silent sky above Goodman Brown. But something fluttered lightly down through the air and caught on the branch of a tree. The young man seized it, and beheld a pink ribbon.

"My Faith is gone!" cried he, after one stupefied moment. "There is no good on earth; and sin is but a name. Come, devil; for to thee is this world given."

And, maddened with despair, so that he laughed loud and long, did Goodman Brown grasp his staff and set forth again, at such a rate that he seemed to fly along the forest path, rather than to walk or run. The road grew wilder and drearier and more faintly traced, and vanished at length, leaving him in the heart of the dark wilderness, still rushing onward with the instinct that guides mortal man to evil. The whole forest was peopled with frightful sounds—the creaking of the trees, the howling of wild beasts, and the yell of Indians; while sometimes the wind tolled like a distant church bell, and sometimes gave a broad roar around the traveller, as if all Nature were laughing him to scorn. But he was himself the chief horror of the scene, and shrank not from its other horrors.

"Ha! ha! ha!" roared Goodman Brown when the wind laughed at him. "Let us hear which will laugh loudest! Think not to frighten me with your deviltry! Come witch, come wizard, come Indian powwow, come devil himself, and here comes Goodman Brown. You may as well fear him as he fear you!"

In truth, all through the haunted forest there could be nothing more frightful than the figure of Goodman Brown. On he flew among the black pines, brandishing his staff with frenzied gestures, now giving vent to an inspiration of horrid blasphemy, and now shouting forth such laughter as set all the echoes of the forest laughing like demons around him. The fiend in his own shape is less hideous than when he rages in the breast of man. Thus sped the demoniac on his course, until, quivering among the trees, he saw a red light before him, as when the felled trunks and branches of a clearing have been set on fire, and throw up their lurid blaze against the sky, at the hour of midnight. He paused, in a lull of the tempest that had driven him onward, and heard the swell of what seemed a hymn, rolling solemnly from a distance with the weight of many voices. He knew the tune; it was a familiar one in the choir of the village meeting-house. The verse died heavily away, and was lengthened by a chorus, not of human voices, but of all the sounds of the benighted wilderness pealing in awful harmony together. Goodman Brown cried out; and his cry was lost to his own ear by its unison with the cry of the desert.

In the interval of silence he stole forward until the light glared full upon his eyes. At one extremity of an open space, hemmed in by the dark wall of the forest, arose a rock, bearing some rude, natural resemblance either to an altar or a pulpit, and surrounded by four blazing pines, their tops aflame, their stems untouched, like candles at an evening meeting. The mass of foliage that had overgrown the summit of the rock was all on fire, blazing high into the night and fitfully illuminating the whole field. Each pendent twig and leafy festoon was in a blaze. As the red light arose and fell, a numerous congregation alternately shone forth, then disappeared in shadow, and again grew, as it were, out of the darkness, peopling the heart of the solitary woods at once.

"A grave and dark-clad company," quoth Goodman Brown.

In truth, they were such. Among them, quivering to-and-fro between gloom and splendor, appeared faces that would be seen next day at the council board of the province, and others which, Sabbath after Sabbath, looked devoutly heavenward, and benignantly over the crowded pews, from the holiest pulpits in the land. Some affirm that the lady of the governor was there. At least there were high dames well known to her, and wives of honored husbands, and widows, a great multitude, and ancient maidens, all of excellent repute, and fair young girls, who trembled lest their mothers should espy them. Either the sudden gleams of light flashing over the obscure field bedazzled Goodman Brown, or he recognized a score of the church-members of Salem village famous for their especial sanctity. Good old Deacon Gookin had arrived, and waited at the skirts of that venerable saint, his revered pastor. But, irreverently consorting with these grave, reputable, and pious people, these elders of the church, these chaste dames and dewy virgins, there were men of dissolute lives and women of spotted fame, wretches given over to all mean and filthy vice, and suspected even of horrid crimes. It was strange to see, that the good shrank not from the wicked, nor were the sinners abashed by the saints. Scattered also among their pale-faced enemies were the Indian priests, or powwows, who had often scared their native forest with more hideous incantations than any known to English witchcraft.

"But, where is Faith?" thought Goodman Brown; and, as hope came into his heart, he trembled.

Another verse of the hymn arose, a slow and mournful strain, such as the pious love, but joined to words which expressed all that our nature can conceive of sin, and darkly hinted at far more. Unfathomable to mere mortals is the lore of fiends. Verse after verse was sung; and still the chorus of the desert swelled between, like the deepest tone of a mighty organ; and, with the final peal of that dreadful anthem there came a sound, as if the roaring wind, the rushing streams, the howling beasts, and every other voice of the unconcerted wilderness were mingling and according with the voice of guilty man in homage to the prince of all. The four blazing pines threw up a loftier flame, and obscurely discovered shapes and visages of horror on the smoke wreaths above the impious assembly. At the same moment the fire on the rock shot redly forth and formed a glowing arch above its base, where now appeared a figure. With reverence be it spoken, the figure bore no slight similitude, both in garb and manner, to some grave divine of the New England church.

"Bring forth the converts!" cried a voice that echoed through the field and rolled into the forest.

At the word, Goodman Brown stepped forth from the shadow of the trees and approached the congregation, with whom he felt a loathful brotherhood by the sympathy of all that was wicked in his heart. He could have well nigh sworn that the shape of his own dead father beckoned him to advance, looking downward from a smoke wreath, while a woman, with dim features of despair, threw out her hand to warn him back. Was it his mother? But he had no power to retreat one step, nor to resist, even in thought, when the minister and good old Deacon Gookin seized his arms and led him to the blazing rock. Thither came also the slender form of a veiled female, led between Goody Cloyse, that pious teacher of the catechism, and Martha Carrier, who had received the devil's promise to be queen of hell. A rampant hag was she. And there stood the proselytes beneath the canopy of fire.

"Welcome, my children," said the dark figure, "to the communion of your race. Ye have found thus young your nature and your destiny. My children, look behind you!"

They turned; and flashing forth, as it were, in a sheet of flame, the fiend worshippers were seen; the smile of welcome gleamed darkly on every visage.

"There," resumed the sable form, "are all whom ye have reverenced from youth. Ye deemed them holier than yourselves, and shrank from your own sin, contrasting it with their lives of righteousness and prayerful aspirations heavenward. Yet here are they all in my worshipping assembly. This night it shall be granted you to know their secret deeds: how hoary-bearded elders of the church have whispered wanton words to the young maids of their households; how many a woman, eager for widow's weeds, has given her husband a drink at bedtime, and let him sleep his last sleep in her bosom; how beardless youths have made haste to inherit their fathers' wealth; and how fair damsels—blush not, sweet ones— have dug little graves in the garden, and bidden me, the sole guest, to an infant's funeral. By the sympathy of your human hearts for sin ye shall scent out all the places—whether in church, bed-chamber, street, field, or forest—where crime has been committed, and shall exult to behold the whole earth one stain of guilt, one mighty blood spot. Far more than this. It shall be yours to penetrate, in every bosom, the deep mystery of sin, the fountain of all wicked arts, and which inexhaustibly supplies more evil impulses than human power—than my power at its utmost—can make manifest in deeds. And now, my, children, look upon each other."

They did so; and, by the blaze of the hell-kindled torches, the wretched man beheld his Faith, and the wife her husband, trembling before that unhallowed altar.

"Lo, there ye stand, my children," said the figure, in a deep and solemn tone, almost sad with its despairing awfulness, as if his once angelic nature could yet mourn for our miserable race. "Depending upon one another's hearts, ye had still hoped that virtue were not all a dream. Now are ye undeceived. Evil is the nature of mankind. Evil must be your only happiness. Welcome, again, my children, to the communion of your race."

"Welcome," repeated the fiend worshippers, in one cry of despair and triumph.

And there they stood, the only pair, as it seemed, who were yet hesitating on the verge of wickedness in this dark world. A basin was hollowed, naturally, in the rock. Did it contain water, reddened by the lurid light? or was it blood? or, perchance, a liquid flame? Herein did the shape of evil dip his hand and prepare to lay the mark of baptism upon their foreheads, that they might be partakers of the mystery of sin, more conscious of the secret guilt of others, both in deed and thought, than they could now be of their own. The husband cast one look at his pale wife, and Faith at him. What polluted wretches would the next glance show them to each other, shuddering alike at what they disclosed and what they saw!

"Faith! Faith!" cried the husband, "look up to heaven, and resist the wicked one."

Whether Faith obeyed he knew not. Hardly had he spoken when he found himself amid calm night and solitude, listening to a roar of the wind which died heavily away through the forest. He staggered against the rock, and felt it chill and damp; while a hanging twig, that had been all on fire, besprinkled his cheek with the coldest dew.

The next morning young Goodman Brown came slowly into the street of Salem village, staring around him like a bewildered man. The good old minister was taking a walk along the graveyard to get an appetite for breakfast and meditate his sermon, and bestowed a blessing, as he passed, on Goodman Brown. He shrank from the venerable saint as if to avoid an anathema. Old Deacon Gookin was at domestic worship, and the holy words of his prayer were heard through the open window. "What God doth the wizard pray to?" quoth Goodman Brown. Goody Cloyse, that excellent old Christian, stood in the early sunshine at her own lattice, catechizing a little girl who had brought her a pint of morning's milk. Goodman Brown snatched away the child as from the grasp of the fiend himself. Turning the corner by the meeting-house, he spied the head of Faith, with the pink ribbons, gazing anxiously forth, and bursting into such joy at sight of him that she skipped along the street and almost kissed her husband before the whole village. But Goodman Brown looked sternly and sadly into her face, and passed on without a greeting.

Had Goodman Brown fallen asleep in the forest and only dreamed a wild dream of a witch-meeting?

Be it so, if you will; but, alas! it was a dream of evil omen for young Goodman Brown. A stern, a sad, a darkly meditative, a distrustful, if not a desperate man did he become from the night of that fearful dream. On the Sabbath day, when the congregation were singing a holy psalm, he could not listen because an anthem of sin rushed loudly upon his ear and drowned all the blessed strain. When the minister spoke from the pulpit with power and fervid eloquence, and, with his hand on the open Bible, of the sacred truths of our religion, and of saint-like lives and triumphant deaths, and of future bliss or misery unutterable, then did Goodman Brown turn pale, dreading lest the roof should thunder down upon the gray blasphemer and his hearers. Often, awakening suddenly at midnight, he shrank from the bosom of Faith; and at morning or eventide, when the family knelt down at prayer, he scowled and muttered to himself, and gazed sternly at his wife, and turned away. And when he had lived long, and was borne to his grave a hoary corpse, followed by Faith, an aged woman, and children and grandchildren, a goodly procession, besides neighbors, not a few, they carved no hopeful verse upon his tombstone, for his dying hour was gloom.

—1835

Questions: Reading, Responding, Arguing

1. Discuss Hawthorne's use of nature imagery. What language does he use? How is nature characterized? How does nature connect with his themes?

2. Explain the significance of the sentence "'Faith! Faith!' cried the husband, 'look up to heaven, and resist the wicked one.'"

3. Discuss Hawthorne's approach to or use of history for thematic purposes. Why did he choose the setting he did?

4. Were the events in the forest a dream or did they really happen? How do you know? Locate passages in the story where Hawthorne tries to make the reader doubtful about what has occurred. Construct an argument about an "alternative" version of what may have actually happened to the protagonist.

Ralph Ellison (1914–1995)

A Party Down at the Square

I don't know what started it. A bunch of men came by my Uncle Ed's place and said there was going to be a party down at the Square, and my uncle hollered for me to come on and I ran with them through the dark and rain and there we were at the Square. When we got there everybody was mad and quiet and standing around looking at the nigger. Some of the men had guns, and one man kept goosing the nigger in his pants with the barrel of a shotgun, saying he ought to pull the trigger, but he never did. It was right in front of the courthouse, and the old clock in the tower was striking twelve. The rain was falling cold and freezing as it fell. Everybody was cold, and the nigger kept wrapping his arms around himself trying to stop the shivers.

Then one of the boys pushed through the circle and snatched off the nigger's shirt, and there he stood, with his black skin all shivering in the light from the fire, and looking at us with a scaired look on his face and putting his hands in his pants pockets. Folks started yelling to hurry up and kill the nigger. Somebody yelled: "Take your hands out of your pockets, nigger; we gonna have plenty heat in a minnit." But the nigger didn't hear him and kept his hands where they were.

I tell you the rain was cold. I had to stick my hands in my pockets they got so cold. The fire was pretty small, and they put some logs around the platform they had the nigger on and then threw on some gasoline, and you could see the flames light up the whole Square. It was late and the streetlights had been off for a long time. It was so bright that the bronze statue of the general standing there in the Square was like something alive. The shadows playing on his moldy green face made him seem to be smiling down at the nigger.

They threw on more gas, and it made the Square bright like it gets when the lights are turned on or when the sun is setting red. All the wagons and cars were standing around the curbs. Not like Saturday though—the niggers weren't there. Not a single nigger was there except this Bacote nigger and they dragged him there tied to the back of Jed Wilson's truck. On Saturday there's as many niggers as white folks.

Everybody was yelling crazy 'cause they were about to set fire to the nigger, and I got to the rear of the circle and looked around the Square to try to count the cars. The shadows of the folks was flickering on the trees in the middle of the Square. I saw some birds that the noise had woke up flying through the trees. I guess maybe they thought it was morning. The ice had started the cobblestones in the street to shine where the rain was falling and freezing. I counted forty cars before I lost count. I knew folks must have been there from Phenix City by all the cars mixed in with the wagons.

God, it was a hell of a night. It was some night all right. When the noise died down I heard the nigger's voice from where I stood in the back, so I pushed my way up front. The nigger was bleeding from his nose and ears, and I could see him all red where the dark blood was running down his black skin. He kept lifting first one foot and then the other, like a chicken on a hot stove. I looked down to the platform they had him on, and they had pushed a ring of fire up close to his feet. It must have been hot to him with the flames almost touching his big black toes. Somebody yelled for the nigger to say his prayers, but the nigger wasn't saying anything now. He just kinda moaned with his eyes shut and kept moving up and down on his feet, first one foot and then the other.

I watched the flames burning the logs up closer and closer to the nigger's feet. They were burning good now, and the rain had stopped and the wind was rising, making the flames flare higher. I looked, and there must have been thirty-five women in the crowd, and I could hear their voices clear and shrill mixed in with those of the men. Then it happened. I heard the noise about the same time everyone else did. It was like the roar of a cyclone blowing up from the gulf, and everyone was looking up into the air to see what it was. Some of the faces looked surprised and scaired, all but the nigger. He didn't even hear the noise. He didn't even look up. Then the roar came closer, right above our heads and the wind was blowing higher and higher and the sound seemed to be going in circles.

Then I saw her. Through the clouds and fog I could see a red and green light on her wings. I could see them just for a second; then she rose up into the low clouds. I looked out for the beacon over the tops of the buildings in the direction of the airfield that's forty miles away, and it wasn't circling around. You usually could see it sweeping around the sky at night, but it wasn't there. Then, there she was again, like a big bird lost in the fog. I looked for the red and green lights, and they weren't there anymore. She was flying even closer to the tops of the buildings than before. The wind was blowing harder, and leaves started flying about, making funny shadows on the ground, and tree limbs were cracking and falling.

It was a storm all right. The pilot must have thought he was over the landing field. Maybe he thought the fire in the Square was put there for him to land by. Gosh, but it scaired the folks. I was scaired too. They started yelling: "He's going to land. He's going to land." And: "He's going to fall." A few started for their cars and wagons. I could hear the wagons creaking and chains jangling and cars spitting and missing as they started the engines up. Off to my right, a horse started pitching and striking his hooves against a car.

I didn't know what to do. I wanted to run, and I wanted to stay and see what was going to happen. The plane was close as hell. The pilot must have been trying to see where he was at, and her motors were drowning out all the sounds. I could even feel the vibration, and my hair felt like it was standing up under my hat. I happened to look over at the statue of the general standing with one leg before the other and leaning back on a sword, and I was fixing to run over and climb between his legs and sit there and watch when the roar stopped some, and I looked up and she was gliding just over the top of the trees in the middle of the Square.

Her motors stopped altogether and I could hear the sound of branches cracking and snapping off below her landing gear. I could see her plain now, all silver and shining in the light of the fire with T.W.A. in black letters under her wings. She was sailing smoothly out of the Square when she hit the high power lines that follow the Birmingham highway through the town. It made a loud crash. It sounded like the wind blowing the door of a tin barn shut. She only hit with her landing gear, but I could see the sparks flying, and the wires knocked loose from the poles were spitting blue sparks and whipping around like a bunch of snakes and leaving circles of blue sparks in the darkness.

The plane had knocked five or six wires loose, and they were dangling and swinging, and every time they touched they threw off more sparks. The wind was making them swing, and when I got over there, there was a crackling and spitting screen of blue haze across the highway. I lost my hat running over, but I didn't stop to look for it. I was among the first and I could hear the others pounding behind me across the grass of the Square. They were yelling to beat all hell, and they came up fast, pushing and shoving, and someone got pushed against a swinging wire. It made a sound like when a blacksmith drops a red hot horseshoe into a barrel of water, and the steam comes up. I could smell the flesh burning. The first time I'd ever smelled it. I got up close and it was a woman. It must have killed her right off. She was lying in a puddle stiff as a board, with pieces of glass insulators that the plane had knocked off the poles lying all around her. Her white dress was torn, and I saw one of her tits hanging out in the water and her thighs. Some woman screamed and fainted and almost fell on a wire, but a man caught her. The sheriff and his men were yelling and driving folks back with guns shining in their hands, and everything was lit up blue by the sparks. The shock had turned the woman almost as black as the nigger. I was trying to see if she wasn't blue too, or if it was just the sparks, and the sheriff drove me away. As I backed off trying to see, I heard the motors of the plane start up again somewhere off to the right in the clouds.

The clouds were moving fast in the wind and the wind was blowing the smell of something burning over to me. I turned around, and the crowd was headed back to the nigger. I could see him standing there in the middle of the flames. The wind was making the flames brighter every minute. The crowd was running. I ran too. I ran back across the grass with the crowd. It wasn't so large now that so many had gone when the plane came. I tripped and fell over the limb of a tree lying in the grass and bit my lip. It ain't well yet I bit it so bad. I could taste the blood in my mouth as I ran over. I guess that's what made me sick. When I got there, the fire had caught the nigger's pants, and the folks were standing around watching, but not too close on account of the wind blowing the flames. Somebody hollered, "Well, nigger, it ain't so cold now, is it? You don't need to put your hands in your pockets now." And the nigger looked up with his great white eyes looking like they was 'bout to pop out of his head, and I had enough. I didn't want to see anymore. I wanted to run somewhere and puke, but I stayed. I stayed right there in the front of the crowd and looked.

The nigger tried to say something I couldn't hear for the roar of the wind in the fire, and I strained my ears. Jed Wilson hollered, "What you say there, nigger?" And it came back through the flames in his nigger voice: "Will one a you gentlemen please cut my throat?" he said. "Will somebody please cut my throat like a Christian?" And Jed hollered back, "Sorry, but ain't no Christians around tonight. Ain't no Jew-boys neither. We're just one hundred percent Americans."

Then the nigger was silent. Folks started laughing at Jed. Jed's right popular with the folks, and next year, my uncle says, they plan to run him for sheriff. The heat was too much for me, and the smoke was making my eyes to smart. I was trying to back away when Jed reached down and brought up a can of gasoline and threw it in the fire on the nigger. I could see the flames catching the gas in a puff as it went in in a silver sheet and some of it reached the nigger, making spurts of blue fire all over his chest.

Well, that nigger was tough. I have to give it to that nigger; he was really tough. He had started to burn like a house afire and was making the smoke smell like burning hides. The fire was up around his head, and the smoke was so thick and black we couldn't see him. And him not moving—we thought he was dead. Then he started out. The fire had burned the ropes they had tied him with, and he started jumping and kicking about like he was blind, and you could smell his skin burning. He kicked so hard that the platform, which was burning too, fell in, and he rolled out of the fire at my feet. I jumped back so he wouldn't get on me. I'll never forget it. Every time I eat barbeque I'll remember that nigger. His back was just like a barbecued hog. I could see the prints of his ribs where they start around from his backbone and curve down and around. It was a sight to see, that nigger's back. He was right at my feet, and somebody behind pushed me and almost made me step on him, and he was still burning.

I didn't step on him though, and Jed and somebody else pushed him back into the burning planks and logs and poured on more gas. I wanted to leave, but the folks were yelling and I couldn't move except to look around and see the statue. A branch the wind had broken was resting on his hat. I tried to push out and get away because my guts were gone, and all I got was spit and hot breath in my face from the woman and two men standing directly behind me. So I had to turn back around. The nigger rolled out of the fire again. He wouldn't stay put. It was on the other side this time. I couldn't see him very well through the flames and smoke. They got some tree limbs and held him there this time and he stayed there till he was ashes. I guess he stayed there. I know he burned to ashes because I saw Jed a week later, and he laughed and showed me some white finger bones still held together with little pieces of the nigger's skin. Anyway, I left when somebody moved around to see the nigger. I pushed my way through the crowd, and a woman in the rear scratched my face as she yelled and fought to get up close.

I ran across the Square to the other side, where the sheriff and his deputies were guarding the wires that were still spitting and making a blue fog. My heart was pounding like I had been running a long ways, and I bent over and let my insides go. Everything came up and spilled in a big gush over the ground. I was sick, and tired, and weak, and cold. The wind was still high, and large drops of rain were beginning to fall. I headed down the street to my uncle's place past a store where the wind had broken a window, and glass lay over the sidewalk. I kicked it as I went by. I remember somebody's fool rooster crowing like it was morning in all that wind.

The next day I was too weak to go out, and my uncle kidded me and called me "the gutless wonder from Cincinnati." I didn't mind. He said you get used to it in time. He couldn't go out himself. There was too much wind and rain. I got up and looked out of the window, and the rain was pouring down and dead sparrows and limbs of trees were scattered all over the yard. There had been a cyclone all right. It swept a path right through the county, and we were lucky we didn't get the full force of it.

It blew for three days steady, and put the town in a hell of a shape. The wind blew sparks and set fire to the white-and-green-rimmed house on Jackson Avenue that had the big concrete lions in the yard and burned it down to the ground. They had to kill another nigger who tried to run out of the county after they burned this Bacote nigger. My Uncle Ed said they always have to kill niggers in pairs to keep the other niggers in place. I don't know though, the folks seem a little skittish of the niggers. They all came back, but they act pretty sullen. They look mean as hell when you pass them down at the store. The other day I was down to Brinkley's store, and a white cropper said it didn't do no good to kill the niggers 'cause things don't get no better. He looked hungry as hell. Most of the croppers look hungry. You'd be surprised how hungry white folks can look. Somebody said that he'd better shut his damn mouth, and he shut up. But from the look on his face he won't stay shut long. He went out of the store muttering to himself and spit a big chew of tobacco right down on Brinkley's floor. Brinkley said he was sore 'cause he wouldn't let him have credit. Anyway, it didn't seem to help things. First it was the nigger and the storm, then the plane, then the woman and the wires, and now I hear the airplane line is investigating to find who set the fire that almost wrecked their plane. All that in one night, and all of it but the storm over one nigger. It was some night all right. It was some party too. I was right there, see. I was right there watching it all. It was my first party and my last. God, but that nigger was tough. That Bacote nigger was some nigger!

—1997

Questions: Reading, Responding, Arguing

1. Jed says, "We're just one hundred percent Americans." Explain the social and cultural context of this story and discuss how this story can be read as a social critique or political commentary.

2. Explain how diction is used to construct the narrator's character, personality, and point of view. Why did Ellison choose this point of view for this story?
3. How does Ellison use the plane incident to suggest or develop the story's themes?
4. Compare Ellison's depiction of racial tensions with another selection from the anthology. How are they similar or different in the treatment of this subject? Which story makes the most effective case about racism? Why?

Ray Bradbury (b. 1920)

The Veldt

"George, I wish you'd look at the nursery."

"What's wrong with it?"

"I don't know."

"Well, then."

"I just want you to look at it, is all, or call a psychologist in to look at it."

"What would a psychologist want with a nursery?"

"You know very well what he'd want." His wife paused in the middle of the kitchen and watched the stove busy humming to itself, making supper for four.

"It's just that the nursery is different now than it was."

"All right, let's have a look."

They walked down the hall of their soundproofed Happylife Home, which had cost them thirty thousand dollars installed, this house which clothed and fed and rocked them to sleep and played and sang and was good to them. Their approach sensitized a switch somewhere and the nursery light flicked on when they came within ten feet of it. Similarly, behind them, in the halls, lights went on and off as they left them behind, with a soft automaticity.

"Well," said George Hadley.

They stood on the thatched floor of the nursery. It was forty feet across by forty feet long and thirty feet high; it had cost half again as much as the rest of the house. "But nothing's too good for our children," George had said.

The nursery was silent. It was empty as a jungle glade at hot high noon. The walls were blank and two dimensional. Now, as George and Lydia Hadley stood in the center of the room, the walls began to purr and recede into crystalline distance, it seemed, and presently an African veldt appeared, in three dimensions, on all sides, in color, reproduced to the final pebble and bit of straw. The ceiling above them became a deep sky with a hot yellow sun.

George Hadley felt the perspiration start on his brow.

"Let's get out of this sun," he said. "This is a little too real. But I don't see anything wrong."

"Wait a moment, you'll see," said his wife.

Now the hidden odorophonics were beginning to blow a wind of odor at the two people in the middle of the baked veldtland. The hot straw smell of lion grass, the cool green smell of the hidden water hole, the great rusty smell of animals, the smell of dust like a red paprika in the hot air. And now the sounds: the thump of distant antelope feet on grassy sod, the papery rustling of vultures. A shadow passed through the sky. The shadow flickered on George Hadley's upturned, sweating face.

"Filthy creatures," he heard his wife say.

"The vultures."

"You see, there are the lions, far over, that way. Now they're on their way to the water hole. They've just been eating," said Lydia. "I don't know what."

"Some animal." George Hadley put his hand up to shield off the burning light from his squinted eyes. "A zebra or a baby giraffe, maybe."

"Are you sure?" His wife sounded peculiarly tense.

"No, it's a little late to be sure," he said amused. "Nothing over there I can see but cleaned bone, and the vultures dropping for what's left."

"Did you hear that scream?" she asked.

"No."

"About a minute ago?"

"Sorry, no."

The lions were coming. And again George Hadley was filled with admiration for the mechanical genius who had conceived this room. A miracle of efficiency selling for an absurdly low price. Every home should have one. Oh, occasionally they frightened you with their clinical accuracy, they startled you, gave you a twinge, but most of the time what fun for everyone, not only your own son and daughter, but for yourself when you felt like a quick jaunt to a foreign land, a quick change of scenery. Well, here it was!

And here were the lions now, fifteen feet away, so real, so feverishly and startlingly real that you could feel the prickling fur on your hand, and your mouth was stuffed with the dusty upholstery smell of their heated pelts, and the yellow of them was in your eyes like the yellow of an exquisite French tapestry, the yellows of lions and summer grass, and the sound of the matted lion lungs exhaling on the silent noontide, and the smell of meat from the panting, dripping mouths.

The lions stood looking at George and Lydia Hadley with terrible green-yellow eyes.

"Watch out!" screamed Lydia.

The lions came running at them.

Lydia bolted and ran. Instinctively, George sprang after her. Outside, in the hall, with the door slammed, he was laughing and she was crying, and they both stood appalled at the other's reaction.

"George!"

"Lydia! Oh, my dear poor sweet Lydia!"

"They almost got us!"

"Walls, Lydia, remember; crystal walls, that's all they are. Oh, they look real, I must admit—Africa in your parlor—but it's all dimensional, superreactionary, supersensitive color film and mental tape film behind glass screens. It's all odorophonics and sonics, Lydia. Here's my handkerchief."

"I'm afraid." She came to him and put her body against him and cried steadily. "Did you *see*? Did you *feel*? It's too real."

"Now, Lydia . . ."

"You've got to tell Wendy and Peter not to read any more on Africa."

"Of course—of course." He patted her.

"Promise?"

"Sure."

"And lock the nursery for a few days until I get my nerves settled."

"You know how difficult Peter is about that. When I punished him a month ago by locking the nursery for even a few hours—the tantrum he threw! And Wendy too. They *live* for the nursery."

"It's got to be locked, that's all there is to it."

"All right." Reluctantly he locked the huge door. "You've been working too hard. You need a rest."

"I don't know—I don't know," she said, blowing her nose, sitting down in a chair that immediately began to rock and comfort her.

"Maybe I don't have enough to do. Maybe I have time to think too much. Why don't we shut the whole house off for a few days and take a vacation?"

"You mean you want to fry my eggs for me?"

"Yes." She nodded.

"And darn my socks?"

"Yes." A frantic, watery-eyed nodding.

"And sweep the house?"

"Yes, yes—oh, yes!"

"But I thought that's why we bought this house, so we wouldn't have to do anything?"

"That's just it. I feel like I don't belong here. The house is wife and mother now, and nursemaid. Can I compete with an African veldt? Can I give a bath and scrub the children as efficiently or quickly as the automatic scrub bath can? I cannot. And it isn't just me. It's you. You've been awfully nervous lately."

"I suppose I have been smoking too much."

"You look as if you didn't know what to do with yourself in this house, either. You smoke a little more every morning and drink a little more every afternoon and need a little more sedative every night. You're beginning to feel unnecessary too."

"Am I?" He paused and tried to feel into himself to see what was really there.

"Oh, George!" She looked beyond him, at the nursery door. "Those lions can't get out of there, can they?"

He looked at the door and saw it tremble as if something had jumped against it from the other side.

"Of course not," he said.

At dinner they ate alone, for Wendy and Peter were at a special plastic carnival across town and had televised home to say they'd be late, to go ahead eating. So George Hadley, bemused, sat watching the dining-room table produce warm dishes of food from its mechanical interior.

"We forgot the ketchup," he said.

"Sorry," said a small voice within the table, and ketchup appeared.

As for the nursery, thought George Hadley, it won't hurt for the children to be locked out of it awhile. Too much of anything isn't good for anyone. And it was clearly indicated that the children had been spending a little too much time on Africa. That *sun*. He could feel it on his neck, still, like a hot paw. And the *lions*. And the smell of blood. Remarkable how the nursery caught the telepathic emanations of the children's minds and created life to fill their every desire. The children thought lions, and there were lions. The children thought zebras, and there were zebras. Sun—sun. Giraffes—giraffes. Death and death.

That *last*. He chewed tastelessly on the meat that the table had cut for him. Death thoughts. They were awfully young, Wendy and Peter, for death thoughts. Or, no, you were never too young, really. Long before you knew what death was you were wishing it on someone else. When you were two years old you were shooting people with cap pistols.

But this—the long, hot African veldt—the awful death in the jaws of a lion. And repeated again and again.

"Where are you going?"

He didn't answer Lydia. Preoccupied, he let the lights glow softly on ahead of him, extinguish behind him as he padded to the nursery door. He listened against it. Far away, a lion roared.

He unlocked the door and opened it. Just before he stepped inside, he heard a faraway scream. And then another roar from the lions, which subsided quickly.

He stepped into Africa. How many times in the last year had he opened this door and found Wonderland, Alice, the Mock Turtle, or Aladdin and his Magical Lamp, or Jack Pumpkinhead of Oz, or Dr. Doolittle, or the cow jumping over a very real-appearing moon—all the delightful contraptions of a make-believe world. How often had he seen Pegasus flying in the sky ceiling, or seen fountains of red fireworks, or heard angel voices singing. But now, this yellow hot Africa, this bake oven with murder in the heat. Perhaps Lydia was right. Perhaps they needed a little vacation from the fantasy which was growing a bit too real for ten-year-old children. It was all right to exercise one's mind with gymnastic fantasies, but when the lively child mind settled on *one* pattern . . .? It seemed that, at a distance, for the past month, he had heard lions roaring, and smelled their strong odor seeping as far away as his study door. But, being busy, he had paid it no attention.

George Hadley stood on the African grassland alone. The lions looked up from their feeding, watching him. The only flaw to the illusion was the open door through which he could see his wife, far down the dark hall, like a framed picture, eating her dinner abstractedly.

"Go away," he said to the lions.

They did not go.

He knew the principle of the room exactly. You sent out your thoughts. Whatever you thought would appear.

"Let's have Aladdin and his lamp," he snapped.

The veldtland remained; the lions remained.

"Come on, room! I demand Aladdin!" he said.

Nothing happened. The lions mumbled in their baked pelts.

"Aladdin!"

He went back to dinner. "The fool room's out of order," he said. "It won't respond."

"Or—"

"Or what?"

"Or it *can't* respond," said Lydia, "because the children have thought about Africa and lions and killing so many days that the room's in a rut."

"Could be."

"Or Peter's set it to remain that way."

"Set it?"

"He may have got into the machinery and fixed something."

"Peter doesn't know machinery."

"He's a wise one for ten. That I. Q. of his—"

"Nevertheless—"

"Hello, Mom. Hello, Dad."

The Hadleys turned. Wendy and Peter were coming in the front door, cheeks like peppermint candy, eyes like bright blue agate marbles, a smell of ozone on their jumpers from their trip in the helicopter.

"You're just in time for supper," said both parents.

"We're full of strawberry ice cream and hot dogs," said the children, holding hands. "But we'll sit and watch."

"Yes, come tell us about the nursery," said George Hadley.

The brother and sister blinked at him and then at each other. "Nursery?"

"All about Africa and everything," said the father with false joviality.

"I don't understand," said Peter.

"Your mother and I were just traveling through Africa with rod and reel; Tom Swift and his Electric Lion," said George Hadley.

"There's no Africa in the nursery," said Peter simply.

"Oh, come now, Peter. We know better."

"I don't remember any Africa," said Peter to Wendy. "Do you?"

"No."

"Run see and come tell."

She obeyed.

"Wendy, come back here!" said George Hadley, but she was gone. The house lights followed her like a flock of fireflies. Too late, he realized he had forgotten to lock the nursery door after his last inspection.

"Wendy'll look and come tell us," said Peter.

"She doesn't have to tell *me*. I've seen it."

"I'm sure you're mistaken, Father."

"I'm not, Peter. Come along now."

But Wendy was back. "It's not Africa," she said breathlessly.

"We'll see about this," said George Hadley, and they all walked down the hall together and opened the nursery door.

There was a green, lovely forest, a lovely river, a purple mountain, high voices singing, and Rima, lovely and mysterious, lurking in the trees with colorful flights of butterflies, like animated bouquets, lingering in her long hair. The African veldtland was gone. The lions were gone. Only Rima was here now, singing a song so beautiful that it brought tears to your eyes.

George Hadley looked in at the changed scene. "Go to bed," he said to the children.

They opened their mouths.

"You heard me," he said.

They went off to the air closet, where a wind sucked them like brown leaves up the flue to their slumber rooms.

George Hadley walked through the singing glade and picked up something that lay in the corner near where the lions had been. He walked slowly back to his wife.

"What is that?" she asked.

"An old wallet of mine," he said.

He showed it to her. The smell of hot grass was on it and the smell of a lion. There were drops of saliva on it, it had been chewed, and there were blood smears on both sides.

He closed the nursery door and locked it, tight.

In the middle of the night he was still awake and he knew his wife was awake. "Do you think Wendy changed it?" she said at last, in the dark room.

"Of course."

"Made it from a veldt into a forest and put Rima there instead of lions?"

"Yes."

"Why?"

"I don't know. But it's staying locked until I find out."

"How did your wallet get there?"

"I don't know anything," he said, "except that I'm beginning to be sorry we bought that room for the children. If children are neurotic at all, a room like that—"

"It's supposed to help them work off their neuroses in a healthful way."

"I'm starting to wonder." He stared at the ceiling.

"We've given the children everything they ever wanted. Is this our reward—secrecy, disobedience?"

"Who was it said, 'Children are carpets, they should be stepped on occasionally'? We've never lifted a hand. They're insufferable—let's admit it. They come and go when they like; they treat us as if we were offspring. They're spoiled and we're spoiled."

"They've been acting funny ever since you forbade them to take the rocket to New York a few months ago."

"They're not old enough to do that alone, I explained."

"Nevertheless, I've noticed they've been decidedly cool toward us since."

"I think I'll have David McClean come tomorrow morning to have a look at Africa."

"But it's not Africa now, it's *Green Mansions* country and Rima."

"I have a feeling it'll be Africa again before then."

A moment later they heard the screams.

Two screams. Two people screaming from downstairs. And then a roar of lions.

"Wendy and Peter aren't in their rooms," said his wife.

He lay in his bed with his beating heart. "No," he said. "They've broken into the nursery."

"Those screams—they sound familiar."

"Do they?"

"Yes, awfully."

And although their beds tried very hard, the two adults couldn't be rocked to sleep for another hour. A smell of cats was in the night air.

"Father?" said Peter.

"Yes."

Peter looked at his shoes. He never looked at his father any more, nor at his mother. "You aren't going to lock up the nursery for good, are you?"

"That all depends."

"On what?" snapped Peter.

"On you and your sister. If you intersperse this Africa with a little variety—oh, Sweden perhaps, or Denmark or China—"

"I thought we were free to play as we wished."

"You are, within reasonable bounds."

"What's wrong with Africa, Father?"

"Oh, so now you admit you have been conjuring up Africa, do you?"

"I wouldn't want the nursery locked up," said Peter coldly. "Ever."

"Matter of fact, we're thinking of turning the whole house off for about a month. Live sort of a carefree one-for-all existence."

"That sounds dreadful! Would I have to tie my own shoes instead of letting the shoe tier do it? And brush my own teeth and comb my hair and give myself a bath?"

"It would be fun for a change, don't you think?"

"No, it would be horrid. I didn't like it when you took out the picture painter last month."

"That's because I wanted you to learn to paint all by yourself, son."

"I don't want to do anything but look and listen and smell; what else *is* there to do?"

"All right, go play in Africa."

"Will you shut off the house sometime soon?"

"We're considering it."

"I don't think you'd better consider it any more, Father."

"I won't have any threats from my son!"

"Very well." And Peter strolled off to the nursery.

"Am I on time?" said David McClean.

"Breakfast?" asked George Hadley.

"Thanks, had some. What's the trouble?"

"David, you're a psychologist."

"I should hope so."

"Well, then, have a look at our nursery. You saw it a year ago when you dropped by; did you notice anything peculiar about it then?"

"Can't say I did; the usual violences, a tendency toward a slight paranoia here or there, usual in children because they feel persecuted by parents constantly, but, oh, really nothing."

They walked down the hall. "I locked the nursery up," explained the father, "and the children broke back into it during the night. I let them stay so they could form the patterns for you to see."

There was a terrible screaming from the nursery.

"There it is," said George Hadley. "See what you make of it."

They walked in on the children without rapping.

The screams had faded. The lions were feeding.

"Run outside a moment, children," said George Hadley. "No, don't change the mental combination. Leave the walls as they are. Get!"

With the children gone, the two men stood studying the lions clustered at a distance, eating with great relish whatever it was they had caught.

"I wish I knew what it was," said George Hadley. "Sometimes I can almost see. Do you think if I brought high-powered binoculars here and—"

David McClean laughed dryly. "Hardly." He turned to study all four walls. "How long has this been going on?"

"A little over a month."

"It certainly doesn't *feel* good."

"I want facts, not feelings."

"My dear George, a psychologist never saw a fact in his life. He only hears about feelings; vague things. This doesn't feel good, I tell you. Trust my hunches and my instincts. I have a nose for something bad. This is very bad. My advice to you is to have the whole damn room torn down and your children brought to me every day during the next year for treatment."

"Is it that bad?"

"I'm afraid so. One of the original uses of these nurseries was so that we could study the patterns left on the walls by the child's mind, study at our leisure, and help the child. In this case, however, the room has become a channel toward—destructive thoughts, instead of a release away from them."

"Didn't you sense this before?"

"I sensed only that you had spoiled your children more than most. And now you're letting them down in some way. What way?"

"I wouldn't let them go to New York."

"What else?"

"I've taken a few machines from the house and threatened them, a month ago, with closing up the nursery unless they did their homework. I did close it for a few days to show I meant business."

"Ah, ha!"

"Does that mean anything?"

"Everything. Where before they had a Santa Claus now they have a Scrooge. Children prefer Santas. You've let this room and this house replace you and your wife in your children's affections. This room is their mother and father, far more important in their lives than their real parents. And now you come along and want to shut it off. No wonder there's hatred here. You can feel it coming out of the sky. Feel that sun. George, you'll have to change your life. Like too many others, you've built it around creature comforts. Why, you'd starve tomorrow if something went wrong in your kitchen. You wouldn't know how to tap an egg. Nevertheless, turn everything off. Start new. It'll take time. But we'll make good children out of bad in a year, wait and see."

"But won't the shock be too much for the children, shutting the room up abruptly, for good?"

"I don't want them going any deeper into this, that's all."

The lions were finished with their red feast.

The lions were standing on the edge of the clearing watching the two men.

"Now *I'm* feeling persecuted," said McClean. "Let's get out of here. I never have cared for these damned rooms. Make me nervous."

"The lions look real, don't they?" said George Hadley. "I don't suppose there's any way—"

"What?"

"—that they could *become* real?"

"Not that I know."

"Some flaw in the machinery, a tampering or something?"

"No."

They went to the door.

"I don't imagine the room will like being turned off," said the father. "Nothing ever likes to die—even a room."

"I wonder if it hates me for wanting to switch it off?"

"Paranoia is thick around here today," said David McClean. "You can follow it like a spoor. Hello." He bent and picked up a bloody scarf. "This yours?"

"No." George Hadley's face was rigid. "It belongs to Lydia."

They went to the fuse box together and threw the switch that killed the nursery.

The two children were in hysterics. They screamed and pranced and threw things. They yelled and sobbed and swore and jumped at the furniture.

"You can't do that to the nursery, you can't't!"

"Now, children."

The children flung themselves onto a couch, weeping.

"George," said Lydia Hadley, "turn on the nursery, just for a few moments. You can't be so abrupt."

"No."

"You can't be so cruel."

"Lydia, it's off, and it stays off. And the whole damn house dies as of here and now. The more I see of the mess we've put ourselves in, the more it sickens me. We've been contemplating our mechanical, electronic navels for too long. My God, how we need a breath of honest air!"

And he marched about the house turning off the voice clocks, the stoves, the heaters, the shoe shiners, the shoe lacers, the body scrubbers and swabbers and massagers, and every other machine he could put his hand to.

The house was full of dead bodies, it seemed. It felt like a mechanical cemetery. So silent. None of the humming hidden energy of machines waiting to function at the tap of a button.

"Don't let them do it!" wailed Peter at the ceiling, as if he was talking to the house, the nursery. "Don't let Father kill everything." He turned to his father. "Oh, I hate you!"

"Insults won't get you anywhere."

"I wish you were dead!"

"We were, for a long while. Now we're going to really start living. Instead of being handled and massaged, we're going to *live*."

Wendy was still crying and Peter joined her again. "Just a moment, just one moment, just another moment of nursery," they wailed.

"Oh, George," said the wife, "it can't hurt."

"All right—all right, if they'll just shut up. One minute, mind you, and then off forever."

"Daddy, Daddy, Daddy!" sang the children, smiling with wet faces.

"And then we're going on a vacation. David McClean is coming back in half an hour to help us move out and get to the airport. I'm going to dress. You turn the nursery on for a minute, Lydia, just a minute, mind you."

And the three of them went babbling off while he let himself be vacuumed upstairs through the air flue and set about dressing himself. A minute later Lydia appeared.

"I'll be glad when we get away," she sighed.

"Did you leave them in the nursery?"

"I wanted to dress too. Oh, that horrid Africa. What can they see in it?"

"Well, in five minutes we'll be on our way to Iowa. Lord, how did we ever get in this house? What prompted us to buy a nightmare?"

"Pride, money, foolishness."

"I think we'd better get downstairs before those kids get engrossed with those damned beasts again."

Just then they heard the children calling, "Daddy, Mommy, come quick—quick!"

They went downstairs in the air flue and ran down the hall. The children were nowhere in sight. "Wendy? Peter!"

They ran into the nursery. The veldtland was empty save for the lions waiting, looking at them. "Peter, Wendy?"

The door slammed.

"Wendy, Peter!"

George Hadley and his wife whirled and ran back to the door.

"Open the door!" cried George Hadley, trying the knob. "Why, they've locked it from the outside! Peter!" He beat at the door. "Open up!"

He heard Peter's voice outside, against the door.

"Don't let them switch off the nursery and the house," he was saying.

Mr. and Mrs. George Hadley beat at the door. "Now, don't be ridiculous, children. It's time to go. Mr. McClean'll be here in a minute and . . ."

And then they heard the sounds.

The lions on three sides of them, in the yellow veldt grass, padding through the dry straw, rumbling and roaring in their throats.

The lions.

Mr. Hadley looked at his wife and they turned and looked back at the beasts edging slowly forward, crouching, tails stiff.

Mr. and Mrs. Hadley screamed.

And suddenly they realized why those other screams had sounded familiar.

"Well, here I am," said David McClean in the nursery doorway. "Oh, hello." He stared at the two children seated in the center of the open glade eating a little picnic lunch. Beyond them was the water hole and the yellow veldtland; above was the hot sun. He began to perspire. "Where are your father and mother?"

The children looked up and smiled. "Oh, they'll be here directly."

"Good, we must get going." At a distance Mr. McClean saw the lions fighting and clawing and then quieting down to feed in silence under the shady trees.

He squinted at the lions with his hand up to his eyes.

Now the lions were done feeding. They moved to the water hole to drink.

A shadow flickered over Mr. McClean's hot face. Many shadows flickered. The vultures were dropping down the blazing sky.

"A cup of tea?" asked Wendy in the silence.

—1951

Questions: Reading, Responding, Arguing

1. What does the phrase "virtual reality" mean, and why is it applicable to this story?
2. Is the story satirical? If so, point out satirical elements, especially those relating to the narrator's tone of voice.
3. How is foreshadowing used in the opening paragraphs of the story?
4. All science fiction depends on a nonexistent technology. What things in this story that were considered far-fetched at the time are now considered commonplace? Argue that the story is or is not dated.

John Updike (b. 1932)

A & P

In walks three girls in nothing but bathing suits. I'm in the third checkout slot, with my back to the door, so I don't see them until they're over by the bread. The one that caught my eye first was the one in the plaid green two-piece. She was a chunky kid, with a good tan and a sweet broad soft-looking can with those two crescents of white just under it, where the sun never seems to hit, at the top of the backs of her legs. I stood there with my hand on a box of HiHo crackers trying to remember if I rang it up or not. I ring it up again and the customer starts giving me hell. She's one of these cash-register-watchers, a witch about fifty with rouge on her cheekbones and no eyebrows, and I know it made her day to trip me up. She'd been watching cash registers for fifty years and probably never seen a mistake before.

By the time I got her feathers smoothed and her goodies into a bag—she gives me a little snort in passing, if she'd been born at the right time they would have burned her over in Salem—by the time I get her on her way the girls had circled around the bread and were coming back, without a pushcart, back my way along the counters, in the aisle between the check-outs and the Special bins. They didn't even have shoes on. There was this chunky one, with the two-piece—it was bright green and the seams on the bra were still sharp and her belly was still pretty pale so I guessed she just got it (the suit)—there was this one, with one of those chubby berry-faces, the lips all bunched together under her nose, this one, and a tall one, with black hair that hadn't quite frizzed right, and one of these sunburns right across under the eyes, and a chin that was too long—you know, the kind of girl other girls think is very "striking" and "attractive" but never quite makes it, as they very well know, which is why they like her so much—and then the third one, that wasn't quite so tall. She was the queen. She kind of led them, the other two peeking around and making their shoulders round. She didn't look around, not this queen, she just walked straight on slowly, on these long white prima-donna legs. She came down a little hard on her heels, as if she didn't walk in her bare feet that much, putting down her heels and then letting the weight move along to her toes as if she was testing the floor with every step, putting a little deliberate extra action into it. You never know for sure how girls' minds work (do you really think it's a mind in there or just a little buzz like a bee in a glass jar?) but you got the idea she had talked the other two into coming in here with her, and now she was showing them how to do it, walk slow and hold yourself straight.

She had on a kind of dirty-pink—beige maybe, I don't know—bathing suit with a little nubble all over it and, what got me, the straps were down. They were off her shoulders looped loose around the cool tops of her arms, and I guess as a result the suit had slipped a little on her, so all around the top of the cloth there was this shining rim. If it hadn't been there you wouldn't have known there could have been anything whiter than those shoulders. With the straps pushed off, there was nothing between the top of the suit and the top of her head except just *her*, this clean bare plane of the top of her chest down from the shoulder bones like a dented sheet of metal tilted in the light. I mean, it was more than pretty.

She had sort of oaky hair that the sun and salt had bleached, done up in a bun that was unravelling, and a kind of prim face. Walking into the A & P with your straps down, I suppose it's the only kind of face you *can* have. She held her head so high her neck, coming up out of those white shoulders, looked kind of stretched, but I didn't mind. The longer her neck was, the more of her there was.

She must have felt in the corner of her eye me and over my shoulder Stokesie in the second slot watching, but she didn't tip. Not this queen.

She kept her eyes moving across the racks, and stopped, and turned so slow it made my stomach rub the inside of my apron, and buzzed to the other two, who kind of huddled against her for relief, and then they all three of them went up the cat and dog food-breakfast-cereal-macaroni-rice-raisins-seasonings-spreads-spaghetti-soft drinks-crackers-and-cookies aisle. From the third slot I look straight up this aisle to the meat counter, and I watched them all the way. The fat one with the tan sort of fumbled with the cookies, but on second thought she put the packages back. The sheep pushing their carts down the aisle—the girls were walking against the usual traffic (not that we have one-way signs or anything)—were pretty hilarious. You could see them, when Queenie's white shoulders dawned on them, kind of jerk, or hop, or hiccup, but their eyes snapped back to their own baskets and on they pushed. I bet you could set off dynamite in an A & P and the people would by and large keep reaching and checking oatmeal off their lists and muttering "Let me see, there was a third thing, began with A, asparagus, no, ah, yes, applesauce!" or whatever it is they do mutter. But there was no doubt, this jiggled them. A few house slaves in pin curlers even look around after pushing their carts past to make sure what they had seen was correct.

You know, it's one thing to have a girl in a bathing suit down on the beach, where what with the glare nobody can look at each other much anyway, and another thing in the cool of the A & P, under the fluorescent lights, against all those stacked packages, with her feet padding along naked over our checker-board green-and-cream rubber-tile floor.

"Oh, Daddy," Stokesie said beside me. "I feel so faint."

"Darling," I said. "Hold me tight." Stokesie's married, with two babies chalked up on his fuselage already, but as far as I can tell that's the only difference. He's twenty-two, and I was nineteen this April.

"Is it done?" he asks, the responsible married man finding his voice. I forgot to say he thinks he's going to be manager some sunny day, maybe in 1990 when it's called the Great Alexandrov and Petrooshki Tea Company or something.

What he meant was, our town is five miles from a beach, with a big summer colony out on the Point, but we're right in the middle of town, and the women generally put on a shirt or shorts or something before they get out of the car into the street. And anyway these are usually women with six children and varicose veins mapping their legs and nobody, including them, could care less. As I say, we're right in the middle of town, and if you stand at our front doors you can see two banks and the Congregational church and the newspaper store and three real estate offices and about twenty-seven old freeloaders tearing up Central

Street because the sewer broke again. It's not as if we're on the Cape; we're north of Boston and there's people in this town haven't seen the ocean for twenty years.

The girls had reached the meat counter and were asking McMahon something. He pointed, they pointed, and they shuffled out of sight behind a pyramid of Diet Delight peaches. All that was left for us to see was old McMahon patting his mouth and looking after them sizing up their joints. Poor kids, I began to feel sorry for them, they couldn't help it.

Now here comes the sad part of the story, at least my family says it's sad, but I don't think it's so sad myself. The store's pretty empty, it being Thursday afternoon, so there was nothing much to do except lean on the register and wait for the girls to show up again. The whole store was like a pinball machine and I didn't know which tunnel they'd come out of. After a while they come around out of the far aisle, around the light bulbs, records at discount of the Caribbean Six or Tony Martin Sings or some such gunk you wonder they waste the wax on, sixpacks of candy bars, and plastic toys done up in cellophane that fall apart when a kid looks at them anyway. Around they come, Queenie still leading the way, and holding a little gray jar in her hand. Slots Three through Seven are unmanned and I could see her wondering between Stokes and me, but Stokesie with his usual luck draws an old party in baggy gray pants who stumbles up with four giant cans of pineapple juice (what do these bums *do* with all that pineapple juice? I've often asked myself) so the girls come to me. Queenie puts down the jar and I take it into my fingers icy cold. Kingfish Fancy Herring Snacks in Pure Sour Cream: 49¢. Now her hands are empty, not a ring or a bracelet, bare as God made them, and I wonder where the money's coming from. Still with that prim look she lifts a folded dollar bill out of the hollow at the center of her nubbled pink top. The jar went heavy in my hand. Really, I thought that was so cute.

Then everybody's luck begins to run out. Lengel comes in from haggling with a truck full of cabbages on the lot and is about to scuttle into that door marked MANAGER behind which he hides all day when the girls touch his eye. Lengel's pretty dreary, teaches Sunday school and the rest, but he doesn't miss that much. He comes over and says, "Girls, this isn't the beach."

Queenie blushes, though maybe it's just a brush of sunburn I was noticing for the first time, now that she was so close. "My mother asked me to pick up a jar of herring snacks." Her voice kind of startled me, the way voices do when you see the people first, coming out so flat and dumb yet kind of tony, too, the way it ticked over "pick up" and "snacks." All of a sudden I slid right down her voice into her living room. Her father and the other men were standing around in ice-cream coats and bow ties and the women were in sandals picking up herring snacks on toothpicks off a big glass plate and they were all holding drinks the color of water with olives and sprigs of mint in them. When my parents have somebody over they get lemonade and if it's a real racy affair Schlitz in tall glasses with "They'll Do It Every Time" cartoons stencilled on.

"That's all right," Lengel said. "But this isn't the beach." His repeating this struck me as funny, as if it had just occurred to him, and he had been thinking all these years the A & P was a great big dune and he was the head lifeguard. He didn't like my smiling—as I say he doesn't miss much—but he concentrates on giving the girls that sad Sunday-school-superintendent stare.

Queenie's blush is no sunburn now, and the plump one in plaid, that I liked better from the back—a really sweet can—pipes up, "We weren't doing any shopping. We just came in for the one thing."

"That makes no difference," Lengel tells her, and I could see from the way his eyes went that he hadn't noticed she was wearing a two-piece before. "We want you decently dressed when you come in here."

"We *are* decent," Queenie says suddenly, her lower lip pushing, getting sore now that she remembers her place, a place from which the crowd that runs the A & P must look pretty crummy. Fancy Herring Snacks flashed in her very blue eyes.

"Girls, I don't want to argue with you. After this come in here with your shoulders covered. It's our policy." He turns his back. That's policy for you. Policy is what the kingpins want. What the others want is juvenile delinquency.

All this while, the customers had been showing up with their carts but, you know, sheep, seeing a scene, they had all bunched up on Stokesie, who shook open a paper bag as gently as peeling a peach, not wanting to miss a word. I could feel in the silence everybody getting nervous, most of all Lengel, who asks me, "Sammy, have you rung up this purchase?"

I thought and said "No" but it wasn't about that I was thinking. I go through the punches, 4, 9, GROC, TOT—it's more complicated than you think, and after you do it often enough, it begins to make a little song, that you hear words to, in my case "Hello *(bing)* there, you *(gung)* happy *peepul (splat)!*"—the splat being the drawer flying out. I uncrease the bill, tenderly as you may imagine, it just having come from between the two smoothest scoops of vanilla I had ever known were there, and pass a half and a penny into her narrow pink palm, and nestle the herrings in a bag and twist its neck and hand it over, all the time thinking.

The girls, and who'd blame them, are in a hurry to get out, so I say "I quit" to Lengel quick enough for them to hear, hoping they'll stop and watch me, their unsuspected hero. They keep right on going, into the electric eye; the door flies open and they flicker across the lot to their car, Queenie and Plaid and Big Tall Goony-Goony (not that as raw material she was so bad), leaving me with Lengel and a kink in his eyebrow.

"Did you say something, Sammy?"

"I said I quit."

"I thought you did."

"You didn't have to embarrass them."

"It was they who were embarrassing us."

I started to say something that came out "Fiddle-de-doo." It's a saying of my grandmother's, and I know she would have been pleased.

"I don't think you know what you're saying," Lengel said.

"I know you don't," I said. "But I do." I pull the bow at the back of my apron and start shrugging it off my shoulders. A couple customers that had been heading for my slot begin to knock against each other, like scared pigs in a chute.

Lengel sighs and begins to look very patient and old and gray. He's been a friend of my parents for years. "Sammy, you don't want to do this to your Mom and Dad," he tells me. It's true, I don't. But it seems to me that once you begin a gesture it's fatal not to go through with it. I fold the apron, "Sammy" stitched in red on the pocket, and put it on the counter, and drop the bow tie on top of it. The bow tie is theirs, if you've ever wondered. "You'll feel this for the rest of your life," Lengel says, and I know that's true, too, but remembering how he made that pretty girl blush makes me so scrunchy inside I punch the No Sale tab and the machine whirs "pee-pul" and the drawer splats out. One advantage to this scene taking place in summer, I can follow this up with a clean exit, there's no fumbling around getting your coat and galoshes, I just saunter into the electric eye in my white shirt that my mother ironed the night before, and the door heaves itself open, and outside the sunshine is skating around on the asphalt.

I look around for my girls, but they're gone, of course. There wasn't anybody but some young married screaming with her children about some candy they didn't get by the door of a powder-blue Falcon station wagon. Looking back in the big windows, over the bags of peat moss and aluminum lawn furniture stacked on the pavement, I could see Lengel in my place in the slot, checking the sheep through. His face was dark gray and his back stiff, as if he'd just had an injection of iron, and my stomach kind of fell as I felt how hard the world was going to be to me hereafter.

—*1962*

Questions: Reading, Responding, Arguing

1. What kind of language, sentence structure, diction, and imagery does the narrator use?
2. Describe this narrator. Why has Updike chosen this kind of narrator for his story?
3. Why does Sammy quit his job? What are the factors that lead up to this action?
4. Explain the significance of the story's final line. How does this line conclude the story? Why does Updike end the story with this line? Argue about its possible implications for Sammy's future.

Raymond Carver (1938–1988)

Cathedral*

This blind man, an old friend of my wife's, he was on his way to spend the night. His wife had died. So he was visiting the dead wife's relatives in Connecticut. He called my wife from his in-laws'. Arrangements were made. He would come by train, a five-hour trip, and my wife would meet him at the station. She hadn't seen him since she worked for him one summer in Seattle ten years ago. But she and the blind man had kept in touch. They made tapes and mailed them back and forth. I wasn't enthusiastic about his visit. He was no one I knew. And his being blind bothered me. My idea of blindness came from the movies. In the movies, the blind moved slowly and never laughed. Sometimes they were led by seeing-eye dogs. A blind man in my house was not something I looked forward to.

That summer in Seattle she had needed a job. She didn't have any money. The man she was going to marry at the end of the summer was in officers' training school. He didn't have any money, either. But she was in love with the guy, and he was in love with her, etc. She'd seen something in the paper: HELP—*Reading to Blind Man*, and a telephone number. She phoned and went over, was hired on the spot. She'd worked with this blind man all summer. She read stuff to him, case studies, reports, that sort of thing. She helped him organize his little office in the county social-service department. They'd become good friends, my wife and the blind man. How do I know these things? She told me. And she told me something else. On her last day in the office, the blind man asked if he could touch her face. She agreed to this. She told me he touched his fingers to every part of her face, her nose—even her neck! She never forgot it. She even tried to write a poem about it. She was always trying to write a poem. She wrote a poem or two every year, usually after something really important had happened to her.

When we first started going out together, she showed me the poem. In the poem, she recalled his fingers and the way they had moved around over her face. In the poem, she talked about what she had felt at the time, about what went through her mind when the blind man touched her nose and lips. I can remember I didn't think much of the poem. Of course, I didn't tell her that. Maybe I just don't understand poetry. I admit it's not the first thing I reach for when I pick up something to read.

Anyway, this man who'd first enjoyed her favors, the officer-to-be, he'd been her childhood sweetheart. So okay. I'm saying that at the end of the summer she let the blind man run his hands over her face, said good-bye to him, married her childhood sweetheart etc., who was now a commissioned officer, and she moved away from Seattle. But they'd kept in touch, she and the blind man. She made the first contact after a year or so. She called him up one night from an Air Force base in Alabama. She wanted to talk. They talked. He asked her to send a tape and tell him about her life. She did this. She sent the tape. On the tape, she told the blind man about her husband and about their life together in the military. She told the blind man she loved her husband but she didn't like it where they lived and she didn't like it that he was part of the military-industrial thing. She told the blind man she'd written a poem and he was in it. She told him that she was writing a poem about what it was like to be an Air Force officer's wife. The poem wasn't finished yet. She was still writing it. The blind man made a tape. He sent her the tape. She made a tape. This went on for years. My wife's officer was posted to one base and then another. She sent tapes from Moody AFB, McGuire, McConnell, and finally Travis, near Sacramento, where one night she got to feeling lonely and cut off from people she kept losing in that moving-around life. She got to feeling she couldn't go it another step. She went in and swallowed all the pills and capsules in the medicine chest and washed them down with a bottle of gin. Then she got into a hot bath and passed out.

But instead of dying, she got sick. She threw up. Her officer—why should he have a name? he was the childhood sweetheart, and what more does he want?—came home from somewhere, found her, and called the ambulance. In time, she put it all on a tape and sent the tape to the blind man. Over the years, she put all kinds of stuff on tapes and sent the tapes off lickety-split. Next to writing a poem every year, I think it was her chief means of recreation. On one tape, she told the blind man she'd decided to live away from her officer for a time. On another tape, she told him about her divorce. She and I began going out, and of course she told her blind man about it. She told him everything, or so it seemed to me. Once she asked me if I'd like to hear the latest tape from the blind man. This was a year ago. I was on the tape, she said. So I said okay, I'd listen to it. I got us drinks and we settled down in the living room. We made ready to listen. First she inserted the tape into the player and adjusted a couple of dials. Then she pushed a lever. The tape squeaked and someone began to talk in this loud voice. She lowered the volume. After a few minutes of harmless chitchat, I heard my own name in the mouth of this stranger, this blind man I didn't even know! And then this: "From all you've said about him, I can only conclude—" But we were interrupted, a knock at the door, something, and we didn't ever get back to the tape. Maybe it was just as well. I'd heard all I wanted to.

Now this same blind man was coming to sleep in my house.

"Maybe I could take him bowling," I said to my wife. She was at the draining board doing scalloped potatoes. She put down the knife she was using and turned around.

"If you love me," she said, "you can do this for me. If you don't love me, okay. But if you had a friend, any friend, and the friend came to visit, I'd make him feel comfortable." She wiped her hands with the dish towel.

"I don't have any blind friends," I said.

"You don't have *any* friends," she said. "Period. Besides," she said, "goddamn it, his wife's just died! Don't you understand that? The man's lost his wife!"

I didn't answer. She'd told me a little about the blind man's wife. Her name was Beulah. Beulah! That's a name for a colored woman.

"Was his wife a Negro?" I asked.

"Are you crazy?" my wife said. "Have you just flipped or something?" She picked up a potato. I saw it hit the floor, then roll under the stove. "What's wrong with you?" she said. "Are you drunk?"

"I'm just asking," I said.

Right then my wife filled me in with more detail than I cared to know. I made a drink and sat at the kitchen table to listen. Pieces of the story began to fall into place.

Beulah had gone to work for the blind man the summer after my wife had stopped working for him. Pretty soon Beulah and the blind man had themselves a church wedding. It was a little wedding—who'd want to go to such a wedding in the first place?—just the two of them, plus the minister and the minister's wife. But it was a church wedding just the same. It was what Beulah had wanted, he'd said. But even then Beulah must have been carrying the cancer in her glands. After they had been inseparable for eight years—my wife's word, *inseparable*—Beulah's health went into a rapid decline. She died in a Seattle hospital room, the blind man sitting beside the bed and holding on to her hand. They'd married, lived and worked together, slept together—had sex, sure—and then the blind man had to bury her. All this without his having ever seen what the goddamned woman looked like. It was beyond my understanding. Hearing this, I felt sorry for the blind man for a little bit. And then I found myself thinking what a pitiful life this woman must have led. Imagine a woman who could never see herself as she was seen in the eyes of her loved one. A woman who could go on day after day and never receive the smallest compliment from her beloved. A woman whose husband could never read the expression on her face, be it misery or something better. Someone who could wear makeup or not—what difference to him? She could, if she wanted, wear green eyeshadow around one eye, a straight pin in her nostril, yellow slacks, and purple shoes, no matter. And then to slip off into death, the blind man's hand on her hand, his blind eyes streaming tears—I'm imagining now—her last thought maybe this: that he never even knew what she looked like, and she on an express to the grave. Robert was left with a small insurance policy and a half of a twenty-peso Mexican coin. The other half of the coin went into the box with her. Pathetic.

So when the time rolled around, my wife went to the depot to pick him up. With nothing to do but wait—sure, I blamed him for that—I was having a drink and watching the TV when I heard the car pull into the drive. I got up from the sofa with my drink and went to the window to have a look.

I saw my wife laughing as she parked the car. I saw her get out of the car and shut the door. She was still wearing a smile. Just amazing. She went around to the other side of the car to where the blind man was already starting to get out. This blind man, feature this, he was wearing a full beard! A beard on a blind man! Too much, I say. The blind man reached into the backseat and dragged out a suitcase. My wife took his arm, shut the car door, and, talking all the way, moved him down the drive and then up the steps to the front porch. I turned off the TV. I finished my drink, rinsed the glass, dried my hands. Then I went to the door.

My wife said, "I want you to meet Robert. Robert, this is my husband. I've told you all about him." She was beaming. She had this blind man by his coat sleeve.

The blind man let go of his suitcase and up came his hand.

I took it. He squeezed hard, held my hand, and then he let it go.

"I feel like we've already met," he boomed.

"Likewise," I said. I didn't know what else to say. Then I said, "Welcome. I've heard a lot about you." We began to move then, a little group, from the porch into the living room, my wife guiding him by the arm. The blind man was carrying his suitcase in his other hand. My wife said things like, "To your left here, Robert. That's right. Now watch it, there's a chair. That's it. Sit down right here. This is the sofa. We just bought this sofa two weeks ago."

I started to say something about the old sofa. I'd liked that old sofa. But I didn't say anything. Then I wanted to say something else, small-talk, about the scenic ride along the Hudson. How going *to* New York, you should sit on the right-hand side of the train, and coming *from* New York, the left-hand side.

"Did you have a good train ride?" I said. "Which side of the train did you sit on, by the way?"

"What a question, which side!" my wife said. "What's it matter which side?" she said.

"I just asked," I said.

"Right side," the blind man said. "I hadn't been on a train in nearly forty years. Not since I was a kid. With my folks. That's been a long time. I'd nearly forgotten the sensation. I have winter in my beard now," he said. "So I've been told, anyway. Do I look distinguished, my dear?" the blind man said to my wife.

"You look distinguished, Robert," she said. "Robert," she said. "Robert, it's just so good to see you."

My wife finally took her eyes off the blind man and looked at me. I had the feeling she didn't like what she saw. I shrugged.

I've never met, or personally known, anyone who was blind. This blind man was late forties, a heavy-set, balding man with stooped shoulders, as if he carried a great weight there. He wore brown slacks, brown shoes, a light-brown shirt, a tie, a sports coat. Spiffy. He also had this full beard. But he didn't use a cane and he didn't wear dark glasses. I'd always thought dark glasses were a must for the blind. Fact was, I wished he had a pair. At first glance, his eyes looked like anyone else's eyes. But if you looked close, there was something different about them. Too much white in the iris, for one thing, and the pupils seemed to move around in the sockets without his knowing it or being able to stop it. Creepy. As I stared at his face, I saw the left pupil turn in toward his nose while the other made an effort to keep in one place. But it was only an effort, for that eye was on the roam without his knowing it or wanting it to be.

I said, "Let me get you a drink. What's your pleasure? We have a little of everything. It's one of our pastimes."

"Bub, I'm a Scotch man myself," he said fast enough in this big voice.

"Right," I said. Bub! "Sure you are. I knew it."

He let his fingers touch his suitcase, which was sitting alongside the sofa. He was taking his bearings. I didn't blame him for that.

"I'll move that up to your room," my wife said.

"No, that's fine," the blind man said loudly. "It can go up when I go up."

"A little water with the Scotch?" I said.

"Very little," he said.

"I knew it," I said.

He said, "Just a tad. The Irish actor, Barry Fitzgerald? I'm like that fellow. When I drink water, Fitzgerald said, I drink water. When I drink whiskey, I drink whiskey." My wife laughed. The blind man brought his hand up under his beard. He lifted his beard slowly and let it drop.

I did the drinks, three big glasses of Scotch with a splash of water in each. Then we made ourselves comfortable and talked about Robert's travels. First the long flight from the West Coast to Connecticut, we covered that. Then from Connecticut up here by train. We had another drink concerning that leg of the trip.

I remembered having read somewhere that the blind didn't smoke because, as speculation had it, they couldn't see the smoke they exhaled. I thought I knew that much and that much only about blind people. But this blind man smoked his cigarette down to the nubbin and then lit another one. This blind man filled his ashtray and my wife emptied it.

When we sat down at the table for dinner, we had another drink. My wife heaped Robert's plate with cube steak, scalloped potatoes, green beans. I buttered him up two slices of bread. I said, "Here's bread and butter for you." I swallowed some of my drink. "Now let us pray," I said, and the blind man lowered his head. My wife looked at me, her mouth agape. "Pray the phone won't ring and the food doesn't get cold," I said.

We dug in. We ate everything there was to eat on the table. We ate like there was no tomorrow. We didn't talk. We ate. We scarfed. We grazed that table. We were into serious eating. The blind man had right away located his foods, he knew just where everything was on his plate. I watched with admiration as he used his knife and fork on the meat. He'd cut two pieces of meat, fork the meat into his mouth, and then go all out for the scalloped potatoes, the beans next, and then he'd tear off a hunk of buttered bread and eat that. He'd follow this up with a big drink of milk. It didn't seem to bother him to use his fingers once in a while, either.

We finished everything, including half a strawberry pie. For a few moments, we sat as if stunned. Sweat beaded on our faces. Finally, we got up from the table and left the dirty plates. We didn't look back. We took ourselves into the living room and sank into our places again. Robert and my wife sat on the sofa. I took the big chair. We had us two or three more drinks while they talked about the major things that had come to pass for them in the past ten years. For the most part, I just listened. Now and then I joined in. I didn't want him to think I'd left the room, and I didn't want her to think I was feeling left out. They talked of things that had happened to them—to them!—these past ten years. I waited in vain to hear my name on my wife's sweet lips: "And then my dear husband came into my life"—something like that. But I heard nothing of the sort. More talk of Robert. Robert had done a little of everything, it seemed, a regular blind jack-of-all-trades. But most recently he and his wife had had an Amway distributorship, from which, I gathered, they'd earned their living, such as it was. The blind man was also a ham radio operator. He talked in his loud voice about conversations he'd had with fellow operators in Guam, in the Philippines, in Alaska, and even in Tahiti. He said he'd have a lot of friends there if he ever wanted to go visit those places. From time to time, he'd turn his blind face toward me, put his hand under his beard, ask me something. How long had I been in my present position? (Three years.) Did I like my work? (I didn't.) Was I going to stay with it? (What were the options?) Finally, when I thought he was beginning to run down, I got up and turned on the TV.

My wife looked at me with irritation. She was heading toward a boil. Then she looked at the blind man and said, "Robert, do you have a TV?"

The blind man said, "My dear, I have two TVs. I have a color set and a black-and-white thing, an old relic. It's funny, but if I turn the TV on, and I'm always turning it on, I turn on the color set. It's funny, don't you think?"

I didn't know what to say to that. I had absolutely nothing to say to that. No opinion. So I watched the news program and tried to listen to what the announcer was saying.

"This is a color TV," the blind man said. "Don't ask me how, but I can tell."

"We traded up a while ago," I said.

The blind man had another taste of his drink. He lifted his beard, sniffed it, and let it fall. He leaned forward on the sofa. He positioned his ashtray on the coffee table, then put the lighter to his cigarette. He leaned back on the sofa and crossed his legs at the ankles.

My wife covered her mouth, and then she yawned. She stretched. She said, "I think I'll go upstairs and put on my robe. I think I'll change into something else. Robert, you make yourself comfortable," she said.

"I'm comfortable," the blind man said.

"I want you to feel comfortable in this house," she said.

"I am comfortable," the blind man said.

After she'd left the room, he and I listened to the weather report and then to the sports roundup. By that time, she'd been gone so long I didn't know if she was going to come back. I thought she might have gone to bed. I wished she'd come back downstairs. I didn't want to be left alone with a blind man. I asked him if he wanted another drink, and he said sure. Then I asked if he wanted to smoke some dope with me. I said I'd just rolled a number. I hadn't, but I planned to do so in about two shakes.

"I'll try some with you," he said.

"Damn right," I said. "That's the stuff."

I got our drinks and sat down on the sofa with him. Then I rolled us two fat numbers. I lit one and passed it. I brought it to his fingers. He took it and inhaled.

"Hold it as long as you can," I said. I could tell he didn't know the first thing.

My wife came back downstairs wearing her pink robe and her pink slippers.

"What do I smell?" she said.

"We thought we'd have us some cannabis," I said.

My wife gave me a savage look. Then she looked at the blind man and said, "Robert, I didn't know you smoked."

He said, "I do now, my dear. There's a first time for everything. But I don't feel anything yet."

"This stuff is pretty mellow," I said. "This stuff is mild. It's dope you can reason with," I said. "It doesn't mess you up."

"Not much it doesn't, bub," he said, and laughed.

My wife sat on the sofa between the blind man and me. I passed her the number. She took it and toked and then passed it back to me. "Which way is this going?" she said. Then she said, "I shouldn't be smoking this. I can hardly keep my eyes open as it is. That dinner did me in. I shouldn't have eaten so much."

"It was the strawberry pie," the blind man said. "That's what did it," he said, and he laughed his big laugh. Then he shook his head.

"There's more strawberry pie," I said.

"Do you want some more, Robert?" my wife said.

"Maybe in a little while," he said.

We gave our attention to the TV. My wife yawned again. She said, "Your bed is made up when you feel like going to bed, Robert. I know you must have had a long day. When you're ready to go to bed, say so." She pulled his arm. "Robert?"

He came to and said, "I've had a real nice time. This beats tapes, doesn't it?"

I said, "Coming at you," and I put the number between his fingers. He inhaled, held the smoke, and then let it go. It was like he'd been doing it since he was nine years old.

"Thanks, bub," he said. "But I think this is all for me. I think I'm beginning to feel it," he said. He held the burning roach out for my wife.

"Same here," she said. "Ditto. Me, too." She took the roach and passed it to me. "I may just sit here for a while between you two guys with my eyes closed. But don't let me bother you, okay? Either one of you. If it bothers you, say so. Otherwise, I may just sit here with my eyes closed until you're ready to go to bed," she said. "Your bed's made up, Robert, when you're ready. It's right next to our room at the top of the stairs. We'll show you up when you're ready. You wake me up now, you guys, if I fall asleep." She said that and then she closed her eyes and went to sleep.

The news program ended. I got up and changed the channel. I sat back down on the sofa. I wished my wife hadn't pooped out. Her head lay across the back of the sofa, her mouth open. She'd turned so that her robe slipped away from her legs, exposing a juicy thigh. I reached to draw her robe back over her, and it was then that I glanced at the blind man. What the hell! I flipped the robe open again.

"You say when you want some strawberry pie," I said.

"I will," he said.

I said, "Are you tired? Do you want me to take you up to your bed? Are you ready to hit the hay?"

"Not yet," he said. "No, I'll stay up with you, bub. If that's all right. I'll stay up until you're ready to turn in. We haven't had a chance to talk. Know what I mean? I feel like me and her monopolized the evening." He lifted his beard and he let it fall. He picked up his cigarettes and his lighter.

"That's all right," I said. Then I said, "I'm glad for the company."

And I guess I was. Every night I smoked dope and stayed up as long as I could before I fell asleep. My wife and I hardly ever went to bed at the same time. When I did go to sleep, I had these dreams. Sometimes I'd wake up from one of them, my heart going crazy.

Something about the church and the Middle Ages was on the TV. Not your run-of-the-mill TV fare. I wanted to watch something else. I turned to the other channels. But there was nothing on them, either. So I turned back to the first channel and apologized.

"Bub, it's all right," the blind man said. "It's fine with me. Whatever you want to watch is okay, I'm always learning something. Learning never ends. It won't hurt me to learn something tonight. I got ears," he said.

We didn't say anything for a time. He was leaning forward with his head turned at me, his right ear aimed in the direction of the set. Very disconcerting. Now and then his eyelids drooped and then they snapped open again. Now and then he put his fingers into his beard and tugged, like he was thinking about something he was hearing on the television.

On the screen, a group of men wearing cowls was being set upon and tormented by men dressed in skeleton costumes and men dressed as devils. The men dressed as devils wore devil masks, horns, and long tails. This pageant was part of a procession. The Englishman who was narrating the thing said it took place in Spain once a year. I tried to explain to the blind man what was happening.

"Skeletons," he said. "I know about skeletons," he said, and he nodded.

The TV showed this one cathedral. Then there was a long, slow look at another one. Finally, the picture switched to the famous one in Paris, with its flying buttresses and its spires reaching up to the clouds. The camera pulled away to show the whole of the cathedral rising above the skyline.

There were times when the Englishman who was telling the thing would shut up, would simply let the camera move around the cathedrals. Or else the camera would tour the countryside, men in fields walking behind oxen. I waited as long as I could. Then I felt I had to say something. I said, "They're showing the outside of this cathedral now. Gargoyles. Little statues carved to look like monsters. Now I guess they're in Italy. Yeah, they're in Italy. There's paintings on the walls of this one church."

"Are those fresco paintings, bub?" he asked, and he sipped from his drink.

I reached for my glass. But it was empty. I tried to remember what I could remember. "You're asking me are those frescoes?" I said. "That's a good question. I don't know."

The camera moved to a cathedral outside Lisbon. The differences in the Portuguese cathedral compared with the French and Italian were not that great. But they were there. Mostly the interior stuff. Then something occurred to me, and I said, "Something has occurred to me. Do you have any idea what a cathedral is? What they look like, that is? Do you follow me? If somebody says cathedral to you, do you have any notion what they're talking about? Do you know the difference between that and a Baptist church, say?"

He let the smoke dribble from his mouth. "I know they took hundreds of workers fifty or a hundred years to build," he said. "I just heard the man say that, of course. I know generations of the same families worked on a cathedral. I heard him say that, too. The men who began their life's work on them, they never lived to see the completion of their work. In that wise, bub, they're no different from the rest of us, right?" He laughed. Then his eyelids drooped again. His head nodded. He seemed to be snoozing. Maybe he was imagining himself in Portugal. The TV was showing another cathedral now. This one was in Germany. The Englishman's voice droned on. "Cathedrals," the blind man said. He sat up and rolled his head back and forth. "If you want the truth, bub, that's about all I know. What I just said. What I heard him say. But maybe you could describe one to me? I wish you'd do it. I'd like that. If you want to know. I really don't have a good idea."

I stared hard at the shot of the cathedral on the TV. How could I even begin to describe it? But say my life depended on it. Say my life was being threatened by an insane guy who said I had to do it or else.

I stared some more at the cathedral before the picture flipped off into the countryside. There was no use. I turned to the blind man and said, "To begin with, they're very tall." I was looking around the room for clues. "They reach way up. Up and up. Toward the sky. They're so big, some of them, they have to have these supports. To help hold them up, so to speak. These supports are called buttresses. They remind me of viaducts, for some reason. But maybe you don't know viaducts, either? Sometimes the cathedrals have devils and such carved into the front. Sometimes lords and ladies. Don't ask me why this is," I said.

He was nodding. The whole upper part of his body seemed to be moving back and forth.

"I'm not doing so good, am I?" I said.

He stopped nodding and leaned forward on the edge of the sofa. As he listened to me, he was running his fingers through his beard. I wasn't getting through to him, I could see that. But he waited for me to go on just the same. He nodded, like he was trying to encourage me. I tried to think what else to say. "They're really big," I said. "They're massive. They're built of stone. Marble, too, sometimes. In those olden days, when they built cathedrals, men wanted to be close to God. In those olden days, God was an important part of everyone's life. You could tell this from their cathedral-building. I'm sorry," I said, "but it looks like that's the best I can do for you. I'm just no good at it."

"That's all right, bub," the blind man said. "Hey, listen. I hope you don't mind my asking you. Can I ask you something? Let me ask you a simple question, yes or no. I'm just curious and there's no offense. You're my host. But let me ask if you are in any way religious? You don't mind my asking?"

I shook my head. He couldn't see that, though. A wink is the same as a nod to a blind man. "I guess I don't believe in it. In anything. Sometimes it's hard. You know what I'm saying?"

"Sure, I do," he said.

"Right," I said.

The Englishman was still holding forth. My wife sighed in her sleep. She drew a long breath and went on with her sleeping.

"You'll have to forgive me," I said. "But I can't tell you what a cathedral looks like. It just isn't in me to do it. I can't do any more than I've done."

The blind man sat very still, his head down, as he listened to me.

I said, "The truth is, cathedrals don't mean anything special to me. Nothing. Cathedrals. They're something to look at on late-night TV. That's all they are."

It was then that the blind man cleared his throat. He brought something up. He took a handkerchief from his back pocket. Then he said, "I get it, bub. It's okay. It happens. Don't worry about it," he said.

"Hey, listen to me. Will you do me a favor? I got an idea. Why don't you find us some heavy paper? And a pen. We'll do something. We'll draw one together. Get us a pen and some heavy paper. Go on, bub, get the stuff," he said.

So I went upstairs. My legs felt like they didn't have any strength in them. They felt like they did after I'd done some running. In my wife's room, I looked around. I found some ballpoints in a little basket on her table. And then I tried to think where to look for the kind of paper he was talking about.

Downstairs, in the kitchen. I found a shopping bag with onion skins in the bottom of the bag. I emptied the bag and shook it. I brought it into the living room and sat down with it near his legs. I moved some things, smoothed the wrinkles from the bag, spread it out on the coffee table.

The blind man got down from the sofa and sat next to me on the carpet.

He ran his fingers over the paper. He went up and down the sides of the paper. The edges, even the edges. He fingered the corners.

"All right," he said. "All right, let's do her."

He found my hand, the hand with the pen. He closed his hand over my hand. "Go ahead, bub, draw," he said. "Draw. You'll see. I'll follow along with you. It'll be okay. Just begin now like I'm telling you. You'll see. Draw," the blind man said.

So I began. First I drew a box that looked like a house. It could have been the house I lived in. Then I put a roof on it. At either end of the roof. I drew spires. Crazy.

"Swell," he said, "Terrific. You're doing fine," he said. "Never thought anything like this could happen in your lifetime, did you, bub? Well, it's a strange life, we all know that. Go on now. Keep it up."

I put in windows with arches. I drew flying buttresses. I hung great doors. I couldn't stop. The TV station went off the air. I put down the pen and closed and opened my fingers. The blind man felt around over the paper. He moved the tips of his fingers over the paper, all over what I had drawn, and he nodded.

"Doing fine," the blind man said.

I took up the pen again, and he found my hand. I kept at it. I'm no artist. But I kept drawing just the same.

My wife opened up her eyes and gazed at us. She sat up on the sofa, her robe hanging open. She said, "What are you doing? Tell me, I want to know."

I didn't answer her.

The blind man said, "We're drawing a cathedral. Me and him are working on it. Press hard," he said to me. "That's right. That's good," he said. "Sure. You got it, bub, I can tell. You didn't think you could. But you can, can't you? You're cooking with gas now. You know what I'm saying? We're going to really have us something here in a minute. How's the old arm?" he said. "Put some people in there now. What's a cathedral without people?"

My wife said, "What's going on? Robert, what are you doing? What's going on?"

"It's all right," he said to her. "Close your eyes now," the blind man said to me.

I did it. I closed them just like he said.

"Are they closed?" he said. "Don't fudge."

"They're closed," I said.

"Keep them that way," he said. He said, "Don't stop now. Draw."

So we kept on with it. His fingers rode my fingers as my hand went over the paper. It was like nothing else in my life up to now.

Then he said, "I think that's it. I think you got it," he said. "Take a look. What do you think?"

But I had my eyes closed. I thought I'd keep them that way for a little longer. I thought it was something I ought to do.

"Well?" he said. "Are you looking?"

My eyes were still closed. I was in my house. I knew that. But I didn't feel like I was inside anything.

"It's really something," I said.

—1983

Questions: Reading, Responding, Arguing

1. Describe the narrator's tone of voice. Is he reliable, or do his preconceptions about blind people limit his reliability?
2. How does jealousy figure as an element in this story? Why, exactly, is the narrator disturbed when he thinks about his wife's long friendship with Robert?
3. What is surprising about Robert as a character? How does his behavior affect the narrator?
4. Why is the story titled "Cathedral" other than the obvious reference to the television show the narrator and Robert "watch"? Does the story's conclusion contain any religious elements? Could it be argued that Carver's intent is primarily religious?

John Donne (1572–1631)

Holy Sonnet 10

Death, be not proud, though some have callèd thee
Mighty and dreadful, for thou art not so;
For those whom thou think'st thou dost overthrow
Die not, poor Death, nor yet canst thou kill me.
From rest and sleep, which but thy pictures be,   5
Much pleasure; then from thee much more must flow,
And soonest our best men with thee do go,
Rest of their bones, and soul's delivery.
Thou'art slave to fate, chance, kings, and desperate men,
And dost with poison, war, and sickness dwell,   10
And poppy° or charms can make us sleep as well
And better than thy stroke; why swell'st thou then?
One short sleep past, we wake eternally,
And death shall be no more; Death, thou shalt die.

—*1633*

Questions: Reading, Responding, Arguing

1. Analyze Donne's use of personification. What is achieved by his personifying Death?
2. How does the final couplet help emphasize Donne's themes? How does he use paradox here?
3. The speaker addresses Death directly. Explain why Donne's speaker says "Death, be not proud."

Holy Sonnet 14*

Batter my heart, three-personed God; for You
As yet but knock, breathe, shine, and seek to mend;
That I may rise, and stand, o'erthrow me, and bend
Your force to break, blow, burn, and make me new.
I, like an usurped town, to another due,   5

11 **poppy** opium

Labor to admit You, but O, to no end;
Reason, Your viceroy in me, me should defend,
But is captived, and proves weak or untrue.
Yet dearly I love You, and would be lovèd fain,°
But am betrothed unto Your enemy.   10
Divorce me, untie or break that knot again;
Take me to You, imprison me, for I,
Except You enthrall me, never shall be free,
Nor ever chaste, except You ravish me.

—1633

Questions: Reading, Responding, Arguing

1. Who is the "you" in the poem? What is the speaker's attitude toward the "you"?
2. Examine Donne's rhythm and syntax. How does the sound of the poem help convey Donne's theme?
3. This sonnet is part of a series called the Holy Sonnets. Connect this sonnet with its religious context. Explain why Donne uses a feminine persona here.

George Herbert (1593–1633)

Love (III)

Love bade me welcome: yet my soul drew back,
    Guilty of dust and sin.
But quick-eyed Love, observing me grow slack
    From my first entrance in,
Drew nearer to me, sweetly questioning   5
    If I lacked anything.

"A guest," I answered, "worthy to be here":
    Love said, "You shall be he."
"I, the unkind, ungrateful? Ah, my dear,
    I cannot look on thee."   10

9 fain gladly

Love took my hand, and smiling did reply,
  "Who made the eyes but I?"

"Truth, Lord, but I have marred them; let my shame
  Go where it doth deserve."
"And know you not," says Love, "who bore the blame?"   15
  "My dear, then I will serve."
"You must sit down," says Love, "and taste my meat."
  So I did sit and eat.

—*1633*

Questions: Reading, Responding, Arguing

1. Herbert uses dialogue in this poem. What does the dialogue contribute to this poem? Why has Herbert used dialogue? What effect does it create?
2. Compare Herbert's treatment of religion and love with another Herbert poem.
3. Construct an argument that Herbert's poem is a good example of an allegory.

Percy Bysshe Shelley (1792–1822)

Ozymandias°

I met a traveler from an antique land
Who said: Two vast and trunkless legs of stone
Stand in the desert. . . . Near them, on the sand,
Half sunk, a shattered visage lies, whose frown,
And wrinkled lip, and sneer of cold command,   5
Tell that its sculptor well those passions read
Which yet survive, stamped on these lifeless things,
The hand that mocked them, and the heart that fed:
And on the pedestal these words appear:
"My name is Ozymandias, king of kings: 10
Look on my works, ye Mighty, and despair!"
Nothing beside remains. Round the decay

Ozymandias Ramses II of Egypt (c. 1250 BC)

Of that colossal wreck, boundless and bare
The lone and level sands stretch far away.

—*1818*

Questions: Reading, Responding, Arguing

1. Why does Shelley take Ozymandias as his subject matter? What themes does he address through this character?
2. How does Shelley's language and diction help to convey his themes?
3. Explain the significance of the lines on the pedestal to the poem's themes. Argue that Shelley effectively uses several kinds of irony in the poem.

Robert Browning (1812–1889)

My Last Duchess*

FERRARA°

That's my last duchess painted on the wall,
Looking as if she were alive. I call
That piece a wonder, now: Frà Pandolf's° hands
Worked busily a day, and there she stands.
Will't please you sit and look at her? I said   5
"Frà Pandolf" by design, for never read
Strangers like you that pictured countenance,
The depth and passion of its earnest glance,
But to myself they turned (since none puts by
The curtain I have drawn for you, but I)   10
And seemed as they would ask me, if they durst,
How such a glance came there; so, not the first
Are you to turn and ask thus. Sir, 'twas not
Her husband's presence only, called that spot
Of joy into the Duchess' cheek: perhaps   15
Frà Pandolf chanced to say "Her mantle laps

Ferrara The speaker is probably Alfonso II d'Este, Duke of Ferrara (1533–158?)   **3 Frà Pandolf** an imaginary painter

Over my lady's wrist too much," or "Paint
Must never hope to reproduce the faint
Half-flush that dies along her throat": such stuff
Was courtesy, she thought, and cause enough   20
For calling up that spot of joy. She had
A heart—how shall I say?—too soon made glad,
Too easily impressed; she liked whate'er
She looked on, and her looks went everywhere.
Sir, 'twas all one! My favor at her breast,   25
The dropping of the daylight in the West,
The bough of cherries some officious fool
Broke in the orchard for her, the white mule
She rode with round the terrace—all and each
Would draw from her alike the approving speech,   30
Or blush, at least. She thanked men—good! but thanked
Somehow—I know not how—as if she ranked
My gift of a nine-hundred-years-old name
With anybody's gift. Who'd stoop to blame
This sort of trifling? Even had you skill   35
In speech—which I have not—to make your will
Quite clear to such an one, and say, "Just this
Or that in you disgusts me; here you miss,
Or there exceed the mark"—and if she let
Herself be lessoned so, nor plainly set   40
Her wits to yours, forsooth, and made excuse,
—E'en then would be some stooping; and I choose
Never to stoop. Oh sir, she smiled, no doubt,
Whene'er I passed her; but who passed without
Much the same smile? This grew; I gave commands;   45
Then all smiles stopped together. There she stands
As if alive. Will't please you rise? We'll meet
The company below, then. I repeat,
The Count your master's° known munificence
Is ample warrant that no just pretense   50
Of mine for dowry will be disallowed;
Though his fair daughter's self, as I avowed
At starting, is my object. Nay, we'll go

---

49 **Count your master's** The auditor is apparently an envoy sent to arrange a marriage between the Duke of Ferrara and a count's daughter.

Together down, sir. Notice Neptune, though,
Taming a sea horse, thought a rarity, 55
Which Claus of Innsbruck cast in bronze for me!

—*1842*

Questions: Reading, Responding, Arguing

1. Browning is a master of the dramatic monologue form. How is "My Last Duchess" a good example of his skill at the form?
2. What is the speaker's attitude toward the Duchess? How does Browning convey this to the reader?
3. Is the speaker in the poem a reliable or an unreliable source of information about the Duchess? Argue why or why not. To whom is he telling the account of his marriage and what are his motives for doing so?

Christina Rossetti (1830–1894)

Up-Hill

Does the road wind up-hill all the way?
    Yes, to the very end.
Will the day's journey take the whole long day?
    From morn to night, my friend.

But is there for the night a resting-place?
    A roof for when the slow dark hours begin.
May not the darkness hide it from my face?
    You cannot miss that inn.

Shall I meet other wayfarers at night?
    Those who have gone before. 10
Then must I knock, or call when just in sight?
    They will not keep you waiting at that door.

Shall I find comfort, travel-sore and weak?
    Of labor you shall find the sum.
Will there be beds for me and all who seek? 15
    Yea, beds for all who come.

—*1858*

Questions: Reading, Responding, Arguing

1. Identify the two voices who speak in the poem. What does each represent?
2. What does the road in this poem represent?
3. Examine Rossetti's use of questions and answers. How do these convey the poem's theme or meaning?
4. Argue that the symbolic significance of the inn must be read in an allegorical context.

William Butler Yeats (1865–1939)

Leda° and the Swan

A sudden blow: the great wings beating still
Above the staggering girl, her thighs caressed
By the dark webs, her nape caught in his bill,
He holds her helpless breast upon his breast.

How can those terrified vague fingers push   5
The feathered glory from her loosening thighs?
And how can body, laid in that white rush,
But feel the strange heart beating where it lies?

A shudder in the loins engenders there
The broken wall, the burning roof and tower   10
And Agamemnon dead.
                Being so caught up,
So mastered by the brute blood of the air,
Did she put on his knowledge with his power
Before the indifferent beak could let her drop?

—1923

Questions: Reading, Responding, Arguing

1. Analyze Yeats's choice of words regarding the swan. What tone does he create?

Leda mortal mother of Helen of Troy and Clytemnestra, wife and assassin of Agamemnon

2. Examine Yeats's rhyme scheme. How does he use it to help develop his themes?
3. Compare Yeats's poem with the myth of Leda. How is Yeats's telling of the story similar? Different?

Wilfred Owen (1893–1918)

Dulce et Decorum Est°

Bent double, like old beggars under sacks,
Knock-kneed, coughing like hags, we cursed through sludge,
Till on the haunting flares we turned our backs
And towards our distant rest began to trudge.
Men marched asleep. Many had lost their boots   5
But limped on, blood-shod. All went lame; all blind;
Drunk with fatigue; deaf even to the hoots
Of tired, outstripped Five-Nines° that dropped behind.

Gas! Gas! Quick, boys!—An ecstasy of fumbling
Fitting the clumsy helmets just in time;   10
But someone still was yelling out and stumbling
And flound'ring like a man in fire or lime . . .
Dim, through the misty panes and thick green light,°
As under a green sea, I saw him drowning.

In all my dreams, before my helpless sight,   15
He plunges at me, guttering, choking, drowning.

If in some smothering dreams you too could pace
Behind the wagon that we flung him in,
And watch the white eyes writhing in his face,
His hanging face, like a devil's sick of sin;   20
If you could hear, at every jolt, the blood
Come gargling from the froth-corrupted lungs,
Obscene as cancer, bitter as the cud
Of vile, incurable sores on innocent tongues,—

Dulce et Decorum Est (pro patria mori) from the Roman poet Horace: "It is sweet and proper to die for one's country"   8 Five-Nines German artillery shells (59 mm)   13 misty panes and thick green light i.e., through the gas mask

My friend,° you would not tell with such high zest   25
To children ardent for some desperate glory,
The old Lie: Dulce et decorum est
Pro patria mori.

—*1920*

Questions: Reading, Responding, Arguing

1. Describe the effect of Owen's title on the mood or tone of the poem.
2. Analyze the way in which Owen's words create rhythm and sound. How does sound help him create and convey theme and meaning?
3. Why does Owen use "I," "me," "you," and "us"?
4. Compare this poem with another selection in this anthology about war. Is that selection similarly antiwar? Or does it contain a justification of war?

---

e. e. cummings (1894–1962)

pity this busy monster,manunkind

pity this busy monster,manunkind,

not. Progress is a comfortable disease:
your victim (death and life safely beyond)

plays with the bigness of his littleness
—electrons° deify one razorblade   5
into a mountainrange; lenses extend

unwish through curving wherewhen till unwish
returns on its unself.
                          A world of made
is not a world of born—pity poor flesh

---

25 **My friend** The poem was originally addressed to Jessie Pope, a writer of patriotic verse.
5 **electrons** in an electron microscope

and trees,poor stars and stones,but never this   10
fine specimen of hypermagical
ultraomnipotence. We doctors know

a hopeless case if—listen: there's a hell
of a good universe next door; let's go

—1944

Questions: Reading, Responding, Arguing

1. How would you describe the poem's language? Characterize how cummings uses or subverts language, punctuation, and language conventions.
2. Compare this poem's style with another of cummings's poems. Are the styles different or similar? How do the styles affect meaning in the poems?
3. How does cummings observe the conventions of the sonnet here?
4. What does the poet mean when he says, "electrons deify one razorblade / into a mountainrange"? What is he describing?
5. The poem contains a key oxymoron: "progress is a comfortable disease." Explain the implications of this statement and how they are supported by cummings's ironic tone of voice.

Stevie Smith (1902–1971)

Our Bog Is Dood

Our Bog is dood, our Bog is dood,
They lisped in accents mild,
But when I asked them to explain
They grew a little wild.
How do you know your Bog is dood   5
My darling little child?

We know because we wish it so
That is enough, they cried,
And straight within each infant eye
Stood up the flame of pride,   10

And if you do not think it so
You shall be crucified.

Then tell me, darling little ones,
What's dood, suppose Bog is?
Just what we think, the answer came,   15
Just what we think it is.
They bowed their heads. Our Bog is ours
And we are wholly his.

But when they raised them up again
They had forgotten me   20
Each one upon each other glared
In pride and misery
For what was dood, and what their Bog
They never could agree.

Oh sweet it was to leave them then,   25
And sweeter not to see,
And sweetest of all to walk alone
Beside the encroaching sea,
The sea that soon should drown them all,
That never yet drowned me.   30

—1950

Questions: Reading, Responding, Arguing

1. What effect would replacing "bog" and "dood" with the
   "real" words have on the poem?
2. Who are the "children" in the poem and in what sense are
   they childlike?
3. Smith once described herself as "an Anglican (Church of
   England) agnostic." How is this oxymoron reflected in the
   poem, especially at its ending? Argue that Smith's view of religion is implicit in the whole poem.

William Stafford (1914–1993)

Traveling Through the Dark

Traveling through the dark I found a deer
dead on the edge of the Wilson River road.
It is usually best to roll them into the canyon:
that road is narrow; to swerve might make more dead.

By glow of the tail-light I stumbled back of the car   5
and stood by the heap, a doe, a recent killing;
she had stiffened already, almost cold.
I dragged her off; she was large in the belly.

My fingers touching her side brought me the reason—
her side was warm; her fawn lay there waiting,   10
alive, still, never to be born.
Beside that mountain road I hesitated.

The car aimed ahead its lowered parking lights;
under the hood purred the steady engine.
I stood in the glare of the warm exhaust turning red;   15
around our group I could hear the wilderness listen.

I thought hard for us all—my only swerving—
then pushed her over the edge into the river.

—*1960*

Questions: Reading, Responding, Arguing

1. Analyze Stafford's choice of diction. How does it convey the speaker's thoughts about the deer?
2. What's the significance of Stafford's lines "I could hear the wilderness listen / I thought hard for us all"?
3. Discuss how themes of life and death are addressed in this poem. Is it possible to argue that the poet did not make the correct decision?

Gwendolyn Brooks (1917–2000)

the mother*

Abortions will not let you forget.
You remember the children you got that you did not get,
The damp small pulps with a little or with no hair,
The singers and workers that never handled the air.
You will never neglect or beat   5
them, or silence or buy with a sweet.
You will never wind up the sucking-thumb
Or scuttle off ghosts that come.
You will never leave them, controlling your luscious sigh,
Return for a snack of them, with gobbling mother-eye.   10

I have heard in the voices of the wind the voices of my dim killed
        children.
I have contracted. I have eased
My dim dears at the breasts they could never suck.
I have said, Sweets, if I sinned, if I seized
Your luck   15
And your lives from your unfinished reach,
If I stole your births and your names,
Your straight baby tears and your games,
Your stilted or lovely loves, your tumults, your marriages, aches, and
        your deaths,
If I poisoned the beginnings of your breaths,   20
Believe that even in my deliberateness I was not deliberate.
Though why should I whine,
Whine that the crime was other than mine?—
Since anyhow you are dead.
Or rather, or instead,   25
You were never made.
But that too, I am afraid,
Is faulty: oh, what shall I say, how is the truth to be said?
You were born, you had body, you died.
It is just that you never giggled or planned or cried.   30

Believe me, I loved you all.
Believe me, I knew you, though faintly, and I loved, I loved you
All.

—*1945*

Questions: Reading, Responding, Arguing

1. Brooks's poem is about a highly emotional subject. How does Brooks convey the speaker's emotions? How does she use detail to create an effect of sadness and loss?
2. What impact does Brooks's use of "I" and "you" have on the poem?
3. What does Brooks attempt to say about motherhood and love in this poem? How does the ironic title emphasize her belief? Construct an argument challenging or defending the persona's definition of love.

Carolyn Kizer (b. 1925)

The Ungrateful Garden

Midas watched the golden crust
That formed over his streaming sores,
Hugged his agues, loved his lust,
But damned to hell the out-of-doors

Where blazing motes of sun impaled   5
The serried° roses, metal-bright.
"Those famous flowers," Midas wailed,
"Have scorched my retina with light."

This gift, he'd thought, would gild his joys,
Silt up the waters of his grief;
His lawns a wilderness of noise,   10
The heavy clang of leaf on leaf.

Within, the golden cup is good
To heft, to sip the yellow mead.
Outside, in summer's rage, the rude   15
Gold thorn has made his fingers bleed.

6 serried crowded in rows

"I strolled my halls in golden shift,
As ruddy as a lion's meat.
Then I rushed out to share my gift,
And golden stubble cut my feet."   20

Dazzled with wounds, he limped away
To climb into his golden bed.
Roses, roses can betray.
"Nature is evil," Midas said.

                                                        —1961

Questions: Reading, Responding, Arguing

1. Who is Midas and what stories are connected with him?
   Why does Kizer choose Midas as her central character?
2. How does Kizer use irony?
3. Why is the garden "ungrateful"?
4. Why has this poem often been read as a parable with ecological overtones? Argue that the last line makes it important to
   do so.

Maxine Kumin (b. 1925)

Woodchucks

Gassing the woodchucks didn't turn out right.
The knockout bomb from the Feed and Grain Exchange
was featured as merciful, quick at the bone
and the case we had against them was airtight,
both exits shoehorned shut with puddingstone,   5
but they had a sub-sub-basement out of range.

Next morning they turned up again, no worse
for the cyanide than we for our cigarettes
and state-store Scotch, all of us up to scratch.
They brought down the marigolds as a matter of course   10
and then took over the vegetable patch
nipping the broccoli shoots, beheading the carrots.

The food from our mouths, I said, righteously thrilling
to the feel of the .22, the bullets' neat noses.
I, a lapsed pacifist fallen from grace   15
puffed with Darwinian pieties for killing,
now drew a bead on the littlest woodchuck's face.
He died down in the everbearing roses.

Ten minutes later I dropped the mother. She
flipflopped in the air and fell, her needle teeth   20
still hooked in a leaf of early Swiss chard.
Another baby next. O one-two-three
the murderer inside me rose up hard,
the hawkeye killer came on stage forthwith.

There's one chuck left. Old wily fellow, he keeps   25
me cocked and ready day after day after day.
All night I hunt his humped-up form. I dream
I sight along the barrel in my sleep.
If only they'd all consented to die unseen
gassed underground the quiet Nazi way.   30

—*1982*

Questions: Reading, Responding, Arguing

1. How does Kumin morally justify trying to exterminate the woodchucks?
2. What does she mean when she describes herself as "a lapsed pacifist fallen from grace / puffed with Darwinian pieties for killing"?
3. How are the victims "humanized" in the poem?
4. Kumin has often written about her identity as a Jew. Is this sense of identity important here? Argue your response.

James Merrill (1926–1995)

Casual Wear

Your average tourist: Fifty. 2.3
Times married. Dressed, this year, in Ferdi Plinthbower°
Originals. Odds 1 to 9^{10}°
Against her strolling past the Embassy

Today at noon. Your average terrorist: 5
Twenty-five. Celibate. No use for trends,
At least in clothing. Mark, though, where it ends.
People have come forth made of colored mist

Unsmiling on one hundred million screens
To tell of his prompt phone call to the station,   10
"Claiming responsibility"—devastation
Signed with a flourish, like the dead wife's jeans.

—*1984*

Questions: Reading, Responding, Arguing

1. Note Merrill's use of rhymes in the poem. Are they effective?
2. What does the phrase "average tourist" mean, especially in "2.3 times married"?
3. What is ironic about the phrase "claiming responsibility"?
4. How can there be such a thing as an "average terrorist"? Does the terrorist fit any cultural or political stereotype? How has this poem grown more relevant in the years since its publication?

---

2 Ferdi Plinthbower a fictional designer   3 1 to 9^{10} pronounced "one to nine to the tenth power"

W. S. Merwin (b. 1927)

The Last One

Well they'd made up their minds to be everywhere because why not.
Everywhere was theirs because they thought so.
They with two leaves they whom the birds despise.
In the middle of stones they made up their minds.
They started to cut.   5

Well they cut everything because why not.
Everything was theirs because they thought so.
It fell into its shadows and they took both away.
Some to have some for burning.

Well cutting everything they came to the water.   10
They came to the end of the day there was one left standing.
They would cut it tomorrow they went away.
The night gathered in the last branches.
The shadow of the night gathered in the shadow on the water.
The night and the shadow put on the same head.   15
And it said Now.

Well in the morning they cut the last one.
Like the others the last one fell into its shadow.
It fell into its shadow on the water.
They took it away its shadow stayed on the water.   20

Well they shrugged they started trying to get the shadow away.
They cut right to the ground the shadow stayed whole.
They laid boards on it the shadow came out on top.
They shone lights on it the shadow got blacker and clearer.
They exploded the water the shadow rocked.   25
They built a huge fire on the roots.
They sent up black smoke between the shadow and the sun.
The new shadow flowed without changing the old one.
They shrugged they went away to get stones.

They came back the shadow was growing.   30
They started setting up stones it was growing.
They looked the other way it went on growing.

They decided they would make a stone out of it.
They took stones to the water they poured them into the shadow.
They poured them in they poured them in the stones vanished.   35
The shadow was not filled it went on growing.
That was one day.

The next day was just the same it went on growing.
They did all the same things it was just the same.
They decided to take its water from under it.   40
They took away water they took it away the water went down.
The shadow stayed where it was before.
It went on growing it grew onto the land.
They started to scrape the shadow with machines.
When it touched the machines it stayed on them.   45
They started to beat the shadow with sticks.
Where it touched the sticks it stayed on them.
They started to beat the shadow with hands.
Where it touched the hands it stayed on them.
That was another day.   50

Well the next day started about the same it went on growing.
They pushed lights into the shadow.
Where the shadow got onto them they went out.
They began to stomp on the edge it got their feet.
And when it got their feet they fell down.   55
It got into eyes the eyes went blind.
The ones that fell down it grew over and they vanished.
The ones that went blind and walked into it vanished.
The ones that could see and stood still
It swallowed their shadows.   60
Then it swallowed them too and they vanished.
Well the others ran.

The ones that were left went away to live if it would let them.
They went as far as they could.
The lucky ones with their shadows.   65

—*1969*

Questions: Reading, Responding, Arguing

1. What is the "last one"? What is significant or symbolic about it? Why is it the title of the poem?
2. Explain why Merwin repeats "Well" and "They."
3. How does Merwin use blindness and shadow? Argue that his uses of these key terms are not just literal.

James Wright (1927–1980)

Saint Judas

When I went out to kill myself, I caught
A pack of hoodlums beating up a man.
Running to spare his suffering, I forgot
My name, my number, how my day began,
How soldiers milled around the garden stone   5
And sang amusing songs; how all that day
Their javelins measured crowds; how I alone
Bargained the proper coins, and slipped away.

Banished from heaven, I found this victim beaten,
Stripped, kneed, and left to cry. Dropping my rope   10
Aside, I ran, ignored the uniforms:
Then I remembered bread my flesh had eaten,
The kiss that ate my flesh. Flayed without hope,
I held the man for nothing in my arms.

—*1959*

Questions: Reading, Responding, Arguing

1. Who is Saint Judas? Why is this the title of the poem?
2. Explain the connections between the first and last lines. What is the progression from the first line to the last line?
3. Is there an example of epiphany in this poem? What is it? How does the speaker arrive at it? What is the result of the epiphany?

Mary Oliver (b. 1935)

The Black Walnut Tree

My mother and I debate:
we could sell
the black walnut tree
to the lumberman,
and pay off the mortgage.   5
Likely some storm anyway
will churn down its dark boughs,
smashing the house. We talk
slowly, two women trying
in a difficult time to be wise.   10
Roots in the cellar drains,
I say, and she replies
that the leaves are getting heavier
every year, and the fruit
harder to gather away.   15
But something brighter than money
moves in our blood—an edge
sharp and quick as a trowel
that wants us to dig and sow.
So we talk, but we don't do   20
anything. That night I dream
of my fathers out of Bohemia
filling the blue fields
of fresh and generous Ohio
with leaves and vines and orchards. 25
What my mother and I both know
is that we'd crawl with shame
in the emptiness we'd made
in our own and our fathers' backyard.
So the black walnut tree   30
swings through another year
of sun and leaping winds,
of leaves and bounding fruit,
and, month after month, the whip-
crack of the mortgage.   35

—1979

Questions: Reading, Responding, Arguing

1. Oliver writes "We talk / slowly, two women / trying in a difficult time to be wise." Why does she describe the women this way?
2. Why does the dream change the speaker's mind? What is the dream telling her?
3. What does the tree represent? Explain why it is symbolic.

Marge Piercy (b. 1936)

What's That Smell in the Kitchen?

All over America women are burning dinners.
It's lambchops in Peoria; it's haddock
in Providence; it's steak in Chicago;
tofu delight in Big Sur; red
rice and beans in Dallas.   5
All over America women are burning
food they're supposed to bring with calico
smile on platters glittering like wax.
Anger sputters in her brainpan, confined
but spewing out missiles of hot fat.   10
Carbonized despair presses like a clinker
from a barbecue against the back of her eyes.
If she wants to grill anything, it's
her husband spitted over a slow fire.
If she wants to serve him anything   15
it's a dead rat with a bomb in its belly
ticking like the heart of an insomniac.
Her life is cooked and digested,
nothing but leftovers in Tupperware.
Look, she says, once I was roast duck   20
on your platter with parsley but now I am Spam.
Burning dinner is not incompetence but war.

—1982

Questions: Reading, Responding, Arguing

1. What is ironic about the poem's title? Under what circumstances and by whom would the question ordinarily be asked?
2. Why is the enjambment at the end of line 6 effective?
3. What are the implications of the poem's final five lines? Argue that the theme of "war" is implied throughout the poem.

Yusef Komunyakaa (b. 1947)

Facing It

My black face fades,
hiding inside the black granite.
I said I wouldn't,
dammit: No tears.
I'm stone. I'm flesh.   5
My clouded reflection eyes me
like a bird of prey, the profile of night
slanted against morning. I turn
this way—the stone lets me go.
I turn this way—I'm inside   10
the Vietnam Veterans Memorial
again, depending on the light
to make a difference.
I go down the 58,022 names,
half-expecting to find   15
my own in letters like smoke.
I touch the name Andrew Johnson;
I see the booby trap's white flash.
Names shimmer on a woman's blouse
but when she walks away   20
the names stay on the wall.
Brushstrokes flash, a red bird's
wings cutting across my stare.
The sky. A plane in the sky.
A white vet's image floats   25
closer to me, then his pale eyes

look through mine. I'm a window.
He's lost his right arm
inside the stone. In the black mirror
a woman's trying to erase names: 30
No, she's brushing a boy's hair.

—*1988*

Questions: Reading, Responding, Arguing

1. The title has several levels to it. What are those levels?
2. How does Komunyakaa describe the Vietnam Veteran's Memorial? How is he able to convey the poem's theme through this description?
3. From this speaker's point of view, what is the impact of war?
4. Compare this poem with another writing about war in this anthology. How do they both reflect the importance of memory? What do they imply about the emotions of war's survivors?

Julie Kane (b. 1952)

Alan Doll Rap

When I was ten
I wanted a Ken
to marry Barbie
I was into patriarchy
for plastic dolls   5
eleven inches tall
cuz the sixties hadn't yet
happened at all
Those demonstrations
assassinations   10
conflagrations across the nation
still nothin but a speck in the imagination
Yeah, Ken was the man
but my mama had the cash
and the boy doll she bought me   15

was ersatz
"Alan" was his name
from the discount store
He cost a dollar ninety-nine
Ken was two dollars more   20
Alan's hair was felt
stuck on with cheap glue
like the top of a pool table
scuffed up by cues
and it fell out in patches   25
when he was brand new
Ken's hair was plastic
molded in waves
coated with paint
no Ken bad-hair days   30
Well they wore the same size
and they wore the same clothes
but Ken was a player
and Alan was a boze
Barbie looked around   35
at all the other Barbies
drivin up in Dream Cars
at the Ken-and-Barbie party
and knew life had dealt her
a jack, not a king   40
knew if Alan bought her
an engagement ring
it wouldn't scratch glass
bet your ass
no class   45
made of cubic zirconia
or cubic Plexiglas
Kens would move Barbies
out of their townhouses
into their dreamhouses   50
Pepto-Bismal pink
from the rugs to the sink
wrap her in mink
but Alan was a bum
Our doll was not dumb   55

She knew a fronter from a chum
Take off that tuxedo
Alan would torpedo
for the Barcalounger
Bye-bye libido   60
Hello VCR
No job, no car
Drinkin up her home bar
Stinkin up her boudoir with his cigar
Shrinkin up the line of cash   65
on her MasterCard
Till she'd be pleading:
"Where's that giant *hand*
used to make him *stand,*
used to make him *walk?*"   70

—*2004*

Questions: Reading, Responding, Arguing

1. How do rhythm and rhyme work in rap? Could this poem
   be rapped effectively?
2. What is the difference between the Alan doll and the other
   dolls mentioned in the poem?
3. Argue that the symbolism of the Alan doll reveals much
   about childhood expectations and adult realities.

Shakespeare (1564–1616)

The Tragedy of Hamlet, Prince of Denmark*

Edited by David Bevington

DRAMATIS PERSONAE

Ghost of Hamlet, *the former King of Denmark*
Claudius, *King of Denmark, the former King's brother*
Gertrude, *Queen of Denmark, widow of the former King and
    now wife of Claudius*
Hamlet, *Prince of Denmark, son of the late King and of Gertrude*
Polonius, *councillor to the King*
Laertes, *his son*
Ophelia, *his daughter*
Reynaldo, *his servant*
Horatio, *Hamlet's friend and fellow student*
Voltimand,
Cornelius,
Rosencrantz,
Guildenstern, } *members of the Danish court*
Osric,
A gentleman,
A lord,
Bernardo,
Francisco, } *officers and soldiers on watch*
Marcellus,
Fortinbras, *Prince of Norway*
Captain in his army
Three or Four players, *taking the roles of Prologue, Player King,
    Player Queen, and Lucianus*
Two messengers
First sailor
Two clowns, *a gravedigger and his companion*
Priest

First ambassador from England
Lords, Soldiers, Attendants, Guards, other Players, Followers of
Laertes, other Sailors, another Ambassador or Ambassadors from
England

ACT I

SCENE I [ELSINORE CASTLE. A GUARD PLATFORM.]

Enter Bernardo and Francisco, two sentinels [meeting].

BERNARDO: Who's there?
FRANCISCO: Nay, answer me.° Stand and unfold yourself.°
BERNARDO: Long live the King!
FRANCISCO: Bernardo?
BERNARDO: He. 5
FRANCISCO: You come most carefully upon your hour.
BERNARDO: 'Tis now struck twelve. Get thee to bed, Francisco.
FRANCISCO: For this relief much thanks. 'Tis bitter cold,
And I am sick at heart.
BERNARDO: Have you had quiet guard? 10
FRANCISCO: Not a mouse stirring.
BERNARDO: Well, good night.
If you do meet Horatio and Marcellus,
The rivals° of my watch, bid them make haste.

Enter Horatio and Marcellus.

FRANCISCO: I think I hear them.—Stand, ho! Who is there? 15
HORATIO: Friends to this ground.°
MARCELLUS: And liegemen to the Dane.°
FRANCISCO: Give° you good night.
MARCELLUS: O, farewell, honest soldier. Who hath relieved you?
FRANCISCO: Bernardo hath my place. Give you good night. 20

Exit Francisco.

MARCELLUS: Holla! Bernardo!
BERNARDO: Say, what, is Horatio there?
HORATIO: A piece of him.
BERNARDO: Welcome, Horatio. Welcome, good Marcellus.
HORATIO: What, has this thing appeared again tonight? 25

2 **me** (Francisco emphasizes that he is the sentry currently on watch.); **unfold yourself** reveal your identity.   14 **rivals** partners.   16 **ground** ground, land.   17 **liegemen to the Dane** men sworn to serve the Danish king.   18 **Give** i.e., may God give.

BERNARDO: I have seen nothing.
MARCELLUS: Horatio says 'tis but our fantasy,°
And will not let belief take hold of him
Touching this dreaded sight twice seen of us.
Therefore I have entreated him along°   30
With us to watch° the minutes of this night,
That if again this apparition come
He may approve° our eyes and speak to it.
HORATIO: Tush, tush, 'twill not appear.
BERNARDO: Sit down awhile,
And let us once again assail your ears,   35
That are so fortified against our story,
What° we have two nights seen.
HORATIO: Well, sit we down,
And let us hear Bernardo speak of this.
BERNARDO: Last night of all,°
When yond same star that's westward from the pole°   40
Had made his° course t' illume° that part of heaven
Where now it burns, Marcellus and myself,
The bell then beating one—

Enter Ghost.

MARCELLUS: Peace, break thee off! Look where it comes again!
BERNARDO: In the same figure like the King that's dead.   45
MARCELLUS: Thou art a scholar.° Speak to it, Horatio.
BERNARDO: Looks 'a° not like the King? Mark it, Horatio.
HORATIO: Most like. It harrows me with fear and wonder.
BERNARDO: It would be spoke to.°
MARCELLUS: Speak to it, Horatio.
HORATIO: What art thou that usurp'st° this time of night,   50
Together with that fair and warlike form
In which the majesty of buried Denmark°
Did sometime° march? By heaven, I charge thee, speak!
MARCELLUS: It is offended.
BERNARDO: See, it stalks away.
HORATIO: Stay! Speak, speak! I charge thee, speak!   *Exit Ghost.* 55

---

27 fantasy imagination.   **30 along** to come along.   **31 watch** keep watch during.   **33 approve** corroborate.   **37 What** with what.   **39 Last . . . all** i.e., this very last night (emphatic).   **40 pole** Pole Star, North Star.   **41 his** its;   **illume** illuminate.   **46 scholar** one learned enough to know how to question a ghost properly.   **47 'a** he.   **49 It . . . to** (It was commonly believed that a ghost could not speak until spoken to.)   **50 usurp'st** wrongfully takes over.   **52 buried Denmark** the buried King of Denmark.   **53 sometime** formerly.

MARCELLUS: 'Tis gone and will not answer.

BERNARDO: How now, Horatio? You tremble and look pale.
Is not this something more than fantasy?
What think you on 't?°

HORATIO: Before my God, I might not this believe 60
Without the sensible° and true avouch°
Of mine own eyes.

MARCELLUS: Is it not like the King?

HORATIO: As thou art to thyself.
Such was the very armor he had on
When he the ambitious Norway° combated. 65
So frowned he once when, in an angry parle,°
He smote the sledded° Polacks° on the ice.
'Tis strange.

MARCELLUS: Thus twice before, and jump° at this dead hour,
With martial stalk° hath he gone by our watch. 70

HORATIO: In what particular thought to work° I know not,
But in the gross and scope° of mine opinion
This bodes some strange eruption to our state.

MARCELLUS: Good now,° sit down, and tell me, he that knows,
Why this same strict and most observant watch 75
So nightly toils° the subject° of the land,
And why such daily cast° of brazen cannon
And foreign mart° for implements of war,
Why such impress° of shipwrights, whose sore task
Does not divide the Sunday from the week. 80
What might be toward,° that this sweaty haste
Doth make the night joint-laborer with the day?
Who is 't that can inform me?

HORATIO: That can I;
At least, the whisper goes so. Our last king,
Whose image even but now appeared to us, 85
Was, as you know, by Fortinbras of Norway,
Thereto° pricked on° by a most emulate° pride,
Dared to the combat; in which our valiant Hamlet—

---

59 **on 't** of it. 61 **sensible** confirmed by the sense; **avouch** warrant evidence. 65 **Norway** King of Norway. 66 **parle** parley. 67 **sledded** traveling on sleds; **Polacks** Poles. 69 **jump** exactly. 70 **stalk** stride. 71 **to work** i.e., to collect my thoughts and try to understand this. 72 **gross and scope** general drift. 74 **Good now** (An expression denoting entreaty or expostulation.) 76 **toils** causes to toil; **subject** subjects. 77 **cast** casting. 78 **mart** buying and selling. 79 **impress** impressment, conscription. 81 **toward** in preparation. 87 **Thereto . . . pride** (Refers to old Fortinbras, not the Danish King.) **pricked on** incited. **emulate** emulous, ambitious

For so this side of our known world° esteemed him—
Did slay this Fortinbras; who by a sealed° compact   90
Well ratified by law and heraldry
Did forfeit, with his life, all those his lands
Which he stood seized° of, to the conqueror;
Against the° which a moiety competent°
Was gagèd° by our king, which had returned°   95
To the inheritance° of Fortinbras
Had he been vanquisher, as, by the same cov'nant°
And carriage of the article designed,°
His fell to Hamlet. Now, sir, young Fortinbras,
Of unimprovèd mettle° hot and full,   100
Hath in the skirts° of Norway here and there
Sharked up° a list° of lawless resolutes°
For food and diet° to some enterprise
That hath a stomach° in 't, which is no other—
As it doth well appear unto our state—   105
But to recover of us, by strong hand
And terms compulsatory, those foresaid lands
So by his father lost. And this, I take it,
Is the main motive of our preparations,
The source of this our watch, and the chief head°   110
Of this posthaste and rummage° in the land.
BERNARDO: I think it be no other but e'en so.
Well may it sort° that this portentous figure
Comes armèd through our watch so like the King
That was and is the question° of these wars.   115
HORATIO: A mote° it is to trouble the mind's eye.
In the most high and palmy° state of Rome,
A little ere the mightiest Julius fell,
The graves stood tenantless, and the sheeted° dead
Did squeak and gibber in the Roman streets;   120

---

89 this . . . world i.e., all Europe, the Western world.   **90 sealed** certified, confirmed.   **93 seized** possessed.   **94 Against the** in return for;   **moiety competent** corresponding portion.   **95 gagèd** engaged, pledged;   **had returned** would have passed.   **96 inheritance** possession.   **97 cov'nant** i.e., the sealed compact on line 90.   **98 carriage . . . designed** carrying out of the article or clause drawn up to cover the point.   **100 unimprovèd mettle** untried, undisciplined spirits.   **101 skirts** outlying regions, outskirts.   **102 Sharked up** gathered up, as a shark takes fish;   **list** i.e., troop;   **resolutes** desperadoes.   **103 For Food and diet** i.e., they are to serve as food, or "means," to some enterprises; also they serve in return for the rations they get.   **104 stomach** (1) a spirit of daring (2) an appetite that is fed by the **lawless resolutes**.   **110 head** source.   **111 rummage** bustle, commotion.   **113 sort** suit.   **115 question** focus of contention.   **116 mote** speck of dust.   **117 palmy** flourishing.   **119 sheeted** shrouded.

As° stars with trains° of fire and dews of blood,
Disasters° in the sun; and the moist star°
Upon whose influence Neptune's° empire stands°
Was sick almost to doomsday° with eclipse.
And even the like precurse° of feared events,   125
As harbingers° preceding still° the fates
And prologue to the omen° coming on,
Have heaven and earth together demonstrated
Unto our climatures° and countrymen.

Enter Ghost.

But soft,° behold! Lo, where it comes again!   130
I'll cross° it, though it blast° me. [*It spreads his° arms.*] Stay, illusion!
If thou hast any sound or use of voice,
Speak to me!
If there be any good thing to be done
That may to thee do ease and grace to me,   135
Speak to me!
If thou art privy to° thy country's fate,
Which, happily,° foreknowing may avoid,
O, speak!
Or if thou hast uphoarded in thy life   140
Extorted treasure in the womb of earth,
For which, they say, you spirits oft walk in death,
Speak of it! [*The cock crows.*] Stay and speak!—Stop it, Marcellus.
MARCELLUS: Shall I strike at it with my partisan?°
HORATIO: Do, if it will not stand.   [*They strike at it.*] 145
BERNARDO: 'Tis here!
HORATIO: 'Tis here!   [*Exit Ghost.*]
MARCELLUS: 'Tis gone.
We do it wrong, being so majestical,
To offer it the show of violence,   150
For it is as the air invulnerable,
And our vain blows malicious mockery.
BERNARDO: It was about to speak when the cock crew.
HORATIO: And then it started like a guilty thing

---

121 As (This abrupt transition suggests that matter is possibly omitted between lines 120 and 121.);
trains trails.   122 Disasters unfavorable signs or aspects;   **moist star** i.e., moon, governing tides.
123 Neptune god of the sea;   **stands** depends.   124 sick . . . doomsday (See Matthew 24:29 and
Revelation 6:12.)   125 precurse heralding, foreshadowing.   126 harbingers forerunners;   **still**
continually.   127 omen calamitous event.   129 climatures regions.   130 soft i.e., enough, break
off.   131 cross stand in its path, confront;   **blast** wither, strike with a curse;   **s.d. his** its.   137
privy to in on the secret of.   138 happily haply, perchance.   144 partisan long-handled spear.

Upon a fearful summons. I have heard   155
The cock, that is the trumpet° to the morn,
Doth with his lofty and shrill-sounding throat
Awake the god of day, and at his warning,
Whether in sea or fire, in earth or air,
Th' extravagant and erring° spirit hies°   160
To his confine; and of the truth herein
This present object made probation.°

MARCELLUS: It faded on the crowing of the cock.
Some say that ever 'gainst° that season comes
Wherein our Savior's birth is celebrated,   165
This bird of dawning singeth all night long,
And then, they say, no spirit dare stir abroad;
The nights are wholesome, then no planets strike,°
No fairy takes,° nor witch hath power to charm,
So hallowed and so gracious° is that time.   170

HORATIO: So have I heard and do in part believe it.
But, look, the morn in russet mantle clad
Walks o'er the dew of yon high eastward hill.
Break we our watch up, and by my advice
Let us impart what we have seen tonight   175
Unto young Hamlet; for upon my life,
This spirit, dumb to us, will speak to him.
Do you consent we shall acquaint him with it,
As needful in our loves, fitting our duty?

MARCELLUS: Let's do 't, I pray, and I this morning know   180
Where we shall find him most conveniently.

Exeunt.

SCENE II [THE CASTLE.]

Flourish. Enter Claudius, King of Denmark, Gertrude the Queen,
[the] Council, as° Polonius and his son Laertes, Hamlet, cum aliis°
[including Voltimand and Cornelius].

KING: Though yet of Hamlet our° dear brother's death
The memory be green, and that it us befitted
To bear our hearts in grief and our whole kingdom
To be contracted in one brow of woe,

---

156 **trumpet** trumpeter.   160 **extravagant and erring** wandering beyond bounds. (The words have similar meaning.);   **hies** hastens.   162 **probation** proof.   164 **'gainst** just before.   168 **strike** destroy by evil influence.   169 **takes** bewitches.   170 **gracious** full of grace.   **s.d. as** i.e., such as, including;   **cum aliis** with others.   1 **our** my. (The royal "we"; also in the following lines.)

Yet so far hath discretion fought with nature 5
That we with wisest sorrow think on him
Together with remembrance of ourselves.
Therefore our sometime° sister, now our queen,
Th' imperial jointress° to this warlike state,
Have we, as 'twere with a defeated joy— 10
With an auspicious and a dropping eye,°
With mirth in funeral and with dirge in marriage,
In equal scale weighing delight and dole°—
Taken to wife: Nor have we herein barred
Your better wisdoms, which have freely gone 15
With this affair along. For all, our thanks.
Now follows that you know° young Fortinbras,
Holding a weak supposal° of our worth,
Or thinking by our late dear brother's death
Our state to be disjoint and out of frame, 20
Co-leaguèd with° this dream of his advantage,°
He hath not failed to pester us with message
Importing° the surrender of those lands
Lost by his father, with all bonds° of law,
To our most valiant brother. So much for him. 25
Now for ourself and for this time of meeting.
Thus much the business is: we have here writ
To Norway, uncle of young Fortinbras—
Who, impotent° and bed-rid, scarcely hears
Of this his nephew's purpose—to suppress 30
His° further gait° herein, in that the levies,
The lists, and full proportions are all made
Out of his subject;° and we here dispatch
You, good Cornelius, and you, Voltimand,
For bearers of this greeting to old Norway, 35
Giving to you no further personal power
To business with the King more than the scope
Of these dilated° articles allow. *[He gives a paper.]*
Farewell, and let your haste commend your duty.°

---

8 **sometime** former.   9 **jointress** woman possessing property with her husband.   11 **With . . . eye** with one eye smiling and the other weeping.   13 **dole** grief.   17 **that you know** what you know already, that; or, that you be informed as follows.   18 **weak supposal** low estimate.   21 **Co-leaguèd with** joined to, allied with;   **dream . . . advantage** illusory hope of having the advantage. (His only ally is this hope.)   23 **Importing** pertaining to.   24 **bonds** contracts.   29 **impotent** helpless.   31 **His** i.e., Fortinbras';   **gait** proceeding.   31–33 **in that . . . subject** since the levying of troops and supplies is drawn entirely from the King of Norway's own subjects.   38 **dilated** set out at length.   39 **let . . . duty** let your swift obeying of orders, rather than mere words, express your dutifulness.

CORNELIUS, VOLTIMAND: In that, and all things, will
   we show our duty.   40
KING: We doubt it nothing.° Heartily farewell.

                              [*Exeunt Voltimand and Cornelius.*]

   And now, Laertes, what's the news with you?
   You told us of some suit; what is 't, Laertes?
   You cannot speak of reason to the Dane°
   And lose your voice.° What wouldst thou beg, Laertes,   45
   That shall not be my offer, not thy asking?
   The head is not more native° to the heart,
   The hand more instrumental° to the mouth,
   Than is the throne of Denmark to thy father.
   What wouldst thou have, Laertes?
LAERTES: My dread lord,   50
   Your leave and favor° to return to France,
   From whence though willingly I came to Denmark
   To show my duty in your coronation,
   Yet now I must confess, that duty done,
   My thoughts and wishes bend again toward France   55
   And bow them to your gracious leave and pardon.°
KING: Have you your father's leave? What says Polonius?
POLONIUS: H'ath,° my lord, wrung from me my slow leave
   By laborsome petition, and at last
   Upon his will I sealed° my hard° consent.   60
   I do beseech you, give him leave to go.
KING: Take thy fair hour,° Laertes. Time be thine,
   And thy best graces spend it at thy will!°
   But now, my cousin° Hamlet, and my son—
HAMLET: A little more than kin, and less than kind.°   65
KING: How is it that the clouds still hang on you?
HAMLET: Not so, my lord. I am too much in the sun.°
QUEEN: Good Hamlet, cast thy nighted color° off,

---

41 nothing not at all.   **44 the Dane** the Danish king.   **45 lose your voice** waste your speech.
47 native closely connected, related.   **48 instrumental** serviceable.   **51 leave and favor** kind
permission.   **56 bow . . . pardon** entreatingly make a deep bow, asking your permission to depart.
58 H'ath he has.   **60 sealed** (As if sealing a legal document.);   **hard** reluctant.   **62 Take thy fair hour**
enjoy your time of youth.   **63 And . . . will** and may your finest qualities guide the way you choose to
spend your time.   **64 cousin** any kin not of the immediate family.   **65 A little . . . kind** i.e., closer
than an ordinary nephew (since I am stepson), and yet more separated in natural feeling (with pun on
kind meaning "affectionate" and "natural," "lawful." This line is often read as an aside, but it need
not be. The King chooses perhaps not to respond to Hamlet's cryptic and bitter remark.)   **67 the sun**
i.e., the sunshine of the King's royal favor (with pun on son).   **68 nighted color** (1) mourning
garments of black (2) dark melancholy.

And let thine eye look like a friend on Denmark.°
Do not forever with thy vailèd lids°   70
Seek for thy noble father in the dust.
Thou know'st 'tis common,° all that lives must die,
Passing through nature to eternity.

HAMLET: Ay, madam, it is common.

QUEEN: If it be,
Why seems it so particular° with thee?   75

HAMLET: Seems, madam? Nay, it is. I know not "seems."
'Tis not alone my inky cloak, good Mother,
Nor customary° suits of solemn black,
Nor windy suspiration° of forced breath,
No, nor the fruitful° river in the eye,   80
Nor the dejected havior° of the visage,
Together with all forms, moods,° shapes of grief,
That can denote me truly. These indeed seem,
For they are actions that a man might play.
But I have that within which passes show;   85
These but the trappings and the suits of woe.

KING: 'Tis sweet and commendable in your nature, Hamlet,
To give these mourning duties to your father.
But you must know your father lost a father,
That father lost, lost his, and the survivor bound   90
In filial obligation for some term
To do obsequious° sorrow. But to persever°
In obstinate condolement° is a course
Of impious stubbornness. 'Tis unmanly grief.
It shows a will most incorrect to heaven,   95
A heart unfortified,° a mind impatient,
An understanding simple° and unschooled.
For what we know must be and is as common
As any the most vulgar thing to sense,°
Why should we in our peevish opposition   100
Take it to heart? Fie, 'tis a fault to heaven,
A fault against the dead, a fault to nature,
To reason most absurd, whose common theme

---

69 **Denmark** the King of Denmark.   70 **vailèd lids** lowered eyes.   72 **common** of universal
occurrence. (But Hamlet plays on the sense of "vulgar" in line 74.)   75 **particular** personal.
78 **customary** (1) socially conventional (2) habitual with me.   79 **suspiration** sighing.   80 **fruitful**
abundant.   81 **havior** expression.   82 **moods** outward expression of feeling.   92 **obsequious** suited
to obsequies or funerals;   **persever** persevere.   93 **condolement** sorrowing.   96 **unfortified** i.e.,
against adversity.   97 **simple** ignorant.   99 **As . . . sense** as the most ordinary experience.

Is death of fathers, and who still° hath cried,
From the first corpse° till he that died today, 105
"This must be so." We pray you, throw to earth
This unprevailing° woe and think of us
As of a father; for let the world take note,
You are the most immediate° to our throne,
And with no less nobility of love 110
Than that which dearest father bears his son
Do I impart toward° you. For° your intent
In going back to school° in Wittenberg,°
It is most retrograde° to our desire,
And we beseech you bend you° to remain 115
Here in the cheer and comfort of our eye,
Our chiefest courtier, cousin, and our son.

QUEEN: Let not thy mother lose her prayers, Hamlet.
I pray thee, stay with us, go not to Wittenberg.

HAMLET: I shall in all my best° obey you, madam. 120

KING: Why, 'tis a loving and a fair reply.
Be as ourself in Denmark. Madam, come.
This gentle and unforced accord of Hamlet
Sits smiling to° my heart, in grace° whereof
No jocund° health that Denmark drinks today 125
But the great cannon to the clouds shall tell,
And the King's rouse° the heaven shall bruit again,°
Respeaking earthly thunder.° Come away.

Flourish. Exeunt all but Hamlet.

HAMLET: O, that this too too sullied° flesh would melt,
Thaw, and resolve itself into a dew! 130
Or that the Everlasting had not fixed
His canon° 'gainst self-slaughter! O God, God,
How weary, stale, flat, and unprofitable
Seem to me all the uses° of this world!
Fie on 't, ah fie! 'Tis an unweeded garden 135
That grows to seed. Things rank and gross in nature

104 **still** always.   105 **the first corpse** (Abel's.)   107 **unprevailing** unavailing, useless.   109 **most immediate** next in succession.   112 **impart toward** i.e., bestow my affection on;   **For** as for. 113 **to school** i.e., to your studies;   **Wittenberg** famous German university founded in 1502. 114 **retrograde** contrary.   115 **bend you** incline yourself.   120 **in all my best** to the best of my ability.   124 **to** i.e., at;   **grace** thanksgiving.   125 **jocund** merry.   127 **rouse** drinking of a draft of liquor;   **bruit again** loudly echo.   128 **thunder** i.e., of trumpet and kettledrum, sounded when the King drinks; see 1.4.8–12.   129 **sullied** defiled. (The early quartos read sallied; the Folio, solid.) 132 **canon** law.   134 **all the uses** the whole routine.

Possess it merely.° That it should come to this!
But two months dead—nay, not so much, not two.
So excellent a king, that was to° this
Hyperion° to a satyr,° so loving to my mother   140
That he might not beteem° the winds of heaven
Visit her face too roughly. Heaven and earth,
Must I remember? Why, she would hang on him
As if increase of appetite had grown
By what it fed on, and yet within a month—   145
Let me not think on 't; frailty, thy name is woman!—
A little month, or ere° those shoes were old
With which she followed my poor father's body,
Like Niobe;° all tears, why she, even she—
O God, a beast, that wants discourse of reason,°   150
Would have mourned longer—married with my uncle,
My father's brother, but no more like my father
Than I to Hercules. Within a month,
Ere yet the salt of most unrighteous tears
Had left the flushing in her gallèd° eyes,   155
She married. O, most wicked speed, to post°
With such dexterity to incestuous° sheets!
It is not, nor it cannot come to good.
But break, my heart, for I must hold my tongue.

Enter Horatio, Marcellus and Bernardo.

HORATIO: Hail to your lordship!
HAMLET: I am glad to see you well.   160
Horatio!—or I do forget myself.
HORATIO: The same, my lord, and your poor servant ever.
HAMLET: Sir, my good friend; I'll change that name° with you.
And what make you from° Wittenberg, Horatio?
Marcellus.   165
MARCELLUS: My good lord.
HAMLET: I am very glad to see you. [*To Bernardo.*] Good even, sir.—

---

137 merely completely.   **139 to** in comparison to.   **140 Hyperion** Titan sun-god, father of Helios;
satyr a lecherous creature of classical mythology, half-human but with a goat's legs, tail, ears, and
horns.   **141 beteem** allow.   **147 or ere** even before.   **149 Niobe** Tantalus' daughter, Queen of Thebes,
who boasted that she had more sons and daughters than Leto; for this, Apollo and Artemis, children of
Leto, slew her fourteen children. She was turned by Zeus into a stone that continually dropped tears.
150 wants . . . reason lacks the faculty of reason.   **155 gallèd** irritated, inflamed.   **156 post** hasten.
157 incestuous (In Shakespeare's day, the marriage of a man like Claudius to his deceased brother's
wife was considered incestuous.)   **163 change that name** i.e., give and receive reciprocally the name of
"friend" (rather than talk of "servant").   **164 make you from** are you doing away from.

But what in faith make you from Wittenberg?

HORATIO: A truant disposition, good my lord.

HAMLET: I would not hear your enemy say so,   170
Nor shall you do my ear that violence
To make it truster of your own report
Against yourself. I know you are no truant.
But what is your affair in Elsinore?
We'll teach you to drink deep ere you depart.   175

HORATIO: My lord, I came to see your father's funeral.

HAMLET: I prithee, do not mock me, fellow student;
I think it was to see my mother's wedding.

HORATIO: Indeed, my lord, it followed hard° upon.

HAMLET: Thrift, thrift, Horatio! The funeral baked meats°   180
Did coldly° furnish forth the marriage tables.
Would I had met my dearest° foe in heaven
Or ever° I had seen that day, Horatio!
My father!—Methinks I see my father.

HORATIO: Where, my lord?

HAMLET: In my mind's eye, Horatio.   185

HORATIO: I saw him once. 'A° was a goodly king.

HAMLET: 'A was a man. Take him for all in all,
I shall not look upon his like again.

HORATIO: My lord, I think I saw him yesternight.

HAMLET: Saw? Who?   190

HORATIO: My lord, the King your father.

HAMLET: The King my father?

HORATIO: Season your admiration° for a while
With an attent° ear till I may deliver,
Upon the witness of these gentlemen,   195
This marvel to you.

HAMLET: For God's love, let me hear!

HORATIO: Two nights together had these gentlemen,
Marcellus and Bernardo, on their watch,
In the dead waste° and middle of the night,
Been thus encountered. A figure like your father,   200
Armèd at point° exactly, cap-à-pie,°
Appears before them, and with solemn march

---

179 **hard** close.   180 **baked meats** meat pies.   181 **coldly** i.e., as cold leftovers.   182 **dearest** closest (and therefore deadliest).   183 **Or ever** before.   186 **'A** he.   193 **Season your admiration** restrain your astonishment.   194 **attent** attentive.   199 **dead waste** desolate stillness.   201 **at point** correctly in every detail;   **cap-à-pie** from head to foot.

Goes slow and stately by them. Thrice he walked
By their oppressed and fear-surprisèd eyes
Within his truncheon's° length, whilst they, distilled°   205
Almost to jelly with the act° of fear,
Stand dumb and speak not to him. This to me
In dreadful° secrecy impart they did,
And I with them the third night kept the watch,
Where, as they had delivered, both in time,   210
Form of the thing, each word made true and good,
The apparition comes. I knew your father;
These hands are not more like.

HAMLET: But where was this?

MARCELLUS: My lord, upon the platform where we watch.

HAMLET: Did you not speak to it?

HORATIO: My lord, I did,   215
But answer made it none. Yet once methought
It lifted up its head and did address
Itself to motion, like as it would speak;°
But even then° the morning cock crew loud,
And at the sound it shrunk in haste away   220
And vanished from our sight.

HAMLET: 'Tis very strange.

HORATIO: As I do live, my honored lord, 'tis true,
And we did think it writ down in our duty
To let you know of it.

HAMLET: Indeed, indeed, sirs. But this troubles me.   225
Hold you the watch tonight?

ALL: We do, my lord.

HAMLET: Armed, say you?

ALL: Armed, my lord.

HAMLET: From top to toe?

ALL: My lord, from head to foot.   230

HAMLET: Then saw you not his face?

HORATIO: O, yes, my lord, he wore his beaver° up.

HAMLET: What° looked he, frowningly?

HORATIO: A countenance more in sorrow than in anger.

HAMLET: Pale or red?   235

HORATIO: Nay, very pale.

---

205 **truncheon** officer's staff;   206 **act** action, operation.   208 **dreadful** full of dread.   217–218
did . . . speak began to move as though it were about to speak.   219 **even then** at that very instant.
232 **beaver** visor on the helmet.   233 **What** how.

HAMLET: And fixed his eyes upon you?
HORATIO: Most constantly.
HAMLET: I would I had been there.
HORATIO: It would have much amazed you.   240
HAMLET: Very like, very like. Stayed it long?
HORATIO: While one with moderate haste might tell° a hundred.
MARCELLUS, BERNARDO: Longer, longer.
HORATIO: Not when I saw 't.
HAMLET: His beard was grizzled°—no?   245
HORATIO: It was, as I have seen it in his life,
    A sable silvered.°
HAMLET: I will watch tonight.
    Perchance 'twill walk again.
HORATIO: I warrant° it will.
HAMLET: If it assume my noble father's person,
    I'll speak to it though hell itself should gape   250
    And bid me hold my peace. I pray you all,
    If you have hitherto concealed this sight,
    Let it be tenable° in your silence still,
    And whatsoever else shall hap tonight,
    Give it an understanding but no tongue.   255
    I will requite your loves. So, fare you well.
    Upon the platform twixt eleven and twelve
    I'll visit you.
ALL: Our duty to your honor.
HAMLET: Your loves, as mine to you. Farewell.

                                         Exeunt [all but Hamlet].

    My father's spirit in arms! All is not well.   260
    I doubt° some foul play. Would the night were come!
    Till then sit still, my soul. Foul deeds will rise,
    Though all the earth o'erwhelm them, to men's eyes.

                                                          Exit.

Scene III [Polonius' Chambers.]

Enter Laertes and Ophelia, his sister.

LAERTES: My necessaries are embarked. Farewell.
    And, sister, as the winds give benefit
    And convoy is assistant,° do not sleep

---

242 tell count.   245 grizzled gray.   247 sable silvered black mixed with white.   248 warrant assure you.   253 tenable held.   distilled dissolved.   261 doubt suspect.   3 convoy is assistant means of conveyance are available.

But let me hear from you.

OPHELIA: Do you doubt that?

LAERTES: For Hamlet, and the trifling of his favor,   5
Hold it a fashion and a toy in blood,°
A violet in the youth of primy° nature,
Forward,° not permanent, sweet, not lasting,
The perfume and suppliance° of a minute—
No more.

OPHELIA: No more but so?

LAERTES: Think it no more.   10
For nature crescent° does not grow alone
In thews° and bulk, but as this temple° waxes
The inward service of the mind and soul
Grows wide withal.° Perhaps he loves you now,
And now no soil° nor cautel° doth besmirch   15
The virtue of his will,° but you must fear,
His greatness weighed,° his will is not his own.
For he himself is subject to his birth.
He may not, as unvalued persons do,
Carve° for himself, for on his choice depends   20
The safety and health of this whole state,
And therefore must his choice be circumscribed
Unto the voice and yielding° of that body
Whereof he is the head. Then if he says he loves you,
It fits your wisdom so far to believe it   25
As he in his particular act and place°
May give his saying deed, which is no further
Than the main voice° of Denmark goes withal.°
Then weigh what loss your honor may sustain
If with too credent° ear you list° his songs,   30
Or lose your heart, or your chaste treasure open
To his unmastered importunity.
Fear it, Ophelia, fear it, my dear sister,
And keep you in the rear of your affection,°
Out of the shot and danger of desire.   35

---

6 toy in blood passing amorous fancy.   **7 primy** in its prime, springtime.   **8 Forward** precocious.
9 suppliance supply, filler.   **11 crescent** growing, waxing.   **12 thews** bodily strength;   **temple** i.e.,
body.   **14 Grows wide withal** grows along with it.   **15 soil** blemish;   **cautel** deceit.   **16 will**
desire.   **17 His greatness weighed** if you take into account his high position.   **20 Carve** i.e., choose.
23 voice and yielding assent, approval.   **26 in . . . place** in his particular restricted circumstances.
28 main voice general assent;   **withal** along with.   **30 credent** credulous;   **list** listen to.   **34 keep**
. . . affection don't advance as far as your affection might lead you (A military metaphor.)

The chariest° maid is prodigal enough
If she unmask her beauty° to the moon.°
Virtue itself scapes not calumnious strokes.
The canker galls° the infants of the spring
Too oft before their buttons° be disclosed,° 40
And in the morn and liquid dew° of youth
Contagious blastments° are most imminent.
Be wary then; best safety lies in fear.
Youth to itself rebels,° though none else near.

OPHELIA: I shall the effect of this good lesson keep 45
As watchman to my heart. But, good my brother,
Do not, as some ungracious° pastors do,
Show me the steep and thorny way to heaven,
Whiles like a puffed° and reckless libertine
Himself the primrose path of dalliance treads, 50
And recks° not his own rede.°

Enter Polonius.

LAERTES: O, fear me not.°
I stay too long. But here my father comes.
A double° blessing is a double grace;
Occasion smiles upon a second leave.°

POLONIUS: Yet here, Laertes? Aboard, aboard, for shame! 55
The wind sits in the shoulder of your sail,
And you are stayed for. There—my blessing with thee!
And these few precepts in thy memory
Look° thou character.° Give thy thoughts no tongue,
Nor any unproportioned° thought his° act. 60
Be thou familiar,° but by no means vulgar.°
Those friends thou hast, and their adoption tried,°
Grapple them unto thy soul with hoops of steel,
But do not dull thy palm° with entertainment
Of each new-hatched, unfledged courage.° Beware 65

36 **chariest** most scrupulously modest.   37 **If she unmask her beauty** if she does no more than show her beauty;   **moon** (Symbol of chastity.)   39 **canker galls** canker-worm destroys.   40 **buttons** buds;   **disclosed** opened.   41 **liquid dew** i.e., time when dew is fresh and bright.   42 **blastments** blights.   44 **Youth . . . rebels** youth is inherently rebellious.   47 **ungracious** ungodly.   49 **puffed** bloated, or swollen with pride.   51 **recks** heeds;   **rede** counsel;   **fear me not** don't worry on my account.   53 **double** (Laertes has already bid his father good-bye.)   54 **Occasion . . . leave** happy is the circumstance that provides a second leave-taking. (The goddess Occasion, or Opportunity, smiles.)   59 **Look** be sure that;   **character** inscribe.   60 **unproportioned** badly calculated, intemperate;   **his** its.   61 **familiar** sociable;   **vulgar** common.   62 **and their adoption tried** and also their suitability for adoption as friends having been tested.   64 **dull thy palm** i.e., shake hands so often as to make the gesture meaningless.   65 **courage** young man of spirit.

Of entrance to a quarrel, but being in,
Bear 't that° th' opposèd may beware of thee.
Give every man thy ear, but few thy voice;
Take each man's censure,° but reserve thy judgment.
Costly thy habit° as thy purse can buy,   70
But not expressed in fancy;° rich, not gaudy,
For the apparel oft proclaims the man,
And they in France of the best rank and station
Are of a most select and generous chief in that.°
Neither a borrower nor a lender be,   75
For loan oft loses both itself and friend,
And borrowing dulleth edge of husbandry.°
This above all: to thine own self be true,
And it must follow, as the night the day,
Thou canst not then be false to any man.   80
Farewell. My blessing season° this in thee!
LAERTES: Most humbly do I take my leave, my lord.
POLONIUS: The time invests° you. Go, your servants tend.°
LAERTES: Farewell, Ophelia, and remember well
What I have said to you.   85
OPHELIA: 'Tis in my memory locked,
And you yourself shall keep the key of it.
LAERTES: Farewell.   *Exit Laertes.*
POLONIUS: What is 't, Ophelia, he hath said to you?
OPHELIA: So please you, something touching the Lord Hamlet.   90
POLONIUS: Marry,° well bethought.
'Tis told me he hath very oft of late
Given private time to you, and you yourself
Have of your audience been most free and bounteous.
If it be so—as so 'tis put on° me,   95
And that in way of caution—I must tell you
You do not understand yourself so clearly
As it behooves° my daughter and your honor.
What is between you? Give me up the truth.
OPHELIA: He hath, my lord, of late made many tenders°   100
Of his affection to me.
POLONIUS: Affection? Pooh! You speak like a green girl,

---

67 **Bear 't that** manage it so that.   69 **censure** opinion, judgment.   70 **habit** clothing.   71 **fancy**
excessive ornament, decadent fashion.   74 **Are . . . that** are of a most refined and well-bred
preeminence in choosing what to wear.   77 **husbandry** thrift.   81 **season** mature.   83 **invests**
besieges, presses upon;   **tend** attend, wait.   91 **Marry** i.e., by the Virgin Mary. (A mild oath.)
95 **put on** impressed on, told to.   98 **behooves** befits.   100 **tenders** offers.

Unsifted° in such perilous circumstance.
Do you believe his tenders, as you call them?
OPHELIA: I do not know, my lord, what I should think.   105
POLONIUS: Marry, I will teach you. Think yourself a baby
That you have ta'en these tenders for true pay
Which are not sterling.° Tender° yourself more dearly,
Or—not to crack the wind° of the poor phrase,
Running it thus—you'll tender me a fool.°   110
OPHELIA: My lord, he hath importuned me with love
In honorable fashion.
POLONIUS: Ay, fashion° you may call it. Go to,° go to.
OPHELIA: And hath given countenance° to his speech, my lord,
With almost all the holy vows of heaven.   115
POLONIUS: Ay, springes° to catch woodcocks.° I do know,
When the blood burns, how prodigal° the soul
Lends the tongue vows. These blazes, daughter,
Giving more light than heat, extinct in both
Even in their promise as it° is a-making,   120
You must not take for fire. From this time
Be something° scanter of your maiden presence.
Set your entreatments° at a higher rate
Than a command to parle.° For Lord Hamlet,
Believe so much in him° that he is young,   125
And with a larger tether may he walk
Than may be given you. In few,° Ophelia,
Do not believe his vows, for they are brokers,°
Not of that dye° which their investments° show,
But mere implorators° of unholy suits,   130
Breathing° like sanctified and pious bawds,
The better to beguile. This is for all:°
I would not, in plain terms, from this time forth
Have you so slander° any moment° leisure
As to give words or talk with the Lord Hamlet.   135

---

103 **Unsifted** i.e., untried.   108 **sterling** legal currency;   **Tender** hold, look after, offer.   109 **crack the wind** i.e., run it until it is broken-winded.   110 **tender me a fool** (1) show yourself to me as a fool (2) show me up as a fool (3) present me with a grandchild. (Fool was a term of endearment for a child.)   113 **fashion** mere form, pretense;   **Go to** (An expression of impatience.)   114 **countenance** credit, confirmation.   116 **springes** snares;   **woodcocks** birds easily caught; here used to connote gullibility.   117 **prodigal** prodigally.   120 **it** i.e., the promise.   122 **something** somewhat.   123 **entreatments** negotiations for surrender. (A military term.)   124 **parle** discuss terms with the enemy. (Polonius urges his daughter, in the metaphor of military language, not to meet with Hamlet and consider giving in to him merely because he requests an interview.)   125 **so . . . him** this much concerning him.   127 **In few** briefly.   128 **brokers** go-betweens, procurers.   129 **dye** color or sort;   **investments** clothes. (The vows are not what they seem.)   130 **mere implorators** out-and-out solicitors.   131 **Breathing** speaking.   132 **for all** once for all, in sum.   134 **slander** abuse, misuse;   **moment** moment's.

Look to 't, I charge you. Come your ways.°
OPHELIA: I shall obey, my lord.   *Exeunt.*

SCENE IV [THE GUARD PLATFORM.]

Enter Hamlet, Horatio, and Marcellus.

HAMLET: The air bites shrewdly,° it is very cold.
HORATIO: It is a nipping and an eager° air.
HAMLET: What hour now?
HORATIO: I think it lacks of° twelve.
MARCELLUS: No, it is struck.
HORATIO: Indeed? I heard it not.
It then draws near the season°   5
Wherein the spirit held his wont° to walk.

A flourish of trumpets, and two pieces° go off [within].

What does this mean, my lord?
HAMLET: The King doth wake° tonight and takes his rouse,°
Keeps wassail,° and the swaggering upspring° reels,°
And as he drains his drafts of Rhenish° down,   10
The kettledrum and trumpet thus bray out
The triumph of his pledge.°
HORATIO: It is a custom?
HAMLET: Ay, marry, is 't,
But to my mind, though I am native here
And to the manner° born, it is a custom   15
More honored in the breach than the observance.°
This heavy-headed revel east and west°
Makes us traduced and taxed of° other nations.
They clepe° us drunkards, and with swinish phrase°
Soil our addition;° and indeed it takes   20
From our achievements, though performed at height,°
The pith and marrow of our attribute.°
So, oft it chances in particular men,
That for° some vicious mole of nature° in them,

---

136 Come your ways come along.   **1 shrewdly** keenly, sharply.   **2 eager** biting.   **3 lacks of** is just
short of.   **5 season** time.   **6 held his wont** was accustomed;   **s.d. pieces** i.e., of ordnance, cannon.
8 wake stay awake and hold revel;   **takes his rouse** carouses.   **9 wassail** carousal;   **upspring** wild
German dance;   **reels** dances.   **10 Rhenish** Rhine wine.   **12 The triumph . . . pledge** i.e., his feat in
draining the wine in a single draft.   **15 manner** custom (of drinking).   **16 More . . . observance** better
neglected than followed.   **17 east and west** i.e., everywhere.   **18 taxed of** censured by.   **19 clepe** call;
with swinish phrase i.e., by calling us swine.   **20 addition** reputation.   **21 at height** outstandingly.
22 The pith . . . attribute the essence of the reputation that others attribute to us.   **24 for** on account
of;   **mole of nature** natural blemish in one's constitution.

As in their birth—wherein they are not guilty,   25
Since nature cannot choose his° origin—
By their o'ergrowth of some complexion,°
Oft breaking down the pales° and forts of reason,
Or by some habit that too much o'erleavens°
The form of plausive° manners, that these men,   30
Carrying, I say, the stamp of one defect,
Being nature's livery° or fortune's star,°
His virtues else,° be they as pure as grace,
As infinite as man may undergo,°
Shall in the general censure° take corruption   35
From that particular fault. The dram of evil
Doth all the noble substance often dout
To his own scandal.°

Enter Ghost.

HORATIO: Look, my lord, it comes!
HAMLET: Angels and ministers of grace° defend us!
Be thou° a spirit of health° or goblin damned,   40
Bring° with thee airs from heaven or blasts from hell,
Be thy intents° wicked or charitable,
Thou com'st in such a questionable° shape
That I will speak to thee. I'll call thee Hamlet,
King, father, royal Dane. O, answer me!   45
Let me not burst in ignorance, but tell
Why thy canonized° bones, hearsèd° in death,
Have burst their cerements;° why the sepulcher
Wherein we saw thee quietly inurned°
Hath oped his ponderous and marble jaws   50
To cast thee up again. What may this mean,
That thou, dead corpse, again in complete steel,°
Revisits thus the glimpses of the moon,°

---

26 **his** its.   27 **their o'ergrowth . . . complexion** the excessive growth in individuals of some natural trait.   28 **pales** palings, fences (as of a fortification).   29 **o'erleavens** induces a change throughout (as yeast works in dough).   30 **plausive** pleasing.   32 **nature's livery** sign of one's servitude to nature; **fortune's star** the destiny that chance brings.   33 **His virtues else** i.e., the other qualities of these men (line 30).   34 **may undergo** can sustain.   35 **general censure** general opinion that people have of him.   36–38 **The dram . . . scandal** i.e., the small drop of evil blots out or works against the noble substance of the whole and brings it into disrepute. To dout is to blot out. (A famous crux.)   39 **ministers of grace** messengers of God.   40 **Be thou** whether you are;   **spirit of health** good angel.   41 **Bring** whether you bring.   42 **Be thy intents** whether your intentions are.   43 **questionable** inviting question.   47 **canonized** buried according to the canons of the church; **hearsèd** coffined.   48 **cerements** grave clothes.   49 **inurned** entombed.   52 **complete steel** full armor.   53 **glimpses of the moon** pale and uncertain moonlight.

Making night hideous, and we fools of nature°
So horridly to shake our disposition°   55
With thoughts beyond the reaches of our souls?
Say, why is this? Wherefore? What should we do?

[The Ghost] beckons [Hamlet].

HORATIO: It beckons you to go away with it,
   As if it some impartment° did desire
   To you alone.
MARCELLUS: Look with what courteous action   60
   It wafts you to a more removèd ground.
   But do not go with it.
HORATIO: No, by no means.
HAMLET: It will not speak. Then I will follow it.
HORATIO: Do not, my lord!
HAMLET: Why, what should be the fear?
   I do not set my life at a pin's fee,°   65
   And for my soul, what can it do to that,
   Being a thing immortal as itself?
   It waves me forth again. I'll follow it.
HORATIO: What if it tempt you toward the flood,° my lord,
   Or to the dreadful summit of the cliff   70
   That beetles o'er° his° base into the sea,
   And there assume some other horrible form
   Which might deprive your sovereignty of reason°
   And draw you into madness? Think of it.
   The very place puts toys of desperation,°   75
   Without more motive, into every brain
   That looks so many fathoms to the sea
   And hears it roar beneath.
HAMLET: It wafts me still.—Go on, I'll follow thee.
MARCELLUS: You shall not go, my lord.   *[They try to stop him.]*
HAMLET: Hold off your hands!   80
HORATIO: Be ruled. You shall not go.
HAMLET: My fate cries out,°
   And makes each petty° artery° in this body

---

54 **fools of nature** mere men, limited to natural knowledge and subject to nature.   55 **So . . .
disposition** to distress our mental composure so violently.   59 **impartment** communication.   65 **fee**
value.   69 **flood** sea.   71 **beetles o'er** overhangs threateningly (like bushy eyebrows);   **his** its.
73 **deprive . . . reason** take away the rule of reason over your mind.   75 **toys of desperation** fancies
of desperate acts, i.e., suicide.   81 **My fate cries out** my destiny summons me.   82 **petty** weak;
artery (through which the vital spirits were thought to have been conveyed).

As hardy as the Nemean lion's° nerve.°
Still am I called. Unhand me, gentlemen.
By heaven, I'll make a ghost of him that lets° me!   85
I say, away!—Go on, I'll follow thee.

Exeunt Ghost and Hamlet.

HORATIO: He waxes desperate with imagination.
MARCELLUS: Let's follow. 'Tis not fit thus to obey him.
HORATIO: Have after.° To what issue° will this come?
MARCELLUS: Something is rotten in the state of Denmark.   90
HORATIO: Heaven will direct it.°
MARCELLUS: Nay, let's follow him.   *Exeunt.*

SCENE V [THE BATTLEMENTS OF THE CASTLE.]

Enter Ghost and Hamlet.

HAMLET: Whither wilt thou lead me? Speak. I'll go no further.
GHOST: Mark me.
HAMLET.   I will.
GHOST: My hour is almost come,
   When I to sulfurous and tormenting flames
   Must render up myself.
HAMLET: Alas, poor ghost!
GHOST: Pity me not, but lend thy serious hearing   5
   To what I shall unfold.
HAMLET: Speak. I am bound° to hear.
GHOST: So art thou to revenge, when thou shalt hear.
HAMLET: What?
GHOST: I am thy father's spirit,   10
   Doomed for a certain term to walk the night,
   And for the day confined to fast° in fires,
   Till the foul crimes° done in my days of nature°
   Are burnt and purged away. But that° I am forbid
   To tell the secrets of my prison house,   15
   I could a tale unfold whose lightest word
   Would harrow up° thy soul, freeze thy young blood,
   Make thy two eyes like stars start from their spheres,°

83 Nemean lion one of the monsters slain by Hercules in his twelve labors; nerve sinew. 85 lets hinders. 89 Have after let's go after him; issue outcome. 91 it i.e., the outcome. 7 bound (1) ready (2) obligated by duty and fate. (The Ghost, in line 8, answers in the second sense.) 12 fast do penance by fasting. 13 crimes sins; of nature as a mortal. 14 But that were it not that.
17 harrow up lacerate, tear. 18 spheres i.e., eye-sockets, here compared to the orbits or transparent revolving spheres in which, according to Ptolemaic astronomy, the heavenly bodies were fixed.

Thy knotted and combinèd locks° to part,
And each particular hair to stand on end   20
Like quills upon the fretful porcupine.
But this eternal blazon° must not be
To ears of flesh and blood. List, list, O, list!
If thou didst ever thy dear father love—

HAMLET: O God!   25

GHOST: Revenge his foul and most unnatural murder.

HAMLET: Murder?

GHOST: Murder most foul, as in the best ° it is,
But this most foul, strange, and unnatural.

HAMLET: Haste me to know't, that I, with wings as swift   30
As meditation or the thoughts of love,
May sweep to my revenge.

GHOST: I find thee apt;
And duller shouldst thou be° than the fat° weed
That roots itself in ease on Lethe° wharf,
Wouldst thou not stir in this. Now, Hamlet, hear.   35
'Tis given out that, sleeping in my orchard,°
A serpent stung me. So the whole ear of Denmark
Is by a forgèd process° of my death
Rankly abused.° But know, thou noble youth,
The serpent that did sting thy father's life   40
Now wears his crown.

HAMLET: O, my prophetic soul! My uncle!

GHOST: Ay, that incestuous, that adulterate° beast,
With witchcraft of his wit, with traitorous gifts°—
O wicked wit and gifts, that have the power   45
So to seduce!—won to his shameful lust
The will of my most seeming-virtuous queen.
O Hamlet, what a falling off was there!
From me, whose love was of that dignity
That it went hand in hand even with the vow°   50
I made to her in marriage, and to decline
Upon a wretch whose natural gifts were poor
To° those of mine!
But virtue, as it° never will be moved,

---

19 **knotted . . . locks** hair neatly arranged and confined.   22 **eternal blazon** revelation of the secrets of eternity.   28 **in the best** even at best.   33 **shouldst thou be** you would have to be;   **fat** torpid, lethargic.   348 **Lethe** the river of forgetfulness in Hades.   36 **orchard** garden.   38 **forgèd process** falsified account.   39 **abused** deceived.   43 **adulterate** adulterous.   44 **gifts** (1) talents (2) presents.   50 **even with the vow** with the very vow.   53 **To** compared to.   54 **virtue, as it** as virtue.

Though lewdness court it in a shape of heaven,° 55
So lust, though to a radiant angel linked,
Will sate itself in a celestial bed°
And prey on garbage.
But soft, methinks I scent the morning air.
Brief let me be. Sleeping within my orchard, 60
My custom always of the afternoon,
Upon my secure° hour thy uncle stole,
With juice of cursèd hebona° in a vial,
And in the porches of my ears° did pour
The leprous distillment,° whose effect 65
Holds such an enmity with blood of man
That swift as quicksilver it courses through
The natural gates and alleys of the body,
And with a sudden vigor it doth posset°
And curd, like eager° droppings into milk, 70
The thin and wholesome blood. So did it mine,
And a most instant tetter° barked° about,
Most lazar-like,° with vile and loathsome crust,
All my smooth body.
Thus was I, sleeping, by a brother's hand 75
Of life, of crown, of queen at once dispatched,°
Cut off even in the blossoms of my sin,
Unhouseled,° disappointed,° unaneled,°
No reckoning° made, but sent to my account
With all my imperfections on my head. 80
O, horrible! O, horrible, most horrible!
If thou hast nature° in thee, bear it not.
Let not the royal bed of Denmark be
A couch for luxury° and damnèd incest.
But, howsoever thou pursues this act, 85
Taint not thy mind nor let thy soul contrive
Against thy mother aught. Leave her to heaven
And to those thorns that in her bosom lodge,

---

55 **shape of heaven** heavenly form.   57 **sate . . . bed** cease to find sexual pleasure in a virtuously lawful marriage.   62 **secure** confident, unsuspicious.   63 **hebona** a poison. (The word seems to be a form of ebony, though it is thought perhaps to be related to benbane, a poison, or to ebenus, "yew.")   64 **porches of my ears** ears as a porch or entrance of the body.   65 **leprous distillment** distillation causing leprosylike disfigurement.   69 **posset** coagulate, curdle.   70 **eager** sour, acid.   72 **tetter** eruption of scabs;   **barked** recovered with a rough covering, like bark on a tree.   73 **lazar-like** leperlike.   76 **dispatched** suddenly deprived.   78 **Unhouseled** without having received the Sacrament;   **disappointed** unready (spiritually) for the last journey;   **unaneled** without having received extreme unction.   79 **reckoning** settling of accounts.   82 **nature** i.e., the promptings of a son.   84 **luxury** lechery.

To prick and sting her. Fare thee well at once.
The glowworm shows the matin° to be near, 90
And 'gins to pale his° uneffectual fire.
Adieu, adieu, adieu! Remember me. [*Exit.*]
HAMLET: O all you host of heaven! O earth! What else?
And shall I couple° hell? O, fie! Hold,° hold, my heart,
And you, my sinews, grow not instant° old, 95
But bear me stiffly up. Remember thee?
Ay, thou poor ghost, whiles memory holds a seat
In this distracted globe.° Remember thee?
Yea, from the table° of my memory
I'll wipe away all trivial fond° records, 100
All saws° of books, all forms,° all pressures° past
That youth and observation copied there,
And thy commandment all alone shall live
Within the book and volume of my brain,
Unmixed with baser matter. Yes, by heaven! 105
O most pernicious woman!
O villain, villain, smiling, damnèd villain!
My tables°—meet it is° I set it down
That one may smile, and smile, and be a villain.
At least I am sure it may be so in Denmark. 110

[*Writing.*]

So uncle, there you are.° Now to my word:
It is "Adieu, adieu! Remember me."
I have sworn 't.

Enter Horatio and Marcellus.

HORATIO: My lord, my lord!
MARCELLUS: Lord Hamlet!
HORATIO: Heavens secure him!° 115
HAMLET: So be it.
MARCELLUS: Hilo, ho, ho, my lord!
HAMLET: Hillo, ho, ho, boy! Come, bird, come.°
MARCELLUS: How is 't, my noble lord? 120
HORATIO: What news, my lord?
HAMLET: O, wonderful!

90 **matin** morning.   91 **his** its.   94 **couple** add;   **Hold** hold together.   95 **instant** instantly.   98 **globe** (1) head (2) world.   99 **table** tablet, slate.   100 **fond** foolish.   101 **saws** wise sayings; **forms** shapes or images copied onto the slate; general ideas;   **pressures** impressions stamped.   108 **tables** writing tablets;   **meet it is** it is fitting.   111 **there you are** i.e., there, I've written that down against you.   116 **secure him** keep him safe.   119 **Hillo . . . come** (A falconer's call to a hawk in air. Hamlet mocks the halloing as though it were a part of hawking.)

HORATIO: Good my lord, tell it.

HAMLET: No, you will reveal it.

HORATIO: Not I, my lord, by heaven.   125

MARCELLUS: Nor I, my lord.

HAMLET: How say you, then, would heart of man once° think it?
But you'll be secret?

HORATIO, MARCELLUS: Ay, by heaven, my lord.

HAMLET: There's never a villain dwelling in all Denmark
But he's an arrant° knave.   130

HORATIO: There needs no ghost, my lord, come from the grave
To tell us this.

HAMLET: Why, right, you are in the right.
And so, without more circumstance° at all,
I hold it fit that we shake hands and part,
You as your business and desire shall point you—   135
For every man hath business and desire,
Such as it is—and for my own poor part,
Look you, I'll go pray.

HORATIO: These are but wild and whirling words, my lord.

HAMLET: I am sorry they offend you, heartily;   140
Yes, faith, heartily.

HORATIO: There's no offense, my lord.

HAMLET: Yes, by Saint Patrick,° but there is, Horatio,
And much offense° too. Touching this vision here,
It is an honest ghost,° that let me tell you.
For your desire to know what is between us,   145
O'ermaster 't as you may. And now, good friends,
As you are friends, scholars, and soldiers,
Give me one poor request.

HORATIO: What is 't, my lord? We will.

HAMLET: Never make known what you have seen tonight.   150

HORATIO, MARCELLUS: My lord, we will not.

HAMLET: Nay, but swear 't.

HORATIO: In faith, my lord, not I.°

MARCELLUS: Nor I, my lord, in faith.

HAMLET: Upon my sword.°   [*He holds out his sword.*]   155

MARCELLUS: We have sworn, my lord, already.°

---

127 **once** ever.   130 **arrant** thoroughgoing.   133 **circumstance** ceremony, elaboration.   142 **Saint Patrick** (The keeper of Purgatory and patron saint of all blunders and confusion.)   143 **offense** (Hamlet deliberately changes Horatio's "no offense against all decency.")   144 **an honest ghost** i.e., a real ghost and not an evil spirit.   153 **In faith . . . I** i.e., I swear not to tell what I have seen. (Horatio is not refusing to swear.)   155 **sword** i.e., the hilt in the form of a cross.   156 **We . . . already** i.e., we swore in faith.

HAMLET: Indeed, upon my sword, indeed.

GHOST [*cries under the stage*]: Swear.

HAMLET: Ha, ha, boy, sayst thou so? Art thou there, truepenny?°
Come on, you hear this fellow in the cellarage.   160
Consent to swear.

HORATIO: Propose the oath, my lord.

HAMLET: Never to speak of this that you have seen,
Swear by my sword.

GHOST [*beneath*]: Swear.   [*They swear.*°]

HAMLET: Hic et ubique?° Then we'll shift our ground.   165

[*He moves to another spot.*]

Come hither, gentlemen,
And lay your hands again upon my sword.
Swear by my sword
Never to speak of this that you have heard.

GHOST [*beneath*]: Swear by his sword.   [*They swear.*] 170

HAMLET: Well said, old mole. Canst work i' th' earth so fast?
A worthy pioneer!°—Once more removed, good friends.

[*He moves again.*]

HORATIO: O day and night, but this is wondrous strange!

HAMLET: And therefore as a stranger° give it welcome.
There are more things in heaven and earth, Horatio,   175
Than are dreamt of in your philosophy.°
But come;
Here, as before, never, so help you mercy,°
How strange or odd soe'er I bear myself—
As I perchance hereafter shall think meet   180
To put an antic° disposition on—
That you, at such times seeing me, never shall,
With arms encumbered° thus, or this headshake,
Or by pronouncing of some doubtful phrase
As "Well, we know," or "We could, an if° we would,"   185
Or "If we list° to speak," or "There be, an if they might,"°
Or such ambiguous giving out,° to note°

159 **truepenny** honest old fellow.   164 **s.d. They swear** (Seemingly they swear here, and at lines 170 and 190, as they lay their hands on Hamlet's sword. Triple oaths would have particular force; these three oaths deal with what they have seen, what they have heard, and what they promise about Hamlet's antic disposition.)   165 **Hic et ubique** here and everywhere (Latin).   172 **pioneer** foot soldier assigned to dig tunnels and excavations.   174 **as a stranger** i.e., needing your hospitality.   176 **your philosophy** this subject called "natural philosophy" or "science" that people talk about.   178 **so help you mercy** as you hope for God's mercy when you are judged.   181 **antic** fantastic.   183 **encumbered** folded.   185 **an if** if.   186 **list** wished;   **There . . . might** i.e., there are people here (we, in fact) who could tell news if we were at liberty to do so.   187 **giving out** intimation;   **note** draw attention to the fact.

That you know aught° of me—this do swear,
So grace and mercy at your most need help you.
GHOST [*beneath*]:   Swear.   [*They swear.*] 190
HAMLET: Rest, rest, perturbèd spirit! So, gentlemen,
With all my love I do commend me to you;°
And what so poor a man as Hamlet is
May do t' express his love and friending° to you,
God willing, shall not lack.° Let us go in together,   195
And still° your fingers on your lips, I pray.
The time° is out of joint. O cursèd spite°
That ever I was born to set it right!

                          [*They wait for him to leave first.*]

Nay, come, let's go together.°   *Exeunt.*

Act II

Scene I [Polonius' Chambers.]

Enter old Polonius with his man [Reynaldo].

POLONIUS: Give him this money and these notes, Reynaldo.

                          [*He gives money and papers.*]

REYNALDO: I will, my lord.
POLONIUS: You shall do marvelous° wisely, good Reynaldo,
Before you visit him, to make inquire°
Of his behavior.
REYNALDO: My lord, I did intend it.   5
POLONIUS: Marry, well said, very well said. Look you, sir,
Inquire me first what Danskers° are in Paris,
And how, and who, what means,° and where they keep,°
What company, at what expense; and finding
By this encompassment° and drift° of question   10
That they do know my son, come you more nearer
Than your particular demands will touch it.°
Take you,° as 'twere, some distant knowledge of him,
As thus, "I know his father and his friends,
And in part him." Do you mark this, Reynaldo?   15

188 **aught** i.e., something secret.   192 **do . . . you** entrust myself to you.   194 **friending** friendliness.
195 **lack** be lacking.   196 **still** always.   197 **The time** the state of affairs;   **spite** i.e., the spite of
Fortune.   199 **let's go together** (Probably they wait for him to leave first, but he refuses this cere-
moniousness.)   3 **marvelous** marvelously.   4 **inquire** inquiry.   7 **Danskers** Danes.   8 **what means**
what wealth (they have);   **keep** dwell.   10 **encompassment** roundabout talking;   **drift** gradual
approach or course.   11–12 **come . . . it** you will find out more this way than by asking pointed
questions (particular demands).   13 **Take you** assume, pretend.

REYNALDO: Ay, very well, my lord.
POLONIUS: "And in part him, but," you may say, "not well.
  But if 't be he I mean, he's very wild,
  Addicted so and so," and there put on° him
  What forgeries° you please—marry, none so rank°   20
  As may dishonor him, take heed of that,
  But, sir, such wanton,° wild, and usual slips
  As are companions noted and most known
  To youth and liberty.
REYNALDO: As gaming, my lord.   25
POLONIUS: Ay, or drinking, fencing, swearing,
  Quarreling, drabbing°—you may go so far.
REYNALDO: My lord, that would dishonor him.
POLONIUS: Faith, no, as you may season° it in the charge.
  You must not put another scandal on him   30
  That he is open to incontinency;°
  That's not my meaning. But breathe his faults so quaintly°
  That they may seem the taints of liberty,°
  The flash and outbreak of a fiery mind,
  A savageness in unreclaimèd blood,   35
  Of general assault.°
REYNALDO: But, my good lord—
POLONIUS: Wherefore should you do this?
REYNALDO: Ay, my lord, I would know that.
POLONIUS: Marry, sir, here's my drift,   40
  And I believe it is a fetch of warrant.°
  You laying these slight sullies on my son,
  As 'twere a thing a little soiled wi' the working,°
  Mark you,
  Your party in converse,° him you would sound,°   45
  Having ever° seen in the prenominate crimes°
  The youth you breathe° of guilty, be assured
  He closes with you in this consequence:°
  "Good sir," or so, or "friend," or "gentleman,"
  According to the phrase or the addition°   50
  Of man and country.

19 **put on** impute to.   20 **forgeries** invented tales;   **rank** gross.   22 **wanton** sportive, unrestrained.
27 **drabbing** whoring.   29 **season** temper, soften.   31 **incontinency** habitual sexual excess.
32 **quaintly** artfully, subtly.   33 **taints of liberty** faults resulting from free living.   35–36 **A savageness
. . . assault** a wildness in untamed youth that assails all indiscriminately.   41 **fetch of warrant**
legitimate trick.   43 **soiled wi' the working** soiled by handling while it is being made, i.e., by involvement in the ways of the world.   45 **converse** conversation;   **sound** i.e., sound out.   46 **Having ever** if
he has ever;   **prenominate crimes** before-mentioned offenses.   47 **breathe** speak.   48 **closes . . .
consequence** takes you into his confidence in some fashion, as follows.   50 **addition** title.

REYNALDO: Very good, my lord.

POLONIUS: And then, sir, does 'a this—'a does—
what was I about to say? By the Mass, I was
about to say something. Where did I leave?

REYNALDO: At "closes in the consequence."   55

POLONIUS: At "closes in the consequence," ay, marry.
He closes thus: "I know the gentleman,
I saw him yesterday," or "th' other day,"
Or then, or then, with such or such, "and as you say,
There was 'a gaming," "there o'ertook in 's rouse,"°   60
"There falling out° at tennis," or perchance
"I saw him enter such a house of sale,"
Videlicet° a brothel, or so forth. See you now,
Your bait of falsehood takes this carp° of truth;
And thus do we of wisdom and of reach,°   65
With windlasses° and with assays of bias,°
By indirections find directions° out.
So by my former lecture and advice
Shall you my son. You have° me, have you not?

REYNALDO: My lord, I have.

POLONIUS: God b'wi'° ye; fare ye well.   70

REYNALDO: Good my lord.

POLONIUS: Observe his inclination in yourself.°

REYNALDO: I shall, my lord.

POLONIUS: And let him ply his music.

REYNALDO: Well, my lord.   75

POLONIUS: Farewell.   *Exit Reynaldo.*

Enter Ophelia.

                      How now, Ophelia, what's the matter?

OPHELIA: O my lord, my lord, I have been so affrighted!

POLONIUS: With what, i' the name of God?

OPHELIA: My lord, as I was sewing in my closet,°
Lord Hamlet, with his doublet° all unbraced,°   80
No hat upon his head, his stockings fouled,
Ungartered, and down-gyvèd° to his ankle,

---

60 **o'ertook in 's rouse** overcome by drink. 61 **falling out** quarreling. 63 **Videlicet** namely.
64 **carp** a fish. 65 **reach** capacity, ability. 66 **windlasses** i.e., circuitous paths. (Literally, circuits
made to head off the game in hunting); **assays of bias** attempts through indirection (like the curving path of the bowling ball, which is biased or weighted to one side). 67 **directions** i.e., the way
things really are. 69 **have** understand. 70 **b' wi'** be with. 72 **in yourself** in your own person
(as well as by asking questions). 79 **closet** private chamber. 80 **doublet** close-fitting jacket;
unbraced unfastened. 82 **down-gyvèd** fallen to the ankles (like gyves or fetters).

Pale as his shirt, his knees knocking each other,
And with a look so piteous in purport°
As if he had been loosèd out of hell   85
To speak of horrors—he comes before me.

POLONIUS: Mad for thy love?

OPHELIA: My lord, I do not know,
But truly I do fear it.

POLONIUS: What said he?

OPHELIA: He took me by the wrist and held me hard.
Then goes he to the length of all his arm,   90
And, with his other hand thus o'er his brow
He falls to such perusal of my face
As° 'a would draw it. Long stayed he so.
At last, a little shaking of mine arm
And thrice his head thus waving up and down,   95
He raised a sigh so piteous and profound
As it did seem to shatter all his bulk°
And end his being. That done, he lets me go,
And with his head over his shoulder turned
He seemed to find his way without his eyes,   100
For out o' doors he went without their helps,
And to the last bended their light on me.

POLONIUS: Come, go with me. I will go seek the King.
This is the very ecstasy° of love,
Whose violent property° fordoes° itself   105
And leads the will to desperate undertakings
As oft as any passion under heaven
That does afflict our natures. I am sorry.
What, have you given him any hard words of late?

OPHELIA: No, my good lord, but as you did command   110
I did repel his letters and denied
His access to me.

POLONIUS: That hath made him mad.
I am sorry that with better heed and judgment
I had not quoted° him. I feared he did but trifle
And meant to wrack° thee. But beshrew my jealousy!°   115
By heaven, it is as proper to our age°
To cast beyond° ourselves in our opinions

---

84 **in purport** in what it expressed.   93 **As** as if (also in line 97).   97 **bulk** body.   104 **ecstasy** madness.   105 **property** nature; **fordoes** destroys.   114 **quoted** observed.   115 **wrack** ruin, seduce; **beshrew my jealousy** a plague upon my suspicious nature.   116 **proper . . . age** characteristic of us (old) men.   117 **cast beyond** overshoot, miscalculate. (A metaphor from hunting.)

As it is common for the younger sort
To lack discretion. Come, go we to the King.
This must be known,° which, being kept close,° might move   120
More grief to hide than hate to utter love.°
Come.   *Exeunt.*

SCENE II [THE CASTLE.]

*Flourish. Enter King and Queen, Rosencrantz, and Guildenstern
[with others].*

KING: Welcome, dear Rosencrantz and Guildenstern.
   Moreover that° we much did long to see you,
   The need we have to use you did provoke
   Our hasty sending. Something have you heard
   Of Hamlet's transformation—so call it,   5
   Sith nor° th' exterior nor the inward man
   Resembles that° it was. What it should be,
   More than his father's death, that thus hath put him
   So much from th' understanding of himself,
   I cannot dream of. I entreat you both   10
   That, being of so young days° brought up with him,
   And sith so neighbored to° his youth and havior,°
   That you vouchsafe your rest° here in our court
   Some little time, so by your companies
   To draw him on to pleasures, and to gather   15
   So much as from occasion° you may glean,
   Whether aught to us unknown afflicts him thus
   That, opened,° lies within our remedy.
QUEEN: Good gentlemen, he hath much talked of you,
   And sure I am two men there is not living   20
   To whom he more adheres. If it will please you
   To show us so much gentry° and good will
   As to expend your time with us awhile
   For the supply and profit of our hope,°
   Your visitation shall receive such thanks   25

120 known made known (to the King); close secret. 120–121 might . . . love i.e., might cause more grief (because of what Hamlet might do) by hiding the knowledge of Hamlet's strange behavior toward Ophelia than unpleasantness by telling it. 2 Moreover that besides the fact that. 6 Sith nor since neither. 7 that what. 11 of . . . days from such early youth. 12 And sith so neighbored to and since you are (or, and since that time you are) intimately acquainted with; havior demeanor. 13 vouchsafe your rest please to stay. 16 occasion opportunity. 18 opened being revealed. 22 gentry courtesy. 24 supply . . . hope aid and furtherance of what we hope for.

As fits a king's remembrance.°

ROSENCRANTZ: Both Your Majesties
Might, by the sovereign power you have of° us,
Put your dread° pleasures more into command
Than to entreaty.

GUILDENSTERN: But we both obey,
And here give up ourselves in the full bent°   30
To lay our service freely at your feet,
To be commanded.

KING: Thanks, Rosencrantz and gentle Guildenstern.

QUEEN: Thanks, Guildenstern and gentle Rosencrantz.
And I beseech you instantly to visit   35
My too much changèd son. Go, some of you,
And bring these gentlemen where Hamlet is.

GUILDENSTERN: Heavens make our presence and our practices°
Pleasant and helpful to him!

QUEEN: Ay, amen!

Exeunt Rosencrantz and Guildenstern [with some attendants].

Enter Polonius.

POLONIUS: Th' ambassadors from Norway, my good lord,   40
Are joyfully returned.

KING: Thou still° hast been the father of good news.

POLONIUS: Have I, my lord? I assure my good liege
I hold° my duty, as° I hold my soul,
Both to my God and to my gracious king;   45
And I do think, or else this brain of mine
Hunts not the trail of policy° so sure
As it hath used to do, that I have found
The very cause of Hamlet's lunacy.

KING: O, speak of that! That do I long to hear.   50

POLONIUS: Give first admittance to th' ambassadors.
My news shall be the fruit° to that great feast.

KING: Thyself do grace° to them and bring them in. [*Exit Polonius.*]
He tells me, my dear Gertrude, he hath found
The head and source of all your son's distemper.   55

---

26 As fits . . . remembrance as would be a fitting gift of a king who rewards true service.   27 of
over.   28 dread inspiring awe.   30 in . . . bent to the utmost degree of our capacity. (An archery
metaphor.)   38 practices doings.   42 still always.   44 hold maintain; as firmly as.   47 policy
sagacity.   52 fruit dessert.   53 grace honor (punning on grace said before a feast, line 52.)

QUEEN: I doubt° it is no other but the main,°
　　His father's death and our o'erhasty marriage.

Enter Ambassadors Voltimand and Cornelius, with Polonius.

KING: Well, we shall sift him.°—Welcome, my good friends!
　　Say, Voltimand, what from our brother° Norway?
VOLTIMAND: Most fair return of greetings and desires.°　　　60
　　Upon our first,° he sent out to suppress
　　His nephew's levies, which to him appeared
　　To be a preparation 'gainst the Polack,
　　But, better looked into, he truly found
　　It was against Your Highness. Whereat grieved　　　65
　　That so his sickness, age, and impotence°
　　Was falsely borne in hand,° sends out arrests°
　　On Fortinbras, which he, in brief, obeys,
　　Receives rebuke from Norway, and in fine°
　　Makes vow before his uncle never more　　　70
　　To give th' assay° of arms against Your Majesty.
　　Whereon old Norway, overcome with joy,
　　Gives him three thousand crowns in annual fee
　　And his commission to employ those soldiers,
　　So levied as before, against the Polack,　　　75
　　With an entreaty, herein further shown,

　　　　　　　　　　　　　　　　　　[giving a paper]

　　That it might please you to give quiet pass
　　Through your dominions for this enterprise
　　On such regards of safety and allowance°
　　As therein are set down.
KING:　　　　　　　　　It likes° us well,　　　80
　　And at our more considered° time we'll read,
　　Answer, and think upon this business.
　　Meantime we thank you for your well-took labor.
　　Go to your rest; at night we'll feast together.
　　Most welcome home!　　　　　　　*Exeunt Ambassadors.*
POLONIUS:　　　　　　This business is well ended.　　　85

---

56 **doubt** fear, suspect;　**main** chief point, principal concern.　58 **sift him** question Polonius closely.
59 **brother** fellow king.　60 **desires** good wishes.　61 **Upon our first** at our first words on the
business.　66 **impotence** helplessness.　67 **borne in hand** deluded, taken advantage of;　**arrests**
orders to desist.　69 **in fine** in conclusion.　71 **give th' assay** make trial of strength, challenge.
78 **On . . . allowance** i.e., with such considerations for the safety of Denmark and permission for
Fortinbras.　80 **likes** pleases.　81 **considered** suitable for deliberation.

My liege, and madam, to expostulate°
What majesty should be, what duty is,
Why day is day, night night, and time is time,
Were nothing but to waste night, day, and time.
Therefore, since brevity is the soul of wit,°   90
And tediousness the limbs and outward flourishes,
I will be brief. Your noble son is mad.
Mad call I it, for, to define true madness,
What is't but to be nothing else but mad?
But let that go.
QUEEN: More matter, with less art.   95
POLONIUS: Madam, I swear I use no art at all.
That he's mad, 'tis true; 'tis true 'tis pity.
And pity 'tis 'tis true—a foolish figure,°
But farewell it, for I will use no art.
Mad let us grant him, then, and now remains   100
That we find out the cause of this effect,
Or rather say, the cause of this defect,
For this effect defective comes by cause.°
Thus it remains, and the remainder thus.
Perpend.°   105
I have a daughter—have while she is mine—
Who, in her duty and obedience, mark,
Hath given me this. Now gather and surmise.°
[*He reads the letter.*] "To the celestial and my soul's idol, the
most beautified Ophelia"—That's an ill phrase, a vile phrase;   110
"beautified" is a vile phrase. But you shall hear. Thus:

                                      [*He reads.*]

"In her excellent white bosom,° these,° etc."
QUEEN: Came this from Hamlet to her?
POLONIUS: Good madam, stay° awhile, I will be faithful.°

                                      [*He reads.*]

    "Doubt thou the stars are fire,   115
      Doubt that the sun doth move,
    Doubt° truth to be a liar,
      But never doubt I love.

---

86 **expostulate** expound, inquire into.   90 **wit** sense or judgment.   98 **figure** figure of speech.
103 **For . . . cause** i.e., for this defective behavior, his madness, has a cause.   105 **Perpend** consider.
108 **gather and surmise** draw your own conclusions.   113 **In . . . bosom** (The letter is poetically
addressed to her heart.);   **these** i.e., the letter.   115 **stay** wait;   **faithful** i.e., in reading the letter
accurately.   118 **Doubt** suspect.

O dear Ophelia, I am ill at these numbers.° I have not art to
reckon° my groans. But that I love thee best, O most best, 120
believe it. Adieu. Thine evermore, most dear lady, whilst this
machine° is to him, Hamlet."
This in obedience hath my daughter shown me,
And, more above,° hath his solicitings,
As they fell out° by° time, by means, and place, 125
All given to mine ear.°

KING: But how hath she
Received his love?

POLONIUS: What do you think of me?

KING: As of a man faithful and honorable.

POLONIUS: I would fain° prove so. But what might you think,
When I had seen this hot love on the wing— 130
As I perceived it, I must tell you that,
Before my daughter told me—what might you,
Or my dear Majesty your queen here, think,
If I had played the desk or table book,°
Or given my heart a winking,° mute and dumb, 135
Or looked upon this love with idle sight?°
What might you think? No, I went round° to work,
And my young mistress thus I did bespeak:°
"Lord Hamlet is a prince out of thy star;°
This must not be." And then I prescripts° gave her, 140
That she should lock herself from his resort,°
Admit no messengers, receive no tokens.
Which done, she took the fruits of my advice;
And he, repellèd—a short tale to make—
Fell into a sadness, then into a fast, 145
Thence to a watch,° thence into a weakness,
Thence to a lightness,° and by this declension°
Into the madness wherein now he raves,
And all we° mourn for.

KING [*to the Queen*]:   Do you think 'tis this?

QUEEN: It may be, very like. 150

---

119 **ill . . . numbers** unskilled at writing verses.   120 **reckon** (1) count (2) number metrically, scan.
121 **machine** i.e., body.   124 **more above** moreover.   125 **fell out** occurred;   **by** according to.
126 **given . . . ear** i.e., told me about.   129 **fain** gladly.   134 **played . . . table book** i.e., remained
shut up, concealing the information.   135 **given . . . winking** closed the eyes of my heart to this.
136 **with idle sight** complacently or incomprehendingly.   137 **round** roundly, plainly.   138 **bespeak**
address.   139 **out of thy star** above your sphere, position.   140 **prescripts** orders.   141 **his resort**
his visits.   146 **watch** state of sleeplessness.   147 **lightness** lightheadedness;   **declension** decline,
deterioration (with a pun on the grammatical sense).   149 **all we** all of us, or, into everything that we.

POLONIUS: Hath there been such a time—I would fain know that—
   That I have positively said "'Tis so,"
   When it proved otherwise?
KING: Not that I know.
POLONIUS: Take this from this,° if this be otherwise.
   If circumstances lead me, I will find   155
   Where truth is hid, though it were hid indeed
   Within the center.°
KING: How may we try° it further?
POLONIUS: You know sometimes he walks four hours together
   Here in the lobby.
QUEEN: So he does indeed.
POLONIUS: At such a time I'll loose° my daughter to him.   160
   Be you and I behind an arras° then.
   Mark the encounter. If he love her not
   And be not from his reason fall'n thereon,°
   Let me be no assistant for a state,
   But keep a farm and carters.°
KING: We will try it.   165

Enter Hamlet [reading on a book].

QUEEN: But look where sadly° the poor wretch comes reading.
POLONIUS: Away, I do beseech you both, away.
   I'll board° him presently.° O, give me leave.°

                    Exeunt King and Queen [with attendants].

   How does my good Lord Hamlet?
HAMLET: Well, God-a-mercy.°   170
POLONIUS: Do you know me, my lord?
HAMLET: Excellent well. You are a fishmonger.°
POLONIUS: Not I, my lord.
HAMLET: Then I would you were so honest a man.
POLONIUS: Honest, my lord?   175
HAMLET: Ay, sir. To be honest, as this world goes, is to be one
   man picked out of ten thousand.

---

154 **Take this from this** (The actor probably gestures, indicating that he means his head from his shoulders, or his staff of office or chain from his hands or neck, or something similar.)   157 **center** middle point of the earth (which is also the center of the Ptolemaic universe); **try** test, judge. 160 **loose** (As one might release an animal that is being mated.)   161 **arras** hanging, tapestry. 163 **thereon** on that account.   165 **carters** wagon drivers.   166 **sadly** seriously.   168 **board** accost; **presently** at once; **give me leave** i.e., excuse me, leave me alone. (Said to those he hurries offstage, including the King and Queen.)   170 **God-a-mercy** God have mercy, i.e., thank you. 172 **fishmonger** fish merchant.

POLONIUS: That's very true, my lord.

HAMLET: For if the sun breed maggots in a dead dog, being a
good kissing carrion°—Have you a daughter? 180

POLONIUS: I have, my lord.

HAMLET: Let her not walk i' the sun.° Conception° is a blessing,
but as your daughter may conceive, friend, look to 't.

POLONIUS [*aside*]: How say you by that? Still harping on my
daughter. Yet he knew me not at first; 'a° said I was a fishmonger. 185
'A is far gone. And truly in my youth I suffered much extremity
for love, very near this. I'll speak to him again.—What do you
read, my lord?

HAMLET: Words, words, words.

POLONIUS: What is the matter,° my lord? 190

HAMLET: Between who?

POLONIUS: I mean, the matter that you read, my lord.

HAMLET: Slanders, sir; for the satirical rogue says here that old
men have gray beards, that their faces are wrinkled, their eyes
purging° thick amber° and plum-tree gum, and that they have a 195
plentiful lack of wit,° together with most weak hams. All
which, sir, though I most powerfully and potently believe, yet I
hold it not honesty° to have it thus set down, for yourself, sir,
shall grow old° as I am, if like a crab you could go backward.

POLONIUS [*aside*]: Though this be madness, yet there is method 200
in 't.—Will you walk out of the air,° my lord?

HAMLET: Into my grave.

POLONIUS: Indeed, that's out of the air. [*Aside.*] How pregnant°
sometimes his replies are! A happiness° that often madness hits
on, which reason and sanity could not so prosperously° be 205
delivered of. I will leave him and suddenly° contrive the means
of meeting between him and my daughter.—My honorable
lord, I will most humbly take my leave of you.

HAMLET: You cannot, sir, take from me anything that I will more
willingly part withal°—except my life, except my life, except 210
my life.

179–180 **a good kissing carrion** i.e., a good piece of flesh for kissing, or for the sun to kiss.
182 **i' the sun** in public (with additional implication of the sunshine of princely favors);
Conception (1) understanding (2) pregnancy. 185 **'a** he. 190 **matter** substance. (But Hamlet
plays on the sense of "basis for a dispute.") 195 **purging** discharging; **amber** i.e., resin, like the
resinous **plum-tree gum.** 196 **wit** understanding. 198 **honesty** decency, decorum. 199 **old** as
old. 201 **out of the air** (The open air was considered dangerous for sick people.) 203 **pregnant**
quick-witted, full of meaning. 204 **happiness** felicity of expression. 205 **prosperously**
successfully. 206 **suddenly** immediately. 210 **withal** with.

Enter Guildenstern and Rosencrantz.

POLONIUS: Fare you well, my lord.
HAMLET: These tedious old fools!°
POLONIUS: You go to seek the Lord Hamlet. There he is.
ROSENCRANTZ [*to Polonius*]:   God save you, sir!   215

[*Exit Polonius.*]

GUILDENSTERN: My honored lord!
ROSENCRANTZ: My most dear lord!
HAMLET: My excellent good friends! How dost thou, Guilden-
stern? Ah, Rosencrantz! Good lads, how do you both?
ROSENCRANTZ: As the indifferent° children of the earth.   220
GUILDENSTERN: Happy in that we are not overhappy.
On Fortune's cap we are not the very button.
HAMLET: Nor the soles of her shoe?
ROSENCRANTZ: Neither, my lord.
HAMLET: Then you live about her waist, or in the middle of her   225
favors?°
GUILDENSTERN: Faith, her privates we.°
HAMLET: In the secret parts of Fortune? O, most true, she is a
strumpet.°
What news?   230
ROSENCRANTZ: None, my lord, but the world's grown honest.
HAMLET: Then is doomsday near. But your news is not true. Let
me question more in particular. What have you, my good
friends, deserved at the hands of Fortune that she sends you to
prison hither?   235
GUILDENSTERN: Prison, my lord?
HAMLET: Denmark's a prison.
ROSENCRANTZ: Then is the world one.
HAMLET: A goodly one, in which there are many confines,° wards,°
and dungeons, Denmark being one o' the worst.   240
ROSENCRANTZ: We think not so, my lord.
HAMLET: Why then 'tis none to you, for there is nothing either
good or bad but thinking makes it so. To me it is a prison.

---

213 **old fools** i.e., old men like Polonius.   220 **indifferent** ordinary, at neither extreme of fortune or
misfortune.   226 **favors** i.e., sexual favors.   227 **her privates we** i.e., (1) we are sexually intimate
with Fortune, the fickle goddess who bestows her favors indiscriminately (2) we are her private
citizens.   229 **strumpet** prostitute. (A common epithet for indiscriminate Fortune; see line 466.)
239 **confines** places of confinement; **wards** cells.

ROSENCRANTZ: Why then, your ambition makes it one. 'Tis too
   narrow for your mind.   245

HAMLET: O God, I could be bounded in a nutshell and count
   myself a king of infinite space, were it not that I have bad dreams.

GUILDENSTERN: Which dreams indeed are ambition, for the very
   substance of the ambitious° is merely the shadow of a dream.

HAMLET: A dream itself is but a shadow.   250

ROSENCRANTZ: Truly, and I hold ambition of so airy and light a
   quality that it is but a shadow's shadow.

HAMLET: Then are our beggars bodies,° and our monarchs and
   outstretched° heroes the beggars' shadows. Shall we to the
   court? For, by my fay,° I cannot reason.   255

ROSENCRANTZ, GUILDENSTERN: We'll wait upon° you.

HAMLET: No such matter. I will not sort° you with the rest of my
   servants, for, to speak to you like an honest man, I am most
   dreadfully attended.° But, in the beaten way° of friendship,
   what make° you at Elsinore?   260

ROSENCRANTZ: To visit you, my lord, no other occasion.

HAMLET: Beggar that I am, I am even poor in thanks; but I thank
   you, and sure, dear friends, my thanks are too dear a halfpenny.°
   Were you not sent for? Is it your own inclining? Is it a free°
   visitation? Come, come, deal justly with me. Come, come. Nay,   265
   speak.

GUILDENSTERN: What should we say, my lord?

HAMLET: Anything but to the purpose.° You were sent for, and
   there is a kind of confession in your looks which your modesties°
   have not craft enough to color.° I know the good King and   270
   Queen have sent for you.

ROSENCRANTZ: To what end, my lord?

HAMLET: That you must teach me. But let me conjure° you, by
   the rights of our fellowship, by the consonancy of our youth,°
   by the obligation of our ever-preserved love, and by what more   275

248–249 **the very . . . ambitious** that seemingly very substantial thing that the ambitious pursue.
253 **bodies** i.e., solid substances rather than shadows (since beggars are not ambitious).
254 **outstretched** (1) far-reaching in their ambition (2) elongated as shadows.   255 **fay** faith.
256 **wait upon** accompany, attend. (But Hamlet uses the phrase in the sense of providing menial
service.)   257 **sort** class, categorize.   259 **dreadfully attended** waited upon in slovenly fashion.
beaten way familiar path, tried-and-true course;   260 **make** do.   263 **too dear a halfpenny** (1) too
expensive at even a halfpenny, i.e., of little worth (2) too expensive by a halfpenny in return for
worthless kindness.   264 **free** voluntary.   268 **Anything but to the purpose** anything except a
straightforward answer. (Said ironically.)   269 **modesties** sense of shame.   270 **color** disguise.
273 **conjure** adjure, entreat.   274 **the consonancy of our youth** our closeness in our younger days.

dear a better° proposer could charge° you withal, be even° and
direct with me whether you were sent for or no.

ROSENCRANTZ [*aside to Guildenstern*]: What say you?

HAMLET [*aside*]: Nay, then, I have an eye of° you.—If you love
me, hold not off.° 280

GUILDENSTERN: My lord, we were sent for.

HAMLET: I will tell you why; so shall my anticipation prevent your
discovery,° and your secrecy to the King and Queen molt no
feather,° I have of late—but wherefore I know not—lost all my
mirth, for-gone all custom of exercises; and indeed it goes so 285
heavily with my disposition that this goodly frame, the earth,
seems to me a sterile promontory; this most excellent canopy, the
air, look you, this brave° o'erhanging firmament, this majestical
roof fretted° with golden fire, why, it appeareth nothing to me
but a foul and pestilent congregation° of vapors. What a piece of 290
work° is a man! How noble in reason, how infinite in faculties,
in form and moving how express° and admirable, in action how
like an angel, in apprehension° how like a god! The beauty of the
world, the paragon of animals! And yet, to me, what is this
quintessence° of dust? Man delights not me—no, nor woman 295
neither, though by your smiling you seem to say so.

ROSENCRANTZ: My lord, there was no such stuff in my thoughts.

HAMLET: Why did you laugh, then, when I said man delights not
me?

ROSENCRANTZ: To think, my lord, if you delight not in man, 300
what Lenten entertainment° the players shall receive from you.
We coted° them on the way, and hither are they coming to offer
you service.

HAMLET: He that plays the king shall be welcome; His Majesty
shall have tribute° of° me. The adventurous knight shall use his 305
foil and target,° the lover shall not sigh gratis,° the humorous
man° shall end his part in peace,° the clown shall make those

---

276 **better** more skillful; **charge** urge. **even** straight, honest. 279 **of** on; 280 **hold not off** don't
hold back. 282–283 **so . . . discovery** in that way my saying it first will spare you from revealing
the truth. 283–284 **molt no feather** i.e., not diminish in the least. 288 **brave** splendid. 279
fretted adorned (with fretwork, as in a vaulted ceiling). 290 **congregation** mass; 290–291 **piece
of work** masterpiece. 292 **express** well-framed, exact, expressive. 293 **apprehension** power of
comprehending. 295 **quintessence** the fifth essence of ancient philosophy, beyond earth, water, air,
and fire, supposed to be the substance of the heavenly bodies and to be latent in all things. 301
Lenten entertainment meager reception (appropriate to Lent); 302 **coted** overtook and passed by.
305 **tribute** (1) applause (2) homage paid in money. **of** from; 306 **foil and target** sword and
shield. **gratis** for nothing; 306–307 **humorous man** eccentric character, dominated by one trait or
"humor"; 307 **in peace** i.e., with full license.

laugh whose lungs are tickle o' the sear,° and the lady shall say
her mind freely, or the blank verse shall halt° for 't. What
players are they?

ROSENCRANTZ: Even those you were wont to take such delight 310
in, the tragedians° of the city.

HAMLET: How chances it they travel? Their residence,° both in
reputation and profit, was better both ways.

ROSENCRANTZ: I think their inhibition° comes by the means of
the late° innovation.° 315

HAMLET: Do they hold the same estimation they did when I was
in the city? Are they so followed?

ROSENCRANTZ: No, indeed are they not.

HAMLET: How comes it? Do they grow rusty?

ROSENCRANTZ: Nay, their endeavor keeps° in the wonted° pace. 320
But there is, sir, an aerie° of children, little eyases,° that cry out
on the top of question° and are most tyrannically° clapped for
't. These are now the fashion, and so berattle° the common
stages°—so they call them—that many wearing rapiers° are
afraid of goose quills° and dare scarce come thither. 325

HAMLET: What, are they children? Who maintains 'em? How are
they escoted?° Will they pursue the quality° no longer than they
can sing?° Will they not say afterwards, if they should grow
themselves to common° players—as it is most like,° if their
means are no better°—their writers do them wrong to make 330
them exclaim against their own succession?°

ROSENCRANTZ: Faith, there has been much to-do° on both sides,
and the nation holds it no sin to tar° them to controversy.
There was for a while no money bid for argument unless the
poet and the player went to cuffs in the question.° 335

307 **tickle o' the sear** easy on the trigger, ready to laugh easily. (A sear is part of a gunlock.)   308 **halt**
limp.   311 **tragedians** actors.   312 **residence** remaining in their usual place, i.e., in the city.
314 **inhibition** formal prohibition (from acting plays in the city);   315 **late** recent;   **innovation** i.e., the
new fashion in satirical plays performed by boy actors in the "private" theaters; or possibly a political
uprising; or the strict limitations set on theaters in London in 1600.   319–345 **How . . . load too** (The
passage, omitted from the early quartos, alludes to the so-called War of the Theaters, 1599–1602, the
rivalry between the children's companies and the adult actors.)   320 **keeps** continues;   **wonted** usual.
321 **aerie** nest;   **eyases** young hawks;   321–322 **cry . . . question** speak shrilly, dominating the controversy (in decrying the public theaters).   322 **tyrannically** outrageously.   323 **berattle** berate, clamor
against;   323–324 **common stages** public theaters.   324 **many wearing rapiers** i.e., many men of
fashion, afraid to patronize the common players for fear of being satirized by the poets writing for the
boy actors;   325 **goose quills** i.e., pens of satirists.   327 **escoted** maintained.   **quality** (acting) profession;   327–328 **no longer . . . sing** i.e., only until their voices change.   329 **common** regular, adult.
329 **like** likely;   329–330 **if . . . better** if they find no better way to support themselves.   331 **succession**
i.e., future careers.   332 **to-do** ado.   333 **tar** set on (as dogs).   333–335 **There . . . question** i.e., for a
while, no money was offered by the acting companies to playwrights for the plot to a play unless the
satirical poets who wrote for the boys and the adult actors came to blows in the play itself.

HAMLET: Is 't possible?

GUILDENSTERN: O, there has been much throwing about of brains.

HAMLET: Do the boys carry it away?°

ROSENCRANTZ: Ay, that they do, my lord—Hercules and his 340 load° too.

HAMLET: It is not very strange; for my uncle is King of Denmark, and those that would make mouths° at him while my father lived give twenty, forty, fifty, a hundred ducats° apiece for his picture in little.° 'Sblood,° there is something in this more than 345 natural, if philosophy° could find it out.

A flourish [of trumpets within].

GUILDENSTERN: There are the players.

HAMLET: Gentlemen, you are welcome to Elsinore. Your hands, come then. Th' appurtenance° of welcome is fashion and ceremony. Let me comply° with you in this garb,° lest my extent° 350 to the players, which, I tell you, must show fairly outwards,° should more appear like entertainment° than yours. You are welcome. But my uncle-father and aunt-mother are deceived.

GUILDENSTERN: In what, my dear lord?

HAMLET: I am but mad north-north-west.° When the wind is 355 southerly I know a hawk from a handsaw.°

Enter Polonius.

POLONIUS: Well be with you, gentlemen!

HAMLET: Hark you, Guildenstern, and you too; at each ear a hearer. That great baby you see there is not yet out of his swaddling clouts.° 360

ROSENCRANTZ: Haply° he is the second time come to them, for they say an old man is twice a child.

HAMLET: I will prophesy he comes to tell me of the players. Mark it.—You say right, sir, o' Monday morning, 'twas then indeed.

---

339 **carry it away** i.e., win the day   340–341 **Hercules . . . load** (Thought to be an allusion to the sign of the Globe Theatre, which was Hercules bearing the world on his shoulders.)   343 **mouths** faces.   344 **ducats** gold coins;   344 **in little** in miniature;   **'Sblood** by God's (Christ's) blood.   346 **philosophy** i.e., scientific inquiry.   349 **appurtenance** proper accompaniment;   350 **comply** observe the formalities of courtesy.   **garb** i.e., manner;   **my extent** that which I extend, i.e., my polite behavior.   351 **show fairly outwards** show every evidence of cordiality;   352 **entertainment** a (warm) reception.   355 **north-north-west** just off true north, only partly.   356 **hawk, handsaw** i.e., two very different things, though also perhaps meaning a mattock (or hack) and carpenter's cutting tools, respectively; also birds, with a play on bernshaw, or heron.   360 **swaddling clouts** cloths in which to wrap a newborn baby.   361 **Haply** perhaps.

POLONIUS: My lord, I have news to tell you.   365
HAMLET: My lord, I have news to tell you. When Roscius° was
an actor in Rome—
POLONIUS: The actors are come hither, my lord.
HAMLET: Buzz,° buzz!
POLONIUS: Upon my honor—   370
HAMLET: Then came each actor on his ass.
POLONIUS: The best actors in the world, either for tragedy,
comedy, history, pastoral, pastoral-comical, historical-pastoral,
tragical-historical, tragical-comical-historical-pastoral, scene
individable,° or poem unlimited.° Seneca° cannot be too heavy,   375
nor Plautus° too light. For the law of writ and the liberty,° these°
are the only men.
HAMLET: O Jephthah, judge of Israel,° what a treasure hadst thou!
POLONIUS: What a treasure had he, my lord?
HAMLET: Why,   380
"One fair daughter, and no more,
The which he lovèd passing° well."
POLONIUS [*aside*]:   Still on my daughter.
HAMLET: Am I not i' the right, old Jephthah?
POLONIUS: If you call me Jephthah, my lord, I have a daughter   385
that I love passing well.
HAMLET: Nay, that follows not.
POLONIUS: What follows then, my lord?
HAMLET: Why,
"As by lot,° God wot,"°   390
and then, you know,
"It came to pass, as most like° it was"—
the first row° of the pious chanson° will show you more, for
look where my abridgement° comes.

Enter the players.

You are welcome, masters; welcome, all. I am glad to see thee   395
well. Welcome, good friends. O, old friend! Why, thy face is

---

366 **Roscius** a famous Roman actor who died in 62 B.C.   369 **Buzz** (An interjection used to denote
stale news.)   374–375 **scene individable** a play observing the unity of place; or perhaps one that is
unclassifiable, or performed without intermission;   375 **poem unlimited** a play disregarding the
unities of time and place; one that is all-inclusive.   **Seneca** writer of Latin tragedies;   376 **Plautus**
writer of Latin comedies.   **law . . . liberty** dramatic composition both according to the rules and
disregarding the rules;   **these** i.e., the actors.   378 **Jephthah . . . Israel** (Jephthah had to sacrifice
his daughter; see Judges 11. Hamlet goes on to quote from a ballad on the theme.)   382 **passing**
surpassingly.   390 **lot** chance;   **wot** knows.   392 **like** likely, probable.   393 **row** stanza;   **chanson**
ballad, song.   394 **my abridgement** something that cuts short my conversation; also, a diversion.

valanced° since I saw thee last. Com'st thou to beard° me in Denmark? What, my young lady° and mistress! By 'r Lady,° your ladyship is nearer to heaven than when I saw you last, by the altitude of a chopine.° Pray God your voice, like a piece of uncurrent° gold, be not cracked within the ring.° Masters, you are all welcome. We'll e'en to 't° like French falconers, fly at anything we see. We'll have a speech straight.° Come, give us a taste of your quality.° Come, a passionate speech.

FIRST PLAYER: What speech, my good lord?

HAMLET: I heard thee speak me a speech once, but it was never acted, or if it was, not above once, for the play, I remember, pleased not the million; 'twas caviar to the general.° But it was—as I received it, and others, whose judgments in such matters cried in the top of° mine—an excellent play, well digested° in the scenes, set down with as much modesty° as cunning.° I remember one said there were no sallets° in the lines to make the matter savory, nor no matter in the phrase that might indict° the author of affectation, but called it an honest method, as wholesome as sweet, and by very much more handsome° than fine.° One speech in 't I chiefly loved: 'twas Aeneas' tale to Dido, and thereabout of it especially when he speaks of Priam's slaughter.° If it live in your memory, begin at this line: let me see, let me see—
"The rugged Pyrrhus,° like th' Hyrcanian beast°"—
'Tis not so. It begins with Pyrrhus:
"The rugged° Pyrrhus, he whose sable° arms,
Black as his purpose, did the night resemble
When he lay couchèd° in the ominous horse,°
Hath now this dread and black complexion smeared

400

405

410

415

420

425

---

397 valanced fringed (with a beard). **beard** confront, challenge (with obvious pun). **398 young lady** i.e., boy playing women's parts; **By 'r Lady** by Our Lady. **400 chopine** thick-soled shoe of Italian fashion. **401 uncurrent** not passable as lawful coinage; **cracked . . . ring** i.e., changed from adolescent to male voice, no longer suitable for women's roles. (Coins featured rings enclosing the sovereign's head; if the coin was cracked within this ring, it was unfit for currency.) **402 e'en to 't** go at it. **403 straight** at once. **404 quality** professional skill. **408 caviar to the general** caviar to the multitude, i.e., a choice dish too elegant for coarse tastes. **410 cried in the top of** i.e., spoke with greater authority than. **411 digested** arranged, ordered; **modesty** moderation, restraint. **412 cunning** skill; **sallets** i.e., something savory, spicy improprieties. **414 indict** convict. **416 handsome** well-proportioned; **fine** elaborately ornamented, showy. **418 Priam's slaughter** the slaying of the ruler of Troy, when the Greeks finally took the city. **420 Pyrrhus** a Greek hero in the Trojan War, also known as Neoptolemus, son of Achilles—another avenging son; **Hyrcanian beast** i.e., tiger. (On the death of Priam, see Virgil, Aeneid, 2.506 ff.; compare the whole speech with Marlowe's Dido Queen of Carthage, 2.1.214. ff. On the Hyrcanian tiger, see Aeneid, 4.366–367. Hyrcania is on the Caspian Sea.) **422 rugged** shaggy, savage; **sable** black (for reasons of camouflage during the episode of the Trojan horse). **424 couchèd** concealed; **ominous horse** fateful Trojan horse, by which the Greeks gained access to Troy.

With heraldry more dismal.° Head to foot   430
Now is he total gules,° horridly tricked°
With blood of fathers, mothers, daughters, sons,
Baked and impasted° with the parching streets,°
That lend a tyrannous° and a damnèd light
To their lord's° murder. Roasted in wrath and fire,   435
And thus o'ersizèd° with coagulate gore,
With eyes like carbuncles,° the hellish Pyrrhus
Old grandsire Priam seeks
So proceed you.

POLONIUS: 'Fore God, my lord, well spoken, with good accent 440
and good discretion.

FIRST PLAYER: "Anon he finds him
Striking too short at Greeks. His antique° sword,
Rebellious to his arm, lies where it falls,
Repugnant° to command. Unequal matched,
Pyrrhus at Priam drives, in rage strikes wide,   445
But with the whiff and wind of his fell° sword
Th' unnervèd° father falls. Then senseless Ilium,°
Seeming to feel this blow, with flaming top
Stoops to his° base, and with a hideous crash
Takes prisoner Pyrrhus' ear. For, lo! His sword,   450
Which was declining° on the milky° head
Of reverend Priam, seemed i' th' air to stick.
So as a painted° tyrant Pyrrhus stood,
And, like a neutral to his will and matter,°
Did nothing.   455
But as we often see against° some storm
A silence in the heavens, the rack° stand still,
The bold winds speechless, and the orb° below
As hush as death, anon the dreadful thunder
Doth rend the region,° so, after Pyrrhus' pause,   460
A rousèd vengeance sets him new a-work

---

430 **dismal** ill-omened.   431 **total gules** entirely red. (A heraldic term);   **tricked** spotted and smeared. (Heraldic.)   433 **impasted** crusted, like a thick paste;   **with . . . streets** by the parching heat of the streets (because of the fires everywhere).   434 **tyrannous** cruel.   435 **their lord's** i.e., Priam's.   436 **o'ersizèd** covered as with size or glue.   437 **carbuncles** large fiery-red precious stones thought to emit their own light.   442 **antique** ancient, long-used.   444 **Repugnant** disobedient, resistant.   446 **fell** cruel.   447 **unnervèd** strengthless;   **senseless Ilium** inanimate citadel of Troy.   417 **his** its.   451 **declining** descending;   **milky** white-haired.   453 **painted** i.e., painted in a picture.   454 **like . . . matter** i.e., as though suspended between his intention and its fulfillment.   456 **against** just before.   457 **rack** mass of clouds.   458 **orb** globe, earth.   460 **region** sky.

And never did the Cyclops'° hammers fall
On Mars's armor forged for proof eterne°
With less remorse° than Pyrrhus' bleeding sword
Now falls on Priam.   465
Out, out, thou strumpet Fortune! All you gods
In general synod° take away her power!
Break all the spokes and fellies° from her wheel,
And bowl the round nave° down the hill of heaven°
As low as to the fiends!"   470

POLONIUS: This is too long.

HAMLET: It shall to the barber's with your beard.—Prithee, say
on. He's for a jig° or a tale of bawdry, or he sleeps. Say on;
come to Hecuba.°

FIRST PLAYER: "But who, ah woe! had° seen the mobled° queen"— 475

HAMLET: "The mobled queen?"

POLONIUS: That's good. "Mobled queen" is good.

FIRST PLAYER: "Run barefoot up and down, threat'ning the flames°
With bisson rheum,° a clout° upon that head
Where late° the diadem stood, and, for a robe,   480
About her lank and all o'erteemd° loins
A blanket, in the alarm of fear caught up—
Who this had seen, with tongue in venom steeped,
'Gainst Fortune's state° would treason have pronounced.°
But if the gods themselves did see her then   495
When she saw Pyrrhus make malicious sport
In mincing with his sword her husband's limbs,
The instant burst of clamor that she made,
Unless things mortal move them not at all,
Would have made milch° the burning eyes of heaven,°   490
And passion° in the gods."

POLONIUS: Look whe'er° he has not turned his color and has
tears in 's eyes. Prithee, no more.

HAMLET: 'Tis well; I'll have thee speak out the rest of this
soon.—Good my lord, will you see the players well bestowed?°   495

---

462 **Cyclops** giant armor makers in the smithy of Vulcan.   463 **proof eterne** eternal resistance to
assault.   464 **remorse** pity.   467 **synod** assembly.   468 **fellies** pieces of wood forming the rim of a
wheel.   469 **nave** hub; **hill of heaven** Mount Olympus.   473 **jig** comic song and dance often given
at the end of a play.   474 **Hecuba** wife of Priam.   475 **who . . . had** anyone who had (also in line
469); **mobled** muffled.   478 **threat'ning the flames** i.e., weeping hard enough to dampen the flames.
479 **bisson rheum** blinding tears; **clout** cloth.   480 **late** lately.   481 **all o'erteemèd** utterly worn
out with bearing children.   494 **state** rule, managing; **pronounced** proclaimed.   490 **milch** milky,
moist with tears; **burning eyes of heaven** i.e., heavenly bodies.   491 **passion** overpowering emotion.
492 **whe'er** whether.   495 **bestowed** lodged.

Do you hear, let them be well used, for they are the abstract°
and brief chronicles of the time. After your death you were
better have a bad epitaph than their ill report while you live.

POLONIUS: My lord, I will use them according to their desert.

HAMLET: God's bodikin,° man, much better. Use every man after   500
his desert, and who shall scape whipping? Use them after° your
own honor and dignity. The less they deserve, the more merit is
in your bounty. Take them in.

POLONIUS: Come, sirs.   [*Exit.*]

HAMLET: Follow him, friends. We'll hear a play tomorrow. [*As   505
they start to leave, Hamlet detains the first player.*] Dost thou
hear me, old friend? Can you play The Murder of Gonzago?

FIRST PLAYER: Ay, my lord.

HAMLET: We'll ha 't° tomorrow night. You could, for a need, study°
a speech of some dozen or sixteen lines which I would set down   510
and insert in 't, could you not?

FIRST PLAYER: Ay, my lord.

HAMLET: Very well. Follow that lord, and look you mock him not.

[*Exeunt players.*]

My good friends, I'll leave you till night. You are welcome to
Elsinore.   515

ROSENCRANTZ: Good my lord!

Exeunt [Rosencrantz and Guildenstern].

HAMLET: Ay, so, goodbye to you.—Now I am alone.
O, what a rogue and peasant slave am I!
Is it not monstrous that this player here,
But° in a fiction, in a dream of passion,   520
Could force his soul so to his own conceit°
That from her working° all his visage wanned,°
Tears in his eyes, distraction in his aspect,°
A broken voice, and his whole function suiting
With forms to his conceit?° And all for nothing!   525
For Hecuba!
What's Hecuba to him, or he to Hecuba,
That he should weep for her? What would he do

496 abstract summary account.   500 God's bodikin by God's (Christ's) little body, bodykin. (Not
to be confused with bodkin, "dagger.")   501 after according to.   509 ha 't have it;   study
memorize.   520 But merely.   521 force . . . conceit bring his innermost being so entirely into
accord with his conception (of the role).   522 from her working as a result of, or in response to,
his soul's activity;   wanned grew pale.   523 aspect look, glance.   524–525 his whole . . . conceit
all his bodily powers responding with actions to suit his thought.

Had he the motive and the cue for passion
That I have? He would drown the stage with tears   600
And cleave the general ear° with horrid° speech,
Make mad the guilty and appall° the free,°
Confound the ignorant,° and amaze° indeed
The very faculties of eyes and ears. Yet I,
A dull and muddy-mettled° rascal, peak°   605
Like John-a-dreams,° unpregnant of° my cause,
And can say nothing—no, not for a king
Upon whose property° and most dear life
A damned defeat° was made. Am I a coward?
Who calls me villain? Breaks my pate° across?   610
Plucks off my beard and blows it in my face?
Tweaks me by the nose? Gives me the lie i' the throat°
As deep as to the lungs? Who does me this?
Ha, 'swounds,° I should take it; for it cannot be
But I am pigeon-livered° and lack gall   615
To make oppression bitter,° or ere this
I should ha' fatted all the region kites°
With this slave's offal.° Bloody, bawdy villain!
Remorseless,° treacherous, lecherous, kindless° villain!
O, vengeance!   620
Why, what an ass am I! This is most brave,°
That I, the son of a dear father murdered,
Prompted to my revenge by heaven and hell,
Must like a whore unpack my heart with words
And fall a-cursing, like a very drab,°   625
A scullion!° Fie upon 't, foh! About,° my brains!
Hum, I have heard
That guilty creatures sitting at a play
Have by the very cunning° of the scene°
Been struck so to the soul that presently°   630
They have proclaimed their malefactions;
For murder, though it have no tongue, will speak

---

601 the general ear everyone's ear;   horrid horrible.   602 appall (Literally, make pale.);
free innocent.   603 Confound the ignorant, i.e., dumbfound those who know nothing of the crime
that has been committed;   amaze stun.   605 muddy-mettled dull-spirited;   peak mope, pine.
606 John-a-dreams a sleepy, dreaming idler;   unpregnant of not quickened by.   608 property i.e.,
the crown; also character, quality.   609 damned defeat damnable act of destruction.   610 pate
head.   612 Gives . . . throat calls me an out-and-out liar.   614 'swounds by his (Christ's) wounds.
615 pigeon-livered (The pigeon or dove was popularly supposed to be mild because it secreted no
gall.)   616 bitter i.e., bitter to me.   617 region kites kites (birds of prey) of the air.   618 offal
entrails.   619 Remorseless pitiless;   kindless unnatural.   621 brave fine, admirable. (Said ironically.)
625 drab whore.   626 scullion menial kitchen servant (apt to be foul-mouthed);   About about it, to
work.   629 cunning art, skill;   scene dramatic presentation.   630 presently at once.

With most miraculous organ. I'll have these players
Play something like the murder of my father
Before mine uncle. I'll observe his looks;   635
I'll tent° him to the quick.° If 'a do blench,°
I know my course. The spirit that I have seen
May be the devil, and the devil hath power
T' assume a pleasing shape; yea, and perhaps,
Out of my weakness and my melancholy,   640
As he is very potent with such spirits,°
Abuses° me to damn me. I'll have grounds
More relative° than this. The play's the thing
Wherein I'll catch the conscience of the King.   *Exit.*

ACT III

SCENE I [THE CASTLE.]

Enter King, Queen, Polonius, Ophelia, Rosencrantz, Lords.

KING: And can you by no drift of conference°
Get from him why he puts on this confusion,
Grating so harshly all his days of quiet
With turbulent and dangerous lunacy?
ROSENCRANTZ: He does confess he feels himself distracted,   5
But from what cause 'a will by no means speak.
GUILDENSTERN: Nor do we find him forward° to be sounded,°
But with a crafty madness keeps aloof
When we would bring him on to some confession
Of his true state.
QUEEN: Did he receive you well?   10
ROSENCRANTZ: Most like a gentleman.
GUILDENSTERN: But with much forcing of his disposition.°
ROSENCRANTZ: Niggard° of question,° but of our demands
Most free in his reply.
QUEEN: Did you assay° him
To any pastime?   15
ROSENCRANTZ: Madam, it so fell out that certain players
We o'erraught° on the way. Of these we told him,

---

636 tent probe; **the quick** the tender part of a wound, the core; **blench** quail, flinch. 641 **spirits** humors (of melancholy). 642 **Abuses** deludes. 643 **relative** cogent, pertinent. 1 **drift of conference** directing of conversation. 7 **forward** willing; **sounded** questioned. 12 **dispositon** inclination. 13 **Niggard** stingy; **question** conversation. 14 **assay** try to win. 17 **o'erraught** overtook.

And there did seem in him a kind of joy
To hear of it. They are here about the court,
And, as I think, they have already order   20
This night to play before him.
POLONIUS: 'Tis most true,
And he beseeched me to entreat Your Majesties
To hear and see the matter.
KING: With all my heart, and it doth much content me
To hear him so inclined.   25
Good gentlemen, give him a further edge°
And drive his purpose into these delights.
ROSENCRANTZ: We shall, my lord.

                Exeunt Rosencrantz and Guildenstern.

KING: Sweet Gertrude, leave us too
For we have closely° sent for Hamlet hither,
That he, as 'twere by accident, may here   30
Affront° Ophelia.
Her father and myself, lawful espials,°
Will so bestow ourselves that seeing, unseen,
We may of their encounter frankly judge,
And gather by him, as he is behaved,   35
If 't be th' affliction of his love or no
That thus he suffers for.
QUEEN: I shall obey you.
And for your part, Ophelia, I do wish
That your good beauties be the happy cause
Of Hamlet's wildness. So shall I hope your virtues   40
Will bring him to his wonted° way again,
To both your honors.
OPHELIA: Madam, I wish it may.   [*Exit Queen.*]
POLONIUS: Ophelia, walk you here.—Gracious,° so please you,
We will bestow° ourselves. [*To Ophelia.*] Read on this book,

                          [*giving her a book*]

That show of such an exercise° may color°   45
Your loneliness.° We are oft to blame in this—
'Tis too much proved°—that with devotion's visage

---

26 edge incitement.   29 closely privately.   31 Affront confront, meet.   32 espials spies.   41 wonted
accustomed.   43 Gracious Your Grace (i.e., the King).   44 bestow conceal.   45 exercise religious
exercise. (The book she reads is one of devotion.);   color give a plausible appearance to.
46 loneliness being alone.   47 too much proved too often shown to be true, too often practiced.

And pious action we do sugar o'er
The devil himself.
KING [*aside*]:   O 'tis too true!   50
How smart a lash that speech doth give my conscience!
The harlot's cheek, beautied with plastering art,
Is not more ugly to° the thing° that helps it
Than is my deed to my most painted word.
O heavy burden!   55
POLONIUS: I hear him coming. Let's withdraw, my lord.

[*The King and Polonius withdraw.*°]

Enter Hamlet. [*Ophelia pretends to read a book.*]

HAMLET: To be, or not to be, that is the question:
Whether 'tis nobler in the mind to suffer
The slings° and arrows of outrageous fortune,
Or to take arms against a sea of troubles   60
And by opposing end them. To die, to sleep—
No more—and by a sleep to say we end
The heartache and the thousand natural shocks
That flesh is heir to. 'Tis a consummation
Devoutly to be wished. To die, to sleep;   65
To sleep, perchance to dream. Ay, there's the rub,°
For in that sleep of death what dreams may come,
When we have shuffled° off this mortal coil,°
Must give us pause. There's the respect°
That makes calamity of so long life.°   70
For who would bear the whips and scorns of time,
Th' oppressor's wrong, the proud man's contumely,°
The pangs of disprized° love, the law's delay,
The insolence of office,° and the spurns°
That patient merit of th' unworthy takes,°   75
When he himself might his quietus° make
With a bare bodkin?° Who would fardels° bear,
To grunt and sweat under a weary life,

---

53 **to** compared to;   **the thing** i.e., the cosmetic.   56 s.d. **withdraw** (The King and Polonius may retire behind an arras. The stage directions specify that they "enter" again near the end of the scene.)   59 **slings** missiles.   66 **rub** (Literally, an obstacle in the game of bowls.)   68 **shuffled** sloughed, cast;   **coil** turmoil.   69 **respect** consideration.   70 **of . . . life** so long-lived, something we willingly endure for so long (also suggesting that long life is itself a calamity).   72 **contumely** insolent abuse.   73 **disprized** unvalued.   74 **office** officialdom;   **spurns** insults.   75 **of . . . takes** receives from unworthy persons.   76 **quietus** acquitance; here, death.   77 **a bare bodkin** a mere dagger, unsheathed;   **fardels** burdens.

But that the dread of something after death,
The undiscovered country from whose bourn°   80
No traveler returns, puzzles the will,
And makes us rather bear those ills we have
Than fly to others that we know not of?
Thus conscience does make cowards of us all;
And thus the native hue° of resolution   85
Is sicklied o'er with the pale cast° of thought,
And enterprises of great pitch° and moment°
With this regard° their currents° turn awry
And lose the name of action.—Soft you° now,
The fair Ophelia. Nymph, in thy orisons°   90
Be all my sins remembered.

OPHELIA: Good my lord,
How does your honor for this many a day?

HAMLET: I humbly thank you; well, well, well.

OPHELIA: My lord, I have remembrances of yours,
That I have longèd long to redeliver.   95
I pray you, now receive them.   [*She offers tokens.*]

HAMLET: No, not I, I never gave you aught.

OPHELIA: My honored lord, you know right well you did,
And with them words of so sweet breath composed
As made the things more rich. Their perfume lost,   100
Take these again, for to the noble mind
Rich gifts wax poor when givers prove unkind.
There, my lord.   [*She gives tokens.*]

HAMLET: Ha, ha! Are you honest?°

OPHELIA: My lord?   105

HAMLET: Are you fair?°

OPHELIA: What means your lordship?

HAMLET: That if you be honest and fair, your honesty° should
admit no discourse to° your beauty

OPHELIA: Could beauty, my lord, have better commerce° than   110
with honesty?

HAMLET: Ay, truly, for the power of beauty will sooner transform
honesty from what it is to a bawd than the force of honesty can

---

80 **bourn** frontier, boundary.   85 **native hue** natural color, complexion.   86 **cast** tinge, shade of color.   87 **pitch** height (as of a falcon's flight.);   **moment** importance.   88 **regard** respect, consideration;   **currents** courses.   89 **Soft you** i.e., wait a minute, gently.   90 **orisons** prayers.   104 **honest** (1) truthful (2) chaste.   106 **fair** (1) beautiful (2) just, honorable.   108 **your honesty** your chastity.   109 **discourse to** familiar dealings with.   110 **commerce** dealings, intercourse.

translate beauty into his° likeness. This was sometime° a
paradox,° but now the time° gives it proof. I did love you once. 115

OPHELIA: Indeed, my lord, you made me believe so.

HAMLET: You should not have believed me, for virtue cannot so
inoculate° our old stock but we shall relish of it.° I loved you not.

OPHELIA: I was the more deceived.

HAMLET: Get thee to a nunnery.° Why wouldst thou be a breeder 120
of sinners? I am myself indifferent honest,° but yet I could
accuse me of such things that it were better my mother had not
borne me: I am very proud, revengeful, ambitious, with more
offenses at my beck° than I have thoughts to put them in,
imagination to give them shape, or time to act them in. What 125
should such fellows as I do crawling between earth and heaven?
We are arrant knaves all; believe none of us. Go thy ways to a
nunnery. Where's your father?

OPHELIA: At home, my lord.

HAMLET: Let the doors be shut upon him, that he may play the 130
fool nowhere but in's own house. Farewell.

OPHELIA: O, help him, you sweet heavens!

HAMLET: If thou dost marry, I'll give thee this plague for thy
dowry: be thou as chaste as ice, as pure as snow, thou shalt not
escape calumny. Get thee to a nunnery, farewell. Or, if thou wilt 135
needs marry, marry a fool, for wise men know well enough
what monsters° you° make of them. To a nunnery, go, and
quickly too. Farewell.

OPHELIA: Heavenly powers, restore him!

HAMLET: I have heard of your paintings too, well enough. God 140
hath given you one face, and you make yourselves another. You
jig,° you amble,° and you lisp, you nickname God's creatures,°
and make your wantonness your ignorance.° Go to, I'll no more
on 't;° it hath made me mad. I say we will have no more
marriage. Those that are married already—all but one—shall 145
live. The rest shall keep as they are. To a nunnery, go.   *Exit.*

OPHELIA: O, what a noble mind is here o'erthrown!
The courtier's, soldier's, scholar's, eye, tongue, sword,

---

114 his its; **sometime** formerly; **115 a paradox** a view opposite to commonly held opinion;
the time the present age. **118 inoculate** graft, be engrafted to. **118 but . . . it** that we do not still
have about us a taste of the old stock, i.e., retain our sinfulness. **120 nunnery** convent (with
possibly an awareness that the word was also used derisively to denote a brothel). **121 indifferent
honest** reasonably virtuous. **124 beck** command. **137 monsters** (An illusion to the horns of a
cuckold.); **you** i.e., you women. **142 jig** dance; **amble** move coyly. **you nickname . . . creatures**
i.e., you give trendy names to things in place of their God-given names. **143 make . . . ignorance**
i.e., excuse your affectation on the grounds of pretended ignorance; **144 on 't** of it.

Th' expectancy° and rose° of the fair state,
The glass of fashion and the mold of form,°   150
Th' observed of all observers,° quite, quite down!
And I, of ladies most deject and wretched,
That sucked the honey of his music° vows,
Now see that noble and most sovereign reason
Like sweet bells jangled out of tune and harsh,   155
That unmatched form and feature of blown° youth
Blasted° with ecstasy.° O, woe is me,
T' have seen what I have seen, see what I see!

Enter King and Polonius.

KING: Love? His affections° do not that way tend;
Nor what he spake, though it lacked form a little,   160
Was not like madness. There's something in his soul
O'er which his melancholy sits on brood,°
And I do doubt° the hatch and the disclose°
Will be some danger; which for to prevent,
I have in quick determination   165
Thus set it down:° he shall with speed to England
For the demand of° our neglected tribute.
Haply the seas and countries different
With variable objects° shall expel
This something-settled matter in his heart,°   170
Whereon his brains still° beating puts him thus
From fashion of himself.° What think you on 't?
POLONIUS: It shall do well. But yet do I believe
The origin and commencement of his grief
Sprung from neglected love.—How now, Ophelia?   175
You need not tell us what Lord Hamlet said;
We heard it all.—My lord, do as you please,
But, if you hold it fit, after the play
Let his queen-mother° all alone entreat him
To show his grief. Let her be round° with him;   180

---

149 **expectancy** hope;   **rose** ornament   150 **The glass . . . form** the mirror of true fashioning and the pattern of courtly behavior.   151 **Th' observed . . . observers** i.e., the center of attention and honor in the court.   153 **music** musical, sweetly uttered.   156 **blown** blooming.   157 **Blasted** withered;   **ecstasy** madness.   159 **affections** emotions, feelings.   162 **sits on brood** sits like a bird on a nest, about to hatch mischief (line 169).   163 **doubt** fear;   **disclose** disclosure, hatching. 166 **set it down** resolved.   167 **For . . . of** to demand.   169 **variable objects** various sights and surroundings to divert him.   170 **This something . . . heart** the strange matter settled in his heart. 171 **still** continually.   172 **From . . . himself** out of his natural manner.   179 **queen-mother** queen and mother.   180 **round** blunt.

And I'll be placed, so please you, in the ear
Of all their conference. If she find him not,°
To England send him, or confine him where
Your wisdom best shall think.

KING: It shall be so.
Madness in great ones must not unwatched go.   185

Exeunt.

SCENE II [THE CASTLE.]

Enter Hamlet and three of the Players.

HAMLET: Speak the speech, I pray you, as I pronounced it to you,
trippingly on the tongue. But if you mouth it, as many of our
players° do, I had as lief° the town crier spoke my lines. Nor do
not saw the air too much with your hand, thus, but use all gently;   5
for in the very torrent, tempest, and, as I may say, whirlwind of
your passion, you must acquire and beget a temperance that may
give it smoothness. O, it offends me to the soul to hear a
robustious° periwig-pated° fellow tear a passion to tatters, to very
rags, to split the ears of the groundlings,° who for the most part   10
are capable of° nothing but inexplicable dumb shows° and noise.
I would have such a fellow whipped for o'erdoing Termagant.° It
out-Herods Herod.° Pray you, avoid it.

FIRST PLAYER: I warrant your honor.

HAMLET: Be not too tame neither, but let your own discretion be   15
your tutor. Suit the action to the word, the word to the action,
with this special observance, that you o'erstep not the modesty°
of nature. For anything so o'erdone is from° the purpose of
playing, whose end, both at the first and now, was and is to
hold as 't were the mirror up to nature, to show virtue her   20
feature, scorn° her own image, and the very age and body of
the time° his° form and pressure.° Now this overdone or come
tardy off,° though it makes the unskillful° laugh, cannot but

---

182 **find him not** fails to discover what is troubling him.   3 **our players** players nowadays.
I had as lief I would just as soon.   8 **robustious** violent, boisterous;   **periwig-pated** wearing a wig.
9 **groundlings** spectators who paid least and stood in the yard of the theater.   10 **capable of** able to
understand;   **dumb shows** mimed performances, often used before Shakespeare's time to precede a
play or each act.   11 **Termagant** a supposed deity of the Mohammedans, not found in any English
medieval play but elsewhere portrayed as violent and blustering.   12 **Herod** Herod of Jewry. (A
character in The Slaughter of the Innocents and other cycle plays. The part was played with great
noise and fury.)   16 **modesty** restraint, moderation.   17 **from** contrary to.   20 **scorn** i.e., something foolish and deserving of scorn.   20–21 **the very . . . time** i.e., the present state of affairs;
21 **his** its;   **pressure** stamp, impressed character;   21–22 **come tardy off** inadequately done.
22 **the unskillful** those lacking in judgment.

make the judicious grieve, the censure of the which one° must
in your allowance° o'erweigh a whole theater of others. O,
there be players that I have seen play, and heard others praise, 25
and that highly, not to speak it profanely,° that, neither having
th' accent of Christians° nor the gait of Christian, pagan, nor
man,° have so strutted and bellowed that I have thought some
of nature's journeymen° had made men and not made them
well, they imitated humanity so abominably.° 30

FIRST PLAYER: I hope we have reformed that indifferently° with
us, sir.

HAMLET: O, reform it altogether. And let those that play your
clowns speak no more than is set down for them; for there be
of them° that will themselves laugh, to set on some quantity of 35
barren° spectators to laugh too, though in the meantime some
necessary question of the play be then to be considered. That's
villainous, and shows a most pitiful ambition in the fool that
uses it. Go make you ready.   [*Exeunt Players.*]

Enter Polonius, Guildenstern and Rosencrantz.

How now, my lord, will the King hear this piece of work? 40

POLONIUS: And the Queen too, and that presently.°

HAMLET: Bid the players make haste.   [*Exit Polonius.*]
Will you two help to hasten them?

ROSENCRANTZ: Ay, my lord.   *Exeunt they two.*

HAMLET: What ho, Horatio!

Enter Horatio.

HORATIO: Here, sweet lord, at your service. 45

HAMLET: Horatio, thou art e'en as just a man
As e'er my conversation coped withal.°

HORATIO: O, my dear lord—

HAMLET: Nay, do not think I flatter,
For what advancement may I hope from thee
That no revenue hast but thy good spirits 50
To feed and clothe thee? Why should the poor be flattered?

---

23 the censure . . . one the judgment of even one of whom;   **24 your allowance** your scale of
values.   **26 not . . . profanely** (Hamlet anticipates his idea in lines 25–27 that some men were not
made by God at all.)   **27 Christians** i.e., ordinary decent folk.   **27–28 nor man** i.e., nor any human
being at all.   **29 journeymen** laborers who are not yet masters in their trade.   **30 abominably**
(Shakespeare's usual spelling, abhominably, suggests a literal though etymologically incorrect
meaning, "removed from human nature.")   **31 indifferently** tolerably.   **35 of them** some among
them.   **36 barren** i.e., of wit.   **41 presently** at once.   **47 my . . . withal** my dealings encountered.

No, let the candied° tongue lick absurd pomp,
And crook the pregnant° hinges of the knee
Where thrift° may follow fawning. Dost thou hear?
Since my dear soul was mistress of her choice 55
And could of men distinguish her election,°
Sh' hath sealed thee° for herself, for thou hast been
As one, in suffering all, that suffers nothing,
A man that Fortune's buffets and rewards
Hast ta'en with equal thanks; and blest are those 60
Whose blood° and judgment are so well commeddled°
That they are not a pipe for Fortune's finger
To sound what stop° she please. Give me that man
That is not passion's slave, and I will wear him
In my heart's core, ay, in my heart of heart, 65
As I do thee.—Something too much of this.—
There is a play tonight before the King.
One scene of it comes near the circumstance
Which I have told thee of my father's death.
I prithee, when thou seest that act afoot, 70
Even with the very comment of thy soul°
Observe my uncle. If his occulted° guilt
Do not itself unkennel° in one speech,
It is a damnéd° ghost that we have seen,
And my imaginations are as foul 75
As Vulcan's stithy.° Give him heedful note,
For I mine eyes will rivet to his face,
And after we will both our judgments join
In censure of his seeming.°
HORATIO: Well, my lord.
If 'a steal aught° the whilst this play is playing 80
And scape detecting, I will pay the theft.

[*Flourish.*] *Enter trumpets and kettledrums, King, Queen, Polonius,
Ophelia,* [*Rosencrantz, Guildenstern, and other lords, with guards
carrying torches*].

52 **candied** sugared, flattering. 53 **pregnant** compliant. 54 **thrift** profit. 56 **could . . . election**
could make distinguishing choices among persons. 57 **sealed thee** (Literally, as one would seal
a legal document to mark possession.) 61 **blood** passion; **commeddled** commingled. 63 **stop**
hole in a wind instrument for controlling the sound. 71 **very . . . soul** your most penetrating
observation and consideration. 72 **occulted** hidden. 73 **unkennel** (As one would say of a fox
driven from its lair.) 74 **damnéd** in league with Satan. 76 **stithy** smithy, place of stiths (anvils).
79 **censure of his seeming** judgment of his appearance or behavior. 80 **If 'a steal aught** if he gets
away with anything.

HAMLET: They are coming to the play. I must be idle.° Get you a place.

[The King, Queen, and courtiers sit.]

KING: How fares our cousin° Hamlet?

HAMLET: Excellent, i' faith, of the chameleon's dish:° I eat the air, 85 promise-crammed. You cannot feed capons° so.

KING: I have nothing with° this answer, Hamlet. These words are not mine.°

HAMLET: No, nor mine now.°

[To Polonius.]

My lord, you played once i' th' university, you say? 90

POLONIUS: That did I, my lord, and was accounted a good actor.

HAMLET: What did you enact?

POLONIUS: I did enact Julius Caesar. I was killed i' the Capitol; Brutus killed me.

HAMLET: It was a brute° part° of him to kill so capital a calf° 95 there.—Be the players ready?

ROSENCRANTZ: Ay, my lord. They stay upon° your patience.

QUEEN: Come hither, my dear Hamlet, sit by me.

HAMLET: No, good Mother, here's metal° more attractive.

POLONIUS *[to the King]*: O, ho, do you mark that? 100

HAMLET: Lady, shall I lie in your lap?

[Lying down at Ophelia's feet.]

OPHELIA: No, my lord.

HAMLET: I mean, my head upon your lap?

OPHELIA: Ay, my lord.

HAMLET: Do you think I meant country matters?° 105

OPHELIA: I think nothing, my lord.

HAMLET: That's a fair thought to lie between maids' legs.

OPHELIA: What is, my lord?

---

82 **idle** (1) unoccupied (2) mad. 84 **cousin** i.e., close relative. 85 **chameleon's dish** (Chameleons were supposed to feed on air. Hamlet deliberately misinterprets the King's *fares* as "feeds." By his phrase *eat the air* he also plays on the idea of feeding himself with the promise of succession, of being the heir.) 86 **capons** roosters castrated and crammed with feed to make them succulent. 87 **have . . . with** make nothing of, or gain nothing from; 87–88 **are not mine** do not respond to what I asked. 89 **nor mine now** (Once spoken, words are proverbially no longer the speaker's own—and hence should be uttered warily.) 95 **brute** (The Latin meaning of *brutus*, "stupid," was often used punningly with the name Brutus.); **part** (1)deed (2) role; **calf** fool. 97 **stay upon** await. 99 **metal** substance that is attractive, i.e., magnetic, but with suggestion also of mettle, "disposition." 105 **country matters** sexual intercourse (making a bawdy pun on the first syllable of country).

HAMLET: Nothing.°

OPHELIA: You are merry, my lord. 110

HAMLET: Who, I?

OPHELIA: Ay, my lord.

HAMLET: O God, your only jig maker.° What should a man do
but be merry? For look you how cheerfully my mother looks,
and my father died within 's° two hours. 115

OPHELIA: Nay, 'tis twice two months, my lord.

HAMLET: So long? Nay then, let the devil wear black, for I'll have
a suit of sables.° O heavens! Die two months ago, and not forgotten yet? Then there's hope a great man's memory may outlive
his life half a year. But, by 'r Lady, 'a must build churches, then, 120
or else shall 'a suffer not thinking on,° with the hobbyhorse,
whose epitaph is "For O, for O, the hobbyhorse is forgot."°

The trumpets sound. Dumb show follows.

*Enter a King and a Queen [very lovingly]; the Queen embracing
him, and he her. [She kneels, and makes show of protestation unto
him.] He takes her up, and declines his head upon her neck. He lies
him down upon a bank of flowers. She, seeing him asleep, leaves
him. Anon comes in another man, takes off his crown, kisses it,
pours poison in the sleeper's ears, and leaves him. The Queen returns, finds the King dead, makes passionate action. The Poisoner
with some three or four come in again, seem to condole with her.
The dead body is carried away. The Poisoner woos the Queen with
gifts; she seems harsh awhile, but in the end accepts love.*

[Exeunt players.]

OPHELIA: What means this, my lord?

HAMLET: Marry, this' miching mallico;° it means mischief.

OPHELIA: Belike° this show imports the argument° of the play. 125

Enter Prologue.

109 **Nothing** the figure zero or naught, suggesting the female sexual anatomy. (Thing not
infrequently has a bawdy connotation of male or female anatomy, and the reference here could
be male.) 113 **only jig maker** very best composer of jigs, i.e., pointless merriment. (Hamlet
replies sardonically to Ophelia's observation that he is merry by saying, "If you're looking for
someone who is really merry, you've come to the right person.") 115 **within 's** within this (i.e.,
these). 118 **suit of sables** garments trimmed with the fur of the sable and hence suited for a
wealthy person, not a mourner (but with a pun on sable, "black," ironically suggesting mourning
once again). 121 **suffer . . . on** undergo oblivion. 122 **For . . . forgot** (Verse of a song occurring
also in Love's Labor's Lost, 3.1.27–28. The hobbyhorse was a character made up to resemble a
horse and rider, appearing in the morris dance and such May-game sports. This song laments the
disappearance of such customs under pressure from the Puritans.) 124 **this' miching mallico** this is
sneaking mischief. 125 **Belike** probably; **argument** plot.

HAMLET: We shall know by this fellow. The players cannot keep counsel;° they'll tell all.

OPHELIA: Will 'a tell us what this show meant?

HAMLET: Ay, or any show that you will show him. Be not you° ashamed to show, he'll not shame to tell you what it means. 130

OPHELIA: You are naught,° you are naught. I'll mark the play.

PROLOGUE: For us, and for our tragedy,
Here stooping° to your clemency,
We beg your hearing patiently.   [*Exit.*]

HAMLET: Is this a prologue, or the posy of a ring?°   135

OPHELIA: 'Tis brief, my lord.

HAMLET: As woman's love.

Enter [two Players as] King and Queen.

PLAYER KING: Full thirty times hath Phoebus' cart° gone round
Neptune's salt wash° and Tellus'° orbèd ground,
And thirty dozen moons with borrowed° sheen   140
About the world have times twelve thirties been,
Since love our hearts and Hymen° did our hands
Unite commutual° in most sacred bands.°

PLAYER QUEEN: So many journeys may the sun and moon
Make us again count o'er ere love be done!   145
But, woe is me, you are so sick of late,
So far from cheer and from your former state,
That I distrust° you. Yet, though I distrust,
Discomfort° you, my lord, it nothing° must.
For women's fear and love hold quantity;°   150
In neither aught, or in extremity.°
Now, what my love is, proof° hath made you know,
And as my love is sized,° my fear is so.
Where love is great, the littlest doubts are fear;
Where little fears grow great, great love grows there. 155

PLAYER KING: Faith, I must leave thee, love, and shortly too;
My operant powers° their functions leave to do.°

---

127 **counsel** secret.   129 **Be not you** provided you are not.   131 **naught** indecent. (Ophelia is reacting to Hamlet's pointed remarks about not being ashamed to show all.)   133 **stooping** bowing.
135 **posy . . . ring** brief motto in verse inscribed in a ring.   138 **Phoebus' cart** the sun-god's chariot, making its yearly cycle.   139 **salt wash** the sea;   **Tellus** goddess of the earth, of the orbèd ground.
140 **borrowed** i.e., reflected.   142 **Hymen** god of matrimony.   143 **commutual** mutually;   **bands** bonds.   148 **distrust** am anxious about.   149 **Discomfort** distress;   **nothing** not at all.   150 **hold quantity** keep proportion with one another.   151 **In . . . extremity** i.e., women fear and love either too little or too much, but the two, fear and love, are equal in either case.   152 **proof** experience.
153 **sized** in size.   157 **operant powers** vital functions;   **leave to do** cease to perform.

And thou shalt live in this fair world behind,°
Honored, beloved; and haply one as kind
For husband shalt thou—
PLAYER QUEEN: O, confound the rest!   160
Such love must needs be treason in my breast.
In second husband let me be accurst!
None° wed the second but who° killed the first.
HAMLET: Wormwood,° wormwood.
PLAYER QUEEN: The instances° that second marriage move°   165
Are base respects of thrift,° but none of love.
A second time I kill my husband dead
When second husband kisses me in bed.
PLAYER KING: I do believe you think what now you speak,
But what we do determine oft we break.   170
Purpose is but the slave to memory,°
Of violent birth, but poor validity,°
Which° now, like fruit unripe, sticks on the tree,
But fall unshaken when they mellow be.
Most necessary 'tis that we forget   175
To pay ourselves what to ourselves is debt.°
What to ourselves in passion we propose,
The passion ending, doth the purpose lose.
The violence of either grief or joy
Their own enactures° with themselves destroy.   180
Where joy most revels, grief doth most lament;
Grief joys, joy grieves, on slender accident.°
This world is not for aye,° nor 'tis not strange
That even our loves should with our fortunes change;
For 'tis a question left us yet to prove,   185
Whether love lead fortune, or else fortune love.
The great man down,° you mark his favorite flies;
The poor advanced makes friends of enemies.°
And hitherto° doth love on fortune tend;°

---

158 **behind** after I have gone.   163 **None** i.e., let no woman; **but who** except the one who.
164 **Wormwood** i.e., how bitter. (Literally, a bitter-tasting plant.)   165 **instances** motives; **move**
motivate.   166 **base . . . thrift** ignoble considerations of material prosperity.   171 **Purpose . . .**
memory our good intentions are subject to forgetfulness.   172 **validity** strength, durability.
173 **Which** i.e., purpose.   175–176 **Most . . . debt** it's inevitable that in time we forget the
obligations we have imposed on ourselves.   180 **enactures** fulfillments.   181–182 **Where . . .**
accident the capacity for extreme joy and grief go together, and often one extreme is instantly
changed into its opposite on the slightest provocation.   183 **aye** ever.   187 **down** fallen in fortune.
188 **The poor . . . enemies** when one of humble station is promoted, you see his enemies suddenly
becoming his friends.   189 **hitherto** up to this point in the argument, or, to this extent; **tend** attend.

For who not needs° shall never lack a friend,   190
And who in want° a hollow friend doth try°
Directly seasons him° his enemy.
But, orderly to end where I begun,
Our wills and fates do so contrary run°
That our devices still° are overthrown;   195
Our thoughts are ours, their ends° none of our own.
So think thou wilt no second husband wed,
But die thy thoughts when thy first lord is dead.

PLAYER QUEEN: Nor° earth to me give food, nor heaven light,
Sport and repose lock from me day and night,°   200
To desperation turn my trust and hope,
An anchor's cheer° in prison be my scope!°
Each opposite that blanks° the face of joy
Meet what I would have well and it destroy!°
Both here and hence° pursue me lasting strife   205
If, once a widow, ever I be wife!

HAMLET: If she should break it now!

PLAYER KING: 'Tis deeply sworn. Sweet, leave me here awhile;
My spirits° grow dull, and fain I would beguile
The tedious day with sleep.

PLAYER QUEEN: Sleep rock thy brain,   210
And never come mischance between us twain!

                        [He sleeps.] Exit [Player Queen].

HAMLET: Madam, how like you this play?

QUEEN: The lady doth protest too much,° methinks.

HAMLET: O, but she'll keep her word.

KING: Have you heard the argument?° Is there no offense° in 't?   215

HAMLET: No, no, they do but jest,° poison in jest. No offense i'
the world.

KING: What do you call the play?

---

190 **who not needs** he who is not in need (of wealth).   191 **who in want** he who, being in need;
try test (his generosity).   192 **seasons him** ripens him into.   194 **Our . . . run** what we want and
what we get go so contrarily.   195 **devices still** intentions continually.   196 **ends** results.   199 **Nor**
let neither.   200 **Sport . . . night** may day deny me its pastimes and night its repose.   202 **anchor's
cheer** anchorite's or hermit's fare;   **my scope** the extent of my happiness.   203 **blanks** causes to
blanch or grow pale.   204 **Each . . . destroy** may every adverse thing that causes the face of joy to
turn pale meet and destroy everything that I desire to see prosper.   205 **hence** in the life hereafter.
209 **spirits** vital spirits.   213 **doth . . . much** makes too many promises and protestations.
215 **argument** plot.   215–216 **offense . . . offense** cause for objection . . . actual injury, crime.
216 **jest** make believe.

HAMLET: *The Mousetrap.* Marry, how? Tropically.° This play is
the image of a murder done in Vienna. Gonzago is the Duke's°   220
name, his wife, Baptista. You shall see anon. 'Tis a knavish piece
of work, but what of that? Your Majesty, and we that have free°
souls, it touches us not. Let the galled jade° wince, our withers°
are unwrung.°

Enter Lucianus.

This is one Lucianus, nephew to the King.   225

OPHELIA: You are as good as a chorus,° my lord.

HAMLET: I could interpret° between you and your love, if I could
see the puppets dallying.°

OPHELIA: You are keen,° my lord, you are keen.

HAMLET: It would cost you a groaning to take off mine edge.   230

OPHELIA: Still better, and worse.°

HAMLET: So° you mis-take° your husbands. Begin, murder; leave
thy damnable faces and begin. Come, the croaking raven doth
bellow for revenge.

LUCIANUS: Thoughts black, hands apt, drugs fit, and time agreeing,   235
Confederate season,° else° no creature seeing,°
Thou mixture rank, of midnight weeds collected,
With Hecate's ban° thrice blasted, thrice infected,
Thy natural magic and dire property°
On wholesome life usurp immediately.   240

[*He pours the poison into the sleeper's ear.*]

HAMLET: 'A poisons him i' the garden for his estate.° His° name's
Gonzago. The story is extant, and written in very choice Italian.
You shall see anon how the murderer gets the love of Gonzago's
wife.

219 **Tropically** figuratively. (The First Quarto reading, trapically, suggests a pun on trap in
Mousetrap.)   220 **Duke's** i.e., King's (A slip that may be due to Shakespeare's possible source, the
alleged murder of the Duke of Urbino by Luigi Gonzaga in 1538.)   222 **free** guiltless.   223 **galled
jade** horse whose hide is rubbed by saddle or harness.   **withers** the part between the horse's shoulder
blades;   224 **unwrung** not rubbed sore.   226 **chorus** (In many Elizabethan plays, the forthcoming
action was explained by an actor known as the "chorus"; at a puppet show, the actor who spoke the
dialogue was known as an "interpreter," as indicated by the lines following.)   227 **interpret** (1)
ventriloquize the dialogue, as in a puppet show (2) act as pander.   228 **puppets dallying** (With
suggestion of sexual play, continued in keen, "sexually aroused," groaning, "moaning in pregnancy,"
and edge, "sexual desire" or "impetuosity.")   229 **keen** sharp, bitter.   231 **Still . . . worse** more keen,
always bettering what other people say with witty wordplay, but at the same time more offensive.
232 **So** even thus (in marriage);   **mis-take** take falseheartedly and cheat on. (The marriage vows say
"for better, for worse.")   236 **Confederate season** the time and occasion conspiring (to assist the
murderer);   **else** otherwise;   **seeing** seeing me.   238 **Hecate's ban** the curse of Hecate, the goddess of
witchcraft.   239 **dire property** baleful quality.   241 **estate** i.e., the kingship;   **His** i.e., the King's.

[Claudius rises.]

OPHELIA: The King rises. 245
HAMLET: What, frighted with false fire?°
QUEEN: How fares my lord?
POLONIUS: Give o'er the play.
KING: Give me some light. Away!
POLONIUS: Lights, lights, lights! 250

Exeunt all but Hamlet and Horatio.

HAMLET:

"Why,° let the strucken deer go weep,
    The hart ungallèd° play.
For some must watch,° while some must sleep;
    Thus runs the world away."°

Would not this,° sir, and a forest of feathers°—if the rest of my 255
fortunes turn Turk with° me—with two Provincial roses° on my
razed° shoes, get me a fellowship in a cry° of players?°
HORATIO: Half a share.
HAMLET: A whole one, I.

"For thou dost know, O Damon° dear, 260
    This realm dismantled° was
Of Jove himself, and now reigns here
    A very, very—pajock."°

HORATIO: You might have rhymed.
HAMLET: O good Horatio, I'll take the ghost's word for a thou- 265
sand pound. Didst perceive?
HORATIO: Very well, my lord.
HAMLET: Upon the talk of the poisoning?
HORATIO: I did very well note him.

---

246 **false fire** the blank discharge of a gun loaded with powder but no shot.   252–255 **Why . . .
away** (Probably from an old ballad, with allusion to the popular belief that a wounded deer retires
to weep and die; compare with As You Like It, 2.1.33–66.)   252 **ungallèd** unafflicted.   253 **watch**
remain awake.   254 **Thus . . . away** thus the world goes.   255 **this** i.e., the play;   **feathers**
(Allusion to the plumes that Elizabethan actors were fond of wearing.)   256 **turn Turk with** turn
renegade against, go back on;   **Provincial roses** rosettes of ribbon, named for roses grown in a part
of France;   257 **razed** with ornamental slashing.   **cry** pack (of hounds);   **fellowship . . . players**
partnership in a theatrical company.   260 **Damon** the friend of Pythias, as Horatio is friend of
Hamlet; or, a traditional pastoral name.   261 **dismantled** stripped, divested.   261–263 **This realm
. . . pajock** i.e., Jove, representing divine authority and justice, has abandoned this realm to its own
devices, leaving in his stead only a peacock or vain pretender to virtue (though the rhyme-word
expected in place of pajock or "peacock" suggests that the realm is now ruled over by an "ass").

Enter Rosencrantz and Guildenstern.

HAMLET: Aha! Come, some music! Come, the recorders.°   270

"For if the King like not the comedy,
Why then, belike, he likes it not, perdy."°

Come, some music.
GUILDENSTERN: Good my lord, vouchsafe me a word with you.
HAMLET: Sir, a whole history.   275
GUILDENSTERN: The King, sir—
HAMLET: Ay, sir, what of him?
GUILDENSTERN: Is in his retirement° marvelous distempered.°
HAMLET: With drink, sir?
GUILDENSTERN: No, my lord, with choler.°   280
HAMLET: Your wisdom should show itself more richer to signify
this to the doctor, for for me to put him to his purgation°
would perhaps plunge him into more choler.
GUILDENSTERN: Good my lord, put your discourse into some
frame° and start° not so wildly from my affair.   285
HAMLET: I am tame, sir. Pronounce.
GUILDENSTERN: The Queen, your mother, in most great afflic-
tion of spirit, hath sent me to you.
HAMLET: You are welcome.
GUILDENSTERN: Nay, good my lord, this courtesy is not of the   290
right breed.° If it shall please you to make me a wholesome
answer, I will do your mother's commandment; if not, your
pardon° and my return shall be the end of my business.
HAMLET: Sir, I cannot.
ROSENCRANTZ: What, my lord?   295
HAMLET: Make you a wholesome answer; my wit's diseased. But,
sir, such answer as I can make, you shall command, or rather,
as you say, my mother. Therefore no more, but to the matter.
My mother, you say—
ROSENCRANTZ: Then thus she says: your behavior hath struck   300
her into amazement and admiration.°

---

270 recorders wind instruments of the flute kind. 272 perdy (A corruption of the French par dieu,
"by God.") 278 retirement withdrawal to his chambers; distempered out of humor. (But Hamlet
deliberately plays on the wider application to any illness of mind or body, as in line 298, especially
to drunkenness.) 280 choler anger. (But Hamlet takes the word in its more basic humoral sense of
"bilious disorder.") 282 purgation (Hamlet hints at something going beyond medical treatment to
bloodletting and the extraction of confession.) 285 frame order; start shy or jump away (like a
horse; the opposite of tame in line 275). 291 breed (1) kind (2) breeding, manners. 293 pardon
permission to depart. 301 admiration bewilderment.

HAMLET: O wonderful son, that can so stonish a mother! But is there no sequel at the heels of this mother's admiration? Impart.

ROSENCRANTZ: She desires to speak with you in her closet° ere you go to bed. 305

HAMLET: We shall obey, were she ten times our mother. Have you any further trade with us?

ROSENCRANTZ: My lord, you once did love me.

HAMLET: And do still, by these pickers and stealers.°

ROSENCRANTZ: Good my lord, what is your cause of distemper? 310 You do surely bar the door upon your own liberty° if you deny° your griefs to your friend.

HAMLET: Sir, I lack advancement.

ROSENCRANTZ: How can that be, when you have the voice of the King himself for your succession in Denmark? 315

HAMLET: Ay, sir, but "While the grass grows"°—the proverb is something° musty.

Enter the Players° with recorders.

O, the recorders. Let me see one. [*He takes a recorder.*] To withdraw° with you: why do you go about to recover the wind° of me, as if you would drive me into a toil?° 320

GUILDENSTERN: O, my lord, if my duty be too bold, my love is too unmannerly.°

HAMLET: I do not well understand that.° Will you play upon this pipe?

GUILDENSTERN: My lord, I cannot. 325

HAMLET: I pray you.

GUILDENSTERN: Believe me, I cannot.

HAMLET: I do beseech you.

GUILDENSTERN: I know no touch of it, my lord.

HAMLET: It is as easy as lying. Govern these ventages° with your 330 fingers and thumb, give it breath with your mouth, and it will discourse most eloquent music. Look you, these are the stops.

GUILDENSTERN: But these cannot I command to any utterance of harmony. I have not the skill.

---

304 **closet** private chamber.   309 **pickers and stealers** i.e., hands. (So called from the catechism, "to keep my hands from picking and stealing.")   311 **liberty** i.e., being freed from distemper, line 297, but perhaps with a veiled threat as well;   **deny** refuse to share.   316 **While . . . grows** (The rest of the proverb is "the silly horse starves"; Hamlet may not live long enough to succeed to the kingdom.);   317 **something** somewhat;   **s.d. Players** actors.   319 **withdraw** speak privately; **recover the wind** get to the windward side (thus driving the game into the toil, or "net").   320 **toil** snare.   321–322 **if . . . unmannerly** if I am using an unmannerly boldness, it is my love that occasions it.   323 **I . . . that** i.e., I don't understand how genuine love can be unmannerly. 330 **ventages** finger-holes or stops (line 319) of the recorder.

HAMLET: Why, look you now, how unworthy a thing you make 335
of me! You would play upon me, you would seem to know my
stops, you would pluck out the heart of my mystery, you would
sound° me from my lowest note to the top of my compass,° and
there is much music, excellent voice, in this little organ,° yet
cannot you make it speak. 'Sblood, do you think I am easier to 340
be played on than a pipe? Call me what instrument you will,
though you can fret° me, you cannot play upon me.

Enter Polonius.

God bless you, sir!

POLONIUS: My lord, the Queen would speak with you, and
presently.° 345

HAMLET: Do you see yonder cloud that's almost in shape of a
camel?

POLONIUS: By the Mass and 'tis, like a camel indeed.

HAMLET: Methinks it is like a weasel.

POLONIUS: It is backed like a weasel. 350

HAMLET: Or like a whale.

POLONIUS: Very like a whale.

HAMLET: Then I will come to my mother by and by.° [*Aside.*]
They fool me° to the top of my bent.°—I will come by and by.

POLONIUS: I will say so. [*Exit.*] 355

HAMLET: "By and by" is easily said. Leave me, friends.

[*Exeunt all but Hamlet.*]

'Tis now the very witching time° of night,
When churchyards yawn and hell itself breathes out
Contagion to this world. Now could I drink hot blood
And do such bitter business as the day 360
Would quake to look on. Soft, now to my mother.
O heart, lose not thy nature!° Let not ever
The soul of Nero° enter this firm bosom.
Let me be cruel, not unnatural;
I will speak daggers to her, but use none. 365
My tongue and soul in this be hypocrites:

---

338 **sound** (1) fathom (2) produce sound in. **compass** range (of voice). 339 **organ** musical instrument. 342 **fret** irritate (with a quibble on fret, meaning the piece of wood, gut, or metal that regulates the fingering on an instrument). 345 **presently** at once. 353 **by and by** quite soon. 354 **fool me** trifle with me, humor my fooling. **top of my bent** limit of my ability or endurance. (Literally, the extent to which a bow may be bent.) 357 **witching time** time when spells are cast and evil is abroad. 362 **nature** natural feeling. 363 **Nero** murderer of his mother, Agrippina.

How in my words soever° she be shent,°
To give them seals° never my soul consent!   *Exit.*

SCENE III [THE CASTLE.]

Enter King, Rosencrantz, and Guildenstern.

KING: I like him° not, nor stands it safe with us
To let his madness range. Therefore prepare you.
I your commission will forthwith dispatch,°
And he to England shall along with you.
The terms of our estate° may not endure   5
Hazard so near 's as doth hourly grow
Out of his brows.°

GUILDENSTERN: We will ourselves provide.
Most holy and religious fear° it is
To keep those many many bodies safe
That live and feed upon Your Majesty.   10

ROSENCRANTZ: The single and peculiar° life is bound
With all the strength and armor of the mind
To keep itself from noyance,° but much more
That spirit upon whose weal depends and rests
The lives of many. The cess° of majesty   15
Dies not alone, but like a gulf° doth draw
What's near it with it; or it is a massy° wheel
Fixed on the summit of the highest mount,
To whose huge spokes ten thousand lesser things
Are mortised° and adjoined, which, when it falls,°   20
Each small annexment, petty consequence,°
Attends° the boisterous ruin. Never alone
Did the King sigh, but with a general groan.

KING: Arm° you, I pray you, to this speedy voyage,
For we will fetters put about this fear,   25
Which now goes too free-footed.

ROSENCRANTZ: We will haste us.

---

367 How . . . soever however much by my words;   shent rebuked.   368 give them seals i.e.,
confirm them with deeds.   1 him i.e., his behavior.   3 dispatch prepare, cause to be drawn up.
5 terms of our estate circumstances of my royal position.   7 Out of his brows i.e., from his brain,
in the form of plots and threats.   8 religious fear sacred concern.   11 single and peculiar individual
and private.   13 noyance harm.   15 cess decease, cessation.   16 gulf whirlpool.   17 massy
massive.   20 mortised fastened (as with a fitted joint);   when it falls i.e., when it descends, like
the wheel of Fortune, bringing a king down with it.   21 Each . . .consequence i.e., every hanger-on
and unimportant person or thing connected with the King.   22 Attends participates in.   24 Arm
prepare.

Exeunt gentlemen [Rosencrantz and Guildenstern].

Enter Polonius.

POLONIUS: My lord, he's going to his mother's closet.
    Behind the arras° I'll convey myself
    To hear the process.° I'll warrant she'll tax him home,°
    And, as you said—and wisely was it said—   30
    'Tis meet° that some more audience than a mother,
    Since nature makes them partial, should o'erhear
    The speech, of vantage.° Fare you well, my liege.
    I'll call upon you ere you go to bed
    And tell you what I know.

KING: Thanks, dear my lord.   35

Exit [Polonius].

O, my offense is rank! It smells to heaven.
It hath the primal eldest curse° upon't,
A brother's murder. Pray can I not,
Though inclination be as sharp as will;°
My stronger guilt defeats my strong intent,   40
And like a man to double business bound°
I stand in pause where I shall first begin,
And both neglect. What if this cursèd hand
Were thicker than itself with brother's blood,
Is there not rain enough in the sweet heavens   45
To wash it white as snow? Whereto serves mercy
But to confront the visage of offense?°
And what's in prayer but this twofold force,
To be forestallèd° ere we come to fall,
Or pardoned being down? Then I'll look up.   50
My fault is past. But O, what form of prayer
Can serve my turn? "Forgive me my foul murder"?
That cannot be, since I am still possessed
Of those effects for which I did the murder:
My crown, mine own ambition, and my Queen.   55

---

28 arras screen of tapestry placed around the walls of household apartments. (On the Elizabethan stage, the arras was presumably over a door or discovery space in the tiring-house facade.)
29 process proceedings;   **tax him home** reprove him severely.   **31 meet** fitting.   **33 of vantage** from an advantageous place, or, in addition.   **37 the primal eldest curse** the curse of Cain, the first murderer; he killed his brother Abel.   **39 Though . . . will** though my desire is as strong as my determination.   **41 bound** (1) destined (2) obliged. (The King wants to repent and still enjoy what he has gained.)   **46–47 Whereto . . . offense** what function does mercy serve other than to meet sin face to face?   **49 forestallèd** prevented (from sinning).

May one be pardoned and retain th' offense?°
In the corrupted currents° of this world
Offense's gilded hand° may shove by° justice,
And oft 'tis seen the wicked prize° itself
Buys out the law. But 'tis not so above.   60
There° is no shuffling,° there the action lies°
In his° true nature, and we ourselves compelled,
Even to the teeth and forehead° of our faults,
To give in° evidence. What then? What rests?°
Try what repentance can. What can it not?   65
Yet what can it, when one cannot repent?
O wretched state, O bosom black as death,
limèd° soul that, struggling to be free,
Art more engaged!° Help, angels! Make assay.°
Bow, stubborn knees, and heart with strings of steel,   70
Be soft as sinews of the newborn babe!
All may be well.   [*He kneels.*]

Enter Hamlet.

HAMLET: Now might I do it pat,° now 'a is a-praying;
And now I'll do 't. [*He draws his sword.*] And so 'a goes to heaven,
And so am I revenged. That would be scanned:°   75
A villain kills my father, and for that,
I, his sole son, do this same villain send
To heaven.
Why, this is hire and salary, not revenge.
'A took my father grossly, full of bread,°   80
With all his crimes broad blown,° as flush° as May;
And how his audit° stands who knows save° heaven?
But in our circumstance and course of thought°
'Tis heavy with him. And am I then revenged,
To take him in the purging of his soul   85
When he is fit and seasoned° for his passage?

---

56 **th' offense** the thing for which one offended.   57 **currents** courses.   58 **gilded hand** hand
offering gold as a bribe;   **shove by** thrust aside.   59 **wicked prize** prize won by wickedness.
61 **There** i.e., in heaven;   **shuffling** escape by trickery;   **the action lies** the accusation is made
manifest. (A legal metaphor.)   62 **his** its.   63 **to the teeth and forehead** face to face, concealing
nothing.   64 **give in** provide;   **rests** remains.   68 **limèd** caught as with birdlime, a sticky substance
used to ensnare birds.   69 **engaged** entangled;   **assay** trial. (Said to himself.)   73 **pat** opportunely.
75 **would be scanned** needs to be looked into, or, would be interpreted as follows.   80 **grossly, full**
of bread i.e., enjoying his worldly pleasures rather than fasting. (See Ezekiel 16:49.)   81 **crimes**
broad blown sins in full bloom;   **flush** vigorous.   82 **audit** account;   **save** except for.   83 **in . . .**
thought as we see it from our mortal perspective.   86 **seasoned** matured, readied.

No!
Up, sword, and know thou a more horrid hent.°

[*He puts up his sword.*]

When he is drunk asleep, or in his rage,°
Or in th' incestuous pleasure of his bed,   90
At game,° a-swearing, or about some act
That has no relish° of salvation in 't—
Then trip him, that his heels may kick at heaven,
And that his soul may be as damned and black
As hell, whereto it goes. My mother stays.°   95
This physic° but prolongs thy sickly days.   *Exit.*

KING: My words fly up, my thoughts remain below.
Words without thoughts never to heaven go.   *Exit.*

Scene IV [The Queen's Private Chamber.]

Enter [Queen] Gertrude and Polonius.

POLONIUS: 'A will come straight. Look you lay home° to him.
Tell him his pranks have been too broad° to bear with,
And that Your Grace hath screened and stood between
Much heat° and him. I'll shroud° me even here.
Pray you, be round° with him.   5

HAMLET [*within*]:   Mother, Mother, Mother!

QUEEN: I'll warrant you, fear me not.
Withdraw, I hear him coming.

[*Polonius hides behind the arras.*]

Enter Hamlet.

HAMLET: Now, Mother, what's the matter?

QUEEN: Hamlet, thou hast thy father° much offended.   10

HAMLET: Mother, you have my father much offended.

QUEEN: Come, come, you answer with an idle° tongue.

HAMLET: Go, go, you question with a wicked tongue.

QUEEN: Why, how now, Hamlet?

HAMLET: What's the matter now?

88 **know . . . hent** await to be grasped by me on a more horrid occasion; **hent** act of seizing.
89 **drunk . . . rage** dead drunk, or in a fit of sexual passions.   91 **game** gambling.   92 **relish** trace,
savor.   95 **stays** awaits (me).   96 **physic** purging (by prayer), or, Hamlet's postponement of the
killing.   1 **lay home** thrust to the heart, reprove him soundly.   2 **broad** unrestrained.   4 **Much
heat** i.e., the King's anger;   **shroud** conceal. (With ironic fitness to Polonius' imminent death. The
word is only in the First Quarto: the Second Quarto and the Folio read "silence.")   5 **round** blunt.
10 **thy father** i.e., your stepfather, Claudius.   12 **idle** foolish.

QUEEN: Have you forgot me?°

HAMLET: No, by the rood,° not so: 15
     You are the Queen your husband's brother's wife,
     And—would it were not so!—you are my mother.

QUEEN: Nay, then, I'll set those to you that can speak.°

HAMLET: Come, come, and sit you down; you shall not budge.
     You go not till I set you up a glass   20
     Where you may see the inmost part of you.

QUEEN: What wilt thou do? Thou wilt not murder me?
     Help, ho!

POLONIUS [*behind the arras*]: What ho! Help!

HAMLET [*drawing*]: How now? A rat? Dead for a ducat,° dead!   25

[*He thrusts his rapier through the arras.*]

POLONIUS [*behind the arras*]: O, I am slain!   [*He falls and dies.*]

QUEEN: O me, what hast thou done?

HAMLET: Nay, I know not. Is it the King?

QUEEN: O, what a rash and bloody deed is this!

HAMLET: A bloody deed—almost as bad, good Mother,
     As kill a King, and marry with his brother.   30

QUEEN: As kill a King!

HAMLET: Ay, lady, it was my word.

[*He parts the arras and discovers Polonius.*]

     Thou wretched, rash, intruding fool, farewell!
     I took thee for thy better. Take thy fortune.
     Thou find'st to be too busy° is some danger.—
     Leave wringing of your hands. Peace, sit you down,   35
     And let me wring your heart, for so I shall,
     If it be made of penetrable stuff,
     If damnèd custom° have not brazed° it so
     That it be proof° and bulwark against sense.°

QUEEN: What have I done, that thou dar'st wag thy tongue   40
     In noise so rude against me?

HAMLET: Such an act
     That blurs the grace and blush of modesty,
     Calls virtue hypocrite, takes off the rose

---

15 forgot me i.e., forgotten that I am your mother; **rood** cross of Christ. **18 speak** i.e., to someone so rude. **25 Dead for a ducat** i.e., I bet a ducat he's dead; or, a ducat is his life's fee. **34 busy** nosey. **38 damnèd custom** habitual wickedness; **brazed** brazened, hardened. **39 proof** armor; **sense** feeling.

From the fair forehead of an innocent love
And sets a blister° there, makes marriage vows 45
As false as dicers' oaths. O, such a deed
As from the body of contraction° plucks
The very soul, and sweet religion makes°
A rhapsody° of words. Heaven's face does glow
O'er this solidity and compound mass 50
With tristful visage, as against the doom,
Is thought-sick at the act.°

QUEEN: Ay me, what act,
That roars so loud and thunders in the index?°

HAMLET [*showing her two likenesses*]:   Look here upon this picture,
and on this, 55
The counterfeit presentment° of two brothers.
See what a grace was seated on this brow:
Hyperion's° curls, the front° of Jove himself,
An eye like Mars° to threaten and command,
A station° like the herald Mercury° 60
New-lighted° on a heaven-kissing hill—
A combination and a form indeed
Where every god did seem to set his seal°
To give the world assurance of a man.
This was your husband. Look you now what follows: 65
Here is your husband, like a mildewed ear,°
Blasting° his wholesome brother. Have you eyes?
Could you on this fair mountain leave° to feed
And batten° on this moor?° Ha, have you eyes?
You cannot call it love, for at your age 70
The heyday° in the blood° is tame, it's humble,
And waits upon the judgment, and what judgment
Would step from this to this? Sense,° sure, you have,
Else could you not have motion, but sure that sense

---

45 **sets a blister** i.e., brands as a harlot.   47 **contraction** the marriage contract.   48 **sweet religion makes** i.e., makes marriage vows.   49 **rhapsody** senseless string.   49–52 **Heaven's . . . act** heaven's face blushes at this solid world compounded of the various elements, with sorrowful face as though the day of doom were near, and is sick with horror at the deed (i.e., Gertrude's marriage).
54 **index** table of contents, prelude or preface.   56 **counterfeit presentment** portrayed representation.   58 **Hyperion's** the sungod's;   **front** brow.   59 **Mars** god of war.   60 **station** manner of standing;   **Mercury** winged messenger of the gods.   61 **New-lighted** newly alighted.   63 **set his seal** i.e., affix his approval.   66 **ear** i.e., of grain.   67 **Blasting** blighting.   68 **leave** cease.
69 **batten** gorge;   **moor** barren or marshy ground (suggesting also "dark-skinned").   71 **heyday** state of excitement;   **blood** passion.   73 **Sense** perception through the five senses (the functions of the middle sensible soul).

Is apoplexed,° for madness would not err,°   75
Nor sense to ecstasy was ne'er so thralled,
But° it reserved some quantity of choice
To serve in such a difference.° What devil was 't
That thus hath cozened° you at hoodman-blind?°
Eyes without feeling, feeling without sight,   80
Ears without hands or eyes, smelling sans° all
Or but a sickly part of one true sense
Could not so mope.° O shame, where is thy blush?
Rebellious hell,
If thou canst mutine° in a matron's bones,   85
To flaming youth let virtue be as wax
And melt in her own fire.° Proclaim no shame
When the compulsive ardor gives the charge,
Since frost itself as actively doth burn,
And reason panders will.°   90
QUEEN: O Hamlet, speak no more!
Thou turn'st mine eyes into my very soul,
And there I see such black and grainèd° spots
As will not leave their tinct.°
HAMLET: Nay, but to live
In the rank sweat of an enseamèd° bed,   95
Stewed° in corruption, honeying and making love
Over the nasty sty!
QUEEN: O, speak to me no more!
These words like daggers enter in my ears.
No more, sweet Hamlet!
HAMLET: A murderer and a villain,   100
A slave that is not twentieth part the tithe°
Of your precedent lord,° a vice° of kings,

---

75 apoplexed paralyzed (Hamlet goes on to explain that, without such a paralysis of will, mere madness would not so err, nor would the five senses so enthrall themselves to ecstasy or lunacy; even such deranged states of mind would be able to make the obvious choice between Hamlet Senior and Claudius.);   **err** so err.   **77 But** but that.   **78 To . . . difference** to help in making a choice between two such men.   **79 cozened** cheated;   **hoodman-blind** blindman's buff. (In this game, says Hamlet, the devil must have pushed Claudius toward Gertrude while she was blind-folded.)   **81 sans** without.   **83 mope** be dazed, act aimlessly.   **85 mutine** incite mutiny. **86–87 be as wax . . . fire** melt like a candle or stick of sealing wax held over the candle flame. **87–90 Proclaim . . . will** call it no shameful business when the compelling ardor of youth delivers the attack, says Hamlet, the devil must have pushed Claudius toward Gertrude while she was blind-and reason perverts itself by fomenting lust rather than restraining it.   **93 grainèd** dyed in grain, indelible.   **94 leave their tinct** surrender their color.   **95 enseamèd** saturated in the grease and filth of passionate lovemaking.   **96 Stewed** soaked, bathed (with a suggestion of "stew," brothel). **101 tithe** tenth part.   **102 precedent lord** former husband;   **vice** buffoon. (A reference to the Vice of the morality plays.)

A cutpurse of the empire and the rule,
That from a shelf the precious diadem stole
And put it in his pocket!   105

QUEEN: No more!

Enter Ghost [in his nightgown].

HAMLET: A king of shreds and patches°—
Save me, and hover o'er me with your wings,
You heavenly guards! What would your gracious figure?

QUEEN: Alas, he's mad!   110

HAMLET: Do you not come your tardy son to chide,
That, lapsed° in time and passion, lets go by
Th' important° acting of your dread command?
O, say!

GHOST: Do not forget. This visitation   115
Is but to whet thy almost blunted purpose.
But look, amazement° on thy mother sits.
O, step between her and her fighting soul!
Conceit° in weakest bodies strongest works.
Speak to her, Hamlet.

HAMLET: How is it with you, lady?   120

QUEEN: Alas, how is 't with you,
That you do bend your eye on vacancy,
And with th' incorporal° air do hold discourse?
Forth at your eyes your spirits wildly peep,
And, as the sleeping soldiers in th' alarm,°   125
Your bedded° hair, like life in excrements,°
Start up and stand on end. O gentle son,
Upon the heat and flame of thy distemper°
Sprinkle cool patience. Whereon do you look?

HAMLET: On him, on him! Look you how pale he glares!   130
His form and cause conjoined,° preaching to stones,
Would make them capable.°—Do not look upon me,
Lest with this piteous action you convert
My stern effects.° Then what I have to do

---

107 **shreds and patches** i.e., motley, the traditional costume of the clown or fool.   112 **lapsed**
delaying.   113 **important** importunate, urgent.   117 **amazement** distraction.   119 **Conceit**
imagination.   123 **incorporal** immaterial.   125 **as . . . alarm** like soldiers called out of sleep
by an alarum.   126 **bedded** laid flat;   **like life in excrements** i.e., as though hair, an outgrowth
of the body, had a life of its own. (Hair was thought to be lifeless because it lacks sensation,
and so its standing on end would be unnatural and ominous.)   128 **distemper** disorder.
131 **His . . . conjoined** his appearance joined to his cause for speaking.   132 **capable** receptive.
133–134 **convert . . . effects** divert me from my stern duty.

Will want true color—tears perchance for blood.° 135
QUEEN: To whom do you speak this?
HAMLET: Do you see nothing there?
QUEEN: Nothing at all, yet all that is I see.
HAMLET: Nor did you nothing hear?
QUEEN: No, nothing but ourselves. 140
HAMLET: Why, look you there, look how it steals away!
My father, in his habit° as° he lived!
Look where he goes even now out at the portal!

Exit Ghost.

QUEEN: This is the very° coinage of your brain.
This bodiless creation ecstasy 145
Is very cunning in.°
HAMLET: Ecstasy?
My pulse as yours doth temperately keep time,
And makes as healthful music. It is not madness
That I have uttered. Bring me to the test, 150
And I the matter will reword,° which madness
Would gambol° from. Mother, for love of grace,
Lay not that flattering unction° to your soul
That not your trespass but my madness speaks.
It will but skin° and film the ulcerous place, 155
Whiles rank corruption, mining° all within,
Infects unseen. Confess yourself to heaven,
Repent what's past, avoid what is to come,
And do not spread the compost° on the weeds
To make them ranker. Forgive me this my virtue;° 160
For in the fatness° of these pursy° times
Virtue itself of vice must pardon beg,
Yea, curb° and woo for leave° to do him good.
QUEEN: O Hamlet, thou hast cleft my heart in twain.
HAMLET: O, throw away the worser part of it, 165
And live the purer with the other half.
Good night. But go not to my uncle's bed;

---

135 want . . . blood lack plausibility so that (with a play on the normal sense of color) I shall shed colorless tears instead of blood. 141 habit clothes; as as when. 144 very mere. 145–146 This . . . in madness is skillful in creating this kind of hallucination. 151 reword repeat word for word. 152 gambol skip away. 153 unction ointment. 155 skin grow a skin for. 156 mining working under the surface. 159 compost manure. 160 this my virtue my virtuous talk in reproving you.\ 161 fatness grossness; pursy flabby, out of shape. 163 curb bow, bend the knee; leave permission.

Assume a virtue, if you have it not.
That monster, custom, who all sense doth eat,°
Of habits devil,° is angel yet in this,   170
That to the use of actions fair and good
He likewise gives a frock or livery°
That aptly° is put on. Refrain tonight,
And that shall lend a kind of easiness
To the next abstinence; the next more easy;   175
For use° almost can change the stamp of nature,°
And either° . . .the devil, or throw him out
With wondrous potency. Once more, good night;
And when you are desirous to be blest,
I'll blessing beg of you.° For this same lord,   180

[*Pointing to Polonius.*]

I do repent; but heaven hath pleased it so
To punish me with this, and this with me,
That I must be their scourge and minister.°
I will bestow° him, and will answer° well
The death I gave him. So, again, good night.   185
I must be cruel only to be kind.
This° bad begins, and worse remains behind.°
One word more, good lady.
QUEEN: What shall I do?
HAMLET: Not this by no means that I bid you do:
Let the bloat° King tempt you again to bed,   190
Pinch wanton° on your cheek, call you his mouse,
And let him, for a pair of reechy° kisses,
Or paddling° in your neck with his damned fingers,
Make you to ravel all this matter out°
That I essentially am not in madness,   195
But mad in craft.° 'Twere good° you let him know,

169 who . . .eat which consumes all proper or natural feeling, all sensibility.   170 Of habits devil
devil-like in prompting evil habits.   172 livery an outer appearance, a customary garb (and hence a
predisposition easily assumed in time of stress).   173 aptly readily.   176 use habit;   the stamp of
nature our inborn traits.   177 And either (A defective line, usually emended by inserting the word
master after either, following the Fourth Quarto and early editors.)   179–180 when . . . you i.e.,
when you are ready to be penitent and seek God's blessing, I will ask your blessing as a dutiful son
should.   183 their scourge and minister i.e., agent of heavenly retribution. (By scourge, Hamlet also
suggests that he himself will eventually suffer punishment in the process of fulfilling heaven's will.)
184 bestow stow, dispose of;   answer account or pay for.   187 This i.e., the killing of Polonius;
behind to come.   190 bloat bloated.   191 Pinch wanton i.e., leave his love pinches on your
cheeks, branding you as wanton.   192 reechy dirty, filthy.   193 paddling fingering amorously.
194 ravel . . . out unravel, disclose.   196 in craft by cunning;   good (Said sarcastically; also the
following eight lines.)

For who that's but a Queen, fair, sober, wise,
Would from a paddock,° from a bat, a gib,°
Such dear concernings° hide? Who would do so?
No, in despite of sense and secrecy,° 200
Unpeg the basket° on the house's top,
Let the birds fly, and like the famous ape,°
To try conclusions,° in the basket creep
And break your own neck down.°

QUEEN: Be thou assured, if words be made of breath, 205
And breath of life, I have no life to breathe
What thou hast said to me.

HAMLET: I must to England. You know that?

QUEEN: Alack,
I had forgot. 'Tis so concluded on.

HAMLET: There's letters sealed, and my two schoolfellows, 210
Whom I will trust as I will adders fanged,
They bear the mandate; they must sweep my way
And marshal me to knavery.° Let it work.°
For 'tis the sport to have the enginer°
Hoist with° his own petard,° and 't shall go hard 215
But I will° delve one yard below their mines°
And blow them at the moon. O, 'tis most sweet
When in one line° two crafts° directly meet.
This man shall set me packing.°
I'll lug the guts into the neighbor room. 220
Mother, good night indeed. This counselor
Is now most still, most secret, and most grave,
Who was in life a foolish prating knave.—
Come, sir, to draw toward an end° with you.—
Good night, Mother. 225

Exeunt [separately, Hamlet dragging in Polonius].

198 **paddock** toad; **gib** tomcat. 199 **dear concernings** important affairs. 200 **sense and secrecy** secrecy that common sense requires. 201 **Unpeg the basket** open the cage, i.e., let out the secret. 202 **famous ape** (In a story now lost.) 203 **try conclusions** test the outcome (in which the ape apparently enters a cage from which birds have been released and then tries to fly out of the cage as they have done, falling to its death). 204 **down** in the fall; utterly. 211–212 **sweep . . . knavery** sweep a path before me and conduct me to some knavery or treachery prepared for me; **work** proceed. 214 **enginer** maker of military contrivances. 215 **Hoist with** blown up by; **petard** an explosive used to blow in a door or make a breach. 215–216 **'t shall . . . will** unless luck is against me, I will; **mines** tunnels used in warfare to undermine the enemy's emplacements; Hamlet will countermine by going under their mines. 218 **in one line** i.e., mines and countermines on a collision course, or the countermines directly below the mines; **crafts** acts of guile, plots. 219 **set me packing** set me to making schemes, and set me to lugging (him), and, also, send me off in a hurry. 224 **draw . . . end** finish up (with a pun on draw, "pull").

ACT IV

SCENE I [THE CASTLE.]

Enter King and Queen,° with Rosencrantz and Guildenstern.

KING: There's matter° in these sighs, these profound heaves.°
    You must translate; 'tis fit we understand them.
    Where is your son?
QUEEN: Bestow this place on us a little while.

                    [Exeunt Rosencrantz and Guildenstern.]

    Ah, mine own lord, what have I seen tonight!   5
KING: What, Gertrude? How does Hamlet?
QUEEN: Mad as the sea and wind when both contend
    Which is the mightier. In his lawless fit,
    Behind the arras hearing something stir,
    Whips out his rapier, cries, "A rat, a rat!"   10
    And in this brainish apprehension° kills
    The unseen good old man.
KING: O heavy° deed!
    It had been so with us,° had we been there.
    His liberty is full of threats to all—
    To you yourself, to us, to everyone.   15
    Alas, how shall this bloody deed be answered?°
    It will be laid to us, whose providence°
    Should have kept short,° restrained, and out of haunt°
    This mad young man. But so much was our love,
    We would not understand what was most fit,   20
    But, like the owner of a foul disease,
    To keep it from divulging,° let it feed
    Even on the pith of life. Where is he gone?
QUEEN: To draw apart the body he hath killed,
    O'er whom his very madness, like some ore°   25
    Among a mineral° of metals base,
    Shows itself pure: 'a weeps for what is done.
KING: O Gertrude, come away!
    The sun no sooner shall the mountains touch
    But we will ship him hence, and this vile deed   30

---

s.d. Enter . . . Queen (Some editors argue that Gertrude never exits in Act III, Scene iv and that the scene is continuous here, as suggested in the Folio, but the Second Quarto marks an entrance for her and at line 35 Claudius speaks of Gertrude's closet as though it were elsewhere. A short time has elapsed, during which the King has become aware of her highly wrought emotional state.)
1 matter significance; **heaves** heavy sighs. **11 brainish apprehension** headstrong conception.
12 heavy grievous. **13 us** i.e., me. (The royal "we"; also in line 15.) **16 answered** explained.
17 providence foresight. **18 short** i.e., on a short tether; **out of haunt** secluded. **22 divulging** becoming evident. **25 ore** vein of gold. **26 mineral** mine.

We must with all our majesty and skill
Both countenance° and excuse.—Ho, Guildenstern!

Enter Rosencrantz and Guildenstern.

Friends both, go join you with some further aid.
Hamlet in madness hath Polonius slain,
And from his mother's closet hath he dragged him.   35
Go seek him out, speak fair, and bring the body
Into the chapel. I pray you, haste in this.

[Exeunt Rosencrantz and Guildenstern.]

Come, Gertrude, we'll call up our wisest friends
And let them know both what we mean to do
And what's untimely done.........°   40
Whose whisper o'er the world's diameter,°
As level° as the cannon to his blank,°
Transports his poisoned shot, may miss our name
And hit the woundless° air. O, come away!
My soul is full of discord and dismay.   *Exeunt.* 45

SCENE II [THE CASTLE.]

Enter Hamlet.

HAMLET: Safely stowed.
ROSENCRANTZ, GUILDENSTERN [*within*]: Hamlet! Lord Hamlet!
HAMLET: But soft, what noise? Who calls on Hamlet? O, here they
come.

Enter Rosencrantz and Guildenstern.

ROSENCRANTZ: What have you done, my lord, with the dead   5
body?
HAMLET: Compounded it with dust, whereto 'tis kin.
ROSENCRANTZ: Tell us where 'tis, that we may take it thence
And bear it to the chapel.
HAMLET: Do not believe it.   10
ROSENCRANTZ: Believe what?
HAMLET: That I can keep your counsel and not mine own.°
Besides, to be demanded of° a sponge, what replication° should
be made by the son of a king?

---

32 **countenance** put the best face on.   40 **And . . . done** (A defective line; conjectures as to the missing words include So, haply, slander [Capell and others]; For, haply, slander [Theobald and others]; and So envious slander [Jenkins].)   41 **diameter** extent from side to side.   42 **As level** with as direct aim;   **his blank** its target at point-blank range.   44 **woundless** invulnerable.
12 **That . . . own** i.e., that I can follow your advice (by telling where the body is) and still keep my own secret.   13 **demanded of** questioned by;   **replication** reply.

ROSENCRANTZ: Take you me for a sponge, my lord?   15

HAMLET: Ay, sir, that soaks up the King's countenance,° his
   rewards, his authorities.° But such officers do the King best
   service in the end. He keeps them, like an ape, an apple, in the
   corner of his jaw, first mouthed to be last swallowed. When he
   needs what you have gleaned, it is but squeezing you, and,   20
   sponge, you shall be dry again.

ROSENCRANTZ: I understand you not, my lord.

HAMLET: I am glad of it. A knavish speech sleeps in° a foolish ear.

ROSENCRANTZ: My lord, you must tell us where the body is and
   go with us to the King.   25

HAMLET: The body is with the King, but the King is not with the
   body.° The King is a thing—

GUILDENSTERN: A thing, my lord?

HAMLET: Of nothing.° Bring me to him. Hide fox, and all after!°

                                              Exeunt [running].

SCENE III [THE CASTLE.]

Enter King, and two or three.

KING: I have sent to seek him, and to find the body.
   How dangerous is it that this man goes loose!
   Yet must not we put the strong law on him.
   He's loved of° the distracted° multitude,
   Who like not in their judgment, but their eyes,°   5
   And where 'tis so, th' offender's scourge° is weighed,°
   But never the offense. To bear all smooth and even,°
   This sudden sending him away must seem
   Deliberate pause.° Diseases desperate grown
   By desperate appliance° are relieved,   10
   Or not at all.

Enter Rosencrantz, Guildenstern, and all the rest.

---

16 **countenance** favor.   17 **authorities** delegated power, influence.   23 **sleeps in** has no meaning to.
26–27 **The . . . body** (Perhaps alludes to the legal commonplace of "the king's two bodies," which
drew a distinction between the sacred office of kingship and the particular mortal who possessed it
at any given time. Hence, although Claudius' body is necessarily a part of him, true kingship is not
contained in it. Similarly, Claudius will have Polonius' body when it is found, but there is no kingship in this business either.)   29 **Of nothing** (1) of no account (2) lacking the essence of kingship, as
in lines 24–25 and note;   **Hide . . . after** (An old signal cry in the game of hide-and-seek, suggesting
that Hamlet now runs away from them.)   4 **of** by;   **distracted** fickle, unstable.   5 **Who . . . eyes**
who choose not by judgment but by appearance.   6 **scourge** punishment. (Literally, blow with a
whip.);   **weighed** sympathetically considered.   7 **To . . . even** to manage the business in an
unprovocative way.   9 **Deliberate pause** carefully considered action.   10 **appliance** remedies.

How now, what hath befall'n?

ROSENCRANTZ: Where the dead body is bestowed, my lord,
We cannot get from him.

KING: But where is he?

ROSENCRANTZ: Without, my lord; guarded, to know your
pleasure.   15

KING: Bring him before us.

ROSENCRANTZ: Ho! Bring in the lord.

They enter [with Hamlet].

KING: Now, Hamlet, where's Polonius?

HAMLET: At supper.

KING: At supper? Where?

HAMLET: Not where he eats, but where 'a is eaten. A certain con-   20
vocation of politic worms° are e'en° at him. Your worm° is
your only emperor for diet.° We fat all creatures else to fat us,
and we fat ourselves for maggots. Your fat king and your lean
beggar is but variable service°—two dishes, but to one table.
That's the end.   25

KING: Alas, alas!

HAMLET: A man may fish with the worm that hath eat° of a king,
and eat of the fish that hath fed of that worm.

KING: What dost thou mean by this?

HAMLET: Nothing but to show you how a king may go a   30
progress° through the guts of a beggar.

KING: Where is Polonius?

HAMLET: In heaven. Send thither to see. If your messenger find
him not there, seek him i' th' other place yourself. But if indeed
you find him not within this month, you shall nose him as you   35
go up the stairs into the lobby.

KING [*to some attendants*]: Go seek him there.

HAMLET: 'A will stay till you come.

[*Exeunt attendants.*]

KING: Hamlet, this deed, for thine especial safety—
Which we do tender,° as we dearly° grieve   40
For that which thou hast done—must send thee hence

---

21 **politic worms** crafty worms (suited to a master spy like Polonius);   **e'en** even now;   **Your worm**
your average worm. (Compare **your fat king** and **your lean beggar** in lines 21–22.);   22 **diet** food,
eating (with a punning reference to the Diet of Worms, a famous convocation held in 1521).
24 **variable service** different courses of a single meal.   27 **eat** eaten. (Pronounced et.)   31 **progress**
royal journey of state.   40 **tender** regard, hold dear;   **dearly** intensely.

With fiery quickness. Therefore prepare thyself.
The bark° is ready, and the wind at help,
Th' associates tend,° and everything is bent°
For England.   45
HAMLET: For England!
KING: Ay, Hamlet.
HAMLET: Good.
KING: So is it, if thou knew'st our purposes.
HAMLET: I see a cherub° that sees them. But come, for England!   50
Farewell, dear mother.
KING: Thy loving father, Hamlet.
HAMLET: My mother. Father and mother is man and wife, man
and wife is one flesh, and so, my mother. Come, for England!

Exit.

KING: Follow him at foot;° tempt him with speed aboard.   55
Delay it not. I'll have him hence tonight.
Away! For everything is sealed and done
That else leans on° th' affair. Pray you, make haste.

[Exeunt all but the King.]

And, England,° if my love thou hold'st at aught°—
As my great power thereof may give thee sense,°   60
Since yet thy cicatrice° looks raw and red
After the Danish sword, and thy free awe°
Pays homage to us—thou mayst not coldly set°
Our sovereign process,° which imports at full,°
By letters congruing° to that effect,   65
The present° death of Hamlet. Do it, England,
For like the hectic° in my blood he rages,
And thou must cure me. Till I know 'tis done,
Howe'er my haps,° my joys were ne'er begun.

Exit.

---

43 **bark** sailing vessel.   44 **tend** wait; **bent** in readiness.   50 **cherub** (Cherubim are angels of
knowledge. Hamlet hints that both he and heaven are onto Claudius' tricks.)   55 **at foot** close
behind, at heel.   58 **leans on** bears upon, is related to.   59 **England** i.e., King of England;
at aught at any value.   60 **As . . . sense** for so my great power may give you a just appreciation of
the importance of valuing my love.   61 **cicatrice** scar.   62 **free awe** voluntary show of respect.
63 **coldly set** regard with indifference.   64 **process** command; **imports at full** conveys specific
directions for.   65 **congruing** agreeing.   66 **present** immediate.   67 **hectic** persistent fever.
69 **haps** fortunes.

SCENE IV [THE COAST OF DENMARK.]

Enter Fortinbras with his army over the stage.

FORTINBRAS: Go, Captain, from me greet the Danish king.
Tell him that by his license° Fortinbras
Craves the conveyance of° a promised march
Over his kingdom. You know the rendezvous.
If that His Majesty would aught with us,   5
We shall express our duty° in his eye;°
And let him know so.

CAPTAIN: I will do 't, my lord.

FORTINBRAS: Go softly° on.

                                    [Exeunt all but the Captain.]

Enter Hamlet, Rosencrantz, [Guildenstern,] etc.

HAMLET: Good sir, whose powers° are these?   10

CAPTAIN: They are of Norway, sir.

HAMLET: How purposed, sir, I pray you?

CAPTAIN: Against some part of Poland.

HAMLET: Who commands them, sir?

CAPTAIN: The nephew to old Norway, Fortinbras.   15

HAMLET: Goes it against the main° of Poland, sir,
Or for some frontier?

CAPTAIN: Truly to speak, and with no addition,°
We go to gain a little patch of ground
That hath in it no profit but the name.   20
To pay° five ducats, five, I would not farm it;°
Nor will it yield to Norway or the Pole
A ranker° rate, should it be sold in fee.°

HAMLET: Why, then the Polack never will defend it.

CAPTAIN: Yes, it is already garrisoned.   25

HAMLET: Two thousand souls and twenty thousand ducats
Will not debate the question of this straw.°
This is th' impostume° of much wealth and peace,
That inward breaks, and shows no cause without
Why the man dies. I humbly thank you, sir.   30

CAPTAIN: God b' wi' you, sir.

                                         [Exit.]

---

2 **license** permission.   3 **the conveyance of** escort during.   6 **duty** respect;   **eye** presence.   9 **softly** slowly, circumspectly.   10 **powers** forces.   16 **main** main part.   18 **addition** exaggeration.   21 **To pay** i.e., for a yearly rental of;   **farm it** take a lease on it.   23 **ranker** higher;   **in fee** fee simple, outright.   27 **debate . . .straw** settle this trifling matter.   28 **impostume** abscess.

ROSENCRANTZ: Will 't please you go, my lord?
HAMLET: I'll be with you straight. Go a little before.

[*Exeunt all except Hamlet.*]

How all occasions do inform against° me
And spur my dull revenge! What is a man,
If his chief good and market of° his time   35
Be but to sleep and feed? A beast, no more.
Sure he that made us with such large discourse,°
Looking before and after,° gave us not
That capability and godlike reason
To fust° in us unused. Now, whether it be   40
Bestial oblivion,° or some craven° scruple
Of thinking too precisely° on th' event°—
A thought which, quartered, hath but one part wisdom
And ever three parts coward—I do not know
Why yet I live to say "This thing's to do,"   45
Sith° I have cause, and will, and strength, and means
To do 't. Examples gross° as earth exhort me:
Witness this army of such mass and charge,°
Led by a delicate and tender° prince,
Whose spirit with divine ambition puffed   50
Makes mouths° at the invisible event,°
Exposing what is mortal and unsure
To all that fortune, death, and danger dare,°
Even for an eggshell. Rightly to be great
Is not to stir without great argument,   55
But greatly to find quarrel in a straw
When honor's at the stake.° How stand I, then,
That have a father killed, a mother stained,
Excitements of° my reason and my blood,
And let all sleep, while to my shame I see   60
The imminent death of twenty thousand men

---

33 inform against denounce, betray; take shape against.   **35 market of** profit of, compensation
for.   **37 discourse** power of reasoning.   **38 Looking before and after** able to review past events
and anticipate the future.   **40 fust** grow moldy.   **41 oblivion** forgetfulness;   **craven** cowardly.
42 precisely scrupulously;   **event** outcome.   **46 Sith** since.   **47 gross** obvious.   **48 charge** expense.
49 delicate and tender of fine and youthful qualities.   **51 Makes mouths** makes scornful faces;
invisible event unforeseeable outcome.   **53 dare** could do (to him).   **54–57 Rightly . . . stake** true
greatness does not normally consist of rushing into action over some trivial provocation; however,
when one's honor is involved, even a trifling insult requires that one respond greatly (?); **at the stake**
(A metaphor from gambling or bear-baiting.)   **59 Excitements of** promptings by.

That for a fantasy° and trick° of fame
Go to their graves like beds, fight for a plot°
Whereon the numbers cannot try the cause,°
Which is not tomb enough and continent°   65
To hide the slain? O, from this time forth
My thoughts be bloody or be nothing worth!

                                                                  Exit.

SCENE V [THE CASTLE.]

Enter Horatio, [Queen] gertrude, and a gentleman.

QUEEN: I will not speak with her.
GENTLEMAN: She is importunate,
   Indeed distract.° Her mood will needs be pitied.
QUEEN: What would she have?
GENTLEMAN: She speaks much of her father, says she hears
   There's tricks° i' the world, and hems,° and beats her heart,°   5
   Spurns enviously at straws,° speaks things in doubt°
   That carry but half sense. Her speech is nothing,
   Yet the unshapèd use° of it doth move
   The hearers to collection;° they yawn° at it,
   And botch° the words up fit to their own thoughts,   10
   Which,° as her winks and nods and gestures yield° them,
   Indeed would make one think there might be thought,°
   Though nothing sure, yet much unhappily.°
HORATIO: 'Twere good she were spoken with, for she may strew
   Dangerous conjectures in ill-breeding° minds.   15
QUEEN: Let her come in.

                                                    [*Exit gentleman.*]

   [*Aside.*]   To my sick soul, as sin's true nature is,
   Each toy° seems prologue to some great amiss.°
   So full of artless jealousy is guilt,
   It spills itself in fearing to be spilt.°   20

---

62 **fantasy** fanciful caprice, illusion;   **trick** trifle, deceit.   63 **plot** plot of ground.   64 **Whereon . . . cause** on which there is insufficient room for the soldiers needed to engage in a military contest. 65 **continent** receptacle; container.   2 **distract** distracted.   5 **tricks** deceptions;   **hems** makes "hmm" sounds;   **heart** i.e., breast.   6 **Spurns . . . straws** kicks spitefully, takes offense at trifles; **in doubt** obscurely.   8 **unshapèd use** incoherent manner.   9 **collection** inference, a guess at some sort of meaning;   **yawn** gape, wonder; grasp. (The Folio reading, aim, is possible.)   10 **botch** patch.   11 **Which** which words;   **yield** deliver, represent.   12 **thought** intended.   13 **unhappily** unpleasantly near the truth, shrewdly.   15 **ill-breeding** prone to suspect the worst and to make mischief.   18 **toy** trifle;   **amiss** calamity.   19–20 **So . . . split** guilt is so full of suspicion that it unskilfully betrays itself in fearing betrayal.

Enter Ophelia° [*distracted*].

OPHELIA: Where is the beauteous majesty of Denmark?
QUEEN: How now, Ophelia?
OPHELIA [*she sings*]:
    "How should I your true love know
      From another one?
    By his cockle hat° and staff,   25
      And his sandal shoon."°
QUEEN: Alas, sweet lady, what imports this song?
OPHELIA: Say you? Nay, pray you, mark.
    "He is dead and gone, lady,   [*Song.*]
      He is dead and gone;   30
    At his head a grass-green turf,
      At his heels a stone."
    O, ho!
QUEEN: Nay, but Ophelia—
OPHELIA: Pray you, mark. [*Sings.*]   35
    "White his shroud as the mountain snow"—

Enter King.

QUEEN: Alas, look here, my lord.
OPHELIA:
    "Larded° with sweet flowers;   [*Song.*]
    Which bewept to the ground did not go
      With true-love showers."°   40
KING: How do you, pretty lady?
OPHELIA: Well, God 'ild° you! They say the owl° was a baker's
    daughter. Lord, we know what we are, but know not what we
    may be. God be at your table!
KING: Conceit° upon her father.   45
OPHELIA: Pray let's have no words of this; but when they ask you
    what it means, say you this:
    "Tomorrow is Saint Valentine's day,   [*Song.*]
      All in the morning betime,°

---

s.d. **Enter Ophelia** (In the First Quarto, Ophelia enters, "playing on a lute, and her hair down, singing.") 25 **cockle hat** hat with cockle-shell stuck in it as a sign that the wearer had been a pilgrim to the shrine of Saint James of Compostela in Spain. 26 **shoon** shoes. 38 **Larded** decorated. 40 **showers** i.e., tears. 42 **God 'ild** God yield or reward; **owl** (Refers to a legend about a baker's daughter who was turned into an owl for being ungenerous when Jesus begged a loaf of bread.) 45 **Conceit** brooding. 49 **betime** early.

And I a maid at your window,   50
To be your Valentine.
Then up he rose, and donned his clothes,
And dupped° the chamber door,
Let in the maid, that out a maid
Never departed more."   55

KING: Pretty Ophelia—

OPHELIA: Indeed, la, without an oath, I'll make an end on 't:
"By Gis° and by Saint Charity,
Alack, and fie for shame!
Young men will do 't, if they come to 't;   60
By Cock,° they are to blame.
Quoth she, 'Before you tumbled me,
You promised me to wed.'"

He answers:
"'So would I ha' done, by yonder sun,   65
An° thou hadst not come to my bed.'"

KING: How long hath she been thus?

OPHELIA: I hope all will be well. We must be patient, but I cannot
choose but weep to think they would lay him i' the cold
ground. My brother shall know of it. And so I thank you for   70
your good counsel. Come, my coach! Good night, ladies, good
night, sweet ladies, good night, good night.   [*Exit.*]

KING [*to Horatio*]:   Follow her close. Give her good watch, I pray
you.   [*Exit Horatio.*]

O, this is the poison of deep grief; it springs   75
All from her father's death—and now behold!
O Gertrude, Gertrude,
When sorrows come, they come not single spies,°
But in battalions. First, her father slain;
Next, your son gone, and he most violent author   80
Of his own just remove;° the people muddied,°
Thick and unwholesome in their thoughts and whispers
For good Polonius' death—and we have done but greenly,°
In hugger-mugger° to inter him; poor Ophelia
Divided from herself and her fair judgment,   85

---

53 **dupped** did up, opened. 58 **Gis** Jesus. 61 **Cock** (A perversion of "God" in oaths; here also
with a quibble on the slang word for penis.) 66 **An** if. 78 **spies** scouts sent in advance of the
main force. 81 **remove** removal; **muddied** stirred up, confused. 83 **greenly** in an inexperienced
way, foolishly. 84 **hugger-mugger** secret haste.

Without the which we are pictures or mere beasts;
Last, and as much containing° as all these,
Her brother is in secret come from France,
Feeds on this wonder, keeps himself in clouds,°
And wants° not buzzers° to infect his ear   90
With pestilent speeches of his father's death,
Wherein necessity,° of matter beggared,°
Will nothing stick our person to arraign
In ear and ear.° O my dear Gertrude, this,
Like to a murdering piece,° in many places   95
Gives me superfluous death.°   *A noise within.*

QUEEN: Alack, what noise is this?

KING: Attend!°
Where is my Switzers?° Let them guard the door.

Enter a Messenger.

What is the matter?

MESSENGER: Save yourself, my lord!   100
The ocean, overpeering of his list,°
Eats not the flats° with more impetuous° haste
Than young Laertes, in a riotous head,°
O'erbears your officers. The rabble call him lord,
And, as° the world were now but to begin,   105
Antiquity forgot, custom not known,
The ratifiers and props of every word,°
They cry, "Choose we! Laertes shall be king!"
Caps,° hands, and tongues applaud it to the clouds,
"Laertes shall be king, Laertes king!"   110

QUEEN: How cheerfully on the false trail they cry!   *A noise within.*
O, this is counter,° you false Danish dogs!

---

87 **as much containing** as full of serious matter.   89 **Feeds . . . clouds** feeds his resentment or shocked grievance, holds himself inscrutable and aloof amid all this rumor.   90 **wants** lacks; **buzzers** gossipers, informers.   92 **necessity** i.e., the need to invent some plausible explanation; **of matter beggared** unprovided with facts.   92–94 **Will . . . ear** will not hesitate to accuse my (royal) person in everybody's ears.   95 **murdering piece** cannon loaded so as to scatter its shot. 96 **Gives . . . death** kills me over and over.   98 **Attend** i.e., guard me.   99 **Switzers** Swiss guards, mercenaries.   101 **overpeering of his list** overflowing its shore, boundary.   102 **flats** i.e., flatlands near shore;   **impetuous** violent. (Perhaps also with the meaning of impiteous [impitious, Q2], "pitiless.")   103 **head** insurrection.   105 **as** as if.   107 **The ratifiers . . . word** i.e., antiquity (or tradition) and custom ought to confirm (ratify) and underprop our every word or promise. 109 **Caps** (The caps are thrown in the air.)   112 **counter** (A hunting term, meaning to follow the trail in a direction opposite to that which the game has taken.)

Enter Laertes with others.

KING: The doors are broke.
LAERTES: Where is this King?—Sirs, stand you all without.
ALL: No, let's come in.   115
LAERTES: I pray you, give me leave.
ALL: We will, we will.
LAERTES: I thank you. Keep the door. [*Exeunt followers.*]
                    O thou vile king, Give me my father!
QUEEN [*restraining him*]: Calmly, good Laertes.
LAERTES: That drop of blood that's calm proclaims me bastard,   120
     Cries cuckold to my father, brands the harlot
     Even here, between° the chaste unsmirchèd brow
     Of my true mother.
KING: What is the cause, Laertes,
     That thy rebellion looks so giantlike?
     Let him go, Gertrude. Do not fear our° person.   125
     There's such divinity doth hedge° a king
     That treason can but peep to what it would,°
     Acts little of his will.° Tell me, Laertes,
     Why thou art thus incensed. Let him go, Gertrude.
     Speak, man.
LAERTES: Where is my father?
KING: Dead.   130
QUEEN: But not by him.
KING: Let him demand his fill.
LAERTES: How came he dead? I'll not be juggled with.°
     To hell, allegiance! Vows, to the blackest devil!
     Conscience and grace, to the profoundest pit!
     I dare damnation. To this point I stand,°   135
     That both the worlds I give to negligence,°
     Let come what comes, only I'll be revenged
     Most throughly° for my father.
KING: Who shall stay you?
LAERTES: My will, not all the world's.°   140

---

122 **between** in the middle of.   125 **fear our** fear for my.   126 **hedge** protect, as with a surrounding barrier.   127 **can ... would** can only peep furtively, as through a barrier, at what it would intend.   128 **Acts ... will** (but) performs little of what it intends.   132 **juggled with** cheated, deceived.   135 **To ... stand** I am resolved in this.   136 **both ... negligence** i.e. both this world and the next are of no consequence to me.   138 **throughly** thoroughly.   140 **My will ... world's** I'll stop (stay) when my will is accomplished, not for anyone else's.

And for° my means, I'll husband them so well
They shall go far with little.

KING: Good Laertes,
If you desire to know the certainty
Of your dear father, is 't writ in your revenge
That, swoopstake,° you will draw both friend and foe,   145
Winner and loser?

LAERTES: None but his enemies.

KING: Will you know them, then?

LAERTES: To his good friends thus wide I'll ope my arms,
And like the kind life-rendering pelican°   150
Repast° them with my blood.

KING: Why, now you speak
Like a good child and a true gentleman.
That I am guiltless of your father's death,
And am most sensibly° in grief for it,
It shall as level° to your judgment 'pear   155
As day does to your eye.   *A noise within.*

LAERTES: How now, what noise is that?

Enter Ophelia.

KING: Let her come in.

LAERTES: O heat, dry up my brains! Tears seven times salt
Burn out the sense and virtue° of mine eye!
By heaven, thy madness shall be paid with weight°   160
Till our scale turn the beam.° O rose of May!
Dear maid, kind sister, sweet Ophelia!
O heavens, is 't possible a young maid's wits
Should be as mortal as an old man's life?
Nature is fine in° love, and where 'tis fine   165
It sends some precious instance° of itself
After the thing it loves.°

OPHELIA:
"They bore him barefaced on the bier,   [*Song.*]

---

141 for as for.   **145 swoopstake** i.e., indiscriminately. (Literally, taking all stakes on the gambling table at once. Draw is also a gambling term, meaning "taken from.")   **150 pelican** (Refers to the belief that the female pelican fed its young with its own blood.)   **151 Repast** feed.   **154 sensibly** feelingly.   **155 level** plain.   **159 virtue** faculty, power.   **160 paid with weight** repaid, avenged equally or more.   **161 beam** crossbar of a balance.   **165 fine in** refined by.   **166 instance** token. **167 After . . . loves** i.e., into the grave, along with Polonius.

Hey non nonny, nonny, hey nonny,
And in his grave rained many a tear—" 170

Fare you well, my dove!

LAERTES: Hadst thou thy wits and didst persuade° revenge,
It could not move thus.

OPHELIA: You must sing "A-down a-down," and you "call him a-
down-a."° 175

O, how the wheel° becomes it! It is the false steward° that stole his
master's daughter.

LAERTES: This nothing's more than matter.°

OPHELIA: There's rosemary,° that's for remembrance; pray you,
love, remember. And there is pansies;° that's for thoughts. 180

LAERTES: A document° in madness, thoughts and remembrance
fitted.

OPHELIA: There's fennel° for you, and columbines.° There's rue°
for you, and here's some for me; we may call it herb of grace o'
Sundays. You must wear your rue with a difference.° There's a 185
daisy.° I would give you some violets,° but they withered all
when my father died. They say 'a made a good end— [*Sings.*]

"For bonny sweet Robin is all my joy."

LAERTES: Thought° and affliction, passion,° hell itself,
She turns to favor° and to prettiness. 190

OPHELIA:

"And will 'a not come again? [*Song.*]
And will 'a not come again?
No, no, he is dead.
Go to thy deathbed,
He never will come again. 195

"His beard was as white as snow,

---

172 persuade argue cogently for.   **175 You . . . a-down-a** (Ophelia assigns the singing of refrains,
like her own "Hey non nonny," to others present.)   **176 wheel** spinning wheel as accompaniment
to the song, or refrain;   **false steward** (The story is unknown.)   **178 This . . . matter** this seeming
nonsense is more eloquent than sane utterance.   **179 rosemary** (Used as a symbol of remembrance
both at weddings and at funerals.)   **180 pansies** (Emblems of love and courtship; perhaps from
French pensées, "thoughts.")   **181 document** instruction, lesson.   **183 fennel** (Emblem of flattery.);
columbines (Emblems of unchastity or ingratitude.);   **rue** (Emblem of repentance—a signification
that is evident in its popular name, herb of grace.)   **185 with a difference** (A device used in heraldry
to distinguish one family from another on the coat of arms, here suggesting that Ophelia and the
others have different causes of sorrow and repentance; perhaps with a play on rue in the sense of
"ruth," "pity.");   **186 daisy** (Emblem of dissembling, faithlessness.)   **violets** (Emblems of
faithfulness.)   **189 Thought** melancholy;   **passion** suffering.   **190 favor** grace, beauty.

All flaxen was his poll.°
   He is gone, he is gone,
   And we cast away moan.
God ha' mercy on his soul!"

And of all Christian souls, I pray God. God b' wi' you.   200

[*Exit, followed by Gertrude.*]

LAERTES: Do you see this, O God?
KING: Laertes, I must commune with your grief,
  Or you deny me right. Go but apart,
  Make choice of whom° your wisest friends you will,   205
  And they shall hear and judge twixt you and me.
  If by direct or by collateral hand°
  They find us touched,° we will our kingdom give,
  Our crown, our life, and all that we call ours
  To you in satisfaction; but if not,   210
  Be you content to lend your patience to us,
  And we shall jointly labor with your soul
  To give it due content.
LAERTES: Let this be so.
  His means of death, his obscure funeral—
  No trophy,° sword, nor hatchment° o'er his bones,   215
  No noble rite, nor formal ostentation°—
  Cry to be heard, as 'twere from heaven to earth,
  That° I must call 't in question.°
KING: So you shall,
  And where th' offense is, let the great ax fall.
  I pray you, go with me.   *Exeunt.* 220

SCENE VI [THE CASTLE.]

Enter Horatio and others.

HORATIO: What are they that would speak with me?
GENTLEMAN: Seafaring men, sir. They say they have letters for you.
HORATIO: Let them come in.   [*Exit gentleman.*]

---

197 poll head. 205 whom whichever of. 207 collateral hand indirect agency. 208 us touched me implicated. 215 trophy memorial; hatchment tablet displaying the armorial bearings of a deceased person. 216 ostentation ceremony. 218 That so that; call 't in question demand an explanation.

I do not know from what part of the world
I should be greeted, if not from Lord Hamlet.   5

Enter Sailors.

FIRST SAILOR: God bless you, sir.
HORATIO: Let him bless thee too.
FIRST SAILOR: 'A shall, sir, an 't° please him. There's a letter for
you, sir—it came from th' ambassador° that was bound for
England—if your name be Horatio, as I am let to know it is.   10

[*He gives a letter.*]

HORATIO [*reads*]:   "Horatio, when thou shalt have overlooked°
this, give these fellows some means° to the King; they have letters
for him. Ere we were two days old at sea, a pirate of very warlike
appointment° gave us chase. Finding ourselves too slow of sail,
we put on a compelled valor, and in the grapple I boarded them.   15
On the instant they got clear of our ship, so I alone became their
prisoner. They have dealt with me like thieves of mercy,° but
they knew what they did: I am to do a good turn for them. Let
the King have the letters I have sent, and repair° thou to me with
as much speed as thou wouldest fly death. I have words to speak   20
in thine ear will make thee dumb, yet are they much too light
for the bore° of the matter. These good fellows will bring thee
where I am. Rosencrantz and Guildenstern hold their course for
England. Of them I have much to tell thee. Farewell.
He that thou knowest thine, Hamlet."   25
Come, I will give you way° for these your letters,
And do 't the speedier that you may direct me
To him from whom you brought them.   *Exeunt.*

SCENE VII [THE CASTLE.]

Enter King and Laertes.

KING: Now must your conscience my acquittance seal,°
And you must put me in your heart for friend,
Sith° you have heard, and with a knowing ear,

8 **an 't** if it.   9 **th' ambassador** (Evidently Hamlet. The sailor is being circumspect.)   11 **overlooked**
looked over.   12 **means** means of access.   14 **appointment** equipage.   17 **thieves of mercy** merciful
thieves.   19 **repair** come.   22 **bore** caliber, i.e., importance.   26 **way** means of access.   1 **my**
acquittance seal confirm or acknowledge my innocence.   3 **Sith** since.

That he which hath your noble father slain
Pursued my life.

LAERTES: It well appears. But tell me   5
Why you proceeded not against these feats°
So crimeful and so capital° in nature,
As by your safety, greatness, wisdom, all things else,
You mainly° were stirred up.

KING: O, for two special reasons,   10
Which may to you perhaps seem much unsinewed,°
But yet to me they're strong. The Queen his mother
Lives almost by his looks, and for myself—
My virtue or my plague, be it either which—
She is so conjunctive° to my life and soul   15
That, as the star moves not but in his° sphere,°
I could not but by her. The other motive
Why to a public count° I might not go
Is the great love the general gender° bear him,
Who, dipping all his faults in their affection,   20
Work° like the spring° that turneth wood to stone,
Convert his gyves° to graces, so that my arrows,
Too slightly timbered° for so loud° a wind,
Would have reverted° to my bow again
But not where I had aimed them.   25

LAERTES: And so have I a noble father lost,
A sister driven into desperate terms,°
Whose worth, if praises may go back° again,
Stood challenger on mount° of all the age
For her perfections. But my revenge will come.   30

KING: Break not your sleeps for that. You must not think
That we are made of stuff so flat and dull
That we can let our beard be shook with danger
And think it pastime. You shortly shall hear more.

6 **feats** acts.   7 **capital** punishable by death.   9 **mainly** greatly.   11 **unsinewed** weak.
15 **conjunctive** closely united. (An astronomical metaphor.)   16 **his** its;   **sphere** one of the
hollow spheres in which, according to Ptolemaic astronomy, the planets were supposed to move.
18 **count** account, reckoning, indictment.   19 **general gender** common people.   21 **Work** operate,
act;   **spring** i.e., a spring with such a concentration of lime that it coats a piece of wood with
limestone, in effect gilding and petrifying it.   22 **gyves** fetters (which, gilded by the people's praise,
would look like badges of honor).   23 **slightly timbered** light;   **loud** (suggesting public outcry on
Hamlet's behalf).   24 **reverted** returned.   27 **terms** state, condition.   28 **go back** i.e., recall what
she was.   29 **on mount** set up on high.

I loved your father, and we love ourself;   35
And that, I hope, will teach you to imagine—

Enter a Messenger with letters.

    How now? What news?
MESSENGER: Letters, my lord, from Hamlet:
This to Your Majesty, this to the Queen.

                                     [He gives letters.]

KING: From Hamlet? Who brought them?
MESSENGER: Sailors, my lord, they say. I saw them not.   40
They were given me by Claudio. He received them
Of him that brought them.
KING: Laertes, you shall hear them.—
Leave us.   *[Exit messenger.]*
[He reads.] "High and mighty, you shall know I am set naked°
on your kingdom. Tomorrow shall I beg leave to see your kingly   45
eyes, when I shall, first asking your pardon,° thereunto recount
the occasion of my sudden and more strange return.   Hamlet."
What should this mean? Are all the rest come back? Or is it
some abuse,° and no such thing?°
LAERTES: Know you the hand?
KING: 'Tis Hamlet's character.° "Naked!"   50
And in a postscript here he says "alone."
Can you devise° me?
LAERTES: I am lost in it, my lord. But let him come.
It warms the very sickness in my heart
That I shall live and tell him to his teeth,   55
"Thus didst thou."°
KING: If it be so, Laertes—
As how should it be so? How otherwise?°—
Will you be ruled by me?
LAERTES: Ay, my lord,
So° you will not o'errule me to a peace.
KING: To thine own peace. If he be now returned,   60

---

44 **naked** destitute, unarmed, without following. 46 **pardon** permission. 49 **abuse** deceit;
no such thing not what it appears. 50 **character** handwriting. 52 **devise** explain to. 56 **Thus
didst thou** i.e., here's for what you did to my father. 57 **As . . . otherwise** how can this (Hamlet's
return) be true? Yet how otherwise than true (since we have the evidence of his letter)? 59 **So**
provided that.

As checking at° his voyage, and that° he means
No more to undertake it, I will work him
To an exploit, now ripe in my device,°
Under the which he shall not choose but fall;
And for his death no wind of blame shall breathe,   65
But even his mother shall uncharge the practice°
And call it accident.

LAERTES: My lord, I will be ruled,
The rather if you could devise it so
That I might be the organ.°

KING: It falls right.
You have been talked of since your travel much,   70
And that in Hamlet's hearing, for a quality
Wherein they say you shine. Your sum of parts°
Did not together pluck such envy from him
As did that one, and that, in my regard,
Of the unworthiest siege.°   75

LAERTES: What part is that, my lord?

KING: A very ribbon in the cap of youth,
Yet needful too, for youth no less becomes°
The light and careless livery that it wears
Than settled age his sables° and his weeds°   80
Importing health and graveness.° Two months since
Here was a gentleman of Normandy.
I have seen myself, and served against, the French,
And they can well° on horseback, but this gallant
Had witchcraft in 't; he grew unto his seat,   85
And to such wondrous doing brought his horse
As had he been incorpsed and demi-natured°
With the brave beast. So far he topped° my thought
That I in forgery° of shapes and tricks
Come short of what he did.

LAERTES: A Norman was 't?   90

KING: A Norman.

---

61 **checking at** i.e., turning aside from (like a falcon leaving the quarry to fly at a chance bird); **that** if. 63 **device** devising, invention. 66 **uncharge the practice** acquit the stratagem of being a plot. 69 **organ** agent, instrument. 72 **Your . . . parts** i.e., all your other virtues. 75 **unworthiest siege** least important rank. 78 **no less becomes** is no less suited by. 80 **his sables** its rich robes furred with sable; **weeds** garments. 81 **Importing . . . graveness** signifying a concern for health and dignified prosperity; also, giving an impression of comfortable prosperity. 84 **can well** are skilled. 87 **As . . . demi-natured** as if he had been of one body and nearly of one nature (like the centaur). 88 **topped** surpassed. 89 **forgery** imagining.

LAERTES: Upon my life, Lamord.

KING: The very same.

LAERTES: I know him well. He is the brooch° indeed
   And gem of all the nation.

KING: He made confession° of you,   95
   And gave you such a masterly report
   For art and exercise in your defense,°
   And for your rapier most especial,
   That he cried out 'twould be a sight indeed
   If one could match you. Th' escrimers° of their nation,   100
   He swore, had neither motion, guard, nor eye
   If you opposed them. Sir, this report of his
   Did Hamlet so envenom with his envy
   That he could nothing do but wish and beg
   Your sudden° coming o'er, to play° with you.   105
   Now, out of this—

LAERTES: What out of this, my lord?

KING: Laertes, was your father dear to you?
   Or are you like the painting of a sorrow,
   A face without a heart?

LAERTES: Why ask you this?

KING: Not that I think you did not love your father,   110
   But that I know love is begun by time,°
   And that I see, in passages of proof,°
   Time qualifies° the spark and fire of it.
   There lives within the very flame of love
   A kind of wick or snuff° that will abate it,   115
   And nothing is at a like goodness still,°
   For goodness, growing to a pleurisy,°
   Dies in his own too much.° That° we would do,
   We should do when we would; for this "would" changes
   And hath abatements° and delays as many   120
   As there are tongues, are hands, are accidents,°
   And then this "should" is like a spendthrift sigh,°

---

93 brooch ornament.   95 confession testimonial, admission of superiority.   97 For . . . defense with respect to your skill and practice with your weapon.   100 escrimers fencers.   105 sudden immediate;   play fence.   111 begun by time i.e., created by the right circumstance and hence subject to change.   112 passages of proof actual instances that prove it.   113 qualifies weakens, moderates.   115 snuff the charred part of a candlewick.   116 nothing . . . still nothing remains at a constant level of perfection.   117 pleurisy excess, plethora. (Literally, a chest inflammation.)   118 in . . . much of its own excess;   That that which.   120 abatements diminutions.   121 As . . . accidents as there are tongues to dissuade, hands to prevent, and chance events to intervene.   122 spendthrift sigh (An allusion to the belief that sighs draw blood from the heart.)

That hurts by easing.° But, to the quick o' th' ulcer:°
Hamlet comes back. What would you undertake
To show yourself in deed your father's son   125
More than in words?

LAERTES: To cut his throat i' the church.

KING: No place, indeed, should murder sanctuarize;°
Revenge should have no bounds. But good Laertes,
Will you do this,° keep close within your chamber.
Hamlet returned shall know you are come home.   130
We'll put on those shall° praise your excellence
And set a double varnish on the fame
The Frenchman gave you, bring you in fine° together,
And wager on your heads. He, being remiss,°
Most generous,° and free from all contriving,   135
Will not peruse the foils, so that with ease,
Or with a little shuffling, you may choose
A sword unbated,° and in a pass of practice°
Requite him for your father.

LAERTES: I will do 't,
And for that purpose I'll anoint my sword.   140
I bought an unction° of a mountebank°
So mortal that, but dip a knife in it,
Where it draws blood no cataplasm° so rare,
Collected from all simples° that have virtue°
Under the moon,° can save the thing from death   145
That is but scratched withal. I'll touch my point
With this contagion, that if I gall° him slightly,
It may be death.

KING: Let's further think of this,
Weigh what convenience both of time and means
May fit us to our shape.° If this should fail,   150
And that our drift look through our bad performance,°
'Twere better not assayed. Therefore this project

---

123 **hurts by easing** i.e., costs the heart blood and wastes precious opportunity even while it affords emotional relief;   **quick o' th' ulcer** i.e., heart of the matter.   127 **sanctuarize** protect from punishment. (Alludes to the right of sanctuary with which certain religious places were invested.)   129 **Will you do this** if you wish to do this.   131 **put on those shall** arrange for some to.   133 **in fine** finally.   134 **remiss** negligently unsuspicious.   135 **generous** noble-minded.   138 **unbated** not blunted, having no button;   **pass of practice** treacherous thrust.   141 **unction** ointment;   **mountebank** quack doctor.   143 **cataplasm** plaster or poultice.   144 **simples** herbs;   **virtue** potency.   145 **Under the moon** i.e., anywhere (with reference perhaps to the belief that herbs gathered at night had a special power).   147 **gall** graze, wound.   150 **shape** part we propose to act.   151 **drift . . . performance** intention should be made visible by our bungling.

Should have a back or second, that might hold
If this did blast in proof.° Soft, let me see.
We'll make a solemn wager on your cunnings°—   155
I ha 't!
When in your motion you are hot and dry—
As° make your bouts more violent to that end—
And that he calls for drink, I'll have prepared him
A chalice for the nonce,° whereon but sipping,   160
If he by chance escape your venomed stuck,°
Our purpose may hold there. [*A cry within.*] But stay, what noise?

Enter Queen.

QUEEN: One woe doth tread upon another's heel,
So fast they follow. Your sister's drowned, Laertes.
LAERTES: Drowned! O, where?   165
QUEEN: There is a willow grows askant° the brook,
That shows his hoar leaves° in the glassy stream;
Therewith fantastic garlands did she make
Of crowflowers, nettles, daisies, and long purples,°
That liberal° shepherds give a grosser name,°   170
But our cold° maids do dead men's fingers call them.
There on the pendent° boughs her crownet° weeds
Clamb'ring to hang, an envious sliver° broke,
When down her weedy° trophies and herself
Fell in the weeping brook. Her clothes spread wide,   175
And mermaidlike awhile they bore her up,
Which time she chanted snatches of old lauds,°
As one incapable of° her own distress,
Or like a creature native and endued°
Unto that element. But long it could not be   180
Till that her garments, heavy with their drink,
Pulled the poor wretch from her melodious lay
To muddy death.
LAERTES: Alas, then she is drowned?
QUEEN: Drowned, drowned.

154 **blast in proof** burst in the test (like a cannon).   155 **cunnings** respective skills.   158 **As** i.e.,
and you should.   160 **nonce** occasion.   161 **stuck** thrust. (From stoccado, a fencing term.)
166 **askant** aslant.   167 **hoar leaves** white or gray undersides of the leaves.   169 **long purples** early
purple orchids.   170 **liberal** free-spoken;   **a grosser name** (The testicle-resembling tubers of the
orchid, which also in some cases resemble dead men's fingers, have earned various slang names like
"dogstones" and "cullions.")   171 **cold** chaste.   172 **pendent** over-hanging;   **crownet** made into a
chaplet or coronet.   173 **envious sliver** malicious branch.   174 **weedy** i.e., of plants.   177 **lauds**
hymns.   178 **incapable of** lacking capacity to apprehend.   179 **endued** adapted by nature.

LAERTES: Too much of water hast thou, poor Ophelia,   185
And therefore I forbid my tears. But yet
It is our trick;° nature her custom holds,
Let shame say what it will. [*He weeps.*] When these are gone,
The woman will be out.° Adieu, my lord.
I have a speech of fire that fain would blaze,   190
But that this folly douts° it.   *Exit.*

KING: Let's follow, Gertrude.
How much I had to do to calm his rage!
Now fear I this will give it start again;
Therefore let's follow.   *Exeunt.*

ACT V

SCENE I [A CHURCHYARD.]

Enter two clowns° [with spades and mattocks].

FIRST CLOWN: Is she to be buried in Christian burial, when she will-
fully seeks her own salvation?°

SECOND CLOWN: I tell thee she is; therefore make her grave
straight.° The crowner° hath sat on her,° and finds it° Christian
burial.   5

FIRST CLOWN: How can that be, unless she drowned herself in
her own defense?

SECOND CLOWN: Why, 'tis found so.°

FIRST CLOWN: It must be se offendendo,° it cannot be else. For
here lies the point: if I drown myself wittingly, it argues an act,   10
and an act hath three branches—it is to act, to do, and to
perform. Argal,° she drowned herself wittingly.

SECOND CLOWN: Nay, but hear you, goodman° delver—

FIRST CLOWN: Give me leave. Here lies the water; good. Here
stands the man; good. If the man go to this water and drown   15
himself, it is, will he, nill he,° he goes, mark you that. But if the
water come to him and drown him, he drowns not himself.

187 It is our trick i.e., weeping is our natural way (when sad).   **188–190 When . . . out** when my tears are all shed, the woman in me will be expended, satisfied.   **191 douts** extinguishes. (The Second Quarto reads "drowns.")   **s.d. Clowns** rustics.   **2 salvation** (A blunder for "damnation," or perhaps a suggestion that Ophelia was taking her own shortcut to heaven.)   **4 straight** straightway, immediately. (But with a pun on strait, "narrow.")   **crowner** coroner;   **sat on her** conducted an inquest on her case;   **finds it** gives his official verdict that her means of death was consistent with.   **8 found so** determined so in the coroner's verdict.   **9 se offendendo** (A comic mistake for se defendendo, a term used in verdicts of justifiable homicide.)   **12 Argal** (Corruption of ergo, "therefore.")   **13 goodman** (An honorific title often used with the name of a profession or craft.)   **16 will he, nill he** whether he will or no, willy-nilly.

Argal, he that is not guilty of his own death shortens not his own life.

SECOND CLOWN: But is this law? 20

FIRST CLOWN: Ay, marry, is 't—crowner's quest° law.

SECOND CLOWN: Will you ha' the truth on 't? If this had not been a gentlewoman, she should have been buried out o' Christian burial.

FIRST CLOWN: Why, there thou sayst.° And the more pity that 25 great folk should have countenance° in this world to drown or hang themselves, more than their even-Christian.° Come, my spade. There is no ancient° gentlemen but gardeners, ditchers, and grave makers. They hold up° Adam's profession.

SECOND CLOWN: Was he a gentleman? 30

FIRST CLOWN: 'A was the first that ever bore arms.°

SECOND CLOWN: Why, he had none.

FIRST CLOWN: What, art a heathen? How dost thou understand the Scripture? The Scripture says Adam digged. Could he dig without arms?° I'll put another question to thee. If thou 35 answerest me not to the purpose, confess thyself°—

SECOND CLOWN: Go to.

FIRST CLOWN: What is he that builds stronger than either the mason, the shipwright, or the carpenter?

SECOND CLOWN: The gallows maker, for that frame° outlives a 40 thousand tenants.

FIRST CLOWN: I like thy wit well, in good faith. The gallows does well.° But how does it well? It does well to those that do ill. Now thou dost ill to say the gallows is built stronger than the church. Argal, the gallows may do well to thee. To 't again, come. 45

SECOND CLOWN: "Who builds stronger than a mason, a shipwright, or a carpenter?"

FIRST CLOWN: Ay, tell me that, and unyoke.°

SECOND CLOWN: Marry, now I can tell.

FIRST CLOWN: To 't. 50

SECOND CLOWN: Mass,° I cannot tell.

Enter Hamlet and Horatio [at a distance].

---

21 **quest** inquest.   25 **there thou sayst** i.e., that's right.   26 **countenance** privilege.   27 **even-Christian** fellow Christians;   28 **ancient** going back to ancient times.   29 **hold up** maintain.
31 **bore arms** (To be entitled to bear a coat of arms would make Adam a gentleman, but as one who bore a spade, our common ancestor was an ordinary delver in the earth.)   35 **arms** i.e., the arms of the body.   36 **confess thyself** (The saying continues, "and be hanged.")   40 **frame** (1) gallows (2) structure.   43 **does well** (1) is an apt answer (2) does a good turn.   48 **unyoke** i.e., after this great effort, you may unharness the team of your wits.   51 **Mass** by the Mass.

FIRST CLOWN: Cudgel thy brains no more about it, for your dull
ass will not mend his pace with beating; and when you are
asked this question next, say "a grave maker." The houses he
makes lasts till doomsday. Go get thee in and fetch me a stoup° 55
of liquor.

> [*Exit second clown. First clown digs.*]
> *Song.*

"In youth, when I did love, did love,°
Methought it was very sweet,
To contract—O—the time for—a—my behove,°
O, methought there—a—was nothing—a—meet."° 60

HAMLET: Has this fellow no feeling of his business, 'a° sings in
gravemaking?
HORATIO: Custom hath made it in him a property of easiness.°
HAMLET: 'Tis e'en so. The hand of little employment hath the
daintier sense.° 65
FIRST CLOWN: *Song.*

"But age with his stealing steps
Hath clawed me in his clutch,
And hath shipped me into the land,°
As if I had never been such."

> [*He throws up a skull.*]

HAMLET: That skull had a tongue in it and could sing once. How 70
the knave jowls° it to the ground, as if 'twere Cain's jawbone,
that did the first murder! This might be the pate of a politician,°
which this ass now o'erreaches,° one that would circumvent
God, might it not?
HORATIO: It might, my lord. 75
HAMLET: Or of a courtier, which could say, "Good morrow,
sweet lord! How dost thou, sweet lord?" This might be my
Lord Such-a-one, that praised my Lord Such-a-one's horse
when 'a meant to beg it, might it not?

---

55 **stoup** two-quart measure.   57 **In . . . love** (This and the two following stanzas, with nonsensical
variations, are from a poem attributed to Lord Vaux and printed in Tottel's Miscellany, 1557. The O
and a [for "ah"] seemingly are the grunts of the digger.)   59 **To contract . . . behove** i.e., to shorten the
time for my own advantage. (Perhaps he means to prolong it.)   60 **meet** suitable, i.e., more suitable.
61 **'a** that he.   63 **property of easiness** something he can do easily and indifferently.   65 **daintier sense**
more delicate sense of feeling.   68 **into the land** i.e., toward my grave (?) (But note the lack of rhyme
in steps, land.)   71 **jowls** dashes (with a pun on jowl, "jawbone").   72 **politician** schemer, plotter;
73 **o'erreaches** circumvents, gets the better of (with a quibble on the literal sense).

HORATIO: Ay, my lord. 80

HAMLET: Why, e'en so, and now my Lady Worm's, chapless,° and knocked about the mazard° with a sexton's spade. Here's fine revolution,° an° we had the trick to see° 't. Did these bones cost no more the breeding but to° play at loggets° with them? Mine ache to think on 't. 85

FIRST CLOWN: *Song.*

"A pickax and a spade, a spade,
For and° a shrouding sheet;
O, a pit of clay for to be made
For such a guest is meet."

[He throws up another skull.]

HAMLET: There's another. Why may not that be the skull of a 90 lawyer? Where be his quiddities° now, his quillities,° his cases, his tenures,° and his tricks? Why does he suffer this mad knave now to knock him about the sconce° with a dirty shovel, and will not tell him of his action of battery?° Hum, this fellow might be in 's time a great buyer of land, with his statutes, his 95 recognizances,° his fines, his double° vouchers,° his recoveries.° Is this the fine of his fines and the recovery of his recoveries, to have his fine pate full of fine dirt?° Will his vouchers vouch him no more of his purchases, and double ones too, than the length and breadth of a pair of indentures?° The very conveyances° of 100 his lands will scarcely lie in this box,° and must th' inheritor° himself have no more, ha?

HORATIO: Not a jot more, my lord.

HAMLET: Is not parchment made of sheepskins?

HORATIO: Ay, my lord, and of calves' skins too. 105

---

81 **chapless** having no lower jaw.   82 **mazard** i.e., head (Literally, a drinking vessel.);   83 **revolution** turn of Fortune's wheel, change;   **an** if.   **trick to see** knack of seeing;   83–84 **cost . . . to** involve so little expense and care in upbringing that we may.   84 **loggets** a game in which pieces of hard wood shaped like Indian clubs or bowling pins are thrown to lie as near as possible to a stake.   87 **For and** and moreover.   91 **quiddities** subtleties, quibbles. (From Latin quid, "a thing.");   **quillities** verbal niceties, subtle distinctions. (Variation of quiddities.);   92 **tenures** the holding of a piece of property or office, or the conditions or period of such holding.   93 **sconce** head.   94 **action of battery** lawsuit about physical assault.   95–96 **statutes, recognizances** legal documents guaranteeing a debt by attaching land and property.   96 **fines, recoveries** ways of converting entailed estates into "fee simple" or freehold;   **double** signed by two signatories;   **vouchers** guarantees of the legality of a title to real estate.   97–98 **fine of his fines . . . fine pate . . . fine dirt** end of his legal maneuvers . . . elegant head . . . minutely sifted dirt.   100 **pair of indentures** legal document drawn up in duplicate on a single sheet and then cut apart on a zigzag line so that each pair was uniquely matched. (Hamlet may refer to two rows of teeth or dentures.)   100 **conveyances** deeds.   101 **box** (1) deed box (2) coffin. ("Skull" has been suggested.);   **inheritor** possessor, owner.

HAMLET: They are sheep and calves which seek out assurance in that.° I will speak to this fellow.—Whose grave's this, sirrah?°

FIRST CLOWN: Mine, sir. [*Sings.*]

"O, pit of clay for to be made
For such a guest is meet." 110

HAMLET: I think it be thine, indeed, for thou liest in 't.

FIRST CLOWN: You lie out on 't, sir, and therefore 'tis not yours. For my part, I do not lie in 't, yet it is mine.

HAMLET: Thou dost lie in 't, to be in 't and say it is thine. 'Tis for the dead, not for the quick;° therefore thou liest. 115

FIRST CLOWN: 'Tis a quick lie, sir; 'twill away again from me to you.

HAMLET: What man dost thou dig it for?

FIRST CLOWN: For no man, sir.

HAMLET: What woman, then? 120

FIRST CLOWN: For none, neither.

HAMLET: Who is to be buried in 't?

FIRST CLOWN: One that was a woman, sir, but, rest her soul, she's dead.

HAMLET: How absolute° the knave is! We must speak by the 125 card,° or equivocation° will undo us. By the Lord, Horatio, this three years I have took° note of it: the age is grown so picked° that the toe of the peasant comes so near the heel of the courtier, he galls his kibe.°—How long hast thou been grave maker?

FIRST CLOWN: Of all the days i' the year, I came to 't that day 130 that our last king Hamlet overcame Fortinbras.

HAMLET: How long is that since?

FIRST CLOWN: Cannot you tell that? Every fool can tell that. It was that very day that young Hamlet was born—he that is mad and sent into England. 135

HAMLET: Ay, marry, why was he sent into England?

FIRST CLOWN: Why, because 'a was mad. 'A shall recover his wits there, or if 'a do not, 'tis no great matter there.

HAMLET: Why?

FIRST CLOWN: 'Twill not be seen in him there. There the men are 140 as mad as he.

---

107 **assurance in that** safety in legal parchments. **sirrah** (A term of address to inferiors.) 115 **quick** living. 125 **absolute** strict, precise; 125-126 **by the card** i.e., with precision. (Literally, by the mariner's compass-card, on which the points of the compass were marked.) 126 **equivocation** ambiguity in the use of terms. 127 **took** taken; **picked** refined, fastidious. 129 **galls his kibe** chafes the courtier's chilblain.

HAMLET: How came he mad?

FIRST CLOWN: Very strangely, they say.

HAMLET: How strangely?

FIRST CLOWN: Faith, e'en with losing his wits. 145

HAMLET: Upon what ground?°

FIRST CLOWN: Why, here in Denmark. I have been sexton here, man and boy, thirty years.

HAMLET: How long will a man lie i' th' earth ere he rot?

FIRST CLOWN: Faith, if 'a be not rotten before 'a die—as we have 150 many pocky° corpses nowadays, that will scarce hold the laying in°—'a will last you° some eight year or nine year. A tanner will last you nine year.

HAMLET: Why he more than another?

FIRST CLOWN: Why, sir, his hide is so tanned with his trade that 155 'a will keep out water a great while, and your water is a sore° decayer of your whoreson° dead body. [He picks up a skull.] Here's a skull now hath lien you° i' th' earth three-and-twenty years.

HAMLET: Whose was it? 160

FIRST CLOWN: A whoreson mad fellow's it was. Whose do you think it was?

HAMLET: Nay, I know not.

FIRST CLOWN: A pestilence on him for a mad rogue! 'A poured a flagon of Rhenish° on my head once. This same skull, sir, was, 165 sir, Yorick's skull, the King's jester.

HAMLET: This?

FIRST CLOWN: E'en that.

HAMLET: Let me see. [He takes the skull.] Alas, poor Yorick! I knew him, Horatio, a fellow of infinite jest, of most excellent 170 fancy. He hath bore° me on his back a thousand times, and now how abhorred in my imagination it is! My gorge rises° at it. Here hung those lips that I have kissed I know not how oft. Where be your gibes now? Your gambols, your songs, your flashes of merriment that were wont° to set the table on a roar? 175 Not one now, to mock your own grinning?° Quite chopfallen?°

146 ground cause. (But, in the next line, the gravedigger takes the word in the sense of "land," "country.") 151 pocky rotten, diseased. (Literally, with the pox, or syphilis.) 151–152 hold the laying in hold together long enough to be interred; 152 last you last. (You is used colloquially here and in the following lines.) 156 sore i.e., terrible, great; 157 whoreson i.e., vile, scurvy. 158 lien you lain. (See the note at line 144.) 165 Rhenish Rhine wine. 171 bore borne. 172 My gorge rises i.e., I feel nauseated. 175 were wont used. 176 mock your own grinning mock at the way your skull seems to be grinning (just as you used to mock at yourself and those who grinned at you); chopfallen (1) lacking the lower jaw (2) dejected.

Now get you to my lady's chamber and tell her, let her paint an inch thick, to this favor° she must come. Make her laugh at that. Prithee, Horatio, tell me one thing.

HORATIO: What's that, my lord? 180

HAMLET: Dost thou think Alexander looked o' this fashion i' th' earth?

HORATIO: E'en so.

HAMLET: And smelt so? Pah! [*He throws down the skull.*]

HORATIO: E'en so, my lord. 185

HAMLET: To what base uses we may return, Horatio! Why may not imagination trace the noble dust of Alexander till 'a find it stopping a bunghole?°

HORATIO: 'Twere to consider too curiously° to consider so.

HAMLET: No, faith, not a jot, but to follow him thither with 190 modesty° enough, and likelihood to lead it. As thus: Alexander died, Alexander was buried, Alexander returneth to dust, the dust is earth, of earth we make loam,° and why of that loam whereto he was converted might they not stop a beer barrel? Imperious° Caesar, dead and turned to clay, 195
Might stop a hole to keep the wind away.
O, that that earth which kept the world in awe
Should patch a wall t' expel the winter's flaw!°

Enter King, Queen, Laertes, and the corpse [*of Ophelia, in procession, with Priest, lords, etc.*].

But soft,° but soft awhile! Here comes the King,
The Queen, the courtiers. Who is this they follow? 200
And with such maimèd° rites? This doth betoken
The corpse they follow did with desperate hand
Fordo° its own life. 'Twas of some estate.°
Couch we° awhile and mark.

[*He and Horatio conceal themselves. Ophelia's body is taken to the grave.*]

LAERTES: What ceremony else? 205

HAMLET [*to Horatio*]: That is Laertes, a very noble youth. Mark.

LAERTES: What ceremony else?

---

178 **favor** aspect, appearance. 188 **bunghole** hole for filling or emptying a cask. 189 **curiously** minutely. 191 **modesty** plausible moderation. 193 **loam** mortar consisting chiefly of moistened clay and straw. 195 **Imperious** imperial. 198 **flaw** gust of wind. 199 **soft** i.e., wait, be careful. 201 **maimèd** mutilated, incomplete. 203 **Fordo** destroy; **estate** rank. 204 **Couch we** let's hide, lie low.

PRIEST: Her obsequies have been as far enlarged
　　As we have warranty.° Her death was doubtful,
　　And but that great command o'ersways the order°　　　　210
　　She should in ground unsanctified been lodged°
　　Till the last trumpet. For° charitable prayers,
　　Shards,° flints, and pebbles should be thrown on her.
　　Yet here she is allowed her virgin crants,°
　　Her maiden strewments,° and the bringing home　　　　215
　　Of bell and burial.°

LAERTES: Must there no more be done?

PRIEST:　　　　　　　　　　　　　No more be done.
　　We should profane the service of the dead
　　To sing a requiem and such rest° to her
　　As to peace-parted souls.°

LAERTES:　　　　　　　　　Lay her i' th' earth,　　　　220
　　And from her fair and unpolluted flesh
　　May violets° spring! I tell thee, churlish priest,
　　A ministering angel shall my sister be
　　When thou liest howling.°

HAMLET [*to Horatio*]:　　　　　What, the fair Ophelia!

QUEEN [*scattering flowers*]: Sweets to the sweet! Farewell.　　　225
　　I hoped thou shouldst have been my Hamlet's wife.
　　I thought thy bride-bed to have decked, sweet maid,
　　And not t' have strewed thy grave.

LAERTES:　　　　　　　　　　O, treble woe
　　Fall ten times treble on that cursèd head
　　Whose wicked deed thy most ingenious sense°　　　　230
　　Deprived thee of! Hold off the earth awhile,
　　Till I have caught her once more in mine arms.

[*He leaps into the grave and embraces Ophelia.*]

　　Now pile your dust upon the quick and dead,
　　Till of this flat a mountain you have made
　　T' o'ertop old Pelion or the skyish head　　　　235
　　Of blue Olympus.°

---

209 warranty i.e., ecclesiastical authority.　**210 great . . . order** orders from on high overrule the prescribed procedures.　**211 She should . . . lodged** she should have been buried in unsanctified ground.　**212 For** in place of.　**213 Shards** broken bits of pottery.　**214 crants** garlands betokening maidenhood.　**215 strewments** flowers strewn on a coffin.　**218 bringing . . . burial** laying the body to rest, to the sound of the bell.　**219 such rest** i.e., to pray for such rest.　**220 peace-parted souls** those who have died at peace with God.　**222 violets** (See 4.5.191 and note.)　**224 howling** i.e., in hell.　**230 ingenious sense** a mind that is quick, alert, of fine qualities.　**235–236 Pelion, Olympus** sacred mountains in the north of Thessaly; see also Ossa, below, at line 248.

HAMLET [*coming forward*]: What is he whose grief
    Bears such an emphasis,° whose phrase of sorrow
    Conjures the wandering stars° and makes them stand
    Like wonder-wounded° hearers? This is I,   240
    Hamlet the Dane.°
LAERTES [*grappling with him*°]: The devil take thy soul!
HAMLET: Thou pray'st not well.
    I prithee, take thy fingers from my throat,
    For though I am not splenitive° and rash,   245
    Yet have I in me something dangerous,
    Which let thy wisdom fear. Hold off thy hand.
KING: Pluck them asunder.
QUEEN: Hamlet, Hamlet!
ALL: Gentlemen!   250
HORATIO: Good my lord, be quiet.

                 [*Hamlet and Laertes are parted.*]

HAMLET: Why, I will fight with him upon this theme
    Until my eyelids will no longer wag.°
QUEEN: O my son, what theme?
HAMLET: I loved Ophelia. Forty thousand brothers   255
    Could not with all their quantity of love
    Make up my sum. What wilt thou do for her?
KING: O, he is mad, Laertes.
QUEEN: For love of God, forbear him.°
HAMLET: 'Swounds,° show me what thou'lt do.   260
    Woo't° weep? Woo't fight? Woo't fast? Woo't tear thyself?
    Woo't drink up° eisel?° Eat a crocodile?°
    I'll do 't. Dost come here to whine?
    To outface me with leaping in her grave?
    Be buried quick° with her, and so will I.   265
    And if thou prate of mountains, let them throw

---

238 emphasis i.e., rhetorical and florid emphasis. (Phrase has a similar rhetorical connotation.)
239 wandering stars planets.   **240 wonder-wounded** struck with amazement.   **241 the Dane** (This title normally signifies the King; see 1.1.17 and note.)   **242 s.d. grappling with him** (The testimony of the First Quarto that "Hamlet leaps in after Laertes" and the "Elegy on Burbage" ("Oft have I seen him leap into the grave") seem to indicate one way in which this fight was staged; however, the difficulty of fitting two contenders and Ophelia's body into a confined space (probably the trapdoor) suggests to many editors the alternative, that Laertes jumps out of the grave to attack Hamlet.)   **245 splenitive** quick-tempered.   **253 wag** move. (A fluttering eyelid is a conventional sign that life has not yet gone.)   **259 forbear him** leave him alone.   **260 'Swounds** by His (Christ's) wounds.   **261 Woo't** wilt thou.   **262 drink up** drink deeply;   **eisel** vinegar;   **crocodile** (Crocodiles were tough and dangerous, and were supposed to shed hypocritical tears.)   **265 quick** alive.

Millions of acres on us, till our ground,
Singeing his pate° against the burning zone,°
Make Ossa° like a wart! Nay, an° thou'lt mouth,°
I'll rant as well as thou.

QUEEN: This is mere° madness,   270
And thus awhile the fit will work on him;
Anon, as patient as the female dove
When that her golden couplets° are disclosed,°
His silence will sit drooping.

HAMLET: Hear you, sir,
What is the reason that you use me thus?   275
I loved you ever. But it is no matter.
Let Hercules himself do what he may,
The cat will mew, and dog will have his day.°

                                        Exit Hamlet.

KING: I pray thee, good Horatio, wait upon him.

                                        [*Exit Horatio.*]

HORATIO [*to Laertes*]: Strengthen your patience in° our last   280
    night's speech;
We'll put the matter to the present push.°—
Good Gertrude, set some watch over your son.—
This grave shall have a living° monument.
An hour of quiet° shortly shall we see;   285
Till then, in patience our proceeding be.   *Exeunt.*

Scene II [The Castle.]

Enter Hamlet and Horatio.

HAMLET: So much for this, sir; now shall you see the other.°
    You do remember all the circumstance?
HORATIO: Remember it, my lord!

---

268 **his pate** its head, i.e., top; **burning zone** zone in the celestial sphere containing the sun's orbit, between the tropics of Cancer and Capricorn. 269 **Ossa** another mountain in Thessaly. (In their war against the Olympian gods, the giants attempted to heap Ossa on Pelion to scale Olympus.); **an** if; **mouth** i.e., rant. 270 **mere** utter. 273 **golden couplets** two baby pigeons, covered with yellow down; **disclosed** hatched. 277–278 **Let . . . day** i.e., (1) even Hercules couldn't stop Laertes' theatrical rant (2) I, too, will have my turn; i.e., despite any blustering attempts at interference, every person will sooner or later do what he or she must do. 280 **in** i.e., by recalling. 282 **present push** immediate test. 284 **living** lasting. (For Laertes' private understanding, Claudius also hints that Hamlet's death will serve as such a monument.) 285 **hour of quiet** time free of conflict. 1 **see the other** hear the other news.

HAMLET: Sir, in my heart there was a kind of fighting
    That would not let me sleep. Methought I lay   5
    Worse than the mutines° in the bilboes.° Rashly,°
    And praised be rashness for it—let us know°
    Our indiscretion° sometimes serves us well
    When our deep plots do pall,° and that should learn° us
    There's a divinity that shapes our ends,   10
    Rough-hew° them how we will—
HORATIO: That is most certain.
HAMLET: Up from my cabin,
    My sea-gown° scarfed° about me, in the dark
    Groped I to find out them,° had my desire,
    Fingered° their packet, and in fine° withdrew   15
    To mine own room again, making so bold,
    My fears forgetting manners, to unseal
    Their grand commission; where I found, Horatio—
    Ah, royal knavery!—an exact command,
    Larded° with many several° sorts of reasons   20
    Importing° Denmark's health and England's too,
    With, ho! such bugs° and goblins in my life,°
    That on the supervise,° no leisure bated,°
    No, not to stay° the grinding of the ax,
    My head should be struck off.
HORATIO: Is't possible?   25
HAMLET [*giving a document*]:   Here's the commission. Read it at
    more leisure.
    But wilt thou hear now how I did proceed?
HORATIO: I beseech you.
HAMLET: Being thus benetted round with villainies—   30
    Ere I could make a prologue to my brains,
    They had begun the play°—I sat me down,
    Devised a new commission, wrote it fair.°
    I once did hold it, as our statists° do,
    A baseness° to write fair, and labored much   35

---

6 **mutines** mutineers; **bilboes** shackles; **Rashly** on impulse. (This adverb goes with lines 12 ff.)
7 **know** acknowledge 8 **indiscretion** lack of foresight and judgment (not an indiscreet act). **9 pall**
fail, falter, go stale; **learn** teach. **11 Rough-hew** shape roughly. **13 sea-gown** seaman's coat;
scarfed loosely wrapped. **14 them** i.e., Rosencrantz and Guildenstern. **15 Fingered** pilfered,
pinched; **in fine** finally, in conclusion. **20 Larded** garnished; **several** different. **21 Importing**
relating to. **22 bugs** bugbears, hobgoblins; **in my life** i.e., to be feared if I were allowed to live.
23 supervise reading; **leisure bated** delay allowed. **24 stay** await. **31–32 Ere . . . play** before I
could consciously turn my brain to the matter, it had started working on a plan. **33 fair** in a clear
hand. **34 statists** statesmen. **35 baseness** i.e., lower-class trait.

How to forget that learning; but, sir, now
It did me yeoman's° service. Wilt thou know
Th' effect° of what I wrote?

HORATIO: Ay, good my lord.

HAMLET: An earnest conjuration° from the King,
As England was his faithful tributary,   40
As love between them like the palm° might flourish,
As peace should still° her wheaten garland° wear
And stand a comma° 'tween their amities,
And many suchlike "as"es° of great charge,°
That on the view and knowing of these contents,   45
Without debatement further more or less,
He should those bearers put to sudden death,
Not shriving time° allowed.

HORATIO: How was this sealed?

HAMLET: Why, even in that was heaven ordinant.°
I had my father's signet° in my purse,   50
Which was the model° of that Danish seal;
Folded the writ° up in the form of th' other,
Subscribed° it, gave 't th' impression,° placed it safely,
The changeling° never known. Now, the next day
Was our sea fight, and what to this was sequent°   55
Thou knowest already.

HORATIO: So Guildenstern and Rosencrantz go to 't.

HAMLET: Why, man, they did make love to this employment.
They are not near my conscience. Their defeat°
Does by their own insinuation° grow.   60
'Tis dangerous when the baser° nature comes
Between the pass° and fell° incensèd points
Of mighty opposites.°

HORATIO: Why, what a king is this!

HAMLET: Does it not, think thee, stand me now upon°—
He that hath killed my king and whored my mother,   65

---

37 **yeoman's** i.e., substantial, faithful, loyal.   38 **effect** purport.   39 **conjuration** entreaty.
41 **palm** (An image of health; see Psalm 92:12.)   42 **still** always;   **wheaten garland** (Symbolic of
fruitful agriculture, of peace and plenty.)   43 **comma** (Indicating continuity, link.)   44 **"as"es**
(1) the "whereases" of a formal document (2) asses;   **charge** (1) import (2) burden (appropriate to
asses).   48 **shriving time** time for confession and absolution.   49 **ordinant** directing.   50 **signet**
small seal.   51 **model** replica.   52 **writ** writing.   53 **Subscribed** signed (with forged signature);
impression i.e., with a wax seal.   54 **changeling** i.e., substituted letter. (Literally, a fairy child
substituted for a human one.)   55 **was sequent** followed.   59 **defeat** destruction.   60 **insinuation**
intrusive intervention, sticking their noses in my business.   61 **baser** of lower social station.
62 **pass** thrust;   **fell** fierce.   63 **opposites** antagonists.   64 **stand me now upon** become incumbent
on me now.

Popped in between th' election° and my hopes,
Thrown out his angle° for my proper° life,
And with such cozenage°—is 't not perfect conscience
To quit° him with this arm? And is 't not to be damned
To let this canker° of our nature come   70
In° further evil?

HORATIO: It must be shortly known to him from England
What is the issue of the business there.

HAMLET: It will be short. The interim is mine,
And a man's life's no more than to say "one."°   75
But I am very sorry, good Horatio,
That to Laertes I forgot myself,
For by the image of my cause I see
The portraiture of his. I'll court his favors.
But, sure, the bravery° of his grief did put me   80
Into a tow'ring passion.

HORATIO: Peace, who comes here?

Enter a Courtier [Osric].

OSRIC: Your lordship is right welcome back to Denmark.

HAMLET: I humbly thank you, sir. [*To Horatio.*] Dost know this
water fly?

HORATIO: No, my good lord.   85

HAMLET: Thy state is the more gracious, for 'tis a vice to know
him. He hath much land, and fertile. Let a beast be lord of
beasts, and his crib° shall stand at the King's mess.° 'Tis a chuff,°
but, as I say, spacious in the possession of dirt.

OSRIC: Sweet lord, if your lordship were at leisure, I should   90
impart a thing to you from His Majesty.

HAMLET: I will receive it, sir, with all diligence of spirit.
Put your bonnet° to his° right use; 'tis for the head.

OSRIC: I thank your lordship, it is very hot.

HAMLET: No, believe me, 'tis very cold. The wind is northerly.   95

OSRIC: It is indifferent° cold, my lord, indeed.

---

66 election (The Danish monarch was "elected" by a small number of high-ranking electors.)
67 angle fishhook;   proper very.   68 cozenage trickery.   69 quit requite, pay back.   70 canker
ulcer.   70–71 come In grow into.   75 a man's . . . "one" one's whole life occupies such a short
time, only as long as it takes to count to 1.   80 bravery bravado.   88 crib manger.   87–88 Let . . .
mess i.e., if a man, no matter how beastlike, is as rich in livestock and possessions as Osric, he may
eat at the King's table.   88 chuff boor, churl. (The Second Quarto spelling, chough, is a variant
spelling that also suggests the meaning here of "chattering jackdaw.")   93 bonnet any kind of cap
or hat;   his its.   96 indifferent somewhat.

HAMLET: But yet methinks it is very sultry and hot for my complexion.°

OSRIC: Exceedingly, my lord. It is very sultry, as 'twere—I cannot tell how. My lord, His Majesty bade me signify to you that 'a 100 has laid a great wager on your head. Sir, this is the matter—

HAMLET: I beseech you, remember.

[Hamlet moves him to put on his hat.]

OSRIC: Nay, good my lord; for my ease,° in good faith. Sir, here is newly come to court Laertes—believe me, an absolute° gentleman, full of most excellent differences,° of very soft society° 105 and great showing.° Indeed, to speak feelingly° of him, he is the card° or calendar° of gentry,° for you shall find in him the continent of what part a gentleman would see.°

HAMLET: Sir, his definement° suffers no perdition° in you,° though I know to divide him inventorially° would dozy° th' 110 arithmetic of memory, and yet but yaw° neither° in respect of° his quick sail. But, in the verity of extolment,° I take him to be a soul of great article,° and his infusion° of such dearth and rareness° as, to make true diction° of him, his semblable° is his mirror and who else would trace° him his umbrage,° nothing more. 115

OSRIC: Your lordship speaks most infallibly of him.

HAMLET: The concernancy,° sir? Why do we wrap the gentleman in our more rawer breath?°

OSRIC: Sir?

HORATIO: Is 't not possible to understand in another tongue?° 120 You will do 't,° sir, really.

HAMLET: What imports the nomination° of this gentleman?

---

98 **complexion** temperament.   103 **for my ease** (A conventional reply declining the invitation to put his hat back on.)   104 **absolute** perfect.   105 **differences** special qualities;   **soft society** agreeable manners;   106 **great showing** distinguished appearance.   **feelingly** with just perception;   107 **card** chart, map;   **calendar** guide.   **gentry** good breeding.   107–108 **the continent . . . see** one who contains in him all the qualities a gentleman would like to see. (A continent is that which contains.)   109 **definement** definition (Hamlet proceeds to mock Osric by throwing his lofty diction back at him);   **perdition** loss, diminution;   **you** your description.   110 **divide him inventorially** enumerate his graces;   **dozy** dizzy.   111 **yaw** swing unsteadily off course. (Said of a ship.);   **neither** for all that;   **in respect of** in comparison with.   112 **in . . . extolment** in true praise (of him).   113 **of great article** one with many articles in his inventory;   **infusion** essence, character infused into him by nature.   **dearth and rareness** rarity;   114 **make true diction** speak truly;   **semblable** only true likeness.   115 **who . . . trace** any other person who would wish to follow;   **umbrage** shadow.   117 **concernancy** import, relevance.   118 **rawer breath** unrefined speech that can only come short in praising him.   120 **to understand . . . tongue** i.e., for you, Osric, to understand when someone else speaks your language. (Horatio twits Osric for not being able to understand the kind of flowery speech he himself uses, when Hamlet speaks in such a vein. Alternatively, all this could be said to Hamlet.);   121 **You will do 't** i.e., you can if you try, or, you may well have to try (to speak plainly).   122 **nomination** naming.

OSRIC: Of Laertes?

HORATIO [*to Hamlet*]: His purse is empty already; all 's golden
words are spent.   125

HAMLET: Of him, sir.

OSRIC: I know you are not ignorant—

HAMLET: I would you did, sir. Yet in faith if you did, it would
not much approve° me. Well, sir?

OSRIC: You are not ignorant of what excellence Laertes is—   130

HAMLET: I dare not confess that, lest I should compare with him
in excellence. But to know a man well were to know himself.°

OSRIC: I mean, sir, for° his weapon; but in the imputation laid on
him by them,° in his meed° he's unfellowed.°

HAMLET: What's his weapon?   135

OSRIC: Rapier and dagger.

HAMLET: That's two of his weapons—but well.°

OSRIC: The King, sir, hath wagered with him six Barbary horses,
against the which he° has impawned,° as I take it, six French
rapiers and poniards,° with their assigns,° as girdle, hangers,°   140
and so.° Three of the carriages,° in faith, are very dear to fancy,°
very responsive° to the hilts, most delicate° carriages, and of
very liberal conceit.°

HAMLET: What call you the carriages?

HORATIO [*to Hamlet*]: I knew you must be edified by the margent°   145
ere you had done.

OSRIC: The carriages, sir, are the hangers.

HAMLET: The phrase would be more germane to the matter if we
could carry a cannon by our sides; I would it might be hangers till
then. But, on: six Barbary horses against six French swords, their   150
assigns, and three liberal-conceited carriages; that's the French bet
against the Danish. Why is this impawned, as you call it?

OSRIC: The King, sir, hath laid,° sir, that in a dozen passes°
between yourself and him, he shall not exceed you three hits.

---

129 **approve** commend.   131–132 **I dare . . . himself** I dare not boast of knowing Laertes'
excellence lest I seem to imply a comparable excellence in myself. Certainly, to know another
person well, one must know oneself.   133 **for** i.e., with;   134 **imputation . . . them** reputation
given him by others.   **meed** merit;   **unfellowed** unmatched.   137 **but well** but never mind.
139 **he** i.e., Laertes;   **impawned** staked, wagered;   140 **poniards** daggers.   **assigns** appurtenances;
hangers straps on the sword belt (girdle), from which the sword hung;   141 **and so** and so on;
carriages (An affected way of saying hangers; literally, gun carriages.)   **dear to fancy** delightful to
the fancy;   142 **responsive** corresponding closely, matching or well adjusted.   **delicate** (i.e., in
workmanship);   143 **liberal conceit** elaborate design.   145 **margent** margin of a book, place for
explanatory notes.   153 **laid** wagered;   **passes** bouts. (The odds of the betting are hard to explain.
Possibly the King bets that Hamlet will win at least five out of twelve, at which point Laertes raises
the odds against himself by betting he will win nine.)

He hath laid on twelve for nine, and it would come to 155
immediate trial, if your lordship would vouchsafe the answer.°

HAMLET: How if I answer no?

OSRIC: I mean, my lord, the opposition of your person in trial.

HAMLET: Sir, I will walk here in the hall. If it please His Majesty, it
is the breathing time° of day with me. Let° the foils be brought, 160
the gentleman willing, and the King hold his purpose. I will win
for him an I can; if not, I will gain nothing but my shame and
the odd hits.

OSRIC: Shall I deliver you° so?

HAMLET: To this effect, sir—after what flourish your nature will. 165

OSRIC: I commend° my duty to your lordship.

HAMLET: Yours, yours. [*Exit Osric.*] 'A does well to commend it
himself; there are no tongues else for 's turn.°

HORATIO: This lapwing° runs away with the shell on his head.

HAMLET: 'A did comply with his dug° before 'a sucked it. Thus 170
has he—and many more of the same breed that I know the
drossy° age dotes on—only got the tune° of the time and, out of
an habit of encounter,° a kind of yeasty° collection,° which
carries them through and through the most fanned and win-
nowed opinions;° and do° but blow them to their trial, the 175
bubbles are out.°

Enter a Lord.

LORD: My lord, His Majesty commended him to you by young
Osric, who brings back to him that you attend him in the hall.
He sends to know if your pleasure hold to play with Laertes, or
that° you will take longer time. 180

---

156 **vouchsafe the answer** be so good as to accept the challenge. (Hamlet deliberately takes the
phrase in its literal sense of replying.)   160 **breathing time** exercise period;   **Let** i.e., if.
164 **deliver you** report what you say.   166 **commend** commit to your favor. (A conventional
salutation, but Hamlet wryly uses a more literal meaning, "recommend," "praise," in line 161.)
168 **for 's turn** for his purposes, i.e., to do it for him.   169 **lapwing** (A proverbial type of youthful
forwardness. Also, a bird that draws intruders away from its nest and was thought to run about
with its head in the shell when newly hatched; a seeming reference to Osric's hat.)   170 **comply . . .
dug** observe ceremonious formality toward his nurse's or mother's teat.   172 **drossy** laden with
scum and impurities, frivolous.   172 **tune** temper, mood, manner of speech;   173 **an habit**
of encounter a demeanor in conversing (with courtiers of his own kind);   **yeasty** frothy.
collection i.e., of current phrases.   174–175 **carries . . . opinions** sustains them right through the
scrutiny of persons whose opinions are select and refined. (Literally, like grain separated from its
chaff. Osric is both the chaff and the bubbly froth on the surface of the liquor that is soon blown
away.)   **and do yet** do.   175–176 **blow . . . out** test them by merely blowing on them, and their
bubbles burst.   180 **that** if.

HAMLET: I am constant to my purposes; they follow the King's
pleasure. If his fitness speaks, mine is ready;° now or when-
soever, provided I be so able as now.

LORD: The King and Queen and all are coming down.

HAMLET: In happy time.°   185

LORD: The Queen desires you to use some gentle entertainment°
to Laertes before you fall to play.

HAMLET: She well instructs me.   [*Exit Lord.*]

HORATIO: You will lose, my lord.

HAMLET: I do not think so. Since he went into France, I have been   190
in continual practice; I shall win at the odds. But thou wouldst
not think how ill all's here about my heart; but it is no matter.

HORATIO: Nay, good my lord—

HAMLET: It is but foolery, but it is such a kind of gaingiving° as
would perhaps trouble a woman.   195

HORATIO: If your mind dislike anything, obey it. I will forestall
their repair° hither and say you are not fit.

HAMLET: Not a whit, we defy augury. There is special providence
in the fall of a sparrow. If it be now, 'tis not to come; if it be not
to come, it will be now; if it be not now, yet it will come. The   200
readiness is all. Since no man of aught he leaves knows, what is
't to leave betimes? Let be.°

A table prepared. [Enter] trumpets, drums, and officers with cush-
ions; King, Queen, [Osric,] and all the state; foils, daggers, [and
wine borne in;] and Laertes.

KING: Come, Hamlet, come and take this hand from me.

[*The King puts Laertes' hand into Hamlet's.*]

HAMLET   [*to Laertes*]: Give me your pardon, sir. I have done you
wrong,   205
But pardon 't as you are a gentleman.
This presence° knows,
And you must needs have heard, how I am punished°
With a sore distraction. What I have done
That might your nature, honor, and exception°   210
Roughly awake, I here proclaim was madness.

---

182 If . . . ready if he declares his readiness, my convenience waits on his.   185 In happy time (A
phrase of courtesy indicating that the time is convenient.)   186 entertainment greeting.   194
gaingiving misgiving.   197 repair coming.   201–202 Since ... Let be since no one has knowledge
of what he is leaving behind, what does an early death matter after all? Enough; don't struggle
against it.   207 presence royal assembly.   208 punished afflicted.   210 exception disapproval.

Was 't Hamlet wronged Laertes? Never Hamlet.
If Hamlet from himself be ta'en away,
And when he's not himself does wrong Laertes,
Then Hamlet does it not, Hamlet denies it. 215
Who does it, then? His madness. If 't be so,
Hamlet is of the faction° that is wronged;
His madness is poor Hamlet's enemy.
Sir, in this audience
Let my disclaiming from a purposed evil 220
Free me so far in your most generous thoughts
That I have° shot my arrow o'er the house
And hurt my brother.

LAERTES: I am satisfied in nature,°
Whose motive° in this case should stir me most
To my revenge. But in my terms of honor 225
I stand aloof, and will no reconcilement
Till by some elder masters of known honor
I have a voice° and precedent of peace°
To keep my name ungored.° But till that time
I do receive your offered love like love, 230
And will not wrong it.

HAMLET: I embrace it freely,
And will this brothers' wager frankly° play.—
Give us the foils. Come on.

LAERTES: Come, one for me.

HAMLET: I'll be your foil,° Laertes. In mine ignorance
Your skill shall, like a star i' the darkest night, 235
Stick fiery off° indeed.

LAERTES: You mock me, sir.

HAMLET: No, by this hand.

KING: Give them the foils, young Osric. Cousin Hamlet,
You know the wager?

HAMLET: Very well, my lord.
Your Grace has laid the odds o'° the weaker side. 240

KING: I do not fear it; I have seen you both.
But since he is bettered,° we have therefore odds.

---

217 faction party.   **222 That I have** as if I had.   **223 in nature** i.e., as to my personal feelings.
224 motive prompting.   **228 voice** authoritative pronouncement;   **of peace** for reconciliation.
229 name ungored reputation unwounded.   **232 frankly** without ill feeling or the burden of rancor.
234 foil thin metal background which sets a jewel off (with pun on the blunted rapier for fencing).
236 Stick fiery off stand out brilliantly.   **240 laid the odds o'** bet on, backed.   **242 is bettered** has
improved; is the odds-on favorite. (Laertes' handicap is the "three hits" specified in line 149.)

LAERTES: This is too heavy. Let me see another.

[*He exchanges his foil for another.*]

HAMLET: This likes me° well. These foils have all a length?

[*They prepare to play.*]

OSRIC: Ay, my good lord.   245

KING: Set me the stoups of wine upon that table.
    If Hamlet give the first or second hit,
    Or quit in answer of the third exchange,°
    Let all the battlements their ordnance fire.
    The King shall drink to Hamlet's better breath,°   250
    And in the cup an union° shall he throw
    Richer than that which four successive kings
    In Denmark's crown have worn. Give me the cups,
    And let the kettle° to the trumpet speak,
    The trumpet to the cannoneer without,   255
    The cannons to the heavens, the heaven to earth,
    "Now the King drinks to Hamlet." Come, begin.

Trumpets the while.

    And you, the judges, bear a wary eye.

HAMLET: Come on, sir.

LAERTES: Come, my lord. [*They play. Hamlet scores a hit.*]   260

HAMLET: One.

LAERTES: No.

HAMLET: Judgment.

OSRIC: A hit, a very palpable hit.

Drum, trumpets, and shot. Flourish.
A piece goes off.

LAERTES: Well, again.

KING: Stay, give me drink. Hamlet, this pearl is thine.   265

[*He drinks, and throws a pearl in Hamlet's cup.*]

    Here's to thy health. Give him the cup.

HAMLET: I'll play this bout first. Set it by awhile.
    Come. [*They play.*] Another hit; what say you?

---

244 **likes me** pleases me.   248 **Or ... exchange** i.e., or requites Laertes in the third bout for having won the first two.   250 **better breath** improved vigor.   251 **union** pearl. (So called, according to Pliny's *Natural History*, 9, because pearls are *unique*, never identical.)   254 **kettle** kettledrum.

LAERTES: A touch, a touch, I do confess 't.

KING: Our son shall win.

QUEEN: He's fat° and scant of breath.   270
　Here, Hamlet, take my napkin,° rub thy brows.
　The Queen carouses° to thy fortune, Hamlet.

HAMLET: Good madam!

KING: Gertrude, do not drink.

QUEEN: I will, my lord, I pray you pardon me.   [*She drinks.*] 275

KING [*aside*]: It is the poisoned cup. It is too late.

HAMLET: I dare not drink yet, madam; by and by.

QUEEN: Come, let me wipe thy face.

LAERTES [*to King*]: My lord, I'll hit him now.

KING: I do not think 't.

LAERTES [*aside*]: And yet it is almost against my conscience.   280

HAMLET: Come, for the third, Laertes. You do but dally.
　I pray you, pass° with your best violence;
　I am afeard you make a wanton of me.°

LAERTES: Say you so? Come on.   [*They play.*]

OSRIC: Nothing neither way.   285

LAERTES: Have at you now!

*[Laertes wounds Hamlet; then, in scuffling, they change rapiers,°
　　　　　　　　　and Hamlet wounds Laertes.]*

KING: Part them! They are incensed.

HAMLET: Nay, come, again.   [*The Queen falls.*]

OSRIC: Look to the Queen there, ho!

HORATIO: They bleed on both sides. How is it, my lord?

OSRIC: How is 't, Laertes?

LAERTES: Why, as a woodcock° to mine own springe,° Osric;   290
　I am justly killed with mine own treachery.

HAMLET: How does the Queen?

KING: She swoons to see them bleed.

QUEEN: No, no, the drink, the drink—O my dear Hamlet—
　The drink, the drink! I am poisoned.   [*She dies.*]

HAMLET: O villainy! Ho, let the door be locked!   290
　Treachery! Seek it out.

---

270 **fat** not physically fit, out of training.   271 **napkin** handkerchief.   272 **carouses** drinks a toast.
282 **pass** thrust.   283 **make** ... **me** i.e., treat me like a spoiled child, trifle with me.   **s.d. in scuffling,
they change rapiers** (This stage direction occurs in the Folio. According to a widespread stage
tradition, Hamlet receives a scratch, realizes that Laertes' sword is unbated, and accordingly forces
an exchange.)   290 **woodcock** a bird, a type of stupidity or as a decoy;   **springe** trap, snare.

[*Laertes falls. Exit Osric.*]

LAERTES: It is here, Hamlet. Hamlet, thou art slain.
No med'cine in the world can do thee good;
In thee there is not half an hour's life.
The treacherous instrument is in thy hand,   295
Unbated° and envenomed. The foul practice°
Hath turned itself on me. Lo, here I lie,
Never to rise again. Thy mother's poisoned.
I can no more. The King, the King's to blame.

HAMLET: The point envenomed too? Then, venom, to thy work.   300

[*He stabs the King.*]

ALL: Treason! Treason!

KING: O, yet defend me, friends! I am but hurt.

HAMLET [*forcing the King to drink*]:
Here, thou incestuous, murderous, damnèd Dane,
Drink off this potion. Is thy union° here?
Follow my mother.   [*The King dies.*]

LAERTES: He is justly served.   305
It is a poison tempered° by himself.
Exchange forgiveness with me, noble Hamlet.
Mine and my father's death come not upon thee,
Nor thine on me!   [*He dies.*]

HAMLET: Heaven make thee free of it! I follow thee.   310
I am dead, Horatio. Wretched Queen, adieu!
You that look pale and tremble at this chance,°
That are but mutes° or audience to this act,
Had I but time—as this fell° sergeant,° Death,
Is strict° in his arrest°—O, I could tell you—   315
But let it be. Horatio, I am dead;
Thou livest. Report me and my cause aright
To the unsatisfied.

HORATIO: Never believe it.
I am more an antique Roman° than a Dane.
Here's yet some liquor left.   320

---

296 **Unbated** not blunted with a button;   **practice** plot.   304 **union** pearl. (See line 240; with grim puns on the word's other meanings: marriage, shared death.)   306 **tempered** mixed.   312 **chance** mischance.   313 **mutes** silent observers. (Literally, actors with nonspeaking parts.)   314 **fell** cruel; **sergeant** sheriff's officer.   315 **strict** (1) severely just (2) unavoidable;   **arrest** (1) taking into custody (2) stopping my speech.   319 **Roman** (Suicide was an honorable choice for many Romans as an alternative to a dishonorable life.)

[*He attempts to drink from the poisoned cup. Hamlet prevents him.*]

HAMLET: As thou'rt a man,
  Give me the cup! Let go! By heaven, I'll ha 't.
  O God, Horatio, what a wounded name,
  Things standing thus unknown, shall I leave behind me!
  If thou didst ever hold me in thy heart,
  Absent thee from felicity awhile,   325
  And in this harsh world draw thy breath in pain
  To tell my story.   *A march afar off* [*and a volley within*].
  What warlike noise is this?

Enter Osric.

OSRIC: Young Fortinbras, with conquest come from Poland,
  To th' ambassadors of England gives   330
  This warlike volley.
HAMLET: O, I die, Horatio!
  The potent poison quite o'ercrows° my spirit.
  I cannot live to hear the news from England,
  But I do prophesy th' election lights
  On Fortinbras. He has my dying voice.°   335
  So tell him, with th' occurents° more and less
  Which have solicited°—the rest is silence.   [*He dies.*]
HORATIO: Now cracks a noble heart. Good night, sweet prince,
  And flights of angels sing thee to thy rest!   [*March within.*]
  Why does the drum come hither?   340

Enter Fortinbras, with the [*English*] *Ambassadors* [*with drum, colors, and attendants*].

FORTINBRAS: Where is this sight?
HORATIO: What is it you would see?
  If aught of woe or wonder, cease your search.
FORTINBRAS: This quarry° cries on havoc.° O proud Death,
  What feast° is toward° in thine eternal cell,
  That thou so many princes at a shot   345
  So bloodily hast struck?
FIRST AMBASSADOR: The sight is dismal,

---

332 **o'ercrows** triumphs over (like the winner in a cockfight).   335 **voice** vote.   336 **occurrents** events, incidents.   337 **solicited** moved, urged. (Hamlet doesn't finish saying what the events have prompted—presumably, his acts of vengeance, or his reporting of those events to Fortinbras.) 343 **quarry** heap of dead; **cries on havoc** proclaims a general slaughter.   344 **feast** i.e., Death feasting on those who have fallen; **toward** in preparation.

And our affairs from England come too late.
The ears are senseless that should give us hearing,
To tell him his commandment is fulfilled,
That Rosencrantz and Guildenstern are dead.   350
Where should we have our thanks?

HORATIO: Not from his° mouth,
Had it th' ability of life to thank you.
He never gave commandment for their death.
But since, so jump° upon this bloody question,°
You from the Polack wars, and you from England,   355
And here arrived, give order that these bodies
High on a stage° be placèd to the view,
And let me speak to th' yet unknowing world
How these things came about. So shall you hear
Of carnal, bloody, and unnatural acts,   360
Of accidental judgments,° casual° slaughters,
Of deaths put on° by cunning and forced cause,°
And, in this upshot, purposes mistook
Fall'n on th' inventors' heads. All this can I
Truly deliver.

FORTINBRAS: Let us haste to hear it,   365
And call the noblest to the audience.
For me, with sorrow I embrace my fortune.
I have some rights of memory° in this kingdom,
Which now to claim my vantage° doth invite me.

HORATIO: Of that I shall have also cause to speak,   370
And from his mouth whose voice will draw on more.°
But let this same be presently° performed,
Even while men's minds are wild, lest more mischance
On° plots and errors happen.

FORTINBRAS: Let four captains
Bear Hamlet, like a soldier, to the stage,   375
For he was likely, had he been put on,°
To have proved most royal; and for his passage,°
The soldiers' music and the rite of war
Speak° loudly for him.

---

351 his i.e., Claudius'.   354 jump precisely, immediately;   question dispute, affair.   357 stage
platform.   361 judgments retributions;   casual occurring by chance.   362 put on instigated;
forced cause contrivance.   368 of memory traditional, remembered, unforgotten.   369 vantage
favorable opportunity.   367 voice ... more vote will influence still others.   368 presently
immediately.   370 On on the basis of; on top of.   372 put on i.e., invested in royal office and so
put to the test.   373 passage i.e., from life to death.   375 Speak let them speak.

Take up the bodies. Such a sight as this   380
Becomes the field,° but here shows much amiss.
Go bid the soldiers shoot.

> *Exeunt [marching, bearing off the dead bodies;*
> *a peal of ordnance is shot off].*

—*c. 1600*

Questions: Reading, Responding, Arguing

1. Describe the play's opening scene. How does it build interest and suspense? What might be the result if Shakespeare had chosen to begin the play, say, with scene 2?
2. After he speaks with the ghost of his father, Hamlet tells Horatio and the others that he may soon put on an "antic disposition"? What does he mean?
3. One of Shakespeare's most famous passages in *Hamlet* is Polonius's speech to the departing Laertes. What advice does he offer? What makes it ironic?
4. How does Polonius act toward Ophelia after he thinks he discovers the cause of Hamlet's madness? What does Hamlet suspect about Ophelia's behavior?
5. The soliloquy in 3.1 is Shakespeare's greatest piece of blank verse. Examine it closely for the logic of Hamlet's inner debate.
6. How does the "play within a play" function as an important plot device?
7. In Hamlet's confrontation scene with his mother, is his madness still a mere act? How do you know?
8. Throughout the play, the presence of Fortinbras is felt, even though he does not appear until the play's final scene. How does Hamlet compare himself to Fortinbras?
9. The scene with the grave diggers is a classic example of comic relief. Why is it important at this point in the play?
10. What are the potential difficulties in staging the fencing scene between Hamlet and Laertes?
11. Laurence Olivier begins his famous film version of *Hamlet* by saying that the play is the tragedy of a "man who could

---

381 **Becomes the field** suits the field of battle.

not make up his mind." Is this an accurate approach to the character of Hamlet? Construct an argument supporting or refuting this statement.

12. Notice that the play has two subplots, one involving Polonius and his children and another involving Fortinbras. How do each of these plots reflect the action and issues of the main plot? How do they reflect the primary themes of this drama? What are the primary themes?

Plato (427–347 B.C.)

The Allegory of the Cave

Next, said I, here is a parable to illustrate the degrees in which our nature may be enlightened or unenlightened. Imagine the condition of men living in a sort of cavernous chamber underground, with an entrance open to the light and a long passage all down the cave. Here they have been from childhood, chained by the leg and also by the neck, so that they cannot move and can see only what is in front of them, because the chains will not let them turn their heads. At some distance higher up is the light of a fire burning behind them; and between the prisoners and the fire is a track with a parapet build along it, like the screen at a puppet-show, which hides the performers while they show their puppets over the top.

I see, said he.

Now behind this parapet imagine persons carrying along various artificial objects, including figures of men and animals in wood or stone or other materials, which project above the parapet. Naturally, some of these persons will be talking, others silent.

It is a strange picture, he said, and a strange sort of prisoners.

Like ourselves, I replied; for in the first place prisoners so confined would have seen nothing of themselves or of one another, except the shadows thrown by the fire-light on the wall of the cave facing them, would they?

Not if all their lives they had been prevented from moving their heads.

And they would have seen as little of the objects carried past.

Of course.

Now, if they could talk to one another, would they not suppose that their words referred only to those passing shadows which they saw?

Necessarily.

And suppose their prison had an echo from the wall facing them? When one of the people crossing behind them spoke, they could only suppose that the sound came from the shadow passing before their eyes.

No doubt.

In every way, then, such prisoners would recognize as reality nothing but the shadows of those artificial objects.

Inevitably.

Now consider what would happen if their release from the chains and the healing of their unwisdom should come about in this way. Suppose one of them set free and forced suddenly to stand up, turn his head, and walk with eyes lifted to the light; all these movements would be painful, and he would be too dazzled to make out the objects whose shadows he had been used to see. What do you think he would say, if someone told him that what he had formerly seen was meaningless illusion, but now, being somewhat nearer to reality and turned towards more real objects, he was getting a truer view? Suppose further that he were shown the various objects being carried by and were made to say, in reply to questions, what each of them was. Would he not be perplexed and believe the objects now shown him to be not so real as what he formerly saw?

Yes, not nearly so real.

And if he were forced to look at the fire-light itself, would not his eyes ache, so that he would try to escape and turn back to the things which he could see distinctly, convinced that they really were clearer than these other objects now being shown to him?

Yes.

And suppose someone were to drag him away forcibly up the steep and rugged ascent and not let him go until he had hauled him out into the sunlight, would he not suffer pain and vexation at such treatment, and, when he had come out into the light, find his eyes so full of its radiance that he could not see a single one of the things that he was now told were real?

Certainly he would not see them all at once.

He would need, then, to grow accustomed before he could see things in that upper world. At first it would be easiest to make out shadows, and then the images of men and things reflected in water, and later on the things themselves. After that, it would be easier to watch the heavenly bodies and the sky itself by night, looking at the light of the moon and stars rather than the Sun and the Sun's light in the daytime.

Yes, surely.

Last of all, he would be able to look at the Sun and contemplate its nature, not as it appears when reflected in water or any alien medium, but as it is in itself in its own domain.

No doubt.

And now he would begin to draw the conclusion that it is the Sun that produces the seasons and the course of the year and controls everything in the visible world, and moreover is in a way the cause of all that he and his companions used to see.

Clearly he would come at last to that conclusion.

Then if he called to mind his fellow prisoners and what passed for wisdom in his former dwelling-place he would surely think himself happy in the change and be sorry for them. They may have had a practice of honouring and commending one another, with prizes for the man who had the keenest eye for the passing shadows and the best memory for the order in which they followed or accompanied one another, so that he could make a good guess as to which was going to come next. Would our released prisoner be likely to covet those prizes or to envy the men exalted to honour and power in the cave? Would he not feel like Homer's Achilles, that he would far sooner be on earth as a hired servant in the house of a landless man or endure anything rather than go back to his old beliefs and live in the old way?

Yes, he would prefer any fate to such a life.

Now imagine what would happen if he went down again to take his former seat in the Cave. Coming suddenly out of the sunlight, his eyes would be filled with darkness. He might be required once more to deliver his opinion on those shadows, in competition with the prisoners who had never been released, while his eyesight was still dim and unsteady; and it might take some time to become used to the darkness. They would laugh at him and say that he had gone up only to come back with his sight ruined; it was worth no one's while even to attempt the ascent. If they could lay hands on the man who was trying to set them free and lead them up, they would kill him.

Yes, they would.

Every feature in this parable, my dear Glaucon, is meant to fit our earlier analysis. The prison dwelling corresponds to the region revealed to us through the sense of sight, and the fire-light within it to the power of the Sun. The ascent to see the things in the upper world you may take as standing for the upward journey of the soul into the region of the intelligible; then you will be in possession of what I surmise, since that is what you wish to be told. Heaven knows whether it is true; but this, at any rate, is how it appears to me. In the world of knowledge the last thing to be perceived and only with great difficulty is the essential Form of Goodness. Once it is perceived, the conclusion must follow that, for all things, this is the cause of whatever is right and good; in the visible world it gives birth to light and to the lord of light, while it is itself sovereign in the intelligible world and the parent of intelligence and truth. Without having had a vision of this Form no one can act with wisdom, either in his own life or in matters of state.

So far as I can understand, I share your belief.

Then you may also agree that it is no wonder if those who have reached this height are reluctant to manage the affairs of men. Their souls long to spend all their time in that upper world—naturally enough, if here once more our parable holds true. Nor, again, is it at all strange that one who comes from the contemplation of divine things to the miseries of human life should appear awkward and ridiculous when, with eyes still dazed and not yet accustomed to the darkness, he is compelled, in a law-court or elsewhere, to dispute about the shadows of justice or the images that cast those shadows, and to wrangle over the notions of what is right in the minds of men who have never beheld Justice itself.

It is not at all strange.

No; a sensible man will remember that the eyes may be confused in two ways—by a change from light to darkness or from darkness to light; and he will recognize that the same thing happens to the soul when he sees it troubled and unable to discern anything clearly, instead of laughing thoughtlessly, he will ask whether, coming from a brighter existence, its unaccustomed vision is obscured by the darkness, in which case he will think its condition enviable and its life a happy one; or whether, emerging from the depths of ignorance, it is dazzled by excess of light. If so, he will rather feel sorry for it; or, if he were inclined to laugh, that would be less ridiculous than to laugh at the soul which has come down from the light.

That is a fair statement.

If this is true, then, we must conclude that education is not what it is said to be by some, who profess to put knowledge into a soul which does not possess it, as if they could put sight into blind eyes. On the contrary, our own account signifies that the soul of every man does possess the power of learning the truth and the organ to see it with;

and that, just as one might have to turn the whole body round in order that the eye should see light instead of darkness, so the entire soul must be turned away from this changing world, until its eye can bear to contemplate reality and that supreme splendour which we have called the Good. Hence there may well be an art whose aim would be to effect this very thing, the conversion of the soul, in the readiest way; not to put the power of sight into the soul's eye, which already has it, but to ensure that, instead of looking in the wrong direction, it is turned the way it ought to be.

Yes, it may well be so.

It looks, then, as though wisdom were different from those ordinary virtues, as they are called, which are not far removed from bodily qualities, in that they can be produced by habituation and exercise in a soul which has not possessed them from the first. Wisdom, it seems, is certainly the virtue of some diviner faculty, which never loses its power, though its use for good or harm depends on the direction towards which it is turned. You must have noticed in dishonest men with a reputation for sagacity, the shrewd glance of a narrow intelligence piercing the objects to which it is directed. There is nothing wrong with their power of vision, but it has been forced into the service of evil, so that the keener its sight, the more harm it works.

Quite true.

And yet if the growth of a nature like this had been pruned from earliest childhood, cleared of those clinging overgrowths which come of gluttony and all luxurious pleasure and, like leaden weights charged with affinity to this mortal world, hang upon the soul, bending its vision downwards; if, freed from these, the soul were turned round towards true reality, then this same power in these very men would see the truth as keenly as the objects it is turned to now.

Yes, very likely.

Is it not also likely, or indeed certain after what has been said, that a state can never be properly governed either by the uneducated who know nothing of truth or by men who are allowed to spend all their days in the pursuit of culture? The ignorant have no single mark before their eyes at which they must aim in all the conduct of their own lives and of affairs of state; and the others will not engage in action if they can help it, dreaming that, while still alive, they have been translated to the Islands of the Blest.

Quite true.

—c. 390 B.C.

Questions: Reading, Responding, Arguing

1. How does Plato use his allegory to urge philosophical education for people? How does he reveal that the men in the cave are ignorant?
2. Explain the allegorical meaning of the chains and cave in Plato's essay.
3. The freed man experiences blindness both when he leaves the cave and again when he returns to it. Why?
4. What argument is Plato attempting to make in his essay? How does the dialogue between a teacher and a student support or convey that argument?

George Orwell (1903–1950)

Politics and the English Language

Most people who bother with the matter at all would admit that the English language is in a bad way, but it is generally assumed that we cannot by conscious action do anything about it. Our civilization is decadent and our language—so the argument runs—must inevitably share in the general collapse. It follows that any struggle against the abuse of language is a sentimental archaism, like preferring candles to electric light or hansom cabs to aeroplanes. Underneath this lies the half-conscious belief that language is a natural growth and not an instrument which we shape for our own purposes.

Now, it is clear that the decline of a language must ultimately have political and economic causes: it is not due simply to the bad influence of this or that individual writer. But an effect can become a cause, reinforcing the original cause and producing the same effect in an intensified form, and so on indefinitely. A man may take to drink because he feels himself to be a failure, and then fail all the more completely because he drinks. It is rather the same thing that is happening to the English language. It becomes ugly and inaccurate because our thoughts are foolish, but the slovenliness of our language makes it easier for us to have foolish thoughts. The point is that the process is reversible.

Modern English, especially written English, is full of bad habits which spread by imitation and which can be avoided if one is willing to take the necessary trouble. If one gets rid of these habits one can think more clearly, and to think clearly is a necessary first step towards political regeneration: so that the fight against bad English is not frivolous and is not the exclusive concern of professional writers. I will come back to this presently, and I hope that by that time the meaning of what I have said here will have become clearer. Meanwhile, here are five specimens of the English language as it is now habitually written.

These five passages have not been picked out because they are especially bad—I could have quoted far worse if I had chosen—but because they illustrate various of the mental vices from which we now suffer. They are a little below the average, but are fairly representative samples. I number them so that I can refer back to them when necessary:

> "(1) I am not, indeed, sure whether it is not true to say that the Milton who once seemed not unlike a seventeenth-century Shelley had not become, out of an experience ever more bitter in each year, more alien *[sic]* to the founder of that Jesuit sect which nothing could induce him to tolerate."
>
> *Professor Harold Laski (Essay in* Freedom of Expression)

> "(2) Above all, we cannot play ducks and drakes with a native battery of idioms which prescribes such egregious collocations of vocables as the Basic *put up with for tolerate or put at a loss for bewilder.*"
>
> *Professor Lancelot Hogben* (Interglossa)

> "(3) On the one side we have the free personality: by definition it is not neurotic, for it has neither conflict nor dream. Its desires, such as they are, are transparent, for they are just what institutional approval keeps in the forefront of consciousness; another institutional pattern would alter their number and intensity; there is little in them that is natural, irreducible, or culturally dangerous. But *on the other side,* the social bond itself is nothing but the mutual reflection of these self-secure integrities. Recall the definition of love. Is not this the very picture of a small academic? Where is there a place in this hall of mirrors for either personality or fraternity?"
>
> *Essay on psychology in* Politics *(New York)*

> "(4) All the 'best people' from the gentlemen's clubs, and all the frantic fascist captains, united in common hatred of Socialism and bestial horror of the rising tide of the mass revolutionary movement, have turned to acts of provocation, to foul incendiarism, to medieval legends of poisoned wells, to legalize their own destruction of proletarian organiza-

tions, and rouse the agitated petty-bourgeoisie to chauvinistic fervour on behalf of the fight against the revolutionary way out of the crisis."

Communist pamphlet

"(5) If a new spirit *is* to be refused into this old country, there is one thorny and contentious reform which must be tackled, and that is the humanization and galvanization of the B.B.C. Timidity here will bespeak cancer and atrophy of the soul. The heart of Britain may be sound and of strong beat, for instance, but the British lion's roar at present is like that of Bottom in Shakespeare's *Midsummer Night's Dream*—as gentle as any sucking dove. A virile new Britain cannot continue indefinitely to be traduced in the eyes or rather ears, of the world by the effete languors of Langham Place, brazenly masquerading as 'standard English'. When the Voice of Britain is heard at nine o'clock, better far and infinitely less ludicrous to hear aitches honestly dropped than the present priggish, inflated, inhibited, school-ma'amish arch braying of blameless bashful mewing maidens!"

Letter in Tribune

Each of these passages has faults of its own, but, quite apart from avoidable ugliness, two qualities are common to all of them. The first is staleness of imagery: the other is lack of precision. The writer either has a meaning and cannot express it, or he inadvertently says something else, or he is almost indifferent as to whether his words mean anything or not. This mixture of vagueness and sheer incompetence is the most marked characteristic of modern English prose, and especially of any kind of political writing. As soon as certain topics are raised, the concrete melts into the abstract and no one seems able to think of turns of speech that are not hackneyed: prose consists less and less of *words* chosen for the sake of their meaning, and more and more of *phrases* tacked together like the sections of a prefabricated henhouse. I list below, with notes and examples, various of the tricks by means of which the work of prose-construction is habitually dodged:

Dying Metaphors

A newly invented metaphor assists thought by evoking a visual image, while on the other hand a metaphor which is technically "dead" (e.g. *iron resolution*) has in effect reverted to being an ordinary word and can generally be used without loss of vividness. But in between these two classes there is a huge dump of worn-out metaphors which have lost all evocative power and are merely used because they save people the trouble of inventing phrases for themselves. Examples are: *Ring the changes on, take up the cudgels for, toe the line, ride roughshod over, stand shoulder to shoulder with, play into the hands of, no axe to grind, grist to the mill, fishing in troubled waters, on the order of the day, Achilles heel, swan song, hotbed.* Many of these are used without knowledge of their meaning (what is a "rift," for instance?), and incompatible metaphors are frequently mixed, a sure sign that the writer is not interested in what he is saying. Some metaphors now current have been twisted out of their original meaning without those who use them even being aware of the fact. For example, *toe the line* is sometimes written *tow the line.* Another example is the *hammer and the anvil,* now always used with the implication that the anvil gets the worst of it. In real life it is always the anvil that breaks the hammer, never the other way about: a writer who stopped to think what he was saying would be aware of this, and would avoid perverting the original phrase.

Operators or Verbal False Limbs

These save the trouble of picking out appropriate verbs and nouns, and at the same time pad each sentence with extra syllables which give it an appearance of symmetry. Characteristic phrases are: *render inoperative, militate against, make contact with, be subjected to, give rise to, give grounds for, have the effect of, play a leading part (role) in, make itself felt, take effect, exhibit a tendency to, serve the purpose of, etc., etc.* The keynote is the elimination of simple verbs. Instead of being a single word, such as *break, stop, spoil, mend, kill,* a verb becomes *a phrase,* made up of a noun or adjective tacked on to some general-purposes verb such as *prove, serve, form, play, render.* In addition, the passive voice is wherever possible used in preference to the active, and noun constructions are used instead of gerunds (*by examination of* instead of *by examining*). The range of verbs is further cut down by means of the -ize and de- formation, and the banal statements are given an appearance of profundity by means of the not un- formation. Simple conjunctions and prepositions are replaced by such phrases as *with respect to, having regard to, the fact that, by dint of, in view of, in the interest of, on the hypothesis that*; and the ends of sentences are saved from anticlimax by such resounding commonplaces *as greatly to be desired, cannot be left out of account, a development to be expected in the near future, deserving of serious consideration, brought to a satisfactory conclusion,* and so on and so forth.

Pretentious Diction

Words like *phenomenon, element, individual* (as noun), *objective, categorical, effective, virtual, basic, primary, promote, constitute, exhibit, exploit, utilize, eliminate, liquidate,* are used to dress up simple statements and give an air of scientific impartiality to biased judgments. Adjectives like *epoch-making, epic, historic, unforgettable, triumphant, age-old, inevitable, inexorable, veritable,* are used to dignity the sordid processes of international politics, while writing that aims at glorifying war usually takes on an archaic colour, its characteristic words being: *realm, throne, chariot, mailed fist, trident, sword, shield, buckler, banner, jackboot, clarion.* Foreign words and expressions such as *cul de sac, ancien régime, deus ex machina, mutatis mutandis, status quo, gleichschaltung, weltanschauung,* are used to give an air of culture and elegance. Except for the useful abbreviations *i.e., e.g.,* and *etc.,* there is no real need for any of the hundreds of foreign phrases now current in English. Bad writers, and especially scientific, political and sociological writers, are nearly aways haunted by the notion that Latin or Greek words are grander than Saxon ones, and unnecessary words like *expedite, ameliorate, predict, extraneous, deracinated, clandestine, subaqueous* and hundreds of others constantly gain ground from their Anglo-Saxon opposite numbers.[1] The jargon peculiar to Marxist writing (*hyena, hangman, cannibal, petty bourgeois, these gentry, lacquey, flunkey, mad dog, White Guard,* etc., consists largely of words and phrases translated from Russian, German or French; but the normal way of coining a new word is to use a Latin or Greek root with the appropriate affix and, where necessary, the *-ize* formation. It is often easier to make up words of this kind (*deregionalize, impermissible, extramarital, nonfragmentatory* and so forth) than to think up the English words that will cover one's meaning. The result, in general, is an increase in slovenliness and vagueness.

MEANINGLESS WORDS

In certain kinds of writing, particularly in art criticism and literary criticism, it is normal to come across long passages which are almost completely lacking in meaning.[2] Words like *romantic, plastic, values, human, dead, sentimental, natural, vitality,* as used in art criticism, are strictly

---

[1]An interesting illustration of this is the way in which the English flower names which were in use till very recently are being ousted by Greek ones, snapdragon becoming *antirrhinum, forget-me-not* becoming *myosotis,* etc. It is hard to see any practical reason for this change of fashion: it is probably due to an instinctive turning-away from the more homely word and a vague feeling that the Greek word is scientific [Orwell's note].

[2]Example: "Comfort's catholicity of perception and image, strangely Whitmanesque in range, almost the exact opposite in aesthetic compulsion, continues to evoke that trembling atmospheric accumulative hinting at a cruel, an inexorably serene timelessness. . . . Wrey Gardiner scores by aiming at simple bull's-eyes with precision. Only they are not so simple, and through this contented sadness runs more than the surface bittersweet of resignation" *Poetry Quarterly*) [Orwell's note].

meaningless in the sense that they not only do not point to any discoverable object, but are hardly ever expected to do so by the reader. When one critic writes, "The outstanding feature of Mr. X's work is its living quality," while another writes, "The immediately striking thing about Mr. X's work is its peculiar deadness," the reader accepts this as a simple difference of opinion. If words like *black* and *white* were involved, instead of the jargon words *dead* and *living*, he would see at once that language was being used in an improper way. Many political words are similarly abused. The word *Fascism* has now no meaning except in so far as it signifies "something not desirable." The words *democracy, socialism, freedom, patriotic, realistic, justice*, have each of them several different meanings which cannot be reconciled with one another. In the case of a word like *democracy*, not only is there no agreed definition, but the attempt to make one is resisted from all sides. It is almost universally felt that when we call a country democratic we are praising it: consequently the defenders of every kind of régime claim that it is a democracy, and fear that they might have to stop using the word if it were tied down to any one meaning. Words of this kind are often used in a consciously dishonest way. That is, the person who uses them has his own private definition, but allows his hearer to think he means something quite different. Statements like *Marshal Pétain was a true patriot, The Soviet Press is the freest in the world, The Catholic Church is opposed to persecution*, are almost always made with intent to deceive. Other words used in variable meanings, in most cases more or less dishonestly, are: *class, totalitarian, science, progressive, reactionary, bourgeois, equality.*

Now that I have made this catalogue of swindles and perversions, let me give another example of the kind of writing that they lead to. This time it must of its nature be an imaginary one. I am going to translate a passage of good English into modern English of the worst sort. Here is a well-known verse from *Ecclesiastes*:

> "I returned and saw under the sun, that the race is not to the swift, nor the battle to the strong, neither yet bread to the wise, nor yet riches to men of understanding, nor yet favour to men of skill; but time and chance happeneth to them all."

Here it is in modern English:

> "Objective consideration of contemporary phenomena compels the conclusion that success or failure in competitive activities exhibits no tendency to be commensurate with innate capacity, but that a considerable element of the unpredictable must invariably be taken into account."

This is a parody, but not a very gross one. Exhibit (3), above, for instance, contains several patches of the same kind of English. It will be seen that I have not made a full translation. The beginning and ending of the sentence follow the original meaning fairly closely, but in the middle the concrete illustrations—race, battle, bread—dissolve into the vague phrase "success or failure in competitive activities." This had to be so, because no modern writer of the kind I am discussing—no one capable of using phrases like "objective consideration of contemporary phenomena"—would ever tabulate his thoughts in that precise and detailed way. The whole tendency of modern prose is away from concreteness. Now analyse these two sentences a little more closely. The first contains forty-nine words but only sixty syllables, and all its words are those of everyday life. The second contains thirty-eight words of ninety syllables: eighteen of its words are from Latin roots, and one from Greek. The first sentence contains six vivid images, and only one phrase ("time and chance") that could be called vague. The second contains not a single fresh, arresting phrase, and in spite of its ninety syllables it gives only a shortened version of the meaning contained in the first. Yet without a doubt it is the second kind of sentence that is gaining ground in modern English. I do not want to exaggerate. This kind of writing is not yet universal, and outcrops of simplicity will occur here and there in the worst-written page. Still, if you or I were told to write a few lines on the uncertainty of human fortunes, we should probably come much nearer to my imaginary sentence than to the one from *Ecclesiastes*.

As I have tried to show, modern writing at its worst does not consist in picking out words for the sake of their meaning and inventing images in order to make the meaning clearer. It consists in gumming together long strips of words which have already been set in order by someone else, and making the results presentable by sheer humbug. The attraction of this way of writing is that it is easy. It is easier—even quicker, once you have the habit—to say *In my opinion it is a not unjustifiable assumption that* than to say *I think*. If you use ready-made phrases, you not only don't have to hunt about for words; you also don't have to bother with the rhythms of your sentences, since these phrases are generally so arranged as to be more or less euphonious. When you are composing in a hurry—when you are dictating to a stenographer, for instance, or making a public speech—it is natural to fall into a pretentious, Latinized style. Tags like *a consideration which we should do well to bear in mind* or *a conclusion to which all of us would readily assent* will save many a sentence from coming down with a bump. By using stale metaphors, similes and idioms, you save much mental effort, at the cost of leaving your meaning vague, not only for your reader but for yourself. This is the significance of mixed metaphors. The sole aim of a metaphor is to call up a visual image. When these images clash—as in *The Fascist octopus has sung its swan song, the jackboot is thrown into the melting pot*—it can be taken as certain that the writer is not seeing a mental image of the objects he is naming; in other words he is not really thinking. Look again at the examples I gave at the beginning of this essay. Professor Laski (1) uses five negatives in fifty-three words. One of these is superfluous, making nonsense of the whole passage, and in addition there is the slip *alien* for akin, making further nonsense, and several avoidable pieces of clumsiness which increase the general vagueness. Professor Hogben (2) plays ducks and drakes with a battery which is able to write prescriptions, and, while disapproving of the everyday phrase *put up with,* is unwilling to look *egregious* up in the dictionary and see what it means. (3), if one takes an uncharitable attitude towards it, is simply meaningless: probably one could work out its intended meaning by reading the whole of the article in which it occurs. In (4), the writer knows more or less what he wants to say, but an accumulation of stale phrases chokes him like tea leaves blocking a sink. In (5), words and meaning have almost parted company. People who write in this manner usually have a general emotional meaning—they dislike one thing and want to express solidarity with another—but they are not interested in the detail of what they are saying. A scrupulous writer, in every sentence that he writes, will ask himself at least four questions, thus: What am I trying to say? What words will express it? What image or idiom will make it clearer? Is this image fresh enough to have an effect? And he will probably ask himself two more: Could I put it more shortly? Have I said anything that is avoidably ugly? But you are not obliged to go to all this trouble. You can shirk it by simply throwing your mind open and letting the ready-made phrases come crowding in. They will construct your sentences for you—even think your thoughts for you, to a certain extent—and at need they will perform the important service of partially concealing your meaning even from yourself. It is at this point that the special connection between politics and the debasement of language becomes clear.

In our time it is broadly true that political writing is bad writing. Where it is not true, it will generally be found that the writer is some kind of rebel, expressing his private opinions and not a "party line." Orthodoxy, of whatever colour, seems to demand a lifeless, imitative style. The political dialects to be found in pamphlets, leading articles, manifestos, White Papers and the speeches of under-secretaries do, of course, vary from party to party, but they are all alike in that one almost never finds in them a fresh, vivid, homemade turn of speech. When one watches some tired hack on the platform mechanically repeating the familiar phrases—*bestial atrocities, iron heel, bloodstained tyranny, free peoples of the world, stand shoulder to shoulder*—one often has a curious feeling that one is not watching a live human being but some kind of dummy: a feeling which suddenly becomes stronger at moments when the light catches the speaker's spectacles and turns them into blank discs which seem to have no eyes behind them. And this is not altogether fanciful. A speaker who uses that kind of phraseology has gone some distance towards turning himself into a machine. The appropriate noises are coming out of his larynx, but his brain is not involved as it would be if he were choosing his words for himself. If the speech he is making is one that he is accustomed to make over and over again, he may be almost unconscious of what he is saying, as one is when one utters the responses in church. And this reduced state of consciousness, if not indispensable, is at any rate favourable to political conformity.

In our time, political speech and writing are largely the defence of the indefensible. Things like the continuance of British rule in India, the Russian purges and deportations, the dropping of the atom bombs on Japan, can indeed be defended, but only by arguments which are too brutal for most people to face, and which do not square with the professed aims of political parties. Thus political language has to consist largely of euphemism, question-begging and sheer cloudy vagueness. Defenceless villages are bombarded from the air, the inhabitants driven out into the countryside, the cattle machine-gunned, the huts set on fire with incendiary bullets: this is called *pacification*. Millions of peasants are robbed of their farms and sent trudging along the roads with no more than they can carry: this is called *transfer of population or rectification of frontiers*. People are imprisoned for years without trial, or shot in the back of the neck or sent to die of scurvy in Arctic lumber camps: this is called *elimination of unreliable elements*. Such phraseology is needed if one wants to name things without calling up mental pictures of them. Consider for instance some comfortable English professor defending Russian totalitarianism. He cannot say outright, "I believe in killing off your opponents when you can get good results by doing so." Probably, therefore, he will say something like this:

"While freely conceding that the Soviet régime exhibits certain features which the humanitarian may be inclined to deplore, we must, I think, agree that a certain curtailment of the right to political opposition is an unavoidable concomitant of transitional periods, and that the rigors which the Russian people have been called upon to undergo have been amply justified in the sphere of concrete achievement."

The inflated style is itself a kind of euphemism. A mass of Latin words falls upon the facts like soft snow, blurring the outlines and covering up all the details. The great enemy of clear language is insincerity. When there is a gap between one's real and one's declared aims, one turns as it were instinctively to long words and exhausted idioms, like a cuttlefish squirting out ink. In our age there is no such thing as "keeping out of politics." All issues are political issues, and politics itself is a mass of lies, evasions, folly, hatred and schizophrenia. When the general atmosphere is bad, language must suffer. I should expect to find—this is a guess which I have not sufficient knowledge to verify—that the German, Russian and Italian languages have all deteriorated in the last ten or fifteen years, as a result of dictatorship.

But if thought corrupts language, language can also corrupt thought. A bad usage can spread by tradition and imitation, even among people who should and do know better. The debased language that I have been discussing is in some ways very convenient. Phrases like *a not unjustifiable assumption, leaves much to be desired, would serve no good purpose, a consideration which we should do well to bear in mind,* are a continuous temptation, a packet of aspirins always at one's elbow. Look back through this essay, and for certain you will find that I have again and again committed the very faults I am protesting against. By this morning's post I have received a pamphlet dealing with conditions in Germany. The author tells me that he "felt impelled" to write it. I open it at random, and here is almost the first sentence that I see: "(The Allies) have an opportunity not only of achieving a radical transformation of Germany's social and political structure in such a way as to avoid a nationalistic reaction in Germany itself, but at the same time of laying the foundations of a co-operative and unified Europe." You see, he "feels impelled" to write—feels, presumably, that he has something new to say—and yet his words, like cavalry horses answering the bugle, group themselves automatically into the familiar dreary pattern. This invasion of one's mind by ready-made phrases (*lay the foundations, achieve a radical transformation*) can only be prevented if one is constantly on guard against them, and every such phrase anaesthetizes a portion of one's brain.

I said earlier that the decadence of our language is probably curable. Those who deny this would argue, if they produced an argument at all, that language merely reflects existing social conditions, and that we cannot influence its development by any direct tinkering with words and constructions. So far as the general tone or spirit of a language goes, this may be true, but it is not true in detail. Silly words and expressions have often disappeared, not through any evolutionary process but owing to the conscious action of a minority. Two recent examples were *explore every avenue and leave no stone unturned,* which were killed by the jeers of a few journalists. There is a long list of fly-blown metaphors which could similarly be got rid of if enough people would interest themselves in the job; and it should also be possible to laugh the *not un-* formation out of existence,[3] to reduce the amount of Latin and Greek in the average sentence, to drive out foreign phrases and strayed scientific words, and, in general, to make pretentiousness unfashionable. But all these are minor points. The defence of the English language implies more than this, and perhaps it is best to start by saying what it does *not* imply.

To begin with it has nothing to do with archaism, with the salvaging of obsolete words and turns of speech, or with the setting up of a "standard English" which must never be departed from. On the contrary, it is especially concerned with the scrapping of every word or idiom which has outworn its usefulness. It has nothing to do with correct grammar and syntax, which are of no importance so long as one makes one's meaning clear, or with the avoidance of Americanisms, or with having what is called a "good prose style." On the other hand it is not concerned with fake simplicity and the attempt to make written English colloquial. Nor does it even imply in every case preferring the Saxon word to the Latin one, though it does imply using the fewest and shortest words that will cover one's meaning. What is above all needed is to let the meaning choose the word, and not the other way about. In prose, the worst thing one can do with words is to surrender to them. When you think of a concrete object, you think wordlessly, and then, if you want to describe the thing you have been visualizing you probably hunt about till you find the exact words that seem to fit. When you think of something abstract you are more inclined to use words from the start, and unless you make a conscious effort to prevent it, the existing dialect will come rushing in and do the job for you, at the expense of blurring or even changing your meaning. Probably it is better to put off using words as long as possible and get one's meaning as clear as one can through pictures or sensations. Afterwards one can choose—not simply *accept*—the phrases that will best cover the meaning, and then switch round and decide what impression one's words are likely to make on

---

[3]One can cure oneself of the *not un-* formation by memorizing this sentence: A *not unblack dog was chasing a not unsmall rabbit across a not ungreen field* [Orwell's note].

another person. This last effort of the mind cuts out all stale or mixed images, all prefabricated phrases, needless repetitions, and humbug and vagueness generally. But one can often be in doubt about the effect of a word or a phrase, and one needs rules that one can rely on when instinct fails. I think the following rules will cover most cases:

(i) Never use a metaphor, simile or other figure of speech which you are used to seeing in print.
(ii) Never use a long word where a short one will do.
(iii) If it is possible to cut a word out, always cut it out.
(iv) Never use the passive where you can use the active.
(v) Never use a foreign phrase, a scientific word or a jargon word if you can think of an everyday English equivalent.
(vi) Break any of these rules sooner than say anything outright barbarous.

These rules sound elementary, and so they are, but they demand a deep change of attitude in anyone who has grown used to writing in the style now fashionable. One could keep all of them and still write bad English, but one could not write the kind of stuff that I quoted in those five specimens at the beginning of this article.

I have not here been considering the literary use of language, but merely language as an instrument for expressing and not for concealing or preventing thought. Stuart Chase and others have come near to claiming that all abstract words are meaningless, and have used this as a pretext for advocating a kind of political quietism. Since you don't know what Fascism is, how can you struggle against Fascism? One need not swallow such absurdities as this, but one ought to recognize that the present political chaos is connected with the decay of language, and that one can probably bring about some improvement by starting at the verbal end. If you simplify your English, you are freed from the worst follies of orthodoxy. You cannot speak any of the necessary dialects, and when you make a stupid remark its stupidity will be obvious, even to yourself. Political language—and with variations this is true of all political parties, from Conservatives to Anarchists—is designed to make lies sound truthful and murder respectable, and to give an appearance of solidity to pure wind. One cannot change this all in a moment, but one can at least change one's own habits, and from time to time one can even, if one jeers loudly enough, send some worn-out and useless phrase—some *jackboot, Achilles' heel, hotbed, melting pot, acid test, veritable inferno* or other lump of verbal refuse—into the dustbin where it belongs.

—*1946*

Questions: Reading, Responding, Arguing

1. When Orwell suggests that "political writing is bad writing," what does he think categorizes political writing?
2. What is the essay cautioning us against in our own writing?
3. According to Orwell, what is "standard language"? Why is he against it?
4. Explain why Orwell provides a parodic translation of *Ecclesiastes*. How does he change the language of the original text?
5. Using newspaper reports of politcal speeches, argue that the situation Orwell describes has grown worse.

John Fitzgerald Kennedy (1917–1963)

Poetry and Power

This day devoted to the memory of Robert Frost offers an opportunity for reflection which is prized by politicians as well as by others, and even by poets, for Robert Frost was one of the granite figures of our time in America. He was supremely two things: an artist and an American. A nation reveals itself not only by the men it produces but also by the men it honors, the men it remembers.

In America, our heroes have customarily run to men of large accomplishments. But today this college and country honors a man whose contribution was not to our size but to our spirit, not to our political beliefs but to our insight, not to our self-esteem, but to our self-comprehension. In honoring Robert Frost, we therefore can pay honor to the deepest sources of our national strength. That strength takes many forms, and the most obvious forms are not always the most significant. The men who create power make an indispensable contribution to the Nation's greatness, but the men who question power make a contribution just as indispensable, especially when that questioning is disinterested, for they determine whether we use power or power uses us.

Our national strength matters, but the spirit which informs and controls our strength matters just as much. This was the special significance of Robert Frost. He brought an unsparing instinct for reality to bear on the platitudes and pieties of society. His sense of the human tragedy fortified him against self-deception and easy consolation. "I have been," he wrote, "one acquainted with the night." And because he knew the midnight as well as the high noon, because he understood the ordeal as well as the triumph of the human spirit, he gave his age strength with which to overcome despair. At bottom, he held a deep faith in the spirit of man, and it is hardly an accident that Robert Frost coupled poetry and power, for he saw poetry as the means of saving power from itself. When power leads man towards arrogance, poetry reminds him of his limitations. When power narrows the areas of man's concern, poetry reminds him of the richness and diversity of his existence. When power corrupts, poetry cleanses. For art establishes the basic human truth which must serve as the touchstone of our judgment.

The artists, however faithful to his personal vision of reality, becomes the last champion of the individual mind and sensibility against an intrusive society and an officious state. The great artist is thus a solitary figure. He has, as Frost said, a lover's quarrel with the world. In pursuing his perceptions of reality, he must often sail against the currents of his time. This is not a popular role. If Robert Frost was much honored in his lifetime, it was because a good many preferred to ignore his darker truths. Yet in retrospect, we see how the artist's fidelity has strengthened the fibre of our national life.

If sometimes our great artist have been the most critical of our society, it is because their sensitivity and their concern for justice, which must motivate any true artist, makes him aware that our Nation falls short of its highest potential. I see little of more importance to the future of our country and our civilization than full recognition of the place of the artist.

If art is to nourish the roots of our culture, society must set the artist free to follow his vision wherever it takes him. We must never forget that art is not a form of propaganda; it is a form of truth. And as Mr. MacLeish once remarked of poets, there is nothing worse for our trade than to be in style. In free society art is not a weapon and it does not belong to the sphere of polemics and ideology. Artists are not engineers of the soul. It may be different elsewhere. But in a democratic society—in it, the highest duty of the writer, the composer, the artist is to remain true to himself and to let the chips fall where they may. In serving his vision of the truth, the artist best serves his nation. And the nation which disdains the mission of art invites the fate of Robert Frost's hired man, the fate of having "nothing to look backward to with pride. And nothing to look forward to with hope."

I look forward to a great future for America, a future in which our country will match its military strength with our moral restraint, its wealth with our wisdom, its power with our purpose. I look forward to an America which will not be afraid of grace and beauty, which will protect the beauty of our natural environment, which will preserve the great old American houses and squares and parks of our national past, and which will build handsome and balanced cities for our future.

I look forward to an America which will reward achievement in the arts as we reward achievement in business or statecraft. I look forward to an America which will steadily raise the standards of artistic accomplishment and which will steadily enlarge cultural opportunities for all our citizens. And I look forward to an America which commands respect throughout the world, not only for its strength but for its civilization as well. And I look forward to a world which will be safe not only for democracy and diversity but also for personal distinction.

—1963

Questions: Reading, Responding, Arguing

1. What are the things about Frost that Kennedy finds most memorable?
2. How does Kennedy feel about Frost's criticism of society?
3. Kennedy repeats the line "I look forward to an America . . ." several times in the essay. Explain how Kennedy uses Frost to put forward his vision of the American future.
4. What is the relationship of poetry to power? Is there a possible counter argument to this?

Martin Luther King, Jr. (1929–1968)

Letter from Birmingham Jail

My Dear Fellow Clergymen:

While confined here in the Birmingham city jail, I came across your recent statement calling my present activities "unwise and untimely." Seldom do I pause to answer criticism of my work and ideas. If I sought to answer all the criticisms that cross my desk, my secretaries would have little time for anything other than such correspondence in the course of the day, and I would have no time for constructive work. But since I feel that you are men of genuine good will and that your criticisms are sincerely set forth, I want to try to answer your statement in what I hope will be patient and reasonable terms.

I think I should indicate why I am here in Birmingham, since you have been influenced by the view which argues against "outsiders coming in." I have the honor of serving as president of the Southern Christian Leadership Conference, an organization operating in every southern state, with headquarters in Atlanta, Georgia. We have some eighty-five affiliated organizations across the South, and one of them is the Alabama Christian Movement for Human Rights. Frequently we share staff, educational, and financial resources with our affiliates. Several months ago the affiliate here in Birmingham asked us to be on call to engage in a nonviolent direct-action program if such were deemed necessary. We readily consented, and when the hour came we lived up to our promise. So I, along with several members of my staff, am here because I was invited here. I am here because I have organizational ties here.

But more basically, I am in Birmingham because injustice is here. Just as the prophets of the eighth century B.C. left their villages and carried their "thus saith the Lord" far beyond the boundaries of their home towns, and just as the Apostle Paul left his village of Tarsus and carried the gospel of Jesus Christ to the far corners of the Greco-Roman world, so am I compelled to carry the gospel of freedom beyond my own home town. Like Paul, I must constantly respond to the Macedonian call for aid.

Moreover, I am cognizant of the interrelatedness of all communities and states. I cannot sit idly by in Atlanta and not be concerned about what happens in Birmingham. Injustice anywhere is a threat to justice everywhere. We are caught in an inescapable network of mutuality, tied in a single garment of destiny. Whatever affects one directly, affects all indirectly. Never again can we afford to live with the narrow, provincial "outside agitator" idea. Anyone who lives inside the United States can never be considered an outsider anywhere within its bounds.

You deplore the demonstrations taking place in Birmingham. But your statement, I am sorry, to say fails to express a similar concern for the conditions that brought about the demonstrations. I am sure that none of you would want to rest content with the superficial kind of social analysis that deals merely with effects and does not grapple with underlying causes. It is unfortunate that demonstrations are taking place in Birmingham, but it is even more unfortunate that the city's white power structure left the Negro community with no alternative.

In any nonviolent campaign there are four basic steps: collection of the facts to determine whether injustices exist; negotiation; self-purification; and direct action. We have gone through all these steps in Birmingham. There can be no gainsaying the fact that racial injustice engulfs this community. Birmingham is probably the most thoroughly segregated city in the United States. Its ugly record of brutality is widely known. Negroes have experienced grossly unjust treatment in the courts. There have been more unsolved bombings of Negro homes and churches in Birmingham than in any other city in the nation. These are the hard, brutal facts of the case. On the basis of these conditions, Negro leaders sought to negotiate with the city fathers. But the latter consistently refused to engage in good-faith negotiation.

Then, last September, came the opportunity to talk with leaders of Birmingham's economic community. In the course of the negotiations, certain promises were made by the merchants—for example, to remove the stores' humiliating racial signs. On the basis of these promises, the Reverend Fred Shuttlesworth and the leaders of the Alabama Christian Movement for Human Rights agreed to a moratorium on all demonstrations. As the weeks and months went by, we realized that we were the victims of a broken promise. A few signs, briefly removed, returned; the others remained.

As in so many past experiences, our hopes had been blasted, and the shadow of deep disappointment settled upon us. We had no alternative except to prepare for direct action, whereby we would present our very bodies as a means of laying our case before the conscience of the local and the national community. Mindful of the difficulties involved, we decided to undertake a process of self-purification. We began a series of workshops on nonviolence, and we repeatedly asked ourselves: "Are you able to accept blows without retaliating?" "Are you able to endure the ordeal of jail?" We decided to schedule our direct-action program for the Easter season, realizing that except for Christmas, this is the main shopping period of the year. Knowing that a strong economic-withdrawal program would be the by-product of direct action, we felt that this would be the best time to bring pressure to bear on the merchants for the needed change.

Then it occurred to us that Birmingham's mayoral election was coming up in March, and we speedily decided to postpone action until after election day. When we discovered that the Commissioner of Public Safety, Eugene "Bull" Connor, had piled up enough votes to be in the run-off, we decided again to postpone action until the day after the run-off so that the demonstrations could not be used to cloud the issues. Like many others, we wanted to see Mr. Connor defeated, and to this end we endured postponement after postponement. Having aided in this community need, we felt that our direct-action program could be delayed no longer.

You may well ask, "Why direct action? Why sit-ins, marches, and so forth? Isn't negotiation a better path?" You are quite right in calling for negotiation. Indeed, this is the very purpose of direct action. Nonviolent direct action seeks to create such a crisis and foster such a tension that a community which has constantly refused to negotiate is forced to confront the issue. It seeks so to dramatize the issue that it can no longer be ignored. My citing the creation of tension as part of the work of the nonviolent-resister may sound rather shocking. But I must confess that I am not afraid of the word "tension." I have earnestly opposed violent tension, but there is a type of constructive, nonviolent tension which is necessary for growth. Just as Socrates felt that it was necessary to create a tension in the mind so that individuals could rise from the bondage of myths and half-truths to the unfettered realm of creative analysis and objective appraisal, so must we see the need for nonviolent gadflies to create the kind of tension in society that will help men rise from the dark depths of prejudice and racism to the majestic heights of understanding and brotherhood.

The purpose of our direct-action program is to create a situation so crisis-packed that it will inevitably open the door to negotiation. I therefore concur with you in your call for negotiation. Too long has our beloved Southland been bogged down in a tragic effort to live in monologue rather than dialogue.

One of the basic points in your statement is that the action that I and my associates have taken in Birmingham is untimely. Some have asked: "Why didn't you give the new city administration time to act?" The only answer that I can give to this query is that the new Birmingham administration must be prodded about as much as the outgoing one, before it will act. We are sadly mistaken if we feel that the election of Albert Boutwell as mayor will bring the millennium to Birmingham. While Mr. Boutwell is a much more gentle person than Mr. Connor, they are both segregationists, dedicated to maintenance of the status quo. I have hoped that Mr. Boutwell will be reasonable enough to see the futility of massive resistance to desegregation. But he will not see this without pressure from devotees of civil rights. My friends, I must say to you that we have not made a single gain in civil rights without determined legal and nonviolent pressure. Lamentably, it is an historical fact that privileged groups seldom give up their privileges voluntarily. Individuals may see the moral light and voluntarily give up their unjust posture, but, as Reinhold Niebuhr has reminded us, groups tend to be more immoral than individuals.

We know through painful experience that freedom is never voluntarily given by the oppressor; it must be demanded by the oppressed. Frankly, I have yet to engage in a direct-action campaign that was "well timed" in the view of those who have not suffered unduly from the disease of segregation. For years now I have heard the word "Wait!" It rings in the ear of every Negro with piercing familiarity. This "Wait" has almost always meant "Never." We must come to see, with one of our distinguished jurists, that "justice too long delayed is justice denied."

We have waited for more than 340 years for our constitutional and God-given rights. The nations of Asia and Africa are moving with jet-like speed toward gaining political independence, but we still creep at horse-and-buggy pace toward gaining a cup of coffee at a lunch counter. Perhaps it is easy for those who have never felt the stinging darts of segregation to say, "Wait." But when you have seen vicious mobs lynch your mothers and fathers at will and drown your sisters and brothers at whim; when you have seen hate-filled policemen curse, kick, and even kill your black brothers and sisters; when you see the vast majority of your twenty million Negro brothers smothering in an airtight cage of poverty in the midst of an affluent society; when you suddenly find your tongue twisted and your speech stammering as you seek to explain to your six-year-old daughter why she can't go to the public amusement park that has just been advertised on television, and see tears welling up in her eyes when she is told that Funtown is closed to colored children, and see ominous clouds of inferiority beginning to form in her little mental sky, and see her beginning to distort her personality by developing an unconscious bitterness toward white people; when you have to concoct an answer for a five-year-old son who is asking, "Daddy, why do white people treat colored people so mean?"; when you take a cross-country drive and find it necessary to sleep night after night in the uncomfortable corners of your automobile because no motel will accept you; when you are humiliated day in and day out by nagging signs reading "white" and "colored"; when your first name becomes "nigger," your middle name becomes "boy" (however old you are) and your last name becomes "John," and your wife and mother are never given the respected title "Mrs."; when you are harried by day and haunted by night by the fact that you are a Negro, living constantly at tiptoe stance, never quite knowing what to expect next, and are plagued with inner fears and outer resentments; when you are forever fighting a degenerating sense of "nobodiness"—then you will understand why we find it difficult to wait. There comes a time when the cup of endurance runs over, and men are no longer willing to be plunged into the abyss of despair. I hope, sirs, you can understand our legitimate and unavoidable impatience.

You express a great deal of anxiety over our willingness to break laws. This is certainly a legitimate concern. Since we so diligently urge people to obey the Supreme Court's decision of 1954 outlawing segregation in the public schools, at first glance it may seem rather paradoxical for us consciously to break laws. One may well ask: "How can you advocate breaking some laws and obeying others?" The answer lies in the fact that there are two types of laws: just and unjust. I would be the first to advocate obeying just laws. One has not only a legal but a moral responsibility to obey just laws. Conversely, one has a moral responsibility to disobey unjust laws. I would agree with St. Augustine that "an unjust law is no law at all."

Now, what is the difference between the two? How does one determine whether a law is just or unjust? A just law is a man-made code that squares with the moral law or the law of God. An unjust law is a code that is out of harmony with the moral law. To put it in the terms of St. Thomas Aquinas: An unjust law is a human law that is not rooted in eternal law and natural law. Any law that uplifts human personality is just. Any law that degrades human personality is unjust. All segregation statutes are unjust because segregation distorts the soul and damages the personality. It gives the segregator a false sense of superiority and the segregated a false sense of inferiority. Segregation, to use the terminology of the Jewish philosopher Martin Buber, substitutes an "I-it" relationship for an "I-thou" relationship and ends up relegating persons to the status of things. Hence segregation is not only politically, economically, and sociologically unsound, it is morally wrong and sinful. Paul Tillich has said that sin is separation. Is not segregation an existential expression of man's tragic separation, his awful estrangement, his terrible sinfulness? Thus it is that I can urge men to obey the 1954 decision of the Supreme Court, for it is morally right; and I can urge them to disobey segregation ordinances, for they are morally wrong.

Let us consider a more concrete example of just and unjust laws. An unjust law is a code that a numerical or power majority group compels a minority group to obey but does not make binding on itself. This is *difference* made legal. By the same token, a just law is a code that a majority compels a minority to follow and that it is willing to follow itself. This is *sameness* made legal.

Let me give another explanation. A law is unjust if it is inflicted on a minority that, as a result of being denied the right to vote, had no part in enacting or devising the law. Who can say that the legislature of Alabama which set up that state's segregation laws was democratically elected? Throughout Alabama all sorts of devious methods are used to prevent Negroes from becoming registered voters, and there are some counties in which, even though Negroes constitute a majority of the population, not a single Negro is registered. Can any law enacted under such circumstances be considered democratically structured?

Sometimes a law is just on its face and unjust in its application. For instance, I have been arrested on a charge of parading without a permit. Now, there is nothing wrong in having an ordinance which requires a permit for a parade. But such an ordinance becomes unjust when it is used to maintain segregation and to deny citizens the First-Amendment privilege of peaceful assembly and protest.

I hope you are able to see the distinction I am trying to point out. In no sense do I advocate evading or defying the law, as would the rabid segregationist. That would lead to anarchy. One who breaks an unjust law must do so openly, lovingly, and with a willingness to accept the penalty. I submit that an individual who breaks a law that conscience tells him is unjust, and who willingly accepts the penalty of imprisonment in order to arouse the conscience of the community over its injustice, is in reality expressing the highest respect for law.

Of course, there is nothing new about this kind of civil disobedience. It was evidenced sublimely in the refusal of Shadrach, Meshach, and Abednego to obey the laws of Nebuchadnezzar, on the ground that a higher moral law was at stake. It was practiced superbly by the early Christians, who were willing to face hungry lions and the excruciating pain of chopping blocks rather than submit to certain unjust laws of the Roman Empire. To a degree, academic freedom is a reality today because Socrates practiced civil disobedience. In our own nation, the Boston Tea Party represented a massive act of civil disobedience.

We should never forget that everything Adolf Hitler did in Germany was "legal" and everything the Hungarian freedom fighters did in Hungary was "illegal." It was "illegal" to aid and comfort a Jew in Hitler's Germany. Even so, I am sure that, had I lived in Germany at the time, I would have aided and comforted my Jewish brothers. If today I lived in a Communist country where certain principles dear to the Christian faith are suppressed, I would openly advocate disobeying that country's anti-religious laws.

I must make two honest confessions to you, my Christian and Jewish brothers. First, I must confess that over the past few years I have been gravely disappointed with the white moderate. I have almost reached the regrettable conclusion that the Negro's great stumbling block in his stride toward freedom is not the White Citizen's Counciler or the Ku Klux Klanner, but the white moderate, who is more devoted to "order" than to justice; who prefers a negative peace which is the absence of tension to a positive peace which is the presence of justice; who constantly says, "I agree with you in the goal you seek, but I cannot agree with your methods of direct action"; who paternalistically believes he can set the timetable for another man's freedom; who lives by a mythical concept of time and who constantly advises the Negro to wait for a "more convenient season." Shallow understanding from people of good will is more frustrating than absolute misunderstanding from people of ill will. Lukewarm acceptance is much more bewildering than outright rejection.

I had hoped that the white moderate would understand that law and order exist for the purpose of establishing justice and that when they fail in this purpose they become the dangerously structured dams that block the flow of social progress. I had hoped that the white moderate would understand that the present tension in the South is a necessary phase of the transition from an obnoxious negative peace, in which the Negro passively accepted his unjust plight, to a substantive and positive peace, in which all men will respect the dignity and worth of human personality. Actually, we who engage in nonviolent direct action are not the creators of tension. We merely bring to the surface the hidden tension that is already alive. We bring it out in the open, where it can be seen and dealt with. Like a boil that can never be cured so long as it is covered up but must be opened with all its ugliness to the natural medicines of air and light, injustice must be exposed, with all the tension its exposure creates, to the light of human conscience and the air of national opinion, before it can be cured.

In your statement you assert that our actions, even though peaceful, must be condemned because they precipitate violence. But is this a logical assertion? Isn't this like condemning a robbed man because his possession of money precipitated the evil act of robbery? Isn't this like condemning Socrates because his unswerving commitment to truth and his philosophical inquiries precipitated the act by the misguided populace in which they made him drink hemlock? Isn't this like condemning Jesus because his unique God-consciousness and never-ceasing devotion to God's will precipitated the evil act of crucifixion? We must come to see that, as the federal courts have consistently affirmed, it is wrong to urge an individual to cease his efforts to gain his basic constitutional rights because the quest may precipitate violence. Society must protect the robbed and punish the robber.

I had also hoped that the white moderate would reject the myth concerning time in relation to the struggle for freedom. I have just received a letter from a white brother in Texas. He writes: "All Christians know that the colored people will receive equal rights eventually, but it is possible that you are in too great a religious hurry. It has taken Christianity almost two thousand years to accomplish what it has. The teachings of Christ take time to come to earth." Such an attitude stems from a tragic misconception of time, from the strangely irrational notion that there is something in the very flow of time that will inevitably cure all ills. Actually, time itself is neutral; it can be used either destructively or constructively. More and more I feel that the people of ill will have used time much more effectively than have the people of good will. We will have to repent in this generation not merely for the hateful words and actions of the bad people, but for the appalling silence of the good people. Human progress never rolls in on wheels of inevitability; it comes through the tireless efforts of men willing to be co-workers with God, and without this hard work, time itself becomes an ally of the forces of social stagnation. We must use time creatively, in the knowledge that the time is always ripe to do right. Now is the time to make real the promise of democracy and transform our pending national elegy into a creative psalm of brotherhood. Now is the time to lift our national policy from the quicksand of racial injustice to the solid rock of human dignity.

You speak of our activity in Birmingham as extreme. At first I was rather disappointed that fellow clergymen would see my nonviolent efforts as those of an extremist. I began thinking about the fact that I stand in the middle of two opposing forces in the Negro community. One is a force of complacency, made up in part of Negroes who, as a result of long years of oppression, are so drained of self-respect and a sense of "somebodiness" that they have adjusted to segregation; and in part of a few middle-class Negroes who, because of a degree of academic and economic security and because in some ways they profit by segregation, have become insensitive to the problems of the masses. The other force is one of bitterness and hatred, and it comes perilously close to advocating violence. It is expressed in the various black nationalist groups that are springing up across the nation, the largest and best-known being Elijah Muhammad's Muslim movement. Nourished by the Negro's frustration over the continued existence of racial discrimination, this movement is made up of people who have lost faith in America, who have absolutely repudiated Christianity, and who have concluded that the white man is an incorrigible "devil."

I have tried to stand between these two forces, saying that we need emulate neither the "do-nothingism" of the complacent nor the hatred and despair of the black nationalist. For there is the more excellent way of love and nonviolent protest. I am grateful to God that, through the influence of the Negro church, the way of nonviolence became an integral part of our struggle.

If this philosophy had not emerged, by now many streets of the South would, I am convinced, be flowing with blood. And I am further convinced that if our white brothers dismiss as "rabblerousers" and "outside agitators" those of us who employ nonviolent direct action, and if they refuse to support our nonviolent efforts, millions of Negroes will, out of frustration and despair, seek solace and security in black-nationalist ideologies—a development that would inevitably lead to a frightening racial nightmare.

Oppressed people cannot remain oppressed forever. The yearning for freedom eventually manifests itself, and that is what has happened to the American Negro. Something within has reminded him of his birthright of freedom, and something without has reminded him that it can be gained. Consciously or unconsciously, he has been caught up by the *Zeitgeist*, and with his black brothers of Africa and his brown and yellow brothers of Asia, South America, and the Caribbean, the United States Negro is moving with a sense of great urgency toward the promised land of racial justice. If one recognizes this vital urge that has engulfed the Negro community, one should readily understand why public demonstrations are taking place. The Negro has many pent-up resentments and latent frustrations, and he must release them. So let him march; let him make prayer pilgrimages to the city hall; let him go on freedom rides—and try to understand why he must do so. If his repressed emotions are not released in nonviolent ways, they will seek expression through violence; this is not a threat but a fact of history. So I have not said to my people, "Get rid of your discontent." Rather, I have tried to say that this normal and healthy discontent can be channeled into the creative outlet of nonviolent direct action. And now this approach is being termed extremist.

But though I was initially disappointed at being categorized as an extremist, as I continued to think about the matter I gradually gained a measure of satisfaction from the label. Was not Jesus an extremist for love: "Love your enemies, bless them that curse you, do good to them that hate you, and pray for them which despitefully use you, and persecute you." Was not Amos an extremist for justice: "Let justice roll down like waters and righteousness like an ever-flowing stream." Was not Paul an extremist for the Christian gospel: "I bear in my body the marks of the Lord Jesus." Was not Martin Luther an extremist: "Here I stand; I cannot do otherwise, so help me God." And John Bunyan: "I will stay in jail to the end of my days before I make a butchery of my conscience." And Abraham Lincoln: "This nation cannot survive half slave and half free." And Thomas Jefferson: "We hold these truths to be self-evident, that all men are created equal. . . ." So the question is not whether we will be extremists, but what kind of extremists we will be. Will we be extremists for hate or for love? Will we be extremists for the preservation of injustice or for the extension of justice? In that dramatic scene on Calvary's hill three men were crucified. We must never forget that all three were crucified for the same crime—the crime of extremism. Two were extremists for immorality, and thus fell below their environment. The other, Jesus Christ, was an extremist for love, truth, and goodness, and thereby rose above his environment. Perhaps the South, the nation, and the world are in dire need of creative extremists.

I had hoped that the white moderate would see this need. Perhaps I was too optimistic; perhaps I expected too much. I suppose I should have realized that few members of the oppressor race can understand the deep groans and passionate yearnings of the oppressed race, and still fewer have the vision to see that injustice must be rooted out by strong, persistent, and determined action. I am thankful, however, that some of our white brothers in the South have grasped the meaning of this social revolution and committed themselves to it. They are still all too few in quantity, but they are big in quality. Some—such as Ralph McGill, Lillian Smith, Harry Golden, James McBridge Dabbs, Ann Braden, and Sarah Patton Boyle—have written about our struggle in eloquent and prophetic terms. Others have marched with us down nameless streets of the South. They have languished in filthy, roach-infested jails, suffering the abuse and brutality of policemen who view them as "dirty nigger-lovers." Unlike so many of their moderate brothers and sisters, they have recognized the urgency of the moment and sensed the need for powerful "action" antidotes to combat the disease of segregation.

Let me take note of my other major disappointment. I have been so greatly disappointed with the white church and its leadership. Of course, there are some notable exceptions. I am not unmindful of the fact that each of you has taken some significant stands on this issue. I commend you, Reverend Stallings, for your Christian stand on this past Sunday, in welcoming Negroes to your worship service on a non-segregated basis. I commend the Catholic leaders of this state for integrating Spring Hill College several years ago.

But despite these notable exceptions, I must honestly reiterate that I have been disappointed with the church. I do not say this as one of those negative critics who can always find something wrong with the church. I say this as a minister of the gospel, who loves the church; who was nurtured in its bosom; who has been sustained by its spiritual blessings and who will remain true to it as long as the cord of life shall lengthen.

When I was suddenly catapulted into the leadership of the bus protest in Montgomery, Alabama, a few years ago, I felt we would be supported by the white church. I felt that the white ministers, priests, and rabbis of the South would be among our strongest allies. Instead, some have been outright opponents, refusing to understand the freedom movement and misrepresenting its leaders; all too many others have been more cautious than courageous and have remained silent behind the anesthetizing security of stainedglass windows.

In spite of my shattered dreams, I came to Birmingham with the hope that the white religious leadership of this community would see the justice of our cause and, with deep moral concern, would serve as the channel through which our just grievances could reach the power structure. I had hoped that each of you would understand. But again I have been disappointed.

I have heard numerous southern religious leaders admonish their worshipers to comply with a desegregation decision because it is the law, but I have longed to hear white ministers declare: "Follow this decree because integration is morally right and because the Negro is your brother." In the midst of blatant injustices inflicted upon the Negro, I have watched white churchmen stand on the sideline and mouth pious irrelevancies and sanctimonious trivialities. In the midst of a mighty struggle to rid our nation of racial and economic injustice, I have heard many ministers say: "Those are social issues, with which the gospel has no real concern." And I have watched many churches commit themselves to a completely otherworldly religion which makes a strange, un-Biblical distinction between body and soul, between the sacred and the secular.

I have traveled the length and breadth of Alabama, Mississippi, and all the other southern states. On sweltering summer days and crisp autumn mornings I have looked at the South's beautiful churches with their lofty spires pointing heavenward. I have beheld the impressive outlines of her massive religious-education buildings. Over and over I have found myself asking: "What kind of people worship here? Who is their God? Where were their voices when the lips of Governor Barnett dripped with words of interposition and nullification? Where were they when Governor Wallace gave a clarion call for defiance and hatred? Where were their voices of support when bruised and weary Negro men and women decided to rise from the dark dungeons of complacency to the bright hills of creative protest?"

Yes, these questions are still in my mind. In deep disappointment I have wept over the laxity of the church. But be assured that my tears have been tears of love. There can be no deep disappointment where there is not deep love. Yes, I love the church. How could I do otherwise? I am in the rather unique position of being the son, the grandson, and the great-grandson of preachers. Yes, I see the church as the body of Christ. But, oh! How we have blemished and scarred that body through social neglect and through fear of being nonconformists.

There was a time when the church was very powerful—in the time when the early Christians rejoiced at being deemed worthy to suffer for what they believed. In those days the church was not merely a thermometer that recorded the ideas and principles of popular opinion; it was a thermostat that transformed the mores of society. Whenever the early Christians entered a town, the people in power became disturbed and immediately sought to convict the Christians for being "disturbers of the peace" and "outside agitators." But the Christians pressed on, in the conviction that they were "a colony of heaven," called to obey God rather than man. Small in number, they were big in commitment. They were too God-intoxicated to be "astronomically intimidated." By their effort and example they brought an end to such ancient evils as infanticide and gladiatorial contests.

Things are different now. So often the contemporary church is a weak, ineffectual voice with an uncertain sound. So often it is an archdefender of the status quo. Far from being disturbed by the presence of the church, the power structure of the average community is consoled by the church's silent—and often even vocal—sanction of things as they are.

But the judgment of God is upon the church as never before. If today's church does not recapture the sacrificial spirit of the early church, it will lose its authenticity, forfeit the loyalty of millions, and be dismissed as an irrelevant social club with no meaning for the twentieth century. Every day I meet young people whose disappointment with the church has turned into outright disgust.

Perhaps I have once again been too optimistic. Is organized religion too inextricably bound to the status quo to save our nation and the world? Perhaps I must turn my faith to the inner spiritual church, the church within the church, as the true *ekklesia* and the hope of the world. But again I am thankful to God that some noble souls from the ranks of organized religion have broken loose from the paralyzing chains of conformity and joined us as active partners in the struggle for freedom. They have left their secure congregations and walked the streets of Albany, Georgia, with us. They have gone down the highways of the South on tortuous rides for freedom. Yes, they have gone to jail with us. Some have been dismissed from their churches, have lost the support of their bishops and fellow ministers. But they have acted in the faith that right defeated is stronger than evil triumphant. Their witness has been the spiritual salt that has preserved the true meaning of the gospel in these troubled times. They have carved a tunnel of hope through the dark mountain of disappointment.

I hope the church as a whole will meet the challenge of this decisive hour. But even if the church does not come to the aid of justice, I have no despair about the future. I have no fear about the outcome of our struggle in Birmingham, even if our motives are at present misunderstood. We will reach the goal of freedom in Birmingham and all over the nation, because the goal of America is freedom. Abused and scorned though we may be, our destiny is tied up with America's destiny. Before the pilgrims landed at Plymouth, we were here. Before the pen of Jefferson etched the majestic words of the Declaration of Independence across the pages of history, we were here. For more than two centuries our forebears labored in this country without wages: they made cotton king; they built the homes of their masters while suffering gross injustice and shameful humiliation—and yet out of a bottomless vitality they continued to thrive and develop. If the inexpressible cruelties of slavery could not stop us, the opposition we now face will surely fail. We will win our freedom because the sacred heritage of our nation and the eternal will of God are embodied in our echoing demands.

Before closing I feel impelled to mention one other point in your statement that has troubled me profoundly. You warmly commended the Birmingham police force for keeping "order" and "preventing violence." I doubt that you would have so warmly commended the police force if you had seen its dogs sinking their teeth into unarmed, nonviolent Negroes. I doubt that you would so quickly commend the policemen if you were to observe their ugly and inhumane treatment of Negroes here in the city jail; if you were to watch them push and curse old Negro women and young Negro girls; if you were to see them slap and kick old Negro men and young boys; if you were to observe them, as they did on two occasions, refuse to give us food because we wanted to sing our grace together. I cannot join you in your praise of the Birmingham police department.

It is true that the police have exercised a degree of discipline in handling the demonstrators. In this sense they have conducted themselves rather "nonviolently" in public. But for what purpose? To preserve the evil system of segregation. Over the past few years I have consistently preached that nonviolence demands that the means we use must be as pure as the ends we seek. I have tried to make clear that it is wrong to use immoral means to attain moral ends. But now I must affirm that it is just as wrong, or perhaps even more so, to use moral means to preserve immoral ends. Perhaps Mr. Connor and his policemen have been rather nonviolent in public, as was Chief Pritchett in Albany, Georgia, but they have used the moral means of nonviolence to maintain the immoral end of racial injustice. As T. S. Eliot has said. "The last temptation is the greatest treason: To do the right deed for the wrong reason."

I wish you had commended the Negro sit-inners and demonstrators of Birmingham for their sublime courage, their willingness to suffer, and their amazing discipline in the midst of great provocation. One day the South will recognize its real heroes. They will be the James Merediths, with the noble sense of purpose that enables them to face jeering and hostile mobs, and with the agonizing loneliness that characterizes the life of the pioneer. They will be old, oppressed, battered Negro women, symbolized in a seventy-two-year-old woman in Montgomery, Alabama, who rose up with a sense of dignity and with her people decided not to ride segregated buses, and who responded with ungrammatical profundity to one who inquired about her weariness: "My feets is tired, but my soul is at rest." They will be the young high school and college students, the young ministers of the gospel and a host of their elders, courageously and nonviolently sitting in at lunch counters and willingly going to jail for conscience' sake. One day the South will know that when these disinherited children of God sat down at lunch counters, they were in reality standing up for what is best in the American dream and for the most sacred values in our Judaeo-Christian heritage, thereby bringing our nation back to those great wells of democracy which were dug deep by the founding fathers in their formulation of the Constitution and the Declaration of Independence.

Never before have I written so long a letter. I'm afraid it is much too long to take your precious time. I can assure you that it would have been much shorter if I had been writing from a comfortable desk, but what else can one do when he is alone in a narrow jail cell, other than write long letters, think long thoughts, and pray long prayers?

If I have said anything in this letter that overstates the truth and indicates an unreasonable impatience, I beg you to forgive me. If I have said anything that understates the truth and indicates my having a patience that allows me to settle for anything less than brotherhood, I beg God to forgive me.

I hope this letter finds you strong in the faith. I also hope that circumstances will soon make it possible for me to meet each of you, not as an integrationist or a civil-rights leader but as a fellow clergyman and a Christian brother. Let us all hope that the dark clouds of racial prejudice will soon pass away and the deep fog of misunderstanding will be lifted from our fear-drenched communities, and in some not too distant tomorrow the radiant stars of love and brotherhood will shine over our great nation with all their scintillating beauty.

Yours for the cause of Peace and Brotherhood,
Martin Luther King, Jr.
—1963

Questions: Reading, Responding, Arguing

1. King connects the actions of Paul, and Jesus, to his own activities in Birmingham. What other Biblical associations or references can be found in the letter?
2. How does King define "tension" and what place does he see for it in political activity?
3. Explain why the argument to "Wait!" is unsatisfactory to King.
4. To whom is this letter addressed and what is its argumentative purpose?

Robert Flynn (b. 1932)

John Wayne Must Die

When I was young, I saw a lot of John Wayne. I watched him kill a lot of people. All of them bad, most of them Indians. He was also pretty good at killing Japanese, but not so good at killing Germans. John Wayne didn't die. Heroes never die. Not in the movies.

When I was in Marine boot camp they showed us John Wayne movies. In Marine boot camp you couldn't leave the base, you couldn't go to the PX, you couldn't buy soft drinks, ice cream, or candy. You couldn't have cigarettes, beer, or women. Instead, we had John Wayne. Usually, he wore a Marine uniform and killed a lot of Japanese.

An eighteen-year-old Marine boot is one of the dumbest things on earth. We didn't think catsup was a vegetable; catsup was an hors d'oeuvre. As a eighteen-year-old boot I didn't understand why we had to use the atomic bomb when we had John Wayne. He could kill as many Japanese as anyone could enjoy seeing die. And he didn't cost much more than the research and development of the atomic bomb. Not if you threw in the research and development of the B-29.

And John Wayne didn't die.

John Wayne didn't do much in Korea. Killing Indians paid better. And John Wayne didn't die.

After Korea, John and I went our separate ways. I was busy going to school, getting married, starting a career. I didn't have time for movies. I didn't see "The Alamo." I don't know how he got out of that one.

John Wayne had his own problems in Vietnam. He killed a lot of Viet Cong but no one enjoyed it. At the drive-in a few people cheered, but they were blowing grass and thought he was killing Indians. The Viet Cong had a Benevolent and Protective Society in Berkeley and other schools of thought. The Japanese didn't have a Benevolent and Protective Society but they had Toyotas. And yen. So John went back to killing Indians. Nobody cared about Indians.

John Wayne didn't die.

John also killed some bad men. They were so bad that watching them curl up and croak was almost as pleasurable as watching the Japanese fry or seeing gut-shot Indians run over by their own horses before being scalped by Christians. Bad men weren't massacred. They died one by one, like men. There was a Benevolent and Protective Society for bad men.

John Wayne didn't kill women. No need to. Some things were lower than Indians. John Wayne didn't marry them either. He wasn't afraid of bad women, although good women gave him a scare or two. Nothing scarier than a good woman when she was breathy and in heat. John Wayne put women in their place. A little higher than a coyote. A little lower than a dead horse.

But John Wayne didn't die.

John Wayne became the hero of America, replacing such impostors as Lindbergh, Clarence Darrow, Albert Einstein, Audie Murphy, William

Faulkner. He became the icon of the west, replacing such impostors as Sam Houston, Chief Joseph, Teddy Roosevelt, Bill Haywood, Will Rogers.

John Wayne was spit and image of the American hero. He was tougher than a longhorn steak until real bullets flew. He was meaner than a side-winder if someone sat on his hat, beat his woman or was discourteous to a horse. But only on film.

John Wayne was charmingly inarticulate. He had only twelve words in his vocabulary other than Winchester, six-shooter, kill, shoot, maim, horse, dog and pilgrim. Six of the remaining words were conjugations of "Wal." Don Quixote may have been addled but he wasn't incoherent. In the theater, even heroes have to speak. In novels, even stupid men have to be able to think. It took movies to give us "yep" heroes. Movies started out silent. They remained dumb; they just added sound.

John Wayne didn't need nobody. He didn't ask favors. He didn't take handouts. He pulled himself up by his own six-shooters.

John Wayne had no self-doubts. His opinion was right and you were welcome to your own as long as it agreed with his. He was on the right road, headed in the right direction and if you didn't get out of his way he'd kill you. Or maybe just maim you if you had made an honest mistake. He sometimes let women and children live. And he didn't die.

John Wayne never broke a sweat for daily bread, toiled at a repetitive and humbling job for minimum wage, or was gainfully employed, except at killing people. His only skill was violence, but it was the skill most honored and most envied by his countrymen. And he didn't die.

John Wayne loved freedom. The freedom to go wherever he wanted to go, do whatever he wanted to do, and kill anyone who wanted the same. He was the quickest to violence. Always. Leaving slower men dead in the street.

Wayne had values. Good horses. Good dogs. Good whiskey. Good violence. He hated bad violence and killed bad-violent men. He was more violent than anyone, but he killed only those he thought needed killing. He had a code that permitted no extenuating circumstances and no exceptions. Except himself.

John Wayne was innocent. No matter how many people he killed, or how much pleasure or satisfaction he got out of it, he maintained innocence about the whole bloody business. Wal, sure, some good men died too. And some women were caught in the crossfire. And some babies. Some babies always die. But when you look up there and see old glory waving in the breeze, high up there, on top of the Savings and

Loan Building, it makes you wish the taxpayers weren't so gol darned cheap and had given you a few more bullets to waste. Someone with.

John Wayne didn't lose. Right means might so John Wayne couldn't lose. John Wayne wasn't at Wake Island or Corregidor because John Wayne didn't lose. He left Vietnam early.

I didn't see "The Alamo." I don't know how he got out of that. Travis died. Crockett and Bowie died. John Wayne didn't die. I've been to the Alamo. I know that John Wayne is in there somewhere. And he's alive.

John Wayne didn't die. His spirit transcended him, passed into the souls of Americans everywhere. The story that St. John bodily ascended into heaven is probably not true. John Wayne passed into the spirit of Americans who died in Beirut, Grenada, Nicaragua, Libya, Panama, Iran, Iraq. John Wayne didn't die.

John gave us the stories that tell us how to be men when women and children don't measure up to our standards for them. When other men don't get out of the way of our ambitions. When teachers, parents or peers try to fence in our egos. When inferiors pretend they have the same rights we have.

St. John taught us, big and powerful is good. Small and weak is bad and must be killed. Or at least, exploited.

St. John taught us that a man should take everything he can get, and the quickest way to get it is with a gun.

St. John taught us that the fastest to the trigger is the hero.

John Wayne lives in the souls of those who believe bullets speak louder than words, who believe a gun, a quick draw and a steady aim are the only Bill of Rights you'll ever need.

John Wayne must die.

—2001

Questions: Reading, Responding, Arguing

1. John Wayne is the satiric focus of the essay, but what is the real target of Flynn's satire?

2. Flynn repeats "John Wayne didn't die" several times throughout the essay. What is the effect of this repetition?

3. Flynn deliberately uses incorrect grammar and writes in sentence fragments several times in the essay. How does this writing style relate to the topic being argued?

Hendrik Hertzberg   (b. 1943)

Bah Humbug

Chestnuts are roasting on an open fire, with Jack Frost nipping at your nose and folks dressed up like Eskimos—or, to update the line for political correctness, with tots in boots just like Aleuts. It's that magical season when lights twinkle and good will abounds. It's time again for the thrill that comes but once a year: the War on Christmas.

The War on Christmas is a little like Santa Claus, in that it (a) comes to us from the sky, beamed down by the satellites of cable news, and (b) does not, in the boringly empirical sense, exist. What does exist is the idea of the War on Christmas, which, though forever new, is a venerable tradition, older even than strip malls and plastic mistletoe. Christmas itself, in something like its recognizably modern form, with gifts and cards and elves, dates from the early nineteenth century. The War on Christmas seems to have come along around a hundred years later, with the publication of "The International Jew," by Henry Ford, the automobile magnate, whom fate later punished by arranging to have his fortune diverted to the sappy, do-gooder Ford Foundation. "It is not religious tolerance in the midst of religious difference, but religious attack that they"—the Jews—"preach and practice," he wrote. "The whole record of the Jewish opposition to Christmas, Easter and certain patriotic songs shows that." Ford's anti-Semitism has not aged well, thanks to the later excesses of its European adherents, but by drawing a connection between Christmasbashing and patriotism-scorning he pointed the way for future Christmas warriors.

Over the next few decades, when the country was preoccupied with the Depression, the Second World War, and going to movies like "It's a Wonderful Life," the W. on C. went into remission. But at the end of the placid nineteen-fifties the John Birch Society, a pioneering organization of the bug-eyed right, took up the Yuletide cudgels. As Michelle Goldberg recalled recently in *Salon*, a 1959 Birch pamphlet warned that "the Reds" and "the U.N. fanatics" had launched an "assault on Christmas" as "part of a much broader plan, not only to promote the U.N., but to destroy *all* religious beliefs and customs." The enemy's strategy, the Birchers warned, was to aim at the soft underbelly and shake it like a bowlful of jelly. "What they now want to put over on the American people is simply this: Department stores throughout the country are to utilize U.N. symbols and emblems as Christmas decorations." The focus on department stores was a prophetic insight, but its full potential as a weapon in Christmas war-fighting was not realized until the next century.

Today's Christmas Pentagon is the Fox News Channel, which during a recent five-day period carried no fewer than fifty-eight different segments about the ongoing struggle, some of them labeled "CHRIST-MAS UNDER ATTACK." One of Fox's on-air warriors is John Gibson, whose new book, "The War on Christmas: How the Liberal Plot to Ban the Sacred Christian Holiday Is Worse Than You Thought," presents itself as the definitive word. So one opens it eagerly with hopes of learning what this war actually consists of. These hopes are soon dashed—or, rather, fulfilled, since it turns out to consist of very little. Gibson provides a half-dozen or so anecdotes, padded out to stupefying length, in which a school board or a city hall renames its Christmas break a winter break or declines to rename its winter break a Christmas break, or removes Christmas trees from the lobbies of government buildings and then restores them after people complain. "The war on Christmas," the author concludes triumphantly, "is joined."

Gibson is a mere grunt in Fox's army. Bill O'Reilly, the network's most prominent religio-political commentator, is its Patton. The shortage of anti-Christmas atrocities (plus the fact that the U.N. fanatics long ago switched to subverting Halloween) may explain why he has concentrated on department stores, many of which, in their ads or via their salespeople, wish people "Happy Holidays" instead of—or in addition to, or more frequently than—"Merry Christmas." (In 1921, Henry Ford attacked from the opposite flank, sneering that "the strange inconsistency of it all is to see the great department stores of the Levys and the Isaacs and the Goldsteins and the Silvermans filled with brilliant Christmas cheer.")

O'Reilly sat out Vietnam. In the war on the War on Christmas, however, he not only has been in the trenches but has gone over the top. "I am not going to let oppressive, totalitarian, anti-Christian forces in this country diminish and denigrate the holiday!" he said the other day. And "I'm going to use all the power that I have on radio and television to bring horror into the world of people who are trying to do that!" And, "There is no reason on this earth that all of us cannot celebrate a public holiday devoted to generosity, peace, and love together!" And, "And anyone who tries to stop us from doing it is gonna face me!"

O'Reilly sees the War on Christmas as part of the "secular progressive agenda," because "if you can get religion out, then you can pass secular progressive programs like legalization of narcotics, euthanasia, abortion at will, gay marriage." Just as Christmas itself evolved as a way to synthesize a variety of winter festivals, so the War on Christmas fantasy is a way of grouping together a variety of enemies, where they can all be rhetorically machine-gunned at once. But the suspicion remains that a truer explanation for Fox's militancy may be, like so much else at Yuletide, business. Christmas is the big retail season. What Fox retails is resentment.

In this war, no weapons of Christmas destruction have been found—just a few caches of linguistic oversensitivity and commercial caution. Christmas remains robust: even Gibson says in his book that in America Christmas celebrators (ninety-six percent) outnumber Christians (eighty-four percent). But the "Happy Holidays" contagion has probably spread too far to be wiped out. "President Bush and I wish everyone a very happy holiday," Laura Bush says sweetly on a video posted on the White House Web site. And even the Fox News online store advertised, until a couple of weeks ago, "The O'Reilly Factor Holiday Ornament." ("Put your holiday tree in 'The No Spin Zone.'")

John Lennon, who died in this city, at this season, twenty-five years ago, didn't bother with "Happy Holidays" and the like. In 1971, he and his wife, Yoko Ono, wrote and recorded a song that has become a classic. Here's its final verse:

A very Merry Christmas
And a happy New Year
Let's hope it's a good one
Without any fear
War is over, if you want it
War is over now.

That's the spirit, John. You bet we want it. And Merry Christmas to all.

—*2001*

Questions: Reading, Responding, Arguing

1. Explain how Hertzberg understands the "War on Christmas." Does he think it is a real war?
2. Explain Hertzberg's use of military terminology in the essay. Is he serious or satiric in his application of military language?
3. The essay ends with a quote from John Lennon. How does this quote relate to the rest of the article?
4. What is the central argument of Hertzberg's essay?

Slavoj Žižek (b. 1949)

Welcome to the Desert of the Real!

SEPTEMBER 17, 2001

The ultimate American paranoiac fantasy is that of an individual living in a small idyllic Californian city, a consumerist paradise, who suddenly starts to suspect that the world he lives in is a fake, a spectacle staged to convince him that he lives in a real world, while all people around him are effectively actors and extras in a gigantic show. The most recent example of this is Peter Weir's *The Truman Show* (1998), with Jim Carrey playing the small town clerk who gradually discovers the truth that he is the hero of a 24-hours permanent TV show: his hometown is constructed on a gigantic studio set, with cameras following him permanently. Among its predecessors, it is worth mentioning Philip Dick's *Time Out of Joint* (1959), in which a hero living a modest daily life in a small idyllic Californian city of the late 50s, gradually discovers that the whole town is a fake staged to keep him satisfied. . . The underlying experience of *Time Out of Joint* and of *The Truman Show* is that the late capitalist consumerist Californian paradise is, in its very hyper-reality, in a way IRREAL, substanceless, deprived of the material inertia.

So it is not only that Hollywood stages a semblance of real life deprived of the weight and inertia of materiality—in the late capitalist consumerist society, "real social life" itself somehow acquires the features of a staged fake, with our neighbors behaving in "real" life as stage actors and extras. . . Again, the ultimate truth of the capitalist utilitarian de-spiritualized universe is the de-materialization of the "real life" itself, its reversal into a spectral show. Among them, Christopher Isherwood gave expression to this unreality of the American daily life, exemplified in the motel room: "American motels are unreal! /. . ./ they are deliberately designed to be unreal. /. . ./ The Europeans hate us because we've retired to live inside our advertisements, like hermits going into caves to contemplate." Peter Sloterdijk's notion of the "sphere" is here literally realized, as the gigantic metal sphere that envelopes and isolates the entire city. Years ago, a series of science-fiction films like *Zardoz* or *Logan's Run* forecasted today's postmodern predicament by extending this fantasy to the community itself: the isolated group living an aseptic life in a secluded area longs for the experience of the real world of material decay.

The Wachowski brothers' hit *Matrix* (1999) brought this logic to its climax: the material reality we all experience and see around us is a virtual one, generated and coordinated by a gigantic mega-computer to which we are all attached; when the hero (played by Keanu Reeves) awakens into the "real reality," he sees a desolate landscape littered with burned ruins—what remained of Chicago after a global war. The resistance leader Morpheus utters the ironic greeting: "Welcome to the desert of the real." Was it not something of the similar order that took place in New York on September 11? Its citizens were introduced to the "desert of the real"—to us, corrupted by Hollywood, the landscape and the shots we saw of the collapsing towers could not but remind us of the most breathtaking scenes in the catastrophe big productions.

When we hear how the bombings were a totally unexpected shock, how the unimaginable Impossible happened, one should recall the other defining catastrophe from the beginning of the XXth century, that of Titanic: it was also a shock, but the space for it was already prepared in ideological fantasizing, since Titanic was the symbol of the might of the XIXth century industrial civilization. Does the same not hold also for these bombings? Not only were the media bombarding us all the time with the talk about the terrorist threat; this threat was also obviously libidinally invested—just recall the series of movies from *Escape From New York* to *Independence Day*. The unthinkable which happened was thus the object of fantasy: in a way, America got what it fantasized about, and this was the greatest surprise.

It is precisely now, when we are dealing with the raw Real of a catastrophe, that we should bear in mind the ideological and fantasmatic coordinates which determine its perception. If there is any symbolism in the collapse of the WTC towers, it is not so much the old-fashioned notion of the "center of financial capitalism," but, rather, the notion that the two WTC towers stood for the center of the VIRTUAL capitalism, of financial speculations disconnected from the sphere of material production. The shattering impact of the bombings can only be accounted for only against the background of the borderline which today separates the digitalized First World from the Third World "desert of the Real." It is the awareness that we live in an insulated artificial universe which generates the notion that some ominous agent is threatening us all the time with total destruction.

Is, consequently, Osama Bin Laden, the suspected mastermind behind the bombings, not the real-life counterpart of Ernst Stavro Blofeld, the master-criminal in most of the James Bond films, involved in the acts of global destruction. What one should recall here is that the only place in Hollywood films where we see the production process in all its intensity is when James Bond penetrates the master-criminal's secret domain and locates there the site of intense labor (distilling and packaging the drugs, constructing a rocket that will destroy New York. . .). When the master-criminal, after capturing Bond, usually takes him on a tour of his illegal factory, is this not the closest Hollywood comes to the socialist-realist proud presentation of the production in a factory? And the function of Bond's intervention, of course, is to explode in firecraks this site of production, allowing us to return to the daily semblance of our existence in a world with the "disappearing working class." Is it not that, in the exploding WTC towers, this violence directed at the threatening Outside turned back at us? The safe Sphere in which Americans live is experienced as under threat from the Outside of terrorist attackers who are ruthlessly self-sacrificing AND cowards, cunningly intelligent AND primitive barbarians. Whenever we encounter such a purely evil Outside, we should gather the courage to endorse the Hegelian lesson: in this pure Outside, we should recognize the distilled version of our own essence. For the last five centuries, the (relative) prosperity and peace of the "civilized" West was bought by the export of ruthless violence and destruction into the "barbarian" Outside: the long story from the conquest of America to the slaughter in Congo. Cruel and indifferent as it may sound, we should also, now more than ever, bear in mind that the actual effect of these bombings is much more symbolic than real. The US just got the taste of what goes on around the world on a daily basis, from Sarajevo to Grozny, from Rwanda and Congo to Sierra Leone. If one adds to the situation in New York snipers and gang rapes, one gets an idea about what Sarajevo was a decade ago.

It is when we watched on TV screen the two WTC towers collapsing, that it became possible to experience the falsity of the "reality TV shows": even if this shows are "for real," people still act in them—they simply play themselves. The standard disclaimer in a novel ("characters in this text are a fiction, every resemblance with the real life characters is purely contingent") holds also for the participants of the reality soaps: what we see there are fictional characters, even if they play themselves for the real. Of course, the "return to the Real" can be given different twists: Rightist commentators like George Will also immediately proclaimed the end of the American "holiday from history"—the impact of reality shattering the isolated tower of the liberal tolerant attitude and the Cultural Studies focus on textuality. Now, we are forced to strike back, to deal with real enemies in the real world. . . However, WHOM to strike? Whatever the response, it will never hit the RIGHT target, bringing us full satisfaction. The ridicule of America attacking Afghanistan cannot but strike the eye: if the greatest power in the world will destroy one of the poorest countries in which peasants barely survive on barren hills, will this not be the ultimate case of the impotent acting out?

There is a partial truth in the notion of the "clash of civilizations" attested here—witness the surprise of the average American: "How is it possible that these people have such a disregard for their own lives?" Is not the obverse of this surprise the rather sad fact that we, in the First World countries, find it more and more difficult even to imagine a public or universal Cause for which one would be ready to sacrifice one's life? When, after the bombings, even the Taliban foreign minister said that he can "feel the pain" of the American children, did he not thereby confirm the hegemonic ideological role of this Bill Clinton's trademark phrase? Furthermore, the notion of America as a safehaven, of course, also is a fantasy: when a New Yorker commented on how, after the bombings, one can no longer walk safely on the city's streets, the irony of it was that, well before the bombings, the streets of New York were well-known for the dangers of being attacked or, at least, mugged—if anything, the bombings gave rise to a new sense of solidarity, with the scenes of young African-Americans helping an old Jewish gentlemen to cross the street, scenes unimaginable a couple of days ago.

Now, in the days immediately following the bombings, it is as if we dwell in the unique time between a traumatic event and its symbolic impact, like in those brief moments after we are deeply cut, and before the full extent of the pain strikes us—it is open how the events will be symbolized, what their symbolic efficiency will be, what acts they will be evoked to justify. Even here, in these moments of utmost tension, this link is not automatic but contingent. There are already the first bad omens; the day after the bombing, I got a message from a journal which was just about to publish a longer text of mine on Lenin, telling me that they decided to postpone its publication—they considered inopportune to publish a text on Lenin immediately after the bombing. Does this not point towards the ominous ideological rearticulations which will follow?

We don't yet know what consequences in economy, ideology, politics, war, this event will have, but one thing is sure: the US, which, till now, perceived itself as an island exempted from this kind of violence, witnessing this kind of things only from the safe distance of the TV screen, is now directly involved. So the alternative is: will Americans decide to fortify further their "sphere," or to risk stepping out of it? Either America will persist in, strengthen even, the attitude of "Why should this happen to us? Things like this don't happen HERE!", leading to more aggressivity towards the threatening Outside, in short: to a paranoiac acting out. Or America will finally risk stepping through the fantasmatic screen separating it from the Outside World, accepting its arrival into the Real world, making the long-overdued move from "A thing like this should not happen HERE!" to "A thing like this should not happen ANYWHERE!" America's "holiday from history" was a fake: America's peace was bought by the catastrophes going on elsewhere. Therein resides the true lesson of the bombings: the only way to ensure that it will not happen HERE again is to prevent it going on ANYWHERE ELSE.

—2001

Questions: Reading, Responding, Arguing

1. Žižek mentions several cinematic examples of "unreal" life in his opening paragraphs. Are there other examples that could compare to Žižek's? How do they relate?
2. The essay compares the 9/11 terrorist attacks to the sinking of the *Titanic*. How are the two related?
3. Explain Žižek's argument against attacking Afghanistan.
4. Žižek's article was written six days after the terrorist attacks. How accurately has he predicted the American response to the attacks? Is his prediction still valid?

Jules Feiffer (b. 1929)

Perfection

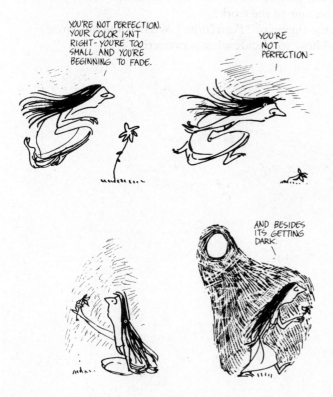

—1958

Questions: Reading, Responding, Arguing

1. How much of the story is told from the illustrations? How much from the actual written text?
2. What direction is the woman facing in different panels? Would changing her direction change the message?
3. How do the pictures of the sun and the moon relate to the overall message of the work?
4. Explain the theme of "Perfection." What is the author saying about how we decide what is perfect?

Where We Stand

The Individual and the Institution

"Whatever my individual desires were to be free, I was not
alone. There were many others who felt the same way."

—Rosa Parks

Some of the earliest writings of humanity reveal the attempts
of individuals to create laws and governing bodies to enforce
those laws—a struggle to find the optimal system for organizing and maintaining the collective lives of people. Until a
perfect system of government is developed, individuals will
always have some dissatisfaction with institutions such as
schools, companies, and governing bodies that surround, and
to some degree control, their actions. Therein lies the paradox of institutions: We create and support them because they
help us—police officers keep criminals off the streets, banks
hold our money in convenient locations—but they also serve
as a nuisance, or problem—police officers give us speeding
tickets, and banks charge us a fee just to get *our own money*
out of the ATM.

The selections in "Where We Stand" all reflect a relationship between the individual and the institution. Some of the
ways that institutions influence us are obvious, such as in a
time of war when the individual desire for self-preservation is
at obvious loggerheads with institutional needs to recruit for
the military to defend the nation. But the negotiation between the individual and the institution doesn't have to be so
obvious. We encounter institutions every day, as soon as we
get up in the morning. The desire to catch a few extra minutes of sleep is thwarted by an institutional demand that we

get to work or class on time. Even standing in front of the mirror and combing our hair is a reflection (literally) of our conformity to institutional demands of beauty and cleanliness, reinforced by countless corporations who sell combs and hair gel, by the dentist who told us to brush our teeth (and the schools that trained her), or even by the "institution" of the family; our parents, for example, spent years of our childhood putting clothes on us and sending us off to school when we would rather have been playing in the backyard. Given the pervasive nature of institutional demands upon our time and upon our lives, it is unlikely that we will resolve the complications of these relationships anytime soon, but the selections of this chapter can help us think about how institutions influence us, and the consequences both of rejecting them, and acceding to their demands.

> "Whoso would be a man must be a non-conformist."
> —Ralph Waldo Emerson, *Self-Reliance*

Franz Kafka (1883–1924)

A Hunger Artist

Translated by Willa and Edwin Muir

During these last decades the interest in professional fasting has markedly diminished. It used to pay very well to stage such great performances under one's own management, but today that is quite impossible. We live in a different world now. At one time the whole town took a lively interest in the hunger artist; from day to day of his fast the excitement mounted; everybody wanted to see him at least once a day; there were people who bought season tickets for the last few days and sat from morning till night in front of his small barred cage; even in the nighttime there were visiting hours, when the whole effect was heightened by torch flares; on fine days the cage was set out in the open air, and then it was the children's special treat to see the hunger artist; for their elders he was often just a joke that happened to be in fashion, but the children stood open mouthed, holding each other's hands for greater security, marveling at him as he sat there pallid in black tights, with his ribs sticking out so prominently, not even on a seat but down among straw on the ground, sometimes giving a courteous nod, answering questions with a constrained smile, or perhaps stretching an arm through the bars so that one might feel how thin it was, and then again withdrawing deep into himself, paying no attention to anyone or anything, not even to the all-important striking of the clock that was the only piece of furniture in his cage, but merely staring into vacancy with half-shut eyes, now and then taking a sip from a tiny glass of water to moisten his lips.

Besides casual onlookers there were also relays of permanent watchers selected by the public, usually butchers, strangely enough, and it was their task to watch the hunger artist day and night, three of them at a time, in case he should have some secret recourse to nourishment. This was nothing but a formality, instituted to reassure the masses, for the initiates knew well enough that during his fast the artist would never in any circumstances, not even under forcible compulsion, swallow the smallest morsel of food; the honor of his profession forbade it. Not every watcher, of course, was capable of understanding this, there were often groups of night watchers who were very lax in carrying out their duties and deliberately huddled together in a retired corner to play cards with great absorption, obviously intending to give the hunger artist the chance of a little refreshment, which they supposed he could draw from some private hoard. Nothing annoyed the artist more than such watchers; they made him miserable; they made his fast seem unendurable; sometimes he mastered his feebleness sufficiently to sing during their watch for as long as he could keep going, to show them just how unjust their suspicions were. But that was of little use; they only wondered at his cleverness in being able to fill his mouth even while singing. Much more to his taste were the watchers who sat close up to the bars, who were not content with the dim night lighting of the hall but focused him in the full glare of the electric pocket torch given them by the impresario. The harsh light did not trouble him at all, in any case he could never sleep properly, and he could always drowse a little, whatever the light, at any hour, even when the hall was thronged with noisy onlookers. He was quite happy at the prospect of spending a sleepless night with such watchers; he was ready to exchange jokes with them, to tell them stories out of his nomadic life, anything at all to keep them awake and demonstrate to them again that he had no eatables in his cage and that he was fasting as not one of them could fast. But his happiest moment was when the morning came and an enormous breakfast was brought them, at his expense, on which they flung themselves with the keen appetite of healthy men after a weary night of wakefulness. Of course there were people who argued that this breakfast was an unfair attempt to bribe the watchers, but that was going rather too far, and when they were invited to take on a night's vigil without a breakfast, merely for the sake of the cause, they made themselves scarce, although they struck stubbornly to their suspicions.

Such suspicions, anyhow, were a necessary accompaniment to the profession of fasting. No one could possibly watch the hunger artist continuously, day and night, and so no one could produce first-hand evidence that the fast had really been rigorous and continuous; only the artist himself could know that, he was therefore bound to be the sole completely satisfied spectator of his own fast. Yet for other reasons he was never satisfied; it was not perhaps mere fasting that had brought him to such skeleton thinness that many people had regretfully to keep away from his exhibitions, because the sight of him was too much for them, perhaps it was dissatisfaction with himself that had worn him down. For he alone knew, what no other initiate knew, how easy it was to fast. It was the easiest thing in the world. He made no secret of this, yet people did not believe him, at the best they set him down as modest, most of them however, thought he was out for publicity or else was some kind of cheat who found it easy to fast because he had discovered a way of making it easy, and then had the impudence to admit the fact, more or less. He had to put up with all that, and in the course of time had got used to it, but his inner dissatisfaction always rankled, and never yet, after any term of fasting— this must be granted to his credit—had he left the cage of his own free will. The longest period of fasting was fixed by his impresario at forty days, beyond that term he was not allowed to go, not even in great cities, and there was good reason for it, too. Experience had proved that for forty days the interest of the public could be stimulated by a steadily increasing pressure of advertisement, but after that the town began to lose interest, sympathetic support began notably to fall off; there were of course local variations as between one town and another or one country and another, but as a general rule forty days marked the limit. So on the fortieth day the flower-bedecked cage was opened, enthusiastic spectators filled the hall, a military band played, two doctors entered the cage to measure the results of the fast, which were announced through a megaphone, and finally two young ladies appeared blissful at having been selected for the honor, to help the hunger artist down the few steps leading to a small table on which was spread a carefully chosen invalid repast. And at this very moment the artist always turned stubborn. True, he would entrust his bony arms to the outstretched helping hands of the ladies bending over him, but stand up he would not. Why stop fasting at this particular moment, after forty days of it? He had held out for a long time, an illimitably long time; why stop now, when he was in his best fasting form, or rather, not yet quite in his best fasting form? Why should he be cheated of the fame he would get for fasting longer, for being not only the record hunger artist of all time, which presumably he was already, but for beating his own record by a performance beyond human imagination, since he felt that there were no limits to his capacity for fasting? His public pretended to admire him so much, why should it have so little patience with him; if he could endure fasting longer, why shouldn't the public endure it? Besides, he was tired, he was comfortable sitting in the straw, and now he was supposed to lift himself to his full height and go down to a meal the very thought of which gave him a nausea that only the presence of the ladies kept him from betraying, and even that with an effort. And he looked up into the eyes of the ladies who were apparently so friendly and in reality so cruel, and shook his head, which felt too heavy on its strengthless neck. But then there happened yet again what always happened. The impresario came forward, without a word—for the band made speech impossible—lifted his arms in the air above the artist, as if inviting Heaven to look down upon its creature here in the straw, this suffering martyr, which indeed he was, although in quite another sense; grasped him around the emaciated waist, with exaggerated caution, so that the frail condition he was in might be appreciated; and committed him to the care of the blenching ladies, not without secretly giving him a shaking so that his legs and body tottered and swayed. The artist now submitted completely; his head lolled on his breast as if it had landed there by chance; his body was hollowed out; his legs in a spasm of self-preservation clung close to each other at the knees, yet scraped on the ground as if it were not really solid ground, as if they were only trying to find solid ground; and the whole weight of his body, a featherweight after all, relapsed onto one of the ladies, who, looking around for help and panting a little—this post of honor was not at all what she had expected it to be—first stretched her neck as far as she could to keep her face at least free from contact with the artist, then finding this impossible, and her more fortunate companion not coming to her aid but merely holding extended in her own trembling hand the little bunch of knucklebones that was the artist's, to the great delight of the spectators burst into tears and had to be replaced by an attendant who had long been stationed in readiness. Then came the food, a little of which the impresario managed to get between the artist's lips, while he sat in a kind of half-fainting trance, to the accompaniment of cheerful patter designed to distract the public's attention from the artist's condition; after that, a toast was drunk to the public, supposedly prompted by a whisper from the artist in the impresario's ear; the band confirmed it with a mighty flourish, the spectators melted away, and no one had any cause to be dissatisfied with the proceedings, no one except the hunger artist himself, he only, as always.

So he lived for many years, with small regular intervals of recuperation, in visible glory, honored by the world, yet in spite of that troubled in spirit, and all the more troubled because no one would take his trouble seriously. What comfort could he possibly need? What more could he possibly wish for? And if some good-natured person, feeling sorry for him, tried to console him by pointing out that his melancholy was probably caused by fasting, it could happen, especially when he had been fasting for some time, that he reacted with an outburst of fury and to the general alarm began to shake the bars of his cage like a wild animal. Yet the impresario had a way of punishing these outbreaks which he rather enjoyed putting into operation. He would apologize publicly for the artist's behavior, which was only to be excused, he admitted, because of the irritability caused by fasting; a condition hardly to be understood by well-fed people; then by natural transition he went on to mention the artist's equally incomprehensible boast that he could fast for much longer than he was doing; he praised the high ambition, the good will, the great self-denial undoubtedly implicit in such a statement; and then quite simply countered it by bringing out photographs, which were also on sale to the public, showing the artist on the fortieth day of a fast lying in bed almost dead from exhaustion. This perversion of the truth, familiar to the artist though it was, always unnerved him afresh and proved too much for him. What was a consequence of the premature ending of his fast was here presented as the cause of it! To fight against this lack of understanding, against a whole world of nonunderstanding, was impossible. Time and again in good faith he stood by the bars listening to the impresario, but as soon as the photographs appeared he always let go and sank with a groan back onto his straw, and the reassured public could once more come close and gaze at him.

A few years later when the witnesses of such scenes called them to mind, they often failed to understand themselves at all. For meanwhile the aforementioned change in public interest had set in; it seemed to happen almost overnight; there may have been profound causes for it, but who was going to bother about that; at any rate the pampered hunger artist suddenly found himself deserted one fine day by the amusement-seekers, who went streaming past him to more-favored attractions. For the last time the impresario hurried him over half Europe to discover whether the old interest might still survive here and there; all in vain; everywhere, as if by secret agreement, a positive revulsion from professional fasting was in evidence. Of course it could not really have sprung up so suddenly as all that, and many premonitory symptoms which had not been sufficiently remarked or suppressed during the rush and glitter of success now came retrospectively to mind, but it was now too late to take any countermeasures. Fasting would surely come into fashion again at some future date, yet that was no comfort for those living in the present. What, then, was the hunger artist to do? He had been applauded by thousands in his time and could hardly come down to showing himself in a street booth at village fairs, and as for adopting another profession, he was not only too old for that but too fanatically devoted to fasting. So he took leave of the impresario, his partner in an unparalleled career, and hired himself to a large circus; in order to spare his own feelings he avoided reading the conditions of his contract.

A large circus with its enormous traffic in replacing and recruiting men, animals, and apparatus can always find a use for people at any time, even for a hunger artist, provided of course that he does not ask too much, and in this particular case anyhow it was not only the artist who was taken on but his famous and long-known name as well, indeed considering the peculiar nature of his performance, which was not impaired by advancing age, it could not be objected that here was an artist past his prime, no longer at the height of his professional skill, seeking a refuge in some quiet corner of a circus; on the contrary, the hunger artist averred that he could fast as well as ever, which was entirely credible, he even alleged that if he were allowed to fast as he liked and this was at once promised him without more ado, he could astound the world by establishing a record never yet achieved, a statement that certainly provoked a smile among the other professionals, since it left out of account the change in public opinion, which the hunger artist in his zeal conveniently forgot.

He had not, however, actually lost his sense of the real situation and took it as a matter of course that he and his cage should be stationed, not in the middle of the ring as a main attraction, but outside, near the animal cages, on a site that was after all easily accessible. Large and gaily painted placards made a frame for the cage and announced what was to be seen inside it. When the public came thronging out in the intervals to see the animals, they could hardly avoid passing the hunger artist's cage and stopping there for a moment, perhaps they might even have stayed longer had not those pressing behind them in the narrow gangway, who did not understand why they should be held up on their way toward the excitements of the menagerie, made it impossible for anyone to stand gazing quietly for any length of time. And that was the reason why the hunger artist, who had of course been looking forward to these visiting hours as the main achievement of his life, began instead to shrink from them. At first he could hardly wait for the intervals; it was exhilarating to watch the crowds come streaming his way, until only too soon—not even the most obstinate self-deception, clung to almost consciously, could hold out against the fact—the conviction was borne in upon him that these people, most of them, to judge from their actions, again and again, without exception, were all on their way to the menagerie. And the first sight of them from the distance remained the best. For when they reached his cage he was at once deafened by the storm of shouting and abuse that arose from the two contending factions, which renewed themselves continuously, of those who wanted to stop and stare at him—he soon began to dislike them more than the others—not out of real interest but only out of obstinate self-assertiveness, and those who wanted to go straight on to the animals. When the first great rush was past, the stragglers came along, and these, whom nothing could have prevented from stopping to look at him as long as they had breath, raced past with long strides, hardly even glancing at him, in their haste to get to the menagerie in time. And all too rarely did it happen that he had a stroke of luck, when some father of a family fetched up before him with his children, pointed a finger at the hunger artist, and explained at length what the phenomenon meant, telling stories of earlier years when he himself had watched similar but much more thrilling performances, and the children, still rather uncomprehending, since neither inside nor outside school had they been sufficiently prepared for this lesson—what did they care about fasting?—yet showed by the brightness of their intent eyes that new and better times might be coming. Perhaps, said the hunger artist to himself many a time, things would be a little better if his cage were not set quite so near the menagerie. That made it too easy for people to make their choice, to say nothing of what he suffered from the stench of the menagerie, the animals' restlessness by night, the carrying past of raw lumps of flesh for the beasts of prety, the roaring at feeding times, which depressed him continually. But he did not dare to lodge a complaint with the management; after all, he had the animals to thank for the troops of people who passed his cage, among whom there might always be one here and there to take an interest in him, and who could tell where they might seclude him if he called attention to his existence and thereby to the fact that, strictly speaking, he was only an impediment on the way to the menagerie.

A small impediment, to be sure, one that grew steadily less. People grew familiar with the strange idea that they could be expected, in times like these, to take an interest in a hunger artist, and with this familiarity the verdict went out against him. He might fast as much as he could, and he did so; but nothing could save him now, people passed him by. Just try to explain to anyone the art of fasting! Anyone who has no feeling for it cannot be made to understand it. The fine placards grew dirty and illegible, they were torn down; the little notice board telling the number of fast days achieved, which at first was changed carefully every day, had long stayed at the same figure, for after the first few weeks even this small task seemed pointless to the staff; and so the artist simply fasted on and on, as he had once dreamed of doing, and it was no trouble to him, just as he had always foretold, but no one counted the days, no one, not even the artist himself knew what records he was already breaking and his heart grew heavy. And when once in a while some leisurely passer-by stopped, made merry over the old figure on the board, and spoke of swindling, that was in its way the stupidest lie ever invented by indifference and inborn malice, since it was not the hunger artist who was cheating, he was working honestly, but the world was cheating him of his reward.

Many more days went by, however, and that too came to an end. An overseer's eye fell on the cage one day and he asked the attendants why this perfectly good cage should be left standing there unused with dirty straw inside it; nobody knew, until one man, helped out by the notice board, remembered about the hunger artist. They poked the straw with sticks and found him in it. "Are you still fasting?" asked the overseer, "when on earth do you mean to stop?" "Forgive me, everybody," whispered the hunger artist; only the overseer, who had his ears to the bars, understood him. "Of course," said the overseer, and tapped his forehead with a finger to let the attendants know what state the man was in, "we forgive you." "I always wanted you to admire my fasting," said the hunger artist. "We do admire it," said the overseer, affably. "But you shouldn't admire it," said the hunger artist. "Well then then we don't admire it," said the overseer, "but why shouldn't we admire it?" "Because I have to fast, I can't help it," the hunger artist. "What a fellow you are," said the overseer, "and why can't you help it?" "Because," said the hunger artist, lifting his head a little and speaking, with his lips pursed, as if for a kiss, right into the overseer's ear, so that no syllable might be lost, "because I couldn't find the food I liked. If I had found it, believe me, I should have made no fuss and stuffed myself like you or anyone else." These were his last words, but in his dimming eyes remained the firm though no longer proud persuasion that he was still continuing to fast.

"Well, clear this out now!" said the overseer, and they buried the hunger artist, straw and all. Into the cage they put a young panther. Even the most insensitive felt it refreshing to see this wild creature leaping around the cage that had so long been dreary. The panther was all right. The food he liked was brought him without hesitation by the attendants; he seemed not even to miss his freedom; his noble body, furnished almost to the bursting point with all that it needed, seemed to carry freedom around with it too; somewhere in his jaws it seemed to lurk; and the joy of life streamed with such ardent passion from his throat that for the onlookers it was not easy to stand the shock of it. But they braced themselves, crowded around the cage, and did not want ever to move away.

—1924

Questions: Reading, Responding, Arguing

1. How do the events of the story match up with the flat, matter-of-fact tone in which it is written?

2. What role does the agent play in the story? And why is the artist's period of starvation set at 40 days?
3. What does the panther at the end of the story symbolize? How does the crowd of people react to it and why?
4. The story is deliberately unrealistic and meant to be an extended fable or allegory. Yet the precise meaning of its symbolic action has been widely debated. Argue some possible interpretations of its meaning.

Shirley Jackson (1919–1965)

The Lottery

The morning of June 27th was clear and sunny, with the fresh warmth of a full-summer day; the flowers were blossoming profusely and the grass was richly green. The people of the village began to gather in the square, between the post office and the bank, around ten o'clock; in some towns there were so many people that the lottery took two days and had to be started on June 26th, but in this village, where there were only about three hundred people, the whole lottery took less than two hours, so it could begin at ten o'clock in the morning and still be through in time to allow the villagers to get home for noon dinner.

The children assembled first, of course. School was recently over for the summer, and the feeling of liberty sat uneasily on most of them; they tended to gather together quietly for a while before they broke into boisterous play, and their talk was still of the classroom and the teacher, of books and reprimands. Bobby Martin had already stuffed his pockets full of stones, and the other boys soon followed his example, selecting the smoothest and roundest stones; Bobby and Harry Jones and Dickie Delacroix—the villagers pronounced this name "Dellacroy"—eventually made a great pile of stones in one corner of the square and guarded it against the raids of the other boys. The girls stood aside, talking among themselves, looking over their shoulders at the boys, and the very small children rolled in the dust or clung to the hands of their older brothers or sisters.

Soon the men began to gather, surveying their own children, speaking of planting and rain, tractors and taxes. They stood together, away from the pile of stones in the corner, and their jokes were quiet and they smiled rather than laughed. The women, wearing faded house dresses and sweaters, came shortly after their menfolk. They greeted one another and exchanged bits of gossip as they went to join their husbands. Soon the women, standing by their husbands, began to call to their children, and the children came reluctantly, having to be called four or five times. Bobby Martin ducked under his mother's grasping hand and ran, laughing, back to the pile of stones. His father spoke up sharply, and Bobby came quickly and took his place between his father and his oldest brother.

The lottery was conducted—as were the square dances, the teenage club, the Halloween program—by Mr. Summers, who had time and energy to devote to civic activities. He was a roundfaced, jovial man and he ran the coal business, and people were sorry for him, because he had no children and his wife was a scold. When he arrived in the square, carrying the black wooden box, there was a murmur of conversation among the villagers and he waved and called, "Little late today, folks." The postmaster, Mr. Graves, followed him, carrying a three-legged stool, and the stool was put in the center of the square and Mr. Summers set the black box down on it. The villagers kept their distance, leaving a space between themselves and the stool, and when Mr. Summers said, "Some of you fellows want to give me a hand?" there was a hesitation before two men, Mr. Martin and his oldest son, Baxter, came forward to hold the box steady on the stool while Mr. Summers stirred up the papers inside it.

The original paraphernalia for the lottery had been lost long ago, and the black box now resting on the stool had been put into use even before Old Man Warner, the oldest man in town, was born. Mr. Summers spoke frequently to the villagers about making a new box, but no one liked to upset even as much tradition as was represented by the black box. There was a story that the present box had been made with some pieces of the box that had preceded it, the one that had been constructed when the first people settled down to make a village here. Every year, after the lottery, Mr. Summers began talking again about a new box, but every year the subject was allowed to fade off without anything's being done. The black box grew shabbier each year; by now it was no longer completely black but splintered badly along one side to show the original wood color, and in some places faded or stained.

Mr. Martin and his oldest son, Baxter, held the black box securely on the stool until Mr. Summers had stirred the papers thoroughly with his hand. Because so much of the ritual had been forgotten or discarded, Mr. Summers had been successful in having slips of paper substituted for the chips of wood that had been used for generations. Chips of wood, Mr. Summers had argued, had been all very well when the village was tiny, but now that the population was more than three hundred and likely to keep on growing, it was necessary to use something that would fit more easily into the black box. The night before the lottery, Mr. Summers and Mr. Graves made up the slips of paper and put them in the box, and it was then taken to the safe of Mr. Summers's coal company and locked up until Mr. Summers was ready to take it to the square next morning. The rest of the year, the box was put away, sometimes one place, sometimes another; it had spent one year in Mr. Graves's barn and another year underfoot in the post office, and sometimes it was set on a shelf in the Martin grocery and left there.

There was a great deal of fussing to be done before Mr. Summers declared the lottery open. There were lists to make up—of heads of families, heads of households in each family, members of each household in each family. There was the proper swearing-in of Mr. Summers by the postmaster, as the official of the lottery; at one time, some people remembered, there had been a recital of some sort, performed by the official of the lottery, a perfunctory, tuneless chant that had been rattled off duly each year; some people believed that the official of the lottery used to stand just so when he said or sang it, others believed that he was supposed to walk among the people, but years and years ago this part of the ritual had been allowed to lapse. There had been, also, a ritual salute, which the official of the lottery had had to use in addressing each person who came up to draw from the box, but this also had changed with time, until now it was felt necessary only for the official to speak to each person approaching. Mr. Summers was very good at all this; in his clean white shirt and blue jeans, with one hand resting carelessly on the black box, he seemed very proper and important as he talked interminably to Mr. Graves and the Martins.

Just as Mr. Summers finally left off talking and turned to the assembled villagers, Mrs. Hutchinson came hurriedly along the path to the square, her sweater thrown over her shoulders, and slid into place in the back of the crowd. "Clean forgot what day it was," she said to Mrs. Delacroix, who stood next to her, and they both laughed softly. "Thought my old man was out back stacking wood," Mrs. Hutchinson went on, "and then I looked out the window and the kids were gone, and then I remembered it was the twenty-seventh and came a-running." She dried her hands on her apron, and Mrs. Delacroix said, "You're in time, though. They're still talking away up there."

Mrs. Hutchinson craned her neck to see through the crowd and found her husband and children standing near the front. She tapped Mrs. Delacroix on the arm as a farewell and began to make her way through the crowd. The people separated good-humoredly to let her through; two or three people said, in voices just loud enough to be heard across the crowd, "Here comes your Missus, Hutchinson," and "Bill, she made it after all." Mrs. Hutchinson reached her husband, and Mr. Summers, who had been waiting, said cheerfully, "Thought we were going to have to get on without you, Tessie." Mrs. Hutchinson said, grinning, "Wouldn't have me leave m'dishes in the sink, now would you, Joe?," and soft laughter ran through the crowd as the people stirred back into position after Mrs. Hutchinson's arrival.

"Well, now," Mr. Summers said soberly, "guess we better get started, get this over with, so's we can go back to work. Anybody ain't here?"

"Dunbar," several people said. "Dunbar, Dunbar."

Mr. Summers consulted his list. "Clyde Dunbar," he said. "That's right. He's broke his leg, hasn't he? Who's drawing for him?"

"Me, I guess," a woman said, and Mr. Summers turned to look at her. "Wife draws for her husband," Mr. Summers said. "Don't you have a grown boy to do it for you, Janey?" Although Mr. Summers and everyone else in the village knew the answer perfectly well, it was the business of the official of the lottery to ask such questions formally. Mr. Summers waited with an expression of polite interest while Mrs. Dunbar answered.

"Horace's not but sixteen yet," Mrs. Dunbar said regretfully. "Guess I gotta fill in for the old man this year."

"Right," Mr. Summers said. He made a note on the list he was holding. Then he asked, "Watson boy drawing this year?"

A tall boy in the crowd raised his hand. "Here," he said. "I'm drawing for m'mother and me." He blinked his eyes nervously and ducked his head as several voices in the crowd said things like "Good fellow, Jack," and "Glad to see your mother's got a man to do it."

"Well," Mr. Summers said, "guess that's everyone. Old Man Warner make it?"

"Here," a voice said, and Mr. Summers nodded.

A sudden hush fell on the crowd as Mr. Summers cleared his throat and looked at the list. "All ready?" he called. "Now, I'll read the names—heads of families first—and the men come up and take a paper out of the box. Keep the paper folded in your hand without looking at it until everyone has had a turn. Everything clear?"

The people had done it so many times that they only half listened to the directions; most of them were quiet, wetting their lips, not looking around. Then Mr. Summers raised one hand high and said, "Adams." A man disengaged himself from the crowd and came forward. "Hi, Steve," Mr. Summers said, and Mr. Adams said, "Hi, Joe." They grinned at one another humorlessly and nervously. Then Mr. Adams reached into the black box and took out a folded paper. He held it firmly by one corner as he turned and went hastily back to his place in the crowd, where he stood a little apart from his family, not looking down at his hand.

"Allen," Mr. Summers said. "Anderson . . . Bentham."

"Seems like there's no time at all between lotteries any more," Mrs. Delacroix said to Mrs. Graves in the back row. "Seems like we got through with the last one only last week."

"Time sure goes fast," Mrs. Graves said.

"Clark . . . Delacroix."

"There goes my old man," Mrs. Delacroix said. She held her breath while her husband went forward.

"Dunbar," Mr. Summers said, and Mrs. Dunbar went steadily to the box while one of the women said, "Go on, Janey," and another said, "There she goes."

"We're next," Mrs. Graves said. She watched while Mr. Graves came around from the side of the box, greeted Mr. Summers gravely, and selected a slip of paper from the box. By now, all through the crowd there were men holding the small folded papers in their large hands, turning them over and over nervously. Mrs. Dunbar and her two sons stood together, Mrs. Dunbar holding the slip of paper.

"Harburt . . . Hutchinson."

"Get up there, Bill," Mrs. Hutchinson said, and the people near her laughed.

"Jones."

"They do say," Mr. Adams said to Old Man Warner, who stood next to him, "that over in the north village they're talking of giving up the lottery."

Old Man Warner snorted. "Pack of crazy fools," he said. "Listening to the young folks, nothing's good enough for *them*. Next thing you know, they'll be wanting to go back to living in caves, nobody work any more, live *that* way for a while. Used to be a saying about 'Lottery in June, corn be heavy soon.' First thing you know, we'd all be eating stewed chickweed and acorns. There's *always* been a lottery," he added petulantly. "Bad enough to see young Joe Summers up there joking with everybody."

"Some places have already quit lotteries," Mrs. Adams said.

"Nothing but trouble in *that*," Old Man Warner said stoutly. "Pack of young fools."

"Martin." And Bobby Martin watched his father go forward. "Overdyke . . . Percy."

"I wish they'd hurry," Mrs. Dunbar said to her older son. "I wish they'd hurry."

"They're almost through," her son said.

"You get ready to run tell Dad," Mrs. Dunbar said.

Mr. Summers called his own name and then stepped forward precisely and selected a slip from the box. Then he called, "Warner."

"Seventy-seventh year I been in the lottery," Old Man Warner said as he went through the crowd. "Seventy-seventh time."

"Watson." The tall boy came awkwardly through the crowd. Someone said, "Don't be nervous, Jack," and Mr. Summers said, "Take your time, son."

"Zanini."

After that, there was a long pause, a breathless pause, until Mr. Summers, holding his slip of paper in the air, said, "All right, fellows." For a minute, no one moved, and then all the slips of paper were opened. Suddenly, all women began to speak at once, saying, "Who is it?" "Who's got it?" "Is it the Dunbars?" "Is it the Watsons?" Then the voices began to say, "It's Hutchinson. It's Bill." "Bill Hutchinson's got it."

"Go tell your father," Mrs. Dunbar said to her older son.

People began to look around to see the Hutchinsons. Bill Hutchinson was standing quiet, staring down at the paper in his hand. Suddenly, Tessie Hutchinson shouted to Mr. Summers, "You didn't give him time enough to take any paper he wanted. I saw you. It wasn't fair!"

"Be a good sport, Tessie," Mrs. Delacroix called, and Mrs. Graves said, "All of us took the same chance."

"Shut up, Tessie," Bill Hutchinson said.

"Well, everyone," Mr. Summers said, "that was done pretty fast, and now we've got to be hurrying a little more to get done in time." He consulted his next list. "Bill," he said, "you draw for the Hutchinson family. You got any other households in the Hutchinsons?"

"There's Don and Eva," Mrs. Hutchinson yelled. "Make *them* take their chance!"

"Daughters draw with their husbands' families, Tessie," Mr. Summers said gently. "You know that as well as anyone else."

"It wasn't fair," Tessie said.

"I guess not, Joe," Bill Hutchinson said regretfully. "My daughter draws with her husband's family, that's only fair. And I've got no other family except the kids."

"Then, as far as drawing for families is concerned, it's you," Mr. Summers said in explanation, "and as far as drawing for households is concerned, that's you, too. Right?"

"Right," Bill Hutchinson said.

"How many kids, Bill?" Mr. Summers asked formally.

"Three," Bill Hutchinson said. "There's Bill, Jr., and Nancy, and little Dave. And Tessie and me."

"All right, then," Mr. Summers said. "Harry, you got their tickets back?"

Mr. Graves nodded and held up the slips of paper. "Put them in the box, then," Mr. Summers directed. "Take Bill's and put it in."

"I think we ought to start over," Mrs. Hutchinson said, as quietly as she could. "I tell you it wasn't *fair*. You didn't give him time enough to choose. *Everybody* saw that."

Mr. Graves had selected the five slips and put them in the box, and he dropped all the papers but those onto the ground, where the breeze caught them and lifted them off.

"Listen, everybody," Mrs. Hutchinson was saying to the people around her.

"Ready, Bill?" Mr. Summers asked, and Bill Hutchinson, with one quick glance around at his wife and children, nodded.

"Remember," Mr. Summers said, "take the slips and keep them folded until each person has taken one. Harry, you help little Dave." Mr. Graves took the hand of the little boy, who came willingly with him up to the box. "Take a paper out of the box, Davy," Mr. Summers said. Davy put his hand into the box and laughed. "Take just *one* paper," Mr. Summers said. "Harry, you hold it for him." Mr. Graves took the child's hand and removed the folded paper from the tight fist and held it while little Dave stood next to him and looked up at him wonderingly.

"Nancy next," Mr. Summers said. Nancy was twelve, and her school friends breathed heavily as she went forward, switching her skirt, and took a slip daintily from the box. "Bill, Jr.," Mr. Summers said, and Billy, his face red and his feet overlarge, nearly knocked the box over as he got a paper out. "Tessie," Mr. Summers said. She hesitated for a minute, looking around defiantly, and then set her lips and went up to the box. She snatched a paper out and held it behind her.

"Bill," Mr. Summers said, and Bill Hutchinson reached into the box and felt around, bringing his hand out at last with the slip of paper in it.

The crowd was quiet. A girl whispered, "I hope it's not Nancy," and the sound of the whisper reached the edges of the crowd.

"It's not the way it used to be," Old Man Warner said clearly. "People ain't the way they used to be."

"All right," Mr. Summers said. "Open the papers. Harry, you open little Dave's."

Mr. Graves opened the slip of paper and there was a general sigh through the crowd as he held it up and everyone could see that it was blank. Nancy and Bill, Jr., opened theirs at the same time, and both beamed and laughed, turning around to the crowd and holding their slips of paper above their heads.

"Tessie," Mr. Summers said. There was a pause, and then Mr. Summers looked at Bill Hutchinson, and Bill unfolded his paper and showed it. It was blank.

"It's Tessie," Mr. Summers said, and his voice was hushed. "Show us her paper, Bill."

Bill Hutchinson went over to his wife and forced the slip of paper out of her hand. It had a black spot on it, the black spot Mr. Summers had made the night before with the heavy pencil in the coal-company office. Bill Hutchinson held it up, and there was a stir in the crowd.

"All right, folks," Mr. Summers said, "let's finish quickly."

Although the villagers had forgotten the ritual and lost the original black box, they still remembered to use stones. The pile of stones the boys had made earlier was ready; there were stones on the ground with the blowing scraps of paper that had come out of the box. Mrs. Delacroix selected a stone so large she had to pick it up with both hands and turned to Mrs. Dunbar. "Come on," she said. "Hurry up."

Mrs. Dunbar had small stones in both hands, and she said, gasping for breath, "I can't run at all. You'll have to go ahead and I'll catch up with you."

The children had stones already, and someone gave little Davy Hutchinson a few pebbles.

Tessie Hutchinson was in the center of a cleared space by now, and she held her hands out desperately as the villagers moved in on her. "It isn't fair," she said. A stone hit her on the side of the head.

Old Man Warner was saying, "Come on, come on, everyone." Steve Adams was in the front of the crowd of villagers, with Mrs. Graves beside him.

"It isn't fair, it isn't right," Mrs. Hutchinson screamed, and then they were upon her.

—1948

Questions: Reading, Responding, Arguing

1. Examine the names Jackson gives her characters. How do they connect to the story's themes or ideas?

2. The story's ending often shocks readers. What stylistic choices does Jackson make to develop shock or surprise?

3. Critics Cleanth Brooks and Robert Penn Warren have noted that "The Lottery" remains a puzzle "not because the story is vague and fuzzy, but rather because its web of observations about human nature is too subtle and too complex to be stated in one or two brief maxims." Discuss this story's "web of observations about human nature."

4. Poe is another masterful storyteller who relies upon suspense. Compare Jackson's style with Poe's. What are differences and similarities between them? Do they use suspense for the same purposes?

Tim O'Brien (b. 1946)

The Things They Carried*

First Lieutenant Jimmy Cross carried letters from a girl named Martha, a junior at Mount Sebastian College in New Jersey. They were not love letters, but Lieutenant Cross was hoping, so he kept them folded in plastic at the bottom of his rucksack. In the late afternoon, after a day's march, he would dig his foxhole, wash his hands under a canteen, unwrap the letters, hold them with the tips of his fingers, and spend the last hour of light pretending. He would imagine romantic camping trips into the White Mountains in New Hampshire. He would sometimes taste the envelope flaps, knowing her tongue had been there. More than anything, he wanted Martha to love him as he loved her, but the letters were mostly chatty, elusive on the matter of love. She was a virgin, he was almost sure. She was an English major at Mount Sebastian, and she wrote beautifully about her professors and roommates and midterm exams, about her respect for Chaucer and her great affection for Virginia Woolf. She often quoted lines of poetry; she never mentioned the war, except to say, Jimmy, take care of yourself. The letters weighed ten ounces. They were signed "Love, Martha," but Lieutenant Cross understood that Love was only a way of signing and did not mean what he sometimes pretended it meant. At dusk, he would carefully return the letters to his rucksack. Slowly, a bit distracted, he would get up and move among his men, checking the perimeter, then at full dark he would return to his hole and watch the night and wonder if Martha was a virgin.

The things they carried were largely determined by necessity. Among the necessities or near-necessities were P-38 can openers, pocket knives, heat tabs, wrist watches, dog tags, mosquito repellent, chewing gum, candy, cigarettes, salt tablets, packets of Kool-Aid, lighters, matches, sewing kits, Military Payment Certificates, C rations, and two or three canteens of water. Together, these items weighed between fifteen and twenty pounds, depending upon a man's habits or rate of metabolism. Henry Dobbins, who was a big man, carried extra rations; he was especially fond of canned peaches in heavy syrup over pound cake. Dave Jensen, who practiced field hygiene, carried a toothbrush, dental floss, and several hotel-size bars of soap he'd stolen on R & R[1] in Sydney, Australia. Ted Lavender, who was scared, carried tranquilizers until he was shot in the head outside the village of Than Khe in mid-April. By necessity, and because it was SOP,[2] they all carried steel helmets that weighed five pounds including the liner and camouflage cover. They carried the standard fatigue jackets and trousers. Very few carried underwear. On their feet they carried jungle boots—2.1 pounds—and Dave Jensen carried three pairs of socks and a can of Dr. Scholl's foot powder as a precaution against trench foot. Until he was shot, Ted Lavender carried six or seven ounces of premium dope, which for him was a necessity. Mitchell Sanders, the RTO,[3] carried condoms. Norman Bowker carried a diary. Rat Kiley carried comic books. Kiowa, a devout Baptist, carried an illustrated New Testament that had been presented to him by his father, who taught Sunday school in Oklahoma City, Okalahoma. As a hedge against bad times, however, Kiowa also carried his grandmother's distrust of the white man, his grandfather's old hunting hatchet. Necessity dictated. Because the land was mined and booby-trapped, it was SOP for each man to carry a steel-centered, nylon-covered flak jacket, which weighed 6.7 pounds, but which on hot days seemed much heavier. Because you could die so quickly, each man carried at least one large compress bandage, usually in the helmet band for easy access. Because the nights were cold, and because the monsoons were wet, each carried a green plastic poncho that could be used as a raincoat or groundsheet or makeshift tent. With its quilted liner, the poncho weighed almost two pounds, but it was worth every ounce. In April, for instance, when Ted Lavender was shot, they used his poncho to wrap him up, then to carry him across the paddy, then to lift him into the chopper that took him away.

[1] R & R rest and rehabilitation.
[2] SOP standard operating procedure.
[3] RTO radio/telephone operator.

They were called legs or grunts.

To carry something was to "hump" it, as when Lieutenant Jimmy Cross humped his love for Martha up the hills and through the swamps. In its intransitive form, "to hump" meant "to walk," or "to march," but it implied burdens far beyond the intransitive.

Almost everyone humped photographs. In his wallet, Lieutenant Cross carried two photographs of Martha. The first was a Kodachrome snapshot signed "Love," though he knew better. She stood against a brick wall. Her eyes were gray and neutral, her lips slightly open as she stared straight-on at the camera. At night, sometimes, Lieutenant Cross wondered who had taken the picture, because he knew she had boyfriends, because he loved her so much, and because he could see the shadow of the picture taker spreading out against the brick wall. The second photograph had been clipped from the 1968 Mount Sebastian yearbook. It was an action shot—women's volleyball—and Martha was bent horizontal to the floor, reaching, the palms of her hands in sharp focus, the tongue taut, the expression frank and competitive. There was no visible sweat. She wore white gym shorts. Her legs, he thought, were almost certainly the legs of a virgin, dry and without hair, the left knee cocked and carrying her entire weight, which was just over one hundred pounds. Lieutenant Cross remembered touching that left knee. A dark theater, he remembered, and the movie was *Bonnie and Clyde,* and Martha wore a tweed skirt, and during the final scene, when he touched her knee, she turned and looked at him in a sad, sober way that made him pull his hand back, but he would always remember the feel of the tweed skirt and the knee beneath it and the sound of the gunfire that killed Bonnie and Clyde, how embarrassing it was, how slow and oppressive. He remembered kissing her goodnight at the dorm door. Right then, he thought, he should've done something brave. He should've carried her up the stairs to her room and tied her to the bed and touched that left knee all night long. He should've risked it. Whenever he looked at the photographs, he thought of new things he should've done.

What they carried was partly a function of rank, partly of field specialty.

As a first lieutenant and platoon leader, Jimmy Cross carried a compass, maps, code books, binoculars, and a .45-caliber pistol that weighed 2.9 pounds fully loaded. He carried a strobe light and the responsibility for the lives of his men.

As an RTO, Mitchell Sanders carried the PRC-25 radio, a killer, twenty-six pounds with its battery.

As a medic, Rat Kiley carried a canvas satchel filled with morphine and plasma and malaria tablets and surgical tape and comic books and all the things a medic must carry, including M & Ms[4] for especially bad wounds, for a total weight of nearly twenty pounds.

As a big man, therefore a machine gunner, Henry Dobbins carried the M-60, which weighed twenty-three pounds unloaded, but which was almost always loaded. In addition, Dobbins carried between ten and fifteen pounds of ammunition draped in belts across his chest and shoulders.

As PFCs or Spec 4s, most of them were common grunts and carried the standard M-16 gas operated assault rifle. The weapon weighed 7.5 pounds unloaded, 8.2 pounds with its full twenty-round magazine. Depending on numerous factors, such as topography and psychology, the riflemen carried anywhere from twelve to twenty magazines, usually in cloth bandoliers, adding on another 8.4 pounds at minimum, fourteen pounds at maximum. When it was available, they also carried M-16 maintenance gear—rods and steel brushes and swabs and tubes of LSA oil—all of which weighed about a pound. Among the grunts, some carried the M-79 grenade launcher, 5.9 pounds unloaded, a reasonably light weapon except for the ammunition, which was heavy. A single round weighed ten ounces. The typical load was twenty-five rounds. But Ted Lavender, who was scared, carried thirty-four rounds when he was shot and killed outside Than Khe, and he went down under an exceptional burden, more than twenty pounds of ammunition, plus the flak jacket and helmet and rations and water and toilet paper and tranquilizers and all the rest, plus the unweighed fear. He was dead weight. There was no twitching or flopping. Kiowa, who saw it happen, said it was like watching a rock fall, or a big sandbag or something—just boom, then down—not like the movies where the dead guy rolls around and does fancy spins and goes ass over teakettle—not like that, Kiowa said, the poor bastard just flat-fuck fell. Boom. Down. Nothing else. It was a bright morning in mid-April. Lieutenant Cross felt the pain. He blamed himself. They stripped off Lavender's canteens and ammo, all the heavy things, and Rat Kiley said the obvious, the guy's dead, and Mitchell Sanders used his radio to report one U.S. KIA[5] and to request a chopper. Then they wrapped Lavender in his poncho. They carried him out to a dry paddy, established security, and sat smoking the dead man's dope until the chopper came. Lieutenant Cross

---

[4] **M & M** medications and morphine.
[5] **KIA** killed in action.

kept to himself. He pictured Martha's smooth young face, thinking he loved her more than anything, more than his men, and now Ted Lavender was dead because he loved her so much and could not stop thinking about her. When the dust-off arrived, they carried Lavender aboard. Afterward they burned Than Khe. They marched until dusk, then dug their holes, and that night Kiowa kept explaining how you had to be there, how fast it was, how the poor guy just dropped like so much concrete. Boom-down, he said. Like cement.

In addition to the three standard weapons—the M-60, M-16, and M-79—they carried whatever presented itself, or whatever seemed appropriate as a means of killing or staying alive. They carried catch-as-catch-can. At various times, in various situations, they carried M-14s and CAR-15s and Swedish Ks and grease guns and captured AK-47s and Chi-Coms and RPGs and Simonov carbines and black-market Uzis and .38-caliber Smith & Wesson handguns and 66 mm LAWs and shotguns and silencers and blackjacks and bayonets and C-4 plastic explosives. Lee Strunk carried a slingshot; a weapon of last resort, he called it. Mitchell Sanders carried brass knuckles. Kiowa carried his grandfather's feathered hatchet. Every third or fourth man carried a Claymore antipersonnel mine—3.5 pounds with its firing device. They all carried fragmentation grenades—fourteen ounces each. They all carried at least one M-18 colored smoke grenade—twenty-four ounces. Some carried CS or tear-gas grenades. Some carried white-phosphorus grenades. They carried all they could bear, and then some, including a silent awe for the terrible power of the things they carried.

In the first week of April, before Lavender died, Lieutenant Jimmy Cross received a goodluck charm from Martha. It was a simple pebble, an ounce at most. Smooth to the touch, it was a milky-white color with flecks of orange and violet, oval-shaped, like a miniature egg. In the accompanying letter, Martha wrote that she had found the pebble on the Jersey shoreline, precisely where the land touched the water at high tide, where things came together but also separated. It was this separate-but-together quality, she wrote, that had inspired her to pick up the pebble and to carry it in her breast pocket for several days, where it seemed weightless, and then to send it through the mail, by air, as a token of her truest feelings for him. Lieutenant Cross found this romantic. But he wondered what her truest feelings were, exactly, and what she meant by separate-but-together. He wondered how the tides and waves had come into play on that afternoon along the Jersey shoreline when Martha saw the pebble and bent down to rescue it from geology. He imagined bare feet. Martha was a poet, with the poet's sensibilities, and her feet would be brown and bare, the toenails unpainted, the eyes chilly and somber like the ocean in March, and though it was painful, he wondered who had been with her that afternoon. He imagined a pair of shadows moving along the strip of sand where things came together but also separated. It was phantom jealousy, he knew, but he couldn't help himself. He loved her so much. On the march, through the hot days of early April, he carried the pebble in his mouth, turning it with his tongue, tasting sea salts and moisture. His mind wandered. He had difficulty keeping his attention on the war. On occasion he would yell at his men to spread out the column, to keep their eyes open, but then he would slip away into daydreams, just pretending, walking barefoot along the Jersey shore, with Martha, carrying nothing. He would feel himself rising. Sun and waves and gentle winds, all love and lightness.

What they carried varied by mission.

When a mission took them to the mountains, they carried mosquito netting, machetes, canvas tarps, and extra bugjuice.

If a mission seemed especially hazardous, or if it involved a place they knew to be bad, they carried everything they could. In certain heavily mined AOs,[6] where the land was dense with Toe Poppers and Bouncing Betties, they took turns humping a twenty-eight-pound mine detector. With its headphones and big sensing plate, the equipment was a stress on the lower back and shoulders, awkward to handle, often useless because of the shrapnel in the earth, but they carried it anyway, partly for safety, partly for the illusion of safety.

On ambush, or other night missions, they carried peculiar little odds and ends. Kiowa always took along his New Testament and a pair of moccasins for silence. Dave Jensen carried night-sight vitamins high in carotin. Lee Strunk carried his slingshot; ammo, he claimed, would never be a problem. Rat Kiley carried brandy and M&Ms. Until he was shot, Ted Lavender carried the starlight scope, which weighed 6.3 pounds with its aluminum carrying case. Henry Dobbins carried his girlfriend's panty hose wrapped around his neck as a comforter. They all carried ghosts. When dark came, they would move out single file across the meadows and paddies to their ambush coordinates, where they would quietly set up the Claymores and lie down and spend the night waiting.

---

[6]AOs areas of operation.

Other missions were more complicated and required special equipment. In mid-April, it was their mission to search out and destroy the elaborate tunnel complexes in the Than Khe area south of Chu Lai. To blow the tunnels, they carried one-pound blocks of pentrite high explosives, four blocks to a man, sixty-eight pounds in all. They carried wiring, detonators, and battery-powered clackers. Dave Jensen carried earplugs. Most often, before blowing the tunnels, they were ordered by higher command to search them, which was considered bad news, but by and large they just shrugged and carried out orders. Because he was a big man, Henry Dobbins was excused from tunnel duty. The others would draw numbers. Before Lavender died there were seventeen men in the platoon, and whoever drew the number seventeen would strip off his gear and crawl in headfirst with a flashlight and Lieutenant Cross's .45-caliber pistol. The rest of them would fan out as security. They would sit down or kneel, not facing the hole, listening to the ground beneath them, imagining cobwebs and ghosts, whatever was down there—the tunnel walls squeezing in—how the flashlight seemed impossibly heavy in the hand and how it was tunnel vision in the very strictest sense, compression in all ways, even time, and how you had to wiggle in—ass and elbows—a swallowed-up feeling—and how you found yourself worrying about odd things—will your flashlight go dead? Do rats carry rabies? If you screamed, how far would the sound carry? Would your buddies hear it? Would they have the courage to drag you out? In some respects, though not many, the waiting was worse than the tunnel itself. Imagination was a killer.

On April 16, when Lee Strunk drew the number seventeen, he laughed and muttered something and went down quickly. The morning was hot and very still. Not good, Kiowa said. He looked at the tunnel opening, then out across a dry paddy toward the village of Than Khe. Nothing moved. No clouds or birds or people. As they waited, the men smoked and drank Kool-Aid, not talking much, feeling sympathy for Lee Strunk but also feeling the luck of the draw. You win some, you lose some, said Mitchell Sanders, and sometimes you settle for a rain check. It was a tired line and no one laughed.

Henry Dobbins ate a tropical chocolate bar. Ted Lavender popped a tranquilizer and went off to pee.

After five minutes, Lieutenant Jimmy Cross moved to the tunnel, leaned down, and examined the darkness. Trouble, he thought—a cave-in maybe. And then suddenly, without willing it, he was thinking about Martha. The stresses and fractures, the quick collapse, the two of them buried alive under all that weight. Dense, crushing love.

Kneeling, watching the hole, he tried to concentrate on Lee Strunk and the war, all the dangers, but his love was too much for him, he felt paralyzed, he wanted to sleep inside her lungs and breathe her blood and be smothered. He wanted her to be a virgin and not a virgin, all at once. He wanted to know her. Intimate secrets—why poetry? Why so sad? Why that grayness in her eyes? Why so alone? Not lonely, just alone—riding her bike across campus or sitting off by herself in the cafeteria. Even dancing, she danced alone—and it was the aloneness that filled him with love. He remembered telling her that one evening. How she nodded and looked away. And how, later, when he kissed her, she received the kiss without returning it, her eyes wide open, not afraid, not a virgin's eyes, just flat and uninvolved.

Lieutenant Cross gazed at the tunnel. But he was not there. He was buried with Martha under the white sand at the Jersey shore. They were pressed together, and the pebble in his mouth was her tongue. He was smiling. Vaguely, he was aware of how quiet the day was, the sullen paddies, yet he could not bring himself to worry about matters of security. He was beyond that. He was just a kid at war, in love. He was twenty-two years old. He couldn't help it.

A few minutes later Lee Strunk crawled out of the tunnel. He came up grinning, filthy but alive. Lieutenant Cross nodded and closed his eyes while the others clapped Strunk on the back and made jokes about rising from the dead.

Worms, Rat Kiley said. Right out of the grave. Fuckin' zombie.

The men laughed. They all felt great relief.

Spook City, said Mitchell Sanders.

Lee Strunk made a funny ghost sound, a kind of moaning, yet very happy, and right then, when Strunk made that high happy moaning sound, when he went *Ah-hooooo,* right then Ted Lavender was shot in the head on his way back from peeing. He lay with his mouth open. The teeth were broken. There was a swollen black bruise under his left eye. The cheekbone was gone. Oh shit, Rat Kiley said, the guy's dead. The guy's dead, he kept saying, which seemed profound—the guys' dead. I mean really.

The things they carried were determined to some extent by superstition. Lieutenant Cross carried his good-luck pebble. Dave Jensen carried a rabbit's foot. Norman Bowker, otherwise a very gentle person, carried a thumb that had been presented to him as a gift by Mitchell Sanders. The thumb was dark brown, rubbery to the touch, and weighed four ounces at most. It had been cut from a VC corpse, a boy of fifteen or sixteen. They'd found him at the bottom of an irrigation ditch, badly burned, flies in his mouth and eyes. They boy wore black shorts and sandals. At the time of his death he had been carrying a pouch of rice, a rifle, and three magazines of ammunition.

You want my opinion, Mitchell Sanders said, there's a definite moral here.

He put his hand on the dead boy's wrist. He was quiet for a time, as if counting a pulse, then he patted the stomach, almost affectionately, and used Kiowa's hunting hatchet to remove the thumb.

Henry Dobbins asked what the moral was.

Moral?

You know. *Moral.*

Sanders wrapped the thumb in toilet paper and handed it across to Norman Bowker. There was no blood. Smiling, he kicked the boy's head, watched the flies scatter, and said, It's like with that old TV show—Paladin. Have gun, will travel.

Henry Dobbins thought about it.

Yeah, well, he finally said. I don't see no moral.

There it *is,* man.

Fuck off.

They carried USO stationery and pencils and pens. They carried Sterno, safety pins, trip flares, signal flares, spools of wire, razor blades, chewing tobacco, liberated joss sticks and statuettes of the smiling Buddha, candles, grease pencils, *The Stars and Stripes,* fingernail clippers, Psy Ops leaflets, bush hats, bolos, and much more. Twice a week, when the resupply choppers came in, they carried hot chow in green Mermite cans and large canvas bags filled with iced beer and soda pop. They carried plastic water containers, each with a two gallon capacity. Mitchell Sanders carried a set of starched tiger fatigues for special occasions. Henry Dobbins carried Black Flag insecticide. Dave Jensen carried empty sandbags that could be filled at night for added protection. Lee Strunk carried tanning lotion. Some things they carried in common. Taking turns, they carried the big PRC-77 scrambler radio, which weighed thirty pounds with its battery. They shared the weight of memory. They took up what others could no longer bear. Often, they carried each other, the wounded or weak. They carried infections. They carried chess sets, basketballs, Vietnamese-English dictionaries, insignia of rank, Bronze Stars and Purple Hearts, plastic cards imprinted with the Code of Conduct. They carried diseases, among them malaria and dysentery. They carried lice and ringworm and leeches and paddy

algae and various rots and molds. They carried the land itself—
Vietnam, the place, the soil—a powdery orange-red dust that covered
their boots and fatigues and faces. They carried the sky. The whole atmosphere, they carried it, the humidity, the monsoons, the stink of fungus and decay, all of it, they carried gravity. They moved like mules. By
daylight they took sniper fire, at night they were mortared, but it was
not battle, it was just the endless march, village to village, without purpose, nothing won or lost. They marched for the sake of the march.
They plodded along slowly, dumbly, leaning forward against the heat,
unthinking, all blood and bone, simple grunts, soldiering with their
legs, toiling up the hills and down into the paddies and across the rivers
and up again and down, just humping, one step and then the next and
then another, but no volition, no will, because it was automatic, it was
anatomy, and the war was entirely a matter of posture and carriage, the
hump was everything, a kind of inertia, a kind of emptiness, a dullness
of desire and intellect and conscience and hope and human sensibility.
Their principles were in their feet. Their calculations were biological.
They had no sense of strategy or mission. They searched the villages
without knowing what to look for, nor caring, kicking over jars of rice,
frisking children and old men, blowing tunnels, sometimes setting fires
and sometimes not, then forming up and moving on to the next village,
then other villages, where it would always be the same. They carried
their own lives. The pressures were enormous. In the heat of early afternoon, they would remove their helmets and flak jackets, walking
bare, which was dangerous but which helped ease the strain. They
would often discard things along the route of march. Purely for comfort, they would throw away rations, blow their Claymores and
grenades, no matter, because by nightfall the resupply choppers would
arrive with more of the same, then a day or two later still more, fresh
watermelons and crates of ammunition and sunglasses and woolen
sweaters—the resources were stunning—sparklers for the Fourth of
July, colored eggs for Easter. It was the great American war chest—the
fruits of sciences, the smokestacks, the canneries, the arsenals at
Hartford, the Minnesota forests, the machine shops, the vast fields of
corn and wheat—they carried like freight trains; they carried it on their
backs and shoulders—and for all the ambiguities of Vietnam, all the
mysteries and unknowns, there was at least the single abiding certainty
that they would never be at a loss for things to carry.

After the chopper took Lavender away, Lieutenant Jimmy Cross led
his men into the village of Than Khe. They burned everything. They

shot chickens and dogs, they trashed the village well, they called in artillery and watched the wreckage, then they marched for several hours through the hot afternoon, and then at dusk, while Kiowa explained how Lavender died, Lieutenant Cross found himself trembling.

He tried not to cry. With his entrenching tool, which weighed five pounds, he began digging a hole in the earth.

He felt shame. He hated himself. He had loved Martha more than his men, and as a consequence Lavender was now dead, and this was something he would have to carry like a stone in his stomach for the rest of the war.

All he could do was dig. He used his entrenching tool like an ax, slashing, feeling both love and hate, and then later, when it was full dark, he sat at the bottom of his foxhole and wept. It went on for a long while. In part, he was grieving for Ted Lavender, but mostly it was for Martha, and for himself, because she belonged to another world, which was not quite real, and because she was a junior at Mount Sebastian College in New Jersey, a poet and a virgin and uninvolved, and because he realized she did not love him and never would.

Like cement, Kiowa whispered in the dark. I swear to God—boom-down. Not a word.

I've heard this, said Norman Bowker.

A pisser, you know? Still zipping himself up. Zapped while zipping.

All right, fine. That's enough.

Yeah, but you had to see it, the guy just—

I *heard*, man. Cement. So why not shut the fuck *up?*

Kiowa shook his head sadly and glanced over at the hole where Lieutenant Jimmy Cross sat watching the night. The air was thick and wet. A warm, dense fog had settled over the paddies and there was the stillness that precedes rain.

After a time Kiowa sighed.

One thing for sure, he said. The lieutenant's in some deep hurt. I mean that crying jag—the way he was carrying on—it wasn't fake or anything, it was real heavy-duty hurt. The man cares.

Sure, Norman Bowker said.

Say what you want, the man does care.

We all got problems.

Not Lavender.

No, I guess not, Bowker said. Do me a favor, though.

Shut up?

That's a smart Indian. Shut up.

Shrugging, Kiowa pulled off his boots. He wanted to say more, just to lighten up his sleep, but instead he opened his New Testament and arranged it beneath his head as a pillow. The fog made things seem hollow and unattached. He tried not to think about Ted Lavender, but then he was thinking how fast it was, no drama, down and dead, and how it was hard to feel anything except surprise. It seemed unchristian. He wished he could find some great sadness, or even anger, but the emotion wasn't there and he couldn't make it happen. Mostly he felt pleased to be alive. He liked the smell of the New Testament under his cheek, the leather and ink and paper and glue, whatever the chemicals were. He liked hearing the sounds of night. Even his fatigue, it felt fine, the stiff muscles and the prickly awareness of his own body, a floating feeling. He enjoyed not being dead. Lying there, Kiowa admired Lieutenant Jimmy Cross's capacity for grief. He wanted to share the man's pain, he wanted to care as Jimmy Cross cared. And yet when he closed his eyes, all he could think was Boom-down, and all he could feel was the pleasure of having his boots off and the fog curling in around him and damp soil and the Bible smells and the plush comfort of night.

After a moment Norman Bowker sat up in the dark.

What the hell, he said. You want to talk, *talk*. Tell it to me.

Forget it.

No, man, go on. One thing I hate, it's a silent Indian.

For the most part they carried themselves with poise, a kind of dignity. Now and then, however, there were times of panic, when they squealed or wanted to squeal but couldn't, when they twitched and made moaning sounds and covered their heads and said Dear Jesus and flopped around on the earth and fired their weapons blindly and cringed and sobbed and begged for the noise to stop and went wild and made stupid promises to themselves and to God and to their mothers and fathers, hoping not to die. In different ways, it happened to all of them. Afterward, when the firing ended, they would blink and peek up. They would touch their bodies, feeling shame, then quickly hiding it. They would force themselves to stand. As if in slow motion, frame by frame, the world would take on the old logic—absolute silence, then the wind, then sunlight, then voices. It was the burden of being alive. Awkwardly, the men would reassemble themselves, first in private, then in groups, becoming soldiers again. They would repair the leaks in their eyes. They would check for casualties, call in dust-offs, light cigarettes, try to smile, clear their throats and spit and begin cleaning their weapons. After a time someone would shake his head and say, No lie, I almost shit my pants, and someone else would laugh, which meant it was bad, yes, but the guy had obviously not shit his pants, it wasn't that bad, and in any case nobody would ever do such a thing and then go ahead and talk about it. They would squint into the dense, oppressive sunlight. For a few moments, perhaps, they would fall silent, lighting a joint and tracking its passage from man to man, inhaling, holding in the humiliation. Scary stuff, one of them might say. But then someone else would grin or flick his eyebrows and say, Roger-dodger, almost cut me a new asshole, *almost.*

There were numerous such poses. Some carried themselves with a sort of wistful resignation, others with pride or still soldierly discipline or good humor or macho zeal. They were afraid of dying but they were even more afraid to show it.

They found jokes to tell.

They used a hard vocabulary to contain the terrible softness. *Greased,* they'd say. *Offed, lit up, zapped while zipping.* It wasn't cruelty, just stage presence. They were actors and the war came at them in 3-D. When someone died, it wasn't quite dying, because in a curious way it seemed scripted, and because they had their lines mostly memorized, irony mixed with tragedy, and because they called it by other names, as if to encyst and destroy the reality of death itself. They kicked corpses. They cut off thumbs. They talked grunt lingo. They told stories about Ted Lavender's supply of tranquilizers, how the poor guy didn't feel a thing, how incredibly tranquil he was.

There's a moral here, said Mitchell Sanders.

They were waiting for Lavender's chopper, smoking the dead man's dope.

The moral's pretty obvious, Sanders said, and winked. Stay away from drugs. No joke, they'll ruin your day every time.

Cute, said Henry Dobbins.

Mind-blower, get it? Talk about wiggy—nothing left, just blood and brains.

They made themselves laugh.

There it is, they'd say, over and over, as if the repetition itself were an act of poise, a balance between crazy and almost crazy, knowing without going. There it is, which meant be cool, let it ride, because oh yeah, man, you can't change what can't be changed, there it is, there it absolutely and positively and fucking well *is.*

They were tough.

They carried all the emotional baggage of men who might die. Grief, terror, love, longing—these were intangibles, but the intangibles had their own mass and specific gravity, they had tangible weight. They carried shameful memories. They carried the common secret of cowardice barely restrained, the instinct to run or freeze or hide, and in many respects this was the heaviest burden of all, for it could never be put down, it required perfect balance and perfect posture. They carried their reputations. They carried the soldier's greatest fear, which was the fear of blushing. Men killed, and died, because they were embarrassed not to. It was what had brought them to the war in the first place, nothing positive, no dreams of glory or honor, just to avoid the blush of dishonor. They died so as not to die of embarrassment. They crawled into tunnels and walked point and advanced under fire. Each morning, despite the unknowns, they made their legs move. They endured. They kept humping. They did not submit to the obvious alternative, which was simply to close the eyes and fall. So easy, really. Go limp and tumble to the ground and let the muscles unwind and not speak and not budge until your buddies picked you up and lifted you into the chopper that would roar and dip its nose and carry you off to the world. A mere matter of falling, yet no one ever fell. It was not courage, exactly; the object was not valor. Rather, they were too frightened to be cowards.

By and large they carried these things inside, maintaining the masks of composure. They sneered at sick call. They spoke bitterly about guys who had found release by shooting off their own toes or fingers. Pussies, they'd say. Candyasses. It was fierce, mocking talk, with only a trace of envy or awe, but even so, the image played itself out behind their eyes.

They imagined the muzzle against flesh. They imagined the quick, sweet pain, then the evacuation to Japan, then a hospital with warm beds and cute geisha nurses.

They dreamed of freedom birds.

At night, on guard, staring into the dark, they were carried away by jumbo jets. They felt the rush of takeoff. *Gone!* they yelled. And then velocity, wings and engines, a smiling stewardess—but it was more than a plane, it was a real bird, a big sleek silver bird with feathers and talons and high screeching. They were flying. The weights fell off, there was nothing to bear. They laughed and held on tight, feeling the cold slap of wind and altitude, soaring, thinking *It's over, I'm gone!*—they were naked, they were light and free—it was all lightness, bright and fast and buoyant, light as light, a helium buzz in the brain, a giddy bubbling in the lungs as they were taken up over the clouds and the war, beyond duty, beyond gravity and mortification and global entan-glements—*Sin loi!*[7] They yelled, *I'm sorry, motherfuckers, but I'm out of it, I'm goofed, I'm on a space cruise, I'm gone!*—and it was a restful, disencumbered sensation, just riding the light waves, sailing that big sil-ver freedom bird over the mountains and oceans, over America, over the farms and great sleeping cities and cemeteries and highways and the Golden Arches of McDonald's. It was flight, a kind of fleeing, a kind of falling, falling higher and higher, spinning off the edge of the earth and beyond the sun and through the vast, silent vacuum where there were no burdens and where everything weighed exactly nothing. *Gone! they screamed, I'm sorry but I'm gone!* And so at night, not quite dreaming, they gave themselves over to lightness, they were carried, they were purely borne.

On the morning after Ted Lavender died, First Lieutenant Jimmy Cross crouched at the bottom of his foxhole and burned Martha's let-ters. Then he burned the two photographs. There was a steady rain falling, which made it difficult, but he used heat tabs and Sterno to build a small fire, screening it with his body, holding the photographs over the tight blue flame with the tips of his fingers.

He realized it was only a gesture. Stupid, he thought. Sentimental, too, but mostly just stupid.

Lavender was dead. You couldn't burn the blame.

Besides, the letters were in his head. And even now, without pho-tographs, Lieutenant Cross could see Martha playing volleyball in her white gym shorts and yellow T-shirt. He could see her moving in the rain.

When the fire died out, Lieutenant Cross pulled his poncho over his shoulders and ate breakfast from a can.

There was no great mystery, he decided.

In those burned letters Martha had never mentioned the war, except to say, Jimmy, take care of yourself. She wasn't involved. She signed the letters "Love," but it wasn't love, and all the fine lines and technicali-ties did not matter.

The morning came up wet and blurry. Everything seemed part of everything else, the fog and Martha and the deepening rain.

It was a war, after all.

Half smiling, Lieutenant Jimmy Cross took out his maps. He shook his head hard, as if to clear it, then bent forward and began planning the day's march. In ten minutes, or maybe twenty, he would rouse the

[7]*Sin loi* sorry

men and they would pack up and head west, where the maps showed the country to be green and inviting. They would do what they had always done. The rain might add some weight, but otherwise it would be one more day layered upon all the other days.

He was realistic about it. There was the new hardness in his stomach.

No more fantasies, he told himself.

Henceforth, when he thought about Martha, it would be only to think that she belonged elsewhere. He would shut down the day-dreams. This was not Mount Sebastian, it was another world, where there were no pretty poems or midterm exams, a place where men died because of carelessness and gross stupidity. Kiowa was right. Boom-down, and you were dead, never partly dead.

Briefly, in the rain, Lieutenant Cross saw Martha's gray eyes gazing back at him.

He understood.

It was very sad, he thought. The things men carried inside. The things men did or felt they had to do.

He almost nodded at her, but didn't.

Instead he went back to his maps. He was now determined to perform his duties firmly and without negligence. It wouldn't help Lavender, he knew that, but from this point on he would comport himself as a soldier. He would dispose of his good-luck pebble. Swallow it, maybe, or use Lee Strunk's slingshot, or just drop it along the trail. On the march he would impose strict field discipline. He would be careful to send out flank security, to prevent straggling or bunching up, to keep his troops moving at the proper pace and at the proper interval. He would insist on clean weapons. He would confiscate the remainder of Lavender's dope. Later in the day, perhaps, he would call the men together and speak to them plainly. He would accept the blame for what had happened to Ted Lavender. He would be a man about it. He would look them in the eyes, keeping his chin level, and he would issue the new SOPs in a calm, impersonal tone of voice, an officer's voice, leaving no room for argument or discussion. Commencing immediately, he'd tell them, they would no longer abandon equipment along the route of march. They would police up their acts. They would get their shit together, and keep it together, and maintain it neatly and in good working order.

He would not tolerate laxity. He would show strength, distancing himself.

Among the men there would be grumbling, of course, and maybe worse, because their days would seem longer and their loads heavier, but Lieutenant Cross reminded himself that his obligation was not to be loved but to lead. He would dispense with love; it was not now a factor. And if anyone quarreled or complained, he would simply tighten his lips and arrange his shoulders in the correct command posture. He might give a curt little nod. Or he might not. He might just shrug and say Carry on, then they would saddle up and form into a column and move out toward the villages west of Than Khe.

—1986

Questions: Reading, Responding, Arguing

1. How does the structure of "The Things They Carried" differ from other stories you are familiar with? Other stories from this anthology?
2. Since much of the text is a catalog of items, in what sense is this a story?
3. Each of the characters carries with him items that reveal something about who he is. What are those items and what do they reveal?
4. Why does Lieutenant Cross burn his photographs and letters? Argue that this action and others are symbolic.

Daniel Orozco (b. 1957)

Orientation

Those are the offices and these are the cubicles. That's my cubicle there, and this is your cubicle. This is your phone. Never answer your phone. Let the Voicemail System answer it. This is your Voicemail System Manual. There are no personal phone calls allowed. We do, however, allow for emergencies. If you must make an emergency phone call, ask your supervisor first. If you can't find your supervisor, ask Phillip Spiers, who sits over there. He'll check with Clarissa Nicks, who sits over there. If you make an emergency phone call without asking, you may be let go.

These are your IN and OUT boxes. All the forms in your IN box must be logged in by the date shown in the upper left-hand corner, initialed by you in the upper right-hand corner, and distributed to the Processing Analyst whose name is numerically coded in the lower left-hand corner.

The lower right-hand corner is left blank. Here's your Processing Analyst Numerical Code Index. And here's your Forms Processing Procedures Manual.

You must pace your work. What do I mean? I'm glad you asked that. We pace our work according to the eight-hour workday. If you have twelve hours of work in your IN box, for example, you must compress that work into the eight-hour day. If you have one hour of work in your IN box, you must expand that work to fill the eight-hour day. That was a good question. Feel free to ask questions. Ask too many questions, however, and you may be let go.

That is our receptionist. She is a temp. We go through receptionists here. They quit with alarming frequency. Be polite and civil to the temps. Learn their names, and invite them to lunch occasionally. But don't get close to them, as it only makes it more difficult when they leave. And they always leave. You can be sure of that.

The men's room is over there. The women's room is over there. John LaFountaine, who sits over there, uses the women's room occasionally. He says it is accidental. We know better, but we let it pass. John LaFountaine is harmless, his forays into the forbidden territory of the women's room simply a benign thrill, a faint blip on the dull flat line of his life.

Russell Nash, who sits in the cubicle to your left, is in love with Amanda Pierce, who sits in the cubicle to your right. They ride the same bus together after work. For Amanda Pierce, it is just a tedious bus ride made less tedious by the idle nattering of Russell Nash. But for Russell Nash, it is the highlight of his day. It is the highlight of his life. Russell Nash has put on forty pounds, and grows fatter with each passing month, nibbling on chips and cookies while peeking glumly over the partitions at Amanda Pierce, and gorging himself at home on cold pizza and ice cream while watching adult videos on TV.

Amanda Pierce, in the cubicle to your right, has a six-year-old son named Jamie, who is autistic. Her cubicle is plastered from top to bottom with the boy's crayon artwork—sheet after sheet of precisely drawn concentric circles and ellipses, in black and yellow. She rotates them every other Friday. Be sure to comment on them. Amanda Pierce also has a husband, who is a lawyer. He subjects her to an escalating array of painful and humiliating sex games, to which Amanda Pierce reluctantly submits. She comes to work exhausted and freshly wounded each morning, wincing from the abrasions on her breasts, or the bruises on her abdomen, or the second-degree burns on the backs of her thighs.

But we're not supposed to know any of this. Do not let on. If you let on, you may be let go.

Amanda Pierce, who tolerates Russell Nash, is in love with Albert Bosch, whose office is over there. Albert Bosch, who only dimly registers Amanda Pierce's existence, has eyes only for Ellie Tapper, who sits over there. Ellie Tapper, who hates Albert Bosch, would walk through fire for Curtis Lance. But Curtis Lance hates Ellie Tapper. Isn't the world a funny place? Not in the ha-ha sense, of course.

Anika Bloom sits in that cubicle. Last year, while reviewing quarterly reports in a meeting with Barry Hacker, Anika Bloom's left palm began to bleed. She fell into a trance, stared into her hand, and told Barry Hacker when and how his wife would die. We laughed it off. She was, after all, a new employee. But Barry Hacker's wife is dead. So unless you want to know exactly when and how you'll die, never talk to Anika Bloom.

Colin Heavey sits in that cubicle over there. He was new once, just like you. We warned him about Anika Bloom. But at last year's Christmas Potluck, he felt sorry for her when he saw that no one was talking to her. Colin Heavey brought her a drink. He hasn't been himself since. Colin Heavey is doomed. There's nothing he can do about it, and we are powerless to help him. Stay away from Colin Heavey. Never give any of your work to him. If he asks to do something, tell him you have to check with me. If he asks again, tell him I haven't gotten back to you.

This is the Fire Exit. There are several on this floor, and they are marked accordingly. We have a Floor Evacuation Review every three months, and an Escape Route Quiz once a month. We have our Biannual Fire Drill twice a year, and our Annual Earthquake Drill once a year. These are precautions only. These things never happen.

For your information, we have a comprehensive health plan. Any catastrophic illness, any unforeseen tragedy is completely covered. All dependents are completely covered. Larry Bagdikian, who sits over there, has six daughters. If anything were to happen to any of his girls, or to all of them, if all six were to simultaneously fall victim to illness or injury—stricken with a hideous degenerative muscle disease or some rare toxic blood disorder, sprayed with semiautomatic gunfire while on a class field trip, or attacked in their bunk beds by some prowling nocturnal lunatic—if any of this were to pass, Larry's girls would all be taken care of. Larry Bagdikian would not have to pay one dime. He would have nothing to worry about.

We also have a generous vacation and sick leave policy. We have an excellent disability insurance plan. We have a stable and profitable pension fund. We get group discounts for the symphony, and block seating at the ballpark. We get commuter ticket books for the bridge. We have Direct Deposit. We are all members of Costco.

This is our kitchenette. And this, this is our Mr. Coffee. We have a coffee pool, into which we each pay two dollars a week for coffee, filters, sugar, and CoffeeMate. If you prefer Cremora or half-and-half to CoffeeMate, there is a special pool for three dollars a week. If you prefer Sweet'n Low to sugar, there is a special pool for two-fifty a week. We do not do decaf. You are allowed to join the coffee pool of your choice, but you are not allowed to touch the Mr. Coffee.

This is the microwave oven. You are allowed to *heat* food in the microwave oven. You are not, however, allowed to *cook* food in the microwave oven.

We get one hour for lunch. We also get one fifteen-minute break in the morning, and one fifteen-minute break in the afternoon. Always take your breaks. If you skip a break, it is gone forever. For your information, your break is a privilege, not a right. If you abuse the break policy, we are authorized to rescind your breaks. Lunch, however, is a right, not a privilege. If you abuse the lunch policy, our hands will be tied, and we will be forced to look the other way. We will not enjoy that.

This is the refrigerator. You may put your lunch in it. Barry Hacker, who sits over there, steals food from this refrigerator. His petty theft is an outlet for his grief. Last New Year's Eve, while kissing his wife, a blood vessel burst in her brain. Barry Hacker's wife was two months pregnant at the time, and lingered in a coma for half a year before dying. It was a tragic loss for Barry Hacker. He hasn't been himself since. Barry Hacker's wife was a beautiful woman. She was also completely covered. Barry Hacker did not have to pay one dime. But his dead wife haunts him. She haunts all of us. We have seen her, reflected in the monitors of our computers, moving past our cubicles. We have seen the dim shadow of her face in our photocopies. She pencils herself in in the receptionist's appointment book, with the notation: To see Barry Hacker. She has left messages in the receptionist's Voicemail box, messages garbled by the electronic chirrups and buzzes in the phone line, her voice echoing from an immense distance within the ambient hum. But the voice is hers. And beneath her voice, beneath the tidal *whoosh* of static and hiss, the gurgling and crying of a baby can be heard.

In any case, if you bring a lunch, put a little something extra in the bag for Barry Hacker. We have four Barrys in this office. Isn't that a co-incidence?

This is Matthew Payne's office. He is our Unit Manager, and his door is always closed. We have never seen him, and you will never see him. But he is here. You can be sure of that. He is all around us.

This is the Custodian's Closet. You have no business in the Custodian's Closet.

And this, this is our Supplies Cabinet. If you need supplies, see Curtis Lance. He will log you in on the Supplies Cabinet Authorization Log, then give you a Supplies Authorization Slip. Present your pink copy of the Supplies Authorization Slip to Ellie Tapper. She will log you in on the Supplies Cabinet Key Log, then give you the key. Because the Supplies Cabinet is located outside the Unit Manager's office, you must be very quiet. Gather your supplies quietly. The Supplies Cabinet is divided into four sections. Section One contains letterhead stationery, blank paper and envelopes, memo and note pads, and so on. Section Two contains pens and pencils and typewriter and printer ribbons, and the like. In Section Three we have erasers, correction fluids, transparent tapes, glue sticks, et cetera. And in Section Four we have paper clips and push pins and scissors and razor blades. And here are the spare blades for the shredder. Do not touch the shredder, which is located over there. The shredder is of no concern to you.

Gwendolyn Stich sits in that office there. She is crazy about penguins, and collects penguin knickknacks: penguin posters and coffee mugs and stationery, penguin stuffed animals, penguin jewelry, penguin sweaters and T-shirts and socks. She has a pair of penguin fuzzy slippers she wears when working late at the office. She has a tape cassette of penguin sounds which she listens to for relaxation. Her favorite colors are black and white. She has personalized license plates that read PEN GWEN. Every morning, she passes through all the cubicles to wish each of us a *good* morning. She brings Danish on Wednesdays for Hump Day morning break, and doughnuts on Fridays for TGIF afternoon break. She organizes the Annual Christmas Potluck, and is in charge of the Birthday List. Gwendolyn Stich's door is always open to all of us. She will always lend an ear, and put in a good word for you; she will always give you a hand, or the shirt off her back, or a shoulder to cry on. Because her door is always open, she hides and cries in a stall in the women's room. And John LaFountaine—who, enthralled when a woman enters, sits quietly in his stall with his knees to his chest—John LaFountaine has heard her vomiting in there. We have come upon

Gwendolyn Stich huddled in the stairwell, shivering in the updraft, sipping a Diet Mr. Pibb and hugging her knees. She does not let any of this interfere with her work. If it interfered with her work, she might have to be let go.

Kevin Howard sits in that cubicle over there. He is a serial killer, the one they call the Carpet Cutter, responsible for the mutilations across town. We're not supposed to know that, so do not let on. Don't worry. His compulsion inflicts itself on strangers only, and the routine established is elaborate and unwavering. The victim must be a white male, a young adult no older than thirty, heavyset, with dark hair and eyes, and the like. The victim must be chosen at random, before sunset, from a public place; the victim is followed home, and must put up a struggle; et cetera. The carnage inflicted is precise: the angle and direction of the incisions; the layering of skin and muscle tissue; the rearrangement of the visceral organs; and so on. Kevin Howard does not let any of this interfere with his work. He is, in fact, our fastest typist. He types as if he were on fire. He has a secret crush on Gwendolyn Stich, and leaves a red-foil-wrapped Hershey's Kiss on her desk every afternoon. But he hates Anika Bloom, and keeps well away from her. In his presence, she has uncontrollable fits of shaking and trembling. Her left palm does not stop bleeding.

In any case, when Kevin Howard gets caught, act surprised. Say that he seemed like a nice person, a bit of a loner, perhaps, but always quiet and polite.

This is the photocopier room. And this, this is our view. It faces southwest. West is down there, toward the water. North is back there. Because we are on the seventeenth floor, we are afforded a magnificent view. Isn't it beautiful? It overlooks the park, where the tops of those trees are. You can see a segment of the bay between those two buildings there. You can see the sun set in the gap between those two buildings over there. You can see this building reflected in the glass panels of that building across the way. There. See? That's you, waving. And look there. There's Anika Bloom in the kitchenette, waving back.

Enjoy this view while photocopying. If you have problems with the photocopier, see Russell Nash. If you have any questions, ask your supervisor. If you can't find your supervisor, ask Phillip Spiers. He sits over there. He'll check with Clarissa Nicks. She sits over there. If you can't find them, feel free to ask me. That's my cubicle. I sit in there.

—1995

Questions: Reading, Responding, Arguing

1. What type of point of view does this story use? How is it unusual?
2. What are the implications of the title? Does "orientation" have more than one meaning?
3. Which characters in the story are stereotypes?
4. Is the story primarily realistic or is it an exaggerated satire? Craft an argument supporting one position.

Art Spiegelman (b. 1948)

From *Maus*

—1986

Questions: Reading, Responding, Arguing

1. Explain why Spiegelman chose different animals to portray different nationalities in the selection.
2. Compare and contrast realistic details of the story (its written narrative) with the graphic, obviously fictional elements.
3. Citing examples from the work, make an argument that Spiegelman uses graphic elements of the selection to reveal new ideas or supplement ideas already found in the written text.
4. What is the narrator's attitude towards the dead soldier? Using examples from the text, make an argument that the narrator is both sympathetic to the soldier and happy that he has died.

William Blake (1757–1827)

London

I wander through each chartered street,
Near where the chartered Thames does flow,
And mark in every face I meet
Marks of weakness, marks of woe.

In every cry of every man,   5
In every Infant's cry of fear,
In every voice, in every ban,
The mind-forged manacles I hear.

How the Chimney-sweeper's cry
Every black'ning Church appalls;   10
And the hapless Soldier's sigh
Runs in blood down Palace walls.

But most through midnight streets I hear
How the youthful Harlot's curse
Blasts the new-born Infant's tear,   15
And blights with plagues the Marriage hearse.

—1794

Questions: Reading, Responding, Arguing

1. Examine Blake's specific word choices, especially "chartered" and the phrase "Marriage hearse." Why do you think he chose these specific words?
2. How does repetition function effectively in the poem?
3. Compare this poem's use of "non-poetic," realistic details to another poem's imagery.?
4. What are the implications of the poem's final stanza? What is the "Harlot's curse"?

Walt Whitman   (1819–1892)

When I Heard the Learn'd Astronomer

When I heard the learn'd astronomer,
When the proofs, the figures, were ranged in columns before me,
When I was shown the charts and diagrams, to add, divide, and
    measure them,
When I sitting heard the astronomer where he lectured with much
    applause in the lecture-room,
How soon unaccountable I became tired and sick,   5
Till rising and gliding out I wander'd off by myself,
In the mystical moist night-air, and from time to time,
Look'd up in perfect silence at the stars.

—*1865*

Questions: Reading, Responding, Arguing

1. What does the astronomer represent to the speaker? Is "learn'd" used ironically?
2. Explain the significance of the last line.
3. How does the speaker use the astronomer in order to argue his own point of view?

Emily Dickinson (1830–1886)

The Soul selects her own Society

The Soul selects her own Society—
Then—shuts the Door—
To her divine Majority—
Present no more—

Unmoved—she notes the Chariots—pausing—   5
At her low Gate—
Unmoved—an Emperor be kneeling
Upon her Mat—

I've known her—from an ample nation—
Choose One—   10
Then—close the Valves° of her attention—
Like Stone—

—*1890*

Questions: Reading, Responding, Arguing

1. Explain how, where, and why Dickinson uses the long dash.
2. Examine Dickinson's poetic structure. Why has she ordered the stanzas in the way she has?
3. Compare this poem with another Dickinson poem in terms of her diction, form, use of punctuation, and subject matter. How does each function convey her theme?

11 **Valves** sliding doors

Thomas Hardy (1840–1928)

The Ruined Maid

"O 'Melia, my dear, this does everything crown!
Who could have supposed I should meet you in Town?
And whence such fair garments, such prosperi-ty?"
"O didn't you know I'd been ruined?" said she.

"You left us in tatters, without shoes or socks,   5
Tired of digging potatoes, and spudding up docks;°
And now you've gay bracelets and bright feathers three!"
"Yes: that's how we dress when we're ruined," said she.

"At home in the barton° you said 'thee' and 'thou,'
And 'thik oon,' and 'theäs oon,'° and 't'other'; but now   10
Your talking quite fits 'ee for high compa-ny!"
"Some polish is gained with one's ruin," said she.

"Your hands were like paws then, your face blue and bleak
But now I'm bewitched by your delicate cheek,
And your little gloves fit as on any la-dy!"   15
"We never do work when we're ruined," said she.

"You used to call home-life a hag-ridden dream,
And you'd sigh, and you'd sock; but at present you seem
To know not of megrims° or melancho-ly!"
"True. One's pretty lively when ruined," said she.   20

"I wish I had feathers, a fine sweeping gown,
And a delicate face, and could strut about Town!"
"My dear—a raw country girl, such as you be,
Cannot quite expect that. You ain't ruined," said she.

—*1866*

Questions: Reading, Responding, Arguing

1. Discuss how Hardy uses dialogue to convey the poem's meaning.

6 docks weeds   9 barton barnyard   10 thik oon and theäs oon dialect: "that one and this one"
19 megrims migraines

2. Compare the two women's views of being ruined. How is "ruined" a good example of verbal irony?
3. Analyze how Hardy uses repetition and stanza breaks to convey meaning.
4. What does this poem say about the theme of where we stand as an individual versus the institution? What kind of "institution" is Hardy satirizing?

A. E. Housman (1859–1936)

Eight O'Clock

He stood, and heard the steeple
    Sprinkle the quarters° on the morning town.
One, two, three, four, to market-place and people
    It tossed them down.

Strapped, noosed, nighing his hour,   5
    He stood and counted them and cursed his luck;
And then the clock collected in the tower
    Its strength, and struck.

                  —1922

Questions: Reading, Responding, Arguing

1. Explain the connections between stanzas one and two. How are the stanzas related?
2. Discuss Housman's use of irony in this poem.
3. How does one determine the dramatic situation of this poem? Is it explicit? Explain why.

---

2 quarters quarter hours

Edwin Arlington Robinson (1869–1935)

Richard Cory*

Whenever Richard Cory went down town,
We people on the pavement looked at him:
He was a gentleman from sole to crown,
Clean favored, and imperially slim.

And he was always quietly arrayed,   5
And he was always human when he talked;
But still he fluttered pulses when he said,
"Good-morning," and he glittered when he walked.

And he was rich—yes, richer than a king—
And admirably schooled in every grace: 10
In fine, we thought that he was everything
To make us wish that we were in his place.

So on we worked, and waited for the light,
And went without the meat, and cursed the bread;
And Richard Cory, one calm summer night,   15
Went home and put a bullet through his head.

—*1896*

Questions: Reading, Responding, Arguing

1. How does Robinson depict Richard Cory in stanzas one through three?
2. What do the rhyme and meter contribute to the poem?
3. Write about this poem in relation to the concepts of appearances and realities. Is it possible to argue that both Richard Cory and the poem's speaker are deluded?

Claude McKay (1889–1948)

If We Must Die

If we must die, let it not be like hogs
Hunted and penned in an inglorious spot,
While round us bark the mad and hungry dogs,
Making their mock at our accursed lot.
If we must die, O let us nobly die,   5
So that our precious blood may not be shed
In vain: then even the monsters we defy
Shall be constrained to honor us though dead!
O kinsmen! we must meet the common foe!
Though far outnumbered let us show us brave,   10
And for their thousand blows deal one deathblow!
What though before us lies the open grave?
Like men we'll face the murderous, cowardly pack,
Pressed to the wall, dying, but fighting back!

—*1919*

Questions: Reading, Responding, Arguing

1. Compare the tone of this sonnet with that of Blake's "London" on page 820.
2. What conventions of the sonnet does McKay observe?
3. Argue that the knowledge that McKay was an African American and that the poem was written after the Harlem race riots of 1919 affects the reading of the poems.

Countee Cullen (1903–1946)

Incident

Once riding in old Baltimore,
  Heart-filled, head-filled with glee,
I saw a Baltimorean
  Keep looking straight at me.

Now I was eight and very small,   5
  And he was no whit bigger,
And so I smiled, but he poked out
  His tongue, and called me, "Nigger."

I saw the whole of Baltimore
  From May until December;   10
Of all the things that happened there
  That's all that I remember.

—1963

Questions: Reading, Responding, Arguing

1. Explain how and where the poem's tone changes. Why is this significant?
2. Why is this poem called "Incident"?
3. How can this poem be read as a commentary on race and racism?

W. H. Auden (1907–1973)

The Unknown Citizen

To JS/07/M/378
This Marble Monument Is Erected by the State

He was found by the Bureau of Statistics to be
One against whom there was no official complaint,

And all the reports on his conduct agree
That, in the modern sense of an old-fashioned word, he was a saint,
For in everything he did he served the Greater Community.   5
Except for the War till the day he retired
He worked in a factory and never got fired,
But satisfied his employers, Fudge Motors Inc.
Yet he wasn't a scab or odd in his views,
For his Union reports that he paid his dues,   10
(Our report on his Union shows it was sound)
And our Social Psychology workers found
That he was popular with his mates and liked a drink.
The Press are convinced that he bought a paper every day
And that his reactions to advertisements were normal in every way. 15
Policies taken out in his name prove that he was fully insured,
And his Health-card shows he was once in hospital but left it cured.
Both Producers Research and High-Grade Living declare
He was fully sensible to the advantages of the Installment Plan
And had everything necessary to the Modern Man,   20
A phonograph, a radio, a car and a frigidaire.
Our researchers into Public Opinion are content
That he held the proper opinions for the time of year;
When there was peace, he was for peace; when there was war, he
      went.
He was married and added five children to the population,   25
Which our Eugenist says was the right number for a parent of
      his generation,
And our teachers report that he never interfered with their education.
Was he free? Was he happy? The question is absurd:
Had anything been wrong, we should certainly have heard.

—1939

Questions: Reading, Responding, Arguing

1. Who is the unknown citizen? What characteristic does he possess? Why is he called a saint?
2. What role does the Eugenist play in the poem? What is eugenics?
3. What does the speaker mean by "Was he free? Was he happy? The question is absurd"? Argue that this line and the next express the poem's ironic theme.

Theodore Roethke (1908–1963)

Dolor°

I have known the inexorable sadness of pencils,
Neat in their boxes, dolor of pad and paper-weight,
All of the misery of manilla folders and mucilage,
Desolation in immaculate public places,
Lonely reception room, lavatory, switchboard,   5
The unalterable pathos of basin and pitcher,
Ritual of multigraph, paper-clip, comma,
Endless duplication of lives and objects.
And I have seen dust from the walls of institutions,
Finer than flour, alive, more dangerous than silica,°   10
Sift, almost invisible, through long afternoons of tedium,
Dropping a fine film on nails and delicate eyebrows,
Glazing the pale hair, the duplicate grey standard faces.

—1948

Questions: Reading, Responding, Arguing

1. Explain the significance of the phrase "I have known the inexorable sadness of pencils."
2. What is the connection between the title and the setting?
3. Why does Roethke choose common, everyday images and objects as his subject?
4. What does this poem say about the individual and the institution?
5. Compare the office setting here with the one in Daniel Orozco's "Orientation" (p. 811).

Dolor sadness   10 silica rock dust, a cause of silicosis, an occupational disease of miners and quarry workers

Elizabeth Bishop (1911–1979)

The Fish

I caught a tremendous fish
and held him beside the boat
half out of water, with my hook
fast in a corner of his mouth.
He didn't fight.   5
He hadn't fought at all.
He hung a grunting weight,
battered and venerable
and homely. Here and there
his brown skin hung in strips   10
like ancient wallpaper,
and its pattern of darker brown
was like wallpaper:
shapes like full-blown roses
stained and lost through age.   15
He was speckled with barnacles,
fine rosettes of lime,
and infested
with tiny white sea-lice,
and underneath two or three   20
rags of green weed hung down.
While his gills were breathing in
the terrible oxygen
—the frightening gills,
fresh and crisp with blood,   25
that can cut so badly—
I thought of the coarse white flesh
packed in like feathers,
the big bones and the little bones,
the dramatic reds and blacks   30
of his shiny entrails,
and the pink swim-bladder
like a big peony.
I looked into his eyes
which were far larger than mine   35
but shallower, and yellowed,

the irises backed and packed
with tarnished tinfoil
seen through the lenses
of old scratched isinglass.°   40
They shifted a little, but not
to return my stare.
—It was more like the tipping
of an object toward the light.
I admired his sullen face,   45
the mechanism of his jaw,
and then I saw
that from his lower lip
—if you could call it a lip—
grim, wet, and weapon-like,   50
hung five old pieces of fish-line,
or four and a wire leader
with the swivel still attached,
with all their five big hooks
grown firmly in his mouth.   55
A green line, frayed at the end
where he broke it, two heavier lines,
and a fine black thread
still crimped from the strain and snap
when it broke and he got away.   60
Like medals with their ribbons
frayed and wavering,
a five-haired beard of wisdom
trailing from his aching jaw.
I stared and stared   65
and victory filled up
the little rented boat,
from the pool of bilge
where oil had spread a rainbow
around the rusted engine   70
to the bailer° rusted orange,
the sun-cracked thwarts,
the oarlocks on their strings,
the gunnels°—until everything

40 isinglass semitransparent material made from fish bladders   **71 bailer** bucket   **74 gunnels**
gunwales

was rainbow, rainbow, rainbow!   75
And I let the fish go.

—*1946*

Questions: Reading, Responding, Arguing

1. Examine Bishop's choice of diction. How does her diction reflect her attitude toward the fish?
2. What makes the speaker set the fish free?
3. Explain the significance of the rainbow references in the final eight lines and how they relate to the term epiphany.

Henry Reed (1914–1986)

Naming of Parts

To-day we have naming of parts. Yesterday,
We had daily cleaning. And to-morrow morning,
We shall have what to do after firing. But to-day,
To-day we have naming of parts. Japonica
Glistens like coral in all of the neighboring gardens,   5
      And to-day we have naming of parts.

This is the lower sling swivel. And this
Is the upper sling swivel, whose use you will see,
When you are given your slings. And this is the piling swivel,
Which in your case you have not got. The branches   10
Hold in the gardens their silent, eloquent gestures,
      Which in our case we have not got.

This is the safety-catch, which is always released
With an easy flick of the thumb. And please do not let me
See anyone using his finger. You can do it quite easy   15
If you have any strength in your thumb. The blossoms
Are fragile and motionless, never letting anyone see
      Any of them using their finger.

And this you can see is the bolt. The purpose of this
Is to open the breech, as you see. We can slide it   20
Rapidly backwards and forwards: we call this

Easing the spring. And rapidly backwards and forwards
The early bees are assaulting and fumbling the flowers:
  They call it easing the Spring.

They call it easing the Spring: it is perfectly easy   25
If you have any strength in your thumb: like the bolt,
And the breech, and the cocking-piece, and the point of balance,
Which in our case we have not got; and the almond-blossom
Silent in all of the gardens and the bees going backwards and forwards,
  For to-day we have naming of parts.   30

—*1942*

Questions: Reading, Responding, Arguing

1. Identify the two voices that speak in the poem. Who are
   they? How are they different?
2. How do the parts of the rifle change when the second
   speaker echoes them? Do they take on additional meanings?
3. Why is setting important in this poem? What is the symbolic
   significance of the garden?

Donalò Juƒtice (1925–2004)

Counting the Mad

This one was put in a jacket,
This one was sent home,
This one was given bread and meat
But would eat none,
And this one cried No No No No   5
All day long.

This one looked at the window
As though it were a wall,
This one saw things that were not there,
This one things that were,   10
And this one cried No No No No
All day long.

This one thought himself a bird,
This one a dog,
And this one thought himself a man,   15
An ordinary man,
And this one cried No No No No
All day long.

—*1960*

Questions: Reading, Responding, Arguing

1. What is the form of the poem based on? What does this allusion contribute to the poem's themes?
2. What's the significance of the man who thought himself "An
   ordinary man"?
3. How is this poem a commentary on madness or mental illness?
   Argue that Justice is implicitly criticizing society's definition
   of madness.

Adrienne Rich (b. 1929)

Rape

There is a cop who is both prowler and father:
he comes from your block, grew up with your brothers,
had certain ideals.
You hardly know him in his boots and silver badge,
on horseback, one hand touching his gun.   5

You hardly know him but you have to get to know him:
he has access to machinery that could kill you.
He and his stallion clop like warlords among the trash,
his ideals stand in the air, a frozen cloud
from between his unsmiling lips.   10

And so, when the time comes, you have to turn to him,
the maniac's sperm still greasing your thighs,
your mind whirling like crazy. You have to confess
to him, you are guilty of the crime
of having been forced.   15

And you see his blue eyes, the blue eyes of all the family
whom you used to know, grow narrow and glisten,
his hand types out the details
and he wants them all
but the hysteria in your voice pleases him best.   20

You hardly know him but now he thinks he knows you:
he has taken down your worst moment
on a machine and filed it in a file.
He knows, or thinks he knows, how much you imagined;
he knows, or thinks he knows, what you secretly wanted.   25

He has access to machinery that could get you put away;
and if, in the sickening light of the precinct,
and if, in the sickening light of the precinct,
your details sound like a portrait of your confessor,
will you swallow, will you deny them, will you lie your way home?   30

—*1972*

Questions: Reading, Responding, Arguing

1. What does the police officer represent? Why does Rich describe him and his actions in the way she does?
2. Examine Rich's use of repetition, especially of "you." Who is being addressed here?
3. Explain the significance of Rich's phrasing of the line "You have to confess / to him, you are guilty of the crime / of having been forced." Use this as a way of examining the bitterly ironic tone of the poem.

Miller Williams (b. 1930)

The Book

I held it in my hands while he told the story.

He had found it in a fallen bunker,
a book for notes with all the pages blank.
He took it to keep for a sketchbook and diary.

He learned years later, when he showed the book 5
to an old bookbinder, who paled, and stepped back
a long step and told him what he held,
what he had laid the days of his life in.
It's bound, the binder said, in human skin.

I stood turning it over in my hands, 10
turning it in my head. Human skin.

What child did this skin fit? What man, what woman?
Dragged still full of its flesh from what dream?

Who took it off the meat? Some other one
who stayed alive by knowing how to do this? 15

I stared at the changing book and a horror grew,
I stared and a horror grew, which was, which is,
how beautiful it was until I knew.

—1989

Questions: Reading, Responding, Arguing

1. How does Williams convey the emotions related to the book?
2. What does the book represent, symbolize, or suggest?
3. How and why does the speaker's attitude/tone change in the last stanza? Compare this revelation to that in another poem in this book.

Linda Pastan (b. 1932)

Ethics

In ethics class so many years ago
our teacher asked this question every fall:
if there were a fire in a museum
which would you save, a Rembrandt° painting

4 **Rembrandt** Rembrandt van Rijn (1606–1669), Dutch painter

or an old woman who hadn't many 5
years left anyhow? Restless on hard chairs
caring little for pictures or old age
we'd opt one year for life, the next for art
and always half-heartedly. Sometimes
the woman borrowed my grandmother's face 10
leaving her usual kitchen to wander
some drafty, half-imagined museum.
One year, feeling clever, I replied
why not let the woman decide herself?
Linda, the teacher would report, eschews 15
the burdens of responsibility.
This fall in a real museum I stand
before a real Rembrandt, old woman,
or nearly so, myself. The colors
within this frame are darker than autumn, 20
darker even than winter—the browns of earth,
though earth's most radiant elements burn
through the canvas. I know now that woman
and painting and season are almost one
and all beyond saving by children. 25

—*1981*

Questions: Reading, Responding, Arguing

1. What does this poem say about the hypothetical, classroom discussion of ethics and how ethics function in the real world?
2. Why does the teacher respond as she does to the speaker's suggestion "why not let the woman decide herself?"
3. How has the speaker's perception of the ethical question deepened and changed with age? How does Pastan use the strategies of argumentation to develop her theme?

Seamus Heaney (b. 1939)

Punishment

I can feel the tug
of the halter at the nape
of her neck, the wind
on her naked front.

It blows her nipples   5
to amber beads,
it shakes the frail rigging
of her ribs.

I can see her drowned
body in the bog,   10
the weighing stone,
the floating rods and boughs.

Under which at first
she was a barked sapling
that is dug up   15
oak-bone, brain-firkin°

her shaved head
like a stubble of black corn,
her blindfold a soiled bandage,
her noose a ring   20

to store
the memories of love.
Little adulteress,
before they punished you

you were flaxen-haired,   25
undernourished, and your
tar-black face was beautiful.
My poor scapegoat,

I almost love you
but would have cast, I know,   30

16 **firkin** a small barrel

the stones of silence.
I am the artful voyeur

of your brain's exposed
and darkened combs,
your muscles' webbing   35
and all your numbered bones:

I who have stood dumb
when your betraying sisters,
cauled in tar,
wept by the railings,   40

who would connive
in civilized outrage
yet understand the exact
and tribal, intimate revenge.

—1975

Questions: Reading, Responding, Arguing

1. Who is the "her" in the poem? How does Heaney depict her?
2. Examine Heaney's choice of diction. How and what does it contribute to the poem?
3. Why does Heaney call this poem "Punishment"? Argue that the idea of punishment informs the poem.

Billy Collins (b. 1941)

The Names*

Yesterday, I lay awake in the palm of the night.
A soft rain stole in, unhelped by any breeze,
And when I saw the silver glaze on the windows,
I started with A, with Ackerman, as it happened,
Then Baxter and Calabro,   5
Davis and Eberling, names falling into place
As droplets fell through the dark.
Names printed on the ceiling of the night.

Names slipping around a watery bend.
Twenty-six willows on the banks of a stream.   10
In the morning, I walked out barefoot
Among thousands of flowers
Heavy with dew like the eyes of tears,
And each had a name—
Fiori inscribed on a yellow petal   15
Then Gonzalez and Han, Ishikawa and Jenkins.
Names written in the air
And stitched into the cloth of the day.
A name under a photograph taped to a mailbox.
Monogram on a torn shirt,   20
I see you spelled out on storefront windows
And on the bright unfurled awnings of this city.
I say the syllables as I turn a corner—
Kelly and Lee,
Medina, Nardella, and O'Connor.   25
When I peer in to the woods,
I see a thick tangle where letters are hidden
As in a puzzle concocted for children.
Parker and Quigley in the twigs of an ash,
Rizzo, Schubert, Torres, and Upton,   30
Secrets in the boughs of an ancient maple.
Names written in the pale sky.
Names rising in the updraft amid buildings.
Names silent in stone
Or cried out behind a door.   35
Names blown over the earth and out to sea.
In the evening—weakening light, the last swallows.
A boy on a lake lifts his oars.
A woman by a window puts a match to a candle,
And the names are outlined on the rose clouds—   40
Vanacore and Wallace,
(let X stand, if it can, for the ones unfound)
Then Young and Ziminsky, the final jolt of Z.
Names etched on the head of a pin.
One name spanning a bridge, another undergoing a tunnel.   45
A blue name needled into the skin.
Names of citizens, workers, mothers and fathers,
The bright-eyed daughter, the quick son.
Alphabet of names in a green field.

Names in the small tracks of birds. 50
Names lifted from a hat
Or balanced on the tip of the tongue.
Names wheeled into the dim warehouse of memory.
So many names, there is barely room on the walls of the heart.

—*2002*

Questions: Reading, Responding, Arguing

1. How, exactly, are the names described as existing in the poem? How are these descriptions appropriate?
2. What is the significance of the letter *X* in the poem?
3. As U.S. poet laureate during 9/11, Collins said that he doubted that he would be able to write a poem about the event. But a year later he wrote this one. Why do you suppose he changed his mind?

Sarah Cortez (b. 1950)

Tu Negrito

She's got to bail me out,
he says into the phone outside the holding cell.
She's going there tomorrow anyway for Mikey.
Tell her she's got to do this for me.

He says into the phone outside the holding cell, 5
Make sure she listens. Make her feel guilty, man.
Tell her she's got to do this for me.
She can have all my money, man.

Make sure she listens. Make her feel guilty, man.
Tell her she didn't bail me out the other times. 10
She can have all my money, man.
She always bails out Mikey.

Tell her she didn't bail me out the other times.
I don't got no one else to call, cousin.
She always bails out Mikey. 15
Make sure you write all this down, cousin.

I don't got no one else to call, cousin.
I really need her now.
Make sure you write this all down, cousin.
Page her. Put in code 333. That's me.   20

I really need her now.
Write down "Mommie." Change it from "Mom."
Page her. Put in code 333. That's me.
Write down "*Tu Negrito*." Tell her I love her.

Write down "Mommie." Change it from "Mom."   25
I'm her littlest. Remind her.
Write down "*Tu Negrito*."
Tell her I love her. She's got to bail me out.

—*2000*

Questions: Reading, Responding, Arguing

1. What does "Tu Negrito" mean, and how does this title explain the relations of the characters to one another?
2. What does Cortez imply about the poem's central character?
3. Examine Cortez's use of voice and point of view; how does
   she use them to convey what is happening in the poem?
4. Several words and phrases, including the title, are used
   repetitively in the poem (an example of a pantoum). Argue
   in favor of the poet's choice of form.

Mary Jo Salter (b. 1954)

Welcome to Hiroshima*

is what you first see, stepping off the train:
a billboard brought to you in living English
by Toshiba Electric. While a channel
silent in the TV of the brain

projects those flickering re-runs of a cloud   5
that brims its risen columnful like beer

and, spilling over, hangs its foamy head,
you feel a thirst for history: what year

it started to be safe to breathe the air,
and when to drink the blood and scum afloat   10
on the Ohta River. But no, the water's clear,
they pour it for your morning cup of tea

in one of the countless sunny coffee shops
whose plastic dioramas advertise
mutations of cuisine behind the glass: 15
a pancake sandwich; a pizza someone tops

with a maraschino cherry. Passing by
the Peace Park's floral hypocenter (where
how bravely, or with what mistaken cheer,
humanity erased its own erasure),   20

you enter the memorial museum
and through more glass are served, as on a dish
of blistered grass, three mannequins. Like gloves
a mother clips to coatsleeves, strings of flesh

hang from their fingertips; or as if tied   25
to recall a duty for us, *Reverence
the dead whose mourners too shall soon be dead,*
but all commemoration's swallowed up

in questions of bad taste, how re-created
horror mocks the grim original,   30
and thinking at last *They should have left it all*
you stop. This is the wristwatch of a child.

Jammed on the moment's impact, resolute
to communicate some message, although mute,
it gestures with its hands at eight-fifteen   35
and eight-fifteen and eight-fifteen again

while tables of statistics on the wall
update the news by calling on a roll
of tape, death gummed on death, and in the case
adjacent, an exhibit under glass   40

is glass itself: a shard the bomb slammed in
a woman's arm at eight-fifteen, but some

three decades on—as if to make it plain
hope's only as renewable as pain,

and as if all the unsung   45
debasements of the past may one day come
rising to the surface once again—
worked its filthy way out like a tongue.

—1985

Questions: Reading, Responding, Arguing

1. What is the historical context of this poem? What commentary is Salter making?
2. Examine Salter's diction. How do the words chosen help to address and advance the themes and ideas in the poems?
3. Explain the role of stanza nine. What does it contribute to the poem?
4. Compare this poem's attitude toward war with another work on a similar subject.

Sophocles (496?–406 B.C.)

Antigonê*

An English Version by Dudley Fitts and Robert Fitzgerald*

LIST OF CHARACTERS

Antigonê
Ismenê
Eurydicê
Creon
Haimon
Teiresias
A Sentry
A Messenger
Chorus

*Explanatory notes are indicated by a degree symbol (°) in the text and are keyed
to the text by line number.

Scene: Before the palace of Creon, *king of Thebes. A central double door, and two lateral doors. A platform extends the length of the façade, and from this platform three steps lead down into the "orchestra," or chorus-ground.*

Time: Dawn of the day after the repulse of the Argive army from the assault on Thebes.

Prologue

Antigonê and Ismenê *enter from the central door of the palace.*

ANTIGONÊ: Ismenê, dear sister,
You would think that we had already suffered enough
For the curse on Oedipus.°
I cannot imagine any grief
That you and I have not gone through. And now—   5
Have they told you of the new decree of our King Creon?
ISMENÊ: I have heard nothing: I know
That two sisters lost two brothers, a double death
In a single hour; and I know that the Argive army
Fled in the night; but beyond this, nothing.   10
ANTIGONÊ: I thought so. And this is why I wanted you
To come out here with me. There is something we must do.
ISMENÊ: Why do you speak so strangely?
ANTIGONÊ: Listen, Ismenê:
Creon buried our brother Eteoclês   15
With military honors, gave him a soldier's funeral,
And it was right that he should; but Polyneicês,
Who fought as bravely and died as miserably,—
They say that Creon has sworn
No one shall bury him, no one mourn for him,   20
But his body must lie in the fields, a sweet treasure
For carrion birds to find as they search for food.
That is what they say, and our good Creon is coming here
To announce it publicly; and the penalty—

3 Oedipus, once King of Thebes, was the father of Antigonê and Ismenê, and of their brothers Polyneicês and Eteoclês. Oedipus unwittingly killed his father, Laïos, and married his own mother, Iocastê. When he learned what he had done, he blinded himself and left Thebes. Eteoclês and Polyneicês quarreled; Polyneicês was driven out but returned to assault Thebes. In the battle each brother killed the other; Creon became king and ordered that Polyneicês be left to rot unburied on the battlefield as a traitor.

Stoning to death in the public square!

There it is,   25

And now you can prove what you are:

A true sister, or a traitor to your family.

ISMENÊ: Antigonê, you are mad! What could I possibly do?

ANTIGONÊ: You must decide whether you will help me or not.

ISMENÊ: I do not understand you. Help you in what?   30

ANTIGONÊ: Ismenê. I am going to bury him. Will you come?

ISMENÊ: Bury him! You have just said the new law forbids it.

ANTIGONÊ: He is my brother. And he is your brother, too.

ISMENÊ: But think of the danger! Think what Creon will do!

ANTIGONÊ: Creon is not strong enough to stand in my way.   35

ISMENÊ: Ah sister!

Oedipus died, everyone hating him

For what his own search brought to light, his eyes

Ripped out by his own hand; and Iocastê died,

His mother and wife at once: she twisted the cords   40

That strangled her life; and our two brothers died,

Each killed by the other's sword. And we are left:

But oh, Antigonê,

Think how much more terrible than these

Our own death would be if we should go against Creon   45

And do what he has forbidden! We are only women,

We cannot fight with men, Antigonê!

The law is strong, we must give in to the law

In this thing, and in worse. I beg the Dead

To forgive me, but I am helpless: I must yield   50

To those in authority. And I think it is dangerous business

To be always meddling.

ANTIGONÊ: If that is what you think,

I should not want you, even if you asked to come.

You have made your choice, you can be what you want to be.

But I will bury him; and if I must die,   55

I say that this crime is holy: I shall lie down

With him in death, and I shall be as dear

To him as he to me.

It is the dead,

Not the living, who make the longest demands:

We die for ever. . . .

You may do as you like.   60

Since apparently the laws of the gods mean nothing to you.

ISMENÊ: They mean a great deal to me; but I have no strength
To break laws that were made for the public good.
ANTIGONÊ: That must be your excuse, I suppose. But as for me,
I will bury the brother I love.
ISMENÊ: Antigonê,   65
I am so afraid for you!
ANTIGONÊ: You need not be:
You have yourself to consider, after all.
ISMENÊ: But no one must hear of this, you must tell no one!
I will keep it a secret, I promise!
ANTIGONÊ: O tell it! Tell everyone!
Think how they'll hate you when it all comes out   70
If they learn that you knew about it all the time!
ISMENÊ: So fiery! You should be cold with fear.
ANTIGONÊ: Perhaps. But I am doing only what I must.
ISMENÊ: But can you do it? I say that you cannot.
ANTIGONÊ: Very well: when my strength gives out,
I shall do no more.   75
ISMENÊ: Impossible things should not be tried at all.
ANTIGONÊ: Go away, Ismenê:
I shall be hating you soon, and the dead will too,
For your words are hateful. Leave me my foolish plan:
I am not afraid of the danger; if it means death,   80
It will not be the worst of deaths—death without honor.
ISMENÊ: Go then, if you feel that you must.
You are unwise,
But a loyal friend indeed to those who love you.
          Exit into the palace. Antigonê *goes off, left. Enter the* Chorus.

Párodos

CHORUS: Now the long blade of the sun, lying   *Strophe 1*
Level east to west, touches with glory
Thebes of the Seven Gates. Open, unlidded
Eye of golden day! O marching light
Across the eddy and rush of Dircê's stream,°   5
Striking the white shields of the enemy
Thrown headlong backward from the blaze of morning!
CHORAGOS.°   Polyneicês their commander
Roused them with windy phrases,

---

5 **Dircê's stream** a stream west of Thebes.   8 **Choragos** leader of the Chorus.

He the wild eagle screaming   10
Insults above our land,
His wings their shields of snow,
His crest their marshalled helms.

CHORUS: Against our seven gates in a yawning ring   *Antistrophe 1*
The famished spears came onward in the night: 15
But before his jaws were sated with our blood,
Or pinefire took the garland of our towers,
He was thrown back; and as he turned, great Thebes—
No tender victim for his noisy power—
Rose like a dragon behind him, shouting war.   20

CHORAGOS: For God hates utterly
The bray of bragging tongues;
And when he beheld their smiling,
Their swagger of golden helms,
The frown of his thunder blasted   25
Their first man from our walls.

CHORUS: We heard his shout of triumph high in the air   *Strophe 2*
Turn to a scream; far out in a flaming arc
He fell with his windy torch, and the earth struck him.
And others storming in fury no less than his   30
Found shock of death in the dusty joy of battle.

CHORAGOS: Seven captains at seven gates
Yielded their clanging arms to the god
That bends the battle-line and breaks it.
These two only, brothers in blood,   35
Face to face in matchless rage.
Mirroring each the other's death,
Clashed in long combat.

CHORUS: But now in the beautiful morning of victory *Antistrophe 2*
Let Thebes of the many chariots sing for joy!   40
With hearts for dancing we'll take leave of war:
Our temples shall be sweet with hymns of praise,
And the long nights shall echo with our chorus.

Scene I

CHORAGOS: But now at last our new King is coming:
Creon of Thebes, Menoikeus' son.
In this auspicious dawn of his reign
What are the new complexities
That shifting Fate has woven for him?   5

What is his counsel? Why has he summoned
The old men to hear him?

Enter Creon *from the palace, center. He addresses the* Chorus *from the top step.*

CREON: Gentlemen: I have the honor to inform you that our Ship
of State, which recent storms have threatened to destroy, has
come safely to harbor at last, guided by the merciful wisdom 10
Heaven. I have summoned you here this morning because I
know that I can depend upon you: your devotion to King Laïos
was absolute; you never hesitated in your duty to our late ruler
Oedipus; and when Oedipus died, your loyalty was transferred
to his children. Unfortunately, as you know, his two sons, the 15
princes Eteoclês and Polyneicês, have killed each other in battle; and I, as the next in blood, have succeeded to the full power
of the throne.

I am aware, of course, that no Ruler can expect complete
loyalty from his subjects until he has been tested in office. 20
Nevertheless, I say to you at the very outset that I have nothing
but contempt for the kind of Governor who is afraid, for
whatever reason, to follow the course that he knows is best for
the State; and as for the man who sets private friendship above
the public welfare,—I have no use for him, either. I call God to 25
witness that if I saw my country headed for ruin, I should not
be afraid to speak out plainly; and I need hardly remind you
that I would never have any dealings with an enemy of the
people. No one values friendship more highly than I: but we
must remember that friends made at the risk of wrecking our 30
Ship are not real friends at all.

These are my principles, at any rate, and that is why I have
made the following decision concerning the sons of Oedipus:
Eteoclês, who died as a man should die, fighting for his country,
is to be buried with full military honors, with all the ceremony 35
that is usual when the greatest heroes die; but his brother
Polyneicês, who broke his exile to come back with fire and
sword against his native city and the shrines of his fathers'
gods, whose one idea was to spill the blood of his blood and
sell his own people into slavery—Polyneicês, I say, is to have no 40
burial: no man is to touch him or say the least prayer for him;
he shall lie on the plain, unburied; and the birds and the
scavenging dogs can do with him whatever they like.

This is my command, and you can see the wisdom behind
it. As long as I am King, no traitor is going to be honored with   45
the loyal man. But whoever shows by word and deed that he is
on the side of the State—he shall have my respect while he is
living and my reverence when he is dead.

CHORAGOS: If that is your will, Creon son of Menoikeus,
   You have the right to enforce it: we are yours.   50

CREON: That is my will. Take care that you do your part.

CHORAGOS: We are old men: let the younger ones carry it out.

CREON: I do not mean that: the sentries have been appointed.

CHORAGOS: Then what is it that you would have us do?

CREON: You will give no support to whoever breaks this law.   55

CHORAGOS: Only a crazy man is in love with death!

CREON: And death it is; yet money talks, and the wisest
   Have sometimes been known to count a few coins too many.

Enter Sentry *from left.*

SENTRY: I'll not say that I'm out of breath from running, King,
   because every time I stopped to think about what I have to tell   60
   you, I felt like going back. And all the time a voice kept saying,
   "You fool, don't you know you're walking straight into trouble?"; and then another voice: "Yes, but if you let somebody
   else get the news to Creon first, it will be even worse than that   65
   for you!" But good sense won out, at least I hope it was good
   sense, and here I am with a story that makes no sense at all; but
   I'll tell it anyhow, because, as they say, what's going to happen's
   going to happen and—

CREON: Come to the point. What have you to say?

SENTRY: I did not do it. I did not see who did it. You must not   70
   punish me for what someone else has done.

CREON: A comprehensive defense! More effective, perhaps, if I
   knew its purpose. Come: what is it?

SENTRY: A dreadful thing ... I don't know how to put it—

CREON: Out with it!

SENTRY: Well, then;   75
   The dead man—

               Polyneicês—

Pause. The Sentry *is overcome, fumbles for words.* Creon *waits impassively.*

out there—

someone,—

New dust on the slimy flesh!

Pause. No sign from Creon.

Someone has given it burial that way, and
Gone. . . .

Long pause. Creon *finally speaks with deadly control.*

CREON: And the man who dared do this?
SENTRY: I swear I   80
Do not know! You must believe me!

Listen:
The ground was dry, not a sign of digging, no,
Not a wheeltrack in the dust, no trace of anyone.
It was when they relieved us this morning: and one of them,
The corporal, pointed to it.

There it was,   85
The strangest—

Look:
The body, just mounded over with light dust: you see?
Not buried really, but as if they'd covered it
Just enough for the ghost's peace. And no sign
Of dogs or any wild animal that had been there.   90

And then what a scene there was! Every man of us
Accusing the other: we all proved the other man did it,
We all had proof that we could not have done it.
We were ready to take hot iron in our hands,
Walk through fire, swear by all the gods,   95
It was not I!
I do not know who it was, but it was not I!

Creon's *rage has been mounting steadily, but the* Sentry *is too intent upon his story to notice it.*

And then, when this came to nothing, someone said
A thing that silenced us and made us stare
Down at the ground: you had to be told the news,   100
And one of us had to do it! We threw the dice,
And the bad luck fell to me. So here I am,
No happier to be here than you are to have me:

Nobody likes the man who brings bad news.

CHORAGOS: I have been wondering, King: can it be that the gods   105
have done this?

CREON [*furiously*]:   Stop!
Must you doddering wrecks
Go out of your heads entirely? "The gods"!
Intolerable!   110
The gods favor this corpse? Why? How had he served them?
Tried to loot their temples, burn their images,
Yes, and the whole State, and its laws with it!
Is it your senile opinion that the gods love to honor bad men?
A pious thought!—
                        No, from the very beginning   115
There have been those who have whispered together,
Stiff-necked anarchists, putting their heads together,
Scheming against me in alleys. These are the men,
And they have bribed my own guard to do this thing.
[*Sententiously.*] Money!   120
There's nothing in the world so demoralizing as money.
Down go your cities,
Homes gone, men gone, honest hearts corrupted.
Crookedness of all kinds, and all for money!
[*To* Sentry.]   But you—!
I swear by God and by the throne of God,   125
The man who has done this thing shall pay for it!
Find that man, bring him here to me, or your death
Will be the least of your problems: I'll string you up
Alive, and there will be certain ways to make you
Discover your employer before you die;   130
And the process may teach you a lesson you seem to have missed:
The dearest profit is sometimes all too dear:
That depends on the source. Do you understand me?
A fortune won is often misfortune.

SENTRY: King, may I speak?

CREON: Your very voice distresses me.   135

SENTRY: Are you sure that it is my voice, and not your conscience?

CREON: By God, he wants to analyze me now!

SENTRY: It is not what I say, but what has been done, that hurts you.

CREON: You talk too much.

SENTRY: Maybe; but I've done nothing.

CREON: Sold your soul for some silver: that's all you've done.   140

SENTRY: How dreadful it is when the right judge judges wrong!
CREON: Your figures of speech
    May entertain you now; but unless you bring me the man,
    You will get little profit from them in the end.

                                    Exit Creon *into the palace.*

SENTRY: "Bring me the man"—!   145
    I'd like nothing better than bringing him the man!
    But bring him or not, you have seen the last of me here.
    At any rate, I am safe!   [*Exit* Sentry.]

Ode I

CHORUS: Numberless are the world's wonders, but not   *Strophe 1*
    More wonderful than man; the stormgray sea
    Yields to his prows, the huge crests bear him high;
    Earth, holy and inexhaustible, is graven
    With shining furrows where his plows have gone   5
    Year after year, the timeless labor of stallions.

    The lightboned birds and beasts that cling to cover, *Antistrophe 1*
    The lithe fish lighting their reaches of dim water,
    All are taken, tamed in the net of his mind;
    The lion on the hill, the wild horse windy-maned,   10
    Resign to him; and his blunt yoke has broken
    The sultry shoulders of the mountain bull.

    Words also, and thought as rapid as air,   *Strophe 2*
    He fashions to his good use; statecraft is his,
    And his the skill that deflects the arrows of snow,   15
    The spears of winter rain: from every wind
    He has made himself secure—from all but one:
    In the late wind of death he cannot stand.

    O clear intelligence, force beyond all measure!   *Antistrophe 2*
    O fate of man, working both good and evil!   20
    When the laws are kept, how proudly his city stands!
    When the laws are broken, what of his city then?
    Never may the anarchic man find rest at my hearth,
    Never be it said that my thoughts are his thoughts.

Scene II

Reenter Sentry *leading* Antigonê.

CHORAGOS: What does this mean? Surely this captive woman
    Is the Princess, Antigonê. Why should she be taken?

SENTRY: Here is the one who did it! We caught her
  In the very act of burying him.—Where is Creon?
CHORAGOS: Just coming from the house.

Enter Creon, *center.*

CREON: What has happened?   5
  Why have you come back so soon?
SENTRY [*expansively*]:   O King,
  A man should never be too sure of anything:
  I would have sworn
  That you'd not see me here again: your anger
  Frightened me so, and the things you threatened me with;   10
  But how could I tell then
  That I'd be able to solve the case so soon?
  No dice-throwing this time: I was only too glad to come!
  Here is this woman. She is the guilty one:
  We found her trying to bury him.   15
  Take her, then; question her; judge her as you will.
  I am through with the whole thing now, and glad of it.
CREON: But this is Antigonê! Why have you brought her here?
SENTRY: She was burying him, I tell you!
CREON [*severely*]:   Is this the truth?
SENTRY: I saw her with my own eyes. Can I say more?   20
CREON: The details: come, tell me quickly!
SENTRY: It was like this:
  After those terrible threats of yours, King,
  We went back and brushed the dust away from the body.
  The flesh was soft by now, and stinking,
  So we sat on a hill to windward and kept guard.   25
  No napping this time! We kept each other awake.
  But nothing happened until the white round sun
  Whirled in the center of the round sky over us:
  Then, suddenly,
  A storm of dust roared up from the earth, and the sky   30
  Went out, the plain vanished with all its trees
  In the stinging dark. We closed our eyes and endured it.
  The whirlwind lasted a long time, but it passed;
  And then we looked, and there was Antigonê!
  I have seen   35
  A mother bird come back to a stripped nest, heard

Her crying bitterly a broken note or two
For the young ones stolen. Just so, when this girl
Found the bare corpse, and all her love's work wasted,
She wept, and cried on heaven to damn the hands
That had done this thing.

40

     And then she brought more dust
And sprinkled wine three times for her brother's ghost.

We ran and took her at once. She was not afraid,
Not even when we charged her with what she had done.
She denied nothing.

     And this was a comfort to me,

45

And some uneasiness: for it is a good thing
To escape from death, but it is no great pleasure
To bring death to a friend.

     Yet I always say
There is nothing so comfortable as your own safe skin!

CREON [*slowly, dangerously*]: And you, Antigonê,

50

You with your head hanging,—do you confess this thing?
ANTIGONÊ: I do. I deny nothing.
CREON [*to* Sentry]:   You may go. [*Exit* Sentry.]
[*to* Antigonê] Tell me, tell me briefly:
Had you heard my proclamation touching this matter?
ANTIGONÊ: It was public. Could I help hearing it?

55

CREON: And yet you dared defy the law.
ANTIGONÊ: I dared.
It was not God's proclamation. That final Justice
That rules the world below makes no such laws.

Your edict, King, was strong.

60

But all your strength is weakness itself against
The immortal unrecorded laws of God.
They are not merely now: they were, and shall be,
Operative for ever, beyond man utterly.
I knew I must die, even without your decree:
I am only mortal. And if I must die

65

Now, before it is my time to die,
Surely this is no hardship: can anyone
Living, as I live, with evil all about me,
Think Death less than a friend? This death of mine
Is of no importance; but if I had left my brother

70

Lying in death unburied, I should have suffered.

Now I do not.
                    You smile at me. Ah Creon,
Think me a fool, if you like; but it may well be
That a fool convicts me of folly.

CHORAGOS: Like father, like daughter: both headstrong, deaf to reason! 75
She has never learned to yield.

CREON: She has much to learn.
The inflexible heart breaks first, the toughest iron
Cracks first, and the wildest horses bend their necks
At the pull of the smallest curb.
                              Pride? In a slave?
This girl is guilty of a double insolence,   80
Breaking the given laws and boasting of it.
Who is the man here,
She or I, if this crime goes unpunished?
Sister's child, or more than sister's child,
Or closer yet in blood—she and her sister   85
Win bitter death for this!
[*To* servants.]   Go, some of you,
Arrest Ismenê. I accuse her equally.
Bring her: you will find her sniffling in the house there.

Her mind's a traitor: crimes kept in the dark
Cry for light, and the guardian brain shudders;   90
But how much worse than this
Is brazen boasting of barefaced anarchy!

ANTIGONÊ: Creon, what more do you want than my death?

CREON: Nothing.
That gives me everything.

ANTIGONÊ: Then I beg you: kill me.
This talking is a great weariness: your words   95
Are distasteful to me, and I am sure that mine
Seem so to you. And yet they should not seem so:
I should have praise and honor for what I have done.
All these men here would praise me
Were their lips not frozen shut with fear of you.   100
[*Bitterly.*] Ah the good fortune of kings,
Licensed to say and do whatever they please!

CREON: You are alone here in that opinion.

ANTIGONÊ: No, they are with me. But they keep their tongues in leash.

CREON: Maybe. But you are guilty, and they are not.   105

ANTIGONÊ: There is no guilt in reverence for the dead.

CREON: But Eteoclês—was he not your brother too?

ANTIGONÊ: My brother too.

CREON: And you insult his memory?

ANTIGONÊ [*softly*]:   The dead man would not say that I insult it.

CREON: He would: for you honor a traitor as much as him.   110

ANTIGONÊ: His own brother, traitor or not, and equal in blood.

CREON: He made war on his country. Eteoclês defended it.

ANTIGONÊ: Nevertheless, there are honors due all the dead.

CREON: But not the same for the wicked as for the just.

ANTIGONÊ: Ah Creon, Creon,   115
   Which of us can say what the gods hold wicked?

CREON: An enemy is an enemy, even dead.

ANTIGONÊ: It is my nature to join in love, not hate.

CREON [*finally losing patience*]:   Go join them then; if you must have your love,
   Find it in hell!   120

CHORAGOS: But see, Ismenê comes:

Enter Ismenê, *guarded.*

   Those tears are sisterly, the cloud
   That shadows her eyes rains down gentle sorrow.

CREON: You too, Ismenê,
   Snake in my ordered house, sucking my blood
   Stealthily—and all the time I never knew   125
   That these two sisters were aiming at my throne!
                                              Ismenê,
   Do you confess your share in this crime, or deny it?
   Answer me.

ISMENÊ: Yes, if she will let me say so. I am guilty.   130

ANTIGONÊ [*coldly*]:   No, Ismenê. You have no right to say so.
   You would not help me, and I will not have you help me.

ISMENÊ: But now I know what you meant: and I am here
   To join you, to take my share of punishment.

ANTIGONÊ: The dead man and the gods who rule the dead   135
   Know whose act this was. Words are not friends.

ISMENÊ: Do you refuse me, Antigonê? I want to die with you:
   I too have a duty that I must discharge to the dead.

ANTIGONÊ: You shall not lessen my death by sharing it.

ISMENÊ: What do I care for life when you are dead?   140

ANTIGONÊ: Ask Creon. You're always hanging on his opinions.

ISMENÊ: You are laughing at me. Why, Antigonê?

ANTIGONÊ: It's a joyless laughter, Ismenê.

ISMENÊ: But can I do nothing?

ANTIGONÊ: Yes. Save yourself. I shall not envy you.
     There are those who will praise you; I shall have honor, too.   145

ISMENÊ: But we are equally guilty!

ANTIGONÊ: No more, Ismenê.
     You are alive, but I belong to Death.

CREON [*to the* Chorus]:   Gentlemen, I beg you to observe these girls:
     One has just now lost her mind; the other,
     It seems, has never had a mind at all.   150

ISMENÊ: Grief teaches the steadiest minds to waver, King.

CREON: Yours certainly did, when you assumed guilt with the guilty!

ISMENÊ: But how could I go on living without her?

CREON: You are.
     She is already dead.

ISMENÊ: But your own son's bride!

CREON: There are places enough for him to push his plow.   155
     I want no wicked women for my sons!

ISMENÊ: O dearest Haimon, how your father wrongs you!

CREON: I've had enough of your childish talk of marriage!

CHORAGOS: Do you really intend to steal this girl from your son?

CREON: No; Death will do that for me.

CHORAGOS: Then she must die?   160

CREON [*ironically*]:   You dazzle me.
     —But enough of this talk!
     [*To* Guards.] You, there, take them away and guard them well:
     For they are but women, and even brave men run
     When they see Death coming.

                         Exeunt Ismenê, Antigonê, *and* Guards.

Ode II

CHORUS: Fortunate is the man who has never tasted   *Strophe 1*
     God's vengeance!
     Where once the anger of heaven has struck, that house is shaken
     For ever: damnation rises behind each child
     Like a wave cresting out of the black northeast,
     When the long darkness under sea roars up   5
     And bursts drumming death upon the windwhipped sand.

I have seen this gathering sorrow from time long past   *Antistrophe 1*
Loom upon Oedipus' children: generation from generation
Takes the compulsive rage of the enemy god.
So lately this last flower of Oedipus' line   10
Drank the sunlight! but now a passionate word
And a handful of dust have closed up all its beauty.

What mortal arrogance   *Strophe 2*
Transcends the wrath of Zeus?
Sleep cannot lull him nor the effortless long months   15
Of the timeless gods: but he is young for ever,
And his house is the shining day of high Olympos.
All that is and shall be,
And all the past, is his.
No pride on earth is free of the curse of heaven.   20

The straying dreams of men   *Antistrophe 2*
May bring them ghosts of joy:
But as they drowse, the waking embers burn them;
Or they walk with fixed eyes, as blind men walk.
But the ancient wisdom speaks for our own time: 25

Fate works most for woe
With Folly's fairest show.

Man's little pleasure is the spring of sorrow.

Scene III

CHORAGOS: But here is Haimon, King, the last of all your sons.
Is it grief for Antigonê that brings him here,
And bitterness at being robbed of his bride?

Enter Haimon.

CREON: We shall soon see, and no need of diviners.

—Son,

You have heard my final judgment on that girl: 5
Have you come here hating me, or have you come
With deference and with love, whatever I do?
HAIMON: I am your son, father. You are my guide.
You make things clear for me, and I obey you.
No marriage means more to me than your continuing wisdom.   10
CREON: Good. That is the way to behave: subordinate
Everything else, my son, to your father's will.

This is what a man prays for, that he may get
Sons attentive and dutiful in his house,
Each one hating his father's enemies,   15
Honoring his father's friends. But if his sons
Fail him, if they turn out unprofitably,
What has he fathered but trouble for himself
And amusement for the malicious?

                                                So you are right
Not to lose your head over this woman.   20
Your pleasure with her would soon grow cold, Haimon,
And then you'd have a hellcat in bed and elsewhere.
Let her find her husband in Hell!
Of all the people in this city, only she
Has had contempt for my law and broken it.   25
Do you want me to show myself weak before the people?
Or to break my sworn word? No, and I will not.
The woman dies.
I suppose she'll plead "family ties." Well, let her.
If I permit my own family to rebel,   30
How shall I earn the world's obedience?
Show me the man who keeps his house in hand,
He's fit for public authority.

                                        I'll have no dealings
With lawbreakers, critics of the government:
Whoever is chosen to govern should be obeyed—   35
Must be obeyed, in all things, great and small,
Just and unjust! O Haimon,
The man who knows how to obey, and that man only,
Knows how to give commands when the time comes.
You can depend on him, no matter how fast   40
The spears come: he's a good soldier, he'll stick it out.

Anarchy, anarchy! Show me a greater evil!
This is why cities tumble and the great houses rain down,
This is what scatters armies!
No, no: good lives are made so by discipline.   45
We keep the laws then, and the lawmakers,
And no woman shall seduce us. If we must lose,
Let's lose to a man, at least! Is a woman stronger than we?

CHORAGOS: Unless time has rusted my wits,
       What you say, King, is said with point and dignity.   50

HAIMON [*boyishly earnest*]:   Father:
   Reason is God's crowning gift to man, and you are right
   To warn me against losing mine. I cannot say—
   I hope that I shall never want to say!—that you
   Have reasoned badly. Yet there are other men   55
   Who can reason, too; and their opinions might be helpful.
   You are not in a position to know everything
   That people say or do, or what they feel:
   Your temper terrifies—everyone
   Will tell you only what you like to hear.   60
   But I, at any rate, can listen; and I have heard them
   Muttering and whispering in the dark about this girl.
   They say no woman has ever, so unreasonably,
   Died so shameful a death for a generous act:
   "She covered her brother's body. Is this indecent? 65
   She kept him from dogs and vultures. Is this a crime?
   Death?—She should have all the honor that we can give her!"

   This is the way they talk out there in the city.

   You must believe me:
   Nothing is closer to me than your happiness.   70
   What could be closer? Must not any son
   Value his father's fortune as his father does his?
   I beg you, do not be unchangeable:
   Do not believe that you alone can be right.
   The man who thinks that,   75
   The man who maintains that only he has the power
   To reason correctly, the gift to speak, the soul—
   A man like that, when you know him, turns out empty.

   It is not reason never to yield to reason!
   In flood time you can see how some trees bend,   80
   And because they bend, even their twigs are safe,
   While stubborn trees are torn up, roots and all.
   And the same thing happens in sailing:
   Make your sheet fast, never slacken,—and over you go,
   Head over heels and under: and there's your voyage. 85
   Forget you are angry! Let yourself be moved!
   I know I am young; but please let me say this:
   The ideal condition
   Would be, I admit, that men should be right by instinct;

But since we are all too likely to go astray,   90
The reasonable thing is to learn from those who can teach.
CHORAGOS: You will do well to listen to him, King,
If what he says is sensible. And you, Haimon,
Must listen to your father.—Both speak well.
CREON: You consider it right for a man of my years and experience   95
To go to school to a boy?
HAIMON: It is not right
If I am wrong. But if I am young, and right,
What does my age matter?
CREON: You think it right to stand up for an anarchist?
HAIMON: Not at all. I pay no respect to criminals.   100
CREON: Then she is not a criminal?
HAIMON: The City would deny it, to a man.
CREON: And the City proposes to teach me how to rule?
HAIMON: Ah. Who is it that's talking like a boy now?
CREON: My voice is the one voice giving orders in this City!   105
HAIMON: It is no City if it takes orders from one voice.
CREON: The State is the King!
HAIMON: Yes, if the State is a desert.

   Pause.

CREON: This boy, it seems, has sold out to a woman.
HAIMON: If you are a woman: my concern is only for you.
CREON: So? Your "concern"! In a public brawl with your father!   110
HAIMON: How about you, in a public brawl with justice?
CREON: With justice, when all that I do is within my rights?
HAIMON: You have no right to trample on God's right.
CREON [*completely out of control*]:   Fool, adolescent fool! Taken in
   by a woman!
HAIMON: You'll never see me taken in by anything vile.   115
CREON: Every word you say is for her!
HAIMON [*quietly, darkly*]:   And for you.
   And for me. And for the gods under the earth.
CREON: You'll never marry her while she lives.
HAIMON: Then she must die.—But her death will cause another.
CREON: Another?   120
   Have you lost your senses? Is this an open threat?
HAIMON: There is no threat in speaking to emptiness.
CREON: I swear you'll regret this superior tone of yours!
   You are the empty one!

HAIMON: If you were not my father,
   I'd say you were perverse.   125
CREON: You girlstruck fool, don't play at words with me!
HAIMON: I am sorry. You prefer silence.
CREON: Now, by God—
   I swear, by all the gods in heaven above us,
   You'll watch it, I swear you shall!
   [*To the* Servants.] Bring her out!
   Bring the woman out! Let her die before his eyes!   130
   Here, this instant, with her bridegroom beside her!
HAIMON: Not here, no; she will not die here, King.
   And you will never see my face again.
   Go on raving as long as you've a friend to endure you. *Exit Haimon.*
CHORAGOS: Gone, gone.   135
   Creon, a young man in a rage is dangerous!
CREON: Let him do, or dream to do, more than a man can.
   He shall not save these girls from death.
CHORAGOS: These girls?
   You have sentenced them both?
CREON:
   No, you are right.
   I will not kill the one whose hands are clean.   140
CHORAGOS: But Antigonê?
CREON. [*somberly*]:   I will carry her far away
   Out there in the wilderness, and lock her
   Living in a vault of stone. She shall have food,
   As the custom is, to absolve the State of her death.
   And there let her pray to the gods of hell: 145
   They are her only gods:
   Perhaps they will show her an escape from death,
   Or she may learn,
         though late,
   That piety shown the dead is piety in vain.   [*Exit* Creon.]

Ode III

CHORUS: Love, unconquerable   *Strophe*
   Waster of rich men, keeper
   Of warm lights and all-night vigil
   In the soft face of a girl:
   Sea-wanderer, forest-visitor!   5
   Even the pure Immortals cannot escape you,

And the mortal man, in his one day's dusk,
Trembles before your glory.

Surely you swerve upon ruin   *Antistrophe*
The just man's consenting heart,
As here you have made bright anger   10
Strike between father and son—
And none has conquered by Love!
A girl's glance working the will of heaven:
Pleasure to her alone who mocks us,
Merciless Aphroditê.°   15

Scene IV

CHORAGOS [*as* Antigonê *enters guarded*]:   But I can no longer stand
   in awe of this,
   Nor, seeing what I see, keep back my tears.
   Here is Antigonê, passing to that chamber
   Where all find sleep at last.

ANTIGONÊ: Look upon me, friends, and pity me   *Strophe 1*   5
   Turning back at the night's edge to say
   Good-by to the sun that shines for me no longer;
   Now sleepy Death
   Summons me down to Acheron,° that cold shore:
   There is no bridesong there, nor any music.   10

CHORUS: Yet not unpraised, not without a kind of honor,
   You walk at last into the underworld;
   Untouched by sickness, broken by no sword.
   What woman has ever found your way to death?

ANTIGONÊ: How often I have heard the story of Niobê,°   15
                                             Antistrophe 1

   Tantalos' wretched daughter, how the stone
   Clung fast about her, ivy-close: and they say
   The rain falls endlessly
   And sifting soft snow; her tears are never done.
   I feel the loneliness of her death in mine.   20

CHORUS: But she was born of heaven, and you
   Are woman, woman-born. If her death is yours,
   A mortal woman's, is this not for you
   Glory in our world and in the world beyond?

---

15 **Aphroditê** goddess of love.   9 **Acheron** a river of the underworld, which was ruled by Hades.
15 **Niobê** Niobê boasted of her numerous children, provoking Leto, the mother of Apollo, to
destroy them. Niobê wept profusely, and finally was turned to stone on Mount Sipylus, whose
streams are her tears.

ANTIGONÊ: You laugh at me. Ah, friends, friends   *Strophe 2*   25
   Can you not wait until I am dead? O Thebes,
   O men many-charioted, in love with Fortune,
   Dear springs of Dircê, sacred Theban grove,
   Be witnesses for me, denied all pity,
   Unjustly judged! and think a word of love   30
   For her whose path turns
   Under dark earth, where there are no more tears.

CHORUS: You have passed beyond human daring and come at last
   Into a place of stone where Justice sits.
   I cannot tell   35
   What shape of your father's guilt appears in this.

ANTIGONÊ: You have touched it at last: *Antistrophe 2*
   That bridal bed
   Unspeakable, horror of son and mother mingling:
   Their crime, infection of all our family!
   O Oedipus, father and brother!   40
   Your marriage strikes from the grave to murder mine.
   I have been a stranger here in my own land:
   All my life
   The blasphemy of my birth has followed me.

CHORUS: Reverence is a virtue, but strength   45
   Lives in established law: that must prevail.
   You have made your choice,
   Your death is the doing of your conscious hand.

ANTIGONÊ: Then let me go, since all your words are bitter. *Epode*
   And the very light of the sun is cold to me.   50
   Lead me to my vigil, where I must have
   Neither love nor lamentation; no song, but silence.

   Creon *interrupts impatiently.*

CREON: If dirges and planned lamentations could put off death,
   Men would be singing for ever.
   [*To the* Servants.]   Take her, go!
   You know your orders: take her to the vault   55
   And leave her alone there. And if she lives or dies,
   That's her affair, not ours: our hands are clean.

ANTIGONÊ: O tomb, vaulted bride-bed in eternal rock,
   Soon I shall be with my own again

Where Persephonê° welcomes the thin ghosts underground: 60
And I shall see my father again, and you, mother,
And dearest Polyneicês—
              dearest indeed
To me, since it was my hand
That washed him clean and poured the ritual wine:
And my reward is death before my time!   65

And yet, as men's hearts know, I have done no wrong,
I have not sinned before God. Or if I have,
I shall know the truth in death. But if the guilt
Lies upon Creon who judged me, then, I pray,
May his punishment equal my own.

CHORAGOS: O passionate heart,   70
Unyielding, tormented still by the same winds!

CREON: Her guards shall have good cause to regret their delaying.

ANTIGONÊ: Ah! That voice is like the voice of death!

CREON: I can give you no reason to think you are mistaken.

ANTIGONÊ: Thebes, and you my fathers' gods,   75
And rulers of Thebes, you see me now, the last
Unhappy daughter of a line of kings,
Your kings, led away to death. You will remember
What things I suffer, and at what men's hands,
Because I would not transgress the laws of heaven.   80
[*To the* Guards, *simply.*] Come: let us wait no longer.

                      [*Exit* Antigonê, *left, guarded.*]

Ode IV

CHORUS: All Danaê's° beauty was locked away   *Strophe 1*
In a brazen cell where the sunlight could not come:
A small room, still as any grave, enclosed her.
Yet she was a princess too,
And Zeus in a rain of gold poured love upon her.   5
O child, child,
No power in wealth or war
Or tough sea-blackened ships
Can prevail against untiring Destiny!

And Dryas' son° also, that furious king,   *Antistrophe 1*
Bore the god's prisoning anger for his pride: 10

---

60 **Persephonê** queen of the underworld.   1 **Danaê** A princess shut into a tower by her father because of a prophecy that the king would be killed by his grandson. Zeus nevertheless entered Danaê's chamber in the form of a shower of gold and impregnated her. She gave birth to Perseus, who accidently killed the king with a discus.   9 **Dryas' son** Lycurgus, King of Thrace.

Sealed up by Dionysos in deaf stone,
His madness died among echoes.
So at the last he learned what dreadful power
His tongue had mocked:
For he had profaned the revels,   15
And fired the wrath of the nine
Implacable Sisters° that love the sound of the flute.

And old men tell a half-remembered tale   *Strophe 2*
Of horror where a dark ledge splits the sea
And a double surf beats on the gray shores: 20
How a king's new woman,° sick
With hatred for the queen he had imprisoned,
Ripped out his two sons' eyes with her bloody hands
While grinning Arês° watched the shuttle plunge
Four times: four blind wounds crying for revenge,   25

Crying, tears and blood mingled.—Piteously born,   *Antistrophe 2*
Those sons whose mother was of heavenly birth!
Her father was the god of the North Wind
And she was cradled by gales,
She raced with young colts on the glittering hills
And walked untrammeled in the open light: 30
But in her marriage deathless Fate found means
To build a tomb like yours for all her joy.

Scene V

Enter blind Teiresias, *led by a boy. The opening speeches of* Teiresias
should be in singsong contrast to the realistic lines of Creon.

TEIRESIAS: This is the way the blind man comes, Princes, Princes,
    Lock-step, two heads lit by the eyes of one.
CREON: What new thing have you to tell us, old Teiresias?
TEIRESIAS: I have much to tell you: listen to the prophet, Creon.
CREON: I am not aware that I have ever failed to listen.   5
TEIRESIAS: Then you have done wisely, King, and ruled well.
CREON: I admit my debt to you. But what have you to say?
TEIRESIAS: This, Creon: you stand once more on the edge of fate.
CREON: What do you mean? Your words are a kind of dread.
TEIRESIAS: Listen, Creon: 10

17 **Sisters** the Muses.   21 **king's new woman** Eidothea, second wife of King Phineus, blinded her
stepsons. Their mother, Cleopatra, had been imprisoned in a cave. Phineus was the son of a king,
and Cleopatra, his first wife, was the daughter of Boreas, the North Wind, but this illustrious
ancestry could not protect his sons from violence and darkness.   24 **Arês** god of war.

I was sitting in my chair of augury, at the place
Where the birds gather about me. They were all a-chatter,
As is their habit, when suddenly I heard
A strange note in their jangling, a scream, a
Whirring fury; I knew that they were fighting,   15
Tearing each other, dying
In a whirlwind of wings clashing. And I was afraid.
I began the rites of burnt-offering at the altar,
But Hephaistos° failed me: instead of bright flame,
There was only the sputtering slime of the fat thigh-flesh   20
Melting: the entrails dissolved in gray smoke,
The bare bone burst from the welter. And no blaze!

This was a sign from heaven. My boy described it,
Seeing for me as I see for others.

I tell you, Creon, you yourself have brought   25
This new calamity upon us. Our hearths and altars
Are stained with the corruption of dogs and carrion birds
That glut themselves on the corpse of Oedipus' son.
The gods are deaf when we pray to them, their fire
Recoils from our offering, their birds of omen   30
Have no cry of comfort, for they are gorged
With the thick blood of the dead.
                                        O my son,
These are no trifles! Think: all men make mistakes,
But a good man yields when he knows his course is wrong,
And repairs the evil. The only crime is pride.   35

Give in to the dead man, then: do not fight with a corpse—
What glory is it to kill a man who is dead?
Think, I beg you:
It is for your own good that I speak as I do.
You should be able to yield for your own good.   40
CREON: It seems that prophets have made me their especial province.
All my life long
I have been a kind of butt for the dull arrows
Of doddering fortune-tellers!
                           No, Teiresias:
If your birds—if the great eagles of God himself   45
Should carry him stinking bit by bit to heaven,

19 Hephaistos god of fire.

I would not yield. I am not afraid of pollution:
No man can defile the gods.

                                    Do what you will,
Go into business, make money, speculate
In India gold or that synthetic gold from Sardis,
Get rich otherwise than by my consent to bury him.   50
Teiresias, it is a sorry thing when a wise man
Sells his wisdom, lets out his words for hire!
TEIRESIAS: Ah Creon! Is there no man left in the world—
CREON: To do what?—Come, let's have the aphorism!   55
TEIRESIAS: No man who knows that wisdom outweighs any wealth?
CREON: As surely as bribes are baser than any baseness.
TEIRESIAS: You are sick, Creon! You are deathly sick!
CREON: As you say: it is not my place to challenge a prophet.
TEIRESIAS: Yet you have said my prophecy is for sale.   60
CREON: The generation of prophets has always loved gold.
TEIRESIAS: The generation of kings has always loved brass.
CREON: You forget yourself! You are speaking to your King.
TEIRESIAS: I know it. You are a king because of me.
CREON: You have a certain skill; but you have sold out.   65
TEIRESIAS: King, you will drive me to words that—
CREON: Say them, say them!
Only remember: I will not pay you for them.
TEIRESIAS: No, you will find them too costly.
CREON: No doubt. Speak:
Whatever you say, you will not change my will.
TEIRESIAS: Then take this, and take it to heart!   70
The time is not far off when you shall pay back
Corpse for corpse, flesh of your own flesh.
You have thrust the child of this world into living night,
You have kept from the gods below the child that is theirs:
The one in a grave before her death, the other,   75
Dead, denied the grave. This is your crime:
And the Furies and the dark gods of Hell
Are swift with terrible punishment for you.

Do you want to buy me now, Creon?

                                    Not many days,
And your house will be full of men and women weeping,   80
And curses will be hurled at you from far
Cities grieving for sons unburied, left to rot

Before the walls of Thebes.

These are my arrows, Creon: they are all for you.
[*To* boy.] But come, child: lead me home.   85
Let him waste his fine anger upon younger men.
Maybe he will learn at last
To control a wiser tongue in a better head.   [*Exit* Teiresias.]
CHORAGOS: The old man has gone, King, but his words
Remain to plague us. I am old, too,   90
But I cannot remember that he was ever false.
CREON: That is true. . . . It troubles me.
Oh it is hard to give in! but it is worse
To risk everything for stubborn pride.
CHORAGOS: Creon: take my advice.
CREON: What shall I do?   95
CHORAGOS: Go quickly: free Antigonê from her vault
And build a tomb for the body of Polyneicês.
CREON: You would have me do this!
CHORAGOS: Creon, yes!
And it must be done at once: God moves
Swiftly to cancel the folly of stubborn men.   100
CREON: It is hard to deny the heart! But I
Will do it: I will not fight with destiny.
CHORAGOS: You must go yourself, you cannot leave it to others.
CREON: I will go.
                —Bring axes, servants:
Come with me to the tomb. I buried her, I   105
Will set her free.
                Oh quickly!
My mind misgives—
The laws of the gods are mighty, and a man must serve them
To the last day of his life!   [*Exit* Creon.]

Paean°

CHORAGOS: God of many names   *Strophe 1*
CHORUS: O Iacchos
                                     son
of Kadmeian Sémelê
                      O born of the Thunder!

Paean a hymn (here dedicated to Iacchos, also called Dionysos. His father was Zeus, his mother was
Sémelê, daughter of Kadmos. Iacchos's worshipers were the Maenads, whose cry was "*Evohé
evohé.*")

Guardian of the West
                    Regent
of Eleusis' plain
                    O Prince of Maenad Thebes
and the Dragon Field by rippling Ismenós:°   5
CHORAGOS: God of many names   *Antistrophe 1*
CHORUS: the flame of torches
flares on our hills
                    the nymphs of Iacchos
dance at the spring of Castalia:°
from the vine-close mountain
                    come ah come in ivy:
Evohé evohé! sings through the streets of Thebes   10
CHORAGOS: God of many names   *Strophe 2*
CHORUS: Iacchos of Thebes
heavenly Child
                    of Sémelê bride of the Thunderer!
The shadow of plague is upon us:
                              come
with clement feet
                    oh come from Parnassos
down the long slopes
                    across the lamenting water   15
CHORAGOS: Iô Fire! Chorister of the throbbing stars! *Antistrophe 2*
O purest among the voices of the night!
Thou son of God, blaze for us!
CHORUS: Come with choric rapture of circling Maenads
Who cry *Iô Iacche!*
                    God of many names!   20

Exodos

Enter Messenger *from left.*

MESSENGER: Men of the line of Kadmos,° you who live
Near Amphion's citadel,°
                    I cannot say
Of any condition of human life "This is fixed,

---

5 **Ismenós** a river east of Thebes (from a dragon's teeth, sown near the river, there sprang men who became the ancestors of the Theban nobility).   8 **Castalia** a spring on Mount Parnassos. 1 **Kadmos,** who sowed the dragon's teeth, was founder of Thebes.   2 **Amphion's citadel** Amphion played so sweetly on his lyre that he charmed stones to form a wall around Thebes.

This is clearly good, or bad." Fate raises up,
And Fate casts down the happy and unhappy alike: 5
No man can foretell his Fate.
                              Take the case of Creon:
Creon was happy once, as I count happiness:
Victorious in battle, sole governor of the land,
Fortunate father of children nobly born.
And now it has all gone from him! Who can say   10
That a man is still alive when his life's joy fails?
He is a walking dead man. Grant him rich,
Let him live like a king in his great house:
If his pleasure is gone, I would not give
So much as the shadow of smoke for all he owns.   15

CHORAGOS: Your words hint at sorrow: what is your news for us?
MESSENGER: They are dead. The living are guilty of their death.
CHORAGOS: Who is guilty? Who is dead? Speak!
MESSENGER: Haimon.
    Haimon is dead; and the hand that killed him
    Is his own hand.
CHORAGOS: His father's? or his own?   20
MESSENGER: His own, driven mad by the murder his father had done.
CHORAGOS: Teiresias, Teiresias, how clearly you saw it all!
MESSENGER: This is my news: you must draw what conclusions you
    can from it.
CHORAGOS: But look: Eurydicê, our Queen:
    Has she overheard us?   25

Enter Eurydicê *from the palace, center.*

EURYDICE: I have heard something, friends:
    As I was unlocking the gate of Pallas'° shrine,
    For I needed her help today, I heard a voice
    Telling of some new sorrow. And I fainted
    There at the temple with all my maidens about me.   30
    But speak again: whatever it is, I can bear it:
    Grief and I are no strangers.
MESSENGER: Dearest Lady,
    I will tell you plainly all that I have seen.
    I shall not try to comfort you: what is the use,
    Since comfort could lie only in what is not true?   35

---

27 **Pallas** Pallas Athene, goddess of wisdom.

The truth is always best.
                    I went with Creon
To the outer plain where Polyneicês was lying,
No friend to pity him, his body shredded by dogs.
We made our prayers in the place to Hecatê
And Pluto,° that they would be merciful. And we bathed   40
The corpse with holy water, and we brought
Fresh-broken branches to burn what was left of it,
And upon the urn we heaped up a towering barrow
Of the earth of his own land.
                        When we were done, we ran
To the vault where Antigonê lay on her couch of stone.   45
One of the servants had gone ahead,
And while he was yet far off he heard a voice
Grieving within the chamber, and he came back
And told Creon. And as the King went closer,
The air was full of wailing, the words lost,   50
And he begged us to make all haste. "Am I a prophet?"
He said, weeping, "And must I walk this road,
The saddest of all that I have gone before?
My son's voice calls me on. Oh quickly, quickly!
Look through the crevice there, and tell me   55
If it is Haimon, or some deception of the gods!"
We obeyed; and in the cavern's farthest corner
We saw her lying:
She had made a noose of her fine linen veil
And hanged herself. Haimon lay beside her,   60
His arms about her waist, lamenting her,
His love lost under ground, crying out
That his father had stolen her away from him.

When Creon saw him the tears rushed to his eyes
And he called to him: "What have you done, child?
Speak to me.   65
What are you thinking that makes your eyes so strange?
O my son, my son, I come to you on my knees!"
But Haimon spat in his face. He said not a word,
Staring—
          And suddenly drew his sword

---

40 Hecatê / And Pluto Hecatê and Pluto (also known as Hades) were deities of the underworld.

And lunged. Creon shrank back, the blade missed; and the boy,   70
Desperate against himself, drove it half its length
Into his own side, and fell. And as he died
He gathered Antigonê close in his arms again,
Choking, his blood bright red on her white cheek.
And now he lies dead with the dead, and she is his   75
At last, his bride in the house of the dead.

                    Exit Eurydicê *into the palace.*

CHORAGOS: She has left us without a word. What can this mean?
MESSENGER:
    It troubles me, too; yet she knows what is best,
    Her grief is too great for public lamentation,
    And doubtless she has gone to her chamber to weep   80
    For her dead son, leading her maidens in his dirge.

    Pause.

CHORAGOS: It may be so: but I fear this deep silence.
MESSENGER: I will see what she is doing. I will go in.

                    Exit Messenger *into the palace.*

    Enter Creon *with attendants, bearing* Haimon's *body.*

CHORAGOS: But here is the king himself: on look at him,
    Bearing his own damnation in his arms.   85
CREON: Nothing you say can touch me any more.
    My own blind heart has brought me
    From darkness to final darkness. Here you see
    The father murdering, the murdered son—
    And all my civic wisdom!   90

    Haimon my son, so young, so young to die,
    I was the fool, not you; and you died for me.
CHORAGOS: That is the truth; but you were late in learning it.
CREON: This truth is hard to bear. Surely a god
    Has crushed me beneath the hugest weight of heaven,   95
    And driven me headlong a barbaric way
    To trample out the thing I held most dear.

    The pains that men will take to come to pain!

    Enter Messenger *from the palace.*

MESSENGER: The burden you carry in your hands is heavy,
    But it is not all: you will find more in your house.   100

CREON: What burden worse than this shall I find there?
MESSENGER: The Queen is dead.
CREON: O port of death, deaf world,
   Is there no pity for me? And you, Angel of evil,
   I was dead, and your words are death again.   105
   Is it true, boy? Can it be true?
   Is my wife dead? Has death bred death?
MESSENGER: You can see for yourself.

   The doors are opened and the body of Eurydicê *is disclosed within.*

CREON: Oh pity!
   All true, all true, and more than I can bear!   110
   O my wife, my son!
MESSENGER: She stood before the altar, and her heart
   Welcomed the knife her own hand guided,
   And a great cry burst from her lips for Megareus° dead,
   And for Haimon dead, her sons; and her last breath   115
   Was a curse for their father, the murderer of her sons.
   And she fell, and the dark flowed in through her closing eyes.
CREON: O God, I am sick with fear.
   Are there no swords here? Has no one a blow for me?
MESSENGER: Her curse is upon you for the deaths of both.   120
CREON: It is right that it should be. I alone am guilty.
   I know it, and I say it. Lead me in,
   Quickly, friends.
   I have neither life nor substance. Lead me in.
CHORAGOS: You are right, if there can be right in so much wrong. 125
   The briefest way is best in a world of sorrow.
CREON: Let it come,
   Let death come quickly, and be kind to me.
   I would not ever see the sun again.
CHORAGOS: All that will come when it will; but we, meanwhile, 130
   Have much to do. Leave the future to itself.
CREON: All my heart was in that prayer!
CHORAGOS: Then do not pray any more: the sky is deaf.
CREON: Lead me away. I have been rash and foolish.
   I have killed my son and my wife.   135
   I look for comfort; my comfort lies here dead.
   Whatever my hands have touched has come to nothing.
   Fate has brought all my pride to a thought of dust.

114 Megareus Megareus, brother of Haimon, had died in the assault on Thebes.

As Creon *is being led into the house, the* Choragos *advances and speaks directly to the audience.*

CHORAGOS: There is no happiness where there is no wisdom;
No wisdom but in submission to the gods. 140
Big words are always punished,
And proud men in old age learn to be wise.

—c. 441 B.C.

Questions: Reading, Responding, Arguing

1. What is the mythic background of *Antigone*? How does it relate to the plot of *Oedipus the Ismenê King*?
2. Discuss the importance of Ismene and Haimon as minor characters who serve as foils for major characters.
3. How does the chorus function in the play? How does each choral ode (*stasimon*) connect to the scene (*episodos*) that precedes it?
4. Antigone and Creon are a classic protagonist and antagonist. If the Greek word *agon* originally meant "debate," what specific issue are they debating? What points does each put forth in their argument?
5. Creon is usually criticized for his inflexibility. Is Antigone equally inflexible? What are each character's reasons for their unwillingness to change?
6. Which character, Antigone or Creon, better fits Aristotle's description of the tragic hero? Which one comes to ruin because of a great error or hamartia?

Plato (c. 427–c. 347 B.C.)

The Apology of Socrates[1]

How you, O Athenians, have been affected by my accusers, I cannot tell; but I know that they almost made me forget who I was—so persuasively did they speak; and yet they have hardly uttered a word of truth. But of the many falsehoods told by them, there was one which

[1]Translated by Benjamin Jowett. *Apology* means "defense."

quite amazed me;—I mean when they said that you should be upon your guard and not allow yourselves to be deceived by the force of my eloquence. To say this, when they were certain to be detected as soon as I opened my lips and proved myself to be anything but a great speaker, did indeed appear to me most shameless—unless by the force of eloquence they mean the force of truth; for if such is their meaning, I admit that I am eloquent. But in how different a way from theirs! Well, as I was saying, they have scarcely spoken the truth at all; but from me you shall hear the whole truth: not, however, delivered after their manner in a set oration duly ornamented with words and phrases. No, by heaven! but I shall use the words and arguments which occur to me at the moment; for I am confident in the justice of my cause: at my time of life I ought not to be appearing before you, O men of Athens, in the character of a juvenile orator—let no one expect it of me. And I must beg of you to grant me a favor:—If I defend myself in my accustomed manner, and you hear me using the words which I have been in the habit of using in the agora,[2] at the tables of the money-changers, or anywhere else, I would ask you not to be surprised, and not to interrupt me on this account. For I am more than seventy years of age, and appearing now for the first time in a court of law, I am quite a stranger to the language of the place; and therefore I would have you regard me as if I were really a stranger, whom you would excuse if he spoke in his native tongue, and after the fashion of his country:—Am I making an unfair request of you? Never mind the manner, which may or may not be good; but think only of the truth of my words, and give heed to that: let the speaker speak truly and the judge decide justly.

And first, I have to reply to the older charges and to my first accusers, and then I will go on to the later ones. For of old I have had many accusers, who have accused me falsely to you during many years; and I am more afraid of them than of Anytus and his associates, who are dangerous, too, in their own way. But far more dangerous are the others, who began when you were children, and took possession of your minds with their falsehoods, telling of one Socrates, a wise man, who speculated about the heaven above, and searched into the earth beneath, and made the worse appear the better cause. The disseminators of this tale are the accusers whom I dread; for their hearers are apt to fancy that such enquirers do not believe in the existence of the gods. And they are many, and their charges against me are of ancient date, and they were made by them in the days when you were more impress-

[2]marketplace

ible than you are now—in childhood, or it may have been in youth—
and the cause when heard went by default, for there was none to answer. And hardest of all, I do not know and cannot tell the names of
my accusers; unless in the chance case of a Comic poet.[3] All who from
envy and malice have persuaded you—some of them having first convinced themselves—all this class of men are most difficult to deal with;
for I cannot have them up here, and cross-examine them, and therefore
I must simply fight with shadows in my own defence, and argue when
there is no one who answers. I will ask you then to assume with me, as
I was saying, that my opponents are of two kinds; one recent, the other
ancient: and I hope that you will see the propriety of my answering the
latter first, for these accusations you heard long before the others, and
much oftener.

Well, then, I must make my defence, and endeavor to clear away, in a
short time, a slander which has lasted a long time. May I succeed, if to
succeed be for my good and yours, or likely to avail me in my cause! The
task is not an easy one; I quite understand the nature of it. And so leaving
the event with God, in obedience to the law I will now make my defence.

I will begin at the beginning, and ask what is the accusation which
has given rise to the slander of me, and in fact has encouraged Meletus
to prefer this charge against me. Well, what do the slanderers say? They
shall be my prosecutors, and I will sum up their words in an affidavit:
'Socrates is an evil-doer, and a curious person, who searches into things
under the earth, and in heaven, and he makes the worse appear the better cause; and he teaches the aforesaid doctrines to others.' Such is the
nature of the accusation: it is just what you have yourselves seen in the
comedy of Aristophanes, who has introduced a man whom he calls
Socrates, going about and saying that he walks in air, and talking a deal
of nonsense concerning matters of which I do not pretend to know
either much or little—not that I mean to speak disparagingly of any
one who is a student of natural philosophy. I should be very sorry if
Meletus could bring so grave a charge against me. But the simple truth
is, O Athenians, that I have nothing to do with physical speculations.
Very many of those here present are witnesses to the truth of this, and
to them I appeal. Speak then, you who have heard me, and tell your
neighbors whether any of you have ever known me hold forth in few
words or in many upon such matters. . . . You hear their answer. And
from what they say of this part of the charge you will be able to judge
of the truth of the rest.

---

[3] Arisophanes, whose comedy *The Clouds* satirized Socrates.

As little foundation is there for the report that I am a teacher, and take money; this accusation has no more truth in it than the other. Although, if a man were really able to instruct mankind, to receive money for giving instruction would, in my opinion, be an honor to him. There is Gorgias of Leontium, and Prodicus of Ceos, and Hippias of Elis, who go the round of the cities, and are able to persuade the young men to leave their own citizens by whom they might be taught for nothing, and come to them whom they not only pay, but are thankful if they may be allowed to pay them. There is at this time a Parian philosopher residing in Athens, of whom I have heard; and I came to hear of him in this way:—I came across a man who has spent a world of money on the Sophists, Callias, the son of Hipponicus, and knowing that he had sons, I asked him: 'Callias,' I said, 'if your two sons were foals or calves, there would be no difficulty in finding some one to put over them; we should hire a trainer of horses, or a farmer probably, who would improve and perfect them in their own proper virtue and excellence; but as they are human beings, whom are you thinking of placing over them? Is there any one who understands human and political virtue? You must have thought about the matter, for you have sons; is there any one?' 'There is,' he said. 'Who is he?' said I; 'and of what country? and what does he charge?' 'Evenus the Parian,' he replied; 'he is the man, and his charge is five minae.' Happy is Evenus, I said to myself; if he really has this wisdom, and teaches at such a moderate charge. Had I the same, I should have been very proud and conceited; but the truth is that I have no knowledge of the kind.

I dare say, Athenians, that some one among you will reply, 'Yes, Socrates, but what is the origin of these accusations which are brought against you; there must have been something strange which you have been doing? All these rumors and this talk about you would never have arisen if you had been like other men: tell us, then, what is the cause of them, for we should be sorry to judge hastily of you.' Now I regard this as a fair challenge, and I will endeavor to explain to you the reason why I am called wise and have such an evil fame. Please to attend then. And although some of you may think that I am joking, I declare that I will tell you the entire truth. Men of Athens, this reputation of mine has come of a certain sort of wisdom which I possess. If you ask me what kind of wisdom, I reply, wisdom such as may perhaps be attained by man, for to that extent I am inclined to believe that I am wise; whereas the persons of whom I was speaking have a superhuman wisdom, which I may fail to describe, because I have it not myself; and he who says that I have, speaks falsely, and is taking away my character.

And here, O men of Athens, I must beg you not to interrupt me, even if I seem to say something extravagant. For the word which I will speak is not mine. I will refer you to a witness who is worthy of credit; that witness shall be the God of Delphi—he will tell you about my wisdom, if I have any, and of what sort it is. You must have known Chaerephon; he was early a friend of mine, and also a friend of yours, for he shared in the recent exile of the people, and returned with you. Well, Chaerephon, as you know, was very impetuous in all his doings, and he went to Delphi and boldly asked the oracle to tell him whether—as I was saying, I must beg you not to interrupt—he asked the oracle to tell him whether any one was wiser than I was, and the Pythian prophetess answered, that there was no man wiser. Chaerephon is dead himself; but his brother, who is in court, will confirm the truth of what I am saying.

Why do I mention this? Because I am going to explain to you why I have such an evil name. When I heard the answer, I said to myself, What can the god mean? and what is the interpretation of his riddle? for I know that I have no wisdom, small or great. What then can he mean when he says that I am the wisest of men? And yet he is a god, and cannot lie; that would be against his nature. After long consideration, I thought of a method of trying the question. I reflected that if I could only find a man wiser than myself, then I might go to the god with a refutation in my hand. I should say to him, 'Here is a man who is wiser than I am; but you said that I was the wisest.' Accordingly I went to one who had the reputation of wisdom, and observed him—his name I need not mention; he was a politician whom I selected for examination—and the result was as follows: When I began to talk with him, I could not help thinking that he was not really wise, although he was thought wise by many, and still wiser by himself; and thereupon I tried to explain to him that he thought himself wise, but was not really wise; and the consequence was that he hated me, and his enmity was shared by several who were present and heard me. So I left him, saying to myself, as I went away: Well, although I do not suppose that either of us knows anything really beautiful and good, I am better off than he is,—for he knows nothing, and thinks that he knows; I neither know nor think that I know. In this latter particular, then, I seem to have slightly the advantage of him. Then I went to another who had still higher pretensions to wisdom, and my conclusion was exactly the same. Whereupon I made another enemy of him, and of many others besides him.

Then I went to one man after another, being not unconscious of the enmity which I provoked, and I lamented and feared this: But necessity was laid upon me,—the word of God, I thought, ought to be considered first. And I said to myself, Go I must to all who appear to know, and find out the meaning of the oracle. And I swear to you, Athenians, by the dog I swear!—for I must tell you the truth—the result of my mission was just this: I found that the men most in repute were all but the most foolish; and that others less esteemed were really wiser and better. I will tell you the tale of my wanderings and of the 'Herculean' labors, as I may call them, which I endured only to find at last the oracle irrefutable. After the politicians, I went to the poets; tragic, dithyrambic, and all sorts. And there, I said to myself, you will be instantly detected; now you will find out that you are more ignorant than they are. Accordingly, I took them some of the most elaborate passages in their own writings, and asked what was the meaning of them—thinking that they would teach me something. Will you believe me? I am almost ashamed to confess the truth, but I must say that there is hardly a person present who would not have talked better about their poetry than they did themselves. Then I knew that not by wisdom do poets write poetry, but by a sort of genius and inspiration; they are like diviners or soothsayers who also say many fine things, but do not understand the meaning of them. The poets appeared to me to be much in the same case; and I further observed that upon the strength of their poetry they believed themselves to be the wisest of men in other things in which they were not wise. So I departed, conceiving myself to be superior to them for the same reason that I was superior to the politicians.

At last I went to the artisans, for I was conscious that I knew nothing at all, as I may say, and I was sure that they knew many fine things; and here I was not mistaken, for they did know many things of which I was ignorant, and in this they certainly were wiser than I was. But I observed that even the good artisans fell into the same error as the poets;—because they were good workmen they thought that they also knew all sorts of high matters, and this defect in them overshadowed their wisdom; and therefore I asked myself on behalf of the oracle, whether I would like to be as I was, neither having their knowledge nor their ignorance, or like them in both; and I made answer to myself and to the oracle that I was better off as I was.

This inquisition has led to my having many enemies of the worst and most dangerous kind, and has given occasion also to many calumnies. And I am called wise, for my hearers always imagine that I myself possess the wisdom which I find wanting in others: but the truth is, O men of Athens, that God only is wise; and by his answer he intends to show that the wisdom of men is worth little or nothing; he is not speaking of Socrates, he is only using my name by way of illustration, as if he said, He, O men, is the wisest, who, like Socrates, knows that his wisdom is in truth worth nothing. And so I go about the world, obedient to the god, and search and make enquiry into the wisdom of any one, whether citizen or stranger, who appears to be wise; and if he is not wise, then in vindication of the oracle I show him that he is not wise; and my occupation quite absorbs me, and I have no time to give either to any public matter of interest or to any concern of my own, but I am in utter poverty by reason of my devotion to the god.

There is another thing:—young men of the richer classes, who have not much to do, come about me of their own accord; they like to hear the pretenders examined, and they often imitate me, and proceed to examine others; there are plenty of persons, as they quickly discover, who think that they know something, but really know little or nothing; and then those who are examined by them instead of being angry with themselves are angry with me: This confounded Socrates, they say; this villainous misleader of youth!—and then if somebody asks them, Why, what evil does he practice or teach? they do not know, and cannot tell; but in order that they may not appear to be at a loss, they repeat the ready-made charges which are used against all philosophers about teaching things up in the clouds and under the earth, and having no gods, and making the worse appear the better cause; for they do not like to confess that their pretence of knowledge has been detected—which is the truth; and as they are numerous and ambitious and energetic, and are drawn up in battle array and have persuasive tongues, they have filled your ears with their loud and inveterate calumnies. And this is the reason why my three accusers, Meletus and Anytus and Lycon, have set upon me; Meletus, who has a quarrel with me on behalf of the poets; Anytus, on behalf of the craftsmen and politicians; Lycon, on behalf of the rhetoricians: and as I said at the beginning, I cannot expect to get rid of such a mass of calumny all in a moment. And this, O men of Athens, is the truth and the whole truth; I have concealed nothing, I have dissembled nothing. And yet, I know that my plainness of speech makes them hate me, and what is their hatred but a proof that I am speaking the truth?—Hence has arisen the prejudice against me; and this is the reason of it, as you will find out either in this or in any future enquiry.

I have said enough in my defence against the first class of my accusers; I turn to the second class. They are headed by Meletus, that good man and true lover of his country, as he calls himself. Against these, too, I must try to make a defence:—Let their affidavit be read: it contains something of this kind: It says that Socrates is a doer of evil, who corrupts the youth; and who does not believe in the gods of the state, but has other new divinities of his own. Such is the charge; and now let us examine the particular counts. He says that I am a doer of evil, and corrupt the youth; but I say, O men of Athens, that Meletus is a doer of evil, in that he pretends to be in earnest when he is only in jest, and is so eager to bring men to trial from a pretended zeal and interest about matters in which he really never had the smallest interest. And the truth of this I will endeavor to prove to you.

Come hither, Meletus, and let me ask a question of you. You think a great deal about the improvement of youth?

Yes, I do.

Tell the judges, then, who is their improver; for you must know, as you have taken the pains to discover their corrupter, and are citing and accusing me before them. Speak, then, and tell the judges who their improver is.—Observe, Meletus, that you are silent, and have nothing to say. But is not this rather disgraceful, and a very considerable proof of what I was saying, that you have no interest in the matter? Speak up, friend, and tell us who their improver is.

The laws.

But that, my good sir, is not my meaning. I want to know who the person is, who, in the first place, knows the laws.

The judges, Socrates, who are present in court.

What, do you mean to say, Meletus, that they are able to instruct and improve youth?

Certainly they are.

What, all of them, or some only and not others?

All of them.

By the goddess Here, that is good news! There are plenty of improvers, then. And what do you say of the audience,—do they improve them?

Yes, they do.

And the senators?

Yes, the senators improve them.

But perhaps the members of the assembly corrupt them?—or do they too improve them?

They improve them.

Then every Athenian improves and elevates them; all with the exception of myself; and I alone am their corrupter? Is that what you affirm?

That is what I stoutly affirm.

I am very unfortunate if you are right. But suppose I ask you a question: How about horses? Does one man do them harm and all the world good? Is not the exact opposite the truth? One man is able to do them good, or at least not many;—the trainer of horses, that is to say, does them good, and others who have to do with them rather injure them? Is not that true, Meletus, of horses, or any other animals? Most assuredly it is; whether you and Anytus say yes or no. Happy indeed would be the condition of youth if they had one corrupter only, and all the rest of the world were their improvers. But you, Meletus, have sufficiently shown that you never had a thought about the young: your carelessness is seen in your not caring about the very things which you bring against me.

And now, Meletus, I will ask you another question—by Zeus I will: Which is better, to live among bad citizens, or among good ones? Answer, friend, I say; the question is one which may be easily answered. Do not the good do their neighbors good, and the bad do them evil?

Certainly.

And is there any one who would rather be injured than benefited by those who live with him? Answer, my good friend, the law requires you to answer—does any one like to be injured?

Certainly not.

And when you accuse me of corrupting and deteriorating the youth, do you allege that I corrupt them intentionally or unintentionally?

Intentionally, I say.

But you have just admitted that the good do their neighbors good, and evil do them evil. Now, is that a truth which your superior wisdom has recognized thus early in life, and am I, at my age, in such darkness and ignorance as not to know that if a man with whom I have to live is corrupted by me, I am very likely to be harmed by him; and yet I corrupt him, and intentionally, too—so you say, although neither I nor any other human being is ever likely to be convinced by you. But either I do not corrupt them, or I corrupt them unintentionally; and on either view of the case you lie. If my offence is unintentional, the law has no cognizance of unintentional offences: you ought to have taken me privately, and warned and admonished me; for if I had been better advised, I should have left off doing what I only did unintentionally—no doubt I should; but you would have nothing to say to me and refused to teach me. And now you bring me up in this court, which is not a place of instruction, but of punishment.

It will be very clear to you, Athenians, as I was saying, that Meletus has no care at all, great or small, about the matter. But still I should like to know, Meletus, in what I am affirmed to corrupt the young. I suppose you mean, as I infer from your indictment, that I teach them not to acknowledge the gods which the state acknowledges, but some other new divinities or spiritual agencies in their stead. These are the lessons by which I corrupt the youth, as you say.

Yes, that I say emphatically.

Then, by the gods, Meletus, of whom we are speaking, tell me and the court, in somewhat plainer terms, what you mean! for I do not as yet understand whether you affirm that I teach other men to acknowledge some gods, and therefore that I do believe in gods, and am not an entire atheist—this you do not lay to my charge,—but only you say that they are not the same gods which the city recognizes—the charge is that they are different gods. Or, do you mean that I am an atheist simply, and a teacher of atheism?

I mean the latter—that you are a complete atheist.

What an extraordinary statement! Why do you think so, Meletus? Do you mean that I do not believe in the godhead of the sun or moon, like other men?

I assure you, judges, that he does not: for he says that the sun is stone, and the moon earth.

Friend Meletus, you think that you are accusing Anaxagoras: and you have but a bad opinion of the judges, if you fancy them illiterate to such a degree as not to know that these doctrines are found in the books of Anaxagoras the Clazomenian, which are full of them. And so, forsooth, the youth are said to be taught them by Socrates, when [they can buy the book in the theater district for one drachma at most] and laugh at Socrates if he pretends to father these extraordinary views. And so, Meletus, you really think that I do not believe in any god?

I swear by Zeus that you believe absolutely in none at all.

Nobody will believe you, Meletus, and I am pretty sure that you do not believe yourself. I cannot help thinking, men of Athens, that Meletus is reckless and impudent, and that he has written this indictment in a spirit of mere wantonness and youthful bravado. Has he not compounded a riddle, thinking to try me? He said to himself:—I shall see whether the wise Socrates will discover my facetious contradiction, or whether I shall be able to deceive him and the rest of them. For he certainly does appear to me to contradict himself in the indictment as much as if he said that Socrates is guilty of not believing in the gods, and yet of believing in them—but this is not like a person who is in earnest.

I should like you, O men of Athens, to join me in examining what I conceive to be his inconsistency; and do you, Meletus, answer. And I must remind the audience of my request that they would not make a disturbance if I speak in my accustomed manner:

Did ever man, Meletus, believe in the existence of human things, and not of human beings? . . . I wish, men of Athens, that he would answer, and not be always trying to get up an interruption. Did ever any man believe in horsemanship, and not in horses? or in flute-playing, and not in flute-players? No, my friend; I will answer to you and to the court, as you refuse to answer for yourself. There is no man who ever did. But now please to answer the next question: Can a man believe in spiritual and divine agencies, and not in spirits or demigods?

He cannot.

How lucky I am to have extracted that answer, by the assistance of the court! But then you swear in the indictment that I teach and believe in divine or spiritual agencies (new or old, no matter for that); at any rate, I believe in spiritual agencies,—so you say and swear in the affidavit; and yet if I believe in divine beings, how can I help believing in spirits or demigods;—must I not? To be sure I must; and therefore I may assume that your silence gives consent. Now what are spirits or demigods? are they not either gods or the sons of gods?

Certainly they are.

But this is what I call the facetious riddle invented by you: the demigods or spirits are gods, and you say first that I do not believe in gods, and then again that I do believe in gods; that is, if I believe in demigods. For if the demigods are the illegitimate sons of gods, whether by the nymphs or by any other mothers, of whom they are said to be the sons—what human being will ever believe that there are no gods if they are the sons of gods? You might as well affirm the existence of mules, and deny that of horses and asses. Such nonsense, Meletus, could only have been intended by you to make trial of me. You have put this into the indictment because you had nothing real of which to accuse me. But no one who has a particle of understanding will ever be convinced by you that the same men can believe in divine and superhuman things, and yet not believe that there are gods and demigods and heroes.

I have said enough in answer to the charge of Meletus: any elaborate defence is unnecessary; but I know only too well how many are the enmities which I have incurred, and this is what will be my destruction if I am destroyed;—not Meletus, nor yet Anytus, but the envy and detraction of the world, which has been the death of many good men, and will probably be the death of many more; there is no danger of my being the last of them.

Some one will say: And are you not ashamed, Socrates, of a course of life which is likely to bring you to an untimely end? To him I may fairly answer: There you are mistaken: a man who is good for anything ought not to calculate the chance of living or dying; he ought only to consider whether in doing anything he is doing right or wrong—acting the part of a good man or of a bad. Whereas, upon your view, the heroes who fell at Troy were not good for much, and the son of Thetis[4] above all, who altogether despised danger in comparison with disgrace; and when he was so eager to slay Hector, his goddess mother said to him, that if he avenged his companion Patroclus, and slew Hector, he would die himself—'Fate,' she said, in these or the like words, 'waits for you next after Hector'; he, receiving this warning, utterly despised danger and death, and instead of fearing them, feared rather to live in dishonor, and not to avenge his friend. 'Let me die forthwith,' he replies, 'and be avenged of my enemy, rather than abide here by the beaked ships, a laughing-stock and a burden of the earth.' Had Achilles any thought of death and danger? For wherever a man's place is, whether the place which he has chosen or that in which he has been placed by a commander, there he ought to remain in hour of danger; he should not think of death or of anything but of disgrace. And this, O men of Athens, is a true saying.

Strange, indeed, would be my conduct, O men of Athens, if I who, when I was ordered by the generals whom you chose to command me at Potidaea and Amphipolis and Delium, remained where they placed me, like any other man, facing death—if now, when, as I conceive and imagine, God orders me to fulfil the philosopher's mission of searching into myself and other men, I were to desert my post through fear of death, or any other fear; that would indeed be strange, and I might justly be arraigned in court for denying the existence of the gods, if I disobeyed the oracle because I was afraid of death, fancying that I was wise when I was not wise. For the fear of death is indeed the pretence of wisdom, and not real wisdom, being a pretence of knowing the unknown; and no one knows whether death, which men in their fear apprehend to be the greatest evil, may not be the greatest good. Is not this ignorance of a disgraceful sort, the ignorance which is the conceit that man knows what he does not know? And in this respect only I believe myself to differ from men in general, and may perhaps claim to be wiser than they

[4]Achilles

are:—that whereas I know but little of the world below, I do not suppose that I know: but I do know that injustice and disobedience to a better, whether God or man, is evil and dishonorable, and I will never fear or avoid a possible good rather than a certain evil. And therefore if you let me go now, and are not convinced by Anytus, who said that since I had been prosecuted I must be put to death (or if not that I ought never to have been prosecuted at all); and that if I escape now, your sons will all be utterly ruined by listening to my words—if you say to me, Socrates, this time we will not mind Anytus, and you shall be let off, but upon one condition, that you are not to enquire and speculate in this way any more, and that if you are caught doing so again you shall die:—if this was the condition on which you let me go, I should reply: Men of Athens, I honor and love you; but I shall obey God rather than you, and while I have life and strength I shall never cease from the practice and teaching of philosophy, exhorting any one whom I meet and saying to him after my manner: You, my friend,—a citizen of the great and mighty and wise city of Athens,—are you not ashamed of heaping up the greatest amount of money and honor and reputation, and caring so little about wisdom and truth and the greatest improvement of the soul, which you never regard or heed at all? And if the person with whom I am arguing, says: Yes, but I do care; then I do not leave him or let him go at once; but I proceed to interrogate and examine and cross-examine him, and if I think that he has no virtue in him, but only says that he has, I reproach him with undervaluing the greater, and overvaluing the less. And I shall repeat the same words to every one whom I meet, young and old, citizen and alien, but especially to the citizens, inasmuch as they are my brethren. For know that this is the command of God; and I believe that no greater good has ever happened in the state than my service to the God. For I do nothing but go about persuading you all, old and young alike, not to take thought for your persons or your properties, but first and chiefly to care about the greatest improvement of the soul. I tell you that virtue is not given by money, but that from virtue comes money and every other good of man, public as well as private. This is my teaching, and if this is the doctrine which corrupts the youth, I am a mischievous person. But if any one says that this is not my teaching, he is speaking an untruth. Wherefore, O men of Athens, I say to you, do as Anytus bids or not as Anytus bids, and either acquit me or not; but whichever you do, understand that I shall never alter my ways, not even if I have to die many times.

Men of Athens, do not interrupt, but hear me; there was an understanding between us that you should hear me to the end: I have something more to say, at which you may be inclined to cry out; but I believe that to hear me will be good for you, and therefore I beg that you will not cry out. I would have you know, that if you kill such an one as I am, you will injure yourselves more than you will injure me. Nothing will injure me, not Meletus nor yet Anytus—they cannot, for a bad man is not permitted to injure a better than himself. I do not deny that Anytus may, perhaps, kill him, or drive him into exile, or deprive him of civil rights; and he may imagine, and others may imagine, that he is inflicting a great injury upon him: but there I do not agree. For the evil of doing as he is doing—the evil of unjustly taking away the life of another—is greater far.

And now, Athenians, I am not going to argue for my own sake, as you may think, but for yours, that you may not sin against the God by condemning me, who am his gift to you. For if you kill me you will not easily find a successor to me, who, if I may use such a ludicrous figure of speech, am a sort of gadfly, given to the state by God; and the state is a great and noble steed who is tardy in his motions owing to his very size, and requires to be stirred into life. I am that gadfly which God has attached to the state, and all day long and in all places am always fastening upon you, arousing and persuading and reproaching you. You will not easily find another like me, and therefore I would advise you to spare me. I dare say that you may feel out of temper (like a person who is suddenly awakened from sleep), and you think that you might easily strike me dead as Anytus advises, and then you would sleep on for the remainder of your lives, unless God in his care of you sent you another gadfly. When I say that I am given to you by God, the proof of my mission is this:—if I had been like other men, I should not have neglected all my own concerns or patiently seen the neglect of them during all these years, and have been doing yours, coming to you individually like a father or elder brother, exhorting you to regard virtue; such conduct, I say, would be unlike human nature. If I had gained anything, or if my exhortations had been paid, there would have been some sense in my doing so; but now, as you will perceive, not even the impudence of my accusers dares to say that I have ever exacted or sought pay of any one; of that they have no witness. And I have a sufficient witness to the truth of what I say—my poverty.

Some one may wonder why I go about in private giving advice and busying myself with the concerns of others, but do not venture to come forward in public and advise the state. I will tell you why. You have heard me speak at sundry times and in divers places of an oracle or sign which comes to me, and is the divinity which Meletus ridicules in the indictment. This sign, which is a kind of voice, first began to come to me when I was a child; it always forbids but never commands me to do anything which I am going to do. This is what deters me from being a politician. And rightly, as I think. For I am certain, O men of Athens, that if I had engaged in politics, I should have perished long ago, and done no good either to you or to myself. And do not be offended at my telling you the truth: for the truth is, that no man who goes to war with you or any other multitude, honestly striving against the many lawless and unrighteous deeds which are done in a state, will save his life; he who will fight for the right, if he would live even for a brief space, must have a private station and not a public one.

I can give you convincing evidence of what I say, not words only, but what you value far more—actions. Let me relate to you a passage of my own life which will prove to you that I should never have yielded to injustice from any fear of death, and that 'as I should have refused to yield' I must have died at once. I will tell you a tale of the courts, not very interesting perhaps, but nevertheless true. The only office of state which I ever held, O men of Athens, was that of senator: the tribe Antiochis, which is my tribe, had the presidency at the trial of the generals who had not taken up the bodies of the slain after the battle of Arginusae; and you proposed to try them in a body, contrary to law, as you all thought afterwards; but at the time I was the only one of the Prytanes who was opposed to the illegality, and I gave my vote against you; and when the orators threatened to impeach and arrest me, and you called and shouted, I made up my mind that I would run the risk, having law and justice with me, rather than take part in your injustice because I feared imprisonment and death. This happened in the days of the democracy. But when the oligarchy of the Thirty was in power, they sent for me and four others into the rotunda, and bade us bring Leon the Salaminian from Salamis, as they wanted to put him to death. This was a specimen of the sort of commands which they were always giving with the view of implicating as many as possible in their crimes; and then I showed, not in word only but in deed, that, if I may be allowed to use such an expression, I cared not a straw for death, and that my great and only care was lest I should do an unrighteous or unholy thing. For the strong arm of that oppressive power did not frighten me into doing wrong; and when we came out of the rotunda the other four went to Salamis and fetched Leon, but I went quietly home. For which I might have lost my life, had not the power of the Thirty shortly afterwards come to an end. And many will witness to my words.

Now do you really imagine that I could have survived all these years, if I had led a public life, supposing that like a good man I had always maintained the right and had made justice, as I ought, the first thing? No indeed, men of Athens, neither I nor any other man. But I have been always the same in all my actions, public as well as private, and never have I yielded any base compliance to those who are slanderously termed my disciples, or to any other. Not that I have any regular disciples. But if any one likes to come and hear me while I am pursuing my mission, whether he be young or old, he is not excluded. Nor do I converse only with those who pay; but any one, whether he be rich or poor, may ask and answer me and listen to my words; and whether he turns out to be a bad man or a good one, neither result can be justly imputed to me; for I never taught or professed to teach him anything. And if any one says that he has ever learned or heard anything from me in private which all the world has not heard, let me tell you that he is lying.

But I shall be asked, Why do people delight in continually conversing with you? I have told you already, Athenians, the whole truth about this matter: they like to hear the cross-examination of the pretenders to wisdom; there is amusement in it. Now this duty of cross-examining other men has been imposed upon me by God; and has been signified to me by oracles, visions, and in every way in which the will of divine power was ever intimated to any one. This is true, O Athenians; or, if not true, would be soon refuted. If I am or have been corrupting the youth, those of them who are now grown up and become sensible that I gave them bad advice in the days of their youth should come forward as accusers, and take their revenge; or if they do not like to come themselves, some of their relatives, fathers, brothers, or other kinsmen, should say what evil their families have suffered at my hands. Now is their time. Many of them I see in the court. There is Crito, who is of the same age and of the same deme[5] with myself, and there is Critobulus his son, whom I also see. Then again there is Lysanias of Sphettus, who is the father of Aeschines—he is present; and also there is Antiphon of Cephisus, who is the father of Epigenes; and there are the brothers of several who have associated with me. There is Nicostratus the son of Theosdotides, and the brother of Theodotus (now Theodotus himself is dead, and therefore he, at any rate, will not seek to stop him); and there is Paralus the son of Demodocus, who had a brother Theages; and Adeimantus the son of Ariston, whose brother Plato is present; and Aeantodorus, who is the brother of Apollodorus,

[5] Precinct

whom I also see. I might mention a great many others, some of whom Meletus should have produced as witnesses in the course of his speech; and let him still produce them, if he has forgotten—I will make way for him. And let him say, if he has any testimony of the sort which he can produce. Nay, Athenians, the very opposite is the truth. For all these are ready to witness on behalf of the corrupter, of the injurer of their kindred, as Meletus and Anytus call me; not the corrupted youth only—there might have been a motive for that—but their uncorrupted elder relatives. Why should they too support me with their testimony? Why, indeed, except for the sake of truth and justice, and because they know that I am speaking the truth, and that Meletus is a liar.

Well, Athenians, this and the like of this is all the defence which I have to offer. Yet a word more. Perhaps there may be some one who is offended at me, when he calls to mind how he himself on a similar, or even a less serious occasion, prayed and entreated the judges with many tears, and how he produced his children in court, which was a moving spectacle, together with a host of relations and friends; whereas I, who am probably in danger of my life, will do none of these things. The contrast may occur to his mind, and he may be set against me, and vote in anger because he is displeased at me on this account. Now if there be such a person among you,—mind, I do not say that there is,—to him I may fairly reply: My friend, I am a man, and like other men, a creature of flesh and blood, and not 'of wood or stone,' as Homer says; and I have a family, yes, and sons, O Athenians, three in number, one almost a man, and two others who are still young; and yet I will not bring any of them hither in order to petition you for an acquittal. And why not? Not from any self-assertion or want of respect for you. Whether I am or am not afraid of death is another question, of which I will not now speak. But, having regard to public opinion, I feel that such conduct would be discreditable to myself, and to you, and to the whole state. One who has reached my years, and who has a name for wisdom, ought not to demean himself. Whether this opinion of me be deserved or not, at any rate the world has decided that Socrates is in some way superior to other men. And if those among you who are said to be superior in wisdom and courage, and any other virtue, demean themselves in this way, how shameful is their conduct! I have seen men of reputation, when they have been condemned, behaving in the strangest manner: they seemed to fancy that they were going to suffer something dreadful if they died, and that they could be immortal if you only allowed them to live; and I think that such are a dishonor to the state, and that any stranger coming in would have said of them that the most eminent men of Athens, to whom the Athenians themselves give honor and command, are no better than women. And I say that these things ought not to be done by those of us who have a reputation; and if they are done, you ought not to permit them; you ought rather to show that you are far more disposed to condemn the man who gets up a doleful scene and makes the city ridiculous, than him who holds his peace.

But, setting aside the question of public opinion, there seems to be something wrong in asking a favor of a judge, and thus procuring an acquittal, instead of informing and convincing him. For his duty is, not to make a present of justice, but to give judgment; and he has sworn that he will judge according to the laws, and not according to his own good pleasure; and we ought not to encourage you, nor should you allow yourself to be encouraged, in this habit of perjury—there can be no piety in that. Do not then require me to do what I consider dishonorable and impious and wrong, especially now, when I am being tried for impiety on the indictment of Meletus. For if, O men of Athens, by force of persuasion and entreaty I could overpower your oaths, then I should be teaching you to believe that there are no gods, and in defending should simply convict myself of the charge of not believing in them. But that is not so—far otherwise. For I do believe that there are gods, and in a sense higher than that in which any of my accusers believe in them. And to you and to God I commit my cause, to be determined by you as is best for you and me.[6]

There are many reasons why I am not grieved, O men of Athens, at the vote of condemnation. I expected it, and am only surprised that the votes are so nearly equal; for I had thought that the majority against me would have been far larger; but now, had thirty votes gone over to the other side, I should have been acquitted. And I may say, I think, that I have escaped Meletus. I may say more; for without the assistance of Anytus and Lycon, any one may see that he would not have had a fifth part of the votes, as the law requires, in which case he would have incurred a fine of a thousand drachmae.

And so he proposes death as the penalty. And what shall I propose on my part, O men of Athens? Clearly that which is my due. And what is my due? What return shall be made to the man who has never had the wit to be idle during his whole life; but has been careless of what the many care for—wealth, and family interests, and military offices, and speaking in the assembly, and magistracies, and plots, and parties. Reflecting that I was really too honest a man to be a politician and live, I did not go where I could do no good to you or to myself; but where I

---

[6]Socrates was found guilty by a vote of 280 to 220.

could do the greatest good privately to every one of you, thither I went, and sought to persuade every man among you that he must look to himself, and seek virtue and wisdom before he looks to his private interests, and look to the state before he looks to the interests of the state; and that this should be the order which he observes in all his actions. What shall be done to such an one? Doubtless some good thing, O men of Athens, if he has his reward; and the good should be of a kind suitable to him. What would be a reward suitable to a poor man who is your benefactor, and who desires leisure that he may instruct you? There can be no reward so fitting as maintenance in the Prytaneum,[7] O men of Athens, a reward which he deserves far more than the citizen who has won the prize at Olympia in the horse or chariot race, whether the chariots were drawn by two horses or by many. For I am in want, and he has enough; and he only gives you the appearance of happiness, and I give you the reality. And if I am to estimate the penalty fairly, I should say that maintenance in the Prytaneum is the just return.

Perhaps you think that I am braving you in what I am saying now, as in what I said before about the tears and prayers. But this is not so. I speak rather because I am convinced that I never intentionally wronged any one, although I cannot convince you—the time has been too short; if there were a law at Athens, as there is in other cities, that a capital cause should not be decided in one day, then I believe that I should have convinced you. But I cannot in a moment refute great slander; and, as I am convinced that I never wronged another, I will assuredly not wrong myself. I will not say of myself that I deserve any evil, or propose any penalty. Why should I? Because I am afraid of the penalty of death which Meletus proposes? When I do not know whether death is a good or an evil, why should I propose a penalty which would certainly be an evil? Shall I say imprisonment? And why should I live in prison, and be the slave of the magistrates of the year—of the Eleven?[8] Or shall the penalty be a fine, and imprisonment until the fine is paid? There is the same objection. I should have to lie in prison, for money I have none, and cannot pay. And if I say exile (and this may possibly be the penalty which you will affix), I must indeed be blinded by the love of life, if I am so irrational as to expect that when you, who are my own citizens, cannot endure my discourses and words, and have found them so grievous and odious that you will have no more of them, others are likely to endure me. No indeed, men of Athens, that is not very likely. And what a life should I lead, at my age, wandering from city to city, ever changing my

---

[7]A place where distinguished persons viewed atheletic events.
[8]A committee in charge of executions.

place of exile, and always being driven out! For I am quite sure that wherever I go, there, as here, the young men will flock to me; and if I drive them away, their elders will drive me out at their request; and if I let them come, their fathers and friends will drive me out for their sakes.

Some one will say: Yes, Socrates, but cannot you hold your tongue, and then you may go into a foreign city, and no one will interfere with you? Now I have great difficulty in making you understand my answer to this. For if I tell you that to do as you say would be a disobedience to the God, and therefore that I cannot hold my tongue, you will not believe that I am serious; and if I say again that daily to discourse about virtue, and of those other things about which you hear me examining myself and others, is the greatest good of man, and that the unexamined life is not worth living, you are still less likely to believe me. Yet I say what is true, although a thing of which it is hard for me to persuade you. Also, I have never been accustomed to think that I deserve to suffer any harm. Had I money I might have estimated the offence at what I was able to pay, and not have been much the worse. But I have none, and therefore I must ask you to proportion the fine to my means. Well, perhaps I could afford a mina, and therefore I propose that penalty: Plato, Crito, Critobulus, and Apollodorus, my friends here, bid me say thirty minae, and they will be the sureties. Let thirty minae be the penalty; for which sum they will be ample security to you.[9]

Not much time will be gained, O Athenians, in return for the evil name which you will get from the detractors of the city, who will say that you killed Socrates, a wise man; for they will call me wise, even although I am not wise, when they want to reproach you. If you had waited a little while, your desire would have been fulfilled in the course of nature. For I am far advanced in years, as you may perceive, and not far from death. I am speaking now not to all of you, only to those who have condemned me to death. And I have another thing to say to them: You think that I was convicted because I had no words of the sort which would have procured my acquittal—I mean, if I had thought fit to leave nothing undone or unsaid. Not so; the deficiency which led to my conviction was not of words—certainly not. But I had not the boldness or impudence or inclination to address you as you would have liked me to do, weeping and wailing and lamenting, and saying and doing many things which you have been accustomed to hear from others, and which, as I maintain, are unworthy of me. I thought at the time that I ought not to do anything common or mean when in

---

[9]The citizens voted for the death penalty 300 to 200.

danger: nor do I now repent of the style of my defence; I would rather die having spoken after my manner, than speak in your manner and live. For neither in war nor yet at law ought I or any man to use every way of escaping death. Often in battle there can be no doubt that if a man will throw away his arms, and fall on his knees before his pursuers, he may escape death; and in other dangers there are other ways of escaping death, if a man is willing to say and do anything. The difficulty, my friends, is not to avoid death, but to avoid unrighteousness; for that runs faster than death. I am old and move slowly, and the slower runner has overtaken me, and my accusers are keen and quick, and the faster runner, who is unrighteousness, has overtaken them. And now I depart hence condemned by you to suffer the penalty of death,—they too go their ways condemned by the truth to suffer the penalty of villainy and wrong; and I must abide by my award—let them abide by theirs. I suppose that these things may be regarded as fated,—and I think that they are well.

And now, O men who have condemned me, I would fain prophesy to you; for I am about to die, and in the hour of death men are gifted with prophetic power. And I prophesy to you who are my murderers, that immediately after my departure punishment far heavier than you have inflicted on me will surely await you. Me you have killed because you wanted to escape the accuser, and not to give an account of your lives. But that will not be as you suppose: far otherwise. For I say that there will be more accusers of you than there are now; accusers whom hitherto I have restrained: and as they are younger they will be more inconsiderate with you, and you will be more offended at them. If you think that by killing men you can prevent some one from censuring your evil lives, you are mistaken; that is not a way of escape which is either possible or honorable; the easiest and the noblest way is not to be disabling others, but to be improving yourselves. This is the prophecy which I utter before my departure to the judges who have condemned me.

Friends, who would have acquitted me, I would like also to talk with you about the thing which has come to pass, while the magistrates are busy, and before I go to the place at which I must die. Stay then a little, for we may as well talk with one another while there is time. You are my friends, and I should like to show you the meaning of this event which has happened to me. O my judges—for you I may truly call judges—I should like to tell you of a wonderful circumstance. Hitherto the divine faculty of which the internal oracle is the source has constantly been in the habit of opposing me even about trifles, if I was going to make a slip or error in any matter; and now as you see there has come upon me that which may be thought, and is generally believed to be, the last and worst evil. But the oracle made no sign of opposition, either when I was leaving my house in the morning, or when I was on my way to the court, or while I was speaking, at anything which I was going to say; and yet I have often been stopped in the middle of a speech, but now in nothing I either said or did touching the matter in hand has the oracle opposed me. What do I take to be the explanation of this silence? I will tell you. It is an intimation that what has happened to me is a good, and that those of us who think that death is an evil are in error. For the customary sign would surely have opposed me had I been going to evil and not to good.

Let us reflect in another way, and we shall see that there is great reason to hope that death is a good; for one of two things—either death is a state of nothingness and utter unconsciousness, or, as men say, there is a change and migration of the soul from this world to another. Now if you suppose that there is no consciousness, but a sleep like the sleep of him who is undisturbed even by dreams, death will be an unspeakable gain. For if a person were to select the night in which his sleep was undisturbed even by dreams, and were to compare with this the other days and nights of his life, and then were to tell us how many days and nights he had passed in the course of his life better and more pleasantly than this one, I think that any man, I will not say a private man, but even the great king will not find many such days or nights, when compared with the others. Now if death be of such a nature, I say that to die is gain; for eternity is then only a single night. But if death is the journey to another place, and there, as men say, all the dead abide, what good, O my friends and judges, can be greater than this? If indeed when the pilgrim arrives in the world below, he is delivered from the professors of justice in this world, and finds the true judges who are said to give judgment there, Minos and Rhadamanthus and Aeacus and Triptolemus, and other sons of God who were righteous in their own life, that pilgrimage will be worth making. What would not a man give if he might converse with Orpheus and Musaeus and Hesiod[10] and Homer? Nay, if this be true, let me die again and again. I myself, too, shall have a wonderful interest in there meeting and conversing with Palamedes, and Ajax the son of Telamon, and any other ancient hero who has suffered death through an unjust judgment; and there will be no small pleasure, as I think, in comparing my own sufferings with theirs. Above all, I shall then be able to continue my search into true and false knowledge; as in this world, so also in the next and I

[10]Greek poets

shall find out who is wise, and who pretends to be wise, and is not. What would not a man give, O judges, to be able to examine the leader of the great Trojan expedition; or Odysseus or Sisyphus, or numberless others, men and women too! What infinite delight would there be in conversing with them and asking them questions! In another world they do not put a man to death for asking questions: assuredly not. For besides being happier than we are, they will be immortal, if what is said is true.

Wherefore, O judges, be of good cheer about death, and know of a certainty, that no evil can happen to a good man, either in life or after death. He and his are not neglected by the gods; nor has my own approaching end happened by mere chance. But I see clearly that the time had arrived when it was better for me to die and be released from trouble; wherefore the oracle gave no sign. For which reason, also, I am not angry with my condemners, or with my accusers; they have done me no harm, although they did not mean to do me any good; and for this I may gently blame them.

Still I have a favor to ask of them. When my sons are grown up, I would ask you, O my friends, to punish them; and I would have you trouble them, as I have troubled you, if they seem to care about riches, or anything more than about virtue; or if they pretend to be something when they are really nothing,—then reprove them, as I have reproved you, for not caring about that for which they ought to care, and thinking that they are something when they are really nothing. And if you do this, both I and my sons will have received justice at your hands.

The hour of departure has arrived, and we go our ways—I to die, and you to live. Which is better God only knows.

—*c. 347 B.C.*

Questions: Reading, Responding, Arguing

1. Explain what Socrates learned from his visits to poets, politicians, and other craftsmen.
2. The essay contains both monologue and dialogue. Why does Plato switch from one to the other?
3. Explain why Athenians will be hurting themselves, according to Socrates, if he is put to death.
4. If Socrates is not simply "apologizing" to his audience for his actions, what else is the essay arguing? Examine the strategies of argumentation he employs, especially his use of *ethos, logos,* and *pathos.*

Henry David Thoreau (1817–1862)

Civil Disobedience

I heartily accept the motto,—"That government is best which governs least;" and I should like to see it acted up to more rapidly and systematically. Carried out, it finally amounts to this, which also I believe,—"That government is best which governs not at all;" and when men are prepared for it, that will be the kind of government which they will have. Government is at best but an expedient; but most governments are usually, and all governments are sometimes, inexpedient. The objections which have been brought against a standing army, and they are many and weighty, and deserve to prevail, may also at last be brought against a standing government. The standing army is only an arm of the standing government. The government itself, which is only the mode which the people have chosen to execute their will, is equally liable to be abused and perverted before the people can act through it. Witness the present Mexican war, the work of comparatively a few individuals using the standing government as their tool; for, in the outset, the people would not have consented to this measure.

This American government—what is it but a tradition, though a recent one, endeavoring to transmit itself unimpaired to posterity, but each instant losing some of its integrity? It has not the vitality and force of a single living man; for a single man can bend it to his will. It is a sort of wooden gun to the people themselves. But it is not the less necessary for this; for the people must have some complicated machinery or other, and hear its din, to satisfy that idea of government which they have. Governments show thus how successfully men can be imposed on, even impose on themselves, for their own advantage. It is excellent, we must all allow. Yet this government never of itself furthered any enterprise, but by the alacrity with which it got out of its way. *It* does not keep the country free. *It* does not settle the West. *It* does not educate. The character inherent in the American people has done all that has been accomplished; and it would have done somewhat more, if the government had not sometimes got in its way. For government is an expedient by which men would fain succeed in letting one another alone; and, as has been said, when it is most expedient, the governed are most let alone by it. Trade and commerce, if they were not made of India rubber, would never manage to bounce over the obstacles which legislators are continually putting in their way: and, if one were to judge these men wholly by the effects of their actions, and not partly by their intentions, they would deserve to be classed and punished with those mischievous persons who put obstructions on the railroads.

But, to speak practically and as a citizen, unlike those who call themselves no-government men, I ask for, not at once no government, but *at once* a better government. Let every man make known what kind of government would command his respect, and that will be one step toward obtaining it.

After all, the practical reason why, when the power is once in the hands of the people, a majority are permitted, and for a long period continue, to rule, is not because they are most likely to be in the right, nor because this seems fairest to the minority, but because they are physically the strongest. But a government in which the majority rule in all cases cannot be based on justice, even as far as men understand it. Can there not be a government in which majorities do not virtually decide right and wrong, but conscience?—in which majorities decide only those questions to which the rule of expediency is applicable? Must the citizen ever for a moment, or in the least degree, resign his conscience to the legislator? Why has every man a conscience, then? I think that we should be men first, and subjects afterward. It is not desirable to cultivate a respect for the law, so much as for the right. The only obligation which I have a right to assume is to do at any time what I think right. It is truly enough said that a corporation has no conscience; but a corporation of conscientious men is a corporation *with* a conscience. Law never made men a whit more just; and, by means of their respect for it, even the well-disposed are daily made the agents of injustice. A common and natural result of an undue respect for law is, that you may see a file of soldiers, colonel, captain, corporal, privates, powder-monkeys, and all, marching in admirable order over hill and dale to the wars, against their wills, ay, against their common sense and consciences, which makes it very steep marching indeed, and produces a palpitation of the heart. They have no doubt that it is a damnable business in which they are concerned; they are all peaceably inclined. Now, what are they? Men at all? or small movable forts and magazines, at the service of some unscrupulous man in power? Visit the Navy Yard, and behold a marine, such a man as an American government can make, or such as it can make a man with its black arts—a mere shadow and reminiscence of humanity, a man laid out alive and standing, and already, as one may say, buried under arms with funeral accompaniments, though it may be

> *"Not a drum was heard, not a funeral note,*
> *As his corse to the rampart we hurried;*
> *Not a soldier discharged his farewell shot*
> *O'er the grave where our hero we buried."*

The mass of men serve the state thus, not as men mainly, but as machines, with their bodies. They are the standing army, and the militia, jailers, constables, *posse comitatus,* etc. In most cases there is no free exercise whatever of the judgment or of the moral sense; but they put themselves on a level with wood and earth and stones; and wooden men can perhaps be manufactured that will serve the purpose as well. Such command no more respect than men of straw or a lump of dirt. They have the same sort of worth only as horses and dogs. Yet such as these even are commonly esteemed good citizens. Others, as most legislators, politicians, lawyers, ministers, and office-holders, serve the state chiefly with their heads; and, as they rarely make any moral distinctions, they are as likely to serve the devil, without *intending* it, as God. A very few, as heroes, patriots, martyrs, reformers in the great sense, and *men,* serve the state with their consciences also, and so necessarily resist it for the most part; and they are commonly treated as enemies by it. A wise man will only be useful as a man, and will not submit to be "clay," and "stop a hole to keep the wind away," but leave that office to his dust at least:—

> *"I am too high-born to be propertied,*
> *To be a secondary at control,*
> *Or useful serving-man and instrument*
> *To any sovereign state throughout the world."*

He who gives himself entirely to his fellow-men appears to them useless and selfish; but he who gives himself partially to them is pronounced a benefactor and philanthropist.

How does it become a man to behave toward this American government to-day? I answer, that he cannot without disgrace be associated with it. I cannot for an instant recognize that political organization as *my* government which is the *slave's* government also.

All men recognize the right of revolution; that is, the right to refuse allegiance to, and to resist, the government, when its tyranny or its inefficiency are great and unendurable. But almost all say that such is not the case now. But such was the case, they think, in the Revolution of '75. If one were to tell me that this was a bad government because it taxed certain foreign commodities brought to its ports, it is most probable that I should not make an ado about it, for I can do without them. All machines have their friction; and possibly this does enough good to counterbalance the evil. At any rate, it is a great evil to make a stir about it. But when the friction comes to have its machine, and oppression and robbery are organized, I say, let us not have such a machine any longer. In other words, when a sixth of the population of a nation which has undertaken to be the refuge of liberty are slaves, and a whole country is unjustly overrun and conquered by a foreign army, and subjected to military law, I think that it is not too soon for honest men to rebel and revolutionize. What makes this duty the more urgent is the fact that the country so overrun is not our own, but ours is the invading army.

Paley, a common authority with many on moral questions, in his chapter on the "Duty of Submission to Civil Government," resolves all civil obligation into expediency; and he proceeds to say "that so long as the interest of the whole society requires it, that is, so long as the established government cannot be resisted or changed without public inconveniency, it is the will of God . . . that the established government be obeyed,—and no longer. This principle being admitted, the justice of every particular case of resistance is reduced to a computation of the quantity of the danger and grievance on the one side, and of the probability and expense of redressing it on the other." Of this, he says, every man shall judge for himself. But Paley appears never to have contemplated those cases to which the rule of expediency does not apply, in which a people, as well as an individual, must do justice, cost what it may. If I have unjustly wrested a plank from a drowning man, I must restore it to him though I drown myself. This, according to Paley, would be inconvenient. But he that would save his life, in such a case, shall lose it. This people must cease to hold slaves, and to make war on Mexico, though it cost them their existence as a people.

In their practice, nations agree with Paley; but does any one think that Massachusetts does exactly what is right at the present crisis?

"A drab of state, a cloth-o'-silver slut,
To have her train borne up, and her soul trail in the dirt."

Practically speaking, the opponents to a reform in Massachusetts are not a hundred thousand politicians at the South, but a hundred thousand merchants and farmers here, who are more interested in commerce and agriculture than they are in humanity, and are not prepared to do justice to the slave and to Mexico, *cost what it may.* I quarrel not with far-off foes, but with those who, near at home, cooperate with, and do the bidding of, those far away, and without whom the latter would be harmless. We are accustomed to say, that the mass of men are unprepared; but improvement is slow, because the few are not materially wiser or better than the many. It is not so important that many should be as good as you, as that there be some absolute goodness somewhere; for that will leaven the whole lump. There are thousands who are *in opinion* opposed to slavery and to the war, who yet in effect do nothing to put an end to them; who, esteeming themselves children of Washington and Franklin, sit down with their hands in their pockets, and say that they know not what to do, and do nothing; who even postpone the question of freedom to the question of free trade, and quietly read the prices-current along with the latest advices from Mexico, after dinner, and, it may be, fall asleep over them both. What is the price-current of an honest man and patriot to-day? They hesitate, and they regret, and sometimes they petition; but they do nothing in earnest and with effect. They will wait, well disposed, for others to remedy the evil, that they may no longer have it to regret. At most, they give only a cheap vote, and a feeble countenance and God-speed, to the right, as it goes by them. There are nine hundred and ninety-nine patrons of virtue to one virtuous man. But it is easier to deal with the real possessor of a thing than with the temporary guardian of it.

All voting is a sort of gaming, like checkers or backgammon, with a slight moral tinge to it, a playing with right and wrong, with moral questions; and betting naturally accompanies it. The character of the voters is not staked. I cast my vote, perchance, as I think right; but I am not vitally concerned that that right should prevail. I am willing to leave it to the majority. Its obligation, therefore, never exceeds that of expediency. Even voting *for the right is doing* nothing for it. It is only expressing to men feebly your desire that it should prevail. A wise man will not leave the right to the mercy of chance, not wish it to prevail through the power of the majority. There is but little virtue in the action of masses of men. When the majority shall at length vote for the abolition of slavery, it will be because they are indifferent to slavery, or because there is but little slavery left to be abolished by their vote. *They* will then be the only slaves. Only *his* vote can hasten the abolition of slavery who asserts his own freedom by his vote.

I hear of a convention to be held at Baltimore, or elsewhere, for the selection of a candidate for the Presidency, made up chiefly of editors, and men who are politicians by profession; but I think, what is it to any independent, intelligent, and respectable man what decision they may come to? Shall we not have the advantage of his wisdom and honesty, nevertheless? Can we not count upon some independent votes? Are there not many individuals in the country who do not attend conventions? But no: I find that the respectable man, so called, has immediately drifted from his position, and despairs of his country, when his country has more reason to despair of him. He forthwith adopts one of the candidates thus selected as the only *available* one, thus proving that he is himself *available* for any purposes of the demagogue. His vote is of not more worth than that of any unprincipled foreigner or hireling native, who may have been bought. O for a *man* who is a man, and, as my neighbor says, has a bone in his back which you cannot pass your hand through! Our statistics are at fault: the population has been returned too large. How many *men* are there to a square thousand miles in this country? Hardly one. Does not America offer any inducement for men to settle here? The American has dwindled into an Odd Fellow,—one who may be known by the development of his organ of gregariousness, and a manifest lack of intellect and cheerful self-reliance; whose first and chief concern, on coming into the world, is to see that the almshouses are in good repair; and, before yet he has lawfully donned the virile garb, to collect a fund for the support of the widows and orphans that may be; who, in short, ventures to live only by the aid of the Mutual Insurance company, which has promised to bury him decently.

It is not a man's duty, as a matter of course, to devote himself to the eradication of any, even the most enormous, wrong; he may still properly have other concerns to engage him; but it is his duty, at least, to wash his hands of it, and, if he gives it no thought longer, not to give it practically his support. If I devote myself to other pursuits and contemplations, I must first see, at least, that I do not pursue them sitting upon another man's shoulders. I must get off him first, that he may pursue his contemplations too. See what gross inconsistency is tolerated. I have heard some of my townsmen say. "I should like to have them order me out to help put down an insurrection of the slaves, or to march to Mexico;—see if I would go;" and yet these very men have each, directly by their allegiance, and so indirectly, at least, by their money, furnished a substitute. The soldier is applauded who refuses to serve in an unjust war by those who do not refuse to sustain the unjust government which makes the war; is applauded by those whose own act and authority he disregards and sets at naught; as if the state were penitent to that degree that it hired one to scourge it while it sinned, but not to that degree that it left off sinning for a moment. Thus, under the name of Order and Civil Government, we are all made at last to pay homage to and support our own meanness. After the first blush of sin comes its indifference; and from immoral it becomes, as it were, *un*moral, and not quite unnecessary to that life which we have made.

The broadest and most prevalent error requires the most disinterested virtue to sustain it. The slight reproach to which the virtue of patriotism is commonly liable, the noble are most likely to incur. Those who, while they disapprove of the character and measures of a government, yield to it their allegiance and support, are undoubtedly its most conscientious supporters, and so frequently the most serious obstacles to reform. Some are petitioning the State to dissolve the Union, to disregard the requisitions of the President. Why do they not dissolve it themselves,—the union between themselves and the State,—and refuse to pay their quota into its treasury? Do not they stand in the same relation to the State that the State does to the Union? And have not the same reasons prevented the State from resisting the Union which have prevented them from resisting the State?

How can a man be satisfied to entertain an opinion merely, and enjoy *it?* Is there any enjoyment in it, if his opinion is that he is aggrieved? If you are cheated out of a single dollar by your neighbor, you do not rest satisfied with knowing that you are cheated, or with saying that you are cheated, or even with petitioning him to pay you your due; but you take effectual steps at once to obtain the full amount, and see that you are never cheated again. Action from principle, the perception and the performance of right, changes things and relations; it is essentially revolutionary, and does not consist wholly with anything which was, It not only divides States and churches, it divides families; ay, it divides the *individual*, separating the diabolical in him from the divine.

Unjust laws exist: shall we be content to obey them, or shall we endeavor to amend them, and obey them until we have succeeded, or shall we transgress them at once? Men generally, under such a government as this, think that they ought to wait until they have persuaded the majority to alter them. They think that, if they should resist, the remedy would be worse than the evil. But it is the fault of the government itself that the remedy is worse than the evil. *It* makes it worse. Why is it not more apt to anticipate and provide for reform? Why does it not cherish its wise minority? Why does it cry and resist before it is hurt? Why does it not encourage its citizens to be on the alert to point out its faults, and *do* better than it would have them? Why does it always crucify Christ, and excommunicate Copernicus and Luther, and pronounce Washington and Franklin rebels?

One would think, that a deliberate and practical denial of its authority was the only offense never contemplated by government; else, why has it not assigned its definite, its suitable and proportionate penalty? If a man who has no property refuses but once to earn nine shillings for the State, he is put in prison for a period unlimited by any law that I know, and determined only by the discretion of those who placed him there; but if he should steal ninety times nine shillings from the State, he is soon permitted to go at large again.

If the injustice is part of the necessary friction of the machine of government, let it go, let it go: perchance it will wear smooth,—certainly the machine will wear out. If the injustice has a spring, or a pulley, or a rope, or a crank, exclusively for itself, then perhaps you may consider whether the remedy will not be worse than the evil; but if it is of such a nature that it requires you to be the agent of injustice to another, then, I say, break the law. Let your life be a counter friction to stop the machine. What I have to do is to see, at any rate, that I do not lend myself to the wrong which I condemn.

As for adopting the ways which the State has provided for remedying the evil, I know not of such ways. They take too much time, and a man's life will be gone. I have other affairs to attend to. I came into this world, not chiefly to make this a good place to live in, but to live in it, be it good or bad. A man has not everything to do, but something; and because be cannot do *everything,* it is not necessary that he should do *something* wrong. It is not my business to be petitioning the Governor or the Legislature any more than it is theirs to petition me; and if they should not hear my petition, what should I do then? But in this case the State has provided no way: its very Constitution is the evil. This may seem to be harsh and stubborn and unconciliatory; but it is to treat with the utmost kindness and consideration the only spirit that can appreciate or deserves it. So is all change for the better, like birth and death, which convulse the body.

I do not hesitate to say, that those who call themselves Abolitionists should at once effectually withdraw their support, both in person and property, from the government of Massachusetts, and not wait till they constitute a majority of one, before they suffer the right to prevail through them. I think that it is enough if they have God on their side, without waiting for that other one. Moreover, any man more right than his neighbors constitutes a majority of one already.

I meet this American government, or its representative, the State government, directly, and face to face, once a year—no more—in the person of its tax-gatherer; this is the only mode in which a man situated as I am necessarily meets it; and it then says distinctly, Recognize me; and the simplest, the most effectual, and, in the present posture of affairs, the indispensablest mode of treating with it on this head, of expressing your little satisfaction with and love for it, is to deny it then. My civil neighbor, the tax-gatherer, is the very man I have to deal with,—for it is, after all, with men and not with parchment that I quarrel,—and he has voluntarily chosen to be an agent of the government. How shall he ever know well what he is and does as an officer of the government, or as a man, until he is obliged to consider whether he shall treat me, his neighbor, for whom he has respect, as a neighbor and well-disposed man, or as a maniac and disturber of the peace, and see if he can get over this obstruction to his neighborliness without a ruder and more impetuous thought or speech corresponding with his action. I know this well, that if one thousand, if one hundred, if ten men whom I could name,—if ten *honest* men only,—ay, if *one* honest man, in this State of Massachusetts, *ceasing to hold slaves*, were actually to withdraw from this copartnership, and be locked up in the county jail therefor, it would be the abolition of slavery in America. For it matters not how small the beginning may seem to be: what is once well done is done forever. But we love better to talk about it: that we say is our mission. Reform keeps many scores of newspapers in its service, but not one man. If my esteemed neighbor, the State's ambassador, who will devote his days to the settlement of the question of human rights in the Council Chamber, instead of being threatened with the prisons of Carolina, were to sit down the prisoner of Massachusetts, that State which is so anxious to foist the sin of slavery upon her sister,—though at present she can discover only an act of inhospitality to be the ground of a quarrel with her,—the Legislature would not wholly waive the subject the following winter.

Under a government which imprisons any unjustly, the true place for a just man is also a prison. The proper place to-day, the only place which Massachusetts has provided for her freer and less desponding spirits, is in her prisons, to be put out and locked out of the State by her own act, as they have already put themselves out by their principles. It is there that the fugitive slave, and the Mexican prisoner on parole, and the Indian come to plead the wrongs of his race should find them; on that separate, but more free and honorable ground, where the State places those who are not *with* her, but *against* her,—the only house in a slave State in which a free man can abide with honor. If any think that their influence would be lost there, and their voices no longer afflict the ear of the State, that they would not be as an enemy within its walls, they do not know by how much truth is stronger than error, nor how much more eloquently and effectively he can combat injustice who has experienced a little in his own person. Cast your whole vote, not a strip of paper merely, but your whole influence. A minority is powerless while it conforms to the majority; it is not even a minority then; but it is irresistible when it clogs by its whole weight. If the alternative is to keep all just men in prison, or give up war and slavery, the State will not hesitate which to choose. If a thousand men were not to pay their tax-bills this year, that would not be a violent and bloody measure, as it would be to pay them, and enable the State to commit violence and shed innocent blood. This is, in fact, the definition of a peaceable revolution, if any such is possible. If the tax gatherer, or any other public officer, asks me, as one has done, "But what shall I do?" my answer is, "If you really wish to do anything, resign your office." When the subject has refused allegiance, and the officer has resigned his office, then the revolution is accomplished. But even suppose blood should flow. Is there not a sort of blood shed when the conscience is wounded? Through this wound a man's real manhood and immortality flow out, and he bleeds to an everlasting death. I see this blood flowing now.

I have contemplated the imprisonment of the offender, rather than the seizure of his goods,—though both will serve the same purpose,—because they who assert the purest right, and consequently are most dangerous to a corrupt State, commonly have not spent much time in accumulating property. To such the State renders comparatively small service, and a slight tax is wont to appear exorbitant, particularly if they are obliged to earn it by special labor with their hands. If there were one who lived wholly without the use of money, the State itself would hesitate to demand it of him. But the rich man—not to make any invidious comparison—is always sold to the institution which makes him rich. Absolutely speaking, the more money, the less virtue; for money comes between a man and his objects, and obtains them for him; and it was certainly no great virtue to obtain it. It puts to rest many questions which he would otherwise be taxed to answer; while the only new question which it puts is the hard but superfluous one, how to spend it. Thus his moral ground is taken from under his feet. The opportunities of living are diminished in proportion as what are called the "means" are increased. The best thing a man can do for his culture when he is rich is to endeavor to carry out those schemes which he entertained when he was poor. Christ answered the Herodians according to their condition. "Show me the tribute money," said he;—and took one penny out of his pocket;—if you use money which has the image of Caesar on it and which he has made current and valuable, that is, *if you are men of the State,* and gladly enjoy the advantages of Caesar's government, then pay him back some of his own when he demands it. "Render therefore to Caesar that which is Caesar's, and to God those things which are God's,"—leaving them no wiser than before as to which was which: for they did not wish to know.

When I converse with the freest of my neighbors, I perceive that, whatever they may say about the magnitude and seriousness of the question, and their regard for the public tranquillity, the long and the short of the matter is, that they cannot spare the protection of the existing government, and they dread the consequences to their property and families of disobedience to it. For my own part, I should not like to think that I ever rely on the protection of the State. But, if I deny the authority of the State when it presents its tax-bill, it will soon take and waste all my property, and so harass me and my children without end. This is hard. This makes it impossible for a man to live honestly, and at the same time comfortably, in outward respects. It will not be worth the while to accumulate property; that would be sure to go again. You must hire or squat somewhere, and raise but a small crop, and eat that soon. You must live within yourself, and depend upon yourself always tucked up and ready for a start, and not have many affairs. A man may grow rich in Turkey even, if he will be in all respects a good subject of the Turkish government. Confucius said: "If a state is governed by the principles of reason, poverty and misery are subjects of shame; if a state is not governed by the principles of reason, riches and honors are the subjects of shame." No: until I want the protection of Massachusetts to be extended to me in some distant Southern port, where my liberty is endangered, or until I am bent solely on building up an estate at home by peaceful enterprise. I can afford to refuse allegiance to Massachusetts, and her right to my property and life. It costs me less in every sense to incur the penalty of disobedience to the State than it would to obey. I should feel as if I were worth less in that case.

Some years ago, the State met me in behalf of the Church, and commanded me to pay a certain sum toward the support of a clergyman whose preaching my father attended, but never I myself. "Pay," it said, "or be locked up in the jail." declined to pay. But, unfortunately, another man saw fir to pay it. I did not see why the schoolmaster should be taxed to support the priest, and not the priest the schoolmaster; for I was not the State's schoolmaster, but I supported myself by voluntary subscription. I did not see why the lyceum should not present its tax-bill, and have the State to back its demand, as well as the Church. However, at the request of the select men, I condescended to make some such statement as this in writing:—"Know all men by these presents, that I, Henry Thoreau, do not wish to be regarded as a member of any incorporated society which I have not joined." This I gave to the town clerk; and he has it. The State, having thus learned that I did not wish to be regarded as a member of that church, has never made a like demand on me since; though it said that it must adhere to its original presumption that time. If I had known how to name them, I should then have signed off in detail from all the societies which I never signed on to; but I did not know where to find a complete list.

I have paid no poll-tax for six years. I was put into a jail once on this account, for one night; and, as I stood considering the walls of solid stone, two or three feet thick, the door of wood and iron, a foot thick, and the iron grating which strained the light, I could not help being struck with the foolishness of that institution which treated me as if I were mere flesh and blood and bones, to be locked up. I wondered that it should have concluded at length that this was the best use it could put me to, and had never thought to avail itself of my services in some way. I saw that, if there was a wall of stone between me and my townsmen, there was a still more difficult one to climb or break through before they could get to be as free as I was. I did not for a moment feel confined, and the walls seemed a great waste of stone and mortar. I felt as if I alone of all my townsmen had paid my tax. They plainly did not know how to treat me, but behaved like persons who are underbred. In every threat and in every compliment there was a blunder; for they thought that my chief desire was to stand the other side of that stone wall. I could not but smile to see how industriously they locked the door on my meditations, which followed them out again without let or hindrance, and *they* were really all that was dangerous. As they could not reach me, they had resolved to punish my body; just as boys, if they cannot come at some person against whom they have a spite, will abuse his dog. I saw that the State was half-witted, that it was timid as a lone woman with her silver spoons, and that it did not know its friends from its foes, and I lost all my remaining respect for it, and pitied it.

Thus the State never intentionally confronts a man's sense, intellectual or moral, but only his body, his senses. It is not armed with superior wit or honesty, but with superior physical strength. I was not born to be forced. I will breathe after my own fashion. Let us see who is the strongest. What force has a multitude? They only can force me who obey a higher law than I. They force me to become like themselves. I do not hear of *men* being *forced* to live this way or that by masses of men. What sort of life were that to live? When I meet a government which says to me, "Your money or your life," why should I be in haste to give it my money? It may be in a great strait, and not know what to do: I cannot help that. It must help itself; do as I do. It is not worth the while to snivel about it. I am not responsible for the successful working of the machinery of society. I am not the son of the engineer. I perceive that, when an acorn and a chestnut fall side by side, the one does not remain inert to make way for the other, but both obey their own laws, and spring and grow and flourish as best they can, till one, perchance, over-shadows and destroys the other. If a plant cannot live according to its nature, it dies; and so a man.

The night in prison was novel and interesting enough. The prisoners in their shirt-sleeves were enjoying a chat and the evening air in the doorway, when I entered. But the jailer said, "Come, boys, it is time to lock up;" and so they dispersed, and I heard the sound of their steps returning into the hollow apartments. My room-mate was introduced to me by the jailer as "a first-rate fellow and a clever man." When the door was locked, he showed me where to hang my hat, and how he managed matters there. The rooms were white-washed once a month; and this one, at least, was the whitest, most simply furnished, and probably the neatest apartment in the town. He naturally wanted to know where I came from, and what brought me there; and, when I had told him, I asked him in my turn how he came there, presuming him to be an honest man, of course; and, as the world goes. I believe he was. "Why," said he, "they accuse me of burning a barn; but I never did it." As near as I could discover, he had probably gone to bed in a barn when drunk, and smoked his pipe there; and so a barn was burnt. He had the reputation of being a clever man, had been there some three months waiting for his trial to come on, and would have to wait as much longer; but he was quite domesticated and contented, since he got his board for nothing, and thought that he was well treated.

He occupied one window, and I the other; and I saw that if one stayed there long, his principal business would be to look out the window. I had soon read all the tracts that were left there, and examined where former prisoners had broken out, and where a grate had been sawed off, and heard the history of the various occupants of that room; for I found that even here there was a history and a gossip which never circulated beyond the walls of the jail. Probably this is the only house in the town where verses are composed, which are afterward printed in circular form, but not published. I was shown quite a long list of verses which were composed by some young men who had been detected in an attempt to escape, who avenged themselves by singing them.

I pumped my fellow-prisoner as dry as I could, for fear I should never see him again; but at length he showed me which was my bed, and left me to blow out the lamp.

It was like traveling into a far country, such as I had never expected to behold, to lie there for one night. It seemed to me that I never had heard the town clock strike before, nor the evening sounds of the village; for we slept with the windows open, which were inside the grating. It was to see my native village in the light of the Middle Ages, and our Concord was turned into a Rhine stream, and visions of knights and castles passed before me. They were the voices of old burghers that I heard in the streets. I was an involuntary spectator and auditor of whatever was done and said in the kitchen of the adjacent village-inn,—a wholly new and rare experience to me. It was a closer view of my native town. I was fairly inside of it. I never had seen its institutions before. This is one of the peculiar institutions; for it is a shire town. I began to comprehend what its inhabitants were about.

In the morning, our breakfasts were put through the hole in the door, in small oblong-square tin pans, made to fit, and holding a pint of chocolate, with brown bread, and an iron spoon. When they called for the vessels again, I was green enough to return what bread I had left; but my comrade seized it, and said that I should lay that up for lunch or dinner. Soon after he was let out to work at haying in a neighboring field, whither he went every day, and would not be back till noon; so he bade me good-day, saying, that he doubted if he should see me again.

When I came out of prison,—for some one interfered, and paid that tax,—I did not perceive that great changes had taken place on the common, such as he observed who went in a youth and emerged a tottering and gray-headed man; and yet a change had to my eyes come over the scene,—the town, and State, and country,—greater than any that mere time could effect. I saw yet more distinctly the State in which I lived. I saw to what extent the people among whom I lived could be trusted as good neighbors and friends; that their friendship was for summer weather only; that they did not greatly propose to do right; that they were a distinct race from me by their prejudices and superstitions, as the Chinamen and Malays are; that in their sacrifices to humanity they ran no risks, not even to their property; that after all they were not so noble but they created the thief as he had treated them, and hoped, by a certain outward observance and a few prayers, and by walking in a particular straight though useless path from time to time, to save their souls. This may be to judge my neighbors harshly; for I believe that many of them are not aware that they have such an institution as the jail in their village.

It was formerly the custom in our village, when a poor debtor came out of jail, for his acquaintances to salute him, looking through their fingers, which were crossed to represent the grating of a jail window, "How do ye do?" My neighbors did not thus salute me, but first looked at me, and then at one another, as if I had returned from a long journey, I was put into jail as I was going to the shoemaker's to get a shoe which was mended. When I was let out the next morning, I proceeded to finish my errand, and, having put on my mended shoe, joined a huckleberry party, who were impatient to put themselves under my conduct; and in half an hour,—for the horse was soon tackled,—was in the midst of a huckleberry field, on one of our highest hills, two miles off, and then the State was nowhere to be seen.

This is the whole history of "My Prisons."

I have never declined paying the highway tax, because I am as desirous of being a good neighbor as I am of being a bad subject; and as for supporting schools, I am doing my part to educate my fellow countrymen now. It is for no particular item in the tax-bill that I refuse to pay it. I simply wish to refuse allegiance to the State, to withdraw and stand aloof from it effectually. I do not care to trace the course of my dollar, if I could, till it buys a man or a musket to shoot one with, the dollar is innocent,—but I am concerned to trace the effects of my allegiance. In fact, I quietly declare war with the State, after my fashion, though I will still make what use and get what advantage of her I can, as is usual in such cases.

If others pay the tax which is demanded of me, from a sympathy with the State, they do but what they have already done in their own case, or rather they abet injustice to a greater extent than the State requires. If they pay the tax from a mistaken interest in the individual taxed, to save his property, or prevent his going to jail, it is because they have not considered wisely how far they let their private feelings interfere with the public good.

This, then, is my position at present. But one cannot be too much on his guard in such a case, lest his action be biased by obstinacy or an undue regard for the opinions of men. Let him see that he does only what belongs to himself and to the hour.

I think sometimes, Why, this people mean well, they are only ignorant; they would do better if they knew how: why give your neighbors this pain to treat you as they are not inclined to? But I think again, This is no reason why I should do as they do, or permit others to suffer much greater pain of a different kind. Again, I sometimes say to myself, When many millions of men, without heat, without ill will, without personal feeling of any kind, demand of you a few shillings only, without the possibility, such is their constitution, of retracting or altering their present demand, and without the possibility, on your side, of appeal to any other millions, why expose yourself to this overwhelming brute force? You do not resist cold and hunger, the winds and the waves, thus obstinately; you quietly submit to a thousand similar necessities. You do not put your head into the fire. But just in proportion as I regard this as not wholly a brute force, but partly a human force, and consider that I have relations to those millions as to so many millions of men, and not of mere brute or inanimate things, I see that appeal is possible, first and instantaneously, from them to the Maker of them, and, secondly, from them to themselves. But if I put my head deliberately into the fire, there is no appeal to fire or to the Maker of fire, and I have only myself to blame. If I could convince myself that I had any right to be satisfied with men as they are, and to treat them accordingly, and not according, in some respects, to my requisitions and expectations of what they and I ought to be, then, like a good Mussulman and fatalist, I should endeavor to be satisfied with things as they are, and say it is the will of God. And, above all, there is this difference between resisting this and a purely brute or natural force, that I can resist this with some effect; but I cannot expect, like Orpheus, to change the nature of the rocks and trees and beasts.

I do not wish to quarrel with any man or nation. I do not wish to split hairs, to make fine distinctions, or set myself up as better than my neighbors. I seek rather, I may say, even an excuse for conforming to the laws of the land. I am but too ready to conform to them. Indeed, I have reason to suspect myself on this head; and each year, as the tax-gatherer comes round, I find myself disposed to review the acts and position of the general and State governments, and the spirit of the people, to discover a pretext for conformity.

> "We must affect our country as our parents,
> And if at any time we alienate
> Our love or industry from doing it honor,
> We must respect effects and teach the soul
> Matter of conscience and religion,
> And not desire of rule or benefit."

I believe that the State will soon be able to take all my work of this sort out of my hands, and then I shall be no better a patriot than my fellow-countrymen. Seen from a lower point of view, the Constitution, with all its faults, is very good; the law and the courts are very respectable; even the State and this American government are, in many respects, very admirable, and rare things, to be thankful for, such as a great many have described them; but seen from a point of view a little higher, they are what I have described them; seen from a higher still, and the highest, who shall say what they are, or that they are worth looking at or thinking of at all?

However, the government does not concern me much, and I shall bestow the fewest possible thoughts on it. It is not many moments that I live under a government, even in this world. If a man is thought-free, fancy-free, imagination-free, that which *is not* never for a long time appearing *to be* to him, unwise rulers or reformers cannot fatally interrupt him.

I know that most men think differently from myself; but those whose lives are by profession devoted to the study of these or kindred subjects content me as little as any. Statesmen and legislators, standing so completely within the institution, never distinctly and nakedly behold it. They speak of moving society, but have no resting-place without it. They may be men of a certain experience and discrimination, and have no doubt invented ingenious and even useful systems, for which we sincerely thank them; but all their wit and usefulness lie within certain not very wide limits. They are wont to forget that the world is not governed by policy and expediency. Webster never goes behind government, and so cannot speak with authority about it. His words are wisdom to those legislators who contemplate no essential reform in the existing government; but for thinkers, and those who legislate for all time, he never once glances at the subject. I know of those whose serene and wise speculations on this theme would soon reveal the limits of his mind's range and hospitality. Yet, compared with the cheap professions of most reformers, and the still cheaper wisdom and eloquence of politicians in general, his are almost the only sensible and valuable words, and we thank Heaven for him. Comparatively, he is always strong, original, and, above all, practical. Still, his quality is not wisdom, but prudence. The lawyer's truth is not Truth, but consistency or a consistent expediency. Truth is always in harmony with herself, and is not concerned chiefly to reveal the justice that may consist with wrong-doing. He well deserves to be called, as he has been called, the Defender of the Constitution. There are really no blows to be given by him but defensive ones. He is not a leader, but a follower. His leaders are the men of '87. "I have never made an effort," he says, "and never propose to make an effort; I have never countenanced an effort, and never mean to countenance an effort, to disturb the arrangement as originally made, by which the various States came into the Union." Still thinking of the sanction which the Constitution gives to slavery, he says, "Because it was a part of the original compact,—let it stand." Notwithstanding his special acuteness and ability, he is unable to take a fact out of its merely political relations, and behold it as it lies absolutely to be disposed of by the intellect,—what, for instance, it behooves a man to do here in America to day with regard to slavery,—but ventures, or is driven, to make some such desperate answer as the following, while professing to speak absolutely, and as a private man,—from which what new and singular code of social duties might be inferred? "The manner," says he, "in which the governments of those States where slavery exists are to regulate it is for their own consideration, under their responsibility to their constituents, to the general laws of propriety, humanity, and justice, and to God. Associations formed elsewhere, springing from a feeling of humanity, or any other cause, have nothing whatever to do with it. They have never received any encouragement from me, and they never will."

They who know of no purer sources of truth, who have traced up its stream no higher, stand, and wisely stand, by the Bible and the Constitution, and drink at it there with reverence and humility; but they who behold where it comes trickling into this lake or that pool, gird up their loins once more, and continue their pilgrimage toward its fountain-head.

No man with a genius for legislation has appeared in America. They are rare in the history of the world. There are orators, politicians, and eloquent men, by the thousand; but the speaker has not yet opened his mouth to speak who is capable of settling the much-vexed questions of the day. We love eloquence for its own sake, and not for any truth which it may utter, or any heroism it may inspire. Our legislators have not yet learned the comparative value of free trade and of freedom, of union, and of rectitude, to a nation. They have no genius or talent for comparatively humble questions of taxation and finance, commerce and manufactures and agriculture. If we were left solely to the wordy wit of legislators in Congress for our guidance, uncorrected by the seasonable experience and the effectual complaints of the people, America would not long retain her rank among the nations. For eighteen hundred years, though perchance I have no right to say it, the New Testament has been written; yet where is the legislator who has wisdom and practical talent enough to avail himself of the light which it sheds on the science of legislation?

The authority of government, even such as I am willing to submit to,—for I will cheerfully obey those who know and can do better than I, and in many things even those who neither know not can do so well,—is still an impure one; to be strictly just, it must have the sanction and consent of the governed. It can have no pure right over my person and property but what I concede to it. The progress from an absolute to a limited monarchy, from a limited monarchy to a democracy, is a progress toward a true respect for the individual. Even the Chinese philosopher was wise enough to regard the individual as the basis of the empire. Is a democracy, such as we know it, the last improvement possible in government? Is it not possible to take a step further towards recognizing and organizing the rights of man? There will never be a really free and enlightened State until the State comes to recognize the individual as a higher and independent power, from which all its own power and authority are derived, and treats him accordingly. I please myself with imagining a State at last which can afford to be just to all men, and to treat the individual with respect as a neighbor; which even would not think it inconsistent with its own repose if a few were to live aloof from it, not meddling with it, not embraced by it, who fulfilled all the duties of neighbors and fellowmen. A State which bore this kind of fruit, and suffered it to drop off as fast as it ripened, would prepare the way for a still more perfect and glorious State, which also I have imagined, but not yet anywhere seen.

—1849

Questions: Reading, Responding, Arguing

1. Explain the basis for Thoreau's argument for disobedience. What strategies does he employ?
2. Thoreau argues that the government is in "each instant losing some of its integrity." How does government lose its integrity, and how does Thoreau propose to fix this problem?
3. In several of his paragraphs, Thoreau asks questions, and then addresses possible answers. How effective is this technique in the essay?
4. The essay is at first argumentative and then becomes descriptive of Thoreau's situation in jail. Why does Thoreau shift from one form to the other?

George Orwell (1903–1950)

Shooting an Elephant

In Moulmein, in Lower Burma, I was hated by large numbers of people—the only time in my life that I have been important enough for this to happen to me. I was sub-divisional police officer of the town, and in an aimless, petty kind of way anti-European feeling was very bitter. No one had the guts to raise a riot, but if a European woman went through the bazaars alone somebody would probably spit betel juice over her dress. As a police officer I was an obvious target and was baited whenever it seemed safe to do so. When a nimble Burman tripped me up on the football field and the referee (another Burman) looked the other way, the crowd yelled with hideous laughter. This happened more than once. In the end the sneering yellow faces of young men that met me everywhere, the insults hooted after me when I was at a safe distance, got badly on my nerves. The young Buddhist priests were the worst of all. There were several thousands of them in the town and none of them seemed to have anything to do except stand on street corners and jeer at Europeans.

All this was perplexing and upsetting. For at that time I had already made up my mind that imperialism was an evil thing and the sooner I chucked up my job and got out of it the better. Theoretically—and secretly, of course—I was all for the Burmese and all against their oppressors, the British. As for the job I was doing, I hated it more bitterly than I can perhaps make clear. In a job like that you see the dirty work of Empire at close quarters. The wretched prisoners huddling in the stinking cages of the lock-ups, the grey, cowed faces of the long-term convicts, the scarred buttocks of the men who had been flogged with bamboos—all these oppressed me with an intolerable sense of guilt. But I could get nothing into perspective. I was young and ill-educated and I had had to think out my problems in the utter silence that is imposed on every Englishman in the East. I did not even know that the British Empire is dying, still less did I know that it is a great deal better than the younger empires that are going to supplant it. All I knew was that I was stuck between my hatred of the empire I served and my rage against the evil-spirited little beasts who tried to make my job impossible. With one part of my mind I thought of the British Raj as an unbreakable tyranny, as something clamped down, in *saecula saeculorum* upon the will of prostrate peoples; with another part I thought that the greatest joy in the world would be to drive a bayonet into a Buddhist priest's guts. Feelings like these are the normal by-products of imperialism; ask any Anglo-Indian official, if you can catch him off duty.

One day something happened which in a roundabout way was enlightening. It was a tiny incident in itself, but it gave me a better glimpse than I had had before of the real nature of imperialism—the real motives for which despotic governments act. Early one morning the sub-inspector at a police station the other end of the town rang me up on the 'phone and said that an elephant was ravaging the bazaar. Would I please come and do something about it? I did not know what I could do, but I wanted to see what was happening and I got on to a pony and started out. I took my rifle, an old .44 Winchester and much too small to kill an elephant, but I thought the noise might be useful *in terrorem*. Various Burmans stopped me on the way and told me about the elephant's doings. It was not, of course, a wild elephant, but a tame one which had gone "must." It had been chained up, as tame elephants always are when their attack of "must" is due, but on the previous night it had broken its chain and escaped. Its mahout, the only person who could manage it when it was in that state, had set out in pursuit, but had taken the wrong direction and was now twelve hours' journey away, and in the morning the elephant had suddenly reappeared in the town. The Burmese population had no weapons and were quite helpless against it. It had already destroyed somebody's bamboo hut, killed a cow and raided some fruit-stalls and devoured the stock; also it had met the municipal rubbish van and, when the driver jumped out and took to his heels, had turned the van over and inflicted violences upon it.

The Burmese sub-inspector and some Indian constables were waiting for me in the quarter where the elephant had been seen. It was a very poor quarter, a labyrinth of squalid bamboo huts, thatched with palm-leaf, winding all over a steep hillside. I remember that it was a cloudy, stuffy morning at the beginning of the rains. We began questioning the people as to where the elephant had gone and, as usual, failed to get any definite information. That is invariably the case in the East; a story always sounds clear enough at a distance, but the nearer you get to the scene of events the vaguer it becomes. Some of the people said that the elephant had gone in one direction, some said that he had gone in another, some professed not even to have heard of any elephant. I had almost made up my mind that the whole story was a pack of lies, when we heard yells a little distance away. There was a loud, scandalized cry of "Go away, child! Go away this instant!" and an old woman with a switch in her hand came round the corner of a hut, violently shooing away a crowd of naked children. Some more women followed, clicking their tongues and exclaiming; evidently there was something that the children ought not to have seen. I rounded the hut and saw a man's dead body sprawling in the mud. He was an Indian, a black Dravidian coolie, almost naked, and he could not have been dead many minutes. The people said that the elephant had come suddenly upon him round the corner of the hut, caught him with its trunk, put its foot on his back and ground him into the earth. This was the rainy season and the ground was soft, and his face had scored a trench a foot deep and a couple of yards long. He was lying on his belly with arms crucified and head sharply twisted to one side. His face was coated with mud, the eyes wide open, the teeth bared and grinning with an expression of unendurable agony. (Never tell me, by the way, that the dead look peaceful. Most of the corpses I have seen looked devilish.) The friction of the great beast's foot had stripped the skin from his back as neatly as one skins a rabbit. As soon as I saw the dead man I sent an orderly to a friend's house nearby to borrow an elephant rifle. I had already sent back the pony, not wanting it to go mad with fright and throw me if it smelt the elephant.

The orderly came back in a few minutes with a rifle and five cartridges, and meanwhile some Burmans had arrived and told us that the elephant was in the paddy fields below, only a few hundred yards away. As I started forward practically the whole population of the quarter flocked out of the houses and followed me. They had seen the rifle and were all shouting excitedly that I was going to shoot the elephant. They had not shown much interest in the elephant when he was merely ravaging their homes, but it was different now that he was going to be shot. It was a bit of fun to them, as it would be to an English crowd; besides they wanted the meat. It made me vaguely uneasy. I had no intention of shooting the elephant—I had merely sent for the rifle to defend myself if necessary—and it is always unnerving to have a crowd following you. I marched down the hill, looking and feeling a fool, with the rifle over my shoulder and an ever-growing army of people jostling at my heels. At the bottom, when you got away from the huts, there was a metalled road and beyond that a miry waste of paddy fields a thousand yards across, not yet ploughed but soggy from the first rains and dotted with coarse grass. The elephant was standing eight yards from the road, his left side towards us. He took not the slightest notice of the crowd's approach. He was tearing up bunches of grass, beating them against his knees to clean them and stuffing them into his mouth.

I had halted on the road. As soon as I saw the elephant I knew with perfect certainty that I ought not to shoot him. It is a serious matter to shoot a working elephant—it is comparable to destroying a huge and costly piece of machinery—and obviously one ought not to do it if it can possibly be avoided. And at that distance, peacefully eating, the elephant looked no more dangerous than a cow. I thought then and I think now that his attack of "must" was already passing off; in which case he would merely wander harmlessly about until the mahout came back and caught him. Moreover, I did not in the least want to shoot him. I decided that I would watch him for a little while to make sure that he did not turn savage again, and then go home.

But at that moment I glanced round at the crowd that had followed me. It was an immense crowd, two thousand at the least and growing every minute. It blocked the road for a long distance on either side. I looked at the sea of yellow faces above the garish clothes—faces all happy and excited over this bit of fun, all certain that the elephant was going to be shot. They were watching me as they would watch a conjurer about to perform a trick. They did not like me, but with the magical rifle in my hands I was momentarily worth watching. And suddenly I realized that I should have to shoot the elephant after all. The people expected it of me and I had got to do it; I could feel their two thousand wills pressing me forward, irresistibly. And it was at this moment, as I stood there with the rifle in my hands, that I first grasped the hollowness, the futility of the white man's dominion in the East. Here was I, the white man with his gun, standing in front of the unarmed native crowd—seemingly the leading actor of the piece; but in reality I was only an absurd puppet pushed to and fro by the will of those yellow faces behind. I perceived in this moment that when the white man turns tyrant it is his own freedom that he destroys. He becomes a sort of hollow, posing dummy, the conventionalized figure of a sahib. For it is the condition of his rule that he shall spend his life in trying to impress the "natives," and so in every crisis he has got to do what the "natives" expect of him. He wears a mask, and his face grows to fit it. I had got to shoot the elephant. I had committed myself to doing it when I sent for the rifle. A sahib has got to act like a sahib; he has got to appear resolute, to know his own mind and do definite things. To come all that way, rifle in hand, with two thousand people marching at my heels, and then to trail feebly away, having done nothing—no, that was impossible. The crowd would laugh at me. And my whole life, every white man's life in the East, was one long struggle not to be laughed at.

But I did not want to shoot the elephant. I watched him beating his bunch of grass against his knees, with that preoccupied grandmotherly air that elephants have. It seemed to me that it would be murder to shoot him. At that age I was not squeamish about killing animals, but I had never shot an elephant and never wanted to. (Somehow it always seems worse to kill a *large* animal.) Besides, there was the beast's owner to be considered. Alive, the elephant was worth at least a hundred pounds; dead, he would only be worth the value of his tusks, five pounds, possibly. But I had got to act quickly. I turned to some experienced-looking Burmans who had been there when we arrived, and asked them how the elephant had been behaving. They all said the same thing: he took no notice of you if you left him alone, but he might charge if you went too close to him.

It was perfectly clear to me what I ought to do. I ought to walk up to within, say, twenty-five yards of the elephant and test his behavior. If he charged, I could shoot; if he took no notice of me, it would be safe to leave him until the mahout came back. But also I knew that I was going to do no such thing. I was a poor shot with a rifle and the ground was soft mud into which one would sink at every step. If the elephant charged and I missed him, I should have about as much chance as a toad under a steam-roller. But even then I was not thinking particularly of my own skin, only of the watchful yellow faces behind. For at that moment, with the crowd watching me, I was not afraid in the ordinary sense, as I would have been if I had been alone. A white man mustn't be frightened in front of "natives"; and so, in general, he isn't frightened. The sole thought in my mind was that if anything went wrong those two thousand Burmans would see me pursued, caught, trampled on and reduced to a grinning corpse like that Indian up the hill. And if that happened it was quite probable that some of them would laugh. That would never do. There was only one alternative. I shoved the cartridges into the magazine and lay down on the road to get a better aim.

The crowd grew very still, and a deep, low, happy sigh, as of people who see the theatre curtain go up at last, breathed from innumerable throats. They were going to have their bit of fun after all. The rifle was a beautiful German thing with cross-hair sights. I did not then know that in shooting an elephant one would shoot to cut an imaginary bar running from ear-hole to ear-hole. I ought, therefore, as the elephant was sideways on, to have aimed straight at his ear-hole; actually I aimed several inches in front of this, thinking the brain would be further forward.

When I pulled the trigger I did not hear the bang or feel the kick— one never does when a shot goes home—but I heard the devilish roar of glee that went up from the crowd. In that instant, in too short a time, one would have thought, even for the bullet to get there, a mysterious, terrible change had come over the elephant. He neither stirred nor fell, but every line of his body had altered. He looked suddenly stricken, shrunken, immensely old, as though the frightful impact of the bullet had paralysed him without knocking him down. At last, after what seemed a long time—it might have been five seconds, I dare say—he sagged flabbily to his knees. His mouth slobbered. An enormous senility seemed to have settled upon him. One could have imagined him thousands of years old. I fired again into the same spot. At the second shot he did not collapse but climbed with desperate slowness to his feet and stood weakly upright, with legs sagging and head drooping. I fired a third time. That was the shot that did for him. You could see the agony of it jolt his whole body and knock the last remnant of strength from his legs. But in falling he seemed for a moment to rise, for as his hind legs collapsed beneath him he seemed to tower upward like a huge rock toppling, his trunk reaching skywards like a tree. He trumpeted, for the first and only time. And then down he came, his belly towards me, with a crash that seemed to shake the ground even where I lay.

I got up. The Burmans were already racing past me across the mud. It was obvious that the elephant would never rise again, but he was not dead. He was breathing very rhythmically with long rattling gasps, his great mound of a side painfully rising and falling. His mouth was wide open—I could see far down into caverns of pale pink throat. I waited a long time for him to die, but his breathing did not weaken. Finally I fired my two remaining shots into the spot where I thought his heart must be. The thick blood welled out of him like red velvet, but still he did not die. His body did not even jerk when the shots hit him, the tortured breathing continued without a pause. He was dying, very slowly and in great agony, but in some world remote from me where not even a bullet could damage him further. I felt that I had got to put an end to that dreadful noise. It seemed dreadful to see the great beast lying there, powerless to move and yet powerless to die, and not even to be able to finish him. I sent back for my small rifle and poured shot after shot into his heart and down his throat. They seemed to make no impression. The tortured gasps continued as steadily as the ticking of a clock.

In the end I could not stand it any longer and went away. I heard later that it took him half an hour to die. Burmans were bringing dahs and baskets even before I left, and I was told they had stripped his body almost to the bones by the afternoon.

Afterwards, of course, there were endless discussions about the shooting of the elephant. The owner was furious, but he was only an

Indian and could do nothing. Besides, legally I had done the right thing, for a mad elephant has to be killed, like a mad dog, if its owner fails to control it. Among the Europeans opinion was divided. The older men said I was right, the younger men said it was a damn shame to shoot an elephant for killing a coolie, because an elephant was worth more than any damn Coringhee coolie. And afterwards I was very glad that the coolie had been killed; it put me legally in the right and it gave me a sufficient pretext for shooting the elephant. I often wondered whether any of the others grasped that I had done it solely to avoid looking a fool.

—1936

Questions: Reading, Responding, Arguing

1. Orwell explains that he shoots the elephant to avoid appearing foolish. What other reasons are explained in the essay?
2. Orwell's essay is a descriptive narrative. How is description used to drive home Orwell's unhappiness in the first paragraph?
3. What is "the real nature of imperialism" that is exposed in Orwell's essay? What is the essence of his argument against imperialism?

Naomi Wolf (b. 1962)

From *The Beauty Myth*

At last, after a long silence, women took to the streets. In the two decades of radical action that followed the rebirth of feminism in the early 1970s, Western women gained legal and reproductive rights, pursued higher education, entered the trades and the professions, and overturned ancient and revered beliefs about their social role. A generation on, do women feel free?

The affluent, educated, liberated women of the First World, who can enjoy freedoms unavailable to any women ever before, do not feel as free as they want to. And they can no longer restrict to the subconscious their sense that this lack of freedom has something to do with—with apparently frivolous issues, things that really should not matter.

Many are ashamed to admit that such trivial concerns—to do with physical appearance, bodies, faces, hair, clothes—matter so much. But in spite of shame, guilt, and denial, more and more women are wondering if it isn't that they are entirely neurotic and alone but rather that something important is indeed at stake that has to do with the relationship between female liberation and female beauty.

The more legal and material hindrances women have broken through, the more strictly and heavily and cruelly images of female beauty have come to weigh upon us. Many women sense that women's collective progress has stalled; compared with the heady momentum of earlier days, there is a dispiriting climate of confusion, division, cynicism, and above all, exhaustion. After years of much struggle and little recognition, many older women feel burned out; after years of taking its light for granted, many younger women show little interest in touching new fire to the torch.

During the past decade, women breached the power structure; meanwhile, eating disorders rose exponentially and cosmetic surgery became the fastest-growing medical specialty. During the past five years, consumer spending doubled, pornography became the main media category, ahead of legitimate films and records combined, and thirty-three thousand American women told researchers that they would rather lose ten to fifteen pounds than achieve any other goal. More women have more money and power and scope and legal recognition than we have ever had before; but in terms of how we feel about ourselves *physically*, we may actually be worse off than our unliberated grandmothers. Recent research consistently shows that inside the majority of the West's controlled, attractive, successful working women, there is a secret "underlife" poisoning our freedom; infused with notions of beauty, it is a dark vein of self-hatred, physical obsessions, terror of aging, and dread of lost control.

It is no accident that so many potentially powerful women feel this way. We are in the midst of a violent backlash against feminism that uses images of female beauty as a political weapon against women's advancement: the beauty myth. It is the modern version of a social reflex that has been in force since the Industrial Revolution. As women released themselves from the feminine mystique of domesticity, the beauty myth took over its lost ground, expanding as it waned to carry on its work of social control.

The contemporary backlash is so violent because the ideology of beauty is the last one remaining of the old feminine ideologies that still has the power to control those women whom second wave feminism would have otherwise made relatively uncontrollable: It has grown stronger to take over the work of social coercion that myths about motherhood, domesticity, chastity, and passivity, no longer can manage. It is seeking right now to undo psychologically and covertly all the good things that feminism did for women materially and overtly.

This counterforce is operating to checkmate the inheritance of feminism on every level in the lives of Western women. Feminism gave us laws against job discrimination based on gender; immediately case law evolved in Britain and the United States that institutionalized job discrimination based on women's appearances. Patriarchal religion declined; new religious dogma, using some of the mind-altering techniques of older cults and sects, arose around age and weight to functionally supplant traditional ritual. Feminists, inspired by Friedan, broke the stranglehold on the women's popular press of advertisers for household products, who were promoting the feminine mystique; at once, the diet and skin care industries became the new cultural censors of women's intellectual space, and because of their pressure, the gaunt, youthful model supplanted the happy housewife as the arbiter of successful womanhood. The sexual revolution promoted the discovery of female sexuality; "beauty pornography"—which for the first time in women's history artificially links a commodified "beauty" directly and explicitly to sexuality—invaded the mainstream to undermine women's new and vulnerable sense of sexual self-worth. Reproductive rights gave Western women control over our own bodies; the weight of fashion models plummeted to 23 percent below that of ordinary women, eating disorders rose exponentially, and a mass neurosis was promoted that used food and weight to strip women of that sense of control. Women insisted on politicizing health; new technologies of invasive, potentially deadly "cosmetic" surgeries developed apace to re-exert old forms of medical control of women.

Every generation since about 1830 has had to fight its version of the beauty myth. "It is very little to me," said the suffragist Lucy Stone in 1855, "to have the right to vote, to own property, etcetera, if I may not keep my body, and its uses, in my absolute right." Eighty years later, after women had won the vote, and the first wave of the organized women's movement had subsided, Virginia Woolf wrote that it would still be decades before women could tell the truth about their bodies. In 1962, Betty Friedan quoted a young woman trapped in the Feminine Mystique: "Lately, I look in the mirror, and I'm so afraid I'm going to look like my mother." Eight years after that, heralding the cataclysmic second wave of feminism, Germaine Greer described "the

Stereotype": "To her belongs all that is beautiful, even the very word beauty itself . . . she is a doll . . . I'm sick of the masquerade." In spite of the great revolution of the second wave, we are not exempt. Now we can look out over ruined barricades: A revolution has come upon us and changed everything in its path, enough time has passed since then for babies to have grown into women, but there still remains a final right not fully claimed.

The beauty myth tells a story: The quality called "beauty" objectively and universally exists. Women must want to embody it and men must want to possess women who embody it. This embodiment is an imperative for women and not for men, which situation is necessary and natural because it is biological, sexual, and evolutionary: Strong men battle for beautiful women, and beautiful women are more reproductively successful. Women's beauty must correlate to their fertility, and since this system is based on sexual selection, it is inevitable and changeless.

None of this is true. "Beauty" is a currency system like the gold standard. Like any economy, it is determined by politics, and in the modern age in the West it is the last, best belief system that keeps male dominance intact. In assigning value to women in a vertical hierarchy according to a culturally imposed physical standard, it is an expression of power relations in which women must unnaturally compete for resources that men have appropriated for themselves.

"Beauty" is not universal or changeless, though the West pretends that all ideals of female beauty stem from one Platonic Ideal Woman; the Maori admire a fat vulva, and the Padung, droopy breasts. Nor is "beauty" a function of evolution: Its ideals change at a pace far more rapid than that of the evolution of species, and Charles Darwin was himself unconvinced by his own explanation that "beauty" resulted from a "sexual selection" that deviated from the rule of natural selection; for women to compete with women through "beauty" is a reversal of the way in which natural selection affects all other mammals. Anthropology has overturned the notion that females must be "beautiful" to be selected to mate: Evelyn Reed, Elaine Morgan, and others have dismissed sociobiological assertions of innate male polygamy and female monogamy. Female higher primates are the sexual initiators; not only do they seek out and enjoy sex with many partners, but "every nonpregnant female takes her turn at being the most desirable of all her troop. And that cycle keeps turning as long as she lives." The inflamed pink sexual organs of primates are often cited by male sociobiologists as analogous to human arrangements relating to female "beauty," when in fact that is a universal, nonhierarchical female primate characteristic.

Nor has the beauty myth always been this way. Though the pairing of the older rich men with young, "beautiful" women is taken to be somehow inevitable, in the matriarchal Goddess religions that dominated the Mediterranean from about 25,000 B.C.E. to about 700 B.C.E., the situation was reversed: "In every culture, the Goddess has many lovers. . . . The clear pattern is of an older woman with a beautiful but expendable youth—Ishtar and Tammuz, Venus and Adonis, Cybele and Attis, Isis and Osiris . . . their only function the service of the divine 'womb.' " Nor is it something only women do and only men watch: Among the Nigerian Wodaabes, the women hold economic power and the tribe is obsessed with male beauty; Wodaabe men spend hours together in elaborate makeup sessions, and compete—provocatively painted and dressed, with swaying hips and seductive expressions—in beauty contests judged by women. There is no legitimate historical or biological justification for the beauty myth; what it is doing to women today is a result of nothing more exalted than the need of today's power structure, economy, and culture to mount a counteroffensive against women.

If the beauty myth is not based on evolution, sex, gender, aesthetics, or God, on what is it based? It claims to be about intimacy and sex and life, a celebration of women. It is actually composed of emotional distance, politics, finance, and sexual repression. The beauty myth is not about women at all. It is about men's institutions and institutional power.

The qualities that a given period calls beautiful in women are merely symbols of the female behavior that that period considers desirable: *The beauty myth is always actually prescribing behavior and not appearance.* Competition between women has been made part of the myth so that women will be divided from one another. Youth and (until recently) virginity have been "beautiful" in women since they stand for experiential and sexual ignorance. Aging in women is "unbeautiful" since women grow more powerful with time, and since the links between generations of women must always be newly broken: Older women fear young ones, young women fear old, and the beauty myth truncates for all the female life span. Most urgently, women's identity must be premised upon our "beauty" so that we will remain vulnerable to outside approval, carrying the vital sensitive organ of self-esteem exposed to the air.

Though there has, of course, been a beauty myth in some form for as long as there has been patriarchy, the beauty myth in its modern form is a fairly recent invention. The myth flourishes when material constraints on women are dangerously loosened. Before the Industrial Revolution, the average woman could not have had the same feelings about "beauty" that modern women do who experience the myth as continual comparison to a mass-disseminated physical ideal. Before the development of technologies of mass production—daguerrotypes, photographs, etc.—an ordinary woman was exposed to few such images outside the Church. Since the family was a productive unit and women's work complemented men's, the value of women who were not aristocrats or prostitutes lay in their work skills, economic shrewdness, physical strength, and fertility. Physical attraction, obviously, played its part; but "beauty" as we understand it was not, for ordinary women, a serious issue in the marriage marketplace. The beauty myth in its modern form gained ground after the upheavals of industrialization, as the work unit of the family was destroyed, and urbanization and the emerging factory system demanded what social engineers of the time termed the "separate sphere" of domesticity, which supported the new labor category of the "breadwinner" who left home for the workplace during the day. The middle class expanded, the standards of living and of literacy rose, the size of families shrank; a new class of literate, idle women developed, on whose submission to enforced domesticity the evolving system of industrial capitalism depended. Most of our assumptions about the way women have always thought about "beauty" date from no earlier than the 1830s, when the cult of domesticity was first consolidated and the beauty index invented.

For the first time new technologies could reproduce—in fashion plates, daguerreotypes, tintypes, and rotogravures—images of how women should look. In the 1840s the first nude photographs of prostitutes were taken; advertisements using images of "beautiful" women first appeared in mid-century. Copies of classical artworks, postcards of society beauties and royal mistresses, Currier and Ives prints, and porcelain figurines flooded the separate sphere to which middle-class women were confined.

Since the Industrial Revolution, middle-class Western women have been controlled by ideals and stereotypes as much as by material constraints. This situation, unique to this group, means that analyses that trace "cultural conspiracies" are uniquely plausible in relation to them. The rise of the beauty myth was just one of several emerging social fictions that masqueraded as natural components of the feminine sphere, the better to enclose those women inside it. Other such fictions arose contemporaneously: a version of childhood that required continual maternal supervision; a concept of female biology that required middle-class women to act out the roles of hysterics and hypochondriacs; a conviction that respectable women were sexually anesthetic; and a definition of women's work that occupied them with repetitive, time-consuming, and painstaking tasks such as needlepoint and lacemaking. All such Victorian inventions as these served a double function—that is, though they were encouraged as a means to expend female energy and intelligence in harmless ways, women often used them to express genuine creativity and passion.

But in spite of middle-class women's creativity with fashion and embroidery and child rearing, and, a century later, with the role of the suburban housewife that devolved from these social fictions, the fictions' main purpose was served: During a century and a half of unprecedented feminist agitation, they effectively counteracted middle-class women's dangerous new leisure, literacy, and relative freedom from material constraints.

Though these time- and mind-consuming fictions about women's natural role adapted themselves to resurface in the post-war Feminine Mystique, when the second wave of the women's movement took apart what women's magazines had portrayed as the "romance," "science," and "adventure" of homemaking and suburban family life, they temporarily failed. The cloying domestic fiction of "togetherness" lost its meaning and middle-class women walked out of their front doors in masses.

So the fictions simply transformed themselves once more: Since the women's movement had successfully taken apart most other necessary fictions of femininity, all the work of social control once spread out over the whole network of these fictions had to be reassigned to the only strand left intact, which action consequently strengthened it a hundredfold. This reimposed onto liberated women's faces and bodies all the limitations, taboos, and punishments of the repressive laws, religious injunctions and reproductive enslavement that no longer carried sufficient force. Inexhaustible but ephemeral beauty work took over from inexhaustible but ephemeral housework. As the economy, law, religion, sexual mores, education, and culture were forcibly opened up to include women more fairly, a private reality colonized female consciousness. By using ideas about "beauty," it reconstructed an alternative female world with its own laws, economy, religion, sexuality, education, and culture, each element as repressive as any that had gone before.

Since middle-class Western women can best be weakened psychologically now that we are stronger materially, the beauty myth, as it has resurfaced in the last generation, has had to draw on more technological sophistication and reactionary fervor than ever before. The modern arsenal of the myth is a dissemination of millions of images of the current ideal; although this barrage is generally seen as a collective sexual fantasy, there is in fact little that is sexual about it. It is summoned out of political fear on the part of male-dominated institutions threatened by women's freedom, and it exploits female guilt and apprehension about our own liberation—latent fears that we might be going too far. This frantic aggregation of imagery is a collective reactionary hallucination willed into being by both men and women stunned and disoriented by the rapidity with which gender relations have been transformed: a bulwark of reassurance against the flood of change. The mass depiction of the modern woman as a "beauty" is a contradiction: Where modern women are growing, moving, and expressing their individuality, as the myth has it, "beauty" is by definition inert, timeless, and generic. That this hallucination is necessary and deliberate is evident in the way "beauty" so directly contradicts women's real situation.

And the unconscious hallucination grows ever more influential and pervasive because of what is now conscious market manipulation: powerful industries—the $33-billion-a-year diet industry, the $20-billion cosmetics industry, the $300-million cosmetic surgery industry, and the $7-billion pornography industry—have arisen from the capital made out of unconscious anxieties, and are in turn able, through their influence on mass culture, to use, stimulate, and reinforce the hallucination in a rising economic spiral.

This is not a conspiracy theory; it doesn't have to be. Societies tell themselves necessary fictions in the same way that individuals and families do. Henrik Ibsen called them "vital lies," and psychologist Daniel Goleman describes them working the same way on the social level that they do within families: "The collusion is maintained by directing attention away from the fearsome fact, or by repackaging its meaning in an acceptable format." The costs of these social blind spots, he writes, are destructive communal illusions. Possibilities for women have become so open-ended that they threaten to destabilize the institutions on which a male-dominated culture has depended, and a collective panic reaction on the part of both sexes has forced a demand for counterimages.

The resulting hallucination materializes, for women, as something all too real. No longer just an idea, it becomes three-dimensional, incorporating within itself how women live and how they do not live: It becomes the Iron Maiden. The original Iron Maiden was a medieval German instrument of torture, a body-shaped casket painted with the limbs and features of a lovely, smiling young woman. The unlucky victim was slowly enclosed inside her; the lid fell shut to immobilize the victim, who died either of starvation or, less cruelly, of the metal spikes embedded in her interior. The modern hallucination in which women are trapped or trap themselves is similarly rigid, cruel, and euphemistically painted. Contemporary culture directs attention to imagery of the Iron Maiden, while censoring real women's faces and bodies.

Why does the social order feel the need to defend itself by evading the fact of real women, our faces and voices and bodies, and reducing the meaning of women to these formulaic and endlessly reproduced "beautiful" images? Though unconscious personal anxieties can be a powerful force in the creation of a vital lie, economic necessity practically guarantees it. An economy that depends on slavery needs to promote images of slaves that "justify" the institution of slavery. Western economies are absolutely dependent now on the continued underpayment of women. An ideology that makes women feel "worth less" was urgently needed to counteract the way feminism had begun to make us feel worth more. This does not require a conspiracy; merely an atmosphere. The contemporary economy depends right now on the representation of women within the beauty myth. Economist John Kenneth Galbraith offers an economic explanation for "the persistence of the view of homemaking as a 'higher calling' ": the concept of women as naturally trapped within the Feminine Mystique, he feels, "has been forced on us by popular sociology, by magazines, and by fiction to disguise the fact that woman in her role of consumer has been essential to the development of our industrial society. . . . Behavior that is essential for economic reasons is transformed into a social virtue." As soon as a woman's primary social value could no longer be defined as the attainment of virtuous domesticity, the beauty myth redefined it as the attainment of virtuous beauty. It did so to substitute both a new consumer imperative and a new justification for economic unfairness in the workplace where the old ones had lost their hold over newly liberated women.

Another hallucination arose to accompany that of the Iron Maiden: The caricature of the Ugly Feminist was resurrected to dog the steps of the women's movement. The caricature is unoriginal; it was coined to ridicule the feminists of the nineteenth century. Lucy Stone herself, whom supporters saw as "a prototype of womanly grace . . . fresh and fair as the morning," was derided by detractors with "the usual report" about Victorian feminists: "a big masculine woman, wearing boots, smoking a cigar, swearing like a trooper." As Betty Friedan put it presciently in 1960, even before the savage revamping of that old caricature: "The unpleasant image of feminists today resembles less the feminists themselves than the image fostered by the interests who so bitterly opposed the vote for women in state after state." Thirty years on, her conclusion is more true than ever: That resurrected caricature, which sought to punish women for their public acts by going after their private sense of self, became the paradigm for new limits placed on aspiring women everywhere. After the success of the women's movement's second wave, the beauty myth was perfected to checkmate power at every level in individual women's lives. The modern neuroses of life in the female body spread to woman after woman at epidemic rates. The myth is undermining—slowly, imperceptibly, without our being aware of the real forces of erosion—the ground women have gained through long, hard, honorable struggle.

The beauty myth of the present is more insidious than any mystique of femininity yet: A century ago, Nora slammed the door of the doll's house; a generation ago, women turned their backs on the consumer heaven of the isolated multiapplianced home; but where women are trapped today, there is no door to slam. The contemporary ravages of the beauty backlash are destroying women physically and depleting us psychologically. If we are to free ourselves from the dead weight that has once again been made out of femaleness, it is not ballots or lobbyists or placards that women will need first; it is a new way to see.

—*1991*

Questions: Reading, Responding, Arguing

1. What is the thesis of Wolf's argument? Why does she want to expose the "myth" of beauty?
2. Explain some of the "hallucinations" Wolf describes in her argument.
3. Wolf argues that "the beauty myth is actually prescribing behavior and not appearance." How does this connect to the rest of her arguments?
4. The essay uses the idea of feminist revolution to ground its main points. What revolutions have occurred for women, and what further revolutions does the essay suggest are possible?
5. How does Wolf use the topic of *authority* to support her argument?

How We Care

Sex, Love, and Hate

> "Love is like a vending machine, eh? Not bad. You insert a coin and press home the lever. There's some mechanical activity inside the bowels of the device. You receive a small sweet, frown at yourself in the dirty mirror, adjust your hat, take a firm grip on your umbrella and walk away, trying to look as though nothing had happened."
>
> —Nathanael West, *The Dream Life of Balso Snell*

We humans are a complicated and contradictory bunch. It is rare that we are singular in our emotional relationships with others. Take the family, for example. While we may love our parents, "Love" does not comprise all aspects of our relationships with them; there is also the frustration and anger we feel when they make us mow the lawn, don't let us borrow the car, or spend all the money that we wanted them to save and give us for our inheritance. Once we grow up and begin to have relationships with others outside of the family, the complications only intensify. The selections that follow all have some connection to three registers of human passions: sex, love, and hate.

Those who think sex is unimportant or overemphasized in the arts can content themselves with all of the great works of painting, music, writing, and sculpture that have been created by eunuchs in this world—but after that empty, silent museum has been thoroughly explored, those people can join the rest of us in reading an endless collection of texts that integrates at least some element of sexual desire, whether insinuated or obvious. It is our job to discover, analyze, or imagine the relationship between sexual desire and love in our reading of these texts. Because *sex* has become such a catch-all phrase for human interaction, it may be difficult to use it either as a term for argument or as a word with any specific meaning whatsoever. However, the beauty of literature lies in the fact that it allows us to clarify and classify exactly what love is, who bears it, and what its objects are. Finally, hate, which may or may not be the necessary shadow side of love, is similarly difficult to define with any precision. Yet the effects of aggression, anger, and despair, all of which contribute to the emotional pit that is hatred, are as pervasive in literature as any other emotion, and a lack of care in studying hate will only make it easier for us to fall prey to its subtle and empowering call.

> "The fickleness of the women I love is only equaled by the infernal constancy of the women who love me."
> —George Bernard Shaw, *The Philanderer*

James Joyce (1882–1941)

Araby*

North Richmond Street, being blind, was a quiet street except at the hour when the Christian Brothers' School set the boys free. An uninhabited house of two stories stood at the blind end, detached from its neighbors in a square ground. The other houses of the street, conscious of decent lives within them, gazed at one another with brown imperturbable faces.

The former tenant of our house, a priest, had died in the back drawing-room. Air, musty from having long been enclosed, hung in all the rooms, and the waste room behind the kitchen was littered with old useless papers. Among these I found a few papercovered books, the pages of which were curled and damp: The Abbot, by Walter Scott, The Devout Communicant and The Memoirs of Vidocq. I liked the last best because its leaves were yellow. The wild garden behind the house contained a central apple-tree and a few straggling bushes under one of which I found the late tenant's rusty bicycle-pump. He had been a very charitable priest; in his will he had left all his money to institutions and the furniture of his house to his sister.

When the short days of winter came dusk fell before we had well eaten our dinners. When we met in the street the houses had grown sombre. The space of sky above us was the colour of everchanging violet and towards it the lamps of the street lifted their feeble lanterns. The cold air stung us and we played till our bodies glowed. Our shouts echoed in the silent street. The career of our play brought us through the dark muddy lanes behind the houses where we ran the gauntlet of the rough tribes from the cottages, to the back doors of the dark dripping gardens where odours arose from the ashpits, to the dark odorous stables where a coachman smoothed and combed the horse or shook music from the buckled harness. When we returned to the street light from the kitchen windows had filled the areas. If my uncle was seen turning the corner we hid in the shadow until we had seen him safely housed. Or if Mangan's sister came out on the doorstep to call her brother in to his tea we watched her from our shadow peer up and down the street. We waited to see whether she would remain or go in and, if she remained, we left our shadow and walked up to Mangan's steps resignedly. She was waiting for us, her figure defined by the light from the half-opened door. Her brother always teased her before he obeyed and I stood by the railings looking at her. Her dress swung as she moved her body and the soft rope of her hair tossed from side to side.

Every morning I lay on the floor in the front parlour watching her door. The blind was pulled down to within an inch of the sash so that I could not be seen. When she came out on the doorstep my heart leaped. I ran to the hall, seized my books and followed her. I kept her brown figure always in my eye and, when we came near the point at which our ways diverged, I quickened my pace and passed her. This happened morning after morning. I had never spoken to her, except for a few casual words, and yet her name was like a summons to all my foolish blood.

Her image accompanied me even in places the most hostile to romance. On Saturday evenings when my aunt went marketing I had to go to carry some of the parcels. We walked through the flaring streets, jostled by drunken men and bargaining women, amid the curses of labourers, the shrill litanies of shop-boys who stood on guard by the barrels of pigs' cheeks, the nasal chanting of street-singers, who sang a come-all-you about O'Donovan Rossa, or a ballad about the troubles in our native land. These noises converged in a single sensation of life for me: I imagined that I bore my chalice safely through a throng of foes. Her name sprang to my lips at moments in strange prayers and praises which I myself did not understand. My eyes were often full of tears (I could not tell why) and at times a flood from my heart seemed to pour itself out into my bosom. I thought little of the future. I did not know whether I would ever speak to her or not or, if I spoke to her, how I could tell her of my confused adoration. But my body was like a harp and her words and gestures were like fingers running upon the wires.

One evening I went into the back drawing-room in which the priest had died. It was a dark rainy evening and there was no sound in the house. Through one of the broken panes I heard the rain impinge upon the earth, the fine incessant needles of water playing in the sodden beds. Some distant lamp or lighted window gleamed below me. I was thankful that I could see so little. All my senses seemed to desire to veil themselves and, feeling that I was about to slip from them, I pressed the palms of my hands together until they trembled, murmuring: O love! O love! many times.

At last she spoke to me. When she addressed the first words to me I was so confused that I did not know what to answer. She asked me was I going to Araby.

I forget whether I answered yes or no. It would be a splendid bazaar, she said; she would love to go.

—And why can't you? I asked.

While she spoke she turned a silver bracelet round and round her wrist. She could not go, she said, because there would be a retreat that week in her convent. Her brother and two other boys were fighting for their caps and I was alone at the railings. She held one of the spikes, bowing her head towards me. The light from the lamp opposite our door caught the white curve of her neck, lit up her hair that rested there and, falling, lit up the hand upon the railing. It fell over one side of her dress and caught the white border of a petticoat, just visible as she stood at ease.

—It's well for you, she said.

—If I go, I said, I will bring you something.

What innumerable follies laid waste my waking and sleeping thoughts after that evening! I wished to annihilate the tedious intervening days. I chafed against the work of school. At night in my bedroom and by day in the classroom her image came between me and the page I strove to read. The syllables of the word Araby were called to me through the silence in which my soul luxuriated and cast an Eastern enchantment over me. I asked for leave to go to the bazaar on Saturday night. My aunt was surprised and hoped it was not some Freemason affair. I answered few questions in class, I watched my master's face pass from amiability to sternness; he hoped I was not beginning to idle. I could not call my wandering thoughts together. I had hardly any patience with the serious work of life which, now that it stood between me and my desire, seemed to me child's play, ugly monotonous child's play.

On Saturday morning I reminded my uncle that I wished to go to the bazaar in the evening. He was fussing at the hallstand, looking for the hat-brush, and answered me curtly:

—Yes, boy, I know.

As he was in the hall I could not go into the front parlour and lie at the window. I left the house in bad humour and walked slowly towards the school. The air was pitilessly raw and already my heart misgave me.

When I came home to dinner my uncle had not yet been home. Still it was early. I sat staring at the clock for some time and, when its ticking began to irritate me, I left the room. I mounted the staircase and gained the upper part of the house. The high cold empty gloomy rooms liberated me and I went from room to room singing. From the front window I saw my companions playing below in the street. Their cries reached me weakened and indistinct and, leaning my forehead against the cool glass, I looked over at the dark house where she lived. I may have stood there for an hour, seeing nothing but the brown-clad figure cast by my imagination, touched discreetly by the lamplight at the curved neck, at the hand upon the railings and at the border below the dress.

When I came downstairs again I found Mrs Mercer sitting at the fire. She was an old garrulous woman, a pawnbroker's widow, who collected used stamps for some pious purpose. I had to endure the gossip of the tea-table. The meal was prolonged beyond an hour and still my uncle did not come. Mrs Mercer stood up to go: she was sorry she couldn't wait any longer, but it was after eight o'clock and she did not like to be out late, as the night air was bad for her. When she had gone I began to walk up and down the room, clenching my fists. My aunt said:

—I'm afraid you may put off your bazaar for this night of Our Lord.

At nine o'clock I heard my uncle's latchkey in the halldoor. I heard him talking to himself and heard the hallstand rocking when it had received the weight of his overcoat. I could interpret these signs. When he was midway through his dinner I asked him to give me the money to go to the bazaar. He had forgotten.

—The people are in bed and after their first sleep now, he said.

I did not smile. My aunt said to him energetically:

—Can't you give him the money and let him go? You've kept him late enough as it is.

My uncle said he was very sorry he had forgotten. He said he believed in the old saying: All work and no play makes Jack a dull boy. He asked me where I was going and, when I had told him a second time he asked me did I know The Arab's Farewell to His Steed. When I left the kitchen he was about to recite the opening lines of the piece to my aunt.

I held a florin tightly in my hand as I strode down Buckingham Street towards the station. The sight of the streets thronged with buyers and glaring with gas recalled to me the purpose of my journey. I took my seat in a third-class carriage of a deserted train. After an intolerable delay the train moved out of the station slowly. It crept onward among ruinous houses and over the twinkling river. At Westland Row Station a crowd of people pressed to the carriage doors; but the porters moved them back, saying that it was a special train for the bazaar. I remained alone in the bare carriage. In a few minutes the train drew up beside an improvised wooden platform. I passed out on to the road and saw by the lighted dial of a clock that it was ten minutes to ten. In front of me was a large building which displayed the magical name.

I could not find any sixpenny entrance and, fearing that the bazaar would be closed, I passed in quickly through a turnstile, handing a shilling to a wearylooking man. I found myself in a big hall girdled at half its height by a gallery. Nearly all the stalls were closed and the greater part of the hall was in darkness. I recognised a silence like that which pervades a church after a service. I walked into the center of the bazaar timidly. A few people were gathered about the stalls which were still open. Before a curtain, over which the words Café Chantant were written in coloured lamps, two men were counting money on a salver. I listened to the fall of the coins.

Remembering with difficulty why I had come I went over to one of the stalls and examined porcelain vases and flowered tea-sets. At the door of the stall a young lady was talking and laughing with two young gentlemen. I remarked their English accents and listened vaguely to their conversation.

—O, I never said such a thing!

—O, but you did!

—O, but I didn't!

—Didn't she say that?

—Yes! I heard her.

—O, there's a . . . fib!

Observing me the young lady came over and asked me did I wish to buy anything. The tone of her voice was not encouraging; she seemed to have spoken to me out of a sense of duty. I looked humbly at the great jars that stood like eastern guards at either side of the dark entrance to the stall and murmured:

—No, thank you.

The young lady changed the position of one of the vases and went back to the two young men. They began to talk of the same subject. Once or twice the young lady glanced at me over her shoulder.

I lingered before her stall, though I knew my stay was useless, to make my interest in her wares seem the more real. Then I turned away slowly and walked down the middle of the bazaar. I allowed the two pennies to fall against the sixpence in my pocket. I heard a voice call from one end of the gallery that the light was out. The upper part of the hall was now completely dark.

Gazing up into the darkness I saw myself as a creature driven and derided by vanity; and my eyes burned with anguish and anger.

—*1905*

Questions: Reading, Responding, Arguing

1. In what sense is this an initiation story? What is the protagonist initiated into?
2. What does Mangan's sister represent for the protagonist? How does he act in her presence?
3. "Araby," the name of the bazaar, has romantic connotations. How do the protagonist's imaginings of it match its reality?
4. What is the epiphany at the end of the story?

Zora Neale Hurston (1891–1960)

Sweat*

I

It was eleven o'clock of a Spring night in Florida. It was Sunday. Any other night, Delia Jones would have been in bed for two hours by this time. But she was a washwoman, and Monday morning meant a great deal to her. So she collected the soiled clothes on Saturday when she returned the clean things. Sunday night after church, she sorted and put the white things to soak. It saved her almost a half-day's start. A great hamper in the bedroom held the clothes that she brought home. It was so much neater than a number of bundles lying around.

She squatted on the kitchen floor beside the great pile of clothes, sorting them into small heaps according to color, and humming a song in a mournful key, but wondering through it all where Sykes, her husband, had gone with her horse and buckboard.[1]

Just then something long, round, limp, and black fell upon her shoulders and slithered to the floor beside her. A great terror took hold of her. It softened her knees and dried her mouth so that it was a full minute before she could cry out or move. Then she saw that it was the big bull whip her husband liked to carry when he drove.

She lifted her eyes to the door and saw him standing there bent over with laughter at her fright. She screamed at him.

"Sykes, what you throw dat whip on me like dat? You know it would skeer me—looks just like a snake, an' you knows how skeered Ah is of snakes."

---
[1]*buckboard*: open wagon with a seat.

"Course Ah knowed it! That's how come Ah done it." He slapped his leg with his hand and almost rolled on the ground in his mirth. "If you such a big fool dat you got to have a fit over a earth worm or a string, Ah don't keer how bad Ah skeer you."

"You ain't got no business doing it. Gawd knows it's a sin. Some day Ah'm gointuh drop dead from some of yo' foolishness. 'Nother thing, where you been wid mah rig? Ah feeds dat pony. He ain't fuh you to be drivin' wid no bull whip."

"You sho' is one aggravatin' nigger woman!" he declared and stepped into the room. She resumed her work and did not answer him at once. "Ah done tole you time and again to keep them white folks' clothes outa dis house."

He picked up the whip and glared at her. Delia went on with her work. She went out into the yard and returned with a galvanized tub and set it on the washbench. She saw that Sykes had kicked all of the clothes together again, and now stood in her way truculently, his whole manner hoping, *praying,* for an argument. But she walked calmly around him and commenced to re-sort the things.

"Next time, Ah'm gointer kick 'em outdoors," he threatened as he struck a match along the leg of his corduroy breeches.

Delia never looked up from her work, and her thin, stooped shoulders sagged further.

"Ah ain't for no fuss t'night Sykes. Ah just come from taking sacrament at the church house."

He snorted scornfully. "Yeah, you just come from de church house on a Sunday night, but heah you is gone to work on them clothes. You ain't nothing but a hypocrite. One of them amen-corner Christians—sing, whoop, and shout, then come home and wash white folks' clothes on the Sabbath."

He stepped roughly upon the whitest pile of things, kicking them helter-skelter as he crossed the room. His wife gave a little scream of dismay, and quickly gathered them together again.

"Sykes, you quit grindin' dirt into these clothes! How can Ah git through by Sat'day if Ah don't start on Sunday?"

"Ah don't keer if you never git through. Anyhow, Ah done promised Gawd and a couple of other men, Ah ain't gointer have it in mah house. Don't gimme no lip neither, else Ah'll throw 'em out and put mah fist up side yo' head to boot."

Delia's habitual meekness seemed to slip from her shoulders like a blown scarf. She was on her feet; her poor little body, her bare knuckly hands bravely defying the strapping hulk before her.

"Looka heah, Sykes, you done gone too fur. Ah been married to you fur fifteen years, and Ah been takin' in washin' fur fifteen years. Sweat, sweat, sweat! Work and sweat, cry and sweat, pray and sweat!"

"What's that got to do with me?" he asked brutally.

"What's it got to do with you, Sykes? Mah tub of suds is filled yo' belly with vittles more times than yo' hands is filled it. Mah sweat is done paid for this house and Ah reckon Ah kin keep on sweatin' in it."

She seized the iron skillet from the stove and struck a defensive pose, which act surprised him greatly, coming from her. It cowed him and he did not strike her as he usually did.

"Naw you won't," she panted, "that ole snaggle-toothed black woman you runnin' with ain't comin' heah to pile up on *mah* sweat and blood. You ain't paid for nothin' on this place, and Ah'm gointer stay right heah till Ah'm toted out foot foremost."

"Well, you better quit gittin' me riled up, else they'll be totin' you out sooner than you expect. Ah'm so tired of you Ah don't know whut to do. Gawd! How Ah hates skinny wimmen!"

A little awed by this new Delia, he sidled out of the door and slammed the back gate after him. He did not say where he had gone, but she knew too well. She knew very well that he would not return until nearly daybreak also. Her work over, she went on to bed but not to sleep at once. Things had come to a pretty pass!

She lay awake, gazing upon the debris that cluttered their matrimonial trail. Not an image left standing along the way. Anything like flowers had long ago been drowned in the salty stream that had been pressed from her heart. Her tears, her sweat, her blood. She had brought love to the union and he had brought a longing after the flesh. Two months after the wedding, he had given her the first brutal beating. She had the memory of his numerous trips to Orlando with all of his wages when he had returned to her penniless, even before the first year had passed. She was young and soft then, but now she thought of her knotty, muscled limbs, her harsh knuckly hands, and drew herself up into an unhappy little ball in the middle of the big feather bed. Too late now to hope for love, even if it were not Bertha it would be someone else. This case differed from the others only in that she was bolder than the others. Too late for everything except her little home. She had built it for her old days, and planted one by one the trees and flowers there. It was lovely to her, lovely.

Somehow, before sleep came, she found herself saying aloud: "Oh well, whatever goes over the Devil's back, is got to come under his belly. Sometime or ruther, Sykes, like everybody else, is gointer reap his sowing." After that she was able to build a spiritual earthworks against her husband. His shells could no longer reach her. AMEN. She went to sleep and slept until he announced his presence in bed by kicking her feet and rudely snatching the covers away.

"Gimme some kivah heah, an' git yo' damn foots over on yo' own side! Ah oughter mash you in yo' mouf fuh drawing dat skillet on me."

Delia went clear to the rail without answering him. A triumphant indifference to all that he was or did.

II

The week was full of work for Delia as all other weeks, and Saturday found her behind her little pony, collecting and delivering clothes.

It was a hot, hot day near the end of July. The village men on Joe Clarke's porch even chewed cane listlessly. They did not hurl the cane-knots as usual. They let them dribble over the edge of the porch. Even conversation had collapsed under the heat.

"Heah come Delia Jones," Jim Merchant said, as the shaggy pony came 'round the bend of the road toward them. The rusty buckboard was heaped with baskets of crisp, clean laundry.

"Yep," Joe Lindsay agreed. "Hot or col', rain or shine, jes'ez reg'lar ez de weeks rool roun' Delia carries 'em an' fetches 'em on Sat'day."

"She better if she wanter eat," said Moss. "Syke Jones ain't wuth de shot an' powder hit would tek tuh kill 'em. Not to *huh* he ain't."

"He sho' ain't," Walter Thomas chimed in. "It's too bad, too, cause she wuz a right pretty li'l trick when he got huh. Ah'd uh mah'ied huh mahself if he hadnter beat me to it."

Delia nodded briefly at the men as she drove past.

"Too much knockin' will ruin *any* 'oman. He done beat huh 'nough tuh kill three women, let 'lone change they looks," said Elijah Moseley. "How Syke kin stommuck dat big black greasy Mogul he's layin' roun' wid, gits me. Ah swear dat eight-rock couldn't kiss a sardine can Ah done thowed out de back do' 'way las' yeah."

"Aw, she's fat, thass how come. He's allus been crazy 'bout fat women," put in Merchant. "He'd a' been tied up wid one long time ago if he could a' found one tuh have him. Did Ah tell yuh 'bout him come sidlin' roun' *mah* wife—bringin' her a basket uh peecans outa his yard fuh a present? Yessir, mah wife! She tol' him tuh take 'em right straight back home, 'cause Delia works so hard ovah dat washtub she reckon everything on de place taste lak sweat an' soapsuds. Ah jus' wisht Ah'd a' caught 'im 'roun' dere! Ah'd a' made his hips ketch on fiah down dat shell road."

"Ah know he done it, too. Ah sees 'im grinnin' at every 'oman dat passes," Walter Thomas said. "But even so, he useter eat some mighty big hunks uh humble pie tuh git dat li'l 'oman he got. She wuz ez pritty ez a speckled pup! Dat wuz fifteen years ago. He useter be so skeered uh losin' huh, she could make him do some parts of a husband's duty. Dey never wuz de same in de mind."

"There oughter be a law about him," said Lindsay. "He ain't fit tuh carry guts tuh a bear."

Clarke spoke for the first time. "Tain't no law on earth dat kin make a man be decent if it ain't in 'im. There's plenty men dat takes a wife lak dey do a joint uh sugar-cane. It's round, juicy, an' sweet when dey gits it. But dey squeeze an' grind, squeeze an' grind an' wring tell dey wring every drop uh pleasure dat's in 'em out. When dey's satisfied dat dey is wrung dry, dey treats 'em jes' lak dey do a cane-chew. Dey thows 'em away. Dey knows whut dey is doin' while dey is at it, an' hates theirselves fuh it but they keeps on hangin' after huh tell she's empty. Den dey hates huh fuh bein' a cane-chew an' in de way."

"We oughter take Syke an' dat stray 'oman uh his'n down in Lake Howell swamp an' lay on de rawhide till they cain't say Lawd a' mussy. He allus wuz uh ovahbearin niggah, but since dat white 'oman from up north done teached 'im how to run a automobile, he done got too beggety to live—an' we oughter kill 'im," Old Man Anderson advised.

A grunt of approval went around the porch. But the heat was melting their civic virtue and Elijah Moseley began to bait Joe Clarke.

"Come on, Joe, git a melon outa dere an' slice it up for yo' customers. We'se all sufferin' wid de heat. De bear's done got *me*!"

"Thass right, Joe, a watermelon is jes' whut Ah needs tuh cure de eppizudicks," Walter Thomas joined forces with Moseley. "Come on dere, Joe. We all is steady customers an' you ain't set us up in a long time. Ah chooses dat long, bowlegged Floridy favorite."

"A god, an' be dough. You all gimme twenty cents and slice away," Clarke retorted. "Ah needs a col' slice m'self. Heah, everybody chip in. Ah'll lend y'all mah meat knife."

The money was all quickly subscribed and the huge melon brought forth. At that moment, Sykes and Bertha arrived. A determined silence fell on the porch and the melon was put away again.

Merchant snapped down the blade of his jackknife and moved toward the store door.

"Come on in, Joe, an' gimme a slab uh sow belly an' uh pound uh coffee—almost fuhgot 'twas Sat'day. Got to git on home." Most of the men left also.

Just then Delia drove past on her way home, as Sykes was ordering magnificently for Bertha. It pleased him for Delia to see.

"Git whutsoever yo' heart desires, Honey. Wait a minute, Joe. Give huh two bottles uh strawberry soda-water, uh quart parched ground-peas, an' a block uh chewin' gum."

With all this they left the store, with Sykes reminding Bertha that this was his town and she could have it if she wanted it.

The men returned soon after they left, and held their watermelon feast.

"Where did Syke Jones git da 'oman from nohow?" Lindsay asked.

"Ovah Apopka. Guess dey musta been cleanin' out de town when she lef'. She don't look lak a thing but a hunk uh liver wid hair on it."

"Well, she sho' kin squall," Dave Carter contributed. "When she gits ready tuh laff, she jes' opens huh mouf an' latches it back tuh de las' notch. No ole granpa alligator down in Lake Bell ain't got nothin' on huh."

III

Bertha had been in town three months now. Sykes was still paying her room-rent at Della Lewis'—the only house in town that would have taken her in. Sykes took her frequently to Winter Park to "stomps." He still assured her that he was the swellest man in the state.

"Sho' you kin have dat li'l ole house soon's Ah git dat 'oman out-adere. Everything b'longs tuh me an' you sho' kin have it. Ah sho' 'bominates uh skinny 'oman. Lawdy, you sho' is got one portly shape on you! You kin git *anything* you wants. Dis is *mah* town an' you sho' kin have it."

Delia's work-worn knees crawled over the earth in Gethsemane[2] and up the rocks of Calvary[3] many, many times during these months. She avoided the villagers and meeting places in her efforts to be blind and deaf. But Bertha nullified this to a degree, by coming to Delia's house to call Sykes out to her at the gate.

Delia and Sykes fought all the time now with no peaceful interludes. They slept and ate in silence. Two or three times Delia had attempted a timid friendliness, but she was repulsed each time. It was plain that the breaches must remain agape.

The sun had burned July to August. The heat streamed down like a million hot arrows, smiting all things living upon the earth. Grass

---

[2]*Gethsemane:* the garden that was the scene of Jesus' arrest (see Matthew 26:36–57); hence, any scene of suffering.
[3]*Calvary:* hill outside Jerusalem where Jesus was crucified.

withered, leaves browned, snakes went blind in shedding, and men and dogs went mad. Dog days!

Delia came home one day and found Sykes there before her. She wondered, but started to go on into the house without speaking, even though he was standing in the kitchen door and she must either stoop under his arm or ask him to move. He made no room for her. She noticed a soap box beside the steps, but paid no particular attention to it, knowing that he must have brought it there. As she was stooping to pass under his outstretched arm, he suddenly pushed her backward, laughingly.

"Look in de box dere Delia, Ah done brung yuh somethin'!"

She nearly fell upon the box in her stumbling, and when she saw what it held, she all but fainted outright.

"Syke! Syke, mah Gawd! You take dat rattlesnake 'way from heah! You *gottuh*. Oh, Jesus, have mussy!"

"Ah ain't got tuh do nuthin' uh de kin'—fact is Ah ain't got tuh do nothin' but die. Tain't no use uh you puttin' on airs makin' out lak you skeered uh dat snake—he's gointer stay right heah tell he die. He wouldn't bite me cause Ah knows how tuh handle 'im. Nohow he wouldn't risk breakin' out his fangs 'gin *yo* skinny laigs."

"Naw, now Syke, don't keep dat thing 'round tryin' tuh skeer me tuh death. You knows Ah'm even feared uh earth worms. Thass de biggest snake Ah evah did see. Kill 'im Syke, please."

"Doan ast me tuh do nothin' fuh yuh. Goin' 'round tryin' tuh be so damn asterperious.[4] Naw, Ah ain't gonna kill it. Ah think uh damn sight mo' uh him dan you! Dat's a nice snake an' anybody doan lak 'im kin jes' hit de grit."

The village soon heard that Sykes had the snake, and came to see and ask questions.

"How de hen-fire did you ketch dat six-foot rattler, Syke?" Thomas asked.

"He's full uh frogs so he cain't hardly move, thass how Ah eased up on 'm. But Ah'm a snake charmer an' knows how tuh handle 'em. Shux, dat ain't nothin'. Ah could ketch one eve'y day if Ah so wanted tuh."

"Whut he needs is a heavy hick'ry club leaned real heavy on his head. Dat's de bes' way tuh charm a rattlesnake."

"Naw, Walt, y'all jes' don't understand dese diamon' backs lak Ah do," said Sykes in a superior tone of voice.

The village agreed with Walter, but the snake stayed on. His box remained by the kitchen door with its screen wire covering. Two or three

---

[4]*asterperious*: haughty.

days later it had digested its meal of frogs and literally came to life. It rattled at every movement in the kitchen or the yard. One day as Delia came down the kitchen steps she saw his chalky-white fangs curved like scimitars hung in the wire meshes. This time she did not run away with averted eyes as usual. She stood for a long time in the doorway in a red fury that grew bloodier for every second that she regarded the creature that was her torment.

That night she broached the subject as soon as Sykes sat down to the table.

"Syke, Ah wants you tuh take dat snake 'way fum heah. You done starved me an' Ah put up widcher, you done beat me an' Ah took dat, but you done kilt all mah insides bringin' dat varmint heah."

Sykes poured out a saucer full of coffee and drank it deliberately before he answered her.

"A whole lot Ah keer 'bout how you feels inside uh out. Dat snake ain't goin' no damn wheah till Ah gits ready fuh 'im tuh go. So fur as beatin' is concerned, yuh ain't took near all dat you gointer take ef yuh stay 'round *me*."

Delia pushed back her plate and got up from the table. "Ah hates you, Sykes," she said calmly. "Ah hates you tuh de same degree dat Ah useter love yuh. Ah done took an' took till mah belly is full up tuh mah neck. Dat's de reason Ah got mah letter fum de church an' moved mah membership tuh Woodbridge—so Ah don't haftuh take no sacrament wid yuh. Ah don't wantuh see yuh 'round me at all. Lay 'round wid dat 'oman all yuh wants tuh, but gwan 'way fum me an' mah house. Ah hates yuh lak uh suck-egg dog."

Sykes almost let the huge wad of corn bread and collard greens he was chewing fall out of his mouth in amazement. He had a hard time whipping himself up to the proper fury to try to answer Delia.

"Well, Ah'm glad you does hate me. Ah'm sho' tiahed uh you hangin' ontuh me. Ah don't want yuh. Look at yuh stringey ole neck! Yo' rawbony laigs an' arms is enough tuh cut uh man tuh death. You looks jes' lak de devvul's doll-baby tuh *me*. You cain't hate me no worse dan Ah hates you. Ah been hatin' *you* fuh years."

"Yo' ole black hide don't look lak nothin' tuh me, but uh passle uh wrinkled up rubber, wid yo' big ole yeahs flappin' on each side lak uh paih uh buzzard wings. Don't think Ah'm gointuh be run 'way fum mah house neither. Ah'm goin' tuh de white folks 'bout *you*, mah young man, de very nex' time you lay yo' han's on me. Mah cup is done run ovah." Delia said this with no signs of fear and Sykes departed from the house, threatening her, but made not the slightest move to carry out any of them.

That night he did not return at all, and the next day being Sunday, Delia was glad she did not have to quarrel before she hitched up her pony and drove the four miles to Woodbridge.

She stayed to the night service—"love feast"—which was very warm and full of spirit. In the emotional winds her domestic trials were borne far and wide so that she sang as she drove homeward,

> *Jurden water,[5] black an' col*
> *Chills de body, not de soul*
> *An' Ah wantah cross Jurden in uh calm time.*

She came from the barn to the kitchen door and stopped.

"Whut's de mattah, ol' Satan, you ain't kickin' up yo' racket?" She addressed the snake's box. Complete silence. She went on into the house with a new hope in its birth struggles. Perhaps her threat to go to the white folks had frightened Sykes! Perhaps he was sorry! Fifteen years of misery and suppression had brought Delia to the place where she would hope *anything* that looked towards a way over or through her wall of inhibitions.

She felt in the match-safe behind the stove at once for a match. There was only one there.

"Dat niggah wouldn't fetch nothin' heah tuh save his rotten neck, but he kin run thew whut Ah brings quick enough. Now he done toted off nigh on tuh haff uh box uh matches. He done had dat 'oman heah in mah house, too."

Nobody but a woman could tell how she knew this even before she struck the match. But she did and it put her into a new fury.

Presently she brought in the tubs to put the white things to soak. This time she decided she need not bring the hamper out of the bedroom; she would go in there and do the sorting. She picked up the pot-bellied lamp and went in. The room was small and the hamper stood hard by the foot of the white iron bed. She could sit and reach through the bedposts—resting as she worked.

"*Ah wantah cross Jurden in uh calm time.*" She was singing again. The mood of the "love feast" had returned. She threw back the lid of the basket almost gaily. Then, moved by both horror and terror, she sprang back toward the door. *There lay the snake in the basket!* He moved sluggishly at first, but even as she turned round and round, jumped up and down in an insanity of fear, he began to stir vigorously. She saw him pouring his awful beauty from the basket upon the bed,

---

[5]*Jurden water:* the River Jordan.

then she seized the lamp and ran as fast as she could to the kitchen. The wind from the open door blew out the light and the darkness added to her terror. She sped to the darkness of the yard, slamming the door after her before she thought to set down the lamp. She did not feel safe even on the ground, so she climbed up in the hay barn.

There for an hour or more she lay sprawled upon the hay a gibbering wreck.

Finally she grew quiet, and after that came coherent thought. With this stalked through her a cold, bloody rage. Hours of this. A period of introspection, a space of retrospection, then a mixture of both. Out of this an awful calm.

"Well, Ah done de bes' Ah could. If things ain't right, Gawd knows tain't mah fault."

She went to sleep—a twitch sleep—and woke up to a faint gray sky. There was a loud hollow sound below. She peered out. Sykes was at the wood-pile, demolishing a wire-covered box.

He hurried to the kitchen door, but hung outside there some minutes before he entered, and stood some minutes more inside before he closed it after him.

The gray in the sky was spreading. Delia descended without fear now, and crouched beneath the low bedroom window. The drawn shade shut out the dawn, shut in the night. But the thin walls held back no sound.

"Dat ol' scratch[6] is woke up now!" She mused at the tremendous whirr inside, which every woodsman knows, is one of the sound illusions. The rattler is a ventriloquist. His whirr sounds to the right, to the left, straight ahead, behind, close under foot—everywhere but where it is. Woe to him who guesses wrong unless he is prepared to hold up his end of the argument! Sometimes he strikes without rattling at all.

Inside, Sykes heard nothing until he knocked a pot lid off the stove while trying to reach the match-safe in the dark. He had emptied his pockets at Bertha's.

The snake seemed to wake up under the stove and Sykes made a quick leap into the bedroom. In spite of the gin he had had, his head was clearing now.

"Mah Gawd!" he chattered, "ef Ah could on'y strack uh light!"

The rattling ceased for a moment as he stood paralyzed. He waited. It seemed that the snake waited also.

"Oh, fuh de light! Ah thought he'd be too sick"—Sykes was muttering to himself when the whirr began again, closer, right underfoot

---

[6]*scratch:* the devil.

this time. Long before this, Sykes' ability to think had been flattened down to primitive instinct and he leaped—onto the bed.

Outside Delia heard a cry that might have come from a maddened chimpanzee, a stricken gorilla. All the terror, all the horror, all the rage that man possibly could express, without a recognizable human sound.

A tremendous stir inside there, another series of animal screams, the intermittent whirr of the reptile. The shade torn violently down from the window, letting in the red dawn, a huge brown hand seizing the window stick, great dull blows upon the wooden floor punctuating the gibberish of sound long after the rattle of the snake had abruptly subsided. All this Delia could see and hear from her place beneath the window, and it made her ill. She crept over to the four o'clocks and stretched herself on the cool earth to recover.

She lay there. "Delia, Delia!" She could hear Sykes calling in a most despairing tone as one who expected no answer. The sun crept on up, and he called. Delia could not move—her legs had gone flabby. She never moved, he called, and the sun kept rising.

"Mah Gawd!" She heard him moan, "Mah Gawd fum Heben!" She heard him stumbling about and got up from her flower-bed. The sun was growing warm. As she approached the door she heard him call out hopefully, "Delia, is dat you Ah heah?"

She saw him on his hands and knees as soon as she reached the door. He crept an inch or two toward her—all that he was able, and she saw his horribly swollen neck and his one open eye shining with hope. A surge of pity too strong to support bore her away from that eye that must, could not, fail to see the tubs. He would see the lamp. Orlando with its doctors was too far. She could scarcely reach the chinaberry tree, where she waited in the growing heat while inside she knew the cold river was creeping up and up to extinguish that eye which must know by now that she knew.

—1926

Questions: Reading, Responding, Arguing

1. Discuss Hurston's treatment of marriage and/or women.
2. Connect this story with its social, cultural, and political context, especially in terms of race and gender.
3. Explore Hurston's thematic use of the snake. What does it represent and how does it relate to her themes?

4. Connect this story's use of language with another story or poem in the anthology that also uses a nonstandard language or dialect. How does the use of language influence the themes of these stories?

John Steinbeck (1902–1968)

The Chrysanthemums

The high grey-flannel fog of winter closed off the Salinas Valley from the sky and from all the rest of the world. On every side it sat like a lid on the mountains and made of the great valley a closed pot. On the broad, level land floor the gang plows bit deep and left the black earth shining like metal where the shares had cut. On the foothill ranches across the Salinas River, the yellow stubble fields seemed to be bathed in pale cold sunshine, but there was no sunshine in the valley now in December. The thick willow scrub along the river flamed with sharp and positive yellow leaves.

It was a time of quiet and of waiting. The air was cold and tender. A light wind blew up from the southwest so that the farmers were mildly hopeful of a good rain before long; but fog and rain do not go together.

Across the river, on Henry Allen's foothill ranch there was little work to be done, for the hay was cut and stored and the orchards were plowed up to receive the rain deeply when it should come. The cattle on the higher slopes were becoming shaggy and rough-coated.

Elisa Allen, working in her flower garden, looked down across the yard and saw Henry, her husband, talking to two men in business suits. The three of them stood by the tractor shed, each man with one foot on the side of the little Fordson. They smoked cigarettes and studied the machine as they talked.

Elisa watched them for a moment and then went back to her work. She was thirty-five. Her face was lean and strong and her eyes were as clear as water. Her figure looked blocked and heavy in her gardening costume, a man's black hat pulled low down over her eyes, clod-hopper shoes, a figured print dress almost completely covered by a big corduroy apron with four big pockets to hold the snips, the trowel and scratcher, the seeds and the knife she worked with. She wore heavy leather gloves to protect her hands while she worked.

She was cutting down the old year's chrysanthemum stalks with a pair of short and powerful scissors. She looked down toward the men by the tractor shed now and then. Her face was eager and mature and handsome; even her work with the scissors was over-eager, over-powerful. The chrysanthemum stems seemed too small and easy for her energy.

She brushed a cloud of hair out of her eyes with the back of her glove, and left a smudge of earth on her cheek in doing it. Behind her stood the neat white farm house with red geraniums close-banked around it as high as the windows. It was a hard-swept looking little house with hard-polished windows, and a clean mud-mat on the front steps.

Elisa cast another glance toward the tractor shed. The strangers were getting into their Ford coupe. She took off a glove and put her strong fingers down into the forest of new green chrysanthemum sprouts that were growing around the old roots. She spread the leaves and looked down among the close-growing stems. No aphids were there, no sowbugs or snails or cutworms. Her terrier fingers destroyed such pests before they could get started.

Elisa started at the sound of her husband's voice. He had come near quietly, and he leaned over the wire fence that protected her flower garden from cattle and dogs and chickens.

"At it again," he said. "You've got a strong new crop coming."

Elisa straightened her back and pulled on the gardening glove again. "Yes. They'll be strong this coming year." In her tone and on her face there was a little smugness.

"You've got a gift with things," Henry observed. "Some of those yellow chrysanthemums you had this year were ten inches across. I wish you'd work out in the orchard and raise some apples that big."

Her eyes sharpened. "Maybe I could do it, too. I've a gift with things, all right. My mother had it. She could stick anything in the ground and make it grow. She said it was having planters' hands that knew how to do it."

"Well, it sure works with flowers," he said.

"Henry, who were those men you were talking to?"

"Why, sure, that's what I came to tell you. They were from the Western Meat Company. I sold those thirty head of three-year-old steers. Got nearly my own price, too."

"Good," she said. "Good for you."

"And I thought," he continued, "I thought how it's Saturday afternoon, and we might go into Salinas for dinner at a restaurant, and then to a picture show—to celebrate, you see."

"Good," she repeated. "Oh, yes. That will be good."

Henry put on his joking tone. "There's fights tonight. How'd you like to go to the fights?"

"Oh, no," she said breathlessly. "No, I wouldn't like fights."

"Just fooling, Elisa. We'll go to a movie. Let's see. It's two now. I'm going to take Scotty and bring down those steers from the hill. It'll take us maybe two hours. We'll go in town about five and have dinner at the Cominos Hotel. Like that?"

"Of course I'll like it. It's good to eat away from home."

"All right, then. I'll go get up a couple of horses."

She said, "I'll have plenty of time to transplant some of these sets, I guess."

She heard her husband calling Scotty down by the barn. And a little later she saw the two men ride up the pale yellow hillside in search of the steers.

There was a little square sandy bed kept for rooting the chrysanthemums. With her trowel she turned the soil over and over, and smoothed it and patted it firm. Then she dug ten parallel trenches to receive the sets. Back at the chrysanthemum bed she pulled out the little crisp shoots, trimmed off the leaves of each one with her scissors and laid it on a small orderly pile.

A squeak of wheels and plod of hoofs came from the road. Elisa looked up. The country road ran along the dense bank of willows and cottonwoods that bordered the river, and up this road came a curious vehicle, curiously drawn. It was an old springwagon, with a round canvas top on it like the cover of a prairie schooner. It was drawn by an old bay horse and a little grey-and-white burro. A big stubble bearded man sat between the cover flaps and drove the crawling team. Underneath the wagon, between the hind wheels, a lean and rangy mongrel dog walked sedately. Words were painted on the canvas, in clumsy, crooked letters. "Pots, pans, knives, sisors, lawn mores, Fixed." Two rows of articles, and the triumphantly definitive "Fixed" below. The black paint had run down in little sharp-points beneath each letter.

Elisa, squatting on the ground, watched to see the crazy, loose-jointed wagon pass by. But it didn't pass. It turned into the farm road in front of her house, crooked old wheels skirling and squeaking. The rangy dog darted from between the wheels and ran ahead. Instantly the two ranch shepherds flew out at him. Then all three stopped, and with stiff and quivering tails, with taut straight legs, with ambassadorial dignity, they slowly circled, sniffing daintily. The caravan pulled up to Elisa's wire fence and stopped. Now the newcomer dog, feeling outnumbered, lowered his tail and retired under the wagon with raised hackles and bared teeth.

The man on the wagon seat called out, "That's a bad dog in a fight when he gets started."

Elisa laughed. "I see he is. How soon does he generally get started?"

The man caught up her laughter and echoed it heartily. "Sometimes not for weeks and weeks," he said. He climbed stiffly down, over the wheel. The horse and the donkey drooped like unwatered flowers.

Elisa saw that he was a very big man. Although his hair and beard were greying, he did not look old. His worn black suit was wrinkled and spotted with grease. The laughter had disappeared from his face and eyes the moment his laughing voice ceased. His eyes were dark, and they were full of the brooding that gets in the eyes of teamsters and of sailors. The calloused hands he rested on the wire fence were cracked, and every crack was a black line. He took off his battered hat.

"I'm off my general road, ma'am," he said. "Does this dirt road cut over across the river to the Los Angeles highway?"

Elisa stood up and shoved the thick scissors in her apron pocket. "Well, yes, it does, but it winds around and then fords the river. I don't think your team could pull through the sand."

He replied with some asperity. "It might surprise you what them beasts can pull through."

"When they get started?" she asked.

He smiled for a second. "Yes. When they get started."

"Well," said Elisa, "I think you'll save time if you go back to the Salinas road and pick up the highway there."

He drew a big finger down the chicken wire and made it sing. "I ain't in any hurry, ma'am. I go from Seattle to San Diego and back every year. Takes all my time. About six months each way. I aim to follow nice weather."

Elisa took off her gloves and stuffed them in the apron pocket with the scissors. She touched the under edge of her man's hat, searching for fugitive hairs. "That sounds like a nice kind of a way to live," she said.

He leaned confidentially over the fence. "Maybe you noticed the writing on my wagon. I mend pots and sharpen knives and scissors. You got any of them things to do?"

"Oh, no," she said quickly. "Nothing like that." Her eyes hardened with resistance.

"Scissors is the worst thing," he explained. "Most people just ruin scissors trying to sharpen 'em, but I know how. I got a special tool. It's a little bobbit kind of thing, and patented. But it sure does the trick."

"No. My scissors are all sharp."

"All right, then. Take a pot," he continued earnestly, "a bent pot, or a pot with a hole. I can make it like new so you don't have to buy no new ones. That's a saving for you."

"No," she said shortly. "I tell you I have nothing like that for you to do."

His face fell to an exaggerated sadness. His voice took on a whining undertone. "I ain't had a thing to do today. Maybe I won't have no supper tonight. You see I'm off my regular road. I know folks on the highway clear from Seattle to San Diego. They save their things for me to sharpen up because they know I do it so good and save them money."

"I'm sorry," Elisa said irritably. "I haven't anything for you to do."

His eyes left her face and fell to searching the ground. They roamed about until they came to the chrysanthemum bed where she had been working. "What's them plants, ma'am?"

The irritation and resistance melted from Elisa's face. "Oh, those are chrysanthemums, giant whites and yellows. I raise them every year, bigger than anybody around here."

"Kind of a long-stemmed flower? Looks like a quick puff of colored smoke?" he asked.

"That's it. What a nice way to describe them."

"They smell kind of nasty till you get used to them," he said.

"It's a good bitter smell," she retorted, "not nasty at all."

He changed his tone quickly. "I like the smell myself."

"I had ten-inch blooms this year," she said.

The man leaned farther over the fence. "Look. I know a lady down the road a piece, has got the nicest garden you ever seen. Got nearly every kind of flower but no chrysanthemums. Last time I was mending a copper bottom wash tub for her (that's a hard job but I do it good), she said to me, 'If you ever run acrost some nice chrysanthemums I wish you'd try to get me a few seeds.' That's what she told me."

Elisa's eyes grew alert and eager. "She couldn't have known much about chrysanthemums. You *can* raise them from seed, but it's much easier to root the little sprouts you see there."

"Oh," he said. "I s'pose I can't take none to her, then."

"Why yes you can," Elisa cried. "I can put some in damp sand, and you can carry them right along with you. They'll take root in the pot if you keep them damp. And then she can transplant them."

"She'd sure like to have some, ma'am. You say they're nice ones?"

"Beautiful," she said. "Oh, beautiful." Her eyes shone. She tore off the battered hat and shook out her dark pretty hair. "I'll put them in a flower pot, and you can take them right with you. Come into the yard."

While the man came through the picket gate Elisa ran excitedly along the geranium-bordered path to the back of the house. And she returned carrying a big red flower pot. The gloves were forgotten now. She kneeled on the ground by the starting bed and dug up the sandy soil with her fingers and scooped it into the bright new flower pot. Then she picked up the little pile of shoots she had prepared. With her strong fingers she pressed them into the sand and tamped around them with her knuckles. The man stood over her. "I'll tell you what to do," she said. "You remember so you can tell the lady."

"Yes, I'll try to remember."

"Well, look. These will take root in about a month. Then she must set them out, about a foot apart in good rich earth like this, see?" She lifted a handful of dark soil for him to look at. "They'll grow fast and tall. Now remember this: In July tell her to cut them down, about eight inches from the ground."

"Before they bloom?" he asked.

"Yes, before they bloom." Her face was tight with eagerness. "They'll grow right up again. About the last of September the buds will start."

She stopped and seemed perplexed. "It's the budding that takes the most care," she said hesitantly. "I don't know how to tell you." She looked deep into his eyes, searchingly. Her mouth opened a little, and she seemed to be listening. "I'll try to tell you," she said. "Did you ever hear of planting hands?"

"Can't say I have, ma'am."

"Well, I can only tell you what it feels like. It's when you're picking off the buds you don't want. Everything goes right down into your fingertips. You watch your fingers work. They do it themselves. You can feel how it is. They pick and pick the buds. They never make a mistake. They're with the plant. Do you see? Your fingers and the plant. You can feel that, right up your arm. They know. They never make a mistake. You can feel it. When you're like that you can't do anything wrong. Do you see that? Can you understand that?"

She was kneeling on the ground looking up at him. Her breast swelled passionately.

The man's eyes narrowed. He looked away self-consciously. "Maybe I know," he said. "Sometimes in the night in the wagon there—"

Elisa's voice grew husky. She broke in on him, "I've never lived as you do, but I know what you mean. When the night is dark—why, the stars are sharp-pointed, and there's quiet. Why, you rise up and up!

Every pointed star gets driven into your body. It's like that. Hot and sharp and—lovely."

Kneeling there, her hand went out toward his legs in the greasy black trousers. Her hesitant fingers almost touched the cloth. Then her hand dropped to the ground. She crouched low like a fawning dog.

He said, "It's nice, just like you say. Only when you don't have no dinner, it ain't."

She stood up then, very straight, and her face was ashamed. She held the flower pot out to him and placed it gently in his arms. "Here. Put it in your wagon, on the seat, where you can watch it. Maybe I can find something for you to do."

At the back of the house she dug in the can pile and found two old and battered aluminum saucepans. She carried them back and gave them to him. "Here, maybe you can fix these."

His manner changed. He became professional. "Good as new I can fix them." At the back of his wagon he set a little anvil, and out of an oily tool box dug a small machine hammer. Elisa came through the gate to watch him while he pounded out the dents in the kettles. His mouth grew sure and knowing. At a difficult part of the work he sucked his under-lip.

"You sleep right in the wagon?" Elisa asked.

"Right in the wagon, ma'am. Rain or shine I'm dry as a cow in there."

"It must be nice," she said. "It must be very nice. I wish women could do such things."

"It ain't the right kind of a life for a woman."

Her upper lip raised a little, showing her teeth. "How do you know? How can you tell?" she said.

"I don't know, ma'am," he protested. "Of course I don't know. Now here's your kettles, done. You don't have to buy no new ones."

"How much?"

"Oh, fifty cents'll do. I keep my prices down and my work good. That's why I have all them satisfied customers up and down the highway."

Elisa brought him a fifty-cent piece from the house and dropped it in his hand. "You might be surprised to have a rival some time. I can sharpen scissors, too. And I can beat the dents out of little pots. I could show you what a woman might do."

He put his hammer back in the oily box and shoved the little anvil out of sight. "It would be a lonely life for a woman, ma'am, and a scarey life, too, with animals creeping under the wagon all night." He climbed over the singletree, steadying himself with a hand on the burro's white rump. He settled himself in the seat, picked up the lines. "Thank you kindly, ma'am," he said. "I'll do like you told me; I'll go back and catch the Salinas road."

"Mind," she called, "if you're long in getting there, keep the sand damp."

"Sand, ma'am? . . . Sand? Oh, sure. You mean around the chrysanthemums. Sure I will." He clucked his tongue. The beasts leaned luxuriously into their collars. The mongrel dog took his place between the back wheels. The wagon turned and crawled out the entrance road and back the way it had come, along the river.

Elisa stood in front of her wire fence watching the slow progress of the caravan. Her shoulders were straight, her head thrown back, her eyes half-closed, so that the scene came vaguely into them. Her lips moved silently, forming the words "Good-bye—good-bye." Then she whispered, "That's a bright direction. There's a glowing there." The sound of her whisper startled her. She shook herself free and looked about to see whether anyone had been listening. Only the dogs had heard. They lifted their heads toward her from their sleeping in the dust, and then stretched out their chins and settled asleep again. Elisa turned and ran hurriedly into the house.

In the kitchen she reached behind the stove and felt the water tank. It was full of hot water from the noonday cooking. In the bathroom she tore off her soiled clothes and flung them into the corner. And then she scrubbed herself with a little block of pumice, legs and thighs, loins and chest and arms, until her skin was scratched and red. When she had dried herself she stood in front of a mirror in her bedroom and looked at her body. She tightened her stomach and threw out her chest. She turned and looked over her shoulder at her back.

After a while she began to dress, slowly. She put on her newest underclothing and her nicest stockings and the dress which was the symbol of her prettiness. She worked carefully on her hair, penciled her eyebrows and rouged her lips.

Before she was finished she heard the little thunder of hoofs and the shouts of Henry and his helper as they drove the red steers into the corral. She heard the gate bang shut and set herself for Henry's arrival.

His step sounded on the porch. He entered the house calling, "Elisa, where are you?"

"In my room, dressing. I'm not ready. There's hot water for your bath. Hurry up. It's getting late."

When she heard him splashing in the tub, Elisa laid his dark suit on the bed, and shirt and socks and tie beside it. She stood his polished shoes on the floor beside the bed. Then she went to the porch and sat primly and stiffly down. She looked toward the river road where the willow-line was still yellow with frosted leaves so that under the high grey fog they seemed a thin band of sunshine. This was the only color in the grey afternoon. She sat unmoving for a long time. Her eyes blinked rarely.

Henry came banging out of the door shoving his tie inside his vest as he came. Elisa stiffened and her face grew tight. Henry stopped short and looked at her. "Why—why, Elisa. You look so nice!"

"Nice? You think I look nice? What do you mean by 'nice'?"

Henry blundered on. "I don't know. I mean you look different, strong and happy."

"I am strong? Yes, strong. What do you mean 'strong'?"

He looked bewildered. "You're playing some kind of a game," he said helplessly. "It's a kind of a play. You look strong enough to break a calf over your knee, happy enough to eat it like a watermelon."

For a second she lost her rigidity. "Henry! Don't talk like that. You didn't know what you said." She grew complete again. "I'm strong," she boasted. "I never knew before how strong."

Henry looked down toward the tractor shed, and when he brought his eyes back to her, they were his own again. "I'll get out the car. You can put on your coat while I'm starting."

Elisa went into the house. She heard him drive to the gate and idle down his motor, and then she took a long time to put on her hat. She pulled it here and pressed it there. When Henry turned the motor off she slipped into her coat and went out.

The little roadster bounced along on the dirt road by the river, raising the birds and driving the rabbits into the brush. Two cranes flapped heavily over the willow-line and dropped into the river-bed.

Far ahead on the road Elisa saw a dark speck. She knew.

She tried not to look as they passed it, but her eyes would not obey. She whispered to herself sadly, "He might have thrown them off the road. That wouldn't have been much trouble, not very much. But he kept the pot," she explained. "He had to keep the pot. That's why he couldn't get them off the road."

The roadster turned a bend and she saw the caravan ahead. She swung full around toward her husband so she could not see the little covered wagon and the mismatched team as the car passed them.

In a moment it was over. The thing was done. She did not look back.

She said loudly, to be heard above the motor, "It will be good, tonight, a good dinner."

"Now you're changed again," Henry complained. He took one hand from the wheel and patted her knee. "I ought to take you in to dinner oftener. It would be good for both of us. We get so heavy out on the ranch."

"Henry," she asked, "could we have wine at dinner?"

"Sure we could. Say! That will be fine."

She was silent for a while; then she said, "Henry, at those prize fights, do the men hurt each other very much?"

"Sometimes a little, not often. Why?"

"Well, I've read how they break noses, and blood runs down their chests. I've read how the fighting gloves get heavy and soggy with blood."

He looked around at her. "What's the matter, Elisa? I didn't know you read things like that." He brought the car to a stop, then turned to the right over the Salinas River bridge.

"Do any women ever go to the fights?" she asked.

"Oh, sure, some. What's the matter, Elisa? Do you want to go? I don't think you'd like it, but I'll take you if you really want to go."

She relaxed limply in the seat. "Oh, no. No. I don't want to go. I'm sure I don't." Her face was turned away from him. "It will be enough if we can have wine. It will be plenty." She turned up her coat collar so he could not see that she was crying weakly—like an old woman.

—*1940*

Questions: Reading, Responding, Arguing

1. How, where, and why does Steinbeck use description to convey his story's theme?
2. What do the chrysanthemums symbolize?
3. Discuss Elisa in relation to constructions of womanhood. How does this story depict women and why does Elisa cry at the end of the story?

John Cheever (1912–1982)

Reunion

The last time I saw my father was in Grand Central Station. I was going from my grandmother's in the Adirondacks to a cottage on the Cape that my mother had rented, and I wrote my father that I would be in New York between trains for an hour and a half, and asked if we could have lunch together. His secretary wrote to say that he would meet me at the information booth at noon, and at twelve o'clock sharp I saw him coming through the crowd. He was a stranger to me—my mother divorced him three years ago and I hadn't been with him since—but as soon as I saw him I felt that he was my father, my flesh and blood, my future and my doom. I knew that when I was grown I would be something like him; I would have to plan my campaigns within his limitations. He was a big, good-looking man, and I was terribly happy to see him again. He struck me on the back and shook my hand. "Hi, Charlie," he said. "Hi, boy. I'd like to take you up to my club, but it's in the Sixties, and if you have to catch an early train I guess we'd better get something to eat around here." He put his arm around me, and I smelled my father the way my mother sniffs a rose. It was a rich compound of whiskey, after-shave lotion, shoe polish, woolens, and the rankness of a mature male. I hoped that someone would see us together. I wished that we could be photographed. I wanted some record of our having been together.

We went out of the station and up a side street to a restaurant. It was still early, and the place was empty. The bartender was quarreling with a delivery boy, and there was one very old waiter in a red coat down by the kitchen door. We sat down, and my father hailed the waiter in a loud voice. "*Kellner!*" he shouted. "*Garçon! Cameriere! You!*" His boisterousness in the empty restaurant seemed out of place. "Could we have a little service here!" he shouted. "Chop-chop." Then he clapped his hands. This caught the waiter's attention, and he shuffled over to our table.

"Were you clapping your hands at me?" he asked.

"Calm down, calm down, *sommelier*," my father said. "If it isn't too much to ask of you—if it wouldn't be too much above and beyond the call of duty, we would like a couple of Beefeater Gibsons."

"I don't like to be clapped at," the waiter said.

"I should have brought my whistle," my father said. "I have a whistle that is audible only to the ears of old waiters. Now, take out your little pad and your little pencil and see if you can get this straight: two Beefeater Gibsons. Repeat after me: two Beefeater Gibsons."

"I think you'd better go somewhere else," the waiter said quietly.

"That," said my father, "is one of the most brilliant suggestions I have ever heard. Come on, Charlie, let's get the hell out of here!"

I followed my father out of that restaurant into another. He was not so boisterous this time. Our drinks came, and he cross-questioned me about the baseball season. He then struck the edge of his empty glass with his knife and began shouting again. *"Garçon! Kellner! Cameriere! You!* Could we trouble you to bring us two more of the same."

"How old is the boy?" the waiter asked.

"That," my father said, "is none of your God-damned business."

"I'm sorry, sir," the waiter said, "but I won't serve the boy another drink."

"Well, I have some news for you," my father said. "I have some very interesting news for you. This doesn't happen to be the only restaurant in New York. They've opened another on the corner. Come on, Charlie."

He paid the bill, and I followed him out of that restaurant into another. Here the waiters wore pink jackets like hunting coats, and there was a lot of horse tack on the walls. We sat down, and my father began to shout again. "Master of the hounds! Tallyhoo and all that sort of thing. We'd like a little something in the way of a stirrup cup. Namely, two Bibson Geefeaters."

"Two Bibson Geefeaters?" the waiter asked, smiling.

"You know damned well what I want," my father said angrily. "I want two Beefeater Gibsons, and make it snappy. Things have changed in jolly old England. So my friend the duke tells me. Let's see what England can produce in the way of a cocktail."

"This isn't England," the waiter said.

"Don't argue with me," my father said. "Just do as you're told."

"I just thought you might like to know where you are," the waiter said.

"If there is one thing I cannot tolerate," my father said, "it is an impudent domestic. Come on, Charlie."

The fourth place we went to was Italian. *"Buon giorno,"* my father said. *"Per favore, possiamo avere due cocktail americani, forti, forti. Molto gin, poco vermut."*[1]

"I don't understand Italian," the waiter said.

---

[1] The father is ordering drinks in Italian.

"Oh, come off it," my father said. "You understand Italian, and you know damned well you do. *Vogliamo due cocktail americani. Subito.*"

The waiter left us and spoke with the captain, who came over to our table and said, "I'm sorry, sir, but this table is reserved."

"All right," my father said. "Get us another table."

"All the tables are reserved," the captain said.

"I get it," my father said. "You don't desire our patronage. Is that it? Well, the hell with you. *Vada all' inferno.* Let's go, Charlie."

"I have to get my train," I said.

"I'm sorry, sonny," my father said. "I'm terribly sorry." He put his arm around me and pressed me against him. "I'll walk you back to the station. If there had only been time to go up to my club."

"That's all right, Daddy," I said.

"I'll get you a paper," he said. "I'll get you a paper to read on the train."

Then he went up to a newsstand and said, "Kind sir, will you be good enough to favor me with one of your God-damned, no-good, ten-cent afternoon papers?" The clerk turned away from him and stared at a magazine cover. "Is it asking too much, kind sir," my father said, "is it asking too much for you to sell me one of your disgusting specimens of yellow journalism?"

"I have to go, Daddy," I said. "It's late."

"Now, just wait a second, sonny," he said. "Just wait a second. I want to get a rise out of this chap."

"Goodbye, Daddy," I said, and I went down the stairs and got my train, and that was the last time I saw my father.

—1962

Questions: Reading, Responding, Arguing

1. Cheever shows us the father through the dialogue. Describe how Cheever constructs his character and what character traits the father possesses.
2. Discuss Cheever's choice of point of view. How does this choice affect how the reader views the father?
3. The narrator writes that his father was "my flesh and blood, my future and my doom." Explain the significance of this statement in terms of the theme of personal and communal identities. How would you compare it to another depiction of father/son relationships in this anthology?

Alice Walker (b. 1944)

Everyday Use*

For your grandmama

I will wait for her in the yard that Maggie and I made so clean and wavy yesterday afternoon. A yard like this is more comfortable than most people know. It is not just a yard. It is like an extended living room. When the hard clay is swept clean as a floor and the fine sand around the edges lined with tiny, irregular grooves anyone can come and sit and look up into the elm tree and wait for the breezes that never come inside the house.

Maggie will be nervous until after her sister goes: she will stand hopelessly in corners homely and ashamed of the burn scars down her arms and legs, eyeing her sister with a mixture of envy and awe. She thinks her sister has held life always in the palm of one hand, that "no" is a word the world never learned to say to her.

You've no doubt seen those TV shows where the child who has "made it" is confronted, as a surprise, by her own mother and father, tottering in weakly from backstage. (A pleasant surprise, of course: What would they do if parent and child came on the show only to curse out and insult each other?) On TV mother and child embrace and smile into each other's faces. Sometimes the mother and father weep, the child wraps them in her arms and leans across the table to tell how she would not have made it without their help. I have seen these programs.

Sometimes I dream a dream in which Dee and I are suddenly brought together on a TV program of this sort. Out of a dark and soft-seated limousine I am ushered into a bright room filled with many people. There I meet a smiling, gray, sporty man like Johnny Carson who shakes my hand and tells me what a fine girl I have. Then we are on the stage and Dee is embracing me with tears in her eyes. She pins on my dress a large orchid, even though she has told me once that she thinks orchids are tacky flowers.

In real life I am a large, big-boned woman with rough, man-working hands. In the winter I wear flannel nightgowns to bed and overalls during the day. I can kill and clean a hog as mercilessly as a man. My fat keeps me hot in zero weather. I can work outside all day, breaking ice to get water for washing. I can eat pork liver cooked over the open fire minutes after it comes steaming from the hog. One winter I knocked a bull calf straight in the brain between the eyes with a sledge hammer and had the meat hung up to chill before nightfall. But of course all this does not show on television. I am the way my daughter would want me to be: a hundred pounds lighter, my skin like an uncooked barley pancake. My hair glistens in the hot bright lights. Johnny Carson has much to do to keep up with my quick and witty tongue.

But that is a mistake. I know even before I wake up. Who ever knew a Johnson with a quick tongue? Who can even imagine me looking a strange white man in the eye? It seems to me I have talked to them always with one foot raised in flight, with my head turned in whichever way is farthest from them. Dee, though. She would always look anyone in the eye. Hesitation was no part of her nature.

"How do I look, Mama?" Maggie says, showing just enough of her thin body enveloped in pink skirt and red blouse for me to know she's there, almost hidden by the door.

"Come out into the yard," I say.

Have you ever seen a lame animal, perhaps a dog run over by some careless person rich enough to own a car, sidle up to someone who is ignorant enough to be kind to him? That is the way my Maggie walks. She has been like this, chin on chest, eyes on ground, feet in shuffle, ever since the fire that burned the other house to the ground.

Dee is lighter than Maggie, with nicer hair and a fuller figure. She's a woman now, though sometimes I forget. How long ago was it that the other house burned? Ten, twelve years? Sometimes I can still hear the flames and feel Maggie's arms sticking to me, her hair smoking and her dress falling off her in little black papery flakes. Her eyes seemed stretched open, blazed open by the flames reflected in them. And Dee. I see her standing off under the sweet gum tree she used to dig gum out of; a look of concentration on her face as she watched the last dingy gray board of the house fall in toward the red-hot brick chimney. Why don't you do a dance around the ashes? I'd wanted to ask her. She had hated the house that much.

I used to think she hated Maggie, too. But that was before we raised the money, the church and me, to send her to Augusta to school. She used to read to us without pity; forcing words, lies, other folks' habits, whole lives upon us two, sitting trapped and ignorant underneath her voice. She washed us in a river of make-believe, burned us with a lot of knowledge we didn't necessarily need to know. Pressed us to her with the serious way she read, to shove us away at just the moment, like dimwits, we seemed about to understand.

Dee wanted nice things. A yellow organdy dress to wear to her graduation from high school; black pumps to match a green suit she'd made from an old suit somebody gave me. She was determined to stare down any disaster in her efforts. Her eyelids would not flicker for minutes at a time. Often I fought off the temptation to shake her. At sixteen she had a style of her own: and knew what style was.

I never had an education myself. After second grade the school was closed down. Don't ask me why: in 1927 colored asked fewer questions than they do now. Sometimes Maggie reads to me. She stumbles along good-naturedly but can't see well. She knows she is not bright. Like good looks and money, quickness passed her by. She will marry John Thomas (who has mossy teeth in an earnest face) and then I'll be free to sit here and I guess just sing church songs to myself. Although I never was a good singer. Never could carry a tune. I was always better at a man's job. I used to love to milk till I was hoofed in the side in '49. Cows are soothing and slow and don't bother you, unless you try to milk them the wrong way.

I have deliberately turned my back on the house. It is three rooms, just like the one that burned, except the roof is tin; they don't make shingle roofs any more. There are no real windows, just some holes cut in the sides, like the portholes in a ship, but not round and not square, with rawhide holding the shutters up on the outside. This house is in a pasture, too, like the other one. No doubt when Dee sees it she will want to tear it down. She wrote me once that no matter where we "choose" to live, she will manage to come see us. But she will never bring her friends. Maggie and I thought about this and Maggie asked me, "Mama, when did Dee ever *have* any friends?"

She had a few. Furtive boys in pink shirts hanging about on washday after school. Nervous girls who never laughed. Impressed with her they worshiped the well-turned phrase, the cute shape, the scalding humor that erupted like bubbles in lye. She read to them.

When she was courting Jimmy T she didn't have much time to pay to us, but turned all her faultfinding power on him. He *flew* to marry a cheap gal from a family of ignorant flashy people. She hardly had time to recompose herself.

When she comes I will meet—but there they are!

Maggie attempts to make a dash for the house, in her shuffling way, but I stay her with my hand. "Come back here," I say. And she stops and tries to dig a well in the sand with her toe.

It is hard to see them clearly through the strong sun. But even the first glimpse of leg out of the car tells me it is Dee. Her feet were always neat-looking, as if God himself had shaped them with a certain style. From the other side of the car comes a short, stocky man. Hair is all over his head a foot long and hanging from his chin like a kinky mule tail. I hear Maggie suck in her breath. "Uhnnnh," is what it sounds like. Like when you see the wriggling end of a snake just in front of your foot on the road. "Uhnnnh."

Dee next. A dress down to the ground, in this hot weather. A dress so loud it hurts my eyes. There are yellows and oranges enough to throw back the light of the sun. I feel my whole face warming from the heat waves it throws out. Earrings, too, gold and hanging down to her shoulders. Bracelets dangling and making noises when she moves her arm up to shake the folds of the dress out of her armpits. The dress is loose and flows, and as she walks closer, I like it. I hear Maggie go "Uhnnnh" again. It is her sister's hair. It stands straight up like the wool on a sheep. It is black as night and around the edges are two long pigtails that rope about like small lizards disappearing behind her ears.

"Wa-su-zo-Tean-o!" she says, coming on in that gliding way the dress makes her move. The short stocky fellow with the hair to his navel is all grinning and he follows up with "Asalamalakim, my mother and sister!" He moves to hug Maggie but she falls back, right up against the back of my chair. I feel her trembling there and when I look up I see the perspiration falling off her chin.

"Don't get up," says Dee. Since I am stout it takes something of a push. You can see me trying to move a second or two before I make it. She turns, showing white heels through her sandals, and goes back to the car. Out she peeks next with a Polaroid. She stoops down quickly and lines up picture after picture of me sitting there in front of the house with Maggie cowering behind me. She never takes a shot without making sure the house is included. When a cow comes nibbling around the edge of the yard she snaps it and me and Maggie and the house. Then she puts the Polaroid in the back seat of the car, and comes up and kisses me on the forehead.

Meanwhile Asalamalakim is going through the motions with Maggie's hand. Maggie's hand is as limp as a fish, and probably as cold, despite the sweat, and she keeps trying to pull it back. It looks like Asalamalakim wants to shake hands but wants to do it fancy. Or maybe he don't know how people shake hands. Anyhow, he soon gives up on Maggie.

"Well," I say. "Dee."

"No, Mama," she says. "Not 'Dee,' Wangero Leewanika Kemanjo!"

"What happened to 'Dee'?" I wanted to know.

"She's dead," Wangero said. "I couldn't bear it any longer being named after the people who oppress me."

"You know as well as me you was named after your aunt Dicie," I said. Dicie is my sister. She named Dee. We called her "Big Dee" after Dee was born.

"But who was *she* named after?" asked Wangero.

"I guess after Grandma Dee," I said.

"And who was she named after?" asked Wangero.

"Her mother," I said, and saw Wangero was getting tired. "That's about as far back as I can trace it," I said. Though, in fact, I probably could have carried it back beyond the Civil War through the branches.

"Well," said Asalamalakim, "there you are."

"Uhnnnh," I heard Maggie say.

"There I was not," I said, "before 'Dicie' cropped up in our family, so why should I try to trace it that far back?"

He just stood there grinning, looking down on me like somebody inspecting a Model A car. Every once in a while he and Wangero sent eye signals over my head.

"How do you pronounce this name?" I asked.

"You don't have to call me by it if you don't want to," said Wangero.

"Why shouldn't I?" I asked. "If that's what you want us to call you, we'll call you."

"I know it might sound awkward at first," said Wangero.

"I'll get used to it," I said. "Ream it out again."

Well, soon we got the name out of the way. Asalamalakim had a name twice as long and three times as hard. After I tripped over it two or three times he told me to just call him Hakim-a-barber. I wanted to ask him was he a barber, but I didn't really think he was, so I didn't ask.

"You must belong to those beef-cattle peoples down the road," I said. They said "Asalamalakim" when they met you, too, but they didn't shake hands. Always too busy: feeding the cattle, fixing the fences, putting up salt-lick shelters, throwing down hay. When the white folks poisoned some of the herd the men stayed up all night with rifles in their hands. I walked a mile and a half just to see the sight.

Hakim-a-barber said, "I accept some of their doctrines, but farming and raising cattle is not my style." (They didn't tell me, and I didn't ask, whether Wangero [Dee] had really gone and married him.)

We sat down to eat and right away he said he didn't eat collards and pork was unclean. Wangero, though, went on through the chitlins and corn bread, the greens and everything else. She talked a blue streak over the sweet potatoes. Everything delighted her. Even the fact that we still used the benches her daddy made for the table when we couldn't afford to buy chairs.

"Oh, Mama!" she cried. Then turned to Hakim-a-barber. "I never knew how lovely these benches are. You can feel the rump prints," she said, running her hands underneath her and along the bench. Then she gave a sigh and her hand closed over Grandma Dee's butter dish. "That's it!" she said. "I knew there was something I wanted to ask you if I could have." She jumped up from the table and went over in the corner where the churn stood, the milk in it clabber by now. She looked at the churn and looked at it.

"This churn top is what I need," she said. "Didn't Uncle Buddy whittle it out of a tree you all used to have?"

"Yes," I said.

"Uh huh," she said happily. "And I want the dasher, too."

"Uncle Buddy whittle that, too?" asked the barber.

Dee (Wangero) looked up at me.

"Aunt Dee's first husband whittled the dash," said Maggie so low you almost couldn't hear her. "His name was Henry, but they called him Stash."

"Maggie's brain is like an elephant's," Wangero said, laughing. "I can use the churn top as a centerpiece for the alcove table," she said, sliding a plate over the churn, "and I'll think of something artistic to do with the dasher."

When she finished wrapping the dasher the handle stuck out. I took it for a moment in my hands. You didn't even have to look close to see where hands pushing the dasher up and down to make butter had left a kind of sink in the wood. In fact, there were a lot of small sinks; you could see where thumbs and fingers had sunk into the wood. It was beautiful light yellow wood, from a tree that grew in the yard where Big Dee and Stash had lived.

After dinner Dee (Wangero) went to the trunk at the foot of my bed and started rifling through it. Maggie hung back in the kitchen over the dishpan. Out came Wangero with two quilts. They had been pieced by Grandma Dee and then Big Dee and me had hung them on the quilt frames on the front porch and quilted them. One was in the Lone Star pattern. The other was Walk Around the Mountain. In both of them were scraps of dresses Grandma Dee had worn fifty and more years ago. Bits and pieces of Grandpa Jarrell's paisley shirts. And one teeny faded blue piece, about the size of a penny matchbox, that was from Great Grandpa Ezra's uniform that he wore in the Civil War.

"Mama," Wangero said sweet as a bird. "Can I have these old quilts?"

I heard something fall in the kitchen, and a minute later the kitchen door slammed.

"Why don't you take one or two of the others?" I asked. "These old things was just done by me and Big Dee from some tops your grandma pieced before she died."

"No," said Wangero. "I don't want those. They are stitched around the borders by machine."

"That's make them last better," I said.

"That's not the point," said Wangero. "These are all pieces of dresses Grandma used to wear. She did all this stitching by hand. Imagine!" She held the quilts securely in her arms, stroking them.

"Some of the pieces, like those lavender ones, come from old clothes her mother handed down to her," I said, moving up to touch the quilts. Dee (Wangero) moved back just enough so that I couldn't reach the quilts. They already belonged to her.

"Imagine!" she breathed again, clutching them closely to her bosom.

"The truth is," I said, "I promised to give them quilts to Maggie, for when she marries John Thomas."

She gasped like a bee had stung her.

"Maggie can't appreciate these quilts!" she said. "She'd probably be backward enough to put them to everyday use."

"I reckon she would," I said. "God knows I been saving 'em for long enough with nobody using 'em. I hope she will!" I didn't want to bring up how I had offered Dee (Wangero) a quilt when she went away to college. Then she had told me they were old-fashioned, out of style.

"But they're *priceless!*" she was saying now, furiously; for she has a temper. "Maggie would put them on the bed and in five years they'd be in rags. Less than that!"

"She can always make some more," I said. "Maggie knows how to quilt."

Dee (Wangero) looked at me with hatred. "You just will not understand. The point is these quilts, *these* quilts!"

"Well," I said, stumped. "What would *you* do with them?"

"Hang them," she said. As if that was the only thing you *could* do with quilts.

Maggie by now was standing in the door. I could almost hear the sound her feet made as they scraped over each other.

"She can have them, Mama," she said, like somebody used to never winning anything, or having anything reserved for her. "I can 'member Grandma Dee without the quilts."

I looked at her hard. She had filled her bottom lip with checker-berry snuff and it gave her face a kind of dopey, hangdog look. It was Grandma Dee and Big Dee who taught her how to quilt herself. She stood there with her scarred hands hidden in the folds of her skirt. She looked at her sister with something like fear but she wasn't mad at her. This was Maggie's portion. This was the way she knew God to work.

When I looked at her like that something hit me in the top of my head and ran down to the soles of my feet. Just like when I'm in church and the spirit of God touches me and I get happy and shout. I did something I never had done before: hugged Maggie to me, then dragged her on into the room, snatched the quilts out of Miss Wangero's hands and dumped them into Maggie's lap. Maggie just sat there on my bed with her mouth open.

"Take one or two of the others," I said to Dee.

But she turned without a word and went out to Hakim-a-barber.

"You just don't understand," she said, as Maggie and I came out to the car.

"What don't I understand?" I wanted to know.

"Your heritage," she said. And then she turned to Maggie, kissed her, and said, "You ought to try to make something of yourself, too, Maggie. It's really a new day for us. But from the way you and Mama still live you'd never know it."

She put on some sunglasses that hid everything above the tip of her nose and her chin.

Maggie smiled; maybe at the sunglasses. But a real smile, not scared. After we watched the car dust settle I asked Maggie to bring me a dip of snuff. And then the two of us sat there just enjoying, until it was time to go in the house and go to bed.

—*1973*

Questions: Reading, Responding, Arguing

1. Compare the characters of Maggie and Dee. How are they different and how does the mother view these differences?
2. What makes the mother see Maggie differently?
3. Explain the irony and significance of Dee's statement that the mother and Maggie don't understand their heritage.
4. Walker's story is about family, heritage, and identity. Choose one or two characters and examine how they approach family, heritage, and identity.

Michael Drayton (1563–1631)

Idea: Sonnet 61

Since there's no help, come let us kiss and part;
Nay, I have done, you get no more of me,
And I am glad, yea glad with all my heart
That thus so cleanly I myself can free;
Shake hands forever, cancel all our vows,   5
And when we meet at any time again,
Be it not seen in either of our brows
That we one jot of former love retain.
Now at the last gasp of love's latest breath,
When, his pulse failing, passion speechless lies,   10
When faith is kneeling by his bed of death,
And innocence is closing up his eyes,
    Now if thou wouldst, when all have given him over,
    From death to life thou mightst him yet recover.

—1619

Questions: Reading, Responding, Arguing

1. Describe Drayton's use of the sonnet form. How does his use of form connect with his thematic concerns?
2. Compare Drayton's treatment of love with that of another poet in the anthology.
3. What's the significance of the final couplet? What does this couplet contribute to his themes?

William Shakespeare (1564–1616)

Sonnet 18*

Shall I compare thee to a summer's day?
Thou art more lovely and more temperate:
Rough winds do shake the darling buds of May,
And summer's lease hath all too short a date:

Sometimes too hot the eye of heaven shines,   5
And often is his gold complexion dimmed;
And every fair from fair° sometimes declines,
By chance or nature's changing course untrimmed;°
But thy eternal summer shall not fade,
Nor lose possession of that fair thou ow'st;°   10
Nor shall death brag thou wander'st in his shade,
When in eternal lines to time thou grow'st:
So long as men can breathe, or eyes can see,
So long lives this, and this gives life to thee.

—*1609*

Questions: Reading, Responding, Arguing

1. Discuss Shakespeare's use of the "summer's day." Why does he choose this image?
2. How does Shakespeare use the final couplet for effect?
3. Analyze Shakespeare's use of nature imagery in relation to love.

Sonnet 20

A woman's face, with nature's own hand painted,
Hast thou, the master mistress of my passion—
A woman's gentle heart, but not acquainted
With shifting change, as is false women's fashion;
An eye more bright than theirs, less false in rolling,°   5
Gilding the object whereupon it gazeth;
A man in hue all hues in his controlling,
Which steals men's eyes and women's souls amazeth.
And for a woman wert thou first created,
Till nature as she wrought thee fell a-doting,   10
And by addition me of thee defeated,
By adding one thing to my purpose nothing.
  But since she pricked thee out for women's pleasure,
  Mine be thy love and thy love's use their treasure.

—*1609*

7 **fair from fair** every fair thing from its fairness   8 **untrimmed** stripped   10 **ow'st** ownest
5 **rolling** wandering

Questions: Reading, Responding, Arguing

1. Analyze Shakespeare's use of rhyme and meter.
2. Describe the speaker's discussion of women and men and the confusion of genders.
3. The speaker uses the word "false" several times. How does Shakespeare address the idea of falseness?

John Donne (1572–1631)

A Valediction:° Forbidding Mourning

As virtuous men pass mildly away,
   And whisper to their souls to go,
Whilst some of their sad friends do say
   The breath goes now, and some say, No;

So let us melt, and make no noise,   5
   No tear-floods, nor sigh-tempests move,
'Twere profanation of our joys
   To tell the laity our love.

Moving of th' earth brings harms and fears,
   Men reckon what it did and meant;   10
But trepidation of the spheres,°
   Though greater far, is innocent.

Dull sublunary° lovers' love,
   (Whose soul is sense) cannot admit
Absence, because it doth remove   15
   Those things which elemented it.

Valediction farewell speech; Donne is addressing his wife before leaving on a diplomatic mission.
11 trepidation of the spheres natural trembling of the heavenly spheres, a concept of Ptolemaic astronomy **13 sublunary** under the moon, hence, changeable (a Ptolemaic concept)

But we by a love so much refined
    That our selves know not what it is,
Inter-assurèd of the mind,
    Care less, eyes, lips, and hands to miss.   20

Our two souls therefore, which are one,
    Though I must go, endure not yet
A breach, but an expansion,
    Like gold to airy thinness beat.

If they be two, they are two so   25
    As stiff twin compasses° are two;
Thy soul, the fixed foot, makes no show
    To move, but doth, if th' other do.

And though it in the center sit,
    Yet when the other far doth roam,   30
It leans and hearkens after it,
    And grows erect, as that comes home.

Such wilt thou be to me, who must
    Like th' other foot, obliquely run;
Thy firmness makes my circle just,°   35
    And makes me end where I begun.

                                —*1633*

Questions: Reading, Responding, Arguing

1. Describe the relationship between the "you" and "I." What is the speaker's attitude toward their relationship?
2. Why, as the title suggests, does the speaker "forbid mourning"?
3. Discuss the elaborate metaphor—or conceit— in the poem's final three stanzas.

26 **stiff twin compasses** drafting compasses   35 **just** complete

Andrew Marvell (1621–1678)

To His Coy Mistress

    Had we but world enough, and time,
This coyness,° lady, were no crime.
We would sit down, and think which way
To walk, and pass our long love's day.
Thou by the Indian Ganges' side   5
Shouldst rubies find; I by the tide
Of Humber° would complain. I would
Love you ten years before the flood,
And you should, if you please, refuse
Till the conversion of the Jews.°   10
My vegetable° love should grow
Vaster than empires, and more slow;
An hundred years should go to praise
Thine eyes, and on thy forehead gaze;
Two hundred to adore each breast,   15
But thirty thousand to the rest;
An age at least to every part,
And the last age should show your heart.
For, lady, you deserve this state,°
Nor would I love at lower rate.   20
    But at my back I always hear
Time's wingèd chariot hurrying near;
And yonder all before us lie
Deserts of vast eternity.
Thy beauty shall no more be found;   25
Nor, in thy marble vault, shall sound
My echoing song; then worms shall try°
That long-preserved virginity,
And your quaint° honor turn to dust,
And into ashes all my lust: 30
The grave's a fine and private place,
But none, I think, do there embrace.

---

2 **coyness** here, artificial sexual reluctance   7 **Humber** an English river near Marvell's home
10 **conversion of the Jews** at the end of time   11 **vegetable** flourishing   19 **state** estate   27 **try** test
29 **quaint** too subtle

Now therefore, while the youthful hue
Sits on thy skin like morning glow,
And while thy willing soul transpires   35
At every pore with instant fires,
Now let us sport us while we may,
And now, like amorous birds of prey,
Rather at once our time devour
Than languish in his slow-chapped° power.   40
Let us roll all our strength and all
Our sweetness up into one ball,
And tear our pleasures with rough strife
Thorough the iron gates of life:
Thus, though we cannot make our sun   45
Stand still, yet we will make him run.

—*1681*

Questions: Reading, Responding, Arguing

1. What is the speaker's attitude toward his mistress's coyness?
   What language does Marvell use to convey the speaker's
   attitude?
2. How does the speaker attempt to convince his mistress to
   abandon her coyness?
3. In what ways is this poem about carpe diem, that is, seizing
   the day?

John Keats (1795–1821)

La Belle Dame sans Merci°

O what can ail thee, Knight at arms,
   Alone and palely loitering?
The sedge has withered from the Lake
   And no birds sing!

---

40 **chapped** jawed
La Belle Dame sans Merci "the beautiful lady without pity"

O what can ail thee, Knight at arms,
    So haggard, and so woebegone?
The squirrel's granary is full
    And the harvest's done.

I see a lily on thy brow
    With anguish moist and fever dew,
And on thy cheeks a fading rose
    Fast withereth too.

"I met a Lady in the Meads,
    Full beautiful, a faery's child,
Her hair was long, her foot was light,
    And her eyes were wild.

"I made a Garland for her head,
    And bracelets too, and fragrant Zone;°
She looked at me as she did love
    And made sweet moan.

"I set her on my pacing steed
    And nothing else saw all day long,
For sidelong would she bend and sing
    A faery's song.

"She found me roots of relish sweet,
    And honey wild, and manna dew,
And sure in language strange she said
    'I love thee true.'

"She took me to her elfin grot°
    And there she wept and sighed full sore,
And there I shut her wild wild eyes
    With kisses four.

"And there she lullèd me asleep,
    And there I dreamed, Ah Woe betide!
The latest dream I ever dreamt
    On the cold hill side.

"I saw pale Kings, and Princes too,
    Pale warriors, death-pale were they all;

5

10

15

20

25

30

35

18 Zone belt   **29 grot** cave

They cried, 'La belle Dame sans merci
   Hath thee in thrall!'   40

"I saw their starved lips in the gloam
   With horrid warning gapèd wide,
And I awoke, and found me here
   On the cold hill's side.

"And this is why I sojourn here   45
   Alone and palely loitering;
Though the sedge is withered from the Lake,
   And no birds sing."

—1819

Questions: Reading, Responding, Arguing

1. The poem has a mythical or otherworldly feel to it. How does Keats create this atmosphere?
2. Examine how Keats describes and creates the Lady and her power.
3. Analyze Keats's structure. How does he use form to help convey meaning and themes?
4. This poem is the subject for numerous nineteenth-century paintings. Imagine what a painted version of this poem would look like. What image or focus do you think would best portray the poem's theme or message? Is there an element to the poem that would be lost in a painting?

Elizabeth Barrett Browning (1806–1861)

Sonnets from the Portuguese, 18

I never gave a lock of hair away
To a man, dearest, except this to thee,
Which now upon my fingers thoughtfully,
I ring out to the full brown length and say
"Take it." My day of youth went yesterday;   5

My hair no longer bounds to my foot's glee,
Nor plant I it from rose or myrtle-tree,
As girls do, any more: it only may
Now shade on two pale cheeks the mark of tears,
Taught drooping from the head that hangs aside   10
Through sorrow's trick. I thought the funeral-shears
Would take this first, but Love is justified,—
Take it thou,—finding pure, from all those years,
The kiss my mother left here when she died.

—*1845–1846*

Questions: Reading, Responding, Arguing

1. To whom is the poem addressed? What is their relationship?
2. What does she mean by the reference to "funeral-shears"?
3. Why does the poet refer to her mother's death?
4. How does Barrett Browning allude to her own age in the
   poem? Argue its importance to the poem's theme.

Edgar Allan Poe (1809–1849)

The Raven

Once upon a midnight dreary, while I pondered, weak and weary,
Over many a quaint and curious volume of forgotten lore—
While I nodded, nearly napping, suddenly there came a tapping,
As of some one gently rapping, rapping at my chamber door.
"'Tis some visitor," I muttered, "tapping at my chamber door—   5
            Only this and nothing more."

Ah, distinctly I remember it was in the bleak December;
And each separate dying ember wrought its ghost upon the floor.
Eagerly I wished the morrow;—vainly I had sought to borrow
From my books surcease of sorrow—sorrow for the lost Lenore—   10
For the rare and radiant maiden whom the angels name Lenore—
            Nameless *here* for evermore.

And the silken, sad, uncertain rustling of each purple curtain
Thrilled me—filled me with fantastic terrors never felt before;

So that now, to still the beating of my heart, I stood repeating   15
"'Tis some visitor entreating entrance at my chamber door;—
Some late visitor entreating entrance at my chamber door;—
            This it is and nothing more."

Presently my soul grew stronger; hesitating then no longer,
"Sir," said I, "or Madam, truly your forgiveness I implore;   20
But the fact is I was napping, and so gently you came rapping,
And so faintly you came tapping, tapping at my chamber door,
That I scarce was sure I heard you"—here I opened wide the door;—
            Darkness there and nothing more.

Deep into that darkness peering, long I stood there wondering,
    fearing,   25
Doubting, dreaming dreams no mortal ever dared to dream before;
But the silence was unbroken, and the stillness gave no token,
And the only word there spoken was the whispered word, "Lenore?"
This I whispered, and an echo murmured back the word, "Lenore!"
            Merely this and nothing more.   30

Back into the chamber turning, all my soul within me burning,
Soon again I heard a tapping somewhat louder than before.
"Surely," said I, "surely that is something at my window lattice;
Let me see, then, what thereat is, and this mystery explore—
Let my heart be still a moment and this mystery explore;—   35
            'Tis the wind and nothing more!"

Open here I flung the shutter, when, with many a flirt and flutter,
In there stepped a stately Raven of the saintly days of yore;
Not the least obeisance made he; not a minute stopped or stayed he;
But, with mien of lord or lady, perched above my chamber door—   40
Perched upon a bust of Pallas° just above my chamber door—
            Perched, and sat, and nothing more.

Then this ebony bird beguiling my sad fancy into smiling,
By the grave and stern decorum of the countenance it wore,
"Though thy crest be shorn and shaven, thou," I said, "art sure no
    craven,   45
Ghastly grim and ancient Raven wandering from the Nightly shore—
Tell me what thy lordly name is on the Night's Plutonian° shore!"
            Quoth the Raven, "Nevermore."

---

41 Pallas Athena, goddess of wisdom   **47 Plutonian** after Pluto, Roman god of the underworld

Much I marvelled this ungainly fowl to hear discourse so plainly,
Though its answer little meaning—little relevancy bore;   50
For we cannot help agreeing that no living human being
Ever yet was blessed with seeing bird above his chamber door—
Bird or beast upon the sculptured bust above his chamber door,
               With such name as "Nevermore."

But the Raven, sitting lonely on the placid bust, spoke only   55
That one word, as if his soul in that one word he did outpour.
Nothing farther then he uttered—not a feather then he fluttered—
Till I scarcely more than muttered, "Other friends have flown before—
On the morrow *he* will leave me, as my Hopes have flown before."
               Then the bird said, "Nevermore."   60

Startled at the stillness broken by reply so aptly spoken,
"Doubtless," said I, "what it utters is its only stock and store
Caught from some unhappy master whom unmerciful Disaster
Followed fast and followed faster till his songs one burden bore—
Till the dirges of his Hope that melancholy burden bore   65
               Of 'Never—nevermore.'"

But the Raven still beguiling all my sad fancy into smiling,
Straight I wheeled a cushioned seat in front of bird and bust and door;
Then, upon the velvet sinking, I betook myself to linking
Fancy unto fancy, thinking what this ominous bird of yore—   70
What this grim, ungainly, ghastly, gaunt, and ominous bird of yore
               Meant in croaking "Nevermore."

This I sat engaged in guessing, but no syllable expressing
To the fowl whose fiery eyes now burned into my bosom's core;
This and more I sat divining, with my head at ease reclining   75
On the cushion's velvet lining that the lamp-light gloated o'er,
But whose velvet-violet lining with the lamp-light gloating o'er,
               She shall press, ah, nevermore!

Then, methought, the air grew denser, perfumed from an unseen
   censer
Swung by seraphim whose foot-falls tinkled on the tufted floor.   80
"Wretch," I cried, "thy God hath lent thee—by these angels he
   hath sent thee.
Respite—respite and nepenthe° from thy memories of Lenore;

---

82 nepenthe drug causing forgetfulness

Quaff, oh quaff this kind nepenthe and forget this lost Lenore!"
            Quoth the Raven, "Nevermore."

"Prophet!" said I, "thing of evil!—prophet still, if bird or devil!—   85
Whether Tempter sent, or whether tempest tossed thee here ashore,
Desolate yet all undaunted, on this desert land enchanted—
On this home by Horror haunted—tell me truly, I implore—
Is there—*is* there balm in Gilead?—tell me—tell me, I implore!"
            Quoth the Raven, "Nevermore."   90

"Prophet!" said I, "thing of evil!—prophet still, if bird or devil!
By that Heaven that bends above us—by that God we both adore—
Tell this soul with sorrow laden if, within the distant Aidenn,°
It shall clasp a sainted maiden whom the angels name Lenore—
Clasp a rare and radiant maiden whom the angels name Lenore."   95
            Quoth the Raven, "Nevermore."

"Be that word our sign of parting, bird or fiend!" I shrieked,
        upstarting—
"Get thee back into the tempest and the Night's Plutonian shore!
Leave no black plume as a token of that lie thy soul hath spoken!
Leave my loneliness unbroken!—quit the bust above my door!   100
Take thy beak from out my heart, and take thy form from off my
        door!"
            Quoth the Raven, "Nevermore."

And the Raven, never flitting, still is sitting, *still* is sitting
On the pallid bust of Pallas just above my chamber door;
And his eyes have all the seeming of a demon's that is dreaming,   105
And the lamp-light o'er him streaming throws his shadow on the floor;
And my soul from out that shadow that lies floating on the floor
            Shall be lifted—nevermore!

—*1845*

Questions: Reading, Responding, Arguing

1. What is the narrative plot of the poem? What, if anything,
   happens to the narrator?
2. Why does the speaker react to the raven the way that he
   does? What is the raven's role in the poem?

93 Aidenn Eden

3. Poe is well known for his use of sound and rhythm for effect. How does he create his compelling rhythm? What effect does it have on the poem?
4. Analyze Poe's use of repetition. Why and when does he repeat certain phrases?
5. Read Poe's "The Philosophy of Composition" (p. 1092). Argue that his account of how he wrote the poem is or is not accurate.

To Helen

Helen, thy beauty is to me
    Like those Nicean° barks of yore,
That gently, o'er a perfumed sea,
    The weary, way-worn wanderer bore
    To his own native shore.   5

On desperate seas long wont to roam,
    Thy hyacinth° hair, thy classic face
Thy Naiad° airs have brought me home
    To the glory that was Greece
And the grandeur that was Rome.   10

Lo! in yon brilliant window-niche
    How statue-like I see thee stand!
    The agate lamp within thy hand,
Ah! Psyche,° from the regions which
    Are Holy Land!   15

—1831

Questions: Reading, Responding, Arguing

1. Describe Poe's style in this poem in terms of syntax and stanzas. How does he use them to create an effect?
2. Who is the speaker addressing and what is his relationship to her?

---

2 Nicean possibly of Nice (in the South of France); or Phoenician   **7 hyacinth** reddish, like the flower of Greek myth   **8 Naiad** water nymph   **14 Psyche** the soul

3. Poe uses allusions to classical mythology. What do they contribute to the poem? Use research on mythological figures in the poem to construct an argument about its meaning.

Robert Browning (1812–1889)

Porphyria's° Lover

The rain set early in tonight,
    The sullen wind was soon awake,
It tore the elm-tops down for spite,
    And did its worst to vex the lake:
    I listened with heart fit to break.   5
When glided in Porphyria; straight
    She shut the cold out and the storm,
And kneeled and made the cheerless grate
    Blaze up, and all the cottage warm;
    Which done, she rose, and from her form   10
Withdrew the dripping cloak and shawl,
    And laid her soiled gloves by, untied
Her hat and let the damp hair fall,
    And, last, she sat down by my side
    And called me. When no voice replied,   15
She put my arm about her waist,
    And made her smooth white shoulder bare,
And all her yellow hair displaced,
    And, stooping, made my cheek lie there,
    And spread, o'er all, her yellow hair,   20
Murmuring how she loved me—she
    Too weak, for all her heart's endeavor,
To set its struggling passion free
    From pride, and vainer ties dissever,
    And give herself to me forever.   25
But passion sometimes would prevail,
    Nor could tonight's gay feast restrain

Porphyria name suggesting purple, the color of nobility and royalty

A sudden thought of one so pale
    For love of her, and all in vain:
    So, she was come through wind and rain.   30
Be sure I looked up at her eyes
    Happy and proud; at last I knew
Porphyria worshipped me; surprise
    Made my heart swell, and still it grew
    While I debated what to do.   35
That moment she was mine, mine, fair,
    Perfectly pure and good: I found
A thing to do, and all her hair
    In one long yellow string I wound
    Three times her little throat around,   40
And strangled her. No pain felt she;
    I am quite sure she felt no pain.
As a shut bud that holds a bee,
    I warily oped her lids: again
    Laughed the blue eyes without a stain.   45
And I untightened next the tress
    About her neck; her cheek once more
Blushed bright beneath my burning kiss:
    I propped her head up as before,
    Only, this time my shoulder bore   50
Her head, which droops upon it still:
    The smiling rosy little head
So glad it has its utmost will,
    That all it scorned at once is fled,
    And I, its love, am gained instead!   55
Porphyria's love: she guessed not how
    Her darling one wish would be heard.
And thus we sit together now,
    And all night long we have not stirred,
    And yet God has not said a word!   60

                               —1842

Questions: Reading, Responding, Arguing

  1. The poem begins and ends differently. What does this shift
     suggest about the narrator?

2. Describe Browning's depiction of Porphyria. How does Browning draw on/subvert the tradition of love poetry?
3. Compare the narrator in this poem with that of "My Last Duchess" on page 579. How is their treatment of the women in their lives similar? How are they different?

Thomas Hardy (1840–1928)

Neutral Tones

We stood by a pond that winter day,
And the sun was white, as though chidden of God,
And a few leaves lay on the starving sod;
  —They had fallen from an ash, and were gray.

Your eyes on me were as eyes that rove   5
Over tedious riddles of years ago;
And some words played between us to and fro
  On which lost the more by our love.

The smile on your mouth was the deadest thing
Alive enough to have strength to die;   10
And a grin of bitterness swept thereby
  Like an ominous bird a-wing . . .

Since then, keen lessons that love deceives,
And wrings with wrong, have shaped to me
Your face, and the God-curst sun, and a tree,   15
  And a pond edged with grayish leaves.

              —*1898*

Questions: Reading, Responding, Arguing

1. About whose relationship is this poem written? How would you describe it?
2. Why is Hardy's stanza form unique? How does it help convey theme and meaning?
3. What does the term "tones" imply besides colors? Argue that the poem's title has several symbolic overtones.

4. Compare Hardy's depiction of love with another poem in this anthology that deals with death. How do the different poems conceive of death differently? Which is the most effective in conceptualizing death?

William Butler Yeats (1865–1939)

The Song of Wandering Aengus°

I went out to the hazel wood,
Because a fire was in my head,
And cut and peeled a hazel wand,
And hooked a berry to a thread;
And when white moths were on the wing,   5
And moth-like stars were flickering out,
I dropped the berry in a stream
And caught a little silver trout.

When I had laid it on the floor
I went to blow the fire aflame,   10
But something rustled on the floor,
And some one called me by my name:
It had become a glimmering girl
With apple blossom in her hair
Who called me by my name and ran   15
And faded through the brightening air.

Though I am old with wandering
Through hollow lands and hilly lands,
I will find out where she has gone,
And kiss her lips and take her hands;   20
And walk among long dappled grass,

Aengus Among the Sidhe (native Irish deities), the god of youth, love, beauty, and poetry. Yeats once also called him the "Master of Love." Here, however, he seems mortal.

And pluck till time and times are done
The silver apples of the moon,
The golden apples of the sun.

—*1899*

Questions: Reading, Responding, Arguing

1. Connect this poem with the myth of Aengus. Why does Yeats choose a Celtic myth for his poem, and how does his poem differ from the myth?
2. Who is the "glimmering girl"? What does she contribute to the poem?
3. Aengus is a Celtic god of love. How does the theme of the poem relate to love, or the loss of love?
4. Compare the rhythm and rhyme in this poem with one other Yeats poem found in a different thematic section. How do the rhythms and rhymes change as the themes change?

Edwin Arlington Robinson (1869–1935)

Firelight

Ten years together without yet a cloud,
They seek each other's eyes at intervals
Of gratefulness to firelight and four walls
For love's obliteration of the crowd.
Serenely and perennially endowed   5
And bowered as few may be, their joy recalls
No snake, no sword; and over them there falls
The blessing of what neither says aloud.

Wiser for silence, they were not so glad
Were she to read the graven° tale of lines   10

---

10 graven engraved

On the wan face of one somewhere alone;
Nor were they more content could he have had
Her thoughts a moment since of one who shines
Apart, and would be hers if he had known.

—*1920*

Questions: Reading, Responding, Arguing

1. Discuss Robinson's use of irony, giving at least two examples.
2. Analyze the relationship between stanzas one and two. Why does Robinson put in a stanza break?
3. Argue that Robinson's treatment of love and relationships in this poem is accurate or inaccurate.

Robert Frost (1874–1963)

Home Burial

He saw her from the bottom of the stairs
Before she saw him. She was starting down,
Looking back over her shoulder at some fear.
She took a doubtful step and then undid it
To raise herself and look again. He spoke   5
Advancing toward her: "What is it you see
From up there always?—for I want to know."
She turned and sank upon her skirts at that,
And her face changed from terrified to dull.
He said to gain time: "What is it you see?"   10
Mounting until she cowered under him.
"I will find out now—you must tell me, dear."
She, in her place, refused him any help,
With the least stiffening of her neck and silence.
She let him look, sure that he wouldn't see,   15
Blind creature; and awhile he didn't see.
But at last he murmured, "Oh," and again, "Oh."

"What is it—what?" she said.

"Just that I see."

"You don't," she challenged. "Tell me what it is."

"The wonder is I didn't see at once.   20
I never noticed it from here before.
I must be wonted to it—that's the reason.
The little graveyard where my people are!
So small the window frames the whole of it.
Not so much larger than a bedroom, is it?   25
There are three stones of slate and one of marble,
Broad-shouldered little slabs there in the sunlight
On the sidehill. We haven't to mind *those*.
But I understand: it is not the stones,
But the child's mound—"

                         "Don't, don't, don't, don't," she cried.   30

She withdrew, shrinking from beneath his arm
That rested on the banister, and slid downstairs;
And turned on him with such a daunting look,
He said twice over before he knew himself:
"Can't a man speak of his own child he's lost?"   35

"Not you!—Oh, where's my hat? Oh, I don't need it!
I must get out of here. I must get air.—
I don't know rightly whether any man can."

"Amy! Don't go to someone else this time.
Listen to me. I won't come down the stairs."   40
He sat and fixed his chin between his fists.
"There's something I should like to ask you, dear."

"You don't know how to ask it."

                         "Help me, then."

Her fingers moved the latch for all reply.

"My words are nearly always an offense.   45
I don't know how to speak of anything
So as to please you. But I might be taught,
I should suppose. I can't say I see how.
A man must partly give up being a man

With womenfolk. We could have some arrangement   50
By which I'd bind myself to keep hands off
Anything special you're a-mind to name.
Though I don't like such things 'twixt those that love.
Two that don't love can't live together without them.
But two that do can't live together with them."   55
She moved the latch a little. "Don't—don't go.
Don't carry it to someone else this time.
Tell me about it if it's something human.
Let me into your grief. I'm not so much
Unlike other folks as your standing there   60
Apart would make me out. Give me my chance.
I do think, though, you overdo it a little.
What was it brought you up to think it the thing
To take your mother-loss of a first child
So inconsolably—in the face of love.   65
You'd think his memory might be satisfied—"

"There you go sneering now!"

                    "I'm not, I'm not!

You make me angry. I'll come down to you.
God, what a woman! And it's come to this,
A man can't speak of his own child that's dead."   70

"You can't because you don't know how to speak.
If you had any feelings, you that dug
With your own hand—how could you?—his little grave;
I saw you from that very window there,
Making the gravel leap and leap in air,   75
Leap up, like that, like that, and land so lightly
And roll back down the mound beside the hole.
I thought, Who is that man? I didn't know you.
And I crept down the stairs and up the stairs
To look again, and still your spade kept lifting.   80
Then you came in. I heard your rumbling voice
Out in the kitchen, and I don't know why,
But I went near to see with my own eyes.
You could sit there with the stains on your shoes
Of the fresh earth from your own baby's grave   85
And talk about your everyday concerns.

You had stood the spade up against the wall
Outside there in the entry, for I saw it."

"I shall laugh the worst laugh I ever laughed.
I'm cursed. God, if I don't believe I'm cursed."   90

"I can repeat the very words you were saying:
'Three foggy mornings and one rainy day
Will rot the best birch fence a man can build.'
Think of it, talk like that at such a time!
What had how long it takes a birch to rot   95
To do with what was in the darkened parlor?
You *couldn't* care! The nearest friends can go
With anyone to death, comes so far short
They might as well not try to go at all.
No, from the time when one is sick to death,   100
One is alone, and he dies more alone.
Friends make pretense of following to the grave,
But before one is in it, their minds are turned
And making the best of their way back to life
And living people, and things they understand.   105
But the world's evil. I won't have grief so
If I can change it. Oh, I won't, I won't!"

"There, you have said it all and you feel better.
You won't go now. You're crying. Close the door.
The heart's gone out of it: why keep it up?   110
Amy! There's someone coming down the road!"

"*You*—oh, you think the talk is all. I must go—
Somewhere out of this house. How can I make you—"

"If—you—do!" She was opening the door wider.
"Where do you mean to go? First tell me that.   115
I'll follow and bring you back by force. I *will!*—"

—*1914*

Questions: Reading, Responding, Arguing

1. A narrative poem is any poem that tells a story. How is this
   poem an example of a narrative poem? What happens in this
   poem?

2. Explain the significance of the grave. How does Frost use it?
3. Describe the relationship between the man and the woman. How does Frost depict this relationship? Discuss the arguments that the characters use to justify their actions.

T. S. Eliot (1888–1965)

The Love Song of J. Alfred Prufrock

S'io credesse che mia risposta fosse
A persona che mai tornasse al mondo,
Questa fiamma staria senza più scosse.
Ma perciocche giammai di questo fondo
Non tornò vivo alcun, s'i'odo il vero,
Senza tema d'infamia ti rispondo.°

Let us go then, you° and I,
When the evening is spread out against the sky
Like a patient etherised upon a table;
Let us go, through certain half-deserted streets,
The muttering retreats   5
Of restless nights in one-night cheap hotels
And sawdust restaurants with oyster-shells:
Streets that follow like a tedious argument
Of insidious intent
To lead you to an overwhelming question . . .   10
Oh, do not ask, "What is it?"
Let us go and make our visit.

In the room the women come and go
Talking of Michelangelo.°

The yellow fog that rubs its back upon the window-panes,   15
The yellow smoke that rubs its muzzle on the window-panes,

S'io credesse . . . rispondo From Dante's *Inferno* (Canto 27). The speaker is Guido da Montefeltro:
"If I thought I spoke to someone who would return to the world, this flame would tremble no
longer. But, if what I hear is true, since no one has ever returned alive from this place I can answer
you without fear of infamy."   **1 you** Eliot said that the auditor of the poem was a male friend of
Prufrock.   **14 Michelangelo** Italian painter and sculptor (1475–1564)

Licked its tongue into the corners of the evening,
Lingered upon the pools that stand in drains,
Let fall upon its back the soot that falls from chimneys,
Slipped by the terrace, made a sudden leap,   20
And seeing that it was a soft October night,
Curled once about the house, and fell asleep.

And indeed there will be time
For the yellow smoke that slides along the street,
Rubbing its back upon the window-panes;   25
There will be time, there will be time
To prepare a face to meet the faces that you meet;
There will be time to murder and create,
And time for all the works and days of hands
That lift and drop a question on your plate: 30
Time for you and time for me,
And time yet for a hundred indecisions,
And for a hundred visions and revisions,
Before the taking of a toast and tea.

In the room the women come and go   35
Talking of Michelangelo.

And indeed there will be time
To wonder, "Do I dare?" and, "Do I dare?"—
Time to turn back and descend the stair,
With a bald spot in the middle of my hair—   40
(They will say: "How his hair is growing thin!")
My morning coat, my collar mounting firmly to the chin,
My necktie rich and modest, but asserted by a simple pin—
(They will say: "But how his arms and legs are thin!")
Do I dare   45
Disturb the universe?
In a minute there is time
For decisions and revisions which a minute will reverse.

For I have known them all already, known them all:
Have known the evenings, mornings, afternoons,   50
I have measured out my life with coffee spoons;
I know the voices dying with a dying fall
Beneath the music from a farther room.
        So how should I presume?

And I have known the eyes already, known them all—   55
The eyes that fix you in a formulated phrase,
And when I am formulated, sprawling on a pin,
When I am pinned and wriggling on the wall,
Then how should I begin
To spit out all the butt-ends of my days and ways?   60
      And how should I presume?

And I have known the arms already, known them all—
Arms that are braceleted and white and bare
(But in the lamplight, downed with light brown hair!)
Is it perfume from a dress   65
That makes me so digress?
Arms that lie along a table, or wrap about a shawl.
    And should I then presume?
    And how should I begin?

   . . . . .

Shall I say, I have gone at dusk through narrow streets,   70
And watched the smoke that rises from the pipes
Of lonely men in shirtsleeves, leaning out of windows? . . .

I should have been a pair of ragged claws
Scuttling across the floors of silent seas.

   . . . . .

And the afternoon, the evening, sleeps so peacefully!   75
Smoothed by long fingers,
Asleep . . . tired . . . or it malingers,
Stretched on the floor, here beside you and me.
Should I, after tea and cakes and ices,
Have the strength to force the moment to its crisis?   80
But though I have wept and fasted, wept and prayed,
Though I have seen my head (grown slightly bald) brought in
    upon a platter,
I am no prophet°—and here's no great matter;
I have seen the moment of my greatness flicker,
And I have seen the eternal Footman hold my coat, and
    snicker,   85
      And in short, I was afraid.

82–83 **my head . . . no prophet** allusion to John the Baptist

And would it have been worth it, after all,
After the cups, the marmalade, the tea,
Among the porcelain, among some talk of you and me,
Would it have been worth while,   90
To have bitten off the matter with a smile,
To have squeezed the universe into a ball
To roll it towards some overwhelming question,
To say: "I am Lazarus,° come from the dead,
Come back to tell you all, I shall tell you all"—   95
If one, settling a pillow by her head,
    Should say: "That is not what I meant at all;
    That is not it, at all."

And would it have been worth it, after all,
Would it have been worth while,   100
After the sunsets and the dooryards and the sprinkled streets,
After the novels, after the teacups, after the skirts that trail
    along the floor—
And this, and so much more?—
It is impossible to say just what I mean!
But as if a magic lantern° threw the nerves in patterns on
    a screen: 105
Would it have been worth while
If one, settling a pillow or throwing off a shawl,
And turning toward the window, should say:
    "That is not it at all,
    That is not what I meant, at all."   110

        . . . . .

No! I am not Prince Hamlet, nor was meant to be;
Am an attendant lord, one that will do
To swell a progress, start a scene or two,
Advise the prince; no doubt, an easy tool,
Deferential, glad to be of use,   115
Politic, cautious, and meticulous;
Full of high sentence, but a bit obtuse;
At times, indeed, almost ridiculous—
Almost, at times, the Fool.°

---

94 **Lazarus** raised from the dead in John 11:1–44   105 **magic lantern** old-fashioned slide projector
111–119 **not Prince Hamlet . . . the Fool** The allusion is probably to Polonius, a character in
Hamlet.

I grow old . . . I grow old . . .   120
I shall wear the bottoms of my trousers rolled.

Shall I part my hair behind? Do I dare to eat a peach?
I shall wear white flannel trousers, and walk upon the beach.
I have heard the mermaids singing, each to each.

I do not think that they will sing to me.   125

I have seen them riding seaward on the waves
Combing the white hair of the waves blown back
When the wind blows the water white and black.
We have lingered in the chambers of the sea
By sea-girls wreathed with seaweed red and brown   130
Till human voices wake us, and we drown.

                                                                                              —1917

Questions: Reading, Responding, Arguing

1. Characterize the speaker. How does Eliot convey character?
2. To whom is the love song directed? How do you know?
3. Give three examples of figures of speech in this poem.
4. Analyze the effect of Eliot's use of repeated phrases, words, and sounds.
5. Critics have found a number of themes for the poem, such as love, alienation, and paralysis. Is there a central theme to the poem? Argue that exploring a different theme can reveal a different meaning to the work.

Edna St. Vincent Millay (1892–1950)

Love Is Not All: It Is Not Meat nor Drink*

Love is not all: it is not meat nor drink
Nor slumber nor a roof against the rain;
Nor yet a floating spar to men that sink
And rise and sink and rise and sink again;

Love can not fill the thickened lung with breath,   5
Nor clean the blood, nor set the fractured bone;
Yet many a man is making friends with death
Even as I speak, for lack of love alone.

It well may be that in a difficult hour,
Pinned down by pain and moaning for release,   10
Or nagged by want past resolution's power,
I might be driven to sell your love for peace,
Or trade the memory of this night for food.
It well may be. I do not think I would.

—*1931*

Questions: Reading, Responding, Arguing

1. How does Millay use negative metaphors to make her point?
2. Does the poem have an auditor? If so, who is it?
3. What is ironic about the decision that the speaker makes at the end of the poem? Argue that the poem prepares the reader for this turn.

Theodore Roethke (1908–1963)

My Papa's Waltz*

The whiskey on your breath
Could make a small boy dizzy;
But I hung on like death:
Such waltzing was not easy.

We romped until the pans   5
Slid from the kitchen shelf;
My mother's countenance
Could not unfrown itself.

The hand that held my wrist
Was battered on one knuckle;   10
At every step you missed
My right ear scraped a buckle.

You beat time on my head
With a palm caked hard by dirt,
Then waltzed me off to bed   15
Still clinging to your shirt.

—*1948*

Questions: Reading, Responding, Arguing

1. What is the "waltz" Roethke's speaker refers to? Why does Roethke choose the word "waltz"?
2. How does Roethke convey the nature of the relationship between the boy and his father and the boy and his mother?
3. How do tone and diction help Roethke advance the poem's central image?
4. Some readers have argued that this poem describes an abusive relationship. What details in the poem support or deny this assertion?

Elizabeth Bishop (1911–1979)

One Art[*]

The art of losing isn't hard to master;
so many things seem filled with the intent
to be lost that their loss is no disaster.

Lose something every day. Accept the fluster
of lost door keys, the hour badly spent.   5
The art of losing isn't hard to master.

Then practice losing farther, losing faster:
places, and names, and where it was you meant
to travel. None of these will bring disaster.

I lost my mother's watch. And look! my last, or   10
next-to-last, of three loved houses went.
The art of losing isn't hard to master.

I lost two cities, lovely ones. And, vaster,
some realms I owned, two rivers, a continent.
I miss them, but it wasn't a disaster.   15

—Even losing you (the joking voice, a gesture
I love) I shan't have lied. It's evident
the art of losing's not too hard to master
though it may look like *(Write* it!) like disaster.

—*1976*

Questions: Reading, Responding, Arguing

1. Describe the speaker's attitude toward the "you." How is this loss related to other losses?
2. In the final stanza, Bishop uses a long dash and two sets of parentheses. Why does she use these only in her final stanzas?
3. What is Bishop's speaker saying about loss and losing? Argue that the theme of *art* is as important as the theme of loss.

Robert Hayden   (1913–1980)

Those Winter Sundays

Sundays too my father got up early
and put his clothes on in the blueblack cold,
then with cracked hands that ached
from labor in the weekday weather made
banked fires blaze. No one ever thanked him.   5

I'd wake and hear the cold splintering, breaking.
When the rooms were warm, he'd call,
and slowly I would rise and dress,
fearing the chronic angers of that house,

Speaking indifferently to him,   10
who had driven out the cold
and polished my good shoes as well.
What did I know, what did I know
of love's austere and lonely offices?°

—*1962*

---

14 offices daily religious ceremonies

Questions: Reading, Responding, Arguing

1. Which of Hayden's adjectives and adverbs contribute most to the poem's themes and ideas? How?
2. What is meant by the phrase "love's austere and lonely offices"?
3. Describe Hayden's treatment of the father/child relationship. What words in the poem help to characterize it? How does his use of past tense affect the poem?

Alan Dugan (1923–2003)

Love Song: I and Thou

Nothing is plumb, level or square:
   the studs are bowed, the joists
are shaky by nature, no piece fits
   any other piece without a gap
or pinch, and bent nails   5
   dance all over the surfacing
like maggots. By Christ
   I am no carpenter. I built
the roof for myself, the walls
   for myself, the floors   10
for myself, and got
   hung up in it myself. I
danced with a purple thumb
   at this house-warming, drunk
with my prime whiskey: rage.   15
   Oh I spat rage's nails
into the frame-up of my work:
   it held. It settled plumb,
level, solid, square and true
   for that great moment. Then   20
it screamed and went on through,
   skewing as wrong the other way.

God damned it. This is hell,
    but I planned it, I sawed it,
I nailed it, and I 25
    will live in it until it kills me.
I can nail my left palm
    to the left-hand cross-piece but
I can't do everything myself.
    I need a hand to nail the right, 30
a help, a love, a you, a wife.

—*1961*

Questions: Reading, Responding, Arguing

1. Explain how Dugan uses the metaphors of carpentry. What ideas does he convey?
2. What is Dugan's speaker saying about the "structure" he built?
3. How is this a "love song"? Connect and compare this poem with other love songs in this anthology. Do they offer different or similar insights into of the nature of "Love"? Of love songs?

Margaret Atwood (b. 1939)

Siren° Song

This is the one song everyone
would like to learn: the song
that is irresistible:

the song that forces men
to leap overboard in squadrons
even though they see the beached skulls 5

the song nobody knows
because anyone who has heard it
is dead, and the others can't remember.

Siren in Greek myth, one of the women whose irresistible song lured sailors onto the rocks

Shall I tell you the secret   10
and if I do, will you get me
out of this bird suit?

I don't enjoy it here
squatting on this island
looking picturesque and mythical   15

with these two feathery maniacs,
I don't enjoy singing
this trio, fatal and valuable.

I will tell the secret to you,
to you, only to you.   20
Come closer. This song

is a cry for help: Help me!
Only you, only you can,
you are unique

at last. Alas   25
it is a boring song
but it works every time.

—1974

Questions: Reading, Responding, Arguing

1. What is a Siren? What is the significance of a siren song?
   How does Atwood use this allusion for her own purposes?
2. Who is the "I"? What clues does Atwood give us about the
   "I's" identity?
3. Why does the song "work every time"? What is the secret?
4. Construct an argument that this poem is an example of feminist satire and compare it to Piercy's "What's That Smell in
   the Kitchen?" (p. 597).

Diane Lockward (b. 1943)

My Husband Discovers Poetry

Because my husband would not read my poems,
I wrote one about how I did not love him.
In lines of strict iambic pentameter,
I detailed his coldness, his lack of humor.
It felt good to do this.   5

Stanza by stanza, I grew bolder and bolder.
Towards the end, struck by inspiration,
I wrote about my old boyfriend,
a boy I had not loved enough to marry
but who could make me laugh and laugh.   10
I wrote about a night years after we parted
when my husband's coldness drove me from the house
and back to my old boyfriend.
I even included the name of a seedy motel
well-known for hosting quickies.   15
I have a talent for verisimilitude.

In sensuous images, I described
how my boyfriend and I stripped off our clothes,
got into bed, and kissed and kissed,
then spent half the night telling jokes,   20
many of them about my husband.
I left the ending deliberately ambiguous,
then hid the poem away
in an old trunk in the basement.

You know how this story ends,   25
how my husband one day loses something,
goes into the basement,
and rummages through the old trunk,
how he uncovers the hidden poem
and sits down to read it.   30

But do you hear the strange sounds
that floated up the stairs that day,
the sounds of an animal, its paw caught
in one of those traps with teeth of steel?
Do you see the wounded creature   35
at the bottom of the stairs,
his shoulders hunched over and shaking,
fist in his mouth and choking back sobs?
It was my husband paying tribute to my art.

                                                —*2003*

Questions: Reading, Responding, Arguing

1. How closely should we identify the poet with the poem's
   persona?
2. This is actually a poem about another poem, one that may
   or may not exist. Explain.
3. If Lockward has said that this poem is her "real" husband's
   favorite, argue that her statement should influence the way
   we read her involvement with the poem's situation.

Dave Morice (b. 1946)

William Shakespeare's "Sonnet 130"*

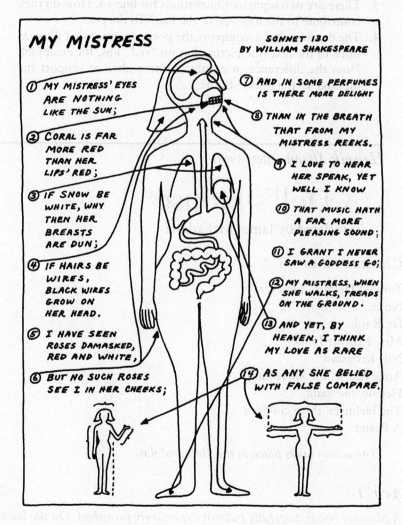

—2002

Questions: Reading, Responding, Arguing

1. How does the graphic content correspond to the details of the poem?
2. When line 6 refers to "cheeks," arrows in the illustration point to two separate areas. Why? How does this relate to the overall theme of the poem?
3. There are two separate illustrations for line 14. How do they contribute to the message of the line? To the poem?
4. The pictures that accompany the poem are not exact illustrations of the text (the picture has no "red" lips, for example). Does the difference in graphic content alter or support the message of the poem? Both?

Henrik Ibsen (1828–1906)

A Doll's House

Translated by James McFarlane

CHARACTERS

Torvald Helmer, *a lawyer*
Nora, *his wife*
Dr. Rank
Mrs. Kristine Linde
Nils Krogstad
Anne Marie, *the nursemaid*
Helene, *the maid*
The Helmers' three children
A Porter

The action takes place in the Helmers' flat.

ACT I

A pleasant room, tastefully but not expensively furnished. On the back wall, one door on the right leads to the entrance hall, a second door on the left leads to Helmer's study. Between these two doors, a piano. In the middle of the left wall, a door; and downstage from it, a window. Near the window a round table with armchairs and a small sofa. In the right wall, upstage, a door; and on the same wall downstage, a porcelain stove with a couple of armchairs and a rocking chair. Between the stove and the door a small table. Etchings on the walls. A whatnot with china and other small objets d'art; a small bookcase with books in handsome bindings. Carpet on the floor; a fire burns in the stove. A winter's day.

The front door-bell rings in the hall; a moment later, there is the sound of the front door being opened. Nora comes into the room, happily humming to herself. She is dressed in her outdoor things, and is carrying lots of parcels which she then puts down on the table, right. She leaves the door into the hall standing open; a Porter can be seen outside holding a Christmas tree and a basket; he hands them to the Maid who has opened the door for them.

NORA: Hide the Christmas tree away carefully, Helene. The children mustn't see it till this evening when it's decorated. [*To the Porter, taking out her purse.*] How much?
PORTER: Fifty öre.
NORA: There's a crown. Keep the change.

[*The Porter thanks her and goes. Nora shuts the door. She continues to laugh quietly and happily to herself as she takes off her things. She takes a bag of macaroons out of her pocket and eats one or two; then she walks stealthily across and listens at her husband's door.*]

NORA: Yes, he's in.

[*She begins humming again as she walks over to the table, right.*]

HELMER [*in his study*]: Is that my little sky-lark chirruping out there?
NORA [*busy opening some of the parcels*]: Yes, it is.
HELMER: Is that my little squirrel frisking about?
NORA: Yes!
HELMER: When did my little squirrel get home?
NORA: Just this minute. [*She stuffs the bag of macaroons in her pocket and wipes her mouth.*] Come on out, Torvald, and see what I've bought.
HELMER: I don't want to be disturbed! [*A moment later, he opens the door and looks out, his pen in his hand.*] 'Bought', did you

say? All that? Has my little spendthrift been out squandering money again?

NORA: But, Torvald, surely this year we can spread ourselves just a little. This is the first Christmas we haven't had to go carefully.

HELMER: Ah, but that doesn't mean we can afford to be extravagant, you know.

NORA: Oh yes, Torvald, surely we can afford to be just a little bit extravagant now, can't we? Just a teeny-weeny bit. You are getting quite a good salary now, and you are going to earn lots and lots of money.

HELMER: Yes, after the New Year. But it's going to be three whole months before the first pay cheque comes in.

NORA: Pooh! We can always borrow in the meantime.

HELMER: Nora! [*Crosses to her and takes her playfully by the ear.*] Here we go again, you and your frivolous ideas! Suppose I went and borrowed a thousand crowns today, and you went and spent it all over Christmas, then on New Year's Eve a slate fell and hit me on the head and there I was. . . .

NORA [*putting her hand over his mouth*]: Sh! Don't say such horrid things.

HELMER: Yes, but supposing something like that did happen . . . what then?

NORA: If anything as awful as that did happen, I wouldn't care if I owed anybody anything or not.

HELMER: Yes, but what about the people I'd borrowed from?

NORA: Them? Who cares about them! They are only strangers!

HELMER: Nora, Nora! Just like a woman! Seriously though, Nora, you know what I think about these things. No debts! Never borrow! There's always something inhibited, something unpleasant, about a home built on credit and borrowed money. We two have managed to stick it out so far, and that's the way we'll go on for the little time that remains.

NORA [*walks over to the stove*]: Very well, just as you say, Torvald.

HELMER [*following her*]: There, there! My little singing bird mustn't go drooping her wings, eh? Has it got the sulks, that little squirrel of mine? [*Takes out his wallet.*] Nora, what do you think I've got here?

NORA [*quickly turning round*]: Money!

HELMER: There! [*He hands her some notes*]. Good heavens, I know only too well how Christmas runs away with the housekeeping.

NORA [*counts*]: Ten, twenty, thirty, forty. Oh, thank you, thank you, Torvald! This will see me quite a long way.

HELMER: Yes, it'll have to.

NORA: Yes, yes, I'll see that it does. But come over here, I want to show you all the things I've bought. And so cheap! Look, some new clothes for Ivar . . . and a little sword. There's a horse and a trumpet for Bob. And a doll and a doll's cot for Emmy. They are not very grand but she'll have them all broken before long anyway. And I've got some dress material and some handkerchiefs for the maids. Though, really, dear old Anne Marie should have had something better.

HELMER: And what's in this parcel here?

NORA [shrieking]: No, Torvald! You mustn't see that till tonight!

HELMER: All right. But tell me now, what did my little spendthrift fancy for herself?

NORA: For me? Puh, I don't really want anything.

HELMER: Of course you do. Anything reasonable that you think you might like, just tell me.

NORA: Well, I don't really know. As a matter of fact, though, Torvald . . .

HELMER: Well?

NORA [toying with his coat buttons, and without looking at him]: If you did want to give me something, you could . . . you could always . . .

HELMER: Well, well, out with it!

NORA [quickly]: You could always give me money, Torvald. Only what you think you could spare. And then I could buy myself something with it later on.

HELMER: But Nora. . . .

NORA: Oh, please, Torvald dear! Please! I beg you. Then I'd wrap the money up in some pretty gilt paper and hang it on the Christmas tree. Wouldn't that be fun?

HELMER: What do we call my pretty little pet when it runs away with all the money?

NORA: I know, I know, we call it a spendthrift. But please let's do what I said, Torvald. Then I'll have a bit of time to think about what I need most. Isn't that awfully sensible, now, eh?

HELMER [smiling]: Yes, it is indeed—that is, if only you really could hold on to the money I gave you, and really did buy something for yourself with it. But it just gets mixed up with the housekeeping and frittered away on all sorts of useless things, and then I have to dig into my pocket all over again.

NORA: Oh but, Torvald. . . .

HELMER: You can't deny it, Nora dear. [*Puts his arm round her waist.*] My pretty little pet is very sweet, but it runs away with an awful lot of money. It's incredible how expensive it is for a man to keep such a pet.

NORA: For shame! How can you say such a thing? As a matter of fact I save everything I can.

HELMER [*laughs*]: Yes, you are right there. Everything you *can*. But you simply can't.

NORA [*hums and smiles quietly and happily*]: Ah, if you only knew how many expenses the likes of us sky-larks and squirrels have, Torvald!

HELMER: What a funny little one you are! Just like your father. Always on the look-out for money, wherever you can lay your hands on it; but as soon as you've got it, it just seems to slip through your fingers. You never seem to know what you've done with it. Well, one must accept you as you are. It's in the blood. Oh yes, it is, Nora. That sort of thing is hereditary.

NORA: Oh, I only wish I'd inherited a few more of Daddy's qualities.

HELMER: And I wouldn't want my pretty little song-bird to be the least bit different from what she is now. But come to think of it, you look rather . . . rather . . . how shall I put it? . . . rather guilty today. . . .

NORA: Do I?

HELMER: Yes, you do indeed. Look me straight in the eye.

NORA [*looks at him*]: Well?

HELMER [*wagging his finger at her*]: My little sweet-tooth surely didn't forget herself in town today?

NORA: No, whatever makes you think that?

HELMER: She didn't just pop into the confectioner's for a moment?

NORA: No, I assure you, Torvald . . . !

HELMER: Didn't try sampling the preserves?

NORA: No, really I didn't.

HELMER: Didn't go nibbling a macaroon or two?

NORA: No, Torvald, honestly, you must believe me . . . !

HELMER: All right then! It's really just my little joke. . . .

NORA [*crosses to the table*]: I would never dream of doing anything you didn't want me to.

HELMER: Of course not, I know that. And then you've given me your word. . . . [*Crosses to her.*] Well then, Nora dearest, you shall keep your little Christmas secrets. They'll all come out tonight, I dare say, when we light the tree.

NORA: Did you remember to invite Dr. Rank?

HELMER: No. But there's really no need. Of course he'll come and have dinner with us. Anyway, I can ask him when he looks in this morning. I've ordered some good wine. Nora, you can't imagine how I am looking forward to this evening.

NORA: So am I. And won't the children enjoy it, Torvald!

HELMER: Oh, what a glorious feeling it is, knowing you've got a nice, safe job, and a good fat income. Don't you agree? Isn't it wonderful, just thinking about it?

NORA: Oh, it's marvellous!

HELMER: Do you remember last Christmas? Three whole weeks beforehand you shut yourself up every evening till after midnight making flowers for the Christmas tree and all the other splendid things you wanted to surprise us with. Ugh, I never felt so bored in all my life.

NORA: I wasn't the least bit bored.

HELMER [smiling]: But it turned out a bit of an anticlimax, Nora.

NORA: Oh, you are not going to tease me about that again! How was I to know the cat would get in and pull everything to bits?

HELMER: No, of course you weren't. Poor little Nora! All you wanted was for us to have a nice time—and it's the thought behind it that counts, after all. All the same, it's a good thing we've seen the back of those lean times.

NORA: Yes, really it's marvellous.

HELMER: Now there's no need for me to sit here all on my own, bored to tears. And you don't have to strain your dear little eyes, and work those dainty little fingers to the bone. . . .

NORA [clapping her hands]: No, Torvald, I don't, do I? Not any more. Oh, how marvellous it is to hear that! [Takes his arm.] Now I want to tell you how I've been thinking we might arrange things, Torvald. As soon as Christmas is over. . . . [The door-bell rings in the hall.] Oh, there's the bell. [Tidies one or two things in the room.] It's probably a visitor. What a nuisance!

HELMER: Remember I'm not at home to callers.

MAID [in the doorway]: There's a lady to see you, ma'am.

NORA: Show her in, please.

MAID [to Helmer]: And the doctor's just arrived, too, sir.

HELMER: Did he go straight into my room?

MAID: Yes, he did, sir.

[*Helmer goes into his study. The Maid shows in Mrs. Linde, who is in travelling clothes, and closes the door after her.*]

MRS. LINDE [*subdued and rather hesitantly*]:   How do you do, Nora?

NORA [*uncertainly*]:   How do you do?

MRS. LINDE: I'm afraid you don't recognize me.

NORA: No, I don't think I . . . And yet I seem to. . . . [*Bursts out suddenly.*] Why! Kristine! Is it really you?

MRS. LINDE: Yes, it's me.

NORA: Kristine! Fancy not recognizing you again! But how was I to, when . . . [*Gently.*] How you've changed, Kristine!

MRS. LINDE: I dare say I have. In nine . . . ten years. . . .

NORA: Is it so long since we last saw each other? Yes, it must be. Oh, believe me these last eight years have been such a happy time. And now you've come up to town, too? All that long journey in wintertime. That took courage.

MRS. LINDE: I just arrived this morning on the steamer.

NORA: To enjoy yourself over Christmas, of course. How lovely! Oh, we'll have such fun, you'll see. Do take off your things. You are not cold, are you? [*Helps her.*] There now! Now let's sit down here in comfort beside the stove. No, here, you take the armchair, I'll sit here on the rocking chair. [*Takes her hands.*] Ah, now you look a bit more like your old self again. It was just that when I first saw you. . . . But you are a little paler, Kristine . . . and perhaps even a bit thinner!

MRS. LINDE: And much, much older, Nora.

NORA: Yes, perhaps a little older . . . very, very little, not really very much. [*Stops suddenly and looks serious.*] Oh, what a thoughtless creature I am, sitting here chattering on like this! Dear, sweet Kristine, can you forgive me?

MRS. LINDE: What do you mean, Nora?

NORA [*gently*]:   Poor Kristine, of course you're a widow now.

MRS. LINDE: Yes, my husband died three years ago.

NORA: Oh, I remember now. I read about it in the papers. Oh, Kristine, believe me I often thought at the time of writing to you. But I kept putting it off, something always seemed to crop up.

MRS. LINDE: My dear Nora, I understand so well.

NORA: No, it wasn't very nice of me, Kristine. Oh, you poor thing, what you must have gone through. And didn't he leave you anything?

MRS. LINDE: No.

NORA: And no children?

MRS. LINDE: No.

NORA: Absolutely nothing?

MRS. LINDE: Nothing at all . . . not even a broken heart to grieve over.

NORA [looks at her incredulously]: But, Kristine, is that possible?

MRS. LINDE [smiles sadly and strokes Nora's hair]: Oh, it sometimes happens, Nora.

NORA: So utterly alone. How terribly sad that must be for you. I have three lovely children. You can't see them for the moment, because they're out with their nanny. But now you must tell me all about yourself. . . .

MRS. LINDE: No, no, I want to hear about you.

NORA: No, you start. I won't be selfish today. I must think only about your affairs today. But there's just one thing I really must tell you. Have you heard about the great stroke of luck we've had in the last few days?

MRS. LINDE: No. What is it?

NORA: What do you think? My husband has just been made Bank Manager!

MRS. LINDE: Your husband? How splendid!

NORA: Isn't it tremendous! It's not a very steady way of making a living, you know, being a lawyer, especially if he refuses to take on anything that's the least bit shady—which of course is what Torvald does, and I think he's quite right. You can imagine how pleased we are! He starts at the Bank straight after New Year, and he's getting a big salary and lots of commission. From now on we'll be able to live quite differently . . . we'll do just what we want. Oh, Kristine, I'm so happy and relieved. I must say it's lovely to have plenty of money and not have to worry. Isn't it?

MRS. LINDE: Yes. It must be nice to have enough, at any rate.

NORA: No, not just enough, but pots and pots of money.

MRS. LINDE [smiles]: Nora, Nora, haven't you learned any sense yet? At school you used to be an awful spendthrift.

NORA: Yes, Torvald still says I am. [Wags her finger.] But little Nora isn't as stupid as everybody thinks. Oh, we haven't really been in a position where I could afford to spend a lot of money. We've both had to work.

MRS. LINDE: You too?

NORA: Yes, odd jobs—sewing, crochet-work, embroidery and things like that. [Casually.] And one or two other things, besides. I suppose you know that Torvald left the Ministry when we got married. There weren't any prospects of promotion in his department, and of course he needed to earn more money than he had before. But the first year he wore himself out completely. He had to take on all kinds of extra jobs, you know, and he found himself working all hours of the day and night. But he couldn't go on like that; and he became seriously ill. The doctors said it was essential for him to go South.

MRS. LINDE: Yes, I believe you spent a whole year in Italy, didn't you?

NORA: That's right. It wasn't easy to get away, I can tell you. It was just after I'd had Ivar. But of course we had to go. Oh, it was an absolutely marvellous trip. And it saved Torvald's life. But it cost an awful lot of money, Kristine.

MRS. LINDE: That I can well imagine.

NORA: Twelve hundred dollars. Four thousand eight hundred crowns. That's a lot of money, Kristine.

MRS. LINDE: Yes, but in such circumstances, one is very lucky if one has it.

NORA: Well, we got it from Daddy, you see.

MRS. LINDE: Ah, that was it. It was just about then your father died, I believe, wasn't it?

NORA: Yes, Kristine, just about then. And do you know, I couldn't even go and look after him. Here was I expecting Ivar any day. And I also had poor Torvald, gravely ill, on my hands. Dear, kind Daddy! I never saw him again, Kristine. Oh, that's the saddest thing that has happened to me in all my married life.

MRS. LINDE: I know you were very fond of him. But after that you left for Italy?

NORA: Yes, we had the money then, and the doctors said it was urgent. We left a month later.

MRS. LINDE: And your husband came back completely cured?

NORA: Fit as a fiddle!

MRS. LINDE: But . . . what about the doctor?

NORA: How do you mean?

MRS. LINDE: I thought the maid said something about the gentleman who came at the same time as me being a doctor.

NORA: Yes, that was Dr. Rank. But this isn't a professional visit. He's our best friend and he always looks in at least once a day. No, Torvald has never had a day's illness since. And the children are fit and healthy, and so am I. [*Jumps up and claps her hands.*] Oh God,

oh God, isn't it marvellous to be alive, and to be happy, Kristine!
. . . Oh, but I ought to be ashamed of myself . . . Here I go on talking
about nothing but myself. [*She sits on a low stool near Mrs. Linde
and lays her arms on her lap.*] Oh, please, you mustn't be angry
with me! Tell me, is it really true that you didn't love your husband? What made you marry him, then?

MRS. LINDE: My mother was still alive; she was bedridden and helpless. And then I had my two young brothers to look after as well. I
didn't think I would be justified in refusing him.

NORA: No, I dare say you are right. I suppose he was fairly wealthy
then?

MRS. LINDE: He was quite well off, I believe. But the business was
shaky. When he died, it went all to pieces, and there just wasn't
anything left.

NORA: What then?

MRS. LINDE: Well, I had to fend for myself, opening a little shop, running a little school, anything I could turn my hand to. These last
three years have been one long relentless drudge. But now it's finished, Nora. My poor dear mother doesn't need me any more, she's
passed away. Nor the boys either; they're at work now, they can
look after themselves.

NORA: What a relief you must find it. . . .

MRS. LINDE: No, Nora! Just unutterably empty. Nobody to live for
any more. [*Stands up restlessly.*] That's why I couldn't stand it any
longer being cut off up there. Surely it must be a bit easier here to
find something to occupy your mind. If only I could manage to find
a steady job of some kind, in an office perhaps. . . .

NORA: But, Kristine, that's terribly exhausting; and you look so worn
out even before you start. The best thing for you would be a little
holiday at some quiet little resort.

MRS. LINDE [*crosses to the window*]: I haven't any father I can fall
back on for the money, Nora.

NORA [*rises*]: Oh, please, you mustn't be angry with me!

MRS. LINDE [*goes to her*]: My dear Nora, you mustn't be angry with
me either. That's the worst thing about people in my position, they
become so bitter. One has nobody to work for, yet one has to be
on the look-out all the time. Life has to go on, and one starts
thinking only of oneself. Believe it or not, when you told me the
good news about your step up, I was pleased not so much for your
sake as for mine.

NORA: How do you mean? Ah, I see. You think Torvald might be able to do something for you.

MRS. LINDE: Yes, that's exactly what I thought.

NORA: And so he shall, Kristine. Just leave things to me. I'll bring it up so cleverly . . . I'll think up something to put him in a good mood. Oh, I do so much want to help you.

MRS. LINDE: It is awfully kind of you, Nora, offering to do all this for me, particularly in your case, where you haven't known much trouble or hardship in your own life.

NORA: When I . . . ? I haven't known much . . . ?

MRS. LINDE [*smiling*]: Well, good heavens, a little bit of sewing to do and a few things like that. What a child you are, Nora!

NORA [*tosses her head and walks across the room*]: I wouldn't be too sure of that, if I were you.

MRS. LINDE: Oh?

NORA: You're just like the rest of them. You all think I'm useless when it comes to anything really serious. . . .

MRS. LINDE: Come, come. . . .

NORA: You think I've never had anything much to contend with in this hard world.

MRS. LINDE: Nora dear, you've only just been telling me all the things you've had to put up with.

NORA: Pooh! They were just trivialities! [*Softly.*] I haven't told you about the really big thing.

MRS. LINDE: What big thing? What do you mean?

NORA: I know you rather tend to look down on me, Kristine. But you shouldn't, you know. You are proud of having worked so hard and so long for your mother.

MRS. LINDE: I'm sure I don't look down on anybody. But it's true what you say: I am both proud and happy when I think of how I was able to make Mother's life a little easier towards the end.

NORA: And you are proud when you think of what you have done for your brothers, too.

MRS. LINDE: I think I have every right to be.

NORA: I think so too. But now I'm going to tell you something, Kristine. I too have something to be proud and happy about.

MRS. LINDE: I don't doubt that. But what is it you mean?

NORA: Not so loud. Imagine if Torvald were to hear! He must never on any account . . . nobody must know about it, Kristine, nobody but you.

MRS. LINDE: But what is it?

NORA: Come over here. [*She pulls her down on the sofa beside her.*] Yes, Kristine, I too have something to be proud and happy about. I was the one who saved Torvald's life.

MRS. LINDE: Saved . . . ? How . . . ?

NORA: I told you about our trip to Italy. Torvald would never have recovered but for that. . . .

MRS. LINDE: Well? Your father gave you what money was necessary. . . .

NORA [*smiles*]: That's what Torvald thinks, and everybody else. But . . .

MRS. LINDE: But . . . ?

NORA: Daddy never gave us a penny. I was the one who raised the money.

MRS. LINDE: You? All that money?

NORA: Twelve hundred dollars. Four thousand eight hundred crowns. What do you say to that!

MRS. LINDE: But, Nora, how was it possible? Had you won a sweepstake or something?

NORA [*contemptuously*]: A sweepstake? Pooh! There would have been nothing to it then.

MRS. LINDE: Where did you get it from, then?

NORA [*hums and smiles secretively*]: H'm, tra-la-la!

MRS. LINDE: Because what you couldn't do was borrow it.

NORA: Oh? Why not?

MRS. LINDE: Well, a wife can't borrow without her husband's consent.

NORA [*tossing her head*]: Ah, but when it happens to be a wife with a bit of a sense for business . . . a wife who knows her way about things, then. . . .

MRS. LINDE: But, Nora, I just don't understand. . . .

NORA: You don't have to. I haven't said I did borrow the money. I might have got it some other way. [*Throws herself back on the sofa.*] I might even have got it from some admirer. Anyone as reasonably attractive as I am. . . .

MRS. LINDE: Don't be so silly!

NORA: Now you must be dying of curiosity, Kristine.

MRS. LINDE: Listen to me now, Nora dear—you haven't done anything rash, have you?

NORA [*sitting up again*]: Is it rash to save your husband's life?

MRS. LINDE: I think it was rash to do anything without telling him. . . .

NORA: But the whole point was that he mustn't know anything. Good heavens, can't you see! He wasn't even supposed to know how desperately ill he was. It was me the doctors came and told his life was in danger, that the only way to save him was to go South for a while. Do you think I didn't try talking him into it first? I began dropping hints about how nice it would be if I could be taken on a little trip abroad, like other young wives. I wept, I pleaded. I told him he ought to show some consideration for my condition, and let me have a bit of my own way. And then I suggested he might take out a loan. But at that he nearly lost his temper, Kristine. He said I was being frivolous, that it was his duty as a husband not to give in to all these whims and fancies of mine—as I do believe he called them. All right, I thought, somehow you've got to be saved. And it was then I found a way. . . .

MRS. LINDE: Did your husband never find out from your father that the money hadn't come from him?

NORA: No, never. It was just about the time Daddy died. I'd intended letting him into the secret and asking him not to give me away. But when he was so ill . . . I'm sorry to say it never became necessary.

MRS. LINDE: And you never confided in your husband?

NORA: Good heavens, how could you ever imagine such a thing! When he's so strict about such matters! Besides, Torvald is a man with a good deal of pride—it would be terribly embarrassing and humiliating for him if he thought he owed anything to me. It would spoil everything between us; this happy home of ours would never be the same again.

MRS. LINDE: Are you never going to tell him?

NORA [*reflectively, half-smiling*]: Oh yes, some day perhaps . . . in many years time, when I'm no longer as pretty as I am now. You mustn't laugh! What I mean of course is when Torvald isn't quite so much in love with me as he is now, when he's lost interest in watching me dance, or get dressed up, or recite. Then it might be a good thing to have something in reserve. . . . [*Breaks off.*] What nonsense! That day will never come. Well, what have you got to say to my big secret, Kristine? Still think I'm not much good for anything? One thing, though, it's meant a lot of worry for me, I can tell you. It hasn't always been easy to meet my obligations when the time came. You know in business there is something called quarterly interest, and other things called instalments, and these are always terribly difficult things to cope with. So what I've had to do is save a little here and there, you see, wherever I could. I couldn't really save anything out of the housekeeping, because Torvald has to live in decent style. I couldn't let the children go about badly dressed either—I felt any money I got for them had to go on them alone. Such sweet little things!

MRS. LINDE: Poor Nora! So it had to come out of your own allowance?

NORA: Of course. After all, I was the one it concerned most. Whenever Torvald gave me money for new clothes and suchlike, I never spent more than half. And always I bought the simplest and cheapest things. It's a blessing most things look well on me, so Torvald never noticed anything. But sometimes I did feel it was a bit hard, Kristine, because it is nice to be well dressed, isn't it?

MRS. LINDE: Yes, I suppose it is.

NORA: I have had some other sources of income, of course. Last winter I was lucky enough to get quite a bit of copying to do. So I shut myself up every night and sat and wrote through to the small hours of the morning. Oh, sometimes I was so tired, so tired. But it was tremendous fun all the same, sitting there working and earning money like that. It was almost like being a man.

MRS. LINDE: And how much have you been able to pay off like this?

NORA: Well, I can't tell exactly. It's not easy to know where you are with transactions of this kind, you understand. All I know is I've paid off just as much as I could scrape together. Many's the time I was at my wit's end. [*Smiles.*] Then I used to sit here and pretend that some rich old gentleman had fallen in love with me. . . .

MRS. LINDE: What! What gentleman?

NORA: Oh, rubbish! . . . and that now he had died, and when they opened his will, there in big letters were the words: 'My entire fortune is to be paid over, immediately and in cash, to charming Mrs. Nora Helmer.'

MRS. LINDE: But my dear Nora—who is this man?

NORA: Good heavens, don't you understand? There never was any old gentleman; it was just something I used to sit here pretending, time and time again, when I didn't know where to turn next for money. But it doesn't make very much difference; as far as I'm concerned, the old boy can do what he likes, I'm tired of him; I can't be bothered any more with him or his will. Because now all my worries are over. [*Jumping up.*] Oh God, what a glorious thought, Kristine! No more worries! Just think of being without a care in the world . . . being able to romp with the children, and making the house nice and attractive, and having things just as Torvald likes to have them! And then spring will soon be here, and blue skies. And maybe we can go away somewhere. I might even see something of the sea again. Oh yes! When you're happy, life is a wonderful thing!

[*The door-bell is heard in the hall.*]

MRS. LINDE [*gets up*]: There's the bell. Perhaps I'd better go.

NORA: No, do stay, please. I don't suppose it's for me; it's probably somebody for Torvald. . . .

MAID [*in the doorway*]: Excuse me, ma'am, but there's a gentleman here wants to see Mr. Helmer, and I didn't quite know . . . because the Doctor is in there. . . .

NORA: Who is the gentleman?

KROGSTAD [*in the doorway*]: It's me, Mrs. Helmer.

[*Mrs. Linde starts, then turns away to the window.*]

NORA [*tense, takes a step towards him and speaks in a low voice*]: You? What is it? What do you want to talk to my husband about?

KROGSTAD: Bank matters . . . in a manner of speaking. I work at the bank, and I hear your husband is to be the new manager. . . .

NORA: So it's . . .

KROGSTAD: Just routine business matters, Mrs. Helmer. Absolutely nothing else.

NORA: Well then, please go into his study.

[*She nods impassively and shuts the hall door behind him; then she walks across and sees to the stove.*]

MRS. LINDE: Nora . . . who was that man?

NORA: His name is Krogstad.

MRS. LINDE: So it really was him.

NORA: Do you know the man?

MRS. LINDE: I used to know him . . . a good many years ago. He was a solicitor's clerk in our district for a while.

NORA: Yes, so he was.

MRS. LINDE: How he's changed!

NORA: His marriage wasn't a very happy one, I believe.

MRS. LINDE: He's a widower now, isn't he?

NORA: With a lot of children. There, it'll burn better now.

[*She closes the stove door and moves the rocking chair a little to one side.*]

MRS. LINDE: He does a certain amount of business on the side, they say?

NORA: Oh? Yes, it's always possible. I just don't know. . . . But let's not think about business . . . it's all so dull.

[*Dr. Rank comes in from Helmer's study.*]

DR. RANK [*still in the doorway*]: No, no, Torvald, I won't intrude. I'll just look in on your wife for a moment. [*Shuts the door and notices Mrs. Linde.*] Oh, I beg your pardon. I'm afraid I'm intruding here as well.

NORA: No, not at all! [*Introduces them.*] Dr. Rank . . . Mrs. Linde.

RANK: Ah! A name I've often heard mentioned in this house. I believe I came past you on the stairs as I came in.

MRS. LINDE: I have to take things slowly going upstairs. I find it rather a trial.

RANK: Ah, some little disability somewhere, eh?

MRS. LINDE: Just a bit run down, I think, actually.

RANK: Is that all? Then I suppose you've come to town for a good rest—doing the rounds of the parties?

MRS. LINDE: I have come to look for work.

RANK: Is that supposed to be some kind of sovereign remedy for being run down?

MRS. LINDE: One must live, Doctor.

RANK: Yes, it's generally thought to be necessary.

NORA: Come, come, Dr. Rank. You are quite as keen to live as anybody.

RANK: Quite keen, yes. Miserable as I am, I'm quite ready to let things drag on as long as possible. All my patients are the same. Even those with a moral affliction are no different. As a matter of fact, there's a bad case of that kind in talking with Helmer at this very moment. . . .

MRS. LINDE [*softly*]: Ah!

NORA: Whom do you mean?

RANK: A person called Krogstad—nobody you would know. He's rotten to the core. But even he began talking about having to *live*, as though it were something terribly important.

NORA: Oh? And what did he want to talk to Torvald about?

RANK: I honestly don't know. All I heard was something about the Bank.

NORA: I didn't know that Krog . . . that this Mr. Krogstad had anything to do with the Bank.

RANK: Oh yes, he's got some kind of job down there. [*To Mrs. Linde.*] I wonder if you've got people in your part of the country too who go rushing round sniffing out cases of moral corruption, and then installing the individuals concerned in nice, well-paid jobs where they can keep them under observation. Sound, decent people have to be content to stay out in the cold.

MRS. LINDE: Yet surely it's the sick who most need to be brought in.

RANK [*shrugs his shoulders*]: Well, there we have it. It's that attitude that's turning society into a clinic.

[*Nora, lost in her own thoughts, breaks into smothered laughter and claps her hands.*]

RANK: Why are you laughing at that? Do you know in fact what society is?

NORA: What do I care about your silly old society? I was laughing about something quite different . . . something frightfully funny. Tell me, Dr. Rank, are all the people who work at the Bank dependent on Torvald now?

RANK: Is that what you find so frightfully funny?

NORA [*smiles and hums*]: Never you mind! Never you mind! [*Walks about the room.*] Yes, it really is terribly amusing to think that we . . . that Torvald now has power over so many people. [*She takes the bag out of her pocket.*] Dr. Rank, what about a little macaroon?

RANK: Look at this, eh? Macaroons. I thought they were forbidden here.

NORA: Yes, but these are some Kristine gave me.

MRS. LINDE: What? I . . . ?

NORA: Now, now, you needn't be alarmed. You weren't to know that Torvald had forbidden them. He's worried in case they ruin my teeth, you know. Still . . . what's it matter once in a while! Don't you think so, Dr. Rank? Here! [*She pops a macaroon into his mouth.*] And you too, Kristine. And I shall have one as well; just a little one . . . or two at the most. [*She walks about the room again.*] Really I am so happy. There's just one little thing I'd love to do now.

RANK: What's that?

NORA: Something I'd love to say in front of Torvald.

RANK: Then why can't you?

NORA: No, I daren't. It's not very nice.

MRS. LINDE: Not very nice?

RANK: Well, in that case it might not be wise. But to us, I don't see why. . . . What is this you would love to say in front of Helmer?

NORA: I would simply love to say: 'Damn.'

RANK: Are you mad!

MRS. LINDE: Good gracious, Nora . . . !

RANK: Say it! Here he is!

NORA [*hiding the bag of macaroons*]:   Sh! Sh!

[*Helmer comes out of his room, his overcoat over his arm and his hat in his hand.*]

NORA [*going over to him*]:   Well, Torvald dear, did you get rid of him?

HELMER: Yes, he's just gone.

NORA: Let me introduce you. This is Kristine, who has just arrived in town. . . .

HELMER: Kristine . . . ? You must forgive me, but I don't think I know . . .

NORA: Mrs. Linde, Torvald dear. Kristine Linde.

HELMER: Ah, indeed. A school-friend of my wife's, presumably.

MRS. LINDE: Yes, we were girls together.

NORA: Fancy, Torvald, she's come all this long way just to have a word with you.

HELMER: How is that?

MRS. LINDE: Well, it wasn't really. . . .

NORA: The thing is, Kristine is terribly clever at office work, and she's frightfully keen on finding a job with some efficient man, so that she can learn even more. . . .

HELMER: Very sensible, Mrs. Linde.

NORA: And then when she heard you'd been made Bank Manager— there was a bit in the paper about it—she set off at once. Torvald please! You *will* try and do something for Kristine, won't you? For my sake?

HELMER: Well, that's not altogether impossible. You are a widow, I presume?

MRS. LINDE: Yes.

HELMER: And you've had some experience in business?

MRS. LINDE: A fair amount.

HELMER: Well, it's quite probable I can find you a job, I think. . . .

NORA [*clapping her hands*]:   There, you see!

HELMER: You have come at a fortunate moment, Mrs. Linde. . . .

MRS. LINDE: Oh, how can I ever thank you . . . ?

HELMER: Not a bit. [*He puts on his overcoat.*] But for the present I must ask you to excuse me. . . .

RANK: Wait. I'm coming with you.

[*He fetches his fur coat from the hall and warms it at the stove.*]

NORA: Don't be long, Torvald dear.

HELMER: Not more than an hour, that's all.

NORA: Are you leaving too, Kristine?

MRS. LINDE [*putting on her things*]: Yes, I must go and see if I can't find myself a room.

HELMER: Perhaps we can all walk down the road together.

NORA [*helping her*]: What a nuisance we are so limited for space here. I'm afraid it just isn't possible. . . .

MRS. LINDE: Oh, you mustn't dream of it! Goodbye, Nora dear, and thanks for everything.

NORA: Goodbye for the present. But . . . you'll be coming back this evening, of course. And you too, Dr. Rank? What's that? If you are up to it? Of course you'll be up to it. Just wrap yourself up well.

[*They go out, talking, into the hall; children's voices can be heard on the stairs.*]

NORA: Here they are! Here they are! [*She runs to the front door and opens it. Anne Marie, the nursemaid, enters with the children.*] Come in! Come in! [*She bends down and kisses them.*] Ah! my sweet little darlings. . . . You see them, Kristine? Aren't they lovely!

RANK: Don't stand here chattering in this draught!

HELMER: Come along, Mrs. Linde. The place now becomes unbearable for anybody except mothers.

[*Dr. Rank, Helmer and Mrs. Linde go down the stairs: the Nursemaid comes into the room with the children, then Nora, shutting the door behind her.*]

NORA: How fresh and bright you look! My, what red cheeks you've got! Like apples and roses. [*During the following, the children keep chattering away to her.*] Have you had a nice time? That's splendid. And you gave Emmy and Bob a ride on your sledge? Did you now! Both together! Fancy that! There's a clever boy, Ivar. Oh, let me take her a little while, Anne Marie. There's my sweet little baby-doll! [*She takes the youngest of the children from the nursemaid and dances with her.*] All right, Mummy will dance with Bobby too. What? You've been throwing snowballs? Oh, I wish I'd been there. No, don't bother, Anne Marie, I'll help them off with their things. No, please, let me—I like doing it. You go on in, you look frozen. You'll find some hot coffee on the stove. [*The nurse-*

maid goes into the room, left. Nora takes off the children's coats and hats and throws them down anywhere, while the children all talk at once.] Really! A great big dog came running after you? But he didn't bite. No, the doggies wouldn't bite my pretty little dollies. You mustn't touch the parcels, Ivar! What are they? Wouldn't you like to know! No, no, that's nasty. Now? Shall we play something? What shall we play? Hide and seek? Yes, let's play hide and seek. Bob can hide first. Me first? All right, let me hide first.

[*She and the children play, laughing and shrieking, in this room and in the adjacent room on the right. Finally Nora hides under the table; the children come rushing in to look for her but cannot find her; they hear her stifled laughter, rush to the table, lift up the tablecloth and find her. Tremendous shouts of delight. She creeps out and pretends to frighten them. More shouts. Meanwhile there has been a knock at the front door, which nobody has heard. The door half opens, and Krogstad can be seen. He waits a little; the game continues.*]

KROGSTAD: I beg your pardon, Mrs. Helmer. . . .

NORA [*turns with a stifled cry and half jumps up*]:   Ah! What do you want?

KROGSTAD: Excuse me. The front door was standing open. Somebody must have forgotten to shut it. . . .

NORA [*standing up*]:   My husband isn't at home, Mr. Krogstad.

KROGSTAD: I know.

NORA: Well . . . what are you doing here?

KROGSTAD: I want a word with you.

NORA: With . . . ? [*Quietly, to the children.*] Go to Anne Marie. What? No, the strange man won't do anything to Mummy. When he's gone we'll have another game. [*She leads the children into the room, left, and shuts the door after them; tense and uneasy.*] You want to speak to me?

KROGSTAD: Yes, I do.

NORA: Today? But it isn't the first of the month yet. . . .

KROGSTAD: No, it's Christmas Eve. It depends entirely on you what sort of Christmas you have.

NORA: What do you want? Today I can't possibly . . .

KROGSTAD: Let's not talk about that for the moment. It's something else. You've got a moment to spare?

NORA: Yes, I suppose so, though . . .

KROGSTAD: Good. I was sitting in Olsen's café, and I saw your husband go down the road . . .

NORA: Did you?

KROGSTAD: . . . with a lady.

NORA: Well?

KROGSTAD: May I be so bold as to ask whether that lady was a Mrs. Linde?

NORA: Yes.

KROGSTAD: Just arrived in town?

NORA: Yes, today.

KROGSTAD: And she's a good friend of yours?

NORA: Yes, she is. But I can't see . . .

KROGSTAD: I also knew her once.

NORA: I know.

KROGSTAD: Oh? So you know all about it. I thought as much. Well, I want to ask you straight: is Mrs. Linde getting a job in the Bank?

NORA: How dare you cross-examine me like this, Mr. Krogstad? You, one of my husband's subordinates? But since you've asked me, I'll tell you. Yes, Mrs. Linde *has* got a job. And I'm the one who got it for her, Mr. Krogstad. Now you know.

KROGSTAD: So my guess was right.

NORA [*walking up and down*]: Oh, I think I can say that some of us have a little influence now and again. Just because one happens to be a woman, that doesn't mean. . . . People in subordinate positions, ought to take care they don't offend anybody . . . who . . . hm . . .

KROGSTAD: . . . has influence?

NORA: Exactly.

KROGSTAD [*changing his tone*]: Mrs. Helmer, will you have the goodness to use your influence on my behalf?

NORA: What? What do you mean?

KROGSTAD: Will you be so good as to see that I keep my modest little job at the Bank?

NORA: What do you mean? Who wants to take it away from you?

KROGSTAD: Oh, you needn't try and pretend to me you don't know. I can quite see that this friend of yours isn't particularly anxious to bump up against me. And I can also see now whom I can thank for being given the sack.

NORA: But I assure you. . . .

KROGSTAD: All right, all right. But to come to the point: there's still time. And I advise you to use your influence to stop it.

NORA: But, Mr. Krogstad, I *have* no influence.

KROGSTAD: Haven't you? I thought just now you said yourself . . .

NORA: I didn't mean it that way, of course. Me? What makes you think I've got any influence of that kind over my husband?

KROGSTAD: I know your husband from our student days. I don't suppose he is any more steadfast than other married men.

NORA: You speak disrespectfully of my husband like that and I'll show you the door.

KROGSTAD: So the lady's got courage.

NORA: I'm not frightened of you any more. After New Year's I'll soon be finished with the whole business.

KROGSTAD [*controlling himself*]:   Listen to me, Mrs. Helmer. If necessary I shall fight for my little job in the Bank as if I were fighting for my life.

NORA: So it seems.

KROGSTAD: It's not just for the money, that's the last thing I care about. There's something else . . . well, I might as well out with it. You see it's like this. You know as well as anybody that some years ago I got myself mixed up in a bit of trouble.

NORA: I believe I've heard something of the sort.

KROGSTAD: It never got as far as the courts; but immediately it was as if all paths were barred to me. So I started going in for the sort of business you know about. I had to do something, and I think I can say I haven't been one of the worst. But now I have to get out of it. My sons are growing up; for their sake I must try and win back what respectability I can. That job in the Bank was like the first step on the ladder for me. And now your husband wants to kick me off the ladder again, back into the mud.

NORA: But in God's name, Mr. Krogstad, it's quite beyond my power to help you.

KROGSTAD: That's because you haven't the will to help me. But I have ways of making you.

NORA: You wouldn't go and tell my husband I owe you money?

KROGSTAD: Suppose I did tell him?

NORA: It would be a rotten shame. [*Half choking with tears.*] That secret is all my pride and joy—why should he have to hear about it in this nasty, horrid way . . . hear about it from *you*. You would make things horribly unpleasant for me. . . .

KROGSTAD: Merely unpleasant?

NORA [*vehemently*]: Go on, do it then! It'll be all the worse for you. Because then my husband will see for himself what a bad man you are, and then you certainly won't be able to keep your job.

KROGSTAD: I asked whether it was only a bit of domestic unpleasantness you were afraid of?

NORA: If my husband gets to know about it, he'll pay off what's owing at once. And then we'd have nothing more to do with you.

KROGSTAD [*taking a pace towards her*]: Listen, Mrs. Helmer, either you haven't a very good memory, or else you don't understand much about business. I'd better make the position a little bit clearer for you.

NORA: How do you mean?

KROGSTAD: When your husband was ill, you came to me for the loan of twelve hundred dollars.

NORA: I didn't know of anybody else.

KROGSTAD: I promised to find you the money. . . .

NORA: And you did find it.

KROGSTAD: I promised to find you the money on certain conditions. At the time you were so concerned about your husband's illness, and so anxious to get the money for going away with, that I don't think you paid very much attention to all the incidentals. So there is perhaps some point in reminding you of them. Well, I promised to find you the money against an IOU which I drew up for you.

NORA: Yes, and which I signed.

KROGSTAD: Very good. But below that I added a few lines, by which your father was to stand security. This your father was to sign.

NORA: Was to . . . ? He did sign it.

KROGSTAD: I had left the date blank. The idea was that your father was to add the date himself when he signed it. Remember?

NORA: Yes, I think. . . .

KROGSTAD: I then gave you the IOU to post to your father. Wasn't that so?

NORA: Yes.

KROGSTAD: Which of course you did at once. Because only about five or six days later you brought it back to me with your father's signature. I then paid out the money.

NORA: Well? Haven't I paid the instalments regularly?

KROGSTAD: Yes, fairly. But . . . coming back to what we were talking about . . . that was a pretty bad period you were going through then, Mrs. Helmer.

NORA: Yes, it was.

KROGSTAD: Your father was seriously ill, I believe.

NORA: He was very near the end.

KROGSTAD: And died shortly afterwards?

NORA: Yes.

KROGSTAD: Tell me, Mrs. Helmer, do you happen to remember which day your father died? The exact date, I mean.

NORA: Daddy died on 29 September.

KROGSTAD: Quite correct. I made some inquiries. Which brings up a rather curious point [*takes out a paper*] which I simply cannot explain.

NORA: Curious . . . ? I don't know . . .

KROGSTAD: The curious thing is, Mrs. Helmer, that your father signed this document three days after his death.

NORA: What? I don't understand. . . .

KROGSTAD: Your father died on 29 September. But look here. Your father has dated his signature 2 October. Isn't that rather curious, Mrs. Helmer? [*Nora remains silent.*] It's also remarkable that the words '2 October' and the year are not in your father's handwriting, but in a handwriting I rather think I recognize. Well, perhaps that could be explained. Your father might have forgotten to date his signature, and then somebody else might have made a guess at the date later, before the fact of your father's death was known. There is nothing wrong in that. What really matters is the signature. And *that* is of course genuine, Mrs. Helmer? It really was your father who wrote his name here?

NORA [*after a moment's silence, throws her head back and looks at him defiantly*]: No, it wasn't. It was me who signed father's name.

KROGSTAD: Listen to me. I suppose you realize that that is a very dangerous confession?

NORA: Why? You'll soon have all your money back.

KROGSTAD: Let me ask you a question: why didn't you send that document to your father?

NORA: It was impossible. Daddy was ill. If I'd asked him for his signature, I'd have to tell him what the money was for. Don't you see, when he was as ill as that I couldn't go and tell him that my husband's life was in danger. It was simply impossible.

KROGSTAD: It would have been better for you if you had abandoned the whole trip.

NORA: No, that was impossible. This was the thing that was to save my husband's life. I couldn't give it up.

KROGSTAD: But did it never strike you that this was fraudulent . . . ?

NORA: That wouldn't have meant anything to me. Why should I worry about you? I couldn't stand you, not when you insisted on going through with all those cold-blooded formalities, knowing all the time what a critical state my husband was in.

KROGSTAD: Mrs. Helmer, it's quite clear you still haven't the faintest idea what it is you've committed. But let me tell you, my own offence was no more and no worse than that, and it ruined my entire reputation.

NORA: You? Are you trying to tell me that you once risked everything to save your wife's life?

KROGSTAD: The law takes no account of motives.

NORA: Then they must be very bad laws.

KROGSTAD: Bad or not, if I produce this document in court, you'll be condemned according to them.

NORA: I don't believe it. Isn't a daughter entitled to try and save her father from worry and anxiety on his deathbed? Isn't a wife entitled to save her husband's life? I might not know very much about the law, but I feel sure of one thing: it must say somewhere that things like this are allowed. You mean to say you don't know that—you, when it's your job? You must be a rotten lawyer, Mr. Krogstad.

KROGSTAD: That may be. But when it comes to business transactions—like the sort between us two—perhaps you'll admit I know something about *them?* Good. Now you must please yourself. But I tell you this: if I'm pitched out a second time, you are going to keep me company.

[*He bows and goes out through the hall.*]

NORA [*stands thoughtfully for a moment, then tosses her head*]: Rubbish! He's just trying to scare me. I'm not such a fool as all that. [*Begins gathering up the children's clothes; after a moment she stops.*] Yet . . . ? No, it's impossible! I did it for love, didn't I?

THE CHILDREN [*in the doorway, left*]: Mummy, the gentleman's just gone out of the gate.

NORA: Yes, I know. But you mustn't say anything to anybody about that gentleman. You hear? Not even to Daddy!

THE CHILDREN: All right, Mummy. Are you going to play again?

NORA: No, not just now.

THE CHILDREN: But Mummy, you promised!

NORA: Yes, but I can't just now. Off you go now, I have a lot to do. Off you go, my darlings. [*She herds them carefully into the other room and shuts the door behind them. She sits down on the sofa, picks up her embroidery and works a few stitches, but soon stops.*] No! [*She flings her work down, stands up, goes to the hall door and calls out.*] Helene! Fetch the tree in for me, please. [*She walks across to the table, left, and opens the drawer; again pauses.*] No, really, it's quite impossible!

MAID [*with the Christmas tree*]: Where shall I put it, ma'am?

NORA: On the floor there, in the middle.

MAID: Anything else you want me to bring?

NORA: No, thank you. I've got what I want.

[*The maid has put the tree down and goes out.*]

NORA [*busy decorating the tree*]: Candles here . . . and flowers here—Revolting man! It's all nonsense! There's nothing to worry about. We'll have a lovely Christmas tree. And I'll do anything you want me to, Torvald; I'll sing for you, dance for you. . . .

[*Helmer, with a bundle of documents under his arm, comes in by the hall door.*]

NORA: Ah, back again already?

HELMER: Yes. Anybody been?

NORA: Here? No.

HELMER: That's funny. I just saw Krogstad leave the house.

NORA: Oh? O yes, that's right. Krogstad was here a minute.

HELMER: Nora, I can tell by your face he's been asking you to put a good word in for him.

NORA: Yes.

HELMER: And you were to pretend it was your own idea? You were to keep quiet about his having been here. He asked you to do that as well, didn't he?

NORA: Yes, Torvald. But . . .

HELMER: Nora, Nora, what possessed you to do a thing like that? Talking to a person like him, making him promises? And then on top of everything, to tell me a lie!

NORA: A lie . . . ?

HELMER: Didn't you say that nobody had been here? [*Wagging his finger at her.*] Never again must my little song-bird do a thing like that! Little song-birds must keep their pretty little beaks out of mischief;

no chirruping out of tune! [*Puts his arm round her waist.*] Isn't that the way we want things to be? Yes, of course it is. [*Lets her go.*] So let's say no more about it. [*Sits down by the stove.*] Ah, nice and cosy here!

[*He glances through his papers.*]

NORA [*busy with the Christmas tree, after a short pause*]: Torvald!

HELMER: Yes.

NORA: I'm so looking forward to the fancy dress ball at the Stenborgs on Boxing Day.

HELMER: And I'm terribly curious to see what sort of surprise you've got for me.

NORA: Oh, it's too silly.

HELMER: Oh?

NORA: I just can't think of anything suitable. Everything seems so absurd, so pointless.

HELMER: Has my little Nora come to *that* conclusion?

NORA [*behind his chair, her arms on the chairback*]: Are you very busy, Torvald?

HELMER: Oh. . . .

NORA: What are all those papers?

HELMER: Bank matters.

NORA: Already?

HELMER: I have persuaded the retiring manager to give me authority to make any changes in organisation or personnel I think necessary. I have to work on it over the Christmas week. I want everything straight by the New Year.

NORA: So that was why that poor Krogstad. . . .

HELMER: Hm!

NORA [*still leaning against the back of the chair, running her fingers through his hair*]: If you hadn't been so busy, Torvald, I'd have asked you to do me an awfully big favour.

HELMER: Let me hear it. What's it to be?

NORA: Nobody's got such good taste as you. And the thing is I do so want to look my best at the fancy dress ball. Torvald, couldn't you give me some advice and tell me what you think I ought to go as, and how I should arrange my costume?

HELMER: Aha! So my impulsive little woman is asking for somebody to come to her rescue, eh?

NORA: Please, Torvald, I never get anywhere without your help.

HELMER: Very well, I'll think about it. We'll find something.

NORA: That's sweet of you. [*She goes across to the tree again; pause.*] How pretty these red flowers look.—Tell me, was it really something terribly wrong this man Krogstad did?

HELMER: Forgery. Have you any idea what that means?

NORA: Perhaps circumstances left him no choice?

HELMER: Maybe. Or perhaps, like so many others, he just didn't think. I am not so heartless that I would necessarily want to condemn a man for a single mistake like that.

NORA: Oh no, Torvald, of course not!

HELMER: Many a man might be able to redeem himself, if he honestly confessed his guilt and took his punishment.

NORA: Punishment?

HELMER: But that wasn't the way Krogstad chose. He dodged what was due to him by a cunning trick. And that's what has been the cause of his corruption.

NORA: Do you think it would . . . ?

HELMER: Just think how a man with a thing like that on his conscience will always be having to lie and cheat and dissemble; he can never drop the mask, not even with his own wife and children. And the children—*that's* the most terrible part of it, Nora.

NORA: Why?

HELMER: A fog of lies like that in a household, and it spreads disease and infection to every part of it. Every breath the children take in that kind of house is reeking with evil germs.

NORA [*closer behind him*]: Are you sure of that?

HELMER: My dear Nora, as a lawyer I know what I'm talking about. Practically all juvenile delinquents come from homes where the mother is dishonest.

NORA: Why mothers particularly?

HELMER: It's generally traceable to the mothers, but of course fathers can have the same influence. Every lawyer knows that only too well. And yet there's Krogstad been poisoning his own children for years with lies and deceit. That's the reason I call him morally depraved. [*Holds out his hands to her.*] That's why my sweet little Nora must promise me not to try putting in any more good words for him. Shake hands on it. Well? What's this? Give me your hand. There now! That's settled. I assure you I would have found it impossible to work with him. I quite literally feel physically sick in the presence of such people.

NORA [*draws her hand away and walks over to the other side of the Christmas tree*]: How hot it is in here! And I still have such a lot to do.

HELMER [*stands up and collects his papers together*]: Yes, I'd better think of getting some of this read before dinner. I must also think about your costume. And I might even be able to lay my hands on something to wrap in gold paper and hang on the Christmas tree. [*He lays his hand on her head.*] My precious little singing bird.

[*He goes into his study and shuts the door behind him.*]

NORA [*quietly, after a pause*]: Nonsense! It can't be. It's impossible. It *must* be impossible.

MAID [*in the doorway, left*]: The children keep asking so nicely if they can come in and see Mummy.

NORA: No, no, don't let them in! You stay with them, Anne Marie.

MAID: Very well, ma'am.

[*She shuts the door.*]

NORA [*pale with terror*]: Corrupt my children . . . ! Poison my home? [*Short pause; she throws back her head.*] It's not true! It could never, never be true!

ACT II

The same room. In the corner beside the piano stands the Christmas tree, stripped, bedraggled and with its candles burnt out. Nora's outdoor things lie on the sofa. Nora, alone there, walks about restlessly; at last she stops by the sofa and picks up her coat.

NORA [*putting her coat down again*]: Somebody's coming! [*Crosses to the door, listens.*] No, it's nobody. Nobody will come today, of course, Christmas Day—nor tomorrow, either. But perhaps. . . . [*She opens the door and looks out.*] No, nothing in the letter box; quite empty. [*Comes forward.*] Oh, nonsense! He didn't mean it seriously. Things like that *can't* happen. It's impossible. Why, I have three small children.

[*The Nursemaid comes from the room, left, carrying a big cardboard box.*]

NURSEMAID: I finally found it, the box with the fancy dress costumes.

NORA: Thank you. Put it on the table, please.

NURSEMAID [*does this*]:   But I'm afraid they are in an awful mess.

NORA: Oh, if only I could rip them up into a thousand pieces!

NURSEMAID: Good heavens, they can be mended all right, with a bit of patience.

NORA: Yes, I'll go over and get Mrs. Linde to help me.

NURSEMAID: Out again? In this terrible weather? You'll catch your death of cold, Ma'am.

NORA: Oh, worse things might happen.—How are the children?

NURSEMAID: Playing with their Christmas presents, poor little things, but . . .

NORA: Do they keep asking for me?

NURSEMAID: They are so used to being with their Mummy.

NORA: Yes, Anne Marie, from now on I can't be with them as often as I was before.

NURSEMAID: Ah well, children get used to anything in time.

NORA: Do you think so? Do you think they would forget their Mummy if she went away for good?

NURSEMAID: Good gracious—for good?

NORA: Tell me, Anne Marie—I've often wondered—how on earth could you bear to hand your child over to strangers?

NURSEMAID: Well, there was nothing else for it when I had to come and nurse my little Nora.

NORA: Yes but . . . how could you *bring* yourself to do it?

NURSEMAID: When I had the chance of such a good place? When a poor girl's been in trouble she must make the best of things. Because *he* didn't help, the rotter.

NORA: But your daughter will have forgotten you.

NURSEMAID: Oh no, she hasn't. She wrote to me when she got confirmed, and again when she got married.

NORA [*putting her arms round her neck*]:   Dear old Anne Marie, you were a good mother to me when I was little.

NURSEMAID: My poor little Nora never had any other mother but me.

NORA: And if my little ones only had you, I know you would. . . . Oh, what am I talking about! [*She opens the box.*] Go in to them. I must . . . Tomorrow I'll let you see how pretty I am going to look.

NURSEMAID: Ah, there'll be nobody at the ball as pretty as my Nora.

[*She goes into the room, left.*]

NORA [*begins unpacking the box, but soon throws it down*]:   Oh, if only I dare go out. If only I could be sure nobody would come.

And that nothing would happen in the meantime here at home. Rubbish—nobody's going to come. I mustn't think about it. Brush this muff. Pretty gloves, pretty gloves! I'll put it right out of my mind. One, two, three, four, five, six. . . . [*Screams.*] Ah, they are coming. . . . [*She starts towards the door, but stops irresolute. Mrs. Linde comes from the hall, where she has taken off her things.*] Oh, it's you, Kristine. There's nobody else out there, is there? I'm so glad you've come.

MRS. LINDE: I heard you'd been over looking for me.

NORA: Yes, I was just passing. There's something you must help me with. Come and sit beside me on the sofa here. You see, the Stenborgs are having a fancy dress party upstairs tomorrow evening, and now Torvald wants me to go as a Neapolitan fisher lass and dance the tarantella. I learned it in Capri, you know.

MRS. LINDE: Well, well! So you are going to do a party piece?

NORA: Torvald says I should. Look, here's the costume, Torvald had it made for me down there. But it's got all torn and I simply don't know. . . .

MRS. LINDE: We'll soon have that put right. It's only the trimming come away here and there. Got a needle and thread? Ah, here's what we are after.

NORA: It's awfully kind of you.

MRS. LINDE: So you are going to be all dressed up tomorrow, Nora? Tell you what—I'll pop over for a minute to see you in all your finery. But I'm quite forgetting to thank you for the pleasant time we had last night.

NORA [*gets up and walks across the room*]: Somehow I didn't think yesterday was as nice as things generally are.—You should have come to town a little earlier, Kristine.—Yes, Torvald certainly knows how to make things pleasant about the place.

MRS. LINDE: You too, I should say. You are not your father's daughter for nothing. But tell me, is Dr. Rank always as depressed as he was last night?

NORA: No, last night it was rather obvious. He's got something seriously wrong with him, you know. Tuberculosis of the spine, poor fellow. His father was a horrible man, who used to have mistresses and things like that. That's why the son was always ailing, right from being a child.

MRS. LINDE [*lowering her sewing*]: But my dear Nora, how do you come to know about things like that?

NORA [*walking about the room*]:   Huh! When you've got three children, you get these visits from . . . women who have had a certain amount of medical training. And you hear all sorts of things from them.

MRS. LINDE [*begins sewing again; short silence*]:   Does Dr. Rank call in every day?

NORA: Every single day. He was Torvald's best friend as a boy, and he's a good friend of *mine,* too. Dr. Rank is almost like one of the family.

MRS. LINDE: But tell me—is he really genuine? What I mean is: doesn't he sometimes rather turn on the charm?

NORA: No, on the contrary. What makes you think that?

MRS. LINDE: When you introduced me yesterday, he claimed he'd often heard my name in this house. But afterwards I noticed your husband hadn't the faintest idea who I was. Then how is it that Dr. Rank should. . . .

NORA: Oh yes, it was quite right what he said, Kristine. You see Torvald is so terribly in love with me that he says he wants me all to himself. When we were first married, it even used to make him sort of jealous if I only as much as mentioned any of my old friends from back home. So of course I stopped doing it. But I often talk to Dr. Rank about such things. He likes hearing about them.

MRS. LINDE: Listen, Nora! In lots of ways you are still a child. Now, I'm a good deal older than you, and a bit more experienced. I'll tell you something: I think you ought to give up all this business with Dr. Rank.

NORA: Give up what business?

MRS. LINDE: The whole thing, I should say. Weren't you saying yesterday something about a rich admirer who was to provide you with money. . . .

NORA: One who's never existed, I regret to say. But what of it?

MRS. LINDE: Has Dr. Rank money?

NORA: Yes, he has.

MRS. LINDE: And no dependents?

NORA: No, nobody. But . . . ?

MRS. LINDE: And he comes to the house every day?

NORA: Yes, I told you.

MRS. LINDE: But how can a man of his position want to pester you like this?

NORA: I simply don't understand.

MRS. LINDE: Don't pretend, Nora. Do you think I don't see now who you borrowed the twelve hundred from?

NORA: Are you out of your mind? Do you really think that? A friend of ours who comes here every day? The whole situation would have been absolutely intolerable.

MRS. LINDE: It *really* isn't him?

NORA: No, I give you my word. It would never have occurred to me for one moment. . . . Anyway, he didn't have the money to lend then. He didn't inherit it till later.

MRS. LINDE: Just as well for you, I'd say, my dear Nora.

NORA: No, it would never have occurred to me to ask Dr. Rank. . . . All the same I'm pretty certain if I were to ask him . . .

MRS. LINDE: But of course you won't.

NORA: No, of course not. I can't ever imagine it being necessary. But I'm quite certain if ever I were to mention it to Dr. Rank. . . .

MRS. LINDE: Behind your husband's back?

NORA: I have to get myself out of that other business. That's also behind his back. I *must* get myself out of that.

MRS. LINDE: Yes, that's what I said yesterday. But . . .

NORA [*walking up and down*]: A man's better at coping with these things than a woman. . . .

MRS. LINDE: Your own husband, yes.

NORA: Nonsense! [*Stops.*] When you've paid everything you owe, you do get your IOU back again, don't you?

MRS. LINDE: Of course.

NORA: And you can tear it up into a thousand pieces and burn it— the nasty, filthy thing!

MRS. LINDE [*looking fixedly at her, puts down her sewing and slowly rises*]: Nora, you are hiding something from me.

NORA: Is it so obvious?

MRS. LINDE: Something has happened to you since yesterday morning. Nora, what is it?

NORA [*going towards her*]: Kristine! [*Listens.*] Hush! There's Torvald back. Look, you go and sit in there beside the children for the time being. Torvald can't stand the sight of mending lying about. Get Anne Marie to help you.

MRS. LINDE [*gathering a lot of the things together*]: All right, but I'm not leaving until we have thrashed this thing out.

[*She goes into the room, left; at the same time Helmer comes in from the hall.*]

NORA [*goes to meet him*]: I've been longing for you to be back, Torvald, dear.

HELMER: Was that the dressmaker . . . ?

NORA: No, it was Kristine; she's helping me with my costume. I think it's going to look very nice . . .

HELMER: Wasn't that a good idea of mine, now?

NORA: Wonderful! But wasn't it also nice of me to let you have your way?

HELMER [*taking her under the chin*]: Nice of you—because you let your husband have his way? All right, you little rogue, I know you didn't mean it that way. But I don't want to disturb you. You'll be wanting to try the costume on, I suppose.

NORA: And I dare say you've got work to do?

HELMER: Yes. [*Shows her a bundle of papers.*] Look at this. I've been down at the Bank. . . .

[*He turns to go into his study.*]

NORA: Torvald!

HELMER [*stopping*]: Yes.

NORA: If a little squirrel were to ask ever so nicely . . . ?

HELMER: Well?

NORA: Would you do something for it?

HELMER: Naturally I would first have to know what it is.

NORA: Please, if only you would let it have its way, and do what it wants, it'd scamper about and do all sorts of marvellous tricks.

HELMER: What is it?

NORA: And the pretty little sky-lark would sing all day long. . . .

HELMER: Huh! It does that anyway.

NORA: I'd pretend I was an elfin child and dance a moonlight dance for you, Torvald.

HELMER: Nora—I hope it's not that business you started on this morning?

NORA [*coming closer*]: Yes, it is, Torvald. I implore you!

HELMER: You have the nerve to bring that up again?

NORA: Yes, yes, you *must* listen to me. You must let Krogstad keep his job at the Bank.

HELMER: My dear Nora, I'm giving his job to Mrs. Linde.

NORA: Yes, it's awfully sweet of you. But couldn't you get rid of somebody else in the office instead of Krogstad?

HELMER: This really is the most incredible obstinacy! Just because you go and make some thoughtless promise to put in a good word for him, you expect me . . .

NORA: It's not that, Torvald. It's for your own sake. That man writes in all the nastiest papers, you told me that yourself. He can do you no end of harm. He terrifies me to death. . . .

HELMER: Aha, now I see. It's your memories of what happened before that are frightening you.

NORA: What do you mean?

HELMER: It's your father you are thinking of.

NORA: Yes . . . yes, that's right. You remember all the nasty insinuations those wicked people put in the papers about Daddy? I honestly think they would have had him dismissed if the Ministry hadn't sent you down to investigate, and you hadn't been so kind and helpful.

HELMER: My dear little Nora, there is a considerable difference between your father and me. Your father's professional conduct was not entirely above suspicion. Mine is. And I hope it's going to stay that way as long as I hold this position.

NORA: But nobody knows what some of these evil people are capable of. Things could be so nice and pleasant for us here, in the peace and quiet of our home—you and me and the children, Torvald! That's why I implore you. . . .

HELMER: The more you plead for him, the more impossible you make it for me to keep him on. It's already known down at the Bank that I am going to give Krogstad his notice. If it ever got around that the new manager had been talked over by his wife. . . .

NORA: What of it?

HELMER: Oh, nothing! As long as the little woman gets her own stubborn way . . . ! Do you want me to make myself a laughing stock in the office? . . . Give people the idea that I am susceptible to any kind of outside pressure? You can imagine how soon I'd feel the consequences of that! Anyway, there's one other consideration that makes it impossible to have Krogstad in the Bank as long as I am manager.

NORA: What's that?

HELMER: At a pinch I might have overlooked his past lapses. . . .

NORA: Of course you could, Torvald!

HELMER: And I'm told he's not bad at his job, either. But we knew each other rather well when we were younger. It was one of those rather rash friendships that prove embarrassing in later life. There's no reason why you shouldn't know we were once on terms of some familiarity. And he, in his tactless way, makes no attempt to hide the fact, particularly when other people are present. On the contrary, he thinks he has every right to treat me as an equal, with his 'Torvald this' and 'Torvald that' every time he opens his mouth. I find it extremely irritating, I can tell you. He would make my position at the Bank absolutely intolerable.

NORA: Torvald, surely you aren't serious?

HELMER: Oh? Why not?

NORA: Well, it's all so petty.

HELMER: What's that you say? Petty? Do you think I'm petty?

NORA: No, not at all, Torvald dear! And that's why . . .

HELMER: Doesn't make any difference! . . . You call my motives petty; so I must be petty too. Petty! Indeed! Well, we'll put a stop to that, once and for all. [*He opens the hall door and calls.*] Helene!

NORA: What are you going to do?

HELMER [*searching among his papers*]: Settle things. [*The Maid comes in.*] See this letter? I want you to take it down at once. Get hold of a messenger and get him to deliver it. Quickly. The address is on the outside. There's the money.

MAID: Very good, sir.

[*She goes with the letter.*]

HELMER [*putting his papers together*]: There now, my stubborn little miss.

NORA [*breathless*]: Torvald . . . what was that letter?

HELMER: Krogstad's notice.

NORA: Get it back, Torvald! There's still time! Oh, Torvald, get it back! Please for my sake, for your sake, for the sake of the children! Listen, Torvald, please! You don't realize what it can do to us.

HELMER: Too late.

NORA: Yes, too late.

HELMER: My dear Nora, I forgive you this anxiety of yours, although it is actually a bit of an insult. Oh, but it is, I tell you! It's hardly flattering to suppose that anything this miserable pen-pusher wrote could frighten *me!* But I forgive you all the same, because it is rather a sweet way of showing how much you love me. [*He takes her in his arms.*] This is how things must be, my own darling Nora. When it comes to the point, I've enough strength and enough courage, believe me, for whatever happens. You'll find I'm man enough to take everything on myself.

NORA [*terrified*]: What do you mean?

HELMER: Everything, I said. . . .

NORA [*in command of herself*]: That is something you shall never, never do.

HELMER: All right, then we'll share it, Nora—as man and wife. That's what we'll do. [*Caressing her.*] Does that make you happy now? There, there, don't look at me with those eyes, like a little frightened dove. The whole thing is sheer imagination.—Why don't you run through the tarantella and try out the tambourine? I'll go into my study and shut both the doors, then I won't hear anything. You can make all the noise you want. [*Turns in the doorway.*] And when Rank comes, tell him where he can find me.

[*He nods to her, goes with his papers into his room, and shuts the door behind him.*]

NORA [*wild-eyed with terror, stands as though transfixed*]: He's quite capable of doing it! He would do it! No matter what, he'd do it.—No, never in this world! Anything but that! Help? Some way out . . . ? [*The door-bell rings in the hall.*] Dr. Rank . . . ! Anything but that, *anything!* [*She brushes her hands over her face, pulls herself together and opens the door into the hall. Dr. Rank is standing outside hanging up his fur coat. During what follows it begins to grow dark.*] Hello, Dr. Rank. I recognized your ring. Do you mind not going in to Torvald just yet, I think he's busy.

RANK: And you?

[*Dr. Rank comes into the room and she closes the door behind him.*]

NORA: Oh, you know very well I've always got time for you.

RANK: Thank you. A privilege I shall take advantage of as long as I am able.

NORA: What do you mean—as long as you are able?

RANK: Does that frighten you?

NORA: Well, it's just that it sounds so strange. Is anything likely to happen?

RANK: Only what I have long expected. But I didn't think it would come quite so soon.

NORA [*catching at his arm*]: What have you found out? Dr. Rank, you must tell me!

RANK: I'm slowly sinking. There's nothing to be done about it.

NORA [*with a sigh of relief*]: Oh, it's *you* you're . . . ?

RANK: Who else? No point in deceiving oneself. I am the most wretched of all my patients, Mrs. Helmer. These last few days I've made a careful analysis of my internal economy. Bankrupt! Within a month I shall probably be lying rotting up there in the churchyard.

NORA: Come now, what a ghastly thing to say!

RANK: The whole damned thing is ghastly. But the worst thing is all the ghastliness that has to be gone through first. I only have one more test to make; and when that's done I'll know pretty well when the final disintegration will start. There's something I want to ask you. Helmer is a sensitive soul; he loathes anything that's ugly. I don't want him visiting me. . . .

NORA: But Dr. Rank. . . .

RANK: On no account must he. I won't have it. I'll lock the door on him.—As soon as I'm absolutely certain of the worst, I'll send you my visiting card with a black cross on it. You'll know then the final horrible disintegration has begun.

NORA: Really, you are being quite absurd today. And here was I hoping you would be in a thoroughly good mood.

RANK: With death staring me in the face? Why should I suffer for another man's sins? What justice is there in that? Somewhere, somehow, every single family must be suffering some such cruel retribution. . . .

NORA [*stopping up her ears*]: Rubbish! Do cheer up!

RANK: Yes, really the whole thing's nothing but a huge joke. My poor innocent spine must do penance for my father's gay subaltern life.

NORA [*by the table, left*]: Wasn't he rather partial to asparagus and *pâté de foie gras*?

RANK: Yes, he was. And truffles.

NORA: Truffles, yes. And oysters, too, I believe?

RANK: Yes, oysters, oysters, of course.

NORA: And all the port and champagne that goes with them. It does seem a pity all these delicious things should attack the spine.

RANK: Especially when they attack a poor spine that never had any fun out of them.

NORA: Yes, that is an awful pity.

RANK [*looks at her sharply*]: Hm. . . .

NORA [*after a pause*]: Why did you smile?

RANK: No, it was you who laughed.

NORA: No, it was you who smiled, Dr. Rank!

RANK [*getting up*]: You are a bigger rascal than I thought you were.

NORA: I feel full of mischief today.

RANK: So it seems.

NORA [*putting her hands on his shoulders*]:   Dear, dear Dr. Rank, you mustn't go and die on Torvald and me.

RANK: You wouldn't miss me for long. When you are gone, you are soon forgotten.

NORA [*looking at him anxiously*]:   Do you think so?

RANK: People make new contacts, then . . .

NORA: Who make new contacts?

RANK: Both you and Helmer will, when I'm gone. You yourself are already well on the way, it seems to me. What was this Mrs. Linde doing here last night?

NORA: Surely you aren't jealous of poor Kristine?

RANK: Yes, I am. She'll be my successor in this house. When I'm done for, I can see this woman. . . .

NORA: Hush! Don't talk so loud, she's in there.

RANK: Today as well? There you are, you see!

NORA: Just to do some sewing on my dress. Good Lord, how absurd you are! [*She sits down on the sofa.*] Now Dr. Rank, cheer up. You'll see tomorrow how nicely I can dance. And you can pretend I'm doing it just for you—and for Torvald as well, of course. [*She takes various things out of the box.*] Come here, Dr. Rank. I want to show you something.

RANK [*sits*]:   What is it?

NORA: Look!

RANK: Silk stockings.

NORA: Flesh-coloured! Aren't they lovely! Of course, it's dark here now, but tomorrow. . . . No, no, no, you can only look at the feet. Oh well, you might as well see a bit higher up, too.

RANK: Hm. . . .

NORA: Why are you looking so critical? Don't you think they'll fit?

RANK: I couldn't possibly offer any informed opinion about that.

NORA [*looks at him for a moment*]:   Shame on you. [*Hits him lightly across the ear with the stockings.*] Take that! [*Folds them up again.*]

RANK: And what other delights am I to be allowed to see?

NORA: Not another thing. You are too naughty. [*She hums a little and searches among her things.*]

RANK [*after a short pause*]:   Sitting here so intimately like this with you, I can't imagine . . . I simply cannot conceive what would have become of me if I had never come to this house.

NORA [*smiles*]:   Yes, I rather think you do enjoy coming here.

RANK [*in a low voice, looking fixedly ahead*]:   And the thought of having to leave it all . . .

NORA: Nonsense. You aren't leaving.

RANK [*in the same tone*]: . . . without being able to leave behind even the slightest token of gratitude, hardly a fleeting regret even . . . nothing but an empty place to be filled by the first person that comes along.

NORA: Supposing I were to ask you to . . . ? No . . .

RANK: What?

NORA: . . . to show me the extent of your friendship . . .

RANK: Yes?

NORA: I mean . . . to do me a tremendous favour. . . .

RANK: Would you really, for once, give me that pleasure?

NORA: You have no idea what it is.

RANK: All right, tell me.

NORA: No, really I can't, Dr. Rank. It's altogether too much to ask . . . because I need your advice and help as well. . . .

RANK: The more the better. I cannot imagine what you have in mind. But tell me anyway. You do trust me, don't you?

NORA: Yes, I trust you more than anybody I know. You are my best and my most faithful friend. I know that. So I will tell you. Well then, Dr. Rank, there is something you must help me to prevent. You know how deeply, how passionately Torvald is in love with me. He would never hesitate for a moment to sacrifice his life for my sake.

RANK [*bending towards her*]: Nora . . . do you think he's the only one who . . . ?

NORA [*stiffening slightly*]: Who . . . ?

RANK: Who wouldn't gladly give his life for your sake.

NORA [*sadly*]: Oh!

RANK: I swore to myself you would know before I went. I'll never have a better opportunity. Well, Nora! Now you know. And now you know too that you can confide in me as in nobody else.

NORA [*rises and speaks evenly and calmly*]: Let me past.

RANK [*makes way for her, but remains seated*]: Nora. . . .

NORA [*in the hall doorway*]: Helene, bring the lamp in, please. [*Walks over to the stove.*] Oh, my dear Dr. Rank, that really was rather horrid of you.

RANK [*getting up*]: That I have loved you every bit as much as anybody? Is *that* horrid?

NORA: No, but that you had to go and tell me. When it was all so unnecessary. . . .

RANK: What do you mean? Did you know . . . ?

[*The Maid comes in with the lamp, puts it on the table, and goes out again.*]

RANK: Nora . . . Mrs. Helmer . . . I'm asking you if you knew?

NORA: How can I tell whether I did or didn't. I simply can't tell you. . . . Oh, how could you be so clumsy, Dr. Rank! When everything was so nice.

RANK: Anyway, you know now that I'm at your service, body and soul. So you can speak out.

NORA [*looking at him*]: After this?

RANK: I beg you to tell me what it is.

NORA: I can tell you nothing now.

RANK: You must. You can't torment me like this. Give me a chance— I'll do anything that's humanly possible.

NORA: You can do nothing for me now. Actually, I don't really need any help. It's all just my imagination, really it is. Of course! [*She sits down in the rocking chair, looks at him and smiles.*] I must say, you are a nice one, Dr. Rank! Don't you feel ashamed of yourself, now the lamp's been brought in?

RANK: No, not exactly. But perhaps I ought to go—for good?

NORA: No, you mustn't do that. You must keep coming just as you've always done. You know very well Torvald would miss you terribly.

RANK: And *you?*

NORA: I always think it's tremendous fun having you.

RANK: That's exactly what gave me wrong ideas. I just can't puzzle you out. I often used to feel you'd just as soon be with me as with Helmer.

NORA: Well, you see, there are those people you love and those people you'd almost rather *be* with.

RANK: Yes, there's something in that.

NORA: When I was a girl at home, I loved Daddy best, of course. But I also thought it great fun if I could slip into the maids' room. For one thing they never preached at me. And they always talked about such exciting things.

RANK: Aha! So it's their role I've taken over!

NORA [*jumps up and crosses to him*]: Oh, my dear, kind Dr. Rank, I didn't mean that at all. But you can see how it's a bit with Torvald as it was with Daddy. . . .

[*The Maid comes in from the hall.*]

MAID: Please, ma'am . . . !

[*She whispers and hands her a card.*]

NORA [*glances at the card*]: Ah!

[*She puts it in her pocket.*]

RANK: Anything wrong?
NORA: No, no, not at all. It's just . . . it's my new costume. . . .
RANK: How is that? There's your costume in there.
NORA: That one, yes. But this is another one. I've ordered it. Torvald mustn't hear about it. . . .
RANK: Ah, so that's the big secret, is it!
NORA: Yes, that's right. Just go in and see him, will you? He's in the study. Keep him occupied for the time being. . . .
RANK: Don't worry. He shan't escape me.

[*He goes into Helmer's study.*]

NORA [*to the maid*]: Is he waiting in the kitchen?
MAID: Yes, he came up the back stairs. . . .
NORA: But didn't you tell him somebody was here?
MAID: Yes, but it was no good.
NORA: Won't he go?
MAID: No, he won't till he's seen you.
NORA: Let him in, then. But quietly. Helene, you mustn't tell anybody about this. It's a surprise for my husband.
MAID: I understand, ma'am. . . .

[*She goes out.*]

NORA: Here it comes! What I've been dreading! No, no, it can't happen, it *can't* happen.

[*She walks over and bolts Helmer's door. The maid opens the hall door for Krogstad and shuts it again behind him. He is wearing a fur coat, over-shoes, and a fur cap.*]

NORA [*goes towards him*]: Keep your voice down, my husband is at home.
KROGSTAD: What if he is?
NORA: What do you want with me?
KROGSTAD: To find out something.
NORA: Hurry, then. What is it?

KROGSTAD: You know I've been given notice.

NORA: I couldn't prevent it, Mr. Krogstad, I did my utmost for you, but it was no use.

KROGSTAD: Has your husband so little affection for you? He knows what I can do to you, yet he dares. . . .

NORA: You don't imagine he knows about it!

KROGSTAD: No, I didn't imagine he did. It didn't seem a bit like my good friend Torvald Helmer to show that much courage. . . .

NORA: Mr. Krogstad, I must ask you to show some respect for my husband.

KROGSTAD: Oh, sure! All due respect! But since you are so anxious to keep this business quiet, Mrs. Helmer, I take it you now have a rather clearer idea of just what it is you've done, than you had yesterday.

NORA: Clearer than *you* could ever have given me.

KROGSTAD: Yes, being as I am such a rotten lawyer. . . .

NORA: What do you want with me?

KROGSTAD: I just wanted to see how things stood, Mrs. Helmer. I've been thinking about you all day. Even a mere money-lender, a hack journalist, a—well, even somebody like me has a bit of what you might call feeling.

NORA: Show it then. Think of my little children.

KROGSTAD: Did you or your husband think of mine? But what does it matter now? There was just one thing I wanted to say: you needn't take this business too seriously. I shan't start any proceedings, for the present.

NORA: Ah, I knew you wouldn't.

KROGSTAD: The whole thing can be arranged quite amicably. Nobody need know. Just the three of us.

NORA: My husband must never know.

KROGSTAD: How can you prevent it? Can you pay off the balance?

NORA: No, not immediately.

KROGSTAD: Perhaps you've some way of getting hold of the money in the next few days.

NORA: None I want to make use of.

KROGSTAD: Well, it wouldn't have been very much help to you if you had. Even if you stood there with the cash in your hand and to spare, you still wouldn't get your IOU back from me now.

NORA: What are you going to do with it?

KROGSTAD: Just keep it—have it in my possession. Nobody who isn't implicated need know about it. So if you are thinking of trying any desperate remedies . . .

NORA: Which I am. . . .

KROGSTAD: . . . if you happen to be thinking of running away . . .

NORA: Which I am!

KROGSTAD: . . . or anything worse . . .

NORA: How did you know?

KROGSTAD: . . . forget it!

NORA: How did you know I was thinking of *that*?

KROGSTAD: Most of us think of *that,* to begin with. I did, too; but I didn't have the courage. . . .

NORA [*tonelessly*]: I haven't either.

KROGSTAD [*relieved*]: So you haven't the courage either, eh?

NORA: No, I haven't! I haven't!

KROGSTAD: It would also be very stupid. There'd only be the first domestic storm to get over. . . . I've got a letter to your husband in my pocket here. . . .

NORA: And it's all in there?

KROGSTAD: In as tactful a way as possible.

NORA [*quickly*]: He must never read that letter. Tear it up. I'll find the money somehow.

KROGSTAD: Excuse me, Mrs. Helmer, but I've just told you. . . .

NORA: I'm not talking about the money I owe you. I want to know how much you are demanding from my husband, and I'll get the money.

KROGSTAD: I want no money from your husband.

NORA: What do you want?

KROGSTAD: I'll tell you. I want to get on my feet again, Mrs. Helmer; I want to get to the top. And your husband is going to help me. For the last eighteen months I've gone straight; all that time it's been hard going; I was content to work my way up, step by step. Now I'm being kicked out, and I won't stand for being taken back again as an act of charity. I'm going to get to the top, I tell you. I'm going back into that Bank—with a better job. Your husband is going to create a new vacancy, just for me. . . .

NORA: He'll never do that!

KROGSTAD: He will do it. I know him. He'll do it without so much as a whimper. And once I'm in there with him, you'll see what's what. In less than a year I'll be his right-hand man. It'll be Nils Krogstad, not Torvald Helmer, who'll be running that Bank.

NORA: You'll never live to see that day!

KROGSTAD: You mean you . . . ?

NORA: Now I have the courage.

KROGSTAD: You can't frighten me! A precious pampered little thing like you. . . .

NORA: I'll show you! I'll show you!

KROGSTAD: Under the ice, maybe? Down in the cold, black water? Then being washed up in the spring, bloated, hairless, unrecognizable. . . .

NORA: You can't frighten me.

KROGSTAD: You can't frighten me, either. People don't do that sort of thing, Mrs. Helmer. There wouldn't be any point to it, anyway, I'd still have him right in my pocket.

NORA: Afterwards? When I'm no longer . . .

KROGSTAD: Aren't you forgetting that your reputation would then be entirely in my hands? [*Nora stands looking at him, speechless.*] Well, I've warned you. Don't do anything silly. When Helmer gets my letter, I expect to hear from him. And don't forget: it's him who is forcing me off the straight and narrow again, your own husband! That's something I'll never forgive him for. Goodbye, Mrs. Helmer.

[*He goes out through the hall. Nora crosses to the door, opens it slightly, and listens.*]

NORA: He's going. He hasn't left the letter. No, no, that would be impossible! [*Opens the door further and further.*] What's he doing? He's stopped outside. He's not going down the stairs. Has he changed his mind? Is he . . .? [*A letter falls into the letter-box. Then Krogstad's footsteps are heard receding as he walks downstairs. Nora gives a stifled cry, runs across the room to the sofa table; pause.*] In the letter-box! [*She creeps stealthily across to the hall door.*] There it is! Torvald, Torvald! It's hopeless now!

MRS. LINDE [*comes into the room, left, carrying the costume*]: There, I think that's everything. Shall we try it on?

NORA [*in a low, hoarse voice*]: Kristine, come here.

MRS. LINDE [*throws the dress down on the sofa*]: What's wrong with you? You look upset.

NORA: Come here. Do you see that letter? *There*, look! Through the glass in the letter-box.

MRS. LINDE: Yes, yes, I can see it.

NORA: It's a letter from Krogstad.

MRS. LINDE: Nora! It was Krogstad who lent you the money!

NORA: Yes. And now Torvald will get to know everything.

MRS. LINDE: Believe me, Nora, it's best for you both.

NORA: But there's more to it than that. I forged a signature. . . .

MRS. LINDE: Heavens above!

NORA: Listen, I want to tell you something, Kristine, so you can be my witness.

MRS. LINDE: What do you mean 'witness'? What do you want me to . . . ?

NORA: If I should go mad . . . which might easily happen . . .

MRS. LINDE: Nora!

NORA: Or if anything happened to me . . . which meant I couldn't be here. . . .

MRS. LINDE: Nora, Nora! Are you out of your mind?

NORA: And if somebody else wanted to take it all upon himself, the whole blame, you understand. . . .

MRS. LINDE: Yes, yes. But what makes you think . . . ?

NORA: Then you must testify that it isn't true, Kristine. I'm not out of my mind; I'm quite sane now. And I tell you this: nobody else knew anything, I alone was responsible for the whole thing. Remember that!

MRS. LINDE: I will. But I don't understand a word of it.

NORA: Why should you? You see something miraculous is going to happen.

MRS. LINDE: Something miraculous?

NORA: Yes, a miracle. But something so terrible as well, Kristine— oh, it must *never* happen, not for anything.

MRS. LINDE: I'm going straight over to talk to Krogstad.

NORA: Don't go. He'll only do you harm.

MRS. LINDE: There was a time when he would have done anything for me.

NORA: Him!

MRS. LINDE: Where does he live?

NORA: How do I know . . . ? Wait a minute. [*She feels in her pocket.*] Here's his card. But the letter, the letter . . . !

HELMER [*from his study, knocking on the door*]: Nora!

NORA [*cries out in terror*]: What's that? What do you want?

HELMER: Don't be frightened. We're not coming in. You've locked the door. Are you trying on?

NORA: Yes, yes, I'm trying on. It looks so nice on me, Torvald.

MRS. LINDE [*who has read the card*]: He lives just round the corner.

NORA: It's no use. It's hopeless. The letter is there in the box.

MRS. LINDE: Your husband keeps the key?

NORA: Always.

MRS. LINDE: Krogstad must ask for his letter back unread, he must find some sort of excuse. . . .

NORA: But this is just the time that Torvald generally . . .

MRS. LINDE: Put him off! Go in and keep him busy. I'll be back as soon as I can.

[*She goes out hastily by the hall door. Nora walks over to Helmer's door, opens it and peeps in.*]

NORA: Torvald!

HELMER [*in the study*]: Well, can a man get into his own living-room again now? Come along, Rank, now we'll see . . . [*In the doorway.*] But what's this?

NORA: What, Torvald dear?

HELMER: Rank led me to expect some kind of marvellous transformation.

RANK [*in the doorway*]: That's what I thought too, but I must have been mistaken.

NORA: I'm not showing myself off to anybody before tomorrow.

HELMER: Nora dear, you look tired. You haven't been practising too hard?

NORA: No, I haven't practised at all yet.

HELMER: You'll have to, though.

NORA: Yes, I certainly must, Torvald. But I just can't get anywhere without your help: I've completely forgotten it.

HELMER: We'll soon polish it up.

NORA: Yes, do help me, Torvald. Promise? I'm so nervous. All those people. . . . You must devote yourself exclusively to me this evening. Pens away! Forget all about the office! Promise me, Torvald dear!

HELMER: I promise. This evening I am wholly and entirely at your service . . . helpless little thing that you are. Oh, but while I remember, I'll just look first . . .

[*He goes towards the hall door.*]

NORA: What do you want out there?

HELMER: Just want to see if there are any letters.

NORA: No, don't, Torvald!

HELMER: Why not?

NORA: Torvald, *please!* There aren't any.

HELMER: Just let me see.

[*He starts to go. Nora, at the piano, plays the opening bars of the tarantella.*]

HELMER [*at the door, stops*]: Aha!

NORA: I shan't be able to dance tomorrow if I don't rehearse it with you.

HELMER [*walks to her*]: Are you really so nervous, Nora dear?

NORA: Terribly nervous. Let me run through it now. There's still time before supper. Come and sit here and play for me, Torvald dear. Tell me what to do, keep me right—as you always do.

HELMER: Certainly, with pleasure, if that's what you want.

[*He sits at the piano. Nora snatches the tambourine out of the box, and also a long gaily-coloured shawl which she drapes round herself, then with a bound she leaps forward.*]

NORA [*shouts*]: Now play for me! Now I'll dance!

[*Helmer plays and Nora dances; Dr. Rank stands at the piano behind Helmer and looks on.*]

HELMER [*playing*]: Not so fast! Not so fast!

NORA: I can't help it.

HELMER: Not so wild, Nora!

NORA: This is how it has to be.

HELMER [*stops*]: No, no, that won't do at all.

NORA [*laughs and swings the tambourine*]: Didn't I tell you?

RANK: Let me play for her.

HELMER [*gets up*]: Yes, do. Then I'll be better able to tell her what to do.

[*Rank sits down at the piano and plays. Nora dances more and more wildly. Helmer stands by the stove giving her repeated directions as she dances; she does not seem to hear them. Her hair comes undone and falls about her shoulders; she pays no attention and goes on dancing. Mrs. Linde enters.*]

MRS. LINDE [*standing as though spellbound in the doorway*]: Ah . . . !

NORA [*dancing*]: See what fun we are having, Kristine.

HELMER: But my dear darling Nora, you are dancing as though your life depended on it.

NORA: It does.

HELMER: Stop, Rank! This is sheer madness. Stop, I say.

[*Rank stops playing and Nora comes to a sudden halt.*]

HELMER [*crosses to her*]:   I would never have believed it. You have forgotten everything I ever taught you.

NORA [*throwing away the tambourine*]:   There you are, you see.

HELMER: Well, some more instruction is certainly needed there.

NORA: Yes, you see how necessary it is. You must go on coaching me right up to the last minute. Promise me, Torvald?

HELMER: You can rely on me.

NORA: You mustn't think about anything else but me until after tomorrow . . . mustn't open any letters . . . mustn't touch the letter-box.

HELMER: Ah, you are still frightened of what that man might . . .

NORA: Yes, yes, I am.

HELMER: I can see from your face there's already a letter there from him.

NORA: I don't know. I think so. But you mustn't read anything like that now. We don't want anything horrid coming between us until all this is over.

RANK [*softly to Helmer*]:   I shouldn't cross her.

HELMER [*puts his arm round her*]:   The child must have her way. But tomorrow night, when your dance is done. . . .

NORA: Then you are free.

MAID [*in the doorway, right*]:   Dinner is served, madam.

NORA: We'll have champagne, Helene.

MAID: Very good, madam.

[*She goes.*]

HELMER: Aha! It's to be quite a banquet, eh?

NORA: With champagne flowing until dawn. [*Shouts.*] And some macaroons, Helene . . . lots of them, for once in a while.

HELMER [*seizing her hands*]:   Now, now, not so wild and excitable! Let me see you being my own little singing bird again.

NORA: Oh yes, I will. And if you'll just go in . . . you, too, Dr. Rank. Kristine, you must help me to do my hair.

RANK [*softly, as they leave*]:   There isn't anything . . . anything as it were, impending, is there?

HELMER: No, not at all, my dear fellow. It's nothing but these childish fears I was telling you about.

[*They go out to the right.*]

NORA: Well?

MRS. LINDE: He's left town.

NORA: I saw it in your face.

MRS. LINDE: He's coming back tomorrow evening. I left a note for him.

NORA: You shouldn't have done that. You must let things take their course. Because really it's a case for rejoicing, waiting like this for the miracle.

MRS. LINDE: What is it you are waiting for?

NORA: Oh, you wouldn't understand. Go and join the other two. I'll be there in a minute.

[*Mrs. Linde goes into the dining-room. Nora stands for a moment as though to collect herself, then looks at her watch.*]

NORA: Five. Seven hours to midnight. Then twenty-four hours till the next midnight. Then the tarantella will be over. Twenty-four and seven? Thirty-one hours to live.

HELMER [*in the doorway, right*]:   What's happened to our little sky-lark?

NORA [*running towards him with open arms*]:   Here she is!

Act III

The same room. The round table has been moved to the centre of the room, and the chairs placed round it. A lamp is burning on the table. The door to the hall stands open. Dance music can be heard coming from the floor above. Mrs. Linde is sitting by the table, idly turning over the pages of a book; she tries to read, but does not seem able to concentrate. Once or twice she listens, tensely, for a sound at the front door.

MRS. LINDE [*looking at her watch*]:   Still not here. There isn't much time left. I only hope he hasn't . . . [*She listens again.*] Ah, there he is. [*She goes out into the hall, and cautiously opens the front door. Soft footsteps can be heard on the stairs. She whispers.*] Come in. There's nobody here.

KROGSTAD [*in the doorway*]:   I found a note from you at home. What does it all mean?

MRS. LINDE: I *had* to talk to you.

KROGSTAD: Oh? And did it have to be here, in this house?

MRS. LINDE: It wasn't possible over at my place, it hasn't a separate entrance. Come in. We are quite alone. The maid's asleep and the Helmers are at a party upstairs.

KROGSTAD [*comes into the room*]: Well, well! So the Helmers are out dancing tonight! Really?

MRS. LINDE: Yes, why not?

KROGSTAD: Why not indeed!

MRS. LINDE: Well then, Nils. Let's talk.

KROGSTAD: Have we two anything more to talk about?

MRS. LINDE: We have a great deal to talk about.

KROGSTAD: I shouldn't have thought so.

MRS. LINDE: That's because you never really understood me.

KROGSTAD: What else was there to understand, apart from the old, old story? A heartless woman throws a man over the moment something more profitable offers itself.

MRS. LINDE: Do you really think I'm so heartless? Do you think I found it easy to break it off.

KROGSTAD: Didn't you?

MRS. LINDE: You didn't really believe that?

KROGSTAD: If that wasn't the case, why did you write to me as you did?

MRS. LINDE: There was nothing else I could do. If I had to make the break, I felt in duty bound to destroy any feeling that you had for me.

KROGSTAD [*clenching his hands*]: So that's how it was. And all that . . . was for money!

MRS. LINDE: You mustn't forget I had a helpless mother and two young brothers. We couldn't wait for you, Nils. At that time you hadn't much immediate prospect of anything.

KROGSTAD: That may be. But you had no right to throw me over for somebody else.

MRS. LINDE: Well, I don't know. Many's the time I've asked myself whether I was justified.

KROGSTAD [*more quietly*]: When I lost you, it was just as if the ground had slipped away from under my feet. Look at me now: a broken man clinging to the wreck of his life.

MRS. LINDE: Help might be near.

KROGSTAD: It was near. Then you came along and got in the way.

MRS. LINDE: Quite without knowing, Nils. I only heard today it's you I'm supposed to be replacing at the Bank.

KROGSTAD: If you say so, I believe you. But now you do know, aren't you going to withdraw?

MRS. LINDE: No, that wouldn't benefit you in the slightest.

KROGSTAD: Benefit, benefit . . . ! I would do it just the same.

MRS. LINDE: I have learned to go carefully. Life and hard, bitter necessity have taught me that.

KROGSTAD: And life has taught me not to believe in pretty speeches.

MRS. LINDE: Then life has taught you a very sensible thing. But deeds are something you surely must believe in?

KROGSTAD: How do you mean?

MRS. LINDE: You said you were like a broken man clinging to the wreck of his life.

KROGSTAD: And I said it with good reason.

MRS. LINDE: And I am like a broken woman clinging to the wreck of her life. Nobody to care about, and nobody to care for.

KROGSTAD: It was your own choice.

MRS. LINDE: At the time there was no other choice.

KROGSTAD: Well, what of it?

MRS. LINDE: Nils, what about us two castaways joining forces.

KROGSTAD: What's that you say?

MRS. LINDE: Two of us on *one* wreck surely stand a better chance than each on his own.

KROGSTAD: Kristine!

MRS. LINDE: Why do you suppose I came to town?

KROGSTAD: You mean, you thought of me?

MRS. LINDE: Without work I couldn't live. All my life I have worked, for as long as I can remember; that has always been my one great joy. But now I'm completely alone in the world, and feeling horribly empty and forlorn. There's no pleasure in working only for yourself. Nils, give me somebody and something to work for.

KROGSTAD: I don't believe all this. It's only a woman's hysteria, wanting to be all magnanimous and self-sacrificing.

MRS. LINDE: Have you ever known me hysterical before?

KROGSTAD: Would you really do this? Tell me—do you know all about my past?

MRS. LINDE: Yes.

KROGSTAD: And you know what people think about me?

MRS. LINDE: Just now you hinted you thought you might have been a different person with me.

KROGSTAD: I'm convinced I would.

MRS. LINDE: Couldn't it still happen?

KROGSTAD: Kristine! You know what you are saying, don't you? Yes, you do. I can see you do. Have you really the courage . . . ?

MRS. LINDE: I need someone to mother, and your children need a mother. We two need each other. Nils, I have faith in what, deep down, you are. With you I can face anything.

KROGSTAD [*seizing her hands*]: Thank you, thank you, Kristine. And I'll soon have everybody looking up to me, or I'll know the reason why. Ah, but I was forgetting. . . .

MRS. LINDE: Hush! The tarantella! You must go!

KROGSTAD: Why? What is it?

MRS. LINDE: You hear that dance upstairs? When it's finished they'll be coming.

KROGSTAD: Yes, I'll go. It's too late to do anything. Of course, you know nothing about what steps I've taken against the Helmers.

MRS. LINDE: Yes, Nils, I do know.

KROGSTAD: Yet you still want to go on. . . .

MRS. LINDE: I know how far a man like you can be driven by despair.

KROGSTAD: Oh, if only I could undo what I've done!

MRS. LINDE: You still can. Your letter is still there in the box.

KROGSTAD: Are you sure?

MRS. LINDE: Quite sure. But . . .

KROGSTAD [*regards her searchingly*]: Is that how things are? You want to save your friend at any price? Tell me straight. Is that it?

MRS. LINDE: When you've sold yourself *once* for other people's sake, you don't do it again.

KROGSTAD: I shall demand my letter back.

MRS. LINDE: No, no.

KROGSTAD: Of course I will, I'll wait here till Helmer comes. I'll tell him he has to give me my letter back . . . that it's only about my notice . . . that he mustn't read it. . . .

MRS. LINDE: No, Nils, don't ask for it back.

KROGSTAD: But wasn't that the very reason you got me here?

MRS. LINDE: Yes, that was my first terrified reaction. But that was yesterday, and it's quite incredible the things I've witnessed in this house in the last twenty-four hours. Helmer must know everything. This unhappy secret must come out. Those two must have the whole thing out between them. All this secrecy and deception, it just can't go on.

KROGSTAD: Well, if you want to risk it. . . . But one thing I can do, and I'll do it at once. . . .

MRS. LINDE [*listening*]: Hurry! Go, go! The dance has stopped. We aren't safe a moment longer.

KROGSTAD: I'll wait for you downstairs.

MRS. LINDE: Yes, do. You must see me home.

KROGSTAD: I've never been so incredibly happy before.

[*He goes out by the front door. The door out into the hall remains standing open.*]

MRS. LINDE [*tidies the room a little and gets her hat and coat ready*]: How things change! How things change! Somebody to work for . . . to live for. A home to bring happiness into. Just let me get down to it. . . . I wish they'd come. . . . [*Listens.*] Ah, there they are. . . . Get my things.

[*She takes her coat and hat. The voices of Helmer and Nora are heard outside. A key is turned and Helmer pushes Nora almost forcibly into the hall. She is dressed in the Italian costume, with a big black shawl over it. He is in evening dress, and over it a black cloak, open.*]

NORA [*still in the doorway, reluctantly*]: No, no, not in here! I want to go back up again. I don't want to leave so early.

HELMER: But my dearest Nora . . .

NORA: Oh, please, Torvald, I beg you. . . . *Please*, just for another hour.

HELMER: Not another minute, Nora my sweet. You remember what we agreed. There now, come along in. You'll catch cold standing there.

[*He leads her, in spite of her resistance, gently but firmly into the room.*]

MRS. LINDE: Good evening.

NORA: Kristine!

HELMER: Why, Mrs. Linde. You here so late?

MRS. LINDE: Yes. You must forgive me but I did so want to see Nora all dressed up.

NORA: Have you been sitting here waiting for me?

MRS. LINDE: Yes, I'm afraid I wasn't in time to catch you before you went upstairs. And I felt I couldn't leave again without seeing you.

HELMER [*removing Nora's shawl*]: Well take a good look at her. I think I can say she's worth looking at. Isn't she lovely, Mrs. Linde?

MRS. LINDE: Yes, I must say. . . .

HELMER: Isn't she quite extraordinarily lovely? That's what everybody at the party thought, too. But she's dreadfully stubborn . . .

the sweet little thing! And what shall we do about that? Would you believe it, I nearly had to use force to get her away.

NORA: Oh Torvald, you'll be sorry you didn't let me stay, even for half an hour.

HELMER: You hear that, Mrs. Linde? She dances her tarantella, there's wild applause—which was well deserved, although the performance was perhaps rather realistic . . . I mean, rather more so than was strictly necessary from the artistic point of view. But anyway! The main thing is she was a success, a tremendous success. Was I supposed to let her stay after that? Spoil the effect? No thank you! I took my lovely little Capri girl—my capricious little Capri girl, I might say—by the arm, whisked her once round the room, a curtsey all round, and then—as they say in novels—the beautiful vision vanished. An exit should always be effective, Mrs. Linde. But I just can't get Nora to see that. Phew! It's warm in here. [*He throws his cloak over a chair and opens the door to his study.*] What? It's dark. Oh yes, of course. Excuse me. . . .

[*He goes in and lights a few candles.*]

NORA [*quickly, in a breathless whisper*]: Well?

MRS. LINDE [*softly*]: I've spoken to him.

NORA: And . . . ?

MRS. LINDE: Nora . . . you must tell your husband everything.

NORA [*tonelessly*]: I knew it.

MRS. LINDE: You've got nothing to fear from Krogstad. But you must speak.

NORA: I won't.

MRS. LINDE: Then the letter will.

NORA: Thank you, Kristine. Now I know what's to be done. Hush . . . !

HELMER [*comes in again*]: Well, Mrs. Linde, have you finished admiring her?

MRS. LINDE: Yes. And now I must say good night.

HELMER: Oh, already? Is this yours, this knitting?

MRS. LINDE [*takes it*]: Yes, thank you. I nearly forgot it.

HELMER: So you knit, eh?

MRS. LINDE: Yes.

HELMER: You should embroider instead, you know.

MRS. LINDE: Oh? Why?

HELMER: So much prettier. Watch! You hold the embroidery like this in the left hand, and then you take the needle in the right hand, like this, and you describe a long, graceful curve. Isn't that right?

MRS. LINDE: Yes, I suppose so. . . .

HELMER: Whereas knitting on the other hand just can't help being ugly. Look! Arms pressed into the sides, the knitting needles going up and down—there's something Chinese about it. . . . Ah, that was marvellous champagne they served tonight.

MRS. LINDE: Well, good night, Nora! And stop being so stubborn.

HELMER: Well said, Mrs. Linde!

MRS. LINDE: Good night, Mr. Helmer.

HELMER [*accompanying her to the door*]: Good night, good night! You'll get home all right, I hope? I'd be only too pleased to. . . . But you haven't far to walk. Good night, good night! [*She goes; he shuts the door behind her and comes in again.*] There we are, got rid of her at last. She's a frightful bore, that woman.

NORA: Aren't you very tired, Torvald?

HELMER: Not in the least.

NORA: Not sleepy?

HELMER: Not at all. On the contrary, I feel extremely lively. What about you? Yes, you look quite tired and sleepy.

NORA: Yes, I'm very tired. I just want to fall straight off to sleep.

HELMER: There you are, you see! Wasn't I right in thinking we shouldn't stay any longer.

NORA: Oh, everything you do is right.

HELMER [*kissing her forehead*]: There's my little sky-lark talking common sense. Did you notice how gay Rank was this evening?

NORA: Oh, was he? I didn't get a chance to talk to him.

HELMER: I hardly did either. But it's a long time since I saw him in such a good mood. [*Looks at Nora for a moment or two, then comes nearer her.*] Ah, it's wonderful to be back in our own home again, and quite alone with you. How irresistibly lovely you are, Nora!

NORA: Don't look at me like that, Torvald!

HELMER: Can't I look at my most treasured possession? At all this loveliness that's mine and mine alone, completely and utterly mine.

NORA [*walks round to the other side of the table*]: You mustn't talk to me like that tonight.

HELMER [*following her*]: You still have the tarantella in your blood, I see. And that makes you even more desirable. Listen! The guests are beginning to leave now. [*Softly.*] Nora . . . soon the whole house will be silent.

NORA: I should hope so.

HELMER: Of course you do, don't you, Nora my darling? You know, whenever I'm out at a party with you . . . do you know why I never talk to you very much, why I always stand away from you and only steal a quick glance at you now and then . . . do you know why I do that? It's because I'm pretending we are secretly in love, secretly engaged and nobody suspects there is anything between us.

NORA: Yes, yes. I know your thoughts are always with me, of course.

HELMER: And when it's time to go, and I lay your shawl round those shapely, young shoulders, round the exquisite curve of your neck . . . I pretend that you are my young bride, that we are just leaving our wedding, that I am taking you to our new home for the first time . . . to be alone with you for the first time . . . quite alone with your young and trembling loveliness! All evening I've been longing for you, and nothing else. And as I watched you darting and swaying in the tarantella, my blood was on fire . . . I couldn't bear it any longer . . . and that's why I brought you down here with me so early. . . .

NORA: Go away, Torvald! Please leave me alone. I won't have it.

HELMER: What's this? It's just your little game isn't it, my little Nora. Won't! Won't! Am I not your husband . . . ?

[*There is a knock on the front door.*]

NORA [*startled*]: Listen . . . !

HELMER [*going towards the hall*]: Who's there?

RANK [*outside*]: It's me. Can I come in for a minute?

HELMER [*in a low voice, annoyed*]: Oh, what does he want now? [*Aloud.*] Wait a moment. [*He walks across and opens the door.*] How nice of you to look in on your way out.

RANK: I fancied I heard your voice and I thought I would just look in. [*He takes a quick glance round.*] Ah yes, this dear, familiar old place! How cosy and comfortable you've got things here, you two.

HELMER: You seemed to be having a pretty good time upstairs yourself.

RANK: Capital! Why shouldn't I? Why not make the most of things in this world? At least as much as one can, and for as long as one can. The wine was excellent. . . .

HELMER: Especially the champagne.

RANK: You noticed that too, did you? It's incredible the amount I was able to put away.

NORA: Torvald also drank a lot of champagne this evening.

RANK: Oh?

NORA: Yes, and that always makes him quite merry.

RANK: Well, why shouldn't a man allow himself a jolly evening after a day well spent?

HELMER: Well spent? I'm afraid I can't exactly claim that.

RANK [*clapping him on the shoulder*]: But I can, you see!

NORA: Dr. Rank, am I right in thinking you carried out a certain laboratory test today?

RANK: Exactly.

HELMER: Look at our little Nora talking about laboratory tests!

NORA: And may I congratulate you on the result?

RANK: You may indeed.

NORA: So it was good?

RANK: The best possible, for both doctor and patient—certainty!

NORA [*quickly and searchingly*]: Certainty?

RANK: Absolute certainty. So why shouldn't I allow myself a jolly evening after that?

NORA: Quite right, Dr. Rank.

HELMER: I quite agree. As long as you don't suffer for it in the morning.

RANK: Well, you never get anything for nothing in this life.

NORA: Dr. Rank . . . you are very fond of masquerades, aren't you?

RANK: Yes, when there are plenty of amusing disguises. . . .

NORA: Tell me, what shall we two go as next time?

HELMER: There's frivolity for you . . . thinking about the next time already!

RANK: We two? I'll tell you. You must go as Lady Luck. . . .

HELMER: Yes, but how do you find a costume to suggest *that?*

RANK: Your wife could simply go in her everyday clothes. . . .

HELMER: That was nicely said. But don't you know what you would be?

RANK: Yes, my dear friend, I know exactly what I shall be.

HELMER: Well?

RANK: At the next masquerade, I shall be invisible.

HELMER: That's a funny idea!

RANK: There's a big black cloak . . . haven't you heard of the cloak of invisibility? That comes right down over you, and then nobody can see you.

HELMER [*suppressing a smile*]: Of course, that's right.

RANK: But I'm clean forgetting what I came for. Helmer, give me a cigar, one of the dark Havanas.

HELMER: With the greatest of pleasure.

[*He offers his case.*]

RANK [*takes one and cuts the end off*]:   Thanks.

NORA [*strikes a match*]:   Let me give you a light.

RANK: Thank you. [*She holds out the match and he lights his cigar.*] And now, goodbye!

HELMER: Goodbye, goodbye, my dear fellow!

NORA: Sleep well, Dr. Rank.

RANK: Thank you for that wish.

NORA: Wish me the same.

RANK: You? All right, if you want me to. . . . Sleep well. And thanks for the light.

[*He nods to them both, and goes.*]

HELMER [*subdued*]:   He's had a lot to drink.

NORA [*absently*]:   Very likely.

[*Helmer takes a bunch of keys out of his pocket and goes out into the hall.*]

NORA: Torvald . . . what do you want there?

HELMER: I must empty the letter-box, it's quite full. There'll be no room for the papers in the morning. . . .

NORA: Are you going to work tonight?

HELMER: You know very well I'm not. Hello, what's this? Somebody's been at the lock.

NORA: At the lock?

HELMER: Yes, I'm sure of it. Why should that be? I'd hardly have thought the maids . . . ? Here's a broken hair-pin. Nora, it's one of yours. . . .

NORA [*quickly*]:   It must have been the children. . . .

HELMER: Then you'd better tell them not to. Ah . . . there . . . I've managed to get it open. [*He takes the things out and shouts into the kitchen.*] Helene! . . . Helene, put the light out in the hall. [*He comes into the room again with the letters in his hand and shuts the hall door.*] Look how it all mounts up. [*Runs through them.*] What's this?

NORA: The letter! Oh no, Torvald, no!

HELMER: Two visiting cards . . . from Dr. Rank.

NORA: From Dr. Rank?

HELMER [*looking at them*]:   Dr. Rank, Medical Practitioner. They were on top. He must have put them in as he left.

NORA: Is there anything on them?

HELMER: There's a black cross above his name. Look. What an uncanny idea. It's just as if he were announcing his own death.

NORA: He is.

HELMER: What? What do you know about it? Has he said anything to you?

NORA: Yes. He said when these cards came, he would have taken his last leave of us. He was going to shut himself up and die.

HELMER: Poor fellow! Of course I knew we couldn't keep him with us very long. But so soon. . . . And hiding himself away like a wounded animal.

NORA: When it has to happen, it's best that it should happen without words. Don't you think so, Torvald?

HELMER [*walking up and down*]: He had grown so close to us. I don't think I can imagine him gone. His suffering and his loneliness seemed almost to provide a background of dark cloud to the sunshine of our lives. Well, perhaps it's all for the best. For him at any rate. [*Pauses.*] And maybe for us as well, Nora. Now there's just the two of us. [*Puts his arms round her.*] Oh, my darling wife, I can't hold you close enough. You know, Nora . . . many's the time I wish you were threatened by some terrible danger so I could risk everything, body and soul, for your sake.

NORA [*tears herself free and says firmly and decisively*]: Now you must read your letters, Torvald.

HELMER: No, no, not tonight. I want to be with you, my darling wife.

NORA: Knowing all the time your friend is dying . . . ?

HELMER: You are right. It's been a shock to both of us. This ugly thing has come between us . . . thoughts of death and decay. We must try to free ourselves from it. Until then . . . we shall go our separate ways.

NORA [*her arms round his neck*]: Torvald . . . good night! Good night!

HELMER [*kisses her forehead*]: Goodnight, my little singing bird. Sleep well, Nora, I'll just read through my letters.

[*He takes the letters into his room and shuts the door behind him.*]

NORA [*gropes around her, wild-eyed, seizes Helmer's cloak, wraps it round herself, and whispers quickly, hoarsely, spasmodically*]: Never see him again. Never, never, never. [*Throws her shawl over her head.*] And never see the children again either. Never, never. Oh, that black icy water. Oh, that bottomless . . . ! If only it were all over! He's got it now.

Now he's reading it. Oh no, no! Not yet! Torvald, goodbye . . . and my children. . . .

[*She rushes out in the direction of the hall; at the same moment Helmer flings open his door and stands there with an open letter in his hand.*]

HELMER: Nora!

NORA [*shrieks*]: Ah!

HELMER: What is this? Do you know what is in this letter?

NORA: Yes, I know. Let me go! Let me out!

HELMER [*holds her back*]: Where are you going?

NORA [*trying to tear herself free*]: You mustn't try to save me, Torvald!

HELMER [*reels back*]: True! Is it true what he writes? How dreadful! No, no, it can't possibly be true.

NORA: It *is* true. I loved you more than anything else in the world.

HELMER: Don't come to me with a lot of paltry excuses!

NORA [*taking a step towards him*]: Torvald . . . !

HELMER: Miserable woman . . . what is this you have done?

NORA: Let me go. I won't have you taking the blame for me. You mustn't take it on yourself.

HELMER: Stop play-acting! [*Locks the front door.*] You are staying here to give an account of yourself. Do you understand what you have done? Answer me! Do you understand?

NORA [*looking fixedly at him, her face hardening*]: Yes, now I'm really beginning to understand.

HELMER [*walking up and down*]: Oh, what a terrible awakening this is. All these eight years . . . this woman who was my pride and joy . . . a hypocrite, a liar, worse than that, a criminal! Oh, how utterly squalid it all is! Ugh! Ugh! [*Nora remains silent and looks fixedly at him.*] I should have realized something like this would happen. I should have seen it coming. All your father's irresponsible ways. . . . Quiet! All your father's irresponsible ways are coming out in you. No religion, no morals, no sense of duty. . . . Oh, this is my punishment for turning a blind eye to him. It was for your sake I did it, and this is what I get for it.

NORA: Yes, this.

HELMER: Now you have ruined my entire happiness, jeopardized my whole future. It's terrible to think of. Here I am, at the mercy of a thoroughly unscrupulous person; he can do whatever he likes with me, demand anything he wants, order me about just as he chooses . . . and I daren't even whimper. I'm done for, a miserable failure, and it's all the fault of a feather-brained woman!

NORA: When I've left this world behind, you will be free.

HELMER: Oh, stop pretending! Your father was just the same, always ready with fine phrases. What good would it do me if you left this world behind, as you put it? Not the slightest bit of good. He can still let it all come out, if he likes; and if he does, people might even suspect me of being an accomplice in these criminal acts of yours. They might even think I was the one behind it all, that it was I who pushed you into it! And it's you I have to thank for this . . . and when I've taken such good care of you, all our married life. Now do you understand what you have done to me?

NORA [*coldly and calmly*]: Yes.

HELMER: I just can't understand it, it's so incredible. But we must see about putting things right. Take that shawl off. Take it off, I tell you! I must see if I can't find some way or other of appeasing him. The thing must be hushed up at all costs. And as far as you and I are concerned, things must appear to go on exactly as before. But only in the eyes of the world, of course. In other words you'll go on living here; that's understood. But you will not be allowed to bring up the children, I can't trust you with them. . . . Oh, that I should have to say this to the woman I loved so dearly, the woman I still. . . . Well, that must be all over and done with. From now on, there can be no question of happiness. All we can do is save the bits and pieces from the wreck, preserve appearances. . . . [*The front door-bell rings. Helmer gives a start.*] What's that? So late? How terrible, supposing. . . . If he should . . . ? Hide, Nora! Say you are not well.

[*Nora stands motionless. Helmer walks across and opens the door into the hall.*]

MAID [*half dressed, in the hall*]: It's a note for Mrs. Helmer.

HELMER: Give it to me. [*He snatches the note and shuts the door.*] Yes, it's from him. You can't have it. I want to read it myself.

NORA: You read it then.

HELMER [*by the lamp*]: I hardly dare. Perhaps this is the end, for both of us. Well, I must know. [*He opens the note hurriedly, reads a few lines, looks at another enclosed sheet, and gives a cry of joy.*] Nora! [*Nora looks at him inquiringly.*] Nora! I must read it again. Yes, yes, it's true! I am saved! Nora, I am saved!

NORA: And me?

HELMER: You too, of course, we are both saved, you as well as me. Look, he's sent your IOU back. He sends his regrets and apologies for what he has done. . . . His luck has changed. . . . Oh, what does it matter what he says. We are saved, Nora! Nobody can do anything to you now. Oh, Nora, Nora . . . but let's get rid of this disgusting thing first. Let me see. . . . [*He glances at the IOU.*] No, I don't want to see it. I don't want it to be anything but a dream. [*He tears up the IOU and both letters, throws all the pieces into the stove and watches them burn.*] Well, that's the end of that. He said in his note you'd known since Christmas Eve. . . . You must have had three terrible days of it, Nora.

NORA: These three days haven't been easy.

HELMER: The agonies you must have gone through! When the only way out seemed to be. . . . No, let's forget the whole ghastly thing. We can rejoice and say: It's all over! It's all over! Listen to me, Nora! You don't seem to understand: it's all over! Why this grim look on your face? Oh, poor little Nora, of course I understand. You can't bring yourself to believe I've forgiven you. But I have, Nora, I swear it. I forgive you everything. I know you did what you did because you loved me.

NORA: That's true.

HELMER: You loved me as a wife should love her husband. It was simply that you didn't have the experience to judge what was the best way of going about things. But do you think I love you any the less for that; just because you don't know how to act on your own responsibility? No, no, you just lean on me, I shall give you all the advice and guidance you need. I wouldn't be a proper man if I didn't find a woman doubly attractive for being so obviously helpless. You mustn't dwell on the harsh things I said in that first moment of horror, when I thought everything was going to come crashing down about my ears. I have forgiven you, Nora, I swear it! I have forgiven you!

NORA: Thank you for your forgiveness.

[*She goes out through the door, right.*]

HELMER: No, don't go! [*He looks through the doorway.*] What are you doing in the spare room?

NORA: Taking off this fancy dress.

HELMER [*standing at the open door*]: Yes, do. You try and get some rest, and set your mind at peace again, my frightened little song-bird. Have a good long sleep; you know you are safe and sound under my wing. [*Walks up and down near the door.*] What a nice, cosy little home we have here, Nora! Here you can find refuge. Here I shall hold you like a hunted dove I have rescued unscathed from the cruel talons of the hawk, and calm your poor beating heart. And that will come, gradually, Nora, believe me. Tomorrow you'll see everything quite differently. Soon everything will be just as it was before. You won't need me to keep on telling you I've forgiven you; you'll feel convinced of it in your own heart. You don't really imagine me ever thinking of turning you out, or even of reproaching you? Oh, a real man isn't made that way, you know, Nora. For a man, there's something indescribably moving and very satisfying in knowing that he has forgiven his wife—forgiven her, completely and genuinely, from the depths of his heart. It's as though it made her his property in a double sense: he has, as it were, given her a new life, and she becomes in a way both his wife and at the same time his child. That is how you will seem to me after today, helpless, perplexed little thing that you are. Don't you worry your pretty little head about anything, Nora. Just you be frank with me, and I'll take all the decisions for you. . . . What's this? Not in bed? You've changed your things?

NORA [*in her everyday dress*]: Yes, Torvald, I've changed.

HELMER: What for? It's late.

NORA: I shan't sleep tonight.

HELMER: But my dear Nora. . . .

NORA [*looks at her watch*]: It's not so terribly late. Sit down, Torvald. We two have a lot to talk about.

[*She sits down at one side of the table.*]

HELMER: Nora, what is all this? Why so grim?

NORA: Sit down. It'll take some time. I have a lot to say to you.

HELMER [*sits down at the table opposite her*]: You frighten me, Nora. I don't understand you.

NORA: Exactly. You don't understand me. And I have never understood you, either—until tonight. No, don't interrupt. I just want you to listen to what I have to say. We are going to have things out, Torvald.

HELMER: What do you mean?

NORA: Isn't there anything that strikes you about the way we two are sitting here?

HELMER: What's that?

NORA: We have now been married eight years. Hasn't it struck you this is the first time you and I, man and wife, have had a serious talk together?

HELMER: Depends what you mean by 'serious.'

NORA: Eight whole years—no, more, ever since we first knew each other—and never have we exchanged one serious word about serious things.

HELMER: What did you want me to do? Get you involved in worries that you couldn't possibly help me to bear?

NORA: I'm not talking about worries. I say we've never once sat down together and seriously tried to get to the bottom of anything.

HELMER: But, my dear Nora, would that have been a thing for you?

NORA: That's just it. You have never understood me . . . I've been greatly wronged, Torvald. First by my father, and then by you.

HELMER: What! Us two! The two people who loved you more than anybody?

NORA [*shakes her head*]: You two never loved me. You only thought now nice it was to be in love with me.

HELMER: But, Nora, what's this you are saying?

NORA: It's right, you know, Torvald. At home, Daddy used to tell me what he thought, then I thought the same. And if I thought differently, I kept quiet about it, because he wouldn't have liked it. He used to call me his baby doll, and he played with me as I used to play with my dolls. Then I came to live in your house. . . .

HELMER: What way is that to talk about our marriage?

NORA [*imperturbably*]: What I mean is: I passed out of Daddy's hands into yours. You arranged everything to your tastes, and I acquired the same tastes. Or I pretended to . . . I don't really know . . . I think it was a bit of both, sometimes one thing and sometimes the other. When I look back, it seems to me I have been living here like a beggar, from hand to mouth. I lived by doing tricks for you, Torvald. But that's the way you wanted it. You and Daddy did me a great wrong. It's your fault that I've never made anything of my life.

HELMER: Nora, how unreasonable . . . how ungrateful you are! Haven't you been happy here?

NORA: No, never. I thought I was, but I wasn't really.

HELMER: Not . . . not happy!

NORA: No, just gay. And you've always been so kind to me. But our house has never been anything but a play-room. I have been your doll wife, just as at home I was Daddy's doll child. And the children in turn have been my dolls. I thought it was fun when you came and played with me, just as they thought it was fun when I went and played with them. That's been our marriage, Torvald.

HELMER: There is some truth in what you say, exaggerated and hysterical though it is. But from now on it will be different. Play-time is over; now comes the time for lessons.

NORA: Whose lessons? Mine or the children's?

HELMER: Both yours and the children's, my dear Nora.

NORA: Ah, Torvald, you are not the man to teach me to be a good wife for you.

HELMER: How can you say that?

NORA: And what sort of qualifications have I to teach the children?

HELMER: Nora!

NORA: Didn't you say yourself, a minute or two ago, that you couldn't trust me with that job.

HELMER: In the heat of the moment! You shouldn't pay any attention to that.

NORA: On the contrary, you were quite right. I'm not up to it. There's another problem needs solving first. I must take steps to educate myself. You are not the man to help me there. That's something I must do on my own. That's why I'm leaving you.

HELMER [*jumps up*]: What did you say?

NORA: If I'm ever to reach any understanding of myself and the things around me, I must learn to stand alone. That's why I can't stay here with you any longer.

HELMER: Nora! Nora!

NORA: I'm leaving here at once. I dare say Kristine will put me up for tonight. . . .

HELMER: You are out of your mind! I won't let you! I forbid you!

NORA: It's no use forbidding me anything now. I'm taking with me my own personal belongings. I don't want anything of yours, either now or later.

HELMER: This is madness!

NORA: Tomorrow I'm going home—to what used to be my home, I mean. It will be easier for me to find something to do there.

HELMER: Oh, you blind, inexperienced . . .

NORA: I must set about *getting* experience, Torvald.

HELMER: And leave your home, your husband and your children? Don't you care what people will say?

NORA: That's no concern of mine. All I know is that this is necessary for *me*.

HELMER: This is outrageous! You are betraying your most sacred duty.

NORA: And what do you consider to be my most sacred duty?

HELMER: Does it take me to tell you that? Isn't it your duty to your husband and your children?

NORA: I have another duty equally sacred.

HELMER: You have not. What duty might *that* be?

NORA: My duty to myself.

HELMER: First and foremost, you are a wife and mother.

NORA: That I don't believe any more. I believe that first and foremost I am an individual, just as much as you are—or at least I'm going to try to be. I know most people agree with you, Torvald, and that's also what it says in books. But I'm not content any more with what most people say, or with what it says in books. I have to think things out for myself, and get things clear.

HELMER: Surely you are clear about your position in your own home? Haven't you an infallible guide in questions like these? Haven't you your religion?

NORA: Oh, Torvald, I don't really know what religion is.

HELMER: What do you say!

NORA: All I know is what Pastor Hansen said when I was confirmed. He said religion was this, that and the other. When I'm away from all this and on my own, I'll go into that, too. I want to find out whether what Pastor Hansen told me was right—or at least whether it's right for *me*.

HELMER: This is incredible talk from a young woman! But if religion cannot keep you on the right path, let me at least stir your conscience. I suppose you do have some moral sense? Or tell me—perhaps you don't?

NORA: Well, Torvald, that's not easy to say. I simply don't know. I'm really very confused about such things. All I know is my ideas about such things are very different from yours. I've also learnt that the law is different from what I thought; but I simply can't get it into my head that that particular law is right. Apparently a woman has no right to spare her old father on his deathbed, or to save her husband's life, even. I just don't believe it.

HELMER: You are talking like a child. You understand nothing about the society you live in.

NORA: No, I don't. But I shall go into that too. I must try to discover who is right, society or me.

HELMER: You are ill, Nora. You are delirious. I'm half inclined to think you are out of your mind.

NORA: Never have I felt so calm and collected as I do tonight.

HELMER: Calm and collected enough to leave your husband and children?

NORA: Yes.

HELMER: Then only one explanation is possible.

NORA: And that is?

HELMER: You don't love me any more.

NORA: Exactly.

HELMER: Nora! Can you say that!

NORA: I'm desperately sorry, Torvald. Because you have always been so kind to me. But I can't help it. I don't love you any more.

HELMER [*struggling to keep his composure*]: Is that also a 'calm and collected' decision you've made?

NORA: Yes, absolutely calm and collected. That's why I don't want to stay here.

HELMER: And can you also account for how I forfeited your love?

NORA: Yes, very easily. It was tonight, when the miracle didn't happen. It was then I realized you weren't the man I thought you were.

HELMER: Explain yourself more clearly. I don't understand.

NORA: For eight years I have been patiently waiting. Because, heavens, I knew miracles didn't happen every day. Then this devastating business started, and I became absolutely convinced the miracle *would* happen. All the time Krogstad's letter lay there, it never so much as crossed my mind that you would ever submit to that man's conditions. I was absolutely convinced you would say to him: Tell the whole wide world if you like. And when that was done . . .

HELMER: Yes, then what? After I had exposed my own wife to dishonour and shame . . . !

NORA: When that was done, I was absolutely convinced you would come forward and take everything on yourself, and say: I am the guilty one.

HELMER: Nora!

NORA: You mean I'd never let you make such a sacrifice for my sake? Of course not. But what would my story have counted for against yours?—That was the miracle I went in hope and dread of. It was to prevent it that I was ready to end my life.

HELMER: I would gladly toil day and night for you, Nora, enduring all manner of sorrow and distress. But nobody sacrifices his *honour* for the one he loves.

NORA: Hundreds and thousands of women have.

HELMER: Oh, you think and talk like a stupid child.

NORA: All right. But you neither think nor talk like the man I would want to share my life with. When you had got over your fright—and you weren't concerned about me but only about what might happen to you—and when all danger was past, you acted as though nothing had happened. I was your little sky-lark again, your little doll, exactly as before; except you would have to protect it twice as carefully as before, now that it had shown itself to be so weak and fragile. [*Rises.*] Torvald, that was the moment I realised that for eight years I'd been living with a stranger, and had borne him three children. . . . Oh, I can't bear to think about it! I could tear myself to shreds.

HELMER [*sadly*]: I see. I see. There is a tremendous gulf dividing us. But, Nora, is there no way we might bridge it?

NORA: As I am now, I am no wife for you.

HELMER: I still have it in me to change.

NORA: Perhaps . . . if you have your doll taken away.

HELMER: And be separated from you! No, no, Nora, the very thought of it is inconceivable.

NORA [*goes into the room, right*]: All the more reason why it must be done.

[*She comes back with her outdoor things and a small travelling bag which she puts on the chair beside the table.*]

HELMER: Nora, Nora, not now! Wait till the morning.

NORA [*putting on her coat*]: I can't spend the night in a strange man's room.

HELMER: Couldn't we go on living here like brother and sister . . . ?

NORA [*tying on her hat*]: You know very well that wouldn't last. [*She draws the shawl round her.*] Goodbye, Torvald. I don't want to see the children. I know they are in better hands than mine. As I am now, I can never be anything to them.

HELMER: But some day, Nora, some day . . . ?

NORA: How should I know? I've no idea what I might turn out to be.

HELMER: But you are my wife, whatever you are.

NORA: Listen, Torvald, from what I've heard, when a wife leaves her husband's house as I am doing now, he is absolved by law of all responsibility for her. I can at any rate free you from all responsibility. You must not feel in any way bound, any more than I shall. There must be full freedom on both sides. Look, here's your ring back. Give me mine.

HELMER: That too?

NORA: That too.

HELMER: There it is.

NORA: Well, that's the end of that. I'll put the keys down here. The maids know where everything is in the house—better than I do, in fact. Kristine will come in the morning after I've left to pack up the few things I brought with me from home. I want them sent on.

HELMER: The end! Nora, will you never think of me?

NORA: I dare say I'll often think about you and the children and this house.

HELMER: May I write to you, Nora?

NORA: No, never. I won't let you.

HELMER: But surely I can send you . . .

NORA: Nothing, nothing.

HELMER: Can't I help you if ever you need it?

NORA: I said 'no.' I don't accept things from strangers.

HELMER: Nora, can I never be anything more to you than a stranger?

NORA [takes her bag]: Ah, Torvald, only by a miracle of miracles. . . .

HELMER: Name it, this miracle of miracles!

NORA: Both you and I would have to change to the point where. . . . Oh, Torvald, I don't believe in miracles any more.

HELMER: But I *will* believe. Name it! Change to the point where . . . ?

NORA: Where we could make a real marriage of our lives together. Goodbye!

[*She goes out through the hall door.*]

HELMER [*sinks down on a chair near the door, and covers his face with his hands*]: Nora! Nora! [*He rises and looks round.*] Empty! She's gone! [*With sudden hope.*] The miracle of miracles . . . ?

[*The heavy sound of a door being slammed is heard from below.*]

—1879

Questions: Reading, Responding, Arguing

1. Analyze Ibsen's use of stage direction, his cues to the actors, and his descriptions. How do these directions help to create dramatic effect, or indicate theme and meaning?

2. Examine the opening dialogue between Helmer and Nora. What kind of relationship does Ibsen set up between them? What issues are set up? How does Ibsen set the scene for the rest of the play?

3. Describe the character of Nora. What are her character traits? What are her strengths and weaknesses? How is she presented to the audience? Compare how Helmer perceives her with how she sees herself.

4. Analyze the role of money. How do the different characters view/use/react to money? What role does money play?

5. Analyze Ibsen's depiction of marriage. How does he present married life in the play?

6. Examine the character of Mrs. Linde. What function does she perform in the play? How does Ibsen contrast her with Nora? What contribution does she make to the play's themes and ideas?

7. Discuss Nora's secret. Why does she do what she does? What is the impact of her actions? What do her actions say about her? Discuss the themes of appearances, deception, and secrecy.

8. Examine the character of Krogstad or Dr. Rank. What function do they play? What issues do they raise?

9. Analyze the play's title and the depiction of Nora as a child. What is Ibsen saying about domesticity, family life, and gender?

10. The play ends with a door slamming. What is signified by this sound? Why is it the final stage direction? How is this sound a commentary about women's lives or womanhood?

11. Research Ibsen's alternate ending to the play. Argue for its effectiveness or its lack thereof.

David Ives (b. 1950]

Sure Thing

CHARACTERS

Betty
Bill

Scene: A café.

Betty, a woman in her late twenties, is reading at a café table. An empty chair is opposite her. Bill, same age, enters.

BILL: Excuse me. Is this chair taken?
BETTY: Excuse me?
BILL: Is this taken?
BETTY: Yes it is.
BILL: Oh. Sorry.
BETTY: Sure thing.

   [*A bell rings softly.*]

BILL: Excuse me. Is this chair taken?
BETTY: Excuse me?
BILL: Is this taken?
BETTY: No, but I'm expecting somebody in a minute.
BILL: Oh. Thanks anyway.
BETTY: Sure thing.

   [*A bell rings softly.*]

BILL: Excuse me. Is this chair taken?
BETTY: No, but I'm expecting somebody very shortly.
BILL: Would you mind if I sit here till he or she or it comes?
BETTY [*glances at her watch*]:   They do seem to be pretty late. . . .
BILL: You never know who you might be turning down.
BETTY: Sorry. Nice try, though.
BILL: Sure thing.

   [*Bell.*]

Is this seat taken?

BETTY: No it's not.

BILL: Would you mind if I sit here?

BETTY: Yes I would.

BILL: Oh.

[*Bell.*]

Is this chair taken?

BETTY: No it's not.

BILL: Would you mind if I sit here?

BETTY: No. Go ahead.

BILL: Thanks. [*He sits. She continues reading.*] Everyplace else seems to be taken.

BETTY: Mm-hm.

BILL: Great place.

BETTY: Mm-hm.

BILL: What's the book?

BETTY: I just wanted to read in quiet, if you don't mind.

BILL: No. Sure thing.

[*Bell.*]

BILL: Everyplace else seems to be taken.

BETTY: Mm-hm.

BILL: Great place for reading.

BETTY: Yes, I like it.

BILL: What's the book?

BETTY: *The Sound and the Fury.*

BILL: Oh. Hemingway.

[*Bell.*]

What's the book?

BETTY: *The Sound and the Fury.*

BILL: Oh. Faulkner.

BETTY: Have you read it?

BILL: Not . . . actually. I've sure read *about* it, though. It's supposed to be great.

BETTY: It is great.

BILL: I hear it's great. [*Small pause.*] Waiter?

[*Bell.*]

What's the book?

BETTY: *The Sound and the Fury.*
BILL: Oh. Faulkner.
BETTY: Have you read it?
BILL: I'm a Mets fan, myself.

[*Bell.*]

BETTY: Have you read it?
BILL: Yeah, I read it in college.
BETTY: Where was college?
BILL: I went to Oral Roberts University.

[*Bell.*]

BETTY: Where was college?
BILL: I was lying. I never really went to college. I just like to party.

[*Bell.*]

BETTY: Where was college?
BILL: Harvard.
BETTY: Do you like Faulkner?
BILL: I love Faulkner. I spent a whole winter reading him once.
BETTY: I've just started.
BILL: I was so excited after ten pages that I went out and bought everything else he wrote. One of the greatest reading experiences of my life. I mean, all that incredible psychological understanding. Page after page of gorgeous prose. His profound grasp of the mystery of time and human existence. The smells of the earth . . . What do you think?
BETTY: I think it's pretty boring.

[*Bell.*]

BILL: What's the book?
BETTY: *The Sound and the Fury.*
BILL: Oh! Faulkner!
BETTY: Do you like Faulkner?
BILL: I love Faulkner.
BETTY: He's incredible.
BILL: I spent a whole winter reading him once.
BETTY: I was so excited after ten pages that I went out and bought everything else he wrote.
BILL: All that incredible psychological understanding.
BETTY: And the prose is so gorgeous.

BILL: And the way he's grasped the mystery of time—

BETTY: —and human existence. I can't believe I've waited this long to read him.

BILL: You never know. You might not have liked him before.

BETTY: That's true.

BILL: You might not have been ready for him. You have to hit these things at the right moment or it's no good.

BETTY: That's happened to me.

BILL: It's all in the timing. [*Small pause.*] My name's Bill, by the way.

BETTY: I'm Betty.

BILL: Hi.

BETTY: Hi. [*Small pause.*]

BILL: Yes I thought reading Faulkner was . . . a great experience.

BETTY: Yes. [*Small pause.*]

BILL: *The Sound and the Fury* . . . [*Another small pause.*]

BETTY: Well. Onwards and upwards. [*She goes back to her book.*]

BILL: Waiter—?

[*Bell.*]

You have to hit these things at the right moment or it's no good.

BETTY: That's happened to me.

BILL: It's all in the timing. My name's Bill, by the way.

BETTY: I'm Betty.

BILL: Hi.

BETTY: Hi.

BILL: Do you come in here a lot?

BETTY: Actually I'm just in town for two days from Pakistan.

BILL: Oh. Pakistan.

[*Bell.*]

My name's Bill, by the way.

BETTY: I'm Betty.

BILL: Hi.

BETTY: Hi.

BILL: Do you come in here a lot?

BETTY: Every once in a while. Do you?

BILL: Not so much anymore. Not as much as I used to. Before my nervous breakdown.

[*Bell.*]

Do you come in here a lot?

BETTY: Why are you asking?

BILL: Just interested.

BETTY: Are you really interested, or do you just want to pick me up?

BILL: No, I'm really interested.

BETTY: Why would you be interested in whether I come in here a lot?

BILL: I'm just . . . getting acquainted.

BETTY: Maybe you're only interested for the sake of making small talk long enough to ask me back to your place to listen to some music, or because you've just rented this great tape for your VCR, or because you've got some terrific unknown Django Reinhardt record, only all you really want to do is fuck—which you won't do very well—after which you'll go into the bathroom and pee very loudly, then pad into the kitchen and get yourself a beer from the refrigerator without asking me whether I'd like anything, and then you'll proceed to lie back down beside me and confess that you've got a girlfriend named Stephanie who's away at medical school in Belgium for a year, and that you've been involved with her—*off and on*—in what you'll call a very "intricate" relationship, for the past *seven YEARS*. None of which *interests* me, mister!

BILL: Okay.

[*Bell.*]

Do you come in here a lot?

BETTY: Every other day, I think.

BILL: I come in here quite a lot and I don't remember seeing you.

BETTY: I guess we must be on different schedules.

BILL: Missed connections.

BETTY: Yes. Different time zones.

BILL: Amazing how you can live right next door to somebody in this town and never even know it.

BETTY: I know.

BILL: City life.

BETTY: It's crazy.

BILL: We probably pass each other in the street every day. Right in front of this place, probably.

BETTY: Yep.

BILL [*looks around*]:   Well the waiters here sure seem to be in some different time zone. I can't seem to locate one anywhere. . . . Waiter! [*He looks back.*] So what do you—[*He sees that she's gone back to her book.*]

BETTY: I beg pardon?

BILL: Nothing. Sorry.

[*Bell.*]

BETTY: I guess we must be on different schedules.
BILL: Missed connections.
BETTY: Yes. Different time zones.
BILL: Amazing how you can live right next door to somebody in this town and never even know it.
BETTY: I know.
BILL: City life.
BETTY: It's crazy.
BILL: You weren't waiting for somebody when I came in, were you?
BETTY: Actually I was.
BILL: Oh. Boyfriend?
BETTY: Sort of.
BILL: What's a sort-of boyfriend?
BETTY: My husband.
BILL: Ah-ha.

[*Bell.*]

You weren't waiting for somebody when I came in, were you?
BETTY: Actually I was.
BILL: Oh. Boyfriend?
BETTY: Sort of.
BILL: What's a sort-of boyfriend?
BETTY: We were meeting here to break up.
BILL: Mm-hm . . .

[*Bell.*]

What's a sort-of boyfriend?
BETTY: My lover. Here she comes right now!

[*Bell.*]

BILL: You weren't waiting for somebody when I came in, were you?
BETTY: No, just reading.
BILL: Sort of a sad occupation for a Friday night, isn't it? Reading here, all by yourself?
BETTY: Do you think so?
BILL: Well sure. I mean, what's a good-looking woman like you doing out alone on a Friday night?

BETTY: Trying to keep away from lines like that.

BILL: No, listen—

[*Bell.*]

You weren't waiting for somebody when I came in, were you?

BETTY: No, just reading.

BILL: Sort of a sad occupation for a Friday night, isn't it? Reading here all by yourself?

BETTY: I guess it is, in a way.

BILL: What's a good-looking woman like you doing out alone on a Friday night anyway? No offense, but . . .

BETTY: I'm out alone on a Friday night for the first time in a very long time.

BILL: Oh.

BETTY: You see, I just recently ended a relationship.

BILL: Oh.

BETTY: Of rather long standing.

BILL: I'm sorry. [*Small pause.*] Well listen, since reading by yourself *is* such a sad occupation for a Friday night, would you like to go elsewhere?

BETTY: No . . .

BILL: Do something else?

BETTY: No thanks.

BILL: I was headed out to the movies in a while anyway.

BETTY: I don't think so.

BILL: Big chance to let Faulkner catch his breath. All those long sentences get him pretty tired.

BETTY: Thanks anyway.

BILL: Okay.

BETTY: I appreciate the invitation.

BILL: Sure thing.

[*Bell.*]

You weren't waiting for somebody when I came in, were you?

BETTY: No, just reading.

BILL: Sort of a sad occupation for a Friday night, isn't it? Reading here all by yourself?

BETTY: I guess I was trying to think of it as existentially romantic. You know—cappuccino, great literature, rainy night . . .

BILL: That only works in Paris. We *could* hop the late plane to Paris. Get on a Concorde. Find a café . . .

BETTY: I'm a little short on plane fare tonight.

BILL: Darn it, so am I.

BETTY: To tell you the truth, I was headed to the movies after I finished this section. Would you like to come along? Since you can't locate a waiter?

BILL: That's a very nice offer, but . . .

BETTY: Uh-huh. Girlfriend?

BILL: Two, actually. One of them's pregnant, and Stephanie—

[*Bell.*]

BETTY: Girlfriend?

BILL: No, I don't have a girlfriend. Not if you mean the castrating bitch I dumped last night.

[*Bell.*]

BETTY: Girlfriend?

BILL: Sort of. Sort of.

BETTY: What's a sort-of girlfriend?

BILL: My mother.

[*Bell.*]

I just ended a relationship, actually.

BETTY: Oh.

BILL: Of rather long standing.

BETTY: I'm sorry to hear it.

BILL: This is my first night out alone in a long time. I feel a little bit at sea, to tell you the truth.

BETTY: So you didn't stop to talk because you're a Moonie, or you have some weird political affiliation—?

BILL: Nope. Straight-down-the-ticket Republican.

[*Bell.*]

Straight-down-the-ticket Democrat.

[*Bell.*]

Can I tell you something about politics?

[*Bell.*]

I like to think of myself as a citizen of the universe.

[*Bell.*]

I'm unaffiliated.

BETTY: That's a relief. So am I.

BILL: I vote my beliefs.

BETTY: Labels are not important.

BILL: Labels are not important, exactly. Take me, for example. I mean, what does it matter if I had a two-point at—

[*Bell.*]

three-point at—

[*Bell.*]

four-point at college? Or if I did come from Pittsburgh—

[*Bell.*]

Cleveland—

[*Bell.*]

Westchester County?

BETTY: Sure.

BILL: I believe that a man is what he is.

[*Bell.*]

A person is what he is.

[*Bell.*]

A person is . . . what they are.

BETTY: I think so too.

BILL: So what if I admire Trotsky?

[*Bell.*]

So what if I once had a total-body liposuction?

[*Bell.*]

So what if I don't have a penis?

[*Bell.*]

So what if I spent a year in the Peace Corps? I was acting on my convictions.

BETTY: Sure.

BILL: You just can't hang a sign on a person.

BETTY: Absolutely. I'll bet you're a Scorpio.

[*Many bells ring.*]

Listen, I was headed to the movies after I finished this section. Would you like to come along?

BILL: That sounds like fun. What's playing?

BETTY: A couple of the really early Woody Allen movies.

BILL: Oh.

BETTY: You don't like Woody Allen?

BILL: Sure. I like Woody Allen.

BETTY: But you're not crazy about Woody Allen.

BILL: Those early ones kind of get on my nerves.

BETTY: Uh-huh.

[*Bell.*]

BILL: Y'know I was headed to the—

BETTY [*simultaneously*]: I was thinking about—

BILL: I'm sorry.

BETTY: No, go ahead.

BILL: I was going to say that I was headed to the movies in a little while, and . . .

BETTY: So was I.

BILL: The Woody Allen festival?

BETTY: Just up the street.

BILL: Do you like the early ones?

BETTY: I think anybody who doesn't ought to be run off the planet.

BILL: How many times have you seen *Bananas*?

BETTY: Eight times.

BILL: Twelve. So are you still interested? [*Long pause.*]

BETTY: Do you like Entenmann's crumb cake . . . ?

BILL: Last night I went out at two in the morning to get one. Did you have an Etch-a-Sketch as a child?

BETTY: Yes! And do you like Brussels sprouts? [*Pause.*]

BILL: No, I think they're disgusting.

BETTY: They *are* disgusting!

BILL: Do you still believe in marriage in spite of current sentiments against it?

BETTY: Yes.

BILL: And children?

BETTY: Three of them.

BILL: Two girls and a boy.

BETTY: Harvard, Vassar, and Brown.

BILL: And will you love me?
BETTY: Yes.
BILL: And cherish me forever?
BETTY: Yes.
BILL: Do you still want to go to the movies?
BETTY: Sure thing.
BILL AND BETTY [*together*]: *Waiter!*

BLACKOUT

—1988

Questions: Reading, Responding, Arguing

1. Discuss the treatment of time in this play.
2. Describe the narrative in the play. How does the author manipulate the narrative?
3. How does the setting contribute to the play? Could it have been set somewhere else? What is the effect of this particular setting on the play's themes and ideas?
4. What is the thematic and/or narrative effect of the repeated and changing dialogue?
5. What is the significance of the title? What is meant by "sure thing"?
6. Identify at least three literary allusions or allusions to popular culture in the play. What do they contribute to the play and its ideas?
7. How would you choose to stage the play? What are your options? Explain your staging choices.
8. Explain how the themes of appearances and façades are presented in the play.
9. What genre is this play? Explain your reasons.
10. Argue that the play's treatment of relationships, love, and dating is an accurate reflection of contemporary society.

Edgar Allan Poe (1809–1849)

The Philosophy of Composition

Charles Dickens, in a note now lying before me, alluding to an examination I once made of the mechanism of "Barnaby Rudge," says—"By the way, are you aware that Godwin wrote his 'Caleb Williams' backwards? He first involved his hero in a web of difficulties, forming the second volume, and then, for the first, cast about him for some mode of accounting for what had been done."

I cannot think this the *precise* mode of procedure on the part of Godwin—and indeed what he himself acknowledges, is not altogether in accordance with Mr. Dickens' idea—but the author of "Caleb Williams" was too good an artist not to perceive the advantage derivable from at least a somewhat similar process. Nothing is more clear than that every plot, worth the name, must be elaborated to its *dénouement* before anything be attempted with the pen. It is only with the *dénouement* constantly in view that we can give a plot its indispensable air of consequence, or causation, by making the incidents, and especially the tone at all points, tend to the development of the intention.

There is a radical error, I think, in the usual mode of constructing a story. Either history affords a thesis—or one is suggested by an incident of the day—or, at best, the author sets himself to work in the combination of striking events to form merely the basis of his narrative—designing, generally, to fill in with description, dialogue, or autorial comment, whatever crevices of fact, or action, may, from page to page, render themselves apparent.

I prefer commencing with the consideration of an *effect*. Keeping originality *always* in view—for he is false to himself who ventures to dispense with so obvious and so easily attainable a source of interest—I say to myself, in the first place, "Of the innumerable effects, or impressions, of which the heart, the intellect, or (more generally) the soul is susceptible, what one shall I, on the present occasion, select?" Having chosen a novel, first, and secondly a vivid effect, I consider whether it can be best wrought by incident or tone—whether by ordinary incidents and peculiar tone, or the converse, or by peculiarity both of incident and tone—afterward looking about me (or rather within) for such combinations of event, or tone, as shall best aid me in the construction of the effect.

I have often thought how interesting a magazine paper might be written by any author who would—that is to say, who could—detail, step by step, the processes by which any one of his compositions attained its ultimate point of completion. Why such a paper has never been given to the world, I am much at a loss to say—but, perhaps, the autorial vanity has had more to do with the omission than any one other cause. Most writers—poets in especial—prefer having it understood that they compose by a species of fine frenzy—an ecstatic intuition—and would positively shudder at letting the public take a peep behind the scenes, at the elaborate and vacillating crudities of thought—at the true purposes seized only at the last moment—at the innumerable glimpses of idea that arrived not at the maturity of full view—at the fully-matured fancies discarded in despair as unmanageable—at the cautious selections and rejections—at the painful erasures and interpolations—in a word, at the wheels and pinions—the tackle for scene-shifting—the step-ladders, and demon-traps—the cock's feathers, the red paint and the black patches, which, in ninety-nine cases out of a hundred, constitute the properties of the literary *histrio*.

I am aware, on the other hand, that the case is by no means common, in which an author is at all in condition to retrace the steps by which his conclusions have been attained. In general, suggestions, having arisen pell-mell are pursued and forgotten in a similar manner.

For my own part, I have neither sympathy with the repugnance alluded to, nor, at any time, the least difficulty in recalling to mind the progressive steps of any of my compositions, and, since the interest of an analysis or reconstruction, such as I have considered a *desideratum*[1], is quite independent of any real or fancied interest in the thing analysed, it will not be regarded as a breach of decorum on my part to show the *modus operandi*[2] by which some one of my own works was put together. I select 'The Raven' as most generally known. It is my design to render it manifest that no one point in its composition is referable either to accident or intuition—that the work proceeded step by step, to its completion, with the precision and rigid consequence of a mathematical problem.

Let us dismiss, as irrelevant to the poem, *per se,* the circumstance—or say the necessity—which, in the first place, gave rise to the intention

---

[1]*desideratum:* a thing desired.
[2]*modus operandi:* method of proceeding.

of composing a poem that should suit at once the popular and the critical taste.

We commence, then, with this intention.

The initial consideration was that of extent. If any literary work is too long to be read at one sitting, we must be content to dispense with the immensely important effect derivable from unity of impression—for, if two sittings be required, the affairs of the world interfere, and everything like totality is at once destroyed. But since, *ceteris paribus*[3], no poet can afford to dispense with *anything* that may advance his design, it but remains to be seen whether there is, in extent, any advantage to counterbalance the loss of unity which attends it. Here I say no, at once. What we term a long poem is, in fact, merely a succession of brief ones—that is to say, of brief poetical effects. It is needless to demonstrate that a poem is such only inasmuch as it intensely excites, by elevating the soul; and all intense excitements are, through a psychal necessity, brief. For this reason, at least, one-half of the "Paradise Lost" is essentially prose—a succession of poetical excitements interspersed, *inevitably*, with corresponding depressions—the whole being deprived, through the extremeness of its length, of the vastly important artistic element, totality, or unity of effect.

It appears evident, then, that there is a distinct limit, as regards length, to all works of literary art—the limit of a single sitting—and that, although in certain classes of prose composition, such as "Robinson Crusoe" (demanding no unity), this limit may be advantageously overpassed, it can never properly be overpassed in a poem. Within this limit, the extent of a poem may be made to bear mathematical relation to its merit—in other words, to the excitement or elevation—again, in other words, to the degree of the true poetical effect which it is capable of inducing; for it is clear that the brevity must be in direct ratio of the intensity of the intended effect—this, with one proviso—that a certain degree of duration is absolutely requisite for the production of any effect at all.

Holding in view these considerations, as well as that degree of excitement which I deemed not above the popular, while not below the critical taste, I reached at once what I conceived the proper *length* for my intended poem—a length of about one hundred lines. It is, in fact, a hundred and eight.

My next thought concerned the choice of an impression, or effect, to be conveyed: and here I may as well observe that throughout the construction, I kept steadily in view the design of rendering the work *universally* appreciable. I should be carried too far out of my immediate

---

[3]*ceteris paribus:* with other things being the same (Latin).

topic were I to demonstrate a point upon which I have repeatedly insisted, and which, with the poetical, stands not in the slightest need of demonstration—the point, I mean, that Beauty is the sole legitimate province of the poem. A few words, however, in elucidation of my real meaning, which some of my friends have evinced a disposition to misrepresent. That pleasure which is at once the most intense, the most elevating, and the most pure is, I believe, found in the contemplation of the beautiful. When, indeed, men speak of Beauty, they mean, precisely, not a quality, as is supposed, but an effect—they refer, in short, just to that intense and pure elevation of *soul—not* of intellect, or of heart—upon which I have commented, and which is experienced in consequence of contemplating the "beautiful." Now I designate Beauty as the province of the poem, merely because it is an obvious rule of Art that effects should be made to spring from direct causes—that objects should be attained through means best adapted for their attainment—no one as yet having been weak enough to deny that the peculiar elevation alluded to is *most readily* attained in the poem. Now the object Truth, or the satisfaction of the intellect, and the object Passion, or the excitement of the heart, are, although attainable to a certain extent in poetry, far more readily attainable in prose. Truth, in fact, demands a precision, and Passion, a *homeliness* (the truly passionate will comprehend me), which are absolutely antagonistic to that Beauty which, I maintain, is the excitement or pleasurable elevation of the soul. It by no means follows, from anything here said, that passion, or even truth, may not be introduced, and even profitably introduced, into a poem for they may serve in elucidation, or aid the general effect, as do discords in music, by contrast—but the true artist will always contrive, first, to tone them into proper subservience to the predominant aim, and, secondly, to enveil them, as far as possible, in that Beauty which is the atmosphere and the essence of the poem.

Regarding, then, Beauty as my province, my next question referred to the tone of its highest manifestation—and all experience has shown that this tone is one of *sadness*. Beauty of whatever kind in its supreme development invariably excites the sensitive soul to tears. Melancholy is thus the most legitimate of all the poetical tones.

The length, the province, and the tone, being thus determined, I betook myself to ordinary induction, with the view of obtaining some artistic piquancy which might serve me as a key-note in the construction of the poem—some pivot upon which the whole structure might turn. In carefully thinking over all the usual artistic effects—or more properly *points,* in the theatrical sense—I did not fail to perceive immediately that no one had been so universally employed as that of the refrain. The universality of its employment sufficed to assure me of its intrinsic value, and spared me the necessity of submitting it to analysis. I considered it, however, with regard to its susceptibility of improvement, and soon saw it to be in a primitive condition. As commonly used, the *refrain,* or burden, not only is limited to lyric verse, but depends for its impression upon the force of monotone—both in sound and thought. The pleasure is deduced solely from the sense of identity—of repetition. I resolved to diversify, and so heighten the effect, by adhering in general to the monotone of sound, while I continually varied that of thought: that is to say, I determined to produce continuously novel effects, by the variation *of the application* of the *refrain*—the *refrain* itself remaining for the most part, unvaried.

These points being settled, I next bethought me of the *nature* of my *refrain.* Since its application was to be repeatedly varied it was clear that the *refrain* itself must be brief, for there would have been an insurmountable difficulty in frequent variations of application in any sentence of length. In proportion to the brevity of the sentence would, of course, be the facility of the variation. This led me at once to a single word as the best *refrain.*

The question now arose as to the *character* of the word. Having made up my mind to a *refrain,* the division of the poem into stanzas was of course a corollary, the *refrain* forming the close to each stanza. That such a close, to have force, must be sonorous and susceptible of protracted emphasis, admitted no doubt, and these considerations inevitably led me to the long o as the most sonorous vowel in connection with r as the most producible consonant.

The sound of the *refrain* being thus determined, it became necessary to select a word embodying this sound, and at the same time in the fullest possible keeping with that melancholy which I had pre-determined as the tone of the poem. In such a search it would have been absolutely impossible to overlook the word "Nevermore." In fact it was the very first which presented itself.

The next *desideratum* was a pretext for the continuous use of the one word "nevermore." In observing the difficulty which I had at once found in inventing a sufficiently plausible reason for its continuous repetition, I did not fail to perceive that this difficulty arose solely from the preassumption that the word was to be so continuously or monotonously spoken by a *human* being—I did not fail to perceive, in short, that the difficulty lay in the reconciliation of this monotony with the exercise of reason on the part of the creature repeating the word. Here, then, immediately arose the idea of a *non*-reasoning creature capable of speech, and very naturally, a parrot, in the first instance, suggested itself, but was superseded forthwith by a Raven as equally capable of speech, and infinitely more in keeping with the intended *tone*.

I had now gone so far as the conception of a Raven, the bird of ill-omen, monotonously repeating the one word "Nevermore" at the conclusion of each stanza in a poem of melancholy tone, and in length about one hundred lines. Now, never losing sight of the object—*supremeness* or perfection at all points, I asked myself—"Of all melancholy topics what, according to the *universal* understanding of mankind, is the *most* melancholy?" Death, was the obvious reply. "And when," I said, "is this most melancholy of topics most poetical?" From what I have already explained at some length the answer here also is obvious—"When it most closely allies itself to *Beauty*: the death then of a beautiful woman is unquestionably the most poetical topic in the world, and equally is it beyond doubt that the lips best suited for such topic are those of a bereaved lover."

I had now to combine the two ideas of a lover lamenting his deceased mistress and a Raven continuously repeating the word "Nevermore." I had to combine these, bearing in mind my design of varying at every turn the *application* of the word repeated, but the only intelligible mode of such combination is that of imagining the Raven employing the word in answer to the queries of the lover. And here it was that I saw at once the opportunity afforded for the effect on which I had been depending, that is to say, the effect of the *variation of application*. I saw that I could make the first query propounded by the lover—the first query to which the Raven should reply "Nevermore"—that I could make this first query a commonplace one, the second less so, the third still less, and so on, until at length the lover, startled from his original *nonchalance* by the melancholy character of the word itself, by its frequent repetition, and by a consideration of the ominous reputation of the fowl that uttered it, is at length excited to superstition, and wildly propounds queries of a far different character—queries whose solution he has passionately at heart—propounds them half in superstition and half in that species of despair which delights in self-torture—propounds them not altogether because he believes in the prophetic or demoniac character of the bird (which reason assures him is merely repeating a lesson learned by rote), but because he experiences a frenzied pleasure in so modelling his questions as to receive from the *expected* "Nevermore" the most delicious because the most intolerable of sorrows. Perceiving the opportunity thus afforded me, or, more strictly, thus forced upon me in the progress of the construction, I first established in my mind the climax or concluding query—that query to which "Nevermore" should be in the last place an answer—that query in reply to which this word "Nevermore" should involve the utmost conceivable amount of sorrow and despair.

Here then the poem may be said to have had its beginning—at the end where all works of art should begin—for it was here at this point of my preconsiderations that I first put pen to paper in the composition of the stanza:

> "Prophet!" said I, "thing of evil! prophet still if bird or devil!
> By that heaven that bends above us—by that God we both adore,
> Tell this soul with sorrow laden, if within the distant Aidenn,
> It shall clasp a sainted maiden whom the angels name Lenore—
> Clasp a rare and radiant maiden whom the angels name Lenore."
>   Quoth the Raven—"Nevermore."

I composed this stanza, at this point, first that, by establishing the climax, I might the better vary and graduate, as regards seriousness and importance, the preceding queries of the lover, and secondly, that I might definitely settle the rhythm, the metre, and the length and general arrangement of the stanza, as well as graduate the stanzas which were to precede, so that none of them might surpass this in rhythmical effect. Had I been able in the subsequent composition to construct more vigorous stanzas I should without scruple have purposely enfeebled them so as not to interfere with the climacteric effect.

And here I may as well say a few words of the versification. My first object (as usual) was originality. The extent to which this has been neglected in versification is one of the most unaccountable things in the world. Admitting that there is little possibility of variety in mere *rhythm*, it is still clear that the possible varieties of metre and stanza are absolutely infinite, and yet, *for centuries, no man, in verse, has ever done, or ever seemed to think of doing, an original thing.* The fact is that originality (unless in minds of very unusual force) is by no means a matter, as some suppose, of impulse or intuition. In general, to be found, it must be elaborately sought, and although a positive merit of the highest class, demands in its attainment less of invention than negation.

Of course I pretend to no originality in either the rhythm or metre of the "Raven." The former is trochaic—the latter is octametre acatalectic, alternating with heptametre catalectic repeated in the *refrain* of the fifth verse, and terminating with tetrametre catalectic. Less pedantically the feet employed throughout (trochees) consist of a long syllable followed by a short, the first line of the stanza consists of eight of these feet, the second of seven and a half (in effect two-thirds), the third of eight, the fourth of seven and a half, the fifth the same, the sixth three and a half. Now, each of these lines taken individually has been employed before, and what originality the "Raven" has, is in their *combination into stanza*; nothing even remotely approaching this has ever been attempted. The effect of this originality of combination is aided by other unusual and some altogether novel effects, arising from an extension of the application of the principles of rhyme and alliteration.

The next point to be considered was the mode of bringing together the lover and the Raven—and the first branch of this consideration was the *locale*. For this the most natural suggestion might seem to be a forest, or the fields—but it has always appeared to me that a *close circumscription of space* is absolutely necessary to the effect of insulated incident—it has the force of a frame to a picture. It has an indisputable moral power in keeping concentrated the attention, and, of course, must not be confounded with mere unity of place.

I determined, then, to place the lover in his chamber—in a chamber rendered sacred to him by memories of her who had frequented it. The room is represented as richly furnished—this in mere pursuance of the ideas I have already explained on the subject of Beauty, as the sole true poetical thesis.

The *locale* being thus determined, I had now to introduce the bird—and the thought of introducing him through the window was inevitable. The idea of making the lover suppose, in the first instance, that the flapping of the wings of the bird against the shutter, is a "tapping" at the door, originated in a wish to increase, by prolonging, the reader's curiosity, and in a desire to admit the incidental effect arising from the lover's throwing open the door, finding all dark, and thence adopting the half-fancy that it was the spirit of his mistress that knocked.

I made the night tempestuous, first to account for the Raven's seeking admission, and secondly, for the effect of contrast with the (physical) serenity within the chamber.

I made the bird alight on the bust of Pallas, also for the effect of contrast between the marble and the plumage—it being understood that the bust was absolutely *suggested* by the bird—the bust of *Pallas* being chosen, first, as most in keeping with the scholarship of the lover, and secondly, for the sonorousness of the word, Pallas, itself.

About the middle of the poem, also, I have availed myself of the force of contrast, with a view of deepening the ultimate impression. For example, an air of the fantastic—approaching as nearly to the ludicrous as was admissible—is given to the Raven's entrance. He comes in "with many a flirt and flutter."

> Not the *least obeisance made* he—not a moment stopped or stayed he,
> But *with mien of lord or lady,* perched above my chamber door.

In the two stanzas which follow, the design is more obviously carried out:—

> Then this ebony bird, beguiling my sad fancy into smiling
> By the *grave and stern decorum of the countenance it wore,*
> "Though thy *crest be shorn and shaven,* thou," I said, "art sure no craven,
> Ghastly grim and ancient Raven wandering from the Nightly shore—
> Tell me what thy lordly name is on the Night's Plutonian shore?"
> Quoth the Raven—"Nevermore."

> Much I marvelled *this ungainly fowl* to hear discourse so plainly,
> Though its answer little meaning—little relevancy bore;
> For we cannot help agreeing that no living human being
> *Ever yet was blessed with seeing bird above his chamber door—*
> *Bird or beast upon the sculptured bust above his chamber door,*
> With such name as "Nevermore."

The effect of the *dénouement* being thus provided for, I immediately drop the fantastic for a tone of the most profound seriousness—this tone commencing in the stanza directly following the one last quoted, with the line,

> But the Raven, sitting lonely on that placid bust, spoke only, etc.

From this epoch the lover no longer jests—no longer sees anything even of the fantastic in the Raven's demeanour. He speaks of him as a "grim, ungainly, ghastly, gaunt, and ominous bird of yore," and feels the "fiery eyes" burning into his "bosom's core." This revolution of thought, or fancy, on the lover's part, is intended to induce a similar one on the part of the reader—to bring the mind into a proper frame for the *dénouement*—which is now brought about as rapidly and as *directly* as possible.

With the *dénouement* proper—with the Raven's reply, "Nevermore," to the lover's final demand if he shall meet his mistress in another world—the poem, in its obvious phase, that of a simple narrative, may be said to have its completion. So far, everything is within the limits of the accountable—of the real. A raven, having learned by rote the single word "Nevermore," and having escaped from the custody of its owner, is driven at midnight, through the violence of a storm, to seek admission at a window from which a light still gleams—the chamber-window of a student, occupied half in poring over a volume, half in dreaming of a beloved mistress deceased. The casement being thrown open at the fluttering of the bird's wings, the bird itself perches on the most convenient seat out of the immediate reach of the student, who amused by the incident and the oddity of the visitor's demeanour, demands of it, in jest and without looking for a reply, its name. The raven addressed, answers with its customary word, "Nevermore" —a word which finds immediate echo in the melancholy heart of the student, who, giving utterance aloud to certain thoughts suggested by the occasion, is again startled by the fowl's repetition of "Nevermore." The student now guesses the state of the case, but is impelled, as I have before explained, by the human thirst for self-torture, and in part by superstition, to propound such queries to the bird as will bring him, the lover, the most of the luxury of sorrow, through the anticipated answer, "Nevermore." With the indulgence, to the extreme, of this self-torture, the narration, in what I have termed its first or obvious phase, has a natural termination, and so far there has been no overstepping of the limits of the real.

But in subjects so handled, however skillfully, or with however vivid an array of incident, there is always a certain hardness or nakedness which repels the artistical eye. Two things are invariably required—first, some amount of complexity, or more properly, adaptation; and, secondly, some amount of suggestiveness—some under-current, however indefinite, of meaning. It is this latter, in especial, which imparts to a work of art so much of that *richness* (to borrow from colloquy a forcible term), which we are too fond of confounding with *the ideal*. It is the excess of the suggested meaning—it is the rendering this the upper instead of the undercurrent of the theme—which turns into prose (and that of the very flattest kind), the so-called poetry of the so-called transcendentalists.

Holding these opinions, I added the two concluding stanzas of the poem—their suggestiveness being thus made to pervade all the narrative which has preceded them. The under-current of meaning is rendered first apparent in the line—

> "Take thy beak from out *my* heart, and take thy form from off my door!"
> Quoth the Raven "Nevermore!"

It will be observed that the words, "from out my heart," involve the first metaphorical expression in the poem. They, with the answer, "Nevermore," dispose the mind to seek a moral in all that has been previously narrated. The reader begins now to regard the Raven as emblematical—but it is not until the very last line of the very last stanza that the intention of making him emblematical of *Mournful and Never ending Remembrance* is permitted distinctly to be seen:

> And the Raven, never flitting, still is sitting, still is sitting,
> On the pallid bust of Pallas just above my chamber door;
> And his eyes have all the seeming of a demon that is dreaming,
> And the lamplight o'er him streaming throws his shadow on the floor;
> And my soul *from out that shadow* that lies floating on the floor
>   Shall be lifted—nevermore.

—1846

Questions: Reading, Responding, Arguing

1. What are the recommendations Poe gives for composing a work, and how does his own essay conform to those recommendations?
2. Poe emphasizes the importance of thinking of "dénouement" when composing an essay. What is the dénouement of his essay?
3. According to Poe, what are the stylistic elements of his poem "The Raven"?
4. Does "The Raven" have elements in common with Poe's essay? What are they?
5. See the questions following "The Raven" (p. 982).

Judy Brady (b. 1937)

I Want a Wife

I belong to that classification of people known as wives. I am a Wife. And, not altogether incidentally, I am a mother.

Not too long ago a male friend of mine appeared on the scene fresh from a recent divorce. He had one child, who is, of course, with his ex-wife. He is obviously looking for another wife. As I thought about him while I was ironing one evening, it suddenly occurred to me that I, too, would like to have a wife. Why do I want a wife?

I would like to go back to school so that I can become economically independent, support myself, and, if need be, support those dependent upon me. I want a wife who will work and send me to school. And while I am going to school I want a wife to take care of my children. I want a wife to keep track of the children's doctor and dentist appointments. And to keep track of mine, too. I want a wife to make sure my children eat properly and are kept clean. I want a wife who will wash the children's clothes and keep them mended. I want a wife who is a good nurturant attendant to my children, who arranges for their schooling, makes sure that they have an adequate social life with their peers, takes them to the park, the zoo, etc. I want a wife who takes care of the children when they are sick, a wife who arranges to be around when the children need special care, because, of course, I cannot miss classes at school. My wife must arrange to lose time at work and not lose the job. It may mean a small cut in my wife's income from time to time, but I guess I can tolerate that. Needless to say, my wife will arrange and pay for the care of the children while my wife is working.

I want a wife who will take care of my physical needs. I want a wife who will keep my house clean. A wife who will pick up after me. I want a wife who will keep my clothes clean, ironed, mended, replaced when need be, and who will see to it that my personal things are kept in their proper place so that I can find what I need the minute I need it. I want a wife who cooks the meals, a wife who is a good cook. I want a wife who will plan the menus, do the necessary grocery shopping, prepare the meals, serve them pleasantly, and then do the cleaning up while I do my studying. I want a wife who will care for me when I am sick and sympathize with my pain and loss of time from school. I want a wife to go along when our family takes a vacation so that someone can continue to care for me and my children when I need a rest and change of scene.

I want a wife who will not bother me with rambling complaints about a wife's duties. But I want a wife who will listen to me when I feel the need to explain a rather difficult point I have come across in my course of studies. And I want a wife who will type my papers for me when I have written them.

I want a wife who will take care of the details of my social life. When my wife and I are invited out by my friends, I want a wife who will take care of the babysitting arrangements. When I meet people at school that I like and want to entertain, I want a wife who will have the house clean, will prepare a special meal, serve it to me and my friends, and not interrupt when I talk about the things that interest me and my friends. I want a wife who will have arranged that the children are fed and ready for bed before my guests arrive so that the children do not bother us. I want a wife who takes care of the needs of my guests so that they feel comfortable, who makes sure that they have an ashtray, that they are passed the hors d'oeuvres, that they are offered a second helping of the food, that their wine glasses are replenished when necessary, that their coffee is served to them as they like it. And I want a wife who knows that sometimes I need a night out by myself.

I want a wife who is sensitive to my sexual needs, a wife who makes love passionately and eagerly when I feel like it, a wife who makes sure that I am satisfied. And, of course, I want a wife who will not demand sexual attention when I am not in the mood for it. I want a wife who assumes the complete responsibility for birth control, because I do not want more children. I want a wife who will remain sexually faithful to me so that I do not have to clutter up my intellectual life with jealousies. And I want a wife who understands that my sexual needs may entail more than strict adherence to monogamy. I must, after all, be able to relate to people as fully as possible.

If, by chance, I find another person more suitable as a wife than the wife I already have, I want the liberty to replace my present wife with another one. Naturally, I will expect a fresh, new life; my wife will take the children and be solely responsible for them so that I am left free.

When I am through with school and have a job, I want my wife to quit working and remain at home so that my wife can more fully and completely take care of a wife's duties.

My God, who wouldn't want a wife?

—1972

Questions: Reading, Responding, Arguing

1. What does the essay suggest about the roles that women and men play in relationships?
2. Explain the real satiric target of Brady's essay.
3. To reveal her argument about wives in society and the tasks they perform, Brady repeatedly uses the phrase, "I want a wife." She also describes wifely duties in a very specific fashion. Are her techniques successful and effective? Why or why not?

David Mamet (b. 1947)

Girl Copy

I sat for a year in a cork-lined office and looked at photos of naked women.

I did it for a living.

I got the job at a party given by a friend of a friend.

A man came up to me, he said he knew my plays, and asked me to come work for him as a contributing editor of his men's magazine.

I told him I had no idea what such a job might be supposed to entail. He said my duties would be these: to come to the office and offer innovative solutions to various problems, and to suggest projects of my own.

This explanation left me no better informed than I had been prior to my question. "Look," I said, "I don't want to mislead or disappoint you. I am not a good 'company' man, I've never worked on a magazine before, and, though I'm flattered by your offer . . . ."

I went on in this vein for a while, warmed by my own candor, until he stopped and assured me that there was nothing in the job beyond my capabilities, that I could make my own hours, and that he would pay me $20,000 a year.

The magazine took up a floor in the Playboy Building.

It was decorated in an informal but serious style; and that, of course, was the manner in which we were supposed to function while in it.

We contributing editors, men and women in our twenties, were being paid to pitch in and be witty and creative promptly, and in service of the Issue and its deadlines.

I wrote my share of letters to the editor. Each letter, either through agreement or through disagreement with the policies of the Rag, was to function as entertainment; and I and the others strove to make it so. We cranked them out, and made up names and hometowns for our faithful correspondents, checking the telephone books of those hometowns to insure that each burg housed at least three people of the name we had appropriated. This tactic, the legal department informed us, lessened the chance of a lawsuit by someone who felt offended seeing his name borrowed by a girlie mag.

I wrote captions for cartoons. Who would have thought it? I'd always assumed that a cartoonist dreamt up the idea whole; but, however it came about, there were these drawings of folks in what would prove to be a comic situation after the caption had been applied, and there I was straining to find a caption.

I wrote "service features"; that is, surveys of a particular gadget or service—toiletries or resorts, for example. The items surveyed were, in the main, sold by our mag's advertisers; and these gratuities I found both easy and enjoyable to write. Perhaps because I felt I was dispensing patronage, I don't know.

I wrote puns and gags, and one-liners, and photo captions; my favorite of the last: We had a shot of a house trailer that had been turned into a helicopter; I titled it "Upwardly mobile homes." I talked on the phone to Henny Youngman. I had coffee and croissants with Eddie Constantine; I created the fictitious craze that was supposedly sweeping the swinging North Side of Chicago: strip darts; I invented the American joke. Yes. This sounds like the pompous posturing of a garrulous old Fool—is he so bereft of kudos that he would stoop to garner that owing to the creator of "How many Americans does it take to change a lightbulb? One." Well, yes. I would so stoop, and there it is in print in 1976. Where did I get the energy for these bons mots? For this, finally, this "humor"? The energy came as a counterirritant to the despair caused by my attempts to write Girl Copy.

Fran Lebowitz wrote that as a child, she detested homework; and then she grew up and became a writer; which, she found, is a life of constant homework.

All over the country adolescent boys and frustrated married men were looking at the sexy photos of the sexy naked women, and these men were having fantasies about them.

Here I was, getting twenty grand a year to look at the same photos and create those fantasies, and it felt to me like work.

I would be given "the blues," blue-and-gray first runs of what would later be glorious color spreads of the said naked women, and I would tack them on the cork-lined walls, and I would strive to have fantasies about them. For it was all a fiction, all that stuff; their names were made up, their biographies, their likes and peeves. It was whole cloth, like the letters to the editor. Someone made it up, and that year, that was my job.

I think my personal best was "Katya with her pants down"; and there was also "Anna is a palindrome," but I'm not sure if that was mine.

I did write: "Tolstoy said that a nap after dinner is silver, a nap before dinner gold. Gretchen prefers a nap to dinner altogether."

Workmanlike, as you see.

Others did better. The office consensus favorite concerned French women, and informed us that French women have eyes like chocolate horses, that they wear white socks and harbor a fear of being frightened by an orangutan that has gained entrance to their flat by means of the chimney. I butcher the above-referenced work, with apologies to its author, whose name I have forgotten. The original can be found in an issue of *Oui,* nineteen seventy-four or -five.

No, I never did better than the acceptable "Katya."

I toyed with "London britches" and "London derriere," neither of which ever progressed beyond the title. I spent too much time staring at the blues—much too much to achieve that effortlessness that, unfortunately, usually denotes lack of effort.

They were my homework. Photos of naked women feigning sexual interest in something or other—their people, the camera, or, in what was considered quite daring in those forgotten times, themselves.

For there were two plateaus, it seems to me, in those bygone days, two Rubiconim[1], which we approached with utmost caution.

My editor, the bloke who gave me the job, was, by the way, good as his word. He was generous and helpful, and made a point of both aiding and appreciating my efforts. Our editor, I say, would come to this meeting or that, and display a copy of some rival and less prestigious men's mag, and say: "They've Gone Pink."

To "Go Pink," was, of course, to reveal, in a photo, the Labia; the existence of which was, one would think, a secret to no one, but to which photographic reference was felt, in that time, to be Non-U[2].

We at the mag considered ourselves gentlemen—and-women. We held to the crypto-British, which is to say wry, self-deprecating, view of our work.

We tried to be funny and smart, and put out a book diverting and honestly, if mildly, erotic. What then of this Going Pink?

But the decision was not ours. It came from on high, and devolved upon the photographic rather than the verbal portion of the floor, and Pink we went—the ensuing consequence of which can be seen all around us in the savage immorality of the American Culture and the general falling-away-from-God.

The second Rubicon was Missing Fingers.

---

[1]*Rubiconim:* after Rubicon, the Roman river crossed by Julius Caesar and his army in 49 BCE.

[2]*Non-U:* a British phrase implying "lower-class"

And what was the intent and what the effect of That Magazine,
Brute that I am?

I am reminded of a passage in a Kurt Vonnegut book. A young man
is admiring the centerfold of some girlie mag. He shows it to an older
man and says, "Look at that woman!" "Son, that's not a woman," the
older man says, "that's a photograph."

And they were lovely, those photographs. And their subjects were
lovely, too.

The models came to the office infrequently; and had I jotted down
my fantasies about the models rather than staring at the blues, I would
have got home earlier all that year.

I always hoped that the gentle collegiality of the office hid a raucous
sexual nightlife, and that in time, I would be invited to share it. I
looked, through the year, for signs that I was being accepted and, in
fact, for signs that such a secret life went on—that the editorial staff,
Chicagoan P. G. Wodehouses[3], when the Lindbergh Beacon[4] went on,
turned to diversions worthy of Arthur Schnitzler[5].

I more than fantasized about it; I *knew* that it happened somewhere
north of Division Street and after midnight. And I knew that I was
never going to be invited.

For I was an interloper; I was a Ringer, brought in by the kindness
of the Editor, and how could I hope to be given the Office to come to a
soiree if I couldn't even get my Girl Copy right?

The invite never came. My closest approach came out of my "strip
darts" gag.

I wrote the copy, and the photo folks set up a shoot.

We went, at nine a.m., to some studio around State Street, and various people took their clothes off and pretended to play darts, and we
drank the warm prop champagne and went home at lunch feeling
foolish.

"Yes," you might say, "that's how you should have felt during that
whole year."

And looking back, I think that I did, and my Schnitzler fantasies
were signals of my *anomie*[6].

I wasn't as funny as the people who were funny, nor as sexy as
those who were gifted in that way; what I chose to recognize as Fantasy

---

[3]*P.G. Wodehouse:* English humorist (1881–1975).
[4]*Lindberg Beacon:* atop the building that housed *Playboy.*
[5]*Arthur Schnitzler:* Austrian playwright (1862–1931).
[6]*anomie:* malaise.

was boring, and my true fantasies never made it past the superego and onto the page.

I made friends with one of the senior editors, and we bummed cigarettes and talked about Poetry.

I rented a room on Lake Shore Drive and saw the sun pop out of the lake most mornings during the Bicentennial summer. The editor still expressed approval of me, and I got offered a gig teaching drama at Yale.

I went to the man who gave me the job, and he congratulated me and said that he'd still like me, at the same salary, that I would only have to work three days a week, which left four for Yale, and that the mag would pay the airfare.

Once again I told him that he had the wrong guy, that I wasn't worth it, and he once again said that he didn't share my feelings.

I was very much surprised by his interest and endorsement after a year of my work. But it never occurred to me to accept his offer.

So I left Chicago, that most wonderful of towns, and went to Yale to discover that teaching writing was yet one more thing that I could not do.

Now, going on twenty years later, I browse sometimes through old magazines in a bookstore, looking for copies of jokes and gags and my Girl Copy, and I remember those long afternoons sitting in my office, looking at the blurred photographs of naked women.

—1996

Questions: Reading, Responding, Arguing

1. Mamet admits to being worse at his job than others around him. What hinders his ability to write good essay copy for the magazine?

2. Mamet never reveals the magazine he worked for, deliberately leaving the question unanswered and unfulfilled for the reader. Why does he do this? How does this deliberate omission relate to the subject of his essay?

3. Mamet suggests satirically that the magazine's "Going Pink" brought about "the savage immorality of the American Culture and the general falling-away-from-God." Explain the target of his satire.

4. Explain Mamet's methods for writing a good essay for a pinup magazine. Argue that this relates to good essay writing in general.

Where We Are Going

Time, Aging, and Death

> "Death is the only god who comes when you call."
> —Roger Zelazny, *24 Views of Mt. Fuji*

If you have had a typical upbringing, you know what it is like to anticipate typical events on your personal timeline. Each year in school you anticipate learning new skills that are necessary for educational advancement. Later in high school you are taught to anticipate college; in college you are taught to anticipate the job market. Eventually, and one might even say mysteriously, your relationship to time also becomes nostalgic instead of just anticipatory. You look back upon the past events, either with joy or sorrow, and when present moments occur they take on a meaning that relates to events of the past. Time, then, encodes our lives at the most basic level. It informs everything we do, and gives meaning both to what has happened to us and to the plans we make for the future. We would not have the same identity without it.

Surely we would not have this fascination with time, however, if we were not so intimately aware of our own mortality. An entire culture industry sustains itself on selling products to forestall the effects of aging, and the idea of death is everywhere in our culture. An alien visitor might very well suspect that we are in love with death, for it is impossible to turn on the television or watch a movie without encountering death in multiple, spectacular repetitions. And it's true that we are obsessed with death, although it might be more appropriate to recognize that the fascination usually stems from a desire to avoid dying, rather than an actual love of deathly manifestations. Our awareness of present and future time is balanced by our sense of the past, for, to tell the truth, we would prefer to be moving backward in the process of aging rather than forward. The selections in this section called "Where We Are Going" all have some connection, explicit or implicit, with these three themes—time, aging, and death. Each of these themes, however, can easily be seen for what it is, a reflection on the question of life itself. How is life to be lived, and what is to be done with it, before it is over?

> "It is quite true what philosophy says: that life must be understood backwards. But then one forgets the other principle: that it must be lived forwards."
>
> —Søren Kierkegaard, *Journals*

Leo Tolstoy (1828–1910)

The Death of Ivan Ilych

Translated by Louise and Aylmer Maude

I

During an interval in the Melvinski trial in the large building of the Law Courts, the members and public prosecutor met in Ivan Egorovich Shebek's private room, where the conversation turned on the celebrated Krasovski case. Fëdor Vasilievich warmly maintained that it was not subject to their jurisdiction, Ivan Egorovich maintained the contrary, while Peter Ivanovich, not having entered into the discussion at the start, took no part in it but looked through the *Gazette* which had just been handed in.

"Gentlemen," he said, "Ivan Ilych has died!"

"You don't say so!"

"Here, read it yourself," replied Peter Ivanovich, handing Fëdor Vasilievich the paper still damp from the press. Surrounded by a black border were the words: "Praskovya Fëdorovna Goloviná, with profound sorrow, informs relatives and friends of the demise of her beloved husband Ivan Ilych Golovin, Member of the Court of Justice, which occurred on February the 4th of this year 1882. The funeral will take place on Friday at one o'clock in the afternoon."

Ivan Ilych had been a colleague of the gentlemen present and was liked by them all. He had been ill for some weeks with an illness said to be incurable. His post had been kept open for him, but there had been conjectures that in case of his death Alexeev might receive his appointment, and that either Vinnikov or Shtabel would succeed Alexeev. So on receiving the news of Ivan Ilych's death the first thought of each of the gentlemen in that private room was of the changes and promotions it might occasion among themselves or their acquaintances.

"I shall be sure to get Shtabel's place or Vinnikov's," thought Fëdor Vasilievich. "I was promised that long ago, and the promotion means an extra eight hundred rubles a year for me besides the allowance."

"Now I must apply for my brother-in-law's transfer from Kaluga," thought Peter Ivanovich. "My wife will be very glad, and then she won't be able to say that I never do anything for her relations."

"I thought he would never leave his bed again," said Peter Ivanovich aloud. "It's very sad."

"But what really was the matter with him?"

"The doctors couldn't say—at least they could, but each of them said something different. When last I saw him I thought he was getting better."

"And I haven't been to see him since the holidays. I always meant to go."

"Had he any property?"

"I think his wife had a little—but something quite trifling."

"We shall have to go to see her, but they live so terribly far away."

"Far away from you, you mean. Everything's far away from your place."

"You see, he never can forgive my living on the other side of the river," said Peter Ivanovich, smiling at Shebek. Then, still talking of the distances between different parts of the city, they returned to the Court.

Besides considerations as to the possible transfers and promotions likely to result from Ivan Ilych's death, the mere fact of the death of a near acquaintance aroused, as usual, in all who heard of it the complacent feeling that "it is he who is dead and not I."

Each one thought or felt, "Well, he's dead but I'm alive!" But the more intimate of Ivan Ilych's acquaintances, his so-called friends, could not help thinking also that they would now have to fulfil the very tiresome demands of propriety by attending the funeral service and paying a visit of condolence to the widow.

Fëdor Vasilievich and Peter Ivanovich had been his nearest acquaintances. Peter Ivanovich had studied law with Ivan Ilych and had considered himself to be under obligations to him.

Having told his wife at dinner-time of Ivan Ilych's death and of his conjecture that it might be possible to get her brother transferred to their circuit, Peter Ivanovich sacrificed his usual nap, put on his evening clothes, and drove to Ivan Ilych's house.

At the entrance stood a carriage and two cabs. Leaning against the wall in the hall downstairs near the cloak-stand was a coffin-lid covered with cloth of gold, ornamented with gold cord and tassels, that had been polished up with metal powder. Two ladies in black were taking off their fur cloaks. Peter Ivanovich recognized one of them as Ivan Ilych's sister, but the other was a stranger to him. His colleague Schwartz was just coming downstairs, but on seeing Peter Ivanovich enter he stopped and winked at him, as if to say: "Ivan Ilych has made a mess of things—not like you and me."

Schwartz's face with his Piccadilly whiskers and his slim figure in evening dress had as usual an air of elegant solemnity which contrasted with the playfulness of his character and had a special piquancy here, or so it seemed to Peter Ivanovich.

Peter Ivanovich allowed the ladies to precede him and slowly followed them upstairs. Schwartz did not come down but remained where he was, and Peter Ivanovich understood that he wanted to arrange where they should play bridge that evening. The ladies went upstairs to the widow's room, and Schwartz with seriously compressed lips but a playful look in his eyes, indicated by a twist of his eyebrows the room to the right where the body lay.

Peter Ivanovich, like everyone else on such occasions, entered feeling uncertain what he would have to do. All he knew was that at such times it is always safe to cross oneself. But he was not quite sure whether one should make obeisances while doing so. He therefore adopted a middle course. On entering the room he began crossing himself and made a slight movement resembling a bow. At the same time, as far as the motion of his head and arm allowed, he surveyed the room. Two young men—apparently nephews, one of whom was a high-school pupil—were leaving the room, crossing themselves as they did so. An old woman was standing motionless, and a lady with strangely arched eyebrows was saying something to her in a whisper. A vigorous, resolute Church Reader, in a frock-coat, was reading something in a loud voice with an expression that precluded any contradiction. The butler's assistant, Gerasim, stepping lightly in front of Peter Ivanovich, was strewing something on the floor. Noticing this, Peter Ivanovich was immediately aware of a faint odor of a decomposing body.

The last time he had called on Ivan Ilych, Peter Ivanovich had seen Gerasim in the study. Ivan Ilych had been particularly fond of him and he was performing the duty of a sick nurse.

Peter Ivanovich continued to make the sign of the cross, slightly inclining his head in an intermediate direction between the coffin, the Reader, and the icons on the table in a corner of the room. Afterwards, when it seemed to him that this movement of his arm in crossing himself had gone on too long, he stopped and began to look at the corpse.

The dead man lay, as dead men always lie, in a specially heavy way, his rigid limbs sunk in the soft cushions of the coffin, with the head forever bowed on the pillow. His yellow waxen brow with bald patches over his sunken temples was thrust up in the way peculiar to the dead, the protruding nose seeming to press on the upper lip. He was much changed and had grown even thinner since Peter Ivanovich had last seen him, but, as is always the case with the dead, his face was handsomer and above all more dignified than when he was alive. The expression on the face said that what was necessary had been accomplished, and accomplished rightly. Besides this there was in that expression a reproach and a warning to the living. This warning seemed to Peter Ivanovich out of place, or at least not applicable to him. He felt a certain discomfort and so he hurriedly crossed himself once more and turned and went out the door—too hurriedly and too regardless of propriety, as he himself was aware.

Schwartz was waiting for him in the adjoining room with legs spread wide apart and both hands toying with his top-hat behind his back. The mere sight of that playful, well-groomed, and elegant figure refreshed Peter Ivanovich. He felt that Schwartz was above all these happenings and would not surrender to any depressing influences. His very look said that this incident of a church service for Ivan Ilych could not be a sufficient reason for infringing the order of the session—in other words, that it would certainly not prevent his unwrapping a new pack of cards and shuffling them that evening while a footman placed four fresh candles on the table: in fact, that there was no reason for supposing that this incident would hinder their spending the evening agreeably. Indeed he said this in a whisper as Peter Ivanovich passed him, proposing that they should meet for a game at Fëdor Vasilievich's. But apparently Peter Ivanovich was not destined to play bridge that evening. Praskovya Fëdorovna (a short, fat woman who despite all efforts to the contrary had continued to broaden steadily from her shoulders downwards and who had the same extraordinarily arched eyebrows as the lady who had been standing by the coffin), dressed all in black, her head covered with lace, came out of her own room with some other ladies, conducted them to the room where the dead body lay, and said: "The service will begin immediately. Please go in."

Schwartz, making an indefinite bow, stood still, evidently neither accepting nor declining this invitation. Praskovya Fëdorovna, recognizing Peter Ivanovich, sighed, went close up to him, took his hand, and said: "I know you were a true friend to Ivan Ilych . . ." and looked at him awaiting some suitable response. And Peter Ivanovich knew that, just as it had been the right thing to cross himself in that room, so what he had to do here was to press her hand, sigh, and say, "Believe me. . . ." So he did all this and as he did it felt that the desired result had been achieved: that both he and she were touched.

"Come with me. I want to speak to you before it begins," said the widow. "Give me your arm."

Peter Ivanovich gave her his arm and they went to the inner rooms, passing Schwartz, who winked at Peter Ivanovich compassionately.

"That does for our bridge! Don't object if we find another player. Perhaps you can cut in when you do escape," said his playful look.

Peter Ivanovich sighed still more deeply and despondently, and Praskovya Fëdorovna pressed his arm gratefully. When they reached the drawing-room, upholstered in pink cretonne and lighted by a dim lamp, they sat down at the table—she on a sofa and Peter Ivanovich on a low pouffe, the springs of which yielded spasmodically under his weight. Praskovya Fëdorovna had been on the point of warning him to take another seat, but felt that such a warning was out of keeping with her present condition and so changed her mind. As he sat down on the pouffe Peter Ivanovich recalled how Ivan Ilych had arranged this room and had consulted him regarding this pink cretonne with green leaves. The whole room was full of furniture and knick-knacks, and on her way to the sofa the lace of the widow's black shawl caught on the carved edge of the table. Peter Ivanovich rose to detach it, and the springs of the pouffe, relieved of his weight, rose also and gave him a push. The widow began detaching her shawl herself, and Peter Ivanovich again sat down, suppressing the rebellious springs of the pouffe under him. But the widow had not quite freed herself and Peter Ivanovich got up again, and again the pouffe rebelled and even creaked. When this was all over she took out a clean cambric handkerchief and began to weep. The episode with the shawl and the struggle with the pouffe had cooled Peter Ivanovich's emotions and he sat there with a sullen look on his face. This awkward situation was interrupted by Sokolov, Ivan Ilych's butler, who came to report that the plot in the cemetery that Praskovya Fëdorovna had chosen would cost two hundred rubles. She stopped weeping and, looking at Peter Ivanovich with the air of a victim, remarked in French that it was very hard for her. Peter Ivanovich made a silent gesture signifying his full conviction that it must indeed be so.

"Please smoke," she said in a magnanimous yet crushed voice, and turned to discuss with Sokolov the price of the plot for the grave.

Peter Ivanovich while lighting his cigarette heard her inquiring very circumstantially into the prices of different plots in the cemetery and finally decide which she would take. When that was done she gave instructions about engaging the choir. Sokolov then left the room.

"I look after everything myself," she told Peter Ivanovich, shifting the albums that lay on the table; and noticing that the table was endangered by his cigarette-ash, she immediately passed him an ashtray, saying as she did so: "I consider it an affectation to say that my grief prevents my attending to practical affairs. On the contrary, if anything can—I won't say console me, but—distract me, it is seeing to everything concerning him." She again took out her handkerchief as if preparing to cry, but suddenly, as if mastering her feeling, she shook herself and began to speak calmly. "But there is something I want to talk to you about."

Peter Ivanovich bowed, keeping control of the springs of the pouffe, which immediately began quivering under him.

"He suffered terribly the last few days."

"Did he?" said Peter Ivanovich.

"Oh, terribly! He screamed unceasingly, not for minutes but for hours. For the last three days he screamed incessantly. It was unendurable. I cannot understand how I bore it; you could hear him three rooms off. Oh, what I have suffered!"

"Is it possible that he was conscious all that time?" asked Peter Ivanovich.

"Yes," she whispered. "To the last moment. He took leave of us a quarter of an hour before he died, and asked us to take Vasya away."

The thought of the sufferings of this man he had known so intimately, first as a merry little boy, then as a school-mate, and later as a grown-up colleague, suddenly struck Peter Ivanovich with horror, despite an unpleasant consciousness of his own and this woman's dissimulation. He again saw that brow, and that nose pressing down on the lip, and felt afraid for himself.

"Three days of frightful suffering and then death! Why, that might suddenly, at any time, happen to me," he thought, and for a moment felt terrified. But—he did not himself know how—the customary reflection at once occurred to him that this had happened to Ivan Ilych and not to him, and that it should not and could not happen to him, and that to think that it could would be yielding to depression which he ought not to do, as Schwartz's expression plainly showed. After which reflection Peter Ivanovich felt reassured, and began to ask with interest about the details of Ivan Ilych's death, as though death was an accident natural to Ivan Ilych but certainly not to himself.

After many details of the really dreadful physical sufferings Ivan Ilych had endured (which details he learnt only from the effect those sufferings had produced on Praskovya Fëdorovna's nerves) the widow apparently found it necessary to get to business.

"Oh, Peter Ivanovich, how hard it is! How terribly, terribly hard!" and she again began to weep.

Peter Ivanovich sighed and waited for her to finish blowing her nose. When she had done so he said, "Believe me . . ." and she again began talking and brought out what was evidently her chief concern with him—namely, to question him as to how she could obtain a grant of money from the government on the occasion of her husband's death. She made it appear that she was asking Peter Ivanovich's advice about her pension, but he soon saw that she already knew about that to the minutest detail, more even than he did himself. She knew how much could be got out of the government in consequence of her husband's death, but wanted to find out whether she could not possibly extract something more. Peter Ivanovich tried to think of some means of doing so, but after reflecting for a while and, out of propriety, condemning the government for its niggardliness, he said he thought that nothing more could be got. Then she sighed and evidently began to devise means of getting rid of her visitor. Noticing this, he put out his cigarette, rose, pressed her hand, and went out into the anteroom.

In the dining-room where the clock stood that Ivan Ilych had liked so much and had bought at an antique shop, Peter Ivanovich met a priest and a few acquaintances who had come to attend the service, and he recognized Ivan Ilych's daughter, a handsome young woman. She was in black and her slim figure appeared slimmer than ever. She had a gloomy, determined, almost angry expression, and bowed to Peter Ivanovich as though he were in some way to blame. Behind her, with the same offended look, stood a wealthy young man, an examining magistrate, whom Peter Ivanovich also knew and who was her fiancé, as he had heard. He bowed mournfully to them and was about to pass into the death-chamber, when from under the stairs appeared the figure of Ivan Ilych's schoolboy son, who was extremely like his father. He seemed a little Ivan Ilych, such as Peter Ivanovich remembered when they studied law together. His tear-stained eyes had in them the look that is seen in the eyes of boys of thirteen or fourteen who are not pureminded. When he saw Peter Ivanovich he scowled morosely and shamefacedly. Peter Ivanovich nodded to him and entered the death-chamber. The service began: candles, groans, incense, tears, and sobs. Peter Ivanovich stood looking gloomily down at his feet. He did not look once at the dead man, did not yield to any depressing influence, and was one of the first to leave the room. There was no one in the anteroom, but Gerasim darted out of the dead man's room, rummaged with his strong hands among the fur coats to find Peter Ivanovich's, and helped him on with it.

"Well, friend Gerasim," said Peter Ivanovich, so as to say something. "It's a sad affair, isn't it?"

"It's God's will. We shall all come to it some day," said Gerasim, displaying his teeth—the even white teeth of a healthy peasant—and, like a man in the thick of urgent work, he briskly opened the front door, called the coachman, helped Peter Ivanovich into the sledge, and sprang back to the porch as if in readiness for what he had to do next.

Peter Ivanovich found the fresh air particularly pleasant after the smell of incense, the dead body, and carbolic acid.

"Where to, sir?" asked the coachman.

"It's not too late even now . . . I'll call round on Fëdor Vasilievich."

He accordingly drove there and found them just finishing the first rubber, so that it was quite convenient for him to cut in.

II

Ivan Ilych's life had been most simple and most ordinary and therefore most terrible.

He had been a member of the Court of Justice, and died at the age of forty-five. His father had been an official who after serving in various ministries and departments in Petersburg had made the sort of career which brings men to positions from which by reason of their long service they cannot be dismissed, though they are obviously unfit to hold any responsible position, and for whom therefore posts are specially created, which though fictitious carry salaries of from six to ten thousand rubles that are not fictitious, and in receipt of which they live on to a great age.

Such was the Privy Councillor and superfluous member of various superfluous institutions, Ilya Epimovich Golovin.

He had three sons, of whom Ivan Ilych was the second. The eldest son was following in his father's footsteps only in another department, and was already approaching that stage in the service at which a similar sinecure would be reached. The third son was a failure. He had ruined his prospects in a number of positions and was now serving in the railway department. His father and brothers, and still more their wives, not merely disliked meeting him, but avoided remembering his existence unless compelled to do so. His sister had married Baron Greff, a

Petersburg official of her father's type. Ivan Ilych was *le phénix de la famille*[1] as people said. He was neither as cold and formal as his elder brother nor as wild as the younger, but was a happy mean between them—an intelligent, polished, lively, and agreeable man. He had studied with his younger brother at the School of Law, but the latter had failed to complete the course and was expelled when he was in the fifth class. Ivan Ilych finished the course well. Even when he was at the School of Law he was just what he remained for the rest of his life: a capable, cheerful, good-natured, and sociable man, though strict in the fulfillment of what he considered to be his duty: and he considered his duty to be what was so considered by those in authority. Neither as a boy nor as a man was he a toady, but from early youth was by nature attracted to people of high station as a fly is drawn to the light, assimilating their ways and views of life and establishing friendly relations with them. All the enthusiasms of childhood and youth passed without leaving much trace on him; he succumbed to sensuality, to vanity, and latterly among the highest classes to liberalism, but always within limits which his instinct unfailingly indicated to him as correct.

At school he had done things which had formerly seemed to him very horrid and made him feel disgusted with himself when he did them; but when later on he saw that such actions were done by people of good position and that they did not regard them as wrong, he was able not exactly to regard them as right, but to forget about them entirely or not be at all troubled at remembering them.

Having graduated from the School of Law and qualified for the tenth rank of the civil service, and having received money from his father for his equipment, Ivan Ilych ordered himself clothes at Scharmer's, the fashionable tailor, hung a medallion inscribed *respice finem*[2] on his watch-chain, took leave of his professor and the prince who was patron of the school, had a farewell dinner with his comrades at Donon's first-class restaurant, and with his new and fashionable portmanteau, linen, clothes, shaving and other toilet appliances, and a traveling rug all purchased at the best shops, he set off for one of the provinces where through his father's influence, he had been attached to the Governor as an official for special service.

In the province Ivan Ilych soon arranged as easy and agreeable a position for himself as he had had at the School of Law. He performed his official tasks, made his career, and at the same time amused himself

[1]*le phénix de la famille*: the family pride and joy.
[2]*respice finem*: regard the end (of life).

pleasantly and decorously. Occasionally he paid official visits to country districts, where he behaved with dignity both to his superiors and inferiors, and performed the duties entrusted to him, which related chiefly to the sectarians, with an exactness and incorruptible honesty of which he could not but feel proud.

In official matters, despite his youth and taste for frivolous gaiety, he was exceedingly reserved, punctilious, and even severe; but in society he was often amusing and witty, and always good-natured, correct in his manner, and *bon enfant*,[3] as the Governor and his wife—with whom he was like one of the family—used to say of him.

In the province he had an affair with a lady who made advances to the elegant young lawyer, and there was also a milliner; and there were carousals with aides-de-camp who visited the district, and after-supper visits to a certain outlying street of doubtful reputation; and there was too some obsequiousness to his chief and even to his chief's wife, but all this was done with such a tone of good breeding that no hard names could be applied to it. It all came under the heading of the French saying: "*Il faut que jeunesse se passe.*"[4] It was all done with clean hands, in clean linen, with French phrases, and above all among people of the best society and consequently with the approval of people of rank.

So Ivan Ilych served for five years and then came a change in his official life. The new and reformed judicial institutions were introduced, and new men were needed. Ivan Ilych became such a new man. He was offered the post of examining magistrate, and he accepted it though the post was in another province and obliged him to give up the connections he had formed and to make new ones. His friends met to give him a send-off; they had a group-photograph taken and presented him with a silver cigarette-case, and he set off to his new post.

As examining magistrate Ivan Ilych was just as *comme il faut*[5] and decorous a man, inspiring general respect and capable of separating his official duties from his private life, as he had been when acting as an official on special service. His duties now as examining magistrate were far more interesting and attractive than before. In his former position it had been pleasant to wear an undress uniform made by Scharmer, and to pass through the crowd of petitioners and officials who were timorously awaiting an audience with the Governor, and who envied him as with free and easy gait he went straight into his chief's private room to have a cup of tea and a cigarette with him. But not many people had

[3]*bon enfant*: a good boy.
[4]"*il faut que jeunesse se passe*": Youth will pass.
[5]*comme il faut*: done correctly.

been directly dependent on him—only police officials and the sectarians when he went on special missions—and he liked to treat them politely, almost as comrades, as if he were letting them feel that he who had the power to crush them was treating them in this simple, friendly way. There were then but few such people. But now, as an examining magistrate, Ivan Ilych felt that everyone without exception, even the most important and self-satisfied, was in his power, and that he need only write a few words on a sheet of paper with a certain heading, and this or that important, self-satisfied person would be brought before him in the role of an accused person or a witness, and if he did not choose to allow him to sit down, would have to stand before him and answer his questions. Ivan Ilych never abused his power; he tried on the contrary to soften its expression, but the consciousness of it and of the possibility of softening its effect, supplied the chief interest and attraction of his office. In his work itself, especially in his examinations, he very soon acquired a method of eliminating all considerations irrelevant to the legal aspect of the case, and reducing even the most complicated case to a form in which it would be presented on paper only in its externals, completely excluding his personal opinion of the matter, while above all observing every prescribed formality. The work was new and Ivan Ilych was one of the first men to apply the new Code of 1864.[6]

On taking up the post of examining magistrate in a new town, he made new acquaintances and connections, placed himself on a new footing, and assumed a somewhat different tone. He took up an attitude of rather dignified aloofness towards the provincial authorities, but picked out the best circle of legal gentlemen and wealthy gentry living in the town and assumed a tone of slight dissatisfaction with the government, of moderate liberalism, and of enlightened citizenship. At the same time, without at all altering the elegance of his toilet, he ceased shaving his chin and allowed his beard to grow as it pleased.

Ivan Ilych settled down very pleasantly in this new town. The society there, which inclined towards opposition to the Governor, was friendly, his salary was larger, and he began to play *vint*,[7] which he found added not a little to the pleasure of life, for he had a capacity for cards, played good-humoredly, and calculated rapidly and astutely, so that he usually won.

After living there for two years he met his future wife, Praskovya Fëdorovna Mikhel, who was the most attractive, clever, and brilliant girl of the set in which he moved, and among other amusements and

[6]*Code of 1864:* wide ranging judicial reforms.
[7]*vint:* a card game.

relaxations from his labors as examining magistrate, Ivan Ilych established light and playful relations with her.

While he had been an official on special service he had been accustomed to dance, but now as an examining magistrate it was exceptional for him to do so. If he danced now, he did it as if to show that though he served under the reformed order of things, and had reached the fifth official rank, yet when it came to dancing he could do it better than most people. So at the end of an evening he sometimes danced with Praskovya Fëdorovna, and it was chiefly during these dances that he captivated her. She fell in love with him. Ivan Ilych had at first no definite intention of marrying, but when the girl fell in love with him he said to himself: "Really, why shouldn't I marry?"

Praskovya Fëdorovna came of a good family, was not bad-looking, and had some little property. Ivan Ilych might have aspired to a more brilliant match, but even this was good. He had his salary, and she, he hoped, would have an equal income. She was well connected, and was a sweet, pretty, and thoroughly correct young woman. To say that Ivan Ilych married because he fell in love with Praskovya Fëdorovna and found that she sympathized with his views of life would be as incorrect as to say that he married because his social circle approved of the match. He was swayed by both these considerations: the marriage gave him personal satisfaction, and at the same time it was considered the right thing by the most highly placed of his associates.

So Ivan Ilych got married.

The preparations for marriage and the beginning of married life, with its conjugal caresses, the new furniture, new crockery, and new linen, were very pleasant until his wife became pregnant—so that Ivan Ilych had begun to think that marriage would not impair the easy, agreeable, gay, and always decorous character of his life, approved of by society and regarded by himself as natural, but would even improve it. But from the first months of his wife's pregnancy, something new, unpleasant, depressing, and unseemly, and from which there was no way of escape, unexpectedly showed itself.

His wife, without any reason—*de gaieté de coeur*[8] as Ivan Ilych expressed it to himself—began to disturb the pleasure and propriety of their life. She began to be jealous without any cause, expected him to devote his whole attention to her, found fault with everything, and made coarse and ill-mannered scenes.

---

[8]*de gaieté de cœur:* for no clear reason.

At first Ivan Ilych hoped to escape from the unpleasantness of this state of affairs by the same easy and decorous relation to life that had served him heretofore: he tried to ignore his wife's disagreeable moods, continued to live in his usual easy and pleasant way, invited friends to his house for a game of cards, and also tried going out to his club or spending his evenings with friends. But one day his wife began upbraiding him so vigorously, using such coarse words, and continued to abuse him every time he did not fulfil her demands, so resolutely and with such evident determination not to give way till he submitted—that is, till he stayed at home and was bored just as she was—that he became alarmed. He now realized that matrimony—at any rate with Praskovya Fëdorovna—was not always conducive to the pleasures and amenities of life, but on the contrary often infringed both comfort and propriety, and that he must therefore entrench himself against such infringement. And Ivan Ilych began to seek for means of doing so. His official duties were the one thing that imposed upon Praskovya Fëdorovna, and by means of his official work and the duties attached to it he began struggling with his wife to secure his own independence.

With the birth of their child, the attempts to feed it and the various failures in doing so, and with the real and imaginary illnesses of mother and child, in which Ivan Ilych's sympathy was demanded but about which he understood nothing, the need of securing for himself an existence outside his family life became still more imperative.

As his wife grew more irritable and exacting and Ivan Ilych transferred the center of gravity of his life more and more to his official work, so did he grow to like his work better and became more ambitious than before.

Very soon, within a year of his wedding, Ivan Ilych had realized that marriage, though it may add some comforts to life, is in fact a very intricate and difficult affair towards which in order to perform one's duty, that is, to lead a decorous life approved of by society, one must adopt a definite attitude just as towards one's official duties.

And Ivan Ilych evolved such an attitude towards married life. He only required of it those conveniences—dinner at home, housewife, and bed—which it could give him, and above all that propriety of external forms required by public opinion. For the rest he looked for light-hearted pleasure and propriety, and was very thankful when he found them, but if he met with antagonism and querulousness he at once retired into his separate fenced-off world of official duties, where he found satisfaction.

Ivan Ilych was esteemed a good official, and after three years was made Assistant Public Prosecutor. His new duties, their importance, the possibility of indicting and imprisoning anyone he chose, the publicity his speeches received, and the success he had in all these things, made his work still more attractive.

More children came. His wife became more and more querulous and illtempered, but the attitude Ivan Ilych had adopted towards his home life rendered him almost impervious to her grumbling.

After seven years' service in that town he was transferred to another province as Public Prosecutor. They moved, but were short of money and his wife did not like the place they moved to. Though the salary was higher the cost of living was greater, besides which two of their children died and family life became still more unpleasant for him.

Praskovya Fëdorovna blamed her husband for every inconvenience they encountered in their new home. Most of the conversations between husband and wife, especially as to the children's education, led to topics which recalled former disputes, and those disputes were apt to flare up again at any moment. There remained only those rare periods of amorousness which still came to them at times but did not last long. These were islets at which they anchored for a while and then again set out upon that ocean of veiled hostility which showed itself in their aloofness from one another. This aloofness might have grieved Ivan Ilych had he considered that it ought not to exist, but he now regarded the position as normal, and even made it the goal at which he aimed in family life. His aim was to free himself more and more from those unpleasantnesses and to give them a semblance of harmlessness and propriety. He attained this by spending less and less time with his family, and when obliged to be at home he tried to safeguard his position by the presence of outsiders. The chief thing, however, was that he had his official duties. The whole interest of his life now centered in the official world and that interest absorbed him. The consciousness of his power, being able to ruin anybody he wished to ruin, the importance, even the external dignity of his entry into court, or meetings with his subordinates, his success with superiors and inferiors, and above all his masterly handling of cases, of which he was conscious—all this gave him pleasure and filled his life, together with chats with his colleagues, dinners, and bridge. So that on the whole Ivan Ilych's life continued to flow as he considered it should do—pleasantly and properly.

So things continued for another seven years. His eldest daughter was already sixteen, another child had died, and only one son was left, a schoolboy and a subject of dissension. Ivan Ilych wanted to put him in the School of Law, but to spite him Praskovya Fëdorovna entered him at the High School. The daughter had been educated at home and had turned out well: the boy did not learn badly either.

III

So Ivan Ilych lived for seventeen years after his marriage. He was already a Public Prosecutor of long standing, and had declined several proposed transfers while awaiting a more desirable post, when an unanticipated and unpleasant occurrence quite upset the peaceful course of his life. He was expecting to be offered the post of presiding judge in a University town, but Happe somehow came to the front and obtained the appointment instead. Ivan Ilych became irritable, reproached Happe, and quarreled both with him and with his immediate superiors—who became colder to him and again passed him over when other appointments were made.

This was in 1880, the hardest year of Ivan Ilych's life. It was then that it became evident on the one hand that his salary was insufficient for them to live on, and on the other that he had been forgotten, and not only this, but that what was for him the greatest and most cruel injustice appeared to others a quite ordinary occurrence. Even his father did not consider it his duty to help him. Ivan Ilych felt himself abandoned by everyone, and that they regarded his position with a salary of 3,500 rubles as quite normal and even fortunate. He alone knew that with the consciousness of the injustices done him, with his wife's incessant nagging, and with the debts he had contracted by living beyond his means, his position was far from normal.

In order to save money that summer he obtained leave of absence and went with his wife to live in the country at her brother's place.

In the country, without his work, he experienced *ennui* for the first time in his life, and not only *ennui* but intolerable depression, and he decided that it was impossible to go on living like that, and that it was necessary to take energetic measures.

Having passed a sleepless night pacing up and down the veranda, he decided to go to Petersburg and bestir himself, in order to punish those who had failed to appreciate him and to get transferred to another ministry.

Next day, despite many protests from his wife and her brother, he started for Petersburg with the sole object of obtaining a post with a salary of five thousand rubles a year. He was no longer bent on any particular department, or tendency, or kind of activity. All he now wanted was an appointment to another post with a salary of five thousand rubles, either in the administration, in the banks, with the railways, in one of the Empress Marya's Institutions, or even in the customs—but it had to carry with it a salary of five thousand rubles and be in a ministry other than that in which they had failed to appreciate him.

And this quest of Ivan Ilych's was crowned with remarkable and unexpected success. At Kursk an acquaintance of his, F. I. Ilyin, got into the first-class carriage, sat down beside Ivan Ilych, and told him of a telegram just received by the Governor of Kursk announcing that a change was about to take place in the ministry: Peter Ivanovich was to be superseded by Ivan Semënovich.

The proposed change, apart from its significance for Russia, had a special significance for Ivan Ilych, because by bringing forward a new man, Peter Petrovich, and consequently his friend Zachar Ivanovich, it was highly favorable for Ivan Ilych, since Zachar Ivanovich was a friend and colleague of his.

In Moscow this news was confirmed, and on reaching Petersburg Ivan Ilych found Zachar Ivanovich and received a definite promise of an appointment in his former department of Justice.

A week later he telegraphed to his wife: "Zachar in Miller's place. I shall receive appointment on presentation of report."

Thanks to this change of personnel, Ivan Ilych had unexpectedly obtained an appointment in his former ministry which placed him two stages above his former colleagues besides giving him five thousand rubles salary and three thousand five hundred rubles for expenses connected with his removal. All his ill humor towards his former enemies and the whole department vanished, and Ivan Ilych was completely happy.

He returned to the country more cheerful and contented than he had been for a long time. Praskovya Fëdorovna also cheered up and a truce was arranged between them. Ivan Ilych told of how he had been feted by everybody in Petersburg, how all those who had been his enemies were put to shame and now fawned on him, how envious they were of his appointment, and how much everybody in Petersburg had liked him.

Praskovya Fëdorovna listened to all this and appeared to believe it. She did not contradict anything, but only made plans for their life in the town to which they were going. Ivan Ilych saw with delight that these plans were his plans, that he and his wife agreed, and that, after a stumble, his life was regaining its due and natural character of pleasant lightheartedness and decorum.

Ivan Ilych had come back for a short time only, for he had to take up his new duties on the 10th of September. Moreover, he needed time to settle into the new place, to move all his belongings from the province, and to buy and order many additional things: in a word, to make such arrangements as he had resolved on, which were almost exactly what Praskovya Fëdorovna too had decided on.

Now that everything had happened so fortunately, and that he and his wife were at one in their aims and moreover saw so little of one another, they got on together better than they had done since the first years of marriage. Ivan Ilych had thought of taking his family away with him at once, but the insistence of his wife's brother and her sister-in-law, who had suddenly become particularly amiable and friendly to him and his family, induced him to depart alone.

So he departed, and the cheerful state of mind induced by his success and by the harmony between his wife and himself, the one intensifying the other, did not leave him. He found a delightful house, just the thing both he and his wife had dreamt of. Spacious, lofty reception rooms in the old style, a convenient and dignified study, rooms for his wife and daughter, a study for his son—it might have been specially built for them. Ivan Ilych himself superintended the arrangements, chose the wallpapers, supplemented the furniture (preferably with antiques which he considered particularly *comme il faut*), and supervised the upholstering. Everything progressed and progressed and approached the ideal he had set himself: even when things were only half completed they exceeded his expectations. He saw what a refined and elegant character, free from vulgarity, it would all have when it was ready. On falling asleep he pictured to himself how the reception-room would look. Looking at the yet unfinished drawing-room he could see the fireplace, the screen, the what-not, the little chairs dotted here and there, the dishes and plates on the walls, and the bronzes, as they would be when everything was in place. He was pleased by the thought of how his wife and daughter, who shared his taste in this matter, would be impressed by it. They were certainly not expecting as much. He had been particularly successful in finding, and buying cheaply, antiques which gave a particularly aristocratic character to the whole place. But in his letters he intentionally understated everything in order to be able to surprise them. All this so absorbed him that his new duties—though he liked his official work—interested him less than he had expected. Sometimes he even had moments of absentmindedness during the Court Sessions, and would consider whether he should have straight or curved cornices for his curtains. He was so interested in it all that he often did things himself, rearranging the furniture, or re-hanging the curtains. Once when mounting a stepladder to show the upholsterer, who did not understand, how he wanted the hangings draped, he made a false step and slipped, but being a strong and agile man he clung on and only knocked his side against the knob of the window frame. The bruised place was painful but the pain soon passed, and he felt particularly bright and well just then. He wrote: "I feel fifteen years younger." He thought he would have everything ready by September, but it dragged on till mid-October. But the result was charming not only in his eyes but to everyone who saw it.

In reality it was just what is usually seen in the houses of people of moderate means who want to appear rich, and therefore succeed only in resembling others like themselves: there were damasks, dark wood, plants, rugs, and dull and polished bronzes—all the things people of a certain class have in order to resemble other people of that class. His house was so like the others that it would never have been noticed, but to him it all seemed to be quite exceptional. He was very happy when he met his family at the station and brought them to the newly fur-nished house all lit up, where a footman in a white tie opened the door into the hall decorated with plants, and when they went on into the drawing-room and the study uttering exclamations of delight. He con-ducted them everywhere, drank in their praises eagerly, and beamed with pleasure. At tea that evening, when Praskovya Fëdorovna among other things asked him about his fall, he laughed and showed them how he had gone flying and had frightened the upholsterer.

"It's a good thing I'm a bit of an athlete. Another man might have been killed, but I merely knocked myself, just there; it hurts when it's touched, but it's passing off already—it's only a bruise."

So they began living in their new home—in which, as always hap-pens, when they got thoroughly settled in they found they were just one room short—and with the increased income, which as always was just a little (some five hundred rubles) too little, but it was all very nice.

Things went particularly well at first, before everything was finally arranged and while something had still to be done: this thing bought, that thing ordered, another thing moved, and something else adjusted. Though there were some disputes between husband and wife, they were both so well satisfied and had so much to do that it all passed off with-out any serious quarrels. When nothing was left to arrange it became rather dull and something seemed to be lacking, but they were then making acquaintances, forming habits, and life was growing fuller.

Ivan Ilych spent his mornings at the law courts and came home to dinner, and at first he was generally in a good humor, though he occasionally became irritable just on account of his house. (Every spot on the tablecloth or the upholstery, and every broken window-blind string, irritated him. He had devoted so much trouble to arranging it all that every disturbance of it distressed him.) But on the whole his life ran its course as he believed life should do: easily, pleasantly, and decorously.

He got up at nine, drank his coffee, read the paper, and then put on his undress uniform and went to the law courts. There the harness in which he worked had already been stretched to fit him and he donned it without a hitch: petitioners, inquiries at the chancery, the chancery itself, and the sittings public and administrative. In all this the thing was to exclude everything fresh and vital, which always disturbs the regular course of official business, and to admit only official relations with people, and then only on official grounds. A man would come, for instance, wanting some information. Ivan Ilych, as one in whose sphere the matter did not lie, would have nothing to do with him: but if the man had some business with him in his official capacity, something that could be expressed on officially stamped paper, he would do everything, positively everything he could within the limits of such relations, and in doing so would maintain the semblance of friendly human relations, that is, would observe the courtesies of life. As soon as the official relations ended, so did everything else. Ivan Ilych possessed this capacity to separate his real life from the official side of affairs and not mix the two, in the highest degree, and by long practice and natural aptitude had brought it to such a pitch that sometimes, in the manner of a virtuoso, he would even allow himself to let the human and official relations mingle. He let himself do this just because he felt that he could at any time he chose resume the strictly official attitude again and drop the human relation. And he did it all easily, pleasantly, correctly, and even artistically. In the intervals between the sessions he smoked, drank tea, chatted a little about politics, a little about general topics, a little about cards, but most of all about official appointments. Tired, but with the feelings of a virtuoso—one of the first violins who has played his part in an orchestra with precision—he would return home to find that his wife and daughter had been out paying calls, or had a visitor, and that his son had been to school, had done his homework with his tutor, and was duly learning what is taught at High Schools. Everything was as it should be. After dinner, if they had no visitors, Ivan Ilych sometimes read a book that was being much discussed at the time, and in the evening settled down to work, that is, read official papers, compared the depositions of witnesses, and noted paragraphs of the Code applying to them. This was neither dull nor amusing. It was dull when he might have been playing bridge, but if no bridge was available it was at any rate better than doing nothing or sitting with his wife. Ivan Ilych's chief pleasure was giving little dinners to which he invited men and women of good social position, and just as his drawing-room resembled all other drawing-rooms so did his enjoyable little parties resemble all other such parties.

Once they even gave a dance. Ivan Ilych enjoyed it and everything went off well, except that it led to a violent quarrel with his wife about the cakes and sweets. Praskovya Fëdorovna had made her own plans, but Ivan Ilych insisted on getting everything from an expensive confectioner and ordered too many cakes, and the quarrel occurred because some of those cakes were left over and the confectioner's bill came to forty-five rubles. It was a great and disagreeable quarrel. Praskovya Fëdorovna called him "a fool and an imbecile," and he clutched at his head and made angry allusions to divorce.

But the dance itself had been enjoyable. The best people were there, and Ivan Ilych had danced with Princess Trufonova, a sister of the distinguished founder of the Society "Bear My Burden."

The pleasures connected with his work were pleasures of ambition; his social pleasures were those of vanity; but Ivan Ilych's greatest pleasure was playing bridge. He acknowledged that whatever disagreeable incident happened in his life, the pleasure that beamed like a ray of light above everything else was to sit down to bridge with good players, not noisy partners, and of course to four-handed bridge (with five players it was annoying to have to stand out, though one pretended not to mind), to play a clever and serious game (when the cards allowed it), and then to have supper and drink a glass of wine. After a game of bridge, especially if he had won a little (to win a large sum was unpleasant), Ivan Ilych went to bed in specially good humor.

So they lived. They formed a circle of acquaintances among the best people and were visited by people of importance and by young folk. In their views as to their acquaintances, husband, wife, and daughter were entirely agreed, and tacitly and unanimously kept at arm's length and shook off the various shabby friends and relations who, with much show of affection, gushed into the drawing-room with its Japanese plates on the walls. Soon these shabby friends ceased to obtrude themselves and only the best people remained in the Golovins' set.

Young men made up to Lisa, and Petrishchev, an examining magistrate and Dmitri Ivanovich Petrischev's son and sole heir, began to be so attentive to her that Ivan Ilych had already spoken to Praskovya Fëdorovna about it, and considered whether they should not arrange a party for them, or get up some private theatricals.

So they lived, and all went well, without change, and life flowed pleasantly.

IV

They were all in good health. It could not be called ill health if Ivan Ilych sometimes said that he had a queer taste in his mouth and felt some discomfort in his left side.

But this discomfort increased and, though not exactly painful, grew into a sense of pressure in his side accompanied by ill humor. And his irritability became worse and worse and began to mar the agreeable, easy, and correct life that had established itself in the Golovin family. Quarrels between husband and wife became more and more frequent, and soon the ease and amenity disappeared and even the decorum was barely maintained. Scenes again became frequent, and very few of those islets remained on which husband and wife could meet without an explosion. Praskovya Fëdorovna now had good reason to say that her husband's temper was trying. With characteristic exaggeration she said he had always had a dreadful temper, and that it had needed all her good nature to put up with it for twenty years. It was true that now the quarrels were started by him. His bursts of temper always came just before dinner, often just as he began to eat his soup. Sometimes he noticed that a plate or dish was chipped, or the food was not right, or his son put his elbow on the table, or his daughter's hair was not done as he liked it, and for all this he blamed Praskovya Fëdorovna. At first she retorted and said disagreeable things to him, but once or twice he fell into such a rage at the beginning of dinner that she realized it was due to some physical derangement brought on by taking food, and so she restrained herself and did not answer, but only hurried to get the dinner over. She regarded this self-restraint as highly praiseworthy. Having come to the conclusion that her husband had a dreadful temper and made her life miserable, she began to feel sorry for herself, and the more she pitied herself the more she hated her husband. She began to wish he would die; yet she did not want him to die because then his salary would cease. And this irritated her against him still more. She considered herself dreadfully unhappy just because not even his death could save her, and though she concealed her exasperation, that hidden exasperation of hers increased his irritation also.

After one scene in which Ivan Ilych had been particularly unfair and after which he had said in explanation that he certainly was irritable but that it was due to his not being well, she said that if he was ill it should be attended to, and insisted on his going to see a celebrated doctor.

He went. Everything took place as he had expected and as it always does. There was the usual waiting and the important air assumed by the doctor, with which he was so familiar (resembling that which he himself assumed in court), and the sounding and listening, and the questions which called for answers that were foregone conclusions and were evidently unnecessary, and the look of importance which implied that "if only you put yourself in our hands we will arrange everything—we know indubitably how it has to be done, always in the same way for everybody alike." It was all just as it was in the law courts. The doctor put on just the same air towards him as he himself put on towards an accused person.

The doctor said that so-and-so indicated that there was so-and-so inside the patient, but if the investigation of so-and-so did not confirm this, then he must assume that and that. If he assumed that and that, then . . . and so on. To Ivan Ilych only one question was important: was his case serious or not? But the doctor ignored that inappropriate question. From his point of view it was not the one under consideration, the real question was to decide between a floating kidney, chronic catarrh, or appendicitis. It was not a question of Ivan Ilych's life or death, but one between a floating kidney and appendicitis. And that question the doctor solved brilliantly, as it seemed to Ivan Ilych, in favor of the appendix, with the reservation that should an examination of the urine give fresh indications the matter would be reconsidered. All this was just what Ivan Ilych had himself brilliantly accomplished a thousand times in dealing with men on trial. The doctor summed up just as brilliantly, looking over his spectacles triumphantly and even gaily at the accused. From the doctor's summing up Ivan Ilych concluded that things were bad, but that for the doctor, and perhaps for everybody else, it was a matter of indifference, though for him it was bad. And this conclusion struck him painfully, arousing in him a great feeling of pity for himself and of bitterness towards the doctor's indifference to a matter of such importance.

He said nothing of this, but rose, placed the doctor's fee on the table, and remarked with a sigh: "We sick people probably often put inappropriate questions. But tell me, in general, is this complaint dangerous, or not? . . . ."

The doctor looked at him sternly over his spectacles with one eye, as if to say: "Prisoner, if you will not keep to the questions put to you, I shall be obliged to have you removed from the court."

"I have already told you what I consider necessary and proper. The analysis may show something more." And the doctor bowed.

Ivan Ilych went out slowly, seated himself disconsolately in his sledge, and drove home. All the way home he was going over what the doctor had said, trying to translate those complicated, obscure, scientific phrases into plain language and find in them an answer to the question: "Is my condition bad? Is it very bad? Or is there as yet nothing much wrong?" And it seemed to him that the meaning of what the doctor had said was that it was very bad. Everything in the streets seemed depressing. The cabmen, the houses, the passers-by, and the shops, were dismal. His ache, this dull gnawing ache that never ceased for a moment, seemed to have acquired a new and more serious significance from the doctor's dubious remarks. Ivan Ilych now watched it with a new and oppressive feeling.

He reached home and began to tell his wife about it. She listened, but in the middle of his account his daughter came in with her hat on, ready to go out with her mother. She sat down reluctantly to listen to this tedious story, but could not stand it long, and her mother too did not hear him to the end.

"Well, I am very glad," she said. "Mind now to take your medicine regularly. Give me the prescription and I'll send Gerasim to the chemist's." And she went to get ready to go out.

While she was in the room Ivan Ilych had hardly taken time to breathe, but he sighed deeply when she left it.

"Well," he thought, "perhaps it isn't so bad after all."

He began taking his medicine and following the doctor's directions, which had been altered after the examination of the urine. But then it happened that there was a contradiction between the indications drawn from the examination of the urine and the symptoms that showed themselves. It turned out that what was happening differed from what the doctor had told him, and that he had either forgotten, or blundered, or hidden something from him. He could not, however, be blamed for that, and Ivan Ilych still obeyed his orders implicitly and at first derived some comfort from doing so.

From the time of his visit to the doctor, Ivan Ilych's chief occupation was the exact fulfillment of the doctor's instructions regarding hygiene and the taking of medicine, and the observation of his pain and his excretions. His chief interests came to be people's ailments and people's health. When sickness, deaths, or recoveries were mentioned in his presence, especially when the illness resembled his own, he listened with agitation which he tried to hide, asked questions, and applied what he heard to his own case.

The pain did not grow less, but Ivan Ilych made efforts to force himself to think that he was better. And he could do this so long as nothing agitated him. But as soon as he had any unpleasantness with his wife, any lack of success in his official work, or held bad cards at bridge, he was at once acutely sensible of his disease. He had formerly borne such mischances, hoping soon to adjust what was wrong, to master it and attain success, or make a grand slam. But now every mischance upset him and plunged him into despair. He would say to himself: "There now, just as I was beginning to get better and the medicine had begun to take effect, comes this accursed misfortune, or unpleasantness. . . ." And he was furious with the mishap, or with the people who were causing the unpleasantness and killing him, for he felt that this fury was killing him but could not restrain it. One would have thought that it should have been clear to him that this exasperation with circumstances and people aggravated his illness, and that he ought therefore to ignore unpleasant occurrences. But he drew the very opposite conclusion: he said that he needed peace, and he watched for everything that might disturb it and became irritable at the slightest infringement of it. His condition was rendered worse by the fact that he read medical books and consulted doctors. The progress of his disease was so gradual that he could deceive himself when comparing one day with another—the difference was so slight. But when he consulted the doctors it seemed to him that he was getting worse, and even very rapidly. Yet despite this he was continually consulting them.

That month he went to see another celebrity, who told him almost the same as the first had done but put his questions rather differently, and the interview with this celebrity only increased Ivan Ilych's doubts and fears. A friend of a friend of his, a very good doctor, diagnosed his illness again quite differently from the others, and though he predicted recovery, his questions and suppositions bewildered Ivan Ilych still more and increased his doubts. A homeopathist diagnosed the disease in yet another way, and prescribed medicine which Ivan Ilych took secretly for a week. But after a week, not feeling any improvement and having lost confidence both in the former doctor's treatment and in this one's, he became still more despondent. One day a lady acquaintance mentioned a cure effected by a wonder-working icon. Ivan Ilych caught himself listening attentively and beginning to believe that it had occurred. This incident alarmed him. "Has my mind really weakened to such an extent?" he asked himself. "Nonsense! It's all rubbish. I mustn't give way to nervous fears but having chosen a doctor must keep strictly to his treatment. That is what I will do. Now it's all settled. I won't think about it, but will follow the treatment seriously till summer, and then we shall see. From now there must be no more of this wavering!" This was easy to say but impossible to carry out. The pain in his side oppressed him and seemed to grow worse and more incessant, while the taste in his mouth grew stranger and stranger. It seemed to him that his breath had a disgusting smell, and he was conscious of a loss of appetite and strength. There was no deceiving himself: something terrible, new, and more important than anything before in his life, was taking place within him of which he alone was aware. Those about him did not understand or would not understand it, but thought everything in the world was going on as usual. That tormented Ivan Ilych more than anything. He saw that his household, especially his wife and daughter who were in a perfect whirl of visiting, did not understand anything of it and were annoyed that he was so depressed and so exacting, as if he were to blame for it. Though they tried to disguise it he saw that he was an obstacle in their path, and that his wife had adopted a definite line in regard to his illness and kept to it regardless of anything he said or did. Her attitude was this: "You know," she would say to her friends, "Ivan Ilych can't do as other people do, and keep to the treatment prescribed for him. One day he'll take his drops and keep strictly to his diet and go to bed in good time, but the next day unless I watch him he'll suddenly forget his medicine, eat sturgeon—which is forbidden—and sit up playing cards till one o'clock in the morning."

"Oh, come, when was that?" Ivan Ilych would ask in vexation. "Only once at Peter Ivanovich's."

"And yesterday with Shebek."

"Well, even if I hadn't stayed up, this pain would have kept me awake."

"Be that as it may you'll never get well like that, but will always make us wretched."

Praskovya Fëdorovna's attitude to Ivan Ilych's illness, as she expressed it both to others and to him, was that it was his own fault and was another of the annoyances he caused her. Ivan Ilych felt that this opinion escaped her involuntarily—but that did not make it easier for him.

At the law courts too, Ivan Ilych noticed, or thought he noticed, a strange attitude towards himself. It sometimes seemed to him that people were watching him inquisitively as a man whose place might soon be vacant. Then again, his friends would suddenly begin to chaff him in a friendly way about his low spirits, as if the awful, horrible, and unheard-of thing that was going on within him, incessantly gnawing at him and irresistibly drawing him away, was a very agreeable subject for jests. Schwartz in particular irritated him by his jocularity, vivacity, and *savoir-faire*, which reminded him of what he himself had been ten years ago.

Friends came to make up a set and they sat down to cards. They dealt, bending the new cards to soften them, and he sorted the diamonds in his hand and found he had seven. His partner said "No trumps" and supported him with two diamonds. What more could be wished for? It ought to be jolly and lively. They would make a grand slam. But suddenly Ivan Ilych was conscious of that gnawing pain, that taste in his mouth, and it seemed ridiculous that in such circumstances he should be pleased to make a grand slam.

He looked at his partner Mikhail Mikhaylovich, who rapped the table with his strong hand and instead of snatching up the tricks pushed the cards courteously and indulgently towards Ivan Ilych that he might have the pleasure of gathering them up without the trouble of stretching out his hand for them. "Does he think I am too weak to stretch out my arm?" thought Ivan Ilych, and forgetting what he was doing he over-trumped his partner, missing the grand slam by three tricks. And what was most awful of all was that he saw how upset Mikhail Mikhaylovich was about it but did not himself care. And it was dreadful to realize why he did not care.

They all saw that he was suffering, and said: "We can stop if you are tired. Take a rest." Lie down? No, he was not at all tired, and he finished the rubber. All were gloomy and silent. Ivan Ilych felt that he had diffused this gloom over them and could not dispel it. They had supper and went away, and Ivan Ilych was left alone with the consciousness that his life was poisoned and was poisoning the lives of others, and that this poison did not weaken but penetrated more and more deeply into his whole being.

With this consciousness, and with physical pain besides the terror, he must go to bed, often to lie awake the greater part of the night. Next morning he had to get up again, dress, go to the law courts, speak, and write; or if he did not go out, spend at home those twenty-four hours a day each of which was a torture. And he had to live thus all alone on the brink of an abyss, with no one who understood or pitied him.

V

So one month passed and then another. Just before the New Year his brother-in-law came to town and stayed at their house. Ivan Ilych was at the law courts and Praskovya Fëdorovna had gone shopping. When Ivan Ilych came home and entered his study he found his brother-in-law there—a healthy, florid man—unpacking his portmanteau himself. He raised his head on hearing Ivan Ilych's footsteps and looked up at him for a moment without a word. That stare told Ivan Ilych everything. His brother-in-law opened his mouth to utter an exclamation of surprise but checked himself, and that action confirmed it all.

"I have changed, eh?"

"Yes, there is a change."

And after that, try as he would to get his brother-in-law to return to the subject of his looks, the latter would say nothing about it. Praskovya Fëdorovna came home and her brother went out to her. Ivan Ilych locked the door and began to examine himself in the glass, first full face, then in profile. He took up a portrait of himself taken with his wife, and compared it with what he saw in the glass. The change in him was immense. Then he bared his arms to the elbow, looked at them, drew the sleeves down again, sat down on an ottoman, and grew blacker than night.

"No, no, this won't do!" he said to himself, and jumped up, went to the table, took up some law papers, and began to read them, but could not continue. He unlocked the door and went into the reception-room. The door leading to the drawing-room was shut. He approached it on tiptoe and listened.

"No, you are exaggerating!" Praskovya Fëdorovna was saying.

"Exaggerating! Don't you see it? Why, he's a dead man! Look at his eyes—there's no light in them. But what is it that is wrong with him?"

"No one knows. Nikolaevich said something, but I don't know what. And Leshchetitsky said quite the contrary . . ."

Ivan Ilych walked away, went to his own room, lay down, and began musing: "The kidney, a floating kidney." He recalled all the doctors had told him of how it detached itself and swayed about. And by an effort of imagination he tried to catch that kidney and arrest it and support it. So little was needed for this, it seemed to him. "No, I'll go to see Peter Ivanovich again." He rang, ordered the carriage, and got ready to go.

"Where are you going, Jean?" asked his wife, with a specially sad and exceptionally kind look.

This exceptionally kind look irritated him. He looked morosely at her.

"I must go to see Peter Ivanovich."

He went to see Peter Ivanovich, and together they went to see his friend, the doctor. He was in, and Ivan Ilych had a long talk with him.

Reviewing the anatomical and physiological details of what in the doctor's opinion was going on inside him, he understood it all.

There was something, a small thing, in the vermiform appendix. It might all come right. Only stimulate the energy of one organ and check the activity of another, then absorption would take place and everything would come right. He got home rather late for dinner, ate his dinner, and conversed cheerfully, but could not for a long time bring himself to go back to work in his room. At last, however, he went to his study and did what was necessary, but the consciousness that he had put something aside—an important, intimate matter which he would revert to when his work was done—never left him. When he had finished his work he remembered that this intimate matter was the thought of his vermiform appendix. But he did not give himself up to it, and went to the drawing-room for tea. There were callers there, including the examining magistrate who was a desirable match for his daughter, and they were conversing, playing the piano, and singing. Ivan Ilych, as Praskovya Fëdorovna remarked, spent that evening more cheerfully than usual, but he never for a moment forgot that he had postponed the important matter of the appendix. At eleven o'clock he said good-night and went to his bedroom. Since his illness he had slept alone in a small room next to his study. He undressed and took up a novel by Zola, but instead of reading it he fell into thought, and in his imagination that desired improvement in the vermiform appendix occurred. There was the absorption and evacuation and the re-establishment of normal activity. "Yes, that's it!" he said to himself. "One need only assist nature, that's all." He remembered his medicine, rose, took it, and lay down on his back watching for the beneficent action of the medicine and for it to lessen the pain. "I need only take it regularly and avoid all injurious influences. I am already feeling better, much better." He began touching his side: it was not painful to the touch. "There, I really don't feel it. It's much better already." He put out the light and turned on his side . . . "The appendix is getting better, absorption is occurring." Suddenly he felt the old, familiar, dull, gnawing pain, stubborn and serious. There was the same familiar loathsome taste in his mouth. His heart sank and he felt dazed. "My God! My God!" he muttered. "Again, again! and it will never cease." And suddenly the matter presented itself in a quite different aspect. "Vermiform appendix! Kidney!" he said to himself. "It's not a question of appendix or kidney, but of life and . . . death. Yes, life was there and now it is going, going and I cannot stop it. Yes. Why deceive myself? Isn't it obvious to everyone but me that I'm dying, and that it's only a question of weeks, days . . . it may happen this moment. There was light and now there is darkness. I was here and now I'm going there! Where?" A chill came over him, his breathing ceased, and he felt only the throbbing of his heart.

"When I am not, what will there be? There will be nothing. Then where shall I be when I am no more? Can this be dying? No, I don't want to!" He jumped up and tried to light the candle, felt for it with trembling hands, dropped candle and candlestick on the floor, and fell back on his pillow.

"What's the use? It makes no difference," he said to himself, staring with wide-open eyes into the darkness. "Death. Yes, death. And none of them know or wish to know it, and they have no pity for me. Now they are playing." (He heard through the door the distant sound of a song and its accompaniment.) "It's all the same to them, but they will die too! Fools! I first, and they later, but it will be the same for them. And now they are merry . . . the beasts!"

Anger choked him and he was agonizingly, unbearably miserable. "It is impossible that all men have been doomed to suffer this awful horror!" He raised himself.

"Something must be wrong. I must calm myself—must think it all over from the beginning." And he again began thinking. "Yes, the beginning of my illness: I knocked my side, but I was still quite well that day and the next. It hurt a little, then rather more. I saw the doctors, then followed despondency and anguish, more doctors, and I drew nearer to the abyss. My strength grew less and I kept coming nearer and nearer, and now I have wasted away and there is no light in my eyes. I think of the appendix—but this is death! I think of mending the appendix, and all the while here is death! Can it really be death?" Again terror seized him and he gasped for breath. He leant down and began feeling for the matches, pressing with his elbow on the stand beside the bed. It was in his way and hurt him, he grew furious with it, pressed on it still harder, and upset it. Breathless and in despair he fell on his back, expecting death to come immediately.

Meanwhile the visitors were leaving. Praskovya Fëdorovna was seeing them off. She heard something fall and came in.

"What has happened?"

"Nothing. I knocked it over accidentally."

She went out and returned with a candle. He lay there panting heavily, like a man who has run a thousand yards, and stared upwards at her with a fixed look.

"What is it, Jean?"

"No . . . o . . . thing. I upset it." ("Why speak of it? She won't understand," he thought.)

And in truth she did not understand. She picked up the stand, lit his candle, and hurried away to see another visitor off. When she came back he still lay on his back, looking upwards.

"What is it? Do you feel worse?"

"Yes."

She shook her head and sat down.

"Do you know, Jean, I think we must ask Leshchetitsky to come and see you here."

This meant calling in the famous specialist, regardless of expense. He smiled malignantly and said "No." She remained a little longer and then went up to him and kissed his forehead.

While she was kissing him he hated her from the bottom of his soul and with difficulty refrained from pushing her away.

"Good-night. Please God you'll sleep."

"Yes."

VI

Ivan Ilych saw that he was dying, and he was in continual despair.

In the depth of his heart he knew he was dying, but not only was he not accustomed to the thought, he simply did not and could not grasp it.

The syllogism he had learnt from Kiezewetter's Logic: "Caius is a man, men are mortal, therefore Caius is mortal," had always seemed to him correct as applied to Caius, but certainly not as applied to himself. That Caius—man in the abstract—was mortal, was perfectly correct, but he was not Caius, not an abstract man, but a creature quite, quite separate from all others. He had been little Vanya, with a mamma and a papa, with Mitya and Volodya, with the toys, a coachman and a nurse, afterwards with Katenka and with all the joys, griefs, and delights of childhood, boyhood, and youth. What did Caius know of the smell of that striped leather ball Vanya had been so fond of? Had Caius kissed his mother's hand like that, and did the silk of her dress rustle so for Caius? Had he rioted like that at school when the pastry was bad? Had Caius been in love like that? Could Caius preside at a session as he did? "Caius really was mortal, and it was right for him to die; but for me, little Vanya, Ivan Ilych, with all my thoughts and emotions, it's altogether a different matter. It cannot be that I ought to die. That would be too terrible."

Such was his feeling.

"If I had to die like Caius I should have known it was so. An inner voice would have told me so, but there was nothing of the sort in me and I and all my friends felt that our case was quite different from that of Caius. And now here it is!" he said to himself. "It can't be. It's impossible! But here it is. How is this? How is one to understand it?"

He could not understand it, and tried to drive this false, incorrect, morbid thought away and to replace it by other proper and healthy thoughts. But that thought, and not the thought only but the reality itself, seemed to come and confront him.

And to replace that thought he called up a succession of others, hoping to find in them some support. He tried to get back into the former current of thoughts that had once screened the thought of death from him. But strange to say, all that had formerly shut off, hidden, and destroyed his consciousness of death, no longer had that effect. Ivan Ilych now spent most of his time in attempting to re-establish that old current. He would say to himself: "I will take up my duties again—after all I used to live by them." And banishing all doubts he would go to the law courts, enter into conversation with his colleagues, and sit carelessly as was his wont, scanning the crowd with a thoughtful look and leaning both his emaciated arms on the arms of his oak chair; bending over as usual to a colleague and drawing his papers nearer he would interchange whispers with him, and then suddenly raising his eyes and sitting erect would pronounce certain words and open the proceedings. But suddenly in the midst of those proceedings the pain in his side, regardless of the stage the proceedings had reached, would begin its own gnawing work. Ivan Ilych would turn his attention to it and try to drive the thought of it away, but without success. *It* would come and stand before him and look at him, and he would be petrified and the light would die out of his eyes, and he would again begin asking himself whether *It* alone was true. And his colleagues and subordinates would see with surprise and distress that he, the brilliant and subtle judge, was becoming confused and making mistakes. He would shake himself, try to pull himself together, manage somehow to bring the sitting to a close, and return home with the sorrowful consciousness that his judicial labors could not as formerly hide from him what he wanted them to hide, and could not deliver him from *It*. And what was worst of all was that *It* drew his attention to itself not in order to make him take some action but only that he should look at *It,* look it straight in the face: look at it and, without doing anything, suffer inexpressibly.

And to save himself from this condition Ivan Ilych looked for consolation—new screens—and new screens were found and for a while seemed to save him, but then they immediately fell to pieces or rather became transparent, as if *It* penetrated them and nothing could veil *It.*

In these latter days he would go into the drawing-room he had arranged—that drawing-room where he had fallen and for the sake of which (how bitterly ridiculous it seemed) he had sacrificed his life—for he knew that his illness originated with that knock. He would enter and see that something had scratched the polished table. He would look for the cause of this and find that it was the bronze ornamentation of an album, that had got bent. He would take up the expensive album which he had lovingly arranged, and feel vexed with his daughter and her friends for their untidiness—for the album was torn here and there and some of the photographs turned upside down. He would put it carefully in order and bend the ornamentation back into position. Then it would occur to him to place all those things in another corner of the room, near the plants. He could call the footman, but his daughter or wife would come to help him. They would not agree, and his wife would contradict him, and he would dispute and grow angry. But that was all right, for then he did not think about *It. It* was invisible.

But then, when he was moving something himself, his wife would say: "Let the servants do it. You will hurt yourself again." And suddenly *It* would flash through the screen and he would see it. It was just a flash, and he hoped it would disappear, but he would involuntarily pay attention to his side. "It sits there as before, gnawing just the same!" And he could no longer forget *It,* but could distinctly see it looking at him from behind the flowers. "What is it all for?"

"It really is so! I lost my life over that curtain as I might have done when storming a fort. Is that possible? How terrible and how stupid. It can't be true! It can't, but it is."

He would go to his study, lie down, and again be alone with *It:* face to face with *It.* And nothing could be done with *It* except to look at it and shudder.

VII

How it happened it is impossible to say because it came about step by step, unnoticed, but in the third month of Ivan Ilych's illness, his wife, his daughter, his son, his acquaintances, the doctors, the servants, and above all he himself, were aware that the whole interest he had for other people was whether he would soon vacate his place, and at last release the living from the discomfort caused by his presence and be himself released from his sufferings.

He slept less and less. He was given opium and hypodermic injections of morphine, but this did not relieve him. The dull depression he experienced in a somnolent condition at first gave him a little relief, but only as something new, afterwards it became as distressing as the pain itself or even more so.

Special foods were prepared for him by the doctors' orders, but all those foods became increasingly distasteful and disgusting to him.

For his excretions also special arrangements had to be made, and this was a torment to him every time—a torment from the uncleanliness, the unseemliness, and the smell, and from knowing that another person had to take part in it.

But just through this most unpleasant matter, Ivan Ilych obtained comfort. Gerasim, the butler's young assistant, always came in to carry the things out. Gerasim was a clean, fresh peasant lad, grown stout on town food and always cheerful and bright. At first the sight of him, in his clean Russian peasant costume, engaged on that disgusting task embarrassed Ivan Ilych.

Once when he got up from the commode too weak to draw up his trousers, he dropped into a soft armchair and looked with horror at his bare, enfeebled thighs with the muscles so sharply marked on them.

Gerasim with a firm light tread, his heavy boots emitting a pleasant smell of tar and fresh winter air, came in wearing a clean Hessian apron, the sleeves of his print shirt tucked up over his strong, bare young arms; and refraining from looking at his sick master out of consideration for his feelings, and restraining the joy of life that beamed from his face, he went up to the commode.

"Gerasim!" said Ivan Ilych in a weak voice.

Gerasim started, evidently afraid he might have committed some blunder, and with a rapid movement turned his fresh, kind, simple young face which just showed the first downy signs of a beard.

"Yes, sir?"

"That must be very unpleasant for you. You must forgive me. I am helpless."

"Oh, why, sir," and Gerasim's eyes beamed and he showed his glistening white teeth, "what's a little trouble? It's a case of illness with you, sir."

And his deft strong hands did their accustomed task, and he went out of the room stepping lightly. Five minutes later he as lightly returned.

Ivan Ilych was still sitting in the same position in the armchair.

"Gerasim," he said when the latter had replaced the freshly washed utensil. "Please come here and help me." Gerasim went up to him. "Lift me up. It is hard for me to get up, and I have sent Dmitri away."

Gerasim went up to him, grasped his master with his strong arms deftly but gently, in the same way that he stepped—lifted him, supported him with one hand, and with the other drew up his trousers and would have set him down again, but Ivan Ilych asked to be led to the sofa. Gerasim, without an effort and without apparent pressure, led him, almost lifting him, to the sofa, and placed him on it.

"Thank you. How easily and well you do it all!"

Gerasim smiled again and turned to leave the room. But Ivan Ilych felt his presence such a comfort that he did not want to let him go.

"One thing more, please move up that chair. No, the other one— under my feet. It is easier for me when my feet are raised."

Gerasim brought the chair, set it down gently in place, and raised Ivan Ilych's legs on to it. It seemed to Ivan Ilych that he felt better while Gerasim was holding up his legs.

"It's better when my legs are higher," he said. "Place that cushion under them."

Gerasim did so. He again lifted the legs and placed them, and again Ivan Ilych felt better while Gerasim held his legs. When he set them down Ivan Ilych fancied he felt worse.

"Gerasim," he said. "Are you busy now?"

"Not at all, sir," said Gerasim, who had learnt from the townsfolk how to speak to gentlefolk.

"What have you still to do?"

"What have I to do? I've done everything except chopping the logs for tomorrow."

"Then hold my legs up a bit higher, can you?"

"Of course I can. Why not?" And Gerasim raised his master's legs higher and Ivan Ilych thought that in that position he did not feel any pain at all.

"And how about the logs?"

"Don't trouble about that, sir. There's plenty of time."

Ivan Ilych told Gerasim to sit down and hold his legs, and began to talk to him. And strange to say it seemed to him that he felt better while Gerasim held his legs up.

After that Ivan Ilych would sometimes call Gerasim and get him to hold his legs on his shoulders, and he liked talking to him. Gerasim did it all easily, willingly, simply, and with a good nature that touched Ivan Ilych. Health, strength, and vitality in other people were offensive to him, but Gerasim's strength and vitality did not mortify but soothed him.

What tormented Ivan Ilych most was the deception, the lie, which for some reason they all accepted, that he was not dying but was simply ill, and that he only need keep quiet and undergo a treatment and then something very good would result. He, however, knew that do what they would nothing would come of it, only still more agonizing suffering and death. This deception tortured him—their not wishing to admit what they all knew and what he knew, but wanting to lie to him concerning his terrible condition, and wishing and forcing him to participate in that lie. Those lies—lies enacted over him on the eve of his death and destined to degrade this awful, solemn act to the level of their visitings, their curtains, their sturgeon for dinner—were a terrible agony for Ivan Ilych. And strangely enough, many times when they were going through their antics over him he had been within a hair-breadth of calling out to them: "Stop lying! You know and I know that I am dying. Then at least stop lying about it!" But he had never had the spirit to do it. The awful, terrible act of his dying was, he could see, reduced by those about him to the level of a casual, unpleasant, and almost indecorous incident (as if someone entered a drawing-room diffusing an unpleasant odor) and this was done by that very decorum which he had served all his life long. He saw that no one felt for him, because no one even wished to grasp his position. Only Gerasim recognized it and pitied him. And so Ivan Ilych felt at ease only with him. He felt comforted when Gerasim supported his legs (sometimes all night long) and refused to go to bed, saying: "Don't you worry, Ivan Ilych. I'll get sleep enough later on," or when he suddenly became familiar and exclaimed: "If you weren't sick it would be another matter, but as it is, why should I grudge a little trouble?" Gerasim alone did not lie; everything showed that he alone understood the facts of the case and did not consider it necessary to disguise them, but simply felt sorry for his emaciated and enfeebled master. Once when Ivan Ilych was sending him away he even said straight out: "We shall all of us die, so why should I grudge a little trouble?"—expressing the fact that he did not think his work burdensome, because he was doing it for a dying man and hoped someone would do the same for him when his time came.

Apart from this lying, or because of it, what most tormented Ivan Ilych was that no one pitied him as he wished to be pitied. At certain moments after prolonged suffering he wished most of all (though he would have been ashamed to confess it) for someone to pity him as a sick child is pitied. He longed to be petted and comforted. He knew he was an important functionary, that he had a beard turning grey, and that therefore what he longed for was impossible, but still he longed for it. And in Gerasim's attitude towards him there was something akin to what he wished for, and so that attitude comforted him. Ivan Ilych wanted to weep, wanted to be petted and cried over, and then his colleague Shebek would come, and instead of weeping and being petted, Ivan Ilych would assume a serious, severe, and profound air, and by force of habit would express his opinion on a decision of the Court of Cassation and would stubbornly insist on that view. This falsity around him and within him did more than anything else to poison his last days.

VIII

It was morning. He knew it was morning because Gerasim had gone, and Peter the footman had come and put out the candles, drawn back one of the curtains, and begun quietly to tidy up. Whether it was morning or evening, Friday or Sunday, made no difference, it was all just the same: the gnawing, unmitigated, agonizing pain, never ceasing for an instant, the consciousness of life inexorably waning but not yet extinguished, the approach of that ever dreaded and hateful Death which was the only reality, and always the same falsity. What were days, weeks, hours, in such a case?

"Will you have some tea, sir?"

"He wants things to be regular, and wishes the gentlefolk to drink tea in the morning," thought Ivan Ilych, and only said "No."

"Wouldn't you like to move onto the sofa, sir?"

"He wants to tidy up the room, and I'm in the way. I am uncleanliness and disorder," he thought, and said only:

"No, leave me alone."

The man went on bustling about. Ivan Ilych stretched out his hand. Peter came up, ready to help.

"What is it, sir?"

"My watch."

Peter took the watch which was close at hand and gave it to his master.

"Half-past eight. Are they up?"

"No, sir, except Vasily Ivanovich" (the son) "who has gone to school. Praskovya Fëdorovna ordered me to wake her if you asked for her. Shall I do so?"

"No, there's no need to." "Perhaps I'd better have some tea," he thought, and added aloud: "Yes, bring me some tea."

Peter went to the door, but Ivan Ilych dreaded being left alone. "How can I keep him here? Oh yes, my medicine." "Peter, give me my medicine." "Why not? Perhaps it may still do me some good." He took a spoonful and swallowed it. "No, it won't help. It's all tomfoolery, all deception," he decided as soon as he became aware of the familiar, sickly, hopeless taste. "No, I can't believe in it any longer. But the pain, why this pain? If it would only cease just for a moment!" And he moaned. Peter turned towards him. "It's all right. Go and fetch me some tea."

Peter went out. Left alone Ivan Ilych groaned not so much with pain, terrible though that was, as from mental anguish. Always and forever the same, always these endless days and nights. If only it would come quicker! If only *what* would come quicker? Death, darkness? . . . No, no! Anything rather than death!

When Peter returned with the tea on a tray, Ivan Ilych stared at him for a time in perplexity, not realizing who and what he was. Peter was disconcerted by that look and his embarrassment brought Ivan Ilych to himself.

"Oh, tea! All right, put it down. Only help me to wash and put on a clean shirt."

And Ivan Ilych began to wash. With pauses for rest, he washed his hands and then his face, cleaned his teeth, brushed his hair, and looked in the glass. He was terrified by what he saw, especially by the limp way in which his hair clung to his pallid forehead.

While his shirt was being changed he knew that he would be still more frightened at the sight of his body, so he avoided looking at it. Finally he was ready. He drew on a dressing-gown, wrapped himself in a plaid, and sat down in the armchair to take his tea. For a moment he felt refreshed, but soon as he began to drink the tea he was again aware of the same taste, and the pain also returned. He finished it with an effort, and then lay down stretching out his legs, and dismissed Peter.

Always the same. Now a spark of hope flashes up, then a sea of despair rages, and always pain; always pain, always despair, and always the same. When alone he had a dreadful and distressing desire to call someone, but he knew beforehand that with others present it would be still worse. "Another dose of morphine—to lose consciousness. I will tell him, the doctor, that he must think of something else. It's impossible, impossible, to go on like this."

An hour and another pass like that. But now there is a ring at the door bell. Perhaps it's the doctor? It is. He comes in fresh, hearty, plump, and cheerful, with that look on his face that seems to say: "There now, you're in a panic about something, but we'll arrange it all for you directly!" The doctor knows this expression is out of place here, but he has put it on once for all and can't take it off—like a man who has put on a frock-coat in the morning to pay a round of calls.

The doctor rubs his hands vigorously and reassuringly.

"Brr! How cold it is! There's such a sharp frost; just let me warm myself!" he says, as if it were only a matter of waiting till he was warm, and then he would put everything right.

"Well now, how are you?"

Ivan Ilych feels that the doctor would like to say: "Well, how are our affairs?" but that even he feels that this would not do, and says instead: "What sort of a night have you had?"

Ivan Ilych looks at him as much as to say: "Are you really never ashamed of lying?" But the doctor does not wish to understand this question, and Ivan Ilych says: "Just as terrible as ever. The pain never leaves me and never subsides. If only something . . ."

"Yes, you sick people are always like that. . . . There, now I think I am warm enough. Even Praskovya Fëdorovna, who is so particular, could find no fault with my temperature. Well, now I can say good-morning," and the doctor presses his patient's hand.

Then, dropping his former playfulness, he begins with a most serious face to examine the patient, feeling his pulse and taking his temperature, and then begins the sounding and auscultation.

Ivan Ilych knows quite well and definitely that all this is nonsense and pure deception, but when the doctor, getting down on his knee, leans over him, putting his ear first higher then lower, and performs various gymnastic movements over him with a significant expression on his face, Ivan Ilych submits to it all as he used to submit to the speeches of the lawyers, though he knew very well that they were all lying and why they were lying.

The doctor, kneeling on the sofa, is still sounding him when Praskovya Fëdorovna's silk dress rustles at the door and she is heard scolding Peter for not having let her know of the doctor's arrival.

She comes in, kisses her husband, and at once proceeds to prove that she has been up a long time already, and only owing to a misunderstanding failed to be there when the doctor arrived.

Ivan Ilych looks at her, scans her all over, sets against her the whiteness and plumpness and cleanness of her hands and neck, the gloss of her hair, and the sparkle of her vivacious eyes. He hates her with his whole soul. And the thrill of hatred he feels for her makes him suffer from her touch.

Her attitude towards him and his disease is still the same. Just as the doctor had adopted a certain relation to his patient which he could not abandon, so had she formed one towards him—that he was not doing something he ought to do and was himself to blame, and that she reproached him lovingly for this—and she could not now change that attitude.

"You see he doesn't listen to me and doesn't take his medicine at the proper time. And above all he lies in a position that is no doubt bad for him—with his legs up."

She described how he made Gerasim hold his legs up.

The doctor smiled with a contemptuous affability that said: "What's to be done? These sick people do have foolish fancies of that kind, but we must forgive them."

When the examination was over the doctor looked at his watch, and then Praskovya Fëdorovna announced to Ivan Ilych that it was of course as he pleased, but she had sent today for a celebrated specialist who would examine him and have a consultation with Michael Danilovich (their regular doctor).

"Please don't raise any objections. I am doing this for my own sake," she said ironically, letting it be felt that she was doing it all for his sake and only said this to leave him no right to refuse. He remained silent, knitting his brows. He felt that he was so surrounded and involved in a mesh of falsity that it was hard to unravel anything.

Everything she did for him was entirely for her own sake, and she told him she was doing for herself what she actually was doing for herself, as if that was so incredible that he must understand the opposite.

At half-past eleven the celebrated specialist arrived. Again the sounding began and the significant conversations in his presence and in another room, about the kidneys and the appendix, and the questions and answers, with such an air of importance that again, instead of the real question of life and death which now alone confronted him, the question arose of the kidney and appendix which were not behaving as they ought to and would now be attacked by Michael Danilovich and the specialist and forced to amend their ways.

The celebrated specialist took leave of him with a serious though not hopeless look, and in reply to the timid question Ivan Ilych, with eyes glistening with fear and hope, put to him as to whether there was a chance of recovery, said that he could not vouch for it but there was a possibility. The look of hope with which Ivan Ilych watched the doctor out was so pathetic that Praskovya Fëdorovna, seeing it, even wept as she left the room to hand the doctor his fee.

The gleam of hope kindled by the doctor's encouragement did not last long. The same room, the same pictures, curtains, wallpaper, medicine bottles, were all there, and the same aching suffering body, and Ivan Ilych began to moan. They gave him a subcutaneous injection and he sank into oblivion.

It was twilight when he came to. They brought him his dinner and he swallowed some beef tea with difficulty, and then everything was the same again and night was coming on.

After dinner, at seven o'clock, Praskovya Fëdorovna came into the room in evening dress, her full bosom pushed up by her corset, and with traces of powder on her face. She had reminded him in the morning that they were going to the theater. Sarah Bernhardt was visiting the town and they had a box, which he had insisted on their taking. Now he had forgotten about it and her toilet offended him, but he concealed his vexation when he remembered that he had himself insisted on their securing a box and going because it would be an instructive and aesthetic pleasure for the children.

Praskovya Fëdorovna came in, self-satisfied but yet with a rather guilty air. She sat down and asked how he was, but, as he saw, only for the sake of asking and not in order to learn about it, knowing that there was nothing to learn—and then went on to what she really wanted to say: that she would not on any account have gone but that the box had been taken and Helen and their daughter were going, as well as Petrishchev (the examining magistrate, their daughter's fiancé), and that it was out of the question to let them go alone; but that she would have much preferred to sit with him for a while; and he must be sure to follow the doctor's orders while she was away.

"Oh, and Fëdor Petrovich" (the fiancé) "would like to come in. May he? And Lisa?"

"All right."

Their daughter came in in full evening dress, her fresh young flesh exposed (making a show of that very flesh which in his own case caused so much suffering), strong, healthy, evidently in love, and impatient with illness, suffering, and death, because they interfered with her happiness.

Fëdor Petrovich came in too, in evening dress, his hair curled *à la Capoul,*[9] a tight stiff collar round his long sinewy neck, an enormous white shirtfront, and narrow black trousers tightly stretched over his strong thighs. He had one white glove tightly drawn on, and was holding his opera hat in his hand.

Following him the schoolboy crept in unnoticed, in a new uniform, poor little fellow, and wearing gloves. Terribly dark shadows showed under his eyes, the meaning of which Ivan Ilych knew well.

His son had always seemed pathetic to him, and now it was dreadful to see the boy's frightened look of pity. It seemed to Ivan Ilych that Vasya was the only one besides Gerasim who understood and pitied him.

They all sat down and again asked how he was. A silence followed. Lisa asked her mother about the opera-glasses, and there was an altercation between mother and daughter as to who had taken them and where they had been put. This occasioned some unpleasantness.

Fëdor Petrovich inquired of Ivan Ilych whether he had ever seen Sarah Bernhardt. Ivan Ilych did not at first catch the question, but then replied: "No, have you seen her before?"

"Yes, in *Adrienne Lecouvreur.*"

Praskovya Fëdorovna mentioned some roles in which Sarah Bernhardt was particularly good. Her daughter disagreed. Conversation sprang up as to the elegance and realism of her acting—the sort of conversation that is always repeated and is always the same.

In the midst of the conversation Fëdor Petrovich glanced at Ivan Ilych and became silent. The others also looked at him and grew silent. Ivan Ilych was staring with glittering eyes straight before him, evidently indignant with them. This had to be rectified, but it was impossible to do so. The silence had to be broken, but for a time no one dared to break it and they all became afraid that the conventional deception would suddenly become obvious and the truth become plain to all. Lisa was the first to pluck up courage and break that silence, but by trying to hide what everybody was feeling, she betrayed it.

"Well, if we are going it's time to start," she said, looking at her watch, a present from her father, and with a faint and significant smile at Fëdor Petrovich relating to something known only to them. She got up with a rustle of her dress.

They all rose, said good-night, and went away.

---

[9] *à la Capoul:* in the style of Capoul, a popular singer.

When they had gone it seemed to Ivan Ilych that he felt better; the falsity had gone with them. But the pain remained—that same pain and that same fear that made everything monotonously alike, nothing harder and nothing easier. Everything was worse.

Again minute followed minute and hour followed hour. Everything remained the same and there was no cessation. And the inevitable end of it all became more and more terrible.

"Yes, send Gerasim here," he replied to a question Peter asked.

IX

His wife returned late at night. She came in on tiptoe, but he heard her, opened his eyes, and made haste to close them again. She wished to send Gerasim away and to sit with him herself, but he opened his eyes and said: "No, go away."

"Are you in great pain?"

"Always the same."

"Take some opium."

He agreed and took some. She went away.

Till about three in the morning he was in a state of stupefied misery. It seemed to him that he and his pain were being thrust into a narrow, deep black sack, but though they were pushed further and further in they could not be pushed to the bottom. And this, terrible enough in itself, was accompanied by suffering. He was frightened yet wanted to fall through the sack, he struggled but yet cooperated. And suddenly he broke through, fell, and regained consciousness. Gerasim was sitting at the foot of the bed dozing quietly and patiently, while he himself lay with his emaciated stockinged legs resting on Gerasim's shoulders; the same shaded candle was there and the same unceasing pain.

"Go away, Gerasim," he whispered.

"It's all right, sir. I'll stay a while."

"No. Go away."

He removed his legs from Gerasim's shoulders, turned sideways onto his arm, and felt sorry for himself. He only waited till Gerasim had gone into the next room and then restrained himself no longer but wept like a child. He wept on account of his helplessness, his terrible loneliness, the cruelty of man, the cruelty of God, and the absence of God.

"Why hast Thou done all this? Why hast Thou brought me here? Why, why dost Thou torment me so terribly?"

He did not expect an answer and yet wept because there was no answer and could be none. The pain grew more acute, but he did not stir and did not call. He said to himself: "Go on! Strike me! But what is it for? What have I done to Thee? What is it for?"

Then he grew quiet and not only ceased weeping but even held his breath and became all attention. It was as though he was listening not to an audible voice but to the voice of his soul, to the current of thoughts arising within him.

"What is it you want?" was the first clear conception capable of expression in words, that he heard.

"What do you want? What do you want?" he repeated to himself. "What do I want? To live and not to suffer," he answered.

And again he listened with such concentrated attention that even his pain did not distract him.

"To live? How?" asked his inner voice.

"Why, to live as I used to—well and pleasantly."

"As you lived before, well and pleasantly?" the voice repeated.

And in imagination he began to recall the best moments of his pleasant life. But strange to say none of those best moments of his pleasant life now seemed at all what they had then seemed—none of them except the first recollections of childhood. There, in childhood, there had been something really pleasant with which it would be possible to live if it could return. But the child who had experienced that happiness existed no longer, it was like a reminiscence of somebody else.

As soon as the period began which had produced the present Ivan Ilych, all that had then seemed joys now melted before his sight and turned into something trivial and often nasty.

And the further he departed from childhood and the nearer he came to the present the more worthless and doubtful were the joys. This began with the School of Law. A little that was really good was still found there—there was lightheartedness, friendship, and hope. But in the upper classes there had already been fewer of such good moments. Then during the first years of his official career, when he was in the service of the Governor, some pleasant moments again occurred: they were the memories of love for a woman. Then all became confused and there was still less of what was good; later on again there was still less that was good, and the further he went the less there was. His marriage, a mere accident, then the disenchantment that followed it, his wife's bad breath and the sensuality and hypocrisy; then the deadly official life and those preoccupations about money, a year of it, and two, and ten, and twenty, and always the same thing. And the longer it lasted the more deadly it became. "It is as if I had been going downhill while I imagined I was going up. And that is really what it was. I was going up in public opinion, but to the same extent life was ebbing away from me. And now it is all done and there is only death."

"Then what does it mean? Why? It can't be that life is so senseless and horrible. But if it really has been so horrible and senseless, why must I die and die in agony? There is something wrong!"

"Maybe I did not live as I ought to have done," it suddenly occurred to him. "But how could that be, when I did everything properly?" he replied, and immediately dismissed from his mind this, the sole solution of all the riddles of life and death, as something quite impossible.

"Then what do you want now? To live? Live how? Live as you lived in the law courts when the usher proclaimed 'The judge is coming!' The judge is coming, the judge!" he repeated to himself. "Here he is, the judge. But I am not guilty!" he exclaimed angrily. "What is it for?" And he ceased crying, but turning his face to the wall continued to ponder on the same question: Why, and for what purpose, is there all this horror? But however much he pondered he found no answer. And whenever the thought occurred to him, as it often did, that it all resulted from his not having lived as he ought to have done, he at once recalled the correctness of his whole life and dismissed so strange an idea.

X

Another fortnight passed. Ivan Ilych now no longer left his sofa. He would not lie in bed but lay on the sofa, facing the wall nearly all the time. He suffered ever the same unceasing agonies and in his loneliness pondered always on the same insoluble question: "What is this? Can it be that it is Death?" And the inner voice answered: "Yes, it is Death."

"Why these sufferings?" And the voice answered, "For no reason—they just are so." Beyond and besides this there was nothing.

From the very beginning of his illness, ever since he had first been to see the doctor, Ivan Ilych's life had been divided between two contrary and alternating moods: now it was despair and the expectation of this uncomprehended and terrible death, and now hope and an intently interested observation of the functioning of his organs. Now before his eyes there was only a kidney or an intestine that temporarily evaded its duty, and now only that incomprehensible and dreadful death from which it was impossible to escape.

These two states of mind had alternated from the very beginning of his illness, but the further it progressed the more doubtful and fantastic became the conception of the kidney, and the more real the sense of impending death.

He had but to call to mind what he had been three months before and what he was now, to call to mind with what regularity he had been going downhill, for every possibility of hope to be shattered.

Latterly during that loneliness in which he found himself as he lay facing the back of the sofa, a loneliness in the midst of a populous town and surrounded by numerous acquaintances and relations but that yet could not have been more complete anywhere—either at the bottom of the sea or under the earth—during that terrible loneliness Ivan Ilych had lived only in memories of the past. Pictures of his past rose before him one after another. They always began with what was nearest in time and then went back to what was most remote—to his childhood—and rested there. If he thought of the stewed prunes that had been offered him that day, his mind went back to the raw shrivelled French plums of his childhood, their peculiar flavor and the flow of saliva when he sucked their stones, and along with the memory of that taste came a whole series of memories of those days: his nurse, his brother, and their toys. "No, I mustn't think of that. . . . It is too painful," Ivan Ilych said to himself, and brought himself back to the present—to the button on the back of the sofa and the creases in its morocco. "Morocco is expensive, but it does not wear well: there had been a quarrel about it. It was a different kind of quarrel and a different kind of morocco that time when we tore father's portfolio and were punished, and mamma brought us some tarts. . . ." And again his thoughts dwelt on his childhood, and again it was painful and he tried to banish them and fix his mind on something else.

Then again together with that chain of memories another series passed through his mind—of how his illness had progressed and grown worse. There also the further back he looked the more life there had been. There had been more of what was good in life and more of life itself. The two merged together. "Just as the pain went on getting worse and worse, so my life grew worse and worse," he thought. "There is one bright spot there at the back, at the beginning of life, and afterwards all becomes blacker and blacker and proceeds more and more rapidly—in inverse ratio to the square of the distance from death," thought Ivan Ilych. And the example of a stone falling downwards with increasing velocity entered his mind. Life, a series of increasing sufferings, flies further and further towards its end—the most terrible suffering. "I am flying. . . ." He shuddered, shifted himself, and tried to resist, but was already aware that resistance was impossible, and again, with eyes weary of gazing but unable to cease seeing what was before them, he stared at the back of the sofa and waited—awaiting that dreadful fall and shock and destruction.

"Resistance is impossible!" he said to himself. "If I could only understand what it is all for! But that too is impossible. An explanation would be possible if it could be said that I have not lived as I ought to. But it is impossible to say that," and he remembered all the legality, correctitude, and propriety of his life. "That at any rate can certainly not be admitted," he thought, and his lips smiled ironically as if someone could see that smile and be taken in by it. "There is no explanation! Agony, death. . . . What for?"

XI

Another two weeks went by in this way and during that fortnight an event occurred that Ivan Ilych and his wife had desired. Petrishchev formally proposed. It happened in the evening. The next day Praskovya Fëdorovna came into her husband's room considering how best to inform him of it, but that very night there had been a fresh change for the worse in his condition. She found him still lying on the sofa but in a different position. He lay on his back, groaning and staring fixedly straight in front of him.

She began to remind him of his medicines, but he turned his eyes towards her with such a look that she did not finish what she was saying; so great an animosity, to her in particular, did that look express.

"For Christ's sake let me die in peace!" he said.

She would have gone away, but just then their daughter came in and went up to say good morning. He looked at her as he had done at his wife, and in reply to her inquiry about his health said dryly that he would soon free them all of himself. They were both silent and after sitting with him for a while went away.

"Is it our fault?" Lisa said to her mother. "It's as if we were to blame! I am sorry for papa, but why should we be tortured?"

The doctor came at his usual time. Ivan Ilych answered "Yes" and "No," never taking his angry eyes from him, and at last said: "You know you can do nothing for me, so leave me alone."

"We can ease your sufferings."

"You can't even do that. Let me be."

The doctor went into the drawing-room and told Praskovya Fëdorovna that the case was very serious and that the only resource left was opium to allay her husband's sufferings, which must be terrible.

It was true, as the doctor said, that Ivan Ilych's physical sufferings were terrible, but worse than the physical sufferings were his mental sufferings, which were his chief torture.

His mental sufferings were due to the fact that one night, as he looked at Gerasim's sleepy, good-natured face with its prominent cheekbones, the question suddenly occurred to him: "What if my whole life has really been wrong?"

It occurred to him that what had appeared perfectly impossible before, namely that he had not spent his life as he should have done, might after all be true. It occurred to him that his scarcely perceptible attempts to struggle against what was considered good by the most highly placed people, those scarcely noticeable impulses which he had immediately suppressed, might have been the real thing, and all the rest false. And his professional duties and the whole arrangement of his life and of his family, and all his social and official interests, might all have been false. He tried to defend all those things to himself and suddenly felt the weakness of what he was defending. There was nothing to defend.

"But if that is so," he said to himself, "and I am leaving this life with the consciousness that I have lost all that was given me and it is impossible to rectify it—what then?"

He lay on his back and began to pass his life in review in quite a new way. In the morning when he saw first his footman, then his wife, then his daughter, and then the doctor, their every word and movement confirmed to him the awful truth that had been revealed to him during the night. In them he saw himself—all that for which he had lived— and saw clearly that it was not real at all, but a terrible and huge deception which had hidden both life and death. This consciousness intensified his physical suffering tenfold. He groaned and tossed about, and pulled at his clothing which choked and stifled him. And he hated them on that account.

He was given a large dose of opium and became unconscious, but at noon his sufferings began again. He drove everybody away and tossed from side to side.

His wife came to him and said:

"Jean, my dear, do this for me. It can't do any harm and often helps. Healthy people often do it."

He opened his eyes wide.

"What? Take communion? Why? It's unnecessary! However . . ." She began to cry.

"Yes, do, my dear. I'll send for our priest. He is such a nice man."

"All right. Very well," he muttered.

When the priest came and heard his confession, Ivan Ilych was softened and seemed to feel a relief from his doubts and consequently from his sufferings, and for a moment there came a ray of hope. He again began to think of the vermiform appendix and the possibility of correcting it. He received the sacrament with tears in his eyes.

When they laid him down again afterwards he felt a moment's ease, and the hope that he might live awoke in him again. He began to think of the operation that had been suggested to him. "To live! I want to live!" he said to himself.

His wife came in to congratulate him after his communion, and when uttering the usual conventional words she added:

"You feel better, don't you?"

Without looking at her he said "Yes."

Her dress, her figure, the expression of her face, the tone of her voice, all revealed the same thing. "This is wrong, it is not as it should be. All you have lived for and still live for is falsehood and deception, hiding life and death from you." And as soon as he admitted that thought, his hatred and his agonizing physical suffering again sprang up, and with that suffering a consciousness of the unavoidable, approaching end. And to this was added a new sensation of grinding shooting pain and a feeling of suffocation.

The expression of his face when he uttered that "yes" was dreadful. Having uttered it, he looked her straight in the eyes, turned on his face with a rapidity extraordinary in his weak state and shouted:

"Go away! Go away and leave me alone!"

XII

From that moment the screaming began that continued for three days, and was so terrible that one could not hear it through two closed doors without horror. At the moment he answered his wife he realized that he was lost, that there was no return, that the end had come, the very end, and his doubts were still unsolved and remained doubts.

"Oh! Oh! Oh!" he cried in various intonations. He had begun by screaming "I won't!" and continued screaming on the letter O.

For three whole days, during which time did not exist for him, he struggled in that black sack into which he was being thrust by an invisible, resistless force. He struggled as a man condemned to death struggles in the hands of the executioner, knowing that he cannot save himself. And every moment he felt that despite all his efforts he was drawing nearer and nearer to what terrified him. He felt that his agony was due to his being thrust into that black hole and still more to his not being able to get right into it. He was hindered from getting into it by his conviction that his life had been a good one. That very justification of his life held him fast and prevented his moving forward, and it caused him most torment of all.

Suddenly some force struck him in the chest and side, making it still harder to breathe, and he fell through the hole and there at the bottom was a light. What had happened to him was like the sensation one sometimes experiences in a railway carriage when one thinks one is going backwards while one is really going forwards and suddenly becomes aware of the real direction.

"Yes, it was all not the right thing," he said to himself, "but that's no matter. It can be done. But what *is* the right thing?" he asked himself, and suddenly grew quiet.

This occurred at the end of the third day, two hours before his death. Just then his schoolboy son had crept softly in and gone up to the bedside. The dying man was still screaming desperately and waving his arms. His hand fell on the boy's head, and the boy caught it, pressed it to his lips, and began to cry.

At that very moment Ivan Ilych fell through and caught sight of the light, and it was revealed to him that though his life had not been what it should have been, this could still be rectified. He asked himself, "What *is* the right thing?" and grew still, listening. Then he felt that someone was kissing his hand. He opened his eyes, looked at his son, and felt sorry for him. His wife came up to him and he glanced at her. She was gazing at him open-mouthed, with undried tears on her nose and cheek and a despairing look on her face. He felt sorry for her too.

"Yes, I am making them wretched," he thought. "They are sorry, but it will be better for them when I die." He wished to say this but had not the strength to utter it. "Besides, why speak? I must act," he thought. With a look at his wife he indicated his son and said: "Take him away . . . sorry for him . . . sorry for you too. . . ." He tried to add, "Forgive me," but said "forgo" and waved his hand, knowing that He whose understanding mattered would understand.

And suddenly it grew clear to him that what had been oppressing him and would not leave him was all dropping away at once from two sides, from ten sides, and from all sides. He was sorry for them, he must act so as not to hurt them: release them and free himself from these sufferings. "How good and how simple!" he thought. "And the pain?" he asked himself. "What has become of it? Where are you, pain?"

He turned his attention to it.

"Yes, here it is. Well, what of it? Let the pain be."

"And death . . . where is it?"

He sought his former accustomed fear of death and did not find it. "Where is it? What death?" There was no fear because there was no death.

In place of death there was light.

"So that's what it is!" he suddenly exclaimed aloud. "What joy!"

To him all this happened in a single instant, and the meaning of that instant did not change. For those present his agony continued for another two hours. Something rattled in his throat, his emaciated body twitched, then the gasping and rattle became less and less frequent.

"It is finished!" said someone near him.

He heard these words and repeated them in his soul.

"Death is finished," he said to himself. "It is no more!"

He drew in a breath, stopped in the midst of a sigh, stretched out, and died.

—1886

Questions: Reading, Responding, Arguing

1. What is the purpose of the opening section of the story? Why did Tolstoy choose to tell his story in an extended flashback?
2. How can Ivan's life be both ordinary and terrible at the same time?
3. The external complication of the plot begins with Ivan's injury. How has Tolstoy set up internal conflicts before this occurs?
4. What is the role of Ivan's wife? His daughter? His son? His servant Gerasim?
5. Does the story contain any satire of the medical profession?
6. What is the significance of the repeated word "it" in the story?
7. What is Ivan's final epiphany? How does it affect the way he dies?

8. Compare the protagonist of this story with Kurt in Jerome Groopman's essay "The Last Deal" on page 000. How are their situations similar and different? How do their deaths differ?

Stephen Crane (1871–1900)

The Open Boat

I.

None of them knew the color of the sky. Their eyes glanced level, and were fastened upon the waves that swept toward them. These waves were of the hue of slate, save for the tops, which were of foaming white, and all of the men knew the colors of the sea. The horizon narrowed and widened, and dipped and rose, and at all times its edge was jagged with waves that seemed thrust up in points like rocks.

Many a man ought to have a bath-tub larger than the boat which here rode upon the sea. These waves were most wrongfully and barbarously abrupt and tall, and each froth-top was a problem in small boat navigation.

The cook squatted in the bottom and looked with both eyes at the six inches of gunwale which separated him from the ocean. His sleeves were rolled over his fat forearms, and the two flaps of his unbuttoned vest dangled as he bent to bail out the boat. Often he said: "Gawd! That was a narrow clip." As he remarked it he invariably gazed eastward over the broken sea.

The oiler, steering with one of the two oars in the boat, sometimes raised himself suddenly to keep clear of water that swirled in over the stern. It was a thin little oar and it seemed often ready to snap.

The correspondent, pulling at the other oar, watched the waves and wondered why he was there.

The injured captain, lying in the bow, was at this time buried in that profound dejection and indifference which comes, temporarily at least, to even the bravest and most enduring when, willy nilly, the firm fails, the army loses, the ship goes down. The mind of the master of a vessel is rooted deep in the timbers of her, though he command for a day or a decade, and this captain had on him the stern impression of a scene in the grays of dawn of seven turned faces, and later a stump of a topmast with a white ball on it that slashed to and fro at the waves, went low and lower, and down. Thereafter there was something strange in his voice. Although steady, it was deep with mourning, and of a quality beyond oration or tears.

"Keep'er a little more south, Billie," said he.

" 'A little more south,' sir," said the oiler in the stern.

A seat in this boat was not unlike a seat upon a bucking broncho, and, by the same token, a broncho is not much smaller. The craft pranced and reared, and plunged like an animal. As each wave came, and she rose for it, she seemed like a horse making at a fence outrageously high. The manner of her scramble over these walls of water is a mystic thing, and, moreover, at the top of them were ordinarily these problems in white water, the foam racing down from the summit of each wave, requiring a new leap, and a leap from the air. Then, after scornfully bumping a crest, she would slide, and race, and splash down a long incline and arrive bobbing and nodding in front of the next menace.

A singular disadvantage of the sea lies in the fact that after successfully surmounting one wave you discover that there is another behind it just as important and just as nervously anxious to do something effective in the way of swamping boats. In a ten-foot dingey one can get an idea of the resources of the sea in the line of waves that is not probable to the average experience, which is never at sea in a dingey. As each slaty wall of water approached, it shut all else from the view of the men in the boat, and it was not difficult to imagine that this particular wave was the final outburst of the ocean, the last effort of the grim water. There was a terrible grace in the move of the waves, and they came in silence, save for the snarling of the crests.

In the wan light, the faces of the men must have been gray. Their eyes must have glinted in strange ways as they gazed steadily astern. Viewed from a balcony, the whole thing would doubtlessly have been weirdly picturesque. But the men in the boat had no time to see it, and if they had had leisure there were other things to occupy their minds. The sun swung steadily up the sky, and they knew it was broad day because the color of the sea changed from slate to emerald-green, streaked with amber lights, and the foam was like tumbling snow. The process of the breaking day was unknown to them. They were aware only of this effect upon the color of the waves that rolled toward them.

In disjointed sentences the cook and the correspondent argued as to the difference between a life-saving station and a house of refuge. The cook had said: "There's a house of refuge just north of the Mosquito Inlet Light, and as soon as they see us, they'll come off in their boat and pick us up."

"As soon as who see us?" said the correspondent.

"The crew," said the cook.

"Houses of refuge don't have crews," said the correspondent. "As I understand them, they are only places where clothes and grub are stored for the benefit of shipwrecked people. They don't carry crews."

"Oh, yes, they do," said the cook.

"No, they don't," said the correspondent.

"Well, we're not there yet, anyhow," said the oiler, in the stern.

"Well," said the cook, "perhaps it's not a house of refuge that I'm thinking of as being near Mosquito Inlet Light. Perhaps it's a life-saving station."

"We're not there yet," said the oiler, in the stern.

II.

As the boat bounced from the top of each wave, the wind tore through the hair of the hatless men, and as the craft plopped her stern down again the spray slashed past them. The crest of each of these waves was a hill, from the top of which the men surveyed, for a moment, a broad tumultuous expanse; shining and wind-riven. It was probably splendid. It was probably glorious, this play of the free sea, wild with lights of emerald and white and amber.

"Bully good thing it's an on-shore wind," said the cook. "If not, where would we be? Wouldn't have a show."

"That's right," said the correspondent.

The busy oiler nodded his assent.

Then the captain, in the bow, chuckled in a way that expressed humor, contempt, tragedy, all in one. "Do you think we've got much of a show, now, boys?" said he.

Whereupon the three were silent, save for a trifle of hemming and hawing. To express any particular optimism at this time they felt to be childish and stupid, but they all doubtless possessed this sense of the situation in their mind. A young man thinks doggedly at such times. On the other hand, the ethics of their condition was decidedly against any open suggestion of hopelessness. So they were silent.

"Oh, well," said the captain, soothing his children, "we'll get ashore all right."

But there was that in his tone which made them think, so the oiler quoth: "Yes! If this wind holds!"

The cook was bailing: "Yes! If we don't catch hell in the surf."

Canton flannel gulls flew near and far. Sometimes they sat down on the sea, near patches of brown sea-weed that rolled over the waves with a movement like carpets on line in a gale. The birds sat comfortably in groups, and they were envied by some in the dingey, for the wrath of the sea was no more to them than it was to a covey of prairie chickens a thousand miles inland. Often they came very close and stared at the men with black bead-like eyes. At these times they were uncanny and sinister in their unblinking scrutiny, and the men hooted angrily at them, telling them to be gone. One came, and evidently decided to alight on the top of the captain's head. The bird flew parallel to the boat and did not circle, but made short sidelong jumps in the air in chicken-fashion. His black eyes were wistfully fixed upon the captain's head. "Ugly brute," said the oiler to the bird. "You look as if you were made with a jack-knife." The cook and the correspondent swore darkly at the creature. The captain naturally wished to knock it away with the end of the heavy painter, but he did not dare do it, because anything resembling an emphatic gesture would have capsized this freighted boat, and so with his open hand, the captain gently and carefully waved the gull away. After it had been discouraged from the pursuit the captain breathed easier on account of his hair, and others breathed easier because the bird struck their minds at this time as being somehow grewsome and ominous.

In the meantime the oiler and the correspondent rowed. And also they rowed.

They sat together in the same seat, and each rowed an oar. Then the oiler took both oars; then the correspondent took both oars; then the oiler; then the correspondent. They rowed and they rowed. The very ticklish part of the business was when the time came for the reclining one in the stern to take his turn at the oars. By the very last star of truth, it is easier to steal eggs from under a hen than it was to change seats in the dingey. First the man in the stern slid his hand along the thwart and moved with care, as if he were of Sevres. Then the man in the rowing seat slid his hand along the other thwart. It was all done with the most extraordinary care. As the two sidled past each other, the whole party kept watchful eyes on the coming wave, and the captain cried: "Look out now! Steady there!"

The brown mats of sea-weed that appeared from time to time were like islands, bits of earth. They were travelling, apparently, neither one way nor the other. They were, to all intents stationary. They informed the men in the boat that it was making progress slowly toward the land.

The captain, rearing cautiously in the bow, after the dingey soared on a great swell, said that he had seen the lighthouse at Mosquito Inlet. Presently the cook remarked that he had seen it. The correspondent was at the oars, then, and for some reason he too wished to look at the lighthouse, but his back was toward the far shore and the waves were important, and for some time he could not seize an opportunity to turn his head. But at last there came a wave more "See it?" said the captain.

"No," said the correspondent, slowly, "I didn't see anything."

"Look again," said the captain. He pointed. "It's exactly in that direction."

At the top of another wave, the correspondent did as he was bid, and this time his eyes chanced on a small still thing on the edge of the swaying horizon. It was precisely like the point of a pin. It took an anxious eye to find a lighthouse so tiny.

"Think we'll make it, captain?"

"If this wind holds and the boat don't swamp, we can't do much else," said the captain.

The little boat, lifted by each towering sea, and splashed viciously by the crests, made progress that in the absence of sea-weed was not apparent to those in her. She seemed just a wee thing wallowing, miraculously, top-up, at the mercy of five oceans. Occasionally, a great spread of water, like white flames, swarmed into her.

"Bail her, cook," said the captain, serenely.

"All right, captain," said the cheerful cook.

III

It would be difficult to describe the subtle brotherhood of men that was here established on the seas. No one said that it was so. No one mentioned it. But it dwelt in the boat, and each man felt it warm him. They were a captain, an oiler, a cook, and a correspondent, and they were friends, friends in a more curiously iron-bound degree than may be common. The hurt captain, lying against the water-jar in the bow, spoke always in a low voice and calmly, but he could never command a more ready and swiftly obedient crew than the motley three of the dingey. It was more than a mere recognition of what was best for the common safety. There was surely in it a quality that was personal and heartfelt. And after this devotion to the commander of the boat there was this comradeship that the correspondent, for instance, who had been taught to be cynical of men, knew even at the time was the best experience of his life. But no one said that it was so. No one mentioned it.

"I wish we had a sail," remarked the captain. "We might try my overcoat on the end of an oar and give you two boys a chance to rest." So the cook and the correspondent held the mast and spread wide the overcoat. The oiler steered, and the little boat made good way with her new rig. Sometimes the oiler had to scull sharply to keep a sea from breaking into the boat, but otherwise sailing was a success.

Meanwhile the light-house had been growing slowly larger. It had now almost assumed color, and appeared like a little gray shadow on the sky. The man at the oars could not be prevented from turning his head rather often to try for a glimpse of this little gray shadow.

At last, from the top of each wave the men in the tossing boat could see land. Even as the light-house was an upright shadow on the sky, this land seemed but a long black shadow on the sea. It certainly was thinner than paper. "We must be about opposite New Smyrna," said the cook, who had coasted this shore often in schooners. "Captain, by the way, I believe they abandoned that life-saving station there about a year ago."

"Did they?" said the captain.

The wind slowly died away. The cook and the correspondent were not now obliged to slave in order to hold high the oar. But the waves continued their old impetuous swooping at the dingey, and the little craft, no longer under way, struggled woundily over them. The oiler or the correspondent took the oars again.

Shipwrecks are apropos of nothing. If men could only train for them and have them occur when the men had reached pink condition, there would be less drowning at sea. Of the four in the dingey none had slept any time worth mentioning for two days and two nights previous to embarking in the dingey, and in the excitement of clambering about the deck of a foundering ship they had also forgotten to eat heartily.

For these reasons, and for others, neither the oiler nor the correspondent was fond of rowing at this time. The correspondent wondered ingenuously how in the name of all that was same could there be people who thought it amusing to row a boat. It was not an amusement; it was a diabolical punishment, and even a genius of mental aberrations could never conclude that it was anything but a horror to the muscles and a crime against the back. He mentioned to the boat in general how the amusement of rowing struck him, and the weary-faced oiler smiled in full sympathy. Previously to the foundering, by the way, the oiler had worked double-watch in the engine-room of the ship.

"Take her easy, now, boys," said the captain. "Don't spend yourselves. If we have to run a surf you'll need all your strength, because we'll sure have to swim for it. Take your time."

Slowly the land arose from the sea. From a black line it became a line of black and a line of white, trees, and sand. Finally, the captain said that he could make out a house on the shore. "That's the house of refuge, sure," said the cook. "They'll see us before long, and come out after us."

The distant light-house reared high. "The keeper ought to be able to make us out now, if he's looking through a glass," said the captain "He'll notify the life-saving people."

"None of those other boats could have got ashore to give word of the wreck," said the oiler, in a low voice. "Else the life-boat would be out hunting us."

Slowly and beautifully the land loomed out of the sea. The wind came again. It had veered from the northeast to the southeast. Finally, a new sound struck the ears of the men in the boat. It was the low thunder of the surf on the shore. "We'll never be able to make the light-house now," said the captain. "Swing her head a little more north, Billie," said the captain.

"'A little more north,' sir," said the oiler.

Whereupon the little boat turned her nose once more down the wind, and all but the oarsman watched the shore grow. Under the influence of this expansion doubt and direful apprehension was leaving the minds of the men. The management of the boat was still most absorbing, but it could not prevent a quiet cheerfulness. In an hour, perhaps, they would be ashore.

Their back-bones had become thoroughly used to balancing in the boat and they now rode this wild colt of a dingey like circus men. The correspondent thought that he had been drenched to the skin, but happening to feel in the top pocket of his coat, he found therein eight cigars. Four of them were soaked with sea-water; four were perfectly scatheless. After a search, somebody produced three dry matches, and thereupon the four waifs rode in their little boat, and with an assurance of an impending rescue shining in their eyes, puffed at the big cigars and judged well and ill of all men. Everybody took a drink of water.

IV

"Cook," remarked the captain, "there don't seem to be any signs of life about your house of refuge."

"No," replied the cook. "Funny they don't see us!"

A broad stretch of lowly coast lay before the eyes of the men. It was of low dunes topped with dark vegetation. The roar of the surf was plain, and sometimes they could see the white lip of a wave as it spun up the beach. A tiny house was blocked out black upon the sky. Southward, the slim light-house lifted its little gray length.

Tide, wind, and waves were swinging the dingey northward. "Funny they don't see us," said the men.

The surf's roar was here dulled, but its tone was, nevertheless, thunderous and mighty. As the boat swam over the great rollers, the men sat listening to this roar. "We'll swamp sure," said everybody.

It is fair to say here that there was not a life-saving station within twenty miles in either direction, but the men did not know this fact and in consequence they made dark and opprobrious remarks concerning the eyesight of the nation's life-savers. Four scowling men sat in the dingey and surpassed records in the invention of epithets.

"Funny they don't see us."

The light-heartedness of a former time had completely faded. To their sharpened minds it was easy to conjure pictures of all kinds of incompetency and blindness and indeed, cowardice. There was the shore of the populous land, and it was bitter and bitter to them that from it came no sign.

"Well," said the captain, ultimately, "I suppose we'll have to make a try for ourselves. If we stay out here too long, we'll none of us have strength left to swim after the boat swamps."

And so the oiler, who was at the oars, turned the boat straight for the shore. There was a sudden tightening of muscles. There was some thinking.

"If we don't all get ashore —" said the captain. "If we don't all get ashore, I suppose you fellows know where to send news of my finish?"

They then briefly exchanged some addresses and admonitions. As for the reflections of the men, there was a great deal of rage in them. Perchance they might be formulated thus: "If I am going to be drowned — if I am going to be drowned — if I am going to be drowned, why, in the name of the seven mad gods who rule the sea, was I allowed to come thus far and contemplate sand and trees? Was I brought here merely to have my nose dragged away as I was about to nibble the sacred cheese of life? It is preposterous. If this old ninny woman, Fate, cannot do better than this, she should be deprived of the management of men's fortunes. She is an old hen who knows not her intention. If she has decided to drown me, why did she not do it in the beginning and save me all this trouble. The whole affair is absurd. . . . But, no, she cannot mean to drown me. She dare not drown me. She cannot drown me. Not after all this work." Afterward the man might have had an impulse to shake his fist at the clouds: "Just you drown me, now, and then hear what I call you!"

The billows that came at this time were more formidable. They seemed always just about to break and roll over the little boat in a turmoil of foam. There was a preparatory and long growl in the speech of them. No mind unused to the sea would have concluded that the dingey could ascend these sheer heights in time. The shore was still afar. The oiler was a wily surfman. "Boys," he said, swiftly, "she won't live three minutes more and we're too far out to swim. Shall I take her to sea again, captain?"

"Yes! Go ahead!" said the captain.

This oiler, by a series of quick miracles, and fast and steady oarsmanship, turned the boat in the middle of the surf and took her safely to sea again.

There was a considerable silence as the boat bumped over the furrowed sea to deeper water. Then somebody in gloom spoke. "Well, anyhow, they must have seen us from the shore by now."

The gulls went in slanting flight up the wind toward the gray desolate east. A squall, marked by dingy clouds, and clouds brick-red, like smoke from a burning building, appeared from the southeast.

"What do you think of those life-saving people? Ain't they peaches?"

"Funny they haven't seen us."

"Maybe they think we're out here for sport! Maybe they think we're fishin'. Maybe they think we're damned fools."

It was a long afternoon. A changed tide tried to force them southward, but wind and wave said northward. Far ahead, where coast-line, sea, and sky formed their mighty angle, there were little dots which seemed to indicate a city on the shore.

"St. Augustine?"

The captain shook his head. "Too near Mosquito Inlet."

And the oiler rowed, and then the correspondent rowed. Then the oiler rowed. It was a weary business. The human back can become the seat of more aches and pains than are registered in books for the composite anatomy of a regiment. It is a limited area, but it can become the theatre of innumerable muscular conflicts, tangles, wrenches, knots, and other comforts.

"Did you ever like to row, Billie?" asked the correspondent.

"No," said the oiler. "Hang it."

When one exchanged the rowing-seat for a place in the bottom of the boat, he suffered a bodily depression that caused him to be careless of everything save an obligation to wiggle one finger. There was cold sea-water swashing to and fro in the boat, and he lay in it. His head, pillowed on a thwart, was within an inch of the swirl of a wave crest, and sometimes a particularly obstreperous sea came in-board and drenched him once more. But these matters did not annoy him. It is almost certain that if the boat had capsized he would have tumbled comfortably out upon the ocean as if he felt sure it was a great soft mattress.

"Look! There's a man on the shore!"

"Where?"

"There! See 'im? See 'im?"

"Yes, sure! He's walking along."

"Now he's stopped. Look! He's facing us!"

"He's waving at us!"

"So he is! By thunder!"

"Ah, now, we're all right! Now we're all right! There'll be a boat out here for us in half an hour."

"He's going on. He's running. He's going up to that house there."

The remote beach seemed lower than the sea, and it required a searching glance to discern the little black figure. The captain saw a floating stick and they rowed to it. A bath-towel was by some weird chance in the boat, and, tying this on the stick, the captain waved it. The oarsman did not dare turn his head, so he was obliged to ask questions.

"What's he doing now?"

"He's standing still again. He's looking, I think. . . . There he goes again. Toward the house. . . . Now he's stopped again."

"Is he waving at us?"

"No, not now! he was, though."

"Look! There comes another man!"

"He's running."

"Look at him go, would you."

"Why, he's on a bicycle. Now he's met the other man. They're both waving at us. Look!"

"There comes something up the beach."

"What the devil is that thing?"

"Why, it looks like a boat."

"Why, certainly it's a boat."

"No, it's on wheels."

"Yes, so it is. Well, that must be the life-boat. They drag them along shore on a wagon."

"That's the life-boat, sure."

"No, by — —, it's — it's an omnibus."

"I tell you it's a life-boat."

"It is not! It's an omnibus. I can see it plain. See? One of these big hotel omnibuses."

"By thunder, you're right. It's an omnibus, sure as fate. What do you suppose they are doing with an omnibus? Maybe they are going around collecting the life-crew, hey?"

"That's it, likely. Look! There's a fellow waving a little black flag. He's standing on the steps of the omnibus. There come those other two fellows. Now they're all talking together. Look at the fellow with the flag. Maybe he ain't waving it."

"That ain't a flag, is it? That's his coat. Why, certainly, that's his coat."

"So it is. It's his coat. He's taken it off and is waving it around his head. But would you look at him swing it."

"Oh, say, there isn't any life-saving station there. That's just a winter resort hotel omnibus that has brought over some of the boarders to see us drown."

"What's that idiot with the coat mean? What's he signaling, anyhow?"

"It looks as if he were trying to tell us to go north. There must be a life-saving station up there."

"No! He thinks we're fishing. Just giving us a merry hand. See? Ah, there, Willie."

"Well, I wish I could make something out of those signals. What do you suppose he means?"

"He don't mean anything. He's just playing."

"Well, if he'd just signal us to try the surf again, or to go to sea and wait, or go north, or go south, or go to hell—there would be some reason in it. But look at him. He just stands there and keeps his coat revolving like a wheel. The ass!"

"There come more people."

"Now there's quite a mob. Look! Isn't that a boat?"

"Where? Oh, I see where you mean. No, that's no boat."

"That fellow is still waving his coat."

"He must think we like to see him do that. Why don't he quit it. It don't mean anything."

"I don't know. I think he is trying to make us go north. It must be that there's a life-saving station there somewhere."

"Say, he ain't tired yet. Look at 'im wave."

"Wonder how long he can keep that up. He's been revolving his coat ever since he caught sight of us. He's an idiot. Why aren't they getting men to bring a boat out. A fishing boat—one of those big yawls—could come out here all right. Why don't he do something?"

"Oh, it's all right, now."

"They'll have a boat out here for us in less than no time, now that they've seen us."

A faint yellow tone came into the sky over the low land. The shadows on the sea slowly deepened. The wind bore coldness with it, and the men began to shiver.

"Holy smoke!" said one, allowing his voice to express his impious mood, "if we keep on monkeying out here! If we've got to flounder out here all night!"

"Oh, we'll never have to stay here all night! Don't you worry. They've seen us now, and it won't be long before they'll come chasing out after us."

The shore grew dusky. The man waving a coat blended gradually into this gloom, and it swallowed in the same manner the omnibus and the group of people. The spray, when it dashed uproariously over the side, made the voyagers shrink and swear like men who were being branded.

"I'd like to catch the chump who waved the coat. I feel like soaking him one, just for luck."

"Why? What did he do?"

"Oh, nothing, but then he seemed so damned cheerful."

In the meantime the oiler rowed, and then the correspondent rowed, and then the oiler rowed. Gray-faced and bowed forward, they mechanically, turn by turn, plied the leaden oars. The form of the lighthouse had vanished from the southern horizon, but finally a pale star appeared, just lifting from the sea. The streaked saffron in the west passed before the all-merging darkness, and the sea to the east was black. The land had vanished, and was expressed only by the low and drear thunder of the surf.

"If I am going to be drowned—if I am going to be drowned—if I am going to be drowned, why, in the name of the seven mad gods, who rule the sea, was I allowed to come thus far and contemplate sand and trees? Was I brought here merely to have my nose dragged away as I was about to nibble the sacred cheese of life?"

The patient captain, drooped over the water-jar, was sometimes obliged to speak to the oarsman.

"Keep her head up! Keep her head up!"

"Keep her head up,' sir." The voices were weary and low.

This was surely a quiet evening. All save the oarsman lay heavily and listlessly in the boat's bottom. As for him, his eyes were just capable of noting the tall black waves that swept forward in a most sinister silence, save for an occasional subdued growl of a crest.

The cook's head was on a thwart, and he looked without interest at the water under his nose. He was deep in other scenes. Finally he spoke. "Billie," he murmured, dreamfully, "what kind of pie do you like best?"

V

"Pie," said the oiler and the correspondent, agitatedly. "Don't talk about those things, blast you!"

"Well," said the cook, "I was just thinking about ham sandwiches, and—"

A night on the sea in an open boat is a long night. As darkness settled finally, the shine of the light, lifting from the sea in the south, changed to full gold. On the northern horizon a new light appeared, a small bluish gleam on the edge of the waters. These two lights were the furniture of the world. Otherwise there was nothing but waves.

Two men huddled in the stern, and distances were so magnificent in the dingey that the rower was enabled to keep his feet partly warmed by thrusting them under his companions. Their legs indeed extended far under the rowing-seat until they touched the feet of the captain forward. Sometimes, despite the efforts of the tired oarsman, a wave came piling into the boat, an icy wave of the night, and the chilling water soaked them anew. They would twist their bodies for a moment and groan, and sleep the dead sleep once more, while the water in the boat gurgled about them as the craft rocked.

The plan of the oiler and the correspondent was for one to row until he lost the ability, and then arouse the other from his sea-water couch in the bottom of the boat.

The oiler plied the oars until his head drooped forward, and the overpowering sleep blinded him. And he rowed yet afterward. Then he touched a man in the bottom of the boat, and called his name. "Will you spell me for a little while?" he said, meekly.

"Sure, Billie," said the correspondent, awakening and dragging himself to a sitting position. They exchanged places carefully, and the oiler, cuddling down to the sea-water at the cook's side, seemed to go to sleep instantly.

The particular violence of the sea had ceased. The waves came without snarling. The obligation of the man at the oars was to keep the boat headed so that the tilt of the rollers would not capsize her, and to preserve her from filling when the crests rushed past. The black waves were silent and hard to be seen in the darkness. Often one was almost upon the boat before the oarsman was aware.

In a low voice the correspondent addressed the captain. He was not sure that the captain was awake, although this iron man seemed to be always awake. "Captain, shall I keep her making for that light north, sir?"

The same steady voice answered him. "Yes. Keep it about two points off the port bow."

The cook had tied a life-belt around himself in order to get even the warmth which this clumsy cork contrivance could donate, and he seemed almost stove-like when a rower, whose teeth invariably chattered wildly as soon as he ceased his labor, dropped down to sleep.

The correspondent, as he rowed, looked down at the two men sleeping under foot. The cook's arm was around the oiler's shoulders, and, with their fragmentary clothing and haggard faces, they were the babes of the sea, a grotesque rendering of the old babes in the wood.

Later he must have grown stupid at his work, for suddenly there was a growling of water, and a crest came with a roar and a swash into the boat, and it was a wonder that it did not set the cook afloat in his life-belt. The cook continued to sleep, but the oiler sat up, blinking his eyes and shaking with the new cold.

"Oh, I'm awful sorry, Billie," said the correspondent, contritely.

"That's all right, old boy," said the oiler, and lay down again and was asleep.

Presently it seemed that even the captain dozed, and the correspondent thought that he was the one man afloat on all the oceans. The wind had a voice as it came over the waves, and it was sadder than the end.

There was a long, loud swishing astern of the boat, and a gleaming trail of phosphorescence, like blue flame, was furrowed on the black waters. It might have been made by a monstrous knife.

Then there came a stillness, while the correspondent breathed with the open mouth and looked at the sea.

Suddenly there was another swish and another long flash of bluish light, and this time it was alongside the boat, and might almost have been reached with an oar. The correspondent saw an enormous fin speed like a shadow through the water, hurling the crystalline spray and leaving the long glowing trail.

The correspondent looked over his shoulder at the captain. His face was hidden, and he seemed to be asleep. He looked at the babes of the sea. They certainly were asleep. So, being bereft of sympathy, he leaned a little way to one side and swore softly into the sea.

But the thing did not then leave the vicinity of the boat. Ahead or astern, on one side or the other, at intervals long or short, fled the long sparkling streak, and there was to be heard the whiroo of the dark fin. The speed and power of the thing was greatly to be admired. It cut the water like a gigantic and keen projectile.

The presence of this biding thing did not affect the man with the same horror that it would if he had been a picnicker. He simply looked at the sea dully and swore in an undertone.

Nevertheless, it is true that he did not wish to be alone with the thing. He wished one of his companions to awaken by chance and keep him company with it. But the captain hung motionless over the water-jar and the oiler and the cook in the bottom of the boat were plunged in slumber.

VI

"IF I am going to be drowned—if I am going to be drowned—if I am going to be drowned, why, in the name of the seven mad gods, who rule the sea, was I allowed to come thus far and contemplate sand and trees?"

During this dismal night, it may be remarked that a man would conclude that it was really the intention of the seven mad gods to drown him, despite the abominable injustice of it. For it was certainly an abominable injustice to drown a man who had worked so hard, so hard. The man felt it would be a crime most unnatural. Other people had drowned at sea since galleys swarmed with painted sails, but still—

When it occurs to a man that nature does not regard him as important, and that she feels she would not maim the universe by disposing of him, he at first wishes to throw bricks at the temple, and he hates deeply the fact that there are no bricks and no temples. Any visible expression of nature would surely be pelleted with his jeers.

Then, if there be no tangible thing to hoot he feels, perhaps, the desire to confront a personification and indulge in pleas, bowed to one knee, and with hands supplicant, saying: "Yes, but I love myself."

A high cold star on a winter's night is the word he feels that she says to him. Thereafter he knows the pathos of his situation.

The men in the dingey had not discussed these matters, but each had, no doubt, reflected upon them in silence and according to his mind. There was seldom any expression upon their faces save the general one of complete weariness. Speech was devoted to the business of the boat.

To chime the notes of his emotion, a verse mysteriously entered the correspondent's head. He had even forgotten that he had forgotten this verse, but it suddenly was in his mind.

A soldier of the Legion lay dying in Algiers,
There was lack of woman's nursing, there was dearth of woman's tears;
But a comrade stood beside him, and he took that comrade's hand
And he said: "I shall never see my own, my native land."

In his childhood, the correspondent had been made acquainted with the fact that a soldier of the Legion lay dying in Algiers, but he had never regarded the fact as important. Myriads of his school-fellows had informed him of the soldier's plight, but the dinning had naturally ended by making him perfectly indifferent. He had never considered it his affair that a soldier of the Legion lay dying in Algiers, nor had it appeared to him as a matter for sorrow. It was less to him than breaking of a pencil's point.

Now, however, it quaintly came to him as a human, living thing. It was no longer merely a picture of a few throes in the breast of a poet, meanwhile drinking tea and warming his feet at the grate; it was an actuality—stern, mournful, and fine.

The correspondent plainly saw the soldier. He lay on the sand with his feet out straight and still. While his pale left hand was upon his chest in an attempt to thwart the going of his life, the blood came between his fingers. In the far Algerian distance, a city of low square forms was set against a sky that was faint with the last sunset hues. The correspondent, plying the oars and dreaming of the slow and slower movements of the lips of the soldier, was moved by a profound and perfectly impersonal comprehension. He was sorry for the soldier of the Legion who lay dying in Algiers.

The thing which had followed the boat and waited had evidently grown bored at the delay. There was no longer to be heard the slash of the cut-water, and there was no longer the flame of the long trail. The light in the north still glimmered, but it was apparently no nearer to the boat. Sometimes the boom of the surf rang in the correspondent's ears, and he turned the craft seaward then and rowed harder. Southward, someone had evidently built a watch-fire on the beach. It was too low and too far to be seen, but it made a shimmering, roseate reflection upon the bluff back of it, and this could be discerned from the boat. The wind came stronger, and sometimes a wave suddenly raged out like a mountain-cat and there was to be seen the sheen and sparkle of a broken crest.

The captain, in the bow, moved on his water-jar and sat erect. "Pretty long night," he observed to the correspondent. He looked at the shore. "Those life-saving people take their time."

"Did you see that shark playing around?"

"Yes, I saw him. He was a big fellow, all right."

"Wish I had known you were awake."

Later the correspondent spoke into the bottom of the boat.

"Billie!" There was a slow and gradual disentanglement. "Billie, will you spell me?"

"Sure," said the oiler.

As soon as the correspondent touched the cold comfortable sea-water in the bottom of the boat, and had huddled close to the cook's life-belt he was deep in sleep, despite the fact that his teeth played all the popular airs. This sleep was so good to him that it was but a moment before he heard a voice call his name in a tone that demonstrated the last stages of exhaustion. "Will you spell me?"

"Sure, Billie."

The light in the north had mysteriously vanished, but the correspondent took his course from the wide-awake captain.

Later in the night they took the boat farther out to sea, and the captain directed the cook to take one oar at the stern and keep the boat facing the seas. He was to call out if he should hear the thunder of the surf. This plan enabled the oiler and the correspondent to get respite together. "We'll give those boys a chance to get into shape again," said the captain. They curled down and, after a few preliminary chatterings and trembles, slept once more the dead sleep. Neither knew they had bequeathed to the cook the company of another shark, or perhaps the same shark.

As the boat caroused on the waves, spray occasionally bumped over the side and gave them a fresh soaking, but this had no power to break their repose. The ominous slash of the wind and the water affected them as it would have affected mummies.

"Boys," said the cook, with the notes of every reluctance in his voice, "she's drifted in pretty close. I guess one of you had better take her to sea again." The correspondent, aroused, heard the crash of the toppled crests.

As he was rowing, the captain gave him some whiskey and water, and this steadied the chills out of him. "If I ever get ashore and anybody shows me even a photograph of an oar—"

At last there was a short conversation.

"Billie. . . . Billie, will you spell me?"

"Sure," said the oiler.

VII

When the correspondent again opened his eyes, the sea and the sky were each of the gray hue of the dawning. Later, carmine and gold was painted upon the waters. The morning appeared finally, in its splendor with a sky of pure blue, and the sunlight flamed on the tips of the waves.

On the distant dunes were set many little black cottages, and a tall white wind-mill reared above them. No man, nor dog, nor bicycle appeared on the beach. The cottages might have formed a deserted village.

The voyagers scanned the shore. A conference was held in the boat. "Well," said the captain, "if no help is coming, we might better try a run through the surf right away. If we stay out here much longer we will be too weak to do anything for ourselves at all." The others silently acquiesced in this reasoning. The boat was headed for the beach. The correspondent wondered if none ever ascended the tall wind-tower, and if then they never looked seaward. This tower was a giant, standing with its back to the plight of the ants. It represented in a degree, to the correspondent, the serenity of nature amid the struggles of the individual—nature in the wind, and nature in the vision of men. She did not seem cruel to him, nor beneficent, nor treacherous, nor wise. But she was indifferent, flatly indifferent. It is, perhaps, plausible that a man in this situation, impressed with the unconcern of the universe, should see the innumerable flaws of his life and have them taste wickedly in his mind and wish for another chance. A distinction between right and wrong seems absurdly clear to him, then, in this new ignorance of the grave-edge, and he understands that if he were given another opportunity he would mend his conduct and his words, and be better and brighter during an introduction, or at a tea.

"Now, boys," said the captain, "she is going to swamp sure. All we can do is to work her in as far as possible, and then when she swamps, pile out and scramble for the beach. Keep cool now and don't jump until she swamps sure."

The oiler took the oars. Over his shoulders he scanned the surf. "Captain," he said, "I think I'd better bring her about, and keep her head-on to the seas and back her in."

"All right, Billie," said the captain. "Back her in." The oiler swung the boat then and, seated in the stern, the cook and the correspondent were obliged to look over their shoulders to contemplate the lonely and indifferent shore.

The monstrous inshore rollers heaved the boat high until the men were again enabled to see the white sheets of water scudding up the slanted beach. "We won't get in very close," said the captain. Each time a man could wrest his attention from the rollers, he turned his glance toward the shore, and in the expression of the eyes during this contemplation there was a singular quality. The correspondent, observing the others, knew that they were not afraid, but the full meaning of their glances was shrouded.

As for himself, he was too tired to grapple fundamentally with the fact. He tried to coerce his mind into thinking of it, but the mind was dominated at this time by the muscles, and the muscles said they did not care. It merely occurred to him that if he should drown it would be a shame.

There were no hurried words, no pallor, no plain agitation. The men simply looked at the shore. "Now, remember to get well clear of the boat when you jump," said the captain.

Seaward the crest of a roller suddenly fell with a thunderous crash, and the long white comber came roaring down upon the boat.

"Steady now," said the captain. The men were silent. They turned their eyes from the shore to the comber and waited. The boat slid up the incline, leaped at the furious top, bounced over it, and swung down the long back of the waves. Some water had been shipped and the cook bailed it out.

But the next crest crashed also. The tumbling boiling flood of white water caught the boat and whirled it almost perpendicular. Water swarmed in from all sides. The correspondent had his hands on the gunwale at this time, and when the water entered at that place he swiftly withdrew his fingers, as if he objected to wetting them.

The little boat, drunken with this weight of water, reeled and snuggled deeper into the sea.

"Bail her out, cook! Bail her out," said the captain.

"All right, captain," said the cook.

"Now, boys, the next one will do for us, sure," said the oiler. "Mind to jump clear of the boat."

The third wave moved forward, huge, furious, implacable. It fairly swallowed the dingey, and almost simultaneously the men tumbled into the sea. A piece of life-belt had lain in the bottom of the boat, and as the correspondent went overboard he held this to his chest with his left hand.

The January water was icy, and he reflected immediately that it was colder than he had expected to find it off the coast of Florida. This appeared to his dazed mind as a fact important enough to be noted at the time. The coldness of the water was sad; it was tragic. This fact was somehow mixed and confused with his opinion of his own situation that it seemed almost a proper reason for tears. The water was cold.

When he came to the surface he was conscious of little but the noisy water. Afterward he saw his companions in the sea. The oiler was ahead in the race. He was swimming strongly and rapidly. Off to the correspondent's left, the cook's great white and corked back bulged out of the water, and in the rear the captain was hanging with his one good hand to the keel of the overturned dingey.

There is a certain immovable quality to a shore, and the correspondent wondered at it amid the confusion of the sea.

It seemed also very attractive, but the correspondent knew that it was a long journey, and he paddled leisurely. The piece of life-preserver lay under him, and sometimes he whirled down the incline of a wave as if he were on a hand-sled.

But finally he arrived at a place in the sea where travel was beset with difficulty. He did not pause swimming to inquire what manner of current had caught him, but there his progress ceased. The shore was set before him like a bit of scenery on a stage, and he looked at it and understood with his eyes each detail of it.

As the cook passed, much farther to the left, the captain was calling to him, "Turn over on your back, cook! Turn over on your back and use the oar."

"All right, sir!" The cook turned on his back, and, paddling with an oar, went ahead as if he were a canoe.

Presently the boat also passed to the left of the correspondent with the captain clinging with one hand to the keel. He would have appeared like a man raising himself to look over a board fence, if it were not for the extraordinary gymnastics of the boat. The correspondent marvelled that the captain could still hold to it.

They passed on, nearer to shore—the oiler, the cook, the captain—and following them went the water-jar, bouncing gayly over the seas.

The correspondent remained in the grip of this strange new enemy—a current. The shore, with its white slope of sand and its green bluff, topped with little silent cottages, was spread like a picture before him. It was very near to him then, but he was impressed as one who in a gallery looks at a scene from Brittany or Algiers.

He thought: "I am going to drown? Can it be possible? Can it be possible? Can it be possible?" Perhaps an individual must consider his own death to be the final phenomenon of nature.

But later a wave perhaps whirled him out of this small deadly current, for he found suddenly that he could again make progress toward the shore. Later still, he was aware that the captain, clinging with one hand to the keel of the dingey, had his face turned away from the shore and toward him, and was calling his name. "Come to the boat! Come to the boat!"

In his struggle to reach the captain and the boat, he reflected that when one gets properly wearied, drowning must really be a comfortable arrangement, a cessation of hostilities accompanied by a large degree of relief, and he was glad of it, for the main thing in his mind for some moments had been horror of the temporary agony. He did not wish to be hurt.

Presently he saw a man running along the shore. He was undressing with most remarkable speed. Coat, trousers, shirt, everything flew magically off him.

"Come to the boat," called the captain.

"All right, captain." As the correspondent paddled, he saw the captain let himself down to bottom and leave the boat. Then the correspondent performed his one little marvel of the voyage. A large wave caught him and flung him with ease and supreme speed completely over the boat and far beyond it. It struck him even then as an event in gymnastics, and a true miracle of the sea. An overturned boat in the surf is not a plaything to a swimming man.

The correspondent arrived in water that reached only to his waist, but his condition did not enable him to stand for more than a moment. Each wave knocked him into a heap, and the under-tow pulled at him.

Then he saw the man who had been running and undressing, and undressing and running, come bounding into the water. He dragged ashore the cook, and then waded toward the captain, but the captain waved him away, and sent him to the correspondent. He was naked, naked as a tree in winter, but a halo was about his head, and he shone like a saint. He gave a strong pull, and a long drag, and a bully heave at the correspondent's hand. The correspondent, schooled in the minor formulae, said: "Thanks, old man." But suddenly the man cried: "What's that?" He pointed a swift finger. The correspondent said: "Go."

In the shallows, face downward, lay the oiler. His forehead touched sand that was periodically, between each wave, clear of the sea.

The correspondent did not know all that transpired afterward. When he achieved safe ground he fell, striking the sand with each particular part of his body. It was as if he had dropped from a roof, but the thud was grateful to him.

It seems that instantly the beach was populated with men with blankets, clothes, and flasks, and women with coffee-pots and all the remedies sacred to their minds. The welcome of the land to the men from the sea was warm and generous, but a still and dripping shape was carried slowly up the beach, and the land's welcome for it could only be the different and sinister hospitality of the grave.

When it came night, the white waves paced to and fro in the moonlight, and the wind brought the sound of the great sea's voice to the men on shore, and they felt that they could then be interpreters.

—*1898*

Questions: Reading, Responding, Arguing

1. What is the narrative point of view for the story? Why did Crane not use first person?
2. What is ironic about the story's dénouement?
3. Why does the narrator keep thinking about the "soldier of the Legion"?
4. How does the story indicate the indifference of nature to human life?
5. Read "Stephen Crane's Own Story" on page 1282, Crane's journalistic account of his ordeal. Why did he choose to base his story on the events that he did not describe there? Craft an argument speculating on his reasons.

Jorge Luis Borges (1899–1986)

The Secret Miracle

Translated by Anthony Kerrigan

> And God made him die during the course of a
> hundred years and then He revived him and said:
> "How long have you been here?"
> "A day, or part of a day," he replied.
> —*The Koran, II 261*

On the night of March 14, 1939, in an apartment on the Zelternergasse in Prague, Jaromir Hladík, author of the unfinished tragedy *The Enemies,* of a *Vindication of Eternity,* and of an inquiry into the indirect Jewish sources of Jakob Boehme, dreamt a long drawn out chess game. The antagonists were not two individuals, but two illustrious families. The contest had begun many centuries before. No one could any longer describe the forgotten prize, but it was rumored that it was enormous and perhaps infinite. The pieces and the chessboard were set up in a secret tower. Jaromir (in his dream) was the first-born of one of the contending families. The hour for the next move, which could not be postponed, struck on all the clocks. The dreamer ran across the sands of a rainy desert—and he could not remember the chessmen or the rules of chess. At this point he awoke. The din of the rain and the clangor of the terrible clocks ceased. A measured unison, sundered by voices of command, arose from the Zelternergasse. Day had dawned, and the armored vanguards of the Third Reich were entering Prague.

On the 19th, the authorities received an accusation against Jaromir Hladík; on the same day, at dusk, he was arrested. He was taken to a barracks, aseptic and white, on the opposite bank of the Moldau. He was unable to refute a single one of the charges made by the Gestapo: his maternal surname was Jaroslavski, his blood was Jewish, his study of Boehme was Judaizing, his signature had helped to swell the final census of those protesting the *Anschluss*.[1] In 1928, he had translated the *Sepher Yezirah*[2] for the publishing house of Hermann Barsdorf; the effusive catalogue issued by this firm had exaggerated, for commercial

---

[1]*Anschluss:* the 1938 German annexation of Austria.
[2]*Sepher Yezirah:* ancient work of Jewish mysticism.

reasons, the translator's renown; this catalogue was leafed through by Julius Rothe, one of the officials in whose hands lay Hladík's fate. The man does not exist who, outside his own specialty, is not credulous: two or three adjectives in Gothic script sufficed to convince Julius Rothe of Hladík's pre-eminence, and of the need for the death penalty, *pour encourager les autres*.[3] The execution was set for the 29th of March, at nine in the morning. This delay (whose importance the reader will appreciate later) was due to a desire on the part of the authorities to act slowly and impersonally, in the manner of planets or vegetables.

Hladík's first reaction was simply one of horror. He was sure he would not have been terrified by the gallows, the block, or the knife; but to die before a firing squad was unbearable. In vain he repeated to himself that the pure and general act of dying, not the concrete circumstances, was the dreadful fact. He did not grow weary of imagining these circumstances: he absurdly tried to exhaust all the variations. He infinitely anticipated the process, from the sleepless dawn to the mysterious discharge of the rifles. Before the day set by Julius Rothe, he died hundreds of deaths, in courtyards whose shapes and angles defied geometry, shot down by changeable soldiers whose number varied and who sometimes put an end to him from close up and sometimes from far away. He faced these imaginary executions with true terror (perhaps with true courage). Each simulacrum lasted a few seconds. Once the circle was closed, Jaromir returned interminably to the tremulous eve of his death. Then he would reflect that reality does not tend to coincide with forecasts about it. With perverse logic he inferred that to foresee a circumstantial detail is to prevent its happening. Faithful to this feeble magic, he would invent, *so that they might not happen,* the most atrocious particulars. Naturally, he finished by fearing that these particulars were prophetic. During his wretched nights he strove to hold fast somehow to the fugitive substance of time. He knew that time was precipitating itself toward the dawn of the 29th. He reasoned aloud: *I am now in the night of the 22nd. While this night lasts (and for six more nights to come) I am invulnerable, immortal.* His nights of sleep seemed to him deep dark pools into which he might submerge. Sometimes he yearned impatiently for the firing squad's definitive volley, which would redeem him, for better or for worse, from the vain compulsion of his imagination. On the 28th, as the final sunset reverberated across the high barred windows, he was distracted from all these abject considerations by thought of his drama, *The Enemies.*

---

[3]*pour encourager les autres:* "to encourage the others" (from Volatire's *Candide*).

Hladík was past forty. Apart from a few friendships and many habits, the problematic practice of literature constituted his life. Like every writer, he measured the virtues of other writers by their performance, and asked that they measure him by what he conjectured or planned. All of the books he had published merely moved him to a complex repentance. His investigation of the work of Boehme, of Ibn Ezra, and of Fludd[4] was essentially a product of mere application; his translation of the *Sepher Yezirah* was characterized by negligence, fatigue, and conjecture. He judged his *Vindication of Eternity* to be perhaps less deficient: the first volume is a history of the diverse eternities devised by man, from the immutable Being of Parmenides to the alterable past of Hinton; the second volume denies (with Francis Bradley) that all the events in the universe make up a temporal series. He argues that the number of experiences possible to man is not infinite, and that a single "repetition" suffices to demonstrate that time is a fallacy. . . . Unfortunately, the arguments that demonstrate this fallacy are not any less fallacious. Hladík was in the habit of running through these arguments with a certain disdainful perplexity. He had also written a series of expressionist poems; these, to the discomfiture of the author, were included in an anthology in 1924, and there was no anthology of later date which did not inherit them. Hladík was anxious to redeem himself from his equivocal and languid past with his verse drama, *The Enemies*. (He favored the verse form in the theater because it prevents the spectators from forgetting unreality, which is the necessary condition of art.)

This opus preserved the dramatic unities (time, place, and action). It transpires in Hradcany, in the library of the Baron Roemerstadt, on one of the last evenings of the nineteenth century. In the first scene of the first act, a stranger pays a visit to Roemerstadt. (A clock strikes seven, the vehemence of a setting sun glorifies the window panes, the air transmits familiar and impassioned Hungarian music.) This visit is followed by others; Roemerstadt does not know the people who come to importune him, but he has the uncomfortable impression that he has seen them before: perhaps in a dream. All the visitors fawn upon him, but it is obvious—first to the spectators of the drama, and then to the Baron himself—that they are secret enemies, sworn to ruin him. Roemerstadt manages to outwit, or evade, their complex intrigues. In the course of the dialogue, mention is made of his betrothed, Julia de Weidenau, and of a certain Jaroslav Kubin, who at one time had been her suitor. Kubin has now lost his mind and thinks he is Roemerstadt. . . .

---

[4]*Boehme . . . Fludd*: philosophers.

The dangers multiply. Roemerstadt, at the end of the second act, is forced to kill one of the conspirators. The third and final act begins. The incongruities gradually mount up: actors who seemed to have been discarded from the play reappear; the man who had been killed by Roemerstadt returns, for an instant. Someone notes that the time of day has not advanced: the clock strikes seven, the western sun reverberates in the high window panes, impassioned Hungarian music is carried on the air. The first speaker in the play reappears and repeats the words he had spoken in the first scene of the first act. Roemerstadt addresses him without the least surprise. The spectator understands that Roemerstadt is the wretched Jaroslav Kubin. The drama has never taken place: it is the circular delirium which Kubin unendingly lives and relives.

Hladík had never asked himself whether this tragicomedy of errors was preposterous or admirable, deliberate or casual. Such a plot, he intuited, was the most appropriate invention to conceal his defects and to manifest his strong points, and it embodied the possibility of redeeming (symbolically) the fundamental meaning of his life. He had already completed the first act and a scene or two of the third. The metrical nature of the work allowed him to go over it continually, rectifying the hexameters, without recourse to the manuscript. He thought of the two acts still to do, and of his coming death. In the darkness, he addressed himself to God. *If I exist at all, if I am not one of Your repetitions and errata, I exist as the author of* The Enemies. *In order to bring this drama, which may serve to justify me, to justify You, I need one more year. Grant me that year, You to whom belong the centuries and all time.* It was the last, the most atrocious night, but ten minutes later sleep swept over him like a dark ocean and drowned him.

Toward dawn, he dreamt he had hidden himself in one of the naves of the Clementine Library. A librarian wearing dark glasses asked him: *What are you looking for?* Hladík answered: *God.* The Librarian told him: *God is in one of the letters on one of the pages of one of the 400,000 volumes of the Clementine. My fathers and the fathers of my fathers have sought after that letter. I've gone blind looking for it.* He removed his glasses, and Hladík saw that his eyes were dead. A reader came in to return an atlas. *This atlas is useless,* he said, and handed it to Hladík, who opened it at random. As if through a haze, he saw a map of India. With a sudden rush of assurance, he touched one of the tiniest letters. An ubiquitous voice said: *The time for your work has been granted.* Hladík awoke.

He remembered that the dreams of men belong to God, and that Maimonides[5] wrote that the words of a dream are divine, when they are all separate and clear and are spoken by someone invisible. He dressed. Two soldiers entered his cell and ordered him to follow them. From behind the door, Hladík had visualized a labyrinth of passageways, stairs, and connecting blocks. Reality was less rewarding: the party descended to an inner courtyard by a single iron stairway. Some soldiers—uniforms unbuttoned—were testing a motorcycle and disputing their conclusions. The sergeant looked at his watch: it was 8:44. They must wait until nine. Hladík, more insignificant than pitiful, sat down on a pile of firewood. He noticed that the soldiers' eyes avoided his. To make his wait easier, the sergeant offered him a cigarette. Hladík did not smoke. He accepted the cigarette out of politeness or humility. As he lit it, he saw that his hands shook. The day was clouding over. The soldiers spoke in low tones, as though he were already dead. Vainly, he strove to recall the woman of whom Julia de Weidenau was the symbol. . . .

The firing squad fell in and was brought to attention. Hladík, standing against the barracks wall, waited for the volley. Someone expressed fear the wall would be splashed with blood. The condemned man was ordered to step forward a few paces. Hladík recalled, absurdly, the preliminary maneuvers of a photographer. A heavy drop of rain grazed one of Hladík's temples and slowly rolled down his cheek. The sergeant barked the final command.

The physical universe stood still.

The rifles converged upon Hladík, but the men assigned to pull the triggers were immobile. The sergeant's arm eternalized an inconclusive gesture. Upon a courtyard flagstone a bee cast a stationary shadow. The wind had halted, as in a painted picture. Hladík began a shriek, a syllable, a twist of the hand. He realized he was paralyzed. Not a sound reached him from the stricken world.

He thought: *I'm in hell, I'm dead.*

He thought: *I've gone mad.*

He thought: *Time has come to a halt.*

Then he reflected that in that case, his thought, too, would have come to a halt. He was anxious to test this possibility: he repeated (without moving his lips) the mysterious Fourth Eclogue of Virgil. He imagined that the already remote soldiers shared his anxiety; he longed

---

[5]*Maimonides*: Jewish philosopher (1135–1204).

to communicate with them. He was astonished that he felt no fatigue, no vertigo from his protracted immobility. After an indeterminate length of time he fell asleep. On awaking he found the world still motionless and numb. The drop of water still clung to his cheek; the shadow of the bee still did not shift in the courtyard; the smoke from the cigarette he had thrown down did not blow away. Another "day" passed before Hladík understood.

He had asked God for an entire year in which to finish his work: His omnipotence had granted him the time. For his sake, God projected a secret miracle: German lead would kill him, at the determined hour, but in his mind a year would elapse between the command to fire and its execution. From perplexity he passed to stupor, from stupor to resignation, from resignation to sudden gratitude.

He disposed of no document but his own memory; the mastering of each hexameter as he added it, had imposed upon him a kind of fortunate discipline not imagined by those amateurs who forget their vague, ephemeral, paragraphs. He did not work for posterity, nor even for God, of whose literary preferences he possessed scant knowledge. Meticulous, unmoving, secretive, he wove his lofty invisible labyrinth in time. He worked the third act over twice. He eliminated some rather too-obvious symbols: the repeated striking of the hour, the music. There were no circumstances to constrain him. He omitted, condensed, amplified; occasionally, he chose the primitive version. He grew to love the courtyard, the barracks; one of the faces endlessly confronting him made him modify his conception of Roemerstadt's character. He discovered that the hard cacaphonies which so distressed Flaubert are mere visual superstitions: debilities and annoyances of the written word, not of the sonorous, the sounding one. . . . He brought his drama to a conclusion: he lacked only a single epithet. He found it: the drop of water slid down his cheek. He began a wild cry, moved his face aside. A quadruple blast brought him down.

Jaromir Hladík died on March 29, at 9:02 in the morning.

—1943

Questions: Reading, Responding, Arguing

1. How does Borges play tricks with time?
2. What is the "secret miracle" of the title?
3. What is the enveloping action of this story? Argue that it helps to explain its events.

Flannery O'Connor (1925–1964)

A Good Man Is Hard to Find[*]

The grandmother didn't want to go to Florida. She wanted to visit some of her connections in east Tennessee and she was seizing every chance to change Bailey's mind. Bailey was the son she lived with, her only boy. He was sitting on the edge of his chair at the table, bent over the orange sports section of the *Journal.* "Now look here, Bailey," she said, "see here, read this," and she stood with one hand on her thin hip and the other rattling the newspaper at his bald head. "Here this fellow that calls himself The Misfit is aloose from the Federal Pen and headed toward Florida and you read here what it says he did to these people. Just you read it. I wouldn't take my children in any direction with a criminal like that aloose in it. I couldn't answer to my conscience if I did."

Bailey didn't look up from his reading so she wheeled around then and faced the children's mother, a young woman in slacks, whose face was as broad and innocent as a cabbage and was tied around with a green headkerchief that had two points on the top like rabbit's ears. She was sitting on the sofa, feeding the baby his apricots out of a jar. "The children have been to Florida before," the old lady said. "You all ought to take them somewhere else for a change so they would see different parts of the world and be broad. They never have been to east Tennessee."

The children's mother didn't seem to hear her, but the eight-year-old boy, John Wesley, a stocky child with glasses, said. "If you don't want to go to Florida, why dontcha stay at home?" He and the little girl, June Star, were reading the funny papers on the floor.

"She wouldn't stay at home to be queen for a day," June Star said without raising her yellow head.

"Yes, and what would you do if this fellow, The Misfit, caught you?" the grandmother said.

"I'd smack his face," John Wesley said.

"She wouldn't stay at home for a million bucks," June Star said. "Afraid she'd miss something. She has to go everywhere we go."

"All right, Miss," the grandmother said. "Just remember that the next time you want me to curl your hair."

June Star said her hair was naturally curly.

The next morning the grandmother was the first one in the car, ready to go. She had her big black valise that looked like the head of a hippopotamus in one corner, and underneath it she was hiding a basket with Pitty Sing, the cat, in it. She didn't intend for the cat to be left alone in the house for three days because he would miss her too much and she was afraid he might brush against one of the gas burners and accidentally asphyxiate himself. Her son, Bailey, didn't like to arrive at a motel with a cat.

She sat in the middle of the back seat with John Wesley and June Star on either side of her. Bailey and the children's mother and the baby sat in front and they left Atlanta at eight forty-five with the mileage on the car at 55890. The grandmother wrote this down because she thought it would be interesting to say how many miles they had been when they got back. It took them twenty minutes to reach the outskirts of the city.

The old lady settled herself comfortably, removing her white cotton gloves and putting them up with her purse on the shelf in front of the back window. The children's mother still had on slacks and still had her head tied up in a green kerchief, but the grandmother had on a navy blue straw sailor hat with a bunch of white violets on the brim and a navy blue dress with a small white dot in the print. Her collars and cuffs were white organdy trimmed with lace and at her neckline she had pinned a purple spray of cloth violets containing a sachet. In case of an accident, anyone seeing her dead on the highway would know at once that she was a lady.

She said she thought it was going to be a good day for driving, neither too hot nor too cold, and she cautioned Bailey that the speed limit was fifty-five miles an hour and that the patrolmen hid themselves behind bill-boards and small clumps of trees and sped out after you before you had a chance to slow down. She pointed out interesting details of the scenery: Stone Mountain; the blue granite that in some places came up to both sides of the highway; the brilliant red clay banks slightly streaked with purple; and the various crops that made rows of green lace-work on the ground. The trees were full of silver-white sunlight and the meanest of them sparkled. The children were reading comic magazines and their mother had gone back to sleep.

"Let's go through Georgia fast so we won't have to look at it much," John Wesley said.

"If I were a little boy," said the grandmother, "I wouldn't talk about my native state that way. Tennessee has the mountains and Georgia has the hills."

"Tennessee is just a hillbilly dumping ground," John Wesley said, "and Georgia is a lousy state too."

"You said it," June Star said.

"In my time," said the grandmother, folding her thin veined fingers, "children were more respectful of their native states and their parents and everything else. People did right then. Oh look at the cute little pickaninny!" she said and pointed to a Negro child standing in the door of a shack. "Wouldn't that make a picture, now?" she asked and they all turned and looked at the little Negro out of the back window. He waved.

"He didn't have any britches on," June Star said.

"He probably didn't have any," the grandmother explained. "Little niggers in the country don't have things like we do. If I could paint, I'd paint that picture," she said.

The children exchanged comic books.

The grandmother offered to hold the baby and the children's mother passed him over the front seat to her. She set him on her knee and bounced him and told him about the things they were passing. She rolled her eyes and screwed up her mouth and stuck her leathery thin face into his smooth bland one. Occasionally he gave her a faraway smile. They passed a large cotton field with five or six graves fenced in the middle of it, like a small island. "Look at the graveyard!" the grandmother said, pointing it out. "That was the old family burying ground. That belonged to the plantation."

"Where's the plantation?" John Wesley asked.

"Gone With the Wind," said the grandmother. "Ha. Ha."

When the children finished all the comic books they had brought, they opened the lunch and ate it. The grandmother ate a peanut butter sandwich and an olive and would not let the children throw the box and the paper napkins out the window. When there was nothing else to do they played a game by choosing a cloud and making the other two guess what shape it suggested. John Wesley took one the shape of a cow and June Star guessed a cow and John Wesley said, no, an automobile, and June Star said he didn't play fair, and they began to slap each other over the grandmother.

The grandmother said she would tell them a story if they would keep quiet. When she told a story, she rolled her eyes and waved her head and was very dramatic. She said once when she was a maiden lady she had been courted by a Mr. Edgar Atkins Teagarden from Jasper, Georgia. She said he was a very good-looking man and a gentleman and that he brought her a watermelon every Saturday afternoon with his initials cut in it, E.A.T. Well, one Saturday, she said, Mr. Teagarden brought the watermelon and there was nobody at home and he left it on the front porch and returned in his buggy to Jasper, but she never got the watermelon, she said, because a nigger boy ate it when he saw the initials, E.A.T.! This story tickled John Wesley's funny bone and he giggled and giggled but June Star didn't think it was any good. She said she wouldn't marry a man that just brought her a watermelon on Saturday. The grandmother said she would have done well to marry Mr. Teagarden because he was a gentleman and had bought Coca-Cola stock when it first came out and that he had died only a few years ago, a very wealthy man.

They stopped at The Tower for barbecued sandwiches. The Tower was a part-stucco and part-wood filling station and dance hall set in a clearing outside of Timothy. A fat man named Red Sammy Butts ran it and there were signs stuck here and there on the building and for miles up and down the highway saying, TRY RED SAMMY'S FAMOUS BARBECUE. NONE LIKE FAMOUS RED SAMMY'S! RED SAM! THE FAT BOY WITH THE HAPPY LAUGH. A VETERAN! RED SAMMY'S YOUR MAN!

Red Sammy was lying on the bare ground outside The Tower with his head under a truck while a gray monkey about a foot high, chained to a small chinaberry tree, chattered nearby. The monkey sprang back into the tree and got on the highest limb as soon as he saw the children jump out of the car and run toward him.

Inside, The Tower was a long dark room with a counter at one end and tables at the other and dancing space in the middle. They all sat down at a broad table next to the nickelodeon and Red Sam's wife, a tall burnt-brown woman with hair and eyes lighter than her skin, came and took their order. The children's mother put a dime in the machine and played "The Tennessee Waltz," and the grandmother said that tune always made her want to dance. She asked Bailey if he would like to dance but he only glared at her. He didn't have a naturally sunny disposition like she did and trips made him nervous. The grandmother's brown eyes were very bright. She swayed her head from side to side and pretended she was dancing in her chair. June Star said play something she could tap to so the children's mother put in another dime and played a fast number and June Star stepped out onto the dance floor and did her tap routine.

"Ain't she cute?" Red Sam's wife said, leaning over the counter. "Would you like to come be my little girl?"

"No, I certainly wouldn't," June Star said. "I wouldn't live in a broken-down place like this for a million bucks!" and she ran back to the table.

"Ain't she cute?" the woman repeated, stretching her mouth politely. "Aren't you ashamed?" hissed the grandmother.

Red Sam came in and told his wife to quit lounging on the counter and hurry with these people's order. His khaki trousers reached just to his hip bones and his stomach hung over them like a sack of meal swaying under his shirt. He came over and sat down at a table nearby and let out a combination sigh and yodel. "You can't win," he said. "You can't win," and he wiped his sweating red face off with a gray handkerchief. "These days you don't know who to trust," he said. "Ain't that the truth?"

"People are certainly not nice like they used to be," said the grandmother.

"Two fellers come in here last week," Red Sammy said, "driving a Chrysler. It was an old beat-up car but it was a good one and these boys looked all right to me. Said they worked at the mill and you know I let them fellers charge the gas they bought? Now why did I do that?"

"Because you're a good man!" the grandmother said at once.

"Yes'm, I suppose so," Red Sam said as if he were struck with this answer.

His wife brought the orders, carrying the five plates all at once without a tray, two in each hand and one balanced on her arm. "It isn't a soul in this green world of God's that you can trust," she said. "And I don't count nobody out of that, not nobody," she repeated, looking at Red Sammy.

"Did you read about that criminal, The Misfit, that's escaped?" asked the grandmother.

"I wouldn't be a bit surprised if he didn't attack this place right here," said the woman. "If he hears about it being here, I wouldn't be none surprised to see him. If he hears it's two cent in the cash register, I wouldn't be a tall surprised if he . . . "

"That'll do," Red Sam said. "Go bring these people their Co'Colas," and the woman went off to get the rest of the order.

"A good man is hard to find," Red Sammy said. "Everything is getting terrible. I remember the day you could go off and leave your screen door unlatched. Not no more."

He and the grandmother discussed better times. The old lady said that in her opinion Europe was entirely to blame for the way things were now. She said the way Europe acted you would think we were made of money and Red Sam said it was no use talking about it, she was exactly right. The children ran outside into the white sunlight and looked at the monkey in the lacy chinaberry tree. He was busy catching fleas on himself and biting each one carefully between his teeth as if it were a delicacy.

They drove off again into the hot afternoon. The grandmother took cat naps and woke up every five minutes with her own snoring. Outside of Toombsboro she woke up and recalled an old plantation that she had visited in this neighborhood once when she was a young lady. She said the house had six white columns across the front and that there was an avenue of oaks leading up to it and two little wooden trellis arbors on either side in front where you sat down with your suitor after a stroll in the garden. She recalled exactly which road to turn off to get to it. She knew that Bailey would not be willing to lose any time looking at an old house, but the more she talked about it, the more she wanted to see it once again and find out if the little twin arbors were still standing. "There was a secret panel in this house," she said craftily, not telling the truth but wishing that she were, "and the story went that all the family silver was hidden in it when Sherman came through but it was never found . . ."

"Hey!" John Wesley said. "Let's go see it! We'll find it! We'll poke all the woodwork and find it! Who lives there? Where do you turn off at? Hey, Pop, can't we turn off there?"

"We never have seen a house with a secret panel!" June Star shrieked. "Let's go to the house with the secret panel! Hey, Pop, can't we go see the house with the secret panel!"

"It's not far from here, I know," the grandmother said. "It wouldn't take over twenty minutes."

Bailey was looking straight ahead. His jaw was as rigid as a horseshoe. "No," he said.

The children began to yell and scream that they wanted to see the house with the secret panel. John Wesley kicked the back of the front seat and June Star hung over her mother's shoulder and whined desperately into her ear that they never had any fun even on their vacation, that they could never do what THEY wanted to do. The baby began to scream and John Wesley kicked the back of the seat so hard that his father could feel the blows in his kidney.

"All right!" he shouted and drew the car to a stop at the side of the road. "Will you all shut up? Will you all just shut up for one second? If you don't shut up, we won't go anywhere."

"It would be very educational for them," the grandmother murmured.

"All right," Bailey said, "but get this. This is the only time we're going to stop for anything like this. This is the one and only time."

"The dirt road that you have to turn down is about a mile back," the grandmother directed. "I marked it when we passed."

"A dirt road," Bailey groaned.

After they had turned around and were headed toward the dirt road, the grandmother recalled other points about the house, the beautiful glass over the front doorway and the candle lamp in the hall. John Wesley said that the secret panel was probably in the fireplace.

"You can't go inside this house," Bailey said. "You don't know who lives there."

"While you all talk to the people in front, I'll run around behind and get in a window," John Wesley suggested.

"We'll all stay in the car," his mother said.

They turned onto the dirt road and the car raced roughly along in a swirl of pink dust. The grandmother recalled the times when there were no paved roads and thirty miles was a day's journey. The dirt road was hilly and there were sudden washes in it and sharp curves on dangerous embankments. All at once they would be on a hill, looking down over the blue tops of trees for miles around, then the next minute, they would be in a red depression with the dust-coated trees looking down on them.

"This place had better turn up in a minute," Bailey said, "or I'm going to turn around."

The road looked as if no one had traveled on it in months.

"It's not much farther," the grandmother said and just as she said it, a horrible thought came to her. The thought was so embarrassing that she turned red in the face and her eyes dilated and her feet jumped up, upsetting her valise in the corner. The instant the valise moved, the newspaper top she had over the basket under it rose with a snarl and Pitty Sing, the cat, sprang onto Bailey's shoulder.

The children were thrown to the floor and their mother, clutching the baby, was thrown out the door onto the ground; the old lady was thrown into the front seat. The car turned over once and landed right-side-up in a gulch on the side of the road. Bailey remained in the driver's seat with the cat—gray-striped with a broad white face and an orange nose—clinging to his neck like a caterpillar.

As soon as the children saw they could move their arms and legs, they scrambled out of the car, shouting, "We've had an ACCIDENT!" The grandmother was curled up under the dashboard, hoping she was injured so that Bailey's wrath would not come down on her all at once. The horrible thought she had had before the accident was that the house she had remembered so vividly was not in Georgia but in Tennessee.

Bailey removed the cat from his neck with both hands and flung it out the window against the side of a pine tree. Then he got out of the car and started looking for the children's mother. She was sitting against the side of the red gutted ditch, holding the screaming baby, but she only had a cut down her face and a broken shoulder. "We've had an ACCIDENT!" the children screamed in a frenzy of delight.

"But nobody's killed," June Star said with disappointment as the grandmother limped out of the car, her hat still pinned to her head but the broken front brim standing up at a jaunty angle and the violet spray hanging off the side. They all sat down in the ditch, except the children, to recover from the shock. They were all shaking.

"Maybe a car will come along," said the children's mother hoarsely.

"I believe I have injured an organ," said the grandmother, pressing her side, but no one answered her. Bailey's teeth were clattering. He had on a yellow sport shirt with bright blue parrots designed in it and his face was as yellow as the shirt. The grandmother decided that she would not mention that the house was in Tennessee.

The road was about ten feet above and they could see only the tops of the trees on the other side of it. Behind the ditch they were sitting in there were more woods, tall and dark and deep. In a few minutes they saw a car some distance away on top of a hill, coming slowly as if the occupants were watching them. The grandmother stood up and waved both arms dramatically to attract their attention. The car continued to come on slowly, disappeared around a bend and appeared again, moving even slower on top of the hill they had gone over. It was a big black battered hearselike automobile. There were three men in it.

It came to a stop just over them and for some minutes, the driver looked down with a steady expressionless gaze to where they were sitting, and didn't speak. Then he turned his head and muttered something to the other two and they got out. One was a fat boy in black trousers and a red sweat shirt with a silver stallion embossed on the front of it. He moved around on the right side of them and stood staring, his mouth partly open in a kind of loose grin. The other had on khaki pants and a blue striped coat and a gray hat pulled down very low, hiding most of his face. He came around slowly on the left side. Neither spoke.

The driver got out of the car and stood by the side of it, looking down at them. He was an older man than the other two. His hair was just beginning to gray and he wore silver-rimmed spectacles that gave him a scholarly look. He had a long creased face and didn't have on any shirt or undershirt. He had on blue jeans that were too tight for him and was holding a black hat and a gun. The two boys also had guns.

"We've had an ACCIDENT!" the children screamed.

The grandmother had the peculiar feeling that the bespectacled man was someone she knew. His face was as familiar to her as if she had known him all her life but she could not recall who he was. He moved away from the car and began to come down the embankment, placing his feet carefully so that he wouldn't slip. He had on tan and white shoes and no socks, and his ankles were red and thin. "Good afternoon," he said. "I see you all had you a little spill."

"We turned over twice!" said the grandmother.

"Oncet," he corrected. "We seen it happen. Try their car and see will it run, Hiram," he said quietly to the boy with the gray hat.

"What you got that gun for?" John Wesley asked. "Whatcha gonna do with that gun?"

"Lady," the man said to the children's mother, "would you mind calling them children to sit down by you? Children make me nervous. I want all you to sit down right together there where you're at."

"What are you telling us what to do for?" June Star asked.

Behind them the line of woods gaped like a dark open mouth. "Come here," said their mother.

"Look here now," Bailey began suddenly, "we're in a predicament! We're in . . ."

The grandmother shrieked. She scrambled to her feet and stood staring. "You're The Misfit!" she said. "I recognized you at once!"

"Yes'm," the man said, smiling slightly as if he were pleased in spite of himself to be known, "but it would have been better for all of you, lady, if you hadn't of reckernized me."

Bailey turned his head sharply and said something to his mother that shocked even the children. The old lady began to cry and The Misfit reddened.

"Lady," he said, "don't you get upset. Sometimes a man says things he don't mean. I don't reckon he meant to talk to you thataway."

"You wouldn't shoot a lady, would you?" the grandmother said and removed a clean handkerchief from her cuff and began to slap at her eyes with it.

The Misfit pointed the toe of his shoe into the ground and made a little hole and then covered it up again. "I would hate to have to," he said.

"Listen," the grandmother almost screamed, "I know you're a good man. You don't look a bit like you have common blood. I know you must come from nice people!"

"Yes ma'm," he said, "finest people in the world." When he smiled he showed a row of strong white teeth. "God never made a finer woman than my mother and my daddy's heart was pure gold," he said. The boy with the red sweat shirt had come around behind them and was standing with his gun at his hip. The Misfit squatted down on the ground. "Watch them children, Bobby Lee," he said. "You know they make me nervous." He looked at the six of them huddled together in front of him and he seemed to be embarrassed as if he couldn't think of anything to say. "Ain't a cloud in the sky," he remarked, looking up at it. "Don't see no sun but don't see no cloud neither."

"Yes, it's a beautiful day," said the grandmother. "Listen," she said, "you shouldn't call yourself The Misfit because I know you're a good man at heart. I can just look at you and tell."

"Hush!" Bailey yelled, "Hush! Everybody shut up and let me handle this!" He was squatting in the position of a runner about to sprint forward but he didn't move.

"I pre-chate that, lady," The Misfit said and drew a little circle in the ground with the butt of his gun.

"It'll take a half a hour to fix this here car," Hiram called, looking over the raised hood of it.

"Well, first you and Bobby Lee get him and that little boy to step over yonder with you," The Misfit said, pointing to Bailey and John Wesley. "The boys want to ask you something," he said to Bailey. "Would you mind stepping back in them woods there with them?"

"Listen," Bailey began, "we're in a terrible predicament! Nobody realizes what this is," and his voice cracked. His eyes were as blue and intense as the parrots in his shirt and he remained perfectly still.

The grandmother reached up to adjust her hat brim as if she were going to the woods with him but it came off in her hand. She stood staring at it and after a second she let it fall on the ground. Hiram pulled Bailey up by the arm as if he were assisting an old man. John Wesley caught hold of his father's hand and Bobby Lee followed. They went off toward the woods and just as they reached the dark edge, Bailey turned and supporting himself against a gray naked pine trunk, he shouted, "I'll be back in a minute, Mamma, wait on me!"

"Come back this instant!" his mother shrilled but they all disappeared into the woods.

"Bailey Boy!" the grandmother called in a tragic voice but she found she was looking at The Misfit squatting on the ground in front of her. "I just know you're a good man," she said desperately. "You're not a bit common!"

"Nome, I ain't a good man," The Misfit said after a second as if he had considered her statement carefully, "but I ain't the worst in the world neither. My daddy said I was a different breed of dog from my brothers and sisters. 'You know,' Daddy said, 'It's some that can live their whole life without asking about it and it's others has to know why it is, and this boy is one of the latters. He's going to be into everything!'" He put on his black hat and looked up suddenly and then away deep into the woods as if he were embarrassed again. "I'm sorry I don't have on a shirt before you ladies," he said, hunching his shoulders slightly. "We buried our clothes that we had on when we escaped and we're just making do until we can get better. We borrowed these from some folks we met," he explained.

"That's perfectly all right," the grandmother said. "Maybe Bailey has an extra shirt in his suitcase."

"I'll look and see terrectly," The Misfit said.

"Where are they taking him?" the children's mother screamed.

"Daddy was a card himself," The Misfit said. "You couldn't put anything over on him. He never got in trouble with the Authorities though. Just had the knack of handling them."

"You could be honest too if you'd only try," said the grandmother. "Think how wonderful it would be to settle down and live a comfortable life and not have to think about somebody chasing you all the time."

The Misfit kept scratching in the ground with the butt of his gun as if he were thinking about it. "Yes'm, somebody is always after you," he murmured.

The grandmother noticed how thin his shoulder blades were just behind his hat because she was standing up looking down on him. "Do you ever pray?" she asked.

He shook his head. All she saw was the black hat wiggle between his shoulder blades. "Nome," he said.

There was a pistol shot from the woods, followed closely by another. Then silence. The old lady's head jerked around. She could hear the wind move through the tree tops like a long satisfied insuck of breath. "Bailey Boy!" she called.

"I was a gospel singer for a while," The Misfit said. "I been most everything. Been in the arm service, both land and sea, at home and abroad, been twict married, been an undertaker, been with the railroads, plowed Mother Earth, been in a tornado, seen a man burnt alive oncet," and he looked up at the children's mother and the little girl who were sitting close together, their faces white and their eyes glassy; "I even seen a woman flogged," he said.

"Pray, pray," the grandmother began, "pray, pray. . . ."

"I never was a bad boy that I remember of," The Misfit said in an almost dreamy voice, "but somewheres along the line I done something wrong and got sent to the penitentiary. I was buried alive," and he looked up and held her attention to him by a steady stare.

"That's when you should have started to pray," she said. "What did you do to get sent up to the penitentiary that first time?"

"Turn to the right, it was a wall," The Misfit said, looking up again at the cloudless sky. "Turn to the left, it was a wall. Look up it was a ceiling, look down it was a floor. I forget what I done, lady. I set there and set there, trying to remember what it was I done and I ain't recalled it to this day. Oncet in a while, I would think it was coming to me, but it never come."

"Maybe they put you in by mistake," the old lady said vaguely.

"Nome," he said. "It wasn't no mistake. They had the papers on me."

"You must have stolen something," she said.

The Misfit sneered slightly. "Nobody had nothing I wanted," he said. "It was a head-doctor at the penitentiary said what I had done was kill my daddy but I known that for a lie. My daddy died in nineteen ought nineteen of the epidemic flu and I never had a thing to do with it. He was buried in the Mount Hopewell Baptist churchyard and you can go there and see for yourself."

"If you would pray," the old lady said, "Jesus would help you."

"That's right," The Misfit said.

"Well then, why don't you pray?" she asked trembling with delight suddenly.

"I don't want no hep," he said. "I'm doing all right by myself."

Bobby Lee and Hiram came ambling back from the woods. Bobby Lee was dragging a yellow shirt with bright blue parrots on it.

"Throw me that shirt, Bobby Lee," The Misfit said. The shirt came flying at him and landed on his shoulder and he put it on. The grandmother couldn't name what the shirt reminded her of. "No, lady," The Misfit said while he was buttoning it up, "I found out the crime don't matter. You can do one thing or you can do another, kill a man or take a tire off his car, because sooner or later you're going to forget what it was you done and just be punished for it."

The children's mother had begun to make heaving noises as if she couldn't get her breath. "Lady," he asked, "would you and that little girl like to step off yonder with Bobby Lee and Hiram and join your husband?"

"Yes, thank you," the mother said faintly. Her left arm dangled helplessly and she was holding the baby, who had gone to sleep, in the other.

"Hep that lady up, Hiram," The Misfit said as she struggled to climb out of the ditch, "and Bobby Lee, you hold onto that little girl's hand."

"I don't want to hold hands with him," June Star said. "He reminds me of a pig."

The fat boy blushed and laughed and caught her by the arm and pulled her off into the woods after Hiram and her mother.

Alone with The Misfit, the grandmother found that she had lost her voice. There was not a cloud in the sky nor any sun. There was nothing around her but woods. She wanted to tell him that he must pray. She opened and closed her mouth several times before anything came out. Finally she found herself saying, "Jesus, Jesus," meaning, Jesus will help you, but the way she was saying it, it sounded as if she might be cursing.

"Yes'm," The Misfit said as if he agreed. "Jesus thown everything off balance. It was the same case with Him as with me except He hadn't committed any crime and they could prove I had committed one because they had the papers on me. Of course," he said, "they never shown me my papers. That's why I sign myself now. I said long ago, you get you a signature and sign everything you do and keep a copy of it. Then you'll know what you done and you can hold up the crime to the punishment and see do they match and in the end you'll have something to prove you ain't been treated right. I call myself The Misfit," he said, "because I can't make what all I done wrong fit what all I gone through in punishment."

There was a piercing scream from the woods, followed closely by a pistol report. "Does it seem right to you, lady, that one is punished a heap and another ain't punished at all?"

"Jesus!" the old lady cried. "You've got good blood! I know you wouldn't shoot a lady! I know you come from nice people! Pray! Jesus, you ought not to shoot a lady. I'll give you all the money I've got!"

"Lady," The Misfit said, looking beyond her far into the woods, "there never was a body that give the undertaker a tip."

There were two more pistol reports and the grandmother raised her head like a parched old turkey hen crying for water and called, "Bailey Boy, Bailey Boy!" as if her heart would break.

"Jesus was the only One that ever raised the dead," The Misfit continued, "and He shouldn't have done it. He thown everything off balance. If He did what He said, then it's nothing for you to do but thow away everything and follow Him, and if He didn't, then it's nothing for you to do but enjoy the few minutes you got left the best way you can—by killing somebody or burning down his house or doing some other meanness to him. No pleasure but meanness," he said and his voice had become almost a snarl.

"Maybe He didn't raise the dead," the old lady mumbled, not knowing what she was saying and feeling so dizzy that she sank down in the ditch with her legs twisted under her.

"I wasn't there so I can't say He didn't," The Misfit said. "I wisht I had of been there," he said, hitting the ground with his fist. "It ain't right I wasn't there because if I had of been there I would of known. Listen lady," he said in a high voice, "if I had of been there I would of known and I wouldn't be like I am now." His voice seemed about to crack and the grandmother's head cleared for an instant. She saw the man's face twisted close to her own as if he were going to cry and she murmured, "Why you're one of my babies. You're one of my own children!" She reached out and touched him on the shoulder. The Misfit sprang back as if a snake had bitten him and shot her three times through the chest. Then he put his gun down on the ground and took off his glasses and began to clean them.

Hiram and Bobby Lee returned from the woods and stood over the ditch, looking down at the grandmother who half sat and half lay in a puddle of blood with her legs crossed under her like a child's and her face smiling up at the cloudless sky.

Without his glasses, The Misfit's eyes were red-rimmed and pale and defenseless-looking. "Take her off and thow her where you thown the others," he said, picking up the cat that was rubbing itself against his leg.

"She was a talker, wasn't she?" Bobby Lee said, sliding down the ditch with a yodel.

"She would of been a good woman," The Misfit said, "if it had been somebody there to shoot her every minute of her life."

"Some fun!" Bobby Lee said.

"Shut up, Bobby Lee," The Misfit said. "It's no real pleasure in life."

—*1953*

Questions: Reading, Responding, Arguing

1. The Southern Gothic tradition uses supernatural, grotesque, or ironic events to explore the values and themes of the American South. Connect this story with the tradition of the Southern Gothic.

2. Analyze how O'Connor describes/conveys the family dynamic.
3. How does the story mix tragic and comic elements?
4. Discuss O'Connor's use of foreshadowing and coincidence.
5. Discuss the concept of "a good man." Why is a good one hard to find? Craft an argument about the central importance of Jesus to the story's theme.

J. G. Ballard (b. 1930)

Time of Passage

Sunlight spilled among the flowers and tombstones, turning the cemetery into a bright garden of sculpture. Like two large gaunt crows, the gravediggers leaned on their spades between the marble angels, their shadows arching across the smooth white flank of one of the recent graves.

The gilt lettering was still fresh and untarnished.

JAMES FALKMAN

1963–1901

"The End is but the Beginning"

Leisurely they began to pare back the crisp turf, then dismantled the headstone and swathed it in a canvas sheet, laying it behind the graves in the next aisle. Biddle, the older of the two, a lean man in a black waistcoat, pointed to the cemetery gates, where the first mourning party approached.

"They're here. Let's get our backs into it."

The younger man, Biddle's son, watched the small procession winding through the graves. His nostrils scented the sweet broken earth. "They're always early," he murmured reflectively. "It's a strange thing, you never see them come on time."

A clock tolled from the chapel among the cypresses. Working swiftly, they scooped out the soft earth, piling it into a neat cone at the grave's head. A few minutes later, when the sexton arrived with the principal mourners, the polished teak of the coffin was exposed, and Biddle jumped down onto the lid and scraped away the damp earth clinging to its brass rim.

The ceremony was brief and the twenty mourners, led by Falkman's sister, a tall white-haired woman with a narrow autocratic face, leaning on her husband's arm, soon returned to the chapel. Biddle gestured to his son. They jerked the coffin out of the ground and loaded it onto a cart, strapping it down under the harness. Then they heaped the earth back into the grave and relaid the squares of turf.

As they pushed the cart back to the chapel the sunlight shone brightly among the thinning graves.

Forty-eight hours later the coffin arrived at James Falkman's large gray-stoned house on the upper slopes of Mortmere Park. The high-walled avenue was almost deserted and few people saw the hearse enter the tree-lined drive. The blinds were drawn over the windows, and huge wreaths rested among the furniture in the hall where Falkman lay motionless in his coffin on a mahogany table. Veiled by the dim light, his square, strong-jawed face seemed composed and unblemished, a short lock of hair over his forehead making his expression less severe than his sister's.

A solitary beam of sunlight, finding its way through the dark sycamores which guarded the house, slowly traversed the room as the morning progressed, and shone for a few minutes upon Falkman's open eyes. Even after the beam had moved away a faint glimmer of light still remained in the pupils, like the reflection of a star glimpsed in the bottom of a dark well.

All day, helped by two of her friends, sharp-faced women in long black coats, Falkman's sister moved quietly about the house. Her quick deft hands shook the dust from the velvet curtains in the library, wound the miniature Louis XV clock on the study desk, and reset the great barometer on the staircase. None of the women spoke to each other, but within a few hours the house was transformed, the dark wood in the hall gleaming as the first callers were admitted.

"Mr. and Mrs. Montefiore . . ."

"Mr. and Mrs. Caldwell . . ."

"Miss Evelyn Jermyn and Miss Elizabeth . . ."

"Mr. Samuel Banbury . . ."

One by one, nodding in acknowledgment as they were announced, the callers trooped into the hall and paused over the coffin, examining Falkman's face with discreet interest, then passed into the dining room where they were presented with a glass of port and a tray of sweetmeats. Most of them were elderly, overdressed in the warm spring weather, one or two obviously ill at ease in the great oak-paneled house, and all unmistakably revealed the same air of hushed expectancy.

The following morning Falkman was lifted from his coffin and carried upstairs to the bedroom overlooking the drive. The winding sheet was removed from his frail body dressed in a pair of thick woolen pajamas. He lay quietly between the cold sheets, his gray face sightless and reposed, unaware of his sister crying softly on the high-backed chair beside him. Only when Dr. Markham called and put his hand on her shoulder did she contain herself, relieved to have given way to her feelings.

Almost as if this were a signal, Falkman opened his eyes. For a moment they wavered uncertainly, the pupils weak and watery. Then he gazed up at his sister's tear-marked face, his head motionless on the pillow. As she and the doctor leaned forward Falkman smiled fleetingly, his lips parting across his teeth in an expression of immense patience and understanding. Then, apparently exhausted, he lapsed into a deep sleep.

After securing the blinds over the windows, his sister and the doctor stepped from the room. Below, the doors closed quietly into the drive, and the house became silent. Gradually the sounds of Falkman's breathing grew more steady and filled the bedroom, overlaid by the swaying of the dark trees outside.

So James Falkman made his arrival. For the next week he lay quietly in his bedroom, his strength increasing hourly, and managed to eat his first meals prepared by his sister. She sat in the blackwood chair, her mourning habit exchanged for a gray woolen dress, examining him critically.

"Now, James, you'll have to get a better appetite than that. Your poor body is completely wasted."

Falkman pushed away the tray and let his long slim hands fall across his chest. He smiled amiably at his sister. "Careful, Betty, or you'll turn me into a milk pudding."

His sister briskly straightened the eiderdown. "If you don't like my cooking, James, you can fend for yourself."

A faint chuckle slipped between Falkman's lips. "Thank you for telling me, Betty, I fully intend to."

He lay back, smiling weakly to himself as his sister stalked out with the tray. Teasing her did him almost as much good as the meals she prepared, and he felt the blood reaching down into his cold feet. His face was still gray and flaccid, and he conserved his strength carefully, only his eyes moving as he watched the ravens alighting on the window ledge.

Gradually, as his conversations with his sister became more frequent, Falkman gained sufficient strength to sit up. He began to take a fuller interest in the world around him, watching the people in the avenue through the French windows and disputing his sister's commentary on them.

"There's Sam Banbury again," she remarked testily as a small leprechaunlike old man hobbled past. "Off to the Swan as usual. When's he going to get a job, I'd like to know."

"Be more charitable, Berry. Sam's a very sensible fellow. I'd rather go to the pub than have a job."

His sister snorted skeptically, her assessment of Falkman's character apparently at variance with this statement. "You've got one of the finest houses in Mortmere Park," she told him. "I think you should be more careful with people like Sam Banbury. He's not in your class, James."

Falkman smiled patiently at his sister. "We're all in the same class, or have you been here so long you've forgotten, Betty."

"We all forget," she told him soberly. "You will too, James. It's sad, but we're in this world now, and we must concern ourselves with it. If the church can keep the memory alive for us, so much the better. As you'll find out though, the majority of folk remember nothing. Perhaps it's a good thing."

She grudgingly admitted the first visitors, fussing about so that Falkman could barely exchange a word with them. In fact, the visits tired him, and he could do little more than pass a few formal pleasantries. Even when Sam Banbury brought him a pipe and tobacco pouch he had to muster all his energy to thank him and had none left to prevent his sister from making off with them.

Only when the Reverend Matthews called did Falkman manage to summon together his strength, for half an hour spoke earnestly to the parson, who listened with rapt attention, interjecting a few eager questions. When the Reverend left he seemed refreshed and confident, and strode down the stairs with a gay smile at Falkman's sister.

Within three weeks Falkman was out of bed, and managed to hobble downstairs and inspect the house and garden. His sister protested, dogging his slow painful foot-steps with sharp reminders of his feebleness, but Falkman ignored her. He found his way to the conservatory, and leaned against one of the ornamental columns, his nervous fingers feeling the leaves of the miniature trees, the scent of flowers flushing his face. Outside, in the grounds, he examined everything around him, as if comparing it with some Elysian paradise[1] in his mind.

---

[1]*Elysian paradise:* The Elysian Fields were inhabited by the dead in Greek mythology.

He was walking back to the house when he twisted his ankle sharply in the crazy paving. Before he could cry for help he had fallen headlong across the hard stones.

"James Falkman, will you never listen?" his sister protested, as she helped him across the terrace. "I warned you to stay in bed!"

Reaching the lounge, Falkman sat down thankfully in an armchair, reassembling his stunned limbs. "Quiet, Betty, do you mind," he admonished his sister when his breath returned. "I'm still here, and I'm perfectly well."

He had stated no more than the truth. After the accident he began to recover spectacularly, his progress toward complete health accelerating without a break, as if the tumble had freed him from the lingering fatigue and discomfort of the previous weeks. His step became brisk and lively, his complexion brightened, a soft pink glow filling out his cheeks, and he moved busily around the house.

A month afterward his sister returned to her own home, acknowledging his ability to look after himself, and her place was taken by the housekeeper. After re-establishing himself in the house, Falkman became increasingly interested in the world outside. He hired a comfortable car and chauffeur, and spent most of the winter afternoons and evenings at his club; soon he found himself the center of a wide circle of acquaintants. He became the chairman of a number of charitable committees, where his good humor, tolerance and shrewd judgment made him well respected. He now held himself erect, his gray hair sprouting luxuriantly, here and there touched by black flecks, jaw jutting firmly from suntanned cheeks.

Every Sunday he attended the morning and evening services at his church, where he owned a private pew, and was somewhat saddened to see that only the older people formed the congregation. However, he himself found that the picture painted by the liturgy became increasingly detached from his own memories as the latter faded, too soon became a meaningless charade that he could accept only by an act of faith.

A few years later, when he became increasingly restless, he decided to accept the offer of a partnership in a leading firm of stock brokers.

Many of his acquaintants at the club were also finding jobs, forsaking the placid routines of smoking room and conservatory garden. Harold Caldwell, one of his closest friends, was appointed Professor of History at the university, and Sam Banbury became manager of the Swan Hotel.

The ceremony on Falkman's first day at the stock exchange was dignified and impressive. Three junior men also joining the firm were introduced to the assembled staff by the senior partner, Mr. Montefiore, and each presented with a gold watch to symbolize the years he would spend with the firm. Falkman received an embossed silver cigar case and was loudly applauded.

For the next five years Falkman threw himself wholeheartedly into his work, growing more extrovert and aggressive as his appetite for the material pleasures of life increased. He became a keen golfer; then, as the exercise strengthened his physique, played his first games of tennis. An influential member of the business community, his days passed in a pleasant round of conferences and dinner parties. He no longer attended the church, but instead spent his Sundays escorting the more attractive of his lady acquaintances to the race tracks and regattas.

He found it all the more surprising, therefore, when a persistent mood of dejection began to haunt him. Although without any apparent source, this deepened slowly, and he found himself reluctant to leave his house in the evenings. He resigned from his committees and no longer visited his club. At the stock exchange he felt permanently distracted, and would stand for hours by the window, staring down at the traffic.

Finally, when his grasp of the business began to slip, Mr. Montefiore suggested that he go on indefinite leave.

For a week Falkman listlessly paced around the huge empty house. Sam Banbury frequently called to see him, but Falkman's sense of grief was beyond any help. He drew the blinds over the windows and changed into a black tie and suit, sat blankly in the darkened library.

At last, when his depression had reached its lowest ebb, he went to the cemetery to collect his wife.

After the congregation had dispersed, Falkman paused outside the vestry to tip the gravedigger, Biddle, and compliment him on his young son, a cherubic three-year-old who was playing among the headstones. Then he rode back to Mortmere Park in the car following the hearse, the remainder of the cortege behind him.

"A grand turnout, James," his sister told him approvingly. "Twenty cars altogether, not including the private ones."

Falkman thanked her, his eyes examining his sister with critical detachment. In the fifteen years he had known her she had coarsened perceptibly, her voice roughening and her gestures becoming broader. A distinct social gap had always separated them, a division which

Falkman had accepted charitably, but it was now widening markedly. Her husband's business had recently begun to fail, and her thoughts had turned almost exclusively to the subjects of money and social prestige.

As Falkman congratulated himself on his good sense and success, a curious premonition, indistinct but nonetheless disturbing, stirred through his mind.

Like Falkman himself fifteen years earlier, his wife first lay in her coffin in the hall, the heavy wreaths transforming it into a dark olive-green bower. Behind the lowered blinds the air was dim and stifled, and with her rich red hair flaring off her forehead, and her broad cheeks and full lips, his wife seemed to Falkman like some sleeping enchantress in a magical arbor. He gripped the silver foot rail of the coffin and stared at her mindlessly, aware of his sister shepherding the guests to the port and whisky. He traced with his eyes the exquisite dips and hollows around his wife's neck and chin, the white skin sweeping smoothly to her strong shoulders. The next day, when she was carried upstairs, her presence filled the bedroom. All afternoon he sat beside her, waiting patiently for her to wake.

Shortly after five o'clock, in the few minutes of light left before the dusk descended, when the air hung motionlessly under the trees in the garden, a faint echo of life moved across her face. Her eyes cleared and then focused on the ceiling.

Breathlessly, Falkman leaned forward and took one of her cold hands. Far within it, the pulse sounded faintly.

"Marion," he whispered.

Her head inclined slightly, lips parting in a weak smile. For several moments she gazed serenely at her husband.

"Hello, Jamie."

His wife's arrival completely rejuvenated Falkman. A devoted husband, he was soon completely immersed in their life together. As she recovered from the long illness after her arrival, Falkman entered the prime of his life. His gray hair became sleek and black, his face grew thicker, the chin firmer and stronger. He returned to the stock exchange, taking up his job with renewed interest.

He and Marion made a handsome couple. At intervals they would visit the cemetery and join in the service celebrating the arrival of another of their friends, but these became less frequent. Other parties continually visited the cemetery, thinning the ranks of graves, and large areas had reverted to open lawn as the coffins were withdrawn and the tombstones removed. The firm of undertakers near the cemetery which was responsible for notifying mourning relatives closed down and was sold. Finally, after the gravedigger, Biddle, recovered his own wife from the last of the graves the cemetery was converted into a children's playground.

The years of their marriage were Falkman's happiest. With each successive summer Marion became slimmer and more youthful, her red hair a brilliant diadem that stood out among the crowds in the street when she came to see him. They would walk home arm in arm, in the summer evenings pause among the willows by the river to embrace each other like lovers.

Indeed, their happiness became such a byword among their friends that over two hundred guests attended the church ceremony celebrating the long years of their marriage. As they knelt together at the altar before the priest, Marion seemed to Falkman like a demure rose.

This was the last night they were to spend together. Over the years Falkman had become less interested in his work at the stock exchange, and the arrival of older and more serious men had resulted in a series of demotions for him. Many of his friends were facing similar problems. Harold Caldwell had been forced to resign his professorship and was now a junior lecturer, taking postgraduate courses to familiarize himself with the great body of new work that had been done in the previous thirty years. Sam Banbury was a waiter at the Swan Hotel.

Marion went to live with her parents, and the Falkman's apartment, to which they had moved some years earlier after the house was closed and sold, was let to new tenants. Falkman, whose tastes had become simpler as the years passed, took a room in a hostel for young men, but he and Marion saw each other every evening. He felt increasingly restless, half conscious that his life was moving toward an inescapable focus, and often thought of giving up his job.

Marion remonstrated with him. "But you'll lose everything you've worked for, Jamie. All those years."

Falkman shrugged, chewing on a stem of grass as they lay in the park during one of their lunch hours. Marion was now a salesgirl in a department store.

"Perhaps, but I resent being demoted. Even Montefiore is leaving. His grandfather has just been appointed chairman." He rolled over and put his head in her lap. "It's so dull in that stuffy office, with all those pious old men. I'm not satisfied with it any longer."

Marion smiled affectionately at his naïveté and enthusiasm. Falkman was now more handsome than she had ever remembered him, his suntanned face almost unlined.

"It's been wonderful together, Marion," he told her on the eve of their thirtieth anniversary. "How lucky we've been never to have had a child. Do you realize that some people even have three or four? It's absolutely tragic."

"It comes to us all, though, Jamie," she reminded him. "Some people say it's a very beautiful and noble experience, having a child."

All evening he and Marion wandered around the town together, Falkman's desire for her quickened by her increasing demureness. Since she had gone to live with her parents Marion had become almost too shy to take his hand.

Then he lost her.

Walking through the market in the town centre, they were joined by two of Marion's friends, Elizabeth and Evelyn Jermyn.

"There's Sam Banbury," Evelyn pointed out as a firework cracked from a stall on the other side of the market. "Playing the fool as usual." She and her sister clucked disapprovingly. Tight-mouthed and stern, they wore dark serge coats buttoned to their necks.

Distracted by Sam, Falkman wandered off a few steps, suddenly found that the three girls had walked away. Darting through the crowd, he tried to catch up with them, briefly glimpsed Marion's red hair.

He fought his way through the stalls, almost knocking over a barrow of vegetables, and shouted at Sam Banbury:

"Sam! Have you seen Marion?"

Banbury pocketed his crackers and helped him to scan the crowd. For an hour they searched. Finally Sam gave up and went home, leaving Falkman to hang about the cobbled square under the dim lights when the market closed, wandering among the tinsel and litter as the stall holders packed up for home.

"Excuse me, have you seen a girl here? A girl with red hair?"

"Please, she was here this afternoon."

"A girl . . ."

". . . called . . ."

Stunned, he realized that he had forgotten her name.

Shortly afterward, Falkman gave up his job and went to live with his parents. Their small red-brick house was on the opposite side of the town; between the crowded chimney pots he could sometimes see the distant slopes of Mortmere Park. His life now began a less carefree phase, as most of his energy went into helping his mother and looking after his sister Betty. By comparison with his own house his parents' home was bleak and uncomfortable, altogether alien to everything

Falkman had previously known. Although kind and respectable people, his parents' lives were circumscribed by their lack of success or education. They had no interest in music or the theater, and Falkman found his mind beginning to dull and coarsen.

His father was openly critical of him for leaving his job, but the hostility between them gradually subsided as he more and more began to dominate Falkman, restricting his freedom and reducing his pocket money, even warning him not to play with certain of his friends. In fact, going to live with his parents had taken Falkman into an entirely new world.

By the time he began to go to school Falkman had completely forgotten his past life, his memories of Marion and the great house where they had lived surrounded by servants altogether obliterated.

During his first term at school he was in a class with the older boys, whom the teacher treated as equals, but like his parents they began to extend their influence over him as the years passed. At times Falkman rebelled against this attempt to suppress his own personality, but at last they entirely dominated him, controlling his activities and molding his thoughts and speech. The whole process of education, he dimly realized, was designed to prepare him for the strange twilight world of his earliest childhood. It deliberately eliminated every trace of sophistication, breaking down, with its constant repetitions and brain-splitting exercises, all his knowledge of language and mathematics, substituting for them a collection of meaningless rhymes and chants, and out of this constructing an artificial world of total infantilism.

At last, when the process of education had reduced him almost to the stage of an inarticulate infant, his parents intervened by removing him from the school, and the final years of his life were spent at home.

"Mama, can I sleep with you?"

Mrs. Falkman looked down at the serious-faced little boy who leaned his head on her pillow. Affectionately she pinched his square jaw and then touched her husband's shoulder as he stirred. Despite the years between father and son, their two bodies were almost identical, with the same broad shoulders and broad heads, the same thick hair.

"Not today, Jamie, but soon perhaps, one day."

The child watched his mother with wide eyes, wondering why she should be crying to herself, guessing that perhaps he had touched upon one of the taboos that had exercised such a potent fascination for all the boys at school, the mystery of their ultimate destination that remained carefully shrouded by their parents and which they themselves were no longer able to grasp.

By now he was beginning to experience the first difficulties in both walking and feeding himself. He tottered about clumsily, his small piping voice tripping over his tongue. Steadily his vocabulary diminished until he knew only his mother's name. When he could no longer stand upright she would carry him in her arms, feeding him like an elderly invalid. His mind clouded, a few constants of warmth and hunger drifting through it hazily. As long as he could, he clung to his mother.

Shortly afterward, Falkman and his mother visited the lying-in hospital for several weeks. On her return Mrs. Falkman remained in bed for a few days, but gradually she began to move about more freely, slowly shedding the additional weight accumulated during her confinement.

Some nine months after she returned from the hospital, a period during which she and her husband thought continually of their son, the shared tragedy of his approaching death, a symbol of their own imminent separation, bringing them closer together, they went away on their honeymoon.

—*1964*

Questions: Reading, Responding, Arguing

1. How early in the story does Ballard tip the reader off about his chronology? Did you notice the inscription on Falkman's tombstone?

2. Is there any inconsistency in the way the author has handled Sam Banbury? Can you detect a possible error here?

3. Compare the use of time in this story with that in "A Rose for Emily" on page 356, "The Secret Miracle" on page 1185, and "Happy Endings" on page 1231. How does each story manipulate time differently from the normal expectations we have for narrative progression?

4. How does this story reflect the traditional structure of the initiation or rite-of-passage story?

5. If the story were told in conventional chronological order, would there really be any story to tell? Would the plot have a complication, rising action, climax, and so forth?

Joyce Carol Oates (b. 1938)

Where Are You Going, Where Have You Been?*

To Bob Dylan

Her name was Connie. She was fifteen and she had a quick nervous giggling habit of craning her neck to glance into mirrors or checking other people's faces to make sure her own was all right. Her mother, who noticed everything and knew everything and who hadn't much reason any longer to look at her own face, always scolded Connie about it. "Stop gawking at yourself, who are you? You think you're so pretty?" she would say. Connie would raise her eyebrows at these familiar complaints and look right through her mother, into a shadowy vision of herself as she was right at that moment: she knew she was pretty and that was everything. Her mother had been pretty once too, if you could believe those old snapshots in the album, but now her looks were gone and that was why she was always after Connie.

"Why don't you keep your room clean like your sister? How've you got your hair fixed—what the hell stinks? Hair spray? You don't see your sister using that junk."

Her sister June was twenty-four and still lived at home. She was a secretary in the high school Connie attended, and if that wasn't bad enough—with her in the same building—she was so plain and chunky and steady that Connie had to hear her praised all the time by her mother and her mother's sisters. June did this, June did that, she saved money and helped clean the house and cooked and Connie couldn't do a thing, her mind was all filled with trashy daydreams. Their father was away at work most of the time and when he came home he wanted supper and he read the newspaper at supper and after supper he went to bed. He didn't bother talking much to them, but around his bent head Connie's mother kept picking at her until Connie wished her mother was dead and she herself was dead and it was all over. "She makes me want to throw up sometimes," she complained to her friends. She had a high, breathless, amused voice which made everything she said sound a little forced, whether it was sincere or not.

There was one good thing: June went places with girlfriends of hers, girls who were just as plain and steady as she, and so when Connie wanted to do that her mother had no objections. The father of Connie's best girlfriend drove the girls the three miles to town and left them off at a shopping plaza, so that they could walk through the stores or go to a movie, and when he came to pick them up again at eleven he never bothered to ask what they had done.

They must have been familiar sights, walking around that shopping plaza in their shorts and flat ballerina slippers that always scuffed the sidewalk, with charm bracelets jingling on their thin wrists; they would lean together to whisper and laugh secretly if someone passed by who amused or interested them. Connie had long dark blond hair that drew anyone's eye to it, and she wore part of it pulled up on her head and puffed out and the rest of it she let fall down her back. She wore a pull over jersey blouse that looked one way when she was at home and another way when she was away from home. Everything about her had two sides to it, one for home and one for anywhere that was not home: her walk that could be childlike and bobbing, or languid enough to make anyone think she was hearing music in her head, her mouth which was pale and smirking most of the time, but bright and pink on these evenings out, her laugh which was cynical and drawling at home—"Ha, ha, very funny"—but high-pitched and nervous anywhere else, like the jingling of the charms on her bracelet.

Sometimes they did go shopping or to a movie, but sometimes they went across the highway, ducking fast across the busy road, to a drive-in restaurant where older kids hung out. The restaurant was shaped like a big bottle, though squatter than a real bottle, and on its cap was a revolving figure of a grinning boy who held a hamburger aloft. One night in midsummer they ran across, breathless with daring, and right away someone leaned out a car window and invited them over, but it was just a boy from high school they didn't like. It made them feel good to be able to ignore him. They went up through the maze of parked and cruising cars to the bright-lit, fly-infested restaurant, their faces pleased and expectant as if they were entering a sacred building that loomed out of the night to give them what haven and what blessing they yearned for. They sat at the counter and crossed their legs at the ankles, their thin shoulders rigid with excitement, and listened to the music that made everything so good: the music was always in the background like music at a church service, it was something to depend upon.

A boy named Eddie came in to talk with them. He sat backward on his stool, turning himself jerkily around in semicircles and then stopping and turning again, and after a while he asked Connie if she would like something to eat. She said she did and so she tapped her friend's arm on her way out—her friend pulled her face up into a brave droll look—and Connie said she would meet her at eleven, across the way. "I just hate to leave her like that," Connie said earnestly, but the boy said that she wouldn't be alone for long. So they went out to his car and on the way Connie couldn't help but let her eyes wander over the windshields and faces all around her, her face gleaming with a joy that had nothing to do with Eddie or even this place; it might have been the music. She drew her shoulders up and sucked in her breath with the pure pleasure of being alive, and just at that moment she happened to glance at a face just a few feet from hers. It was a boy with shaggy black hair, in a convertible jalopy painted gold. He stared at her and then his lips widened into a grin. Connie slit her eyes at him and turned away, but she couldn't help glancing back and there he was still watching her. He wagged a finger and laughed and said, "Gonna get you, baby," and Connie turned away again without Eddie noticing anything.

She spent three hours with him, at the restaurant where they ate hamburgers and drank Cokes in wax cups that were always sweating, and then down an alley a mile or so away, and when he left her off at five to eleven only the movie house was still open at the plaza. Her girlfriend was there, talking with a boy. When Connie came up the two girls smiled at each other and Connie said, "How was the movie?" and the girl said, "You should know." They rode off with the girl's father, sleepy and pleased, and Connie couldn't help but look at the darkened shopping plaza with its big empty parking lot and its signs that were faded and ghostly now, and over at the drive-in restaurant where cars were still circling tirelessly. She couldn't hear the music at this distance.

Next morning June asked her how the movie was and Connie said, "So-so."

She and that girl and occasionally another girl went out several times a week that way, and the rest of the time Connie spent around the house—it was summer vacation—getting in her mother's way and thinking, dreaming, about the boys she met. But all the boys fell back and dissolved into a single face that was not even a face, but an idea, a feeling, mixed up with the urgent insistent pounding of the music and the humid night air of July. Connie's mother kept dragging her back to the daylight by finding things for her to do or saying, suddenly, "What's this about the Pettinger girl?"

And Connie would say nervously, "Oh, her. That dope." She always drew thick clear lines between herself and such girls, and her mother was simple and kindly enough to believe her. Her mother was so simple, Connie thought, that it was maybe cruel to fool her so much. Her mother went scuffling around the house in old bedroom slippers and complained over the telephone to one sister about the other, then the other called up and the two of them complained about the third one. If June's name was mentioned her mother's tone was approving, and if Connie's name was mentioned it was disapproving. This did not really mean she disliked Connie and actually Connie thought that her mother preferred her to June because she was prettier, but the two of them kept up a pretense of exasperation, a sense that they were tugging and struggling over something of little value to either of them. Sometimes, over coffee, they were almost friends, but something would come up—some vexation that was like a fly buzzing suddenly around their heads—and their faces went hard with contempt.

One Sunday Connie got up at eleven—none of them bothered with church—and washed her hair so that it could dry all day long, in the sun. Her parents and sister were going to a barbecue at an aunt's house and Connie said no, she wasn't interested, rolling her eyes to let her mother know just what she thought of it. "Stay home alone then," her mother said sharply. Connie sat out back in a lawn chair and watched them drive away, her father quiet and bald, hunched around so that he could back the car out, her mother with a look that was still angry and not at all softened through the windshield, and in the back seat poor old June all dressed up as if she didn't know what a barbecue was, with all the running yelling kids and the flies. Connie sat with her eyes closed in the sun, dreaming and dazed with the warmth about her as if this were a kind of love, the caresses of love, and her mind slipped over onto thoughts of the boy she had been with the night before and how nice he had been, how sweet it always was, not the way someone like June would suppose but sweet, gentle, the way it was in movies and promised in songs; and when she opened her eyes she hardly knew where she was, the back yard ran off into weeds and a fence line of trees and behind it the sky was perfectly blue and still. The asbestos "ranch house" that was now three years old startled her—it looked small. She shook her head as if to get awake.

It was too hot. She went inside the house and turned on the radio to drown out the quiet. She sat on the edge of her bed, barefoot, and listened for an hour and a half to a program called XYZ Sunday Jamboree, record after record of hard, fast, shrieking songs she sang along with, interspersed by exclamations from "Bobby King": "An' look here you girls at Napoleon's—Son and Charley want you to pay real close attention to this song coming up!"

And Connie paid close attention herself, bathed in a glow of slow-pulsed joy that seemed to rise mysteriously out of the music itself and lay languidly about the airless little room, breathed in and breathed out with each gentle rise and fall of her chest.

After a while she heard a car coming up the drive. She sat up at once, startled, because it couldn't be her father so soon. The gravel kept crunching all the way in from the road—the driveway was long—and Connie ran to the window. It was a car she didn't know. It was an open jalopy, painted a bright gold that caught the sunlight opaquely. Her heart began to pound and her fingers snatched at her hair, checking it, and she whispered "Christ, Christ," wondering how bad she looked. The car came to a stop at the side door and the horn sounded four short taps as if this were a signal Connie knew.

She went into the kitchen and approached the door slowly, then hung out the screen door, her bare toes curling down off the step. There were two boys in the car and now she recognized the driver: he had shaggy, shabby black hair that looked crazy as a wig and he was grinning at her.

"I ain't late, am I?" he said.

"Who the hell do you think you are?" Connie said.

"Toldja I'd be out, didn't I?"

"I don't even know who you are."

She spoke sullenly, careful to show no interest or pleasure, and he spoke in a fast bright monotone. Connie looked past him to the other boy, taking her time. He had fair brown hair, with a lock that fell onto his forehead. His sideburns gave him a fierce, embarrassed look, but so far he hadn't even bothered to glance at her. Both boys wore sunglasses. The driver's glasses were metallic and mirrored everything in miniature.

"You wanta come for a ride?" he said.

Connie smirked and let her hair fall loose over one shoulder.

"Don'tcha like my car? New paint job," he said. "Hey."

"What?"

"You're cute."

She pretended to fidget, chasing flies away from the door.

"Don'tcha believe me, or what?" he said.

"Look, I don't even know who you are," Connie said in disgust.

"Hey, Ellie's got a radio, see. Mine's broke down." He lifted his friend's arm and showed her the little transistor the boy was holding, and now Connie began to hear the music. It was the same program that was playing inside the house.

"Bobby King?" she said.

"I listen to him all the time. I think he's great."

"He's kind of great," Connie said reluctantly.

"Listen, that guy's *great*. He knows where the action is."

Connie blushed a little, because the glasses made it impossible for her to see just what this boy was looking at. She couldn't decide if she liked him or if he was just a jerk, and so she dawdled in the doorway and wouldn't come down or go back inside. She said, "What's all that stuff painted on your car?"

"Can'tcha read it?" He opened the door very carefully, as if he was afraid it might fall off. He slid out just as carefully, planting his feet firmly on the ground, the tiny metallic world in his glasses slowing down like gelatine hardening and in the midst of it Connie's bright green blouse. "This here is my name, to begin with," he said. ARNOLD FRIEND was written in tarlike black letters on the side, with a drawing of a round grinning face that reminded Connie of a pumpkin, except it wore sunglasses. "I wanta introduce myself, I'm Arnold Friend and that's my real name and I'm gonna be your friend, honey, and inside the car's Ellie Oscar, he's kinda shy." Ellie brought his transistor radio up to his shoulder and balanced it there. "Now these numbers are a secret code, honey," Arnold Friend explained. He read off the numbers 33, 19, 17 and raised his eyebrows at her to see what she thought of that, but she didn't think much of it. The left rear fender had been smashed and around it was written, on the gleaming gold background—DONE BY CRAZY WOMAN DRIVER. Connie had to laugh at that. Arnold Friend was pleased at her laughter and looked up at her. "Around the other side's a lot more—you wanta come and see them?"

"No."

"Why not?"

"Why should I?"

"Don'tcha wanta see what's on the car? Don'tcha wanta go for a ride?"

"I don't know."

"Why not?"

"I got things to do."

"Like what?"

"Things."

He laughed as if she had said something funny. He slapped his thighs. He was standing in a strange way, leaning back against the car as if he were balancing himself. He wasn't tall, only an inch or so taller than she would be if she came down to him. Connie liked the way he was dressed, which was the way all of them dressed: tight faded jeans stuffed into black, scuffed boots, a belt that pulled his waist in and showed how lean he was, and a white pullover shirt that was a little soiled and showed the hard small muscles of his arms and shoulders. He looked as if he probably did hard work, lifting and carrying things. Even his neck looked muscular. And his face was a familiar face, somehow—the jaw and chin and cheeks slightly darkened, because he hadn't shaved for a day or two, and the nose long and hawklike, sniffing as if she were a treat he was going to gobble up and it was all a joke.

"Connie, you ain't telling the truth. This is your day set aside for a ride with me and you know it," he said, still laughing. The way he straightened and recovered from his fit of laughing showed that it had been all fake.

"How do you know what my name is?" she said suspiciously.

"It's Connie."

"Maybe and maybe not."

"I know my Connie," he said, wagging his finger. Now she remembered him even better, back at the restaurant, and her cheeks warmed at the thought of how she sucked in her breath just at the moment she passed him—how she must have looked to him. And he had remembered her. "Ellie and I come out here especially for you," he said. "Ellie can sit in back. How about it?"

"Where?"

"Where what?"

"Where're we going?"

He looked at her. He took off the sunglasses and she saw how pale the skin around his eyes was, like holes that were not in shadow but instead in light. His eyes were like chips of broken glass that catch the light in an amiable way. He smiled. It was as if the idea of going for a ride somewhere, to some place, was a new idea to him.

"Just for a ride, Connie sweetheart."

"I never said my name was Connie," she said.

"But I know what it is. I know your name and all about you, lots of things," Arnold Friend said. He had not moved yet but stood still leaning back against the side of his jalopy. "I took a special interest in you, such a pretty girl, and found out all about you like I know your parents and sister are gone somewheres and I know where and how long they're going to be gone, and I know who you were with last night, and your best girlfriend's name is Betty. Right?"

He spoke in a simple lilting voice, exactly as if he were reciting the words to a song. His smile assured her that everything was fine. In the car Ellie turned up the volume on his radio and did not bother to look around at them.

"Ellie can sit in the back seat," Arnold Friend said. He indicated his friend with a casual jerk of his chin, as if Ellie did not count and she should not bother with him.

"How'd you find out all that stuff?" Connie said.

"Listen: Betty Schultz and Tony Fitch and Jimmy Pettinger and Nancy Pettinger," he said, in a chant. "Raymond Stanley and Bob Hutter—"

"Do you know all those kids?"

"I know everybody."

"Look, you're kidding. You're not from around here."

"Sure."

"But—how come we never saw you before?"

"Sure you saw me before," he said. He looked down at his boots, as if he were a little offended. "You just don't remember."

"I guess I'd remember you," Connie said.

"Yeah?" He looked up at this, beaming. He was pleased. He began to mark time with the music from Ellie's radio, tapping his fists lightly together. Connie looked away from his smile to the car, which was painted so bright it almost hurt her eyes to look at it. She looked at that name, ARNOLD FRIEND. And up at the front fender was an expression that was familiar—MAN THE FLYING SAUCERS. It was an expression kids had used the year before, but didn't use this year. She looked at it for a while as if the words meant something to her that she did not yet know.

"What're you thinking about? Huh?" Arnold Friend demanded. "Not worried about your hair blowing around in the car, are you?"

"No."

"Think I maybe can't drive good?"

"How do I know?"

"You're a hard girl to handle. How come?" he said. "Don't you know I'm your friend? Didn't you see me put my sign in the air when you walked by?"

"What sign?"

"My sign." And he drew an X in the air, leaning out toward her. They were maybe ten feet apart. After his hand fell back to his side the X was still in the air, almost visible. Connie let the screen door close and stood perfectly still inside it, listening to the music from her radio and the boy's blend together. She stared at Arnold Friend. He stood there so stiffly relaxed, pretending to be relaxed, with one hand idly on the door handle as if he were keeping himself up that way and had no intention of ever moving again. She recognized most things about him, the tight jeans that showed his thighs and buttocks and the greasy leather boots and the tight shirt, and even that slippery friendly smile of his, that sleepy dreamy smile that all the boys used to get across ideas they didn't want to put into words. She recognized all this and also the singsong way he talked, slightly mocking, kidding, but serious and a little melancholy, and she recognized the way he tapped one fist against the other in homage to the perpetual music behind him. But all these things did not come together.

She said suddenly, "Hey, how old are you?"

His smile faded. She could see then that he wasn't a kid, he was much older—thirty, maybe more. At this knowledge her heart began to pound faster.

"That's a crazy thing to ask. Can'tcha see I'm your own age?"

"Like hell you are."

"Or maybe a coupla years older, I'm eighteen."

"Eighteen?" she said doubtfully.

He grinned to reassure her and lines appeared at the corners of his mouth. His teeth were big and white. He grinned so broadly his eyes became slits and she saw how thick the lashes were, thick and black as if painted with a black tarlike material. Then he seemed to become embarrassed, abruptly, and looked over his shoulder at Ellie. "*Him*, he's crazy," he said. "Ain't he a riot, he's a nut, a real character." Ellie was still listening to the music. His sunglasses told nothing about what he was thinking. He wore a bright orange shirt unbuttoned halfway to show his chest, which was a pale, bluish chest and not muscular like Arnold Friend's. His shirt collar was turned up all around and the very tips of the collar pointed out past his chin as if they were protecting him. He was pressing the transistor radio up against his ear and sat there in a kind of daze, right in the sun.

"He's kinda strange," Connie said.

"Hey, she says you're kinda strange! Kinda strange!" Arnold Friend cried. He pounded on the car to get Ellie's attention. Ellie turned for the first time and Connie saw with shock that he wasn't a kid either—he had a fair, hairless face, cheeks reddened slightly as if the veins grew too close to the surface of his skin, the face of a forty-year-old baby. Connie felt a wave of dizziness rise in her at this sight and she stared at him as if waiting for something to change the shock of the moment, make it all right again. Ellie's lips kept shaping words, mumbling along, with the words blasting in his ear.

"Maybe you two better go away," Connie said faintly.

"What? How come?" Arnold Friend cried. "We come out here to take you for a ride. It's Sunday." He had the voice of the man on the radio now. It was the same voice, Connie thought. "Don'tcha know it's Sunday all day and honey, no matter who you were with last night today you're with Arnold Friend and don't you forget it!—Maybe you better step out here," he said, and this last was in a different voice. It was a little flatter, as if the heat was finally getting to him.

"No. I got things to do."

"Hey."

"You two better leave."

"We ain't leaving until you come with us."

"Like hell I am—"

"Connie, don't fool around with me. I mean, I mean, don't fool *around*," he said, shaking his head. He laughed incredulously. He placed his sunglasses on top of his head, carefully, as if he were indeed wearing a wig, and brought the stems down behind his ears. Connie stared at him, another wave of dizziness and fear rising in her so that for a moment he wasn't even in focus but was just a blur, standing there against his gold car, and she had the idea that he had driven up the driveway all right but had come from nowhere before that and belonged nowhere and that everything about him and even about the music that was so familiar to her was only half real.

"If my father comes and sees you—"

"He ain't coming. He's at the barbecue."

"How do you know that?"

"Aunt Tillie's. Right now they're—uh—they're drinking. Sitting around," he said vaguely, squinting as if he were staring all the way to town and over to Aunt Tillie's back yard. Then the vision seemed to get clear and he nodded energetically. "Yeah. Sitting around. There's your sister in a blue dress, huh? And high heels, the poor sad bitch—nothing like you, sweetheart! And your mother's helping some fat woman with the corn, they're cleaning the corn—husking the corn—"

"What fat woman?" Connie cried.

"How do I know what fat woman. I don't know every goddam fat woman in the world!" Arnold Friend laughed.

"Oh, that's Mrs. Hornby . . . Who invited her?" Connie said. She felt a little light-headed. Her breath was coming quickly.

"She's too fat. I don't like them fat. I like them the way you are, honey," he said, smiling sleepily at her. They stared at each other for a while, through the screen door. He said softly, "Now what you're going to do is this: you're going to come out that door. You're going to sit up front with me and Ellie's going to sit in the back, the hell with Ellie, right? This isn't Ellie's date. You're my date. I'm your lover, honey."

"What? You're crazy—"

"Yes, I'm your lover. You don't know what that is but you will," he said. "I know that too. I know all about you. But look: it's real nice and you couldn't ask for nobody better than me, or more polite. I always keep my word. I'll tell you how it is, I'm always nice at first, the first time. I'll hold you so tight you won't think you have to try to get away or pretend anything because you'll know you can't. And I'll come inside you where it's all secret and you'll give in to me and you'll love me—"

"Shut up! You're crazy!" Connie said. She backed away from the door. She put her hands against her ears as if she'd heard something terrible, something not meant for her. "People don't talk like that, you're crazy," she muttered. Her heart was almost too big now for her chest and its pumping made sweat break out all over her. She looked out to see Arnold Friend pause and then take a step toward the porch lurching. He almost fell. But, like a clever drunken man, he managed to catch his balance. He wobbled in his high boots and grabbed hold of one of the porch posts.

"Honey?" he said. "You still listening?"

"Get the hell out of here!"

"Be nice, honey. Listen."

"I'm going to call the police—"

He wobbled again and out of the side of his mouth came a fast spat curse, an aside not meant for her to hear. But even this "Christ!" sounded forced. Then he began to smile again. She watched this smile come, awkward as if he were smiling from inside a mask. His whole face was a mask, she thought wildly, tanned down onto his throat but then running out as if he had plastered makeup on his face but had forgotten about his throat.

"Honey—? Listen, here's how it is. I always tell the truth and I promise you this: I ain't coming in that house after you."

"You better not! I'm going to call the police if you—if you don't—"

"Honey," he said, talking right through her voice, "honey, I'm not coming in there but you are coming out here. You know why?"

She was panting. The kitchen looked like a place she had never seen before, some room she had run inside but which wasn't good enough, wasn't going to help her. The kitchen window had never had a curtain, after three years, and there were dishes in the sink for her to do—probably—and if you ran your hand across the table you'd probably feel something sticky there.

"You listening, honey? Hey?"

"—going to call the police—"

"Soon as you touch the phone I don't need to keep my promise and can come inside. You won't want that."

She rushed forward and tried to lock the door. Her fingers were shaking. "But why lock it," Arnold Friend said gently, talking right into her face. "It's just a screen door. It's just nothing." One of his boots was at a strange angle, as if his foot wasn't in it. It pointed out to the left, bent at the ankle. "I mean, anybody can break through a screen door and glass and wood and iron or anything else if he needs to, anybody at all and specially Arnold Friend. If the place got lit up with a fire honey you'd come runnin' out into my arms, right into my arms an' safe at home—like you knew I was your lover and'd stopped fooling around. I don't mind a nice shy girl but I don't like no fooling around." Part of those words were spoken with a slight rhythmic lilt, and Connie somehow recognized them—the echo of a song from last year, about a girl rushing into her boyfriend's arms and coming home again—

Connie stood barefoot on the linoleum floor, staring at him. "What do you want?" she whispered.

"I want you," he said.

"What?"

"Seen you that night and thought, that's the one, yes sir. I never needed to look any more."

"But my father's coming back. He's coming to get me. I had to wash my hair first—" She spoke in a dry, rapid voice, hardly raising it for him to hear.

"No, your Daddy is not coming and yes, you had to wash your hair and you washed it for me. It's nice and shining and all for me, I thank you, sweetheart," he said, with a mock bow, but again he almost lost his balance. He had to bend and adjust his boots. Evidently his feet did not go all the way down; the boots must have been stuffed with something so that he would seem taller. Connie stared out at him and behind him Ellie in the car, who seemed to be looking off toward Connie's right, into nothing. This Ellie said, pulling the words out of the air one after another as if he were just discovering them, "You want me to pull out the phone?"

"Shut your mouth and keep it shut," Arnold Friend said, his face red from bending over or maybe from embarrassment because Connie had seen his boots. "This ain't none of your business."

"What—what are you doing? What do you want?" Connie said. "If I call the police they'll get you, they'll arrest you—"

"Promise was not to come in unless you touch that phone, and I'll keep that promise," he said. He resumed his erect position and tried to force his shoulders back. He sounded like a hero in a movie, declaring something important. He spoke too loudly and it was as if he were speaking to someone behind Connie. "I ain't made plans for coming in that house where I don't belong but just for you to come out to me, the way you should. Don't you know who I am?"

"You're crazy," she whispered. She backed away from the door but did not want to go into another part of the house, as if this would give him permission to come through the door. "What do you . . . You're crazy, you . . ."

"Huh? What're you saying, honey?"

Her eyes darted everywhere in the kitchen. She could not remember what it was, this room.

"This is how it is, honey: you come out and we'll drive away, have a nice ride. But if you don't come out we're gonna wait till your people come home and then they're all going to get it."

"You want that telephone pulled out?" Ellie said. He held the radio away from his ear and grimaced, as if without the radio the air was too much for him.

"I toldja shut up, Ellie," Arnold Friend said, "you're deaf, get a hearing aid, right? Fix yourself up. This little girl's no trouble and's gonna be nice to me, so Ellie keep to yourself, this ain't your date—right? Don't hem in on me. Don't hog. Don't crush. Don't bird dog. Don't trail me," he said in a rapid meaningless voice, as if he were running through all the expressions he'd learned but was no longer sure which one of them was in style, then rushing on to new ones, making them up with his eyes closed, "Don't crawl under my fence, don't squeeze in my chipmunk hole, don't sniff my glue, suck my popsicle, keep your own greasy fingers on yourself!" He shaded his eyes and peered in at Connie, who was backed against the kitchen table. "Don't mind him honey he's just a creep. He's a dope. Right? I'm the boy for you and like I said you come out here nice like a lady and give me your hand, and nobody else gets hurt, I mean, your nice old bald-headed daddy and your mummy and your sister in her high heels. Because listen: why bring them in this?"

"Leave me alone," Connie whispered.

"Hey, you know that old woman down the road, the one with the chickens and stuff—you know her?"

"She's dead!"

"Dead? What? You know her?" Arnold Friend said.

"She's dead—"

"Don't you like her?"

"She's dead—she's—she isn't here any more—"

"But don't you like her, I mean, you got something against her? Some grudge or something?" Then his voice dipped as if he were conscious of a rudeness. He touched the sunglasses perched on top of his head as if to make sure they were still there. "Now you be a good girl."

"What are you going to do?"

"Just two things, or maybe three," Arnold Friend said. "But I promise it won't last long and you'll like me the way you get to like people you're close to. You will. It's all over for you here, so come on out. You don't want your people in any trouble, do you?"

She turned and bumped against a chair or something, hurting her leg, but she ran into the back room and picked up the telephone. Something roared in her ear, a tiny roaring, and she was so sick with fear that she could do nothing but listen to it—the telephone was clammy and very heavy and her fingers groped down to the dial but were too weak to touch it. She began to scream into the phone, into the roaring. She cried out, she cried for her mother, she felt her breath start jerking back and forth in her lungs as if it were something Arnold Friend were stabbing her with again and again with no tenderness. A noisy sorrowful wailing rose all about her and she was locked inside it the way she was locked inside the house.

After a while she could hear again. She was sitting on the floor with her wet back against the wall.

Arnold Friend was saying from the door, "That's a good girl. Put the phone back."

She kicked the phone away from her.

"No, honey. Pick it up. Put it back right."

She picked it up and put it back. The dial tone stopped.

"That's a good girl. Now, you come outside."

She was hollow with what had been fear, but what was now just an emptiness. All that screaming had blasted it out of her. She sat, one leg cramped under her, and deep inside her brain was something like a pinpoint of light that kept going and would not let her relax. She thought, I'm not going to see my mother again. She thought, I'm not going to sleep in my bed again. Her bright green blouse was all wet.

Arnold Friend said, in a gentle-loud voice that was like a stage voice, "The place where you came from ain't there any more, and where you had in mind to go is canceled out. This place you are now—

inside your daddy's house—is nothing but a cardboard box I can knock down any time. You know that and always did know it. You hear me?"

She thought, I have got to think. I have to know what to do.

"We'll go out to a nice field, out in the country here where it smells so nice and it's sunny," Arnold Friend said. "I'll have my arms tight around you so you won't need to try to get away and I'll show you what love is like, what it does. The hell with this house! It looks solid all right," he said. He ran a fingernail down the screen and the noise did not make Connie shiver, as it would have the day before. "Now put your hand on your heart, honey. Feel that? That feels solid too but we know better, be nice to me, be sweet like you can because what else is there for a girl like you but to be sweet and pretty and give in?—and get away before her people come back?"

She felt her pounding heart. Her hand seemed to enclose it. She thought for the first time in her life that it was nothing that was hers, that belonged to her, but just a pounding, living thing inside this body that wasn't really hers either.

"You don't want them to get hurt," Arnold Friend went on. "Now get up, honey. Get up all by yourself."

She stood.

"Now turn this way. That's right. Come over here to me—Ellie, put that away, didn't I tell you? You dope. You miserable creepy dope," Arnold Friend said. His words were not angry but only part of an incantation. The incantation was kindly. "Now come out through the kitchen to me honey, and let's see a smile, try it, you're a brave sweet little girl and now they're eating corn and hot dogs cooked to bursting over an outdoor fire, and they don't know one thing about you and never did and honey you're better than them because not a one of them would have done this for you."

Connie felt the linoleum under her feet; it was cool. She brushed her hair back out of her eyes. Arnold Friend let go of the post tentatively and opened his arms for her, his elbows pointing in toward each other and his wrists limp, to show that this was an embarrassed embrace and a little mocking, he didn't want to make her self-conscious.

She put out her hand against the screen. She watched herself push the door slowly open as if she were safe back somewhere in the other doorway, watching this body and this head of long hair moving out into the sunlight where Arnold Friend waited.

"My sweet little blue-eyed girl," he said, in a half-sung sigh that had nothing to do with her brown eyes but was taken up just the same by the vast sunlit reaches of the land behind him and on all sides of him, so much land that Connie had never seen before and did not recognize except to know that she was going to it.

—*1966*

Questions: Reading, Responding, Arguing

1. Analyze the character of Connie. What does Oates mean by "Everything about her had two sides to it"?
2. Oates uses the characters of Connie's mother and sister to explore her themes. What are those themes and how does Oates achieve this?
3. Oates is noted for her ability to create stories with terror. How is she able to convey terror in this story? What strategies does she use?
4. Compare Oates's use of terror with Ray Bradbury's use of terror in "The Veldt" on page 543. Are there differences or similarities in the ways that each author creates suspense and fear? How are these stories meaningful for us even if we aren't faced with the same dangers that threaten these protagonists?

Margaret Atwood (b. 1939)

Happy Endings

John and Mary meet.
What happens next?
If you want a happy ending, try A.

A

John and Mary fall in love and get married. They both have worthwhile and remunerative jobs which they find stimulating and challenging. They buy a charming house. Real estate values go up. Eventually, when they can afford live-in help, they have two children, to whom they are devoted. The children turn out well. John and Mary have a stimulating and

challenging sex life and worthwhile friends. They go on fun vacations together. They retire. They both have hobbies which they find stimulating
and challenging. Eventually they die. This is the end of the story.

B

Mary falls in love with John but John doesn't fall in love with Mary.
He merely uses her body for selfish pleasure and ego gratification of a
tepid kind. He comes to her apartment twice a week and she cooks him
dinner, you'll notice that he doesn't even consider her worth the price
of a dinner out, and after he's eaten the dinner he fucks her and after
that he falls asleep, while she does the dishes so he won't think she's
untidy, having all those dirty dishes lying around, and puts on fresh lipstick so she'll look good when he wakes up, but when he wakes up he
doesn't even notice, he puts on his socks and his shorts and his pants
and his shirt and his tie and his shoes, the reverse order from the one in
which he took them off. He doesn't take off Mary's clothes, she takes
them off herself, she acts as if she's dying for it every time, not because
she likes sex exactly, she doesn't, but she wants John to think she does
because if they do it often enough surely he'll get used to her, he'll come
to depend on her and they will get married, but John goes out the door
with hardly so much as a good-night and three days later he turns up at
six o'clock and they do the whole thing over again.

Mary gets run-down. Crying is bad for your face, everyone knows
that and so does Mary but she can't stop. People at work notice. Her
friends tell her John is a rat, a pig, a dog, he isn't good enough for her, but
she can't believe it. Inside John, she thinks, is another John, who is much
nicer. This other John will emerge like a butterfly from a cocoon, a Jack
from a box, a pit from a prune, if the first John is only squeezed enough.

One evening John complains about the food. He has never complained about the food before. Mary is hurt.

Her friends tell her they've seen him in a restaurant with another
woman, whose name is Madge. It's not even Madge that finally gets to
Mary: it's the restaurant. John has never taken Mary to a restaurant.
Mary collects all the sleeping pills and aspirins she can find, and takes
them and a half a bottle of sherry. You can see what kind of a woman
she is by the fact that it's not even whiskey. She leaves a note for John.
She hopes he'll discover her and get her to the hospital in time and repent and then they can get married, but this fails to happen and she dies.

John marries Madge and everything continues as in A.

C

John, who is an older man, falls in love with Mary, and Mary, who is only twenty-two, feels sorry for him because he's worried about his hair falling out. She sleeps with him even though she's not in love with him. She met him at work. She's in love with someone called James, who is twenty-two also and not yet ready to settle down.

John on the contrary settled down long ago: this is what is bothering him. John has a steady, respectable job and is getting ahead in his field, but Mary isn't impressed by him, she's impressed by James, who has a motorcycle and a fabulous record collection. But James is often away on his motorcycle, being free. Freedom isn't the same for girls, so in the meantime Mary spends Thursday evenings with John. Thursdays are the only days John can get away.

John is married to a woman called Madge and they have two children, a charming house which they bought just before the real estate values went up, and hobbies which they find stimulating and challenging, when they have the time. John tells Mary how important she is to him, but of course he can't leave his wife because a commitment is a commitment. He goes on about this more than is necessary and Mary finds it boring, but older men can keep it up longer so on the whole she has a fairly good time.

One day James breezes in on his motorcycle with some top-grade California hybrid and James and Mary get higher than you'd believe possible and they climb into bed. Everything becomes very underwater, but along comes John, who has a key to Mary's apartment. He finds them stoned and entwined. He's hardly in any position to be jealous, considering Madge, but nevertheless he's overcome with despair. Finally he's middle-aged, in two years he'll be bald as an egg and he can't stand it. He purchases a handgun, saying he needs it for target practice—this is the thin part of the plot, but it can be dealt with later—and shoots the two of them and himself.

Madge, after a suitable period of mourning, marries an understanding man called Fred and everything continues as in A, but under different names.

D

Fred and Madge have no problems. They get along exceptionally well and are good at working out any little difficulties that may arise. But their charming house is by the seashore and one day a giant tidal wave approaches. Real estate values go down. The rest of the story is about what caused the tidal wave and how they escape from it. They do, though thousands drown, but Fred and Madge are virtuous and lucky. Finally on high ground they clasp each other, wet and dripping and grateful, and continue as in A.

E

Yes, but Fred has a bad heart. The rest of the story is about how kind and understanding they both are until Fred dies. Then Madge devotes herself to charity work until the end of A. If you like, it can be "Madge," "cancer," "guilty and confused," and "bird watching."

F

If you think this is all too bourgeois, make John a revolutionary and Mary a counterespionage agent and see how far that gets you. Remember, this is Canada. You'll still end up with A, though in between you may get a lustful brawling saga of passionate involvement, a chronicle of our times, sort of.

You'll have to face it, the endings are the same however you slice it. Don't be deluded by any other endings, they're all fake, either deliberately fake, with malicious intent to deceive, or just motivated by excessive optimism if not by downright sentimentality.

The only authentic ending is the one provided here:

John and Mary die. John and Mary die. John and Mary die.

So much for endings. Beginnings are always more fun. True connoisseurs, however, are known to favor the stretch in between, since it's the hardest to do anything with.

That's about all that can be said for plots, which anyway are just one thing after another, a what and a what and a what.

Now try How and Why.

—1983

Questions: Reading, Responding, Arguing

1. Atwood's narrator writes, "True connoisseurs, however, are known to favor the stretch in between, since it's the hardest to do anything with." Discuss this comment about fiction in relation to Atwood's form and structure.

2. "Remember, this is Canada," writes the narrator. What is Atwood saying about the Canadian identity?

3. What is Atwood saying about writing fiction when she says "That's about all that can be said for plots . . . How and Why"?

William Shakespeare (1564–1616)

Sonnet 73*

That time of year thou mayst in me behold
When yellow leaves, or none, or few, do hang
Upon those boughs which shake against the cold,
Bare ruined choirs, where late the sweet birds sang.
In me thou see'st the twilight of such day   5
As after sunset fadeth in the west;
Which by and by black night doth take away,
Death's second self, that seals up all in rest.
In me thou see'st the glowing of such fire,
That on the ashes of his youth doth lie,   10
As the deathbed whereon it must expire,
Consumed with that which it was nourished by.
This thou perceiv'st, which makes thy love more strong,
To love that well which thou must leave ere long.

—*1609*

Questions: Reading, Responding, Arguing

1. Shakespeare opens his sonnet with the line "That time of year thou mayst in me behold." What time of year is he referring to? Why is this season significant? How does his diction convey this time of year?

2. The tone in this sonnet is different from "Sonnet 18" on page 974. Compare his use of language to convey tone and meaning. How does it change with the theme?

3. Discuss Shakespeare's treatment of time and season. Why is this important to the sonnet's overall message?

John Keats (1795–1821)

Bright Star!*

Bright star! would I were steadfast as thou art—
   Not in lone splendour hung aloft the night
And watching, with eternal lids apart,
   Like nature's patient, sleepless Eremite,
The moving waters at their priestlike task   5
   Of pure ablution round earth's human shores,
Or gazing on the new soft-fallen mask
   Of snow upon the mountains and the moors—
No—yet still steadfast, still unchangeable,
   Pillowed upon my fair love's ripening breast,   10
To feel for ever its soft swell and fall,
   Awake for ever in a sweet unrest,
Still, still to hear her tender-taken breath,
   And so live ever—or else swoon to death.

—*1820*

Questions: Reading, Responding, Arguing

1. How does Keats negate the first line of the poem as it proceeds?
2. Keats wrote this poem in the final year of his life after separation from his fiancée. How does the poem reflect this situation?
3. What other metaphors from nature does Keats use here?
4. How does Keats use the sonnet form? Argue that the sonnet form is appropriate for this subject.

Alfred, Lord Tennyson (1809–1892)

Ulysses°

It little profits that an idle king,
By this still hearth, among these barren crags,
Matched with an aged wife, I mete and dole
Unequal laws unto a savage race,
That hoard, and sleep, and feed, and know not me.   5
I cannot rest from travel; I will drink
Life to the lees. All times I have enjoyed
Greatly, have suffered greatly, both with those
That loved me, and alone; on shore, and when
Through scudding drifts the rainy Hyades°   10
Vexed the dim sea. I am become a name;
For always roaming with a hungry heart
Much have I seen and known—cities of men
And manners, climates, councils, governments,
Myself not least, but honored of them all—   15
And drunk delight of battle with my peers,
Far on the ringing plains of windy Troy.
I am a part of all that I have met;
Yet all experience is an arch wherethrough
Gleams that untraveled world whose margin fades   20
For ever and for ever when I move.
How dull it is to pause, to make an end,
To rust unburnished, not to shine in use!
As though to breathe were life! Life piled on life
Were all too little, and of one to me   25
Little remains; but every hour is saved
From that eternal silence, something more,
A bringer of new things; and vile it were
For some three suns to store and hoard myself,
And this gray spirit yearning in desire   30
To follow knowledge like a sinking star,
Beyond the utmost bound of human thought.
      This is my son, mine own Telemachus,

Ulysses Homer's *Odyssey* ends with the return of Odysseus (Ulysses) to his island kingdom, Ithaca.
Tennyson's poem takes place some years later.   **10 Hyades** a constellation thought to predict rain

To whom I leave the scepter and the isle,
Well-loved of me, discerning to fulfill   35
This labor, by slow prudence to make mild
A rugged people, and through soft degrees
Subdue them to the useful and the good.
Most blameless is he, centered in the sphere
Of common duties, decent not to fail   40
In offices of tenderness, and pay
Meet adoration to my household gods,
When I am gone. He works his work, I mine.
　　There lies the port; the vessel puffs her sail;
There gloom the dark, broad seas. My mariners,   45
Souls that have toiled, and wrought, and thought with me,
That ever with a frolic welcome took
The thunder and the sunshine, and opposed
Free hearts, free foreheads—you and I are old;
Old age hath yet his honor and his toil.   50
Death closes all; but something ere the end,
Some work of noble note, may yet be done,
Not unbecoming men that strove with gods.
The lights begin to twinkle from the rocks;
The long day wanes; the low moon climbs; the deep   55
Moans round with many voices. Come, my friends,
'Tis not too late to seek a newer world.
Push off, and sitting well in order smite
The sounding furrows; for my purpose holds
To sail beyond the sunset, and the baths   60
Of all the western stars, until I die.
It may be that the gulfs will wash us down;
It may be we shall touch the Happy Isles,°
And see the great Achilles, whom we knew.
Though much is taken, much abides; and though   65
We are not now that strength which in old days
Moved earth and heaven, that which we are, we are,
One equal temper of heroic hearts,
Made weak by time and fate, but strong in will
To strive, to seek, to find, and not to yield.   70

　　　　　　　　　　　　　　　　　　　　　　—*1833*

---

63 **Happy Isles** Elysium, the resting place of dead heroes

Questions: Reading, Responding, Arguing

1. Tennyson's poem takes place some years after Ulysses returns to Ithaca. What is his attitude toward the past and the present?
2. What does Ulysses mean by the phrase "I am become a name"?
3. How does Tennyson's poem relate to Homer's *Odyssey*? How does it use the story? Where is it innovative?
4. Tennyson apparently views Ulysses as a heroic character. Is it possible to argue that he is not?

Walt Whitman (1819–1892)

Song of Myself, 6

A child said *What is the grass?* fetching it to me with full hands;
How could I answer the child? I do not know what it is any more than he.

I guess it must be the flag of my disposition, out of hopeful green stuff woven.

Or I guess it is the handkerchief of the Lord,
A scented gift and remembrancer designedly dropped,   5
Bearing the owner's name someway in the corners, that we may see and remark, and say *Whose?*

Or I guess the grass is itself a child, the produced babe of the vegetation.

Or I guess it is a uniform hieroglyphic,
And it means, Sprouting alike in broad zones and narrow zones,
Growing among black folks as among white,   10
Kanuck,° Tuckahoe,° Congressman, Cuff,° I give them the same, I receive them the same.

And now it seems to me the beautiful uncut hair of graves.

Tenderly will I use you curling grass,
It may be you transpire from the breasts of young men,

11 **Kanuck** French-Canadian **Tuckahoe** coastal Virginian **Cuff** a black slave

It may be if I had known them I would have loved them,   15
It may be you are from old people, or from offspring taken
   soon out of their mothers' laps,
And here you are the mothers' laps.

This grass is very dark to be from the white heads of old mothers.
Darker than the colorless beards of old men.
Dark to come from under the faint red roofs of mouths.   20

O I perceive after all so many uttering tongues,
And I perceive they do not come from the roofs of mouths for
   nothing.

I wish I could translate the hints about the dead young men
   and women,
And the hints about old men and mothers, and the offspring
   taken soon out of their laps.

What do you think has become of the young and old men?   25
And what do you think has become of the women and children?

They are alive and well somewhere,
The smallest sprout shows there is really no death,
And if ever there was it led forward life, and does not wait at
   the end to arrest it.
And ceased the moment life appeared.   30

All goes onward and outward, nothing collapses.
And to die is different from what anyone supposed, and luckier.

—*1855*

Questions: Reading, Responding, Arguing

1. How does Whitman use grass as a central image? What is it
   symbolic of? Representative of?
2. This poem makes reference to children, the elderly, and the
   dead. How does Whitman connect these groups with the image of grass?
3. Explain the significance of the line "All goes onward and
   outward, nothing collapses." How does this line contribute
   to the poem's themes and meanings? What is Whitman's
   overall argument about death?
4. Compare this poem to Donne's "Holy Sonnet 10" on page 576.

Matthew Arnold (1822–1888)

Dover Beach

The sea is calm tonight.
The tide is full, the moon lies fair
Upon the straits; on the French coast the light
Gleams and is gone; the cliffs of England stand,
Glimmering and vast, out in the tranquil bay.   5
Come to the window, sweet is the night-air!
Only, from the long line of spray
Where the sea meets the moon-blanched land,
Listen! you hear the grating roar
Of pebbles which the waves draw back, and fling,   10
At their return, up the high strand,
Begin, and cease, and then again begin,
With tremulous cadence slow, and bring
The eternal note of sadness in.

Sophocles° long ago   15
Heard it on the Aegean, and it brought
Into his mind the turbid ebb and flow
Of human misery; we
Find also in the sound a thought,
Hearing it by this distant northern sea.   20

The Sea of Faith
Was once, too, at the full, and round earth's shore
Lay like the folds of a bright girdle° furled.
But now I only hear
Its melancholy, long, withdrawing roar,   25
Retreating, to the breath
Of the night-wind, down the vast edges drear
And naked shingles° of the world.

Ah, love, let us be true
To one another! for the world, which seems   30
To lie before us like a land of dreams,

---

15 Sophocles Athenian tragic poet (496–406 BC)   **23 girdle** sash   **28 shingles** beach pebbles

So various, so beautiful, so new,
Hath really neither joy, nor love, nor light,
Nor certitude, nor peace, nor help for pain;
And we are here as on a darkling plain   35
Swept with confused alarms of struggle and flight,
Where ignorant armies clash by night.

—*1867*

Questions: Reading, Responding, Arguing

1. The sea is not only the setting for the poem but it is also the poem's central image. Explain Arnold's use of the sea.
2. Who is the "you" in the poem? How does this person relate to the poem's central themes and ideas?
3. Analyze Arnold's description of the ocean. What does he say about the ocean and how does it reflect the section's theme of time, aging, and death?
4. Argue that this poem is thematically similar to Marvell's "To His Coy Mistress" on page 978.

Emily Dickinson (1830–1886)

Because I could not stop for Death*

Because I could not stop for Death—
He kindly stopped for me—
The Carriage held but just Ourselves—
And Immortality.

We slowly drove—He knew no haste   5
And I had put away
My labor and my leisure too,
For His Civility—

We passed the School, where Children strove
At Recess—in the Ring—   10
We passed the Fields of Gazing Grain—
We passed the Setting Sun—

Or rather—He passed Us—
The Dews drew quivering and chill—
For only Gossamer, my Gown—   15
My Tippet°—only Tulle°—

We paused before a House that seemed
A Swelling of the Ground—
The Roof was scarcely visible—
The Cornice—in the Ground—   20

Since then—'tis Centuries—and yet
Feels shorter than the Day
I first surmised the Horses' Heads
Were toward Eternity—

—1890

Questions: Reading, Responding, Arguing

1. Examine Dickinson's use of the long dash. Why and how
   does she use these for effect?
2. What is happening in the final stanza? How do you know?
3. Dickinson personifies Death. Compare her treatment of
   Death and Eternity with the depiction offered in John
   Donne's poem, "Holy Sonnet 10" on page 576. How are
   they similar? Different?

Gerard Manley Hopkins (1844–1889)

Spring and Fall

to a young child

Márgarét, are you gríeving?
Over Goldengrove unleaving?
Leáves, líke the things of man, you
With your fresh thoughts care for, can you?
Ah! ás the heart grows older   5

16 Tippet shawl Tulle net-like fabric

It will come to such sights colder
By and by, nor spare a sigh
Though worlds of wanwood leafmeal lie;
And yet you will weep and know why.
Now no matter, child, the name: 10
Sórrow's spríngs áre the same.
Nor mouth had, no nor mind, expressed
What heart heard of, ghost guessed:
It ís the blight man was born for,
It is Margaret you mourn for.   15

—1880

Questions: Reading, Responding, Arguing

1. What is unusual about Hopkins's diction and syntax in this poem? Why are his sound patterns important?
2. What does this poem have to say about "spring"?
3. What does Hopkins mean by "what heart heard of, ghost guessed"?
4. Compare the theme of this poem with that of other poems which use the *carpe diem* theme (such as Marvell's "To His Coy Mistress"). How does Hopkins avoid the implicit sexual content of such poems?

A. E. Housman (1859–1936)

Loveliest of Trees, the Cherry Now

Loveliest of trees, the cherry now
Is hung with bloom along the bough,
And stands about the woodland ride
Wearing white for Eastertide.

Now, of my threescore years and ten,
Twenty will not come again,   5

And take from seventy springs a score,
It only leaves me fifty more.

And since to look at things in bloom
Fifty springs are little room,   10
About the woodlands I will go
To see the cherry hung with snow.

—*1896*

Questions: Reading, Responding, Arguing

1. What's the significance of the cherry tree?
2. Compare Housman's depiction of nature with another poet in this anthology. Do the two have different visions of nature, or nature's influence?
3. Examine the theme of age and time in this poem.

Wallace Stevens (1879–1955)

The Emperor of Ice-Cream

Call the roller of big cigars,
The muscular one, and bid him whip
In kitchen cups concupiscent° curds.
Let the wenches dawdle in such dress
As they are used to wear, and let the boys   5
Bring flowers in last month's newspapers.
Let be be finale of seem.
The only emperor is the emperor of ice-cream.

Take from the dresser of deal,°
Lacking the three glass knobs, that sheet   10
On which she embroidered fantails° once
And spread it so as to cover her face.

3 concupiscent lustful   9 deal cheap wood   11 fantails pigeons

If her horny feet protrude, they come
To show how cold she is, and dumb.
Let the lamp affix its beam.   15
The only emperor is the emperor of ice-cream.

—*1923*

Questions: Reading, Responding, Arguing

1. Who is the "she" referred to in the poem? What is the dramatic situation here?
2. Discuss how Stevens blends commands and statements in the poem.
3. What are the symbolic implications of ice-cream and other items in the poem? What does it mean to be "the emperor of ice-cream"? How is this phrase central to Stevens's argument about death?

William Carlos Williams (1883–1963)

The Last Words of My English Grandmother

There were some dirty plates
and a glass of milk
beside her on a small table
near the rank, disheveled bed—

Wrinkled and nearly blind   5
she lay and snored
rousing with anger in her tones
to cry for food,

Gimme something to eat—
They're starving me—   10
I'm all right—I won't go
to the hospital. No, no, no

Give me something to eat!
Let me take you

to the hospital, I said   15
and after you are well

you can do as you please.
She smiled, Yes
you do what you please first
then I can do what I please—   20

Oh, oh, oh! she cried
as the ambulance men lifted
her to the stretcher—
Is this what you call

making me comfortable?   25
By now her mind was clear—
Oh you think you're smart
you young people,

she said, but I'll tell you
you don't know anything.   30
Then we started.
On the way

We passed a long row
of elms. She looked at them
awhile out of   35
the ambulance window and said,

What are all those
fuzzy-looking things out there?
Trees? Well, I'm tired
of them and rolled her head away.   40

                                                      —1920

Questions: Reading, Responding, Arguing

1. Discuss the importance of setting in this poem.
2. How does dialogue function in the poem? What does it reveal about the characters and their relationship?
3. What is the significance of the grandmother's last words?
4. Argue that this poem reflects aging as a serious problem in
   society.

W. H. Auden (1907–1973)

As I Walked Out One Evening

As I walked out one evening,
　　Walking down Bristol Street,
The crowds upon the pavement
　　Were fields of harvest wheat.

And down by the brimming river　　　　　　　　5
　　I heard a lover sing
Under an arch of the railway:
　　"Love has no ending.

"I'll love you, dear, I'll love you
　　Till China and Africa meet,　　　　　　　　10
And the river jumps over the mountain
　　And the salmon sing in the street.

"I'll love you till the ocean
　　Is folded and hung up to dry,
And the seven stars go squawking　　　　　　　15
　　Like geese about the sky.

"The years shall run like rabbits,
　　For in my arms I hold
The Flower of the Ages,
　　And the first love of the world."　　　　　　20

But all the clocks in the city
　　Began to whirr and chime:
"O let not Time deceive you,
　　You cannot conquer Time.

"In the burrows of the Nightmare　　　　　　　25
　　Where Justice naked is,
Time watches from the shadow
　　And coughs when you would kiss.

"In headaches and in worry
    Vaguely life leaks away,
And Time will have his fancy
    Tomorrow or to-day.

"Into many a green valley
    Drifts the appalling snow;
Time breaks the threaded dances
    And the diver's brilliant bow.

"O plunge your hands in water,
    Plunge them in up to the wrist;
Stare, stare in the basin
    And wonder what you've missed.

"The glacier knocks in the cupboard,
    The desert sighs in the bed,
And the crack in the tea-cup opens
    A lane to the land of the dead.

"Where the beggars raffle the banknotes
    And the Giant is enchanting to Jack,
And the Lily-white Boy is a Roarer,
    And Jill goes down on her back.

"O look, look in the mirror,
    O look in your distress;
Life remains a blessing
    Although you cannot bless.

"O stand, stand at the window
    As the tears scald and start;
You shall love your crooked neighbor
    With your crooked heart."

It was late, late in the evening,
    The lovers they were gone;
The clocks had ceased their chiming,
    And the deep river ran on.

—*1940*

Questions: Reading, Responding, Arguing

1. What is the "I's" role in the poem?
2. Describe Auden's depiction of love. How do the lovers differ from the clocks?
3. Much of the poem is in quotations from two speakers. Compare the language they use. How does the diction convey differences between the speakers and the ideas that they are "debating"?

Dylan Thomas (1914–1953)

Do Not Go Gentle into That Good Night

Do not go gentle into that good night,
Old age should burn and rave at close of day;
Rage, rage against the dying of the light.

Though wise men at their end know dark is right,
Because their words had forked no lightning they   5
Do not go gentle into that good night.

Good men, the last wave by, crying how bright
Their frail deeds might have danced in a green bay,
Rage, rage against the dying of the light.

Wild men who caught and sang the sun in flight,   10
And learn, too late, they grieved it on its way,
Do not go gentle into that good night.

Grave men, near death, who see with blinding sight
Blind eyes could blaze like meteors and be gay,
Rage, rage against the dying of the light.   15

And you, my father, there on the sad height,
Curse, bless, me now with your fierce tears, I pray,
Do not go gentle into that good night.
Rage, rage against the dying of the light.

—1952

Questions: Reading, Responding, Arguing

1. Describe the relationship among the wise men, the good men, the wild men, the grave men, and the speaker's father.
2. Examine the language used to describe life and death. How would you describe this language? Is it effective? Why or why not?
3. Argue that Thomas uses repetition to emphasize a particular message.

Richard Wilbur (b. 1921)

Year's End

Now winter downs the dying of the year,
And night is all a settlement of snow;
From the soft street the rooms of houses show
A gathered light, a shapen atmosphere,
Like frozen-over lakes whose ice is thin   5
And still allows some stirring down within.

I've known the wind by water banks to shake
The late leaves down, which frozen where they fell
And held in ice as dancers in a spell
Fluttered all winter long into a lake;   10
Graved on the dark in gestures of descent,
They seemed their own most perfect monument.

There was perfection in the death of ferns
Which laid their fragile cheeks against the stone
A million years. Great mammoths overthrown   15
Composedly have made their long sojourns,
Like palaces of patience, in the gray
And changeless lands of ice. And at Pompeii°

The little dog lay curled and did not rise
But slept the deeper as the ashes rose   20

---

18 **Pompeii** Roman city destroyed by volcanic eruption in AD 79.

And found the people incomplete, and froze
The random hands, the loose unready eyes
Of men expecting yet another sun
To do the shapely thing they had not done.

These sudden ends of time must give us pause.   25
We fray into the future, rarely wrought
Save in the tapestries of afterthought.
More time, more time. Barrages of applause
Come muffled from a buried radio.
The New-year bells are wrangling with the snow.   30

—*1950*

Questions: Reading, Responding, Arguing

1. Analyze Wilbur's rhyme and meter. How do rhyme and meter affect the mood or tone of the poem?
2. Explain the significance of the phrase "There was perfection in the death of ferns."
3. Why does Wilbur refer to the volcanic eruption that destroyed Pompeii?
4. Compare Wilbur's description of winter with that of another poet (for example, Robert Frost). Do the two have different visions of what winter offers, or of the meaning of winter to those who experience it?

Philip Larkin   (1922–1985)

Next, Please

Always too eager for the future, we
Pick up bad habits of expectancy.
Something is always approaching; every day
Till then we say,

Watching from a bluff the tiny, clear,   5
Sparkling armada of promises draw near.
How slow they are! And how much time they waste,
Refusing to make haste!

Yet still they leave us holding wretched stalks
Of disappointment, for, though nothing balks   10
Each big approach, leaning with brasswork prinked,
Each rope distinct,

Flagged, and the figurehead with golden tits
Arching our way, it never anchors; it's
No sooner present than it turns to past.   15
Right to the last

We think each one will heave to and unload
All good into our lives, all we are owed
For waiting so devoutly and so long.
But we are wrong: 20

Only one ship is seeking us, a black-
Sailed unfamiliar, towing at her back
A huge and birdless silence. In her wake
No waters breed or break.

                                                —*1951*

Questions: Reading, Responding, Arguing

1. Discuss the way Larkin uses the ship metaphor in the poem.
2. What are the implications of the poem's last two lines?
3. Explain why "expectancy" is considered a bad habit in this poem?

W. S. Merwin (b. 1927)

For the Anniversary of My Death

Every year without knowing it I have passed the day
When the last fires will wave to me
And the silence will set out
Tireless traveller
Like the beam of a lightless star   5

Then I will no longer
Find myself in life as in a strange garment
Surprised at the earth

And the love of one woman
And the shamelessness of men   10
As today writing after three days of rain
Hearing the wren sing and the falling cease
And bowing not knowing to what

—*1969*

Questions: Reading, Responding, Arguing

1. How does the speaker address death? What does death represent to him? What is his attitude toward death?
2. Why does Merwin break the stanza at line 5? What is the relationship between stanzas one and two?
3. Explain the significance of the wren.
4. Argue for this poem as an unusual example of an occasional poem.

Thom Gunn (1929–2004)

Terminal

The eight years difference in age seems now
Disparity so wide between the two
That when I see the man who armoured stood
Resistant to all help however good
Now helped through day itself, eased into chairs,   5
Or else led step by step down the long stairs
With firm and gentle guidance by his friend,
Who loves him, through each effort to descend,
Each wavering, each attempt made to complete
An arc of movement and bring down the feet   10
As if with that spare strength he used to enjoy,
I think of Oedipus, old, led by a boy.

—*1992*

Questions: Reading, Responding, Arguing

1. What is being described in this poem? What language choices convey Gunn's subject?

2. How is the man of eight years ago different from the man today?
3. What does the allusion to Oedipus contribute to the poem's meaning?
4. Argue that this poem may be fully understood only in light of the AIDS epidemic.

Rhina P. Espaillat (b. 1932)

Reservation

As if he has decided on a nap
but feels too pressed for time to find his bed
or even shift the napkin from his lap,
the man across the table drops his head
mid-anecdote, just managing to clear   5
a basket of warm rolls and butter stacked
like little golden dice beside his ear.
The lady seems embarrassed to attract
such swift attention from the formal stranger
who leaves his dinner, bends as if to wake   10
the sleeper, seeks a pulse. Others arrange her
coat about her, gather round to take
the plates, the quiet form, her name, her hand.
Now slowly she begins to understand.

—1998

Questions: Reading, Responding, Arguing

1. What does the title of the poem imply? Does "reservation" have multiple meanings here?
2. Discuss the indirect way the poet unfolds the events of the poem.
3. How is the sonnet form used here? Is it effective and appropriate for the subject? Argue this point.

Sylvia Plath (1932–1963)

Lady Lazarus°

I have done it again.
One year in every ten
I manage it—

A sort of walking miracle, my skin
Bright as a Nazi lampshade,   5
My right foot

A paperweight,
My face a featureless, fine
Jew linen.

Peel off the napkin   10
O my enemy.
Do I terrify?—

The nose, the eye pits, the full set of teeth?
The sour breath
Will vanish in a day.   15

Soon, soon the flesh
The grave cave ate will be
At home on me

And I a smiling woman.
I am only thirty.   20
And like the cat I have nine times to die.

This is Number Three.
What a trash
To annihilate each decade.

What a million filaments.   25
The peanut-crunching crowd
Shoves in to see

Them unwrap me hand and foot—
The big strip tease.
Gentleman, ladies,   30

Lazarus in the New Testament, man raised from the dead by Jesus.

These are my hands,
My knees.
I may be skin and bone,

Nevertheless, I am the same, identical woman.
The first time it happened I was ten.   35
It was an accident.

The second time I meant
To last it out and not come back at all.
I rocked shut

As a seashell.   40
They had to call and call
And pick the worms off me like sticky pearls.

Dying
Is an art, like everything else.
I do it exceptionally well.   45

I do it so it feels like hell.
I do it so it feels real.
I guess you could say I've a call.

It's easy enough to do it in a cell.
It's easy enough to do it and stay put.   50
It's the theatrical

Comeback in broad day
To the same place, the same face, the same brute
Amused shout:

"A miracle!"   55
That knocks me out.
There is a charge

For the eyeing of my scars, there is a charge
For the hearing of my heart—
It really goes.   60

And there is a charge, a very large charge,
For a word or a touch
Or a bit of blood

Or a piece of my hair or my clothes.
So, so, Herr° Doktor.   65
So, Herr Enemy.

I am your opus,
I am your valuable,
The pure gold baby

That melts to a shriek.   70
I turn and burn.
Do not think I underestimate your great concern.

Ash, ash—
You poke and stir.
Flesh, bone, there is nothing there—   75

A cake of soap,
A wedding ring,
A gold filling.

Herr God, Herr Lucifer,
Beware   80
Beware.

Out of the ash
I rise with my red hair
And I eat men like air.

                                              —1965

Questions: Reading, Responding, Arguing

1. Who was Lazarus? Why is he alluded to?
2. What kind of unpleasant imagery does Plath use? Is it effective?
3. Read the biographical sketch of Plath on page 1348. Argue that it is clear why this poem is usually cited as an example of confessional poetry.

65 Herr (German), Mister

Ai (b. 1947)

She Didn't Even Wave

For Marilyn Monroe

I buried Mama in her wedding dress
and put gloves on her hands,
but I couldn't do much about her face,
blue-black and swollen,
so I covered it with a silk scarf.   5
I hike my dress up to my thighs
and rub them,
watching you tip the mortuary fan back and forth.
Hey. Come on over. Cover me all up
like I was never here. Just never.   10
Come on. I don't know why I talk like that.
It was a real nice funeral. Mama's.
I touch the rhinestone heart pinned to my blouse.
Honey, let's look at it again.
See. It's bright like the lightning that struck her.   15

I walk outside
and face the empty house.
You put your arms around me. Don't.
Let me wave goodbye.
Mama never got a chance to do it.   20
She was walking toward the barn
when it struck her. I didn't move;
I just stood at the screen door.
Her whole body was light.
I'd never seen anything so beautiful.   25

I remember how she cried in the kitchen
a few minutes before.
She said, *God. Married.*
I don't believe it, Jean, I won't.
He takes and takes and you just give.   30
At the door, she held out her arms
and I ran to her.

She squeezed me so tight:
I was all short of breath.
And she said, don't do it. 35
In ten years, your heart will be eaten out
and you'll forgive him, or some other man, even that
and it will kill you.
Then she walked outside.
And I kept saying, I've got to, Mama, 40
hug me again. Please don't go.

—*1979*

Questions: Reading, Responding, Arguing

1. Who is the persona in the poem? What is her relationship
   with her mother like?
2. What is implied about the mother's experiences in marriage by
   the poem's description and the advice she gives her daughter?
3. The poem is dedicated to Marilyn Monroe. Why? How does
   the persona reflect the troubled life of the movie star?

Dana Gioia (b. 1950)

Planting a Sequoia

All afternoon my brothers and I have worked in the orchard,
Digging this hole, laying you into it, carefully packing the soil.
Rain blackened the horizon, but cold winds kept it over the Pacific,
And the sky above us stayed the dull gray
Of an old year coming to an end. 5

In Sicily a father plants a tree to celebrate his first son's birth—
An olive or a fig tree—a sign that the earth has one more life to bear.
I would have done the same, proudly laying new stock into my
     father's orchard,
A green sapling rising among the twisted apple boughs,
A promise of new fruit in other autumns. 10

But today we kneel in the cold planting you, our native giant,
Defying the practical custom of our fathers,

Wrapping in your roots a lock of hair, a piece of an infant's birth cord,
All that remains above earth of a first-born son,
A few stray atoms brought back to the elements.   15

We will give you what we can—our labor and our soil,
Water drawn from the earth when the skies fail,
Nights scented with the ocean fog, days softened by the circuit of bees.
We plant you in the corner of the grove, bathed in western light,
A slender shoot against the sunset.   20

And when our family is no more, all of his unborn brothers dead,
Every niece and nephew scattered, the house torn down,
His mother's beauty ashes in the air,
I want you to stand among strangers, all young and ephemeral to you,
Silently keeping the secret of your birth.   25

—1991

Questions: Reading, Responding, Arguing

1. What does the sequoia signify? Why are the characters in the poem planting it?
2. What is the connection between the older traditions and this tree?
3. What is this poem arguing for about life, death, and generations?

Gahon Wilson (b. 1930), Illustrator

Edgar Allan Poe's "The Haunted Palace"

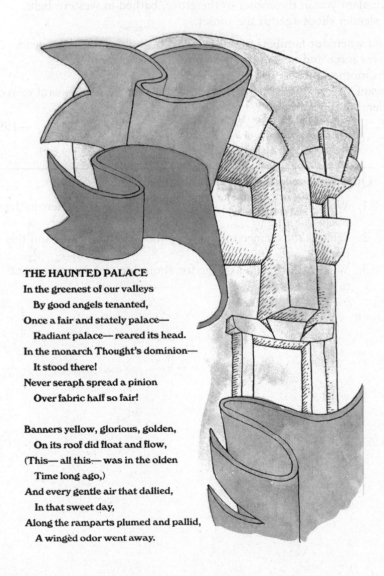

THE HAUNTED PALACE

In the greenest of our valleys
    By good angels tenanted,
Once a fair and stately palace—
    Radiant palace— reared its head.
In the monarch Thought's dominion—
    It stood there!
Never seraph spread a pinion
    Over fabric half so fair!

Banners yellow, glorious, golden,
    On its roof did float and flow,
(This— all this— was in the olden
    Time long ago,)
And every gentle air that dallied,
    In that sweet day,
Along the ramparts plumed and pallid,
    A wingèd odor went away.

Wanderers in that happy valley,
    Through two luminous windows, saw
Spirits moving musically,
    To a lute's well tunèd law,
Round about a throne where, sitting
    (Porphyrogene!)
In state his glory well befitting,
    The ruler of the realm was seen.

And all with pearl and ruby glowing
    Was the fair palace-door,
Through which came flowing, flowing, flowing,
    And sparkling evermore,
A troop of Echoes, whose sweet duty
    Was but to sing,
In voices of surpassing beauty,
    The wit and wisdom of their king.

But evil things, in robes of sorrow,
   Assailed the monarch's high estate.
(Ah, let us mourn!— for never morrow
   Shall dawn upon him desolate!)
And round about his home, the glory
   That blushed and bloomed
Is but a dim-remembered story
   Of the old time entombed.

And travellers now, within that valley,
   Through the red-litten windows see
Vast forms, that move fantastically
   To a discordant melody,
While, like a ghastly rapid river,
   Through the pale door
A hideous throng rush out forever
   And laugh— but smile no more.

—1990

Questions: Reading, Responding, Arguing

1. How does the graphic content relate the details of the poem?
2. How does music relate to the message of the poem? Do the poem's rhyme and meter contribute to that message?
3. What is the difference between the "good angels" of the palace, and the "vast forms" that later occupy it? Does the illustration add meaning to the poem's description of the two?

John Millington Synge (1871–1909)

Riders to the Sea

CHARACTERS

Maurya, *an old woman*
Bartley, *her son*
Cathleen, *her daughter*
Nora, *a younger daughter*
Men and Women

SCENE.   *An Island off the West of Ireland.*

Cottage kitchen, with nets, oil-skins, spinning-wheel, some new boards standing by the wall, etc. Cathleen, a girl of about twenty, finishes kneading cake, and puts it down in the pot-oven by the fire; then wipes her hands, and begins to spin at the wheel. Nora, a young girl, puts her head in at the door.

NORA [*in a low voice*]:   Where is she?
CATHLEEN: She's lying down, God help her, and may be sleeping, if she's able.

Nora comes in softly, and takes a bundle from under her shawl.

CATHLEEN [*spinning the wheel rapidly*]:   What is it you have?
NORA: The young priest is after bringing them. It's a shirt and a plain stocking were got off a drowned man in Donegal.

Cathleen stops her wheel with a sudden movement, and leans out to listen.

NORA: We're to find out if it's Michael's they are, some time herself will be down looking by the sea.

CATHLEEN: How would they be Michael's, Nora? How would he go the length of that way to the far north?

NORA: The young priest says he's known the like of it. "If it's Michael's they are," says he, "you can tell yourself he's got a clean burial by the grace of God, and if they're not his, let no one say a word about them, for she'll be getting her death," says he, "with crying and lamenting."

The door which Nora half-closed is blown open by a gust of wind.

CATHLEEN [*looking out anxiously*]: Did you ask him would he stop Bartley going this day with the horses to the Galway fair?

NORA: "I won't stop him," says he, "but let you not be afraid. Herself does be saying prayers half through the night, and the Almighty God won't leave her destitute," says he, "with no son living."

CATHLEEN: Is the sea bad by the white rocks, Nora?

NORA: Middling bad, God help us. There's a great roaring in the west, and it's worse it'll be getting when the tide's turned to the wind.

She goes over to the table with the bundle.

Shall I open it now?

CATHLEEN: Maybe she'd wake up on us, and come in before we'd done. [*Coming to the table.*] It's a long time we'll be, and the two of us crying.

NORA [*goes to the inner door and listens*]: She's moving about on the bed. She'll be coming in a minute.

CATHLEEN: Give me the ladder, and I'll put them up in the turf-loft, the way she won't know of them at all, and maybe when the tide turns she'll be going down to see would he be floating from the east.

They put the ladder against the gable of the chimney; Cathleen goes up a few steps and hides the bundle in the turf-loft. Maurya comes from the inner room.

MAURYA [*looking up at Cathleen and speaking querulously*]: Isn't it turf enough you have for this day and evening?

CATHLEEN: There's a cake baking at the fire for a short space [*throwing down the turf*] and Bartley will want it when the tide turns if he goes to Connemara.

Nora picks up the turf and puts it round the pot-oven.

MAURYA [*sitting down on a stool at the fire*]: He won't go this day with the wind rising from the south and west. He won't go this day, for the young priest will stop him surely.

NORA: He'll not stop him, mother, and I heard Eamon Simon and Stephen Pheety and Colum Shawn saying he would go.

MAURYA: Where is he itself?

NORA: He went down to see would there be another boat sailing in the week, and I'm thinking it won't be long till he's here now, for the tide's turning at the green head, and the hooker's tacking from the east.

CATHLEEN: I hear some one passing the big stones.

NORA [*looking out*]: He's coming now, and he in a hurry.

BARTLEY [*comes in and looks round the room. Speaking sadly and quietly*]: Where is the bit of new rope, Cathleen, was bought in Connemara?

CATHLEEN [*coming down*]: Give it to him, Nora; it's on a nail by the white boards. I hung it up this morning, for the pig with the black feet was eating it.

NORA [*giving him a rope*]: Is that it, Bartley?

MAURYA: You'd do right to leave that rope, Bartley, hanging by the boards. [*Bartley takes the rope.*] It will be wanting in this place. I'm telling you, if Michael is washed up to-morrow morning, or the next morning, or any morning in the week, for it's a deep grave we'll make him by the grace of God.

BARTLEY [*beginning to work with the rope*]: I've no halter the way I can ride down on the mare, and I must go now quickly. This is the one boat going for two weeks or beyond it, and the fair will be a good fair for horses I heard them saying below.

MAURYA: It's a hard thing they'll be saying below if the body is washed up and there's no man in it to make the coffin, and I after giving a big price for the finest white boards you'd find in Connemara.

She looks round at the boards.

BARTLEY: How would it be washed up, and we after looking each day for nine days, and a strong wind blowing a while back from the west and south?

MAURYA: If it wasn't found itself, that wind is raising the sea, and there was a star up against the moon, and it rising in the night. If it was a hundred horses, or a thousand horses you had itself, what is the price of a thousand horses against a son where there is one son only?

BARTLEY [*working at the halter, to Cathleen*]: Let you go down each day, and see the sheep aren't jumping in on the rye, and if the jobber comes you can sell the pig with the black feet if there is a good price going.

MAURYA: How would the like of her get a good price for a pig?

BARTLEY [*to Cathleen*]: If the west wind holds with the last bit of the moon let you and Nora get up weed enough for another cock for the kelp. It's hard set we'll be from this day with no one in it but one man to work.

MAURYA: It's hard set we'll be surely the day you're drownd'd with the rest. What way will I live and the girls with me, and I an old woman looking for the grave?

Bartley lays down the halter, takes off his old coat, and puts on a newer one of the same flannel.

BARTLEY [*to Nora*]: Is she coming to the pier?

NORA [*looking out*]: She's passing the green head and letting fall her sails.

BARTLEY [*getting his purse and tobacco*]: I'll have half an hour to go down, and you'll see me coming again in two days, or in three days, or maybe in four days if the wind is bad.

MAURYA [*turning round to the fire, and putting her shawl over her head*]: Isn't it a hard and cruel man won't hear a word from an old woman, and she holding him from the sea?

CATHLEEN: It's the life of a young man to be going on the sea, and who would listen to an old woman with one thing and she saying it over?

BARTLEY [*taking the halter*]: I must go now quickly. I'll ride down on the red mare, and the gray pony'll run behind me. . . . The blessing of God on you.

He goes out.

MAURYA [*crying out as he is in the door*]: He's gone now, God spare us, and we'll not see him again. He's gone now, and when the black night is falling I'll have no son left me in the world.

CATHLEEN: Why wouldn't you give him your blessing and he looking round in the door? Isn't it sorrow enough is on every one in this house without your sending him out with an unlucky word behind him, and a hard word in his ear?

Maurya takes up the tongs and begins raking the fire aimlessly without looking round.

NORA [*turning towards her*]: You're taking away the turf from the cake.

CATHLEEN [*crying out*]: The Son of God forgive us, Nora, we're after forgetting his bit of bread.

She comes over to the fire.

NORA: And it's destroyed he'll be going till dark night, and he after eating nothing since the sun went up.

CATHLEEN [*turning the cake out of the oven*]: It's destroyed he'll be, surely. There's no sense left on any person in a house where an old woman will be talking for ever.

Maurya sways herself on her stool.

CATHLEEN [*cutting off some of the bread and rolling it in a cloth; to Maurya*]: Let you go down now to the spring well and give him this and he passing. You'll see him then and the dark word will be broken, and you can say "God speed you," the way he'll be easy in his mind.

MAURYA [*taking the bread*]: Will I be in it as soon as himself?

CATHLEEN: If you go now quickly.

MAURYA [*standing up unsteadily*]: It's hard set I am to walk.

CATHLEEN [*looking at her anxiously*]: Give her the stick, Nora, or maybe she'll slip on the big stones.

NORA: What stick?

CATHLEEN: The stick Michael brought from Connemara.

MAURYA [*taking a stick Nora gives her*]: In the big world the old people do be leaving things after them for their sons and children, but in this place it is the young men do be leaving things behind for them that do be old.

She goes out slowly. Nora goes over to the ladder.

CATHLEEN: Wait, Nora, maybe she'd turn back quickly. She's that sorry, God help her, you wouldn't know the thing she'd do.

NORA: Is she gone around by the bush?

CATHLEEN [*looking out*]: She's gone now. Throw it down quickly, for the Lord knows when she'll be out of it again.

NORA [*getting the bundle from the loft*]: The young priest said he'd be passing tomorrow, and we might go down and speak to him below if it's Michael's they are surely.

CATHLEEN [*taking the bundle*]: Did he say what way they were found?

NORA [*coming down*]: "There were two men," says he, "and they rowing round with poteen before the cocks crowed, and the oar of one of them caught the body, and they passing the black cliffs of the north."

CATHLEEN [*trying to open the bundle*]: Give me a knife, Nora, the strings perished with the salt water, and there's a black knot on it you wouldn't loosen in a week.

NORA [*giving her a knife*]: I've heard tell it was a long way to Donegal.

CATHLEEN [*cutting the string*]: It is surely. There was a man in here a while ago—the man sold us that knife—and he said if you set off walking from the rock beyond, it would be seven days you'd be in Donegal.

NORA: And what time would a man take, and he floating?

Cathleen opens the bundle and takes out a bit of a stocking. They look at them eagerly.

CATHLEEN [*in a low voice*]: The Lord spare us, Nora! Isn't it a queer hard thing to say if it's his they are surely?

NORA: I'll get his shirt off the hook the way we can put the one flannel on the other. [*She looks through some clothes hanging in the corner.*] It's not with them, Cathleen, and where will it be?

CATHLEEN: I'm thinking Bartley put it on him in the morning, for his own shirt was heavy with the salt in it. [*Pointing to the corner.*] There's a bit of a sleeve was of the same stuff. Give me that and it will do.

Nora brings it to her and they compare the flannel.

CATHLEEN: It's the same stuff, Nora; but if it is itself aren't there great rolls of it in the shops of Galway, and isn't it many another man may have a shirt of it as well as Michael himself?

NORA [*who has taken up the stocking and counted the stitches, crying out*]: It's Michael, Cathleen, it's Michael; God spare his soul, and what will herself say when she hears this story, and Bartley on the sea?

CATHLEEN [*taking the stocking*]: It's a plain stocking.

NORA: It's the second one of the third pair I knitted, and I put up three score stitches, and I dropped four of them.

CATHLEEN [*counts the stitches*]: It's that number is in it. [*Crying out.*] Ah, Nora, isn't it a bitter thing to think of him floating that way to the far north, and no one to keen him but the black hags that do be flying on the sea?

NORA [*Swinging herself round, and throwing out her arms on the clothes*]: And isn't it a pitiful thing when there is nothing left of a man who was a great rower and fisher, but a bit of an old shirt and a plain stocking?

CATHLEEN [*after an instant*]: Tell me is herself coming, Nora? I hear a little sound on the path.

NORA [*looking out*]: She is, Cathleen. She's coming up to the door.

CATHLEEN: Put these things away before she'll come in. Maybe it's easier she'll be after giving her blessing to Bartley, and we won't let on we've heard anything the time he's on the sea.

NORA [*helping Cathleen to close the bundle*]: We'll put them here in the corner.

They put them into a hole in the chimney corner. Cathleen goes back to the spinning-wheel.

NORA: Will she see it was crying I was?

CATHLEEN: Keep your back to the door the way the light'll not be on you.

Nora sits down at the chimney corner, with her back to the door. Maurya comes in very slowly, without looking at the girls, and goes over to her stool at the other side of the fire. The cloth with the bread is still in her hand. The girls look at each other, and Nora points to the bundle of bread.

CATHLEEN [*after spinning for a moment*]: You didn't give him his bit of bread?

Maurya begins to keen softly, without turning round.

CATHLEEN: Did you see him riding down?

Maurya goes on keening.

CATHLEEN [*a little impatiently*]: God forgive you; isn't it a better thing to raise your voice and tell what you seen, than to be making lamentation for a thing that's done? Did you see Bartley, I'm saying to you.

MAURYA [*with a weak voice*]: My heart's broken from this day.

CATHLEEN [*as before*]: Did you see Bartley?

MAURYA: I seen the fearfulest thing.

CATHLEEN [*leaves her wheel and looks out*]: God forgive you; he's riding the mare now over the green head, and the gray pony behind him.

MAURYA [*starts, so that her shawl falls back from her head and shows her white tossed hair. With a frightened voice*]:   The gray pony behind him.

CATHLEEN [*coming to the fire*]:   What is it ails you, at all?

MAURYA [*speaking very slowly*]:   I've seen the fearfulest thing any person has seen, since the day Bride Dara seen the dead man with the child in his arms.

CATHLEEN AND NORA: Uah.

They crouch down in front of the old woman at the fire.

NORA: Tell us what it is you seen.

MAURYA: I went down to the spring well, and I stood there saying a prayer to myself. Then Bartley came along, and he riding on the red mare with the gray pony behind him. [*She puts up her hands, as if to hide something from her eyes.*] The Son of God spare us, Nora!

CATHLEEN: What is it you seen?

MAURYA: I seen Michael himself.

CATHLEEN [*speaking softly*]:   You did not Mother; it wasn't Michael you seen, for his body is after being found in the far north, and he's got a clean burial by the grace of God.

MAURYA [*a little defiantly*]:   I'm after seeing him this day, and he riding and galloping. Bartley came first on the red mare; and I tried to say "God speed you," but something choked the words in my throat. He went by quickly; and "the blessing of God on you," says he, and I could say nothing. I looked up then, and I crying, at the gray pony, and there was Michael upon it—with fine clothes on him, and new shoes on his feet.

CATHLEEN [*begins to keen*]:   It's destroyed we are from this day. It's destroyed, surely.

NORA: Didn't the young priest say the Almighty God wouldn't leave her destitute with no son living?

MAURYA [*in a low voice, but clearly*]:   It's little the like of him knows of the sea. . . . Bartley will be lost now, and let you call in Eamon and make me a good coffin out of the white boards, for I won't live after them. I've had a husband, and a husband's father, and six sons in this house—six fine men, though it was a hard birth I had with every one of them and they coming to the world—and some of them were found and some of them were not found, but they're gone now the lot of them. . . . There were Stephen, and Shawn, were lost in the great wind, and found after in the Bay of Gregory of the Golden Mouth, and carried up the two of them on the one plank, and in by that door.

She pauses for a moment, the girls start as if they heard something through the door that is half open behind them.

NORA [*in a whisper*]: Did you hear that, Cathleen? Did you hear a noise in the north-east?

CATHLEEN [*in a whisper*]: There's some one after crying out by the seashore.

MAURYA [*continues without hearing anything*]: There was Sheamus and his father, and his own father again, were lost in a dark night, and not a stick or sign was seen of them when the sun went up. There was Patch after was drowned out of a curagh that turned over. I was sitting here with Bartley, and he a baby, lying on my two knees, and I seen two women, and three women, and four women coming in, and they crossing themselves, and not saying a word. I looked out then, and there were men coming after them, and they holding a thing in the half of a red sail, and water dripping out of it—it was a dry day, Nora—and leaving a track to the door.

She pauses again with her hand stretched out towards the door. It opens softly and old women begin to come in, crossing themselves on the threshold, and kneeling down in front of the stage with red petticoats over their heads.

MAURYA [*half in a dream, to Cathleen*]: Is it Patch, or Michael, or what is it at all?

CATHLEEN: Michael is after being found in the far north, and when he is found there how could he be here in this place?

MAURYA: There does be a power of young men floating round in the sea, and what way would they know if it was Michael they had, or another man like him, for when a man is nine days in the sea, and the wind blowing, it's hard set his own mother would be to say what man was it.

CATHLEEN: It's Michael, God spare him, for they're after sending us a bit of his clothes from the far north.

She reaches out and hands Maurya the clothes that belonged to Michael. Maurya stands up slowly and takes them in her hand. Nora looks out.

NORA: They're carrying a thing among them and there's water dripping out of it and leaving a track by the big stones.

CATHLEEN [*in a whisper to the women who have come in*]:   Is it Bartley it is?

ONE OF THE WOMEN: It is surely, God rest his soul.

Two younger women come in and pull out the table. Then men carry in the body of Bartley, laid on a plank, with a bit of sail over it, and lay it on the table.

CATHLEEN [*to the women, as they are doing so*]:   What way was he drowned?

ONE OF THE WOMEN: The gray pony knocked him into the sea, and he was washed out where there is a great surf on the white rocks.

Maurya has gone over and knelt down at the head of the table. The women are keening softly and swaying themselves with a slow movement. Cathleen and Nora kneel at the other end of the table. The men kneel near the door.

MAURYA [*raising her head and speaking as if she did not see the people around her*]:   They're all gone now, and there isn't anything more the sea can do to me. . . . I'll have no call now to be up crying and praying when the wind breaks from the south and you can hear the surf is in the east, and the surf is in the west, making a great stir with the two noises, and they hitting one on the other. I'll have no call now to be going down and getting Holy Water in the dark nights after Samhain, and I won't care what way the sea is when the other women will be keening. [*To Nora*] Give me the Holy Water, Nora, there's a small cup still on the dresser.

Nora gives it to her.

MAURYA [*drops Michael's clothes across Bartley's feet, and sprinkles the Holy Water over him.*]:   It isn't that I haven't prayed for you, Bartley, to the Almighty God. It isn't that I haven't said prayers in the dark night till you wouldn't know what I'ld be saying; but it's a great rest I'll have now, and it's time surely. It's a great rest I'll have now, and great sleeping in the long nights after Samhain, if it's only a bit of wet flour we do have to eat, and maybe a fish that would be stinking.

She kneels down again, crossing herself, and saying prayers under her breath.

CATHLEEN [*to an old man*]:   Maybe yourself and Eamon would make a coffin when the sun rises. We have fine white boards herself bought, God help her, thinking Michael would be found, and I have a new cake you can eat while you'll be working.

THE OLD MAN [*looking at the boards*]: Are there nails with them?

CATHLEEN: There are not, Colum; we didn't think of the nails.

ANOTHER MAN: It's a great wonder she wouldn't think of the nails, and all the coffins she's been made already.

CATHLEEN: It's getting old she is, and broken.

Maurya stands up again very slowly and spreads out the pieces of Michael's clothes beside the body, sprinkling them with the last of the Holy Water.

NORA [*in a whisper to Cathleen*]: She's quiet now and easy; but the day Michael was drowned you could hear her crying out from this to the spring well. It's fonder she was of Michael, and would any one have thought that?

CATHLEEN [*slowly and clearly*]: An old woman will be soon tired with anything she will do, and isn't it nine days herself is after crying and keening, and making great sorrow in the house?

MAURYA [*puts the empty cup mouth downwards on the table, and lays her hands together on Bartley's feet*]: They're all together this time, and the end is come. May the Almighty God have mercy on Bartley's soul, and on Michael's soul, and on the souls of Sheamus and Patch, and Stephen and Shawn [*bending her head*]; and may He have mercy on my soul, Nora, and on the soul of every one is left living in the world.

She pauses, and the keen rises a little more loudly from the women, then sinks away.

MAURYA [*continuing*]: Michael has a clean burial in the far north, by the grace of the Almighty God. Bartley will have a fine coffin out of the white boards, and a deep grave surely. What more can we want than that? No man at all can be living for ever, and we must be satisfied.

She kneels down again and the curtain falls slowly.

—*1904*

Questions: Reading, Responding, Arguing

1. Why do the daughters initially hide the clothing from Maurya at the beginning of the play?

2. It isn't revealed until later in the narrative what has happened to all the other men of the family. Why does Synge delay in revealing that information? Does the delay affect how the audience receives the news?

3. Much of the impact in the play lies in understanding what happens elsewhere, or what has happened in the past. What actions happen on stage? Cite passages to create an argument for what you feel are the most important actions that happen during the play itself.

4. Besides many references to Catholicism (holy water, etc.), there are references to Celtic traditions, such as "Samhain," in the play. Research Celtic traditions and mythology and make an argument about how Synge uses them to explore his themes.

Terrence McNally (b. 1939)

Andre's Mother

CHARACTERS

Cal, *a young man*
Arthur, *his father*
Penny, *his sister*
Andre's Mother

Time. Now

Place. New York City, Central Park

Four people—Cal, Arthur, Penny, and Andre's Mother—enter. They are nicely dressed and each carries a white helium-filled balloon on a string.

CAL: You know what's really terrible? I can't think of anything terrific to say. Goodbye. I love you. I'll miss you. And I'm supposed to be so great with words!

PENNY: What's that over there?

ARTHUR: Ask your brother.

CAL: It's a theatre. An outdoor theatre. They do plays there in the summer. Shakespeare's plays. [*To Andre's Mother.*] God, how much he wanted to play Hamlet again. He would have gone to Timbuktu to have another go at that part. The summer he did it in Boston, he was so happy!

PENNY: Cal, I don't think she . . . ! It's not the time. Later.

ARTHUR: Your son was a . . . the Jews have a word for it . . .

PENNY [*quietly appalled*]: Oh my God!

ARTHUR: Mensch, I believe it is, and I think I'm using it right. It means warm, solid, the real thing. Correct me if I'm wrong.

PENNY: Fine, Dad, fine. Just quit while you're ahead.

ARTHUR: I won't say he was like a son to me. Even my son isn't always like a son to me. I mean . . . ! In my clumsy way, I'm trying to say how much I liked Andre. And how much he helped me to know my own boy. Cal was always two handsful but Andre and I could talk about anything under the sun. My wife was very fond of him, too.

PENNY: Cal, I don't understand about the balloons.

CAL: They represent the soul. When you let go, it means you're letting his soul ascend to Heaven. That you're willing to let go. Breaking the last earthly ties.

PENNY: Does the Pope know about this?

ARTHUR: Penny!

PENNY: Andre loved my sense of humor. Listen, you can hear him laughing. [*She lets go of her white balloon.*] So long, you glorious, wonderful, I-know-what-Cal-means-about-words . . . *man!* God forgive me for wishing you were straight every time I laid eyes on you. But if any man was going to have you, I'm glad it was my brother! Look how fast it went up. I bet that means something. Something terrific.

ARTHUR [*lets his balloon go*]: Goodbye. God speed.

PENNY: Cal?

CAL: I'm not ready yet.

PENNY: Okay. We'll be over there. Come on, Pop, you can buy your little girl a Good Humor.

ARTHUR: They still make Good Humor?

PENNY: Only now they're called Dove Bars and they cost twelve dollars.

[*Penny takes Arthur off. Cal and Andre's Mother stand with their balloons.*]

CAL: I wish I knew what you were thinking. I think it would help me. You know almost nothing about me and I only know what Andre told me about you. I'd always had it in my mind that one day we would be friends, you and me. But if you didn't know about Andre and me . . . If this hadn't happened, I wonder if he would have ever told you. When he was sick, if I asked him once I asked him a thousand times, tell her. She's your mother. She won't mind. But he was so afraid of hurting you and of your disapproval. I don't know which was worse. [*No response. He sighs.*] God, how many of us live in this city because we don't want to hurt our mothers and live in mortal terror of their disapproval. We lose ourselves here. Our lives aren't furtive, just our feelings toward people like you are! A city of fugitives from our parents' scorn or heartbreak. Sometimes he'd seem a little down and I'd say, "What's the matter, babe?" and this funny sweet, sad smile would cross his face and he'd say, "Just a little homesick, Cal, just a little bit." I always accused him of being a country boy just playing at being a hotshot, sophisticated New Yorker. [*He sighs.*]

It's bullshit. It's all bullshit. [*Still no response.*]

Do you remember the comic strip *Little Lulu*? Her mother had no name, she was so remote, so formidable to all the children. She was just Lulu's mother. "Hello, Lulu's Mother," Lulu's friends would say. She was almost anonymous in her remoteness. You remind me of her. Andre's mother. Let me answer the questions you can't ask and then I'll leave you alone and you won't ever have to see me again. Andre died of AIDS. I don't know how he got it. I tested negative. He died bravely. You would have been proud of him. The only thing that frightened him was you. I'll have everything that was his sent to you. I'll pay for it. There isn't much. You should have come up the summer he played Hamlet. He was magnificent. Yes, I'm bitter. I'm bitter I've lost him. I'm bitter what's happening. I'm bitter even now, after all this, I can't reach you. I'm beginning to feel your disapproval and it's making me ill. [*He looks at his balloon.*] Sorry, old friend. I blew it. [*He lets go of the balloon.*]

Good night, sweet prince, and flights of angels sing thee to thy rest! [*Beat.*]

Goodbye, Andre's mother.

[*He goes. Andre's Mother stands alone holding her white balloon. Her lips tremble. She looks on the verge of breaking down. She is about to let go of the balloon when she pulls it down to her. She looks at it awhile before she gently kisses it. She lets go of the balloon. She follows it with her eyes as it rises and rises. The lights are beginning to fade. Andre's Mother's eyes are still on the balloon. The lights fade.*]

—1988

Questions: Reading, Responding, Arguing

1. What is the significance of the balloons in the play? Do the balloons mean something different for different characters?
2. Several references, some direct and some indirect, are made to the play *Hamlet*. What connections, if any, can you find between these two plays?
3. Compare this play with the 1990 television production *Andre's Mother*, also written by McNally. What changes did McNally make to the production and why?
4. Andre's mother has no speaking role in the play, but is obviously the most important character. Citing examples, reveal where the mother is influential and argue for her importance in the play.

From *The Bible*

Ecclesiastes

To every *thing there is* a season, and a time to every purpose under the heaven:

A time to be born, and a time to die; a time to plant, and a time to pluck up *that which is* planted;

A time to kill, and a time to heal; a time to break down, and a time to build up;

A time to weep, and a time to laugh; a time to mourn, and a time to dance;

A time to cast away stones, and a time to gather stones together; a time to embrace, and a time to refrain from embracing; 5

A time to get, and a time to lose; a time to keep, and a time to cast away;

A time to rend, and a time to sew; a time to keep silence, and a time to speak;

A time to love, and a time to hate; a time of war, and a time of peace.

What profit hath he that worketh in that wherein he laboureth?

I have seen the travail, which God hath given to the sons of men to be exercised in it. 10

He hath made every *thing* beautiful in his time: also he hath set the
world in their heart, so that no man can find out the work that
God maketh from the beginning to the end.

I know that *there is* no good in them, but for a *man* to rejoice, and to
do good in his life.

And also that every man should eat and drink, and enjoy the good of
all his labour, it *is* the gift of God.

I know that, whatsoever God doeth, it shall be for ever: nothing can
be put to it, nor any thing taken from it: and God doeth *it,* that
men should fear before him.

That which hath been is now; and that which is to be hath already
been; and God requireth that which is past.   15

And moreover I saw under the sun the place of judgment, *that*
wickedness *was* there; and the place of righteousness, *that*
iniquity *was* there.

I said in mine heart, God shall judge the righteous and the wicked: for
there is a time there for every purpose and for every work.

I said in mine heart concerning the estate of the sons of men, that
God might manifest them, and that they might see that they
themselves are beasts.

For that which befalleth the sons of men befalleth beasts; even one
thing befalleth them: as the one dieth, so dieth the other; yea,
they have all one breath; so that a man hath no preeminence
above a beast: for all *is* vanity.

All go unto one place; all are of the dust, and all turn to dust again. 20

Who knoweth the spirit of man that goeth upward, and the spirit of
the beast that goeth downward to the earth?

Wherefore I perceive that *there is* nothing better, than that a man
should rejoice in his own works; for that *is* his portion: for who
shall bring him to see what shall be after him?

—*c. 250* BCE

Questions: Reading, Responding, Arguing

1. What metaphors are used in this passage?
2. The selection often uses antithesis—placing words, or ideas,
   in contrast or opposition to one another. Why is the device
   of antithesis so important here?
3. What does the passage imply about negative aspects of human conduct?

Stephen Crane (1871–1900)

Stephen Crane's Own Story

JACKSONVILLE, FLA., Jan. 6.—It was the afternoon of New Year's. The *Commodore* lay at her dock in Jacksonville and negro stevedores processioned steadily toward her with box after box of ammunition and bundle after bundle of rifles. Her hatch, like the mouth of a monster, engulfed them. It might have been the feeding time of some legendary creature of the sea. It was in broad daylight and the crowd of gleeful Cubans on the pier did not forbear to sing the strange patriotic ballads of their island.

Everything was perfectly open. The *Commodore* was cleared with a cargo of arms and munitions for Cuba. There was none of that extreme modesty about the proceeding which had marked previous departures of the famous tug. She loaded up as placidly as if she were going to carry oranges to New York, instead of Remingtons to Cuba. Down the river, furthermore, the revenue cutter *Boutwell,* the old isosceles triangle that protects United States interests in the St. Johns, lay at anchor, with no sign of excitement aboard her.

On the decks of the *Commodore* there were exchanges of farewells in two languages. Many of the men who were to sail upon her had many intimates in the old Southern town, and we who had left our friends in the remote North received our first touch of melancholy on witnessing these strenuous and earnest good-bys.

It seems, however, that there was more difficulty at the custom house. The officers of the ship and the Cuban leaders were detained there until a mournful twilight settled upon the St. Johns, and through a heavy fog the lights of Jacksonville blinked dimly.

Then at last the *Commodore* swung clear of the dock, amid a tumult of good-bys. As she turned her bow toward the distant sea the Cubans ashore cheered and cheered. In response the *Commodore* gave three long blasts of her whistle, which even to this time impressed me with their sadness. Somehow they sounded as wails.

Then at last we began to feel like filibusters. I don't suppose that the most stolid brain could contrive to believe that there is not a mere trifle of danger in filibustering, and so as we watched the lights of Jacksonville swing past us and heard the regular thump, thump, thump of the engines we did considerable reflecting.

But I am sure that there was no hifalutin emotions visible upon any of the faces which fronted the speeding shore. In fact, from cook's boy to captain, we were all enveloped in a gentle satisfaction and cheerfulness.

But less than two miles from Jacksonville this atrocious fog caused the pilot to ram the bow of the *Commodore* hard upon the mud, and in this ignominious position we were compelled to stay until daybreak.

It was to all of us more than a physical calamity. We were now no longer filibusters. We were men on a ship stuck in the mud. A certain mental somersault was made once more necessary. But word had been sent to Jacksonville to the captain of the revenue cutter *Boutwell*, and Captain Kilgore turned out promptly and generously fired up his old triangle and came at full speed to our assistance. She dragged us out of the mud and again we headed for the mouth of the river. The revenue cutter pounded along a half mile astern of us, to make sure that we did not take on board at some place along the river men for the Cuban army.

This was the early morning of New Year's Day, and the fine golden Southern sunlight fell full upon the river. It flashed over the ancient *Boutwell* until her white sides gleamed like pearl and her rigging was spun into little threads of gold. Cheers greeted the old *Commodore* from passing ships and from the shore. It was a cheerful, almost merry, beginning to our voyage.

At Mayport, however, we changed our river pilot for a man who could take her to open sea, and again the *Commodore* was beached. The *Boutwell* was fussing around us in her venerable way, and, upon seeing our predicament, she came again to assist us, but this time with engines reversed the *Commodore* dragged herself away from the grip of the sand and again the *Commodore* headed for the open sea.

The captain of the revenue cutter grew curious. He hailed the *Commodore*: "Are you fellows going to sea to-day?"

Captain Murphy of the *Commodore* called back: "Yes, sir." And then as the whistle of the *Commodore* saluted him Captain Kilgore doffed his cap and said: "Well, gentlemen, I hope you have a pleasant cruise," and this was our last words from shore.

When the *Commodore* came to the enormous rollers that flee over the bar, a certain light-heartedness departed from the throats of the ship's company. The *Commodore* began to turn handsprings, and by the time she had gotten fairly to sea and turned into the eye of the roaring breeze that was blowing from the southeast there was an almost general opinion on board the vessel that a life on the rolling wave was not the finest thing in the world. On deck amidships lay five or six Cubans, limp, forlorn and infinitely depressed. In the bunks below lay more Cubans, also limp, forlorn and infinitely depressed. In the captain's quarters, back of the pilot house, the Cuban leaders were stretched out in postures of complete contentment to this terrestrial realm of their stomachs.

The *Commodore* was heavily laden and in this strong sea she rolled like a rubber ball. She appeared to be a gallant sea boat and bravely flung off the waves that swarmed over her bow. At this time the first mate was at the wheel, and I remember how proud he was of the ship as she dashed the white foaming waters aside and arose to the swells like a duck.

"Ain't she a daisy?" said he. But she certainly did do a remarkable lot of pitching and presently even some American seamen were made ill by the long wallowing motion of the ship. A squall confronted us dead ahead and in the impressive twilight of this New Year's Day the *Commodore* steamed sturdily toward a darkened part of the horizon. The State of Florida is very large when you look at it from an airship, but it is as narrow as a sheet of paper when you look at it sideways. The coast was merely a faint streak.

As darkness came upon the waters the *Commodore*'s wake was a broad, flaming path of blue and silver phosphorescence, and as her stout bow lunged at the great black waves she threw flashing, roaring cascades to either side. And all that was to be heard was the rhythmical and mighty pounding of the engines.

Being an inexperienced filibuster, the writer had undergone considerable mental excitement since the starting of the ship, and consequently he had not yet been to sleep, and so I went to the first mate's bunk to indulge myself in all the physical delights of holding one's self in bed. Every time the ship lurched I expected to be fired through a bulkhead, and it was neither amusing nor instructive to see in the dim light a certain accursed valise aiming itself at the top of my stomach with every lurch of the ship.

The cook was asleep on a bench in the galley. He was of a portly and noble exterior, and by means of a checker board he had himself wedged on this bench in such a manner that the motion of the ship would be unable to dislodge him. He awoke as I entered the galley, and, feeling moved, he delivered himself of some dolorous sentiments. "God," he said, in the course of his observations, "I don't feel right about this ship somehow. It strikes me that something is going to happen to us. I don't know what it is, but the old ship is going to get it in the neck, I think."

"Well, how about the men on board of her?" said I. "Are any of us going to get out, prophet?"

"Yes," said the cook, "sometimes I have these damned feelings come over me, and they are always right, and it seems to me somehow that you and I will both get out and meet again somewhere, down at Coney Island, perhaps, or some place like that."

Finding it impossible to sleep, I went back to the pilot house. An old seaman named Tom Smith, from Charleston, was then at the wheel. In the darkness I could not see Tom's face, except at those times when he leaned forward to scan the compass and the dim light from the box came upon his weather-beaten features.

"Well, Tom," said I, "how do you like filibustering?"

He said: "I think I am about through with it. I've been in a number of these expeditions, and the pay is good, but I think if I ever get back safe this time I will cut it."

I sat down in the corner of the pilot house and went almost to sleep. In the meantime the captain came on duty and he was standing near me when the chief engineer rushed up the stairs and cried hurriedly to the captain that there was something wrong in the engine room. He and the captain departed swiftly. I was drowsing there in my corner when the captain returned, and, going to the door of the little room directly back of the pilot house, cried to the Cuban leader:

"Say, can't you get those fellows to work? I can't talk their language and I can't get them started. Come on and get them going."

The Cuban leader turned to me then and said: "Go help in the fire-room. They are going to bail with buckets."

The engine room, by the way, represented a scene at this time taken from the middle kitchen of hades. In the first place, it was insufferably warm, and the lights burned faintly in a way to cause mystic and grewsome shadows. There was a quantity of soapish sea water swirling and sweeping and swishing among machinery that roared and banged and clattered and steamed, and in the second place, it was a devil of a ways down below.

Here I first came to know a certain young oiler named Billy Higgins. He was sloshing around this inferno filling buckets with water and passing them to a chain of men that extended up to the ship's side. Afterward we got orders to change our point of attack on the water and to operate through a little door on the windward side of the ship that led into the engine room.

During this time there was much talk of pumps out of order and many other statements of a mechanical kind, which I did not altogether comprehend, but understood to mean that there was a general and sudden ruin in the engine room.

There was no particular agitation at this time, and even later there was never a panic on board the *Commodore*. The party of men who worked with Higgins and me at this time were all Cubans, and we were under the direction of the Cuban leaders. Presently we were ordered again to the afterhold, and there was some hesitation about going into the abominable fire-room again, but Higgins dashed down the companionway with a bucket.

The heat and hard work in the fire-room affected me and I was obliged to come on deck again. Going forward I heard as I went talk of lowering the boats. Near the corner of the galley the mate was talking with a man.

"Why don't you send up a rocket?" said this unknown person. And the mate replied: "What the hell do we want to send up a rocket for? The ship is all right."

Returning with a little rubber and cloth overcoat, I saw the first boat about to be lowered. A certain man was the first person in this first boat, and they were handing him in a valise about as large as a hotel. I had not entirely recovered from my astonishment and pleasure in witnessing this noble deed, when I saw another valise go to him. This valise was not perhaps so large as a hotel, but it was a big valise anyhow. Afterward there went to him something which looked to me like an overcoat.

Seeing the chief engineer leaning out of his little window, I remarked to him: "What do you think of that blank, blank, blank?"

"Oh, he's a bird," said the old chief.

It was now that was heard the order to get away the lifeboat, which was stowed on top of the deckhouse. The deckhouse was a mighty slippery place, and with each roll of the ship the men there thought themselves likely to take headers into the deadly black sea. Higgins was on top of the deckhouse, and, with the first mate and two colored stokers, we wrestled with that boat, which I am willing to swear weighed as much as a Broadway cable car. She might have been spiked to the deck. We could have pushed a little brick schoolhouse along a corduroy road as easily as we could have moved this boat. But the first mate got a tackle to her from a leaward davit, and on the deck below the captain corralled enough men to make an impression upon the boat. We were ordered to cease hauling then, and in this lull the cook of the ship came to me and said: "What are you going to do?"

I told him of my plans, an he said: "Well, my God, that's what I am going to do."

Now the whistle of the *Commodore* had been turned loose, and if there ever was a voice of despair and death it was the voice of this whistle. It had gained a new tone. It was as if its throat was already choked by the water, and this cry on the sea at night, with a wind blowing the spray over the ship, and the waves roaring over the bow, and swirling white along the decks, was to each of us probably a song of man's end.

It was now that the first mate showed a sign of losing his grip. To us who were trying in all stages of competence and experience to launch the lifeboat he raged in all terms of fiery satire and hammer-like abuse. But the boat moved at last and swung down toward the water.

Afterward when I went aft I saw the captain standing with his arm in a sling, holding on to a stay with his one good hand and directing the launching of the boat. He gave me a five-gallon jug of water to hold, and asked me what I was going to do. I told him what I thought was about the proper thing, and he told me then that the cook had the same idea, and ordered me to go forward and be ready to launch the ten-foot dingy. I remember very well that he turned then to swear at a colored stoker who was prowling around, done up in life preservers until he looked like a feather bed.

I went forward with my five-gallon jug of water, and when the captain came we launched the dingy, and they put me over the side to fend her off from the ship with an oar.

They handed me down the water jug, and then the cook came into the boat, and we sat there in the darkness, wondering why, by all our hopes of future happiness, the captain was so long in coming over the side and ordering us away from the doomed ship.

The captain was waiting for the other boat to go. Finally he hailed in the darkness: "Are you all right Mr. Graines?"

The first mate answered: "All right, sir."

"Shove off then," cried the captain. The captain was just about to swing over the rail when a dark form came forward and a voice said: "Captain, I go with you."

The captain answered: "Yes, Billy; get in."

It was Billy Higgins, the oiler. Billy dropped into the boat and a moment later the captain followed, bringing with him an end of about forty yards of lead line. The other end was attached to the rail of the ship. As we swung back to leaward the captain said: "Boys, we will stay right near the ship till she goes down."

This cheerful information, of course, filled us with glee. The line kept us headed properly into the wind and as we rode over the monstrous roarers we saw upon each rise the swaying lights of the dying *Commodore*.

When came the gray shade of dawn, the form of the *Commodore* grew slowly clear to us as our little ten-foot boat rose over each swell. She was floating with such an air of buoyancy that we laughed when we had time, and said: "What a guy it would be on those other fellows if she didn't sink at all."

But later we saw men aboard of her, and later still they began to hail us. I had forgotten to mention that previously we had loosened the end of the lead line and dropped much further to leaward. The men on board were a mystery to us, of course, as we had seen all the boats leave the ship. We rowed back to the ship, but did not approach too near, because we were four men in a ten-foot boat, and we knew that the touch of a hand on our gunwale would assuredly swamp us.

The first mate cried out from the ship that the third boat had foundered alongside. He cried that they had made rafts and wished us to tow them. The captain said: "All right."

Their rafts were floating astern.

"Jump in," cried the captain, but here was singular and most harrowing hesitation. There were five white men and two negroes. This scene in the gray light of morning impressed one as would a view into some place where ghosts move slowly. These seven men on the stern of the sinking *Commodore* were silent. Save the words of the mate to the captain there was no talk. Here was death, but here also was a most singular and indefinable kind of fortitude.

Four men, I remember, clambered over the railing and stood there watching the cold, steely sheen of the sweeping waves.

"Jump," cried the captain again. The old chief engineer first obeyed the order. He landed on the outside raft and the captain told him how to grip the raft, and he obeyed as promptly and as docilely as a scholar in riding school.

A stoker followed him, and then the first mate threw his hands over his head and plunged into the sea. He had no life belt, and for my part, even when he did this horrible thing, I somehow felt that I could see in the expression of his hands, and in the very toss of his head, as he leaped thus to death, that it was rage, rage, rage unspeakable that was in his heart at the time.

And then I saw Tom Smith, the man who was going to quit filibustering after this expedition, jump to a raft and turn his face toward us. On board the *Commodore* three men strode, still in silence and with their faces turned toward us. One man had his arms folded and was learning against the deckhouse. His feet were crossed, so that the toe of his left foot pointed downward. There they stood gazing at us, and neither from the deck nor from the rafts was a voice raised. Still was there this silence.

The colored stoker on the first raft threw us a line and we began to tow. Of course, we perfectly understood the absolute impossibility of any such thing; our dingy was within six inches of the water's edge, there was an enormous sea running, and I knew that under the circumstances a tugboat would have no light task in moving these rafts. But we tried it, and would have continued to try it indefinitely, but that something critical came to pass. I was at an oar and so faced the rafts. The cook controlled the line. Suddenly the boat began to go backward, and then we saw this negro on the first raft pulling on the line hand over hand and drawing us to him.

He had turned into a demon. He was wild, wild as a tiger. He was crouched on this raft and ready to spring. Every muscle of him seemed to be turned into an elastic spring. His eyes were almost white. His face was the face of a lost man reaching upward, and we knew that the weight of his hand on our gunwale doomed us. The cook let go of the line.

We rowed around to see if we could not get a line from the chief engineer, and all this time, mind you, there was no shrieks, no groans, but silence, silence and silence, and then the *Commodore* sank. She lurched to windward, then swung afar back, righted and dove into the sea, and the rafts were suddenly swallowed by this frightful maw of the ocean. And then by the men on the ten-foot dingy were words said that were still not words, something far beyond words.

The lighthouse of Mosquito Inlet stuck up above the horizon like the point of a pin. We turned our dingy toward the shore. The history of life in an open boat for thirty hours would no doubt be very instructive for the young, but none is to be told here now. For my part I would prefer to tell the story at once, because from it would shine the splendid manhood of Captain Edward Murphy and of William Higgins, the oiler, but let it suffice at this time to say that when we were swamped in the surf and making the best of our way toward the shore the captain gave orders amid the wildness of the breakers as clearly as if he had been on the quarterdeck of a battleship.

John Kitchell of Daytona came running down the beach, and as he ran the air was filled with clothes. If he had pulled a single lever and undressed, even as the fire horses harness, he could not to me seem to have stripped with more speed. He dashed into the water and grabbed the cook. Then he went after the captain, but the captain sent him to me, and then it was that we saw Billy Higgins lying with his forehead on sand that was clear of the water, and he was dead.

—*1897*

Questions: Reading, Responding, Arguing

1. What style or tone does Crane use in this descriptive piece?
2. This journalistic essay was the inspiration for Crane's "The Open Boat" (see page 1163). How are the two pieces different from one another, and why?
3. Explain why Crane chooses to focus on Billy Higgins as a character so frequently in the essay. Though it is nonfiction, what is Crane's argument or agenda in presenting the essay as he does?

Jessica Mitford (1917–1996)

The Embalming of Mr. Jones

Embalming is indeed a most extraordinary procedure, and one must wonder at the docility of Americans who each year pay hundreds of millions of dollars for its perpetuation, blissfully ignorant of what it is all about, what is done, how it is done. Not one in ten thousand has any idea of what actually takes place. Books on the subject are extremely hard to come by. They are not to be found in most libraries or bookshops.

In an era when huge television audiences watch surgical operations in the comfort of their living rooms, when, thanks to the animated cartoon, the geography of the digestive system has become familiar territory even to the nursery school set, in a land where the satisfaction of curiosity about almost all matters is a national pastime, the secrecy surrounding embalming can, surely, hardly be attributed to the inherent gruesomeness of the subject. Custom in this regard has within this century suffered a complete reversal. In the early days of American embalming, when it was performed in the home of the deceased, it was almost mandatory for some relative to stay by the embalmer's side and witness the procedure. Today, family members who might wish to be in attendance would certainly be dissuaded by the funeral director. All others, except apprentices, are excluded by law from the preparation room.

A close look at what does actually take place may explain in large measure the undertaker's intractable reticence concerning a procedure that has become his major *raison d'être*. Is it possible he fears that public information about embalming might lead patrons to wonder if they really want this service? If the funeral men are loath to discuss the subject outside the trade, the reader may, understandably, be equally loath to go on reading at this point. For those who have the stomach for it, let us part the formaldehyde curtain. . . .

The body is first laid out in the undertaker's morgue—or rather, Mr. Jones is reposing in the preparation room—to be readied to bid the world farewell.

The preparation room in any of the better funeral establishments has the tiled and sterile look of a surgery, and indeed the embalmer-restorative artist who does his chores there is beginning to adopt the term "dermasurgeon" (appropriately corrupted by some mortician-writers as "demisurgeon") to describe his calling. His equipment, consisting of scalpels, scissors, augers, forceps, clamps, needles, pumps, tubes, bowls and basins, is crudely imitative of the surgeon's as is his technique, acquired in a nine- or twelve-month post-high-school course in an embalming school. He is supplied by an advanced chemical industry with a bewildering array of fluids, sprays, pastes, oils, powders, creams, to fix or soften tissue, shrink or distend it as needed, dry it here, restore the moisture there. There are cosmetics, waxes and paints to fill and cover features, even plaster of Paris to replace entire limbs. There are ingenious aids to prop and stabilize the cadaver: a Vari-Pose Head Rest, the Edwards Arm and Hand Positioner, the Repose Block (to support the shoulders during the embalming), and the Throop Foot Positioner, which resembles an old-fashioned stocks.

Mr. John H. Eckels, president of the Eckels College of Mortuary Science, thus describes the first part of the embalming procedure: "In the hands of a skilled practitioner, this work may be done in a comparatively short time and without multilating the body other than by slight incision—so slight that it scarcely would cause serious inconvenience if made upon a living person. It is necessary to remove all the blood, and doing this not only helps in the disinfecting, but removes the principal cause of disfigurements due to discoloration."

Another textbook discusses the all-important time element: "The earlier this is done, the better, for every hour that elapses between death and embalming will add to the problems and complications encountered. . . ." Just how soon should one get going on the embalming? The author tells us, "On the basis of such scanty information made available to this profession through its rudimentary and haphazard system of technical research, we must conclude that the best results are to be obtained if the subject is embalmed before life is completely extinct—that is, before cellular death has occurred. In the average case, this would mean within an hour after somatic death." For those who feel that there is something a little rudimentary, not to say haphazard, about this advice, a comforting thought is offered by another writer. Speaking of fears entertained in early days of premature burial, he points out, "One of the effects of embalming by chemical injection, however, has been to dispel fears of live burial." How true; once the blood is removed, chances of live burial are indeed remote.

To return to Mr. Jones, the blood is drained out through the veins and replaced by embalming fluid pumped in through the arteries. As noted in *The Principles and Practices of Embalming*, "every operator has a favorite injection and drainage point—a fact which becomes a handicap only if he fails or refuses to forsake his favorites when conditions demand it." Typical favorites are the carotid artery, femoral artery, jugular vein, subclavian vein. There are various choices of embalming fluid. If Flextone is used, it will produce a "mild, flexible rigidity. The skin retains a velvety softness, the tissues are rubbery and pliable. Ideal for women and children." It may be blended with B. and G. Products Company's Lyf-Lyk tint, which is guaranteed to reproduce "nature's own skin texture . . . the velvety appearance of living tissue." Suntone comes in three separate tints: Suntan; Special Cosmetic Tint, a pink shade "especially indicated for young female subjects"; and Regular Cosmetic Tint, moderately pink.

About three to six gallons of a dyed and perfumed solution of formaldehyde, glycerin, borax, phenol, alcohol and water is soon circulating through Mr. Jones, whose mouth has been sewn together with a "needle directed upward between the upper lip and gum and brought out through the left nostril," with the corners raised slightly "for a more pleasant expression." If he should be buck-toothed, his teeth are cleaned with Bon Ami and coated with colorless nail polish. His eyes, meanwhile, are closed with flesh-tinted eye caps and eye cement.

The next step is to have at Mr. Jones with a thing called a trocar. This is a long, hollow needle attached to a tube. It is jabbed into the abdomen, poked around the entrails and chest cavity, the contents of which are pumped out and replaced with "cavity fluid." This is done, and the hole in the abdomen sewed up, Mr. Jones's face is heavily creamed (to protect the skin from burns which may be caused by leakage of the chemicals), and he is covered with a sheet and left unmolested for a while. But not for long—there is more, much more, in store for him. He has been embalmed, but not yet restored, and the best time to start restorative work is eight to ten hours after embalming, when the tissues have become firm and dry.

The object of all this attention to the corpse, it must be remembered, is to make it presentable for viewing in an attitude of healthy repose. "Our customs require the presentation of our dead in the semblance of normality . . . unmarred by the ravages of illness, disease or mutilation," says Mr. J. Sheridan Mayer in his *Restorative Art*. This is rather a large order since few people die in the full bloom of health, unravaged by illness and unmarked by some disfigurement. The funeral industry is equal to the challenge: "In some cases the gruesome appearance of a mutilated or disease-ridden subject may be quite discouraging. The task of restoration may seem impossible and shake the confidence of the embalmer. This is the time for intestinal fortitude and determination. Once the formative work is begun and affected tissues are cleaned or removed, all doubts of success vanish. It is surprising and gratifying to discover the results which may be obtained."

The embalmer, having allowed an appropriate interval to elapse, returns to the attack, but now he brings into play the skill and equipment of sculptor and cosmetician. Is a hand missing? Casting one in plaster of Paris is a simple matter. "For replacement purposes, only a cast of the back of the hand is necessary; this is within the ability of the average operator and is quite adequate." If a lip or two, a nose or an ear should be missing, the embalmer has at hand a variety of restorative waxes with which to model replacements. Pores and skin texture are simulated by stippling with a little brush, and over this cosmetics are laid on. Head off? Decapitation cases are rather routinely handled. Ragged edges are trimmed, and head joined to torso with a series of splints, wires and sutures. It is a good idea to have a little something at the neck—a scarf or high collar—when time for viewing comes. Swollen mouth? Cut out tissue as needed from inside the lips. If too much is removed, the surface contour can easily be restored by padding with cotton. Swollen necks and cheeks are reduced by removing tissue through vertical incisions made down each side of the neck. "When the deceased is casketed, the pillow will hide the suture incisions . . . as an extra precaution against leakage, the suture may be painted with liquid sealer."

The opposite condition is more likely to be present itself—that of emaciation. His hypodermnic syringe now loaded with massage cream, the embalmer seeks out and fills the hollowed and sunken areas by injection. In this procedure the backs of the hands and fingers and the under-chin area should not be neglected.

Positioning the lips is a problem that recurrently challenges the ingenuity of the embalmer. Closed too tightly, they tend to give a stern, even disapproving expression. Ideally, embalmers feel, the lips should give the impression of being ever so slightly parted, the upper lip protruding slightly for a more youthful appearance. This takes some engineering, however, as the lips tend to drift apart. Lip drift can sometimes be remedied by pushing one or two straight pins through the inner margin of the lower lip and then inserting them between the two front upper teeth. If Mr. Jones happens to have no teeth, the pins can just as easily be anchored in his Armstrong Face Former and Denture Replacer. Another method to maintain lip closure is to dislocate the lower jaw, which is then held in its new position by a wire run through holes which have been drilled through the upper jaws at the midline. As the French are fond of saying, *il faut souffrir pour être belle.*[1]

If Mr. Jones has died of jaundice, the embalming fluid will very likely turn him green. Does this deter the embalmer? Not if he has intestinal fortitude. Masking pastes and cosmetics are heavily laid on, burial garments and casket interiors are color-correlated with particular care, and Jones is displayed beneath rose-colored lights. Friends will say, "How *well* he looks." Death by carbon monoxide, on the other hand, can be rather a good thing from the embalmer's viewpoint: "One advantage is the fact that this type of discoloration is an exaggerated form of a natural pink coloration." This is because the healthy glow is already present and needs but little attention.

The patching and filling completed, Mr. Jones is now shaved, washed and dressed. Cream-based cosmetic, available in pink, flesh, suntan, brunette and blonde, is applied to his hands and face, his hair is shampooed and combed (and, in the case of Mrs. Jones, set), his hands manicured. For the horny-handed son of toil special care must be taken; cream should be applied to remove ingrained grime, and the nails cleaned. "If he were not in the habit of h'ving them manicured in life, trimming and shaping is advised for better appearance—never questioned by kin."

[1] It is necessary to suffer in order to be beautiful.

Jones is now ready for casketing (this is the present participle of the verb "to casket"). In this operation his right shoulder should be depressed slightly "to turn the body a bit to the right and soften the appearance of lying flat on the back." Positioning the hands is a matter of importance, and special rubber positioning blocks may be used. The hands should be cupped slightly for a more lifelike, relaxed appearance. Proper placement of the body requires a delicate sense of balance. It should lie as high as possible in the casket, yet not so high that the lid, when lowered, will hit the nose. On the other hand, we are cautioned, placing the body too low "creates the impression that the body is in a box."

Jones is next wheeled into the appointed slumber room where a few last touches may be added—his favorite pipe placed in his hand or, if he was a great reader, a book propped into position. (In the case of little Master Jones a Teddy bear may be clutched.) Here he will hold open house for a few days, visiting hours 10 a.m. to 9 p.m.

—1963

Questions: Reading, Responding, Arguing

1. Presumably, Mitford focuses on death to present an argument. What is that argument?
2. Why, as Mitford says, is it so hard to "part the formaldehyde curtain"? What limits our desire to discuss or read about death?
3. What is accomplished by describing embalming so systematically? Why does Mitford write the essay as she does?
4. The essay presents itself as a set of problems (for the embalmer) followed by solutions. How does this format relate to the topic of death?

Jerome Groopman (b. 1939)

The Last Deal

"I won't take no for an answer. It's bullshit. I'm fifty-four. I'm not ready to just pack it up and die. I'm a fighter. I don't buy that *nothing* can be done."

As he spoke, Kirk Bains locked his jaundiced eyes on mine. He was obviously studying my face, looking for clues, trying to read my response in advance. I imagined that it was a style he adopted in his business meetings, where he would face down clients by looking hard into their eyes, to gauge whether the project and the people before him were worth his resources. This time, though, the roles were reversed.

"You've seen my records from Yale and Sloan-Kettering and M. D. Anderson," he went on. "They think I'm too sick for their research studies. So you cook up some new magic. Make me a guinea pig. I take risks all the time—that's my business. I won't sue you. My cousin Grant says you're a medical genius, a wizard."

"That's kind of Grant to say, but I'm not a genius or a wizard, Mr. Bains."

"Well, Dr. Groopman, I need you to be. Because you're my last hope."

Sitting at my desk in the oncology clinic at Harvard's Beth Israel Deaconess Medical Center, where I work, I had read Kirkland Bains's records, all ninety-six photocopied pages, and had no thoughts of magic, just cold despair. I had searched for some detail that might have been overlooked or incompletely investigated, hoping it might guide me to devise a rational and possibly effective treatment. But the cat scans, operative reports, and blood tests left no basis for hope. The oncologists at Yale, Sloan-Kettering, and M. D. Anderson had quickly reached their conclusions, telegraphed in the records in disinterested clinical syntax: "Diffusely metastatic renal carcinoma. Multiple sites including liver, bones, and lungs involved. No effective therapy. Palliative care advised."

I imagined how they had translated this in private to his wife, Catherine, in order to dissuade him from pursuing treatment: the kidney cancer has spread throughout his body; the few drugs we have don't work at this stage; he will only be hurt by their toxicities; his expected survival is no more than several weeks; it's best for your husband to be at home, made comfortable, and allowed to die.

I looked at Kirk Bains—his jet-black hair, sharp, aquiline nose, and square jaw: a handsome and decisive face and wondered how long it would take him to accept his condition. I took an unused tablet of lined white paper from my desk drawer, put it where the records had been, and sat poised to write.

"I've read the reports, Mr. Bains."

"Call me Kirk, Dr. Groopman."

"Then call me Jerry. Let's start fresh. I want to hear the story directly from you—not from the records—and in detail, from the time you first noticed something was wrong. Then I'll examine you. From top to bottom. After that, we'll think this through together." (Bains's name, like certain others in this article, has been changed.)

I knew he'd been through this three times before, but I wasn't performing a perfunctory ritual. Even if I discovered no new fact or physical finding, there was a journey taken when I listened to a patient recount his history and when I palpated his body. It was a journey of the senses—hearing, touching, seeing—which carried me into another dimension, that of intuition.

I planned to walk deliberately along the milestones of Kirk's life—the character of his parents and his siblings, the extent of his education, the nature of his occupation, the details of his travel, the status of his personal relationships, the vicissitudes of his prior and current illnesses and treatments—and for brief but illuminating moments I would become integrated into his experience.

After imagining his past, I would be prepared to enter his present through the physical examination. My hands would press deeply into his abdomen to outline the breadth and texture of his inner organs; my eyes would peer behind his pupils to read the barometers of cerebral pressure and blood flow displayed on his retinas; my ears, linked by the stethoscope, would hear the timbre of his heart. In Kirk's case, though, I feared that I might not reach the dimension of intuition. The cat scans and blood tests and operative findings—the consensus of my medical colleagues in New Haven, New York, and Houston—were like shackles on the imagination.

"I was on the golf course in Palm Beach," Kirk began. "The morning of September 20th. With two Jap investors. They had come in from Osaka. They were considering buying out my share in a refinery in the Gulf, off Galveston. I'm the lead investor. The refinery is expanding operations, betting that oil will recover. Good time to get in—early, before it becomes obvious to every maiden aunt with a pension fund. Anyway, we got up early to play and beat the heat. Japs are crazy for golf. Did you know that? If you ever want something from a Jap, first play golf with him. It doesn't hurt if you let him win, either."

I nodded uncomfortably, disturbed by his brazen attitude but considering how it might prove useful in the fight against his cancer.

"And at the first tee I felt this . . . this tug in my back. It wasn't really a pain. Not like sciatica, which I had once, years ago. Not sharp, like a knife cutting into me. But more a dull, heavy ache, like a charley horse that wouldn't let up. It was on my right side. I tried to ignore it, but it pulled at me through the morning. A lot of my shots went wide, into the rough. I played all eighteen holes. This time, I didn't have to let the Japs win."

Kirk stopped for a moment, in order to regain his breath. I noticed that his lips had assumed a faint bluish tinge of cyanosis, an indication that even the minimal exertion of speaking entirely consumed the limited oxygen carried by his blood.

"Did they buy out your share in the refinery?"

"Not yet. But they will. They're coming back after Christmas. Actually, after the New Year, which is a big deal in Japan. So by January you have to have this fucking tumor gone. I'll take them out again. Depending on the final terms of the buyout, I'll beat them or let them win—but only by a few strokes either way." Kirk gave me a sly, knowing smile, counting me as a co-conspirator in his plan.

His medical history contained no clue to why Kirkland Bains developed kidney cancer at the age of fifty-four. He was born and reared on an estate in Newport, Rhode Island. No one in the family was known to have suffered from diseases of the kidney or the bladder. The Bainses, over several generations, had owned shipbuilding facilities along the southern New England coast, but Kirk and his father rarely visited them. They were managed by intermediaries, and as long as the balance sheets showed healthy yearly profits his father was content to live the detached life of a man born to considerable wealth. Kirk and his mother moved in tow with his father through the ebb and flow of the social seasons: autumn in Manhattan, summer on Mt. Desert Island, in Maine, and a spring tour through the Continent.

Kidney cancer is known to be associated with a variety of environmental toxins. Cadmium, a metal used in batteries, is one of the best known of these pollutants. It had contaminated the water table surrounding many factories that carelessly dumped their spent charges into nearby rivers or buried them in the earth without putting them in sealed containers. Cadmium precipitated in the kidney, and traces of the metal could sometimes be found in the malignant cells that formed the initial seed of a cancer. Other factory materials, including petroleum products and asbestos, are also associated with kidney cancer. But when I asked Kirk about such exposures he reaffirmed that he had never "dirtied his hands" in his father's shipyards. His father had instructed him in how the business was financed, its margins and beneficial capital depreciations, asserting it was "foolish to pretend to be a worker when you're the owner's son." Anyway, Kirk went on, after his father's death, in the late nineteen-fifties, his estate had liquidated the shipbuilding interests, which was fortunate since the industry in New England had dropped way off by then.

In the past two decades, cadmium, asbestos, and petroleum products had become unusual causes of kidney cancer, thanks to stricter regulation of their industrial uses. Tobacco was now the most common predisposing factor: it increased the risk for the disease two- to three-fold. The tars from cigarette smoke leached from the lungs into the bloodstream, and then were deposited in the kidneys. Kirk told me he had smoked, but only for a short time, at boarding school, and, even then, just a few cigarettes a day.

"Everyone did in the fifties at prep school," he said. "But I stopped smoking when I left for Dartmouth. Which is a bit of a blur, really. Because I majored in drinking. The diploma said 'economics,' but it was really beer. Beer doesn't cause kidney cancer, does it?"

"Not to my knowledge."

"Too bad. We could short the beer companies, then let out the bad news, and make a bundle."

"And go to jail together."

"Hospital, jail—not much difference that I can see."

He had travelled all over the world, using the funds he inherited after his father's death to establish an independent investment company that focussed on venture capital and commodities trading. Kirk had first worked out of Lagos, in the early days of Nigerian oil, when "anyone who didn't leave Africa with a few gold bars in his luggage had to be an idiot." He had spent time in Egypt and in the Lower Nile Valley, but had not contracted schistosomiasis, a parasite that infests the genitourinary system, causing inflammation and scarring of the tissues, and predisposes to bladder cancer. He had never had radiation exposure, or even kidney stones. He disliked medicines, and avoided over-the-counter analgesics for headache, which could accumulate in the kidneys and had been linked, when used regularly and in high doses, with kidney cancer.

"We Bainses are disgustingly hardy," Kirk told me. "Good proto-plasm. That's why it's worth trying some magic on me."

But much magic had been tried for this particular cancer, and none of it had worked. Every known chemotherapy drug had been tested against the disease at one time or another, and the "response rates"—meaning the percentages of treated patients who had meaningful shrinkage of the tumor after therapy—were minimal. This had led researchers to ask what made renal carcinoma so resistant to the poisons that worked well against other cancers, including those arising in the neighboring ureter and bladder. Why was kidney cancer so intractable?

The weight of evidence suggested that the malignant cell that multiplies to form kidney cancer has an overactive pump on its surface. A pump called the P-glycoprotein is a normal component of the cells of the kidney. It works to expel unwanted substances that regularly cross the kidney-cell membrane and enter the inner cytoplasm. One could understand why cells whose job was to filter unwanted and toxic wastes from our blood to form the excreted urine would be equipped with active pumps that prevented the retention of noxious molecules.

But in cancerous cells this protective armor had been made even thicker and more resilient. When the toxic molecules known as chemotherapy were sent to assault the tumor, they were easily repelled by the cancer cells—quickly pumped back into the bloodstream by the P-glycoprotein. No one had yet devised a strategy to deactivate the cancer's overzealous pump without destroying the normal one. This maddening disregard by kidney cancer of virtually all chemotherapeutic agents had led it to be labelled, in oncological jargon, M.D.R., for "multidrug resistant."

Kirk and I finished reviewing his medical history—how he returned from Palm Beach to see his internist in Tarrytown, New York, who thought the ache in his flank was a pulled muscle from too much golf. But a week later Kirk developed a fever and his urine became tea-colored, prompting the internist to investigate his complaint further.

The tea color proved to be from small amounts of blood in his urine, and he was sent to a urologist to identify the source of bleeding. A cystoscopy was then performed—a procedure involving the insertion of an instrument like a telescope through the urethra into the bladder. This had revealed nothing abnormal. So a dye study of the kidneys and then a cat scan of his abdomen were done, to look for a site of bleeding within the kidney proper.

The urologist had broken the news to Kirk with a long preamble, explaining that kidney cancer was insidious and hard to detect, because, as in Kirk's case, it often grew up and into the abdomen, so it couldn't be easily palpated on physical exam. There was a mass, some twelve centimetres in maximum diameter, extending from the upper pole of the right kidney to the base of the liver, with tentacles of cancer that had invaded and extended along the channels of the major veins. One tentacle of cancer had tracked so far upward that it had passed the diaphragm and entered into the venous circulation of the chest. If its progress was not checked, it would soon invade the right atrium of the heart.

Kirk had been operated on during the second week of October at Yale–New Haven Hospital. The primary tumor and adjoining kidney had been successfully excised from his abdomen, and so had the malignant tentacles invading the veins. But numerous deposits of cancer had to be left behind, in the liver, the intestines, and the pelvic bones. Those deposits were too extensive to yield to the surgeon's scalpel.

"I had hoped it would be a replay of 'The Exorcist,' " Kirk said dryly. "Remember how the priest took the demon out of the child—a bloody, ugly creature? I thought the surgeon would do the same. Maybe I'd have been better off with a priest than with a doctor. Never thought I'd need the clergy. But that's what everyone is recommending now."

"Are you affiliated with a church?" I always try to learn the scope of religious feeling, the ties of the patient and his family to faith.

"Episcopalian. I celebrate Christmas. The food. The music. Decorating the tree. Giving gifts. That's fun. But the religion—I can't put much stock in a church founded because Henry VIII wanted a younger wife."

My response was a skeptical look.

"Let me put it in my own terms. I'm not a long-term investor. I like quick returns. I don't believe in working for dividends paid only in Heaven."

It was time to move to the examining room. Kirk paused and looked down sheepishly. "I need my wife to help undress me," he said. "I can't manage the belt and the pants anymore. Can your secretary call her from the waiting room?"

His wife, Cathy, a large-boned woman with rich-blue eyes, brunette hair in a pageboy cut, and a flowing flower-print dress, readily removed Kirk's navy blazer and pine-green club tie—for Dartmouth, she informed me. But the buttons on his starched white oxford shirt stubbornly resisted her trembling fingers, his ballooned, cancer-filled abdomen locking them in the taut slits of the buttonholes. "I was inexperienced when I married Kirk," Cathy said. "I guess I never really learned how to undress men."

Kirk failed to laugh with her, and a heavy silence fell over the room. Cathy finally removed Kirk's last article of clothing, a pair of blue cotton boxer shorts, and briefly exposed his fluid-filled genitals before I covered him with a hospital gown. I tied the neck string of the gown loosely, so I could maneuver my stethoscope to listen to his lungs and heart without exposing him unnecessarily.

"I'm a bag of water. Even my balls are bathed in this sewage from the cancer."

Cathy waved goodbye, with a forced smile, as she left the room. Kirk did not acknowledge her exit.

There is no avoiding the feelings of shame and humiliation caused by the forced dependency of disease. These emotions are raw at moments like this, exposed before another, even a physician. But as much as possible I wanted Kirk to feel like a person with worth and substance, not just a patient.

"Tell me more about Galveston," I said as I adjusted the head of my stethoscope and prepared to listen to his lungs.

"You invest?"

"Not like you. Fidelity mutual funds. But I'm interested in venture capital."

"Why?"

"Because it has similarities to scientific research. You try to capitalize on unique ideas by mobilizing technology, people, resources. And you need to be rigorously critical with yourself—facing all problems and set-backs head on, because there's no room for delusion."

Kirk nodded sagely. He elaborated on the deal—how he was the first one in after he realized that oil demand would increase sharply, partly because Iraq was still shut out of the market, and partly because there was continued expansion in the economy. And now, only five months later, a lot of people wanted in, including the Japanese. Which meant it was time to get out. He was counting on a tidy twofold return.

"But there's a difference between what I do and what you do," Kirk said. "I don't give a damn about the product. In your world, it's the product that matters—new knowledge that can lead to curing a disease. For me, the product means nothing. It can be oil or platinum or software or widgets. It's all a shell game played for big money, and once I win enough I wave goodbye."

I continued my physical examination as he explained what drove him in his work: the delicious pleasure of seeing where to go before the crowd does; the challenge of making fast decisions; the fun of everyone trying to outsmart everyone else. I palpated almond-size rock hard lumps behind his left ear—certainly deposits of his kidney cancer growing outward from the mastoid bone. His breath sounds were harsh and wheezy throughout his chest from the masses of cancer. His abdomen was bulging as if he were in the last month of pregnancy. It was filled with malignant ascites, a mixed brew of protein-rich fluid that had seeped from his liver, spleen, and lymph nodes and nourished schools of swimming cancer cells. By pressing down over his liver, I could outline the stony metastatic nodules growing out from its surface. There were several tender areas in his pelvis corresponding to the tumors seen on the cat scan. His legs were elephantine—columns of retained fluid that flared outward at the ankles as gravity settled the edema under the weight of his upper body.

It was easy to understand why Kirk had been turned away from so many medical centers. I had to agree with the prognosis he had been given: his remaining life span was very likely no more than a few weeks. He would soon die of oxygen deprivation as the tumor replaced his lungs, or lapse into coma from liver or kidney failure as the cancer strangled these organs. As I examined him, I could feel death in the coolness of his flesh, in the sunken, jaundiced eyes, in the mottled color of his skin and lips.

But Kirk was not prepared to die. He had pleaded to be given the chance to fight. And I was his last hope. But was there really any hope to be offered?

I backtracked in my mind and looked for any opening, any opportunity to devise a therapy that might help him, even in some small way. Although chemotherapy was rarely effective, one drug, vinblastine, had been reported to work in some cases. Vinblastine is a poison from the periwinkle plant, which disrupts the cell during its mitosis, or process of division. I put its chance of working in Kirk at about one in a hundred, at best. And if it partly shrank the cancer the benefit would probably be transient, while the side effects of vinblastine could be lasting: lowering of blood counts, with predisposition to infection, and paralysis of intestinal movement, causing painful expansion of the bowel from the pressure of its retained contents. This intestinal paralysis is called an ileus, and, with Kirk's abdomen riddled with cancer and bathed in the ascites, an ileus would be a particularly excruciating side effect.

Because men develop kidney cancer from three to five times as frequently as women, it is postulated that male hormones promote its growth and female hormones limit it. The female hormone progesterone has been reported to shrink kidney cancer in some cases. But the chances of a meaningful effect on an extensive disease like Kirk's were even smaller than those I had estimated for vinblastine. The major side effect of progesterone is hyperventilation. Because his lungs were filled with metastases, hyperventilation would be poorly tolerated: it might even precipitate respiratory collapse as his chest muscles became fatigued from the hormone-induced drive to breathe faster.

I was well acquainted with the limitations of the available therapies for metastatic kidney cancer because, four years earlier, the Food and Drug Administration's advisory committee on biological therapies, of which I was chairman, had been asked to evaluate a new approach to the disease.

In the nineteen-eighties, a naturally occurring protein called interleukin-2 was discovered to activate so-called killer T cells; in a healthy immune system, the killer cells are always on patrol, ready to destroy cancer cells should they be detected. Pioneering work at the National Cancer Institute, in Bethesda, indicated that treatment with interleukin-2 could result in regression of some cases of kidney cancer. That finding prompted widespread resting of interleukin-2, and ultimately an application to the F.D.A. requesting its approval in the disease.

It was our advisory committee that the F.D.A. convened to act as an independent assessor of the benefits and risks of interleukin-2 treatment for kidney cancer. The assessment provoked a heated and trying debate. All of us on the committee were acutely aware of the absence of good therapy for this particular malignancy. But interleukin-2, though a natural product, proved to have severe side effects when it was given in the large doses apparently needed to stimulate killer T cells. Most patients who were treated developed spiking fevers, whole-body rash, and severe cardiac and pulmonary toxicities, with leakage of fluid from the circulation and precipitous falls in blood pressure, causing shock. And the tumor responses, although occasionally dramatic, were generally of short duration. Moreover, regressions of the cancer were usually seen in people with limited metastatic deposits, and not in people with the kind of extensive disease and organ failure Kirk had. Only a small subset of kidney-cancer patients was likely to benefit from the treatment, though, with the high cost of toxicities. The initial optimism about interleukin-2 had waned.

Our advisory committee finally decided to approve interleukin-2 in the United States but to recommend its use only in that small subset of patients without extensive disease, and to emphasize the necessity of careful monitoring. We felt it important to provide access to the protein for those who might benefit, even if the chances were small, because there were no other real options. By recommending its limited use, we intended to spare the larger population of kidney-cancer patients the protein's toxic effects and unlikely benefits.

"Make me a guinea pig," Kirk had said.

Did he really understand what that meant? Clinical experimentation was a powerful engine of progress in modern medicine. It was necessary for success fully translating basic-research discoveries from the laboratory into bedside treatments. "Informed consent" was the underpinning of ethical clinical experimentation: the free consent of an understanding patient was required before any trial test of unproved therapies. But could Kirk soberly assess the considerable risks and minimal benefits? How rational can our decisions be when we are desperate and feel unprepared to die? What's more, Kirk didn't fit into any ethically and scientifically reviewed research protocol at my Harvard hospital or at any of the prestigious cancer centers he had already visited. He was too sick, too advanced in his disease—a so-called outlier, in the crude terminology of clinical trials, who was unlikely to benefit, and would very likely suffer side effects. His failure to qualify as an appropriate research subject was the reason that others had turned him away.

I looked at Kirk's jaundiced, bloated form before me, trying to read something beyond the obvious, beyond what the laboratory tests and the cat scans and the physical exams had already written. And I saw in his eyes a deep determination not to give in, despite what he must have realized long ago—that his situation was terminal, that there was no known effective treatment. I didn't know yet why he wanted so much to live. It was too early in our relationship for me to probe. But I felt the energy that remained within his failing body—the force he had tried to convey when he shook my hand, the intensity in his voice when he detailed the Galveston deal, and even the powerful resentment of Cathy's efforts to undo his clothes.

And I looked hard into myself, trying to make sure that what I might do would be for him, not for me. A real chance of helping Kirk was needed to justify treating him. But what kind of odds constituted "a real chance"? Was one in fifty enough? What if Kirk's chances were one in a hundred or one in a thousand? Where was the end-point in this calculus? Kirk was right: I *was* his last hope. And his chances were not zero. But I had to be sure that he understood—as well as a frightened and desperate person, facing death, could understand—what treatment meant. I called Cathy back to make sure, and we convened in my office. This time I didn't sit removed, behind my desk, but, rather, at the apex of a triangle formed by our three chairs.

"Kirk, remember my telling you that I'm not a magician or a wizard."

I saw his face drop with the anticipation that what would follow was another rejection, an exile into hopelessness and certain death. Cathy reached to hold his hand, but he withdrew from her attempt at comfort.

"I wish I were. I wish I could be the alchemist who makes gold from lead, who could transform your cancer cells back to normal. But I'm not. No one is. We, together, have to weigh what is known and what is unknown, and come to the best decision for you. And a wizard's smoke and mirrors couldn't hide the conclusion that there is no effective therapy for most people."

I paused, to make sure that he and Cathy were taking it in, and then went on; "The treatments that are given work only rarely in cases like yours, because your disease is so extensive and your organ function severely impaired. The treatments can have terrible side effects. They can increase your pain without benefitting you. They might even shorten your life. Bluntly said, the treatments might kill you without helping you."

Cathy winced at this statement. Kirk did not react.

"And, if you are treated, then it's outside any scientifically and ethically reviewed and approved protocol. We will, of course, follow the principles of such protocols, but you take unknown risks and have to realize we're flying by the seat of our pants without much precedent."

"May I interrupt?" Kirk asked politely.

"Of course."

"Jerry, I'm a damn successful venture capitalist. And I know what a lousy investment I am. The time on my mortgage is almost up. I have no inventory left. And this fucking cancer is taking my market share, meaning my life."

Cathy's eyes filled with tears. I reached over for a box of tissues on my desk and handed them to her.

Kirk gave her time to compose herself, and then went on, "But I'm willing to fight, to my last breath, to try and make it. If you will help me, I'll undergo anything. The worst side effects. They can't be worse to me than"—he paused—"than being dead. I'm tough as nails, in business and most other matters. My whole life, I haven't really depended on anyone but myself. Cathy can tell you that I'm a pain in the ass, full of piss and vinegar. I'll hear you out, Jerry, if it makes you feel better. But my mind is made up to go for it. What the hell? What other options do I have—consult with William?"

"William? Who's William?"

"William is an Englishman in his seventies in Jupiter, Florida— where my mother and her rich-widow cronics live. He's a faith healer, a charlatan. He's also a gigolo. First he sprinkles herbal powders on the widows, then he screws them. That cures their aches and pains. Mother is insisting William come to heal me. She wants to fly him to New York if you turn me down. Are you going to force me to see William?" Kirk smiled.

I smiled, too, and realized, at that incongruous moment, that Kirk was capable of making rational choices, that it was his right to fight, despite the odds.

I admitted Kirk directly to the hospital from my office. He was too sick to return home to Tarrytown, and if we were going to treat him we needed to start immediately.

The battle was now joined, and I could feel between us the electric exhilaration that flows through soldiers who decide to charge forward together into the unknown. We pumped each other up with the medical equivalents of war cries. We would fight with all the weapons in our armamentarium, using a strategy to maximize their meagre benefits and minimize their considerable risks. I would give Kirk interleukin-2 for five days, which was the schedule approved by the F.D.A., but would give it in lower doses; I hoped that they would still be enough to activate his killer T cells but would not send him into shock. And with the first dose of interleukin-2 we would give him a single dose of vinblastine. Again, because of his condition, I calculated a modification of the dose to avoid side effects. If these first two treatments went well, he would begin daily progesterone.

Later that night, when I decided to return to Kirk's hospital room, my euphoria had begun to wane. Perhaps I had endorsed unrealistic hopes, despite what Kirk said about understanding the odds and the likelihood of side effects.

I returned to check that everything I had ordered for the treatment had been set in motion, and to speak with Kirk once more about our decision. Cathy had already left for Tarrytown, to bring back things Kirk wanted for the hospital stay. I assumed that he would have finished dinner and would be preparing to sleep after such an exhausting day. But when I looked into his room I saw all the lights on, the TV playing, and Kirk sitting upright in bed, wide-eyed.

"Ready for tomorrow?" I asked.

"Absolutely, partner."

I suggested that he go to sleep after we talked. I had prescribed a sleeping pill if he needed one. Should I ring the nurse to leave it at his bedside?

Kirk vigorously shook his head. I saw his hand begin to tremble, and reached for it, noting that it had a cool, clammy texture, despite the warmth of the room and the blankets that were pulled around him.

We sat together without speaking. Finally, I asked, "Are you thinking you could die tonight? You won't, Kirk."

Kirk pursed his lips, containing his emotion. I gripped his hand more tightly.

"So you're a prophet, not a wizard. Shall I call you St. Jerome? I like that name. St. Jerome."

I smiled uncomfortably. "I'm hardly a saint. And certainly no prophet. But you're in a hospital, being closely monitored. We won't let you slip away."

"I didn't expect to be so afraid, Jerry." He paused. "I'm not sure why. I rarely feel afraid. Maybe it's because I know that this is my last chance and I'll probably die, and after death . . . It's just nothingness."

Now I thought I understood why he had insisted on treatment. "So then it would be the same as before we were born," I said. "Is that terrifying, to be unborn? That's what my father used to say to comfort me as a child when I asked him about death."

Kirk said, "See if you still find that enough comfort when you're the one in this bed. Nothingness. No time. No place. No form. I don't ask for Heaven. I'd take Hell. Just to be."

I thought again about those words the next morning, as an amber autumn sun filtered through Kirk's window and warmed the room. Tricia McGann, a vivacious, curly-haired chemotherapy nurse, was reviewing with Kirk and Cathy the details of interleukin-2, vinblastine, and progesterone—the schedule we had devised—for their combined use and their expected side effects.

"I'm ready to be deep-fried," Kirk answered when I asked once again for a clear statement that would constitute his informed consent, with Tricia as a witness. I created an ad-hoc document and inserted it in his medical chart, written in the style of an informed consent that would ordinarily accompany a formal clinical-research protocol.

The unknowns of biology and medicine exist at every moment for every patient and every doctor. But here, in Kirk's case, they were present in the extreme. We would be mixing together three drugs that had never been mixed together before—not in this way, at these doses, on this schedule, and certainly never in this individual, in whom the metabolism and circulation of the drugs would be unpredictably altered by a failing liver, a rising level of serum calcium, a single functioning kidney, and a slowed circulation.

But while he was in Tricia's hands it was safe for me to detach myself from the issues of his disease and its impending treatment, and to return to the scene of the night before. I thought again about how much I had experienced of death, from the moment I watched my father die to now, each day in my work. I thought about how we all develop our own inner pictures of death and an afterlife, from the stories and words we hear as children, which form our first image. As we pass through life, we redraw these images, hoping that at the end we will be prepared for what awaits.

My childhood concept of death, as I'd told Kirk, came from conversations with my father. He had subscribed to the most ancient Jewish concept—that there is no Heaven or Hell, no state of conscious existence similar to the one we enjoy in this life, and that what awaits us on the other side of life is vague and indescribable, a sense that in some way we are reunited with the divine energy of God that permeates the universe, but in a form that we cannot imagine or grasp. My father's focus was on memory—that existence is perpetuated in the hearts and minds of the people who remember those who are gone. That was the only notion of immortality he could conceive. "I will live on in my children," he would say.

After my father died, it was impossible for me to imagine him as disintegrated into nothingness. Perhaps for that reason, I rarely visited his grave. It was too painful, too stark an image in my mind, that his body, the warm, expansive body that had snuggled me in bed when I was fearing the shadows of the night, had held me up in the water when I was learning to swim, had embraced me with surprising strength when I succeeded and with even greater strength when I failed—that that body was now inanimate matter, dispersed in the soil as atoms of carbon and nitrogen, hydrogen and sulfur. And nothing more.

I hoped that when my time came I would not lie terrified in bed, like Kirk. I hoped that my intimate relationship with death, beginning with the death of my father and extending through the deaths of so many of the patients I had cared for, would somehow lessen the fear, and allow me to face the unknown with the sense that others had gone before me, and that all those I now knew would follow. At some future time, I might talk about some of these thoughts and feelings with Kirk. But this was not such a moment, because we had stubbornly "decided" not to surrender to the inevitable. I needed to help Kirk concentrate his energies on the battle that loomed, and bolster him to resist the toxic blows of his treatment—particularly the interleukin-2.

"Ready to fight, Kirk?"

"Absolutely. I'll surprise you. There'll be a tenfold return on your investment."

"I like that kind of payout. Much better than my Fidelity funds."

When I care for a patient, I have noticed, a metaphor sometimes emerges that draws on a unique element in the patient's work or family or cultural heritage. Throughout the relationship, when we assess an option or embark upon it, when it succeeds or it fails, when we enter remission and resume living or acknowledge that our therapy has not succeeded and that the end is near—at each critical point, we invoke our metaphor. It becomes our intimate form of communication, drawing us closer, like children who invent a secret language, or siblings with special words and phrases that have resonance for them and no one else.

Kirk and I had created our metaphor after only two days, and I believed at this moment that it was a good one for his condition. He would gain strength from returning to the images that had spelled success in his life. He could again be the triumphant contrarian, betting against the market's prevailing wisdom, and proving to the world that the commodity of his life had a future.

As expected, Kirk developed a high fever and severe shaking chills from the interleukin-2. On the third day of treatment, his blood pressure dropped precipitously, and we had to infuse fluids to support his circulation. He developed a blistering rash as well, and needed steroids to calm his angry skin. On the fourth day, his wheezing worsened. A chest X-ray showed seepage of fluid from his circulation into his lungs—a state called pulmonary edema. I feared we would need to insert a breathing tube and place him on a respirator to support his oxygenation, but, luckily, we did not need that invasive measure, managing instead to provide oxygen through a face mask and to relieve the spasms in his airways with adrenalinelike drugs and high doses of diuretics.

I had been extremely careful about his dose of vinblastine, because that drug is excreted from the body through the bile, and, with his jaundice and liver dysfunction, there was a risk of its accumulating to very toxic levels in his system. Despite the modified dose, his blood count fell from the vinblastine, so we had to administer the white-cell booster G-CSF, and it gradually returned his neutrophil count to safe levels.

On the fourth day, Kirk had copious bleeding from his colon. A vessel had probably been eroded by a growing deposit of kidney cancer penetrating the bowel. He needed to receive a transfusion of six units of red blood cells before his anemia was reversed. Shortly thereafter, he developed an ileus—the ballooning of paralyzed intestine from the vinblastine—and we were forced to pass a long tube through his nose, down his esophagus, and into his bowel to decompress his painfully swollen abdomen.

Through all this, he did not complain. Cathy sat at his bedside, occasionally trying to distract him with idle chatter but more often in silence, reading a novel or working on needlepoint. I visited him several times a day, both for emotional support and to keep close track of his tenuous medical state.

Kirk and Cathy had two children, Roanna and Paul—one a docent at a museum in Philadelphia, the other working at a small marketing firm in Chicago that was run by a Dartmouth classmate of Kirk's. I offered to speak with them by phone, but Cathy said that wasn't necessary. In private, I emphasized to Cathy again that Kirk could die at any time, from the side effects of the treatment or from the rapidly advancing cancer, and that there might not be another opportunity for their children to visit him. Cathy said she knew that, and so did the children, but dropping everything would disrupt their schedules and probably only upset Kirk, leaving him to think they'd been summoned for a final deathwatch.

Kirk slowly recovered from the toxicities of the interleukin-2 and the vinblastine, and after seven days he was discharged from the hospital. He began the daily progesterone. He was even more debilitated than he had been before he began the treatment. We decided that it was prudent for him to stay close by for regular monitoring, so he and Cathy moved in with Kirk's cousin Grant, in Cambridge.

When I examined Kirk the week after his discharge—some fourteen days after he took his first dose of interleukin 2—I thought he looked less jaundiced, but indoor fluorescent lighting often distorts the true intensity of jaundice. His liver seemed smaller. Its rock-hard nodular edges were softer, more plaint to the palpation of my fingers. And his edema was definitely reduced. His abdomen was less distended, and I could now encircle his ankles with my hands. Kirk confirmed that he hadn't taken any diuretics to reduce his edema since his discharge from the hospital.

I felt a growing excitement that the treatment might be working—that this massive, aggressive monster of a cancer was yielding, retreating just a few inches, from its onslaught.

"Let's get a chest X-ray and a full panel of blood work today," I said to my secretary as I finished my exam.

"I thought you were going to wait until next Friday for the tests," Kirk interjected.

"I sense a drift in the market," I replied. He waited for me to elaborate. "You know, Kirk, I follow your lead. I'm a momentum player. If there's going to be a change, why not find it out earlier rather than later? We'll better leverage our options that way, don't you think?"

Kirk tried to contain his growing smile, like a poker player opening his cards and seeing that the first two are aces, and wondering how much luck he has had. "Sure, we should play it at max leverage," he said. "No other way to play with odds like this. But I thought, Jerry, that we did it all on the first tranche—there was nothing left in the kitty."

"Do you think I can't find some new capital? We don't need to stick to the exact plan if there's some news to make a fast move. So let's increase the doses of interleukin-2 and vinblastine, and give them both ahead of schedule."

"That's what you meant before by upping the leverage? I'm game. Let's go for it all."

An hour later, Kirk and Cathy stood beside me as I mounted his new chest X-ray on the view box next to the one taken fourteen days earlier. The opaque circles that had filled the black space of Kirk's lungs still hung like moons frozen in orbit, but they had become smaller. No question about it. I took a ruler and a pen, and measured each metastasis. Most were reduced by more than half. I also pointed out to Kirk and Cathy that the mountain of cancer-filled fluid above his diaphragm was almost gone—just a trace lip remaining, which curved up in a weak snarl. The objective evidence was indisputable.

"It's melting away!" I called out. I surprised myself and Kirk and Cathy by drawing them into a three-way hug, almost knocking an unsteady Kirk off his feet with the sudden and forceful pull.

"Wasps aren't used to so much emotion," Kirk said after wiping his tear-stained cheeks with the sleeve of his shirt. "Well, St. Jerome, there you are. A miracle before our eyes."

It felt like a miracle. The cancer had seemed invincible, but had fallen like Goliath before our hastily made sling-shot. What could explain this stunning outcome?

Kirk's immune system might be exquisitely sensitive to the interleukin-2, his killer T cells activated to the extreme of biological potency. The cancer might have an unexpectedly feeble P-glycoprotein pump, and have become stuffed full of vinblastine, unable to expel the toxic agent. Or the surface proteins that trap progesterone might be robustly displayed on the kidney-cancer cells, rendering the cells unusually susceptible to inhibition by this hormone. Additional study of Kirk's T cells and his tumor in the laboratory might shed light on these possibilities or give entirely new insights into kidney cancer and its therapy. Medical science delights in understanding the exceptions to the rule and, from such new knowledge, broadening the scope of its effective treatments. Kirk's case could serve as more than an anecdote.

Kirk underwent three more courses of interleukin-2 and vinblastine while continuing the progesterone. He gradually regained his healthy form, as though he had been living in a funhouse mirror and had now stepped out of it. The protuberant abdomen filled with malignant ascites resumed its normal flat contour, the accumulated edema in his legs disappeared, and the stonelike nodularities of his liver melted into the smooth and compliant edge of a healthy organ. We repeated his X-rays and cat scans. The dozen metastatic deposits that had studded his lungs were entirely gone. The ragged lacunae where the cancer had been eating into his pelvis were being filled with healthy, calcified bone. He had entered a complete remission, with no evidence of residual disease.

Kirk's case became the talk of the hospital. The internes, in their monthly clinical-case conference, presented him to the chairman of the Department of Medicine as a "fascinoma." A fascinoma is medical slang for a fascinating case that, because of its rarity, its course, or its outcome, lies outside the usual boundaries of medical experience.

After the case presentation, I received choruses of praise from my colleagues and the medical team. Although I rejoiced in the result, of course, I took no real credit for it, because what had occurred was not the product of wisdom. It was more like playing a slot machine with one silver dollar left in your pocket, figuring that you were going to lose but that you had lost so much already you might as well play it down to the last. I deserved no praise for being lucky. If I could go back to the laboratory and determine why this wildly aggressive cancer in this particular man had melted away, and then use the knowledge to create new treatment strategies that would help others, then congratulations really would be in order.

As Kirk and Cathy prepared to move back to Tarrytown after two months of recuperation in Cambridge, we sat in my office again, reviewing the schedule of return outpatient visits interspersed with weekly checkups by his internist at home.

"Ready to return to real life?" I asked.

Cathy forced a smile.

"I guess so," Kirk offered, without much conviction.

"It's natural to feel unsettled at this juncture," I assured them. "You've been umbilically tied to me and the hospital for months, and now you worry that the cord is being cut. It's not really being cut—just stretched a bit, from Boston to New York. Each day, it will become easier. You'll gain confidence that you're stable and that no catastrophe will occur out of the blue."

Kirk looked glumly away.

"You're still shell-shocked, Kirk," I said. "You've been entirely focussed on one thing, the war with your cancer and living in the trenches of the hospital and the outpatient clinic. Everything else—your work, your social life, your recreation—was suspended. And, frankly, no one thought you would so quickly and so completely eradicate the cancer. It's normal to feel unsettled. But now you'll return home and see that you can resume your prior life."

I spoke with them every day for their first week at home, and then spaced out the calls to every other day during the following week. We would try to speak just before lunch, because, as had been expected, Kirk was still exhausted from the hospitalization, and couldn't make it much past noon without a long nap. Cathy and Kirk were always both on the phone. We would first go through a checklist of symptoms and, once satisfied that nothing new or worrisome had occurred, discuss how much exercise Kirk had been able to tolerate that morning. He was making good progress—taking daily walks, negotiating the three flights of stairs in their home, and sitting for an hour at the breakfast table. When Kirk expressed frustration at how little he could do compared with his former schedule, I reemphasized the point that this would be a long recuperation. He had absorbed many body blows, first from the cancer and then from the therapy.

"He won't read the newspapers," Cathy said as we were closing the call at the end of his second week home. "Kirk used to devour them. We

take three—the *Times,* the *Wall Street Journal,* and *Investor's Daily.*
Now I bundle them unread for recycling."

I asked Kirk if the reason he couldn't concentrate on the papers
was that he was inattentive or felt slow of thought—possible signs of
depression.

"Not at all," be replied.

I probed further, because depression is common after severe illness.
Was he waking up early in the morning, anxious and unable to return
to sleep? Were his bowels irregular or his appetite poor?

"No, none of that, Jerry. I don't think I'm depressed. It's just that
the information in the papers doesn't seem important anymore."

I saw Kirk every two weeks for the next three months. His physical
functioning returned more quickly than I had expected. He was able to
travel from Tarrytown to Manhattan a few times for business meetings
to close deals, was playing nine holes of golf on weekends, and was
planning his first trip away over Easter, to visit his mother in Florida.

All seemed in order, an uncomplicated recovery. But I did note that
in our conversation his tone was less assertive: the piss and vinegar had
given way to bland, disconnected phrases.

A month after Easter, I saw Kirk at a scheduled appointment. After
talking about the fine weather they had enjoyed in Jupiter, he said, almost in passing, that he had a persistent pain in his back.

"I played a set of tennis the last day I was there, on a hard court, and
twisted my back going for a down-the-line return. I thought it would
pass with a warm compress and a few shots of bourbon. But it hasn't."

I noticed then that his face was drawn and his tan not as rich as you
would expect in someone who had spent several weeks in Florida.

In the physical exam, I could not hear breath sounds at the base of
his right lung. On his inner left thigh I felt a hard nodule, the size of a
quarter, that was fixed to the underlying muscle. When I pressed on his
lower spine, he winced. After having him lie supine, I extended his
right leg and lifted it in the air. This maneuver triggered an electric pain
radiating down to his toes.

Even before the blood tests and X-rays were done, I knew that the
cancer had returned. I sensed that Kirk knew it as well.

"The back pain came on three weeks ago? Why didn't you call me
from Florida?"

"And ruin the vacation for Cathy and the kids? And scare the shit
out of my mother? It won't matter, waiting to see you and being told
it's back."

"It likely is," I cautiously replied, not having direct confirmation by tests or biopsy but being unable to think of an alternative explanation—particularly for the nodule in the soft tissue of his thigh. "But we need to be sure by X-ray. And it does matter. If it's pressing on the nerves in your spine, you could lose strength in your legs."

"Legs working, legs not working—it doesn't much matter if you're dead."

I looked at Kirk in surprise. His attitude was a hundred and eighty degrees from what it had been at the onset of his disease. Had we both struggled so hard just to reach this state of despair?

I explained that it did matter if his spinal cord became compressed, even if we couldn't ultimately defeat the cancer. To spend the time that was left paralyzed and incontinent would be a miserable end. Remember, I argued, the biology of your kidney cancer is capricious. Its quirky character might once more play out in our favor. It had an Achilles' heel that we should try to hit again. It was premature to surrender without a fight.

"O.K., Jerry, run the tests. Do what you have to do. I'll humor you."

I didn't have time to explore the causes for his resignation further. I needed to arrange an M.R.I. scan quickly, to assess his spinal cord and brain. In the face of a possible spinal-cord compression, every hour is critical, since the paralysis and the incontinence can be permanent. I was also concerned about his brain. I wondered if his apathy was caused by a metastasis to the frontal lobe, which can blunt the sharpness of one's personality like a surgical lobotomy.

I alerted the staff in radiation therapy that my patient might need emergency treatment. Should the M.R.I. show metastases to the spinal cord, we would have to deliver high-dose radiation to burn the tumor and release its strangling grip on his nerves.

That evening, I visited Kirk in his hospital room—No. 706, the same one he had occupied during his treatments. He was lying on his side, in a fetal position, his knees drawn up to his chest so as to avoid stretching the inflamed nerves from his spine by extending his legs.

He had already received his first radiation treatment. Cathy had just left to spend the night in Cambridge with Grant and his family. I had talked with her by phone briefly, and she had seemed to understand that we'd reached the limits of hope. I explained that, while there were no brain metastases, the cancer had grown through his vertebrae and begun to wrap itself around his spinal cord. Radiation would, if we were lucky, prevent paralysis and incontinence, but there was no chemotherapy or biological treatment that was likely to arrest the cancer in the central nervous system permanently. I asked if she wanted to be present when I gave Kirk the news.

"You tell him alone," she said. "Kirk is more candid about this with you than with me."

Now I sat by his bedside, my eyes level with his, and for a long time we were silent, absorbing the indistinct sounds that filtered into the room from the hospital corridor.

"I'm sorry the magic didn't work longer," I finally offered.

"It did more than anyone expected, Jerry. But you shouldn't feel sorry. There was no reason to live anyway."

What had happened to the Kirk Bains who was so desperate to live that he had tried to persuade every consulting oncologist to treat him?

"You closed a few more deals," I said. "Cathy and the children and your mother had you for four pretty healthy months."

"You read newspapers?" Kirk asked abruptly. I recalled Cathy's comment that Kirk had used to devour them but stopped reading them when he returned home. I didn't know where Kirk was headed, but knew I had to follow.

"Sure."

"I don't read newspapers anymore. I don't know how to. Or why I should." Kirk paused and his voice lowered. "Newspapers used to be a gold mine for me. They're filled with disconnected bits of information—a blizzard in the Midwest, the immigration debate in California, the problems of West Germany absorbing East Germany. For you, Jerry, those articles might be about the lives or fortunes of individuals and nations. For me, they mean nothing beyond information for deals and commodity trading. I never really cared about the world's events or its people. Not deep down inside."

Kirk stared coldly into my eyes.

"And when I went into remission I couldn't read the papers because my deals and trades seemed pointless, because I was a short-term investor. Like I told you, Jerry, I had no patience for the long term. I had no interest in creating something—not a product in business or a partnership with a person. And now I have no equity. No dividends coming in. Nothing to show in my portfolio." Kirk grimaced with pain. "How do you like my great epiphany? No voice of God or holy star but a newspaper left unread in its wrapper."

I tried to say that he was being too harsh with himself, and that people often find it difficult to readjust after the shock of severe illness.

"Don't try to soften it, Jerry. And don't write me off as depressed, because I'm not."

I asked about Cathy and the kids. Hadn't he enjoyed the time with them?

"They'll be fine without me," he said.

I was at a loss for words, because I feared he might be right. I had been amused by his biting wit and sarcasm, but beneath those quips I had never been able to see what he truly believed in.

"Jerry, you realize I'm right," Kirk said. "The remission meant nothing, because it was too late to relive my life. I once asked for Hell. Maybe God made this miracle to have me know what it will feel like."

I felt the crushing weight of Kirk's burden. There is no more awful death than to die with regret, feeling that you have lived a wasted life—death delivering this shattering final sentence on your empty soul. For a moment, I was gripped by the fear that I, too, might one day feel this way. I believed that my life was richer than Kirk's, my love and appreciation of my family, my friends, my work giving it substance and meaning. But there was much that lay ahead—children to bring up, work to do. And I had witnessed countless times how so much that had been created and enjoyed could be destroyed or lost.

But how could I help Kirk at this stage? What more could I say? I thought about my father's belief in memory as our one trump card against death, and realized that Kirk could still redefine himself with words even if there was no time for deeds.

"Have you thought about telling Cathy and the children what you've told me?" I gently suggested.

Kirk recoiled. "Why? So they can hear what they already know? That I was a self-absorbed, uncaring shit? That's really going to be a comforting deathbed interchange."

"Kirk, you can't relive your life. There is no time. But Cathy and Roanna and Paul can learn from you. And when you're gone the memory of your words may help guide them."

Kirkland Bains died in a hospice in Tarrytown on May 8, 1995. A private funeral service at the Episcopal church in Hastings-on-Hudson was planned. Cathy called and explained that it was to be strictly family. She thanked me for everything I had done, and said that I had been very important to Kirk. She and the children would travel to Florida and, with Kirk's mother, inter his ashes there. She said she had been at his bedside through the night, and she sounded drained. She didn't volunteer anything more, and I didn't probe further into what was said before Kirk's passing.

After Cathy's call, I put aside the paperwork on my desk and took a moment to offer a prayer, as I always do when a patient of mine dies. I prayed that, before his passing, Kirk's soul had found some comfort, and that if there is a beyond it would be at pence. Then I composed in my mind a eulogy—addressed, as eulogies are, to the living. The words I chose were not from a holy text but from Kierkegaard: "It is perfectly true, as philosophers say, that life must be understood backward. But they forget the other proposition, that it must be lived forward."

—*1998*

Questions: Reading, Responding, Arguing

1. How does Groopman introduce his central character? Suppose he had begun instead with paragraph six. Would the essay be as effective?
2. What does Kirk Bains mean when he says, "I take risks all the time—that's my business."? How does this statement and others about his work reveal his character and subsequent actions?
3. After examining Kirk, how does Groopman apply logical methods to determine the best (and perhaps only) method of treating him?
4. What ethical issues does Groopman have to confront before he decides to treat Kirk?
5. How does Kirk's attitude toward death force Groopman to examine his own beliefs?
6. Even though Kirk's chemotherapy is initially successful, he has obviously suffered psychologically from it. How does he diagnose his own changes?
7. See the questions following Tolstoy's "The Death of Ivan Ilyich" on page 1113. How are Tolstoy's protagonist and Kirk Bains similar? How do they differ as they approach death?

Appendix

Using Critical Approaches to Craft Arguments

The first three chapters of this book address many specific ways to formulate and organize your arguments about literature. The more advanced your arguments become, the more focused and specific they will be, and eventually you may find that you fall into a particular critical school, or critical approach, one with its own tenants and assumptions about what literature is and how it works—either an approach of your own making or more likely an approach that, whether you knew it or not, has a history of scholars and advocates. While good arguments very often involve multiple approaches and methodologies to make their points, it is still useful to understand the different critical schools and styles that have developed in the history of argumentation.

Formalist Criticism

Formalism assumes as a fundamental tenant that form and content cannot be separated in determining meaning. A paraphrase of a work cannot have the same meaning as the work itself. Therefore, it is the job of the critic not just to argue for the meaning of a given work, but to demonstrate the mechanisms by which a text accomplishes that meaning. A good formalist analysis would almost necessarily begin by addressing elements of structure and genre. For example, the critic first determines structural continuities in the work (rhyme scheme and meter in a poem, narrative voice in a novel, etc.), then determines whether those structural elements are consistent throughout or whether there are any lapses or alterations. Apparent meaning, that is content, in a text could then be analyzed in relation to structure to create an overall understanding of how the work operates. Formalism is useful for explaining what might otherwise be considered "flaws" by some other methodology, in that flaws can be explained as a formal means of generating contrast or tension between various parts of a work. In a typical formalist analysis, tensions are discovered either in the explicit content and message of a work, or in formal qualities such as changes in meter or sentence structure. The critic then proceeds to explain how those tensions become resolved. The resulting explication demonstrates how various attitudes or formal elements combine in order to produce an overall meaning. An example of a work that lends itself to formalist analysis is Andrew Marvell's "To His Coy Mistress." The first stanza of the poem is grammatically punctuated with a number of commas and periods. In contrast, the final stanza of the poem flows much more quickly, with fewer grammatical pauses and breaks. A formalist analysis explains the change in punctuation as one formal element in the poem's overall meaning. In the stanza where formal structure forces the reader to proceed slowly, the narrator praises the beauty of his coy mistress, taking time to allow his love and praise to be accepted. However, later in the poem, when the narrator aggressively pursues a narrative of physical seduction, the poem proceeds quickly, and the repetitive demands that the mistress react "now" are supplemented by the grammar of the poem, which has fewer pauses and hence gives much less time for an auditor or reader to refute the arguments. According to a formalist approach, Marvell's seductive argument cannot be fully understood without taking into account how elements such as grammar, form, meter, and rhyme contribute to its overall effect. Formalism begins by establishing a formal set of expectations, including expectations of genre (poetry, prose, drama, etc.) or subgenre (the ballad, detective fiction, tragedy, etc.) and then reading the work within the context of those expectations.

- In a poem, what are the patterns of rhyme or meter in the work, and how, if at all, does the poem deviate from those expected patterns?
- In a novel, is there a single or multiple narrator? Is the narrative voice presented as a consistent person throughout the work?
- How many acts or scenes are there in a drama, and are those divisions consistent in length and organization to one another?
- Does a drama maintain the traditional Aristotelian rules of dramatic presentation (unity of time, place, etc.)?

Biographical Criticism

Biographical criticism relies on biographies, interviews, and other sources of information about an author's life to offer explanation and insight into an author's work. Obviously, works by anonymous authors, or works such as fairy tales or ancient epics, where no single author exists to scrutinize, do not lend themselves easily to biographical criticism. Texts that most lend themselves to biographical criticism are usually those where the author has, either implicitly or explicitly, put him- or herself into the text, in effect inviting biographical comparison—texts where the narrator shares obvious points of tangency with the author. But even where the narrator and author of a given work are not so clearly comparative, biographical criticism can be performed to good end, particularly when it can shed light on some aspect of a work that would be otherwise obscure or less meaningful. For example, Robert Browning's "My Last Duchess" is a difficult poem to understand without placing it in the historical context of the sixteenth century, when the narrator of the poem is speaking. But a historical reading of the poem, and its obsessive, patriarchal speaker, can be supplemented by understanding the nineteenth-century life of the author, Robert Browning. Browning had many personal reasons to be critical of dominant male figures, because his own wife spent her early years controlled by her father—a man who forbid their marriage. Lines of the poem such as "none puts by / The curtain I have drawn for you, but I" are enriched when one associates them with the hardships the Brownings must have faced in cultivating their love underneath the watchful eyes of a discouraging father. Biographical readings are strongest when they offer explanations for a work that enrich and support readings already available in the work itself. The narrator in "My Last Duchess" is a controlling, murderous tyrant, but biographical criticism allows us to see that Browning is not simply criticizing sixteenth-century Italian political intrigue, but rather is revealing the dangers of male control of women in the present age. Biographical criticism always centers its reading around the author of the work in generating its arguments.

- Is the author clearly implicated in the work, either as an explicit or implicit narrator?
- Do events, settings, or situations in the work mirror elements of the author's own life?
- Are characters in the work related somehow to significant figures (parents, loved ones, enemies, etc.) in the author's life?
- Has the author given interviews or produced other work that relates directly or indirectly to the work in question?

Historical and Sociological Criticism

Historical and sociological criticism uses historical information and sociological analysis to explain what a text means, or (with a "New Historical" approach) what it might have meant to an audience in its own time and culture. Typically, a historical approach necessitates research into the culture and community out of which a text arose, or in which it takes place. Louise Erdrich's "The Red Convertible," for example, lends itself well to this kind of criticism both because the Vietnam War figures heavily in the narrative and because the Indian heritage of the narrator suggests that a knowledge of contemporary Indian reservation life could add meaning to the story. An argument about the story, for example, could compare studies of mental health problems experienced by Vietnam veterans with the descriptions given of character Henry Lamartine. Or, an analysis could use studies of contemporary poverty and depression on Native American reservations to provide a further development of the story's themes. A more elaborate account of the story might address the red convertible that lends the story its title. In such a reading, the convertible is a symbol of white American (i.e., non-Indian) consumer capitalism, the representation of wealth itself, with all the possibilities and hopes that American success represents. Although the convertible serves therefore as a vehicle of escape from the reservation, and similarly as a means of resurrecting Lamartine from his depression, the narrator's renunciation of it at the end suggests a refusal of the temptations and hopes that it offers, in favor of another kind of life. Historical and sociological criticism uses specific details of history, or the material or economic conditions surrounding the writing and reading of a text in order to argue a meaning for it. Although some genres and stories might lend themselves obviously to this kind of criticism (texts situated in specific historical locals, war poetry, etc.), it is worth remembering that virtually all texts relate to historic or sociological concerns, even those texts (fairy tales, science fiction, etc.) that seem entirely divorced from contemporary civilization, because even those texts were either written in some specific locale, or at the very least they are published or transmitted to their readers in specific times and cultures. Historical and sociological criticism always asks questions that are relevant to the material conditions of a story's production and consumption.

- When was the text produced, and how does that time and setting contribute to understanding its meaning?
- Has the text been received differently by readers from different, times, cultures, classes, or political systems?
- Does the text comment, implicitly or explicitly, on the cultural or historical conditions that surround its characters?
- Is money, or some other symbol of value, exchanged?
- Are the characters alienated from, or do they feel connected to, their own labor, their own community, or themselves?

Feminist and Gender Criticism

Feminist and gender criticism works by addressing texts from the perspective that the gender and sexuality of writers, readers, or characters are important in determining meaning. Virtually any text can be addressed in this fashion, even those that ostensibly have nothing whatsoever to do with gender issues (where a critic can then pursue the question of why gender is being excised from the work). Texts that lend themselves easily to feminist readings are those that have explicit conflicts or tensions within them divided along sexual or gendered lines. Critics can use these texts to ask how stereotypes and assumptions about human sexuality are being examined, and whether those models are being strengthened or subverted by the text. Among the many ways to pursue a feminist or gender analysis is to examine the sex or sexual orientation of the author, and ask whether that has any relevance to the meaning of the work as a whole. Similarly, a critic can ask the same of the narrator or the characters, including asking whether an exclusively male or female agenda is being pursued in the writing. Critics can also address whether there is a difference between sex and gender in a work, where the former is understood as natural (biological) sexual difference in a character, while the latter is cultural or social difference (appropriate clothing, behavior, etc., for different sexes). A number of critics in the 1970s and beyond began to theorize a "feminine écriture," the idea of a style of writing that is exclusively female and does not support masculine ideology or power. Many feminist readings of texts address the "political" ramifications of writing texts from either feminine, masculine, or "queered" perspectives. Sylvia Plath's "Daddy" fits many of the qualities that make it an ideal text for a feminist analysis. With a female narrator and author who are often understood as one and the same, the text deals with the narrator's struggle to overcome the oppressive figure of her father. Through the narrator's perception of her father, masculinity is associated in the poem with God, the devil, the color black, war, and ultimately with the horrors of the German holocaust in World War II. The narrator's femininity receives somewhat less description, but is "pretty" and she sees herself, in contrast to her German father, as a Jew, as the target of aggression, and as a victim. Her victimization ends, however, with the voicing of the poem itself, which in a feminist reading could be seen as a proclamation of the poet's victory over her father and the man who served as a substitute for him in her life. Feminist and gender criticism approach texts with an understanding that sex, gender, and sexuality are central to meaning.

- Does the sex or sexual orientation of the author have any bearing on the apparent meaning or agenda of the text?
- Does the sex or sexual orientation of the characters have any bearing on the meaning of the text?
- Does the text reinforce or subvert traditional ideas about sex and gender?
- Regardless of the sex or gender of the author, is the text itself feminine or masculine writing, and what does that mean?
- Is conflict in the text the result of sexual inequality, or related to issues of sexual orientation?

Structuralism: Mythological and Psychological Approaches

Structuralist arguments about texts are, in the most general sense, readings that reveal universal, or at least repetitive, patterns in the world and in texts. Structural criticism works well on texts that other methodologies may not be able to address, such as fairy tales, anonymous works, myths, and other texts without clear historical settings or authorial sources. Many readings of texts are "structuralist" on a simple level, just in their initial explanation of the basic patterns that make up a narrative. It is a structuralist reading, for example, to view Shakespeare's "Sonnet 73" as a metaphor associating the poet's life with seasonal change, specifically autumn representing his fading youth. More specific structuralist readings, such as those found in mythological and psychological criticism, usually attempt to explain the content of a text in terms of its relation to a given structural constant that has been already discovered elsewhere. For example, Sophocles's drama "Oedipus the King," where Oedipus sleeps with his mother and murders his father, was influential enough to inspire the term "Oedipal complex." The pattern of apparent infantile aggression and desire from Sophocles's play has been applied as a means of understanding childhood development, but more important as a pattern used to argue about literature. Richard Wright's "The Man Who Was Almost a Man," can be read in an Oedipal fashion, where the protagonist searches to find his own place in a world with both maternal and paternal figures, and where his departure at the story's end can be seen as a defiance of paternal authority. A different mythological approach may be seen in reading Nathaniel Hawthorne's "Young Goodman Brown." The protagonist undergoes a journey into and out of a dark forest, which can be read as a reflection of traditional "hero" narratives, found in the myths of many cultures, with their descent into an underworld and subsequent return. Structuralist readings always attempt to explain texts in terms of their relation to given patterns. Searching for repetitive "archetypes" and discovering how a given text replicates similar ancient or often repeated myths, patterns, or sign systems is the hallmark of the structuralist approach.

- Does the text contain a protagonist with clear maternal or paternal figures?
- Are there identifiable "archetypes" in the text, such as heroes, shadow characters, trickster characters, or other consistent characters, settings or events that can be found in other works?
- Does the text reflect "seasonal" patterns, such as cycles of winter (and/or death) followed by spring or summer (renewal and rebirth)?
- Does the protagonist undergo trials to be endured or surpassed? Is there a cycle of transgression followed by redemption?

- Are there any numbers in the text (three, seven, or other numbers that occur repetitively in mythologies and cultures) that suggest a universal rather than local significance?

Post-Structuralism: Reader Response Theory and Deconstruction

If structuralism treats every element of a text as a sign that has a place within a given sign system, and it is the job of the critic to find and elaborate on that system, the post-structuralist response has been to find the ways that all signs eventually lead nowhere but to the breakdown of systems themselves. Correspondingly, post-structuralist arguments tend to emphasize how texts do not have unequivocal, or singular meanings, but rather any given text exists as an unstable nexus of competing possibilities, every conflict revealing a fundamental undecidability. Reader response theory accomplishes this task in part by emphasizing how the meanings of texts change, depending on assumptions readers hold as they interpret a given text, a fact that opens the possibility for multiplicity and ambiguity in every reading experience. Reader response theories also emphasize that texts do not exist outside of the experience of reading them, a fact which can reveal several otherwise overlooked details in a text. For example, take the e.e. cummings poem "pity this busy monster, manunkind." Upon seeing the term "manunkind," the immediate reaction of a reader is probably confusion—the word was coined by cummings and is unlikely to have been encountered anywhere else. While initially confused, upon reflection a reader will likely define the word as a combination of the terms "mankind" and "man, unkind." However, those associations are only available after a reader pauses and thinks about the text. Reader response arguments would assert that someone who simply defines the new word only as that combination of terms is missing the point. Part of the meaning of the poem is the confusion that occurs when first seeing the new term—confusion that is a deliberate effect of the poem. This detail, and the subtlety of the poem, will be lost on someone who simply thinks that "manunkind" is a combination of terms. Reader response analysis of the text acknowledges that the meaning of the text is bound in the moment of reading. Deconstructive readings, which have become another mainstay of contemporary post-structuralist criticism, employ any number of methods to explain and reveal the otherwise unnoticed mechanics of how texts operate. A deconstructive reading is one that does not allow a text to perpetuate a single meaning or agenda, and often employs a technique of "reading against the grain," discovering counter narratives within a text that run against traditionally accepted readings. Although you may not have enough critical background to recognize and react against traditional, historical readings of literature, another way to employ deconstructive readings is to look for repetitive themes or symbols in multiple texts, and hence reveal the ways that one text can serve to deconstruct another. For example, Robert Flynn's "John Wayne Must Die" makes repetitive references to John Wayne movies, revealing the ways that those films can be understood was not only simple entertainment but also as racist, sexist, or politically motivated, elements often overlooked in the mythological approval that John Wayne has received as a cultural icon. Post-structuralist accounts of texts employ many of the same questions that would be invoked in performing a structuralist or formalist reading, but with an agenda of discovering different answers, or revealing how formalist claims of unity and resolution may be impossible to achieve. A reader response analysis asks how different readers might react to texts differently, and how meaning changes within those differing contexts. A deconstructionist might begin an analysis by asking what is not being said in a given text, and then attempting to find that message despite its apparent unavailability.

- Would a different audience react to a text differently?
- Does the text deliberately establish or upset reader's expectations?
- What are the implicit, as opposed to explicit, arguments of a text, and what agenda do they serve?
- How does the text compare to other texts with similar icons, symbols, or characters, and what do those differences, similarities, or repetitions mean?

Biographical Notes

CHINUA ACHEBE *(b. 1930)*

Chinua Achebe was born in Ogidi, Nigeria, and, after graduation from University College in Ibadan and study at London University, was employed by the Nigerian Broadcasting Service, where he served for years as a producer. After the appearance of his first novel, *Things Fall Apart* (1958), he became one of the most widely acclaimed writers to emerge from the former British colonies of Africa. The author of several novels as well as a collection of short stories, Achebe has taught at several universities in the United States. While drawing heavily on the oral traditions of his native country, he has been successful in adapting European fictional techniques to deal with subjects like the degradations imposed by colonialism and the relative failure of most post-colonial governments to improve living conditions for their citizens.

AI *(b. 1947)*

Born in Tuscon, Arizona, of mixed ethnic heritage, a Japanese father and a mother who was part black, native american, and Irish, Ai (a pseudonym which means "love") was educated at the University of Arizona, where she majored in Japanese. Ai's realistic dramatic monologues often reveal the agonies of characters trapped in unfulfilling or even dangerous lives. With her gallery of social misfits, she is the contemporary heir to the tradition begun by Robert Browning. Her books have appropriately grim titles—*Cruelty, Dread,* and *Vice,* her collection of new and selected poems.

JULIA ALVAREZ *(b. 1953)*

Julia Alvarez was born in New York City but grew up in the Dominican Republic before being forced to flee with her family at the age of 10 when her father became involved in a plot to overthrow dictator Rafael Trujillo. Her first collection of poetry, *Homecoming* (1984), contains both free verse and "33," a sequence of 33 sonnets on the occasion of the poet's thirty-third birthday. She has gained acclaim for *In the Time of the Butterflies,* a

work of fiction, and *The Other Side/El Otro Lado,* a collection of poems.

MATTHEW ARNOLD *(1822–1888)*

Matthew Arnold was the son of the headmaster of the Rugby School and himself served as an inspector of schools during much of his adult life. An influential essayist as well as a poet, Arnold was unsparing in his criticism of middle-class "Philistinism." At least part of "Dover Beach" is thought to date from his honeymoon in 1851.

MARGARET ATWOOD *(b. 1939)*

Margaret Atwood is a leading figure among Canadian writers, and she is equally skilled as a poet and fiction writer. She is also an internationally known feminist spokesperson, and was named by *Ms.* magazine as Woman of the Year for 1986. Born in Ottawa, Ontario, she graduated from University of Toronto in 1962, the same year that her first book appeared, and she later did graduate work at Radcliffe and Harvard. She has published two volumes of selected poems, over a dozen novels and collections of short stories, and a book of literary criticism, and has edited two anthologies of Canadian literature.

W. H. AUDEN *(1907–1973)*

W. H. Auden was already established as an important younger British poet before he moved to America in 1939 (he later became a U.S. citizen). As a transatlantic link between two literary cultures, Auden was one of the most influential literary figures and cultural spokespersons in the English-speaking world for almost forty years, giving a name to the postwar era when he dubbed it "The Age of Anxiety" in a poem. In his last years he returned briefly to Oxford, where he occupied the poetry chair.

J. G. BALLARD *(b. 1930)*

J.G. Ballard was born in Shanghai, China, into the prosperous community of Europeans who represented international firms doing business in that city's busy port. At the beginning of World War II, Ballard was separated from his parents during the Japanese occupation but later joined them at an internment camp for foreign citizens, where he remained until the end of the war. These experiences were the basis of his bestselling novel, *Empire of the Sun*, which became a 1987 Steven Spielberg film. After coming to England, Ballard studied medicine for a time and then began to write while serving in the Royal Air Force in Canada. Like H.G. Wells a century earlier, Ballard has carved out a reputation as a master of both science fiction, the genre in which he first wrote, and mainstream work. He has also experimented with a variety of unusual storytelling techniques. "Time of Passage" is among the works from four decades collected in *The Complete Short Stories*, which was published in 2001. In 2003, Ballard turned down the Commander of the British Empire award, stating that "as a republican, I can't accept an honour awarded by the monarch."

TONI CADE BAMBARA *(1939–1995)*

Toni Cade Bambara grew up in Harlem and was educated both in the United States and in France, where she studied dance. She took her last name from a signature on a sketch she found among her great-grandmother's possessions. Her first book of stories, *Gorilla, My Love*, was published in 1972 and was followed by more stories and novels. A dedicated activist for African American and feminist causes, she once said, "The dream is real, my friends. The failure to realize it is the only unreality."

ELIZABETH BISHOP *(1911–1979)*

Elizabeth Bishop for most of her life was highly regarded as a "poet's poet," winning the Pulitzer Prize for *North and South* in 1956, but in the years since her death she has gained a wider readership. She traveled widely and lived in Brazil for a number of years before returning to the United States to teach at Harvard during the last years of her life. She is now considered the foremost American woman poet of the second half of the twentieth century.

WILLIAM BLAKE *(1757–1827)*

William Blake was a poet, painter, engraver, and visionary. Blake does not fit easily into any single category, although his political sympathies link him to the later romantic poets. His poetry attracted little attention in his lifetime, but his mature works, starting with *Songs of Innocence* (1789) and *Songs of Experience* (1793), combine poetry with his own remarkable illustrations and are unique in English literature. Blake anticipated many future directions of both literature and modern psychology.

JORGE LUIS BORGES *(1899–1986)*

Jorge Luis Borges is perhaps the most original writer in Spanish of the twentieth century. Born in Buenos Aires, Borges was caught with his parents in Switzerland during World War I. Equally fluent in English (he was an expert in Anglo-Saxon literature) and his native Spanish, Borges also learned French, German, and Latin. His fiction contains paradoxical allegories of time and being and, although widely discussed, was never aimed at large popular audiences. A vocal opponent of the Nazis (who had many supporters in Argentina) and of the Perón dictatorship, Borges was dismissed from several positions because of his politics. After the fall of Perón in 1955, Borges served a distinguished term as director of Argentina's national library, despite progressive deterioration of his sight, which left him almost totally blind.

RAY BRADBURY *(b. 1920)*

Ray Bradbury was born in Waukegan, Illinois, and has spent the majority of the twentieth century being recognized as one of the most prolific and talented science fiction and fantasy authors in the Western world, producing novels, short stories, plays, screenplays, poetry, children's stories, and work in a great number of other genres and forms of media. Bradbury began writing at the age of twelve and had published his first story at eighteen. His first collection of stories, *Dark Carnival* (1947), has been followed by fifty more novels and collections in his lifetime. Bradbury's reputation first began to grow with the publication of *The Martian Chronicles* (1950), a set of stories about the colonization of Mars. These stories, like much of Bradbury's fiction, are less focused on technological development and gadgetry than they are on the impacts and influences that such things can have on human lives and human conflicts. Another influential collection followed, *The Illustrated Man* (1951), followed by *Fahrenheit 451* (1953), which is considered today one of the most compelling anti-censorship works produced by an American author. Other popular works include *Something Wicked This Way Comes* (1962) and *S is for Space* (1962). The past decades have also seen numerous works of his turned into films, including the seminal story "A Sound of Thunder" (1952), a morality tale of unforeseen consequences that has arguably become the structural model for most time travel fiction that has followed it. Although occasionally troubled by failing health in his later years and by the death of his wife Maggie in 2003, Bradbury remains extraordinarily prolific and is today considered one of the most highly respected authors in his field.

JUDY BRADY (b. 1937)

Judy Brady was born in San Francisco, California. She worked as an essayist for a number of publications in the 1960s and 1970s, primarily writing on topics related to the women's movement. After being diagnosed with cancer in 1980 and fighting a second, subsequent cancer, she has focused much of her work as a writer and editor to raise cancer awareness and criticize the medical and political communities for their cancer policies.

GWENDOLYN BROOKS (1917–2000)

Gwendolyn Brooks was the first African American to win a Pulitzer Prize for poetry. Brooks reflected many changes in black culture during her long career, and she wrote about the stages of her own life candidly in *In the Mecca* (1968), her literary autobiography. Brooks was the last poetry consultant of the Library of Congress before that position became Poet Laureate of the United States. At the end of her life, Brooks was one of the most honored and beloved of American poets.

ELIZABETH BARRETT BROWNING
(1806–1861)

Elizabeth Barrett Browning was already a famous poet when she met her husband-to-be, Robert Browning, who had been corresponding with her on literary matters. She originally published her famous sonnet sequence, written in the first years of her marriage, in the guise of a translation of Portuguese poems, perhaps to mask their personal revelations.

ROBERT BROWNING (1812–1889)

Robert Browning wrote many successful dramatic monologues that are his lasting legacy, for he brings the genre to a level of achievement rarely equaled. Less regarded during his lifetime than his contemporary Tennyson, he has consistently risen in the esteem of modern readers. Often overlooked in his gallery of often grotesque characters are his considerable metrical skills and ability to simulate speech while working in demanding poetic forms.

CHRISTOPHER BUCKLEY (b. 1952)

Christopher Buckley is the son of William F. Buckley, political commentator, novelist, and founder of the *National Review*. After working as an editor for *Esquire* and writing a successful book based on his adventures as a merchant seaman, Buckley served for a time as a speechwriter for then–Vice President George H. W. Bush. A frequent contributor to *The New Yorker*, Buckley is regarded as one of the most potent satirists writing today.

GLADYS CARDIFF (b. 1942)

Gladys Cardiff is a member of the Cherokee nation. She grew up in Seattle and studied at the University of Washington and Western Michigan University. She teaches creative writing and literature at Oakland University. "Combing" is taken from her first collection, *To Frighten a Storm*, which was originally published in 1976.

RAYMOND CARVER (1938–1988)

Raymond Carver has a reputation as a master of the contemporary short story that has only grown since his death. A native of Clatskanie, Oregon, Carver was married and a father of two before he was twenty, and worked at a number of unskilled jobs in his early years. He worked his way through Humboldt State College, was a graduate of the Writers' Workshop of the University of Iowa, and taught at several universities. His earliest publications were poems, and *A New Path to the Waterfall* appeared posthumously in 1989. His later years included several personal victories, including the receipt of a prestigious MacArthur Foundation Fellowship and a successful struggle against alcoholism. Carver died only a few months after his marriage to his second wife, poet Tess Gallagher.

JOHN CHEEVER *(1912–1982)*

John Cheever's examinations of the tensions of life in white-collar suburbia are suffused with a melancholy that is often fueled by marital tensions, failed social aspirations, and what one story aptly calls "the sorrows of gin." Born in Quincy, Massachusetts, Cheever worked almost exclusively as a writer of fiction, often associated with *The New Yorker*, for most of his life, with occasional periods spent teaching at universities and writing for television. In recent years his daughter, Susan Cheever, has published a memoir, *Home Before Dark*, and an edition of her father's journals, both of which chronicle Cheever's long struggles with alcoholism and questions of sexual identity.

KATE CHOPIN *(1851–1904)*

Kate Chopin was virtually forgotten for most of the twentieth century. Remembered primarily as a chronicler of life among the Louisiana Creoles and Cajuns, her works had long been out of print when they were rediscovered in recent decades, initially by feminist critics and subsequently by general readers. Her most important novel, *The Awakening* (1899), today appears frequently on college reading lists. Born in St. Louis, Chopin spent the 1870s in rural Louisiana, the wife of a cotton broker from New Orleans. After her husband's death in 1883, Chopin returned to St. Louis with her six children and began her literary career, placing stories and regional pieces in popular magazines. Much of her later writing is remarkable for its frank depiction of women's sexuality, a subject rarely broached in the literature of the era, which resulted in negative reception of her work and effectively ended her literary career.

SANDRA CISNEROS *(b. 1954)*

Sandra Cisneros received a MacArthur Foundation Fellowship in 1995. A native of Chicago and longtime resident of San Antonio, she is a graduate of the University of Iowa

Writers' Workshop. *My Wicked, Wicked Ways* (1987), a collection of poetry that contains several poems about Cisneros's experiences as the only daughter among her parents' seven children, has gone through several editions and was followed by a second collection, *Loose Woman* (1994). Her two collections of short fiction are *The House on Mango Street* (1984) and *Woman Hollering Creek* (1991), which is named after a real creek in the Texas Hill Country. Two nonfiction books on which Cisneros collaborated with other writers, *Days and Nights of Love and War* and *The Future Is Mestizo: Life Where Cultures Meet*, were published in 2000, and *Caramelo*, a new novel, appeared in 2003.

LUCILLE CLIFTON *(b. 1936)*

Lucille Clifton, a native of Depew, New York, was educated at SUNY– Fredonia and Howard University, and has taught at several colleges, including American University in Washington, D.C. About her own work, she has commented succinctly, "I am a Black woman poet, and I sound like one." Clifton won a National Book Award in 2000.

JUDITH ORTIZ COFER *(b. 1952)*

Judith Ortiz Cofer was born in Puerto Rico, the daughter of a member of the U.S. Navy, and came to the United States at the age of 4, when her father was posted to the Brooklyn Naval Yard. After college, she studied at Oxford and began her teaching career in the United States. A skilled writer of fiction and autobiography, she published *The Year of Our Revolution: New and Selected Stories and Poems* in 1998.

BILLY COLLINS *(b. 1941)*

Billy Collins was born in New York City and continues to teach there. One of the few contemporary poets to reach a wide popular audience, Collins has been an enthusiastic performer, commentator on National Public Radio, and advocate for poetry. Beginning in 2001, he served two years as U.S. poet laureate, establishing the online anthology "Poetry 180," a website that presents a poem for every day in the school year. *Sailing Alone Around the Room: New and Selected Poems* was published in 2001.

SARAH CORTEZ *(b. 1950)*

Sarah Cortez grew up in Houston, Texas, and holds degrees in psychology and religion, classical studies, and accounting. She also serves as Visiting Scholar at the University of Houston's Center for Mexican-American Studies. She is a deputy constable in Harris County, Texas.

STEPHEN CRANE *(1871–1900)*

Stephen Crane was born in Newark, New Jersey, the son of a Methodist minister who died when the author was still a boy. His first novel, *Maggie: A Girl of the Streets* (1893), did not sell well, but was noticed by some critics who welcomed his subsequent work, *The Red Badge of Courage* (1895), which was celebrated at the time and recognized today as one of the greatest Civil War novels. Crane continued work as a journalist and, in January 1897, after being shipwrecked while aboard a ship running contraband arms to Cuban revolutionaries, he published his account of the events in the *New York Press*, followed by his fictional version of the same event, titled "The Open Boat." Moving to England, Crane enjoyed brief but intense literary friendships with Henry James, Joseph Conrad, H.G. Wells, and Ford Madox Ford. Ravaged by tuberculosis and malaria, he died in a German sanitarium at the age of 28, leaving the legacy of a brief but incredibly influential career as an experimental poet, novelist, and short fiction writer.

R. CRUMB *(b. 1943)*

Robert Crumb was born in Philadelphia, Pennsylvania, and has a reputation as a major comic-book artist and social satirist. He first achieved recognition outside of the comics world when his work *Fritz the Cat* (1968) was turned into a film of the same name. His work has frequently been accused of sexism and racism, though Crumb's self-proclaimed goal has been to lampoon the repressive middle-class values that are the source of his sexist and racist stereotypes. Known for the popularity of *Fritz the Cat* and the "Keep on Truckin'" image, his growing critical respect led to the production of a biographical documentary movie, *Crumb*, in 1990. He currently lives and works in southern France with his wife and daughter.

COUNTEE CULLEN *(1903–1946)*

Countee Cullen, among black writers of the first half of the twentieth century, crafted poetry representing a more conservative style than that of his contemporary, Langston Hughes. Although he wrote a number of lyrics on standard poetic themes, he is best remembered for his eloquent poems on racial subjects.

E. E. CUMMINGS *(1894–1962)*

e. e. cummings was the son of a Harvard professor and Unitarian clergyman. Edward Estlin Cummings served as a volunteer ambulance driver in France during World War I. cummings's experimentation with the typographical aspects of poetry reveals his serious interest in cubist painting, which he studied in Paris in the 1920s. A brilliant satirist, he also excelled as a writer of lyrical poems whose unusual appearance and idiosyncratic grammar, spelling, and punctuation often overshadow their traditional themes.

EMILY DICKINSON *(1830–1886)*

Emily Dickinson has been reinvented with each generation, and readers' views of her have ranged between two extremes—one perceiving her as the abnormally shy "Belle of Amherst" making poetry out of her own neuroses and another seeing her as a proto-feminist carving out a world of her own in self-willed isolation. What remains is her brilliant poetry—unique, original, and marked with the stamp of individual talent. Dickinson published only seven poems during her lifetime, but left behind hundreds of poems in manuscript at her death. Published by her relatives, they were immediately popular, but it was not until the edition of Thomas Johnson in 1955 that they were read with Dickinson's unusual punctuation and capitalization intact.

JOHN DONNE *(1572–1631)*

John Donne was trained in the law for a career in government service, but he became the greatest preacher of his day, ending his life as dean of St. Paul's Cathedral in London. Only two of Donne's poems and a handful of his sermons were printed during his life, but both circulated widely in manuscript and his literary reputation among his contemporaries was considerable. His poetry falls into two distinct periods: the witty love poetry of his youth and the sober religious meditations of his maturity. In both, however, Donne shows remarkable originality in rhythm, diction, and the use of metaphor and conceit, which marks him as the chief poet of what has become commonly known as the metaphysical style.

MICHAEL DRAYTON *(1563–1631)*

Michael Drayton, like his contemporary, Shakespeare, excelled in several literary genres. He collaborated on plays with Thomas Dekker and wrote long poems on English history, biography, and topography. Drayton labored almost three decades on the sixty-three sonnets in *Idea*, publishing them in their present form in 1619.

ALAN DUGAN *(1923–2003)*

Alan Dugan received the 1961 Yale Younger Poets Award, leading to the publication of his first collection as he neared forty. His plain-spoken poetic voice, often with sardonic overtones, is appropriate for the antiromantic stance of his most characteristic poems. For many years Dugan was associated with the Fine Arts Work Center in Provincetown, Massachusetts, on Cape Cod.

PAUL LAURENCE DUNBAR *(1872–1906)*

Paul Laurence Dunbar, a native of Dayton, Ohio, was one of the first black poets to make a mark in American literature. Many of his dialect poems reflect a sentimentalized view of life in the South, which he did not know directly. However, he was also capable of powerful expressions of racial protest. He died at 33 of tuberculosis.

T. S. ELIOT *(1888–1965)*

T. S. Eliot was the author of *The Waste Land,* one of the most famous and difficult modernist poems, and became an international figure. Born in St. Louis and educated at Harvard, he moved to London in 1914, where he remained for the rest of his life becoming a British subject in 1927. This chief prophet of modern despair turned to the Church of England in later life and wrote suc-

cessful dramas on religious themes. As a critic and influential editor, Eliot dominated poetic taste in England and America for over twenty-five years. He was awarded the Nobel Prize in 1948.

RALPH ELLISON *(1914–1994)*

Ralph Ellison was born in Oklahoma City, where his early interests were primarily musical; he played trumpet and knew many prominent jazz musicians of the Depression era. In 1933 he attended Tuskegee Institute, intending to study music, but he was drawn to literature through his study of contemporary writers (especially the poet T. S. Eliot). Tuskegee and, later, Harlem provided him with material for *Invisible Man* (1952), a brilliant picaresque novel of African American life that established him as a major force in American fiction and won the National Book Award in 1953. Although none of his subsequent works have had the impact of his first novel, Ellison also published two collections of essays, *Shadow and Act* (1964) and *Going to the Territory* (1986), and readers now have access to a posthumous volume of collected stories and an unfinished novel, *Juneteenth* (1999).

LOUISE ERDRICH *(b. 1954)*

Louise Erdrich was born in Little Falls, Minnesota, and grew up in North Dakota. Her father was a teacher with the Bureau of Indian Affairs, and both he and her mother encouraged her to write stories from an early age. Erdrich holds degrees from Dartmouth and Johns Hopkins, where she studied creative writing. Her novel *Love Medicine,* from which "The Red Convertible" is taken, is a sequence of fourteen connected stories told by seven narrators. *Love Medicine* won the National Book Critics Circle Award for 1984. Much of Erdrich's fiction draws on her childhood on the Great Plains and her mixed cultural heritage (her ancestry is German American and Chippewa). In addition to *Love Medicine,* she has published novels, including *The Beet Queen* (1986) and *Tracks* (1988), several prize-winning short stories, and three books of poetry. Erdrich and her late husband Michael Dorris, another Native American writer, appeared in two documentary films shown on PBS and collaborated on a novel, *The Crown of Columbus* (1991). Along with James Welch and Leslie Marmon Silko, Erdrich has helped to redefine Native American fiction. According to the Columbia Literary History of the United States, "These authors have had to resist the formulaic approaches favored by the publishing industry, which has its own opinions about what constitutes the 'proper' form and content of minority fiction." *The Birchbark House,* a novel for young readers, and *The Antelope Wife,* a novel employing the techniques of magic realism, both appeared in 1999. Her most recent novels are *The Last Report on the Miracles at Little No Horse* (2001) and *The Master Butchers Singing Club* (2003).

RHINA P. ESPAILLAT *(b. 1932)*

Rhina P. Espaillat published her first poetry collection at age sixty. Born in the Dominican Republic, she has lived in the United States since 1939, and writes in both English and Spanish. Her first publication, *Lapsing to Grace,* was published by Bennett & Kitchel in 1992, and her second, *Where Horizons Go,* received the 1998 T. S. Eliot Prize and was published by New Odyssey Press. Espaillat runs The Powow River Poets, a monthly workshop, and conducts a reading series and poetry contest sponsored by the Newburyport Art Association, in Massachusetts. A past winner of the Howard Nemerov Award and the *Sparrow* Sonnet Award, she writes intimate, carefully-crafted poems in traditional poetic forms.

WILLIAM FAULKNER *(1897–1962)*

William Faulkner came from a family whose name was originally spelled "Falkner," but a misprint in an early book led him to change it. Faulkner had some success as a screenwriter in Hollywood, but always returned to Oxford, Mississippi, the site of his fictional Jefferson and Yoknapatawpha County. Despite success and critical esteem for early works like *The Sound and the Fury* (1929) and *As I Lay Dying* (1930), Faulkner failed to attract large audiences for what are now considered his best novels. By the late 1940s most of his books were out of print. His reputation was revived when *The Portable Faulkner* appeared in 1946, but he was still not well known when he won the Nobel Prize in 1950. A brilliant innovator of unusual narrative techniques in his novels, Faulkner created complex genealogies of characters to inhabit the world of his mythical South.

JULES FEIFFER *(b. 1929)*

One of the most honored of American cartoonists, Jules Feiffer won a Pulitzer Prize in 1986 and was inducted into the Comic Book Hall of Fame in 2004. Born in the Bronx, Feiffer has published his cartoons in the *Village Voice* for over four decades and is an astute chronicler of American neuroses. He is also known for his successful play, *Little Murders,* and his screenplays. In 1961 Feiffer won an Oscar for his animated film *Munro.*

ROBERT FLYNN *(b. 1932)*

Robert Flynn was born in Chillicothe, Texas. He dropped out of Baylor University after two years to serve in the Marine Corps. After the military, he completed his degree and began teaching. When Baylor closed down a production of Eugene O'Neill's *Long Day's Journey into Night* in 1962, Flynn and the other members of the drama department moved to Trinity University in San Antonio, where he taught until retirement. The author of many novels, Flynn went to Vietnam as a war correspondent in 1970, which later led to a memoir, *A Personal War in Vietnam,* and a novel, *The Last Klick.*

ROBERT FROST *(1874–1963)*

Robert Frost, during the second half of his long life, was a public figure who attained a popularity unmatched by any American poet of the last century. His reading at the inauguration of John F. Kennedy in 1961 capped an impressive career that included four Pulitzer Prizes. Unattracted by the more exotic aspects of modernism, Frost nevertheless remains a poet who speaks eloquently to contemporary uncertainties about humanity's place in a universe that does not seem to care much for its existence. While Frost is rarely directly an autobiographical poet ("Home Burial" may reflect the death of Frost's son Elliot at three), his work always bears the stamp of his powerful personality and identification with the New England landscape.

CHARLOTTE PERKINS GILMAN
(1860–1935)

Charlotte Perkins Gilman was born in Hartford, Connecticut. Gilman's father abandoned the family when she was an infant, and early in life she received a poor education before eventually studying at the Rhode Island School of Design. Following marriage and the birth of a daughter, she suffered from severe depression, an experience that she recreates in "The Yellow Wallpaper." In later life, Gilman became an important public spokesperson for feminist causes. After she discovered that she had inoperable breast cancer, she chose to end her own life.

DANA GIOIA *(b. 1950)*

Dana Gioia grew up in the suburbs of Los Angeles. He took a graduate degree in English from Harvard but made a successful career in business before devoting his full time to writing. The editor of several textbooks and anthologies, he is also an influential critic whose essay "Can Poetry Matter?" stimulated much discussion when it appeared in *The Atlantic. Interrogations at Noon*, his third collection of poetry, appeared in 2001. Gioia became chairman of the National Endowment for the Arts in 2002.

SUSAN GLASPELL *(1882–1948)*

Susan Glaspell was born in Iowa and educated at Drake University. Glaspell was one of the founders, with her husband George Cram Cook, of the Provincetown Players. This company, founded in the Cape Cod resort village, was committed to producing experimental drama, an alternative to the standard fare playing in Broadway theaters. Eventually it was relocated to New York. Along with Glaspell, Eugene O'Neill, America's only Nobel Prize–winning dramatist, wrote plays for this group. Trained as a journalist and the author of short stories and novels, Glaspell wrote *Trifles* (1916), her first play, shortly after the founding of the Players, basing her plot on an Iowa murder case she had covered. The one-act play, with both Glaspell and her husband in the cast, premiered during the Players' second season and also exists in a short story version. Glaspell won the Pulitzer Prize for Drama in 1930 for *Alison's House*, basing the title character on poet Emily Dickinson. A socialist and feminist, Glaspell lived in Provincetown in her last years, writing *The Road to the Temple*, a memoir of her husband's life, and novels.

JEROME GROOPMAN *(b. 1939)*

Jerome Groopman received his M.D. degree from Columbia College of Physicians and Surgeons and currently holds the Dina and Raphael Recanati Chair of Medicine at the Harvard Medical School. The author of many articles on medicine aimed at general readers, his first book, *The Measure of Our Days*, was published in 1997. For some years he has been a staff writer in medicine and biology for *The New Yorker*.

THOM GUNN *(1929–2004)*

Thom Gunn was a British expatriate who lived in San Francisco for over four decades. Gunn managed to retain his ties to the traditions of British literature while writing about motorcycle gangs, surfers, gay bars, and drug experiences. *The Man with Night Sweats*, his 1992 collection, contains a number of forthright poems on AIDS, of which "Terminal" is one.

JIM HALL *(b. 1947)*

Jim Hall is one of the most brilliantly inventive comic poets in recent years. He has also written a successful series of crime novels set in his native south Florida, beginning with *Under Cover of Daylight* in 1987.

LORRAINE HANSBERRY *(1930–1965)*

Lorraine Hansberry was the first African American playwright to rise to prominence in the New York theater and, until recent decades, one of only a handful of women dramatists to have Broadway successes. A victim of cancer in her mid-thirties, Hansberry saw only one of her other plays, *The Sign in Sidney Brustein's Window*, produced. Originally staged in 1959, *A Raisin in the Sun* may seem somewhat dated in its racial attitudes today, but it is well to recall that at the time of its production Martin Luther King was still an obscure southern minister and the major events of the civil rights movement were still several years in the future. *A Raisin in the Sun* has been filmed successfully twice.

THOMAS HARDY *(1840–1928)*

Thomas Hardy, after the disappointing response to his novel *Jude the Obscure* in 1895, returned to his first love, writing poetry for the last thirty years of his long life. The language and life of Hardy's native Wessex inform both his novels and poems. His subject matter is very much of the nineteenth century, but his ironic, disillusioned point of view marks him as one of the chief predecessors of modernism.

JOY HARJO *(b. 1951)*

Joy Harjo, a member of the Creek tribe, is one of the leading voices of contemporary Native American poetry. She is a powerful performer and was one of the poets featured on Bill Moyers's television series, *The Power of the Word.*

NATHANIEL HAWTHORNE *(1804–1864)*

Nathaniel Hawthorne was born in Salem, Massachusetts, and could trace his heritage back to the earliest settlers of New England. For twelve years after his 1825 graduation, Hawthorne lived at his parents' home, devoting himself solely to writing. An early novel attracted scant attention, but a collection of short stories, *Twice-Told Tales* (1837), was the subject of an enthusiastic review by Edgar Allan Poe. Hawthorne traveled in Europe and served as American consul at Liverpool during the Pierce administration. He was a moralist who did not shrink from depicting the dark side of human nature; his often painful examinations of American history and conscience have set the tone for many subsequent generations of writers. His ambivalent attitude toward his Puritan ancestors' religious beliefs supplied material for his novel *The Scarlet Letter* (1850) and many of his short stories.

ROBERT HAYDEN *(1913–1980)*

Robert Hayden named Countee Cullen as one of the chief early influences on his poetry. A native of Michigan, he taught for many years at Fisk University in Nashville and at the University of Michigan. Although many of Hayden's poems are on African American subjects, he wished to be considered a poet with strong links to the mainstream English-language tradition.

SEAMUS HEANEY *(b. 1939)*

Seamus Heaney was born in the troubled country of Northern Ireland. Heaney has largely avoided the type of political subjects that have divided his homeland. Instead, he has chosen to focus on the landscape of the rural Ireland he knew while growing up as a farmer's son. Since 1982, Heaney has taught part of the year at Harvard. He was awarded the Nobel Prize for Literature in 1995.

ERNEST HEMINGWAY *(1899–1961)*

Ernest Hemingway lived an eventful life. Born the son of a doctor in a middle-class suburb of Chicago, he was wounded as an volunteer ambulance driver in Italy during World War I, trained as a reporter on the *Kansas City Star,* and moved to Paris in the early 1920s, where he was at the center of a brilliant generation of American expatriates that included Gertrude Stein and F. Scott Fitzgerald. He spent much time in Spain, which provided material for his first novel, *The Sun Also Rises* (1926), and his many later articles on bullfighting. In the 1930s he covered the Spanish Civil War, the backdrop for his most popular novel, *For Whom the Bell Tolls* (1940). Hemingway won the Nobel Prize in 1954. The decades since his suicide have seen the release of much unpublished material, including a memoir of his Paris years, *A Moveable Feast* (1964), two novels, and a "fictional memoir" of his final African safari. It is difficult to separate the celebrity from the serious artist whose influence on the short story and novel continues to be felt.

GEORGE HERBERT *(1593–1633)*

George Herbert was the great master of the English devotional lyric. Herbert was born into a distinguished family that included his mother, the formidable literary patroness Lady Magdalen Herbert, and his brother, the poet and statesman Edward, Lord Herbert of Cherbury. Like John Donne, with whom he shares the metaphysical label, Herbert early aimed at a political career but turned to the clergy, spending several happy years as rector of Bemerton before his death at age 40. *The Temple,* which contains most of his poems, was published posthumously in 1633.

HENDRICK HERTZBERG *(b. 1945)*

Hendrick Hertzberg was born in New York, New York. Son of a journalist and historian, Hertzberg has followed in the footsteps of his parents by becoming a leading American journalist and political writer, including work as a speech writer for President Jimmy Carter and correspondent and editor for a number of magazines, including *Newsweek, The New Republic,* and *The New Yorker.* His publications are primarily non-fiction, including the book *One Million* (1970), which consists of 200 pages of 5000 dots—literally one million points given with other statistics and data— as well as *Politics, Observations and Arguments: 1966–2004* (2005), a collection of his notable essays and editorials.

GERARD MANLEY HOPKINS *(1844–1889)*

Gerard Manley Hopkins was an English Jesuit priest who developed elaborate theories of poetic meter (what he called "sprung rhythm") and language to express his own spiritual ardor. Most of his work was posthumously printed through the efforts of his Oxford friend and later correspondent Robert Bridges, who was poet laureate.

A. E. HOUSMAN *(1859–1936)*

Educated in the classics at Oxford and a longtime professor at University College, London, and later at Cambridge, Housman was almost forty before he began to write verse seriously. His ballad-like poems of Shropshire (an area in which he never actually lived) were first collected in *A Shropshire Lad* (1896) and have proven some of the most popular lyrics in English, despite their pervasive mood of bittersweet pessimism.

LANGSTON HUGHES *(1902–1967)*

Langston Hughes was a leading figure in the Harlem Renaissance of the 1920s, and he became the most famous black writer of his day. Phrases from his poems and other writings have become deeply ingrained in the American consciousness. An important experimenter with poetic form, Hughes is credited with incorporating the rhythms of jazz into poetry.

ZORA NEALE HURSTON *(1891–1960)*

Zora Neale Hurston was born in Eatonville, Florida, one of eight children of a father who was a carpenter and Baptist preacher and became mayor of the first all-black town incorporated in the United States. After her mother's death, Hurston moved north, eventually attending high school and taking courses at Howard University and Barnard College, where she earned a B.A. in anthropology, and Columbia University, where she did graduate work. Hurston published her first story while a student and became an important member of the Harlem Renaissance. The expert handling of African American dialect would become a trademark of her style. Hurston achieved only modest success during her lifetime, despite the publication of her controversial novel, *Their Eyes Were Watching God* (1937). She also made many contributions to the study of African American folklore, traveling through the Caribbean and the South to transcribe black myths, fables, and folktales, which were collected in *Mules and Men* (1935).

HENRIK IBSEN *(1828–1906)*

Henrik Ibsen, universally acknowledged as the first of the great modern playwrights, was born in Skien, a small town in Norway, the son of a merchant who went bankrupt during Ibsen's childhood. Ibsen first trained for a medical career, but drifted into the theater, gaining, like Shakespeare and Molière, important dramatic training through a decade's service as a stage manager and director. Ibsen was unsuccessful in establishing a theater in Oslo, and he spent almost thirty years living and writing in Germany and Italy. The fame he won through early poetic dramas like *Peer Gynt* (1867), which is considered the supreme exploration of the Norwegian national character, was overshadowed by the realistic prose plays he began writing with *Pillars of Society* (1877). *A Doll's House* (1879) and *Ghosts* (1881), which deal, respectively, with a woman's struggle for independence and self-respect and with the taboo subject of venereal disease, made Ibsen an internationally famous, if controversial, figure. Although Ibsen's type of realism, displayed in "problem plays" such as these and later psychological dramas like *The Wild Duck* (1885) and

Hedda Gabler (1890), has become so fully assimilated into our literary heritage that now it is difficult to think of him as an innovator, his marriage of the tightly constructed plots of the conventional "well-made play" to serious discussion of social issues was one of the most significant developments in the history of drama. Interestingly, the conclusion of *A Doll's House* proved so unsettling that Ibsen was forced to write an alternate ending in which Nora states her case but does not slam the door on her marriage. His most influential advocate in English-speaking countries was George Bernard Shaw, whose *The Quintessence of Ibsenism* (1891) is one of the earliest and most influential studies of Ibsen's dramatic methods and ideas.

DAVID IVES (b. 1950)

David Ives grew up on Chicago's South Side, the son of working-class parents, writing his first play at the age of nine: "But then I realized you had to have a copy of the script for each person in the play, so that was the end of it." Impressed by theatrical productions he saw in his teens, Ives entered Northwestern University and after graduation attended Yale Drama School. After several attempts to become a "serious writer" he decided to "aspire to silliness on a daily basis" and began creating the short comic plays on which his reputation rests. An evening of six one-act comedies, *All in the Timing*, had a successful off-Broadway production in 1994, running over two years. In 1996 it was the most performed contemporary play in the nation, and *Sure Thing*, its signature piece, remains popular, especially with student drama groups. A second collection of one acts, *Mere Mortals*, had a successful run at Primary Stages in 1997, and a third collection, *Lives of Saints*, was produced in 1999. Two of his collections, *All in the Timing* (1995) and *Time Flies* (2001), have been published. Ives's comedic skills range from a hilarious parody of David Mamet's plays (presented at an event honoring Mamet) to his witty revision of a legendary character in the full-length *Don Juan in Chicago*. His short plays, in many cases, hinge on brilliant theatrical conceits; in *Time Flies*, a boy mayfly and girl mayfly must meet, court, and consummate their relationship before dying as their one day of life ends. *Sure Thing*, a piece that plays witty tricks with time, resembles a scene in the Bill Murray film

Groundhog Day, the script of which was written some years after Ives's play. In an article titled "Why I Shouldn't Write Plays," Ives notes, among other reasons, "All reviews should carry a Surgeon General's warning. The good ones turn your head, the bad ones break your heart."

SHIRLEY JACKSON (1919–1965)

Shirley Jackson was born in San Francisco and educated at Syracuse University. With her husband, the literary critic Stanley Edgar Hyman, she lived in Bennington, Vermont. There she produced three novels and the popular *Life Among the Savages* (1953), a "disrespectful memoir" of her four children, and a sequel to it, *Raising Demons* (1957). "The Lottery," which created a sensation when it appeared in *The New Yorker* in 1948, remains a fascinating example of an allegory whose ultimate meaning is open to debate. Many readers at the time, for obvious reasons, associated it with the Holocaust, although it should not be approached in such a restrictive manner. "The Lottery" is the only one of Jackson's many short stories that has been widely reprinted (it was also dramatized for television), but she was a versatile writer of humorous articles for popular magazines, psychological novels, and a popular gothic horror novel, *The Haunting of Hill House* (1959), which was made into a motion picture called *The Haunting* (1963). Jackson published two collections of short stories, *The Lottery* (1949) and *The Magic of Shirley Jackson* (1966).

ROBINSON JEFFERS (1887–1962)

Robinson Jeffers lived with his wife and children for many years in Carmel, California, in a rock house that he built himself by the sea. Many of his ideas about man's small place in the larger world of nature have gained in relevance through the years since his death. Largely forgotten for many years, his poetry, particularly his book-length verse narratives, is once more regaining the attention of serious readers.

SARAH ORNE JEWETT (1849–1909)

Sarah Orne Jewett was born in the harbor village of South Berwick, Maine, the granddaughter of a sea captain and daughter of a doctor who taught at Bowdoin College and also served as a general practitioner among the local fishermen and farmers. Jewett's early sketches of Maine people and places owe much to the popular "local color" tradition of the nineteenth century, but her stories largely avoid the moralizing and sentimentality common to popular fiction of its day. Although she traveled widely in later life, Jewett remained throughout her career a writer inextricably connected with her region.

JAMES JOYCE *(1882–1941)*

James Joyce is best known for his masterpiece *Ulysses,* the difficult modernist novel of a single day in the life of Dublin that shortly after its appearance in 1922 became both a classic and the subject of a landmark censorship case, which its publishers eventually won. Joyce's lifelong quarrel with the provincial concerns of Irish religious, cultural, and literary life led him to permanent continental self-exile in Zürich and Paris. Most readers associate Joyce with his pioneering of experimental techniques such as his use of interior monologue and stream of consciousness, and the complicated linguistic games of *Finnegans Wake* (1939), forgetting that his earlier works lie squarely in the realm of traditional fiction. *Dubliners* (1914), his collection of short stories of life in his native city, remains an imposing achievement, as does his autobiographical novel *A Portrait of the Artist as a Young Man* (1916).

DONALD JUSTICE *(1925–2004)*

Donald Justice published more selectively than most of his contemporaries. His Pulitzer Prize–winning volume of selected poems displays considerable literary sophistication and reveals the poet's familiarity with the traditions of contemporary European and Latin American poetry. As an editor, he was responsible for rescuing the important work of Weldon Kees from obscurity.

PAULINE KAEL *(1919–2001)*

Pauline Kael was born on a farm in California and began reviewing films on the Berkeley radio station KPFA in the 1950s. A contributor of outspoken reviews to many magazines (her negative notice of *The Sound of Music* resulted in her being fired by *McCall's*), she became the resident film critic at *The New Yorker* in 1967. Her collection of reviews, *Deeper into Movies* (1973), won a National Book Award. A critic of wide-ranging tastes who enjoyed both European films and the "great trash" productions of Hollywood, Kael contributed to making film criticism an intellectually respectable form of literature.

FRANZ KAFKA *(1883–1924)*

Franz Kafka was born in Prague, in the Czech Republic (then part of the Austro-Hungarian empire), into a Jewish family, where he learned to speak both Czech and German as a child. Raised primarily by staff rather than his often absent working parents, Kafka began writing at an early age, an occupation that he saw as a release from the troubles and burdens of his other responsibilities. He took a law degree in his 20s and took a job in an insurance office, but also continued to write. Though successful and somewhat upwardly mobile in his profession, he felt harassed by work responsibilities and the constant turmoil of his family life, and he eventually moved from his parents' house in 1914. While he published a small number of stories in his life, much of his work remained either unfinished or unpublished, and Kafka himself ordered that his writings be burnt upon his death—it is only the refusal of his literary executors to do so that created the rich legacy we now have. After his death from tuberculosis, he achieved an enormous posthumous popularity and is considered one of the founders of modern literature. Some of his most famous works include the short story "Metamorphosis," published in 1936 (Also known as "The Metamorphosis," first published as "Die Verwandlung" in 1915) an apparently allegorical tale of a man who awakens to find that the has become a large insect, and "The Trial" (1937, first published as *Der Prozeß: Roman,* 1925), a narrative of a man caught in an illogical bureaucracy that seems to represent the impossibilities of existing in any comfortable relation to law or government. Kafka is known for paradox and confusion in his writing, and the term "Kafkaesque" has come to symbolize strange and inexplicable, or contradictory events in narrative. Several of his works have been turned into films and he continues to be celebrated and studied as one the most important and influential writers of the early twentieth century.

JULIE KANE (b. 1952)

Julie Kane was born and raised in New Jersey and studied creative writing with Anne Sexton. For many years a resident of Louisiana, she has a Ph. D. from Louisiana State University and currently teaches at Northwest Louisiana State University. *Rhythm & Booze* (2003) was selected for the National Poetry Series by Maxine Kumin. Skilled in such difficult forms as the villanelle (the subject of her dissertation), Kane is also readying for publication a translation of selected poems of Victor Hugo.

JOHN KEATS (1795–1821)

John Keats is now perhaps the most admired of all the major romantics. Certainly his tragic death from tuberculosis in his twenties gives poignancy to thoughts of the doomed young poet writing feverishly in a futile race against time; "Here lies one whose name was writ in water" are the words he chose for his own epitaph. Many of Keats's poems are concerned with glimpses of the eternal, whether a translation of an ancient epic poem or a pristine artifact of a vanished civilization.

JOHN F. KENNEDY (1917–1963)

John Fitzgerald Kennedy was born in Brookline, Massachusetts, and served as a U.S. representative, U.S. senator, and eventually as the 35th U.S. President. Before his political service, he had a distinguished record in military service during World War II, earning several medals for heroism, including the Navy and Marine Corps medal for towing a wounded soldier over three miles in the ocean. Aided by his charisma and diplomatic ability, his political career helped make the Kennedy family one of the most prominent American political families of the 20th century. Although his administration faced the embarrassment of the failed Bay of Pigs Invasion in Cuba, Kennedy was responsible for founding the Peace Corps, for the peaceful resolution of the Cuban Missile Crisis, for greatly improving America's funding of space exploration, for early support of the civil rights movement, and for signing into law a partial test ban of nuclear weapons. With such success stories, the Kennedy administration (sometimes called "Camelot") has been often praised. Though in later years there have been revelations of marital infidelity and troubled health, substantial criticism of Kennedy usually comes only from those who doubt whether he could have possibly lived up to the enormous promise and hope that his personality provided the nation. He was also known for giving several memorable speeches, including his 1961 inaugural address with the famed phrase "ask not what your country can do for you; ask what you can do for your country," and his 1963 "Ich bin ein Berliner" speech, supporting West Berlin against communism. As a writer, Kennedy published a number of books, the most prominent of which is *Profiles in Courage*, which won the Pulitzer Prize for Biography in 1957. His assassination in 1963, in Dallas, Texas, was an incalculable blow to the nation, and sparked decades of controversy and a veritable industry of conspiracy theories. It is difficult even today to judge the enormity of his influence and legacy in American politics and culture.

SUJI KWOCK KIM (b. 1968)

Suji Kwock Kim received the 2002 Walt Whitman Award, for *Notes from the Divided Country*, an exploration of the Japanese occupation of Korea, and of the Korean War and its aftermath. Kim's family emigrated to Poughkeepsie, New York, in the 1970s. She studied at Yale, the Iowa Writers' Workshop, Seoul National University, where she was a Fulbright Scholar, and Stanford University, where she was a Stegner Fellow. Kim is coauthor of *Private Property*, a multimedia play produced at the Edinburgh Festival Fringe and featured on BBC-TV. She lives in San Francisco and New York.

MARTIN LUTHER KING, JR. (1929–1968)

Martin Luther King, Jr., was born in Atlanta, Georgia, and is known as the most influential leader of the civil rights movement. Famous for spearheading politically charged protests such as the 1955 Montgomery bus boycott, King won the Nobel Peace Prize in 1964, and was one of the most influential political organizers and leaders of the twentieth century. He received death threats, was monitored by the FBI, accused of supporting communism, and eventually assassinated by an apparent white supremacist, but he has since become one of the most revered figures of American history. King was an astute writer and is known for his famous "I Have A Dream" speech (1963), as well as other writings such as his "Letter from Birmingham Jail" (1963). A pacifist who believed that civil disobedience was necessary to confront unjust laws, King's legacy is substantial, and not even posthumous accusations of marital infidelity and plagiarism have sullied his enormous influence and reputation.

CAROLYN KIZER (b. 1925)

Carolyn Kizer has led a fascinating career that includes a year's study in Taiwan and another year in Pakistan, where she worked for the U.S. State Department. Her first collection, *The Ungrateful Garden* (1961), demonstrates an equal facility with formal and free verse, but her subsequent books (including the Pulitzer Prize–winning *Yin* of 1985) have tended more toward the latter. A committed feminist, Kizer anticipated many of today's women's issues as early as the mid-1950s, just as the poem "The Ungrateful Garden" was published a decade before "ecology" became a household word.

YUSEF KOMUNYAKAA (b. 1947)

Yusef Komunyakaa is a native of Bogalusa, Louisiana. Komunyakaa has written memorably on a wide range of subjects, including jazz and his service during the Vietnam War. *Neon Vernacular: New and Selected Poems* (1993) won the Pulitzer Prize in 1994, and *Pleasure Dome: New and Collected Poems* appeared in 2001.

TED KOOSER (b. 1939)

Ted Kooser, who lives in Nebraska, writes plainspoken poems about life in America's heartland. Born in Iowa, Kooser studied at Iowa State University and the University of Nebraska. His poetry collections include *Winter Morning Walks: One Hundred Postcards to Jim Harrison*, which received the 2001 Nebraska Book Award for poetry and was written during recovery from cancer surgery and radiation treatment. Kooser is editor and publisher of Windflower Press, a small press specializing in contemporary poetry. A retired vice president of Lincoln Benefit Life, an insurance company, Kooser was appointed U.S. Poet Laureate in 2004.

MAXINE KUMIN (b. 1925)

Maxine Kumin was born in Philadelphia and educated at Radcliffe. Kumin was an early literary ally and friend of Anne Sexton, with whom she coauthored several children's books. The winner of the 1973 Pulitzer Prize, Kumin has preferred a rural life raising horses for some years. Her increased interest in the natural world has paralleled the environmental awareness of many of her readers.

PHILIP LARKIN (1922–1985)

Philip Larkin was perhaps the latest British poet to establish a significant body of readers in the United States. The general pessimism of his work is mitigated by a wry sense of irony and brilliant formal control. For many years he was a librarian at the University of Hull, and he was also a dedicated fan and critic of jazz.

EMMA LAZARUS (1849–1887)

Emma Lazarus was born in New York City, one of seven children of a wealthy Jewish American sugar refiner. Her famous sonnet "The New Colossus" was written in 1883 for an art auction raising money to build a pedestal for the Statue of Liberty, which had been given to the United States by France. During Lazarus's short life she became a powerful spokesperson for the rights of immigrants and called on Jews to claim a homeland in Palestine. Sixteen years after her death, "The New Colossus" was engraved on a plaque for the statue's base.

SHIRLEY GEOK-LIN LIM (b. 1944)

Shirley Geok-lin Lim writes poetry, fiction, and criticism. Born in Malacca, Malaya, she grew up in poverty and was abandoned by her mother. Her love of the English language over her native tongue earned her the disapproval of the teachers at the Catholic convent school she attended. Lim, who won a scholarship to the University of Malaysia, went on to earn a Ph.D. in English and American literature from Brandeis University. *Among the White Moon Faces: An Asian-American Memoir of Homelands* (1996) won her attention both in the United States and Asia. Like her poetry, her prose explores questions of identity and national origin.

DIANE LOCKWARD *(b. 1943)*

Diane Lockward is a former high school English teacher who now works as a poet-in-the-schools for both the New Jersey State Council on the Arts and the Geraldine R. Dodge Foundation. She has received numerous awards for her poetry, which has appeared in many literary journals, but her first full-length collection, *Eve's Red Dress* did not appear until 2003. "My Husband Discovers Poetry" has been read by Garrison Keillor several times on NPR's *The Writer's Almanac.*

DAVID MAMET *(b. 1947)*

David Mamet is one of the most successful and honored of American playwrights, and he has also distinguished himself as an essayist, novelist, film writer, and director. His 1984 play *Glengarry Glen Ross* won a Pulitzer Prize and was successfully revived on Broadway in 2005. A master of brutal, realistic dialogue, Mamet has also written poetry, children's books, and several works on acting technique in which he goes against the grain of many modern teachers of "method" acting. His advice to actors is summed up in the quote "Invent Nothing. Deny Nothing."

ANDREW MARVELL *(1621–1678)*

Andrew Marvell is widely known for the playful sexual wit of this most famous example of the carpé diem poem in English. Marvell was a learned Latin scholar who moved in high circles of government under both the Puritans and Charles II, serving as a member of parliament for two decades. Oddly, Marvell was almost completely forgotten as a lyric poet for almost two hundred years after his death, although today he is considered the last of the great exemplars of the metaphysical style.

BOBBIE ANN MASON *(b. 1940)*

Bobbie Ann Mason was born in Mayfield, Kentucky, and grew up on a dairy farm run by her parents. The rural background of her youth figures in many of her best stories, and one of Mason's favorite subjects is the assimilation of the countryside and the South into a larger American culture. Mason's characters may dream of living in log cabins, but they also take adult education courses, watch TV talk shows, and shop in supermarkets and malls. After taking degrees from the University of Kentucky and the University of Connecticut, Mason published her first two books, both works of literary criticism, in the mid 1970s. One of them, *The Girl Sleuth,* was a feminist guide to the exploits of fictional detectives like *Nancy Drew* that Mason read as a child. After years of attempts, Mason's stories began to appear in prestigious magazines, most prominently *The New Yorker,* and the publication of *Shiloh and Other Stories* (1982) established her as an important new voice in American fiction. She has since published a second collection of short stories and four novels, one of which, *In Country* (1985), was filmed in 1989. *Shiloh,* like several of the stories in the collection from which it is taken, gains considerable immediacy from Mason's use of present tense and her sure sense of regional speech patterns. In recent years, Mason has published a story collection, *Zigzagging Down a Wild Trail* (2001), and the biography *Elvis Presley* (2003).

FLORENCE CASSEN MAYERS *(b. 1940)*

Florence Cassen Mayers is a widely published poet and children's author. Her "ABC" books include children's guides to baseball and to the National Basketball Association.

CLAUDE MCKAY *(1889–1948)*

Claude McKay, one of the central figures in the Harlem Renaissance, was born in Jamaica and published his first two books of poetry, one of them based on his experiences as a police officer, before emigrating to the United States in 1912 to study at the Tuskeegee Institute. McKay came to New York in 1914, working as a railway-car waiter and continuing to publish poetry and short fiction. His novel *Home to Harlem* (1928) was widely praised, though W. E. B. DuBois (whom McKay considered a mentor) criticized it for its sexual explicitness. McKay published novels, autobiographical books, and short stories. His *Selected Poems* appeared posthumously in 1953.

TERRENCE MCNALLY *(b. 1939)*

Terrence McNally was born in St. Petersburg, Florida, and is recognized as one of the central American playwrights of the latter half of the

20th century. McNally had his first play, *The Lady of the Camellias,* produced on Broadway in 1963, and has enjoyed a steady growth of commercial and critical success since that time. His work *Frankie and Johnny in the Claire de Lune* (1987) was turned into a successful motion picture, *Frankie and Johnny* in 1991.

JAMES MERRILL *(1926–1995)*

James Merrill wrote *The Changing Light at Sandover,* a long poem that resulted from many years of sessions with a Ouija board. The book became his major work and, among many other things, a remarkable memoir of a long-term gay relationship. Merrill's shorter poems, collected in 2001, reveal meticulous craftsmanship and a play of wit unequaled among contemporary American poets.

W. S. MERWIN *(b. 1927)*

W. S. Merwin often displays environmental concerns that have motivated much poetry in recent years. Even in earlier work his fears of the results of uncontrolled destruction of the environment are presented allegorically. Born in New York City, he currently resides in Hawaii.

EDNA ST. VINCENT MILLAY *(1892–1950)*

Raised in the coastal village of Camden, Maine, Edna St. Vincent Millay was extremely popular in the 1920s, when her sonnets seemed the ultimate expression of the liberated sexuality of what was then called the New Woman. Neglected for many years, her poems have recently generated renewed interest, and it seems likely that she will eventually regain her status as one of the most important female poets of the twentieth century.

JESSICA MITFORD *(1917–1996)*

Jessica Mitford was born in Batsford, Gloucestershire, England. She spent the first half of her life in a variety of jobs before finding her calling as a writer of exposes, finding acclaim with the publication of *The American Way of Death* (1963), criticizing the American funeral industry. Much of her later life was similarly engaged in muckraking, revealing the dubious practices of various businesses and industries, and she was known for witty, unpretentious prose. Mitford died of lung cancer in Oakland, California.

ROBERT MORGAN *(b. 1944)*

Robert Morgan is a native of the mountains of North Carolina and has retained a large measure of regional ties in his poetry. One of his collections, *Sigodlin,* takes its title from an Appalachian word for things that are built slightly out of square. *Gap Creek: The Story of a Marriage,* a novel of turn-of-the-century mountain life, was a bestseller in 2000.

DAVE MORICE *(b. 1946)*

Dave Morice is a poet, writer and illustrator, who has published numerous books for children and adults including *The Dictionary of Wordplay* and *The Adventures of Dr. Alphabet.* Dave's Shakespeare cartoon is reprinted from the second volume of his *Poetry Comics,* a series *The Boston Globe* says "will surely irk the hell out of professors and self-glorious grad students everywhere."

TIMOTHY MURPHY *(b. 1950)*

Timothy Murphy, a former student of Robert Penn Warren at Yale, returned to his native North Dakota to make a career as a venture capitalist in the agricultural field. Unpublished until his midforties, Murphy has brought four collections to print during the last decade.

JOYCE CAROL OATES *(b. 1938)*

Joyce Carol Oates is a prolific writer who has published over sixty books since her first appeared in 1963, and she shows few signs of slowing her output. Her new books—whether novels, books of poems, collections of stories, or nonfiction memoirs on subjects like boxing—always draw serious critical attention and more often than not land on the bestseller lists, and she has even written suspense novels pseudonymously as Rosamond Smith. Born in Lockport, New York, she holds degrees from Syracuse and the University of Wisconsin, and she is writer-in-residence at Princeton, where she also codirects, with her husband, the Ontario Review Press. Oates's work is often violent, a fact for which she has been criticized on numerous occasions. In response, she has remarked that these comments are "always ignorant, always sexist," implying that different standards are often applied to the work of women authors whose realism may be too strong for some tastes. Few readers would argue that her stories and novels exceed the violence of the society they depict. *Them,* a novel of African American life in Detroit, won a National Book Award in 1970, and Oates has since garnered many other honors. "Where Are You Going, Where Have You Been?" is based on a *Life* magazine story about a serial rapist and killer known as "The Pied Piper of Tucson." In 1985 Oates's story was filmed by Joyce Chopra as *Smooth Talk,* starring Laura Dern and Treat Williams. Indicating the long popularity of this story, Oates published a collection of prose pieces in 1999 titled *Where I've Been, and Where I'm Going.* Her thirtieth novel, *Blonde* (2000), took as its subject the life of Marilyn Monroe.

TIM O'BRIEN *(b. 1946)*

Tim O'Brien was born in Minnesota. Immediately after graduating from Macalester College, he was drafted and served in Vietnam, rising to the rank of sergeant. After his discharge, he studied government at Harvard but did not complete his Ph.D. His third book, *Going After Cacciato,* won the National Book Award and is generally considered the finest American novel about the Vietnam War.

FLANNERY O'CONNOR *(1925–1964)*

Flannery O'Connor was one of the first of many important writers to emerge from the Writers' Workshop of the University of Iowa, where she received an M.F.A. in creative writing. Born in Savannah, Georgia, she attended Georgia State College for Women, graduating in 1945. Plagued by disseminated lupus, the same incurable illness that killed her father in 1941, O'Connor spent most of the last decade of her life living with her mother on a dairy farm near Milledgeville, Georgia, where she wrote and raised peacocks. Unusual among modern American writers in the seriousness of her Christianity (she was a devout Roman Catholic in the largely Protestant South), O'Connor focuses an uncompromising moral eye on the violence and spiritual disorder of the modern world. She is sometimes called a "southern gothic" writer because of her fascination with the grotesque, although today she seems far ahead of her time in depicting a region in which the social and religious certainties of the past are becoming extinct almost overnight. O'Connor's published work includes two short novels, *Wise Blood* (1952) and *The Violent Bear It*

Away (1960), and two collections of short stories, *A Good Man Is Hard to Find* (1955) and *Everything That Rises Must Converge,* published posthumously in 1965. A collection of essays and miscellaneous prose, *Mystery and Manners* (1961), and her selected letters, *The Habit of Being* (1979), reveal an engaging social side of her personality that is not always apparent in her fiction.

SHARON OLDS *(b. 1942)*

Sharon Olds displays a candor in dealing with the intimacies of family romance covering three generations that has made her one of the chief contemporary heirs to the confessional tradition. A powerful and dramatic reader, she is much in demand on the lecture circuit. Born in San Francisco, she currently resides in New York City.

MARY OLIVER *(b. 1935)*

Mary Oliver was born in Cleveland, Ohio, and educated at Ohio State University and Vassar. She has served as a visiting professor at a number of universities and at the Fine Arts Work Center in Provincetown, Massachusetts. She has won both the Pulitzer Prize and the National Book Award for her work, which first appeared in *No Voyage and Other Poems* in 1965.

DANIEL OROZCO *(b.1957)*

Daniel Orozco studied writing at the University of Washington and Stanford University, and currently teaches at the University of Idaho. He has not yet published a full-length collection, but his stories have appeared in many journals and in the *Best American Short Stories* and Pushcart Prize anthologies. "Orientation" has been performed on public radio and has been translated into several foreign languages, an indication, perhaps, of how little office culture varies from country to country.

GEORGE ORWELL *(1903–1950)*

George Orwell was born Eric Arthur Blair, in Bengal, India. Although his family moved to England when he was an infant and lived there for much of his education and later life, he also lived and worked in many other places in Europe and India. Politically active throughout his life, he is best known for his novels *Animal Farm* (1945) and *Nineteen*

Eighty-Four (1949). Both works are extremely critical of government control and suspicious of the tendency of institutions to limit human freedom and basic human values. Orwell died of complications resulting from tuberculosis.

WILFRED OWEN *(1893–1918)*

Wilfred Owen was killed in the trenches only a few days before the armistice that ended World War I. Owen showed more promise than any other English poet of his generation. A decorated officer whose nerves broke down after exposure to battle, he met poet Siegfried Sassoon at Craiglockhart military hospital. His work was posthumously collected by his friend. A novel by Pat Barker, *Regeneration* (also made into a film), deals with their poetic and personal relationship.

GRACE PALEY *(b. 1922)*

Grace Goodside Paley was born in the Bronx, the child of Russian Jewish immigrants. Her political, feminist, and antiwar activism often reveals itself in her fiction. Paley was married in the early 1940s and had two children; she and her husband were divorced in the late 1960s after living separately for over twenty years. Early in her career she wrote poetry, studying with W. H. Auden, and turned to fiction only in her midthirties, publishing her first collection, *The Little Disturbances of Man*, in 1959. The book gained in reputation over time and established Paley as a local colorist with a remarkable ear for urban Jewish speech and aphorisms. A subsequent publication, *The Collected Stories* (1994), became a finalist for the National Book Award. Paley currently lives with her second husband in Greenwich Village and Vermont.

LINDA PASTAN *(b. 1932)*

Linda Pastan served as poet laureate of Maryland, where she has lived and taught for many years. Her first book, *A Perfect Circle of Sun*, appeared in 1971, and a dozen more collections have been published since.

HARVEY PEKAR *(b. 1939)*

Harvey Pekar was born in Cleveland, Ohio. A writer and essayist, he has achieved moderate fame for his autobiographical comic work *American Splendor* (1976), which was even-

tually turned into a movie with the same title in 2003. Pekar focuses on the bleak and mundane aspects of life, and the protagonist of his work is often a self-absorbed and aggravating version of himself, reveling in a mixture of bitterness and poignant humanity.

MARGE PIERCY *(b. 1936)*

Marge Piercy was a political radical during her student days at the University of Michigan. Piercy has continued to be outspoken on political, cultural, and sexual issues. Her phrase "to be of use" has become a key measure by which feminist writers and critics have gauged the meaning of their own life experiences.

SYLVIA PLATH *(1932–1963)*

Sylvia Plath, whose troubled personal life is often difficult to separate from her poetry, is almost always read as an autobiographical and confessional poet. Brilliant and precocious, she served a long apprenticeship to the tradition of modern poetry before attaining her mature style in the final two years of her life. Only one collection, *The Colossus* (1960), appeared in her lifetime, and her fame has mainly rested on her posthumous books of poetry and the success of her lone novel, *The Bell Jar* (1963). She committed suicide in 1963. Plath has been the subject of a half-dozen biographical studies and a feature film, *Sylvia* (2003), reflecting the intense interest that readers have in her life and work.

PLATO *(c. 428–348 B.C.E.)*

Plato is the founder of the philosophical tradition in the western world. He has had incalculable and profound influence in every subsequent era. Born of a wealthy family in Athens, Greece, Plato fell under the tutelage of Socrates. After the death of Socrates at the hands of the Athens community, Plato traveled extensively before eventually establishing a famous academy outside the walls of Athens, training other philosophers, including his greatest pupil Aristotle. Plato is best known through his *Dialogues*, narrative lessons on philosophy wherein the character of Socrates teaches a principle or idea through the process of dialogue with another person or persons. The philosophical principles proposed in Plato's works, such as the superiority of eternal Ideas, or forms, over the transient things of the material world, influenced countless subsequent thinkers. Plato is famous for the "Allegory of the Cave," found in the *Republic*, where he argues that literature and poetry ought to be excluded from study because of their negative influence on the populace.

EDGAR ALLAN POE *(1809–1849)*

Edgar Allan Poe was born in Boston. Although the child of actors and orphaned at age 2, he lived a privileged childhood as a ward of a wealthy merchant. After a profligate year at the University of Virginia, successful military service (under an assumed name), and an abortive stay at West Point, Poe broke with his foster father, married his young cousin, and set about a literary career, succeeding as editor of several prominent magazines and becoming a meticulous craftsman of criticism, fiction, and poetry whose impact on world literature has been immense; genres like the horror tale and the detective story list Poe stories like "Ligeia" or "The Murders in the Rue Morgue" among their earliest important examples. Poe's irregular habits and a drinking problem, which grew more pronounced following the death of his wife in 1847, led to his mysterious death in Baltimore at the age of 39.

EZRA POUND *(1885–1972)*

Ezra Pound was the greatest international proponent of modernist poetry. Born in Idaho and reared in Philadelphia, he emigrated to England in 1909, where he befriended Yeats, promoted the early work of Frost, and discovered Eliot. Pound's early promotion of the imagist movement assisted a number of important poetic principles and reputations, including those of H. D. (Hilda Doolittle) and, later, William Carlos Williams. Pound's support of Mussolini during World War II, expressed in controversial radio broadcasts, caused him to be held for over a decade after the war as a mental patient in the United States, after which he returned to Italy for the final years of his long and controversial life.

DUDLEY RANDALL *(1914–2000)*

Dudley Randall was the founder of Broadside Press, a black-owned publishing firm that eventually attracted important writers like Gwendolyn Brooks and Don L. Lee. For most of his life a resident of Detroit, Randall spent many years working in that city's library system before taking a similar position at the University of Detroit.

HENRY REED *(1914–1986)*

Henry Reed was a multitalented English literary figure, known as much for his translations and radio work as his poetry. Born in Birmingham and educated there, he served in the army as a Japanese translator during World War II. After the war he worked as a journalist and scriptwriter for the BBC and had a successful career as a playwright.

ADRIENNE RICH *(b. 1929)*

Adrienne Rich's most recent books of poetry are *The School Among The Ruins: Poems 2000–2004*, and *Fox: Poems 1998–2000*. A selection of her essays, *Arts Of The Possible: Essays and Conversations*, was published in 2001. A new edition of *What Is Found There: Notebooks on Poetry and Politics*, appeared in 2003. She is a recipient of the Lannan Foundation Lifetime Achievement Award, the Lambda Book Award, the Lenore Marshall/*Nation* Prize, the Wallace Stevens Award, and the Bollingen Prize in Poetry, among other honors. She lives in California.

EDWIN ARLINGTON ROBINSON *(1869–1935)*

Edwin Arlington Robinson wrote many poems set in "Tilbury," a recreation of his hometown of Gardiner, Maine. These poems continue to present readers with a memorable cast of eccentric characters who somehow manifest universal human desires. Robinson languished in poverty and obscurity for many years before his reputation began to flourish as a result of the interest taken in his work by President Theodore Roosevelt, who obtained a government job for Robinson and wrote a favorable review of one of his books.

THEODORE ROETHKE *(1908–1963)*

Theodore Roethke was born in Michigan. Roethke was an influential teacher of poetry at the University of Washington for many years. His father was the owner of a greenhouse, and Roethke's childhood closeness to nature was an important influence on his mature poetry. His periodic nervous breakdowns, the result of bipolar manic-depression, presaged his early death.

CHRISTINA ROSSETTI *(1830–1894)*

Christina Rossetti was the younger sister of Dante Gabriel and William, also distinguished writers, and was the author of numerous devotional poems and prose works. Her collected poems, edited by her brother William, appeared posthumously in 1904.

MARY JO SALTER *(b. 1954)*

Mary Jo Salter has traveled widely with her husband, poet and novelist Brad Leithauser, and has lived in Japan, Italy, and Iceland. A student of Elizabeth Bishop at Harvard, Salter brings to her art a devotion to the poet's craft that mirrors that of her mentor. She has published five collections of poetry and *The Moon Comes Home,* a children's book.

MARJANE SATRAPI *(b. 1969)*

Marjane Satrapi was born in Rasht, Iran, and grew up in Tehran, before moving to Vienna, Strasbourg, and ultimately Paris, where she still lives and writes. She is best known for her autobiographical graphic novel *Persepolis,* an account that includes her childhood in Tehran during the 1979 Iranian revolution.

WILLIAM SHAKESPEARE *(1564–1616)*

William Shakespeare, the supreme writer of English, was born, baptized, and buried in the market town of Stratford-on-Avon, eighty miles from London. Son of a glove maker and merchant who was high bailiff (or mayor) of the town, he probably attended grammar school and learned to read Latin authors in the original. At eighteen he married Anne Hathaway, twenty-six, by whom he had three children, including twins. By 1592 he had become well known and envied as an actor and playwright in London. From 1594 until he retired, he belonged to the same theatrical company, the Lord Chamberlain's Men (later renamed the King's Men in honor of their patron, James I), for whom he wrote thirty-six plays—some of them, such as *Hamlet* and *King Lear,* profound reworkings of old plays. As an actor, Shakespeare is believed to have played supporting roles, such as Hamlet's father's ghost. The company prospered, moved into the Globe Theater in 1599, and in 1608 bought the fashionable Blackfriars as well; Shakespeare owned an interest in both theaters. When plagues shut down the theaters

from 1592 to 1594, Shakespeare turned to poems; his great sonnets (published only in 1609) probably also date from the 1590s. Plays were regarded as entertainments of little literary merit and Shakespeare did not bother to supervise their publication. After *The Tempest* (1611), the last play entirely from his hand, he retired to Stratford, where since 1597 he had owned the second largest house in town. Most critics agree that when he wrote *Hamlet* (c. 1600), Shakespeare was at the height of his powers.

PERCY BYSSHE SHELLEY *(1792–1822)*

Percy Bysshe Shelley, like his friend Byron, has not found as much favor in recent eras as the other English romantics, although his political liberalism anticipates many currents of our own day. Perhaps his unbridled emotionalism is sometimes too intense for modern readers. His wife, Mary Wollstonecraft Shelley, will be remembered as the author of the classic horror novel *Frankenstein.*

STEVIE SMITH *(1902–1971)*

Stevie (Florence Margaret) Smith worked for many years as a secretary to a London publisher and first attracted attention with the autobiographical *Novel on Yellow Paper* in 1936. Always something of a literary outsider who nevertheless found popular success with her highly original and idiosyncratic fiction, poetry, and drawings, Smith was brilliantly portrayed by Glenda Jackson in the 1978 film *Stevie.*

CATHY SONG *(b. 1955)*

Cathy Song was born in Honolulu, Hawaii, and holds degrees from Wellesley College and Boston University. Her first book, *Picture Bride,* won the Yale Series of Younger Poets Award in 1983. *The Land of Bliss,* her fourth collection, appeared in 2001.

SOPHOCLES *(c. 496–406 B.C.E.)*

Sophocles lived in Athens in the age of Pericles, during the city's greatest period of culture, power, and influence. Sophocles distinguished himself as an athlete, a musician, a military advisor, a politician and, most important, a dramatist. At sixteen, he was chosen to lead a chorus in reciting a poem on the Greek naval victory over the Persians at Salamis, and he won his first prizes as a playwright before he was thirty. Although both Aeschylus, his senior, and Euripides, his younger rival, have their champions, Sophocles, whose career spanned so long a period that he competed against both of them, is generally considered to be the most important Greek writer of tragedies; his thirty victories in the City Dionysia surpass the combined totals of his two great colleagues. Of his 123 plays, only seven survive intact, including two other plays relating to Oedipus and his children, *Antigone* and *Oedipus at Colonus*, which was produced after Sophocles's death by his grandson. He is generally credited with expanding the technical possibilities of drama by introducing a third actor in certain scenes (Aeschylus used only two) and by both reducing the number of lines given to the chorus and increasing its integration into his plays. Sophocles was intimately involved in both civic and military affairs, twice serving as a chief advisor to Pericles, and his sense of duty to the polis (Greek for city) is apparent in many of his plays. *Oedipus the King* was first performed in Athens in about 430 B.C.E. Its importance can be judged by the many references that Aristotle makes to it in his discussion of tragedy in the Poetics.

ART SPIEGELMAN (b. 1948)

Art Spiegelman was born in Stockholm, Sweden, though he has lived much of his life in New York City. A major figure of the underground comics movement, Spiegelman achieved larger critical recognition with the publication of *Maus* (1985), a graphic novel retelling his parents' Holocaust survival narrative in allegorical form. The story, with its sequel, *Maus II* (1991), almost single handedly brought critical respect to the comics medium, demonstrating that serious themes could be addressed by an art form typically reserved for children. Spiegelman has gained continued respect for *In the Shadow of No Towers* (2004), an autobiographical response to the September 11th terrorist attacks.

WILLIAM STAFFORD (1914–1993)

William Stafford was one of the most prolific poets of the postwar era. Stafford published in virtually every magazine in the United States. Raised in Kansas as a member of the pacifist Church of the Brethren, Stafford served in a camp for conscientious objectors during World War II. His first book did not appear until he was in his forties, but he published over thirty collections before his death at seventy-nine.

JOHN STEINBECK (1902–1968)

John Steinbeck was another American winner of the Nobel Prize. Born in Salinas, California, he drew throughout his career on his familiarity with the farming country, ranches, and fishing communities of his native state, especially in novels like *Tortilla Flat* (1935), *Of Mice and Men* (1937), and *Cannery Row* (1945). Steinbeck's short fiction is less well known, although he excelled at the novella form in *The Pearl* (1947). "The Chrysanthemums" comes from *The Long Valley* (1938), a collection of short stories set in the Salinas Valley. Future generations may view *The Grapes of Wrath* (1939), his epic novel of the Depression and the Oklahoma dust bowl, as one of his greatest works.

WALLACE STEVENS (1879–1955)

Wallace Stevens was a lawyer specializing in surety bonds and rose to be a vice president of the Hartford Accident and Indemnity Company. His poetry was collected for the first time in *Harmonium* when he was forty-five, and while he published widely during his lifetime, his poetry was only slowly recognized as the work of a major modernist whose originality has not been surpassed. Stevens's idea of poetry as a force taking the place of religion has had a profound influence on poets and critics of this century.

LEON STOKESBURY (b. 1945)

Leon Stokesbury, as an undergraduate at Lamar State College of Technology (now Lamar University), published a poem in *The New Yorker*. The author of three collections of poetry, including *Autumn Rhythm: New and Selected Poems*, Stokesbury has also edited anthologies of contemporary Southern poetry and the poetry of World War II.

MARK STRAND (b. 1934)

Mark Strand displays a simplicity in his best poems that reveals the influence of Spanish-language poets like Nicanor Parra, the father of "anti-poetry," and Rafael Alberti, whom

Strand has translated. Strand was named U.S. poet laureate in 1990.

JONATHAN SWIFT *(1667–1745)*

Jonathan Swift, the author of *Gulliver's Travels,* stands unchallenged as the greatest English prose satirist, but his poetry too is remarkable in the unsparing realism of its best passages. Like many poets of the neoclassical era, Swift adds tension to his poetry by ironically emphasizing parallels between the heroic past and the familiar characters and scenes of contemporary London. A native of Dublin, Swift returned to Ireland in his maturity as dean of St. Patrick's Cathedral.

JOHN MILLINGTON SYNGE *(1871–1909)*

John Millington Synge was born in Newton Little, Ireland, near Dublin, and in a relatively short life became one of the most proclaimed playwrights of the Irish literary renaissance. A gifted musician who also wrote poetry, literary criticism, and essays, Synge wrote his first play, *When the Moon Has Set,* in 1901, but its controversial themes involving love between an atheist and a nun made it unproduceable in Ireland at the time. Synge achieved a great deal of success with later plays, including *In the Shadow of the Glen* (1903) and *Riders to the Sea* (1904), but may be best known for the violent riots and controversy that occurred with the first production of *The Playboy of the Western World* in 1907, in Dublin, a play whose offenses included, among others, the mentioning of undergarments. Although attacked by many in his time, Synge had the support of a number of literary greats in his time, such as William Butler Yeats, and he has a solid reputation as a playwright today.

AMY TAN *(b. 1952)*

Amy Tan is the only child of Chinese immigrants and grew up in Oakland, California. Her hugely successful first novel, *The Joy Luck Club* (1989), from which "Two Kinds" is taken, is an example of frame-tale fiction, telling sixteen interconnected stories of four Chinese-American mothers and their daughters as they adjust to the cultural mixture of life in San Francisco. *The Joy Luck Club* was made into a successful film. Tan's other books include two novels, *The Kitchen God's Wife* and *The Hundred Secret Senses,* and two books for children, *The Moon Lady* and *The Chinese Siamese Cat.* A new novel set in China and the United States, *The Bonesetter's Daughter,* appeared in 2001.

ALFRED, LORD TENNYSON *(1809–1892)*

Tennyson became the most famous English poet with the 1850 publication of *In Memoriam,* a sequence of poems on the death of his friend A.H. Hallam. The same year he became Poet Laureate on the death of Wordsworth. Modern critical opinion has focused more favorably on Tennyson's lyrical gifts than on his talents for narrative or drama. T. S. Eliot and W. H. Auden, among other critics, praised Tennyson's rhythms and sound patterns but had reservations about his depth of intellect, especially when he took on the role of official apologist for Victorian England.

DYLAN THOMAS *(1914–1953)*

Dylan Thomas was a legendary performer of his and others' poetry. His popularity in the United States led to several collegiate reading tours, punctuated with outrageous behavior and self-destructive drinking that led to his early death in New York City, the victim of what the autopsy report labeled "insult to the brain." The Wales of his childhood remained a constant source of inspiration for his poetry and for radio dramas like *Under Milk Wood,* which was turned into a film by fellow Welshman Richard Burton and his then wife, Elizabeth Taylor.

HENRY DAVID THOREAU *(1817–1862)*

Henry David Thoreau was born in Concord, Massachusetts, and educated at Harvard, where he first read Ralph Waldo Emerson, who would later become his friend and mentor. His work reveals a dedicated naturalist and Thoreau's masterpiece, *Walden,* details the two years he spent living in a cabin on Walden Pond. As a protest against the Mexican War, Thoreau refused to pay his poll tax and was briefly imprisoned. Out of this experience came his essay "Civil Disobedience," which was cited as an inspiration by both Gandhi and Martin Luther King, Jr. Along with Emerson, he remains the chief spokesperson for the transcendentalist movement.

LEO TOLSTOY (1828–1910)

Leo Tolstoy was born into an aristocratic family in central Russia and studied law at Kazan University. He returned to his family estate, where he unsuccessfully attempted to educate the serfs. For a time he lived a profligate life in St. Petersburg and Moscow, then entered the army in 1851 and saw action in the Crimean War. Tolstoy decided to become a writer in his late twenties and eventually produced two of the world's greatest novels, *War and Peace* (1863–1869) and *Anna Karenina* (1877). A lifelong reformer and critic of the Russian middle class and civil service, in later life he turned increasingly to Christianity and attempted to carry out reforms that would aid the Russian peasants. In "The Death of Ivan Ilyich," he implicitly accuses the middle class of living by values that render them spiritually dead and desperately in need of redemption.

JOHN UPDIKE (b. 1932)

John Updike is a writer whose novels so consistently appear on the bestseller lists that his brilliant forays into light verse, serious poetry, the literary essay, and the short story are often overshadowed by his achievement in longer forms. Born in Shillingford, in rural Pennsylvania, he attended Harvard, where he contributed humor and cartoons to the *Lampoon*, and he later studied art in England. After his return to the United States, he worked for three years for *The New Yorker*, to which he remains a regular contributor of book reviews on a wide range of subjects. Updike is a prolific writer who has won many awards, including the National Book Award in 1963 and both the Pulitzer Prize and an American Book Award in 1982, yet he remains a talent so protean that he is difficult to classify. Still, his bestselling novels about the life of a contemporary American "everyman," Harry "Rabbit" Angstrom—*Rabbit, Run* (1960), *Rabbit Redux* (1971), *Rabbit Is Rich* (1981), and *Rabbit at Rest* (1990), for which he received his second Pulitzer Prize—have solidified his reputation as one of the most astute observers of the American middle class. His novel *The Witches of Eastwick* (1984) was made into a popular motion picture starring Jack Nicholson, Cher, and Michelle Pfeiffer. "A & P," one of his most widely reprinted works, comes from his 1962 collection of short stories, *Pigeon Feathers*.

AMY UYEMATSU (b. 1956)

Amy Uyematsu is the granddaughter of Japanese immigrants. Raised in Los Angeles's Little Tokyo neighborhood, she majored in mathematics as UCLA where she helped pioneer an Asian American studies program. She has published two poetry collections: *Nights of Fire, Nights of Rain* (1998) and *30 Miles from J-Town* (1992), for which she received the Nicholas Roerich Poetry Prize. Uyematsu's 1969 essay "The Emergence of Yellow Power in America" drew connections between the burgeoning Asian American struggle for political power and the more established Black Power movement.

ALICE WALKER (b. 1944)

Alice Walker wrote the Pulitzer Prize–winning epistolary novel, *The Color Purple* (1982). The book and its 1985 film version have made her the most famous living African American woman writer, perhaps the most widely read of any American woman of color. A native of Eatonton, Georgia, Walker was the eighth child of an impoverished farm couple. She attended Spelman College in Atlanta and Sarah Lawrence College on scholarships, graduating in 1965. Walker began her literary career as a poet, eventually publishing six volumes of verse. Walker's short story collections and novels, including *The Temple of My Familiar* (1989) and *Possessing the Secret of Joy* (1992), which takes as its subject the controversial practice of female circumcision among African tribes, have continued to reach large audiences and have solidified her reputation as one of the major figures in contemporary literature. Walker has coined the term "womanist" to stand for the black feminist concerns of much of her fiction. "Everyday Use," a story from the early 1970s, is simultaneously a satisfying piece of realistic social commentary and a subtly satirical variation on the ancient fable of "The City Mouse and the Country Mouse." Her most recent collection of stories, *The Way Forward Is with a Broken Heart* (2000), was described by Booklist as "part memoir, part fiction, and part bibliotherapy."

WALT WHITMAN *(1819–1892)*

Walt Whitman pioneered the use of free verse, which established him as one of the forebears of modern poetry, but his subject matter, often dealing with sexual topics, and his unsparing realism were equally controversial in his day. An admirer of Emerson, he adapted many of the ideas of transcendentalism in *Song of Myself*, his first major sequence, and also incorporated many of Emerson's calls for poets to use American subjects and patterns of speech. *Leaves of Grass*, which he revised from 1855 until his death, expanded to include virtually all of his poems, including the graphic poems he wrote while serving as a volunteer in Civil War army hospitals.

JOHN EDGAR WIDEMAN *(b. 1941)*

John Edgar Wideman was reared in Pittsburgh and attended the University of Pennsylvania where he won a Rhodes Scholarship and was an All Ivy League forward in basketball. A writer since his teens, Wideman has published novels, short stories, memoirs, and essays on a wide range of subjects. He is professor of English at the University of Massachusetts—Amherst. His son is also a writer and his daughter has played professional basketball.

RICHARD WILBUR *(b. 1921)*

Richard Wilbur will be remembered by posterity as perhaps the most skillful metricist and exponent of wit that American poetry has produced. His highly polished poetry—against the grain of much contemporary writing—is a monument to his craftsmanship and intelligence. Perhaps the most honored of all living American poets, Wilbur served as poet laureate of the United States in 1987. His translations of the verse dramas of Molière and Racine are regularly performed throughout the world.

MILLER WILLIAMS *(b. 1930)*

Miller Williams won the Poets' Prize in 1990 for *Living on the Surface*, a volume of selected poems. The author of poems, stories, and critical essays, Williams served as a faculty member at the Breadloaf Writers' Conference for seven years, and has taught at the University of Chile and the National University of Mexico. A skillful translator of both Giuseppe

Belli, a Roman poet of the early nineteenth century, and of Nicanor Parra, a contemporary Chilean, Williams has written many poems about his travels throughout the world, yet has retained the relaxed idiom of his native Arkansas. Father of acclaimed singer-songwriter Lucinda Williams, he is himself no stranger to the national spotlight, having read his poem "Of History and Hope" at Bill Clinton's 1997 presidential inauguration.

WILLIAM CARLOS WILLIAMS *(1883–1963)*

William Carlos Williams, like his friend Wallace Stevens, followed an unconventional career for a poet, working until his death as a pediatrician in Rutherford, New Jersey. Williams is modern poetry's greatest proponent of the American idiom. His plainspoken poems have been more widely imitated than those of any other American poet of this century, perhaps because he represents a homegrown modernist alternative to the intellectualized Europeanism of T.S. Eliot and Ezra Pound (a friend of his from college days). In his later years, Williams assisted many younger poets, among them Allen Ginsberg, for whose controversial book *Howl* he wrote an introduction.

AUGUST WILSON *(1945–2005)*

August Wilson, whose birth name was Frederick August Kittel, was born in Pittsburgh's predominantly African American Hill District, the setting of many of his plays. The child of a mixed-race marriage, he grew up fatherless and credited his real education in life and, incidentally, in language to the older men in his neighborhood, whose distinctive voices echo memorably in his plays. A school dropout at fifteen after a teacher unjustly accused him of plagiarism, he joined in the Black Power movement of the 1960s, eventually founding the Black Horizons on the Hill, an African American theater company. Wilson admitted to having had little confidence in his own ability to write dialogue during his early career, and his first publications were poems. A move to St. Paul, Minnesota, led to work with the Minneapolis Playwrights' Center. After his return to Pittsburgh he wrote *Jitney* and *Fullerton Street*, which were staged by regional theaters. His career hit full stride with the successful debut of *Ma Rainey's*

Black Bottom (1984), which was first produced at the Yale Repertory Theater and later moved to Broadway. *Joe Turner's Come and Gone* (1986) was his next success, and *Fences* (1987) and *The Piano Lesson* (1990) both won Pulitzer Prizes and other major awards, establishing Wilson as the most prominent African American dramatist. In most of Wilson's plays a historical theme is prominent, as Wilson attempted to piece together the circumstances that led African Americans to northern cities, depicting how they remain united and sometimes divided by a common cultural heritage that transcends even the ties of friendship and family. But to these social concerns Wilson brought a long training in the theater and a poet's love of language. As he said to an interviewer in 1991, "[Poetry] is the bedrock of my playwriting. . . . The idea of metaphor is a very large idea in my plays and something that I find lacking in most contemporary plays. I think I write the kinds of plays that I do because I have twenty-six years of writing poetry underneath all of that." *Two Trains Running* (1992), *Seven Guitars* (1995), *King Hedley II* (2001), and *Gem of the Ocean* (2003) were his more recent plays.

GAHAN WILSON *(b. 1930)*

Gahan Wilson was born in Evanston, Illinois. He has spent his life primarily as a cartoonist and illustrator. His work has appeared in a number of magazines and journals, and he is the illustrator for many novels and story collections, usually producing work for science fiction or fantasy genres and employing some element of the macabre or grotesque in his depictions. Known for his twisted but comic approach to his art, Wilson is celebrated as one of the America's leading illustrators.

NAOMI WOLF *(b. 1962)*

Born in San Francisco and educated at Yale and Oxford, Wolf came to prominence with the publication of *The Beauty Myth* in 1991 and lectured widely on how the cosmetics and fashion industries manipulate and exploit women. A controversial figure who has written about politics, sexuality, and childbirth, Wolf has also penned an affectionate memoir of her father, a teacher and poet.

JAMES WRIGHT *(1927–1980)*

James Wright showed compassion for losers and underdogs of all types, an attitude evident everywhere in his poetry. A native of Martins Ferry, Ohio, he often described lives of quiet desperation in the blue-collar towns of his youth. Like many poets of his generation, Wright wrote formal verse in his early career and shifted to open forms during the 1960s.

WILLIAM BUTLER YEATS *(1865–1939)*

William Butler Yeats is considered the greatest Irish poet and provides an important link between the late romantic era and early modernism. His early poetry, focusing on Irish legend and landscape, is regional in the best sense of the term, but his later work, with its prophetic tone and symbolist texture, moves on a larger stage. Yeats lived in London for many years and was at the center of British literary life. He was awarded the Nobel Prize in 1923.

SLAVOJ ŽIŽEK *(b. 1949)*

Slavoj Žižek was born in Ljubljana, Slovenia. A philosopher, cultural critic, and one-time presidential candidate for the Republic of Slovenia, Žižek is a colorful, controversial academic, usually promoting some version of postmodernism and psychoanalysis in his work. The author of numerous articles and books, Žižek was the recent subject of a documentary biography film entitled *Žižek!* (2005).

Credits

Index of Critical Terms

Index of Authors, Titles, and First Lines of Poems

Note: Author's names appear in boldface type. Titles of short stories appear in double quotation marks and italics. Titles of poems appear in double quotation marks. Titles of plays appear in italics.

Additional Titles of Interest

Note to Instructors: Any of these Penguin-Putnam, Inc. titles can be packaged with this book at a special discount. Contact your local Allyn & Bacon Longman sales representative for details on how to create a Value Package.

Aeschylus, *The Oresteia*
Albee, *Three Tall Women*
Allison, *Bastard Out of Carolina*
Alvarez, *How the García Girls Lost Their Accents*
Anonymous, *The Koran*
Arendt, *On Revolution*
Aristotle, *The Politics*
Austen, *Pride and Prejudice*
Cather, *My Antonia*
Chaucer, *The Canterbury Tales*
Chopin, *The Awakening and Selected Stories*
Conrad, *Heart of Darkness*
Cuddon, *The Penguin Dictionary of Literary Terms and Literary Theory*
de Cervantes, *Don Quixote*
Defoe, *Robinson Crusoe*
de Tocqueville, *Democracy in America*
Dickens, *Great Expectations*
Doctorow, *Ragtime*
Douglass, *Narrative of the Life of Frederick Douglass, An American Slave*
Du Bois, *The Souls of Black Folk*
Flaubert, *Madame Bovary*
Franklin, *The Autobiography and Other Writings*
Golding, *Lord of the Flies*
Gore, *Earth in the Balance: Ecology and the Human Spirit*
Griffin, *Black Like Me*
Grimm and Grimm, *Grimms' Fairy Tales*
Hamilton, *The Federalist Papers*
Hardy, *Jude the Obscure*
Hwang, *M. Butterfly*
Ibsen, *A Doll's House and Other Plays*
James, *The Portrait of a Lady*
James, *The Varieties of Religious Experience*
Jefferson, *Notes on the State of Virginia*
Jen, *Typical American*
Karr, *The Liars' Club*

Kerouac, *On the Road*
Kesey, *One Flew Over the Cuckoo's Nest*
Le Guin, *The Left Hand of Darkness*
Lipstadt, *Denying the Holocaust*
MacArthur, *The Penguin Book of 20th-Century Speeches*
Macchiavelli, *The Prince*
Mann, *Death in Venice*
Marx, *The Communist Manifesto*
Miller, *Death of a Salesman*
More, *Utopia*
Orwell, *1984*
Orwell, *Animal Farm*
Parker, *The Portable Dorothy Parker*
The Penguin Book of Historic Speeches
Plato, *Great Dialogues of Plato*
Plato, *The Republic*
The Portable Harlem Renaissance Reader
Rushdie, *Midnight's Children*
Shakespeare, *Four Great Comedies*
Shakespeare, *Four Great Tragedies*
Shelley, *Frankenstein*
Sinclair, *The Jungle*
Solzhenitsyn, *One Day in the Life of Ivan Denisovich*
Sophocles, *The Three Theban Plays*
St. Augustine of Hippo, *The Confessions of St. Augustine*
Steinbeck, *The Grapes of Wrath*
Stoker, *Dracula*
Stowe, *Uncle Tom's Cabin*
Swift, *Gulliver's Travels*
Thoreau, *Walden and Civil Disobedience*
Twain, *The Adventures of Huckleberry Finn*
Voltaire, *Candide, Zadig, and Selected Stories*
Washington, *Up from Slavery*
Wharton, *Ethan Frome*
Wilde, *The Picture of Dorian Gray*
Williams, *A Streetcar Named Desire*
Wilson, *Fences*
Wilson, *Joe Turner's Come and Gone*
Woolf, *Jacob's Room*